Mass Communication and American Social Thought

D1597504

CRITICAL MEDIA STUDIES
INSTITUTIONS, POLITICS, AND CULTURE
Andrew Calabrese, University of Colorado, *Series Editor*

Advisory Board

Recent Titles in the Series

Forthcoming

Entertaining the Citizen: When Politics and Popular Culture Converge
Liesbet van Zoonen

Globalizing Politics
Gerald Sussman

The Blame Game: Why Television Is Not Our Fault
Eileen R. Meehan

Film Industries and Cultures in Transition
Dina Iordanova

Raymond Williams
Alan O'Connor

Mass Communication and American Social Thought

Key Texts, 1919–1968

Edited by
John Durham Peters and Peter Simonson

ROWMAN & LITTLEFIELD PUBLISHERS, INC.
Lanham • Boulder • New York • Toronto • Oxford

ROWMAN & LITTLEFIELD PUBLISHERS, INC.

Published in the United States of America
by Rowman & Littlefield Publishers, Inc.
A wholly owned subsidary of The Rowman & Littlefield Publishing Group, Inc.
4501 Forbes Boulevard, Suite 200, Lanham, Maryland 20706
www.rowmanlittlefield.com

P.O. Box 317, Oxford OX2 9RU, UK

British Library Cataloguing in Publication Information Available

Library of Congress Cataloging-in-Publication Data
Mass communication and American social thought : key texts, 1919–1968 /
[edited by] John Durham Peters and Peter Simonson.
    p. cm.
  Includes bibliographical references and index.
  ISBN 0-7425-2838-3 (cloth : alk. paper) — ISBN 0-7425-2839-1 (pbk. : alk. paper)
  1. Mass media—Social aspects.   2. Mass media—Social aspects—United States.
  3. Communication—Social aspects—United States.   4. Mass media and culture—United States.
  I. Peters, John Durham.   II. Simonson, Peter.

  HM1206.M36   2004
  302.23—dc22
                                         2004002451

Printed in the United States of America

⊗™ The paper used in this publication meets the minimum requirements of American National
Standard for Information Sciences—Permanence of Paper for Printed Library Materials,
ANSI/NISO Z39.48-1992.

For the true collector, every single thing in [the collection] becomes an encyclopedia of all knowledge of the epoch, the landscape, the industry, and the owner from which it comes. . . . Collecting is a form of practical memory.
—Walter Benjamin, *The Arcades Project*

There was no hope of my having a casual conversation with an English professor about what a cool book *Tristam Shandy* was.
—Dave Hickey, *Air Guitar*

Brief Contents

Introduction: Mass Communication and American Social Thought: Key Texts, 1919–1968   1

Part I: From Hope to Disillusionment: Mass Communication Theory Coalesces, 1919–1933   13

Part II: The World in Turmoil: Communications Research, 1933–1949   79

Part III: The American Dream and Its Discontents: Mass Communication Theory, 1949–1968   263

Afterword and Acknowledgments   495

Other Readers and Historical Collections in American Mass Communication Study and Related Subjects   499

Suggested Films   501

Select Supplementary Reading List   505

The Intellectual History of North American Media Studies, 1919–1968: A Selected Bibliography (Including Works Cited in Interpretive Essays)   509

Credits   519

Index   525

About the Editors   531

Contents

Introduction: Mass Communication and American Social Thought: Key Texts,
1919–1968   1

**Part I: From Hope to Disillusionment: Mass Communication Theory
Coalesces, 1919–1933**

Introduction   13

1 "The Process of Social Change," from *Political Science Quarterly* (1897)   21
   Charles Horton Cooley

2 "The House of Dreams," from *The Spirit of Youth and the City Streets* (1909)   25
   Jane Addams

3 From *Winesburg, Ohio* (1919)   30
   Sherwood Anderson

4 From the *Introduction to the Science of Sociology* (1921)   31
   Robert Ezra Park and Ernest W. Burgess

5 "Nature, Communication, and Meaning," from *Experience and Nature* (1925)   35
   John Dewey

6 "The Disenchanted Man," from *The Phantom Public* (1925)   36
   Walter Lippmann

7 "Criteria of Negro Art," from *Crisis Magazine* (1926)   42
   W. E. B. Du Bois

8 "The Results of Propaganda," from *Propaganda Technique in the
   World War* (1927)   47
   Harold Dwight Lasswell

9 "Manipulating Public Opinion: The Why and the How" (1928)   51
   Edward L. Bernays

10   From *Middletown: A Study in Contemporary American Culture* (1929)   58
     Robert S. Lynd and Helen Merrell Lynd

11   "Communication," from *Encyclopaedia of the Social Sciences* (1931)   74
     Edward Sapir

Part II: The World in Turmoil: Communications Research, 1933–1949

Introduction   79

12   "Conclusion," from *Movies and Conduct* (1933)   91
     Herbert Blumer

13   "The Integration of Communication," from *Communication Agencies
     and Social Life* (1933)   95
     Malcolm M. Willey and Stuart A. Rice

14   "Toward a Critique of Negro Music," from *Opportunity* (1934)   98
     Alain Locke

15   From *Technics and Civilization* (1934)   102
     Lewis Mumford

16   "The Business Nobody Knows," from *Our Master's Voice* (1934)   106
     James Rorty

17   "The Influence of Radio upon Mental and Social Life," from
     The Psychology of Radio (1935)   110
     Hadley Cantril and Gordon W. Allport

18   "Foreword," from *Public Opinion Quarterly* (1937)   116
     Editors, *Public Opinion Quarterly*

19   "Human Interest Stories and Democracy," from
     Public Opinion Quarterly (1937)   118
     Helen MacGill Hughes

20   From *The Fine Art of Propaganda* (1939)   124
     Alfred McClung Lee and Elizabeth Briant Lee

21   "A Powerful, Bold, and Unmeasurable Party?" from
     The Pulse of Democracy (1940)   128
     George Gallup and Saul Rae

22   "Democracy in Reverse," from *Public Opinion Quarterly* (1940)   134
     Robert S. Lynd

23   "Needed Research in Communication," from the *Rockefeller Archives* (1940)   136
     *Lyman Bryson, Lloyd A. Free, Geoffrey Gorer, Harold D. Lasswell, Paul F.
     Lazarsfeld, Robert S. Lynd, John Marshall, Charles A. Siepmann,
     Donald Slesinger, and Douglas Waples*

24   "On Borrowed Experience: An Analysis of Listening to Daytime Sketches,"
     from *Studies in Philosophy and Social Science* (1941)   139
     Herta Herzog

25 "Art and Mass Culture," from *Studies in Philosophy and Social Science* (1941)   157
    Max Horkheimer

26 "Administrative and Critical Communications Research," from
    Studies in Philosophy and Social Science (1941)   166
    Paul F. Lazarsfeld

27 "The Popular Music Industry," from *Radio Research 1941* (1942)   174
    Duncan MacDougald Jr.

28 From *Dialectic of Enlightenment* (1944)   180
    Max Horkheimer and Theodor Adorno

29 "Nazi Propaganda and Violence," from *German Radio Propaganda* (1944)   182
    Ernst Kris and Hans Speier

30 "Biographies in Popular Magazines," from *Radio Research 1942–1943* (1944)   188
    Leo Lowenthal

31 "The Negro Press," from *An American Dilemma: The Negro Problem
    and Modern Democracy* (1944)   206
    Gunnar Myrdal

32 "A Social Critique of Radio Music," from the *Kenyon Review* (1945)   210
    Theodor W. Adorno

33 "The Social and Cultural Context," from *Mass Persuasion* (1946)   215
    Robert K. Merton

34 "The Requirements," from *A Free and Responsible Press* (1947)   218
    Hutchins Commission

35 "Mass Media," from *UNESCO: Its Philosophy and Purpose* (1947)   222
    Julian Sorrell Huxley

36 "The Enormous Radio," from *The Enormous Radio and Other Stories* (1947)   224
    John Cheever

37 "Mass Communication, Popular Taste, and Organized Social Action," from
    The Communication of Ideas (1948)   230
    Paul F. Lazarsfeld and Robert K. Merton

38 Table from "Communication Research and the Social Psychologist," from
    Current Trends in Social Psychology (1948)   242
    Paul F. Lazarsfeld

39 "Information, Language, and Society," from *Cybernetics: Control and
    Communication in the Animal and the Machine* (1948)   243
    Norbert Wiener

40 "Consensus and Mass Communication," from *American Sociological
    Review* (1948)   249
    Louis Wirth

41 "What 'Missing the Newspaper' Means," from *Communications
    Research* (1949)   254
    Bernard Berelson

Part III: The American Dream and Its Discontents: Mass Communication Theory, 1949–1968

Introduction 263

42 "Industrialism and Cultural Values," from *The Bias of Communication* (1950) 275
   Harold A. Innis

43 "Emerging from Magic," from *Hollywood: The Dream Factory* (1950) 280
   Hortense Powdermaker

44 "Storytellers as Tutors in Technique," from *The Lonely Crowd* (1950) 293
   David Riesman, with Reuel Denney and Nathan Glazer

45 "Our Next Frontier . . . Transoceanic TV," from *Look* (1950) 309
   David Sarnoff

46 "Communication in the Sovietized State, as Demonstrated in Korea," from
   Public Opinion Quarterly (1951) 310
   Wilbur Schramm and John W. Riley Jr.

47 "The Consumer's Stake in Radio and Television," from *Quarterly of Film,
   Radio and Television* (1951) 318
   Dallas Smythe

48 "The Unique Perspective of Television and Its Effect: A Pilot Study," from
   American Sociological Review (1952) 328
   Kurt Lang and Gladys Engel Lang

49 "Technology and Political Change," from *International Journal* (1952) 338
   Marshall McLuhan

50 "A Theory of Mass Culture," from *Diogenes* (1953) 343
   Dwight Macdonald

51 "Sight, Sound, and Fury," from *Commonweal* (1954) 353
   Marshall McLuhan

52 "Between Media and Mass," from *Personal Influence* (1955) 358
   Elihu Katz and Paul F. Lazarsfeld

53 "The Theory of Mass Society: A Critique," from *Commentary* (1956) 364
   Daniel Bell

54 "Mass Communication and Para-Social Interaction: Observations on
   Intimacy at a Distance," from *Psychiatry* (1956) 373
   Donald Horton and R. Richard Wohl

55 "The Mass Society," from *The Power Elite* (1956) 387
   C. Wright Mills

56 "FDR and the White House Mail," from *Public Opinion Quarterly* (1956) 401
   Leila A. Sussmann

57 "Notes on a Natural History of Fads," from *American Journal
   of Sociology* (1957) 409
   Rolf Meyersohn and Elihu Katz

58   "Mass Communication and Socio-cultural Integration," from
Social Forces (1958)   417
Warren Breed

59   "Modernizing Styles of Life: A Theory," from *The Passing of Traditional
Society* (1958)   426
Daniel Lerner

60   "The Social-Anatomy of the Romance-Confession Cover Girl," from
Journalism Quarterly (1959)   434
George Gerbner

61   "The State of Communication Research," from *Public Opinion
Quarterly* (1959)   440
Bernard Berelson

62   "The State of Communication Research: Comments," from *Public Opinion
Quarterly* (1959)   446
Wilbur Schramm, David Riesman, and Raymond Bauer

63   "What Is Mass Communication?" from *Mass Communication: A Sociological
Perspective* (1959)   454
Charles R. Wright

64   "Social Theory and Mass Media," from *Canadian Journal of Economics and
Political Science* (1961)   457
Thelma McCormack

65   "Television and the Public Interest" (1961)   465
Newton Minow

66   "The Kennedy Assassination and the Nature of Political Commitment,"
from *The Kennedy Assassination and the American Public* (1965)   472
Sidney Verba

67   "TV Overseas: The U.S. Hard Sell," from *The Nation* (1966)   480
Herbert Schiller

68   "Aggressiveness in Advanced Industrial Societies," from *Negations* (1968)   485
Herbert Marcuse

Afterword and Acknowledgments   495

Other Readers and Historical Collections in American Mass Communication
Study and Related Subjects   499

Suggested Films   501

Select Supplementary Reading List   505

The Intellectual History of North American Media Studies, 1919–1968: A Selected
Bibliography (Including Works Cited in Interpretive Essays)   509

Credits   519

Index   525

About the Editors   531

Introduction

Mass Communication and American Social Thought: Key Texts, 1919–1968

Though most complex societies in human history have had means for sending messages to many people at once—whether the stained glass of medieval Europe, the pyramids of ancient Egypt, the great wall of China, or the oral networks of folklore and rumor—only in the twentieth century did the mass media become named as such. From the 1920s to the 1960s, a cluster of media dominated the cultural and political landscape: radio, film, television, newspapers, and magazines. The "Big Five" were genuinely *mass* media in every context: in their content, which was aimed at middle-range cultural tastes; in their audiences, ranging in the millions; and in their mode of production, which was industrialized, bureaucratized, and organized in output. National programs, audiences, and industries were all aligned.

In the heyday of the Big Five, the notion of mass communication grew into one of the dominant concepts for naming and interpreting this new cultural complex. In both popular and higher-brow imaginations, mass communication attached itself to some of the most important hopes and anxieties of the twentieth century. Would it enhance democracy or breed totalitarianism and other despotisms? Would it consolidate power or challenge it? Bring us closer together or isolate us? Educate and uplift us or degrade us and make us stupider? Was it a way to bring art to the masses or to kill art as we know it? Could it be a force to eliminate prejudice and increase cross-cultural understanding, or would it maintain stereotypes, divisions, and dominances? Did it create new and liberating or pathological and distorted forms of social life? Perceptive observers asked all of these questions and believed the stakes were high. Mass communication was one of the core concepts of the twentieth century, a central social experience through which three generations understood their lives and times.

Our media landscape is different today, but the problems of mass communication are still very much with us. Owing to changes in business practices, technology, regulatory climate, and broader political and social environments, mass communication of the sort common from the 1930s through the 1960s is no longer the daily norm. We now live in a postbroadcast age—of cable and satellite television, the Internet, narrowcast musical styles and radio formats, highly sophisticated demographic analysis, niche marketing, and decreased readership of daily newspapers. But mass communication is still with us, and some is global in scope. It is now a cliché to point out that the hijackings of September 11, 2001, formed a worldwide event of mass communication, coordinated by satellite and digital media technologies—the latest in a very important series of live global media events initiated by the Apollo moon landing in 1969. Such media forms, which call on and structure the lives of millions or even billions, will persist into the twenty-first century and beyond. Nationally focused forms of mass communication also remain—news and sports channels, the networks' nightly news, some prime-time television. Media still command huge audiences, and some of their products—hit television shows, Hollywood blockbusters, wide-recognition popular music and literature—still take up broad, and in some cases central, cultural space. Mass communication is not an extinct species, only different from what it was in its formative era.

Like our media, our conceptual landscape is also different from what it was during the high point of the broadcast era. Historically speaking, the postbroadcast era is also the postmodernist era: just as the central forums of mass communication broke apart after the 1970s, so too did many of the central theories of social, political, and cultural life. While it is a mistake to project back too much uniformity in midcentury social thought, it is fair to say that since the 1970s, there has developed a rich new array of vocabularies for understanding media, culture, and society—from feminism, cultural studies, poststructuralism, and critical race theory to revived theories of political economy, psychoanalysis, and media effects. Together, these have added considerably to our collective ability to analyze, interpret, and evaluate media. They have helped create a far more varied and interesting intellectual space than what generally existed in the academic field of communications research from the 1950s through the late 1970s. At the same time, while the new orientations have sometimes brought new questions and areas of interest, they have also continued to address many of the same issues that troubled the first generations of intellectuals who reflected on the world of mass communications around them. There is both continuity and discontinuity in the tradition.

This collection represents a set of intelligent observers bearing witness to mass-mediated worlds that would grow into our own. These observers hold unique historical positions as part of the first generations to live with commercially supported, national-scope broadcast technologies. They are at once informants, ancestors, and teachers. As informants, they tell us about experiencing and studying "mass communication" as a generation new to it. As ancestors, they speak languages we recognize but in dialects different than our own. As teachers, their role is more complex. Often they speak with more clarity and conceptual insight than do the journals and books of our own day, and thus they teach by precept and example. At other times, they display their blind spots, weaknesses, or arrogance in such a way that we either swear never to follow their lead or perhaps see something better because of their failure.

Each historical section of this reader is preceded by an interpretive introduction, but here we want to explain the bounds of the project and our principles of selection; make a short case for the continued relevance of the idea of mass communication; and reflect on the relation between classic works and contemporary thinking. We hope to make our comments in this introduction and elsewhere accessible to upper-level undergraduates but also useful to graduate students, teachers, and researchers. Every collection like this one is constructed from a particular point of view, with its characteristic patterns of insight and blindness. We aim to represent a plurality of voices and approaches, broaden the range of texts and authors considered important in the history of media and mass communication study, and write something of use and interest to both first-time readers of this tradition and those who are already knowledgeable in it.

Bounds of the Project: Principles of Selection and Organization

For most of the twentieth century, mass media in the industrialized world were something like the weather—always there and always a subject of conversation. Just about everyone who wrote or thought about life in that century had something to say about the radically new world of communication—the sights and sounds, the voices and faces, the words and slogans that populated public life. And for a much longer time, from at least Plato and Confucius, there have been smart people who have said smart things about communication, including that special type of communication directed toward the popular classes. So there is a world of writing one could draw on to construct a full intellectual history of the idea of mass communication. This reader represents one segment of this much larger body of thought—the ideas generated in the United States and Canada from 1919 to 1968. We should begin by explaining—and justifying—our focus, historical cutoff points, and principles of selection.

Geographical Focus

First, what of our geographical focus on American social thought? We do not offer this collection in the spirit of Wilbur Schramm, an earlier anthologizer in the field of communication, who sometimes seemed to present communication research in his books as a beacon from the free world. The United States has a more ambivalent place in the world now than it did when Schramm was writing, in the immediate post–World War II period. Throughout the world America is simultaneously loved, hated, and influential. A curious mix of anti-American politics and pro-American culture has long defined attitudes to the United States worldwide. People protest its imperialism in Levis and to the sound of rock and roll—though recent American policy and international action have exacerbated the disjunction between cultural fascination and political unease to new heights.

In a global age, one cannot assert nationality as a simple container, especially a national identity as fraught as the American. To organize a reader on national lines somehow seems narrow, problematic, or politically retrograde. But in this case, we believe it makes good sense, for a number of reasons. First, we take "American" to mean essays written in America, in contact with American media and society. This broadens our focus well beyond "things written by American citizens," which would indeed be narrow and politically retrograde. It allows us to include, rightly, work done by German émigré scholars in exile during the 1930s and 1940s as well as by Canadian intellectuals peering down, sometimes uneasily, at the commercialized behemoth to the south. Hitler drove an amazingly talented group of intellectuals to exile into the United States. If one thinks of the critical theory of the Frankfurt School as an exotic German strain, it is important to remember that it grew to maturity in New York and Los Angeles, coming to terms with American cultural matters like jazz and Mickey Mouse. Due to the centrality of the United States in the global cultural economy in the twentieth century, the country's status as a place of refuge for European intellectuals, and its native variety in styles of media analysis, an American focus turns out to be rather cosmopolitan.

Not only does the American focus prove fertile, but it also turns out to spotlight much of the most significant thought about communication between the 1920s and 1960s. The social and cultural impacts of twentieth-century media were quickly felt in the United States, which had for a longer time attached almost millennial hopes to technologies of communication. With Weimar Germany (1919–1933), the United States was the richest early site for thinking about the meaning and consequences of a media-dominated society.

The debates and studies that took place in the United States from the 1920s to the 1960s have served as a baseline for theoretical argument, even among their avowed enemies, in studies of media and communication since. Indeed, the very idea of offering theories of communication and mass media arose in this era. One can find in it roots or precursors for nearly everything that has followed in media studies. This was a formative intellectual period that continues to haunt and inform the present. The encounter with American culture has been a decisive experience for thinking about communication in every part of the globe where American modernity has spread—and that process began in the United States itself.

Despite their significance, these classic texts have been out of print or hard to get for some time now. Despite the presence of anthologies of almost every theoretical strand in media studies, this institutionally and intellectually central set of texts has been out of circulation—worshipped, criticized, ignored, or forgotten, but not often read. In the end, we put this book together primarily to get these important and interesting texts back in wider readership.

Time Frame

Our time frame, from 1919 to 1968, was determined on the basis of historiographical thinking and practical constraint. It runs basically from World War I to the Vietnam War, two turning points in twentieth-century intellectual history. We realize that, like any such historical cutoff points, our beginning and ending years have strengths and weaknesses. On the negative side, starting in the 1920s risks missing two crucial developments. One is the long nineteenth-century tradition of grappling with the modern world of communication. Though they obviously knew no Hollywood and no broadcasting, nineteenth-century thinkers faced many of the issues we associate with the mass media today. The popular press, the publicity stunts of a P. T. Barnum, the condensation of time and space by the railroad and telegraph, and the blur of capitalist culture in the modern city all gave intellectuals much to consider. Walt Whitman's *Leaves of Grass*, which was published in many editions from 1855 to 1892, was partly inspired by the popular mass communication of his day; Henry David Thoreau's *Walden* (1854) is in large part an analysis of the media and commotion of his time; and more than one person has marveled that Tocqueville's *Democracy in America* (two volumes, 1835 and 1840) seems at times to be describing a society dominated by television. And it goes without saying that the ideas of late-nineteenth- and early-twentieth-century figures such as Marx, Weber, Durkheim, and Freud have long inspired media scholars.

The second danger of starting in the 1920s is that of overlooking the critically important social thought of the American progressive era (roughly 1890 to 1919). In many ways, progressive thought about communication and democracy sets the baseline, acknowledged or unacknowledged, for the rest of the century. John Dewey, Charles Horton Cooley, and George Herbert Mead all wrote rich and highly influential treatments of the idea of communication and its role in constituting group life, individual identity, and democratic society. One could make the argument that theirs was collectively the most important American contribution to social thought about communication.

While we are deeply committed to taking the longer view of the intellectual history of communication, we cut off most of the pre-1920s era—though we do discuss the progressives extensively in the introduction to part I and we do include several short and representative selections of their writings. This decision was partly a matter of sheer size. Including the progressives more fully, much less extending back into the nineteenth century, would have made this book too big to hold without breaking one's wrists! It was also partly a reflection of the fact that there are several fine pragmatism readers now in print, as well as Charles Lemert's excellent collection *Social Theory* (1999), which provides an overview of the deep nineteenth-century background. These provide excerpts that provide some of the intellectual backdrop for the selections in this book, and we hope that students and teachers will draw from them to fill out their understanding.

We also decided to start in the 1920s for historiographical reasons. It was not until the broadcast age of national, commercially sponsored radio that mass communication and mass media were conceptualized as such. To be sure, no one thought of communications research as a coherent enterprise until the late 1930s and 1940s, but starting in the 1920s— again with clear roots in the progressive era—a more or less coherent set of problems and objects started to emerge. In the air was a new sense of a distinctive intellectual field to which students of modern society needed to attend, even if they called it by fairly different names. Although there were countless precursors to the hopes and worries of the broadcast era, earlier thinkers were using different terms without the concept of mass media, a term that became so important in the middle third of the twentieth century. In addition, the post–World War I thinkers operated in a different sociointellectual context than the progressives. The brutality of the war and its unparalleled loss of life made it much harder to maintain the optimistic hopes of the progressive era. The bald use of new propaganda techniques by all sides in the dispute made it harder to think that modern communication would bring the world's citizens closer together. The 1920s generation was hard-boiled in its sentiments, which some among them supplemented with hard-edged empirical techniques for studying the processes of mass communication and propaganda. As a consequence, mass communication study as we know it was born in the period between the two World Wars, a development mapped by this reader.

The other historical cutoff, the 1960s, carries analogous downsides, but we believe it is equally justified. What gets eliminated are the rich variety of approaches to media studies that emerged—or reemerged—in the 1970s and 1980s. In the 1970s a flood of new theories and perspectives broke the dam and have helped to make media studies so richly plural today. Since it represents the birth of the intellectual era we still live in, its key texts and figures remain more alive and vibrant within the collective memory of the field. As that moment fades, the post-1970s period will need its own reader (or perhaps this collection will need to be expanded into the wrist-breaking scope needed to include the new era), though abundant readers in cultural studies, feminism, effects research, and other approaches already represent work done since then. For now, we did not see the same kind of practical need to include texts from the 1970s and after.

So this reader stops with the 1960s, which interestingly look rather like the 1950s. To exaggerate only a little, the 1960s did not happen intellectually in the field of communication and media studies until the 1970s. What took place on the streets to raise consciousness about class, race, gender, and the global responsibility (or irresponsibility) of rich nations did not affect the academic field in any significant way until the 1970s. Classic works of Frankfurt critical theory were not translated until the early 1970s, at a time when feminist and cultural Marxian studies only began to achieve a significant place in academia. Anyone who looks through 1960s scholarly journals and anthologies for tie-dyes and dropouts or critical assaults on everything existing will be sorely disappointed. Work of the 1960s resembles that of the 1950s, at least tonally. Modernization theory occupies pride of place. Empirical studies carry on blithely, without a sense of having to defend themselves against attack for mindless quantification or "value neutrality." Though many things happen of note in the 1960s—especially in the annus mirabilis of 1962, when works still central to communication studies poured forth from a great variety of fields and authors—the central tendencies of 1960s social thought about communication carry on from the 1950s (and, curiously, in a manner often less angst-ridden than that of the earlier decade).

The 1960s inhabits a certain purgatory, a zone betwixt and between something dying and something being born. In 1959, Bernard Berelson gave his funeral oration for communication research, suggesting that all the great ideas and great people had gone. Though rebutted in a lively way, Berelson's declaration was in a sense right (his talk and three responses to it are included in part III [p. 440]). The founding generation of thinkers and analysts, mostly born around the turn of the century, had all faced the shock and exhilaration of the mass media in their young adulthood. By the 1960s, many of the most vibrant figures in this generation—Adorno and Horkheimer, Lazarsfeld and Merton, Mills and Riesman, Allport and Arendt—had moved on to other areas of thought (or, in Mills's case, to an early death). Scholars of the next generation, such as Elihu Katz, remained productive and interesting, but the most creative impulses of the founding generation were played out by the early 1960s. In 1961, FCC commissioner Newton Minow gave a similar indictment of television, calling it a "vast wasteland." In both academic and public life, burial rites for communication research were held at the beginning of the 1960s, but birth pangs did not come until a decade later. The efflorescence of innovative work began, once more, in the 1970s, when the current world of media studies started to come into focus. This reader takes us to the cusp of that new era.

Within our book, we have divided the selections into three chronologically ordered sections: 1919–1933, 1933–1949, and 1949–1968. This periodization reflects our belief that 1933 and 1948–49 are significant hinge years in the intellectual history of mass communication in the twentieth century. The first marked the beginning of the exodus of the European émigré intellectuals who would play such a central role in mass communication study through the 1940s, as well as the start of the Roosevelt administration, with its new levels of commitment to social science, applied empirical research, and intellectuals working in government bureaucracies. The years 1948–49 in turn mark the start of the Cold War era, the founding of the United Nations, and the new growth in big government-funded social science and communications research. If World War I and the Vietnam War anchor the far ends of this collection, Hitler's rise and the start of the Cold War mark different eras within it.

Principles of Selection

Even within the geographical and temporal boundaries, it has been difficult to decide what to keep and what to discard. Nearly every old journal we consulted, including those such as *Public Opinion Quarterly*, *Quarterly of Film, Radio and Television* or the *AV Communication Review,* had something interesting in it that begged mutely to be pulled out of obscurity. At the same time, we found vast oceans of boring print matter that only an antiquarian could love. More than once we as editors felt fortunate not to have lived in the academic field of mass communications research during this period, but then again, one need only glance through our own journals today to know that the 1950s and 1960s had no monopoly on the dull and soon forgotten.

We have chosen texts both for their individual qualities and for their value in adding to a collective portrait of American media and mass communication studies before the 1970s. For individual texts, we have used a variety of criteria for selection. Some pieces have been steadily and demonstrably influential since their publication, while others have reemerged as signal works after years of relatively forgotten or underground status. Others are forgotten gems, included because they address issues of contemporary interest. Still others are specimens of debates or schools of thought that are further from the centers of current attention, but they find place both because of their significance in the history of the field and because their day of revival might come as well.

Necessity has obliged us in several cases to offer excerpts and abridgements, but we believe that much of the historical interest is lost with an overly aggressive abridging policy, and our preference has been to provide the entire original document where possible. The historical charm, the window into the media and culture of the moment, and even the occasionally offensive language (by contemporary standards) are all highly relevant for our understanding. Such dimensions and intangibles are not a crust to be sliced off, but rather they provide important clues and garnishments to the arguments. Our editing policy has been to preserve much of the historical flavor and texture of the original, even at the risk of too much detail. Lazarsfeld and Merton's reference to the "girlish" attitude that many people hold toward propaganda, for instance, is obviously embarassing now, but if we excised it, we would deprive our readers of the opportunity to understand something about how these influential figures thought about propaganda—and about gender. What does it mean that fear of propaganda was associated with women? No one should be surprised to discover a subtext of gender norms in thinking about communication, and little throwaway lines such as this open up larger inquiries into the communicative imagination that feminist-based interpretations and other reading methods have taught us to consider. A famous bit of advice about how to read a classic work goes like this: read along until you find something that doesn't seem to belong or make sense, and then use the part you don't understand as a lens for reading the whole thing. The point is to look for what surprises you, not for confirmation of what you think you already know. If we slice off the parts that do not fit today's fashions and sensibilities, we make rich reading and interpretation more difficult, and deprive history of its ability to teach by surprising us.

Collectively, we have selected texts that display some of the variety found in the study of mass communication in America from the 1920s through the 1960s. We do this partly in response to what we see as a too narrowly remembered history of the field and its dominant paradigms. A rather pinched view of the past seems to us characteristic of media studies in many of its various contemporary manifestations, and we hope this volume might provide a corrective lens. Mass communication and media studies have from the beginning been multidisciplinary affairs marked by rival and competing conceptualizations, methods, styles, and political orientations. This is not to say that competing views have been equally powerful, equally represented within particular organizational formations, or equally supported by the mechanisms of professional or economic reward. At any given time, some voices were lonelier and more marginal than others, and we do not suggest otherwise. Still, at no time did any paradigm stand unchallenged. Alternatives have always existed, as have debates about the nature of mass media and how best to study and talk about them. Our aim has been to present these debates and alternatives in a relatively pluralistic light so that contemporary readers might judge for themselves the stakes and stakeholders.

There are limits to our broadening and leveling impulses, however. The majority of our selections come from professional teachers and scholars in university settings, many of whom were instrumental in starting—and also abandoning—the field of communication research. Many others—including painters, poets, filmmakers, novelists, literary critics, politicians, and businesspeople—had provocative and insightful things to say about media and society in the mid-twentieth century. We offer occasional excerpts from such figures by way of context and background, but a full survey of everything of intellectual interest would exhaust our resources. Serving as a filter for the majority of our materials are links, whether conceptual or historical, to the ongoing fields of communication and media studies—especially at the twin foci of mid-twentieth-century American mass communication theory, the University of Chicago and Columbia University. Most of our texts stand in some kind of direct lineage to current or historically important work in media studies and have had, or could have had, institutional effectiveness in shaping the field. In this sense, we treat media and mass communication studies as *fields,* in the double sense of that term: as ground of intellectual inquiry and as institutional turf.

One unintended by-product of our choice of period is the relative dearth of selections by women and people of color. To put things mildly, this was not a good era to be a female or a member of a racial or ethnic minority who aspired to be a college professor. Through much of the twentieth century, American professors were overwhelmingly white, male, socially privileged, and Protestant. Within that context, though, there have been a large proportion of social "outsiders" writing about media and mass communication—often in the most interesting ways. We have found and included some excellent work by female researchers who faced systematic disadvantages in hiring practices and who often worked from the institutional margins. A great number of our selections were composed by émigré or American Jews marginalized by ethnicity in American universities before the 1950s. Far fewer African Americans found leading positions in academic debates about mass media, but a significant number of children of working-class parents grew up to be opinion leaders in communication and its cognate fields. In addition, Canadian thinkers, peering down on the great cultural behemoth to the south, have made some of the more original and insightful observations about modern mass media. In short, despite the abundance of white Protestant men of privilege who wrote about mass media in midcentury America, relative outsiders have long weighed in, operating from the vexing and intellectually rich border zones that communication theory has always taken advantage of.

Readers may quibble with some of our choices, but, hey, we quibbled with some of our choices. Everyone with more than a passing acquaintance with the history of American media research will be able to name something important we have left out. We know. We couldn't include everything. The word *anthology* originally meant a gathering of flowers. In this spirit we offer this bouquet not as a complete record but as the best representation we could assemble. We do not endorse everything here nor all of the habits of thought, but we do find the body of work here assembled a tradition worthy of engagement on its own terms. The point is not to monumentalize or fix a new pantheon of immortals but to present a rich era of thought to students and scholars so that we may transcend the clichés used by both the enemies and defenders of American mass communication theory. The project aims, in short, to offer genealogies for much of the current work in media studies and to imagine what it would mean for our present projects to connect themselves to alternate pasts.

On the Idea of "Mass Communication"

One of these alternate pasts revolves around the idea of mass communication, a concept central for most of the authors represented here but one that has fallen into partial disfavor in the last three decades. We believe it is time to reexplore the intellectual history of the concept, both because it reveals a great deal about social thought in the twentieth century and because it offers a fresh examination of many of the most fundamental questions in communication theory. As a whole, this reader provides resources for such rethinking, but here it is worth sketching, in broad outline, the rise and fall of the idea of mass communication.

In the years from the end of World War I to the end of World War II, a number of new expressions involving *mass* appeared, including *mass appeal, art, audience, behavior, buying, communication, consciousness, consumer, culture, democracy, education, hysteria, illusion, media, mind, movement, murder, persuasion, production, selling, society, suicide, thinking,* and *unemployment* (*Oxford English Dictionary* 1989, 433). Global warfare and depression, assembly-line industrialism, fascism, Hollywood, broadcasting, national advertising, consumerism, political upheaval, and the Holocaust are all implicit in this list, as is the new field of mass communications research. This collection of crises has continued to shape the destiny of the concept of mass communication, a concept that seems to have first been used in the late 1920s and quite likely coined by David Sarnoff, the long-term leader of NBC. The *New York Times* records four mentions of the term before 1930, all of them between 1927 and 1928, and three of them from speeches or quotations by David Sarnoff, who usually equated the term with *broadcasting*. "Radio encompasses telegraphic communication," he observed, "as exemplified in our transoceanic wireless system; sound communication, as accomplished in telephony; mass communication, as inherent in broadcasting; sight communication, as promised by television" (*New York Times,* April 22, 1928, 146). It was clearly in wider circulation by the early 1930s, even though previous scholars have placed its birth somewhat later, such as in the late 1930s or 1940s.[1]

In a way, these scholars are right. In the late 1920s, *mass communication* was not used in any crucial way and simply suggests message dispersion on a large scale, usually via some "agency," or medium. As the war clouds broke over Europe and Asia in the late 1930s, *mass communication* was given new force by researchers who attended the Rockefeller Communications Seminar, conducted monthly between 1939 and 1940 (see Gary 1999; see p. 136 of this volume). It became a field-defining and field-covering term that was solidly in place by the late 1940s as the general name for the propagation of symbols via radio, film, and the press to vast, spatially scattered audiences. The earlier field of radio research—pioneered in the mid- to late-1930s by Hadley Cantril, Paul Lazarfeld, Frank Stanton, and their associates—gave way to the more spacious (if less focused) *communications research.* Sociologists such as Lazarsfeld and Merton (1948) and Wirth (1948) used the concept easily in the immediate postwar period, while journalism teachers and researchers were drawn to the idea as a way to represent their own burgeoning field and growth of doctorate-granting programs (Dickson 2000, 60; Rogers 1994, 24–27). The term even made an appearance in a 1949 Supreme Court opinion by Justice Felix Frankfurter, who exchanged letters with David Sarnoff: "The various forms of modern so-called 'mass communications' raise issues that were not implied in the means of communication known or contemplated by Franklin and Jefferson and Madison" (*Kovacs v. Cooper* 336 US 77 [1949], 96).

In the 1950s and beyond, *mass communication* remained a relatively stable term in American thought, defined in similar ways in works as different as C. Wright Mills's *The Power Elite* (p. 000) and Charles R. Wright's *Mass Communication: A Sociological Approach* (p. 000). Despite the contrast of Mills's grumpy mass-society theory and Wright's functionalism, both saw mass communication as the sending of impersonal, technically or institutionally mediated messages to vast, anonymous audiences without offering the opportunity for interaction or response. With scholars as diverse as Katz and Lazarsfeld (1955) and Habermas ([1962] 1989), Mills and Wright agreed that mass communication and interpersonal communication were two fundamentally different beasts whose relation was, at best, one of supplementation or coordination and, at worst, one of suffocation. Mass communication was a new species of its own.

Since its postwar solidification, the concept of mass communication has undergone three waves of attack. The first came in the late 1950s, when British cultural theorist Raymond Williams (1958, 301–19) saw the concept as an attack on democratic life that objectified audiences and provided a natural ideology to the captains of the commercial media business. "The whole theory of mass-communication depends, essentially, on a minority in some way exploiting a majority" (314); he thought that the concept reeked of a manipulative attitude, whether with benevolent or malevolent intent. The adjective *mass* implied dysfunctional democracy, poor levels of taste, large indefinite numbers, and homogeneity and standardization. "There are in fact no masses," he famously wrote, "but only ways of seeing people as masses." The second wave of attack came in the mid-1970s, with the argument that the term distorted the field intellectually and politically: *mass communication* meant the study of the conventional mass media to the neglect of a much wider array of forms and practices. Here, too, Williams (1974) led the charge, seconded by Stuart Hall and James Carey (Carey 1989b, 40–42). By the 1990s, *mass communication* had been attacked on the very different grounds that it was an obsolete concept in a multichannel media environment with targeted programming and audience selectivity. Perhaps masses once were the target, the argument goes, but segmentation or even individualization of content is now the order of the day (but see Turow 1992, for a defense of the concept's continuing relevance). More recently, the curious name change of a leading journal in the field revealed the ongoing distaste for the term—*Critical Studies in Mass Communication* morphed into *Critical Studies in Media Communication* (though an exact definition of *media communication* was left unclear.) In each case, attacks on the idea of mass communication concerned the latent meanings of *mass*— whether as an insult to popular taste, a hindrance to theory and research, or an index of eclipsed media technologies and practices. *Communication* has rarely been the problematic of the two terms.

As editors, we are somewhat divided: one of us has problematized *mass communication* and its traditional contrast with interpersonal communication (Peters 1996, 1999), and the other has argued for its extension beyond the broadcast paradigm from which it emerged (Simonson 2003). At the same time, we are agreed that the institutionally distinct subfields sometimes gathered under the umbrella term *media studies*—for example, mass communication research; radio, television, and film (sometimes together, often separated); cultural studies; and journalism—can all trace at least part of their ancestry through the texts reprinted in this reader. Like members of any extended clan, all of us will feel closer to some relatives than others, and many of us will find authors here who are the equivalent of the weird old uncles we would be just as happy to disown. But no multigenerational get-together is complete without the old weird uncles or for that matter the previously unknown second cousins with whom we find a lot in common. Extended family reunions are opportunities to find similarities within differences, and differences within similarities. Sometimes they make us want to run and hide, but other times we find that some of our relatives are cooler than we had been led to believe.

In a sense, this reader is a reunion of the dead and the living. We do not offer it up as a shrine to dead white manhood or as revenge of the rejected fathers, nor do we want to overly burden it with the weight of the term *classics*. Instead, we offer it as a pluralistic resource for retroactive enrichment and reconciliation with a tradition that deserves to be better known. We do so guided by the spirit of pragmatist reader-response criticism—that past texts are, at least in part, what we make of them in the present. Readerly minds prepared in different ways will find different dimensions and dynamics in these writings—ideas that illuminate, opinions that anger, conclusions that seem warranted or opportunity-filled occasions for analogy and comparison. Ours is a different cultural moment, with its own preferences and prejudices, insights and blind spots, questions and concerns. There are enduring issues that link these earlier texts to our own moment, as well as genealogical connections between them and our own intellectual frameworks. But there is also distance that stands ready to be bridged by both sympathetic and critical engagement. Too often, points are made about past authors or schools of thought without anyone going back to reread (or even read!) the works themselves. We ritualistically call out the names of the dead in the spirit of praise or blame, but too seldom do we actually make meaningful contact with the printed words they left behind. We hope this reader makes such contact easier for the current generation of students and researchers.

Some of the thinking about mass communication from the 1920s to the 1960s might, at first glance, seem quaint or simplistic today—and sometimes it is, though simplicity has its lessons and appeal as well. But early theory can also be breathtakingly brilliant and beat later and flashier doctrines to the punch. The readings we have gathered still have much to teach. They do so by their freshness and originality, by their anticipation of later traditions of thought, by their innocence to our current dogmas, and even by the clarity of their mistakes. Reading the history of social thought need not be only an antiquarian enterprise of looking for lost treasures in dusty attics. At its best, it is a consideration both of our academic field's core questions and of our fate as humans and citizens in a media age.

Note

1. The *Oxford English Dictionary* gives the first use of *mass communication* in 1941. However, Czitrom (1982, 131) finds it in a 1940 document from the Rockefeller Communications Seminar, and Rogers (1994, 222) suggests a 1939 letter from John Marshall to I. A. Richards: "In the last couple of years, it has been increasingly clear to me that most of my work has been in a field which for lack of a better name I have come to call mass communications." Morrison (1988, 206) also traces the phrase *mass communication research* to Marshall.

Part I

~

From Hope to Disillusionment
Mass Communication Theory
Coalesces, 1919–1933

Though many thinkers in history and in diverse cultures have wondered about communication in the large sense, only in the late nineteenth century did the particular style, spirit, and set of concerns emerge that are characteristic of American social thought about mass communication. In both Europe and North America many nineteenth-century writers had offered suggestive comments about the convulsions of modernity and communication. Some complained that business made words cheap and image everything, whereas others exulted in the swirl and excitement of the modern city, with its posters, theater, and cheap newspapers. It was intellectuals such as Charles Horton Cooley, John Dewey, and Jane Addams who made the concept of communication a centerpiece in the analysis of what was wrong with society and how to fix it. For them the secret of modern social organization was communication. In the words of Dewey's famous 1916 declaration: "Society not only continues to exist *by* transmission, *by* communication, but it may be fairly said to exist *in* transmission, *in* communication." With many of his colleagues and students, Dewey saw social life as a web of *symbolic interactions* (a term coined by Herbert Blumer). As Cooley and others had written in the 1890s, communication was the means by which communities were made and sometimes the means by which they were destroyed.

Scholarly discussion of communication in the United States dates to the 1890s, pushed by sociologists and social philosophers who typically operated with an organic view of society and were often under the sway of philosophical idealism. Such idealism drips off the page of Dewey's early writings and would remain a feature of his thought even after his shift to naturalism in the early 1890s. Communication would serve as a climactic principle in many of Dewey's mature works, from *Reconstruction in Philosophy* (1921) and *Experience and Nature* (1925) to *The Public and Its Problems* (1927) and *Art as Experience* (1934). For him, communication was at once a moral, political, social, and aesthetic principle. For thinkers such as Dewey, Cooley, and Robert Park, communication and its technologies provided the social and moral base for a democratic collective life. Their writing and that of their colleagues was not typically informed by ideals of objectivity or value neutrality—ideals that would later characterize much U.S. social science in general and mass communication research in particular—but was instead part of a broadly reformist, social democratic impulse that coursed through American public life at the time. For the most part, they were hopeful that modern technologies of large-scale communication could be brought to serve the causes of democracy and social progress.

Some clarifications are in order. The progressive era usually refers to the period in American history from about 1890 to around 1919, the term *progressive* referring to the widespread view that intelligent social planning and government intervention can help to achieve a more just and democratic society. As the name implies, progressives believed in progress, and they saw society's application of reason as the way to achieve it. They tended to admire social engineering and planning as useful ways of improving society. "Pragmatist" is a more specific term to refer to a philosophical school that emerged roughly in the same period in the United States. Pragmatism can be defined in many ways, but central is the belief that ideas and actions are experimental efforts to grasp hold of the world. Whereas other philosophical systems claim to explain how things really are, pragmatism more modestly tries to refine the methods by which people adapt to the ever-evolving cosmos. Many pragmatists were also progressives, with John Dewey as the chief exemplar; however, many were not. William James, for instance, had his doubts about both reason and progress. Finally, many progressives were also communitarians—people who believe in the moral and social indispensability of associated living and community. Here again, Dewey is a prime candidate and James a dissident.

As within progressive social thought, pragmatism too had important internal differences. The Harvard strain of pragmatism, associated with William James, Josiah Royce, and Charles Sanders Peirce, was not afraid to be transcendental and to explore the mysteries of the universe. In Royce and Peirce, *community* became a term that conjured multiple images: it was not only a name for associated living but also a picture of the good life and a model of how scientific inquiry ought to be conducted. At the University of Chicago, pragmatism took a more sociological and less metaphysical bent. James may have been interested in the meaning of truth and Peirce in evolutionary love, but Dewey and Mead tended to focus their philosophical energies on more this-worldly topics, such as democracy, communication, and the social opportunities or injustices of modern life. (To be fair, they could weave magic with the term *community* as well as anyone, often expressing it in quasi-spiritual language). Politically speaking, James was an anarchist and Peirce a Christian communitarian, whereas Dewey and Mead each held to versions of socialism or social democracy throughout their careers. (Dewey's "Ethics of Democracy," for instance, treats economic wealth as something as equally subject to democratization as the vote). All pragmatists were friendly to scientific inquiry and believed in the possibility of social reform, and all thought of communication in some sense as a critical category, so one should perhaps not overemphasize their differences.

The full story of pragmatism, in all its wrinkles, is becoming clearer over the years. Peirce's thought, for instance, had little influence during his lifetime beyond a small circle of discerning friends, such as James and Supreme Court justice Oliver Wendell Holmes Jr.; but since publication of his collected papers in the 1930s, Peirce's reputation as one of America's most original and imaginative thinkers has continued to grow. The tensions within pragmatism still resonate in American social philosophy and sociological theory, and can be detected among thinkers included in this reader, such as W. E. B. Du Bois and Alain Locke, Robert Lynd and C. Wright Mills, Walter Lippmann and Harold Lasswell, all of whom had important but sometimes strained relationships to pragmatism. Louis

Menand's Pulitzer-Prize-winning *The Metaphysical Club* (2002) sketches a colorful story of pragmatist thought and its legacies.

Whether borne by newspapers, books, fads, word of mouth, telephone, or railroad, communication that burst the bounds of the small town was for the progressives simultaneously emancipating and unnerving: it could lead both to the dreams of the great community and to the nightmares of the irrational mob. Not only was Chicago the setting and the laboratory for developing such ideas and arguments, it was also the disciplinary seedbed for the young field of sociology. Thinkers associated with the University of Chicago, this unusual and important university founded by John D. Rockefeller in 1892, have played a disproportionate role in the historical development of American thought about communication. As a new university in a time of major social and intellectual transformation (the 1890s), the University of Chicago was free to innovate beyond traditional models of how knowledge should be organized in favor of the German-style research university, first introduced in the United States at Johns Hopkins, where Peirce briefly and unhappily taught and Dewey received his doctorate. The University of Chicago had the first department of sociology in the United States, under the leadership of Albion Small, whose 1894 *Introduction to the Science of Society* offered one of the earliest treatments of the place of "communication" in society. Investing in a department whose subject was society in the 1890s was a daring act not unlike founding a department of communication studies in the 1970s—something traditionalists might scorn and students might find relevant. Small nursed fears about his department being shut down and fretted about the lack of intellectual respect it received—familiar worries for the field of communication studies later.

In Chicago sociology, not only was communication treated as a topic of study within sociology, but it was also the thing that made society possible in the first place. For Robert Park, a dominant figure at the University of Chicago from 1913 to 1933, sociology was implicitly the study of communication. If you wanted to understand how modern social order was made, you had to turn to processes of communication, whether they are found in the press, face-to-face contacts, or the more subtle rivalries and competitions that people always play out. Communication was not only a principle of social interaction but also a norm of democratic community. The notion of communication not only described the sum total of human relationships, it also implied how people *should* relate.

Cooley (p. 21) set the tone in 1897 with the announcement that "communication is the precise measure of the possibility of social organization, of good understanding among men." In their *Introduction to the Science of Sociology* (p. 31)—a massive anthology of European and American social thought so central and influential in the years between the wars that students called it the "green bible"—Robert Park and Ernest Burgess extended this thinking and helped make it canonical. For them, "the limits of society are coterminous with the limits of interaction, that is, of the participation of persons in the life of society. One way of measuring the wholesome or the normal life of a person is by the sheer external fact of his membership in the social groups of the community in which his lot is cast" (1921, 341). Note how the idea that communication defines social order quickly turns into an ideal of participation and normality. Though they professed to be social scientists—who could study race relations with the same detachment that a biologist studies the potato bug, as Park memorably put it—there is clearly a yearning in Chicago sociology: "a hope for the Great Community" (in the words of Josiah Royce). They never gave up the dream that social inquiry could help form a better society. (Many of the University of Chicago faculty and students were, at some point at least, deeply sympathetic to either socialism or communism, including Mead and Louis Wirth). As the key to society, communication played a clear role in its studies and its dreams. Concepts of communication and community provided both a protest against modern urban life and a formula for how those developments might be steered more humanely.

Several features characterize sociology at the University of Chicago, the most prestigious and influential center for the social sciences in the United States between the two World Wars. First is its interest in social difference. The city of Chicago was a laboratory of ethnic neighborhoods, and scholars and reformers fanned out into the city, trying to make sense of the gangs, "taxi dancers," Poles, African Americans, and many others coping in their urban environment. Robert Park worked for nearly a decade as the personal secretary to Booker T. Washington at the Tuskegee Institute and always had a keen interest in the outsider and the underdog. Many Chicago sociologists, such as Louis Wirth or Franklin Frazier, were themselves ethnic minorities, and interest in socially marginalized groups long informed the school's theory and research. The school served as something of a refuge for outcasts, radicals, and misfits who wanted to ask critical questions about the nature of modern society.

Second is Chicago's characteristic belief that human identity is created in interaction. Self and society, as University of Michigan sociologist Charles Horton Cooley said, are born twins. Cooley, often considered a kind of honorary member of the Chicago School, saw the "primary group"—whether it be family, church, school, or gang—as the cradle of human nature. People are radically social animals, and communication provides us, said Cooley, with our higher development. On scales larger than the primary group, interaction was also held to be crucial. *The Polish Peasant in Europe and America* (1918), the massive five-volume study by W. I. Thomas and Florian Znaniecki, shows how patterns of distant and local interaction helped to enable the immigrants' transition from the old world to the new, as people corresponded and used newspapers not only to stay in touch with each other across the ocean but also to create new kinds of association fit for novel conditions. Chicago sociology faced new forms of social relations in the limboland between personal and distant communications. Cooley welcomed "modern communication," in part because he thought it facilitated interaction on a large scale and at a distance. For him, place had waned as a principle of social life, allowing new kinds of distant association that were based on shared interests rather than shared birth or space (people have been saying similar things for the hundred years since Cooley!). In a way, Cooley is the prophet of virtual reality—of social life that operates fully through the sharing of symbols without any need for physical presence. In general, Chicago thinkers prized interaction as the moral capacity of taking the viewpoint of the other and as the political capacity to deal democratically with strangers.

The concept of symbolic interaction suggests that human relations rest as much or more on shared significance than on physical presence. Human interaction, in other words, takes place not just when people are within touching distance but also when they exchange meaningful gestures. The emphasis on sharing symbols over physical contact meant that Chicago sociology was friendly to forms of community at a distance (the public), though one strong strain of thought emphasizes the importance of assembly and personal interaction (the milling crowd, or the face-to-face public, a theme in Blumer's, Lang and Lang's, and Katz's work). German sociologist Georg Simmel, with whom Park had studied in Germany, had a strong but subtle influence on Chicago sociologists in their interest in sociability with strangers and their sense that the modern city, with its bombardment of stimuli, can make people morally and aesthetically dead (Simmel called it "the blasé attitude"). Chicagoans loved the grace of incidental public contact and disdained the private fantasies of mass society. Imagined sociability makes Chicago social thinkers nervous, from Jane Addams's critique of the theater (p. 25) through Blumer's studies of movies (p. 91) to Horton and Wohl's concept of parasocial interaction (p. 373) up to very recent work.

Third, the Chicago School had an omnivorous intellectual appetite and worked in the long horizon of European social thought. Park once said that what led him to study sociology was the reading of Goethe's *Faust*, a work that dramatizes an intellectual's desire to know everything that holds the world together. For Dewey, Hegel was an always-looming intellectual presence, even after Dewey tried to divorce idealism. Emerson likewise influenced Cooley. This presence of what one might call a "classical tradition" gave Chicago sociology an intellectual flair and flavor that set it apart from later, more hard-edged empirical work. An entire generation of budding Chicago sociologists were sent to listen to the lectures of George Herbert Mead (1863–1931), teaching in the philosophy department. To study society, you were supposed to know your Aristotle, Scottish moralism, and Thorstein Veblen, among a host of other theorists.

Even so, it is false to paint Chicago sociology in terms of later fights between humanists and number crunchers. Classic Chicago sociology is best known for the life-history method, explored most fully in Thomas and Znaniecki's *The Polish Peasant* and echoed in later works, such as Blumer's *Movies and Conduct* (1933), and is hence often correctly seen as a forerunner of qualitative, or ethnographic, modes of social research. But from the beginning, there was also a strong quantitative thrust at Chicago, beginning with early social surveys conducted at Jane Addams's Hull House in the 1890s. In the post–World War I era, Ernest Burgess encouraged his students to use quantitative methods, a trend that accelerated after the department hired William Fielding Ogburn in 1927 (Bulmer 1981). In political science in the early 1920s, Charles Merriam, Harold Gosnell, and others furiously studied a relatively new phenomenon, brought on in part by progressive political reforms: nonvoting. Using questionnaires, random sampling, and other techniques of modern statistical surveys, Chicago political scientists conducted classic studies, such as Merriam and Gosnell's *Non-Voting* (1924), which prefigured the kind of work Paul Lazarsfeld would do two decades later. They also trained a cohort of graduate students that included Harold Lasswell, whose 1927 *Propaganda Technique in the World War* (p. 47) was a signal text in the social scientific study of propaganda. The famous quote by Kelvin engraved on the Social Science Research Building at Chicago reads, "When you cannot measure, your knowledge is meager and unsatisfactory." The subtitle of Frederic Milton Thrasher's *The Gang: A Study of 1,313 Gangs in Chicago* (1927) is so numerically precise that it seems almost satirical. Chicago sociologists were not afraid to count.

Finally, though Chicago sociology successfully emancipated itself from the moral squeamishness of an earlier generation of social reformers—that is, the task was to understand, not to judge—there remained a strong normative core that manifested itself in attitudes toward different kinds of mass communication. We've already seen the implicit normative color of communication as a conceptual tool for advancing social criticism. The political scientists who studied nonvoting also wrote about how to get people to participate as well. Chicago social thought was somewhat nervous about forms of culture and communication that trafficked in entertainment instead of information. Jane Addams's treatment of the turn-of-the-century playhouse as "The House of Dreams" (p. 25) is blatantly moralistic about unchaperoned socializing and the whetting of young women's appetites for fantasy. Though later Chicago theorists are more subtle in their preferences, the sense remains that media that enable empathy and interaction with one's neighbors are worthy whereas those that stimulate solipsistic fantasies about imaginary people are bad. Thus, in the 1930s

Helen McGill Hughes endorsed the human interest story as good for democracy (p. 118), and Herbert Blumer treated the movies as a potential cause of "emotional possession" (p. 91). News stories, even gossipy ones, aroused our curiosity about our neighbors and hence had a social benefit, but fantastical forays into lives of sin and crime via film lowered us into the private recesses of our hearts. The tradition lives on: University of Chicago legal theorist Cass Sunstein (2001) has recently attacked the Internet in just these terms, seeing it as depriving citizens of serendipitous contact with strangers and alternate opinions in public places. He makes no reference to the Chicago sociological tradition, but it is not hard to see ancestral moves being repeated in new generations.

Running parallel to Chicago in the study of mass communication, from the first decades of the twentieth century through the 1950s, was New York's Columbia University. Dewey had moved to Columbia's philosophy department in 1904, where he published nearly all his writings on "communication." In 1912, Columbia opened its School of Journalism (with an endowment bestowed ten years earlier by Joseph Pulitzer), and it quickly became one of the leading such programs in the nation. Meanwhile, in sociology, Columbia's Franklin Giddings rivaled Chicago's Albion Small as early institution builder and theorist, and like his counterpart in the Midwest, he turned his graduate students out into the urban laboratory around them. Though more statistically minded than the early Chicagoans, Giddings and his colleagues, including Alvan A. Tenney, were driven by a similar progressive politics of liberal reform and enlightened social development. During the 1910s and 1920s, they channeled their interests, among other places, into what Tenney called "the scientific analysis of the press," whereby students measured newspaper column inches devoted to different subjects as a way to discover "how to obtain the best means for public discussion" (Tenney 1912, 895). In the 1920s, Columbia sociology students such as Stuart Rice and Malcolm Willey (see p. 95) used this and other methods to develop early alternatives to Chicago's approaches to mass communication. Still, before the 1930s, New York was the Second City of communication and media study, lagging significantly behind its rival to the west.

Although Chicago and Michigan were the main centers of thinking about communication from the 1890s to the 1920s, there were other important and historically influential thinkers in this era who were not university professors but rather what are today called "public intellectuals." From Walter Lippmann and W. E. B. Du Bois to Alain Locke, James Rorty, Lewis Mumford, and Kenneth Burke, a number of individuals were unaffiliated with or only intermittently working in colleges (a trend that would continue less robustly into the next generation). Not surprisingly, one key focus of discussion was the newspaper, the medium par excellence for public debate and criticism. As Lippmann and many others noted, high hopes about the political role of the free press go back to the founding era of the United States and to the Enlightenment. Interest in the immigrant press was high at Chicago, but others also studied it, in different ways. For instance, in his pathbreaking sociological study *The Philadelphia Negro* (1899), Du Bois treats the black press not only as a source for news and views but also as a voice for a different way of being. Thus, Du Bois helped to found the tradition of studying alternative media. As activist, editor, and writer, Du Bois helped inspire the Harlem renaissance of the 1920s, which combined literature, art, music, and philosophy in a remarkable outburst of creativity that still remains a landmark in American intellectual history. In the excerpts by Du Bois (p. 42) and Alain Locke (p. 98), philosopher and publicist of the "New Negro" aesthetic, we see an issue that was a hot topic for all leftist social movements in the period: the place of art in a social world driven by injustice and abuse. Similar concerns would appear in writings by members of the

Frankfurt School, as well as in mass culture debates of the 1950s, though the latter were rarely so explicit about the racial aspect of injustice in modern society.

One of the signal debates about the press and the public occurred in the 1920s between Walter Lippmann and John Dewey. Progressive faith in social democracy had been challenged before, particularly in the wake of World War I, just as the utopia of small-town community life seemed squashed by modern media and mobility (as the brief excerpt from Sherwood Anderson's 1919 novel *Winesburg, Ohio* shows [p. 30]). But into the 1920s, full-throated progressives such as Dewey remained essentially optimistic about the democratic possibilities of favored modes of communication—newspapers, public art, and face-to-face conversation. One wonders how much Dewey knew of the Harlem renaissance, which took place a taxi ride away from his office at Columbia University and which seems precisely to follow his recipe of art and communication serving as vehicles of public debate and consciousness raising.

The relative constancy of Dewey's faith in twentieth-century communication separated him and other progressives of his generation from the harder-edged analysis that came to dominate study in the 1920s and 1930s. Shifting the terms of discussion from *communication* to *propaganda*, writers such as Lippmann (p. 36) and Lasswell (p. 47) influentially drew attention to the ways modern agencies and channels of mass communication could manipulate public opinion. Lippmann's withering critique of the foundations of the democratic faith in the rational public and the well-informed citizen was less an attack on the Founding Fathers (who, Jefferson excepted, were rarely philosophical democrats) than it was on progressives such as Dewey, whose ideas dominated the culture Lippmann grew up in. Lippmann and Lasswell both prided themselves on their realism. Neither had much faith in the intellectual capacity of the masses, yet both entertained occasionally grandiose expectations about what could be achieved by the quantitative methods of the social sciences.

Working in a number of disciplines in the social sciences, many propaganda analysts maintained the progressive era's commitment to democratic reform, but they now expressed it in a manner consonant with postwar attitudes of disillusionment and distrust. The mainstream of propaganda analysis operated through case studies that revealed social and institutional forces threatening democratic life. Such studies were often accompanied by a warning, explicit or assumed, that citizens need to maintain a critical skepticism about news, advertising, education, religion, and other forms of widely disseminated public communication (see part II, p. 79). Edward Bernays, in contrast, argued that public relations did not abuse gullible masses but did a public service by organizing popular thinking in a confusing world (p. 51). His argument had more than a touch of self-interest, since he stood to gain if his new invention of public relations was legitimized as a public service; but Bernays did tap into both a mood of disillusionment with the public and a sense that social engineering could be benign (a sense that would only grow in the 1930s). This mood created ripe conditions for public relations agents to step in and puff the vast social potentials of new media, such as radio. As sociologist Marshall D. Beuick wrote in 1927, "In the past five years Jules Vernian impressions of radio and radio broadcasting have been driven into people's minds by the active publicity man with his circus ballyhooing about the romance of radio and the wonders of wireless. The press agent has convinced many of us that there is practically nothing that radio cannot do." Ever since, social research on media effects has been trying to undo popular impressions about the power of media effects (but note that Beuick had a pretty substantial conception of the persuasive powers of public relations agents).

The 1920s, in short, saw the first flowering of analysis, of many kinds, about the brave new world of worries and powers embodied in the term *mass media,* a phrase first used, according to *The Oxford English Dictionary*, in 1923. Such notions as *broadcasting, mass communication, public relations*, and *instrumentalities of communication* were also in fresh circulation in the 1920s. Though a national communication network had been laid down by the wire services in the late nineteenth century (Blondheim 1994), the scale and scope of the new culture complex was unprecedented. The Hollywood studio system started to coalesce around 1915, thereby forming one key social precondition to the concept of mass communication as a nationally oriented system of production, distribution, and exhibition aimed at the largest possible audience. World War I was also clearly something of a watershed for communication practice and theory. Communication played a key role in military operations thanks to the logistical support of the radio and telephone on the battlefield, but it played an equally large role on the domestic front via the cultural persuasion of propaganda. As Lasswell's teacher Charles Merriam (1919) wrote: "The great war developed many new weapons—the submarine, the aeroplane, the long range gun, the deadly gas; but one of the most novel and deadly was the propaganda—the psychological working on the war will of the enemy." The rise of the modern persuasion and entertainment industries in the wake of World War I led to new kinds of questions and inquiries. American media studies originated in a mix of interests: the economic need by the broadcasting industry to measure its audiences; the political need to manufacture or combat propaganda in times of war; and the human need to understand the curious ways in which modern men and women found themselves enmeshed in new webs of word, image, and sound. Though the progressive era had seen many of the new phenomena in embryo, the 1920s offered a qualitatively different set of problems. The "lost generation," as Gertrude Stein famously called American writers of the 1920s, had to grapple with the new facts of modern communication. One of the fullest summary statements, still prescient today, flowed in 1930 from the pen of anthropologist Edward Sapir (who four years earlier had moved to the University of Chicago). The multiplication of communication channels, he said, only added to the obstacles and lack of communication between people (p. 74). Such gloomy conclusions about the prospects of communication, heard with increasing frequency since the 1930s, signaled the decisive end of the most cherished hopes of the progressive era.

1

The Process of Social Change

From *Political Science Quarterly* (1897)

Charles Horton Cooley

Charles Horton Cooley (1864–1929) was one of the leading figures in the first generation of professional sociology in the United States. He was born and spent his entire life in Ann Arbor, Michigan, where his overbearing father was a brilliant and successful jurist and law professor. He attended the University of Michigan, where he studied broadly before graduating with a degree in mechanical engineering. He studied briefly in Germany, worked as a surveyor in Colorado, and did statistical work and transportation studies of streetcar systems for the Interstate Commerce Commission in Washington before returning to Michigan to take his doctorate in political economy. His dissertation, "The Theory of Transportation," served as a bridge between his Washington research and his subsequent sociological writings on communication and "the social self" (an idea he drew from William James). Cooley developed his ideas most fully in *Human Nature and the Social Order* (1902) and *Social Organization* (1909)—in the former, contributing the influential idea of "the looking glass self," created through social interaction; and, in the latter, offering one of the first extended treatments of "communication" as a central component of social life.

This excerpt, from Cooley's early essay "The Process of Social Change" (1897), gives a good indication of the central place afforded "communication" in his work and that of other classic progressive social theorists. He sets the tone for the grander-style North American social theorists of communication who followed, such as Lewis Mumford, Harold Innis, and Marshall McLuhan. As they would do in succeeding generations, Cooley suggests here that social, cultural, and political life all change when new media of communication are introduced. He displays the characteristic progressive belief in the moral and political superiorities of print over the more "prehistoric" oral tradition, as well as the belief that the written word connects people rather than isolates them.

We know that man is a sympathetic, communicating animal; and I have urged that this is what makes him amenable, plastic, fit to be formed by a social environment. But what forms the environment? The evolution of environment is the most momentous change in history.

A man's social environment embraces all persons with whom he has intelligence or sympathy, all influences that reach him. If I read Aristotle, my environment extends back two thousand years; if I read the dispatches from Japan, it takes in the antipodes. That I can be influenced by the Iliad, the New Testament and other utterances of men distant from me in time and place, is due to the arts of writing, printing and transportation, just as the fact that I can receive a complex thought from my neighbor is due to the art of speech. In other words, the social influences act through a mechanism; and the character their action depends up the character of the mechanism. The existing system of communication determines the reach of the environment. Society is a matter of the incidence of men upon one another; and since this incidence is a matter of communication, the history of the latter is the foundation of all history. It is perhaps worth while to recall some of the more obvious facts of this history, and to make some suggestions as to what they mean.

The mechanism of communication includes, of course, gesture, speech, writing, printing, mails, telephones, telegraphs, photography, the technique of the arts and sciences—all the ways through which thought and feeling can pass from man to man.

Speech no doubt knit prehistoric men into groups and enabled them to emerge into history with a social nature and social institutions. But as an instrument of social organization speech has great defects; it lacks range in both time and place. It can go only where the man goes; and though it can pass from man to man, and so from generation to generation, it flows in a slender and wandering stream, limited in capacity, and diverted in direction by every mind through which it passes. What would the New Testament or the works of Plato now be if they had come down to us by this route?

For the precarious strand of oral tradition writing substitutes strong bonds, numerous and indestructible, reaching all times and countries where the art is practiced and binding history firmly together. It makes possible wide political sway, which cannot well be organized and maintained without recorded laws and precise instructions;[1] it permits the advance of science, which is a cumulative achievement that implies the hoarding of knowledge in dusty manuscripts; it is the condition of diversified literature, for tradition, which cannot carry much, limits itself to what is most prized, chiefly stories: writing, in short, may without much exaggeration be said to underlie all social enlargement and individual specialization. It extends immeasurably the environment of all persons who can read and can get hold of the manuscripts; and it permits one to form his own environment by retaining what suits him from a variety of material, and by opening communication with congenial minds in remote times and places. In so doing each individual, of course, becomes a center for the distribution of what he receives, and extends the environment of many others. Mankind thus attains cooperation, continuity and the capacity for rational and enduring progress.

The particular function of printing is to make communication general or democratic. So long as handwriting was the only means of record, books were costly, newspapers were not to be thought of and direct access to the stores of thought and feeling was the privilege of a few. Under such conditions opportunity was like the early sun: it lit up a hilltop here and there, but left the plain in shadow. Printing, to put it otherwise, may not make the stream of knowledge deeper or improve the taste of the water, but it does open a path along the margin and give every one a cup from which to drink. With popular education, which is its natural complement, it forms the principal free institution, without which no other sort of freedom could long endure, and by the aid of which we may hope to gain more freedom than we have.

It is well worth while to reflect what these changes mean to the individual man, born with the aptitude for indefinite development through an imitative an sympathetic nature. Consider, for instance, a group of our ancestors of several thousand years ago, comparatively small, without the art of writing and with little knowledge of other groups. Primitive life is a field fertile in controversy and one not likely to be exhausted; but most students will admit the probability that our distant forefathers lived in small societies, were unlettered and had the vaguest notions about the rest of mankind. Such groups carried on with one another a true struggle for existence; but within each of them—that is, within the range of possible good understanding—there was an active social life. Mothers loved their children and men fought for their chiefs; the thoughts and acts of all were bound together by imitation, the need of approbation and the communicative motive in general. In this social medium were propagated such movements of change as its dimensions permitted. But think of the narrowness of those dimensions, of the paucity of models for imitation, of the extreme vagueness of knowledge regarding the great men of the past and of the total ignorance regarding those of other societies! A meager environment limited the development of innate tendencies and capacities, and the comparative sameness of thought and action reflected the narrowness of the general life.

In such a state of things all the wider social relations must be either hostile or authoritative. Since communication is the precise measure of the possibility of social organization, of good understanding among men, relations that are beyond its range are not truly social, but mechanical. In justice to the past we must recognize that before the rise of printing and telegraphy it was impossible for the mass of people in any large state to have a free and conscious relation to the social whole. The basis for a social consciousness did not exist. People in general could not comprehend what was going on, and their actions were necessarily regulated by authority. The peasant, the common soldier, could not cooperate in the large social movements except as a truck horse cooperates in movements of trade.

If two persons who cannot understand each other come in contact, three things are possible: they can separate, they can fight or one can enslave the other. In the same way, the social groups of the ancient world could ignore one another, wage war or be bound by coercion into a mechanical whole. As the first was usually impracticable, and as mechanical union proved stronger than none, it was the third course that commonly prevailed. This was especially the case after communication was advanced to such a point that the organization of extensive military despotism became practicable. In antiquity a large free state could not be formed, and a small one could not maintain itself.

If we put together these things, this poverty of influences and this habit of war that could be replaced only by something in the way of servitude, we have gone far in explaining the known differences between our remote forefathers and ourselves. They may have been very unlike us, but it is not necessary to suppose that they were, in order to explain their leading unlike lives.

To the man of to-day society, tending now to become a cooperating whole through that extension of knowledge and sympathy which has come with the rise of communication, offers a selection among many environments. In the relation between himself and the rest of mankind he takes more and more an active part, accumulating the elements of a characteristic environment by the working of elective affinity. One may be an imitator—as indeed all must be—and yet unfold, through imitation, a character different from that of every one else. The breadth and diversity of life, dependent upon communication and daily widening before our eyes, ends, in short, to set man free by opening to his sympathetic and conforming nature a "proud choice of influences." He is not merely, as in primitive times, a member of a social group which tends to shape his thought and action; he is the point of intersection of many groups, each of which, though dispersed in time and place, has a real and definite influence upon him. Nowadays one is not less dependent upon social influences than formerly, but he is less dependent upon the particular ones that happen to be nearest him. Every book, every newspaper, every work of sculpture, painting or music to which one has access, every person or lace brought within his reach by the facility of travel, is a shop which he may enter to examine the goods and buy if he will. A million environments solicit him; there is a eager competition in place of monopoly.

It is upon this multiplicity of accessible influences, and not upon any radical change in human nature, that the present variety and comparative freedom of individual development chiefly rest. If one looks at the circle of his acquaintances he sees nothing of the sameness that prevails among savages; each man has distinctive opinions and modes of action, and so appears to stand by himself. This deceptive appearance is due to the fact that social relations are no longer controlled by mere contiguity. Through the arts of intercourse association is throwing off the gross and oppressive bonds of time and place, and substituting congenial relations of sympathy and choice. So, if a man seems to stand alone, it is mostly because he stands with those who are not visible; if he seems not to keep step with the procession, it is probably because, as Thoreau said, he hears a different drummer. We know little of the influences that formed his early imaginations, or of those persons whose approval he now desires and to whose examples and opinions he tries to conform his actions. They are often far distant—his parents and early friends, perhaps, or the leaders of his profession, or book-people—but the fact remains that character and conduct are nourished upon social influences. A reading of autobiographies, or a perusal of those private records which people carry in their memories, would show that mean are still imitators and hero-worshippers. This is particularly true of children, who spend much of their mental life imagining scenes wherein by glorious actions they gain the applause of some persons they admire. And of course the modes of thinking and acting that originate in sympathy and admiration tend, like everything else we do, to become habit, and to persist amid circumstances very different from those in which they began, seeming then to come from self-sufficient personality.

The same conditions favor also the more conspicuous forms of individuality—that is, originality and genius. Originality is not something independent of surroundings, but rather a characteristic way of reacting upon them. Let a man be as original as you please, he can unfold and express his originality only through such influences and materials as are accessible, and the number and variety of these are matters of communication. "We are indeed born with faculties," said Goethe, who gave lifelong study to this matter, "but we owe our development to a thousand influences of the great world, from which we appropriate to ourselves what we can and what is suitable to us." In order to have genius it is essential that a remarkable child shall be born into the world; but an outfit of natural faculties, however remarkable, is only one of two sets of factors whose product is a career. A gifted child, like an acorn, has indeed the capacity of marvelous growth, but can come to nothing unless it finds fit nutriment. The idea of necessary antagonism, between individuality and association is an illusion. The two are mutually dependent: they have always developed, and always must develop, side by side. As a rule, it is not too much association that cramps us, but the wrong kind.

Finally, it is not hard to see how this enlargement of intercourse has affected the processes of social change. Let us go back to the comparison with waves, which, after all, is better than none. As regards the transmission of influences, primitive societies may be likened to narrow strips of water. They extended more in time than in place, but even in the former direction were liable to be cut off by conquest or decay; they were connected with one another by the shallows and marshes of occasional intercourse and by quickly subsiding freshets of federation. Social change was necessarily local, like the waves of such small waters. Modern society, on the other hand, is more like the uninterrupted ocean, upon which the waves of change meet with no obstacles except one another, and roll as high and as far as the propagating impulse can carry them. Thus, to take a conspicuous instance, certain movements in art, letters and philosophy, originating we scarcely know how or where, but attaining great height among the Greeks, rolled on over the unconscious Middle Ages till they struck the contemporaries of Petrarch and thence were propagated in widening circles to the present time. The invention of writing opened the world to the competition of social institutions very much as maritime navigation opened it to the competition of races. The field was enlarged, and all movements proceeded on a great scale.[2]

This extension of the medium of change is accompanied by an equally remarkable differentiation within it, implied in what I have already said about the growth of individuality. There are as many social media as there are specialized groups of sympathetic and communicating individuals, and in choosing his environment a man chooses what groups he will belong to. Each of these groups or media is subject to movements more or less peculiar to itself; it has in some measure its own opinions, institutions and traditions. So, if one wishes to liken modern social movements to waves, he must conceive an indefinite number of wave-transmitting fluids, interpenetrating one another as the light-bearing ether interpenetrates the sound-bearing air; each of these transmitting most readily undulations originating in itself; yet feeling the influence of those originating in the others; each fluid by itself, as well as the united whole, traversed continually by a multitude of waves having every imaginable difference in force, period and direction. Even when so stated the comparison is still inadequate in various ways, chiefly in that it does not suggest the active part that may be taken by individuals. It represents what would happen if each one were in equilibrium, with very congenial relation established; when in fact each of us is continually stirring about more or less in search of the congenial-resisting, refracting or augmenting the social impulse in a way peculiar to himself. Yet, so far as men have like natures that come into sympathy through communication, they really form a sort of fluid in which impulses are propagated by simple suggestion or contact. If two persons of like feeling for form and color stand before a painting, they and the artists are one through the picture.

The freer development of individuals involves, of course, a freer development of the social order; inasmuch as relations of choice—relations that suit the feelings of men—to spread and to prevail over those of hostility or coercion. It is the tendency of communication to give human nature a fair chance, leveling before it the barriers of ignorance, blind hostility and constraint of place, and permitting man to organize his higher sympathetic and aesthetic impulses.

Within the past fifty years there have been developed new means of communication,—fast mails, telegraphs, telephones, photography and the marvels of the daily newspaper,—all tending to hasten and diversify the flow of thought and feeling to multiply the possibilities of social relation. The working of these agencies is too important to be discussed hastily, and to discuss it fully would carry me too far; I shall therefore only point out that they make all influences quicker in transmission and more general in their incidence, accessible at a greater distance and to a larger proportion of people. So far as concerns the general character of social change, the effect may be described as a more perfect liquefaction of the social medium. A thick, inelastic liquid, like tar or molasses, will transmit only comparatively large waves; but in water the large waves bear upon their surface countless wavelets and ripple of all sizes and directions. So if we were to compare the society of to-day with that of fifty years ago, we should find that great changes are somewhat facilitated, and that there is added to them a multitude of small changes which in former times could not have extended beyond the reach of personal contact. Light ripples now run far: the latest fashion in coats or books permeates the back counties and encircles the earth.

The process of change that I have described involves selection, and is perhaps as natural as anything else. Hence we may, if we choose, call it natural selection. It comes about through the competition of influences and the propagation of opportune innovations in thought and action. The selective principle, the arbiter of competition, is ever human nature—but human nature conditioned in its choices by the state of communication, which determines what influences are accessible, as well as by the constraining momentum of its own past.

Notes

1. I believe there is no instance of a people which has attained a definite, extended and stable political organization without the use of some form of writing. Compare Gibbon's observation in the Decline and Fall, vol. i p. 354 (Milman-Smith edition).

2. There is no better illustration of this than the rise of vast religious systems based upon the recorded lives and maxims of their founders. It is quite possible that individuals of transcendent character appeared in prehistoric times; but the imitation of them could not be organized into extensive and enduring systems without the aid of authentic records.

2

The House of Dreams

From *The Spirit of Youth and the City Streets* (1909)

Jane Addams

Jane Addams (1860–1935) was one of the most important American social reformers of the late nineteenth and early twentieth centuries. From 1889 to her death, she ran Hull House, a settlement house in Chicago for newly arrived immigrants and the downtrodden, designed to combat social disorganization and the disruptions of modernity. A suffragist, feminist, antiracist, pacificist, and cofounder of the American Civil Liberties Union, she shared the Nobel Peace Prize in 1931. A contemporary and friend of John Dewey, she worked in close collaboration with the first generation of University of Chicago sociologists and even declined a position in the university's department of sociology, offered to her by its founder, Albion Small. A prolific author, she was both a social activist and a social theorist. She fought for compulsory education and against child labor laws.

Like most progressives and first-generation Chicago sociologists, Addams's vision of the good society was both intensely democratic and somewhat moralistic. In this selection, from her book *The Spirit of Youth and the City Streets* (1909), Addams explores the dangers of the theater for the moral welfare of girls and young women who were allowed to give themselves over to fantasy without supervision (cf. Peiss 1987). Her concern about popular entertainment and youth is, of course, part of a much longer tradition that continues into our own day. Like many others after her, Addams distrusted media that she believed to promote antisocial behavior by encouraging flights of fancy among socially vulnerable audience members. At the same time, like other progressives, she valued newspapers as democratic and socially enlarging forces that fostered community among different classes.

To the preoccupied adult who is prone to use the city street as a mere passageway from one hurried duty to another, nothing is more touching than his encounter with a group of children and young people who are emerging from a theater with the magic of the play still thick upon them. They look up and down the familiar street scarcely recognizing it and quite unable to determine the direction of home. From a tangle of "make believe" they gravely scrutinize the real world which they are so reluctant to reenter, reminding one of the absorbed gaze of a child who is groping his way back from fairly-land whither the story has completely transported him.

"Going to the show" for thousands of young people in every industrial city is the only possible road to the realms of mystery and romance; the theater is the only place where they can satisfy that craving for a conception of life higher than that which the actual world offers them. In a very real sense the drama and the drama alone performs for them the office of art as is clearly revealed in their blundering demand stated in many forms for "a play unlike life." The theater becomes to them a "veritable house of dreams" infinitely more real than the noisy streets and the crowded factories.

This first simple demand upon the theater for romance is closely allied to one more complex which might be described as a search for solace and distraction in those moments of first awakening from the glamour of a youth's interpretation of life to the sterner realities which are thrust upon his consciousness. These perceptions which inevitably "close around" and imprison the spirit of youth are perhaps never so grim as in the case of the wage-earning child. We can all recall our own moments of revolt against life's actualities, our reluctance to admit that all life was to be as unheroic and uneventful as that which we saw about us, it was too unbearable that "this was all there was" and we tried every possible avenue of escape. As we made an effort to believe, in spite of what we saw, that life was noble and harmonious, as we stubbornly clung to poesy in contradiction to the testimony of our senses, so we see thousands of young people thronging the theaters bent in their turn upon the same quest. The drama provides a transition between the romantic conceptions which they vainly struggle to keep intact and life's cruelties and trivialities which they refuse to admit. A child whose imagination has been cultivated is able to do this for himself through reading and reverie, but for the overworked city youth of meager education, perhaps nothing but the theater is able to perform this important office.

The theater also has a strange power to forecast life for the youth. Each boy comes from our ancestral past not "in entire forgetfulness," and quite as he unconsciously uses ancient war-cries in his street play, so he longs to reproduce and to see set before him the valors and vengeances of a society embodying a much more primitive state of morality than that in which he finds himself. Mr. Patten has pointed out that the elemental action which the stage presents, the old emotions of love and jealousy, of revenge and daring take the thoughts of the spectator back into deep and well worn channels in which his mind runs with a sense of rest afforded by nothing else. The cheap drama brings cause and effect, will power and action, once more into relation and gives a man the thrilling conviction that he may yet be master of his fate. The youth of course, quite unconscious of this psychology, views the deeds of the hero simply as a forecast of his own future and it is this fascinating view of his own career which draws the boy to "shows" of all sorts. They can scarcely be too improbable for him, portraying, as they do, his belief in his own prowess. A series of slides which has lately been very popular in the five-cent theaters of Chicago, portrayed five masked men breaking into a humble dwelling, killing the father of the family and carrying away the family treasure. The golden-haired son of the house, aged seven, vows eternal vengeance on the spot, and follows one villain after another to his doom. The execution of each is shown in lurid detail, and the last slide of the series depicts the hero, aged ten, kneeling upon his father's grave counting on the fingers of one hand the number of men that he has killed, and thanking God that he has been permitted to be an instrument of vengeance.

In another series of slides, a poor woman is wearily bending over some sewing, a baby is crying in the cradle, and two little boys of nine and ten are asking for food. In despair the mother sends them out into the street to beg, but instead they steal a revolver from a pawn shop and with it kill a Chinese laundryman, robbing him of $200. They rush home with the treasure which is found by the mother in the baby's cradle, whereupon she and her sons fall upon their knees and send up a prayer of thankfulness for this timely and heaven-sent assistance.

Is it not astounding that a city allows thousands of its youth to fill their impressionable minds with these absurdities which certainly will become the foundation for their working moral codes and the data from which they will judge the properties of life?

It is as if a child, starved at home, should be forced to go out and search for food, selecting, quite naturally, not that which is nourishing but that which is exciting and appealing to his outward sense, often in his ignorance and foolishness blundering into substances which are filthy and poisonous.

Out of my twenty years' experience at Hull-House I can recall all sorts of pilferings, petty larcenies, and even burglaries, due to that never ceasing effort on the part of boys to procure theater tickets. I can also recall indirect efforts towards the same end which are most pitiful. I remember the remorse of a young girl of fifteen who was brought into the Juvenile Court after a

night spent weeping in the cellar of her home because she had stolen a mass of artificial flowers with which to trim a hat. She stated that she had taken the flowers because she was afraid of losing the attention of a young man whom she had heard say that "a girl has to be dressy if she expects to be seen." This young man was the only one who had ever taken her to the theater and if he failed her, she was sure that she would never go again, and she sobbed out incoherently that she "couldn't live at all without it." Apparently the blankness and grayness of life itself had been broken for her only by the portrayal of a different world.

One boy whom I had known from babyhood began to take money from his mother from the time he was seven years old, and after he was ten she regularly gave him money for the play Saturday evening. However, the Saturday performance, "starting him off like," he always went twice again on Sunday, procuring the money in all sorts of illicit ways. Practically all of his earnings after he was fourteen were spent in this way to satisfy the insatiable desire to know of the great adventures of the wide world which the more fortunate boy takes out in reading Homer and Stevenson.

In talking with his mother, I was reminded of my experience one Sunday afternoon in Russia when the employees of a large factory were seated in an open-air theater, watching with breathless interest the presentation of folk stories. I was told that troupes of actors went from one manufacturing establishment to another presenting the simple elements of history and literature to the illiterate employees. This tendency to slake the thirst for adventure by viewing the drama is, of course, but a blind and primitive effort in the direction of culture, for "he who makes himself its vessel and bearer thereby acquires a freedom from the blindness and soul poverty of daily existence."

It is partly in response to this need that more sophisticated young people often go to the theater, hoping to find a clue to life's perplexities. Many times the bewildered hero reminds one of Emerson's description of Margaret Fuller, "I don't know where I am going, follow me"; nevertheless, the stage is dealing with the moral themes in which the public is most interested.

And while many young people go to the theater if only to see represented, and to hear discussed, the themes which seem to them so tragically important, there is no doubt that what they hear there, flimsy and poor as it often is, easily becomes their actual moral guide. In moments of moral crisis they turn to the sayings of the hero who found himself in a similar plight. The sayings may not be profound, but at least they are applicable to conduct. In the last few years scores of plays have been put upon the stage whose titles might be easily translated into proper headings for sociological lectures or sermons, without including the plays of Ibsen, Shaw and Hauptmann, which deal so directly with moral issues that the moralists themselves wince under their teachings and declare them brutal. But it is this very brutality which the over-refined and complicated city dwellers often crave. Moral teaching has become so intricate, creeds so metaphysical, that in a state of absolute reaction they demand definite instruction for daily living. Their whole-hearted acceptance of the teaching corroborates the statement recently made by an English playwright that "The theater is literally making the minds of our urban populations today. It is a huge factory of sentiment, of character, of points of honor, of conceptions of conduct, of everything that finally determines the destiny of a nation. The theater is not only a place of amusement, it is a place of culture, a place where people learn how to think, act, and feel." Seldom, however, do we associate the theater with our plans for civic righteousness, although it has become so important a factor in city life.

* * *

Already some American cities are making a beginning toward more adequate public recreation. Boston has its municipal gymnasiums, cricket fields, and golf grounds. Chicago has seventeen parks with playing fields, gymnasiums and baths, which at present enroll thousands of young people. These same parks are provided with beautiful halls which are used for many purposes, rent free, and are given over to any group of young people who wish to conduct dancing parties subject to city supervision and chaperonage. Many social clubs have deserted neighboring saloon halls for these municipal drawing rooms beautifully decorated with growing plants supplied by the park greenhouses, and flooded with electric lights supplied by the park power house. In the saloon halls the young people were obliged to "pass money freely over the bar," and in order to make the most of the occasion they usually stayed until morning. At such times

the economic necessity itself would override the counsels of the more temperate, and the thrifty door keeper would not insist upon invitations but would take in any one who had the "price of a ticket." The free rent in the park hall, the good food in the park restaurant, supplied at cost, have made three parties closing at eleven o'clock no more expensive than one party breaking up at daylight, too often in disorder.

Is not this an argument that the drinking, the late hours, the lack of decorum, are directly traceable to the commercial enterprise which ministers to pleasure in order to drag it into excess because excess is more profitable? To thus commercialize pleasure is as monstrous as it is to commercialize art. It is intolerable that the city does not take over this function of making provision for pleasure, as wise communities in Sweden and South Carolina have taken the sale of alcohol out of the hands of enterprising publicans.

We are only beginning to understand what might be done through the festival, the street procession, the band of marching musicians, orchestral music in public squares or parks, with the magic power they all possess to formulate the sense of companionship and solidarity. The experiments which are being made in public schools to celebrate the national holidays, the changing seasons, the birthdays of heroes, the planting of trees, are slowly developing little ceremonials which may in time work out into pageants of genuine beauty and significance. No other nation has so unparalleled an opportunity to do this through its schools as we have, for no other nation has so wide-spreading a school system, while the enthusiasm of children and their natural ability to express their emotions through symbols, gives the securest possible foundation to this growing effort.

The city schools of New York have effected the organization of high school girls into groups for folk dancing. These old forms of dancing which have been worked out in many lands and through long experiences, safeguard unwary and dangerous expression and yet afford a vehicle through which the gaiety of youth may flow. Their forms are indeed those which lie at the basis of all good breeding, forms which at once express and restrain, urge forward and set limits.

One may also see another center of growth for public recreation and the beginning of a pageantry for the people in the many small parks and athletic fields which almost every American city is hastening to provide for its young. These small parks have innumerable athletic teams, each with its distinctive uniform, with track meets and match games arranged with the teams from other parks and from the public schools; choruses of trade unionists or of patriotic societies fill the park halls with eager listeners. Labor Day processions are yearly becoming more carefully planned and more picturesque in character, as the desire to make an overwhelming impression with mere size gives way to a growing ambition to set forth the significance of the craft and the skill of the workman. At moments they almost rival the dignified showing of the processions of the German Turn Vereins which are also often seen in our city streets.

The many foreign colonies which are found in all American cities afford an enormous reserve of material for public recreation and street festival. They not only celebrate the feasts and holidays of the fatherland, but have each their own public expression for their mutual benefit societies and for the observance of American anniversaries. From the gay celebration of the Scandinavians when war was averted and two neighboring nations were united, to the equally gay celebration of the centenary of Garibaldi's birth; from the Chinese dragon cleverly trailing its way through the streets, to the Greek banners flung out in honor of immortal heroes, there is an infinite variety of suggestions and possibilities for public recreation and for the corporate expression of stirring emotions. After all, what is the function of art but to preserve in permanent and beautiful form those emotions and solaces which cheer life and make it kindlier, more heroic and easier to comprehend; which lift the mind of the worker from the harshness and loneliness of his task, and, by connecting him with what has gone before, free him from a sense of isolation and hardship?

Were American cities really eager for municipal art, they would cherish as genuine beginnings the tarantella danced so interminably at Italian weddings; the primitive Greek pipe played throughout the long summer nights; the Bohemian theaters crowded with eager Slavophiles; the Hungarian musicians strolling from street to street; the fervid oratory of the young Russian preaching social righteousness in the open square.

Many Chicago citizens who attended the first annual meeting of the National Playground Association of America, will never forget the long summer day in the large playing field filled during the morning with hundreds of little children romping through the kindergarten game, in the afternoon with the young men and girls contending in athletic sports; and the evening light made gay by the bright colored garments of Italians, Lithuanians, Norwegians, and a dozen other nationalities, reproducing their old dances and festivals for the pleasure of the more stolid Americans. Was this a forecast of what we may yet see accomplished through a dozen agencies promoting public recreation which are springing up in every city of America, as they already are found in the large towns of Scotland and England?

Let us cherish these experiments as the most precious beginnings of an attempt to supply the recreational needs of our industrial cities. To fail to provide for the recreation of youth, is not only to deprive all of them of their natural form of expression, but is certain to subject some of them to the overwhelming temptation of illicit and soul-destroying pleasures. To insist that young people shall forecast their rose-colored future only in a house of dreams, is to deprive the real world of that warmth and reassurance which it so sorely needs and to which it is justly entitled; furthermore, we are left outside with a sense of dreariness, in company with that shadow which already lurks only around the corner for most of us—a skepticism of life's value.

3

From *Winesburg, Ohio* (1919)

Sherwood Anderson

Not only was Sherwood Anderson (1876–1941) a master of the short-story form, but he was also one of the most influential writers of early-twentieth-century America. His *Winesburg, Ohio* (1919) was a breakthrough in its format—several interlinked narratives of diverse characters in one small town—and its poignant picture of yearning and struggle among ordinary people. This brief excerpt from the story called "Godliness" provides one of the most compressed accounts of the historical transformations that American society lived through during the progressive era, and—quite like the work of Addams, Cooley, Dewey, and others—it places mass media at the center of those transformations.

In the last fifty years a vast change has taken place in the lives of our people. A revolution has in fact taken place. The coming of industrialism, attended by all the roar and rattle of affairs, the shrill cries of millions of new voices that have come among us from overseas, the going and coming of trains, the growth of cities, the building of the interurban car lines that weave in and out of towns and past farmhouses, and now in these later days the coming of the automobiles has worked a tremendous change in the lives and in the habits of thought of our people of Mid-America. Books, badly imagined and written though they may be in the hurry of our times, are in every household, magazines circulate by the millions of copies, newspapers are everywhere. In our day a farmer standing by the stove in the store in his village has his mind filled to overflowing with the words of other men. The newspapers and the magazines have pumped him full. Much of the old brutal ignorance that had in it also a kind of beautiful childlike innocence is gone forever. The farmer by the stove is brother to the men of the cities, and if you listen you will find him talking as glibly and as senselessly as the best city man of us all.

4

From the *Introduction to the Science of Sociology* (1921)

Robert Ezra Park and Ernest W. Burgess

Robert Ezra Park (1864–1944) was a man of both the small town and the great city. Park was raised in Red Wing, Minnesota, and his father was a successful small-business owner. Although Park ran with a gang that roamed the rougher sections of town, he also voraciously consumed dime novels and was a sympathetic reader of the religious freethinker Robert Ingersoll. He graduated from the University of Michigan, where he studied with John Dewey, and then, in the late 1880s, he entered the rough-and-tumble world of urban journalism, first in Denver and then in New York. A great admirer of Walt Whitman, Park loved strolling the city streets, and his firsthand experience gave him a sense of the city as a living organism. In 1898, Park went to Harvard, where he took classes from William James, and from 1899 to 1904 he studied in Berlin, where he heard lectures from the great sociologist Georg Simmel and wrote an important dissertation, *Masse und Publikum* (Crowd and Public; 1904). Disillusioned with academic life and seeking something other than a university position, Park became active in African American reform efforts before moving to Tuskegee, Alabama, and becoming the press and publicity agent for Booker T. Washington and his Tuskegee Institute. In 1913, at the age of forty-nine, Park took his first academic job, in the sociology department of the University of Chicago. He remained there until his retirement in 1933, training some of the leading social scientists of the next generation, including Louis Wirth, E. Franklin Frazier, Everett Hughes, and Harold Lasswell (the latter of whom Park considered to be one of the best students he ever taught). Park wrote widely on race and ethnicity, urban life, "social ecology" (a term he coined), newspapers, and the place of communication in society.

Ernest W. Burgess (1886–1966) was born in Tilbury, Ontario, but he came to the United States in 1888, where, as the son of a Congregational minister, he grew up in the Southwest and later in the Midwest. He took his bachelor of arts from Kingfisher College in Oklahoma before going to the University of Chicago, where he took his doctorate in 1913. After teaching stints at the University of Kansas and Ohio State, Burgess returned to Chicago in 1916, where he remained until he became an emeritus professor in 1957. Burgess was an eclectic researcher with strong empirical interests who believed that social sciences should aim at prediction. A genial man who played important institutional roles in the development of American sociology, Burgess wrote broadly on family, criminology, recreation, and urban ecology.

These excerpts come from Park and Burgess's *Introduction to the Science of Sociology* (1921), known as the "green bible" to two generations of students at the University of Chicago and elsewhere. It is at once a compendium of short selections from other writers, a textbook, and an interpretive synthesis of sociology in the immediate post–World War I era. A thousand-plus-page book, it sold more than thirty thousand copies before it went out of print in 1943. Secondhand copies were passed from one generation to the next, in the United States and abroad, and wherever it was taught, it came to represent Chicago sociology. It was

Park who was the leader in planning and writing the book, and the first chapter presents his vision of sociology and social research. The first excerpt, "Publicity as a Form of Secondary Contact," provides suggestive thumbnail interpretations of press agents, research bureaus, educational campaigns, public opinion, and newspapers; and their role in "social control," as the maintenance of social order was called in those days. It also offers an early agenda for public opinion research. The second excerpt shows the central place accorded to "communication" in classic Chicago sociology and provides a basic map for what later became known as "symbolic interactionism" (showing its roots in Simmel and not just George Herbert Mead). It also gives a sense of the cosmopolitan intellectual flavor of the green bible—with references to Simmel, Darwin, Durkheim, and many others who were excerpted (among hundreds of others) in the book—and of the central place accorded printing, books, and newspapers by much progressive social thought.

Publicity as a Form of Secondary Contact[1]

In contrast with the political machine, which has founded its organized action on the local, personal, and immediate interest represented by the different neighborhoods and localities, the good-government organizations, the bureaus of municipal research, and the like have sought to represent the interests of the city as a whole and have appealed to a sentiment and opinion neither local nor personal. These agencies have sought to secure efficiency and good government by the education of the voter, that is to say, by investigating and publishing the facts regarding the government.

In this way publicity has come to be a recognized form of social control, and advertising—"social advertising"—has become a profession with an elaborate technique supported by a body of special knowledge.

It is one of the characteristic phenomena of city life and of society founded on secondary relationships that advertising should have come to occupy so important a place in its economy.

In recent years every individual and organization which has had to deal with the public, that is to say, the public outside the smaller and more intimate communities of the village and small town, has come to have its press agent, who is often less an advertising man than a diplomatic man accredited to the newspapers, and through them to the world at large. Institutions like the Russell Sage Foundation, and to a less extent the General Education Board, have sought to influence public opinion directly through the medium of publicity. The Carnegie Report upon Medical Education, the Pittsburgh Survey, the Russell Sage Foundation Report on Comparative Costs of Public-School Education in the Several States, are something more than scientific reports. They are rather a high form of journalism, dealing with existing conditions critically, and seeking through the agency of publicity to bring about radical reforms. The work of the Bureau of Municipal Research in New York had a similar practical purpose. To these must be added the work accomplished by the child-welfare exhibits, by the social surveys undertaken in different parts of the country, and by similar propaganda in favor of public health.

As a source of social control public opinion becomes important in societies founded on secondary relationships of which great cities are a type. In the city every social group tends to create its own milieu, and, as these conditions become fixed, the mores tend to accommodate themselves to the conditions thus created. In secondary groups and in the city, fashion tends to take the place of custom, and public opinion rather than the mores becomes the dominant force in social control.

In any attempt to understand the nature of public opinion and its relation to social control, it is important to investigate, first of all, the agencies and devices which have come into practical use in the effort to control, enlighten, and exploit it.

The first and most important of these is the press, that is, the daily newspaper and other forms of current literature, including books classed as current.

After the newspaper, the bureaus of research which are now springing up in all the large cities are the most interesting and the most promising devices for using publicity as a means of control.

The fruits of these investigations do not reach the public directly, but are disseminated through the medium of the press, the pulpit and other sources of popular enlightenment.

In addition to these, there are the educational campaigns in the interest of better health conditions, the child-welfare exhibits, and the numerous "social advertising" devices which are now employed, sometimes upon the initiative of private societies, sometimes upon that of popular magazines or newspapers, in order to educate the public and enlist the masses of the people in the movement for the improvement of conditions of community life.

The newspaper is the great medium of communication within the city, and it is on the basis of the information which it supplies that public opinion rests. The first function which a newspaper supplies is that which was formerly performed by the village gossip.

In spite, however, of the industry with which newspapers pursue facts of personal intelligence and human interest, they cannot compete with the village gossips as a means of social control. For one thing, the newspaper maintains some reservations not recognized by gossip, in the matters of personal intelligence. For example, until they run for office or commit some other overt act that brings them before the public conspicuously, the private life of individual men or women is a subject that is for the newspaper taboo. It is not so with gossip, partly because in a small community no individual is so obscure that his private affairs escape observation and discussion; partly because the field is smaller. In small communities there is a perfectly amazing amount of personal information afloat among the individuals who compose them.

The absence of this in city is what, in large part, makes the city what it is.

Classification of the Materials

The material in this chapter will be considered here under three main heads: (*a*) society as interaction, (*b*) communication as the medium of interaction, and (*c*) imitation and suggestion as mechanisms of interaction.

(*a*) *Society as interaction.* Society stated in mechanistic terms reduces to interaction. A person is a member of society so long as he responds to social forces; when interaction ends, he is isolated and detached; he ceases to be a person and becomes a "lost soul." This is the reason that the limits of society are coterminous with the limits of interaction, that is, of the participation of persons in the life of society. One way of measuring the wholesome or the normal life of a person is by the sheer external fact of his membership in the social groups of the community in which his lot is cast.

Simmel has illustrated in a wide survey of concrete detail how interaction defines the group in time and space. Through contacts of historical continuity, the life of society extends backward to prehistoric eras. More potent over group behavior than contemporary discovery and invention is the control exerted by the "dead hand of the past" through the inertia of folkways and mores, through the revival of memories and sentiments and through the persistence of tradition and culture. Contacts of mobility, on the other hand, define the area of the interaction of the members of the group in space. The degree of departure from accepted ideas and modes of behavior and the extent of sympathetic approach to the strange and the novel largely depend upon the rate, the number, and the intensity of the contacts of mobility.

(*b*) *Communication as the medium of social interaction.* Each science postulates its own medium of interaction. Astronomy and physics assume a hypothetical substance, the ether. Physics has its principles of molar action and reaction; chemistry studies molecular interaction. Biology and medicine direct their research to the physiological interaction of organisms. Psychology is concerned with the behavior of the individual organism in terms of the interaction of stimuli and responses. Sociology, as collective psychology, deals with communication. Sociologists have referred to this process as intermental stimulation and response.

The readings on communication are so arranged as to make clear the three natural levels of interaction: (*x*) that of the senses; (*y*) that of the emotions; and (*z*) that of sentiments and ideas.

Interaction through sense-perceptions and emotional responses may be termed the natural forms of communication since they are common to man and to animals. Simmel's interpretation of interaction through the senses is suggestive of the subtle, unconscious, yet profound, way in which personal attitudes are formed. Not alone vision, but hearing, smell and touch exhibit in varying degrees the emotional responses of the type of appreciation. This means understanding other persons or objects on the perceptual basis.

The selections from Darwin and from Morgan upon emotional expression in animals indicate how natural expressive signs become a vehicle for communication. A prepossession for speech and ideas blinds man to the important role in human conduct still exerted by emotional communication, facial expression, and gesture. Blushing and laughter are peculiarly significant, because these forms of emotional response are distinctively human. To say that a person blushes when he is self-conscious, that he laughs when he is detached from, and superior to, and yet interested in, an occurrence means that blushing and laughter represent contrasted attitudes to a social situation. The relation of blushing and laughter to social control, as an evidence of the emotional dependence of the person upon the group, is at its apogee in adolescence.

Interaction through sensory impressions and emotional expression is restricted to the communication of attitudes and feelings. The selections under the heading "Language and the Communication of Ideas" bring out the uniquely human character of speech. Concepts, as Max Müller insists, are the common symbols wrought out in social experience. They are more or less conventionalized, objective, and intelligible symbols that have been defined in terms of a common experience or, as the logicians say, of a universe of discourse. Every group has its own universe of discourse. In short, to use Durkheim's phrase, concepts are "collective representations."

History has been variously conceived in terms of great events, epoch-making personalities, social movements, and cultural changes. From the point of view of sociology social evolution might profitably be studied in its relation to the development and perfection of the means and technique of communication. How revolutionary was the transition from word of mouth and memory to written records! The beginnings of ancient civilization with its five independent centers in Egypt, the Euphrates River Valley, China, Mexico, and Peru appear to be inextricably bound up with the change from pictographs to writing, that is to say from symbols representing words to symbols representing sounds. The modern period began with the invention of printing and the printing press. As books became the possession of the common man the foundation was laid for experiments in democracy. From the sociological standpoint the book is an organized objective mind whose thoughts are accessible to all. The role of the book in social life has long been recognized but not fully appreciated. The Christian church, to be sure, regards the Bible as the word of God. The army does not question the infallibility of the Manual of Arms. Our written Constitution has been termed "the ark of the covenant." The orthodox Socialist appeals in unquestioning faith to the ponderous tomes of Marx.

World-society of today, which depends upon the almost instantaneous communication of events and opinion around the world, rest upon the invention of telegraphy and the laying of the great ocean cables. Wireless telegraphy and radio have only perfected these earlier means and render impossible a monopoly or a censorship of inter-communication between peoples. The traditional cultures, the social inheritances of ages of isolation, are now in a world-process of interaction and modification as a result of the rapidity and the impact of these modern means of the circulation of ideas and sentiments. At the present time it is so popular to malign the newspaper that few recognize the extent to which news has freed mankind from the control of political parties, social institutions, and. It may be added, from the "tyranny" of books.

Note

1. From Robert E. Park, "The City," in the *American Journal of Sociology* XX (1914–1915): 604–7.

5

Nature, Communication, and Meaning

From *Experience and Nature* (1925)

John Dewey

John Dewey (1859–1852) was probably America's most influential philosopher in the first half of the twentieth century. One of his students, Randolph Bourne, wrote that Dewey's teaching seemed like "the American religion." Dewey's characteristic themes of democracy, science, progress, experimentation fit well (too well, for some of his critics) with the social changes and hustle-bustle of America in the industrial era. During his long and prolific life, Dewey taught at the University of Michigan, the University of Chicago, and Columbia University. One of his most consistent interests was communication, a theme he explored in his early educational philosophy and one that blossomed in the 1920s and 1930s in such works as *Reconstruction in Philosophy* (1921), *Experience and Nature* (1925), *The Public and Its Problems* (1927), and *Art as Experience* (1934).

For Dewey, communication is a social, political, and aesthetic principle. Communication joins people in community associations; it works not by transporting the private thoughts of people's minds but by making people share in the making of a common life. Not only is it an instrumental activity aimed at getting things done, but it is a pleasurable end in itself, a way of simply enjoying the experience of being alive together. In his view that art is a form of communication and communication is a form of art, Dewey provides us with one of the lasting ideals of how communication ought to work. This brief excerpt provides a few pieces of the puzzle of how communication, art, experience, community, and democracy fit together.

A useful resource on Dewey is the John Dewey Center at Southern Illinois University, available at www.siu.edu/~deweyctr/.

Of all affairs, communication is the most wonderful. That things should be able to pass from the plane of external pushing and pulling to that of revealing themselves to man, and thereby to themselves; and that the fruit of communication should be participation, sharing, is a wonder by the side of which transubstantiation pales. When communication occurs, all natural events are subject to reconsideration and revision; they are re-adapted to meet the requirements of conversation, whether it be public discourse or that preliminary discourse termed thinking. Events turn into objects, things with a meaning. They may be referred to when they do not exist, and thus be operative among things distant in space and time, through vicarious presence in a new medium. Brute efficiencies and inarticulate consummations as soon as they can be spoken of are liberated from local and accidental contexts, and are eager for naturalization in any non-insulated, communicating, part of the world. Events when once they are named lead an independent and double life. In addition to their original existence, they are subject to ideal experimentation: their meanings may be infinitely combined and re-arranged in imagination, and the outcome of this inner experimentation—which is thought—may issue forth in interaction with crude or raw events. Meanings having been deflected from the rapid and roaring stream of events into a calm

35

and traversable canal, rejoin the main stream, and color, temper and compose its course. Where communication exists, things in acquiring meaning, thereby acquire representatives, surrogates, signs and implicates, which are infinitely more amenable to management, more permanent and more accommodating, than events in their first estate.

By this fashion, qualitative immediacies cease to be dumbly rapturous, a possession that is obsessive and an incorporation that involves submergence: conditions found in sensations and passions. They become capable of survey, contemplation, and ideal or logical elaboration; when something can be said of qualities they are purveyors of instruction. Learning and teaching come into being, and there is no event which may not yield information. A directly enjoyed thing adds to itself meaning, and enjoyment is thereby idealized. Even the dumb pang of an ache achieves a significant existence when it can be designated and descanted upon; it ceases to be merely oppressive and becomes important; it gains importance, because it becomes representative; it has the dignity of an office.

In view of these increments and transformations, it is not surprising that meanings, under the name of forms and essences, have often been hailed as modes of Being beyond and above spatial and temporal existence, invulnerable to vicissitude; nor that thought as their possession has been treated as a nonnatural spiritual energy, disjoined from all that is empirical. Yet there is a natural bridge that joins the gap between existence and essence; namely communication, language, discourse. Failure to acknowledge the presence and operation of natural interaction in the form of communication creates the gulf between existence and essence, and that gulf is factitious and gratuitous.

6

The Disenchanted Man

From *The Phantom Public* (1925)

Walter Lippmann

Walter Lippmann (1889–1974) helped to define the role of public intellectual in twentieth-century America. Born in New York City to a well-to-do family of second-generation German-Jewish immigrants, Lippmann graduated from Harvard in the class of 1909, which included the modernist poet T. S. Eliot and the radical journalist John Reed. After studying with Harvard philosophers William James and George Santayana, Lippmann entered the world of journalism, helping to found the *New Republic*, where he served as associate editor from 1914 to 1921. From the 1920s through the 1960s, he was one of the leading voices in American life as a newspaper correspondent, syndicated columnist, and author of a number of books that drew audiences of scholars, political leaders, and the broader public. Younger than the first-generation progressives, Lippmann was part of a generation of "democratic realists" who in the 1920s helped to debunk the classic ideals of the rational, engaged, and well-informed citizen as the basis of democratic politics.

In *Public Opinion* (1922), his most famous and influential work, Lippmann argues that the ideal of a citizenry well informed through the news was unrealistic, and he shifts burdens of governance onto experts and decision makers. *The Phantom Public* (1925) extends that critique and reveals Lippmann's growing cynicism about a democracy of popular information and the media that are supposed to underwrite it. Lippmann's style shines in this excerpt from that latter work where he depicts bystander citizens disconnected from the affairs of public life, barely able to stay awake yet barraged by eclectic information.

The private citizen today has come to feel rather like a deaf spectator in the back row, who ought to keep his mind on the mystery off there, but cannot quite manage to keep awake. He knows he is somehow affected by what is going on. Rules and regulations continually, taxes annually and wars occasionally remind him that he is being swept along by great drifts of circumstance.

Yet these public affairs are in no convincing way his affairs. They are for the most part invisible. They are managed, if they are managed at all, at distant centers, from behind the scenes, by unnamed powers. As a private person he does not know for certain what is going on, or who is doing it, or where he is being carried. No newspaper reports his environment so that he can grasp it; no school has taught him how to imagine it; his ideals, often, do not fit with it; listening to speeches, uttering opinions and voting do not, he finds, enable him to govern it. He lives in a world which he cannot see, does not understand and is unable to direct.

In the cold light of experience he knows that his sovereignty is a fiction. He reigns in theory, but in fact he does not govern. Contemplating himself and his actual accomplishments in public affairs, contrasting the influence he exerts with the influence his is supposed according to democratic theory to exert, he must say of his sovereignty what Bismarck said of Napoleon III: "At a distance it is something, but close to it is nothing at all."[1] When, during an agitation of some sort, say a political campaign, he hears himself and some thirty million others described as the source of all wisdom and power and righteousness, the prime mover and the ultimate goal, the remnants of sanity in him protest. He cannot all the time play Chanticleer who was so dazzled and delighted because he himself had caused the sun to rise.

For when the private man has lived through the romantic age in politics and is no longer moved by the stale echoes of its hot cries, when he is sober and unimpressed, his own part in public affairs appears to him a pretentious thing, a second rate, an inconsequential. You cannot move him then with a good straight talk about service and civic duty, nor by waving a flag in his face, nor by sending a boy scout after him to make him vote. He is a man back home from a crusade to make the world something or other it did not become; he has been tantalized too often by the foam of events, has seen the gas go out of it, and, with sour derision for the stuff, he is saying with the author of *Trivia:*[2]

"'Self-determination,' one of them insisted.

"'Arbitration,' cried another.

"'Cooperation,' suggested the mildest of the party.

"'Confiscation,' answered an uncompromising female.

"I, too became intoxicated with the sound of these vocables. And were they not the cure for all our ills?

"'Inoculation!' I chimed in. 'Transubstantiation, alliteration, inundation, flagellation, and afforestation!'"

It is well known that nothing like the whole people takes part in public affairs. Of the eligible voters in the United States less than half go to the polls even in a presidential year.[3] During the campaign of 1924 a special effort was made to bring out more voters. They did not come out. The Constitution, the nation, the party system, the presidential succession, private property, all were supposed to be in danger. One party prophesied red ruin, another black corruption, a third tyranny and imperialism if the voters did not go to the polls in greater numbers. Half the citizenship was unmoved.

The students used to write books about voting. They are now beginning to write books about nonvoting. At the University of Chicago Professor Merriam and Mr. Gosnell have made an elaborate inquiry[4] into the reason why, at the typical Chicago mayoral election of 1923, there were, out of 1,400,000 eligible electors, only 9000,000 who registered, and out of those who registered there were only 723,000 who finally managed to vote. Thousands of persons were interviewed. About 30 per cent of the abstainers had, or at least claimed to have had, an insuperable difficulty about going to the polls. They were ill, they were absent from the city, they were women detained at home by a child or an invalid, they had had insufficient legal residence. The other 70 per cent, representing about half a million free and sovereign citizens of the Republic, did not even pretend to have a reason for not voting, which, in effect, was not an admission that they did not care about voting. They were needed at their work, the polls were crowded, the polls were inconveniently located, they were afraid to tell their age, they did not believe in woman suffrage, the husband objected, politics is rotten, elections are rotten, they were afraid to vote, they did not know there was an election. About a quarter of those who were interviewed had the honesty to say they were wholly uninterested.

Yet Bryce is authority for the statement that "the will of the sovereign people is expressed . . . in the United States . . . by as large a proportion of the registered voters as in any other country."[5] And certainly Mr. Lowell's tables on the use of the initiative and referendum in Switzerland in the main support the view that the indifference of the American voter is not unique.[6] In fact, realistic political thinkers in Europe long ago abandoned the notion that the collective mass of the people direct the course of public affairs. Robert Michels, himself a Socialist, says flatly that "the majority is permanently incapable of self-government,"[7] and quotes approvingly the remark of a Swedish Socialist Deputy, Gustaf F. Steffen, that "even after the victory there will always remain in political life the leaders and the led." Michels, who is a political thinker of great penetration, unburdens himself finally on the subject by printing a remark of Hertzen's that the victory of an opposition party amounts to "passing from the sphere of envy to the sphere of avarice."

There is then nothing particularly new in the disenchantment which the private citizen expresses by not voting at all, by voting only for the head of the ticket, by staying away from the primaries, by not reading speeches and documents, by the whole list of sins of omission for which he is denounced. I shall not denounce him further. My sympathies are with him, for I believe that he has been saddled with an impossible task and that he is asked to practice an unattainable ideal. I find it so myself for, although public business is my main interest and I give most of my time to watching it, I cannot find time to do what is expected of me in the theory of democracy; that is, to know what is going on and to have an opinion worth expressing on every question which confronts a self-governing community. And I have not happened to meet anybody, from a President of the United States to a professor of political science, who came anywhere near to embodying the accepted ideal of the sovereign and omnicompetent citizen.

Agents and Bystanders

When a citizen has qualified as a voter he finds himself one of the theoretical rulers of a great going concern. He has not made the complicated machine with its five hundred thousand federal officers and its uncounted local offices. He has not seen much of it. He is bound by contracts, by debts, by treaties, by laws, made before he was aware of them. He does not from day to day decide who shall do what in the business of government. Only some small fraction of it comes intermittently to his notice. And in those episodic moments when he stands in the polling booth he is a highly intelligent and public-spirited voter indeed who can discover two real alternatives and enlist his influence for a party which promises something he can understand.

The actual governing is made up of a multitude of arrangements on specific questions by particular individuals. These rarely become visible to the private citizen. Government, in the long intervals between elections, is carried on by politicians, officeholders and influential men who make settlements with other politicians, officeholders and influential men. The mass of people see these settlements, judge them, and affect them only now and then. They are altogether too numerous, to complicated, too obscure in their effects to become the subject of any continuing exercise of public opinion.

Nor in any exact and literal sense are those who conduct the daily business of government accountable after the fact to the great mass of the voters. They are accountable only, except in spectacular cases, to the other politicians, officeholders and influential men directly interested in the particular act. Modern society is not visible to anybody, nor intelligible continuously and as a whole. One section is visible to another section; one series of acts is intelligible to this group and another to that.

Even this degree of responsible understanding is attainable only by the development of fact-finding agencies of great scope and complexity.[8] These agencies give only a remote and incidental assistance to the general public. Their findings are too intricate for the casual reader. They are also almost always much too uninteresting. Indeed the popular boredom and contempt for the expert and for statistical measurement are such that the organization of intelligence to administer modern affairs would probably be entirely neglected were it not that departments of government, corporations, trade unions and trade associations are being compelled by their own internal necessities of administration, and by compulsion of other corporate groups, to record their own acts, measure them, publish them and stand accountable for them.

The need in the Great Society not only for publicity but for uninterrupted publicity is indisputable. But we shall misunderstand the need seriously if we imagine that the purpose of the publication can possibly be the informing of every voter. We live at the mere beginnings of public accounting. Yet the facts far exceed our curiosity. The railroads, for example, make an accounting. Do we read the results? Hardly. A few executives here and there, some bankers, some regulating officials, some representatives of shippers and the like read them. The rest of us ignore them for the good and sufficient reason that we have other things to do.

For the man does not live who can read all the reports that drift across his doorstep or all the dispatches in his newspaper. And if by some development of the radio every man could see and hear all that was happening everywhere, if publicity, in other words, became absolute, how much time could or would he spend watching the Sinking Fund Commission and the Geological Survey? He would probably tune in on the Prince of Wales, or, in desperation, throw off the switch and seek peace in ignorance. It is bad enough today—with morning newspapers published in the evening and evening newspapers in the morning, with October magazines in September, with the movies and the radio—to be condemned to live under a barrage of eclectic information, to have one's mind made the receptacle for a hullabaloo of speeches, arguments and unrelated episodes.

General information for the informing of public opinion is altogether too general for intellectual decency. And life is too short for the pursuit of omniscience by the counting in a state of nervous excitement of all the leaves on all the trees.

If all men had to conceive the whole process of government all the time the worlds work would obviously never be carried on. Men make no attempt to consider society as a whole. The farmer decides whether to plant wheat or corn, the mechanic whether to take the job offered at the Pennsylvania or the Erie shops, whether to buy a Ford or a piano, and, if a Ford, whether to buy it from the garage on Elm Street or from the dealer who sent him a circular. These decisions are among fairly narrow choices offered to him; he can no more choose among all the jobs in the world than he can consider marrying any woman in the world. These choices in detail are in their cumulative mass the government of society. They may rest on ignorant or enlightened opinions, but, whether he comes to them by accident or scientific instruction, they are specific and particular among at best a few concrete alternatives and they lead to a definite, visible result.

But men are supposed also to hold public opinions about the general conduct of society. The mechanic is supposed not only to choose between working for the Pennsylvania or the Erie but to decide how in the interests of the nation all the railroads of the country shall be regulated. The two kinds of opinion merge insensibly one into the other; men have general notions which influence their individual decisions and their direct experiences unconsciously govern their general notions. Yet it is useful to distinguish between the two kinds of opinion, the specific and direct, the general and the indirect.

Specific opinions give rise to immediate executive acts; to take a job, to do a particular piece of work, to hire or fire, to buy or sell, to stay here or go there, to accept or refuse, to command or obey. General opinions give rise to delegated, indirect, symbolic, intangible results: to a vote, to a resolution, to applause, to criticism, to praise or dispraise, to audiences, circulations, followings, contentment or discontent. The specific opinion may lead to a decision to act within the area where a man has personal jurisdiction; that is, within the limits set by law and custom, his personal power and his personal desire. But general opinions lead only to some sort of expression, such as voting, and do not result in executive acts except in cooperation with the general opinions of large numbers of other persons.

Since the general opinions of large numbers of persons are almost certain to be a vague and confusing medley, action cannot be taken until these opinions have been factored down, canalized, compressed and made uniform. The making of one general will out of a multitude of general wishes is not an Hegelian mystery, as so many social philosophers have imagined, but an art well known to leaders, politicians and steering committees.[9] It consists essentially in the use of symbols which assemble emotions after they have been detached from their ideas. Because feelings are much less specific than ideas, and yet more poignant, the leader is able to make a homogeneous will out of a heterogeneous mass of desires. The process, therefore, by which general opinions are brought to cooperation consists of an intensification of feeling and a degradation of significance. Before a mass of general opinions can eventuate in executive action, the choice is narrowed down to a few alternatives. The victorious alternative is executed not by the mass but by individuals in control of its energy.

A private opinion may be quite complicated, and may issue in quite complicated actions, in a whole train of subsidiary opinions, as when a man decides to build a house and then makes a hundred judgments as to how it shall be built. But a public opinion has no such immediate responsibility or continuous result. It leads in politics to the making of a pencil mark on a piece of paper, and then to a period of waiting and watching as to whether one or two years hence the mark shall be made in the same column or in the adjoining one. The decision to make the mark may be for reasons $a^1, a^2, a^3 \ldots a^n$: the result, whether an idiot or genius has voted, is A.

For great masses of people, though each of them may have more or less distinct views, must when they act converge to an identical result. And the more complex the collection of men the more ambiguous must be the unity and the simpler the common ideas.

In English-speaking countries during the last century the contrast between the action of men individually and in the mass has been much emphasized, and yet greatly misunderstood. Macaulay, for example, speaking on the Reform Bill of 1832, drew the conventional distinction between private enterprise and public action:

In all those things which depend on the intelligence, the knowledge, the industry, the energy of individuals, this country stands preeminent among all countries of the world ancient and modern. But in those things which it belongs to the state to direct we have no such claim to superiority ... can there be a stronger contrast than that which exists between the beauty, the completeness, the speed, the precision with which every process is performed in our factories, and the awkwardness, the crudeness, the slowness, the uncertainty of the apparatus by which offenses are punished and rights vindicated? ...

Surely we see the barbarism of the Thirteenth Century and the highest civilization of the Nineteenth Century side by side, and we see that the barbarism belongs to the government, and the civilization to the people.[10]

Macaulay was, of course, thinking of the contrast between factory production and government as it existed in England under Queen Victoria's uncles and the hard-drinking, hardriding squirearchy. But the Prussian bureaucracy amply demonstrated that there is no such necessary contrast between governmental and private action. There is a contrast between action by and through great masses of people and action that moves without them.

The fundamental contrast is not between public and private enterprises, between "crowd" psychology and individual, but between men doing specific things and men attempting to command general results. The work of the world is carried on by men in their executive capacity, by an infinite number of concrete acts, plowing and planting and reaping, building and destroying, fitting this to that, going from here to there, transforming A into B and moving B from X to Y. The relationships between the individuals doing these specific things are balanced by a most intricate mechanism of exchange, of contract, of custom and of implied promises. Where men are performing their work they must learn to understand the process and the substance of these obligations if they are to do it at all. But in governing the work of other men by votes or by the expression of opinion they can only reward or punish a result, accept or reject alternatives presented to them. They can say yes or no to something which has been done, yes or no to a proposal, but they cannot create, administer and actually perform the act they have in mind. Persons uttering public opinions may now and then be able to define the acts of men, but their opinions do not execute these acts.

To the realm of executive acts, each of us, as a member of the public, remains always external. Our public opinions are always and forever, by their very nature, an attempt to control the actions of others from the outside. If we can grasp the full significance of that conclusion we shall, I think, have found a way of fixing the role of public opinion in its true perspective; we shall know how to account for the disenchantment of democracy, and we shall begin to see the outline of an ideal of public opinion which, unlike that accepted in the dogma of democracy, may be really attainable.

The Main Value of Debate

The individual whose action is governed by a rule is interested in its substance. But in those rules which do not control his own action his chief interest is that there should be workable rules.

It follows that the membership of the public is not fixed. It changes with the issue: the actors in one affair are the spectators of another, and men are continually passing back and forth between the field where they are executives and the field where they are members of a public. The distinction between the two is not, as I said in Chapter III, an absolute one: there is a twilight zone where it is hard to say whether a man is acting executively on his opinions or merely acting to influence the opinion of some one else who is acting executively. There is often a mixture of the two types of behavior. And it is this mixture, as well as the lack of a clear line of distinction in all cases, which permits a very large confusion in affairs between a public and a private attitude toward them. The public point of view on a question is muddied by the presence in the public of spurious members, persons who are really acting to bend the rule in their favor while pretending or imagining that they are moved only by the common public need that there shall be an acceptable rule.

At the outset it is important, therefore, to detect and to discount the self-interested group. In saying this I do not mean to cast even the slightest reflection on a union of men to promote their self-interest. It would be futile to do so, because we may take it as certain that men will act to benefit themselves whenever they think they conveniently can. A political theory based on the expectation of self-denial and sacrifice by the run of men in any community would not be worth considering. Nor is it at all evident that the work of the world could be done unless men followed their private interest and contributed to affairs that direct inner knowledge which they thus obtain. Moreover, the adjustments are likely to be much more real if they are made from fully conscious and thoroughly explored special points of view.

Thus the genius of any illuminating public discussion is not to obscure and censor private interest but to help it to sail and to make it sail under its own colors. The true public, in my definition of that term, has to purge itself of the self-interested groups who become confused with it. It must purge itself not because private interests are bad but because private interests cannot successfully be adjusted to each other if any one of them acquires a counterfeit strength. If the true public, concerned only in the fact of adjustment, becomes mobilized behind a private interest seeking to prevail, the adjustment is false; it does not represent the real balance of forces in the affair and the solution will break down. It will break down because the true public will not stay mobilized very long for anything, and when it demobilizes the private interest which was falsely exalted will find its privileges unmanageable. It will be like a man placed on Jack Dempsey's chest by six policemen, and then left there after the policemen have gone home to dinner. It will be like France placed by the Allies upon a prostrate Germany and then left there after the Allies have departed from Europe.

The separation of the public from the self-interested group will not be assisted by the self-interested group. We may be sure that any body of farmers, business men, and trade unionists will always call themselves the public if they can. How then is their self-interest to be detected? No ordinary bystander is equipped to analyze the propaganda by which a private interest seeks to associate itself with the disinterested public. It is a perplexing matter, perhaps the most perplexing in popular government, and the bystander's only recourse is to insist upon debate. He will not be able, we may assume, to judge the merits of the arguments. But if he does insist upon full freedom of discussion, the advocates are very likely to expose one another. Open debate may lead to no conclusion and throw no light whatever on the problem or its answer, but it will tend to betray the partisan and the advocate. And if it has identified them for the true public, debate will have served its main purpose.

The individual not directly concerned may still choose to join the self-interested group and support its cause. But at least he will know that he has made himself a partisan, and thus perhaps he may be somewhat less likely to mistake a party's purpose for the aim of mankind.

Notes

1. Cited Philip Guedalla, *The Second Empire*.
2. Logan Pearsall Smith, *More Trivia*, p. 41.
3. *Cf.* Simon Michelet, *Stay-at-Home Vote and Absentee Voters*, pamphlet of the National Get Out the Vote Club; also A. M. Schlesinger and E. M. Erickson, "The Vanishing Voters," *New Republic*, Oct. 15, 1924. The percentage of the popular to the eligible vote from 1865 to 1920 declined from 83.51 per cent to 52.36 per cent.

4. Charles Edward Merriam and Harvey Foote Gosnell, *Non-voting: Causes and Methods of Control*.

5. James Bryce, *Modern Democracies*, Vol. II, p. 52.

6. A. Lawrence Lowell, *Public Opinion and Popular Government. Cf.* Appendices.

7. Robert Michels, *Political Parties*, p. 390.

8. *Cf., my Public Opinion,* Chapters XXV and XXVI.

9. *Cf. my Public Opinion*, Chapters XIII and XIV.

10. Speech on the Reform Bill of 1832, quoted in the *Times* (London), July 12, 1923.

7

Criteria of Negro Art

From *Crisis Magazine* (1926)

W. E. B. Du Bois

William Edward Burghardt Du Bois (1868–1963) was a civil rights leader and the leading African American intellectual in the twentieth century. He studied at Harvard, where he was influenced by William James and became the first African American to receive a Ph.D. Like many late-nineteenth-century Americans, he also studied in Germany, where he reveled in the intellectual stimulation and relative lack of antiblack prejudice. He had an extraordinarily long life of activism, teaching, and writing. His works included history, philosophy, and fiction. Du Bois was also one of the first sociologists of black life in the United States, as demonstrated in his *The Philadelphia Negro* (1899), which includes an analysis of the press. He died in Ghana at the age of ninety-five, on the same day as Martin Luther King's "I Have a Dream" speech.

In this selection, Du Bois takes up a vexed question in much of twentieth-century social thought: the role of art in society, especially as it relates to the struggle for emancipation and social justice. Very much like Dewey's work, or that of Horkheimer and Adorno,

Du Bois's thesis is that distortions in the aesthetic sphere are symptoms of social inequities. The white public entertains only distorted depictions of black life. For Du Bois, an emancipated race would not only participate fully as citizens but would also enjoy a fullness of art. In the struggle for emancipation, art leads: "until the art of the black folk compels recognition they will not be rated as human." For Du Bois—as for Dewey and for Horkheimer and Adorno—the flame of German idealism, which had envisioned freedom and beauty as inseparable, continues to burn.

I do not doubt but there are some in this audience who are a little disturbed at the subject of this meeting, and particularly at the subject I have chosen. Such people are thinking something like this: "How is it that an organization like this, a group of radicals trying to bring new things into the world, a fighting organization which has come up out of the blood and dust of battle, struggling for the right of black men to be ordinary human beings—how is it that an organization of this kind can turn aside to talk about art? After all, what have we who are slaves and black to do with art?"

Or perhaps there are others who feel a certain relief and are saying, "After all it is rather satisfactory after all this talk about rights and fighting to sit and dream of something which leaves a nice taste in the mouth."

Let me tell you that neither of these groups is right. The thing we are talking about tonight is part of the great fight we are carrying on and it represents a forward and an upward look— a pushing onward. You and I have been breasting hills; we have been climbing upward; there has been progress and we can see it day by day looking back along blood-filled paths. But as you go through the valleys and over the foothills, so long as you are climbing, the direction—north, sought, east or west—is of less importance. But when gradually the vista widens and you begin to see the world at your feet and the far horizon, then it is time to know more precisely whether you are going and what you really want.

What do we want? What is the thing we are after? As it was phrased last night it had a certain truth: We want to be Americans, full-fledged Americans, with all the rights of other American citizens. But is that all? Do we want simply to be Americans? Once in a while through all of us there flashes some clairvoyance, some clear idea, of what America really is. We who are dark can see America in a way that white Americans cannot. And seeing our country thus, are we satisfied with its present goals and ideals? . . .

If you tonight suddenly should become full-fledged Americans; if your color faded, or the color line here in Chicago was miraculously forgotten; suppose, too, you became at the same time rich and powerful—what is it that you would want? What would you immediately seek? Would you buy the most elaborate estate on the North Shore? Would you be a Rotarian or a Lion or a What-not of the very last degree? Would you wear the most striking clothes, give the richest dinners, and buy the longest press notices?

Even as you visualize such ideals you know in your hearts that these are not the things you really want. You realize this sooner than the average white American because, pushed aside as we have been in America, there has come to us not only a certain distaste for the tawdry and flamboyant but a vision of what the world could be if it were really a beautiful world; if we had the true spirit; if we had the seeing eye, the cunning hand, the feeling heart; if we had, to be sure, not perfect happiness, but plenty of good hard work, the inevitable suffering that always comes with life; sacrifice and waiting, all that—but nevertheless lived in a world where men know, where men create, where they realize themselves and where they enjoy life. It is that sort of a world we want to create for ourselves and for all America.

After all, who shall describe Beauty? What is it? I remember tonight four beautiful things: the cathedral at Cologne, a forest in stone, set in light and changing shadow, echoing with sunlight and solemn song; a village of the Veys in West Africa, a little thing of mauve and purple, quiet, lying content and shining in the sun; a black and velvet room where on a throne rests, in old and yellowing marble, the broken curves of the Venus de Milo; a single phrase of music in the South— utter melody, haunting and appealing, suddenly arising out of night and eternity, beneath the moon.

Such is beauty. Its variety is infinite, its possibility is endless. In normal life all may have it and have it yet again. The world is full of it; and yet today the mass of human beings are choked away from it, and their lives distorted and made ugly. This is not only wrong, it is silly. Who shall right this well-nigh universal failing? Who shall let this world be beautiful? Who shall restore to men the glory of sunsets and the peace of quiet sleep?

We black folk may help for we have within us as a race new stirrings; stirrings of the beginning of a new appreciation of joy, of a new desire to create, of a new will to be; as though in this morning of group life we had awakened from some sleep that at once dimly mourns the past and dreams a splendid future; and there has come the conviction that the youth that is here today, the Negro youth, is a different kind of youth, because in some new way it bears this mighty prophecy on its breast, with a new realization of itself, with new determination for all mankind.

What has this beauty to do with the world? What has beauty to do with truth and goodness—with the facts of the world and the right actions of men? "Nothing," the artists rush to answer. They may be right. I am but an humble disciple of art and cannot presume to say. I am one who tells the truth and exposes evil and seeks with beauty and for beauty to set the world right. That somehow, somewhere eternal and perfect beauty sits above truth and right I can conceive, but here and now and in the world in which I work they are for me unseparated and inseparable.

This is brought to us peculiarly when as artists we face our own past as a people. There has come to us—and it has come especially through the man we are going to honor tonight [Carter Godwin Woodson, 12th Spingarn Medalist]—a realization of that past, of which for long years we have been ashamed, for which we have apologized. We thought nothing could come out of that past which we wanted to remember; which we wanted to hand down to our children. Suddenly, this same past is taking on form, color, and reality, and in a half shame-faced way we are beginning to be proud of it. We are remembering that the romance of the world did not die and lie forgotten in the Middle Ages; that if you want romance to deal with you must have it here and now and in your own hands. . . .

Have you heard the story of the conquest of German East Africa? Listen to the untold tale: There were 40,000 black men and 4,000 white men who talked German. There were 20,000 black men and 12,000 white men who talked English.

There were 10,000 black men and 400 white men who talked French. In Africa then where the Mountains of the Moon raised their white and snowcapped heads into the mouth of the tropic sun, where Nile and Congo rise and the Great Lakes swim, these men fought; they struggled on mountain, hill and valley, in river, lake and swamp, until in masses they sickened, crawled and died; until the 4,000 white Germans had become mostly bleached bones; until nearly all the 12,000 white Englishmen had returned to South Africa, and the 400 Frenchmen to Belgium and heaven; all except a mere handful of the white men died; but thousands of black men from East, West and South Africa, from Nigeria and the Valley of the Nile, and from the West Indies still struggled, fought and died. For four years they fought and won and lost German East Africa; and all you hear about it is that England and Belgium conquered German Africa for the allies!

Such is the true and stirring stuff of which romance is born and from this stuff come the stirrings of men who are beginning to remember that this kind of material is theirs; and this vital life of their own kind is beckoning them on.

The question comes next as to the interpretation of these new stirrings, of this new spirit: Of what is the colored artist capable? We have had on the part of both colored and white people singular unanimity of judgment in the past. Colored people have said: "This work must be inferior because it comes from colored people." White people have said: "It is inferior because it is done by colored people." But today there is coming to both the realization that the work of the black man is not always inferior. Interesting stories come to us. . . .

With the growing recognition of Negro artists in spite of the severe handicaps, one comforting thing is occurring to both white and black. They are whispering, "Here is a way out. Here is the real solution of the color problem. The recognition accorded Cullen, Hughes, Fauset, White and others shows there is no real color line. Keep quiet! Don't complain! Work! All will be well!"

I will not say that already this chorus amounts to a conspiracy. Perhaps I am naturally too suspicious. But I will say that there are today a surprising number of white people who are getting great satisfaction out of these younger Negro writers because they think it is going to stop agitation of the Negro question. They say, "What is the use of your fighting and complaining; do the great thing and the reward is there." And many colored people are all too eager to follow this advice; especially those who weary of the eternal struggle along the colorline, who are afraid to fight and to whom the money of philanthropists and the alluring publicity are subtle and deadly bribes. They say, "What is the use of fighting? Why not show simply what we deserve and let the reward come to us?"

And it is right here that the National Association for the Advancement of Colored People comes upon the field, comes with its great call to a new battle, a new fight and new things to fight before the old things are wholly won; and to say that the beauty of truth and freedom which shall some day be our heritage and the heritage of all civilized men is not in our hands yet and that we ourselves must not fail to realize.

There is in New York tonight a black woman molding clay by herself in a little bare room, because there is not a single school of sculpture in New York where she is welcome. Surely there are doors she might burst through, but when God makes a sculptor He does not always make the pushing sort of person who beats his way through doors thrust in his face. This girl is working her hands off to get out of this country so that she can get some sort of training.

There was Richard Brown. If he had been white he would have been alive today instead of dead of neglect. Many helped him when he asked but he was not the kind of boy that always asks. He was simply one who made colors sing.

This is a colored woman in Chicago who is a great musician. She thought she would like to study at Fontainebleau this summer where Walter Damrosch and a score of leaders of art have an American school of music. But the application blank of this school says: "I am a white American and I apply for admission to the school."

We can go on the stage; we can be just as funny as white Americans wish us to be; we can play all the sordid parts that America likes to assign to Negroes; but for anything else there is still small place for us.

And so I might go on. But let me sum up with this: Suppose the only Negro who survived some centuries hence was the Negro painted by white Americans in the novels and essays they have written. What would people in a hundred years say of black Americans? Now turn it around. Suppose you were to write a story and put in it the kind of people you know and like and imagine. You might get it published and you might

not. And the "might not" is still far bigger than the "might." The white publishers catering to white folk would say, "It is not interesting"—to white folk, naturally not. They want Uncle Toms, Topsies, good "darkies" and clowns. I have in my office a story with all the earmarks of truth. A young man says that he started out to write and had his stories accepted. Then he began to write about the things he knew best about, that is, about his own people. He submitted a story to a magazine which said, "We are sorry, but we cannot take it." "I sat down and revised my story, changing the color of the characters and the locale and sent it under an assumed name with a change of address and it was accepted by the same magazine that had refused it, the editor promising to take anything else I might send in providing it was good enough."

We have, to be sure, a few recognized and successful Negro artists; but they are not all those fit to survive or even a good minority. They are but the remnants of that ability and genius among us whom the accidents of education and opportunity have raised on the tidal waves of chance. We black folk are not altogether peculiar in this. After all, in the world at large, it is only the accident, the remnant, that gets the chance to make the most of itself; but if this is true of the white world it is infinitely more true of the colored world. It is not simply the great clear tenor of Roland Hayes that opened the ears of America. We have had many voices of all kinds as fine as his and America was and is as deaf as she was for years to him. Then a foreign land heard Hayes and puts its imprint on him and immediately America with all its imitative snobbery woke up. We approved Hayes because London, Paris and Berlin approved him and not simply because he was a great singer.

Thus it is the bounden duty of black America to begin this great work of the creation of beauty, of the preservation of beauty, of the realization of beauty, and we must use in this work all the methods that men have used before. And what have been the tools of the artist in times gone by? First of all, he has used the truth—not for the sake of truth, not as a scientist seeking truth, but as one upon whom truth eternally thrusts itself as the highest handmaid of imagination, as the one great vehicle of universal understanding. Again artists have used goodness—goodness in all its aspects of justice, honor, and right—not for sake of an ethical sanction but as the one true method of gaining sympathy and human interest.

The apostle of beauty thus becomes the apostle of truth and right not by choice but by inner and outer compulsion. Free he is but his freedom is ever bounded by truth and justice; and slavery only dogs him when he is denied the right to tell the truth or recognize an ideal of justice.

Thus all art is propaganda and ever must be, despite the wailing of the purists. I stand in utter shamelessness and say that whatever art I have for writing has been used always for propaganda for gaining the right of black folk to love and enjoy. I do not care a damn for any art that is not used for propaganda. But I do care when propaganda is confined to one side while the other is stripped and silent. . . .

You know the current magazine story: a young white man goes down to Central America and the most beautiful colored woman there falls in love with him. She crawls across the whole isthmus to get to him. The white man says nobly, "No." He goes back to his white sweetheart in New York.

In such cases, it is not the positive propaganda of people who believe white blood divine, infallible, and holy to which I object. It is the denial of a similar right of propaganda to those who believe black blood human, lovable, and inspired with new ideals for the world. White artists themselves suffer from this narrowing of their field. They cry for freedom in dealing with Negroes because they have so little freedom in dealing with whites. DuBose Heywood writes "Porgy" and writes beautifully of the black Charleston underworld. But why does he do this? Because he cannot do a similar thing for the white people of Charleston, or they would drum him out of town. The only chance he had to tell the truth of pitiful human degradation was to tell it of colored people. I should not be surprised if Octavius Roy Cohen had approached the *Saturday Evening Post* and asked permission to write about a different kind of colored folk than the monstrosities he has created; but if he has, the *Post* has replied, "No. You are getting paid to write about the kind of colored people you are writing about."

In other words, the white public today demands from its artists, literary and pictorial, racial prejudgment which deliberately distorts truth and justice, as far as colored races are concerned, and it will pay for no other.

On the other hand, the young and slowly growing black public still wants its prophets almost equally unfree. We are bound by all sorts of customs that have come down as second-hand soul clothes of white patrons. We are ashamed of sex and we lower our eyes when people will talk of it. Our religion holds us in superstition. Our worst side has been so shamelessly emphasized that we are denying we have or ever had a worst side. In all sorts of ways we are hemmed in and our new young artists have got to fight their way to freedom.

The ultimate judge has got to be you and you have got to build yourselves up into that wide judgment, that catholicity of temper which is going to enable the artist to have his widest chance for freedom. We can afford the truth. White folk today cannot. As it is now we are handing everything over to a white jury. If a colored man wants to publish a book, he has got to get a white publisher and a white newspaper to say it is great; and then you and I say so. We must come to the place where the work of art when it appears is reviewed and acclaimed by our own free and unfettered judgment. And we are going to have a real and valuable and eternal judgment only as we make ourselves free of mind, proud of body and just of soul to all men.

And then do you know what will be said? It is already saying. Just as soon as true art emerges; just as soon as the black artist appears, someone touches the race on the shoulder and says, "He did that because he was an American, not because he was a Negro; he was born here; he was trained here; he is not a Negro—what is a Negro anyhow? He is just human; it is the kind of thing you ought to expect."

I do not doubt that the ultimate art coming from black folk is going to be just as beautiful, and beautiful largely in the same ways, as the art that comes from white folk, or yellow, or red; but the point today is that until the art of the black folk compels recognition they will not be rated as human. And when through art they compel recognition then let the world discover if it will that their art is as new as it is old and as old as new.

I had a classmate once who did three beautiful things and died. One of them was a story of folk who found fire and then went wandering in the gloom of night seeking again the stars they had once known and lost; suddenly out of blackness they looked up and there loomed the heavens; and what was it that they said? They raised a mighty cry: "It is the stars, it is the ancient stars, it is the young and everlasting stars!"

8

The Results of Propaganda

From *Propaganda Technique in the World War* (1927)

Harold Dwight Lasswell

Harold Lasswell (1902–1978) was an intellectual polymath—a theorist, methodologist, and empirical researcher who contributed to the fields of political science, international relations, philosophy, law, and propaganda and communications research. The son of a Presbyterian minister, he entered the University of Chicago at sixteen, already well read in Kant, Freud, Marx, and other modern social theorists. He took a doctorate in political science, studying with Charles Merriam, Robert Park, George Herbert Mead, and the psychologist Elton Mayo; and he considered John Dewey to be a deep influence. Lasswell taught at the University of Chicago from 1924 to 1938, during which time he became the chief authority on the study of propaganda. His varied work was marked by a strange mix of psychoanalysis, behaviorism, and pragmatism, combined with methodological sophistication and obtuseness of language. Lasswell's dictum that the job of communication researchers is to determine "who said what to whom in what channel and with what effect" played an important role in the development of the field, as did his codification of the method of content analysis.

The following selection is from *Propaganda Technique in the World War* (1927), one of Lasswell's earliest publications (and one which he later condemned as too impressionistic). As a former champion debater and encyclopedia salesman, Lasswell had firsthand experience in the arts of persuasion, and his teacher Merriam had directed American propaganda efforts in Italy during World War I. Unlike many propaganda critics, Lasswell did not condemn propaganda; rather, he saw it as an indifferent instrument to be used for good or evil. Into the 1940s, he argued for the necessity of "myths" that might be used for democratic purposes or to achieve new-world unity. He offered a cold verdict on the possibilities of modern democracy: "If the mass will be free of chains of iron, it must accept its chains of silver."

After this rapid review of the means and conditions of war propaganda we are in a position to undertake an appraisal of its results. The history of the late War shows that modern war must be fought on three fronts: the military front, the economic front, and the propaganda front. The economic blockade strangles, the propaganda confuses, and the armed force delivers the *coup de grace*. Employed in conjunction with the other arms of offence, propaganda saps the stamina of the armed and civilian forces of the enemy, and smoothes the path for the mailed fist of men and metal. The economic blockade slowly squeezes the vitality out of a nation, and depends for its maximum effect upon a prolonged struggle. Propaganda is likewise a passive and contributory weapon, whose chief function is to demolish the enemy's will to fight by intensifying depression, disillusionment and disagreement.

As the U.S. Military Intelligence described the function of propaganda, it

attacks the whole army at its base; threatens to cut it off from its base, to stop the flow of reinforcements, supplies, ammunition, equipment, food, comforts, and above all, to weaken the moral support that sustains the troops in the hardships and cruelties of war far from home.

"Armies fight as the people think" was the wise epigram of the British General Applin. It might be extended to say that armies fight as armies think, for, as George William Curtis said: "Thoughts are Bullets."[1]

Notable successes in which propaganda had an important and perhaps a decisive part were scored in the last War. In common with every other weapon of attack, propaganda has a surprise value, which the Central Powers realized to the full, in the ingenious propaganda offensive, which preceded their attack upon the Italians in 1917 at Caporetto. The spirit of the Italian armies was dissipated, and their lines cracked and broken. In reply, the Allies won a striking success in 1917, when they forced the postponement of the Austro-Hungarian offensive against Italy, from April until June, by sowing demoralization among the troops of the subject nationalities. Mutinous troops blew up ammunition dumps behind the lines, and sabotaged the whole military plan.

One of the gravest triumphs of the War was won when the Germans put the Russians out of the running. They strained every muscle to complete the disintegration which culminated in the second Revolution. They permitted the famous "sealed car" to convey Lenin and forty associates from Switzerland, across Germany on their way to Russia. The ruthless Bolshevists accepted aid from any quarter and completed the job, in spite of all the frantic work of the American Red Cross and the special propaganda services of the Entente group.

But the crowning victory of the War was at the expense of the Germans. German moral depended upon the hope that the victory which had been so many times within their grasp, was just over the horizon. Strained to the breaking point by the inexorable clutch of the economic blockade, their great hopes of the spring and summer of 1918 crumpled into rubbish, the German army and the German people were ready to lend an ear to the seductive voice of Mr. Wilson.

If the great generalissimo on the military front was Foch, the great generalissimo on the propaganda front was Wilson. His monumental rhetoric, epitomizing the aspirations of all humanity in periods at once lucid and persuasive, was scattered far and wide over Germany. He declared war upon autocracies everywhere, and solemnly adhered to his distinction between the German people and the German rulers. His speeches were one prolonged instigation to revolt. He and Lenin were the champion revolutionists of the age. Throughout the entire War his pronouncements had won a substantial measure of confidence and respect in the minds of that minority of democratically-minded men, who longed to transform the pre-war Germany of class discrimination and special privilege. And when the clouds of adversity darkened the sky in 1918, they were joined by immense numbers of their compatriots, pinched by privation and despair, anxiously searching the heavens for portents of a soft peace. They turned, not to Clemenceau— hard, relentless vulture, poised like an avenging coincidence, to tear at the vitals of a fallen adversary, nor to Lloyd George—nimble, unstable and uncertain, but to this mysterious figure in the White House, aloof from the ordinary passions of petty men, who spoke in elegiac prose of a better world, when wars should be no more and a brotherhood of democratic peoples should bury their heritage of ancestral rancour, and march toward a world of fellowship and reconciliation. It was to this man, mercilessly ridiculed and caricatured from one end of Germany to another through long years of hesitation and then of belligerency, that the Germans turned in their extremity.

Could it be that at last a statesman had arisen to lead the peoples of the world in the path of friendship and peace? Had a great prophet at last soared above vindictiveness and animosity to bring understanding to a harassed universe? This butt of ribald jest was transformed at a stroke in those closing months of hunger, insecurity, foreboding and hallucination into a saviour. The people grasped at straws and saw deliverers where they had seen but pedantic fools before.

Such matchless skill as Wilson showed in propaganda has never been equaled in the world's history. He spoke to the heart of the people as no statesman has ever done. For a few brief months he embodied the faith of the idealists in a better world, and the last desperate hope of the defeated peoples for a soft peace. He was raised to a matchless pinnacle of prestige and power, and his name was spoken with reverence in varied accents in the remotest corners of the earth.

Just how much of Wilsonism was rhetorical exhibitionism and how much was the sound fruit of sober reflection will be in debate until the World War is a feeble memory. From a propaganda point of view it was a matchless performance, for Wilson brewed the subtle poison, which industrious men injected into the veins of a staggering people, until the smashing powers of the Allied armies knocked them into submission. While he fomented discord abroad, Wilson fostered unity at home. A nation of one hundred million people, sprung from many alien and antagonistic stocks, was welded into a fighting whole, "to make the world safe for democracy." And the magic of his eloquence soothed the suspicions which Central and South America cherished toward the mighty colossus of the North, and brought most of them into the War on the Allied side.

The propaganda of disintegration which was directed against the tottering realm of the Hapsburgs bore fruit in disaffection and ultimate secession among the Czechs, Slovaks-Rumanians, Croats, Poles and Italians. The Balfour Declaration hastened the reversal of Jewish sympathies in 1917.

Some of the triumphs of propaganda were in the field of recruiting. In the race for Allies, the Germans won in Bulgaria and Turkey, but the honours went to the Allies in the United States, Italy, Rumania, Greece and in a wide array of lesser countries, and Germany stood isolated in sympathy, except for Spain and Sweden. The hand of the whole world was raised against the Teuton. The great tug of war in America was only won by the British and the French after a desperate struggle against the German propaganda. The French were admirable in the very simplicity of their appeal. They invoked the sacred name of Lafayette, implored the gods of democracy, blackguarded the Germans and advertised the Americans who had enlisted on the side of the French. The British had less traditional affection to draw upon, and much more to explain away, but they had the powerful asset of the cables and the good sense to work, not secretly, but just outside the glare of publicity. And neither the British nor the French were severely handicapped by a military-diplomatic programme, which hurled all their fine pretensions in their teeth.[2]

Now a formidable list could be drawn up of the propaganda drives which failed or which accomplished their objective after a long period of waiting. Not all the propagandas to instigate defeat, Revolution, or succession and to preserve friendship succeeded. After all, India, Egypt, Ireland and Morocco did not respond to the proddings of German agents to rise up as one man to cast off the yoke of the Englishman and the Frenchman; Austria-Hungary, Germany, Bulgaria and Turkey did hold out for four long years. France, Great Britain, and most of the Allies persisted through all discouragement to victory, in spite of the dangerous German peace offensive of 1916–17. But before regarding these negative results as a defeat for propaganda, it must be remembered that propaganda was not only an offensive weapon; it was a powerful means of defence as well. Unity could be preserved just as it could be demolished by propaganda. Indeed, propaganda was present on both sides of every hotly-contested sector, and though it is one of those weapons whose precise effect is largely a matter of surmise, it is one which it would be foolhardy to neglect.

A defeated country naturally exaggerates the influence of propaganda. The Italians sought to save their faces after the Caporetto disaster[3] by complaining of the terrible and insidious German propaganda, and Ludendorff devotes a great many pages to explaining just how it was that he did not lose the War, and how the Alien and Radical riff-raff in the population collapsed behind the lines, leaving a sort of vacuum, in which the German troops fell, victorious to the end.

It is especially difficult to extricate the strands of propaganda influence from the means of control which are closely allied to it. When the Nivelle offensive drowned in a sea of blood in 1917, no less than twelve army corps were tainted by mutinous demonstrations. Soldiers began to start home, infuriated by the insensate butchery of their comrades. It was the remarkable work of General Petain which restored orderly enthusiasm to the front and thwarted the ominous diversion of hatred which threatened to turn the French soldiery against their own leaders and away from the enemy. He relied by no means exclusively upon propaganda.[4]

But when all allowances have been made, and all extravagant estimates pared to the bone, the fact remains that propaganda is one of the most powerful instrumentalities in the modern world.[5] It has arisen to its present eminence in response to a complex of changed circumstances which have altered the nature of society. Small, primitive tribes can weld their heterogeneous members into a fighting whole by the beat of the tom-tom and the tempestuous rhythm of the dance. It is in orgies of physical exuberance that young men are brought to the boiling point of war, and that old and young, men and women, are caught in the suction of tribal purpose.

In the Great Society it is no longer possible to fuse the waywardness of individuals in the furnace of the war dance; a new and subtler instrument must weld thousands and even millions of human beings into one amalgamated mass of hate and will and hope. A new flame must burn out the canker of dissent and temper the steel of bellicose enthusiasm. The name of this new hammer and anvil of social solidarity is propaganda. Talk must take the place of drill; print must supplant the dance. War dances live in literature and at the fringes of the modern earth; war propaganda breathes and fumes in the capitals and provinces of the world.

Propaganda is a concession to the rationality of the modern world. A literate world, a reading world, a schooled world prefers to thrive on argument and news. It is sophisticated to the extent of using print; and he that takes to print shall live or perish by the Press. All the apparatus of diffused erudition popularizes the symbols and forms of pseudo-rational appeal; the wolf of propaganda does not hesitate to masquerade in the sheepskin. All the voluble men of the day— writers, reporters, editors, preachers, lecturers, teachers, politicians—are drawn into the service of propaganda to amplify a master voice. All is conducted with the decorum and the trappery of intelligence, for this is a rational epoch, and demands its raw meat cooked and garnished by adroit and skillful chefs.

Propaganda is a concession to the wilfulness of the age. The bonds of personal loyalty and affection which bound a man to his chief have long since dissolved. Monarchy and class privilege have gone the way of all flesh, and the idolatry of the individual passes for the official religion of democracy. It is an atomized world, in which individual whims have wider play than ever before, and it requires more strenuous exertions to co-ordinate and unify than formerly. The new antidote to wilfulness is propaganda. If the mass will be free of chains of iron, it must accept its chains of silver. If it will not love, honour and obey, it must not expect to escape seduction.

Propaganda is a reflex to the immensity, the rationality and wilfulness of the modern world. It is the new dynamic of society, for power is subdivided and diffused, and more can be won by illusion than by coercion. It has all the prestige of the new and provokes all the animosity of the baffled. To illuminate the mechanisms of propaganda is to reveal the secret springs of social action, and to expose to the most searching criticism our prevailing dogmas of sovereignty, of democracy, of honesty, and of the sanctity of individual opinion. The study of propaganda will bring into the open much that is obscure, until, indeed, it may no longer be possible for an Anatole France to observe with truth that "Democracy (and, indeed, all society) is run by an unseen engineer."

Notes

1. *Propaganda in its Military and Legal Aspects*, Introduction.

2. The importance of propaganda in neutral countries has been illustrated, of course, in many other wars before the last one. President Lincoln tried every expedient to stimulate the pro-North sentiment in England's industrial wage earners during the Civil War. He sent Henry Ward Beecher and perhaps a hundred other agents to England to plead the cause of the anti-slavery side. One of the most effective and original stunts was to send a ship loaded with foodstuffs, to relieve the suffering in the cities.

3. The report of the special commission of inquiry into the Caporetto disaster which was appointed by the Italian Government is not now available, and complete judgment cannot be made upon the whole affair.

4. For a description of his methods, see Mayer, *La psychologie du commandement*, and, in general, the reference in the section upon moral and military psychology in the bibliography.

5. Sir Thomas More foreshadows the extensive use of propaganda in Utopia. He records how the Utopians spread distrust among their enemies by offering a reward for the capture or the voluntary surrender of prominent enemy leaders, and how they seek to divide the enemy by fostering the ambition of a rival to the reigning prince.

9

Manipulating Public Opinion: The Why and the How (1928)

Edward L. Bernays

Edward L. Bernays (1891–1995) was born in Vienna, a nephew (on two sides) to Sigmund Freud, and grew up in the United States. The self-appointed father of public relations (a fact that he applied all his public relations zeal to proclaiming), he helped broker the alliance of psychological theory and mass persuasion techniques from the 1920s on. He never claimed that public relations was the manipulation of images: his aim was much more ambitious, the shaping of reality itself. Thanks to a series of successful campaigns in "engineering consent," Bernays has to be counted as one of the most influential theorists and practitioners of public communication in the twentieth century and thus one of the key figures in laying the groundwork for the promotional culture in which we live.

"Propaganda" did not carry the negative connotation to Bernays that it did to many others in the 1920s and 1930s. Dripping from his pages is confidence that propaganda is a good thing—a necessary intervention in the communicative chaos of modern life, a service to the public that helps them intrepet and act in a confusing world. "Manipulating public opinion" was as necessary to reduce prejudice as it was to sell fashion and fur hats. It was part of the necessary "mass distribution of ideas" upon which progress would rest. His analysis parallels that of contemporaneous, culturally oriented Marxist thinkers such as Antonio Gramsci, Max Horkheimer, and Theodor Adorno (see Horkheimer and Adorno's brief treatment of "propaganda" in this volume, p. 180). Like Bernays, these thinkers saw the subtle leadership of opinion all around them, but unlike Bernays, they were repulsed by it. Bernays's critics have often implicitly agreed with his analysis—but not his evaluation—of the managed nature of public communication in the modern world. Until the end of his long and fascinating life, Bernays remained convinced of the public necessity and benefit of the engineering of consent.

Public opinion is subject to a variety of influences that develop and alter its views on nearly every phase of life today. Religion, science, art, commerce, industry are in a state of motion. The inertia of society and institutions is constantly combated by the activity of individuals with strong convictions and desires.

Civilization, however, is limited by inertia. We repeat constantly our beliefs and habits until they become a cumulative retrogressive force.

Our attitude toward social intercourse, toward economics, toward national and international politics continues past attitudes and strengthens them under the force of tradition. Comstock lets his mantle of proselytizing morality fall on a willing Sumner; Penrose lets fall his mantle on Butler; Carnegie his on Schwab; and so *ad infinitum.* Opposing this traditional acceptance of existing ideas is an active public opinion that has been directed consciously into movement against inertia. Public opinion was made or changed formerly by tribal chiefs, by kings, by religious leaders Today the privilege of attempting to sway public opinion is everyone's. It is one of the manifestations of democracy that anyone may try to convince others and to assume leadership on behalf of his own thesis.

Narrowly defined, public opinion represents the thought of any given group of society at any given time toward a given object. Looked at from the broadest standpoint, it is the power of the group to sway the larger public in its attitude toward ideas.

New ideas, new precedents, are continually striving for a place in the scheme of things. Very often these ideas are socially sound and constructive and put an end to worn-out notions. Usually they are minority ideas, for naturally, but regrettably, majority ideas are most often old ones. Public opinion is slow and reactionary, and does not easily accept new ideas.

The innovator, the leader, the special pleader for new ideas, has through necessity developed a new technique—the psychology of public persuasion. Through the application of this new psychology he is able to bring about changes in public opinion that will make for the acceptance of new doctrines, beliefs, and habits. The manipulation of the public mind, which is so marked a characteristic of society today, serves a social purpose. This manipulation serves to gain acceptance for new ideas. It is a species of education in that it presents new problems for study and consideration to the public, and leaves it free to approve or reject them. Never before was so broad a section of the general public so subjected to facts on both sides of so many problems of life. Honest education and honest propaganda have much in common. There is this dissimilarity: Education attempts to be disinterested, while propaganda is frankly partisan.

What are the various motives for the manipulation of public opinion? They are the motives which dominate man in our society today. The basic instincts of self-preservation, procreation, and love are the more complex social motives. People attempt to sway other people for social motives—ethical, philanthropic, educational—for political, for international, for economic, and for motives of personal ambition.

From a social motive a special pleader may wage a campaign against tuberculosis or cancer, or to raise the standard of business ethics, or to secure support for a philanthropic institution. From the political standpoint, he may strive to make the public accept the idea of specific efficiency or economy in government. Internationally a special pleader may be seeking peace among the nations. Or in economics he may try to create a new market for an old product, or a market for a new product. Personal ambition to succeed, to convince others, to win recognition are basic motives that have activated most of the leaders of the world.

There is, of course, one danger inherent in this essential machinery of dealing with public opinion. It is a danger so grave that editors and publicists shy from the subject rather than discuss it.

Where shall we end, they say, in this welter of conflicting ideas? What will come from this chaos? And cannot the man who has manipulated his public opinion and won it to his side misuse it for his own purpose? Possibly he can. There are Ku Klux Klans, there are Mussolinis, there are tyrannies of every sort; but a public that learns more and more how to express itself will learn more and more how to overthrow tyranny of every sort. So that every man who teaches the public how to ask for what it wants is at the same time teaching the public how to safeguard itself against his own possible tyrannous aggressiveness.

How is public opinion manipulated? The technique of measuring and recording human relations has not been perfected as has the technique of measuring physical relations. No Bureau of Standards with micrometers exists for the expert on human or public relations. Experimental psychology has provided some yardsticks, but they are not clearly defined and are more easily applied to one field of manipulated public opinion—advertising—than to the broader field of propaganda or public relations.

It is comparatively simple to test out the comparative efficacy of a page advertisement with white space and an advertisement which is printed solidly, or of a colored billboard and a black-and-white billboard. But the method of the experimental psychological laboratories hardly meets the requirements of the technician who deals with public opinion in the broad.

Here the specialist in swaying public opinion avails himself of the findings of introspective psychology. He knows in general the basic emotions and desires of the public he intends to reach, and their prevalence and intensity. Analysis is the first step in dealing with a problem that concerns the public. He employs the technique of statistics, field-surveying, and the various methods of eliciting facts and opinions in examining both the public, and the idea or product he seeks to propagandize.

Diagnostic ability enters into this question of manipulating public opinion; a diagnostic ability that is perhaps a greater essential in manipulating public opinion effectively today than it will be later, when the technique has been more scientifically developed.

Sociology also contributes to his technique. The group cleavages of society, the importance of group leaders, and the habits of their followers are part of the technical background of his work. He has methods adapted to educating the public to new ideas, to articulating minority ideas and strengthening them, to making latent majority ideas active, to making an old principle apply to a new idea, to substituting ideas by changing *clichés*, to overcoming prejudices, to making a part stand for the whole, and to creating events and circumstances that stand for his ideas. He must know the physical organs of approach to his public: the radio, the lecture platform, the motion picture, the letter, the advertisement, the pamphlet, the newspaper. He must know how an idea can be translated into terms that fit any given form of communication, and that his public can understand.

An interesting experiment is being conducted in New York in an endeavor to chart these human relationships along scientific lines. The first study of this group was to trace the development and functioning of given attitudes toward given subjects, such as religion, sex, race, morality, nationalism, internationalism, and so forth. The conclusion was established that attitudes were often created by a circumstance or circumstances of dramatic moment.

Very often the propagandist is called upon to create circumstance that will eventuate in the desired reaction on the part of the public he is endeavoring to reach.

So much for principle; how, in practice, does this manipulating process work out?

Take the question of the fight against lynching, Jim Crowism, and the civil discriminations against the Negro below the Mason and Dixon line. How was public opinion manipulated after the war to bring about a change, or at least a modification for the better, in the public attitude toward the Negro? The National Association for the Improvement of the Colored People had the fight in hand. As a matter of technique they decided to dramatize the year's campaign in an annual convention which would center attention at one time and at one place upon the ideas they stood for and upon the men who stood for these ideas. The purpose of this convention was to build up for the question and for its proponents the support of all those who would necessarily learn of the conference.

The first step in the technique settled, the next step was to decide how to make it most effective.

Should it be held in the North, South, West, or East? Since the purpose was to affect the entire country, the association was advised to hold it in the South. For, said the propagandist, a point of view on a southern question, emanating from a southern center, would have a greater force of authority than the same point of view issuing from any other locality, particularly when that point of view was at odds with the traditional southern point of view. Atlanta was chosen.

The third step was to surround the conference with people who were stereotypes for ideas that carried weight all over the country. The support of leaders of diversified groups was sought. Telegrams and letters were dispatched to leaders of religious, political, social, and educational groups, asking for their point of view on the purpose of the conference. But in addition to these group leaders of national standing it was particularly important from the technical standpoint to secure the opinions of group leaders of the South, even from Atlanta itself, to emphasize the purposes of the conference to the entire public. There was one group in Atlanta which could be approached. A group of ministers, on the basis of Christianity, had been bold enough to come out for a greater interracial amity. This group was approached and agreed to co-operate in the conference.

Here, then, were main factors of a created circumstance; a conference to be held in a southern city, with the participation of national leaders and especially with the participation of southern gentlemen.

The scene had been set. The acts of the play followed logically.

And the event ran off as scheduled. The program itself followed the general scheme. Negroes and white men from the South on the same platform, expressing the same point of view.

A dramatic element spotlighted here and there. A national leader from Massachusetts, descendant of an Abolitionist, agreeing in principle and in practice with a Baptist preacher from the South.

If the radio had been in effect, the whole country would have heard and been moved by the speeches and the principles expressed.

But the public read the words and the ideas in the press of the country. For the event had been created of such important component parts as to awaken interest throughout the country and to gain support for its ideas even in the South.

The editorials in the southern press, reflecting the public opinion of their communities, showed that the subject had become one of interest to the editors because of the participation by southern leaders.

The event naturally gave the Association itself substantial weapons with which to appeal to an increasingly wider circle. Futher expansion of these thoughts was attained by mailing reports, letters, and other documents to selected groups of the public. Who can tell what homes, what smoking-rooms in Pullman cars and hotels, what schoolrooms, what churches, what Rotary and Kiwanis clubs responded to the keynote struck by these men and women speaking in Atlanta!

As for the practical results, the immediate one was a change in the minds of many southern editors who realized that the question at issue was not an emotional one, but a discussable one; and that this point of view was immediately reflected to their readers. As for the results, these are hard to measure with a slide rule. The conference had its effect in changing the attitude of southerners; it had its definite effect in building up the racial consciousness and solidarity of the Negroes; it had its effect in bringing to the South in a very dramatic way a realization of the problems it was facing, with the consequent desire among its leaders to face them more ably. It is evident that the decline in lynching is an effect of this and other efforts of the association.

But let us touch another field, that of industry. The millinery industry two years ago was hanging by a thread. The felt hat had arrived and was crowding out the manufacture of all those kinds of hats and hat ornaments upon which an industry and thousands of men and women employed in it had subsisted. What to do to prevent débâcle?

A public-relations counsel was called in by the association of the millinery trade, both wholesale and retail. He analyzed the hat situation and found that the hats made by the manufacturer could roughly be classified into six groups: the lace hat, the ribbon hat, the straw and feather-trimmed and other ornamented hats, and so on.

The public relations counsel tabulated the elements of the social structure that dominated the hat-using habits of women. These he found comprised four classes: First, the society leader, the woman at the fountain-head of style who made the fashion by her approval. Second, there was the style expert, the writer or publicist who enunciated fashion facts and information. Third was the artist, who was needed to give artistic approval to the styles. Fourth, and not unimportant either, were beautiful women to wear the embodied ideas sanctioned by other groups. The problem, then, was to bring into juxtaposition all of these groups, and preferably at one time and at one place, before an audience of those most concerned, the buyers of hats.

With that as a working plan of how to shape events to bring about the desired result, the remainder of the work was simply filling in the outline with real people.

A committee of prominent artists was organized to choose the six most beautiful girls in New York to wear, in a series of six tableaux, the six most beautiful hats of the six style classifications at a fashion fête to be held at the Hotel Astor. Heyworth Campbell, art editor of the Condé Nast publications, was head of the committee. Leo Lentelli, the sculptor; Charles Dana Gibson; Henry Creange, the art director; Ray Greenleaf joined the group and toiled mightily to choose from among hundreds of applicants the six most desirable candidates.

In the meantime there was organized a style committee of distinguished American women who, on a basis of their interest in the development of an American industry, were willing to add the authority of their names to the idea. And, simultaneously, there was organized a style committee consisting of Carmel White, of *Vogue*, and other prominent fashion authorities who were willing to support the idea because of its style value. The girls had been chosen. Now they chose the hats.

On the evening of the fashion show everything had been arranged for the dramatic juxtaposition of all of these elements for molding public opinion. The girls—beautiful girls—in their lovely hats and costumes paraded on the running board before an audience of the entire trade.

The news of the event affected not only the buying habits of the onlookers, but also of the women throughout the country. The story of the event was flashed to the consumer by the news service of her newspaper as well as by the advertisement of her favorite store. Broadsides went to the millinery buyer from the manufacturer, and the rotogravure of the lovely women in the lovely hats went to the consumer in the smallest town. In ten days the industry was humming. One manufacturer stated that whereas before the show he had not sold any large trimmed hats, after it he sold thousands. The felt hat was put to rout; not by Paris immediately, but by the women in this country, who quite rightly accepted the leadership of the fashion groups who had created the circumstances as they are outlined here.

If large trimmed hats could put to rout the small felt *cloche*, then perhaps velvet could also make its inroads upon the style habits of twenty-three million women. Analysis showed that the velvet manufacturers could not start their fashion here. Fashion came from Paris. That Lyons, home of silk manufactories, and Paris, home of *couturières* and milliners, influenced the American markets, both of manufacture and distribution, there was no doubt. The attack had to be made at the source. It was determined to substitute purpose for chance, and to utilize the regular sources for fashion distribution, and to influence the public from the sources. A velvet fashion service, openly supported by the manufacturers, was organized. Its first function was to establish contact with the Lyons manufactories and the Paris *couturières* to find out what they were doing, to encourage them to act on behalf of velvet, and to help in the proper exploitation of their wares. An intelligent Parisian was enlisted into their work. It was he who visited Lanvin and Worth, Agnes and Patou, etc., and induced them to use velvet in their gowns and hats. It was he who arranged for the distinguished Countess this or Duchess that to wear the hat or the gown. And as for the presentation of the idea to the public, the American buyer or the American woman of fashion was simply shown the velvet creations in the atelier of the dressmaker or the milliner. She bought the velvet because she liked it and because it was in fashion. The editor of the American newspaper magazine and the fashion reporter of the American newspaper, likewise subjected to the actual (though created) circumstance, reflected it in her news, which, in turn, subjected the consumer and the buyer here to the same influences. The result was that what was at first a trickle of velvet became a flood. A demand was slowly being created, not fortuitously, but consciously. A big department store, aiming to be a style leader, advertised velvet gowns and hats on the authority of French *couturières* and quoted original cables received from them. The echo of the new style note resounded from hundreds of department stores throughout the country who wanted to be style leaders too.

Broadside followed broadside, the mail followed the cables, and the American woman traveler appeared before ship news photographers in velvet gown and hat.

The created circumstances had their effect. Velvet was the fashion. "Fickle fashion had veered to velvet," was one newspaper comment. And the industry in South Manchester and Patterson again kept thousands busy.

The fields in which public opinion can be manipulated to conform to a desired result are as varied as life itself.

In politics, for instance, in order to humanize an individual: When President Coolidge was running for office the question was brought up of how the hitherto unknown personality of the man in the White House could be projected to the country.

It was suggested that an event in which the most human groups would be brought into juxtaposition with the president would have the desired results. Actors and actresses were invited to breakfast with Mr. Coolidge at the White House. The country felt that a man in the White House who could laugh with Al Jolson and the Dolly sisters was not frigid and unsympathetic.

An interesting example of international propaganda is the campaign that was waged to make 110,000,000 people in America realize that a small country on the Baltic was not simply a spot on the map. Lithuania was reflected to this country in its drama, music, literature, habits, economics, and agriculture. The printed word and events created to symbolize facts and ideas made America aware of the conditions in Lithuania and of its just aspirations. Ignorance was dissipated and sympathies strengthened to a point where these feelings became translated into action. Lithuania received economic aid and political recognition.

From Lithuania to silks is a long distance. Yet the same technique of creating circumstance which freed the Lithuanians helped to create a market for more beautiful silks. Although the silks made in America were inspired by France, the American woman refused to recognize their style of beauty until Paris had put its stamp of approval on them. That was the problem: to develop public opinion to accept the idea that American silk was artistic, and to use French authority in accomplishing that end. The silks were authentic in beauty, workmanship, and style. A plan was developed to have the silks exhibited in the Louvre, because that stands for the idea of accredited beauty in the American mind. It was suggested that the American ambassador officially open the exhibition, as a fitting recognition of America's leadership in the field. He felt legitimately that he was doing his duty in encouraging American industry. Leading men and women in the French capital were invited to the exhibition, with the consequence that by cable, by motion picture, by mail, the American public was soon made conscious of the fact that its own silk had received the recognition of the French art authorities. It must be good, therefore! And the best index of the success of the plan was the fact that the leading cities of the United States vied with each other for the honor of exhibiting what the Louvre had shown, whereas before they had regarded the productions of America's looms simply as so much merchandise.

As for the companies interested in gaining acceptance for new inventions, how can they overcome the inertia of the public without applying some stimulus to public opinion? The panatrope, an instrument which is the result of years of painstaking experimentation in the electrical and acoustical laboratories of four great corporations—the Westinghouse, the General Electric, the Radio Corporation, and the Brunswick-Balke-Collender companies—was perfected and ready for general sale. A definite technique must be used to launch it to affect the minds of millions who presumably are much more interested in football scores and Lindbergh than in a new mechanical principle in music-making machinery. Group adherence is the fulcrum around which broad acceptance for new ideas can most rapidly be moved. Certain small groups are important enough to influence the attitudes of large groups that overlap them. First were the music lovers and critics, whose acceptance of this new idea carried weight with the average buyer of musical instruments, who without their aid could not formulate an opinion as to the quality of this machine. Scientists were selected to join the committee of sponsorship

that had been formed. Their support of the idea meant to the public that it was scientifically correct. Third was the stereotype of the Metropolitan Opera House, which stands in the public mind for achievement in music. It was decided to gather all of these elements together at a single dramatic event in a place which should further symbolize the idea. The patrons of music were chosen: Mrs. Vincent Astor and Mr. Otto Kahn joined the committee. The scientists, John Hays Hammond and Doctor Alfred N. Goldsmith, were happy to give their authority to the idea and joined the committee. Benjamino Gigli, a tenor of the Metropolitan Opera Company, gave the artistic stamp of approval to the event. And quite naturally Aeolian Hall, the nucleus of music, was chosen as the place at which the event was to be held. A representative audience responded to the invitation. The event was important and interesting and took a prominent place among the competitive ideas and events of the day. The consequence was that the Panatrope immediately received acceptance as an important musical instrument. Without the definite procedure of implanting a new idea in the public mind, the inertia of society might have retarded the acceptance of this invention in the musical field for many years.

Public opinion may be marshaled for or against even salad dressings: Here the American's sense of humor was made the basis of a plan to make large numbers of the public receptive to a new product. Reciprocal relations between the palate and the palette in terms of harmonies in oil were made the basis of a picturesque joke. The public, more seriously occupied with Chinese revolutions and Nicaraguan questions, responded immediately to the idea that art galleries are fitting places, not only for still-lifes of salads as painted by famous artists, but also of examples of art in cooking. Beautifully prepared salads dedicated to famous artists were therefore displayed underneath canvases painted by famous artists. The exhibit was colorful and spirited and had its effect in focusing attention on salad dressing. That newspapers offer space in their columns and devote time and attention to such an exhibit is not the relevant point. What is relevant is that an idea may strike the fancy and arrest the attention of hundreds of thousands of people, and as such can be communicated to them through every form of thought-transmission of which modern business avails itself.

Analysis of the problem and its causes is the first step toward shaping the public mind on any subject. Occasionally the analysis points to a basic change in the policy of a manufacturer.

Take the case of a certain vegetable shortening. There was no sale of this food product in certain sections of the public. A careful research was made. It was found that orthodox Jews would not buy it because it did not conform to the dietary requirements of their religion. The manufacturer altered the product itself to make it conform to the dietary strictures of this market. The problem that lay before him then was to acquaint this sector of the population with the change. This problem was handled with success. The stamp of approval was given the product by religious leaders and special dietary officials. Institutions such as hospitals, that were known to conform scrupulously to the dietary rules, were asked to convince themselves of the character and quality of the product. Their approval bore weight with the thousands of people who respected their authority.

One method of changing people's ideas has been often used, and that is to substitute new ideas for old by changing *clichés*. The evacuation hospitals during the war came in for a certain amount of criticism because of the summary way in which they handled their wounded. The name was changed to "evacuation post," thus changing the *cliché*. No one expected more than adequate emergency treatment of an institution so named. This story, which was told to me by a reliable authority, is a clear illustration of the principle.

Before 1925 few people in America felt that industry had any connection with art. Few manufacturers thought seriously of the artistic ramifications of their work. A small group of people, however, realizing the importance of this phase of American industry, approached Herbert Hoover, secretary of commerce, and suggested that he appoint a commission to visit and report on the International Exposition of Industrial and Decorative Arts at Paris in 1925. I was appointed associate commissioner. We appointed about 150 delegates from different industries to study the exposition at Paris. A report was made. Industry itself became conscious of the new *cliché* of themselves that had been made in this way. Since then a determined progress toward authentic beauty has been made in large industries around the country.

Soap found a new market and a new use when the public-relations counsel of a large soap corporation called upon the desire for beauty of a strong minority of the population and introduced soap as a medium for sculpture as a pastime for children and as an educational aid for schools. An annual contest has been held for several years in a leading art gallery, and exhibits of the works of thousands of professional and amateur sculptors shown in the leading galleries and museums of the country.

Instantaneous attention was given to the financial articles of W. Z. Ripley, asking for full publicity in financial reports of stock corporations. He articulated an idea that was latent in the minds of a large majority of the public. The next step was to convert this new awareness into action. Public opinion, aroused by Ripley, forced the New York Stock Exchange to take action.

Occasionally, the manipulation of the public mind entails the removal of a prejudice. Prejudices are often the application of old taboos to new conditions. They are illogical, emotional, and hampering to progress. Take, for example, the feeling that used to exist against margarine. In its early stages of manufacture in this country, margarine was, like as not, made of impure animal matter. Its state of wholesomeness was not apparent. Today margarine is made of pure vegetable or animal ingredients that have been scientifically determined upon as wholesome and passed as pure by the government. Yet the prejudice carried over, and a difficult campaign is still being waged to remove this prejudice. Correspondence is carried on with officials and leaders in the field of medicine, hygiene, and dietetics, and the result of their manifold study given out to the public. The prejudice remained long after its cause had been altered.

This is an age of mass production. In the mass production of materials a broad technique has been developed and applied to their distribution. In this age, too, there must be a technique for the mass distribution of ideas. Public opinion can be moved, directed, and formed by such a technique. But at the core of this great heterogeneous body of public opinion is a tenacious will to live, to progress, to move in the direction of ultimate social and individual benefit. He who seeks to manipulate public opinion must always heed it.

10

From *Middletown: A Study in Contemporary American Culture* (1929)

Robert S. Lynd and Helen Merrell Lynd

Robert S. Lynd (1892–1970) was one of the leading sociologists and observers of American culture in the 1930s and 1940s. Born in small-town Indiana, he attended Princeton and worked briefly in the publishing industry before enrolling at the liberal Union Theological Seminary with the intent of becoming a minister. After spending a summer at an isolated oil camp in Wyoming, where he was appalled at the working conditions of the men, he became radicalized. He wrote a well-documented, muckraking account of the camp, which was connected to John D. Rockefeller's Standard Oil Company. His piece was published in *Survey* magazine and excerpted by thousands of newspapers across the country. Ironically, two years later, Lynd and his wife, Helen, received a grant from Rockefeller's Institute of Social and Religious Research to undertake a study of religion in an American community. That project grew into *Middletown* (1929), which with its sequel, *Middletown in Transition* (1937), portrayed a changing America by offering a portrait of one "typical" city—Muncie, Indiana (see Fox 1983). In addition to the *Middletown* books, Robert also wrote a valuable entry on the emerging American consumer culture in *Recent Social Trends* (1933) and in *Knowledge for What* (1940), which was an important critique of disengaged, "value-neutral" social science.

Helen Merrell Lynd was the daughter of an Illinois newspaper publisher. She studied at Wellesley before taking a master's degree in philosophy at Columbia (1922). She introduced her husband to the writings of Thorstein Veblen as well as that of John Dewey, the Lynds' two greatest intellectual influences. She took a doctorate in history from Columbia (1944), where Robert was a professor of sociology from 1931 to 1960. Among other works, Helen published *England in the Eighteen-Eighties* (1945), an important social history of labor, education, politics, and change.

In *Middletown*, the Lynds set out to study Muncie as anthropologists might study a "primitive" tribe. Based on field research the Lynds conducted while living in Muncie from 1924 to 1925, *Middletown* addresses the rise of consumer culture and the changes wrought on work and leisure by industrialization. It ties the Lynds back to Thorstein Veblen's critiques of "conspicuous consumption" and John Dewey's belief that social science could serve as a means of social reflection and criticism. Their community study methods were influential and copied by a young Paul Lazarsfeld, working on his own community study in Austria with Marie Jahoda and Hans Zeisel, *Die Arbeitslosen von Marienthal* (1933). *Middletown*, widely mentioned in the popular press, made steady comparisons to a preconsumerist, preindustrial Muncie of 1890, which the Lynds preferred to the culture they observed. They documented the way Middletowners worked, lived at home, educated their young, practiced religion, conducted their civic life, and spent their leisure time. The three chapters on the reorganization of leisure, from which we have excerpted the following sections, offer a small treasure trove of details about Middletown's patterns of communication and media use and thus offer one window into the experience of American media audiences in the twentieth century.

Traditional Ways of Spending Leisure

Some of Middletown's waking hours escape the routinization of getting a living, home-making, receiving training in school, or carrying on religious or communal practices; in contrast to more strictly marshaled pursuits, such hours are called "leisure time," and this precious time, quite characteristically in a pecuniary society, is "spent."

The manner of spending leisure is perforce conditioned by the physical environment of the city and by the rest of its culture. Its location in the flat ex-prairie known as the Corn Belt precludes such variety of activity as cities adjacent to mountains, lakes, of forests know; Middletown, according to a local editorial, "is unfortunate in not having many natural beauty spots." There is rolling country to the south, but no real hills nearer than one hundred miles. Equally distant to the north are "the lakes," large prairie ponds scattered through flat farming country. A small river wanders through Middletown, and in 1890 when timber still stood on its banks, White River was a pleasant stream for picnics, fishing, and boating, but it has shrunk today to a creek discolored by industrial chemicals and malodorous with the city's sewage. The local chapter of the Isaak Walton League aspires to "Make White River white," "This Corn Belt . . . is not a land to thrill one who loves hills, wild landscape, mountain panorama, waterfalls, babbling brooks, and nature undisturbed. In this flat land of food crops and murky streams rich with silt, man must find thrills in other things, perhaps in travel, print, radio, or movie."[1]

Middletown people today enjoy a greater variety of these alternate other things than their parents knew a generation ago. The lessening of the number of hours spent daily in getting a living and in home-making and the almost universal habit of the Saturday half-holiday combine with these new possibilities for spending an extra hour to make leisure a more generally expected part of every day rather than a more sporadic, semi-occasional event. The characteristic leisure-time pursuits of the city tend to be things done with others rather than by individuals alone;[2] and except for the young males, they are largely passive,

i.e., looking at or listening to something or talking or playing cards or riding in an auto; the leisure of virtually all women and of most of the men over thirty is mainly spent sitting down. Its more striking aspects relate to the coming of inventions, the automobile, the movies, the radio, that have swept through the community since 1890, dragging the life of the city in their wake. Yet these newer forms of leisure must be viewed against an underlying groundwork of folk-play and folk-talk that makes up a relatively less changing human tradition.

Middletown has always delighted in talk. The operation of its business as well as of many of its professional institutions depends upon talk; honored among those who get its living are those puissant in talking. The axis upon which the training of its children turns is teaching them to use language according to the rules of the group and to understand the talk of others, whether spoken or written. Talking is the chief feature of its religious services. Much of its leisure time it spends in talking or listening to talk.

The habit of thinking no occasion, from an ice cream social to the burial of the dead, complete without a speech, is nearly as strong as in the nineties when, on a characteristic occasion, it took no less than eight speakers to dedicate a public building:

> "The evening's exercises were begun by placing Rev. O. M. T——— in the chair. Rev. G——— then delivered a very fine prayer and was followed by the regular address of the evening by Mr. T———. He was succeeded by Mr. J. W. R———. . . . Then came Glenn M———, Charley K———, Charley M———, and George M———. Mrs. P——— then delivered a short address, after which the meeting adjourned."

The dedication of two new buildings at the local college in 1925 included in its morning, afternoon, and evening programs six formal "addresses" and five other "talks." Indeed, as the author of *The American Commonwealth* pointed out forty years ago, "there is scarcely an occasion in life which brings forty or fifty people together on which a prominent citizen or a stranger . . . is not called upon 'to offer a few remarks.'"

And today, as in the nineties, the oratory of the speaker is nearly, if not quite, as important as the subject of his speech. "No matter what it's about, there's nothing I like better than a real good speech," remarked a leading citizen in 1924. In 1890 it was not necessary to announce the subject of a "lecture" to draw a crowd; "Rev. C. R. Bacon of W——— will deliver a free lecture at the Methodist Church Wednesday night. . . . Everybody invited" ran a characteristic announcement in the 1890 press. Another minister was invited to repeat his lecture on "Sunshine." The lecture has been delivered here before," said the press notice, "and yet so well pleased was the audience that the church was well filled to hear the eminent divine a second time."[3]The relative unimportance of lecture subjects today appears in the civic clubs which are kept alive week after week by an endless succession of speeches on almost every subject from Gandhi to the manufacture of a local brand of gas burners for coffee roasters. One of the most popular speakers frequently paid by Middletown to talk to it is a woman travel lecturer described by the local press as one who "delights in superlatives and whose fluency of expression has won for her an enthusiastic group of admirers in this city." "No subject is prescribed for him," continues Lord Bryce in the passage cited above; ". . . he is simply put on his legs to talk upon anything in heaven or earth which may rise to his mind."

If the subject of the address is one with which the hearers are unfamiliar or upon which they have no fixed views, they frequently adopt bodily not only the speaker's opinion but its weighting of emotion. It is not uncommon to hear a final judgment on "the Philippine problem," "economic fundamentals," "the cause of cancer," or "the future of the white race," delivered with the preamble, "Well, I heard ——— say at Chautauqua [or at Rotary] two years ago. . . ."[4] Heckling is unknown; people think with the speaker; rarely do they challenge his thought.[5]

Changes are, however, apparent in this complex of speech habits. Speeches are getting shorter; the long, general public lecture bringing its "message" is disappearing as a form of entertainment. At the Farmers and Knights of Labor picnic in 1890, the feature of the afternoon was "an address lasting two hours" to "a great crowd." This sort of thing would not draw a crowd today. "A large and cultured audience" no longer "crowds the Opera House" to hear "a pol-ished gentleman of pleasant presence and happy manner, thoroughly at ease before an audience," deliver a lecture at once "eloquent and humorous, logical, and pathetic" on the subject of "Nicknames of Prominent Americans," "Milton as an Educator," or "The Uses of Ugliness." The humorous lecture, so popular in 1890 when the great Riley-Nye combination rocked the Middletowns of America, has almost disappeared today. Likewise have all but vanished the heavy crop of moral and religious lectures by visiting ministers and denominational college presidents on "That Boy," "Strange Things and Funny People," "Backbone," "The Trials of Jesus." The secularization of lectures and lecturers is marked and includes the increasing supplanting of such lectures as the above by short talks to club groups, more and more of them talks on specific subjects to specialized groups such as the Advertising Club, Poultry Raisers, Bar Association, and Medical Association. The one-time popular money-raising device of Sunday School classes and Young Peoples' Societies of sponsoring a public lecture or winter lyceum is almost unknown today.[6] The lecture at which an admission fee is charged is in general a losing proposition in these days of radio and movies. The teachers have abandoned their effort to conduct a winter lyceum, and the lyceum conducted by the Ministerial Association, after strenuous city-wide efforts to drum up audiences, lost $6.00 on a course of five lectures in 1923 and made $15.00 in 1924. The local Chautauqua, lasting less than a week, is rapidly ceasing to be popular with the business group and achieves only a precarious support, likewise after hard pushing by the churches. A cleavage between business and working class groups is apparent in the greater tendency of the latter to support the earlier type of general discourse.

Among the activities tending to displace listening to talk is another form of this complex of speech habits, the reading of printed matter. Most of Middletown's reading matter originates elsewhere.[7] Through the development of devices for producing and distributing this material, the city now has access to a range and variety of reading matter unknown to its parents.[8] Book reading in Middletown today means overwhelmingly, if we exclude school-books and Bibles, the reading of public library books.[9] Over 40,000 volumes are available in the library, roughly fifteen volumes for every one to be had in the early nineties. Middletown drew out approximately

6,500 public library books for each thousand of its population during 1924, as against 850 for each thousand of population during 1890. Four hundred and fifty-eight persons in each 1,000 were library card holders in 1923, whereas even as late as 1910 only 199 people in each 1,000 had cards.[10]

The buying of current books is almost entirely confined to a limited number of the business class. The rest of the population buy few books, chiefly religious books, children's books, and Christmas gifts, in the order indicated. Only twenty-four housewives out of the 100 working class families from whom family expenditures were secured reported expenditures for books other than school-books by members of their families during the past twelve months. The totals for the year ranged from $0.50 to $52.50; twelve of the twenty-four had each spent less than $5.00, six between $5.00 and $10.00, and six $10.00 or more.[11]

Even more marked than the greater availability of books is the increase in the number of weekly or monthly periodicals since the days of *"The Pansy* for Sunday and weekday reading" and *"The Household* sent free to every newly-married couple upon receipt of ten cents in stamps." Today the Middletown library offers 225 periodicals as against nineteen periodicals in 1890. Heavy, likewise, has been the increase in the number of magazines coming into Middletown homes.[12] Into the 9,200 homes of the city, there came in 1923, as a rough estimate, 20,000 copies of each issue of commercially published weekly and monthly periodicals, excluding denominational church papers, Sunday School papers distributed free weekly to most of the 6-7,000 attending Sunday School, and lodge and civic club magazines.[13] Forty-seven of the 122 working class families and one of the thirty-nine business class families giving information on this point subscribe to or purchase regularly no periodical; thirty-seven of the former and four of the latter subscribe to or purchase regularly only one of two periodicals; and thirty-eight (three in ten) of the workers' families and thirty-four (nine in ten) of this business group take three or more periodicals. In both groups additional periodicals are bought from the news-stand sporadically by certain families.

The significance of such a ceaseless torrent of printed matter in the process of diffusing new tools and habits of thought can scarcely be overstated. Does this greater accessibility and wider diffusion of books and periodicals today mean, however, that Middletown is spending more time in reading? Library and periodical records suggest a marked increase, but other evidence necessitates qualification of this conclusion. The type of intellectual life that brought anywhere from two dozen to a hundred people, chiefly men, together Sunday after Sunday for an afternoon of discussing every subject from "Books, What to Read and How to Read Them" to the *Origin of the Species* and "Nature of God" has almost disappeared among the males; men are almost never heard discussing books in Middletown today.[14] The impulse in the local labor movement represented in the statement in trade union constitutions, "Each labor union should found libraries, [and] hold lectures," and which eventuated in 1900 in the organization of an independent Workingmen's Library, has gone.[15] The "reading circles" of the nineties have all but disappeared, the women's clubs of today fill much the same place they occupied as stimuli to reading. Although groups of ten or twelve women no longer meet weekly to gain "the college outlook" by following the four-year cycle of Chautauqua readings, at least one business class woman is still reading for her "diploma" and more than one points to the rows of her mother's "Chautauqua books," saying that they are her chief help in preparing her club programs.[16] When teachers come together today it is not to read and discuss books as in the old state reading circles; nor do young people meet to read books suggested by the state for Young People's Reading Circles, although according to some of the teacher, State Young People's Reading Circles were never organized very extensively in Middletown and the required supplementary reading now being done in connection with English classes in the high school more than makes up for their decline.[17] No longer do a Young Ladies' Reading Circle, a Christian Literary Society (of fifty), a Literary League, a Literary Home Circle, a Literary Fireside Club meet weekly or bi-weekly as in 1890, nor are reading circles formed in various sections of the city, nor does a group young women meet to study the classics."[18] The young people's societies of the various churches do not form Dickens Clubs or have "literary evenings," as, for example, "an evening with Robert Burns," with the singing and recitation of Burns' poems and the reading of the poet's biography— a program of eleven numbers, concluding with "a discussion of Burns and his writings." "Young ladies'" clubs in Middletown are more likely now to play bridge; the attenuated church young people's societies follow mission study or other programs sent out from denominational headquarters; men do not talk books; chiefly in women's clubs does the earlier tradition persist.

* * *

The different levels of diffusion within the city appear in the fact that fifty-four periodicals drawing 115 subscriptions from the thirty-nine business class families giving information on this point have not one from the 122 workers' families, while forty-eight periodicals drawing ninety-six subscriptions from seventy-five working class families have none of this group of business class families as a subscriber; in between is a narrow group of twenty periodicals with 128 subscriptions from thirty-eight business class families and 105 from seventy-five workers' families. Nine of the 122 workers and seventeen of this business class group take the *Literary Digest*; seven of the former and twenty of the latter the *Saturday Evening Post*; forty-four of the workers' wives subscribe to women's magazines, scattering a total of 101 subscriptions among twenty-one different women's magazines, while the twenty-seven of the business class wives who take women's magazines bunch their forty-eight subscriptions among only nine magazines, almost entirely recognized leading magazines;[19] thirteen of the workers and nineteen of this business group subscribe to the *American Magazine*; there are only seven subscriptions to juvenile magazines among 122 workers' families, as against twenty-six among the thirty-nine business class families; none of the sample of workers takes a magazine of the *Atlantic, Harper's, World's Work* type, as against a total of twenty-two such subscriptions among less than one-third as many of the business group.

A cleavage between the reading habits of the two sexes is possibly suggested by the answers of 310 boys and 391 girls in the three upper years of the high school to the question, "What magazines other than assigned school magazines do you usually read every month?" Forty-four boys and 367 girls read women's magazines;[20] ninety-five boys and fifteen girls read scientific magazines; 114 boys and seventy-six girls read the *Saturday Evening Post, Collier's* and *Liberty* group of weeklies; thirty-five boys and two girls read outdoor magazines; seventy-two boys and sixteen girls

read juvenile magazines; other smaller groups were more evenly balanced.

Although, according to the city librarian, increased interest in business and technical journals has been marked, as in its reading of books Middletown appears to read magazines primarily for the vicarious living in fictional form they contain. Such reading centers about the idea of romance underlying the institution of marriage; since 1890 there has been a trend toward franker "sex adventure" fiction. It is noteworthy that a culture which traditionally taboos any discussion of sex in its systems of both religious and secular training and even until recently in the home training of children should be receiving such heavy diffusion of this material through its periodical reading matter. The aim of these sex adventure magazines, diffusing roughly 3,500 to 4,000 copies monthly throughout the city, is succinctly stated in the printed rejection slip received by a Middletown author from the New Fiction Publishing Corporation:

"*Live Stories* is interested in what we call 'sex adventure' stories told in the first person. The stories should embody picturesque settings for action; they should also present situations of high emotional character, rich in sentiment. A moral conclusion is essential."

"Until five years ago," said a full-page advertisement in a Middletown paper in 1924, "there was nowhere men and women, boys and girls could turn to get a knowledge of the rules of life. They were sent out into the world totally unprepared to cope with life. . . . Then came *True Story*, a magazine that is different from any ever published. Its foundation is the solid rock of truth. . . . It will help you , too. In five years it has reached the unheard-of circulation of two million copies monthly, and is read by five million of more appreciative men and women."

In these magazines Middletown reads "The Primitive Lover" ("She wanted a caveman husband"), "Her Life Secret," "Can a Wife Win with the Other Woman's Weapons?" "How to Keep the Thrill in Marriage," "What I Told My Daughter the Night before Her Marriage," ("Every girl on the ever of her marriage becomes again a little frightened child").

While four leading motion picture houses were featuring synchronously four sex adventure films, *Telling Tales* on the Middletown

news-stands was featuring on its cover four stories, "Indolent Kisses," "Primitive Love," Watch
Your Step-Ins!" ("Irene didn't and you should
have seen what happened!") and "Innocents
Stray." The way Middletown absorbs this culture
about (to quote the advertisement of a local film)
"things you've always wanted to do and never
DARED" was suggested by the coverless, thumb-
marked condition of the January, 1925, *Motion
Picture Magazine* in the Public Library a fortnight
after its arrival. One page, captioned "Under the
Mistletoe," depicted several "movie kisses" with
such captions as:

> "Do you recognize your little friend, Mae
> Busch? She's had lots of kisses, but never
> seems to grow blasé. At least, you'll agree
> that she's giving a good imitation of a person
> enjoying this one," and "If some one should
> catch you beneath the mistletoe and hold
> you there like this, what would you do?
> Struggle? But making live divinely is one
> of the best things Monte Blue does. Can't
> you just hear Marie Prevost's heart going
> pitty-pat?"

And a Middletown mother complained to the
interviewer, "Children weren't bold like they are
today when we were young!"

Music, like literature, is a traditional leisure activity regarded as of sufficient importance to be
made compulsory for the young. The emergence
of music to a prominent place in the school curriculum has already been described. It seems
probable from informal local testimony that the
taking of music lessons is a generally accepted essential in a child's home training among a wider
group of the city's families than in the nineties.
In forty-one of the 124 working class families,
all of whom, it will be recalled, have children of
school age, one or more children had taken music lessons during the preceding year; in twenty-
seven of the group of forty business class families interviewed, one or more children had taken
lessons.[21] Of fifty-four workers' wives reporting
on the amount of time their children spend on
music, forty-four said that they themselves spent
less time on music as children than do their children today, while only five spent more time, and
five "about the same." Among the business class,
sixteen reported that they had spent less time on
music than do their children, three that they spent
more time, and three "about the same." In answer

to the question to the three upper classes in the
high school, "In what thing that you are doing at
home this fall are you most interested?" "music"
led the list with the 341 girls, being named by
26 per cent of them, with "sewing" next most
often mentioned, by 15 per cent; among the
274 boys "radio" led the list being mentioned by
20 per cent, while "music" followed with 15 per
cent. The current interest arises in part from the
muscularity injected into music by jazz, the diffusion of instruments other than the piano, and the
social and sometimes financial accompaniments
of knowing how to "play." The one musical club
among women of the business class maintains a
Junior and a Juvenile section with social meetings at which children play for an audience of
their mothers; in addition to the two high school
bands and three orchestras, Middletown has a
boys' band, a girls' band, and a band of both boys
and girls from nine to thirteen years.[22]

Mechanical inventions such as the phonograph
and radio are further bringing to Middletown
more contacts with more kinds of music than
ever before. Thirty-five years ago diffusion of musical knowledge was entirely in the handicraft
stage; today it has entered a machine stage. The
first phonograph was exhibited locally in 1890
and was reported as "drawing large crowds. The
Edison invention is undoubtedly the most wonderful of the age."[23] Now these phonographs
have become so much a part of living that, for
example, a family of three, when the father was
laid off in the summer of 1923, "strapped a trunk
on the running board of the Ford, put the Victrola
in the back with the little girl, and went off job-
hunting. Wherever we lived all summer we had
our music with us."[24]

And yet, although more music is available to
Middletown than ever before and children are
taught music with more organized zeal than formerly, the question arises, as in the case of reading, as to whether music actually bulks larger
as a form of leisure-time enjoyment than in the
nineties. If one boy in each six or seven in high
school enjoys music more than any other leisure-
time home activity, this enthusiasm evaporates
between high school and his active life as one
of those getting Middletown's living. Music, like
poetry and the other arts, is almost non-existent
among the men. As noted elsewhere, "having
a love of music and poetry" was ranked ninth
among the qualities desirable in a father by
369 high school boys and seventh by 415 girls,

only 4 per cent of the boys and 6 per cent of the girls ranking it as one of two qualities in the list of ten that they considered most desirable.[25] Music for adults has almost ceased to be a matter of spontaneous, active participation and has become largely a passive matter of listening to others. The popular singing societies of the nineties have disappeared, with one working class exception. One such group in the nineties, composed of workers, met every Sunday afternoon and Thursday evening with a "keg of beer" and a hired "instructor." Another singing society celebrated its sixty-fourth anniversary in 1890. Still another group of forty of the city's male social leaders, calling themselves the Apollo Club and dubbed "dudes" by the others, met every Friday evening, "instructed by Professor B_____" who came over from a neighboring city; its three concerts each year were widely attended and received enthusiastic reports in the press. Even schoolboys apparently enjoyed chorus singing for as late as 1900, 300 of them gave a concert at the Opera House. The program including Gounod's "Praise Ye the Father, "The Lord's Prayer," and "Follow On" from *Der Freischiitz*. In commenting upon the rehearsals, the local press said, "The boys are enjoying the practicing and are attending well despite the fine marble weather."

Even more characteristic of the nineties was spontaneous singing as a part of the fun of any and all gatherings. When a family reunion was held it began with prayer and ended with the inevitable address and singing; at the lawn fêtes of the day some of those present would sing or play while the others sat in the windows or on the porch rail and listened. "Lay awake awhile last night," says a local diary, "listening to serenaders." The diary of a young baker mentions music of all sorts as an informal part of his "banging around town" night after night:

> "Went to L_____s' and serenaded them," "Gang over at N_____s'. Singing, guitar, mouth harp, piano, cake, bananas, oranges and lemonade. Had a time!" "Yesterday _____'s birthday, so he set up cigars and a keg at the union meeting. After the meeting we played cards and sang till eleven."

Even at an "elegant party" of "some of our society young men" of the Success Club in 1900 the press states that "an entertainment of vocal solos and readings was enjoyed by those present."

Solo singing or group singing to jazz accompaniment still appears occasionally at small parties but is far less common than a generation ago. Serenading is a thing of the past. Chorus choirs are disappearing in the churches most frequented by the business class. There is today no chorus of business class men. In the city of today, nearly three and one-half times as large as that of 1890, there are only two adult musical societies in which the earlier tradition survives, as over against four in 1890.[26] The first is a chorus of working class men. This, together with the chorus choirs in working class churches and the frequent appearance of songs and recitations in the 1890 manner in the "socials" of these churches, suggests the relatively greater place of singing and playing in the play life of working class adults. It suggests, too, the tendency noted elsewhere for many of the workers' habits to lag roughly a generation behind those of the business class.

A second group participating actively in music is composed of women of the business class. This group, responsible for most of the organized musical life of the city, began in 1889 with a membership of thirty of the city's leading women, each of whom appeared on the program at every third meeting. Today it has 249 members, sixty-seven of them active, forty-eight professional, and ten chorus members, with many even of these taking no active part in the meetings. "The interest in the club and participation in its programs is not as great today as in the nineties," lamented one member. "Now there are so many clubs and other diversions to occupy people's time." Those most active in the club complain of continual lack of interest on the part of the members. The sophistication of a few of the more privileged women in the city tends to make them impatient of a less cultivated group to whom the club affords a more satisfying form of social and artistic expression. There was a net drop in membership of fifty-nine from 1923-24 to 1924-25. A possible indication of what the mass of the members prefer is furnished by the fact that a recitation to music of Eugene Field's "the dear little boy, the sweet little boy, the pretty little bow-legged boy" will be greeted with more applause on a program of American music than characteristic examples of Negro and Indian music. Leaders complain of lack of support for the various concerts which they bring to the city, although they say that Middletown is "music hungry"' the concert of an organization like the Letz Quartet barely pays for itself, but some song recitals receive more support.

It is an open question whether the devotion of Middletown to music as a personal art, as opposed to listening to music, today is not more a part of tradition and the institutional relationships kept alive as part of the adult social system than of the spontaneous play life of the city. Music seems to serve in part as a symbol that one belongs, and much of the musical activity of the women appears as a rather self-conscious appendage of the city's club life. An incipient trend away from the ritual of music lessons for children may be apparent in the remark of a prominent mother: "My children are not interested in music and there are so many things children can be interested in today that we are not going to waste time and money on them until they really want it. I had five years of lessons as a girl and can't play a thing today. I'm not going to make this mistake with my children." The mothers of the present generation of children were brought up in a culture without Victrola and radio when the girl in the crowd who could play while the others sang or danced was in demand. In their insistence upon music lessons for their children they may be reliving a world that no longer exists. Today when great artists or dance orchestras are in the cabinet in the corner of one's living room or "on the air," the ability to "play a little" may be in increasingly less demand. It seems not unlikely that, within the next generation, this habit of taking music lessons may become more selective throughout the entire population as music is made available to all through instruction in the schools and wide diffusion of Victrolas, radios, and other instruments in the home, while other abilities supplant it as the ritualistic social grace it so often is today.

* * *

Like the automobile, the motion picture is more to Middletown than simply a new way of doing an old thing; it has added new dimensions to the city's leisure. To be sure, the spectacle-watching habit was strong upon Middletown in the nineties. Whenever they had a chance people turned out to a "show," but chances were relatively fewer. Fourteen times during January, 1890, for instance, the Opera House was opened for performances ranging from *Uncle Tom's Cabin* to *The Black Crook*, before the paper announced that "there will not be any more attractions at the Opera House for nearly two weeks." In July

there were no "attractions," a half dozen were scattered through August and September; there were twelve in October.[27]

Today nine motion picture theaters operate from 1 to 11 P.M. seven days a week summer and winter; four of the nine give three different programs a week, the other five having two a week; thus twenty-two different programs with a total of over 300 performances are available to Middletown every week in the year. In addition, during January, 1923, there were three plays in Middletown and four motion pictures in other places than the regular theaters, in July three plays and one additional movie, in October two plays and one movie.

About two and three-fourths times the city's entire population attended the nine motion picture theaters during the month of July, 1923, the "valley" month of the year, and four and one-half times the total population in the "peak" month of December.[28] Of 395 boys and 457 girls in the three upper years of the high school who stated how many times they had attended the movies in "the last seven days," a characteristic week in mid-November, 30 per cent of the boys and 39 per cent of the girls had not attended, 31 and 29 per cent, respectively had been only once, 22 and 21 per cent respectively two times, 10 and 7 per cent three times, and 7 and 4 per cent four or more times. According to the housewives interviewed regarding the custom in their own families, in three of the forty business class families interviewed and in thirty-eight of the 122 working class families no member "goes at all" to the movies.[29] One family in ten in each group goes as an entire family once a week or oftener; the two parents go together without their children once a week or oftener in four business class families (one in ten), and in two working class families (one in sixty); in fifteen business class families and in thirty-eight working class families the children were said by their mothers to go without their parents one or more times weekly.

In short, the frequency of movie attendance of high school boys and girls is about equal, business class families tend to go more often than do working class families, and children of both groups attend more often without their parents than do all the individuals or other combinations of family members put together. The decentralizing tendency of the movies upon the family, suggested by this last, is further indicated by the fact that only 21 per cent of 337 boys and 33 per cent of 423 girls in the three upper years of the high school go to the movies more often with their parents than without them. On the other hand, the comment is frequently heard in Middletown that movies have cut into lodge attendance, and it is probable that time formerly spent in lodges, saloons, and unions is now being spent in part at the movies, at leas occasionally with other members of the family.[30] Like the automobile and radio, the movies, by breaking up leisure time into an individual, family, or small group affair, represent a counter movement to the trend toward organization so marked in clubs and other leisure-time pursuits.

How is life being quickened by the movies for the youngsters who bulk so large in the audiences, for the punch press operator at the end of his working day, for the wife who goes to a "picture" every week or so "while he stays home with the children," for those business class families who habitually attend?

> "Go to a motion picture ... and let yourself go," Middletown reads in a *Saturday Evening Post* advertisement. "Before you know it you are *living* the story—laughing, loving, hating, struggling, winning! All the adventure, all the romance, all the excitement you lack in your daily life are in—Pictures. They take you completely out of yourself into a wonderful new world.... Out of the cage of everyday existence! If only for an afternoon or an evening—escape!"

The program of the five cheaper houses is usually a "Wild West" feature, and a comedy; of the four better houses, one feature film, usually a "society" film but frequently Wild West or comedy, one short comedy, or if the feature is a comedy, an educational film (e.g., *Laying an Ocean Cable* or *Making a Telephone*), and a news film. In general, people do not go to the movies to be instructed; the Yale Press series of historical films, as noted earlier, were a flat failure and the local exhibitor discontinued them after the second picture.

As in the case of the books it reads, comedy, heart interest, and adventure compose the great bulk of what Middletown enjoys in the movies. Its heroes, according to the manager of the leading theater, are, in the order named, Harold Lloyd, comedian; Gloria Swanson, heroine in modern society films; Thomas Meighan, hero in modern society films; Colleen Moore,

ingénue; Douglas Fairbanks, comedian and adventurer; Mary Pickford, ingénue; and Norma Talmadge, heroine in modern society films. Harold Lloyd comedies draw the largest crowds. "Middletown is amusement hungry," says the opening sentence in a local editorial; at the comedies Middletown lives for an hour in a happy sophisticated make-believe world that leaves it, according to the advertisement of one film, "happily convinced that Life is very well worth living."

Next largest are the crowds which come to see the sensational society films. The kind of vicarious living brought to Middletown by these films may be inferred from such titles as: "*Alimony*—brilliant men, beautiful jazz babies, champagne bathes, midnight revels, petting parties in the purple dawn, all ending in one terrific smashing climax that makes you gasp"; "*Married Flirts—Husbands*: Do you flirt? Does your wife always know where you are? Are you faithful to your vows? *Wives*: What's your hubby doing? Do you know? Do you worry? Watch out for *Married Flirts*." So fast do these flow across the silver screen that, e.g., at one time *The Daring Years, Sinners in Silk, Women Who Give*, and *The Price She Paid* were running synchronously, and at another "*Name the Man*—a story of betrayed womanhood," *Rouged Lips*, and *The Queen of Sin*.[31] While Western "action" films and a million-dollar spectacle like *The Covered Wagon* or *The Hunchback of Notre Dame* draw heavy houses, and while managers lament that there are too few of the popular comedy films, it is the film with burning "heart interest," that packs Middletown's motion picture houses week after week. Young Middletown enters eagerly into the vivid experience of *Flaming Youth:* "neckers, petters, white kisses, red kisses, pleasure-mad daughters, sensation-craving mothers, by an author who didn't dare sign his name; the truth bold, naked, sensational"—so ran the press advertisement—under the spell of the powerful conditioning medium of pictures presented with music and all possible heightening of the emotional content, and the added factor of sharing this experience with a "date" in a darkened room. Meanwhile, *Down to the Sea in Ships*, a costly spectacle of whaling adventure, failed at the leading theater "because," the exhibitor explained, "the whale is really the hero in the film and there wasn't enough 'heart interest' for the women."

Over against these spectacles which Middletown watches today stand the pale "sensations" of the nineties, when *Sappho* was the apogee of daring at the Opera House: "*The Telephone Girl*—Hurricane hits, breezy dialogue, gorgeous stage setting, dazzling dancing, spirited repartee, superb music, opulent costumes," *Over the Garden Wall, Edith's Burglar, East Lynne, La Belle Maria,* or *Women's Revenge, The Convict's Daughter, Joe, a Mountain Fairy, The Vagabond Heroine, Guilty Without Crime, The World Against Her* (which the baker pronounced in his diary, "good, but too solemn"), *Love Will Find a Way, Si. Plankard.* These, it must be recalled, were the great days when *Uncle Tom's Cabin*, with "fifty men, women, and children, a pack of genuine bloodhounds, grandest street parade ever given, and two bands," packed the Opera House to capacity.

Actual changes of habits resulting from the week-after-week witnessing of these films can only be inferred. Young Middletown is finding discussion of problems of mating in this new agency that boasts in large illustrated advertisements, "Girls! You will learn how to handle 'em!" and "Is it true that marriage kills love? If you want to know what love really means, its exquisite torture, its overwhelming raptures, see _____."

> "Sheiks and their 'shebas,'" according to the press account of the Sunday opening of one film, "...sat without a movement or a whisper through the presentation.... It was a real exhibition of love-making and the youths and maidens of [Middletown] who thought that they knew something about the art found that they still had a great deal to learn."

Some high school teachers are convinced that the movies are a powerful factor in bringing about the "early sophistication" of the young and the relaxing of social taboos. One working class mother frankly welcomes the movies as an aid in child rearing, saying, "I send my daughter because a girl has to learn the ways of the world somehow and the movies are a good safe way." The judge of the juvenile court lists the movies as one of the "big four" causes of local juvenile delinquency,[32] believing that the disregard of group mores by the young is definitely related to the witnessing week after week of fictitious behavior sequences that habitually link the taking of long chances and the happy

ending. While the community attempts to safeguard its schools from commercially intent private hands, this powerful new educational instrument, which has taken Middletown unawares, remains in the hands of a group of men—an ex-peanut-stand proprietor, an ex-bicycle racer and race promoter, and so on—whose primary concern is making money.[33]

Middletown in 1890 was not hesitant in criticizing poor shows at the Opera house. The "morning after" reviews of 1890 bristle with frank adjectives: "Their version of the play is incomplete. Their scenery is limited to one drop. The women are ancient, the costumes dingy and old. Outside of a few specialties, the show was very 'bum.'" When *Sappho* struck town in 1900, the press roasted it roundly, concluding, "[Middletown] has had enough of naughtiness of the stage. Manager W_____ will do well to fumigate his pretty playhouse before one of the clean, instructive, entertaining plays he has billed comes before the footlights." The newspapers of today keep their hands off the movies, save for running free publicity stories and cuts furnished by the exhibitors who advertise. Save for some efforts among certain of the women's clubs to "clean up the movies" and the opposition of the Ministerial Association to "Sunday movies," Middletown appears content in the main to take the movies at their face value—"a darned good show"—and largely disregard their educational or habit forming aspects.

Though less widely diffused as yet than automobile owning or movie attendance, the radio nevertheless is rapidly crowding its say in among the necessities in the family standard of living. Not the least remarkable feature of this new invention is its accessibility. Here skill and ingenuity can in part offset money as an open sesame to swift sharing of the enjoyments of the wealthy. With but little equipment one can call the life of the rest of the world from the air, and this equipment can be purchased piecemeal at the ten-cent store. Far from being simply one more means of passive enjoyment, the radio has given rise to much ingenious manipulative activity. In a count of representative sections of Middletown, it was found that, of 303 homes in twenty-eight blocks in the "best section" of town, inhabited almost entirely by the business class, 12 per cent had radios; of 518 workers' homes in sixty-four blocks, 6 per cent had radios.[34]

As this new tool is rolling back the horizons of Middletown for the bank clerk or the mechanic sitting at home and listening to a Philharmonic concert or a sermon by Dr. Fosdick, or to President Collidge bidding his father good night on the eve of election,[35] and as it is wedging its way with the movie, the automobile, and other new tools into the twisted mass of habits that are living for the 38,000 people of Middletown, readjustments necessarily occur. Such comments as the following suggest their nature:

"I use time evenings listening in that I used to spend in reading."

"The radio is hurting movie going, especially Sunday evening." (From a leading movie exhibitor.)

"I don't use my car so much any more. The heavy traffic makes it less fun. But I spend seven nights a week on my radio. We hear fine music from Boston." (From a shabby man of fifty.)

"Sundays I take the boy to Sunday School and come straight home and tune in. I get first an eastern service, then a Cincinnati one. Then there's nothing doing till about two-thirty, when I pick up an eastern service again and follow 'em across the country till I wind up with California about ten-thirty. Last night I heard a ripping sermon from Westminster church somewhere in California. We've no preachers here that can compare with any of them"

"One of the bad features of radio," according to a teacher, "is that children stay up late at night and are not fit for school next day."

"We've spent close on to $100 on our radio, and we built it ourselves at that," commented one of the worker's wives. "Where'd we get the money? Oh, out of our savings, like everybody else."

In the flux of competing habits that are oscillating the members of the family now towards and now away from the home, radio occupies and intermediate position. Twenty-five per cent of 337 high school boys and 22 per cent of 423 high school girls said that they listen more often to the radio with their parents than without them,[36] and, as pointed out above, 20 per cent of 274 boys in the three upper years of the high school answered "radio" to the question, "In what thing that you are doing at home this fall are you most interested?"—more than gave any other answer.[37] More than one mother said that her family used to scatter in the evening— "but now we all sit around and listen to the radio."

Likewise the place of the radio in relation to Middletown's other leisure habits is not wholly clear. As it becomes more perfected, cheaper, and a more accepted part of life, it may cease to call forth so much active, constructive ingenuity and become one more form of passive enjoyment. Doubtless it will continue to play a mighty role in lifting Middletown out of the humdrum of every day; it is beginning to take over that function of the great political rallies or the trips by the trainload to the state capital to hear a noted speaker or to see a monument dedicated that a generation ago helped to set the average man in a wide place. But it seems not unlikely that while furnishing a new means of diversified enjoyment, it will at the same time operate, with national advertising, syndicated newspapers, and other means of large-scale diffusion, as yet another means of standardizing many of Middletown's habits. Indeed, at no point is one brought up more sharply against the impossibility of studying Middletown as a self-contained, self-starting community than when one watches these space-binding leisure-time inventions imported from without—automobile, motion picture, and radio—reshaping the city.

* * *

With greater organization has come increasing standardization of leisure-time pursuits; men and women dance, play cards, and motor as the crowd does; business men play golf with their business associates; some men in both groups tinker with their cars and tune in their radios; a decreasing number of men are interested in gardening, a few turn to books, one or two surreptitiously write a little; a few women "keep up music" and two or three paint or write; among the wealthy are a few who collect paintings and prints, two who collect rare books, and one who collects rugs. Interest in drama as in music, art, and poetry, centers mainly in the high school. In 1877 there was even a Mechanics' Dramatic Club," "a local group of amateurs" but today an occasional lodge revue is put on with much labor to raise needed funds, and now and then a sorority gives a revue, but the giving of plays is confined to the high school and to a few women in the Dramatic Department of the Woman's Club. For those who look wistfully beyond the horizon a hobby tends to be like an heretical opinion, something to be kept concealed from the eyes of the world. One family, unusually rich in personal resources, has recently built a home a little way out of town, set back from the road almost hidden in trees. So incomprehensible is such a departure that rumors are afloat as to what secret motive can have prompted such unprecedented action. Hobbies appear to be somewhat more prevalent among high school pupils than among their elders. Of 275 boys and 341 girls in the last three years of the high school answering the question, "In what thing that you are doing at home this fall are you most interested?" one boy was publishing a small magazine, one studying aviation, one practicing mental telepathy, fourteen doing scientific experiments, one girl was collecting books, one studying photography, one collecting linen handkerchiefs, two doing botanical experiments, and three girls and one boy writing.[38] But most of their answers show that standardized pursuits are the rule; with little in their environment to stimulate originality and competitive social life to discourage it, being "different" is rare even among the young.

Men have adopted more rapidly than their wives the activities growing out of new leisure-time inventions: it is largely they who drive and tinker about the car, who build the radio set and "get San Francisco," who play golf, who first use such new play devices as gymnasium and swimming pool. Meanwhile, such new leisure as Middletown women have acquired tends to go largely into doing more of the same kinds of things as before. The answers of the two groups of women interviewed to the question, "What use would you make of an extra hour in your day?" bear witness to the narrowness of the range of leisure-time choices which present themselves to Middletown women. Both groups spoke of wanting time for reading more often than anything else, but as noted in Chapter XVII, this desire to read was both more marked and more specific among the business class. Only one of the thirty-two business class wives answering would use the time to rest, while approximately one in seven of the ninety-six working class wives gave such answers as "Rest," "Go to bed," "Lie down and rest, something I hardly ever do." More than a third of the working class group answered blankly, "I don't know." One in sixteen of each group answered, "Fancy work or crocheting," but in the case of both of the two business class women so answering, in a tone of apology. In both groups a number mentioned getting out more with people, but the answers indicate different kinds

of pressure. Among the working class it was frequently: "I'd go anywhere to get away from the house. I went to the store last night. I've been out of the house only twice in the three months since we moved here, both times to the store." "I have two daughters. One lives only a block away and I've been over to see her only twice in the last two months. The other lives ten miles out on the interurban and I never see her. If I had an hour I'd use it to see them." The pressure upon the group of business class women is apparently much less at this point; some of them say vaguely, "I'd like an hour in the afternoon for bridge or the movies," or "I'd like more time for reading, calling, visiting, and social life." Not one of these business class women answering referred to church work or Bible reading as a possible way of spending an extra hour, although to seven of the working class women answering, such work was their chief desire; two business class women, however, mentioned civic work among other things. No worker's wife spoke of more time with her children, but four of the other group felt this as their chief desire. No woman of either group spoke of wanting to spend more time with her husband. One woman perhaps summed up the situation of the business class mother whose children are not below school age: "I am busy most of the time, but I can always get out when I want to." Another expressed herself as actually having time to spare: "I am not pressed for time, I really have time for more civic activity than the community wants me to do." For a large proportion of the working class wives, on the other hand, each day is a race with time to compass the essentials.[39]

Much may be learned regarding a culture by scrutiny of the things people do when they do not have to engage in prescribed activities, as these leisure pursuits are frequently either extensions of customary occupations to which they contribute or contrasts to the more habitual pursuits. In Middletown both aspects of leisure appear. The reading Middletown people most enjoy, the spectacles of romance and adventure they witness on the screen, the ever-speedier and more extended auto trips, many—perhaps even today the majority—of the women's club papers, would seem to be valued in large part because of their contrast to the humdrum routine of everyday life. This seems to be particularly true of the working class. On the other hand, the whole system of business men's clubs is apparently valued in part for its instrumental character, its usefulness to the main business of getting a living, and even such an apparently spontaneous activity as golf is utilized increasingly as a business asset; this use of leisure-time groups as an extension of the main activities of life is appearing to a minor but seemingly increasing extent in the women's study clubs.

Finally, the greater organization of leisure is not altogether a substitute for the informal contacts of a generation ago; opportunities to touch elbows with people are multiplied in the mobile and organized group life of today, but these contacts appear to be more casual and to leave the individual somewhat more isolated from the close friends of earlier days. In view of the tightening of social and economic lines in the growing city, it is not surprising that the type of leisure-time organization which dominates today tends in the main to erect barriers to keep others out.

Notes

1. Smith, *op. cit.*, pp. 298–9.

2. Cf. Ch. XIX for a discussion of the basis of person-to-person association around which these activities are built.

3. "Judge —— of Rushville will speak on the political issues of the day at the opera house Saturday at 2 P.M.," read the vague announcement of yet another lecture. "The judge is an able and eloquent speaker and you will be well entertained if you hear him."

Nothing is more characteristic of the early interest in speeches than the commencement exercises of the high school in 1890. Every graduate wrote and delivered an essay and people discussed certain essays for years afterwards. On the great night "everybody in town" gathered to hear these talks on such subjects as "We Sinais Climb and Know It Not"; "Whence, What, and Whither"; "Timon of Athens"; "Pandora's Box"; "Flowers," discussed as "aids in making life pleasant for rich and poor"; and a new type of "Germs" filling the body, whose action on mind and heart causes the impulses for good and bad."

4. One such popular speaker told Rotarians: "My friends, we've been asleep as a nation! But we are waking up. We always have waked up in time. We've been in just as bad holes as any of the nations of Europe, but there is always this difference, we always wake in time. . . . That's a characteristic of us Anglo-Saxons. Babylonia went into

a hole—and stayed there. Rome went down—and never came up. Greece—swept away. Spain went down, and we don't see her getting out. But we somehow always do and always will!" And the Rotary Club cheered him to the echo and went home to bring its wives to his evening lecture, the school authorities sending special word for all teachers to turn out. At the evening lecture, speaking on "The Eagle and the Oyster," the speaker lauded the American business individualist as the eagle and decried the radical and socialist as the "colony-hugging non-individualist." According to an enthusiastic business class citizen, "He showed how some things we don't think much about are really socialism creeping in. He said that all these attempts to regulate wages and hours are a mistake—getting away from the law of supply and demand. It is just the sort of sound logic that puts you back on your feet again!"

5. The prominence of oratory as well as this docility of the audience is probably not unrelated to the authority of the evangelical Protestant preaching tradition in the community.

6. Only one in six of the public lectures in Middletown during 1924 was delivered in a church auditorium, as against more than half in 1890. This is in part due to the development of available auditoriums outside of churches, but it carries with it the incidental loss by the religious agencies of their former close place-association with this phase of group activity.

7. See Ch. XXVII for discussion of newspapers, which are, however, only in part written in Middletown.

8. "In 1887 typesetting was essentially the same art as in the sixteenth century. Since 1890 machine composition has been rapidly supplanting typesetting by hand. The average rate of composition on the linotype is estimated . . . at between 4,000 and 5,000 ems per hour. The rate of hand composition does not exceed 1,000 ems per hour on the average." George E. Barnett, "The Introduction of the Linotype" (*Yale Review*, November 1994). The first linotype machine was introduced into Middletown in the late nineties.

Book production in the United States has virtually doubled in the last generation, increasing from 4,559 in 1890 to 8,863 in 1923. (See the files of *The Publishers' Weekly*.)

9. The religious organizations of the city, many of which maintained small separate libraries in 1890 which are said to have been a

boon, have for the most part ceased to perform this service, though free Sunday School papers are the rule today. On the other hand, the public library has entered the schools of the city with sixty libraries and maintains a book truck carrying books to the outlying sections. Seven full-time librarians and a part-time assistant have displaced the single untrained librarian who received $45.00 a month for conducting the public library tucked away in upstairs rooms in 1890.

10. Figures on card-holders in 1890 are not available. Such figures as these must be used carefully. Any literate resident can obtain a card today by merely asking for one, without references or delay of any kind, whereas cards were issued in 1890 only to those ten years of age and over and after more red tape than today. Branch deposits in school buildings, the use of the book truck, and the "supplementary reading" required of children, particularly in the high school, tend to diffuse the card-holding habit. The number of books withdrawn is influenced by the fact that more books may be taken out on a single card today, thereby allowing the borrower to take more books home and read the one that turns out to be most interesting. There is no way of estimating the circulation of Sunday School library books a generation ago.

11. The following books were bought by these twenty-four families, the purchases of each family being set off by semicolons: *Lives of Great Men* and *University Encyclopedia* (total $5.00); a Bible for daughter; a $5.00 book on Sunday School work; a Bible and, for little son, A B C Books, and Bible stories; a fifty-cent *History of the Methodist Church*; Fox's *Book of Martyrs*, Hurlburt's *Story of the Bible*; technical books, ten-cent little leather library books for the children; a family doctor book; a New Testament and *Four Thousand Questions and Answers on the Bible*; two Bibles, and five or six Christmas books; a set of the *World's Wonder Books* ($57.00); Williams' *Tinsmith's Helper and Pattern Book* ($3.00—a book for the husband's trade); Bible stories; family doctor books; religious books ($14.00); a Bible with encyclopaedia and concordance ($7.00) and a Prayer Book; boys' books for Christmas; the set of books studied by the Delphian Chapter of local club women, though the wife was not a member, and also some sociology books in connection with her club work; a Bible and a pamphlet; story books at Christmas time; *Human Interest Library* ($29.00, five volumes); *Beautiful Story of the Bible*;

story books at Christmas time; *Human Interest Library*.

Data were not secured on the book purchases of the business group.

12. Of a given issue of the *Literary Digest* 939 copies reached Middletown in 1923, as over against thirty-one in 1900. Three hundred and fifty-five copies of the *National Geographic* went into local homes in 1923 as against twenty-five in 1910. Both the number of different periodicals and their efficient distribution have increased notably. As many as seventy different current periodicals may be seen displayed in a single drug store window in Middletown today.

There were no national circulations in 1890 like the 2,000,000 circulations of today. The *Atlantic Monthly* had a circulation of only about 10,000 in the entire United States in 1890, as against twelve times that today. In 1898 the *Saturday Evening Post* had a national circulation of 33,069, whereas nearly 1,500 copies of each issue go to Middletown alone today.

13. Based upon subscription and news-stand totals. The circulation of one issue, whether weekly or monthly, is here taken as the unit.

14. Few male leaders in Middletown read except in a desultory manner. Social workers and ministers complain that their outstanding problem is lack of leadership. "There is no group of intelligentsia here," said a leading minister, "only the bourgeoisie of the Rotary Club." One never hears book-talk around the tables at civic club luncheons. Even the ministers, as noted elsewhere, have little time to read.

15. The working men employed one of their number as librarian at $600.00 a year. Among the purchases for the library recorded in 1900 are the *American Statesmen Series*, John B. Clark's *Distribution of Wealth*, Charlotte Perkins Stetson's *Women and Economics*, David A. Wells' *Recent Economic Changes*, "seven books on religion," and 210 volumes of fiction, including Thackeray and Dickens. This was before the day of the automobile and movies. The library has long since disappeared.

16. See Ch. XIX for discussion of the Delphian Chapter, which probably corresponds most closely to these early reading circles, and for an account of the other women's study clubs. In these days of multiplied periodicals, public libraries, motion pictures at every cross-road, and no farm house or village too isolated to "tune in" on a metropolitan lecture or symphony concert,

it is difficult to appreciate the vigor and enthusiasm aroused by the Chautauqua and Bay View circles. By 1903, says the Chautauqua booklet on *Literature and the Larger Life*, "more than 11,000 Chautauqua circles" had been conducted in "about 6,000" different localities. To these eager groups that met "around the study lamp" week after week, "Mehr Licht," the motto of the Bay View Circle, and Bishop Vincent's quotation of "Knowledge is power" at the opening of the Chautauqua Circle, were no mere mottos but promises of fuller life. In Middletown a number of women, after having followed the "readings" on German literature or Greek life, one year on each country through four years, took examinations and received their "diplomas," a few going on to Chautauqua, New York, for the graduation exercises.

17. State Teachers' Reading Circles were active in the nineties. Earlier figures are not available, but in 1902–3, 180 of 286 teachers in the county are listed as members of the state reading circles, and of the 10,566 children enrolled in the schools of the county, 1,817 belonged to state reading circles owning 3,412 books.

18. Such a group as this last did not meet in 1890, but in 1895, the press reported a class of ten young women organized two years earlier which "meets Saturday afternoon, and has read Ruskin's *Essays*, Dante's *Vision*, Pope's Homer's *Iliad*, and is now reading the *Odyssey*, a new prose translation by George Herbert Palmer, professor of philosophy in Harvard College. This little society is a class of students, not a club, and enjoys the distinction of having no officers."

19. The import of this fact that, by and large, the poorer grades of women's magazines go to the workers and the better grades to the business group cannot be overlooked in its significance for the differential rate of diffusion of modern habits of making a home to the two groups.

20. The groups given here are, of course, not mutually exclusive. The predominance of the reading of magazines on making a home among girls of this age and the fact that, aside from this negligible fringe of boys, the males of the group neither here nor elsewhere come in contact with any discussion of home-making problems is suggestive in connection with the concentration of the males upon matters divorced from the home and the fact that habits of management are still in vogue in the homes of Middletown that are becoming obsolete in Middletown's industries.

21. Of the 100 working class families for whom income distribution was secured, twenty-four reported money spent on music lessons for children. The amounts ranged from $2.50 to $104.00, averaging $44.75. See Table VI.

Comments by various parents reveal how seriously many of them take this training in music; witness a working class family of five in which mother teaches one son to play the piano and the father teaches another son the drums, the mother explaining that "there is so much bad in life to keep children away from that we've decided it's hopeless to try, and the only thing to do is to make them love so many good things that they'll never pay attention to the bad things." Another worker's wife said that her sister criticized them for spending so much on their son's music, "but I feel his talent should be developed and want him to have a musical education if that's what he wants." The ubiquitous clash between having more children and maintaining a higher standard for fewer children came out in the remark of a modest-salaried business man's wife, "Our oldest boy takes music lessons and they cost us a good deal—$1.85 a week. That's why you can't have more children when everything you do for them costs so much."

22. Those familiar with the local musical life express the belief that the orchestral and other musical work in the high schools is recruiting an entirely new crop of musicians rather than reducing the number playing the piano. This is probably less true in the case of girls than of boys. Boys are more attracted to other instrumental work than to the piano because of the prestige of playing in one of the high school bands or in the well-known local boys' band, and more particularly because of the money they can earn playing in small dance orchestras. The energetic jazz aggregation of four or five boys, featuring the easily learned saxophone, presents a new and relatively distinguished occupation by which sons of working class parents are seeking in some cases to escape from the industrial level. The city has several of these small groups seeking engagements playing for dances.

23. As late as 1900 "graphophones" were still curiosities. "The graphophone is rapidly superseding the piano in Middletown saloons. Fully fifty are being used and they never fail to draw large crowds," says the press.

24. The ownership of radios in Middletown is noted elsewhere. No check was made of

the ownership of phonographs and of pianolas. Of 100 working class families from whom expenditures were secured, however, twenty-three had bought phonograph records during the last twelve months. Eleven had bought less than $5.00 worth each; the amounts ranged from $1.05 to $50.00, averaging $11.17. Three had spent money for pianola records, each less than $4.00 worth. More than twenty-three phonographs were owned by these 100 families, however, as a number of others spoke of owning but of having no money to spend on records. There was a marked tendency to sacrifice phonograph records both to the cost of installing a radio and to the cost of children's music lessons.

In the study of Zanesville, Ohio, in 1925 there were discovered phonographs in 54 per cent of the homes, pianos in 43 per cent, organs in 3 per cent and other musical instruments in 8 per cent; the figures for the thirty-six cities, including Middletown, compared with Zanesville, were 59 per cent, 51 per cent, 1 per cent, and 11 per cent, respectively. (*Op.cit.*, p. 112.)

25. See Table XV.

26. The war brought "community singing" and it survives today principally in the civic clubs. Here it has relatively little life *qua* singing, aside from the stunts or novelties that the pianist or leader injects into it.

27. Exact counts were made for only January, July, and October. There were less than 125 performances, including matinees, for the entire year.

28. These figures are rough estimates based upon the following data: The total Federal amusement tax paid by Middletown theaters in July was $3,002.04 and in December $4,781.47. The average tax paid per admission is about $0.0325, and the population in 1923 about 38,000. Attendance estimates secured in this way were raised by one-sixth to account for children under twelve who are tax-free. The proprietor of three representative houses said that he had seven admissions over twelve years to one aged twelve or less, and the proprietor of another house drawing many children has four over twelve to one aged twelve or less.

These attendance figures include, however, farmers and others from outlying districts.

29. The question was asked in terms of frequency of attendance "in an average month" and was checked in each case by attendance during the month just past.

Lack of money and young children needing care in the home are probably two factors influencing these families that do not attend at all; of the forty-one working class families in which all the children are twelve years or under, eighteen never go to the movies, while of the eighty-one working class families in which one or more of the children is twelve or older, only twenty reported that no member of the family ever attends.

"I haven't been anywhere in two years," said a working class wife of thirty-three, the mother of six children, the youngest twenty months. "I went to the movies once two years ago. I was over to see Mrs._____, and she says, 'Come on, let's go to the movies.' I didn't believe her. She is always ragging the men and I thought she was joking. 'Come on,' she says 'put your things on and we'll see a show.' I thought, well, if she wanted to rag the men, I'd help her, so I got up and put my things on. And, you know, she really meant it. She paid my carfare uptown and paid my way into the movies. I was never so surprised in my life. I haven't been anywhere since."

30. Cf. N. 10 above.

The ex-proprietor of one of the largest saloons in the city said, "The movies killed the saloon. They cut our business in half overnight."

31. It happens frequently that the title overplays the element of "sex adventure" in a picture. On the other hand, films less luridly advertised frequently portray more "raw situations."

32. Cf. Ch. XI.

Miriam Van Waters, referee of the juvenile court of Los Angeles and author of *Youth in Conflict*, says in a review of Cyril Burt's *The Young Delinquent*: "The cinema is recognized for what it is, the main source of excitement and of moral education for city children. Burt finds that only mental defectives take the movies seriously enough to imitate the criminal exploits portrayed therein, and only a small proportion of thefts can be traced to stealing to gain money for admittance. In no such direct way does the moving picture commonly demoralize youth. It is in the subtle way of picturing the standards of adult life, action and emotion, cheapening, debasing, distorting adults until they appear in the eyes of the young people perpetually bathed in a moral atmosphere of intrigue, jealousy, wild emotionalism, and cheap sentimentality. Burt realizes that these exhibitions stimulate children prematurely." (*The Survey*, April 15, 1926)

33. One exhibitor in Middletown is a college-trained man interested in bringing "good films" to the city. He, like the others, however, is caught in the competitive game and matches his competitors' sensational advertisements.

34. Both percentages have undoubtedly increased notably since 1924, when the counts were made.

35. In 1890 the local press spoke of an occasional citizen's visiting "Paris, France," and "London, England," and even in 1924 a note in one of the papers recording the accident of some Middletown people finding themselves in a box at a New York theater with a group of Englishmen was captioned "Lucky they weren't Chinese!" The rest of the world is still a long way from Middletown, but movies and radio are doing much to break down this isolation: "I've got 120 stations on my radio," gleefully announced a local working man. Meanwhile, the president of the Radio Corporation of America proclaims an era at hand when "the oldest and newest civilizations will throb together at the same intellectual appeal, and to the same artistic emotions."

36. Cf. N. 10 above.

37. Less than 1 per cent of the 341 girls answered "radio."

38. Cf. Ch. XVII.

39. To summarize: Of the ninety-six working class wives answering the question, twenty-seven answered, "I don't know." Sixteen would use it for housework or sewing, fourteen for rest, eighteen for reading, seven for getting away from home and seeing people, seven for church work, two to write letters, one to earn money, and four said that they are not pressed for time and might therefore use the time in various ways.

Of the thirty-two out of this group of forty business class wives answering this question, fourteen want time for reading, three for housework, two for fancy work, four for their children, three for social activities, one for rest, and five stated that they are not pressed for time and might use it in various ways.

11

Communication

From *Encyclopaedia of the Social Sciences* (1931)

Edward Sapir

Edward Sapir (1884–1939) was born in Germany (what is today Poland) but was raised mostly in New York City, where he attended Columbia University. With Ruth Benedict and Margaret Mead, Sapir was one of the most brilliant students of the founding anthropologist Franz Boas. Sapir was probably the most important American linguistic anthropologist of the first half of the twentieth century. His *Language: An Introduction to the Study of Speech* (1921) is perhaps his best-known work and a classic text in linguistics. Sapir did important fieldwork in the United States and Canada, recording and analyzing Native American languages, and he spent fifteen years based in Ottawa as Canada's chief anthropologist. Drawing from that research, Sapir argued that people observe the world through categories embedded in their language, thus introducing an element of cultural specificity to human experience, a notion that lives on as "the Sapir-Whorf hypothesis."

Sapir taught at the University of Chicago between 1925 and 1931, where, until 1929, sociology and anthropology were still housed in a single department. He was a close friend and conversation partner of Harold Lasswell. Beginning in 1931, he spent his last years at Yale University, where he remained not only a leader in linguistic anthropology but also a facilitator of interdisciplinary discussions in the social sciences, especially among anthropology, sociology, linguistics, and psychiatry (see Darnell 1990).

This piece was written for *The Encyclopedia of the Social Sciences*, a fifteen-volume project published between 1930 and 1935, and a monument to 1930s confidence in the importance and potential integration of the social sciences. Sapir wrote a gem of a piece that can stand in the lineage of grander-style North American theory of media and communication that runs from Cooley and Park to Mumford, Innis, and McLuhan. He takes a large view of communication and gives it a central place in human life. "The multiplication of far-reaching techniques of communication," he writes, "for certain purposes [makes] the whole civilized world ... the psychological equivalent of a primitive tribe." The passages on language, gesture, imitation, social suggestion, and groups all deserve careful reading and translation into contemporary idioms.

It is obvious that for the building up of society, its units and subdivisions, and the understandings which prevail between its members some processes of communication are needed. While we often speak of society as though it were a static structure defined by tradition, it is, in the more intimate sense, nothing of the kind, but a highly intricate network of partial or complete understandings between the members of organizational units of every degree of size and complexity, ranging from a pair of lovers or a family to a league of nations or that ever increasing portion of humanity which can be reached by the press through all its transnational ramifications. It is only apparently a static sum of social institutions; actually it is being reanimated or creatively reaffirmed from day to day by particular acts of a communicative nature which obtain among individuals participating in it. Thus the Republican party cannot be said to exist as such, but only to the extent that its tradition is being constantly added to and upheld by such simple acts of communication as that John Doe votes the Republican ticket, thereby communicating a certain kind of message, or that a half dozen individuals meet at a certain time and place, formally or informally, in order to communicate ideas to one another and eventually to decide what points of national interest, real or supposed, are to be allowed to come up many months later for discussion in a gathering of members of the party. The Republican party as a historic entity is merely abstracted from thousands upon thousands of such single acts of communication, which have in common

certain persistent features of reference. If we extend this example into every conceivable field in which communication has a place we soon realize that every cultural pattern and every single act of social behavior involve communication in either an explicit or an implicit sense.

One may conveniently distinguish between certain fundamental techniques, or primary processes, which are communicative in character and certain secondary techniques which facilitate the process of communication. The distinction is perhaps of no great psychological importance but has a very real historical and sociological significance, inasmuch as the fundamental processes are common to all mankind, while the secondary techniques emerge only at relatively sophisticated levels of civilization. Among the primary communicative processes of society may be mentioned: language; gesture, in its widest sense; the imitation of overt behavior; and a large and ill defined group of implicit processes which grow out of overt behavior and which may be rather vaguely referred to as "social suggestion."

Language is the most explicit type of communicative behavior that we know of. It need not here be defined beyond pointing out that it consists in every case known to us of an absolutely complete referential apparatus of phonetic symbols which have the property of locating every known social referent, including all the recognized data of perception which the society that it serves carries in its tradition. Language is the communicative process par excellence in every known society, and it is exceedingly important to observe that whatever may be the shortcomings of a primitive society judged from the vantage point of civilization its language inevitably forms as sure, complete and potentially creative an apparatus of referential symbolism as the most sophisticated language that we know of. What this means for a theory of communication is that the mechanics of significant understanding between human beings are as sure and complex and rich in overtones in one society as in another, primitive or sophisticated.

Gesture includes much more than the manipulation of the hands and other visible and movable parts of the organism. Intonations of the voice may register attitudes and feelings quite as significantly as the clenched fist, the wave of the hand, the shrugging of the shoulders or the lifting of the eyebrows. The field of gesture interplays constantly with that of language proper, but there are many facts of a psychological and historical order which show that there are subtle yet firm lines of demarcation between them. Thus, to give but one example, the consistent message delivered by language symbolism in the narrow sense, whether by speech or by writing, may flatly contradict the message communicated by the synchronous system of gestures, consisting of movements of the hands and head, intonations of the voice and breathing symbolisms. The former system may be entirely conscious, the latter entirely unconscious. Linguistic, as opposed to gesture, communication tends to be the official and socially accredited one; hence one may intuitively interpret the relatively unconscious symbolisms of gesture as psychologically more significant in a given context than the words actually used. In such cases as these we have a conflict between explicit and implicit communications in the growth of the individual's social experience.

The primary condition for the consolidation of society is the imitation of overt behavior. Such imitation, while not communicative in intent, has always the retroactive value of a communication, for in the process of falling in with the ways of society one in effect acquiesces in the meanings that inhere in these ways. When one learns to go to church, for instance, because other members of the community set the pace for this kind of activity, it is as though a communication had been received and acted upon. It is the function of language to articulate and rationalize the full content of these informal communications in the growth of the individual's social experience.

Even less directly communicative in character than overt behavior and its imitation is "social suggestion" as the sum total of new acts and new meanings that are implicitly made possible by these types of social behavior. Thus, the particular method of revolting against the habit of church going in a given society, while contradictory, on the surface, of the conventional meanings of that society, may nevertheless receive all its social significance from hundreds of existing prior communications that belong to the culture of the group as a whole. The importance of the unformulated and unverbalized communications of society is so great that one who is not intuitively familiar with them is likely to be baffled by the significance of certain kinds of behavior, even if he is thoroughly aware of their external forms and of the verbal symbols that accompany them. It is largely the function of the artist to make articulate these more subtle intentions of society.

Communicative processes do not merely apply to society as such; they are indefinitely varied as to form and meaning for the various types of personal relationships into which society resolves itself. Thus, a fixed type of conduct or a linguistic symbol has not by any means necessarily the same communicative significance within the confines of the family, among the members of an economic group and in the nation at large. Generally speaking, the smaller the circle and the more complex the understandings already arrived at within it, the more economical can the act of communication afford to become. A single word passed between members of an intimate group, in spite of its apparent vagueness and ambiguity, may constitute a far more precise communication than volumes of carefully prepared correspondence interchanged between two governments.

There seem to be three main classes of techniques which have for their object the facilitation of the primary communicative processes of society. These may be referred to as: language transfers; symbolisms arising from special technical situations; and the creation of physical conditions favorable for the communicative act. Of language transfers the best known example is writing. The Morse telegraph code is another example. These and many other communicative techniques have this in common, that while they are overtly not at all like one another their organization is based on the primary symbolic organization which has arisen in the domain of speech.

Psychologically, therefore, they extend the communicative character of speech to situations in which for one reason or another speech is not possible.

In the more special class of communicative symbolism one cannot make a word to word translation, as it were, back to speech but can only paraphrase in speech the intent of the communication. Here belong such symbolic systems as wigwagging, the use of railroad lights, bugle calls in the army and smoke signals. It is interesting to observe that while they are late in developing in the history of society they are very much less complex in structure than language itself. They are of value partly in helping out a situation where neither language nor any form of language transfer can be applied, partly where it is desired to encourage the automatic nature of the desired response. Thus, because language is extraordinarily rich in meaning it sometimes becomes a little annoying or even dangerous to rely upon it where only a simple this or that, or yes or no, is expected to be the response.

The importance of extending the physical conditions allowing for communication is obvious. The railroad, the telegraph, the telephone, the radio and the airplane are among the best examples. It is to be noted that such instruments as the railroad and the radio are not communicative in character as such; they become so only because they facilitate the presentation of types of stimuli which act as symbols of communication or which contain implications of communicative significance. Thus a telephone is of no use unless the party at the other end understands the language of the person calling up. Again, the fact that a railroad runs me to a certain point is of no real communicative importance unless there are fixed bonds of interest which connect me with the inhabitants of the place. The failure to bear in mind these obvious points has tended to make some writers exaggerate the importance of the spread in modern times of such inventions as the railroad and the telephone.

The history of civilization has been marked by a progressive increase in the radius of communication. In a typically primitive society communication is reserved for the members of the tribe and at best a small number of surrounding tribes with whom relations are intermittent rather than continuous and who act as a kind of buffer between the significant psychological world—the world of one's own tribal culture—and the great unknown or unreal that lies beyond. Today, in our own civilization, the appearance of a new fashion in Paris is linked by a series of rapid and necessary events with the appearance of the same fashion in such distant places as Berlin, London, New York, San Francisco and Yokohama. The underlying reason for this remarkable change in the radius and rapidity of communication is the gradual diffusion of cultural traits or, in other words, of meaningful cultural reactions. Among the various types of cultural diffusion that of language itself is of paramount importance. Secondary technical devices making for ease of communication are also, of course, of great importance.

The multiplication of far-reaching techniques of communication has two important results. In the first place, it increases the sheer radius of communication, so that for certain purposes the whole civilized world is made the psychological equivalent of a primitive tribe. In the second place, it lessens the importance of mere geographical contiguity. Owing to the technical nature of these sophisticated communicative devices, parts of the world that are geographically remote may, in terms of behavior, be actually much closer to one another than adjoining regions, which, from the historical standpoint, are supposed to share a larger body of common understandings. This means, of course, a tendency to remap the world both sociologically and psychologically. Even now it is possible to say that the scattered "scientific world" is a social unity which has no clear cut geographical location. Further, the world of urban understanding in America contrasts rather sharply with the rural world. The weakening of the geographical factor in social organization must in the long run profoundly modify our attitude toward the meaning of personal relations and of social classes and even nationalities.

The increasing ease of communication is purchased at a price, for it is becoming increasingly difficult to keep an intended communication within the desired bounds. A humble example of this new problem is the inadvisability of making certain kinds of statement on the telephone. Another example is the insidious cheapening of literary and artistic values due to the foreseen and economically advantageous "widening of the appeal." All effects which demand a certain intimacy of understanding tend to become difficult and are therefore avoided. It is a question whether the obvious increase of overt communication is not constantly being corrected, as it were, by the creation of new obstacles to communication. The fear of being too easily understood may, in many cases, be more aptly defined as the fear of being understood by too many—so many, indeed, as to endanger the psychological reality of the image of the enlarged self confronting the not-self.

On the whole, however, it is rather the obstacles to communication that are felt as annoying or ominous. The most important of these obstacles in the modern world is undoubtedly the great diversity of languages. The enormous amount of energy put into the task of translation implies a passionate desire to make as light of the language difficulty as possible. In the long run it seems almost unavoidable that the civilized world will adopt some one language of intercommunication, say English or Esperanto, which can be set aside for denotive purposes pure and simple.

Part II

∼

The World in Turmoil
Communications Research, 1933–1949

In 1945, the sociologist Robert K. Merton surveyed the world around him. The United States and its allies were winning the war in Europe and the Pacific, but all was not well. "American adults have now lived through three decades of turmoil," he wrote.

> The World War of 1914–1918 was followed by the longest and most severe economic depression since industrialism began which, in turn, was only a prelude to the worst war in history. It is easy to see why some old verities have been shaken and some time-honored creeds have lost their hold. Along with new inventions in communication and transportation have come new demands upon government. At the turn of the century, almost every industrial nation assumed that capitalism would and should be its dominant economic framework. Now Russia, one of the great powers of the world and our ally, has traveled the road to Communism. Two others— Australia and New Zealand—are Labor governments with strongly socialist trends. In Canada a Cooperative Commonwealth Federation is growing rapidly. ... The traditional answers no longer seem to be the accepted ones.

To Merton and many others in the 1930s and 1940s, the traditional answers had indeed been thrown into question. The worldwide depression strained the credibility of capitalism and free-market economics. Millions lost their jobs and struggled to feed themselves and their families. Those from an earlier generation had taken democracy as an article of faith and the seemingly inevitable culmination of human social progress, but it now faced serious challenges from two sides. Communism had triumphed in Russia, fascism in Germany, Italy, and Japan. Intellectuals looked in different directions for answers. Some rallied around the ideals and techniques of science, which found defenders across the spectrum of political ideology. Others revived the philosophical classics and saw Aristotle, Aquinas, and the Western humanist tradition as a source of secure knowledge and moral stability. Folk traditions found apologists who saw depth and moral orientation in the music and folkways of a nation's people, while others were drawn toward higher, modernist art and literature for guiding visions. Freud and psychoanalysis provided yet another intellectual orientation, as did Marxism, socialism, and trade unionism—the last of which often brought intellectuals into solidarity with workers who in the 1930s were organizing successfully, in part through huge strikes. Hope lay in various directions for those trying to navigate a landscape that seemed alternately chaotic and highly regimented.

Increasingly central to this landscape were "the new agencies of mass impression," as radio, motion pictures, advertising, public relations, and mass-circulation print were collectively termed. By 1933, two-thirds of American homes owned a radio and most were linked to the broadcast networks (NBC and CBS) which had formed in the late 1920s and could deliver identical content in real time to nationwide audiences listening in their homes. Like movies, recorded music, mass-circulation photography, and print, radio could bring distant personalities close to the geographically scattered masses. This helped create celebrities, entertainment stars, and political figures who could speak directly to audiences of unprecedented size. Fan clubs were created around the nation's popular icons—the singer Kate Smith, for instance, perhaps the most-listened-to radio personality in the early 1930s, had more than four hundred such clubs. More sinisterly, the right-wing radio personality Father Coughlin had an equally powerful network; he was the subject of analysis in Alfred Lee and Elizabeth Lee's 1939 *Fine Art of Propaganda* (p. 124). Political leaders found new avenues of communicative power, which they used in different ways. Franklin Roosevelt famously drew on radio to address the nation in seemingly intimate terms through his *Fireside Chats,* thus bypassing a largely Republican mainstream press solidly against his New Deal initiatives. Instead of old-time political orations delivered to an assembled crowd, these radio speeches were conversations with friends, who responded with political fan mail often addressed in similarly familiar style (see Sussmann, p. 401). Adolph Hitler used the radio in different, though no less impression-creating ways, broadcasting impassioned speeches delivered at massive rallies, one of which reportedly left a deep impression on Marshall McLuhan, who heard it broadcast, in German, over loudspeakers in Canada.

Just as it did for political leaders and entertainers, so too did radio give advertisers new power to reach mass audiences. After significant debate in the 1920s over how to organize and finance radio (see McChesney 1993), American broadcasters had successfully engineered a for-profit, commercial model, which depended on selling audiences to advertisers who sponsored and typically helped produce individual programs. Advertising of consumer goods had been widespread since the late nineteenth century, but commercial broadcasting helped to organize and sell a distinctively national market and to extend the messages and habits of a still-developing consumerism into the new mass medium. After early rating systems indicated the size and demographics of unseen radio audiences, advertisers responded by producing shows that would appeal to the greatest number of potential consumers without offending any socially powerful groups (see Baughman 1997). Evening shows were typically aimed at the general population—the mass in its totality—while daytime shows were produced for the women listening at home. Hoping to capture this latter audience, sponsors in the 1930s developed the dramatic serials that became known as soap operas (see Herzog, p. 139). In many shows, entertainers and actors made direct pitches for their sponsor's products in the middle of broadcasts, helping lead to what Susan Douglas calls "the shameless, blaring commercialization of radio" by the mid-1930s (1999, 121). This commercial substrate helped radio, like other American media, be a force that upheld the capitalist status quo, as Lazarsfeld and Merton observe in the final pages of their classic 1948 essay (p. 230; see also Lazarsfeld 1942). It was part of the greater world of advertising that James Rorty eloquently attacks in his 1934 book *Our Master's Voice* (p. 106).

Miss Lonelyhearts, Nathanel West's haunting 1933 novella about a hard-boiled reporter posing as a female advice columnist, captures one feeling about the new forces of mass communication and industrialized entertainment:

> Crowds of people moved through the street with a dream-like violence. As he looked at their broken hands and torn mouths he was overwhelmed by the desire to help them, and because this desire was sincere, he was happy despite the feeling of guilt which accompanied it.
>
> He saw a man who appeared to be on the verge of death stagger into a movie theater that was showing a picture called *Blonde Beauty.* He saw a ragged woman with an enormous goiter pick a love story magazine out of a garbage can and seem very excited by her find.
>
> Prodded by his conscience, he began to generalize. Men have always fought their misery with their dreams. Although dreams were once powerful, they have been made puerile by the movies, radio, and newspapers. Among many betrayals, this one is the worst. (West [1933] 1975, 115)

The sentiments expressed by West's narrator were by no means universal, but they did capture one of several moods that underlay intellectuals' thinking about mass communication in the interwar period. The democratic faith of the progressive era, which had often attached itself to the techniques and technologies of modern communication, was not extinguished, but it was increasingly challenged by harder-edged skeptics of several varieties. The promise of new media was no longer so clear as it had been to Charles Cooley and his progressive fellow-believers.

Propaganda Analysis and Objectivist Social Science

Advertising was one part of what in the 1930s became known as "the propaganda menace" that weighed heavily on the minds of Americans. Worries about propaganda had escalated after World War I, when all the major combatants rallied their populations through coordinated and organized efforts to vilify their enemies and celebrate their own nation and cause. In the 1920s and 1930s, publicists who had worked on the war effort moved into the general population, where they used their methods of "organized publicity" to create favorable images of the individuals and organizations that hired them. After World War I, there were said to be more than five thousand publicists in New York City alone. They staged events and distributed press releases to cast their clients in the most favorable possible light.

Some analysts suggested that propaganda was everywhere. Politicians, government publicists, interest groups, advertisers, religious leaders, educators, and journalists all contributed to what Violet Edwards of the Institute for Propaganda Analysis called "the bombardment of propaganda which penetrates every aspect of [modern] living" and left us "tragically confused" (Edwards 1938, 5). Some believed that the propaganda threatened democracy from within by circulating information of questionable truth-value, which undermined citizens' abilities to deliberate clearly and effectively. Others were more worried about threats from abroad, such as the propaganda generated by the Nazis or the Communists, which infiltrated the United States with "alien ideas and points of view" (Riegel 1934, 201). Some in this latter camp, championing a "100% Americanism," warned of foreign "agitators" among immigrant groups, who spread communism and other dangerous propaganda to the laboring classes. They were part of a broader moment that severely limited immigration, put limits on the number of Jews who could attend elite colleges, and helped drive members of ethnic minorities to assimilate and "Americanize" themselves.

Though it could sometimes be politically conservative or reactionary, the majority of propaganda analysis was broadly reformist, as J. Michael Sproule (1997) and Brett Gary (1999) have shown. Often through case studies, it drew attention to the workings of propaganda, called news editors to better practices, and counseled ordinary Americans to use critical-thinking skills and be skeptical of what they read and heard (see, e.g., Alfred Lee and Elizabeth Lee's 1939 *Fine Art of Propaganda* [p. 124]). In this regard, propaganda analysis represents a continuation of the democratically oriented social criticism of muckraking journalists and progressive intellectuals such as Jane Addams and John Dewey. At the same time, 1920s and 1930s propaganda analysis was typically harder edged, more skeptical, and often more cynical than the classic, hopeful thought about communication, as exemplified by progressives such as Charles Cooley (see Cmiel 1996; Simonson 1996).

Some of the hope of the progressive generation continued in 1930s communication study, often attaching itself to science as a source of methods and ideals. This was a clear continuation of the Deweyan project, though neo-pragmatists such as Richard Rorty downplay Dewey's scientific side; but it also reflected a much broader turn to science, one that transcended national borders and political ideologies. Marxists were as drawn to science as liberals and democrats were. Diego Rivera, for instance, the Mexican muralist with Marxist and populist sensibilities, frequently depicted science as a liberating force that would guide humanity toward a more enlightened and socially progressive future. With less dramatic flair, propaganda analysts and their fellow travelers turned in similar directions and counseled that, by using the disciplined skepticism and careful inquiry of the scientific method, citizens could defend themselves against the perils of propaganda (see, e.g., Edwards 1938, 25–32).

Developing alongside explicitly reformist propaganda analysis was a more rigorously empirical social science with more technical methodologies and less obvious, though still sometimes animating, reform impulses. This objectivist social scientific paradigm was more professionalized than propaganda analysis, and developed at both Columbia University and the University of Chicago, with roots extending back before World War I.

At Columbia, A. A. Tenney and Franklin Giddings had trained a generation of graduate students to use quantitative and statistical methods for what Tenney called "scientific analysis of the press" (1912). Two of these students, Malcolm Willey and Stuart Rice, developed and applied these methods in the 1920s and early 1930s. Their book *Communication Agencies and Social Life* (1933; p. 95 in this volume) was part of a collection entitled *Recent Social Trends,* which had been commissioned by the Hoover administration and funded by the Rockefeller Foundation as "a comprehensive survey of the many social changes which are proceeding simultaneously" in the United States (Willey and Rice 1933, vi). Its lead researcher was the University of Chicago's W. F. Ogburn, who was busy training his own group of statistically oriented American social scientists, including Samuel Stouffer, who later became a professor at Harvard and a key figure in mass communications and propaganda research during the Second World War. Ogburn was one of several important figures at the University of Chicago in the 1920s and 1930s who collectively formed what Harold Lasswell called "a newer generation, more concerned with elegant methodology" than their predecessors (quoted in Bulmer 1981, 323). Lasswell himself was another key player, who in the 1920s and 1930s studied propaganda with a more detached, scientific style than the more explicitly critical propaganda analysts (see p. 47). In the 1930s, he codified the method of content analysis and compiled massive bibliographies of propaganda and public opinion research, both of which contributed to the emerging field of communications research. Also working on communications at Chicago was Douglas Waples, a professor of library science who studied the effects of reading on Americans and was an important figure in the field in the late 1930s and early 1940s; and Helen MacGill Hughes, a student of Robert Park who extended Park's and Cooley's research on newspaper communication and democratic life (see p. 118).

The most ambitious early application of the newer, social scientific methods to the study of mass communication came in the Payne Fund Studies of American motion pictures, published in twelve volumes, beginning in 1933. Among the original research team named by Ohio State's W. W. Charters were five University of Chicago social scientists, including Robert Park, Herbert L.L. Thurstone, and Herbert Blumer (see p. 91). The researchers aimed to determine the effects of motion pictures on young viewers. They marshaled a variety of social scientific methods—including questionnaires, physiological experiments, interviews, and basic content analyses—to discover the impact movies had on the information, attitudes, emotions, behavior, and health of the children who viewed them. The Payne Fund findings were excerpted in popular magazines and reviewed in the press, where they drew a good deal of attention to a question that runs from at least Jane Addams to the present—what are the effects of media and popular entertainments on children?

Like Deweyan social philosophy, much of the newer, objectivist social science was fueled by interest in democratic reform and renewal. We see this for instance in Hadley Cantril and Gordon Allport's 1935 *Psychology of Radio* (p. 110), which blends laboratory experiments and other disciplined empirical inquiry with pronouncements about radio's democratic potential that were as grand as anything Cooley had written. Quantitative studies and empirically grounded social scientific research also found widespread application in Roosevelt's New Deal agencies, where reformist researchers such as Stuart Rice (see p. 95) and Dallas Smythe (see p. 318), working for the Federal Communications Commission and other agencies, drew on surveys and statistical research to advance an activist agenda supported by a great swath of left-leaning intellectuals of the era. A similar reformist sensibility could also animate another new sort of empirical research, public opinion polling. This impulse is evident in Gallup and Rae's 1940 *Pulse of Democracy* (p. 128), a bold apologetic for the power of opinion polls to cut through the power of special interests and political elites and allow the will of the people to shine through. Gallup had founded his American Institute of Public Opinion in 1935 and through newspaper columns effectively publicized for himself new polling methods that others were using as well. Two years later, *Public Opinion Quarterly* was founded and immediately became the field's flagship journal. In the first issue, its editors breathlessly described the new situation ("*mass* opinion is the final determinant of political, and economic, action") and promised to fill the need of decision makers and researchers for precise information while maintaining "a wholly scientific and objective point of view" (see p. 118). In this respect, it was reminiscent of the *Recent Social Trends* volumes, which saw "objective data" and "the severe requirements of scientific method" as the best hopes for dealing with a rapidly changing world. "If men and women of all shades of opinion from extreme conservatism to extreme radicalism can find a common basis of secure knowledge to build upon," the *Recent Social Trends* researchers wrote, "the social changes of the future may be brought in larger measure under the control of social intelligence" (Willey and Rice 1933, vi–vii).

It is perhaps most accurate to view propaganda analysis and objectivist social science in the 1930s as two branches growing from the same progressive trunk. Both were typically reform minded and guided by questions of how to shore up democratic society during a time of crisis. In varying degrees, both looked hopefully to science as a source of ideals and practices that could enlighten, protect, and control, thus creating a world better than the present. Objectivist social science, with its elegant methods, disciplined empiricism, and increasingly technical vocabularies, may have sometimes seemed a world removed from the turbulence of the 1930s, but it can also be understood as a means to deal with that turbulence and create new order and social good. These were ends Dewey had been advocating for more than three decades, and in the 1930s they were pursued in parallel, sometimes overlapping ways by American propaganda critics and social scientists.

"The Unintended Benevolence of Hitler"

After 1933, North American intellectual life benefited from what Robert Merton once called "the unintended benevolence of Hitler": scores of émigré scholars, many of them German and Austrian Jews, were forced to flee to North America, where they made enormous contributions to fields ranging from atomic physics to art history. In the still ill-defined area of mass communications, their impact was huge. In the short run, they played key roles in establishing the field and problematics of communications research in the 1940s. Over the longer haul, they wrote what remain some of the best and most provocative documents in the intellectual history of communication in the twentieth century. Paul Lazarsfeld, Herta Herzog, Max Horkheimer, Theodor Adorno, Leo Lowenthal, Hans Speier, Ernest Kris, Kurt Lang, Rolf Meyersohn, George Gerbner, and Hannah Arendt all came to the United States during the 1930s or 1940s, and all undertook classic studies in the 1940s or 1950s. Over the course of long careers, some of which have continued into the present century, these émigrés did very different kinds of work, not all equally central to the ongoing conversation about modern media. In varying degrees of contact with American society and its ways of thought, these exile scholars broadened the conceptual apparatus of mass communication study and established baseline positions that the field of media studies continues to build on and refute today.

The most important of these figures for the history of mass communication research is Paul Lazarsfeld. After his death in 1976, Lazarsfeld became a kind of symbolic lightning rod, attracting the blame and praise of competing schools of media studies, who were fighting contemporary battles over the body of the dead father. Lazarsfeld was a cultural outsider who came to inhabit a central place in the field, both institutionally and intellectually. A Viennese Jew who spoke with a thick accent, he long remained self-conscious of his social identity within the context of the overwhelmingly Protestant culture of American universities before midcentury. This was an era of ethnic assimilation and WASP hegemony, and Lazarsfeld did not fit the mold. As he used to say at the beginning of talks with new audiences, "Well, I obviously didn't come over on the Mayflower."

Instead, Lazarsfeld had come to the United States in 1933 as a visiting scholar funded by the Rockefeller Foundation. He was trained as a mathematician, but, as a young socialist in his native Vienna, he had quickly branched out to psychology and social research. Before coming to the United States, his most important study was *The Unemployed of Marienthal*, a collaborative examination of the effects of unemployment on an Austrian mill town. Begun in 1930, it was conducted by Lazarsfeld's Economic and Psychological Research Group

(Wirtschaftspsychologisch Forschungsstelle), the first of four such organized research institutes he founded between 1927 and 1943. At the time, they represented a new form for social investigation—the university-based applied social research institute, which received funding from outside sources to conduct empirical research that was typically conducted by a team of social scientists (see Barton 1982; Morrison 1998). *Marienthal* drew some of its bearings from Robert Lynd and Helen Lynd's 1929 *Middletown* (p. 58), the classic community study conducted by the leading, socially reforming American sociologists of the 1930s. Through *Marienthal* and other work conducted in Vienna, Lazarsfeld established himself as a "managerial scholar," well schooled in new social scientific methodologies and capable of overseeing a research team. He also developed special expertise in the analysis of decision making and individual action, which he applied to areas ranging from marketing behavior and occupational choice to voting.

In the United States, Lazarsfeld initially established himself as an expert in marketing research, before moving into radio research in 1936. He had stayed in the United States after the fascists had come to power in Austria in 1934, detaining many members of his family. Robert Lynd had helped him find work at the University of Newark, where Lazarsfeld established a small research institute in 1936. Strapped financially (as was the case with many of Lazarsfeld's institutes), the Newark center received financial assistance from another set of émigré scholars, Max Horkheimer and the Frankfurt Institute of Social Research (Wiggershaus 1994, 165–68).

Oftentimes, Lazarsfeld and the Frankfurt School are seen as polar opposites, in a historical morality play whose favored protagonist varies depending on who tells the tale. Despite the relative truth in these narratives, they overlook the long and significant connections between so-called critical and administrative research (see Lazarsfeld, p. 166) and the similarities between Lazarsfeld's and Horkheimer's institutes. These connections date back to Lazarsfeld's Vienna days, when Horkheimer enlisted Lazarsfeld to conduct an empirical study of young workers in Austria, and they continued until 1935, when Lazarsfeld helped analyze data for the Frankfurt School's *Studies on Authority and the Family* (Wiggershaus 1994, 167). Horkheimer was grateful for Lazarsfeld's help, and demonstrated his gratitude by enlisting Lazarsfeld's Newark institute and paying the financially challenged Austrian. Lazarsfeld then returned the favor in 1938 by appointing Horkheimer's colleague Theodor Adorno to be head of the music section of Lazarsfeld's large radio research project.

Like propaganda analysis and objectivist social science, the work produced by Lazarsfeld's and Horkheimer's institutes display clear stylistic and methodological differences, but they also overlap and have some interesting similarities. Horkheimer had come to New York in 1934 and quickly brought several of his institute associates to join him, including Herbert Marcuse and Leo Lowenthal. Like Lazarsfeld, he was a German-speaking, Jewish outsider who had to scramble to create a place for himself in a foreign land gripped by the Great Depression. Like Lazarsfeld, he came out of a central European leftist–socialist political tradition, and he took "science" as a positive category for orienting his thought. Like Lazarsfeld, he benefited from the assistance of Robert Lynd, who helped the Frankfurt Institut für Sozialforschung (IfS) secure a building on the Columbia University campus (Wiggershaus 1994, 144–48). Soon after, Horkheimer enlisted Lazarsfeld's Newark institute, a move that signaled the beginning of a collaborative process among scholars in the two émigré's institutes and one that lasted for more than a decade in the United States. (In the next generation, this cross-fertilization continued via Rolf Meyersohn [see p. 409], a Columbia-trained sociologist invited by Horkheimer to bring his empirical expertise to Frankfurt, which conducted "administrative" studies much like Columbia did).

The collaboration was not without friction, a reflection on the personalities involved and the different intellectual orientations of the two institutes. Adorno was a difficult person, as was Lazarsfeld to a lesser degree, and their conflicts are famous (see Adorno 1969; Morrison 1978). Intellectually, Horkheimer's group was developing a nonorthodox Marxian analysis, what the group called "critical theory," that drew on Freud and the idealist tradition of German philosophy. While Lazarsfeld was drawn to questions of individual decision making, believing that any social phenomena could be explained in terms of its smaller, component parts, Horkheimer's group worked on a grander scale. Though they conducted empirical studies, they put their findings in the service of a larger, dialectic social theory that took individual phenomena as part of a broader, sociohistorical context. Moreover, whereas Lazarsfeld was always hesitant to bring critical or normative arguments onto the pages of his objectivist social science—his social conscience, he once told Robert Lynd, began after five o'clock (quoted in M. Smith 1994, 150)—Horkheimer and company saw such arguments as central components of sound intellectual work. This in part reflected the two leaders' differing understandings of "science," which for Horkheimer was intimately connected to humanist philosophy and to questions of ultimate social value. "Each study," a member of the Frankfurt group wrote, "while conforming to the highest scientific standards, should at the same time have a philosophical orientation. It should be intended as a contribution to the ultimate motives of social activity" (Institute for Social Research n.d., 11). In their studies of mass media, this meant drawing attention to positive moral ideals—such as individuality, inwardness, and spontaneity—that modern capitalist society and its industrialized production of culture threatened to eliminate.

To Adorno and his colleagues, Lazarsfeld was conducting research that served the cultural industries of domination. This was certainly true of Lazarsfeld's marketing research as well as his Princeton Radio Project, which he conducted with Hadley Cantril and Frank Stanton, the latter a CBS researcher and later its president. Beginning in 1936, Lazarsfeld, through his newly formed Office of Radio Research, administered a Rockefeller Foundation grant aimed at studying the impact of radio on American society, though in the end it produced more an empirical portrait of the unseen audience—who they were; what they listened to; and, to a limited extent, the role radio played in their lives. This kind of "administrative research" (so named because it operated in the service of an administrative agency who paid for it) had obvious commercial application since it was precisely the sort of information broadcasters wanted to provide to potential advertisers.

But like the émigré scholar who oversaw it, Lazarsfeldian administrative research straddled several worlds. It was often funded by marketing departments and other agencies of capitalism who had pressing interests in dissecting the still-murky recesses of the consumer psyche and its collective decision making; but it also served organizations who wanted to promote racial and ethnic tolerance and educational broadcasters who were looking to appeal to broader audiences. Although his methodologically sophisticated survey research was itself a marketable commodity, Lazarsfeld never got rich; his institutes regularly ran deficits; and he often engaged in what he called "Robin Hooding"—taking money designated for one project to fund others. Administrative research served the needs of the agencies that funded it, but it also allowed Lazarsfeld to develop methodologies and generate knowledge whose significance extended far beyond those needs, leading to important contributions in academic fields ranging from sociology and communications to political science, psychology, and others.

Moreover, Lazarsfeld brought Adorno on board the Princeton Radio Project because he thought the two approaches could be complementary. "I intend to make the musical section . . . the hunting ground for the 'European approach,'" Lazarsfeld told Adorno in 1937, by which he meant "a more theoretical attitude toward the research problem, and a more pessimistic attitude toward an instrument of technical progress" (quoted in Wiggershaus 1994, 238). Though Adorno quit the project after two often-frustrating years, he composed four provocative essays on radio and popular music while associated with the Office of Radio Research (see p. 210). Lazarsfeld's desire to cross-fertilize the two institutes' approaches persisted, however, as clearly evidenced in his 1941 "Administrative and Critical Communications Research" (p. 166), published in the IfS journal *Studies in Philosophy and Social Science* (which also included articles by Harold Lasswell, Margaret Mead, and other American social scientists). Over the next several years, Lazarsfeld was active in helping the IfS secure funding from the American Jewish Committee and in trying to find a more permanent place for the Frankfurt scholars at Columbia. In short, the two institutes had a number of important ties.

When Lazarsfeld moved his Office of Radio Research to Columbia in 1940, it signaled the clear ascendance of New York City as the geographical center for social thought on mass communication. John Dewey was still affiliated with Columbia, though he was well past his peak influence. Robert Lynd was a commanding presence in the university's sociology department, which the next year would hire both Lazarsfeld and Robert Merton, the latter who was soon writing about mass communication as well. Herta Herzog, Lazarsfeld's second wife, was an important presence in radio research and had been since the Newark days. Horkheimer and Adorno were there, until they moved to Los Angeles in 1941, leaving Leo Lowenthal to stay in New York and work closely with the Office of Radio Research through the war years. Meanwhile downtown, the New School for Social Research was becoming known as the "University in Exile" by attracting its own collection of émigré scholars—among them, Ernst Kris and Hans Speier, whose 1943 *German War Propaganda* we have excerpted here (p. 182), as well as Hannah Arendt, one of the leading thinkers of the twentieth century. In addition, two of the most important funding sources of the period were also in New York—CBS's Frank Stanton and the Rockefeller Foundation's John Marshall—as were the headquarters for many of the central media industries: radio networks, publishing houses, and advertising and public relations agencies.

The War Years

After 1939, when war again broke out in Europe, the social scientific study of mass communication quickened in pace and sharpened in focus. The Rockefeller Foundation and Marshall played an important role in this process, as Brett Gary (1999, chap. 3) has carefully argued. Marshall, a Harvard-trained medievalist with deep sympathies for science as an enlightening social force, was chief funding officer for the foundation's numerous communications projects, for which he convened an important monthly seminar that drew together key figures in the nascent field. Among those in attendance were Lasswell, Lazarsfeld, Cantril, Lynd, and Waples, as well as the literary theorist and critic I. A. Richards and the adult-education specialist Lyman Bryson, who edited the important 1948 collection *The Communication of Ideas*. Before the war, the group's goal was to generate a more disciplined model for the study of mass communications and, in particular, what Marshall called "mass influence" (Gary 1999, 87). As the European situation degenerated and Americans debated what role the United States should play, the Rockefeller Communications Group conducted their own discussions about the aims and methods of communications research and the roles it might play in the unfolding crisis (see p. 136).

The Rockefeller Seminar played several important roles. It brought together a network of scholars who together shaped the mainstream of mass communication study through the 1940s, both in their own work and in their training of graduate students. Just as important, it gave them a common conceptual focus by developing what Marshall called a "general theory" (Gary 1999, 100) but what more accurately was a research agenda—that "the job of research in mass communication is to determine who, and with what intentions, said what, to whom, and with what effects." The concept of effects had already been a prominent feature of the Payne Fund Studies, Lasswell's propaganda studies, and Waples's reading research, but the seminar gave the concept a more codified and more central place. Still, one can overstate the degree to which the seminar's formulation made "effects" the central question for the field, as is apparent in Lazarsfeld's 1948 elaboration on the Rockefeller group's question (p. 242).

After the United States entered the war, a number of émigré and native-born scholars volunteered their services for wartime communications research that helped to build the intellectual and institutional structure of the field as it emerged in the late 1940s and 1950s. The Rockefeller Foundation funded some of this contribution, including Nazi propaganda studies by Kris and Speier (p. 182) and by Siegfried Kracauer. A great deal more research was conducted for government agencies such as the Office of War Information, the Office of Strategic Services, and the Library of Congress. Liberal democrats and Marxians alike went to work in the propaganda battle against totalitarianism. Lasswell, Lazarsfeld, Merton, Herzog, Stouffer, Lowenthal, Marcuse, Wilbur Schramm, Gladys Engel Lang, and many others studied the propaganda efforts of Germany and other U.S. enemies and helped plan and evaluate U.S. print, film, and radio propaganda. In the process, they assisted in codifying content analysis and the focused-interview technique (a precursor of today's focus groups), and they wrote several studies of lasting importance, including Lazarsfeld and Merton's "Studies in Radio and Film Propaganda" (1943; reprinted in Merton 1949) and Merton's *Mass Persuasion* (1946; p. 215 of this reader). Finally, the war also boosted the postwar study of communication by allowing former soldiers to go to college or graduate school on the GI Bill, an opportunity seized by a number of authors in this volume.

Though not war-related research, both the Hutchins Commission's *A Free and Responsible Press* and Gunnar Myrdal's *An American Dilemma* were researched and written during World War II, and each continued the longer tradition of reform-minded studies of communication in American society. Myrdal, a Swedish economist and social scientist, was brought in as an outsider to compile the most exhaustive study yet of what he called "the Negro problem and modern democracy." He pursued it by both marshaling scores of empirical studies and by drawing critical attention to moral issues raised by the gap between the American creed and the treatment of African Americans, calling up John Dewey to justify his approach (Myrdal [1944] 1962, lxix). The Negro press was one of the many subjects Myrdal discussed (p. 206). Hutchins, who helped institute the Great Books program as president of the University of Chicago, also explicitly raised moral issues, not only offering a classic liberal defense of a free communication of ideas, but also a warning against dangers posed by monopolization of ownership, censorship, sensationalism, and commercialism (see p. 218).

In the immediate postwar period, there were several intellectual paradigms for the study and understanding of mass communication, none of which was clearly dominant. One, later known as the *limited-effects paradigm,* was spelled out in the last pages of Lazarsfeld and Merton's "Mass Communication, Popular Taste, and Organized Social Action" (p. 230). Growing out of Lazarsfeld's early 1940s radio and voting studies, it held that mass communications rarely have powerful direct effects on audiences, who are generally protected by mediating social and psychological factors. Proponents of limited effects argued that media are most influential when supplemented by face-to-face communication, when not significantly challenged by countervailing ideas, and when drawing on and channeling existing values and beliefs. Since these three conditions are rarely met, mass media tend to have limited effects.

Distinct from the limited-effects paradigm but developed alongside it at Columbia was gratifications research. Pioneered in the late 1930s by Herta Herzog, in consultation with Hadley Cantril, the gratifications approach took media not as a causal agent but rather as a social experience from which audience members took varied meanings and sociopsychological gratifications. Many of the 1940s gratification studies, including Herzog's "On Borrowed Experience" (p. 139) and Katherine Wolf and Marjorie Fiske's "The Children Look at Comics" (1949), were conducted by female researchers concerned not with marketing, political campaigns, or propaganda for social objectives but rather with entertainment media and the roles they played in the everyday lives of audiences. Typically using broadly Freudian categories, gratification studies often examined politically marginal audiences (women and children) and culturally marginal genres (soap operas, quiz shows, comics), though other studies, such as Berelson's "What 'Missing the Newspaper' Means" (p. 253), looked at mainstream media forms.

Gratifications and effects studies at Columbia often focused on psychological experience or behavioral effects and neglected the larger historical and social contexts of mass media, but this was not true of either the critical theorists or the less atomistically oriented American sociologists. In the 1940s, critical theory showed two of its faces, in Lowenthal's 1944 "Biographies in Popular Magazines" (p. 188) and in Horkheimer and Adorno's 1944 *Dialectic of Enlightenment* (p. 180). Horkheimer and Adorno had moved to Los Angeles, where between 1942 and 1944 they lived among other German-speaking émigrés (including Bertolt Brecht and Thomas Mann) and worked out their high-theoretical critique of instrumental rationality, advanced capitalism, and culture industries. Lowenthal, meanwhile, who had stayed in New York, toiled in the more empirically oriented world of Lazarsfeld's institutes, and his study represents probably the happiest marriage of critical theory with the methods of American social science (though Herzog's "On Borrowed Experience" (p. 139) and Merton's *Mass Persuasion* (p. 215) also display hybrid vigor). Meanwhile, American sociologists such as Louis Wirth (p. 249) and Merton (see Lazarsfeld and Merton p. 230, especially pp. 233–38) were also viewing mass media from a larger sociopolitical perspective, though not with the same explicit critical edge as the Frankfurt group.

In the immediate postwar period, one era was coming to an end. The idea of communication appealed to thinkers across a broad range of disciplines—as Lyman Bryson observed, "nearly every thoughtful student of human behavior today, no matter what he calls his field, is likely to find something which he will have to call 'communication'" (1948, 1–2). At the same time, émigré scholars who had contributed some of the most important work to the young research area either moved on to other fields or left the country. By 1949, the bulk of Lazarsfeld's mass communications research was behind him, as it was for his colleagues Merton and Herzog. Horkheimer and Adorno returned to Germany, where they established the IfS on its home turf (though Horkheimer also taught at the University of Chicago in the mid-1950s). This generation's work would be extended by its students, particularly Elihu Katz from Columbia and Jürgen Habermas from Frankfurt—whose respective classic works *Personal Influence* (1955; see p. 358 of this reader) and *Structural Transformation of the Public Sphere* (1962) were landmark texts of the next generation. But the political and intellectual orientation of the field had changed by the time those works were published.

The landscape of mass communications research changed in the Cold War era. Columbia research had basically been cosmopolitan, with a political axis running from liberal and left-liberal to radical. Lazarsfeld, Merton, Herzog, Lowenthal, Adorno, and Horkheimer all looked in important ways to European thought, one dimension that gave their best work breadth and elegance. When this era at Columbia broke up, the institutional center of the field shifted to the far less-cosmopolitan world of Urbana, Illinois, and Wilbur Schramm. Schramm had different politics and a different intellectual compass and never sunk a tap-root into the deeper waters of continental social theory. While Merton and Lazarsfeld were rallying the forces of academic freedom during the McCarthy era, Schramm was busy jetting to Korea and other strategic sites around the globe as an ardent cold warrior doing his part to hold back the Communists (see p. 310). In Urbana, he incorporated Claude Shannon's mathematical theory of communication into the graduate curriculum and guided his students into development communications and its corresponding theories of modernization (see Schramm 1997).

Internationalism cut in different directions during the Cold War, and this helped shape thinking about mass communication. The newly formed United Nations Educational, Social, and Cultural Organization (UNESCO) expressed renewed social hopes in using mass communication for "advancing the mutual knowledge and understanding of peoples, through all means of mass communication" ("UNESCO's Program" 1946–1947, 518). Julian Huxley's piece on UNESCO (p. 222) captures some of this hope, along with the hubris that often accompanied development initiatives from the West. In that same document, we also see the other side of the postwar ideological landscape, namely, the escalating worldwide tensions between the United States and the Soviet Union. Simpson (1994) overstates the influence of the Cold War on communication study in the 1950s (as the variety of readings in this Reader indicate), but there is no doubt that certain sectors of the field benefited from institutional and intellectual proximity to the Cold War's multifront ideological campaign. This group includes Columbia's Bureau of Applied Social Research, which in 1950 received government money to conduct surveys of seven Muslim nations in the Middle East (Turkey, Lebanon, Syria, Egypt, Syria, Jordan, and Iran) and which provided part of the empirical base for Daniel Lerner's *Passing of Traditional Society* (p. 426). The studies were partly coordinated by Leo Lowenthal, then head of the research division of the Voice of America and an important figure on the propaganda front of the Cold War.

The radical democratic and socialist politics that gave the 1930s some of their characteristic tone was in the 1950s supplanted by what Christopher Lasch (1991) resonantly termed "the politics of the civilized minority." Centrist liberalism dominated 1950s communication study, as it did other elements of American intellectual life. In retrospect, we can say that in the late 1940s and 1950s the ties between communications research and the state became morally questionable in a way not seen during World War II, when propaganda researchers served a less-ambiguous national cause. In the 1950s and 1960s, the study of communication was also more native-born than in the previous generation, and more the product of cultural insiders than of the outsiders who had originally made it interesting. As a topic of social thought, mass communication remained vibrant in the 1950s and 1960s, but as an institutionalized field, communication research did not live up to the promise of the previous decade.

12

Conclusion

From *Movies and Conduct* (1933)

Herbert Blumer

Herbert Blumer (1900–1987) was a sociologist best known for his work in *symbolic interactionism,* a term he coined to define a central idea about the nature of social life that he found in the thought of George Herbert Mead. Blumer taught at the University of Chicago from 1925 to 1952 and afterward at the University of California, Berkeley. In the 1930s and 1940s Blumer wrote a number of fine, often-provocative studies of mass media and public life, including "Public Opinion and Public Opinion Polling" (*American Sociological Review,* 13 [1948]: 542–54), a critique still referenced in the field of public opinion studies.

Blumer wrote two book-length studies commissioned by the Payne Fund on the social meaning of motion pictures: *Movies and Conduct* (1933); and *Movies, Delinquency, and Crime* (1933), with Philip Hauser. Blumer employed the Chicago School "biographical method" by inviting young people in schools—and prisons—to write "movie autobiographies," which reflected on the influence that movies had on their actions or attitudes. He found that young people learned many things from the movies—from general attitudes about life, to hairstyles, how to kiss, and how to pickpocket. In this excerpt from *Movies and Conduct,* Blumer reviews the major conclusions of his book, sometimes in charmingly quaint language, and gives a taste of the intense state of social concern about the effects of film in the early 1930s, prior to the film industry's being disciplined by the Hays Office from 1934 on. Though he remains a detached observer to some extent, it is not hard to detect a touch of moralistic censure about "emotional possession" that is not unlike Jane Addams's earlier worries about the effects of the theater on young girls in the city.

Some Remarks on Method

This study is regarded by the author as exploratory in character. It arose in response to an effort to see what could be learned about the influence of motion pictures by inquiring into personal experiences. The procedure employed has been as simple as possible, for the only task involved was that of inducing people to write or relate their motion-picture experiences in an honest and trustworthy fashion. Efforts were always made to secure the frank and sincere cooperation of the informants.

The writer is not unaware of the criticisms which are often made of autobiographical statements. Without seeking to treat categorically these criticisms in so far as the present study is concerned, in the writer's judgment they do not apply significantly to the material which has been collected. The accounts of experiences which have been secured are numerous. They have been written independently of one another. The fact, therefore, that on major items they substantiate one another can be taken, in the writer's judgment, as a substantial indication of their reliability and accuracy.

The study has been confined to experiences with motion pictures. No effort has been made to compare or to contrast these experiences with those which arise through other influences. We

91

are not in a position, consequently, to make any remarks of an evaluative character concerning the role of motion pictures in comparison with other agencies playing upon the lives of people.

The writer feels that the statement of findings in this report errs, if at all, on the side of caution and conservatism. To an appreciable extent the people who have furnished their experiences represent a sophisticated and cultured group. This is perhaps not altogether true of the high-school students who have furnished autobiographies, but it is quite true of the university and college people whose experiences have been employed. Our findings suggest that motion pictures are less influential in the case of people who have had access to higher institutions of learning. To this extent the picture which is presented by this study is underdrawn if it be regarded as depicting the action of motion pictures on the lives of the greater mass of the American population. However, these remarks are not meant to imply any substantial differences in the kinds of experience which people of different strata of our society have as a result of witnessing motion pictures; they are meant merely to suggest that the degree of influence of motion pictures is less in the cultured classes than it is in the case of others. With this one qualification the writer believes that his findings apply to the bulk of movie-goers.

Statement of Findings

A summary of the more important of the specific findings of this study is given here. We have indicated the great influence of motion pictures on the play of children. We have shown that motion pictures serve as a source for considerable imitation. Forms of beautification, mannerisms, poses, ways of courtship and ways of love-making, especially, are copied. We have shown the influence of motion pictures on fantasy and day-dreaming. We have treated at some length the ways in which motion pictures may influence the emotions of the spectators, showing in particular how they may arouse terror and fright in children, sorrow and pathos among people in general, excitement and passions of love chiefly among adolescents. We have indicated how motion pictures provide people with schemes of life, fixed images, and stereotyped conceptions of different characters and modes of conduct. We have called attention

to the way in which motion pictures may furnish people with ideas as to how they should act, notions of their rights and privileges, and conceptions of what they would like to enjoy. We have indicated, finally, how motion pictures may implant attitudes.

Interpretation of Findings

These effects which have been discovered are not to be considered as separate and discreet. They invite interpretation. We have introduced some statement of their significance while treating them in the separate chapters. Here we may endeavor to offer a more embracing explanation.

Since the overwhelming bulk of our material has been drawn from adolescents, or young men and young women, it will be convenient to view our findings with respect to their situation and problems.

In our society, the girl or boy of adolescent age is usually being ushered into a life which is new and strange. It is frequently at this period that the boy or girl begins to feel the attractions and the pressure of more adult conduct. New situations arise in their experience for which they are not likely to be prepared in the way of previous instruction. It is a time when new personal ambitions and hopes and new interests appear, particularly those which involve association with the opposite sex. In the case of the girl, in particular, desires for beauty, for sophistication, for grace and ease, for romance, for adventure, and for love are likely to come to the fore.

The influence of motion pictures upon the mind and conduct of the adolescent is more understandable if we appreciate this condition—to wit, that he is confronted with a new life to whose demands he is not prepared to respond in a ready and self-satisfying way; and that he is experiencing a new range of desires and interests which are pressing for some form of satisfaction.

In the light of this situation it is not strange that motion pictures should exert on the adolescent the kinds of influences which have been specified. Motion pictures show in intimate detail and with alluring appeal forms of life in which he is interested.[1] Before his eyes are displayed modes of living and schemes of conduct which are of the character of his desires and which offer possibilities of instructing him in his own behavior. In a sense, motion pictures organize his needs and suggest lines of conduct useful for their satisfaction.

It is not surprising that the boy or girl should copy from motion pictures forms of conduct which promise to serve immediate interests. Some attractive way of dressing, some effective form of make-up, some gracious mannerism, some skillful form of making love may catch his or her attention and be imitated because of the possibilities which it promises. When such forms of conduct are clothed with romance and attended by successful consequence, as they are likely to be in motion pictures, their appeal is apt to be particularly strong. Further, since these forms of life represent experiences which the adolescent yearns for, that they should profoundly incite and color his fantasy is to be expected. Likewise one can understand how life as it is displayed in the movies may yield the adolescent a picture of the world as he would like to experience it and so give direction and focus to desires and ambitions. And finally, that motion pictures should grip the attention of the adolescent and stir profoundly certain of his emotions, as that of love, is not puzzling in the light of our remarks.

These considerations establish motion pictures as an incitant to conduct as well as a pacifier of feelings. It is insufficient to regard motion pictures simply as a fantasy world by participating in which an individual softens the ardor of his life and escapes its monotony and hardships, nor to justify their content and "unreality" on this basis. For to many the pictures are authentic portrayals of life, from which they draw patterns of behavior, stimulation to overt conduct, content for a vigorous life of imagination, and ideas of reality. They are not merely a device for surcease; they are a form of stimulation. Their content does not merely serve the first purpose, but incites the latter results. What might be intended to have the harmless effect of the former may, on occasion, have the striking influence of the latter.

These remarks should make clear that motion pictures are a genuine educational institution; not educational in the restricted and conventional sense of supplying to the adolescent some detached bit of knowledge, some detail of geography or history, some custom, or some item of dress of a foreign people—but educational in the truer sense of actually introducing him to and acquainting him with a type of life which has immediate, practical, and momentous significance.[2] In a genuine sense, motion pictures define his role,

elicit and direct his impulses, and provide substance for his emotions and ideas. Their modes of life are likely to carry an authority and sanction which make them formative of codes of living. Despite their gay and entertaining character, motion pictures seem to enter seriously into the life of young men and women, particularly of high-school age.

Because motion pictures are educational in this sense, they may conflict with other educational institutions. They may challenge what other institutions take for granted. The schemes of conduct which they present may not only fill gaps left by the school, by the home, and by the church, but they may also cut athwart the standards and values which these latter institutions seek to inculcate. What is presented as entertainment, with perhaps no thought of challenging established values, may be accepted as sanctioned conduct, and so enter into conflict with certain of these values. This is peculiarly likely in the case of motion pictures because they often present the extremes as if they were the norm. For the young moviegoer little discrimination is possible. He probably could not *understand* or even *read* a sophisticated book, but he can *see* the thing in the movies and be stirred and possibly misled. This is likely to be true chiefly among those with least education and sophisticated experience.

Where, as in disorganized city areas, the school, the home, or the community are most ineffective in providing adolescents with knowledge adequate for the new world into which they are entering, the reliance on motion pictures seems to become distinctly greater. Where the molding of thought and attitude by established institutions is greater, a condition of emotional detachment seems to be formed which renders the individual immune to the appeal of much that is shown in motion pictures.

It seems clear that the forte of motion pictures is in their emotional effect. This is to be expected since in the last analysis they are a form of art—even though popular art—and their appeal and their success reside ultimately in the emotional agitation which they induce. To fascinate the observer and draw him into the drama so that he loses himself is the goal of a successful production. As we have sought to show, while in this condition the observer becomes malleable to the touch of what is shown. Ordinary self-control is lost. Impulses and feelings are aroused, and the individual develops a readiness to certain forms of action which are foreign in some degree to his ordinary conduct. Precisely because the individual is in this crucible state what is shown to him may become the mold for a new organization of his conduct. This organization, of course, may be quite temporary, as it frequently is. However, as our cases have shown, occasionally it may be quite abiding.

Another observation is in point, an observation which, in the judgment of the writer, is of major importance in seeking to estimate the role of motion pictures. We refer to the conspicuous tendency of commercial motion pictures to dull discrimination and to confuse judgments. One of the chief reasons for this effect lies in the variety, the inconsistency, and the loose organization among the emotional states which are stimulated. This is to be expected in view of the fact that the aim of motion-picture productions is merely that of provoking emotion whether it be done by playing on the themes of horror, excitement, romance, adventure, particularly passionate love, or what not. In contrast to other educational institutions motion pictures have no definite goal of conduct. They are not seeking to establish any definite set of values. They are not endeavoring to provide a consistent philosophy of life. Their aim, as stated, is essentially mere emotional stimulation.

Just because they have at hand in such an effective fashion the implements of emotional stimulation yet do not employ them consistently towards any conscious goal, their effects, ultimately, are likely to be of confusion. The movies generally play upon the whole range of human emotions, frequently with such realism and intensity as to leave the youthful person emotionally exhausted. The kaleidoscopic change that is involved in mood and receptivity of the spectator is so great that emotionally it may put demands on him which make him callous, or leave him indifferent to the ordinary requirements of emotional response made upon him in his workaday world. As far as his mind is concerned the result of this scattered emotional indulgence is confusion. A variety of impulses may be awakened, a medley of feelings aroused, a multiplicity of daydreams engendered, a mass of ideas suggested—all of which, at best, are likely to hang together in a loose organization. It seems that such a multiple and loosely integrated reaction is typical of the impressions left by the ordinary movie—more typical when movies are considered collectively. In so far as one may seek to cover in a

single proposition the more abiding effect of motion pictures upon the minds of movie-goers, it would be, in the judgment of the writer, in terms of a medley of vague and variable impressions—a disconnected assemblage of ideas, feelings, vagaries, and impulses.

We recognize two other conspicuous ways in which motion pictures confound discrimination and dissolve moral judgment into a maze of ambiguous definitions. One is the sanctioning of questionable or unexpected conduct by running a moral through it. Although the general tenor of a movie, or even its *leitmotif*, may be of an "idealistic" sort, so much often has to be taken into the bargain in the way of trimmings that discrimination becomes confused and the effect is lost. The ideal of the theme may stamp its character on the details of the setting which are meant to be kept apart.[3]

We conclude by directing attention to the other source of confused discrimination and judgment—the possible divergence between the standards of the directors of the picture and the perspective of movie-goers. What may be intended by the producer and the director as art, may be accepted by the movie public, or significant portions of it, as pornography. The difference, if it exist[s], is obviously a matter of interpretation. But the standards and codes of art which transform things into aesthetic objects may be limited to a select number. Other people with different standards can scarcely be expected to view these things in the same light. To justify the depiction on the ground of aesthetic character, or "art for art's sake," seems to overlook the major premise of the situation. It circumscribes the area of judgment to the perspective of the director and those whose attitudes he represents. What may evoke aesthetic satisfaction on the part may stimulate others in an unmistakenly contrary fashion. Unless the aesthetic values and interpretation of the movie public are changed to conform to those of the directing personnel, it is anomalous to defend commercial depictions on the basis of their art value, and to charge unfortunate effects to the base mindedness of people.

Notes

1. It is important to consider that the movies do not come merely as a film that is thrown on a screen; their witnessing is an experience

which is undergone in a very complex setting. There is the darkened theater—itself of no slight significance, especially in case of love or sex pictures; there is the music which is capable not merely of being suggestive and in some degree interpretive of the film but is also designed to raise the pitch of excitement, to facilitate shock and to heighten the emotional effect of the picture; there are the furnishings—sometimes gaudy and gorgeous, which help to tone the experience.

2. The movies may also acquaint the person with aspects of life which, in his own age group, he probably would not have any notion about until later. Their promotion of premature sophistication seems significant.

3. A good example of a picture of this sort was *Our Dancing Daughters* where, in the experience of many, the qualities of fair play and good sportsmanship tended to envelop and give sanction to forms of conduct such as freedom in relations between the sexes, smoking, drinking, petting, etc.

13

The Integration of Communication

From *Communication Agencies and Social Life* (1933)

Malcolm M. Willey and Stuart A. Rice

Malcolm Willey (1897–1974) and Stuart A. Rice (1889–1969) both studied sociology at Columbia University in the 1920s, where they worked with Alvan A. Tenney and Franklin Giddings, who trained them in statistics and quantitative methods. Since at least 1911, Tenney and his students had conducted "scientific analyses of the press" that generated quantitative data about the degree of attention the press paid to its topics. Willey used this and other qualitative and statistical methods in *The Country Newspaper: A Study of Socialization and Newspaper Content* (1926), based on his 1922 dissertation. Columbia paralleled Chicago, where Park and his students conducted their more well-known newspaper studies. Willey spent most of his career at the University of Minnesota (which Paul Lazarsfeld identified in the late 1930s as one of the institutional centers of communications research), where he commissioned a house by Frank Lloyd Wright that is said to have revived the architect's then-faltering career. In the 1930s and 1940s, Willey wrote on higher education, communication, and the press while serving as vice president of the university.

After publishing his dissertation, *Farmers and Workers in American Politics* (1924), Rice wrote two important books on method: *Quantitative Methods in Politics* (1928) and *Methods in Social Science* (1931). He taught sociology and statistics at the University of Pennsylvania and the University of Chicago before moving to Washington in 1935 to work as a statistician in Franklin Roosevelt's New Deal government. He stayed in government until 1952, having worked in Japan during the occupation and serving as assistant director of the Census Bureau. When he retired from government, he began conducting advisory statistical work for business and foreign governments, and from 1958 to 1963, he organized a census for the South Korean government.

This excerpt comes from Willey and Rice's *Communication Agencies and Social Life* (1933), one book in the landmark statistical collection *Recent Social Trends in the United States*, commissioned in 1929 by President Hoover to survey the social changes and social problems confronting the nation. The studies addressed everything from population trends and the growth of federal government to the arts in American life and the manner in which people spent their leisure time. Willey and Rice's book is significant in part for what it designates as "communication": transportation, telecommunication, and "media of mass impression" all find a place in the authors' survey (thus reminding us that transportation and communication were not forever torn apart by the telegraph, as is sometimes suggested). Their spacious understanding of communication and its place in social life resonates with the similarly broad views of Cooley, Sapir, Mumford, Innis, McLuhan, and Park and Burgess; but Willey and Rice address the issue in quantitative and statistical ways that are distinct among the grander theorists.

The preceding pages have traced the changes of three decades in some of the conspicuous agencies of communication, and suggested the influences of these upon human behavior. The presentation has necessarily been schematic. In actuality, each individual is the center of a converging web of communication media, which in turn extend his touch to all the world.

Nor has the presentation been complete. The existence and continuity of social life depend on communication. Its most rudimentary forms in face to face contact have received but scant attention, and only as they have been incidental to the utilization of mediating agencies. The interchange of ideas, attitudes and emotions in the family, on the playground, in the neighborhood, the office and shop, at the corner store, and across the tea table, has passed unmentioned, and is present only by implication. Yet it is such interchanges which are of fundamental importance in setting the personality of the growing child and in giving meaning to the life of the adult. More formal agencies of fact to face contact such as the conference, the club, the fraternal meeting, the "round table," the fair, the picnic, the auction, the "social," the "party," the "reception," are institutionalized devices for furthering communication of the elemental kind. The school, the pulpit, the lecture and "speech," the theatre, the ceremony, are still more highly institutionalized agencies of mass impression which nevertheless preserve their face to face character and values. They receive no further mention here.

Apart from face to face contacts, there are forms of mediated communication, not hitherto mentioned, which cannot entirely escape attention. In 1927, 470,375,000 copies of books and pamphlets were published in the United States. Nearly one-half of these were books, of which more than one-third were texts for school use, and about one-sixth were fiction.[1] In 1929, there were 6,429 libraries of more than 3,000 volumes each, with 154,310,000 volumes.[2] The functions of the library have been extended by the growth of states and other circulating and traveling libraries, and by the development of the special library, particularly in industry and business. No summary can be made of the use of the billboard, the bulletin board, the circular, the hand bill, the placard, the mail announcement, the "catalogue," the road map, and other forms of printed non-periodical communication devices. The costs of printing and publishing books and pamphlets in 1927 were exceeded nearly five-fold by the cost of commercial printing.[3]

Non-printed forms of communication, not mentioned before, are various: The exposition and the exhibit have been of far-reaching influence in disseminating knowledge, establishing social norms, and modifying production and consumption habits. Before the introduction of the radio, many of its functions were performed by the phonograph. Speeches and dialogue as well as music have had wide dissemination through the medium. In 1927, 104,766,000 disc phonograph records were produced in the United States, as compared with 92,855,000 in 1923.[4] The neon table has increased the importance of the electric sign. "Sky-writing" is at least spectacular. Television, still largely experimental, has aroused wide popular interest, and may become a major medium of mass impression comparable to the radio, the moving picture, and the newspaper.

The processes of change are accompanied at every step by integration and adjustment. Old agencies give way to new, and the new appear in quick succession, engendering situations in which competition, supplementation and mutual dependence are inextricably combined. Illustrations have been numerous in the preceding pages, and they could be augmented indefinitely. The surface picture is one of conflict: railroad competing with bus; bus competing with street car; street car competing with private automobile; newspapers concerned over radio advertising; moving picture competing with radio; wireless competing with cable; telephone competing with telegraph. Out of the conflict emerges displacement or adjustment: the horse cab disappears, but trolley car and bus are combined in a single local transportation system; river transportation loses its passenger significance, but railroad and airplane untie their facilities in joint service. One learns of road conditions by the radio; the newspaper advertises the motion picture, which in turn presents the news reel; phonograph and radio corporations merge, and combine techniques in a single instrument.

It is inevitable that the presence of a communication system so all-pervading should lead to its use for the deliberate control of individual behavior. Propaganda, publicity, and mass education are terms expressing the fact of purposive mass impression, which may be designed to effect either private or public ends. The function of the "public relations counsel" has already been mentioned. His success results from his ability to instill within the individual, and to reinforce continually, through a *variety* of communication channels, a suggestion that will engender, consciously or unconsciously, the behavior that he desires. It is the omnipresence of the communication network that makes it so effective.

How intensively the agencies of communication may similarly be knit together for a peace time *public* purpose is illustrated by the extension activities of the United States Department of Agriculture. In furthering the economic and social well being of the agricultural population, it employs general and demonstration, meetings, farm and home visits, newspaper publicity, bulletins on special topics, and circular and personal letters, the radio (both commercial and educational stations), exhibits and posters, telephone calls, the motional picture, and study courses. In 1930 the Department distributed 34,294,000 copies of printed materal.[5]

The residential impression gained from this survey, is of individuals at the focal points of interrelated social stimuli that are continuously impinging upon them from the world about. During thirty years the number and intensity of these stimuli increased, the boundaries within which they arose expanded, while the speed with which they were transmitted accelerated. A vast and intricate system of communication provides for the individual, in the shortest possible time, over the widest possible areas, contacts with a maximum number of other human beings.

Among these interwoven stimuli there appear to be two contradictory tendencies: on the one hand are *reinforcements of community patterns* of attitude and behavior, resulting from the multiplication of contact with others in the same community; these make for the perpetuation and intensification of localism. The increased proportions of local mail and local telephone calls, the intensification of local mobility through the use of the automobile, the fostering of local spirit by the local newspaper and local organizations, are among the factors which seem to be working in this direction. On the other hand are contacts contributing to *standardization over wider national and international regions*. The motion picture, radio broadcasting, national advertising, increasing travel, the growth and utilization of long distance wire and wireless facilities—these are factors which appear to undermine localism, and obviously do so in certain externals.

There is reason to believe that these opposing factors are concurrently effective because they are selective in their operation. Individuals north, south, east, and west, may all wear garments of Hollywood. At the same time each may hold with undiminished vigor to certain local attitudes, traditions, and beliefs. An increase in *overt standardization* may be accompanied by retention of *inward differences*. Therein, perhaps, is one explanation of the local and regional perpetuation of certain political, economic and social doctrines which are anomalous in the face of increasing external social resemblance.

The content of communication is beyond the scope of the present investigation. Further study may disclose what meanings and values are transmitted by each of the agencies that have been considered. Only such study would permit a confident forecast of the ultimate balance between the localizing and the standardizing tendencies.

Notes

1. *Census of Manufactures: Printing and Publishing and Allied Industries,* 1927, Table 5, p. 14.

2. As reported to the United States Office of Education, *World Almanac,* 1931, p. 135.

3. *Census of Manufactures, op. cit.,* Table 3, p. 11.

4. *Statistical Abstract of the United States,* 1930, Table 824, p. 843.

5. Data supplied by the Department. *Cf.* M. C. Wilson, *Extension Methods and Their Relative Effectiveness,* Technical Bulletin No. 106, United States Department of Agriculture, 1929.

14

Toward a Critique of Negro Music,

From *Opportunity* (1934)

Alain Locke

Alain Locke (1886–1954) was one of the most important African American intellectuals of the twentieth century. Born in Philadelphia to a well-educated family with three generations of freedom, Locke studied philosophy with William James at Harvard (B.A. 1907; Ph.D. 1918); became the first African American to earn a Rhodes Scholarship; taught at Howard University; and wrote widely on race, art, culture, and theories of value. In 1925, he was fired from Howard for advocating equity in pay among blacks and whites, and in the same year he published *The New Negro,* the work for which he is best known. One of the central texts of the "Harlem Renaissance"—Locke's label for a somewhat diverse array of literary and artistic productions by the Negro avant-garde—the *New Negro* was a race-proud appreciation of traditional black folkways grafted onto the sophisticated urban sensibility of Harlem, the center point of African American culture.

The 1920s and 1930s were a time when black musical and artistic culture captured the imagination of the white mass audience. Locke saw it as an opportunity for collective self-expression of the Negro and for contribution to a broader, multicultural American identity. At the same time, as the following excerpt indicates, he was alert to the complexities of popularization and the tensions involved in grafting the Negro folk tradition onto the mainstream of American and Western music.

Things Negro have been and still are the victims of two vicious extremes,—uncritical praise or calculated disparagement. Seldom, if ever, do they achieve the golden mean and by escaping both over-praise and belittlement receive fair appraisal and true appreciation. Of no field is this more true than Negro music. I have read nearly all that has been written on the subject, and do not hesitate to rate most of it as platitudinous piffle—repetitious bosh; the pounds of praise being, if anything, more hurtful and damning than the ounces of disparagement. For from the enthusiasts about Negro music comes little else than extravagant superlatives and endless variations on certain half-true commonplaces about our inborn racial musicality, our supposed gift of spontaneous harmony, the uniqueness of our musical idioms and the infectious power and glory of our transmuted suffering.

True—or rather half-true as these things undoubtedly are, the fact remains that it does Negro music no constructive service to have them endlessly repeated by dilettante enthusiasts, especially without the sound correctives of their complementary truths. The state of Negro music, and especially the state of mind of Negro musicians needs the bitter tonic of criticism more than unctuous praise and the soothing syrups of flattery. While the Negro musician sleeps on his much-extolled heritage, the commercial musical world, reveling in its prostitution, gets rich by exploiting it popularly, while the serious musical world tries only half-successfully to imitate and develop a fundamentally alien idiom. Nothing of course can stop this but the exhaustion of the vogue upon which it thrives; still the sound progress of our music depends more upon the independent development of its finer and deeper values than upon the curtailing of the popular and spurious output. The real damage of the popular vogue rests in the corruption and misguidance of the few rare talents that might otherwise make heroic and lasting contributions. For their sake and guidance, constructive criticism and discriminating appreciation must raise a standard far above the curb-stone values of the market-place and far more exacting than the easy favor of the multitude.

Indeed for the sound promotion of its future, we must turn from the self-satisfying glorification of the past of Negro music to consider for their salutary effect the present short-comings of Negro music and musicians. It is time to realize that though we may be a musical people, we have produced few, if any, great musicians,—that though we may have evolved a folk music of power and potentiality, it has not yet been integrated into a musical tradition,—that our creativeness and originality on the folk level has

not yet been matched on the level of instrumental mastery or that of creative composition,—and that with a few exceptions, the masters of Negro musical idiom so far are not Negro. Bitter, disillusioning truths, these: but wholesome if we see them as danger-signs against the popular snares and pitfalls and warnings against corruption and premature decadence. This is why, although sanguine as ever about its possibilities, I entitle my article, *Toward a Critique of Negro Music*.

These shortcomings, however, are not entirely the fault of internal factors; they are due primarily to external influences. Those Negro musicians who are in vital touch with the folk traditions of Negro music are the very ones who are in commercial slavery to Tin Pan Alley and subject to the corruption and tyranny of the ready cash of our dance halls and the vaudeville stage. On the other hand, our musicians with formal training are divorced from the people and their vital inspiration by the cloister-walls of the conservatory and the taboos of musical respectability. Musical criticism for the most part ignores these lamentable conditions, wasting most of its energies in banal praise. Of the four to five thousand pages I have read on the subject of Negro music, four-fifths could be consigned to the flames to the everlasting benefit of the sound appraisal of Negro music and of constructive guidance for the Negro musician. For myself, I would rescue from the bonfire not much more than these few: W. F. Allen's early comment on the *Slave Songs,* Thomas W. Higginson's essay on them, Krehbeil's definitive treatise on *Afro-American Folk Song,* (still the best after thirty years), the few paragraphs on Negro music in Weldon Johnson's *Anthology,* the essays on Negro music in the *New Negro,* the comments on Negro folk-music by W. C. Handy and Abbe Niles, pertinent commentary on the "blues" by Carl Van Vechten and Langston Hughes, Dorothy Scarborough's *On the Trail of Negro Folk Songs,* Handy's *Beale Street,* certain pages of Isaac Goldberg's *Tin Pan Alley,* R. D. Darell's essay on Duke Ellington, some of the penetrating and constructive criticisms of Olin Downes, and interpretations of jazz by Irving Schwerke and Robert Goffin—especially the latter's *On the Frontiers of Jazz.* Fifty pages of real value, certainly not more, may have escaped my memory, but I strongly recommend these few gleanings to the serious reader. One should also include, of course, what little is said on the subject of Negro music in Henry Cowell's *American Composers on American Music,* a projected review of which was the initial cause of this article. But disappointment at what could have been said in this volume sent me into a turtle-shell of silence and brooding from which the editor of Opportunity, who has patiently prodded me for a year or so, will be surprised to see me emerge. It is not that a good deal of importance on this subject is not said in this volume, but here again it is odd to find the best of it coming from two talented Cuban composers and the rest of it from one or two modernists like Cowell and Theodore Chandler. But it is just as odd to find the best criticism of jazz coming from foreign critics like Schwerké and Goffin. Indeed the whole field is full of paradoxes, for after all the most original and pioneering creative use of Negro musical idioms still goes to the credit of white composers from Dvorak down to Aaron Copeland, Alden Carpenter, George Gershwin, Paul Whiteman, and Sesana.

What does this mean? Primarily that Negro musicians have not been first to realize the most genuine values of Negro music, and that the Negro audience has not pioneered in the recognition and intelligent appreciation of the same. Familiarity has bred contempt and nearness induced a myopia of judgment. With our music thus at the mercy of outside recognition and support, the first flow of Negro creative genius has been unusually subject to commercial control, cheap imitation and easy plagiarism. In fact Negro music, like the seed-sower's in the parable, has chiefly fallen by the wayside and has been picked up by musical scavengers and devoured by the musical birds of the air. But lest we charge all of this to outside factors, let us remember that much has also fallen upon our own stony ground of shallow appreciation or been choked by the hostile thorns of a false and blighting academic tradition. No musical idiom that has arisen from the people can flourish entirely cut off from the ground soil of its origin. Even in the sun of popular favor it is baked to an early death unless it has deep under it roots of vital nourishment. Nor can it be effectively developed by the timid and artificial patronage of arid academicians. Vital musical idioms have not been taken up sufficiently by our trained musicians; most of them have been intimidated by their academic training. Many of them are also aesthetic traitors in their heart of hearts. True, they accept

the spirituals and other forms of the folk-tradition in the face of an overwhelming vogue, because they must,—but with half-hearted appreciation, often inner contempt. At the beginning of the vogue, I remember when an urgent appeal had to be sent afield to Coleridge Taylor to transcribe a group of spirituals. In that day our trained musicians disdained the effort. And until quite recently, the Negro composers' treatment of the spirituals has resulted in the most sophisticated and diluted arrangements:—witness a good deal of the work of Burleigh, Rosamond Johnson and Nathaniel Dett. And even those centers which have the avowed purpose of preserving and developing Negro music have ulterior and far from musical motives. To them too often it is a matter of bread-and-butter propaganda, with a fine tradition prostituted to institutional begging and the amusement of philanthropists.

To this must be added the surprising lack of the theoretical study of music beyond conservatory requirements and the resulting paucity of an original vein of composition. This with the tardy development of instrumental virtuosity except in a limited range of instruments, has resulted, despite the efforts of Jim Europe and Marion Cook, in our having almost no orchestral tradition. These facts have blocked the fusion of classical forms with the Negro musical idiom when they have not resulted in an actual watering-down of these idioms by the classical tradition. So except in choral singing,— the one vein of Negro music inherently orchestral, there is yet a deep divide between our folk music and the main stream of formal music.

I ask the reader's patience with these negative but incontestable statements. Encouragingly enough at certain historical stages this same state of affairs has existed with other musical traditions,—with Russian music before Glinka, with Hungarian music before Liszt and Brahms, and with Bohemian music before Dvorak and Smetana.

However, if we would draw consolation from these parallels, we must remember that it took revolutionary originality and native genius to transform the situation, lift the level and break the path to the main-stream for each of these musical traditions. It is inevitable that this should eventually happen with Negro folk-music for it is not only the most vivid and vital and universally appealing body of folk-music in American, there is little in fact that can compete with it. Yet it is far from being much more as yet than the raw material of a racial or national tradition in music in spite of Weldon Johnson's famous statement of its claims. This is, after all a statement of promise, not realization. Mr. W. J. Henderson is right in a recent article, "Why No Great American Music," when he says,—"Where there is no unification of race, as in this country, the folk idiom does not exist except as that of some fraction of the people." He is equally right in saying,—"the potent spell of the Negro spiritual is a deep-rooted, almost desperate grasp of religious belief. It is the song of the Negro soul. It not only interests, but even arouses, the white man because of its innate eloquence," but,—he continues, "the Negro spiritual tells no secret of the wide American soul; it is the creation of black humans crushed under slavery and looking to eternity for their only joy." For the present, this is quite true. But the very remedy that Mr. Henderson prescribes for the creation of a great national music is the same of the proper universalization of the spirituals and other Negro folk-music. What is needed is genius, as he says, and still more genius. That is to say, the same transforming originality that in the instances cited above widened the localisms of Russian, Hungarian and Czech music to a universal language, but in breaking the dialect succeeded in preserving the rare raciness and unique flavor. Certainly the Negro idioms will never become great music nor representative national music over the least common denominators of popular jazz or popular ballads. And perhaps there is more vital originality and power in our secular folk music than even in our religious folk music. It remains for real constructive genius to develop both in the direction which Dvorak clairvoyantly saw.

But the *New World Symphony* stands there a largely unheeded musical sign-post pointing the correct way to Parnassus, while the main procession has followed the lowly but well-paved jazz road. Not that the jazz-road cannot lead to Parnassus; it can and has,—for the persistent few. But the producers of good jazz still produce far too much bad jazz, and the distinction between them is blurred to all but the most discriminating. Jazz must be definitely rid of its shoddy superficiality and it repetitious vulgar gymnastics. Further it must be concentrated nearer to the Negro idioms from which it has been derived. Even good diluted jazz of the sort that is now so much in vogue does a dis-service to the ultimate best development of this great folk tradition. Only true genius and almost consecrated devotion can properly fuse art-music and folk-music. Stimulating and well-intentioned as Gershwin's work has been, I question very seriously the ultimate success of his easy-going formula of superimposing one upon the other. "Jazz," he says, "I regard as an American folk music; not the only one, but a very powerful one which is probably in the blood and feeling of the American people more than any other style of folk-music. I believe that it can be made the basis of serious symphonic works of lasting value in the hands of a composer with talent for both jazz and symphonic music." True,—but out of the union of the two a new style and a new tradition must be forged. Only rare examples of this have appeared as yet, and there is just as much promise of it in Louis Armstrong's and Ellington's best, perhaps more—than in the labored fusions of Carpenter, Gruenberg, Gershwin and Grofe. The late Otto Kahn said, with instinctive intuition: "I look upon modern jazz as a phase, as a transition, not as a completed process." The final jazz will be neither Copeland's bizarre hybrid of European neo-impressionism and jazz rhythms, nor Gruenberg's fusion, however deft, of jazz themes with German and Central European modernisms of style, nor Gershwin's pastiche of American jazz mixed with Liszt, Puccini, Stravinski, and Wagner.

This is not said ungratefully, for each of the above has done yeoman service in the vindication of the higher possibilities of jazz and the education of the popular taste out of the mere ruck of popular song and dance. *Rhapsody in Blue* opened a new era; Alden Carpenter's work brought the first touches of sophistication to jazz, Whiteman and Grofe together broadened the whole instrumental scope of the jazz orchestra; Copeland's *Concerto* carried jazz idiom as far as it could go by sheer intellectual push into the citadel of the classical tradition; Gruenberg has taken jazz to the chamber music level and lately has adapted it more than half-successfully to the dramatic possibilities of opera. However, more remains to be done,—and I hope and expect it from the Negro musician in spite of his present handicaps and comparatively poor showing. Already a newer type of jazz, at one and the same time more intimate to the Negro style and with more originality is coming to the fore, witness Dana Suess's *Jazz*

Nocturne, Constant Lambert's *Rio Grande,* and Otto Sesana's brilliant *Negro Heaven.* Unlike the first phase of classical jazz, these are not artificial hybrids but genuine developments from within the intimate idiom of jazz itself. A still further step may be expected from the growing mastery of the Negro jazz composers, who in the last few years have reached a new plane, and also from those brilliant mulatto composers of Latin America who may roughly be called the Afro-Cuban school even though some of them are from Mexico, Central America and Brazil.

Much indeed is to be expected of the geniuses of the South, Amateo Roldan and Garcia Caturla, who since 1925–26 have been developing a serious school of Negro music out of the Afro-Cuban material. Caturla says: "The so-called Afro-Cuban native music is our most original type of folk song and is a mixture of African primitive music with early Spanish influences. It employs many percussion instruments which have been developed in Cuba and are to be found nowhere else, although they have their origin in African primitive instruments." The manuscript works of these composers for orchestra show greater instrumental originality than has yet appeared in the American school of serious jazz. For its counterpart, we have to go to the unacademic and unwritten but creative jazz technique of our own Negro jazz orchestras.

But with these South Americans, it is a matter of deliberate path-breaking. Roldan expresses his creed by saying "indigenous instruments, both melodic and percussion, should be used not in order to obtain an easy local color, but with the purpose of widening their significance beyond the national boundaries. The sound of a banjo must not always bring jazz to our minds, nor should the rhythm of our guiro always recall a rhumba." Accordingly his *Poema Negro* for string quartet and his *Motivos de Son,* based on native song-motifs with unusual combinations of instruments, and his Afro-Cuban ballet represent, like a good deal of Caturla's work, high points in the serious conquest of a new Negro music.

15

From *Technics and Civilization* (1934)

Lewis Mumford

Lewis Mumford (1895–1990) was a member of an extinct species, the independent man of letters. Famous as an architecture critic and analyst of urban planning from his column in the *New Yorker,* Mumford was also much more: he was one of the most prolific and thoughtful commentators on human experience in the modern age. Literary critic, humanist, historian of American culture, student of cities, regionalist and green, foe of the military-industrial complex, moralist and theorist of civilization, Mumford long had an interest in what happened to communication and human relations in the modern world. This selection, from Mumford's classic and still highly readable *Technics and Civilization* (1934), shows his prescient understanding of the mixed meaning of new communication technologies. Mumford remains among the most subtle and historically imaginative of all twentieth-century students of technologies.

The Paradox of Communication

Communication between human beings begins with the immediate physiological expressions of personal contact, from the howlings and cooings and head-turnings of the infant to the more abstract gestures and signs and sounds out of which language, in its fullness, develops. With hieroglyphics, painting, drawing, the written alphabet, there grew up during the historic period a series of abstract forms of expression which deepened and made more reflective and pregnant the intercourse of men. The lapse of time between expression and reception had something of the effect that the arrest of action produced in making thought itself possible.

With the invention of the telegraph a series of inventions began to bridge the gap in time between communication and response despite the handicaps of space: first the telegraph, then the telephone, then the wireless telegraph, then the wireless telephone, and finally television. As a result, communication is now on the point of returning with the aid of mechanical devices, to that instantaneous reaction of person to person with which it began; but the possibilities of this immediate meeting, instead of being limited by space and time, will be limited only by the amount of energy available and the mechanical perfection and accessibility of the apparatus. When the radio telephone is supplemented by television communication will differ from direct intercourse only to the extent that immediate physical contact will be impossible: the hand of sympathy will not actually grasp the recipient's hand, nor the raised fist fall upon the provoking head.

What will be the outcome? Obviously, a widened range of intercourse: more numerous contacts: more numerous demands on attention and time. But unfortunately, the possibility of this type of immediate intercourse on a worldwide basis does not necessarily mean a less trivial or a less parochial personality. For over against the convenience of instantaneous communication is the fact that the great economical abstractions of writing, reading, and drawing, the media of reflective thought and deliberate action, will be weakened. Men often tend to be more socialized at a distance, than they are in their immediate, limited and local selves: their intercourse sometimes proceeds best, like barter among savage peoples, when neither group is visible to the other. That the breadth and too-frequent repetition of personal intercourse may be socially inefficient is already plain through the abuse of the telephone: a dozen five minute conversations can frequently be reduced in essentials to a dozen notes whose reading, writing, and answering takes less time and effort and nervous energy than the more personal calls. With the telephone the flow of interest and attention, instead of being self-directed, is at the mercy of any strange person who seeks to divert it to his own purposes.

One is faced here with a magnified form of a danger common to all inventions: a tendency to use them whether or not the occasion demands. Thus our forefathers used iron sheets for the fronts of buildings, despite the fact that iron is a notorious conductor of heat: thus people gave up learning the violin, the guitar, and the piano when the phonograph was introduced, despite the fact that the passive listening to records is not in the slightest degree the equivalent of active performance; thus the introduction of anesthetics increased fatalities from superfluous operations. The lifting of restrictions upon close human intercourse has been, in its first stages, as dangerous as the flow of populations into new lands: it has increased the areas of friction. Similarly, it has mobilized and hastened mass-reactions, like those which occur on the eve of a war, and it has increased the dangers of international conflict. To ignore these facts would be to paint a very falsely over-optimistic picture of the present economy.

Nevertheless, instantaneous personal communication over long distances is one of the outstanding marks of the neotechnic phase: it is the mechanical symbol of those world-wide cooperations of thought and feeling which must emerge, finally, if our whole civilization is not to sink into ruin. The new avenues of communication have the characteristic features and advantages of the new technics; for they imply, among other things, the use of mechanical apparatus to duplicate and further organic operations: in the long run, they promise not to displace the human being but to re-focus him and enlarge his capacities. But there is a proviso attached to this promise: namely, that the culture of the personality shall parallel in refinement the mechanical development of the machine. Perhaps the greatest social effect of radio-communication, so far, has been a political one: the restoration of direct contact between the leader and the group. Plato defined the limits of the size of a city as the number of people who could hear the voice of a single orator: today those limits do not define a city but a civilization. Wherever neotechnic instruments exist and a common language is used there are now the elements of almost as close a political unity as that which once was possible in the tiniest cities of Attica. The possibilities for good and evil here are immense: the secondary personal contact with voice and image may increase the amount of mass regimentation, all the more because the opportunity for individual members reacting directly upon the leader himself, as in a local meeting, becomes farther and farther removed. At the present moment, as with so many other neotechnic benefits, the dangers of the radio and the talking picture seem greater than the benefits. *As with all the instruments of multiplication the critical question is as to the function and quality of the object one is multiplying.* There is no satisfactory answer to this on the basis of technics alone: certainly nothing to indicate, as the earlier exponents of instantaneous communication seem pretty uniformly to have thought, that the results will automatically be favorable to the community.

The New Permanent Record

Man's culture depends for its transmission in time upon the permanent record: the building, the monument, the inscribed word. During the early neotechnic phase, vast changes were made here, as important as those brought about five hundred years earlier through the invention of wood-engraving, copper-etching, and printing. The black-and-white image, the color-image, the sound, and the moving image were translated into permanent records, which could be manifolded, by mechanical and chemical means. In the invention of the camera, the phonograph, and the moving picture the interplay of science and mechanical dexterity, which has already been stressed, was again manifested.

While all these new forms of permanent record were first employed chiefly for amusement, and while the interest behind them was esthetic rather than narrowly utilitarian, they had important uses in science, and they even reacted upon our conceptual world as well. The photograph, to begin with, served as an independent objective check upon observation. The value of a scientific experiment lies partly in the fact that it is repeatable and thus verifiable by independent observers: but in the case of astronomical observations, for example, the slowness and fallibility of the eye can be supplemented by the camera, and the photograph gives the effect of repetition to what was, perhaps, a unique event, never to be observed again. In the same fashion, the camera gives an almost instantaneous cross-section of history—arresting images in their flight through time. In the case of architecture this mechanical copying on paper led to unfortunately similar artifices in actual buildings, and instead of enriching the mind left a trail of arrested images in the form of buildings all over the landscape. For history is non-repeatable, and the only thing that can be rescued from history is the note that one takes and preserves at some moment of its evolution. To divorce an object from its integral time-sequence is to rob it of its complete meaning, although it makes it possible to grasp spatial relations which may otherwise defy observation. Indeed, the very value of the camera as a reproducing device is to present a memorandum, as it were, of that which cannot in any other fashion be reproduced.

In a world of flux and change, the camera gave a means of combating the ordinary processes of deterioration and decay, not by "restoration" or "reproduction" but by holding in convenient form the lean image of men, places, buildings, landscapes: thus serving as an extension of the collective memory. The moving picture, carrying a succession of images through time, widened the scope of the camera and essentially altered its function; for it could telescope the slow movement of growth, or prolong the fast movement of jumping, and it could keep in steady focus events which could not otherwise be held in consciousness with the same intensity and fixity. Heretofore records had been confined to snatches of time, or, when they sought to move with time itself, they were reduced to abstractions. Now they could become continuous images of the events they represented. So the flow of time ceased to be representable by the successive mechanical ticks of the clock: its equivalent—and Bergson was quick to seize this image—was the motion picture reel.

One may perhaps over-rate the changes in human behavior that followed the invention of these new devices; but one or two suggest themselves.

Whereas in the eotechnic phase one conversed with the mirror and produced the biographical portrait and the introspective biography, in the neotechnic phase one poses for the camera, or still more, one acts for the motion picture. The change is from an introspective to a behaviorist psychology, from the fulsome sorrows of Werther to the impassive public mask of an Ernest Hemingway. Facing hunger and death in the midst of a wilderness, a stranded aviator writes in his notes: "I built another raft, and this time took off my clothes to try it. I must have looked good, carrying the big logs on my back in my underwear." Alone, he still thinks of himself as a public character, *being watched*: and to a greater or less degree everyone, from the crone in a remote hamlet to the political dictator on his carefully prepared stage is in the same position. This constant sense of a public world would seem in part, at least, to be the result of the camera and the camera-eye that developed with it. If the eye be absent in reality, one improvises it wryly with a fragment of one's consciousness. The change is significant: not self-examination but self-exposure: not tortured confession but easy open candor: not the proud soul wrapped in his cloak, pacing the lonely beach at midnight, but the matter-of-fact soul, naked, exposed to the sun on the beach at noonday, one of a crowd of naked people. Such reactions are, of course, outside the realm of proof; and even if the influence of the camera were directly demonstrable, there is little reason to think that it is final. Need I stress again that nothing produced by technics is more final than the human needs and interests themselves that have created technics?

Whatever the psychal reactions to the camera and the moving picture and the phonograph may be, there is no doubt, I think, as to their contribution to the economic management of the social heritage. Before they appeared, sound could only be imperfectly represented in the conventions of writing: it is interesting to note that one of the best systems, Bell's Visible Speech, was invented by the father of the man who created the telephone. Other than written and printed documents and paintings on paper, parchment, and canvas, nothing survived of a civilization except its rubbish heaps and its monuments, buildings, sculptures, works of engineering—all bulky, all interfering more or less with the free development of a different life in the same place.

By means of the new devices this vast mass of physical impedimenta could be turned into paper leaves, metallic or rubber discs, or celluloid films which could be far more completely and far more economically preserved. It is no longer necessary to keep vast middens of material in order to have contact, in the mind, with the forms and expressions of the past. These mechanical devices are thus an excellent ally to that other new piece of social apparatus which became common in the nineteenth century: the public museum. They gave modern civilization a direct sense of the past and a more accurate perception of its memorials than any other civilization had, in all probability, had. Not alone did they make the past more immediate: they made the present more historic by narrowing the lapse of time between the actual events themselves and their concrete record. For the first time one might come face to face with the speaking likenesses of dead people and recall in their immediacy forgotten scenes and actions. Faust bartered his soul with Mephistopheles to see Helen of Troy: on much easier terms it will be possible for our descendants to view the Helens of the twentieth century. Thus a new form of immortality was effected; and a late Victorian writer, Samuel Butler, might well speculate upon how completely a man was dead when his words, his image, and his voice were still capable of being resurrected and could have a direct effect upon the spectator and listener.

At first these new recording and reproducing devices have confused the mind and defied selective use: no one can pretend that we have yet employed them, in any sufficient degree, with wisdom or even with ordered efficiency. But they suggest a new relationship between deed and record, between the movement of life and its collective enregistration: above all, they demand a nicer sensitiveness and a higher intelligence. If these inventions have so far made monkeys of us, it is because we are still monkeys.

16

The Business Nobody Knows

From *Our Master's Voice* (1934)

James Rorty

James Rorty (1890–1973) was a poet, political activist, social critic, and editor. He was also an adman-turned-radical, having worked for several years in advertising during the 1920s. Like Jane Addams, he worked in settlement houses; and like Ernest Hemingway, he drove an ambulance in France during World War I. He was one of the founders of the radical magazine the *New Masses,* in 1925. He wrote with a witty, pungent style that seems to have served him well as a copywriter and was a gift he gave to his more famous son, philosopher Richard Rorty. The senior Rorty also won awards for his poetry, and his wife, Winifred Raushenbush, was a social critic and activist who studied sociology at the University of Chicago and wrote a biography of Robert Park. His son Richard also studied at Chicago, though mostly philosophy. The degrees of separation are indeed small in American social theories of mass communication!

This selection, from *Our Master's Voice* (1934), provides one of the earliest criticisms of the communication business in general and the advertising industry in particular. Rorty was one of the first critics to point to the parasitic relationship of advertising to all other forms of mass communication. His notion—that advertising, like propaganda and education, is an "instrument of rule"—parallels the idea being developed in Marxist cultural theory at the time: that the media are part of a larger, consciousness industry. Rorty's "reconnaissance" of commercial culture deserves to be better known and read.

The title of this chapter was chosen, not so much to parody the title of Mr. Bruce Barton's widely-read volume of New Testament exegesis, as to suggest that, in the lack of serious critical study, we really know very little about advertising: how the phenomenon happened to achieve its uniquely huge and grotesque dimensions in America; how it has affected our individual and social psychology as a people; what its role is likely to be in the present rapidly changing pattern of social and economic forces.

The advertising business is quite literally the business nobody knows; nobody, including, or perhaps more especially, advertising men. As evidence of this general ignorance, one has only to cite a few of the misapprehensions which have confused the very few contemporary economists, sociologists and publicists who have attempted to treat the subject.

Perhaps the chief of these misapprehensions is that of regarding advertising as merely the business of preparing and placing advertisements in the various advertising media: the daily and periodical press, the mails, the radio, motion picture, car cards, posters, etc. The error here is that of mistaking a function of the thing for the thing itself. It would be much more accurate to say that our daily and periodical press, plus the radio and other lesser media, *are* the advertising business. The commercial press is supported primarily by advertising—roughly the ratio as between advertising income and subscription and news-stand sales income averages about two to one. It is quite natural, therefore, that the publishers of newspapers and magazines should regard their enterprises as *advertising business*. As a matter of fact, every advertising man knows that they do so regard them and so conduct them. These publishers are business men, responsible to their stockholders, and their proper and necessary concern is to make a maximum of profit out of these business properties. They do this by using our major instruments of social communication, whose free and disinterested functioning is embodied in the concept of a democracy, to serve the profit interests of the advertisers who employ and pay them. Within certain limits they give their readers and listeners the sort of editorial content which experience proves to be effective in building circulations and audiences, these to be sold in turn at so much a head to advertisers. The limits are that regardless of the readers' or listeners' true interests, nothing can be given them which seriously conflicts with the profit-interests of the advertisers, or of the vested industrial and financial powers back of these; also nothing can be given them which seriously conflicts with the use and wont, embodied in law and custom, of the competitive capitalist economy and culture.

In defining the advertising business it must be remembered also that newspapers and magazines use paper and ink: a huge bulk of materials, a ramified complex of services by printers, lithographers, photographers, etc. Radio uses other categories of materials and services—the whole art of radio was originally conceived of as a sales device to market radio transmitters and receiving sets. All these services are necessary to advertising and advertising is necessary to them. These are also the advertising business. Surely it is only by examining this business as a whole that we can expect to understand anything about it.

The second misapprehension is that invidious moral value judgments are useful in appraising the phenomena. Advertising is merely an instrument of sales promotion. Good advertising is efficient advertising—advertising which promotes a maximum of sales for a minimum of expenditure. Bad advertising is inefficient advertising, advertising which accomplishes its purpose wastefully or not at all. All advertising is obviously special pleading. Why should it be considered pertinent or useful to express surprise and indignation because special pleading, whether in a court of law, or in the public prints, is habitually disingenuous, and frequently unscrupulous and deceptive? Yet liberal social critics, economists and sociologists, have wasted much time complaining that advertising has "elevated mendacity to the status of a profession." The pressure of competition forces advertisers and the advertising agencies who serve them to become more efficient; to advertise more efficiently frequently means to advertise more mendaciously. Do these liberal critics want advertising to be less efficient? Do they want advertisers to observe standards of ethics, morals and taste which would, under our existing institutional setup, result either in depriving stockholders of dividends, or in loading still heavier costs on the consumer?

There is, of course, a third alternative, which is neither good advertising nor bad advertising, but no advertising. But that is outside the present institutional setup. It should be obvious that in the present (surplus economy) phase of American capitalism, advertising is an industry no less essential than steel, coal, or electric power. If one defines advertising as the total apparatus of American publishing and broadcasting, it is in fact among the twelve greatest industries in the country. It is moreover, one of the most strategically placed industries. Realization of this fact should restrain us from loose talk about "deflating the advertising business." How would one go about organizing "public opinion" for such an enterprise when the instruments of social communication by which public opinion must be shaped and organized are themselves the advertising business?

As should be apparent from the foregoing, the writer has only a qualified interest in "reforming" advertising. Obviously it cannot be reformed without transforming the whole institutional context of our civilization. The bias of the writer is frankly in favor of such a transformation. But the immediate task in this book is one of description and analysis. Although advertising is forever in the public's eye—and in its ear too, now that we have radio—the average layman confines himself either to applauding the tricks of the ad-man, or to railing at what he considers to be more or less of a public nuisance. In neither case does he bother to understand what is being done to him, who is doing it, and why.

The typical view of an advertisement is that it is a selling presentation of a product or service, to be judged as "good" or "bad" depending upon whether the presentation is accurate or inaccurate, fair or deceptive. But to an advertising man, this seems a very shallow view of the matter.

Advertising has to do with the shaping of the economic, social, moral and ethical patterns of the community into serviceable conformity with the profit-making interests of advertisers and of the advertising business. Advertising thus becomes a body of doctrine. Veblen defined advertisements as "doctrinal memoranda," and the phrase is none the less precise because of its content of irony. It is particularly applicable to that steadily increasing proportion of advertising classified as "inter-industrial advertising": that is to say, advertising competition between industries for the consumer's dollar. What such advertising boils down to is special pleading, directed at the consumer by vested property interests, concerning the material, moral and spiritual content of the Good Life. In this special pleading the editorial contents of the daily and periodical press, and the sustaining programs of the broadcasters, are called upon to do their bit, no less manfully, though less directly than the advertising columns or the sponsor's sales talk. Such advertising, as Veblen pointed out, is a lineal descendant of the "Propaganda of the Faith." It is a less unified effort, and less efficient because of the conflicting pressure groups involved; also because of the disruptive stresses of the underlying economic forces of our time. Yet it is very similar in purpose and method.

An important point which the writer develops in detail in later chapters is that advertising is an effect resulting from the unfolding of the economic processes of modern capitalism, but becomes in turn a cause of sequential economic and social phenomena. The earlier causal chain is of course apparent. Mass production necessitated mass distribution which necessitated mass literacy, mass communication and mass advertising. But the achieved result, mass advertising, becomes in turn a generating cause of another sequence. Mass advertising perverts the integrity of the editor-reader relationship essential to the concept of a democracy. Advertising doctrine—always remembering that the separation of the editorial and advertising contents of a modern publication is for the most part formal rather than actual—is a doctrine of material emulation, keeping up with the Joneses, conspicuous waste. Mass advertising plus, of course, the government mail subsidy, makes possible the five-cent price for national weeklies, the ten- to thirty-five-cent price for national monthlies. Because of this low price and because of the large appropriations for circulation-promotion made possible by advertising income, the number of mass publications and the volume of their circulation has hugely increased. These huge circulations are maintained by editorial policies dictated by the requirements of the advertisers. Such policies vary widely but have certain elements in common. Articles, fiction, verse, etc., are conceived of as "entertainment." This means that controversial subjects are avoided. The contemporary social fact is not adequately reported, interpreted, or criticized; in fact the run of commercial magazines and newspapers are extraordinarily empty of social content. On the positive side, their content, whether fiction, articles or criticism, is definitely shaped toward the promotion and fixation of mental and emotional patterns which predispose the reader to an acceptance of the advertiser's doctrinal message.

This secondary causal chain therefore runs as follows: Mass advertising entails the perversion of the editor-reader relationship; it entails reader-exploitation, cultural malnutrition and stultification.

This situation came to fruition during the period just before, during and after the war; a period of rapid technical, economic and social change culminating in the depression of 1929. At precisely the moment in our history when we needed a maximum of open-minded mobility in public opinion, we found a maximum of inertia embodied in our instruments of social communication. Since these have become advertising businesses, and competition is the life of advertising, they have a vested interest in maintaining and promoting the competitive acquisitive economy and the competitive acquisitive social psychology. Both are essential to advertising, but both are becoming obsolete in the modern world. In contemporary sociological writing we find only vague and passing reference to this crucial fact, which is of incalculable influence in determining the present and future movement of social forces in America.

In later chapters the writer will be found dealing coincidentally with advertising, propaganda and education. Contemporary liberal criticism tends to regard these as separate categories, to be separately studied and evaluated. But in the realm of contemporary fact, no such separation exists. All three are *instruments of rule*. Our ruling class, representing the vested interests of business and finance, has primary access to and control over all these instruments. One supplements the other and they are frequently used coordinately. Liberal sociologists would attempt to set up the concept of education, defined as a disinterested objective effort to release capacity, as a contrasting opposite to propaganda and advertising. In practice no such clear apposition obtains, or can obtain, as is in fact acknowledged by some of our most distinguished contemporary educators.

There is nothing unique, isolate or adventitious about the contemporary phenomena of advertising. Your ad-man is merely the particular kind of eccentric cog which the machinery of a competitive acquisitive society required at a particular moment of its evolution. He is, on the average, much more intelligent than the average business man, much more sophisticated, even much more socially minded. But in moving day after day the little cams and gears that he has to move, he inevitably empties himself of human qualities. His daily traffic in half-truths and outright deceptions is subtly and cumulatively degrading. No man can give his days to barbarous frivolity and live. And ad-men don't live. They become dull, resigned, hopeless. Or they become daemonic fantasts and sadists. They are, in a sense, the intellectuals, the male hetaerae of our American commercial culture. Merciful nature makes some of them into hale, pink-fleshed, speech-making morons. Others become gray-faced cynics and are burned out at forty. Some "unlearn hope" and jump out of high windows. Others become extreme political and social radicals, either secretly while they are in the business, or openly, after they have left it.

This, then, is the advertising business. The present volume is merely a reconnaissance study. In addition to what is indicated by the foregoing, some technical material is included on the organization and practices of the various branches of the business. Some attempt is made to answer the questions: how did it happen that America offered a uniquely favorable culture-bed for the development of the phenomena described? What

are the foreign equivalents of our American rule-by-advertising? How will advertising be affected by the present trend toward state capitalism, organized in the corporative forms of fascism, and how will the social inertias nourished and defended by advertising condition that trend?

The writer also attempts tentative measurements of the mental levels of various sections of the American population, using the criteria provided by our mass and class publications. Advertising men are obliged to make such measurements as a part of their business; they are frequently wrong, but since their conclusions are the basis of more or less successful business practice they are worthy of consideration.

The one conclusion which the writer offers in all seriousness is that the advertising business is in fact the Business Nobody Knows. The trails marked out in this volume are brief and crude. It is hoped that some of our contemporary sociologists may be tempted to clear them a little further. Although, of course, there is always the chance that the swift movement of events may eliminate or rather transform that particular social dilemma, making all such studies academic, even archaic. In that case it might happen that ad-men would be preserved chiefly as museum specimens, to an appreciation of which this book might then serve as a moderately useful guide.

Advertising has, of course, a very ancient history. But since the modern American phenomenon represents not merely a change in degree but a change in kind, the chronological tracing of its evolution would be only confusing. It has seemed better first to survey the contemporary phenomena in their totality and then present in a later chapter the limited amount of historical data that seemed necessary and pertinent.

17

The Influence of Radio upon Mental and Social Life

From *The Psychology of Radio* (1935)

Hadley Cantril and Gordon W. Allport

Gordon W. Allport (1897–1967) was one of the leading social psychologists of twentieth-century America. He was the younger brother of social psychologist Floyd Allport, who was an important critic of John Dewey as well as a theorist of public opinion research. Allport spent most of his teaching career at Harvard University. Though best known as a student of personality, racial prejudice, and religious belief, Allport made important contributions to communication theory in *The Psychology of Radio* (1935; excerpted here) and *The Psychology of Rumor* (with Leo Postman, 1946), both of which repay reading today. His life and work were based on the humanistic belief that knowledge of human psychology can advance freedom and happiness.

Hadley Cantril (1906–1969) was a leader in the development of public opinion polling and survey research. Like Paul Lazarsfeld, whom he regarded as his rival, Cantril worked at the intersection of commercial polling and academic social science. He taught at Princeton University, the original home for the Rockefeller Radio Project. In communication research, Cantril is best known for his study *The Invasion from Mars* (1940), written with Hazel Gaudet and Herta Herzog, which examines the social effects of Orson Welles's 1938 broadcast of *The War of the Worlds*.

Cantril and Allport's book *The Psychology of Radio* (1935) still yields fresh insights as an analysis of a new medium. Written in the early New Deal, the book is marked by a confidence in the value of experimental inquiry and considers how the powers of radio can be used for democratic purposes rather than corporate control. The book is filled with diverse experiments, some of them rather quaint, some ingenious. The following excerpt is taken from chapter 2, "The Influence of Radio upon Mental and Social Life," with a few additional paragraphs from the concluding chapter, "Extending the Social Environment." Here Cantril and Allport offer a sweeping agenda for studying the broad social meaning of a new medium that students today might try applying to personal computers, cell phones, or MP3 players. It is an interesting question whether the authors' enthusiasm for the extended horizons of radio is reminiscent of the hype that we have seen in the past decade regarding the Internet.

Apart from the invention of spoken and written language, which took place in some dim prehistoric time, there have been five major innovations of method in human communication: printing, telegraphy, the telephone, the cinema, and the radio.[1] Each innovation has been followed by social and psychological changes of a revolutionary character. These changes, so far as the printing press, the telegraph, and the telephone are concerned, are already a matter of record, chronicled and celebrated by historians and sociologists. To a certain extent, although much less adequately, the epochal significance of the cinema has been studied. But the changes wrought by radio are virtually unrecorded, primarily, no doubt, because they are not yet fully understood.

Many of the trends that followed the earlier inventions are being speeded and augmented by the radio. The world has become even smaller. The time elapsing between an event of public importance and the popular response it arouses has become still shorter. The clamor for higher standards of living has been increased through more widely disseminated knowledge of the world's goods. And yet, as the preceding chapter showed, radio is in principle a novel method of communication and has brought many effects peculiar to itself. It reaches a larger population of people at greater distances than the other mediums, and it reaches them both instantaneously and cheaply. Through its own peculiar blend of personal and impersonal characteristics it relates the speaker and the auditor in a novel way. These circumstances give it an original character and produce social effects which in part are different from those obtained by the older methods of communication.

The scientists who first mastered the acoustical properties of ether did not know they were preparing a device that within one short generation would bind the earth in a universal network of sound, that would be the greatest single democratizing agent since the invention of printing. Nor could they have foreseen to what extent they were placing public opinion and private taste at the mercy of entrepreneurs. Even now we do not know the ultimate consequences of radio for civilization. We do know, however, that certain important changes have already been accomplished and that others are under way. But what will happen after years of adaptation and as a consequence of future inventions is a matter only for speculation. In the present chapter we will record those social-psychological changes for which there seems to be good evidence, although for some there is as yet no demonstrated proof.[2]

The Democracy of Radio

Any device that carries messages instantaneously and inexpensively to the farthest and most inaccessible regions of the earth, that penetrates all manner of social, political, and economic barriers, is by nature a powerful agent of democracy. Millions of people listen to the same thing at the same time—and they themselves are aware of the fact. Distinctions between rural and urban communities, men and women, age and youth, social classes, creeds, states, and nations are abolished. As if by magic the barriers of social stratification disappear and in their place comes a consciousness of equality and of a community of interest.

This consciousness is enhanced by the fact that the radio voice enters directly into our homes, and has a personal appeal lacking in newspapers and magazines. It is enhanced, too, by the informality of the voice, by its conversational rather than oratorical qualities. Although bright lights and bombast in assembly halls have had their place in democracy, they are artificial and do not create, as the radio voice does, the impression of natural equality among men.

When a million or more people hear the same subject matter, the same arguments and appeals, the same music and humor, when their attention is held in the same way and at the same time to the same stimuli, it is psychologically inevitable that they should acquire in some degree common interests, common tastes, and common attitudes. In short, it seems to be the nature of radio to encourage people to think and feel alike.

It is true, of course, that mental differences between people are not easy to eliminate. Nature itself has a way of preferring individuality to uniformity, and the broadcaster knows that his unseen audience is not, after all, of a single mind. Blandishments that will be meat to some of his listeners will be poison to others. This fact creates a problem for the broadcaster. He knows that he is dealing with a *heterogeneous* audience and that in order to make his message effective for all listeners alike he must discover and exploit the common denominator of their interests. He cannot afford to be either high-brow or low-brow, he must aim at the average intelligence, avoid subtlety and sophistication, and yet if possible flatter his listeners. If he can please them, they will accept his message. His problem is to please everyone if possible, and if he can't do this, to please the majority. Music is one of the solutions to his problem, since music has universal charm. For the rest, he learns how to use phrases and words as inoffensively as possible. He avoids controversy, subtlety, and spiciness. He steers a middle course and appeals to the middle class. He respects the principle of majority rule. His technique is the technique of democracy.

One of the characteristics of a democracy is the ease with which individuals acquire a "crowd mind." The radio, more than any other medium of communication, is capable of forming a crowd mind among individuals who are physically separated from one another. (To a lesser degree, of course, the newspaper does the same thing. But newspaper readers do not have as marked an "impression of universality.") The daily experience of hearing the announcer say "This program is coming to you over a coast-to-coast network" inevitably increases our sense of membership in the national family. It lays the foundation for homogeneity. In times of potential social disruption the radio voice of someone in authority, speaking to millions of citizens as "my friends," tends to decrease their sense of insecurity. It diminishes the mischievous effects of rumor and allays dread and apprehension of what is unknown. Through the use of the radio on March 4 and 5, 1933, President Roosevelt unquestionably diminished the force of the financial panic.

Heretofore "crowds" meant chiefly congregate clusters of people sharing and giving expression to a common emotion. But now, as never before, crowd mentality may be created and sustained without the contagion of personal contact. Although such "consociate" crowds are less violent and less dangerous than congregate crowds—the radio can create racial hatred but not itself achieve a lynching—still to a degree the fostering of the mob spirit must be counted as one of the byproducts of radio.

It is the federal and national type of democracy to which radio contributes, rather than to the older form exemplified politically in the town meeting and culturally in the church and grange. In underprivileged communities the radio offers superior opportunities, not only for following the events of the world, but also for hearing national and educational programs of greater variety and better quality than the community itself can provide. Every city dweller who has suffered that familiar boredom which comes after a few days in a rural community has only to turn on the radio to realize how much stimulation it brings into the cultural wastelands of America. On the other hand, in cities where theaters, symphonies, libraries, and universities are found, the radio offers—as a rule—inferior spiritual nourishment. If it keeps the city dweller from participating in these activities, it has a tendency to level down his cultural outlook. And so radio reflects another of the peculiarities of democracy: it equalizes the opportunity of enjoying art, education, and entertainment, and at the same time makes their level everywhere the same.

In a yet wider sense radio is an agent of democracy. It promotes the interpenetration of national cultures. Canadians tune to American broadcasts; the French may listen to Italians, Germans, and English as readily as to their own countrymen. One continent hears another with increasing ease. When the opinions, the songs, the dramas of another nation are a matter of daily acquaintance, its culture seems less foreign. Radio is no respecter of boundaries. Inherently it is a foe of Fascism and of cultural nationalism. It presses always toward internationalism, toward universal democracy. Dictators, it is true, and nationalists of every description, may exploit the ether to their own ends, but in so doing they are unquestionably perverting the natural properties of radio.

Radio and the Standardization of Life

Now we encounter a paradox. Radio brings greater variety into the lives of men, and yet at the same time tends to standardize and to stereotype mental life. Many topics have been introduced into men's circles of interest; they hear a great variety of opinion. There is entertainment and education for all, and those who benefit most are those whose lives are otherwise narrow. The resources of the theater, the university, and the concert hall are made available to the poor, to those who live in remote places, and even to the illiterate. Yet for all the new horizons that it opens, for all its varied and stimulating diversion, radio, for several reasons, is an agency that makes for standardization.

Not every shade of opinion can be put on the air, nor can every variety of cultural interest be represented, although, as we shall see in the next chapter, the degree of standardization varies in different contexts. If I am to enjoy my radio, I must adjust my personal taste to the program that most nearly approximates it. I may choose to listen to a political opinion that is somewhat, though in all probability not exactly, like my own. I may choose music that is more or less agreeable, but not exactly as I would have it. I constantly sacrifice my individuality so that I may fit into one of the common molds that radio offers.

If I insist on remaining an individualist, I shall dislike nearly all radio programs. I may, on the other hand, choose my own books, phonograph records, and lectures.

In its attempt to cater to the greatest possible number of individuals, radio generally provides typical or modal programs. Music is played because it is "jazz," "sentimental," or "classical"; opinions are given because they are either "pro" or "con." Everything tends to be categorical. The broadcaster attempts to provide a coarse net with which to capture the favorable attention of many listeners at once. Subtle shades of appeal are forfeited.

Suppose war is the subject chosen for broadcast, the chances are that the speech will be one that is clear-cut in its support of militarism ("preparedness") or of pacifism. Think of the shadings of analysis which the subject invites. There might be a dispassionate study of war in terms of biological, psychological, economic, or historical concepts. It might be discussed as a problem in instinct, conscience, propaganda, or patriotism. All such subtler issues are submerged in favor of clear-cut positions. It is as though people were capable of perceiving only two colors, black and white, and were blind to all the shades of gray. Left to themselves the listeners would evolve a large number of attitudes, but under the guidance of radio the potential variety becomes limited through sharply drawn points of view. One must take sides: prohibition or repeal, Republican or Democrat, prostrike or antistrike, Americanism or Communism, *this* or *that*. One would think that the universe were dichotomous. Wherever sharp lines are drawn, the complexities of life become oversimplified.

When both sides of an issue are given equal weight, this stereotyping is serious enough, but in practice the radio often favors the emphasis upon only one opinion (for example, in the case of Communism *versus* Americanism). On many issues the radio is not expected to be impartial, but to favor one view only. This tendency grows more marked, of course, in proportion as the mentality of Fascism displaces the liberal tradition. The Nazi "evening hour" in Germany is an example of the standardizing pressure of the radio carried to its logical extreme.

The radio is likewise responsible, no one can possibly deny, for further standardization of our habits of living. Experts tell us what to eat, what

to read, what to buy, what exercise to take, what to think of the music we hear, and how to treat our colds. When the expert signs off, the advertiser takes up the assault on individuality in taste and conduct. (Over the air the distinction between the expert and the advertiser is often intentionally vague.) Radio further emphasizes our time habits. One of the outstanding characteristics of broadcasting is its punctuality. Like train despatching, it is on time. This doubtless has an effect on the already conspicuous habits of punctuality and efficiency in American life and will encourage such habits wherever radio penetrates.

Radio is perhaps our chief potential bulwark of social solidarity. It stems the tide of disrupting influences, and strengthens the ties that are socially binding. It can organize for action in a few hours the emotions of sympathy and indignation. It assists in the apprehension of criminals, in the raising of funds for relief, and in allaying fear. It is such capacities of radio as these that prompted a broadcasting official to declare it to be "one of the greatest solvents of the social problems of the American people." There can be no doubt that broadcasting, by virtue of its standardizing influence, tends to counteract disintegrative forces.

Take the case of the family, the institution that sociologists have always regarded as the keystone of any society. In recent years its functions have obviously been weakened. In a modest and unwitting way radio has added a psychological cement to the threatened structure. A radio in the home relieves an evening of boredom and is an effective competitor for entertainment outside. Children troop home from their play an hour earlier than they would otherwise, simply because Little Orphan Annie has her copyrighted adventures at a stated hour. Young people receive many homilies from the radio, the like of which have not been heard in most American homes for a generation. The adolescent boy frequently prefers to stay home and listen to his favorite comedian than to take a chance on the local movie. Even when father wants to listen to a speech, mother to a symphony, brother to a comedian, and sister to jazz, the resulting conflict is "all within the family," and constitutes an exercise in family adjustment.

One of the abilities of the radio is its reliable and relatively objective news service. Since rumors can be authoritatively denied or converted into fact by the announcer, they are not so likely to become widespread and distorted. To a considerable extent, of course, newspapers have already standardized our information, but radio seems even more decisive. Whereas newspapers sometimes prolong rumors and heighten the suggestion of conflict in order to increase their sales, the radio has more to gain by crisp and conclusive reports. The announcer has little time to waste on innuendo and the creation of atmosphere. Wood-pulp paper is cheap but time is precious. Just as radio allays rumor it may also discourage gossip. The housewife may find the loud-speaker more entertaining than the back fence as her mind becomes occupied with affairs of the outside world rather than with those of her neighbors.

The Radio and Auditory Habits

The ease of tuning in, together with the lack of obligation to listen, has created a new type of auditory background for life within the home. The housewife performs her household duties to the accompaniment of music, advice and advertising: in the afternoon she may sew, read or play bridge with the same background of sound; in the evening, if she is not exhausted, the radio may provide a setting against which dinner is served and guests are entertained. The same auditory ground may be found in restaurants, barbershops, stores, hospitals, hotels, prisons, and dormitories. Students often prepare their assignments to the muted tune of a jazz orchestra (cf. pp. 104ff). The question naturally arises whether such persistent use of the radio is having an effect upon our powers of concentration, upon our habits of listening, and upon our nerves.

Take, first, the case of the housewife or the student who is completely preoccupied with work. The loud-speaker emits its stream of sound, but it falls on deaf ears. The distraction is completely inhibited. As long as attention does not shift, the radio's effect, if it has any at all, is entirely subliminal. In such a case the effort required (and unconsciously exerted) to overcome the distraction may actually enhance concentration on the task in hand. The story is told of a French mathematician who in the war selected a ruined house within sound of guns at the front because he found that his attention to his problems became sharper. Inattention to one stimulus always means attention to some other; inhibition of one

response requires concentration on another. The stronger the potential distraction the greater is the compensatory attention.

But even when distractions are inhibited they may be nerve-racking in the long run. A selection between competing stimuli can be made only at the cost of effort. Recent studies of noise have shown that although it may be unperceived, as in traffic, factories, and offices, it has nevertheless an appreciable effect upon physiological processes.[3] The incessant use of the radio, inhibited though its sounds may be from consciousness, probably causes similar tension. The conclusion must be, then, that working "against the radio" may enhance the degree of attention given to a chosen task, but only at the cost of strain and fatigue.

However, attention is at best a restless thing, always waxing and waning, and shifting from one focus to another. The sounds of the radio are seldom inhibited for more than a few minutes at a time. The mind wanders from the task in hand to the distracting sound, and then returns again. The radio provides a secondary focus of attention. The housewife listens "in snatches," and the student divides his attention between "math" and melody. This agreeable diversion is not harmful in those types of work where the task is something so simple and so habitual that its performance does not require the maximum of concentration. Obviously the sounds are not likely to reduce the efficiency of the housewife as greatly as that of the student. In certain lines of manual work such as are required by household duties and in some types of manufacturing, a background of music such as the radio provides has been demonstrated to be actually beneficial.[4]

There is also the phenomenon of accommodation and fatigue in attention. It is possible to keep the radio plugged in until one scarcely hears it at all. From long continued alternations of attention and protracted distraction, irritation is felt, and when at last the radio is turned off, it is with a sense of great relief. Some people reach the point of radio-fatigue sooner than others. Addicts who seldom sign off find themselves, unreasonably enough, ultimately complaining of the lack of originality in programs.

Radio is probably improving the capacity of the average man to listen intelligently to what he hears. In the experiments reported in Chapter IX it was discovered that the college student, with his long training in listening to lectures, is far better able than the untrained listener to understand and to recall what he hears. His advantage, furthermore, is discovered to be greater for *auditory* than for *visual* material. It appears, therefore, that intelligent listening is *par excellence* the mark of the educated man. Although there is a prevailing tendency to use the radio as a background for other tasks, when the dial is turned to a specific program and when attention is directed fully to its message, an auditory training is provided for millions of people and its long-range effects may be exceedingly important. For increasing the world's population of "good listeners" radio deserves an extra star in its crown.

* * *

Until the advent of radio the social environment of the vast majority of the earth's inhabitants was limited and cramped. Only kings, millionaires, and lucky adventurers were able to include within their mental horizons experiences that the average man has long desired but never obtained. Now at last the average man may also participate. He may attend the best operas and concerts, may assist at important hearings and trials, at inaugurations, coronations, royal weddings and jubilees. A turn of the wrist immeasurably expands his personal world. The poor man escapes the confines of his poverty; the country dweller finds refuge from local gossip; the villager acquires cosmopolitan interests; the invalid forgets his loneliness and pain; the city dweller enlarges his personal world through contact with strange lands and peoples. It is the middle classes and the underprivileged whose desires to share in the world's events have been most persistently thwarted, and it is these classes, therefore, that are the most loyal supporters of radio. For them radio is a gigantic and invisible net which each listener may cast thousands of miles into the sea of human affairs and draw in teeming with palpable delights from which he may select according to his fancy.

There are other means for broadening the social environment; for example, books, moving pictures, and newspapers. But each lacks the quality of contemporaneity. What is heard on the air is transitory, as fleeting as time itself, and it therefore seems *real*. That this sense of the living present is important to the listener is shown by his resentment of broadcasts from electrical transcriptions. Even though such transcriptions cannot be distinguished by the majority of people from real performances, listeners feel dissatisfied. The thought of a whirling disk cannot create the sense of participation in actual events that is radio's chief psychological characteristic. It is not merely words and melodies that the listener craves. These he can obtain from a variety of mechanical contraptions. When he turns his dial he wants to enter the stream of life as it is actually lived.

Notes

1. Excluded from this list are the agencies of transportation, e.g., the locomotive, the automobile, and the airplane, for these are primarily concerned not with the communication of ideas but with the mobility of people.

2. The symposium *Recent Social Trends* (edit. by W. C. Mitchell, *et al.*, New York: McGraw-Hill, 1933) lists without discussion (Vol. I, 152–157) several social changes for which the radio is in part responsible. The present chapter represents a critical sifting and an elaboration of this earlier work.

3. M. S. Viteles, *Industrial Psychology.* New York: Norton, 1932, 506–511.

4. C. M. Diserens, *The Influence of Music on Behavior.* Princeton: Princeton University Press, 1926.

18

Foreword

From *Public Opinion Quarterly* (1937)

Editors, *Public Opinion Quarterly*

Public Opinion Quarterly was started in 1937, a year after the widely publicized failure of the respected *Literary Digest* poll to accurately predict Franklin Roosevelt's landslide reelection victory (its polltakers had said Alf Landon would win). The new journal quickly became one of the central forums for the publication of research on "the agencies of mass impression," running articles by Paul Lazarsfeld, Harold Lasswell, Robert Lynd, and most of the other key figures in the emerging field of communications. Based at Princeton University, *Public Opinion Quarterly* was initially edited by some of the leading figures in propaganda and public opinion research, including Dewitt Pool, Harwood Childs, Hadley Cantril, O. W. Riegel, and Lasswell. This short piece is the editors' foreword, written for the first issue. It captures the sometimes-breathless feel of an era witnessing new powers of public appeal, public relations, and public opinion, as well as the cautious optimism that science could provide reliable knowledge for both "students and leaders of opinion."

A new situation has arisen throughout the world, created by the spread of literacy among the people of the miraculous improvement of the means of communication. Always the opinions of relatively small publics have been a prime force in political life, but now, for the first time in history, we are confronted nearly everywhere by *mass* opinion as the final determinant of political, and economic, action. Today public opinion operates in quite new dimensions and with new intensities; its surging impact upon events becomes the characteristic of the current age—and its ruin or salvation?

For some time the phenomena of public opinion have been an object of scholarly attention. The quantity of published material dealing with the subject has increased tremendously since the early writings of Alexis de Tocqueville, James Bryce, Albert V. Dicey, Wilhelm Bauer, Ferdinand Tonnies, and A. Lawrence Lowell. A recently published bibliography of public opinion studies lists more than five thousand titles; but the attack has not much more than begun. Scholarship is developing new possibilities of scientific approach as a means of verifying hypotheses and of introducing greater precision of thought and treatment.

Meantime practical exigencies created by the mounting power and activity of mass opinion have constrained the agencies of government to set up special offices for contact with the press and to give increasing attention to their direct relations with the public. Today no important executive branch is without its press bureau under one name or another. Senators and congressmen must maintain sizeable staffs to handle their correspondence with great numbers of constituents. Private polls are taken on public questions. The fate of representative government grows uncertain. Lobbies have become almost a part of government. Governments have their ministries of propaganda.

Business has been similarly affected. In the case of large enterprises, the manufacturer can no longer concern himself solely with manufacturing nor the merchant with merchandising in a narrow sense. A wide and active public must be dealt with. Advertising becomes a science and an art. Beyond advertising, business finds it necessary to retain expert counsel on questions of its general relations with the public, and those counselors grow influential in the general conduct of business affairs.

More than ever the press must be reckoned the Fourth Estate, but two new agencies of mass impression—the radio and motion picture—have appeared. The radio facilitates still further the spread of news and opinion, overleaping boundaries, creating new personal contacts, and raising difficult problems of private editorship and governmental control. Motion picture and radio alike stamp the mind with vivid flashes, and the full educational effect of this bombardment has yet to be experienced.

Under these conditions the clearest possible understanding of what public opinion is, how it generates, and how it acts becomes a vital need touching both public and private interest. The editorial staff of THE PUBLIC OPINION QUARTERLY undertakes to serve that need by creating a convenient medium for regularly bringing together from all the sources indicated above—scholarship, government, business, advertising, public relations, press, radio, motion pictures—the latest available information on the phenomena and problems of public opinion and the developing thought, in connection with those phenomena and problems, of scholars, governmental officials, business men, public relations counsel, and the rest.

Of course the most active and intense interest in public opinion is usually displayed by political leaders, group leaders, advertisers, and others who wish to promote some cause—who have objectives the carrying out of which necessitates the cooperation of many minds. THE PUBLIC OPINION QUARTERLY will not attempt the delicate task of evaluating these proffered causes or of discovering new ones. It will seek rather to satisfy the need of students and leaders of opinion, irrespective of their social, economic, religious, and political beliefs, for more precise information regarding the phenomena of public opinion itself. The editors will endeavor to maintain a wholly objective and scientific point of view.

The editors will not restrict their effort to publishing the data and ideas which become available as the result of existing research activities. In addition they will survey continuously the field of public opinion problems, seek out where new research might be useful, and actively promote that research. In this the editorial staff will have the support of the School of Public Affairs at Princeton and of the other institutions with which its several members are connected.

The QUARTERLY does not yet have at its disposal a specially trained corps of research workers. For the present it must rely in very large part upon voluntary assistance in bringing together the vast amount of material on the subject of public opinion which is scattered throughout the academic laboratories of the country and filed away in the offices or minds of those whose personal experience gives them special knowledge of the subject. The success of the QUARTERLY will depend in part upon the extent and quality of this voluntary cooperation. The editors undertake to make the QUARTERLY a clearing house of information and a meeting ground of thought for all interested in public opinion; to gather and systematize the relevant data; and, as the means become available, to promote and direct specific researches. They expect that their activities will contribute substantially to the more enlightened comprehension of a controlling but obscure force.

* * *

The editorial staff whishes to express at this time grateful appreciation of the generous assistance given by many during the launching of the venture. Until the QUARTERLY can support itself from subscriptions and advertising it will owe its existence to the generosity of those whose contributions have made possible the establishment of an underwriting fund, and to Princeton University and the School of Public Affairs in particular, for assuming a large part of the editorial costs. Although the editorial staff shares the financial responsibility with numerous friends, its members realize that they cannot place upon others the burden of editorial guidance and enterprise. Upon them alone rests the responsibility for editorial policy and the carting of an emerging program of public opinion research.

19

Human Interest Stories and Democracy

From *Public Opinion Quarterly* (1937)

Helen MacGill Hughes

Helen MacGill Hughes (1903–1992) lived a life whose broad pattern was repeated by a number of other talented, intellectual women of her generation. She was born to a well-educated professional family in Vancouver, British Columbia—in fact, her mother was a correspondent for the *Atlantic Monthly*, a newspaper editor, a suffragist, and a friend of Jane Addams. Hughes attended the University of British Columbia and then the University of Toronto, where she was influenced by a human geography course taught by Harold Innis. As a consequence of hearing Robert Park lecture at the University of British Columbia, she went to the University of Chicago in 1925 to pursue graduate work in sociology. There, she was one of just two female graduate students, in a class that included Louis Wirth and Everett Hughes, the latter of whom she married after her second year. Everett taught at the University of Montreal, before the couple returned to Chicago in 1938. In 1944, Herbert Blumer offered Helen an editorial position at the *American Journal of Sociology*—"part time work," she later wrote, "the only kind I have ever had." She worked for the journal for seventeen years, receiving exactly one raise, though she rose from editorial assistant to managing editor; afterward, she took adjunct teaching positions and did freelance writing. She also published several articles on mass media, popular culture, and the status of women in academia.

This fine piece was published in the second issue of *Public Opinion Quarterly* (1937). It came out of Hughes's dissertation, written under the direction of Park and later published as *News and the Human Interest Story* (1940). Park's influence is clear in Hughes's historical approach to the human-interest story, which she views in a generally favorable light. Like Walter Lippmann, Hughes recognizes that the news simplifies and sensationalizes. Like Leo Lowenthal, she sees that popular media bring the personal lives of distant figures up close to the masses. But Hughes also retains a solid, late-progressive faith in the people, and she notes the way big, sensationalized stories become "the talking-point for the day" in countless conversations where "the demos" tests its moral values against what is portrayed in the media. One may also compare her take on confession magazines to that of George Gerbner (p. 434). Hughes's article is an interesting lens through which to view contemporary human-interest news spectacles that get the broad population talking, as almost all news spectacles seem to have some element of human interest.

Charles Merz, speculating on the state of the Union, once remarked that it is doubtful whether anything really unifies the country like its murders. Like so many outrageous and undocumented assertions, particularly the more cynical ones, this statement is probably the simple truth. He refers, of course, to murders as made public in the newspapers, and so, eventually, to something that Cooley has commented upon: that the press, by acquainting people with each others' lives, has implemented the democracy.[1] Like other liberals, Cooley looked upon the newspaper as an indispensable condition of government by the people. But, paradoxically, it is not the political news that informs people about one another. It is the revelations of private life and those inconsequential items that in the newspaper office are known as human interest stories. Now historians of the press maintain that it was this type of "copy" that, in America, made newspaper reading a universal habit. And so the question arises, Does the personal news which characterizes the popular newspaper play a part in welding the American Democracy? The question is all the more pertinent because the forms of the totalitarian state which are threatening democratic structures are invariably opposed to this aspect of journalism.

From its beginning in the penny dailies of a century ago, the popular press has envisaged its reader as a plain man of brief schooling who, as Mencken says, "misses the hard words."[2] As soon as newspapermen recognized that the great difference between the educated and others lies in vocabulary, they found it possible to tell substantially the same news in such a way that the uneducated comprehended and enjoyed it.

The conversion of news into stories told in the language of the street, but "written up" like fiction, brought new classes of readers, described by Whitelaw Reid as "men who can't read or at least had not been habitual and regular readers of the high-priced daily newspapers."[3] Day and Bennett, editors of the first penny papers, the *New York Sun* and the *New York Herald,* referred to their readers of the 1830's as "artisans and mechanics," "the man of labor," and "the small merchant." The Yellow Press in the 'nineties delved into other new strata of readers when it enlisted women and immigrants, the former by love stories and department store advertisements, the latter by pictures and words of one syllable. All this time, and continuing into the present, cities were growing by draining population from the rural regions, so there have always been new recruits to be enrolled as metropolitan newspaper readers.[4] For the first time these classes were brought imaginatively into the orbit of city and ultimately national life. For them, the newspaper offers a view of a magical world. A working girl who read Hearst's *New York Evening Journal* once wrote:

It is very exciting to read of a girl who has disappeared from home, no one knowing where she has gone and in about three days a de-

scription of the girl will appear in the *Journal* and the way the detectives disguise themselves and go in search for this wayward girl. . . . Take for example the strange disappearance of Miss Dorothy Arnold, this is a case that I have followed up ever since I first saw its appearance in the *Journal* and I expect to follow it to its end. I am very anxious to know where Miss Arnold is and whether she has become the bride of Mr. George Griscom. The way I hope it will end is where she will return to her parents and they will welcome her with open heart and hands.[5]

To just such literate but unsophisticated city-dwellers—the demos[6]—the newspaper was a collection of stories. Reading matter like the *Journal's* makes them readers and establishes the reading habit. To do so it must, it seems, have the character of a fairy tale. It transports the reader into another world, but, like the Negro folk-play, *Green Pastures,* it conceives the new world invariably in terms of the known. Sophisticate literature has at all times explored people and places that are unfamiliar and intriguing but there is always the familiar core of private sentiments, ambitions, and passions that humanizes even the bizarre and the outlandish. But *popular* literature, though it revolves about the small circle of personal vicissitudes, is realistic; the scenes of action hardly venture further than the reader's curiosity.[7]

The newspaper's stories reflected the popular mind, that is to say the way the demos thought about the things that came within its comprehension. Like the movies and *Saturday Evening Post* fiction they frequently turned out to be stories of young love and its trials.[8] But within this range of experiences known to the demos, the stories were the medium for presenting the unfamiliar and strange. For the human interest story invaded a succession of areas of life for its settings. To that extent the penny press and later the Yellow Press contributed to the education of simple-minded people in some of the facts of contemporary social life. In this the cheap press was joined by the dime novel, the story weekly and the confession magazine. The great growth of the popular newspaper in the last century accompanied by the urbanization of the demos, whose burgeoning curiosity about the world was the beginning of sophistication. The interesting thing is that such a mission was far from the publisher's intention: it all came about as an irrelevant and unforeseen effect of the compulsion put upon the reporter to provide attractive copy in order to sell the paper.

Before the penny press, the newspapers confined their news to business and politics. Benjamin Day unconventionally hunted news in the police court. The *Sun's* intriguing accounts of vicious, violent, and uproarious life as it paraded before minor magistrates in the night sessions were, for thousands of obscure citizens, hitherto without a newspaper, the first impressions of the city to supplement their own direct experiences of sight and hearing. Day's discovery that mechanics and artisans could be readily interested in them is initially responsible for the fact that present-day trial have become public circuses and criminals public characters.

Day's competitor, James Gordon Bennett, was shrewd enough to appreciate the fact that the size of New York prevented the oral circulation of news that everyone would find worth telling if he knew of it, and he announced in his *Herald:*[9]

We shall give a correct picture of the world—in Wall Street—in the Exchange—in the Post Office—at the Theaters—in the Opera—in short, wherever human nature or real life best displays its freaks and vagaries.

The "collector of news" was employed to write up incidents of the city streets and tell New Yorkers about each other. The doings of the rich, for one thing, had become a subject of excited speculation among the poor. On this interest Bennett founded an important innovation, society news. He sent reporters to balls and banquets, printed a list of guests (designated tantalizingly by the first and last letters of their names) and told what they wore. Later on, Hearst reported fashionable functions on a heroic scale, giving as much as five pages to the Bradley-Martin masquerade, copiously illustrated by staff artists.[10]

Then there developed an interest in the contrary direction; the middle-class and the wealthy became curious about the poor. This was evinced in the vogue of slumming parties and of books like Jake Riis's *How the Other Half Lives.* Hearst's *Sunday Journal* ran illustrated sketches by Stephen Crane of his experiences in the Tenderloin. New York was dotted with little worlds like Chinatown, the Bowery, Little Italy, and other exotic neighborhoods which were a perpetual source of wonder for those on the outside.[11] A great volume of "feature stuff" brought the life of the immigrant and the poor into the newspaper. At this time, too, "Annie Laurie" (Winifred Black) was engaged to write accounts of women's lives

and she produced features on such subjects as *The Strange Things Women Do For Love*, that were not police court news, but simply a commentary on the newer and freer careers that young women in particular were pursuing in the city. The shop girl who had inspired some of O. Henry's short stories, the business girl, and the "bachelor girl" began to exist for newspaper readers. For purposes of the newspaper the city became a laboratory for the concoction of stories.

These new departures were accompanied by a change in the balance of power in the editorial rooms, for when the newspaper office became the admitting ward for anything at all that the readers found interesting, local news, which the older papers had almost ignored, became actually more important than any other. Writing in 1879, Whitelaw Reid of the *Tribune* prophesied that city, national, and world news would be revalued in accordance with their relative interest for the reader, and that "the City Department may then cease to be the place where raw beginners wreak their will."[12] His astuteness as a prophet is acknowledged in a more modern pronouncement: "A dog fight in Champa Street is better than a war abroad.[13] What was called the City Desk now represents the largest department in a newspaper's organization. "The trend unmistakably in New York," writes Stanley Walker, "is toward complete coverage.... The space devoted to local news in most New York papers has increased 50 per cent in the last fifteen years."[14]

Dog fights, lovesick girls and masked balls—"the interesting" rather than "the important," to use Hearst's distinction—provoke spontaneous comment and the newspaper did no more than make their area of diffusion wider. The knowledge of the city that it disseminated corresponded to what the readers found acceptable. And on this gossipy level the newspaper made a beginning of creating those conditions of close communication whose absence denies the city the social cohesion that the village possesses.

For sixty years the penny papers contented themselves with an orbit of news-coverage that surveyed with a fair measure of completeness, the small daily world of "the mechanic and the man of labor." The news the *Sun* enumerated in 1882 as causing temporary increases in circulation was of Presidential and civic elections, the last days of walking matches, great fires, and hangings in or near the city.[15] It was Hearst who took his readers out of the State of New York and caused them to move imaginatively in a larger sphere.

A despatch was sent from Havana reporting that a seventeen-year old Cuban girl, Evangelina Cisneros, was to be imprisoned for twenty-years off the African coast for a political offense. Hearst seized upon it, exclaiming to his editor, Chamberlain, "We can make a national issue of this case. It will do more to open the eyes of the country to Spanish cruelty and oppression than a thousand editorials or political speeches." This unknown girl's misfortune, because of its human interest, caught the readers' imagination and it did become a national issue in a more profound sense than any prior question between the United States and Spain. The *Journal* launched a crusade to free her. Petitions with thousands of signatures, at first from such notable women as Julia Ward Howe and the widow of Jefferson Davis, and then from any woman who wanted to sign, were sent to the Pope and the Queen-Regent of Spain. The *Journal* gave more than two pages a day to the campaign, heading them: "The Whole Country Rising to the Rescue: More than Ten Thousand Women Petition for the Release of Miss Cisneros." As the *Journal's* readers saw it, the Cisneros case was one of monstrous persecution that any human being would naturally want to prevent. To their simple thinking the question of the invasion of Spanish jurisdiction did not exist. The diplomatic game has its own set of conventions; they are not those of plain people.

That a small local incident became public business was an unplanned effect of newspaper competition. Hearst had just bought the *New York Journal* and was trying desperately to seize for it the market of Pulitzer's *New York World*. During the Spanish-American War which soon followed, the two papers vied with each other not so much in reporting as in exploiting the news as a means to ensnare buyers. The streamer headline came into regular use for the first time. Its purpose was to force attention upon the inflammatory reports which soon earned them the name, the Yellow Press. To Pulitzer the war brought "an opportunity," as he put it, "to test the effect on circulation."[16] To readers of the Yellow Press it appeared as a thrilling, but at the same time a simplified affair; complicated issues like the sugar market and the location of naval bases were not discussed—no one would enjoy reading that. The campaign was made personal and epic. The *Journal* referred to the Spanish commander of Cuba as "Butcher" Weyler. A private comment of the Spanish Ambassador was headlined "The worst Insult to the United States in its History." The next day the withdrawal of the Ambassador was an-

nounced as "*Journal's* Letter Gets De Lome His Walking Papers."[17] Later came the news: "Spain Refuses to Apologize." This went on for weeks until war was finally declared.

The diplomatic gestures were, of course, reported in all newspapers, but the Yellow Press construed events in terms of the recognizable and informal rules of a street fight. They indulged in the habit of making categorical moral distinctions and calling names that unsophisticated people—and others—fall into in trying to picture the relations between nation and nation.[18] As Godkin of the sober *New York Post* complained, they treated the war like a prize-fight and begot "in hundreds of thousands of the class that enjoys prize-fights an eager desire to read about it." Famous editorial writer that he was, Godkin found it hard to believe that real political power—which, as Merriam has recently said, lies in a "definite common pattern of impulse[19]—is exerted, not by the editorial but by interesting news. Whether there is truth or not in the legend that Hearst made it, this war at all events was wrested from the hands of diplomats. It became popular in the sense that the people entered into it enthusiastically and that they identified themselves wholly with it. The Yellow Press, by its jingo patriotism and its conversion of the news into dramatic concepts, led the attention of the demos from the local scene to the world of international relations. It also created *national* heroes and villains.

The popular newspaper continued the informal education of the demos into the formidable fields of business and science. Here again the familiar gave the entrée to the unknown and, because the commonest object of spontaneous interest is man himself, all copy tended to take the form of personal stories. Business news appeared in the guise of success stories. As expounded to him by politicians and soapbox haranguers, men of power and property are likely to strike the common man as predatory monsters called "The Milk Trust" or "The Traction Interests," and so, among the masses who have no business affairs of their own and no interest in the routine news of business and finance, any understanding there is of the difficulties, the temptations, and the triumphs of merchants and financiers will come from the reading of a personal revelation. For there the *man* is recognized and perhaps forgiven; the *magnate* is feared and hated, envied, or simply disregarded.[20]

One of the best instances of a concentration of general attention on a technical matter occurred when the *New York Sun* put human interest into a report of the convention of the Sanitary Conference of American Republics. The news that Dr. C. W. Stiles had identified the hookworm as the mysterious destroyer of southern "white trash" was facetiously headed "Germ of Laziness Found?"[21] The account below it was sober enough, but the reference to a universal human failing caught immediate attention and gave rise to innumerable jokes and cartoons. Yet the effect of the hubbub was, as Mark Sullivan put it, "to make Stiles the target for newspaper and stage humorists the world over; next, the object of scorn and vituperation in all the region south of the Potomac River and east of the Mississippi; and finally, years later, one of the heroes of medical science in his generation."[22]

All this time newspapermen were making the more obviously personal crises—elopement, murders, bereavements—the occasion for laying bare some obscure individual's inmost thought. The popular press enlivened *everything*. As its scope enlarged,[23] it led the demos through the human interest in a personal story toward an acquaintanceship with a simplified and trivialized, but none the less a wider world. The newspaper implemented this knowledge in perhaps the only possible way. Just what is the effect of this expansion of understanding which the newspaper expedites is a question newspapermen never ask, because it is beyond them. And social philosophers do not ask it because it is beneath them.

It is a matter of common observation that a "big story" in the newspapers becomes, as Northcliffe put it, the talking-point for the day. The Leopold-Loeb trial, one suspects, brought homosexuality into common conversation; the romance of King Edward and Mrs. Simpson animated the subject of morganatic marriage. And, as Merz said of murder, it gives the nation a set of facts on which to test its moral values.[24] Letters like these below are a symptom of general speculation:

> Brooklyn: If any person went through a Hell on earth, that person was Mary Nolan. She has been treated cruelly and needs a helping hand. May she be successful in staging her comeback. She deserves all the success in the world. —Well Wisher.

> Bronx: I have read with interest the story of Mary Nolan's life. From my experience as a social worker I have concluded that she is more sinned against than sinning. Why is it always made so difficult for a woman to stage a comeback? This "Mr. X" is probably living in security and respectability. Mary

Nolan's only chance is to take the public into her confidence. When will the double standard of morality give the woman a fair chance? Through Mary Nolan's story, the *Mirror* has given society a great indictment.
> —Helen E. Martin, President Bronx Civic Study Club.[25]

Moral speculations are not evoked by news of court procedure; they take form on the reading of an intimate story that shows what the impact of law and convention means as a private experience. A popular literature of true stories, by making the local and the remote world human, may be a substitute on an extended scale for those intimate encounters of direct perception which are the basis of any understanding men have of each other. But this, in the end, puts the reader in the position of a confidant. The difference that intimacy makes in passing judgment is expressed in the aphorism: What's the Constitution between friends? It seems to be always the difference between impersonal news of the external facts and this popular literature that reveals the inner experience, that the *news* raises practical questions of ways and means with the appropriate code taken for granted, but *literature*, like all art, exhibits the inhumanity of doctrine, law, and custom. For literature does more than provoke a plea for exceptional treatment. It induces reverie about oneself and the remote, rather than the immediate objectives of one's own career, and it questions the traditional premises of social life.[26] And since the readers read the news as a pastime and rarely feel called upon to intervene, reverie is free to venture beyond the mores.

Such painful cogitation is the particular burden of uprooted people. Greenhorn immigrants, women entering a freer life, and recent arrivals from the country,[27] in becoming incorporated with the life that extends beyond the local community, are confronted with conflicting patterns of behavior and suffer miseries and uncertainties that are new and, it may seem, incurable. They experience cultural divergencies internally as private moral dilemmas. Indeed, in periods of rapid change, like the present, doubts assail all classes of people and become epidemic. "It is a chief use of social institutions," writes Cooley, "to make up our minds for us, and when in time of confusion they fail to do this, there is more mind-work than most of us are capable of."[28] True and contemporary analogues in the news are at once a comfort and a definition, for human interest stories dramatize for them the opposition between the "right," the legitimate, and the doctrinaire on the one hand, and the "human" on the other.[29] Their protests against the mores may be restated as an aspect of social change of which their own mobility is an expression. The vogue of confessional literature among the demos and of biography among sophisticates may signalize the dissolution of local culture and the emergence of a more inclusive consciousness.

One wonders whether a popular literature of true stories is not perhaps a phenomenon of change *in a free society*. The democratic state, as Hobhouse noted, rests more and more on the personality of its citizens. But under an oppressive and autocratic rule, like the totalitarian state, the citizen may not be his own moral judge. Nor is the press free to be interesting when dedicated to the service of the state. Dictators strive to make discipline absolute by contracting the sympathies and they are suspicious of human interest in newspapers because they fear the unconstrained speculation to which it gives rise.

Notes

1. Cooley, C. H., *Social Organization* (New York: Scribner's, 1929), pp. 177–8.

2. Mencken, H. L., *The American Language* (New York: Knopf, 1919), pp. 185–6. The common failure to understand abstract words is well exhibited in chapter 1 of Wembridge, E., *Life Among the Lowbrows* (Boston: Houghton Mifflin, 1931). "A song-writer," says Sigmund Spaeth, "would hardly dare to use whom in a sentence. ... 'Who are you with tonight?' sounds both proper and provocative and the song could not possibly have achieved popularity with the burden of a 'whom' on its neck."—*The Facts of Life in Popular Song* (New York: McGraw-Hill, 1935), p. 24.

3. "Recent Changes in the Press," *American and English Studies* (New York: Scribner's, 1913), Vol, 11, pp. 297–8. Reid was speaking of the year 1901.

4. *True Story Magazine* regards itself as the spokesman of country people, transplanted to the city. Promotion material depicts the reader as a woman who, in her home town knew all the neighbors, but who lives now in a small city flat and knows no one. *Vide* advertisement, *Chicago Tribune*, April 22, 1930.

5. Symposium on "The American Newspaper, "*Collier's Weekly*, September 2, 1911, p. 22.

6. *Demos* is not an economic term like *proletariat*. Summer divides the *classes*, who initiate custom, from the *masses* who conserve it. (*Folkways*, Ginn, 1906, p. 45). Redfield distinguishes the tribal *folk* that sings folk-songs from the city *demos* that buys jazz songs (*Tepoztlan*, University of Chicago Press, 1930, p. 6). The American demos is not purely urban. Blumer describes the *mass*, referring to those of all classes who follow fashions, murder stories, land booms, etc., and so take part in mass behavior ("Molding of Mass Behavior through the Motion Picture," *Publications of the American Sociological Society*, 1935, p. 116). In this discussion of popular literature the demos means the readers—at first artisans, then immigrants, then women—who find in the newspaper the enjoyment that others find in books.

7. A *True Story Magazine* advertisement, discussing the question: "How does a group of people first acquire its reading habit?" answers that it is through "simple stories, simply told, of people like the readers themselves; stories with the same problems that the readers themselves are constantly meeting."—Macfadden advertisement in the *New York Times*, December 3 and 18, 1935.

8. According to Colonel Joy of the Hays organization, "the best movie story concerns a man and a maid who are going some place, encounter difficulties, overcome them, and are rewarded."—Pew, M., "Shop Talk at Thirty," *Editor and Publisher*, March 12, 1932, p. 46.

9. May 11, 1835.

10. An account of the repercussions of this publicity appears in Brown, H. C., *Brownstone Fronts and Saratoga Trunks* (New York: Dutton, 1935), pp. 330 ff.

11. Sightseeing bus conductors in New York have discovered that what middle-aged country visitors want is a version of the Bowery that was true forty years ago, but not true now. They hope to see the dives of the "sinful city" as the earlier legends in popular literature depicted it—Berger, M., "O. Henry Returns to His Bagdad," *New York Times Magazine*, November 24, 1935.

12. "Practical Issues in a Newspaper Office," *American and English Studies* (New York: Scribner's, 1913) Vol. II, p. 256.

13. Credited to Bonfils and Tammen of the *Denver Post*, whose office is on Champa Street.—Walker, S., *City Editor* (New York: Stokes, 1934), p. 87.

14. *Ibid.*, pp. 45–6 and 52–6. Fifteen years ago a New York morning paper might have 40 local items; now it has 100, some illustrated.

15. O'Brien, F. M., *The Story of "The Sun"* (New York: Doran, 1918), pp. 324–5.

16. Seitz, D. *Joseph Pulitzer: His Life and Letters* (New York: Simon and Schuster, 1924), p. 238.

17. February 9, 1898.

18. "In sophisticated people participation (in a drama) may not be the fate of the hero, but in the fate of the whole idea to which hero and villain are essential. . . . In popular representation the handles for identification are almost always marked. You know who the hero is at once. And no work promises to be easily popular where the marking is not definite and the choice clear, . . . a fact which bears heavily on the character of news."—Lippmann, W., *Public Opinion* (New York: Harcourt Brace, 1922), pp. 1162–3.

19. Merriam, C. E., *Political Power: Its Composition and Incidence* (New York: McGraw-Hill, 1935), p. 7.

20. Perceiving this, J. P. Morgan's advisers permitted wide circulation of a photograph, taken during the Senate hearing on munitions, that showed him talking with a circus midget who had climbed into his lap. The Senators wanted the picture destroyed—*Vide* Walker, *op. cit.*, p. 106.

When the steel magnates of the country had a banquet years ago, a reporter put human interest into the news by reciting the menu of extravagant foreign dishes, followed by what each actually ate. One had a little gruel; another had prunes and milk; in short, all were elderly sick men, denied the plain man's luxury of enjoying a full meal.

21. December 5, 1902.

22. *Our Times: Pre-War America* (New York: Scribner's, 1930), Vol. II, p. 293.

23. This is reflected in a growth in staff. The first penny papers had an editor, police reporter, and local news collector. But the present Hearst papers nearly equal the coverage of standard dailies, using press franchises and a variety of reporters, correspondents, department editors, and columnists.

24. *The Great Bandwagon* (New York: John Day, 1928), p. 71.

25. These appeared, following a completely commonplace and unexceptional news story, in Hearst's *New York Mirror* (a tabloid), November 25, 1933.

26. Blumer, H., *op. cit.*, pp. 115–27. Blumer holds the movies invoke reverie that is an attack on the mores, since it reaffirms the basic human values in a novel ("newsy") setting. This could be well taken to describe the human interest story.

27. *True Story* promotion material, picturing the reader as a lonely newcomer to the city continues: "Do you wonder that these people turn to *True Story Magazine* for parallels of their own experience? For some yardstick to measure by in this changing order of a world that is never at rest?"—Advertisement in *Chicago Tribune*, April 22, 1930. The Voice of Experience, a radio counselor on "Your Personal Problems," reports that the most popular of his ten-cent booklets is the one on the inferiority complex.

28. *Life and the Student* (New York: Knopf, 1927), p. 219.

29. The attitude of the tabloid *New York Daily News*, when a Democratic boss made his son a State Supreme Court Justice was: "What could be more natural than for a father to give his son the break?"—Walker, *op. cit.*, p. 70.

20

From *The Fine Art of Propaganda* (1939)

Edited by Alfred McClung Lee and Elizabeth Briant Lee

Alfred McClung Lee (1906–1992) and Elizabeth Briant Lee (1908–) are two of the handful of figures in this reader without connections to Chicago or Columbia. Born and acquainted in Pittsburgh, each took a master's degree in sociology from the University of Pittsburgh (1931). They went to Yale for their doctorates, where Alfred, like his father, worked as a journalist (albeit briefly). Alfred eventually wrote a dissertation, which became *The Daily Newspaper in America,* a nearly encyclopedic study of the history, types, and institutional workings of the press. He taught at New York University (1938–1942), Wayne State (1942–1949), and Brooklyn College (1949–1992); and from 1940 to 1942, he was executive director at the Institute for Propaganda Analysis in New York. As a single author and as a coauthor with his wife, Alfred published numerous studies of newspapers, propaganda, and public opinion; he also edited important collections in sociology, leading a vigorous and active life as a reform-minded public intellectual who wrote for broader audiences.

Elizabeth Lee was less fortunate than her husband. One of the first women in the graduate program at Yale, she wrote an innovative feminist dissertation, which was belittled by some members of her committee: "Eminent Women: A Cultural Study" (see Galliher and Galliher 1995). Like Helen MacGill Hughes and Herta Herzog, she never secured a full-time, tenure-track position at any university, ostensibly because of "antinepotism" rules that prevented spouses from working on the same faculty. Like the other well-trained and talented women connected with this reader (e.g., Alva Myrdal, Helen Lynd, and Gladys Engel Lang), Elizabeth suffered from the widespread and systemic discrimination against women in the academy, which only began to loosen in the 1960s and 1970s, slowly and often grudgingly. Although her husband received most of the credit, Elizabeth also wrote her own scholarship, including a series of articles, some of which examined the place of women in universities.

The Fine Art of Propaganda (1939), from which the following excerpt comes, is a study organized by the Institute for Propaganda Analysis, a democratically oriented reform and adult-education organization founded by members of Columbia's Teachers' College in 1937. Originally titled *The Fine Art of Rabble-Rousing,* it is a critical case study of the populist radio orator Father Charles Coughlin, whom the Lees saw as an antidemocratic danger comparable to the European dictators. This excerpt nicely illustrates the Lees' diagnosis and proposed defenses against propaganda. Quotes from the book continue to circulate widely on contemporary websites whose purposes range from promoting understanding of Islam to fostering college students' critical thinking.

II. Our Bewildering Maze of Propaganda

The World is beset today by a confusion of conflicting propagandas, a Babel of voices in many tongues shouting charges, counter-charges, assertions, and contradictions that assail us continually.

These propagandas are spread broadcast by spokesmen for political parties, labor unions, business associations, farm organizations, patriotic societies, churches, schools, and other agencies. And they are repeated in conversation by millions of individuals.

If American citizens are to have a clear understanding of conditions and what to do about them, they must be able to recognize propaganda, to analyze it, and to appraise it. They must be able to discover whether it is propaganda in line with their own interests and the interests of our

civilization or whether it is propaganda that may distort our views and threaten to undermine our civilization.

Propaganda more than ever is an instrument of aggression, a new means for rendering a country defenseless in the face of an invading army. While it has been used in a halting way for centuries, within the past few years we have seen it prepare the way for Hitler to seize the Saar, Austria, the Sudetenland and Czechoslovakia. It is called a new instrument of aggression because development has given it an effectiveness never before experienced in the history of the world.

Never before has there been so much propaganda. Never before have there been so many propagandas of such great importance to the lives of all of us. And never before have there been such powerfully implemented propagandas. The modern news-gathering systems of the newspapers and the gigantic radio broadcasting facilities of the world have made the chief differences, but refinements in propagandist methods have kept pace.

As generally understood, *propaganda is opinion expressed for the purpose of influencing actions of individuals or groups.* More formally, the Institute for Propaganda Analysis has defined propaganda as "expression of opinion or action by individuals or groups deliberately designed to influence opinions or actions of other individuals or groups with reference to predetermined ends."

Propaganda thus differs fundamentally from scientific analysis. The propagandist tries to "put something across," good or bad. The scientist does not try to put anything across; he devotes his life to the discovery of new facts and principles. The propagandist seldom wants careful scrutiny and criticism; his object is to bring about a specific action. The scientist, on the other hand, is always prepared for and wants the most careful scrutiny and criticism of his facts and ideas. Science flourishes on criticism. Dangerous propaganda crumbles before it.

Because the action sought by a propagandist may be beneficial or harmful to millions of people, it is necessary to focus upon his activities the same searchlight of scientific scrutiny that the scientist invites. This requires a considerable effort. We all have tendency to make a virtue of defending opinions or propagandas that apparently fit in with our own opinions and of opposing as vigorously any others. But socially desirable views and proposals will not suffer from examination, and the opposite type will be detected and revealed for what it is.

Propaganda which concern us most are those which alter public opinion on matters of large social consequence—often to the detriment of large sections and even the majority of the people. Such propagandas, for example, are involved in these issues:

Hitler, Mussolini, and many dignitaries of the Roman Catholic Church *are right or wrong* in supporting Franco.

Chamberlain and Daladier *saved or undermined further* the peace of Europe through their efforts at appeasement—at "buying off" the dictators of Germany and Italy; and

The C.I.O., the A.F. of L., and the National Association of Manufacturers *are or are not* obstructing efforts to merge the C.I.O. and the A.F. of L.

Any effort to analyze the propagandas involved in the public discussion of such cases as these confronts us first with the seven ABC's of Propaganda Analysis. We must have the feel of these seven ABC's before we can fully appreciate the uses made by propagandists of the seven Propaganda Devices, the "Tricks of the Trade" described in the next chapter. Our seven ABC's are:

*A*SCERTAIN the conflict element in the propaganda you are analyzing. All propaganda contains a conflict element in some form or other—either as cause, or as effect, or as both cause and effect.

*B*EHOLD your own reaction to this conflict element. It is always necessary to know and to take into consideration our own opinions with regard to a conflict situation about which we feel strongly, on which we are prone to take sides. This information permits us to become more objective in our analysis.

*C*ONCERN yourself with *today's* propagandas associated with *today's* conflicts. These are the ones that affect directly our income, business, working conditions, health, education, and religious, political, and social responsibilities. It is all too easy to analyze some old example of propaganda, now having little relation to vital issues.

*D*OUBT that your opinions are "your very own." They usually aren't. Our opinions, even with respect to today's propagandas, have been largely determined for us by inheritance and environment. We are born white or black, Catholic, Protestant, Jewish, or "pagan"; rich or poor; in the North or East, South or West; on a farm or in a city. Our beliefs and actions mirror the conditioning influences of home and neighborhood, church and school, vocation and political party, friends and associates. We resemble others with similar inheritance and environment and are bound to them by ties of common experience. We tend to respond favorably to their opinions and propagandas because they are "our kind of people." We tend to distrust the opinions of those who differ from us in inheritance and environment. Only drastic changes in our life conditions, with new and different experiences, associations, and influences, can offset or cancel out the effect of inheritance and long years of environment.

*E*VALUATE, therefore, with the greatest care, *your own propagandas.* We must learn clearly *why*

we act and believe as we do with respect to various conflicts and issues—political, economic, social, and religious. Do we believe and act as we do because our fathers were strong Republicans or lifelong Democrats; because our fathers were members of labor unions or were employers who fought labor unions; because we are Methodists, Seventh Day Adventists, Catholics, or Jews? This is very important.

FIND THE FACTS before you come to any conclusion. There is usually plenty of time to form a conclusion and believe in it later on. Once we learn how to recognize propaganda, we can most effectively deal with it *by suspending our judgment until we have time to learn the facts and the logic or trickery involved in the propaganda in question.* We must ask:

Who is this propagandist?

How is he trying to influence our thoughts and actions?

For what purpose does he use the common propaganda devices?

Do we like his purposes?

How does he use words and symbols?

What are the exact meanings of his words and symbols?

What does the propagandist try to make these words and symbols appear to mean?

What are the basic interests of this propagandist?

Do his interests coincide with the interests of most citizens, of our society as we see it?

GUARD always, finally, against *omnibus words*. They are the words that make us the easy dupes of propagandists. Omnibus or carryall words are words that are extraordinarily difficult to define. They carry all sorts of meanings to the various sorts of men. Therefore, the best test for the truth or falsity of propaganda lies in specific and concrete definitions of the words and symbols used by the propagandist. Moreover, sharp definition is the best antidote against words and symbols that carry a high charge of emotion.

Our seven Propaganda Devices make the application of these seven ABC's of Propaganda Analysis somewhat easier. Before describing these devices, however, let us discuss the nature of propaganda further by answering some pertinent questions regarding it:

When does a propaganda conform to democratic principles? It conforms when it tends to preserve and extend democracy; it is antagonistic when it undermines or destroys democracy.

"What is truly vicious," observed the New York *Times* in an editorial on September 1, 1937, "is not propaganda but a monopoly of it." Any propaganda or act that tends to reduce our freedom in discussing important issues—that tends to promote a monopoly of propaganda—is anti-democratic.

How broadly should we define democracy? Democracy has the four following aspects, set forth or definitely implied in the Constitution and the Federal statutes:

1. *Political*—Freedom to discuss fully and effectively and to vote on public issues.
2. *Economic*—Freedom to work and to participate in organizations and discussions to promote better working standards and higher living conditions.
3. *Social*—Freedom from oppression based on theories of superiority or inferiority of group, class, or race.
4. *Religious*—Freedom of worship, with separation of church and state.

With all such general freedoms and the specific freedoms implied by them are associated definite responsibilities. Thus, with freedom of the press goes the responsibility for accuracy in news and honesty and representativeness in editorials. These responsibilities were summed up once and for all by Jesus Christ in His Sermon on the Mount as follows:

Therefore all things whatsoever ye would that men should do to you, do ye even so to them: for this is the law and the prophets.

In short, democracy is the one political, economic, and social philosophy which permits the free expression and development of the individual in a culture.

Why are we sometimes misled by propaganda antagonistic to democracy? Few people have had the opportunity to learn how to detect and analyze propaganda. Most books on propaganda are for the benefit of the propagandist or the academic specialist rather than of the public. They are frequently in such technical terms that they may be understood only by persons familiar with the nomenclature of psychology and sociology.

Furthermore, most of these treatises deal with the propagandas of the past, not of today. It is *today's propagandas, flowing from today's conflicts,* which interest and concern us most.

Is there any popular recognition of the need to analyze facts, alleged facts, opinions, propagandas? Yes. It is implied in the public forum movement; in the privately printed letters for business men prepared by such as the Kiplinger Washington Agency, and Harland Allen; in the New York *Herald Tribune* Annual Forum on Current Problems; in various college conferences on economics, politics, and world issues; in reports and programs of the Foreign Policy Association; in the privately circulated reports of the Consumers' Union; in the addresses and discussions of educators, clergymen, and editors at the Williamstown Institute of Human Relations; and in various radio programs, including the "University of Chicago Round Table," "The Town Meeting of the Air," and the "People's Platform."

"Propaganda," said an editorial in the Springfield (Mass.) *Republican,* September 3, 1937, "is good as well as bad. 'We are surrounded by clouds of propaganda.'... It is up to each of us to precipitate from those clouds the true and the false, the near-true and the near-false, identifying and giving to each classification its correct label."

How nearly right are our answers? The Institute lays no claim to infallibility. It tries to be scientific, objective, and accurate. When it makes mistakes, it acknowledges them. It asks the readers of this book as well as the subscribers for its regular bulletin, *Propaganda Analysis,* to check its work further and also to co-operate with it by supplying documented evidence on the sources of propaganda and on censorship or distortion of essential news in press, radio, and newsreels. Chiefly the Institute seeks to acquaint its subscribers and other readers of its materials with methods whereby they may become proficient in making their own analyses.

21

A Powerful, Bold, and Unmeasurable Party?

From *The Pulse of Democracy* (1940)

George Gallup and Saul Rae

George H. Gallup (1901–1984) was America's best-known pollster. Raised in small-town Iowa, he took undergraduate and graduate degrees in psychology and journalism, respectively, from the University of Iowa, where he was first introduced to basic survey research. After receiving his doctorate in 1928, Gallup taught briefly at Drake University and Northwestern University before becoming director of research and marketing in 1932 for the famous New York advertising firm Young and Rubicam. Like other early market researchers, Gallup applied his techniques to politics, and in 1935 he founded the American Institute of Public Opinion. He gained notoriety in 1936 by correctly picking the winner of the presidential election, when the better-known poll conducted by the *Literary Digest* wrongly predicted that Alf Landon would win (Landon carried two states). It was a victory for scientific sampling of small but representative populations (the *Literary Digest* relied on large numbers of responses), and it was also a public relations victory for Gallup (though one of three pollsters who predicted FDR's victory, he generally got the credit).

Saul Forbes Rae (1915–1999) grew up one of the "Three Raes of Sunshine," a vaudeville act run by his mother—of Scottish descent, who had been abandoned by her gambling-obsessed husband—and featuring the five Rae children (his sister, Jackie Rae, went on to become an early variety star on Canadian television). Rae attended the University of Toronto, and he took his doctorate in philosophy from the University of London in 1938. He was a legendary diplomat who served as Canada's secretary to the Paris Peace Conference of 1946 and as ambassador to the United Nations, Mexico, Guatemala, and the Netherlands. Rae's international experience must have had an influence on his son Bob, as he eventually became premier of Ontario.

This selection, from Gallup and Rae's 1940 *The Pulse of Democracy,* displays the heroic rhetoric that sometimes accompanied early, scientifically guided public opinion polls (note the images of "the shock troops of public-opinion research," in the opening paragraphs). Against the backdrop of twin threats to democracy, posed by totalitarianism in Europe and by supposed representatives purporting to speak for "the common man" in the United States, Gallup and Rae offer the public opinion poll as the true voice of the people. While public opinion polls are today sometimes viewed as part of the problem of political life, for Gallup and Rae in 1940 they were very much part of the solution.

On State Street in downtown Boston early in May, 1940, a stockbroker stops to answer the questions of a young man with a sheaf of ballots and a lead pencil:

"Whom would you like to see elected President in November?" the young man asks.

"Well, my first choice would be for Wendell Willkie," says the stockbroker, "but I don't know whether or not the politicians would take to him. In any case, put *me* down for Willkie."

"What do you think is the most important problem before the American people today?"

"As I see it—this country must try to avoid getting mixed up in this war in Europe. I'm strongly against our looking for trouble overseas."

The scene shifts to a backwoods road in Arkansas. The man who asks the questions wears a cap; the man who answers them wears the faded overalls of a back-country farmer. But the questions are the same. Both the stockbroker and the farmer agree that keeping the United States out of war is the crucial problem facing Americans today. The Arkansas farmer wants a third term for President Roosevelt. Both men are chance cogs in an endlessly functioning machine that samples public opinion. Both were selected on the initiative of the field investigator, but only after careful and detailed directions had come from the office of the American Institute of Public Opinion in Princeton. Multiplied hundreds of times, these interviews provide continuous descriptions of what Americans are thinking about unemployment, relief, agriculture, the President's

popularity, the third-term issue, labor problems, the Wagner Act, child labor, about the war in Europe, reciprocal trade treaties, conscription, rearmament, birth control, disease prevention, capital punishment, prohibition, the Dies Committee, and the prospects of rival candidates, parties and pressure groups.

In thousands of week-to-week conversations with the men and women voters of America, such issues are presented to the public by the shock troops of public-opinion research. These interviewers know what it is to drive through a Maine snowstorm to make a farm interview; to trudge across Kansas wheat fields on a blistering day to interview a thresher on the job; to travel through the red-clay mud of Georgia in a drenching rainstorm. Their assignments may take them into a third-floor tenement in New York City's East Side, or require them to argue their way past a uniformed doorman guarding a smart Park Avenue apartment. They talk to the prominent industrialist who runs a huge factory employing thousands of employees, just as they talk to the old lady who silently mops his office when everyone else has gone home. As vital issues emerge from the fast-flowing stream of modern life, the public-opinion polls conducted by such organizations as the American Institute and the *Fortune* Survey enable the American people to speak for themselves. Nor is this new phenomenon exclusively confined to the United States. Similar Institutes of Public Opinion have been organized in Great Britain and in France, directly affiliated with the American Institute. From 1938 to the present day, continuing throughout the course of the war, the *News Chronicle* of London has regularly published the results of frequent sampling surveys made by the British Institute. The findings of the French Institute were reported in the French newspaper, *Paris-Soir,* until the present European conflict began.

When the shadow of war fell across Europe in late August, 1939, an instrument was in readiness to test America's attitudes and reactions. Even before the outbreak of hostilities, selected interviewers in every state had received ballots especially designed to test public opinion objectively. In 1917, it was necessary to rely on impression and speculation to assess the reactions of public opinion. In 1939, a more reliable method was ready to be placed in operation. As German troops advanced into western Poland, interviewers went out to talk to the man in the street, and listened closely to what he had to say to such questions as:

Do you think the United States will go into this war?
    Should the United States allow its citizens to travel on ships of countries which are now at war?
    Do you think the United States should declare war on Germany at once and send our Army and Navy abroad to held England, France, and Poland?

Replies were swiftly returned to the Institute, which tabulated the final results and distributed them to its subscribing newspapers throughout the country.

Such a test taken at a moment when the attention of every citizen was riveted on events abroad is typical of hundreds. For in our own day, the study of public opinion has developed from a glorified kind of fortune telling into a practical way of learning what the nation thinks. The surveys of the last five years chart the main alignments and changes in public opinion. Their basic principle is simply this: by sounding the opinions of a relatively small number of persons, proportionate to each major population group in every section of the country, the opinions of the whole population can be determined with a high degree of accuracy.

Is this sampling instrument merely a passing fad or does it fill a genuine need in American public life? Many signs suggest that opinion sampling has come to stay. Not only have the polls demonstrated by their accuracy that public opinion *can* be measured; there is a

growing conviction that public opinion *must* be measured. What the mass of people thinks puts governments in and out of office, starts and stops wars, sets the tone of morality, makes and breaks heroes. We know that democrats think public opinion is important because continuous efforts have been made throughout the history of popular government to improve and clarify its expression. We know, too, that autocrats think public opinion is important because they devote vast sums and careful attention to curbing and controlling it.

Throughout the history of politics this central problem has remained: shall the common people be free to express their basic needs and purposes, or shall they be dominated by a small ruling clique? Shall the goal be the free expression of public opinion, or shall efforts be made to ensure its repression? In the democratic community, the attitudes of the mass of the people determine policy. "With public opinion on its side," said Abraham Lincoln in the course of his famous contest with Douglas, "everything succeeds. With public opinion against it, nothing succeeds." But public opinion is also important in the totalitarian state. Contemporary dictators must inevitably rule through the minds of their people—otherwise they would quickly dispense with their elaborate propaganda machines. "Our ordinary conception of public opinion," Adolf Hitler has written in *Mein Kampf,* "depends only in very small measure on our personal experience or knowledge, but mainly, on the other hand, on what we are told; and this is presented to us in the form of so-called 'enlightenment,' persistent and emphatic." Whether his ultimate goal is to encourage the clear and honest expression of public opinion, or merely to create an "enlightened" majority, no ruler can stay in power without having some measure of the mind of the mass of the people.

What channels are open in a dictatorship? How can public opinion be known? Immediately after Herr Hitler had made his spectacular entry into Vienna on the occasion of the *Anschluss* with Austria, the National Socialist party held a lightning plebiscite and presently informed the world that 99.7 per cent of the electorate had voted in favor of the Führer's action. Election returns from Soviet Russia tell us from time to time that Joseph Stalin has been re-elected by the Moscow Soviet with 99.4 per cent or 99.6 per cent of the total vote.

But when elections merely confirm the *status quo,* when the opportunity to oppose the official candidate or regime must be weighed against the rigors of the concentration camp, such expressions of "public opinion" merit considerable skepticism. The artificial creation of an apparent majority, whether in a vote which allows no freedom of choice, or in the organized enthusiasm of a popular rally supervised by the secret police, provides a poor index of public opinion. Not only does the outside world remain unconvinced that the people have really spoken; the dictator himself can never be certain whether he is hearing the people's voice or the echo of his own. For if there is opinion which is static, controlled, stamped with the seal of official approval, there is another kind of opinion as well. To find it one must go into the concentration camps, and visit the distant wastes of Siberia. It is not voiced at party rallies, but behind locked doors. It is expressed in whispers and jokes, grumbling and curses, when uniforms are hung in closets and men gather together to talk furtively in small groups. One can hear this opinion in fugitive radio messages; one can read it between the lines of letters which from time to time drift past the rigid censorship. It is intangible, but it is always present.

The kind of public opinion implied in the democratic ideal is tangible and dynamic. It springs from many sources deep in the day-to-day experience of individuals who constitute the political public, and who formulate these opinions as working guides for their political representatives. This public opinion listens to many propagandas, most of them contradictory. It tries in the clash and conflict of argument and debate to separate the true from the false. It needs criticism for its very existence, and through criticism it is constantly being modified and molded. It acts and learns by action. Its truths are relative and contingent upon the results which its action achieves. Its chief faith is a faith in experiment. It believes in the value of every individual's contribution to political life, and in the right of ordinary human beings to have a voice in deciding their fate. Public opinion, in this sense, is the pulse of democracy.

Between these two points of view there can be no compromise. For the past decade, the democratic faith in public opinion has been challenged by totalitarian critics. Signor Mussolini insists that Fascism has "thrown on the dump heap" the "lifeless theories" of democracy; Comrade Stalin decries the democratic way as a sham and a delusion, and in the name of liberty has strengthened his dictatorship over the Russian people. Herr Hitler scoffs at the "foolish masses," the "granite stupidity of mankind"; he regards the common people as "mere ballot cattle."

This name-calling has been echoed in contemporary America by the would-be imitators of this triumvirate. Even in our own midst we can hear the pseudo autocrats argue that dictatorship is a better way of life than democracy, because dictatorship rests on the will and action of a single, all-powerful individual. Unhampered by "critics" and "obstructionists," responsible only to his own iron will, the Leader, it is maintained, can take immediate and decisive action in domestic as well as in foreign affairs. "Democracy is cumbersome and slow-moving," we have been told. "The twentieth century belongs to the swift. You must either copy the tactics of the Strong Men, or go to the wall."

This attack on democracy, with the crisis which has swiftly developed in world affairs, has inevitably led to self-questioning. It strikes both at the basis and the methods of popular government. From this challenge spring two fundamental questions to which an answer must be given. *Is democracy really inferior to dictatorship? Can democracy develop new techniques to meet the impact of this strange new decade?* Such questions are not academic. They have long been matters of profound concern to many thinking persons in this country and in all countries where faith in free institutions still runs high.

Remarkably few people in the United States really believe that dictatorship is superior to democracy as a way of life. In spite of the prophets of calamity, propaganda condemning the methods and purposes of popular government has received an extremely cool reception. The challenge of dictatorship, whether of foreign or domestic origin, has made only minor dents on the surface of America's political consciousness. Even the Dies Committee on un-American activities failed to discover that the lure of totalitarianism had seduced Americans in the mass from their fundamental democratic allegiance. The following excerpt from the 15,000-word report that the Committee laid before Congress on January 4, 1940, makes the point clear:

> One of the greatest fact of all that should be recorded in the report of this Committee is that, on the basis of evidence presented to the Committee, not over 1,000,000 people in the United States can be said to have been seriously affected by these essentially foreign or un-American activities. That leaves about 131,000,000 Americans who in spite of Nazis, Fascists, Communists, self-styled saviors of America and all the rest and in spite of the

suffering and distress of ten years of unemployment and depression, are still as sound and loyal to American institutions and the democratic way of life as they ever were.

All the signs point to a growing immunity to the virulent attack which insists that democracy is doomed, that this country must follow the totalitarian pattern, that ordinary citizens must resign in favor of the dictator and the bureaucrat. For the vast majority of the American people feel in their bones that the case for dictatorship is riddled with weaknesses. They believe that the "unity" about which we hear so much is synthetic rather than real; that it disguises but fails to solve, fundamental conflicts within the state itself. They are aware that the great flaw in the dictator's armor lies in his inability to know the real mind of his people, and that when he tries to get a true measure of public opinion, he is like a blind man groping in a dark room for a light that isn't there. They know that, having cut the communication lines on which political stability ultimately rests, the self-chosen are driven to rely on propaganda and brute force to ensure outward conformity.

What of the second question: "Can democracy develop new techniques and be made more efficient?"

To the charge that some of the machinery of democratic government is archaic and unfitted for the speed-up of the twentieth century, Americans have lent a more sympathetic ear. Always an inventive people, they have not confined their ingenuity to building automobiles and radios, bridges and skyscrapers. They have also applied it, although far more gradually, to their political system, and to their methods of living together. They have learned by experience to preserve an open mind to inventions which might make democracy work more effectively. They have met new needs by creating new techniques.

To the solution of the problem of making democracy work more effectively, single or simple answers will be wholly inadequate. Democracy can function efficiently only when the economic system is doing its best to provide for the needs of all its citizens. It can work well only when education and literacy are widespread, and when the people have reliable facts and information on which to base their opinions. It demands the exposure of pressure groups and powerful interests (and the Dies Committee has by no

means covered them all) who speak in the name of democracy while abusing its freedom to destroy its structure. Above all, democracy recognizes the essential dignity of the individual citizen as such; it assumes that our economic, political, and cultural institutions must be geared to the fundamental right of every person to give free expression to the worth that is in him.

What has been obvious these past few years is that the right to vote, to choose between this party or that, is by itself not true democracy. Democracy is more than a legal right which the citizen exercises on a certain day of the year when he enters a tiny polling booth to mark and anonymous "X" on a ballot form. It is a process of constant thought and action on the part of the citizen. It is self-educational. It calls for participation, information, the capacity to make up one's own mind. "The people," it has been truly said, "must understand and participate in the basic ideals of democracy if these ideals are to be defended against attack. They must learn that it is not shibboleth but a vital truth that the state is their own, that they are free citizens with rights and responsibilities.[1]

In an enormous community of more than 130,000,000 persons, this goal has not always been easy to attain. We are not living in an age like that of the Founding Fathers of the American Republic, when "participation in the basic ideals of democracy" was limited exclusively to the "wise, the rich, and the good." Public opinion is not today, as it was then, the opinion of a small and exclusive minority of educated persons enjoying a monopoly of economic and political power. Nor can we restore the practice of direct democracy which operated in the early town-hall meetings of New England, or revive the political intimacy of the rural corner store with its cracker barrel.

For good or evil, public opinion today plays its role on a stage as vast as the American scene itself. The impetus of a growing industrialism, the revolutions in transport and communication, the emergence of factories, towns, and great cities destroyed for all time the rural localism of early America. A new kind of public opinion appeared. It was no longer the opinion of a small, exclusive class; it embraced all classes and sections of the community.

The enormous expansion of social and political life broke down the old face-to-face relationships of the small governing class. The rise of what the late Graham Wallas once called the Great Society occurred only because political parties, nation-wide associations, newspapers, the telephone, the motion picture, and radio came upon the scene. Ideas and information had to be disseminated to an ever-growing public. To reach the outlying districts of the country, to bring the immigrant and the newly franchised groups closer to their government, the newspaper and the school fought a continuous battle.

Inevitably, these new agencies of communication gave those who controlled them the power to influence as well as to express public opinion. More and more voices claimed they spoke for the people. Powerful newspapers called themselves the true *vox populi.* Glib party leaders declared that their policies were inscribed in the hearts of the American workingman. Motion-picture and radio executives asserted their belief that at last "the public was getting what it wanted." As the old equality of participation gradually disappeared, the voice of the common man grew faint in the din and clatter of other voices speaking in his name. Basically that is why Walter Lippmann in his search for "public opinion" found only a "phantom public." It is the background of his gloomy picture of the disenchanted man living in a world "which he cannot see, does not understand, and is unable to direct."

The problem of building machinery for directly approaching the mass of the people and hearing what they have to say demands solution. Between infrequent elections, legislators must depend on all sorts of indirect and impressionistic ways of learning the popular will, and finding out how the mass of the people are reacting to the events and propaganda of the day. Unless the ordinary citizen can find channels of self-expression, the common man may become the forgotten man. When such a situation develops, when public opinion cannot get itself expressed, democracy lays itself open to its hostile critics. For public opinion can be a satisfactory guide only if we can hear it and, what is equally important, if it can hear itself.

The following pages tell the story of a new instrument which may help to bridge the gap between the people and those who are responsible for making decisions in their name. The public-opinions polls provide a swift and efficient method by which legislators, educators, experts, and editors, as well as ordinary citizens throughout the length and breadth of the country, can have a more reliable measure of the pulse of democracy. The study of public opinion is still in the experimental stage. But the blueprints for a new technique of investigation have been drawn up and real working models are already in operation. The public-opinion polls represent but one attempt to give an answer to these vital questions. When many more efforts have been made, all of us who believe in democracy will be in a better position to give sound reasons—based upon evidence—for the faith that is in us. One thing is certain: we cannot avoid the problem of trying to get a better measure of public opinion, for our failure to solve it would be a step in the direction which finally identifies the wishes of the people with the hysterical speeches of a "minister of enlightenment."

"Public Opinion," wrote Montaigne, "is a powerful, bold, and unmeasurable party." It is precisely *because* it is powerful and bold that we must try to devise better instruments for measuring it. In a democratic society the views of the majority must be regarded as the ultimate tribunal for social and political issues. Moreover, a large-scale democracy like our own has a special incentive to improve its knowledge of public opinion because of the fundamental need to combine maintenance of popular government with more decisive and efficient legislative action. It is far too late in the day to take refuge in blanket condemnations or in eulogies of the common man. It is not sufficient to do as some mystical democrats have done and urge that public opinion is some kind of supernatural force which will automatically operate to make democracy create the best of all possible worlds. The voice of the people is not the voice of God—at all times and under all conditions. Public opinion is not a deity, neither is it infallible. It is not something above and superior to the opinions of ordinary men and women organized in a political community. It is as good, or as bad, as the human beings whose ideas and aspirations make up the total stream of opinion. It is not the product of an omniscient group mind, but rather a dynamic process resulting from the communication and interaction of individuals in an ever-moving society. Having chosen a way of life which consults the mass of the people in the formulation of policy, we must listen to what the people themselves have to say, for public opinion can only be of service to democracy if it can be heard.

Note

1. Lederer, E., "Public Opinion," in *Political and Economic Democracy* ed. Ascoli, M., and Lehmann, F., New York, 1937. p. 291.

Democracy in Reverse

From *Public Opinion Quarterly* (1940)

Robert S. Lynd

This short article extends arguments Robert Lynd had made in *Knowledge for What* (1940), an important late-progressive call for engaged social science that would inspire intelligent social change in a world marked by irrationality, complexity, and huge disparities of power. Here Lynd both recognizes and questions the value of public opinion polls. He echoes both Walter Lippmann's claim that ordinary people are limited in their capacity to judge the issues of the day and John Dewey's pragmatist belief that techniques should be judged on the basis of how they are used. Lynd's skepticism serves as a counterweight to Gallup and Rae's almost messianic rhetoric about opinion polls, and his short critique of commercial polling remains timely today. For Lynd's bio, see p. 58.

[*Original abstract—Ed.*] *In this article, one of America's leading sociologists criticizes the fundamental assumptions upon which public opinion polls operate, and suggests that they may impede necessary social change by encouraging the public's belief in its own omni-competence to judge complex social issues, and thereby interfere with a desirable trend toward expert direction and trained intelligence in public affairs.*

No social scientist can view the recent rapid development of public opinion polls without considerable enthusiasm. Here social science is at work on the basic proposition that our institutions are not abstract Mohammed's coffins, suspended between sky and earth, but are rather grounded in and made up of the reactions of common people. And if one wants to deal realistically with what the United States is, more and more of the work of social scientists must drive straight through to the level of the habits of thought, sentiment and action of individual Americans of all types. So the public opinion polls are performing an important service, to science as well as to practical affairs, in forcing attention to the basic importance of the reactions of individuals.

Any new technique, however, is not complete in itself. Its efficacy depends on how and where and why it is used. And these last depend upon the fundamental assumptions and propositions of its users. Professor Gardner Murphy, in his presidential address to the Society for the Psychological Study of Social Issues in 1938, said: "Undoubtedly a large part of our trouble has been an over-rapid development of research techniques which can be applied to the surface aspects of almost any social response and are reasonably sure to give a publishable numerical answer to almost any casual question."

The point I want to make is that the perfecters and users of public opinion polls have thrown this important new technique into gear too rapidly and uncritically, without considering discriminatingly the framework of assumptions they are employing. Polls are news and they are also useful manipulative devices on the level of propaganda; but they may also have serious social effects which their manipulators fail to see or choose to overlook.

To be specific, our democratic institutions were formed in an era in which men had an oversimplified view of human behavior. Men were supposed to "act rationally" and men were supposed to be "free" and "equal." Such assumptions made the individual citizen a prime mover: he knew what was good for him; hedonism taught him that what was good for him was good for others; he knew the facts involved in a given matter, or, if he didn't, being rational, he went and got them before acting; and he could count on other persons' building this same sort of continuously canny behavior into all that they did. But modern psychology has taught us (a) that men are rational only fragmentarily, sporadically, and with great difficulty; (b) that they are not free, but heavily and coercively conditioned by their past and by their surroundings; and (c) that in capacity they run the gamut from imbecility to genius.

Now, unless I am mistaken, the current public opinion polls take over naively the assumptions of the Founding Fathers about human nature and about democracy. They assume that men are rational, free, and equal, and that each citizen's opinion therefore has, and should have, a weighting of one, equal to any other man's. A "majority" becomes in some mysterious sense "right." And, as the individual citizen reads the results of a poll in *Fortune* or in his morning paper, he gets a comfortable sense that *vox populi* is in the saddle and all's right with democracy.

Our Complex World

Actually, we live in a world of rapidly increasing complexity. Science, invention, the shrinking of time and space through communication, are undercutting earlier assumed simplicities as to how things work. Diet, health, family life, business, industry, foreign trade, democratic government, and all the rest of living are being transformed into a bristling array of technical formulae and expert choices. As a result, a major problem democracy faces is to persuade the individual citizen that things are not as simple as he has been wont to believe, that he is not as competent as he thinks he is, and that many issues cannot be solved simply by people's taking positions "for" or "against" them and then totaling up "the truth."

Whether we like it or not, the central issue this generation faces is the change-over from *laissez faire* individualism to the centralized coordination of complex things important to the living of the mass of the people. This entails the relinquishment by the mass of citizens of their traditionally assumed omni-competence, their recognition that complex matters require expert direction, and the re-structuring of democratic action to give clearance to trained intelligence, providing at the same time adequate democratic

controls periodically over broad matters of policy. In other words, we must persuade our citizens to take their hands off the *details* of intricate public matters and to recognize the need of delegating decisions in the highly specialized and intricate world of today to expert surrogates.

A close but sturdy line must be drawn between such a course and the quit-claiming of democratic rights under some form of fascism. But to say this is simply to state the problem we perforce face: the discovery of how to use trained intelligence and centralized direction within a framework of genuine democracy. Too much of our current democracy, operating uncritically under naïve assumptions inherited from the past, is a deceptively spurious cloak for highly undemocratic power tactics.

Now, as regards any such goal, the public opinion polls are working in reverse. They operate actually to confirm the citizen's false sense of security in totaling up "what the majority think." As such, they often obstruct the necessary line of movement ahead in public affairs. And the false sense of the public's being "boss" that they encourage operates to narcotize public awareness of the seriousness of problems and of the drastic social changes many contemporary situations require. In Chapters III and VI of *Knowledge for What?* I have tried to state my own sense of the log-jams in our American culture and of necessary lines of action ahead. Whether that particular statement is right or wrong in detail, the following generalization is certainly in order: We Americans have a false, and therefore dangerous, sense of complacency about ourselves and about the rightness of many of our inherited ways of doing things; and a crucial need today is to encourage an attitude of hospitality toward intelligent change.

Truth By Nose-Counting?

The danger in the popularization of public opinion polls is not that the technicians who operate them have an axe to grind and therefore introduce an active bias. Rather, the danger is that, in their eagerness to be "objective," they eschew all effort to formulate social propositions about public opinion. And this tends to mean too often that a basically useful device is allowed to operate as an ally of outworn and obstructive popular assumptions. The men who take the polls do not for a minute assume that they total up "the truth" about an issue. But their published results, operating within the gong matrix of naïve popular beliefs about the relation of the individual citizen to democratic action, aid and abet the citizen in his propensity to believe that the truth somehow mystically lies with "the majority."

Our American traditions discourage our government from a systematic, long-term policy of reducing lags through continuous application of intelligent education and propaganda at all points in current living where intelligence suggests the wisdom of social change. Sooner or later we will forsake *laissez faire*. Meanwhile, public opinion polls can help to that end by an active policy of polling people satisfied by competence on a

given problem, aimed at disclosing and hammering home to the public the operational poverty of mass opinion on the details of many public matters involving social change. Mass conservatism as regards intelligent things that must be done is irrelevant save as an obstacle to be removed.

A major barrier to such a socially constructive use of public opinion polls is that these polls are in private hands for private profit and Dr. Gallup and *Fortune* live and grow rich by perpetuating the public's sense of the competence of its opinions. The bigger and more complex an issue, the more does it clamor to them for a poll. And, as the world of business is run, those who live by taking polls can hardly be expected to disabuse the public of its false confidence.

23

Needed Research in Communication

From the *Rockefeller Archives* (1940)

Lyman Bryson, Lloyd A. Free, Geoffrey Gorer, Harold D. Lasswell, Paul F. Lazarsfeld, Robert S. Lynd, John Marshall, Charles A. Siepmann, Donald Slesinger, and Douglas Waples

The Rockefeller Communications Group was one of the first efforts to study mass communication in a systematic, interdisciplinary way. Led by John Marshall, who directed the Rockefeller Foundation's work on communication in the late 1930s, this group gathered a diverse set of experts that included Harold Lasswell, Paul Lazarsfeld, and Robert Lynd (who are all represented in this reader), as well as anthropologists, library scientists, film critics, broadcasters, and even I. A. Richards, the literary critic and coinventor of Basic English (a collection of 850 English words that were supposed to cover the needs of everyday life). These discussions took place in New York City from September 1939 to June 1940. "Needed Research on Communication" is the group's summary statement and is, in a sense, the founding document of mass communication research. This excerpt conveys the urgent mission envisioned for communication research, as war clouds loomed on the American horizon. It also clearly predicts empirical social research as serving a clear democratic function in providing two-way interaction between the rulers and the ruled. In the conviction that gathering knowledge about society is not merely description but also communication—that is, a way of opening two-way communication—the group clearly shows a spiritual debt to the thought of John Dewey, who taught Lynd, influenced Lasswell, and was associated with Columbia University at this time. Administrative research is in many respects one of the legacies of John Dewey's instrumentalist philosophy, yet the Rockefeller Group's faith in facts and expertise also led them away from Dewey's radical democracy and toward more technocratic solutions to social problems. In its conflicted elitist and democratic vision of social science, the Rockefeller Communications Group embodies many of the tensions inherent to mid-twentieth-century liberalism, as Gary's *The Nervous Liberals* (1999) demonstrates.

This memorandum asserts, first, that facts, not now available, are urgently needed to provide a basis for more effective communication. Second, that the means of getting the needed facts are ready to hand. Third, that getting them must be closely geared to making communication more effective. It recommends that the work of getting them be begun at once.

Section I (pp. 3–6) gives the background of these assertions. Section II (pp. 7–17) attempts to show by concrete illustration what research in communication is now ready and able to contribute. Section III (pp. 18–22) indicates how that contribution can be promptly realized.

This memorandum grows out of a series of informal discussions over a period from September, 1939, to June, 1940. During these discussions several memoranda were presented by members of the group, or by invitation. At one time it was thought that these several documents might be joined together, at leisure, and circulated to a wider audience. However, the problems of national defense have become so urgent that it was agreed that a briefer statement would be of interest. The general remarks in the present statement are fortified at all points by the more technical material that was considered by the conferees.

The present memorandum took shape in a final discussion held in June, in which those signing the memorandum participated. In the course of the year, however, a number of others took part in the discussions, the most regular participants in addition to the signers of this memorandum being Stacy May and I. A. Richards.

The views expressed in the memorandum are, of course, only the personal views of those signing it and can in no way be regarded as representative of the organizations or institutions to which they are attached. They are now sending the memorandum to a few of their acquaintances to whom they think it may be of interest, with the understanding that it is for private circulation only and not to be quoted or made public in any way. They would, of course, welcome any comments or criticisms which readers of the memorandum may care to offer.

I. A Background of Public Policy

This memorandum proceeds from two assumptions. First, that events are obliging our central government to take on wider and wider responsibility for the welfare of the people. Second, that, if the exercise of that responsibility is to be democratic, more effective ways of keeping the government and the people in communication with each other will have to be created.

Decisions crucial for the general welfare must today be made with a maximum of speed. That the central government must assume a wider responsibility for decision, few will question. But few, likewise, will doubt that this widening of its responsibility may endanger our democracy.

Democracy, after all, cannot survive without two-way communication. In other forms of government, only the government has authority to propose and to decide. It may perhaps explain; but the people can only give assent. From democratic government comes a stream of proposal, explanation, and decision. From the people comes an answering stream of counter-proposal, explanation, and consent, which the government takes into account in final decision and administration. If this two-way process of communication does not function, democracy *is* endangered.

Already, the pace of governmental decision in this country, particularly in foreign affairs and national defense, is outstripping that of explanation. Adequate explanation is not reaching all the people whose lives, even now, are being changed by decisions already made. The gap between the government and the people is widening. Indicative of that gap is the growth of interest, both among the people and in the government, in the national polls of public opinion. For the polls, whatever else they do, enable the people to make known their answers to such questions as are put to them.

If the government and the people are to keep in touch, more effective ways of communicating will have to be created. The government must have better ways of explaining to the people what it proposes or decides. And the people must have better ways of explaining to the government how they feel themselves affected by its proposals or decisions.

Clearly, a more effective use of the available means of communication—print, radio and film—will be necessary. Presumably measures to ensure this use will shortly have to be decided on. What these will be—reliance on private enterprise alone, private enterprise with varying degrees of government supervision and control, or government control and operation—is not here in question.

It is the thesis of this memorandum that whatever form those measures take, research will be essential to make communication a two-way process. More effective communication from the government will require getting promptly to the people adequate explanations of proposals or decisions which change their lives. In this, existing skill in communication will play its part. But skill alone will not suffice. Skill will require new facts to work with. Who is affected, and in what ways? How can they be reached, and promptly reached? What types of explanation are adequate, for whom, and on what subject? Research to provide the factual answers to such questions will be essential, if explanation is to be both prompt and adequate.

Research will also be essential to report how the people feel themselves affected by proposals or decisions thus explained. To what extent do they consent to what the government proposes or decides? What underlies their consent, dissent, or indifference, and among what sections of the people? What have they to say of the proposal that may make advisable its modification or even its withdrawal? Research, by answering such

questions, can give the people a more effective way of communicating with their government than now exists.

Research, then, will be doubly essential to two-way communication, first, to supply facts needed to make explanation both prompt and adequate; and, second, to bring back from the people an equally prompt and adequate response. With such research, the present gap between the government and the people can be closed. The government can then exercise its wider responsibility without risking loss of confidence and impaired morale. The people then can sanction changes in their lives with the assurance that their government has taken their responses into account, and that, in its view, the costs of change are justified by other gains.

Techniques for such research have long since been developed and tested in marketing, in advertising, and in managing public relations for private purposes. In scientific inquiry, particularly in psychology, sociology, and political science, these techniques have been the means of reaching findings which are no longer open to serious question. Research using these techniques has now for some time been providing facts of acknowledged value for private and scientific purposes. The same techniques can be regularly used in the public interest to provide facts of equal value for making communication the vital two-way process the times require.

Comparable facts are now recognized as indispensable in fields of public interest other than communication. Skill in economic policy, for example, now depends on the reliable reporting of facts about finance, trade, production, and consumption. As yet, skill in the use of our means of communication has too few facts on which it can depend. It will need new facts, whatever measures are decided on to ensure a two-way flow of communication. Research can quickly supply those facts, if existing facilities for research—techniques and personnel—are put to work.

What is meant by such research, and what facts it can supply, the following section attempts to make concrete.

24

On Borrowed Experience: An Analysis of Listening to Daytime Sketches

From *Studies in Philosophy and Social Science* (1941)

Herta Herzog

Herta Herzog Massing (b. 1910) was a pioneer in early radio studies in her native Vienna and in the United States. Fascinated by Freudianism but interested in empirical research methods, she studied at Karl and Charlotte Bühler's influential Psychological Institute at the University of Vienna, where she produced one of the first studies (1933) of the perception of voices over the radio and where she also met her future husband, Paul Lazarsfeld (she was the second of three talented and intellectual women who married Lazarsfeld, after Marie Jahoda and before Patricia Kendall). In the United States, Herzog found work as an assistant on communications research projects—a typical fate for female scholars in that time—and she later became one of the authors of *The Invasion from Mars* (1940). She worked for many years in New York City at the advertising agency McCann-Erickson and now lives in Austria. She is remembered as one of the most important and pioneering students of media audiences (Liebes, 2003).

Herzog's research on radio audiences, including those of quiz shows and Iowa farmwives, helped answer one of the puzzles facing the early radio industry: just who is listening and why do they do so? She conducted the first of what later became known as "gratification studies," using lightly Freudian categories to identify the psychological pleasures generated through spectatorship. She argues that listeners make use of sympathy, catharsis, or *Schadenfreude* (enjoyment obtained through the troubles of others) to project themselves into or away from the radio world. In contrast to later students of media audiences, Herzog does not give a favorable picture of the audience or of its intelligence; her psychoanalytic language and relative lack of sympathy for popular media genres such as soap operas tend to unmask people's motives rather than praise them for their active ingenuity, as is more common in audience research today.

If, on an average weekday, one could see at a glance what all the women throughout the country are doing at a specific time, he would find at least two million of them listening to a so-called "daytime serial." Some of these women would just be sitting in front of the radio; most of them would be doing some housework at the same time; but all of these two millions would attentively follow the day's installment of a dramatization which mirrors scenes from the everyday life of middle class people. A number of these stories have gone on for eight years. Each day's episode is introduced by a short summary of the previous day's events, and winds up with questions preparing for the coming sequel. "What will Mrs. X do tomorrow?" "Will Fate catch up with Mr. Y?"

A program of this kind lasts fifteen minutes, and when it is finished another serial comes on the air. Often eight or ten such programs follow one another without interruption other than the voice of the announcer who tells about the product and the company sponsoring the particular dramatization. There are between two and three hundred stories broadcast over American stations during the day, and in one of the larger cities a woman can listen to a score or two of them between morning and evening without more effort than an occasional switch of the dial from one station to another.

Since the life of very many middle class and lower middle class people is uneventful, the variety of incidents in these programs is many times greater than anything which these women could live through or observe themselves. Thus the question comes up of whether, through daytime serials, radio is likely to have a great influence upon the attitude of these listeners toward their own lives and the problems they have to meet.

To determine the effect of these programs seems an urgent, but by no means easy task of contemporary social research. One would have to study their content very carefully. One would have to know which women listen and which women do not listen. Most of all, one would have to check periodically, with a great variety of listeners, to see whether there are any changes in their way of thinking and living which could be traced to the programs.

The present study has tried to prepare the way for such a larger enterprise by reporting on interviews with a number of women who listen regularly and were asked about what these programs mean to them, why they listen, and what they do with what they hear. It is intended to give a picture of these women's reactions and to develop a conceptual framework which would be helpful for future, more elaborate analysis.

The Material

The report is based on personal interviews obtained within the last two years with 100 women living in Greater New York. An effort was made to cover women in various age and income groups. Most of the persons interviewed were housewives, some had worked previous to their marriage, others had not. Among them were also a few high school students and a number of maids. All the women interviewed listened to at least two daytime serials regularly,[1] the number actually listened to varying from two to 22 programs daily. Thus, the study must be considered an analysis of fan listeners.

The first twenty interviews were made as "open" interviews to cover the ground thoroughly. From these discussions a questionnaire was developed which, in its final form, was used for the second half of the sample. The questionnaire covered the listening habits of the respondents, a detailed discussion of the favorite programs of each, a number of questions trying to get at the general appeal of the programs, and finally, some information about the listeners themselves, such as their reading habits, social activities, hobbies or special interests, favorite movies, and the things they wanted most in life. The questionnaire is attached in the Appendix.

"Getting into Trouble and Out Again"

The listeners' reports on the content of their favorite stories boils down almost invariably to one stereotyped formula. Contents of various programs are described as "getting into trouble and out again." Following are a few answers given by the people studied when they were asked to describe their favorite story.

I like DAVID HARUM. It is about a town philosopher who solves everyone's problems, even his enemies'. He is also in the races. Right now his horse has been poisoned and someone stole the body. They are trying to figure out why. *He always is in trouble and out again.*

My favorite is SOCIETY GIRL. The story is about a young man who marries the boss's daughter. The boss buys them a beautiful estate on Long Island. They are *going to have some kind of trouble* about the old graveyard and a tombstone which has been tampered with. They *will find a way out,* though.

I like the O'NEILLS. It is about a widowed mother and her children and grandchildren. The twins offer many problems. The son gets into riots, and the daughter may go to Chicago. But Ma O'Neill will *settle everything,* and *something else will come up.*

The average number of daytime serials listened to regularly by the women in this study is 6.6 programs. Very few of the listeners said "yes" to the question whether they were only listening "because there was nothing else on at this particular time of the day," When asked whether they selected the programs to fit their daily work-schedule or whether they adjusted their schedule to fit the programs, 31 per cent said the latter. Three-fourths of the listeners claimed they had never been "bored" with their favorite story, while 57 per cent could not mention any incident in the stories listened to which they had disliked in any way.

These data indicate an intensive and obviously quite satisfactory consumption of radio stories. How does this tie in with the fact that the "getting into trouble and out again" formula is applied to all the sketches? Why is it that people do not get tired of stories with the same theme?

Programs Picked to Match the Listener's Problems

The listeners studied do not experience the sketches as fictitious or imaginary. They take them as reality and listen to them in terms of their own personal problems. Listeners to the same sketch agree about its "trouble" content, but find it realized in quite different ways. The following comments were made by women who listened to the same program, namely, ROAD OF LIFE.

It is concerning a doctor, his life and how he always tries to do the right thing. Sometimes he gets left out in the cold too.

Dr. Brent is a wonderful man, taking such good care of a poor little orphan boy. He is doing God's work.

It is a drama, Jim Brent and Dr. Parsons—jealousy, you know. There are several characters, but Jim Brent is the important one. He will win out in the end.

It is about a young doctor in Chicago. I like to hear how he cures sick people. It makes me wonder whether he could cure me too.

All of these listeners look for the "troubles" in the story and how they are solved, but each interprets the "trouble" situation according to her own problems. Thus, for example, a sick listener stresses the sick people cured by the doctor in the story. The young high school girl, who wishes she knew interesting people like Dr. Brent, picks the jealousy aspect of the story and the way Dr. Brent stands up to it. The woman over forty, with the memory of a sad childhood, insists that Dr. Brent "is doing God's work." And the mother sacrificing herself for an unappreciative family feels a common bond in the fact that "sometimes he (Dr. Brent) is left out in the cold too."

Each of these women also listens to a number of other programs. In picking the programs she likes, she selects those presenting problems which are to her mind most intimately related to her own. Sometimes all the stories listened to have the same central theme to the listener. Thus the woman quoted above, who likes Dr. Brent because of his kindness to the orphan boy, listens to four other programs which have a "kind adult" for one of their leading characters. Her comment on RIGHT TO HAPPINESS is: "The mother is a fine woman. She gave her life up for her child." Of HILLTOP HOUSE she says: "The woman there is not getting married because she has to take care of the orphanage." She also listens to MYRT AND MARGE and THE O'NEILLS, which she describes in similar terms as having a "kind mother" as the leading character.

Similarly, the young high school girl who would like to know a person like Dr. Brent listens, in addition to ROAD OF LIFE, to two more programs, which she describes as "love stories." They are OUR GAL SUNDAY and HELEN TRENT.

Sometimes the listeners go through quite a complicated process of shifting and exchanging incidents and characters in their favorite stories to suit their own particular needs. This behavior was brought out clearly in the case of a middle aged quite balanced woman whose chief interest in life is her family. She listens to only two radio programs because she claims she has "no time for more." Listening for her has the function of keeping alive the contact with the various members of her family when the real members are at work or in school. Her favorite story is PEPPER YOUNG'S FAMILY. She is interested in it because "the son there acts against his father just the way our son does." But she doesn't care for the mother in this sketch because "she is too submissive"; so she turns to a second program, THE WOMAN IN WHITE, for there "the woman is boss." By scrambling the mother in the one sketch with the father and son in the other she establishes a family situation which she considers most "similar" to her own. To use her own words, the programs "help keep her company" when she is at home alone.

The more complex the listener's troubles are or the less able she is to cope with them, the more programs she seems to listen to. Thus we find on the one hand the woman quoted above who listens to only two programs because she has "no time" for more—that is, probably "no need" for more. On the other hand is the extreme case of a colored maid in a home with no fewer than five radios in it, who listens to twenty-two stories daily. To this person of very little education, with no friends or relatives and few opportunities for a normal life, the radio stories are practically everything. "Sunday," she said, "is a very bad day for me. I don't know what to do with myself. During the week I have the stories." When asked how long, in her opinion, a story should last, misunderstanding the reason for the question she said anxiously, "They're not going to stop them, are they? I'd be lost without them!"

Having no life apart from the stories, this listener wants to listen to as many of them and as long as she possibly can. Since all the stories have the common theme of getting into trouble and out again, it is possible for the listener to combine aspects of various stories into a sort of patchwork of "reality" which best fits her particular needs.

Three Main Types of Gratification

Basically the various stories mean the same thing to all the listeners. They appeal to their insecurity and provide them in one way or another with remedies of a substitute character. This occurs in, roughly, three types of reactions, which are differentiated as modes of experience but not in terms of their function.

1. Listening to the stories offers an emotional release.
2. Listening to the stories allows for a wishful remodelling of the listener's "drudgery."
3. Listening provides an ideology and recipes for adjustment.

Some of the listeners enjoy the stories primarily as a means of letting themselves go emotionally. Others enjoy them because they provide the opportunity to fill their lives with happenings which they would like to experience for themselves. Still others enjoy them in a more realistic way because they furnish them with formulas to bear the kind of life they are living.

Following is a detailed description of how these various types of gratification come about.[2]

I. Listening as an Emotional Release

Many of the listeners become emotionally excited when listening to the stories. When asked whether they had ever been "very excited" about a story, 50 per cent of them said yes. A number

also claimed they could not work while listening. Said one of them: "I can't even do my crocheting when I am listening. I just have to sit still, they get me so excited." The claims of excitement aroused by listening were corroborated by actual observations of some of the respondents while they listened to a story. Such observations were made in a casual and thus quite reliable manner. If for instance a woman complained that the interview interfered with her favorite story, the interviewer politely offered to listen with her and postponed the interview until afterward. In this way it was actually observed how excited some of the listeners became, how they were talking back to the radio, warning the heroes, and so on.

Listening to the stories provides for emotional release in various forms. It provides an outlet for the pent-up anxieties in giving the listener a "chance to cry." It provides, secondly, emotional stimuli and excitement to a listener who is temperamentally unable to have such emotional experiences otherwise or who lives a kind of life which just does not provide such stimuli. Third, it gives the listener a chance to compensate for her own hardships through aggressiveness against other people. Sometimes such tendencies of aggressiveness are satisfied within the stories themselves by giving the listener the opportunity to enjoy "other people's troubles." Sometimes the stories serve as a means to feel vastly superior to people in the actual environment of the listener. Building a "union of sufferers" with the characters of the story, the listener becomes contemptuous and aggressive against members of the world actually surrounding her.

A Chance to Cry Several of the respondents like the sketches because they give them a chance to let themselves go and to release the anxiety stored up in them. This is what the crippled listener already quoted said:

> In a case like mine you can go crazy just sitting and thinking, thinking. Sometimes the stories get me and I cry. I think I am a fool, but it makes me feel better.

Another case is that of a newly married young woman. She used to work before she was married; now she has to live with her in-laws and is quite upset over the narrowness of her new life. She turned to the radio stories originally in order to have something to talk about with her mother-in-law. She said:

There is no one program I like particularly well. They all tug at the heart-strings, they are so sad. I am very nervous sometimes, but my troubles are such stupid ones. I love to listen to the programs; I can cry with them.

The sketches, in their *specific* sad content, serve as an outlet for the *unspecific* anxiety of this listener. They give her a chance to cry, which is gratifying for two reasons. First, many adults would deny themselves the "right" to cry over themselves. Having outgrown the status of the child who could come and cry on its mother's lap, they have lost the comfort of an emotional release in spite of the increase in problems demanding such release. In the second place, the stories allow for crying without the listener's having to reveal the real reasons for her wanting to cry.

In other instances the programs are enjoyed not as an outlet but as a stimulus for an emotional excitement which the listener misses in actual life.

"Surprise, Happy or Sad" The above is the comment of a woman who says she has always enjoyed life. She mentions nothing that she would like to have. She feels that the troubles in radio stories are about the same as her own. "But," as she says, "they can make more of it. They can put them on a big scale." She herself is middle aged, excessively fat, placid, and barely able to read or write. Anything that moves her is "fine." She wants the stories to "go on forever." She likes HELEN TRENT because:

She has hundreds of experiences with her designing, and all. There is always a surprise coming up. Happy or sad, I love it.

When asked whether she would prefer to have her favorite story happen to her in actual life she answered with a decided no. "I am too old," she said. "When you get older you give all that (romance) up."

Similarly, the young woman quoted before, who finds relief in crying over the stories, says she would rather lead a "peaceful life" than have the actual experiences as told in the stories. The listeners prefer the release of being moved to the moving experience itself. They accept the stories as a substitute for reality, just as they identify themselves with the content of the stories and take, as will be seen, the success of the heroine as a substitute for their own success.

The stories make for a short-lived pseudo-catharsis. The laughing or crying produced by them makes the listeners feel better only as long as the story lasts. They keep asking for new "surprises" and new "chances to cry," in the realization that their actual lives will not give them the emotional experiences they crave. "I am too old for romance," says one woman. "My life would make a stupid story," says another. Thus the question might be raised of whether the temporary emotional release obtained from listening to other people's troubles will not, in the long run, have to be paid for by an intensified sense of frustration and by the listener's having been rendered still more incapable of realizing emotional experiences outside the stories.

"If I'm Blue it Makes Me Feel Better ..." A number of the listeners said they felt a sense of relief in knowing that "other people had their troubles too." In a few cases this relief is tied up with the fact that in finding out about other people's troubles the listener loses the sense of having been singled out for trouble herself. In a few others it seems related to the stories' helpfulness in focusing a general sense of frustration upon events or things which "happen." If one knows what is wrong, and if this happens to be a particular "event," rather than the structure of the society one lives in, it makes for a release of anxiety. Most frequently, however, the listeners enjoy the troubles of other people as a means to compensate for their own misery through aggressiveness against others. The stories provide the listeners with subjects to be aggressive against.

Some of the respondents find a particular relief in listening to the troubles of other people who are supposedly "smarter" than they are. In the words of one of them:

If I am gloomy it makes me feel better to know that other people have hardships too. They are so smart and still they have to suffer.

The listeners also enjoy the stories as an outlet for feelings of aggressiveness which they would not allow themselves otherwise. An example is the reaction of a listener describing herself as a "religous" woman. She reads no other book but the Bible and dislikes the movies because they are not "clean." She approves, however, of the radio stories because the people in them "are so brave about their own troubles and in helping other people. They teach you to be good." Although she claims she listens to "learn to be still more helpful," the episode she liked best was one which dealt with a catastrophe suffered by the heroine:

> I liked it best when they were so happy before the husband got murdered and so sad afterwards.

The interest in other people's misfortunes was also brought out in the answers to the question whether and about which incidents the respondents had ever been very much excited. Forty-one per cent of those who answered in the affirmative referred to murders, violent accidents, gangsters, and fires; 15 per cent more mentioned illness and dying; 26 per cent spoke of psychological conflicts, while only 18 per cent named incidents of a non-violent or non-catastrophic kind. The aggressive meaning of these answers was exemplified rather strikingly in the following comment of a listener who explained why she never had been really excited. Referring to WOMAN IN WHITE she said:

> I thought the murder *would* be exciting. But it was not. It happened abroad somewhere.

How closely the aggressiveness against the radio characters is tied up with the listener's desire to find compensation for her own troubles is demonstrated in the following remark of a listener. She has had a hard time bringing up her children after her husband's death. She chooses programs which have as their heroine a self-sacrificing woman. Her comment about one of them is:

> I like HILLTOP HOUSE. The woman there is always doing things for children . . . I wonder whether she will ever get married. Perhaps it isn't right for her to do it and give up the orphanage. She is doing such a wonderful thing. I really don't think she should get married.

This listener compensates for her resented fate by wishing a slightly worse one upon her favorite radio character. In return for the death of her own husband she wants the heroine to have no husband at all. She expects her to sacrifice herself for orphan children, whereas she herself is sacrificing herself for her own.

In the examples given so far the listeners found scapegoats for aggressiveness within the stories themselves. In the cases which will be reported below the stories serve as a means to bolster up tendencies of aggressiveness which are directed against people in the listeners' actual environment.

The Union of Sufferers   Some of the listeners use the stories to magnify their own "suffering." In identifying their sacrifices with those in the stories they find a means to label and to enhance their own. When one of the respondents was asked the routine question about whether she was married and whether she had any children, she gave the following information. She was a widow and she had been living with her only son. Recently, however, she had moved away from her son's apartment so as "not to be in his way." She was induced to make this sacrifice by her favorite story, STELLA DALLAS. Her comment on the heroine which was made at some other point of the interview, was:

> She is like me. She also does not want to be in her daughter's way . . . How does she look? Well, she is a regular person, one in a thousand, always doing the right thing. She is getting tired and haggard. She has just spent herself.

It is possible that this listener did move away from her son's apartment to be like "Stella Dallas." We do not know how voluntary this act of hers was or how much it was appreciated. In any case, her identification with the radio heroine who has "spent herself" gives the listener a chance to make the most of her own act of tolerance and self-sacrifice.

Such identified tolerance sometimes gives the listener a feeling of superiority. She feels different from other people. Admiring the radio characters excessively, she imagines she is like them. While rising to new heights of "tolerance" in this identification, she becomes at the same time contemptuous and critical of the world around her. An example of this may be found in the following two remarks by a woman who listens to the programs because the people in them are so "wonderful":

> They teach you how to be good. I have gone through a lot of suffering, but I still can learn from them.

Yet this same woman, when asked whether she disliked any program, answered:

> I don't listen to THE GOLDBERGS. Why waste electricity on the Jews?

Obviously her "tolerance" wasn't wide enough to include the Jews. It seems rather a means to feel superior to them.

An example of the manner in which the stories are used as an excuse for being critical of people in the listener's actual environment is the case of a woman living in the neighborhood known as Greenwich Village. She "loathes it." When asked what she wanted most in life she said: "A home in the country, just for me and my family, with a *white fence* around it."

She admires the programs because they portray the "clean American life," as contrasted to the hated "Village." Admiration for the radio people is for her a means to exaggerate her contempt against the world surrounding her while at the same time providing for a fence against it.

II. Listening As a Means of Remodelling One's Drudgery

In the various forms of gratification characterized as "emotional release," listening makes for the stimulation or the release of emotions which the listener would not be able to feel or allow herself to enjoy otherwise. The story content is only indirectly important insofar as it provides a sufficiently strong emotional appeal.

In the cases to be described now the connection between the radio stories and the listener's situation is of a much more comprehensive character. Emphasis is on the specific content of the story rather than on its emotional appeal. The listener pretends that what is happening in the stories is happening to her. She not only feels *with* the radio characters, like the person who gets emotional release from listening; she *is* the characters. Accepting the story content as a substitute for reality, she uses it to remodel her life. In this type of experience the distinction between "story" reality and actual reality is destroyed by wishful thinking.

Drowning One's Troubles In the most radical form of identification the listener escapes into the story quite consciously. She makes use of the stories to superimpose upon her life another, more desirable life. Listening works as a potent drug making her forget her own troubles while listening to those described in the stories. One of these listeners said:

> I can hardly wait from Friday till Monday, when the stories come on again. They make me forget my own troubles. I have only

money problems. They don't. Their troubles are more complicated, but also more exciting. Also, they can solve them. For instance, they just hop into a plane when they want to go to Washington. Money doesn't seem to matter to them. In the stories there is real romance. I love to hear about romance. I keep waiting for David to propose.

The stories are as real to the listener as an actual experience. She experiences the romance of MARY MARLIN as if it were her own.

A romance experienced by means of the story is a satisfactory substitute for a real life experience, because of two conditions which do not exist in reality. For one, happenings in the stories are to a large extent determined by the listener's desires. If she wants a romance she selects a program which gives it to her. Within the story, the listener still has a choice in terms of "how it ought to be." If MARY MARLIN in the story does not get enough romance the listener may still feel:

> *I* would have made David propose months ago. They don't have to make him the perfect bachelor. I would have made him slip.

If the listener feels the story is not going to develop at all the way she wants it to, she may even discontinue listening and look for another story. Such discontinuation of listening to a program which had been listened to regularly before was reported by 63 per cent. In two-thirds of the cases the reasons were external, such as the program having gone off the air. In one-third the program was no longer listened to because of the listeners' disapproval. The most frequent reasons were that it was "too improbable," or "too monotonous." Both these objections in most cases meant merely that the program was not developing fast enough or not in the direction the listener hoped it would. This is brought out quite clearly in the comment of a listener who stopped listening to HELEN TRENT:

> I stopped listening when Helen Trent went to Hollywood. It was so improbable. I have been in Hollywood myself. It is an awful place. Wives lose their husbands there. Why did she not go to some nice, safe place? There are a lot of them in this country.

The program was considered "improbable" because its expected course threatened to interfere with the listener's desire to hear about "nice," that is, "safe" places and relationships.

Secondly, listening provides the chance to live "exciting lives" while one "relaxes" and "smokes a cigarette." As mentioned already, hardly any of the listeners would prefer to have the incidents of the stories actually happen to them instead of hearing them over the radio. They enjoy a condition in which they may lose themselves in an excitement related to borrowed rather than to their own experiences.

Examples of complete escape into the stories, such as the one quoted above, were not frequent among the women studied. This is probably due to the character of the stories. They supposedly portray everyday life and contain at least so many allusions to it that they do not allow very easily for a complete forgetting of the listeners' own drudgery. For the most part the listeners studied select certain aspects of the stories to fit into their lives in such a way as to make them more interesting or more agreeable. Such glorification of the listeners' own life goes all the way from finding fulfillment of desires which are not fully satisfied in life to finding compensation for personal failure in borrowing the story-character's success.

Cultivating the "Happy" Aspects   Some of the respondents use the radio programs to get more of the kind of experiences which they claim to enjoy in real life. An example is the case of a young married woman who likes to listen to "some other happy marriages." She says:

> I just love to listen to those programs. Dr. Brent is like a second husband. After all, I can get married only once. I would love to have some more husbands.

We cannot tell from our data whether the listener is as happily married as she claims to be. The Dr. Brent in the story is not an admitted substitute for her real husband. Very likely, however, the desires for her marriage are greater than their fulfillment and listening to Dr. Brent as a "second husband" is used to make up for it.

Similarly, another "happily married" woman says: "I like to snatch romance wherever I can get more of it."

In both instances there is the desire to use the stories as a means of duplicating what one already has. The added quantity provides a substitute for an intensity of experience which is probably lacking in real life.

Filling in the Gaps   Still others use the programs to inject into their lives elements which they admittedly miss in actual life. Here belongs the woman married to a sick husband whom she loves very much. Her favorite program is VIC AND SADE and she especially likes the "funny episodes" in it. She says:

> Since my husband got sick we haven't had much fun. I love to listen to VIC AND SADE. They are like us. Vic looks like my husband. Many funny things happen to them. I always tell my husband about them.

The episode she liked best was the one in which Sade mixed up her shoes at a friend's party and came home with one shoe that was hers and one that was not. This listener probably feels tied down in a marriage which, at the moment, seems to be based primarily on loyalty. Telling her husband about the funny episodes happening to the couple in the story serves as a substitute for their actual occurrence.

One of the gratifications of this type most interesting from a sociological point of view is tied up with stories of doctors as the leading characters. Listening to such stories is a source of extreme gratification not only for the old spinster or the widow:

> Dr. Brent is such a lovely man. He takes care of physical and spiritual problems of all the people who come to him. He reminds me a little bit of my own doctor, but I think Dr. Brent is a younger and more lovable man.

> My husband died and my brother had a stroke. I really don't have anybody to talk to, and I would have needed advice in the tragedy which happened to my daughter. Dr. Brent is such a fine man. It helps me to listen to him. I really have him right in my room.

The kind and efficient Dr. Brent is enjoyed also by the woman who said, at one point in the interview: "At home *I* am the boss," indicating that she does not consider her husband qualified to be. Dr. Brent is loved, too, by the girl who wishes she knew "another person like him." Women in all phases of life seem to have a frequently unfulfilled need for the kind and able male who is protector rather than economic provider or competitor. The doctor of the story fits into this gap. He acquires a kind of father-role for the listener.[3]

Reviving Things Past   Some listeners use the stories to revive things that are past and gone. The associations provided by the stories serve to carry them back to other, more pleasant times. Thus a woman, who was brought up in a small town and feels homesick for it, finds in DAVID HARUM a chance to get back to the small-town life she once knew. Says this listener:

> I like to listen to DAVID HARUM and his homely philosophy. It is about a small town. I was brought up in one too, and I loved it.

Another woman likes OUR GAL SUNDAY because she herself grew up in a mining town. Listening to the story reminds her of "home." She says:

> OUR GAL SUNDAY is about a poor girl found on a doorstep. She is raised by two men in a mining town, and when she grows up she marries a lord. The part about the mining town reminds me of my own life, for I was brought up in one too. I am so far away and there's nobody here to remind me of it otherwise.

Sometimes it is persons, and not situations, that are remembered, as in the case of a listener who said, referring to THE GOLDBERGS:

> Ma Goldberg reminds me of a woman I used to know as a kid. She lived right next door. She was always finding excuses when we didn't behave well. She was always saying good things.

Thirty-nine per cent of the listeners stated they had known "similar" people, while 27 per cent said they had come across "similar" situations to those described in some of the stories. The difference between the two figures must first be proven in a larger sample before an interpretation ought to be ventured. Even in the small sample tested, both figures were significantly higher than the number of cases whose primary source of gratification was related to the familiarity with the persons or situations depicted in the program. Associations with the past account for the primary enjoyment of a program only if the memories evoked are a highly suitable substitute for a less desirable present. This is illustrated in the following comment of a respondent:

> I like to listen to HELEN TRENT. Her romance sounds like mine. My husband was always so lovable and affectionate. He never squab-bled. We were very happy, and still are. This story brings back my romance after nineteen years.

This woman was probably not aware that in telling her story she invariably used the past tense. Her "we are still happy" exemplifies exactly the kind of gratification she gets from listening. There is probably more "squabbling" now between herself and her husband. She enjoys HELEN TRENT as the chance to relive her own early love experiences by pretending that what was true nineteen years ago is still true today.

For the listener it seems more important that the story evokes a memory which allows for wishful thinking than that the similarity between story situation and remembered situation is a complete one. If the listener would like very much that what happens in the story would actually happen to her, she is likely to construct "similarities" in an artificial manner. This is exemplified in the comment of a 55 year old woman who also listens to the romance of HELEN TRENT because it reminds her of experiences of her youth. When she was asked whether she had ever used any product of a sponsoring company, she said:

> I use the face cream advertised by HELEN TRENT because she is using it and she is over 35 years herself and still has all those romances.

This listener does not seem quite convinced about the applicability of the story. By using the beautifying cream that her heroine uses she adds supporting evidence to the rather weak and wishful analogy between herself and Helen Trent. The product, particularly if tied up with the story in such an intricate manner, is the link between the world of story happenings and reality. Through the real face cream the fictitious happenings of the stories are brought within the realm of possible occurrences.[4]

Compensating for Failure through Identification with Success   A great number of the women use the stories to compensate for specific personal failures. They enjoy listening to the success the radio heroine is having in the field where they themselves have failed. When one of the women was asked what she wanted most in life she said, "A happy marriage." She also said that she didn't like to have company because her husband might be "rude" to them. This woman picks as her favorites stories in which "a woman puts things over." Her comment is interesting:

> I like EASY ACES. There is a dumb woman and she puts things over. I also like HILLTOP HOUSE. The woman in it is always doing things. She has no time to marry.

This listener's comment on HILLTOP HOUSE is very different from the comments of other listeners to the same program. Instead of stressing the self-sacrificing and "doing good" elements she interprets the story in terms of her own difficulties and failures. According to her, the heroine "has no time to marry," and she sees in her the "independent" rather than the "good" woman.

Still another of the listeners seems to have been a failure in her family relations. Her daughter has run away from home to marry, and of her husband she says, "He is away from home five nights of the week." She picks programs like THE GOLDBERGS or THE O'NEILLS, each portraying a successful mother or wife. She says:

> I like the O'NEILLS. It stresses harmony and yet it portrays the individuality of family members.

At the same time she is quite critical of Ma O'Neill and says:

> No woman can be that divine and keep her ideals that long.

And of Ma Goldberg she says:

> I have no such hysteria and excitement as Ma Goldberg has. I would never butt into other people's lives as she does.

Why does she go on listening if she disapproves of the leading characters? Obviously she would not be able to bear the thought that other women are so much more successful than she if she could not find any fault with them. She has to tell herself that the stories are not quite true to life or that MA GOLDBERG is not a pleasant personality type if she wants to enjoy listening to them. Her superficial criticism of the stories is the condition for her being able to use them as fully as substitutes as she actually does.

Betting on Outcomes as a Means of Feeling Superior A few of the better educated among the respondents disclaimed any personal interest in the stories and said they listened only for entertainment. They were interested in seeing "how problems are treated" or "how things come out." One of them said:

> I used to go to work previously. This always gave me a lift. I have nothing to keep me busy now. I listen to the programs for no personal reasons. I want to see how problems are treated. I'm usually right in my predictions.

These listeners do not have a "personal" interest in the stories in the sense that they want to identify with, or escape into, the content of the stories. They use the stories chiefly as a means to demonstrate to themselves or some of their co-listeners that they were right in predicting the outcome.[5] If things do not turn out as they predicted, they can always claim that the stories aren't true to life. In passing judgment on script writers and actors they consider themselves superior to those who "take such stories seriously." They feel on a level with powerful people who are controlling things rather than being controlled.

The feeling of superiority connected with such a "detached" appraisal of the stories is illustrated in the following comment:

> I like SCATTERGOOD BAINES. It is a New England situation. He is one of Clarence Budington Kelland's best characters. He has possibility and flexibility . . . I bet with my daughter on the endings. It all fits into my interest in social work. Of course, I would never take anything seriously in them, but I suppose some people do.

The stories provide this listener with substitutes just as they do the more naive listener. Betting on the outcome is a chance to be right. Thus it works as compensation for the listener's lack of success in other fields. Judging the characters of the script writer seems to be a substitute for being a real friend of his or of other "interesting" people.

III. Listening for Recipes Making for Adjustment

In the types of gratification described as "remodelling of drudgery" the story content serves as a means wishfully to change the listener's life. Many listeners, however, do not identify themselves with the stories to the extent of accepting them as substitutes for reality. They identify themselves with them only insofar as they provide adjustment to the kind of life they are living. The stories provide such adjustment in three main forms. They give meaning to a world which seems nothing but a humdrum existence by offering a continuous sequence of events. Second, they give the listener a sense that the world is not as threatening as it might seem by supplying them with formulas of behaviour for various troublesome situations. Third, they explain things by providing labels for them. Happenings in a marriage, in a family, in a community are verbalized in the programs and the listeners are made to feel that they understand better what is going on around them. Listening provides them with an ideology to be applied in the appraisal of the world which is actually confronting them.

The following analysis aims to show in greater detail how each of these "recipes for adjustment" comes about and with what elements in the stories they tie up particularly.

"I Don't Feel Empty any Longer" A number of respondents claimed that the stories had filled their "empty lives" with content. The mere fact that something is scheduled to occur every day provides an element of adventure[6] in their daily drudgery. Life becomes meaningful as a sequence of daily fifteen minute broadcasts.

> . . . the stories have really given me something. I don't feel empty any longer.

> Nothing ever happens in my life, but I have the sketches. It is something to look forward to every day.

But for the sketches, this listener feels she would have nothing to look forward to from one day to the next. The stories make for adjustment to an otherwise empty and meaningless life because of their continued character.

When asked how long a radio story should last, only 12 per cent of the respondents placed a limit in terms of months. The rest wanted them to last at least a year or longer. Some suggested that a story should go on "as long as it was interesting," or "forever." Here are some comments on this aspect:

> I want the story to go on for years so that my family can grow up right along with it.

> They should go on as long as they are interesting. One gets to know the people and they

are like one of the family. I would hate to lose them.

The listeners do not want to lose the story-family which is the model for their actual family. They do not want to lose the story characters they have grown to consider as belonging to their family. They want the stories to go on because they hate to lose the sense of an eventful life they built up listening to them. This is true even for the women who wanted a limit put on the length of the stories. Their objections are not directed against "serial" stories as such; they want a limited length only to avoid "dragging." Thus:

> If they keep them too long they have to drag them. They should get things settled once in a while so they can get a fresh start.

By "dragging," the listeners mean too much talking, as interfering with the progress of the action. They dislike it because it spoils the illusion of a life full of happenings. Here is a typical comment of a woman who was "bored" by too much talking:

> Last time I listened to BIG SISTER they wanted to get somebody to help this boy who has a tumor. They wanted to get a specialist. It wasn't so interesting. The two of them (Ruth and John) just sat and talked. They didn't do anything. I thought the boy might die in the meantime. Why didn't they get going?

The listener disliked the lengthy discussion between Ruth and John because she feared "the boy might die in the meantime." This would have put a sudden end to his part in the story and thus destroyed the sense of a continuously eventful life she had enjoyed in listening.

The desire to have things "go on" seems really a desire to have them continue in the expected way, along accepted patterns. In a culture which represses curiosity, first of all in the sexual sphere, people are made to cling to stereotyped solutions. The deeper the frustrations the greater the needs for such stereotypes.

An interesting corroboration of this hypothesis was found in correlating the desired length of the stories with the total number of stories listened to. Among the women listening to fewer than five programs a day, for each ten who gave any limitation for the stories or said they had no opinion, there were three who wanted the stories to go on "forever" or "as long as they were good." Among those who listened to five or more programs the number rose to seven.

If, in this connection, we take the number of programs listened to as an index of the listener's insecurity and needs, we can then say that the more troubles the listener has the longer she wants the stories to last. And it is probably no mere coincidence that the movie most frequently mentioned as best liked should be GONE WITH THE WIND, the longest of all the most recent pictures. As one woman put it, when asked how long a story should last:

It should just go on like GONE WITH THE WIND. It can have no end.

"They Teach Me What to Do" Another form of listening which makes for adjustment of the listener to her own life is related to the advice obtained from hearing the various stories. Many of the respondents explained spontaneously that they liked listening because the stories taught them what to do or how to behave. Following are a few comments:

I listen for what good it will do me. The end of the story in AUNT JENNY always settles problems and sometimes the way they settle them would help me if the same thing happened to me.

If you listen to these programs and something turns up in your own life, you would know what to do about it.

I like to listen to Ma Goldberg and see how she goes about fixing things. It gives me something to think about when I am sewing. She teaches me what to do.

The listeners feel prepared for the complexities of their own lives in the conviction that there are formulas of behavior ready for all situations and that they can acquire them from listening to the stories. This conviction is closely tied up with the assumption that the stories are "true stories." This is a "claim made by some of the programs and accepted by the listeners.

I like AUNT JENNIE'S STORIES because they are real everyday people that you might meet. They even tell you so—that they are real-life stories. I think they could happen.

The following incident shows that such a claim fits into the desires of the listeners who want the stories to be "true stories." A hypothetical question was posed: A new sponsor wants to introduce some changes in a program. Should he change the actors and leave the story the same, or would the respondent prefer to have him change the story but keep the same actors on the program?

A very great number of the women interviewed could not answer the question. They were unable to differentiate between the actor as a character and the actor as a person. The strength of the listeners' desire to believe that the stories are real is indicated even in the answer of a woman who supposedly understood the question and voted against a change in actors. She said:

The Youngs, Mr. and Mrs., used to have these long talks in bed, and now when they do I can't stand it. She is in bed with another man, now that they have changed actors.

The "truth" of the stories is defined in those terms which are most comforting to the listener. This is illustrated in the following comment of a listener who explained why she preferred listening to the stories to going to the movies:

I am not so crazy about the movies. The sketches are more real, more like my own life. The things that happen in the movies seldom happen to people that I know. I like to listen about plain, everyday people.

She considers the stories more "real" because they concern "average" people similar to herself so that she can identify herself with them. At the same time, however, she wants them to be sufficiently superior to herself to make the identification worth while. The characters in the stories have to be "plain" and at the same time exercise a "wonderful philosophy." The stories have to concern things which happen in "everyday life" while at the same time following the pattern of "getting into trouble *and out* again." In their demands upon the story contents the listeners fluctuate between the two desires of wanting to learn from the stories and to use them as a means of escape. For learning's sake they want them to portray reality. As a means of escape they want them to picture a "better world." These two demands are not contradictory, as it seems at first. They have a common root in the insecurity of the listeners.

The Need for Advice The listeners would not seek advice in the stories if they did not need it and if the advice obtained did not, in a way, fit into their needs. A great number of the regular listeners to serial stories are lower income group housewives who see it as their duty to manage the home on what their husbands make. Many of them seem extremely insecure. This was brought out most strikingly in the answers to a question as to what three things they most wanted to have. In only 12% of the answers were such things as interesting friends, travel, sports, etc., important. All the rest wished for a secure home.

Advice, on the other hand, seems to be particularly inaccessible to the listeners studied. The husband shows up in the interviews as the economic provider rather than as a consultant in family affairs. Only one-fifth of the respondents mentioned that they see a great many friends. Various reasons are given for this. Seeing friends "costs money," which is not available. Seeing friends is an "effort," while listening to the stories is not. Friends have the same troubles as the listener, and since they cannot take care of their own, they wouldn't be of any help to the listener.

Lots of people have problems like mine or the ones told in the stories, but they would not be able to explain them.

Finally, the listener does not ask advice from friends because she would be ashamed to admit that she needs it.

It is altogether different with the radio. The listeners feel they have a right to expect and accept help because they patronize the companies which sponsor the programs. Of the women interviewed, 61% said that they used some of the products of sponsoring companies. Said one of them:

I am kidded by everybody because my pantry shelf is full of radio brands. The programs help me, so I've got to help the products.

In a way the radio seems to have taken the place of the neighbor. The neighbor as a competitor has become the stranger, while the radio in its aloofness is the thing humanly near to the listener. It offers friends who are "wonderful and kind," and the listeners tend to forget that this kindness is designed to make them buy. They are enchanted by a one-sided relationship which fits into their isolationist desires. The radio people give advice and never ask for it, they provide help

without the listeners having to reveal their need for it.

Last, but not least, the radio people and the occupations they portray are frequently socially superior to the listener. The listener enjoys their company because it raises her own social level. This was illustrated in the following comment of a lower income group housewife:

If you have friends in, you have to go down to their level. They are sometimes so dumb. The radio people are more interesting. I love being with them.

For many a listener actual friends seem to have acquired a new function. They are the people with whom she talks over the programs. The study shows that 41 per cent of the listeners discuss the stories with their friends.[7] This discussion is of great psychological importance to the listener in that it allows for the transformation of the stories into something that is her own property. Thus, one of the respondents makes an out-of-town call every day to New Jersey to tell her girl friend about "her sketches." Very likely the girl friend in this case listens to the same stories. However, the respondent feels she discusses "her" stories with her. In a world which offers so few chances for real experiences, any happening must be made immediately into something owned. "Try to live today so tomorrow you can say what a wonderful yesterday," a sentiment expressed by a theme song, embodies the same desire to live so as to have memories.

"Potential"Advice The great majority of listeners spontaneously stated that they had learned something from listening to the stories. However, when asked whether any of the stories had ever indicated to them what to do in a particular situation or how to get along with people, only one-third said that they had. The reason for the drop lies in the listeners' preference for "potential" advice rather than a concrete application.

The listeners enjoy getting a kind of advice which allows for wishful thinking. We happened to interview one woman on the day that the heroine in her favorite story had come into a lot of money. She was concerned with how she might keep her children from throwing it away. The listener felt that there was no chance of ever getting so much money herself, but still felt that she had learned from the program. She said:

It is a good idea to know and to be prepared for what I would do with so much money.

Although this listener knew the need for this advice would never come up, she enjoyed playing around with the idea. The advice works as a substitute for the condition of its applicability.

Similarly, a number of listeners claimed they enjoyed seeing how other people solved their troubles because it made them feel that "if the radio people can manage their troubles I might be able to also." In drawing the parallel they liked to overlook that the story situation might not be quite so complicated as their own, and that the story's heroine had more resources available than they had.

In line with this, the listeners are all in favor of a "beautiful philosophy" as long as they are not really expected to use it themselves. Thus, when asked why they liked the programs their answers were frequently like the following:

> I like David Harum. He lives in the country and is a philosopher. He settles the problems of all the people who come to him. He helps those who have not against those who have. There are still good people left in the world.

> I like THE GUIDING LIGHT. The minister there takes care of everybody who needs him. He keeps a light burning at night for people in distress to find him.

Listening to such kind people fills the respondents with the hope that a "guiding light" may burn for them also. That they are interested in the benefits of kindness rather than in its performance was brought out quite clearly in the answers to the question as to whether the listeners, at any point in their favorite story, would have acted differently from the characters in the story. They were split into two groups, those who talked about what "they would have done" and those who talked about what "the actors should have done." The former group disagreed on the ground of too much sacrifice in words like the following:

> I would not have forgiven my husband that often. One has a right to happiness.

The latter group disagreed on the ground of too little sacrifice and said, for instance:

> She went on the stage after her second marriage. The children did not like her new husband. She should not have done it. It was her fault they did not like him; she should have stayed at home.

The seriousness of the desire to learn paired with the desire for a comfortable solution is also demonstrated in the comments made in answer to the question whether the listeners knew of any problems they would like to have presented in a story. About one-third of the listeners answered in the affirmative. Here are a few quotations:

> When a man's disposition changes suddenly after being married for a long time. He starts gambling and to be unfaithful. What's the explanation?

> I should like to know how much a daughter should give her mother from the money she makes. I give everything I earn to my mother. Do I have to?

> Whether I should marry if I have to live with my mother-in-law.

> A story which would teach people not to put things over.

> About religious and racial differences.

> About mixed marriages.

The comments indicate a very great faith put in radio. People want the stories to solve their most specific and private problems. In the omission of controversial issues, the stories probably leave unsatisfied just those people who are the most eager searchers for means of adjustment. The comments also indicate that the listeners hope for a comforting solution. They would like to be told, for instance, that it is not necessary to give one's whole salary to the family. They would like a story which teaches "other people" not to put things over.

"They Explain Things to Me" Listening not only provides the respondents with formulas for behaviour in various situations, it also gives them sets of explanations with which they may appraise happenings. In following a story and hearing the characters discuss what occurs to them and how they feel about it, the listener feels she is made to "see things."

> I like Papa David in LIFE CAN BE BEAUTIFUL. He always uses very much psychology.

> I do not know much about life and I am sometimes scared seeing how things happen to people. It does me good to listen to these stories. They explain things to you.

I like family stories best. If I get married I want to get an idea of how a wife should be to a husband. Some of the stories show how a wife butts into everybody's business, and the husband gets mad and they start quarrelling. The stories make you see things.

In listening to the stories the often inarticulate listener finds that feelings can be expressed. She is made aware of a meaning to things which goes beyond the mere surface appearance. She realizes the existence of causal relations between happenings. There is, however, the danger that such "understanding" is paired with the illusion of a simple and ready explanation being available for every situation and every happening. The listener quoted last, for instance, seems satisfied with labelling a "good marriage" as one where the wife "does not butt into everybody's business."

Thus the question of what the listeners do with the knowledge acquired from listening become of paramount importance.

The Application of the Stories

As mentioned above, one-third of the listeners stated that the stories had helped them "in indicating what to do in a particular situation or how to get along with other people." Following are some of the comments which show how the "advice" obtained has actually been applied by the listeners.

Listening to AUNT JENNIE'S STORIES today was very important for me. The fellow had an argument with the uncle and he blamed it on the girl. That was wrong of him. It was just like my boy friend. The other night I went to a wedding in the neighborhood where there were a lot of girl friends. Some of the boys told my boy friend. He has been mad at me every since. Listening to the stories lets me know how other girls act, and listening to the way that girl argued today, I know how to tell my boy friend where he can get off. Life is so confusing sometimes.

Bess Johnson shows you how to handle children. She handles all ages. Most mothers slap their children. She deprives them of something. That is better. I use what she does with my own children.

When my lawsuit was on, it helped me to listen to Dr. Brent and how calm he was.

When my boy did not come home till late one night from the movies and I was so worried it helped me to remember how they had been worried in the story and he came home safely.

When Clifford's wife died in childbirth the advice Paul gave him I used for my nephew when his wife died.

The spheres of influence of the stories are quite diversified. The respondents feel they have been helped by being told how to get along with other people, how to handle their boy friends or bring up their children. They feel they have learned how to express themselves in a particular situation. They have learned how to comfort themselves if worried.

In many cases these seem to be potential rather than fulfilled goals. The stories obviously released the worries of a mother by helping her pretend that everything will turn out all right and that her young son will come home safely; they have provided for an escape into calmness for a highly upset listener.

It is doubtful whether the girl's relationship to her boy friend is put on a sounder basis and a "confusing life" really understood when she has learned "how to tell her boy friend where he can get off." The woman who has learned to deprive her children rather than slap them seems to do the first thing in substitution for the other without understanding the underlying pedagogical doctrine. One might wonder how much the bereaved nephew appreciated the speech his aunt had borrowed from her favorite story.

Without a careful content analysis and a more elaborate study of the effects of listening upon the psychological make-up of the listeners it is impossible to give a final interpretation of the comments quoted above. It can not be decided from this material whether the stories are qualified to awaken or increase the psychological articulateness of the listener and have just been misunderstood or abused in some cases, or whether they themselves tend to foster a superficial orientation rather than true psychological understanding.

The analysis of gratifications, which was the problem of this study, has shown that the stories have become an integral part of the lives of many listeners. They are not only successful means of temporary emotional release or escape from a disliked reality. To many listeners they seem to have become a model of reality by which one is to be taught how to think and how to act. As such they must be written not only with an eye to their entertainment value, but also in the awareness of a great social responsibility.

Notes

1. Sixty-five different programs were mentioned as listened to. The programs most frequently referred to were: ROAD OF LIFE, WOMAN IN WHITE, LIFE CAN BE BEAUTIFUL, AND THE GOLDBERGS.

2. The material was not sufficiently large to study the important problem of the correlation of listener characteristics and type of gratification obtained from listening.

3. Whether the importance of the doctor as a father substitute is fostered by the story contents or due to a particular attitude among the listeners cannot be decided without a careful content analysis. Such an analysis is at present under way at the Office of Radio Research at Columbia University. Be it either way, the stress on doctors as psychological consultants might indicate a declining importance of the minister as the helper in spiritual matters. It seems as if, for many people, health has become a substitute for salvation.

4. The kind of advertising in which the product is built into the events of the story in such a manner that it seemingly accounts for some of the "nice" things in the stories is probably more efficient than a promotion of the product which is independent of the story. The respondents occasionally stressed that they disliked such advertising because it "takes time away from the story."

5. A similar reaction was also found among listeners to the Professor Quiz program. See Paul F. Lazarsfeld, *Radio and the Printed Page*, page 87. There it took the form of the listeners' selecting the potential winner from among all the contestants right after the beginning of the program and following it through like a race.

6. In a way the radio stories have taken up the old epic form which describes life as a series of adventures. This form is also still alive in the "funnies."

7. Only 14 per cent discussed them with their husbands. 10 per cent talk them over with their children. 37 per cent do not discuss them with anyone. The percentages refer to the number of respondents mentioning each category.

Appendix

Interviewer's Name:_____ Number of Interview:_____
Women's Daytime Serial Programs.

I. GENERAL LISTENING HABITS
    1. To which daytime serial programs do you listen fairly regularly? Since when? How did you start listening to each of them?
       Name of Program   *Listened to since when*   *How started*
    2. How does listening to them fit into respondent's daily schedule?
       a. Generally speaking, which of the following is true for you:
          Programs are selected to fit into your daily work schedule_____
          Efforts are made to fit your work into the program schedule_____
          Neither is entirely true_____
       Details:
       b. (*Interviewer:* Find out on what station and at what time each of the programs listed under #1 is heard: then fill in.)
          Programs come one after the other, without interruption_____
          with interruption_____
          How many switches of stations are made during total listening period?_____
          If any switches of station: does respondent know about programs following? What is her opinion about them?

3. Do you listen to other daytime serial programs occasionally?
   Yes_____ No_____
4. If you could listen to just one, or a limited number of the programs listed under #1, which would be your first choice? Second? Third? Fourth? Fifth?
   1._____ 2._____ 3._____
   4._____ 5._____
5. What is the content of the three best liked programs? (*Interviewer:* Get description of the three best liked programs by saying that you do not happen to know them.)
   1. _____:
   2. _____:
   3. _____:
6. Have you listened fairly regularly to any serials before to which you do not listen now?
   Yes_____ No_____
   If Yes: Which programs? Why did you give up listening to them? (*Interviewer:* Differentiate between objective reasons, such as programs going off the air, and subjective ones, such as dislike or being bored. If the latter, find out why.)
   Programs no longer listened to   *Reasons*
7. (Ask this question only if #6 was answered with "No," or "Yes, programs went off the air.") Are there any programs which you dislike or would not be at all interested in listening to?
   Yes_____ No_____
   If Yes: Which programs are they and why do you not care to listen to them?
8. Can you remember how long ago you first started listening to any daytime series? What first made you interested in them?

II. WHY LISTENING: GENERAL APPEAL
  1. Various people listen to serials for various reasons. Which of the following points would you say are important to you? (*Interviewer:* Use free space on right hand side for respondent's comments.)
     a. To have company when nobody else is around
     b. To hear about somebody else's problems rather than your own for a while
     c. To keep informed about how your radio friends are making out
     d. Because you can count on something to happen every day
     e. Because the people in the stories are a nice sort of people with a philosophy you approve of
     f. Because you like to see how other people with problems similar to your own are making out
     g. Because you like to hear about romance and family life and other things which have happened to you or might happen to you
     h. Because it is a good way to find out what other people are concerned with
     i. Because there is nothing else you can get at this time of the day
     j. Because being at home a great deal of the day, you like to have your mind occupied.
  2. Which do you like better: Listening to serials over the radio_____;
     Going to the movies_____; Why?
  3. Which do you like better: Listening to serials over the radio_____;
     Reading a magazine_____; Why?
  4. Which do you like better: Listening to serials over the radio_____;
     Being invited out or having company in_____; Why?
  5. Which would you prefer: Having the stories told over the radio_____;
     Having the things told happen to you in real life_____; Why?

III. WHY LISTENING: APPEAL IN TERMS OF SPECIFIC EPISODES
  A. FAVORITE PROGRAM
     Ask the following in terms of the favorite program. Only when the question cannot be answered for the favorite program should it be asked for another serial. Be sure always to mention the name of the serial to which the answer refers.

1. Can you describe any events in your favorite story which you liked particularly?
   Yes_____   No_____   Details.
2. Can you describe any events for which you did not care at all?
3. Have you ever been bored at any point? Yes_____   No_____
   If Yes: When?
4. Do you find it hard to visualize the actors? Yes_____   No_____
   How do you picture them?
   a. Does any of them remind you of a person you know? Yes_____   No_____
      If Yes: Get details.
   b. *If No:* Does any actor in any other story remind you of somebody you know?
      Yes_____   No_____
      If Yes to 4b, get details.
5. If there was a change in your favorite program, which of the following would you mind less:
   If the story remained the same but the actors changed_____
   If the story changed but the actors remained_____
   Why?
6. How do you think your favorite story is going to continue (In the next week? Later on?)
7. What product do they advertise?_____
   Do you use it? Not at all_____; Use since started listening_____;
   Used before already_____
   a. Do you use the products of other stories you listen to?_____
      All_____;   Some_____;   None_____

B. Any Serial Program

8. In this or any other program, was there ever a situation where you would have acted differently from how it happened in the story?
   Yes_____   No_____   Explain.
9. Can you mention a story or episode which meant a great deal to you in indicating what to do in a particular situation or how to get along with people?
   Yes_____   No_____   Details.
10. Did you ever come across a problem or a situation in any of the stories which had occurred to somebody you know, or to yourself?
    Yes_____   No_____   Details.
11. Do you remember ever having gotten quite excited about a story?
    Yes_____   No_____   *If Yes:* When, and which story?

IV. General Appraisal

1. As a rule, which of the following is more true: The various stories are quite similar_____; rather different from each other_____.   Explain:
2. Which of the following is true, as a rule: The people in the various stories have about the same amount of troubles as you have_____; more troubles_____; less troubles_____. Explain:
3. How do you like the episodes to end: Happily_____; sad_____; mixed_____.
   Explain:
4. What do you prefer: Stories with problems similar to your own_____; stories with problems quite different from you own_____? Explain:
5. Is there any particular problem you would want to have treated in a story? Which?
6. Do you have any definite opinion about how many months or years a serial story should last?
7. Would you like a new station to bring out one complete half-hour story every day?
   Yes_____   No_____   Explain:
8. Do you talk about the stories with your friends_____; your husband_____; your children_____; nobody_____?

V. DESCRIPTION OF RESPONDENT

Address_____ Age_____ Education_____
Single_____ Married_____ If married: Number and age range of children_____
Occupation: (Own or husband's if she is a housewife)_____
Phone: Yes_____ No_____ Car: Yes_____ No_____ Description of type
of place she lives in_____
Last book read_____ When finished_____
Magazines read_____
Does she read serial stories there? Yes_____ No_____
Newspapers read fairly regularly_____
Attends meetings of any clubs or organizations_____
Do friends visit her: During the day: A great deal_____ Sometimes_____
   Rarely_____
   Evenings: A great deal_____ Sometimes_____ Rarely_____
Any hobbies or special interests?_____
What radio programs liked best?_____
Three movies liked very well_____
What are the three things she would be most interested to have_____
If not working now: Every worked before? Yes_____ No_____ *If Yes:* Would she
   like to return to it? Why?_____
Additional data:

25

Art and Mass Culture

From *Studies in Philosophy and Social Science* (1941)[1]

Max Horkheimer

Max Horkheimer (1895–1973) was the leader of the Frankfurt School of Social Research. A philosopher with strong interests in the social sciences, his life's project was to formulate a renewed and humane basis for science in society. Famous for his notion of a critical theory opposed to traditional theory, Horkheimer believed that the vast world-changing potentials of science could be harnessed to make the world a place of social justice and beauty, instead of one of industrial blight and fascist violence. He was a strong believer in what would today be called *interdisciplinary studies,* and he lamented the specialization and mutual separation of knowledge. Like many Frankfurt theorists, he was born into a well-to-do, assimilated German-Jewish family, and spent much of his life and thought both rebelling against the smugness of that world and mourning its destruction by the Nazis. He lived in exile from Germany from 1933 to 1949, in Geneva, Paris, New York and Los Angeles, spending his last decades as a professor at the University of Frankfurt and as a retiree in Switzerland. In the late 1950s, he held a visiting appointment in the University of Chicago's department of sociology. He was author of *Eclipse of Reason* (1947) and of numerous studies of the history of philosophy. He also wrote books of aphorisms.

Because of his close colleague Adorno, and Adorno's more prolific and sustained writings on the culture industries, Horkheimer's own interests and insights are often overshadowed. This essay shows him in his own right to be a perceptive and measured analyst of the curious place of art in modern society. For Horkheimer, as for his close friend and coconspirator Adorno, art is not just a bit of frosting that can make life sweeter: it is both a symptom of the sociological health of a culture and a foretaste of a better world. (American thinkers such as Dewey and Du Bois who were influenced by German thought likewise shared this conviction.) Mass culture, therefore, is not just silly; it is dangerous.

At times in history, art was intimately associated with other avenues of social life. The plastic arts, in particular, were devoted to the production of objects for daily use, secular as well as religious. In the modern period, however, sculpture and painting were dissociated from town and building, and the creation of these arts reduced to a size suitable to any interior; during the same historic process, esthetic feeling acquired independent status, separate from fear, awe, exuberance, prestige, and comfort. It became "pure." The purely esthetic feeling is the reaction of the private atomic subject, it is the judgment of an individual who abstracts from prevailing social standards. The definition of the beautiful as an object of disinterested pleasure had its roots in this relation. The subject expressed himself in the esthetic judgment without consulting social values and ends. In his esthetic behavior, man so to speak divested himself of his functions as a member of society and reacted as the isolated individual he had become. Individuality, the true factor in artistic creation and judgment, consists not in idiosyncrasies and crotchets, but in the power to withstand the plastic surgery of the prevailing economic system which carves all men to one pattern. Human beings are free to recognize themselves in works of art in so far as they have not succumbed to the general leveling. The individual's experience embodied in a work of art has no less validity than the organized experience society brings to bear for the control of nature. Although its criterion lies in itself alone, art is knowledge no less than science is.

Kant examines the justification of this claim. How, he inquires, can the esthetic judgment, in which subjective feelings are made known, become a collective or "common" judgment?[2] Science rejects feeling as evidence, how then can one explain the community of feeling evoked by art works? Current feelings among the masses, to be sure, are easy to explain; they have always been the effect of social mechanisms. But what is that hidden faculty in every individual to which art appeals? What is that unmistakable feeling on which it relies time and again despite all contradicting experiences? Kant attempts to answer this question by introducing the notion of a *sensus communis aestheticus* to which the individual assimilates his esthetic judgment. This notion must be carefully distinguished from "common sense" in its usual meaning. Its principles are those of a kind of thinking that is "unprejudiced," "consecutive," and "enlarged," that is, inclusive of the viewpoints of others.[3] In other words, Kant thinks that every man's esthetic judgment is suffused with the humanity he has in himself. Despite the deadly competition in business culture, men are in accord concerning the possibilities they envision. Great art, says Pater, must "have something of the human soul in it,"[4] and Guyau declares that art occupies itself with the possible,[5] erecting a "new world above the familiar world . . . a new society which by force of imagination it adds to the society in which we really live." An element of resistance is inherent in the most aloof art.

Resistance to the restraints imposed by society, now and then flooding forth in political revolution, has been steadily fermenting in the private sphere. The middle class family, though it has frequently been an agency of obsolescent social patterns, has made the individual aware of other potentialities than his labor or vocation opened to him. As a child, and later as a lover, he saw reality not in the hard light of its practical biddings but in a distant perspective which lessened the force of its commandments. This realm of freedom, which originated outside the workshop, was adulterated with the dregs of all past cultures, yet it was man's private preserve in the sense that he could there transcend the function society imposed upon him by way of its division of labor. Seen at such a distance, the appurtenances of reality fuse into images that are foreign to the conventional systems of ideas, into esthetic experience and production. To be sure, the experiences of the subject as an individual are not absolutely different from his normal experiences as a member of society. Yet works of art—objective products of the mind detached from the context of the practical world— harbor principles through which the world that bore them appears alien and false. Not only Shakespeare's wrath and melancholy, but the detached humanism of Goethe's poetry as well, and even Proust's devoted absorption in ephemeral features of *mondanité*, awaken memories of a freedom that makes prevailing standards appear narrow-minded and barbarous. Art, since it became autonomous, has preserved the Utopia that evaporated from religion.

The private realm, however, to which art is related, has been steadily menaced. Society tends to liquidate it. Ever since Calvinism sanctified man's calling in this world, poverty, contrary to the accepted notion, has in practice been a taint to be washed away only by toil. The same process that freed each man from slavery and serfdom, and returned him to himself, also broke him into two parts, the private and the social, and burdened the private with a mortgage. Life outside the office and shop was appointed to refresh a man's strength for office and shop; it was thus a mere appendage, a kind of tail to the comet of labor, measured, like labor, by time, and termed "free time." Free time calls for its own curtailment, for it has no independent value. If it goes beyond recreation of expended energies, it is regarded as wasteful, unless it is utilized to train men for work. The children of the early 19th century who were taken from workshop to dormitory and from dormitory to workshop, and fed while at work, lived exclusively for their calling, like Japanese factory girls of today. The labor contract, in which this condition was grounded, proved itself a mere formality. Later in the 19th century, the chains became looser, but self-interest subordinated private life to business even more effectively than before, until the structural unemployment of the 20th century shook the whole order. The permanently unemployed cannot reproduce a labor power that is useless, and training cannot improve a career that is closed in advance. The contrast between the social and private is blurred when mere waiting becomes a calling and when work is nothing but waiting for work.

For a few decades broad strata in industrial countries were able to have some measure of private life, though within strict limits. In the 20th century, the population is surrounded by large trusts and bureaucracies; the earlier division of man's existence between his occupation and family (always valid only with reservations so far as the majority was concerned) is gradually melting away. The family served to transmit social demands to the individual, thus assuming responsibility not only for his natural birth but for his social birth as well. It was a kind of second womb, in whose warmth the individual gathered the strength necessary to stand alone outside it. Actually, it fulfilled this function adequately only among the well-to-do. Among the lower strata the process was generally frustrated; the child was left only too early to his own devices. His aptitudes were prematurely hardened, and the shock he suffered brought in its wake stunted mental growth, pent-up rage, and all that went with it. Behind the "natural" behavior of ordinary folk, so frequently glorified by intellectuals, there lurk fear, convulsion and agony. The juvenile sex crimes as well as national outbursts of our time are indices of the same process. Evil does not stem from nature, but from the violence committed by society against human nature striving to develop.

In the last stages of industrial society even well-to-do parents educate their children not so much as their heirs as for a coming adjustment to mass culture. They have experienced the insecurities of fortune and draw the consequences. Among the lower strata, the protective authority of the parents, which was always menaced, has worn away entirely, until finally the Balilla has slipped into its place. Totalitarian governments are themselves taking in hand the preparation of the individual for his role as a member of the masses. They pretend that the conditions of urbanized life clamor for it. The problem so brutally solved by Fascism has existed in modern society for the last hundred years. A straight line runs from the children's groups of the Camorra to the cellar clubs of New York,[6] except that the Camorra still had an educational value.

Today, in all strata, the child is intimately familiar with economic life. He expects of the future not a kingdom, but a living, calculated in dollars and cents, from some profession which he considers promising. He is as tough and shrewd as an adult. The modern make-up of society sees to it that the utopian dreams of childhood are cut short in earliest youth, that the much praised "adjustment" replaces the defamed Oedipus complex. If it is true that family life has at all times reflected the baseness of public life, the tyranny, the lies, the stupidity of the existing reality, it is also true that it has produced the forces to resist these. The experiences and images which gave inner direction to the life of every individual could not be acquired outside. They flashed forth when the child hung on his mother's smile, showed off in front of his father, or rebelled against him, when he felt someone shared his experiences— in brief, they were fostered by that cozy and snug warmth which was indispensable for the development of the human being.

The gradual dissolution of the family, the transformation of personal life into leisure and of leisure into routines supervised to the last detail, into the pleasures of the ball park and the movie, the best seller and the radio, has brought about the disappearance of the inner life. Long before culture was replaced by these manipulated pleasures, it had already assumed an escapist character. Men had fled into a private conceptual world and rearranged their thoughts when the time was ripe for rearranging reality. The inner life and the ideal had become conservative factors. But with the loss of his ability to take this kind of refuge—an ability that thrives neither in slums nor in modern settlements—man has lost his power to conceive a world different from that in which he lives. This other world was that of art. Today it survives only in those works which uncompromisingly express the gulf between the monadic individual and his barbarous surrounding—prose like Joyce's and paintings like Picasso's Guernica. The grief and horror such works convey are not identical with the feelings of those who, for rational reasons, are turning away from reality or rising against it. The consciousness behind them is rather one cut off from society as it is, and forced into queer, discordant forms. These inhospitable works of art, by remaining loyal to the individual as against the infamy of existence, thus retain the true content of previous great works of art and are more closely related to Raphael's madonnas and Mozart's operas than is anything that harps on the same harmonies today, at a time when the happy countenance has assumed the mask of frenzy and only the melancholy faces of the frenzied remain a sign of hope.

Today art is no longer communicative. In Guyau's theory, the esthetic quality arises from the fact that a man recognizes the feelings expressed by a work of art as his own.[7] The "life analogous to our own," however, in the portrayal of which our own life becomes visible, is no longer the conscious and active life of the nineteenth century middle class. Today, persons merely appear to be persons; both "elites" and masses obey a mechanism that leaves them only one single reaction in any given situation. Those elements of their nature which have not yet been canalized have no possibility of understandable expression. Under the surface of their organized civic life, of their optimism and enthusiasm, men are apprehensive and bewildered and lead a miserable, almost prehistoric existence. The last works of art are symbols of this, cutting through the veneer of rationality that covers all human relationships. They destroy all superficial unanimity and conflict, which are all in truth clouded and chaotic, and it is only in such sagas as those of Galsworthy or Jules Romains, in white papers and in popular biographies, that they attain an artificial coherence. The last substantial works of art, however, abandon the idea that real community exists; they are the monuments of a solitary and despairing life that finds no bridge to any other or even to its own consciousness. Yet they are monuments, not mere symptoms. The despair is also revealed outside the field of pure art, in so-called entertainment and the world of "cultural goods," but this can only be inferred from without, through the means of psychological or sociological theory. The work of art is the only adequate objectification of the individual's deserted state and despair.

Dewey says that art is "the most universal and freest form of communication."[8] But the gulf between art and communication is perforce wide in a world in which accepted language only intensifies the confusion, in which the dictators speak the more gigantic lies the more deeply they appeal to the heart of the masses. "Art breaks through barriers, . . . which are impermeable in ordinary association."[9] These barriers consist precisely in the accepted forms of thought, in the show of unreserved adjustment, in the language of propaganda and marketable literature. Europe has reached the point where all the highly developed means of communication serve constantly to strengthen the barriers "that divide human beings";[10] in this, radio and cinema in no way yield the palm to airplane and gun. Men as they are today understand each other. If they were to cease to understand either themselves or others, if the forms of their communication were to become suspect to them, and the natural unnatural, then at least the terrifying dynamic would come to a standstill. To the extent that the last works of art still communicate, they denounce the prevailing forms of communication as instruments of destruction, and harmony as a delusion of decay.

The present world, denounced though it is by its last works of art, may change its course. The omnipotence of technics, the increasing independence of production from its location, the transformation of the family, the socialization of existence, all these tendencies of modern society may enable men to create the conditions for eradicating the misery these processes have brought over the earth. Today, however, the substance of the individual remains locked up in himself. His intellectual acts are no longer intrinsically connected with his human essence. They take whatever course the situation may dictate. Popular judgment, whether true or false, is directed from above, like other social functions. No matter how expertly public opinion may be inquired into, no matter how elaborate the statistical or psychological soundings, what they reach is always a mechanism, never the human essence. What comes to the fore when men most candidly reveal their inner selves, is precisely the predatory, evil, cunning beings whom the demagogue knows so well how to handle. A pre-established harmony prevails between his outward purposes and their crumbled inner lives. Everybody knows himself to be wicked and treacherous, and those who confirm this, Freud, Pareto and others, are quickly forgiven. Yet, every new work of art makes the masses draw back in horror. Unlike the Führers, it does not appeal to their psychology, nor, like psychoanalysis, does it contain a promise to guide this psychology towards "adjustment." In giving downtrodden humans a shocking awareness of their own despair, the work of art professes a freedom which makes them foam at the mouth. The generation that

allowed Hitler to become great takes its adequate pleasure in the convulsions which the animated cartoon imposes upon its helpless characters, not in Picasso, who offers no recreation and cannot be "enjoyed" anyhow. Misanthropic, spiteful creatures, who secretely know themselves as such, like to be taken for the pure, childish souls who applaud with innocent approval when Donald Duck gets a cuffing. There are times when faith in the future of mankind can be kept alive only through absolute resistance to the prevailing responses of men. Such a time is the present.

At the end of his book on esthetic problems, Mortimer Adler defines the external marks of the great work of art: gross popularity at any one time or over a period of time, and the ability to satisfy the most varied levels of taste.[11] Consistently with this, Adler praises Walt Disney as the great master because he reaches a perfection in his field that surpasses our best critical capacity to analyze and at the same time pleases children and simple folk.[12] Adler has tried like few other critics for a view of art independent of time. But his unhistorical method makes him fall a prey to time all the more. While undertaking to raise art above history and keep it pure, he betrays it to the contemptible trash of the day. Elements of culture isolated and dissevered from the historical process may appear as similar as drops of water; yet they are as different as Heaven and Hell. For a long time now, Raphael's blue horizons have been quite properly a part of Disney's landscapes, in which *amoretti* frolic more unrestrainedly than they ever did at the feet of the Sistine Madonna. The sunbeams almost beg to have the name of a soap or a toothpaste emblazoned on them; they have no meaning except as a background for such advertising. Disney and his audiences, as well as Adler, unswervingly stand for the purity of the blue horizon, but perfect loyalty to principles isolated from the concrete situation makes them turn into their very opposite and finally results in perfect relativism.

Adler's book is devoted to the film which he loyally measures according to Aristotle's esthetic principles, thereby professing his faith in the supra-historical validity of philosophy. The essence of art, he says, is imitation that combines the greatest similarity of form with the greatest difference of content.[13] This Aristotelian doctrine has become a *cliché*, the opposite of which—the greatest similarity of content with the greatest difference of form—would do as well. Both belong to those axioms which are so calculated that they can easily be adjusted to the conventional doctrine in each field. The content of such principles, whether favored by metaphysicians or empiricists, will not hurt anybody's feelings. If, for instance, science is defined as the aggregate of all verifiable statements, one may be certain of every scientist's approval. But even an empty generality such as this discloses its double-dealing potency as soon as it is related to the real world, which "verifies" the judgment of the powerful and gives the lie to the powerless. A dogmatic definition of the beautiful protects philosophy no better from capitulating to the powers-that-be than a concept of art derived from the uncritical applause of the masses, to which it bows only too readily.

The dogmatists succumb to relativism and conformism not only in their discussions of abstract esthetic problems, but also in their views of the moral significance of art. "There is no question," says Adler, "that prudence should govern art to whatever extent the work of art or the artist comes within the sphere of morality."[14] One of the main purposes of Adler's book is to discover principles for art education. The concept of morality which he advances for this is, however, as unhistorical as his concept of art. "Crime is only one kind of anti-social behavior. Any behavior which does not conform to established customs is anti-social in essentially the same sense.... Men who act anti-socially, whether criminally or contrary to the customs generally prevailing, are in the same sense morally vicious."[15] He recognizes the difficulty arising from the fact that different views and customs prevail in different social strata. But he thinks that the resulting practical difficulties do not impair his principle. The problem simply becomes one of fixing upon which mores are more and which less desirable for society as a whole. This problem, moreover, only exists for him when there is a conflict between the prevailing habits of different social groups; and not when there is a conflict between an individual and all the groups, a situation which incidentally contains within itself the most serious moral problem of all. Thus, with regard to morality, the disparity is obliterated between the principles of metaphysics and those of positivism. Adler is irresistibly led to conclusions drawn long ago by Lévy-Bruhl[16] and other sociologists: what is moral is determined by the positive content of existing customs and habits, and morality

consists in formulating and approving what is accepted by the prevailing social order. But even if the whole of a society, such as the coordinated German nation, is of one mind in this regard, it still does not follow that its judgment is true. Error has no less often united men than truth.

Even though truth, of its nature, coincides with the common interest, it has usually been at loggerheads with the sentiment of the community at large. Socrates was put to death for asserting the rights of his conscience against the accepted Athenian religion. According to Hegel, the sentence was just, for the individual "must bend before the general power, and the real and noblest power is the Nation."[17] And yet, according to Hegel, the principle Socrates upheld was superior to this one. Contrariety is even more pronounced in Christianity, which came to the world as a "scandal." The first Christians impugned "the generally prevailing customs" and were therefore persecuted in line with the prevailing law and mores. But this did not make them "morally depraved," as would follow from Adler's definition; on the contrary, *they* were the ones to unmask the depravity of the Roman world. Just as the essence of art cannot be arrested through rigid supra-temporal principles, ideas such as justice, morality, and public cannot be interconnected through rigid, supra-temporal relations. Kierkegaard's doctrine that the spread of Christianity in the public consciousness has nowise overcome the true Christian's wary attitude to the state is more valid today than ever. "For the concept of the Christian is a polemical concept; it is possible to be a Christian only in opposition to others, or in a manner opposed to that of others."[18] Those modern apologists were ill-advised who attempted to validate the attitude of the Church toward witch-burning as a concession to popular ideas.[19] Truth can make no pacts with "prevailing customs." It finds no guiding thread in them. In the era of witch hunts, opposition to the public spirit would have been moral.

Adler's book breathes the conviction that mankind must orient to fixed values, as these have been set forth by great teachers, above all by Aristotle and St. Thomas. To positivism and relativism he opposes sturdy Christian metaphysics. It is true that modern disbelief does find its theoretical expression in scientivism, which explains that binding values exist for "psychological" reasons, because there is need for them.[20] Success, which in Calvinism was not the same as being a member of the Elect, but was only an indication that one might be, becomes the only standard of human life. In this way, according to Adler, positivism grants a charter to Fascism. For, if there can be no meaningful discussion of questions of value, action alone decides. Metaphysics draws from this a conclusion advantageous to itself: since the denial of eternal principles handicaps the struggle against the new barbarism, the old faith must be reestablished. Men are asked to risk their lives for freedom, democracy, the nation. Such a demand seems absurd when there are no binding values. Metaphysics alone, Adler supposes, can give humanity the hold it has lost, metaphysics makes true community possible.

Such ideas misconstrue the present historical situation. Positivism, indeed, articulates the state of mind of the unbelieving younger generation, and it does so as adequately as sport and jazz. The young no longer have faith in anything, and for this reason they are able to shift to any belief. But the fault lies just as much with the dogmatism they have forgotten as with themselves. The middle class confined religion to a kind of reservation. Following Hobbes' advice, they swallowed its doctrines whole, like pills, and never concretely questioned its truth. Religion for modern men tended to be a memory of childhood. With the disintegration of the family, the experiences that have invigorated religion also lose their power. Today, men exercise restraints not out of belief but out of hard necessity. That is why they are so saddened. The weaker they are and the more deeply disappointed, the more violently do they espouse brutality. They have cast aside all ties to the principle of heavenly love. Any demand that they should return to it for reasons of state is not tenable in religious terms. Religion has a claim on faith not insofar as it is useful but insofar as it is true. Agreement between political and religious interests is by no means guaranteed. The naive presupposition of such agreement, made by those who defend absolute values, confutes their doctrines. Positivism is as strongly in conformity with our time as Adler thinks, but it contains an element of honesty for that very reason. The young who adopt this philosophy exhibit greater probity of mind than those who out of pragmatic motives bow to an absolute in which they do not quite believe. Uncritical return to religion and metaphysics is as questionable today as the road back to the beautiful paintings and compositions of classicism, no matter how enticingly

such havens may beckon. The revivals of Greek and medieval philosophers, such as Adler recommends, are not so far remote from certain revivals of melodies by Bach, Mozart and Chopin in current popular music.

Adler denounces in impressive passages the hopeless spiritual plight of the young.[21] He unmasks "the religion of science and the religion of the state." But it would be a fatal misunderstanding to summon the young away from these doctrines and lead them back to older authorities. What is to be deplored is not that scientific thought has replaced dogmatism, but rather that such thought, still pre-scientific in the literal sense, is always confined within the limits of the various specialized disciplines. It is wrong to rely on science so long as the formulation of its problems is conditioned by an obsolete division into disciplines. Economy of thought and technique alone do not exhaust the meaning of science, which is also will to truth. The way toward overcoming positivistic thinking does not lie in a regressive revision of science, but in driving this will to truth further until it conflicts with present reality. Illuminating insights are not to be found in high and eternal principles, with which everybody agrees anyway (who does not profess faith in freedom and justice!), or in the routine arrangement of facts into customary patterns.

Preference for static principles was the great delusion of Husserl's original "Eidetics," one of the precursors of Neo-Thomism. Adler seems to fall into the same error. Sublime principles are always abstract—positivism is right in speaking here of fictions or auxiliary constructions—but insights always refer to the particular. In the process of cognition, each concept, which in isolation has its conventional meaning, takes part in forming new configurations, in which it acquires a new and specific logical function. Aristotle's metaphysics taken as a whole marks such a configuration, as do the doctrines of St. Thomas on whom Adler draws. The categories become distorted or meaningless unless they enter new, more adequate structures that are required by the particular historical situation in which they play a part. The reason for this is not that each period has its own truth assigned to it, as historical and sociological relativism would like us to believe, or that one can dispense with philosophic and religious traditions, but rather that intellectual loyalty, without which truth cannot exist, consists both in preserving past insights and contradicting and transforming them. Abstract formulations of the highest values are always adjustable to the practice of stake and guillotine. Knowledge really concerned with values does not look to higher realms. It rather tries to penetrate the cultural pretences of its time, in order to distinguish the features of a frustrated humanity. Values are to be disclosed by uncovering the historical practice that destroys them.

In our time thinking is endangered not so much by the wrong paths it may pursue as by its being prematurely cut short. Positivism rests content with the prearranged routines of official science, whereas metaphysics invites intuitions that have their content in the prevailing modes of consciousness. The demand for purity and clarity, applicability and matter-of-factness which is immediately raised to challenge any act of thinking that is not free from imagination, expresses a repugnance to going beyond the limitations of the "statement," to intellectual restlessness and "negativism," all of which are indispensable elements of thought. The truth of ideas is demonstrated not when they are held fast but when they are driven further.

The pedantry of matter-of-factness produces, conversely, a fetishism of ideas. Today ideas are approached with a sullen seriousness; each as soon as it appears is regarded as either a ready-made prescription that will cure society or as a poison that will destroy it. All the ambivalent traits of obedience assert themselves in the attitude to ideas. People desire to submit to them or to rebel against them, as if they were gods. Ideas begin by playing the role of professional guides, and end as authorities and Fuehrers. Whoever articulates them is regarded as a prophet or a heretic, as an object to be adored by the masses or as a prey to be hunted by the Gestapo. This taking of ideas only as verdicts, directives, signals, characterizes the enfeebled man of today. Long before the era of the Gestapo, his intellectual function had been reduced to statements of fact. The movement of thought stops short at slogans, diagnoses and prognoses. Every man is classified: bourgeois, communist, fascist, Jew, alien or "one of us." And this determines the attitude once and for all. According to such patterns dependent masses and dependable sages throughout the world history have always thought. They have been united under "ideas," mental products that have become fetishes. Thinking, faithful to itself, in contrast to this, knows itself at any

moment to be a whole and to be uncompleted. It is less like a sentence spoken by a judge than like the prematurely interrupted last words of a condemned man. The latter looks upon things under a different impulsion than that of dominating them.

Adler appreciates the public as it is, and in consequence popularity is a positive criterion to him. He treats the film as popular poetry and compares it with the theater of the Elizabethan period, when for the first time "writers had the double role of artist and merchant competing in a free market for both plaudits and profits."[22] According to him the middle class theater has been determined by market economy and democracy. Communists or sentimental aristocrats may regret commercialization, says Adler, but its influence on Shakespeare was not so bad. The film must please not merely the masses, but beyond them "the organized groups which have become the unofficial custodians of public manners and the common good."[23] Adler does realize the difficulties encountered by the film, as compared with the theater, because of the size of its public and the differentiated needs of modern society, but he overlooks the dialectics of popularity. Quite against his intention to differentiate and evaluate social phenomena, his static way of thinking tends to level everything. Just as he is tempted to confuse Raphael's and Disney's scenic backgrounds, he seems to identify the Hays Office and the guardians of the Platonic Republic.

His whole approach to the film as an art bears witness to the confusion of entirely different cultural orders. He defends the movies against the accusation that they are not art because of the collective character of their production.[24] But the discrepancy between art and film, which exists despite the potentialities of the motion picture, is not the result of the surface phenomenon of the number of people employed in Hollywood as much as of the economic circumstances. The economic necessity for rapid return of the considerable capital invested in each picture forbids the pursuit of the inherent logic of each work of art—of its own autonomous necessity. What today is called popular entertainment is actually demands evoked, manipulated and by implication deteriorated by the cultural industries. It has little to do with art, least of all where it pretends to be such.

Popularity has to be understood with reference to social change, not merely as a quantitative but as a qualitative process. It was never directly determined by the masses, but always by their representatives in other social strata. Under Elizabeth and even as late as the 19th century, the educated were the spokesmen for the individual. Since the interests of the individual and those of the rising middle classes did not fully coincide, the works of art always contained a critical element. Ever since that time, the concepts of individual and society have been reciprocal ones. The individual developed in harmony with and in opposition to society: society developed when individuals did, and it developed when individuals didn't. In the course of this process, social mechanisms, such as the national and international division of labor, crisis and prosperity, war and peace, strengthened their own independence of the individual, who became increasingly alien to them and faced them with growing impotence. Society slipped away from individuals and individuals from society.

The cleavage between private and social existence has taken on catastrophic proportions toward the end of the liberalistic period. New forms of social life are announcing themselves in which the individual, as he is, will be transshaped unless he is destroyed. But the educated are still indissolubly bound up with man as he existed in the past. They still have in mind the individual's harmony and culture, at a time when the task is no longer to humanize the isolated individual, which is impossible, but to realize humanity as a whole. Even Goethe had to concede that his ideal of the harmonious personality had foundered; in our own time, the pursuit of this ideal presupposes not only indifference toward the general suffering, but the very opposite of the ideal, a distorted personality.

In Europe, representation and leadership of the masses has shifted from the educated to powers more conscious of their task. Criticism in art and theory has been replaced by actual hatred or by the wisdom of obedience. The opposition of individual and society, and of private and social existence, which gave seriousness to the pastime of art, has become obsolete. The so-called entertainments, which have taken over the heritage of art, are today nothing but popular tonics, like swimming or football. Popularity no longer has anything to do with the specific content or the truth of artistic productions. In the democratic countries, the final decision no longer rests with the educated but with the amusement industry.

Popularity consists of the unrestricted accommodation of the people to what the amusement industry thinks they like. For the totalitarian countries, the final decision rests with the managers of direct and indirect propaganda, which is by its nature indifferent to truth. Competition of artists in the free market, a competition in which success was determined by the educated, has become a race for the favor of the powers-that-be, the outcome of which is influenced by the secret police. Supply and demand are no longer regulated by social need but by reasons of state. Popularity, in these countries, is as little a result of the free play of forces as any other prize; in other countries it shows a similar tendency.

In a beautiful passage of his book, Dewey explains that communication is the consequence and not the intention of the artistic work. "Indifference to response of the immediate audience is a necessary trait of all artists that have something new to say."[25] Today even the imaginary future audience has become questionable, because, once again, man within humanity is as solitary and abandoned as humanity within the infinite universe. But the artists, continues Dewey, "are animated by a deep conviction that since they can only say what they have to say, the trouble is not with their work but those who, having eyes, see not, and having ears, hear not."[26] The only hope remaining is that the deaf ears in Europe imply an opposition to the lies that are being hammered at men from all sides and that men are following their leaders with their eyes tight shut. One day we may learn that in the depths of their hearts, the masses, even in fascist countries, secretly knew the truth and disbelieved the lie, like katatonic patients who make known only at the end of their trance that nothing has escaped them. Therefore it may not be entirely senseless to continue speaking a language that is not easily understood.

Notes

1. These remarks have been provoked by Mortimer J. Adler's book, *Art and Prudence,* New York and Toronto 1937.

2. Kant, *Critique of Judgment,* translated by F. H. Bernard. §22, p. 94.

3. *Ibid.,* §40, p. 171.

4. Walter Pater, *Appreciations,* London 1918, p. 38.

5. J. M. Guyau, *L'art au point de vue soci-ologique*, Paris 1930, p. 21.

6. On the subject of cellar clubs, cf. Brill and Payne, *The Adolescent Court and Crime Prevention*, New York 1938.

7. Cf. J. M. Guyau, *op. cit.*, pp. 18–19.

8. John Dewey, *Art as Experience*, New York 1934, p. 270.

9. *Ibid.*, p. 244.

10. *Ibid.*

11. *Op. cit.*, p. 581.

12. *Ibid.*

13. *Ibid.*, pp. 24–25 and 450f.

14. *Ibid.*, p. 448.

15. *Ibid.*, p. 165.

16. L. Lévy-Bruhl, *La Morale et La Science des Moeurs*, Paris 1904.

17. Hegel, *History of Philosophy*, translated by E. S. Haldane (our version), Vol. I, p. 441.

18. Soeren Kierkegaard, *Angriff auf die Christenheit*, herausgegeben von A. D. Dorner und Christoph Schrempf, Stuttgart 1896, p. 239.

19. Cf., e.g., Johannes Janssen, *Kulturzustände des Deutschen Volkes*, 4. Buch, Freiburg i.B. 1903, p. 546.

20. Cf. R. v. Mises, *Kleines Lehrbuch des Positivismus*, The Hague 1939, pp. 368f.

21. Cf. Mortimer Adler, "This Pre-War Generation" in: *Harpers Magazine*, Oct. 1940, p. 524f.

22. *Op. cit.*, pp. 131–32.

23. *Op. cit.*, p. 145.

24. *Op. cit.*, pp. 483–4.

25. *Op. cit.*, p. 104.

26. *Ibid.*

26

Administrative and Critical Communications Research

From *Studies in Philosophy and Social Science* (1941)

Paul F. Lazarsfeld

Paul Lazarsfeld (1901–1976) was one of the central figures in the study of twentieth-century mass communication. Lazarsfeld was born in Vienna to a cultured, Jewish family with socialist sentiments. His mother was a practicing psychologist trained by Alfred Adler, and she wrote an early advice column in the newspaper. Lazarsfeld received his doctorate in applied mathematics in 1925 and that same year established an institute devoted to the application of psychology to social and economic problems. This was the first of four such applied research institutes Lazarsfeld founded. He came to the United States as a Rockefeller fellow in 1933, and he stayed while the political crisis in Europe intensified. Lazarsfeld worked at the University of Newark and at Princeton University, where in 1937 he teamed with psychologist Hadley Cantril on some of the earliest empirical social-scientific studies of the radio audience. They formed the Office of Radio Research (ORR), which Lazarsfeld later moved to Columbia. In 1941, Lazarsfeld was hired as associate professor of sociology, the same year the department hired Robert K. Merton. Over the next three decades, Lazarsfeld and Merton anchored a department that established the tenor for

American sociology from the 1950s until the student protests of 1968. While Lazarsfeld's interests were varied, he was best known as a brilliant methodologist who formulated and helped codify a number of important research techniques, from the panel study to latent structure analysis. However, he was also known as a somewhat inept administrator whose projects ran over budget and never made any money.

"Administrative and Critical Research" (1941) was originally published in the Frankfurt Institute's *Studies in Philosophy and Social Science*. It was written during Lazarsfeld's period of collaboration with the Frankfurt School's Theodor Adorno, at the Office of Radio Research. In it, Lazarsfeld draws examples from some of Adorno's studies. The essay offers one of the most lucid short descriptions of critical theory and its approach to mass communication, even offering a four-step method for putting it into practice. This abridged selection is taken from a later collection, *Qualitative Analysis* (1972).

During the last two decades the media of mass communication, notably radio, print and film, have become some of the best-known and best documented spheres of modern society. Careful studies have revealed the size of the audiences of all major radio programs and the composition of this audience in respect to sex, income, and a few other criteria. The circulations of newspapers and magazines are recorded by specially organized research outfits, and others report currently on which magazine stories and which advertisements are read week by week. Books, radio programs, and movies are tested as to the difficulty of the language they use and as to how adequate they are for the different educational levels of the population. The types of entertainment that different groups of people prefer are being investigated all the time, and many promotional campaigns are tested currently as to their success. A number of important new techniques have been developed in the course of all these research efforts. Modern sampling techniques, for instance, have made great progress because it has been realized that the practical value of a study would be lost if it were conducted among a group of people who are not representative of those sections of the population which the sponsoring agency wants to reach. Interviewing techniques have been greatly refined for similar reasons. The competitive character of much of this work has led to ever better methods of recording facts as to the extent of listening and reading. Where a subject matter doesn't lend itself to simple recording devices, great progress has been made in developing indices for complex attitudes and reactions.[1]

Behind the idea of such research is the notion that modern media of communication are tools handled by people or agencies for given purposes. The purpose may be to sell goods, or to raise the intellectual standards of the population, or to secure an understanding of governmental policies; but in all cases, to someone who uses a medium for something, it is the task of research to make the tool better known, and thus to facilitate its use.

As a result, all communications research centers around a standard set of problems. Who are the people exposed to the different media? What are their specific preferences? What are the effects of different methods of presentation? One who uses media of communication is in competition with other agencies whose purposes are different, and thus research must also keep track of what is communicated by others. Finally, communications research has to be aware that the effect of radio, print, or the movie, does not end with the purposive use which is made of it by administrative agencies. If advertisers, for example, feel that radio is an especially powerful selling device, then printed media will receive less money, and research will have to see whether radio brings about a general deterioration of the reading habits of the population.

Studies of this kind are conducted partly by the major publishing organizations and radio networks and party by academic agencies supported by universities or foundations.[2] Considerable thought has been given during the past years to clarifying the social and political implications of this new branch of social research. Its relationship to the present crisis is very interestingly discussed in a new study by Harold Lasswell.[3] One who has not participated in work of this kind can get a good picture of its atmosphere from a "fable" written by participants in the course of a series of discussions which took place during

1939 and 1940. We quote:

In the interest of concreteness, let us attempt to state the job of research in mass communication in a situation which, though purely hypothetical, serves to illustrate what that job involves.

Let us suppose that government leaders and those responsible for mass communication are in agreement with respect to policy toward alien groups in this country. (This public, they believe, should be made aware of the dangers of subversive activities on the part of aliens, but popular antipathy toward aliens in general should be minimized, and, above all, outbreaks of anti-alien sentiment should be avoided.) The policy that the channels of mass communication must serve, then, becomes one of increasing public awareness of specific dangers of subversive action, while, at the same time, building tolerance toward aliens in general.

Suppose that some popular evening radio program, known to attract a considerable portion of the total listening audience, includes an address dealing with the dangers of subversive activities on the part of aliens. News dispatches of the next day or two, however, bring reports from various parts of the country of outbreaks of feeling against alien groups. Reports of local utterances in connection with these outbreaks carry allusions to the broadcast address of the evening. As a result, there is at least a strong suspicion that some connection exists between them and what was said on the evening broadcast.

Conscientious effort to repair the damage, it is clear, involves learning more of what the damage was. The comment it occasioned in the press makes clear that its effects were felt not through the radio alone, but through reports of the unfortunate address which the newspapers carried, in the local utterances which alluded to it, and even in some widely distributed newsreel reports of the local outbreak that followed. What people then must be reached if the untoward effects of the broadcast are to be remedied?

Something in what was said evidently combined with the predispositions of the listeners and with the current circumstances—with the force of events, and probably with other widely disseminated communications—to set the stage for what ensued.

Each station is asked to assign the best qualified members of its staff to interviewing listeners to determine as best they can what in the address led to the unanticipated outbreaks. Particularly are they urged to have their interviewers talk with individuals who took an active part in the outbreaks in questions.

With the help of specialists in such research, the audience originally affected is redetermined. Types of radio programs, press releases, and newsreel treatments are worked out, calculated on the basis of the best evidence available to get a new hearing for the subject, adequate to counter the effects of the original address. Undoubtedly an explanation would be prepared for delivery by the original speaker, but other speakers would be enlisted whose position and identification in the public mind are likely to make their parts most widely influential. All materials prepared are pre-tested at relatively slight expense—indeed, far less expense, proportionately, than merchandisers ordinarily incur in testing the market for new products. Conscientious effort having taken them so far, those responsible agree in wishing now to have some further test of the actual affects of what they have planned by way of remedy. Accordingly, arrangements are made in advance of their campaign to gauge its progress.

A happy ending to this fable can probably take the form of a series of charts which subsequently ease the conscience of all concerned by showing, as their campaign proceeds, a consistent decline in all indices of overt hostility toward the groups against which outbreaks of feeling were directed.

The original speaker, the sponsors, and the broadcasters are still convinced of their initial innocence. But they are plagued a bit by certain recollections. One of them remembers, for example, suggesting extra publicity for the broadcast on the ground that the address to be included was particularly timely. Another recalls that the topic of the address was suggested by an acquaintance prominent in an organization which presumably on patriotic grounds had for some time been advocating stricter control of aliens in the country. In the end, their feeling is that however innocent their conscious purposes, they too, as Americans of their time, shared the same predispositions in planning the broadcast, and responded to the force of the same circumstances, as did the listeners to it.

Research of the kind described so far could be called *administrative research*. It is carried through in the service of some kind of administrative agency of public or private character. Administrative research is subject to objections from two sides. On the one hand, there are the sponsors themselves, some of whom feel that they have not really got their money's worth. One good guess, so the argument goes, is of more practical importance than all the details which might be brought to light by an empirical study. There is, however, a fallacy behind this objection. Although speculation is indispensable for guidance in any kind of empirical work, if honestly carried through it will usually lead to a number of alternative conclusions which cannot all be true at the same time. Which one corresponds to the real situation can be decided only by empirical studies.[4] From another side comes an objection directed against the aims which prevail in the majority of current studies. They solve little problems, generally of a business character, when the same methods could be used to improve the life of the community if only they were applied to forward-looking projects related to the pressing economic and social problems of our time. Robert S. Lynd, in his *Knowledge for What,* has vigorously taken this point of view and has shown many ways whereby research could be made more vital.

Neither of these two arguments doubts that research can and should be done at the service of certain well-defined purposes. But at this point a third argument comes up. The objection is raised that one cannot pursue a single purpose and study the means of its realization isolated from the total historical situation in which such planning and studying goes on. Modern media of communication have become such complex instruments that wherever they are used they do much more to people than those who administer them mean them to do, and they may have a momentum of their own which leaves the administrative agencies much less choice than they believe they have. The idea of *critical research* is posed against the practice of administrative research, requiring that, prior and in addition to whatever special purpose is to be served, the general role of our media of communication in the present social system should be studied. The rest of these remarks are devoted to a formulation of this conception and to a short appraisal of its possible contributions to current communication research.

The idea of critical research has been developed in many studies by Max Horkheimer.[5] It seems to be distinguished from administrative research in two respects: it develops a theory of the prevailing social trends of our times, general trends which yet require consideration in any concrete research problem; and it seems to imply ideas of basic human values according to which all actual or desired effects should be appraised.

As to prevailing trends, everyone will agree that we live in a period of increasing centralization of ownership. Yet, although large economic organizations plan their production to the minutest detail, the distribution of their products is not planned systematically. Their success depends upon the outcome of a competition among a few large units which must rally sizeable proportions of the population as their customers. Thus promotion in every form becomes one of the main forces in contemporary society. The technique of manipulating large masses of people is developed in the business world and from there permeates our whole culture. In the end everything, be it good or bad, is promoted; we are living more and more in an "advertising culture." This whole trend is accentuated still more by the fact that it has to disguise itself. A salesman who has only one line to sell has to explain to each customer why this line suits just his individual purposes. The radio announcer who serves one national advertiser identifies himself to millions of listeners as "your" announcer.

Such an analysis becomes an element of strong concern and solicitude if it is felt that these trends impair basic values in human life. The idea that our times are engulfed by a multitude of promotional patterns is coupled with the feeling that human beings, as a result, behave more and more like pawns upon a chessboard, losing the spontaneity and dignity which is the basic characteristic of the human personality. In order to understand clearly the idea of critical research, one must realize that it is being urged by men who have the idea ever present before them that what we need most is to do and think what we consider true and not to adjust ourselves to the seemingly inescapable.

The theory of a trend toward promotional culture leads to the conclusion that certain tendencies of our time jeopardize basic human values because people are kept from developing their own potentialities to the full. To be fit for the daily competition, we do not spend our leisure time developing a rich range of interests and abilities, but we use it, willingly or unwillingly, to reproduce our working capacity. Thus, not having acquired any criteria of our own, we succumb to and support a system of promotion in all areas of life, which, in turn, puts us in ever-increasing dependence upon such a system; it gives us more and more technical devices and takes away from us any valuable purposes for which they could be used.[6]

Thus the stage is set for the procedures of critical research. A critical student who analyzes modern media of communication will look at radio, motion pictures, the press, and will ask the following kinds of questions: How are these media organized and controlled? How, in their institutional set-up, is the trend toward centralization, standardization and promotional pressure expressed? In what form, however disguised, are they threatening human values? He will feel that the main task of research is to uncover the unintentional (for the most part) and often very subtle ways in which these media contribute to living habits and social attitudes that he considers deplorable.

What are the operations into which critical communication research could be broken down? The answer is not easy and a first attempt might be made by visualizing how a student would be trained to make observations in everyday life and to try to interpret them in terms of their social meaning. You sit in a movie and look at an old newsreel showing fashions of ten years ago. Many people laugh. Why do those things which we admired just a little while ago seem so ridiculous now? Could it be that we avenge ourselves for having submitted to them under general pressure, and now that the pressure in favor of these particular styles has been lifted, we compensate by deriding the idols of yesteryear? At the same time, we submit to the style-promotion of today only to laugh at it a few years from now. Could it be that by laughing at past submission, we gather strength to submit to the present pressure upon us? Thus, what looks to an ordinary observer like an incident in a movie theater, becomes, from this point of view, a symptom of great social significance.

Or you find that a large brewery advertises its beer by showing a man disgustedly throwing aside a newspaper full of European war horrors while the caption says that in times like these the only place to find peace, strength, and courage is at your own fireside drinking beer. What will be the result if symbols referring to such basic human wants as that for peace become falsified into expressions of private comfort and are rendered habitual to millions of magazine readers as merchandising slogans? Why should people settle their social problems by action and sacrifice if they can serve the same ends by drinking a new brand of beer? To the casual observer the advertisement is nothing but a more or less clever sales trick. From the aspect of a more critical analysis, it becomes a dangerous sign of what a promotional culture might end up with.

A next step in trying to explain this approach could be taken by applying it not only to an observation of daily life, but to problems we meet in textbooks current in the social sciences. A text on the family, for example, would not be likely to contain a detailed analysis showing how one of the functions of the family in our society might be that of maintaining the authoritarian structure necessary for our present economic system, that the predominant position of the father might prepare the child to accept the privations he will suffer as an adult, and to do so without questioning their necessity. Applying this to a study of the family in the depression we might depart from the traditional question of what changes the depression has brought about in family life. Couldn't it be that the family has influenced the depression? Interesting research problems would come up: what was the effect of different family constellations upon people's ability to find out-of-the-way jobs, to use initiative in organizations of unemployed, and so on?

Another example could arise from a well-known observation which can be found in every text on social psychology, to the effect that the way we look at the world and react to the problems of the day is determined by our previous experience. The notion of experience is taken as a psychological concept which does not need much further elucidation. But could it not be that what we call "experience" undergoes historical changes? Visualize what experience meant for a man who lived in a rather stable, small community, reading in his newspaper elaborate accounts of events he considered news because they happened a few weeks before, spending many an hour walking through the countryside, experiencing nature as something eternally changeless, and as so rich that years were needed to observe all its details. Today we live in an environment where skyscrapers shoot up and elevateds disappear overnight; where news comes like shock every few hours; where continually new news programs keep us from ever finding out the details of previous news; and where nature is something we drive past in our car, perceiving a few quickly changing flashes which turn the majesty of a mountain range into the impression of a motion picture. Might it not be that we do not build up experiences the way it was possible to do decades ago, and if so wouldn't that have bearing upon all our educational efforts? Studies of smaller American communities have shown that since the turn of the century there has been a steady decrease of efforts in adult education of the old style. Now radio with its Professor Quiz program brings up new forms of mass education which, in their differences from the old reading and discussion circles, show a striking parallel to the development sketched here.[7]

Omitting a number of details and specifications, the "operation" basic to this approach consists of four steps.

a) A theory about the prevailing trends toward a "promotional culture" is introduced on the basis of general observation. Although efforts are steadily being made to refine and corroborate this theory it is taken for granted prior to any special study.

b) A special study of any phenomenon consists in determining how it expresses these prevailing trends (introduced in (a)) and in turn contributes to reinforcing them.

c) The consequences of (b) in stamping human personalities in a modern, industrial society are brought to the foreground and scrutinized from the viewpoint of more or less explicit ideas of what endangers and what preserves the dignity, freedom and cultural values of human beings.

d) Remedial possibilities, if any, are considered.

Before we turn to the value which such an approach can have for the specific field of communications research, it is first necessary to meet an objection to the idea of critical research which may be raised against it on its own ground, to wit, that so much of its effort is spent on what might

be called "showing up" things, rather than on fact-finding or constructive suggestions. It must be admitted that being constructive is a rather relative concept, and that the question of what are relevant facts cannot be decided only according to established procedures. The situation is somewhat similar to the wave of criticism which started with the reports of the Royal Commission in the British Parliament and with the English social literature of the Dickens type in the first half of the last century. Then, the task was to discover and to denounce the material cruelties of the new industrial system: child labor, slum conditions, and so on. Not that all these horrors have now been eliminated, but at least there is enough public consciousness of them so that whenever a student finds similar conditions, for instance among migrant workers or sharecroppers, some steps toward improvement are taken. The trend of public opinion and public administration is toward better social conditions. In cultural matters, a similar development has not yet taken place. The examples given above will be taken by many readers as rather insignificant in a field which is not of great practical importance. It might very well be, however, that we are all so busy finding our place in society according to established standards of success that nothing is more important at this moment than to remind ourselves of basic cultural values which are violated, just as it was of decisive historic importance a hundred years ago to remind the English middle classes that they were overlooking the sacrifices which the new strata of industrial laborers underwent when the modern industrial world was built. As Waller has pointed out,[8] the moral standards of tomorrow are due to the extreme sensitiveness of a small group of intellectual leaders of today. A few decades ago the artist who was destined to be the classic of the succeeding generation was left to starve in his own time. Today we are very eager not to overlook any growing talent, and we have fellowships and many other institutions which try to assist the growth of any seed of artistic development. Why should we not learn to be more hospitable to criticism and find forms in which more patience can be exercised to wait and, in the end, to see what is constructive and what is not.[9]

And now for the specific contributions which the idea of critical research can make to the student who is engaged in the administrative research side of the problem. As long as there is so little experience in the actual cooperation of critical and administrative research, it is very difficult to be concrete. One way to put it is to point to the strong intellectual stimulation which derives from such joint efforts. There will be hardly a student in empirical research who does not sometimes feel a certain regret or impatience about the vast distance between problems of sampling and probable errors on the one hand, and the significant social problems of our times on the other. Some have hit upon the solution of making their social interests their private avocation, and keeping that separate from their research procedures, hoping that one day in the future the two will again merge. If it were possible in the terms of critical research to formulate an actual research operation which could be integrated with empirical work, the people involved, the problems treated and, in the end, the actual utility of the work would greatly profit.

Such a vitalization of research might well occur in a variety of forms which can only be exemplified and not stated in a systematic way. Quite likely, for instance, more attention will be given to problems of control. If we study the effects of communication, however fine methods we use, we will be able to study only the effects of radio programs or printed material that is actually being distributed. Critical research will be especially interested in such material as never gets access to the channels of mass communication: What ideas and what forms are killed before they ever reach the general public, whether because they would not be interesting enough for large groups, or because they would not pay sufficient returns on the necessary investment, or because no traditional forms of presentation are available?

Once a program is on the air or a magazine is printed, critical research is likely to look at the content in an original way. A number of examples are available in the field of musical programs.[10] Serious music on the radio is not unconditionally accepted as good. The promotion of special conductors, which exaggerates the existing differences and detracts from attention to more important aspects of music, is pointed to as another intrusion of an advertising mentality into an educational sphere. The ceaseless repetition of a comparatively small number of recognized "master works" is derived from the necessity to keep public service programs more in line with commercial fare of the radio. From such an analysis concrete suggestions evolve as to how music

programs on the radio should be conducted to make them really serve a more widespread music appreciation. A discussion of the social significance and the probable effect of popular music, to which almost 50 per cent of all radio time is given, is also available and so far represents the most elaborate analysis of a type of mass communication from the point of view of critical social research.[11] Similar studies of printed matter can be made. For instance, what is the significance of the great vogue of biographies during the last decade? A study of their content shows that they all talk in terms of sweeping laws of society, or mankind or the human soul to which every individual is submitted and at the same time point up the unique greatness and importance of the one hero they are treating.[12] The success of this kind of literature among middle class readers is taken as an indication that many of them have lost their bearing in regard to their social problems. These biographies reflect a feeling that we are swept by waves of events over which the ordinary human being has no control and which call for leadership by people with super-human abilities. By such analysis anti-democratic implications are carved out in a literary phenomenon which otherwise would not attract the attention of the social scientist.

On the other end, upon studying the actual effects of communication, larger vistas are opened to someone whose observations are influenced by the critical attitude here discussed. To give only one example: We praise the contribution which radio makes by enlarging so greatly the world of each single individual, and undoubtedly the praise is deserved. But is the matter quite so simple? A farmer might be very well equipped to handle all the problems which his environment brings up, able to distinguish what makes sense and what doesn't, what he should look out for and what is unimportant. Now the radio brings in a new world with new problems which don't necessarily grow out of the listener's own life. This world has a character of magic, where things happen and are invisible at the same time; many listeners have no experience of their own which would help them to appraise it. We know that that sometimes has very disturbing effects, as witnessed by the attitude of women listeners to daytime serials, by the attitude of millions of letter writers who try to interfere with the world of radio without really believing that their efforts will make any difference. It certainly should be worthwhile not to stop at such incidental observations but to see whether people's attitudes toward reality are not more profoundly changed by radio than we usually find with more superficial observations of their daily habits.

Notes

1. For a general orientation in the field see Douglas Waples, *What Reading Does to People*, University of Chicago Press, 1940 and Paul F. Lazarsfeld, *Radio and the Printed Page*, Duell, Sloan and Pearce, 1940. For more current and specific information the *Public Opinion Quarterly*, published by the Princeton University Press, is the best source of articles and bibliography.

2. Among the universities, the University of Chicago Library School and the University of Minnesota Journalism School are especially active in the field of communications research. Organizations doing similar work with foundation funds are the Adult Education Association, the American Film Center, the Columbia University Office of Radio Research, the Library of Congress and the Princeton Public Opinion Research Project. In the magazine field, *Life* and *McCall's* are currently publishing valuable information. Material on radio can best be obtained through the research directors of the Columbia Broadcasting System and the National Broadcasting Company.

3. Harold Lasswell, *Democracy Through Public Opinion*, George Banta Publishing Co. 1941.

4. There is a rather suggestive way to overcome the argument of the futility of empirical research. One might, for instance, tell such an opponent that according to studies which have been done people who make up their minds during a political campaign as to how to vote are influenced by very different factors than those who have more permanent political affiliations. The opponent will find that immediately understandable and will say that he could have come to this conclusion by using good common sense. It so happens that the opposite is true and that it is possible to predict to a high degree the vote of originally undecided people by means of the same characteristics which describe people with actual party affiliations. There are many other examples by which common sense first can be led to conclusions which then are proved by actual data to be incorrect.

5. Cf. especially "Traditional and Critical Theory" in the *Zeitschrift für Sozialforschung*, VI (1937), pp. 245–295; "Philosophy and Critical Theory" pp. 625–631. The examples used here in presenting the idea of critical social research were taken from studies done by Dr. T. W. Adorno.

6. It might help to clarify these ideas by comparing them briefly with other trends of thought, such as the consumer movement on the one hand and propaganda analysis on the other. The consumer movement is concerned with concrete wrongs in current advertising and might even denounce all advertising as economically wasteful. For the critical approach, business advertisement is only one of the many promotional forms by which present society is maintained and its cultural rather than its economic implications are discussed. A similar difference appears in comparison with propaganda analysis. The problem is not that people are misled in regard to certain isolated facts, but that they have less and less opportunity to develop standards of judgment of their own because wherever they turn they are caught by some kind of promotion.

7. Cf. W. Benjamin's study on Baudelaire in this periodical, Vol. VIII (1939-40), pp. 50 ff.

8. *The Family*, Dryden Press, 1931.

9. It is quite possible that the radio industry could lead in releasing some of the pressure which, at this time, keeps much social research in conventional forms and cuts it off from expanding into new fields. Already, in the field of politics, the radio industry has proved itself more neutral and more balanced than any other large business institution. The necessity of keeping in touch with the large masses of the population might also make them more amenable to trying methods of research even if, at first, they seem less innocuous. An honest analysis of program contents and program policies might be the first testing ground.

10. See T. W. Adorno, "On a Social Critique of Radio Music," on file at the Office of Radio Research, Columbia University.

11. See T. W. Adorno, "On Popular Music," in this issue.

12. Such an analysis has been carried through by L. Lowenthal of the Institute of Social Research and is now being extended to the many biographies which are currently appearing in American magazines with mass circulation.

27

The Popular Music Industry

From *Radio Research 1941* (1942)

Duncan MacDougald Jr.

Duncan MacDougald Jr. (1913–1969) was born in Atlanta, Georgia. His career was spent in freelance writing, including work on popular music. He was a protégé of Theodor Adorno, and this study reads like an extended application of Adorno's theory of popular music. It is also a slice of 1930s musical life, thanks to its heavy documentation. We excerpt from the beginning and from the conclusion of the rather lengthy essay. His analysis of the business of producing hits in popular music seems remarkably similar to today's merchandising of music, even though he is talking about the "plugging" of sheet music rather than pop acts being both promoted by Top 40 radio and exposed by MTV, as is the norm today. MacDougald believed that taste was manufactured into people rather than developed spontaneously from their preferences; in other words, his model of cultural production was "supply driven" not "demand driven." The degree to which taste is a by-product of the culture industries remains one of the great debates in American life, with obvious implications for democracy; it is also not accidentally one of the key debates in social thought about mass communication, from Dewey and Du Bois to the Frankfurt School and Dwight Macdonald.

General Background[1]

The "Industry"

The object of this study is to contribute coherent and specific information about the way in which the popularity of hit songs is determined by the agencies controlling the popular music business. The method of ascertaining these factors has largely been to trace the life of a typical hit from its creation to the sale of the commercial piano copy, and to point out in the steps of this life story those forces which come into play for the purpose of enforcing the acceptance of the song. The study develops the thesis that the making of the majority of "hits" is largely predetermined by and within the industry.

It is in direct contrast to the general opinion of Tin Pan Alley which clings to the ideology that the success of songs represents the spontaneous, free-will acceptance of the public because of the inherent merit of the number. However, it will be seen in the following pages that in the case of most hits many factors other than the song's actual merit are responsible for its "popularity."

Before going into the details of how songs become hits, it is necessary to discuss the business setting which plays such an important role in predetermining the success of song—the broader aspects of the popular music industry known as Tin Pan Alley.

It is essential first of all to explain what is meant by the term "industry." The term is not to be taken literally, but metaphorically. What, then, is the basis of using it at all?

The word industry is used primarily because all this music[2]—"production numbers" from musical revues and films excepted—is produced in terms of direct consumer consumption. In other words, this is music designed expressly for the market, as shown by the confession of almost every song writer that he definitely tries to "*write a hit*," that is, write a song that will *sell*. This is something which contemporary popular music has in common with all the "light music" that has been written since the establishment of a gulf between serious and light music production and does not necessarily constitute a criterion for industrial production, where concepts such as mass-production and use of machines, etc., are necessarily involved. Secondly, when speaking of the music industry one often thinks of the division of labor which outwardly manifests itself in the fact that practically every song hit has at least two writers, and moreover that the actual composing is quite apart from the "arrangement." This seems to suggest on the surface industrial "rationalized" methods. However, the fact that many hands contribute to creating the song actually points more to a manufactural than to an industrial production. Division of labor alone does not constitute an industrial process and has been a familiar method of production throughout the manufactural era.

It should be stated further that the practice of including a number of people in song production—usually at least two writers (the lyric writer and the composer), and frequently other persons (the inventor of the title or lyric idea, the man who writes down the music, the harmonizer, and so on) is not due to an actual rationalization of production. The reason most often suggested is the deficiency of the half amateur who has an idea but cannot write it down or dramatize it. The many musicians incapable of scoring are also cited. However, the fact that Tin Pan Alley stuff is written by men without sound musical training and that Irving Berlin, for instance, must use a specially constructed piano because he can work in only one key, has already become part of the great American legend. An expert on the musical scene in America, Miss Minna Lederman, suggests that it is the "Broadway tradition" that is important here rather than the well-plugged "ignorance" of the supposedly naive composers. There is a kind of vested interest in running the "industry" this way. For several generations Broadway has nurtured a tradition of musical as well as other types of illiteracy; the association of lowbrowism with success is still a vigorous faith on the Main Stem and appears today to be artificially promoted rather than genuine. It is quite probable that a number of the composers can "score," "arrange," and do all the necessary things involved in writing a serious composition; yet they do not do it because of the

traditional set-up of the industry.[3] In any case, the division of labor in the production of song hits is itself of a largely irrational character and leads in many instances to an overlapping of functions and to conflicts between the different agencies involved in song production. It is certainly not a question of a well-planned and systematic idea of dividing labor in order to facilitate the process, reduce overhead costs and operate at maximum capacity. Thus it must be discounted as an index of "industrialization."

There is still a third point of view involved in the use of the term industry, and the last one offers mere justification to the use of the term. Roughly speaking, *the methods of distribution used in the popular music business are largely borrowed from those used by any industry producing consumer goods which do not strictly belong to the necessities of life.* The promotion and distribution of popular songs is not left to chance nor to the spontaneous success or failure of the offered material in the market. What makes this process so similar to the industrial one is its highly developed *"system,"* all of whose parts are directed toward one end: the enforcement of the material upon the customer. As a result of various circumstances, this systematic character today has reached a stage where the exploitation of songs has become largely automatic. An appreciable analogy is to be found in women's fashions, which are manipulated and determined by the producer, i.e., the designer or style expert.

The "Market"

A rough estimate, based upon information gathered in interviews within the industry and open to further investigation, reveals that there are some sixty popular music publishers.[4] These sixty publishers audition an estimated 50,000 songs annually—many of them "repeats," i.e., the same song auditioned by different publishers—and publish and work on some 2,000 popular numbers. Of these some 350 to 400 songs benefit by extensive radio exploitation, while the others are "knocked around," receiving several performances here and there and selling a few hundred copies of sheet music. A computation of "Air Performance Lists" compiled by the Accurate Reporting Service, an organization that checks and reports upon the number of performances of all popular songs broadcast over radio stations WABC, WEAF, WJZ and WHN, WNEW and WOR, reveals that there are at least 300 songs currently "on the market." This figure includes, of course, "standards" (such songs as "Sweet Sue" and "St. Louis Blues") and the so-called "old favorites" (selections such as "Londonderry Air" and swing arrangements of the songs of Stephen Foster) which comprise 10 to 15 per cent of all popular songs heard on the air.

The industry estimates that an average of 35 to 40 new songs are placed on the market each week. Of these numbers, however, only some five to eight new songs receive enough air performances via New York radio stations to be included in the plug lists of the trade press.

The Hit

The business ideal of the industry is to create a "hit."

A song is classified as a hit when it sells 75,000 copies of sheet music, and it is estimated that not more than twenty songs reach sales of 100,000 copies each year. A figure of 300,000 is now considered phenomenal for a popular song, and rarely do more than five numbers attain this popularity annually. Although record sales have increased 500 per cent since 1932, the low year of the industry, few songs ever reach a sale of 500,000 records, while an average hit sells some 250,000 recordings.[5]

The average life of a popular song may be estimated at some twelve weeks. Spectacular novelties such as "The Music Goes Round and Round," or so-called "rhythm numbers," for example "Flat Foot Floogie," enjoy an extensive though short-lived popularity of six to eight weeks, while less sensational material such as waltzes and ballads may remain in favor for ten to twenty weeks.

It is pertinent here to cite comparative figures concerning the life and popularity of songs twenty years ago before radio became the principal medium of exploitation. Songs considered "good sellers" sold 500,000 sheet music copies, as compared to 50,000 sheet music copies now; "smash hits" sold as many as 2,000,000 sheet music copies to a corresponding sale of 300,000 copies under present conditions. Before radio, a best-selling song was popular for as long as eighteen months; now, however, the life of a hit is rarely more than four months.

Thus will be seen the tremendous changes which have taken place in the popular music industry. Twenty years ago songs were "plugged"

by the song pluggers themselves, vaudeville entertainers, singers and traveling bands for a period of several months before they became hits. Now a song is introduced, exploited[6] and "played to death" all within a corresponding period of a few months. A listener then probably heard less than three performances of a hit in a week; listeners now may hear a hit from three to six times daily. Publishers then could count on the popularity of a song lasting for one to two years; now a publisher knows that his song will last only three to five months.

In attempting to ascertain what factors are chiefly responsible for these important changes in the popular music industry, it is natural to assume as do publishers, that radio has been the principal agent. In a certain sense this is probably true. Nevertheless, there are other very important factors which have contributed to these changes, among which are: (1) the significant price differential—most sheet music now is priced at 30 or 35 cents as compared with 10 cents and 25 cents in pre-radio days, (2) preference for other forms of recreational interest such as the movies, automobiles in place of pianos, etc., and (3) curtailed recreational budget due to economic reasons (the 1929 depression). Accordingly, one must not oversimplify the matter. The total and general effect of radio upon popular songs may be summarized as follows: While the length of a song's popularity has been materially shortened, the extent (number of listeners) of its popularity has been greatly increased. In absolute terms, i.e., the number of people who hear and may remember a song at all, the popularity of a song hit has been increased by intensive radio plugging, whereas in relative terms the opposite is true: its life cycle is very much shorter (three months as compared to eighteen months), its sheet sales have materially decreased (50,000–100,000 as compared with 500,000–1,000,000), and it is probably less known (as an *individual* song) than the pre-radio hit.

High Pressure Plugging of Songs and Entertainers on the Radio

Exploitation by means of artificial build-up not only includes plugging in the literal sense of the ceaseless repetition of the same number but also to the way of presentation, to announcement, name plugging, build-up of orchestra leaders, all-star polls, and so on. The following examples may illustrate some of these aspects of plugging.

A very important psychological effect is the build-up by radio announcers of certain songs and featured performers. Frequently songs are presented to the radio audience as "the latest smash hit" or "one of Tin Pan Alley's most outstanding contributions."

As publishers seize every possible opportunity to spread favorable propaganda for their songs, it would be logical to assume that they would concentrate on getting announcers to introduce songs in this pseudo-enthusiastic manner. However, as far as could be ascertained from interviews with the announcing staffs of the two major networks, announcers are rarely approached by publishers requesting favorable introductions of this nature. Such "build-ups" are prohibited at NBC by a regulation which requires announcers to present sustaining programs of dance music as simply as possible and without any unnecessary plugs concerning the popularity or "outstanding" character of any song. CBS has no specific ruling against announcements which might serve to influence listeners favorably toward a particular song, but according to information obtained, the network would be quick to act against any excessive plugging on the part of its announcers. When such build-ups do occur, they are usually interpolated by the announcer to inject some element of "human interest" in the necessarily monotonous routine of announcing a number of similar dance tunes.

On the other hand, there are commercial programs that make definite attempts to popularize and "glamourize" the performers (orchestras, orchestra leaders, singers and song writers) and the material (renditions and songs) featured on these programs.

In industrial civilization there is a tremendous temptation to be interested in "the best," "the biggest," or "the finest." It is particularly true that the American is irresistibly lured by superlatives and is drawn into favoring "the best," "the newest," or "the king" of this or that. Thus Jimmy Dorsey, who was only recently labeled "The World's Greatest Saxophonist" was named by both "All-Star Polls" sponsored by *Metronome*[7] and *Down Beat*[8]—as "The Greatest Alto Saxophonist," receiving 975 votes in *Metronome's* mythical band of stars and 5,109 in the contest conducted by *Down Beat*. Johnny Hodges, who is regarded by musicians and jazz experts as a vastly superior musician, received, as a comparatively obscure member of Duke Ellington's

orchestra, only 594 votes for second place in *Metronome's* poll and 1,219 ballots for third place in the *Down Beat* voting.

The influence of prestige-reputation and build-up upon producer and consumer may be illustrated at this point by a brief history of the song "Day In—Day Out" from manuscript to hit-dom. Johnny Mercer and Rube Bloom are recognized by the industry as outstanding "consistent writers" with a number of past successes to their credit. Any song that they write, therefore, is certain to be given favorable consideration by publishers, consciously or unconsciously, reflecting an attitude of "this-may-be-another-terrific-hit," or "if-I-don't-take-it, some-other-publisher-will."

Once this song has been published by a Big Publisher (in this case B-V-C), it is extensively exploited by leading performers.

Now comes the build-up on the part of the program announcer as the song is introduced on the Camel Caravan[9] featuring Bob Crosby's orchestra, Helen Ward and Johnny Mercer:

CROSBY: Yes sir! Where else in the country can you get this *sensational* two-for-one. Our *lovely* singer Helen Ward, and in the same package, a *brand-new song with words by our versatile verser, Johnny Mercer.*

"CUSTOMER" in the Dixieland Music Shop: Sounds *swell* to me.

CROSBY: It's a Dixieland Music Shop *Exclusive*, because it's *the first performance on the air.*

CUSTOMER: That Johnny Mercer certainly keeps busy. Just give him a pad and pencil, and the first thing you know Johnny comes out with a lyric like "Jeepers Creepers"[10] or "You Must Have Been a Beautiful Baby."[10]

CROSBY: That's right, and "Cuckoo in the Clock," "Could Be" and "And the Angels Sing."[10]

CUSTOMER: That's a *lot of hits for any man in one year.*

CROSBY: It sure is, and *we know you're all going to sing, dance and whistle this new one into another winner.* So here it comes, *words by Johnny Mercer,* music by Rube Bloom, sung by Helen Ward, and Johnny calls it "Day In—Day Out."

As predicted, the song "Day In—Day Out" was "sung, danced and whistled into another winner," and October 21, 1939 it was the Number

One song on the Hit Parade. On October 24, 1939 this selection was again featured on the Camel Caravan with the following build-up:

CROSBY: Not long ago we gave *a new song its first demonstration*, and I remember I said to Johnny Mercer, who wrote the words, "John T," I said, *"that is a lallapalooza of a lyric. That,"* I said, *"will be the nation's number one hit before Hallowe'en,"* end quote. And sure enough it is, with music by Rube Bloom and *words by Johnny Mercer.*[11]

The new song now bears close resemblance to a "bestseller" on the book market. Just as it is "the thing to do" to read the most publicized book of the day, it is correspondingly advantageous from the prestige standpoint to know—and very often to like—"the most popular song in the country."

Listeners who heard the first presentation of "Day In—Day Out" in all probability feel that they are "in on" an important introduction, and are likely to be interested in following the career of the song to see whether it will really become a hit or will turn out to be just another song. Theirs is a "personal interest," and on rehearing it as the country's most popular song, they are in a position to tell friends with a feeling of pride and prestige: *"I heard that song the first time it was played on the radio."*

Such pseudo-enthusiastic plugging is not limited to songs, as performers of this music are frequently heavily plugged in a similar fashion in an attempt to convince the listener that the program in question features "the greatest" performers on the air. Of special interest are the following samples of "build-up" given Benny Goodman during the past four years—plugging which has had an incalculable effect in making the radio audience accept him and his orchestra unconditionally as "the greatest swing-band" of all time:

ANNOUNCER: Ladies and gentlemen: It is my pleasure and my privilege to introduce a man whose soaring genius marks him not as a mortal man, but as a man among tens of millions of mortal—Benny Goodman, Capital B-E-N-N-Y G-O-O-D-M-A-N.[12]
ANNOUNCER: The makers of Camel Cigarettes present the Saturday night Camel Caravan with Benny Goodman, and *the greatest assembly of swing artists in the world.*

. . . And here he is—The King of Swing—Benny Goodman.[13]
ANNOUNCER: And now—one of those early rockeroos *that put Benny Goodman on the throne, and made him the King of Swing.*[14]

In similar fashion featured singers and instrumentalists are enthusiastically plugged:

JOHNNY MERCER: And one of the *main reasons it's really going places is the way Bob Crosby sings it.*[15]
ANNOUNCER: Yeah, you're right. She's here. *The Queen herself*—Mildred Bailey. *The one who started a style of singing no one's ever been able to copy. We hear that Bailey style at its best tonight as Mildred sings one of the most beautiful ballads of recent months*—"The Lamp Is Low."[16]
GOODMAN: And incidentally, Charlie Christian, who was unknown six months ago, is being named in this same poll ("All-Star Band Contest" in *Down Beat* Magazine) *as the best swing guitarist in the country.*[17]

Not directly connected with this investigation of popular music on the air, but still of great interest and importance are the "All-Star Polls" conducted by various trade journals. These yearly contests purport to present a composite all-star dance band, as selected by the magazines' readers. Although the magazines stress the fact that the voting is done chiefly by "musicians," i.e., qualified judges of instrumentalists, the results indicate that a large number of votes are cast by jitterbugs, who could in no way be called discriminating appraisers of genuine, outstanding musicianship. It is, of course, significant that of the sixteen performers named on *Down Beat's* "1939 All-American Band,"[18] eleven are name band leaders[19] in their own right, four are featured instrumentalists with name bands (three with Goodman, one with Bob Crosby), while the remaining position was filled by the highly publicized Bing Crosby.

It may be safely assumed that important among the dominant factors motivating the preference of jitterbugs for certain bands and performers are: (1) the hero-celebrity lure of certain leaders, (2) (largely overlapping the first point) the prestige-popularity influence of name bands, and (3) sensationalism of performers.

Probably the most important factor in influencing ignorant and undiscerning jitterbugs to vote for certain musicians is the prestige and reputation of favorite name bands and leaders. *Metronome* comments as follows upon the prestige influence:

> Note throughout that in all departments, *men playing with name bands drew large votes, greater in many instances than their musicianship warrants.*[20]

In this statement lies the explanation of countless ballots—the "glamorous" mass-appeal of the celebrity.

Even more convincing evidence of the irresistible lure of prestige and the positive effects of plugging is found in the record of Charlie Christian in *Down Beat's* "1939 All-American Band."[21] Until Christian joined the Benny Goodman band in the summer of 1939, he was a totally unknown musician in Oklahoma. Six months later, as a heavily plugged feature member of Goodman's orchestra, he was named "The Best Guitarist in the Country" with a total of 2,665 to 1,877 votes for his nearest competitor.

As far as sensationalism of performers is concerned, one must have a rather primitive idea of this sensationalism. Its criterion is not based upon instrumental virtuosity or artistry, but upon— "the louder the better." This can be confirmed by a comparison of the applause of broadcasting studio audiences—made up largely of jitterbugs— following solo performances by Gene Krupa (drums), Harry James (trumpet), and Jess Stacy (piano) of the Benny Goodman orchestra. In each case it was noted that the loud and spectacular soli of Krupa and James were received with much more ostentatious enthusiasm than those of Stacy, although there are few jazz experts who would admit that Krupa and James are superior musicians.

The result of the whole plugging mechanism in all its different aspects may be summed up as follows: The public at large—more specifically the radio audience—has been led more and more to the point of merely accepting these songs as standardized (musical) products, with less and less active resentment and critical interest. While the accepted songs are being incessantly hammered into the listeners' heads, the prestige build-up strives to make the audience believe that this constant repetition is due to the inherent qualities of the song, rather than to the will to sell it—either for prestige or for profits. Thus it may be assumed that this controlled repetition and manipulated recommendation seem to tend to the standard-ization of the tastes of the listener and the subsequent gradual eradication of these tastes.

Notes

1. The present study was completed prior to the conflict between The American Society of Composers, Authors and Publishers and Broadcast Music, Incorporated. This controversy has created a completely irregular situation in the popular song industry which has not been studied because obviously, once the two copyright agencies have come to an understanding, things will revert to normal. Also, it seemed desirable to avoid taking any stand in the matter.

The author wishes to acknowledge the continual help he has received from Dr. T. W. Adorno in the theoretical organization of his observations in the field, and in the formulation of his final report.

2. An analysis of the lists of radio performances of popular songs in the trade press reveals that some 8 per cent are from musical revues, approximately 25 per cent from films, and the remaining 67 per cent are "pops."

3. An analogy may be found in Hollywood, where certain very well-trained European composers working for the film companies actually were forbidden to score their own works because that was considered exclusively the arranger's job.

4. Bruce and Silver (*How to Write and Sell a Song Hit*, New York, 1939, p. 193) give a list of 50 well-known publishers, while some 40 popular music firms are listed in the New York Classified Telephone Directory. It must be assumed, however, that there are additional firms engaged in publishing popular music that are not given in these sources.

5. It is impossible to arrive at an accurate ratio between the sale of sheet music and of records, this being due to the fact that the record may be purchased for the sake of the rendition by a favorite performer, or for the selection on the other side. In the case of some songs— particularly novelties and rhythm numbers—the sale of records may greatly exceed the sale of sheet music. It may be noted here that in 1939 some 16,000,000 copies of sheet music were sold (*Variety*, April 9, 1941, p. 1), as compared with an estimated 45,000,000 popular records (*Musical Merchandise*, January 1940, p. 50).

6. To what extent the highly organized plugging mechanism of the industry has succeeded may be seen in the following figures. According to statistics compiled by the Federal Communications Commission for 1938 (latest available data), some 40 per cent of all station time is devoted to popular music—more than any other classification of program—on all radio stations in the country. A breakdown of the 1938 performance records of the American Society of Composers, Authors and Publishers made by Broadcast Music, Inc., reveals that 388 songs performed more than 10,000 times (1.8 per cent of the total of 21,038 selections tabulated) accounted for 8,604,894 performances (47.1 per cent of all performances), while an additional 2,121 songs performed up to 10,000 times (10.l per cent of the 21,038 selections tabulated) accounted for an additional 6,678,359 performances (36.6 per cent of performances). Thus the relatively small number of 2,509 selections accounted for 83.7 per cent of all performances. A specific example of this concentrated plugging may be found in the case of the song "Says My Heart" which was performed over WABC, WJZ and WEAF 258 times during the four week period June 22, 1938, to July 13, 1938—an average of 9.2 times daily.

7. *Metronome,* January 1940, p. 12.

8. *Down Beat,* January 1, 1940, p. 12.

9. Camel Caravan, August 22, 1939, 9:30 E.S.T. over WABC. Wm. Esty Agency.

10. Listed as one of the 20 Best Sellers for 1939 (*Variety,* January 3, 1940, p. 124),

11. Camel Caravan, October 24, 1939 (9:30 E.S.T.), over WABC.

12. Camel Caravan, October 7, 1939, at 10:00 over WEAF.

13. Camel Caravan, October 21, 1939, at 10:00 over WEAF.

14. Camel Caravan, October 21, 1939, at 10:00 over WEAF.

15. Camel Caravan, October 3, 1939, 9:30 E.S.T. over WABC.

16. Camel Caravan, October 7, 1939, 10:00 E.S.T. over WEAF.

17. Camel Caravan, December 2, 1939, 10:00 E.S.T. over WEAF.

18. *Down Beat,* January 7, 1940, p. 13.

19. It is revealing to note that *Down Beat* was forced to eliminate the choice of band leaders in subsequent polls, as it was obvious that a great many votes were cast solely because of the leaders' prestige and reputation.

20. *Metronome,* January 1939, p. 14.

21. *Down Beat,* January 1, 1940, p. 13.

28

From *Dialectic of Enlightenment* (1944)

Max Horkheimer and Theodor Adorno

In 1944 Horkheimer and Adorno completed *Dialectic of Enlightenment*, a wide-ranging text treating the catastrophe of Western civilization, in which the blandishments of the "culture industry" play a central part. Subtitling it *Philosophical Fragments,* these longtime collaborators wrote an astonishing, difficult, and profound modernist text that treats such disparate themes as the *Odyssey,* the history of civilization, and Donald Duck. Both Horkheimer and Adorno were practicioners of the art of the aphorism, and these brief sections, from an appendix of "notes and drafts" to the book, feature some of their ideas on the social meaning of mass communication. The fulfillment of such dreams as communication or consumer abundance has created nightmares; the authors always have a keen eye for the dark, ironic side of events (see Peters 2003). For biographies, see pages 157 (Horkheimer) and 210 (Adorno).

Isolation by Communication

Modern communications media have an isolating effect; this is not a mere intellectual paradox. The lying words of the radio announcer become firmly imprinted on the brain and prevent men from speaking to each other; the advertising slogans for Pepsi-Cola sound out above the collapse of continents; the example of movie stars encourages young children to experiment with sex and later leads to broken marriages. Progress literally keeps men apart. The little counters in railroad stations or banks enabled clerks to talk and joke with their colleagues. The glass windows of modern offices and the great halls in which innumerable employees sit down together and can easily be supervised by the public and managers prevent private conversations and moments out of time. In administrative offices the taxpayer is now protected against time wasting by employees. They are isolated in the collective system. But means of communication also isolate men physically. Railroads have given way to private automobiles, which reduce acquaintanceships made during journeys to contacts with hitchhikers— which may even be dangerous. Men travel on rubber tires in complete isolation from each other. The conversations in their vehicles are always identical and regulated by practical interests. The families in specific income brackets spend the same percentage on housing, movies, and cigarettes as the statistics prescribe; the themes of conversation vary with the category of vehicle. When visitors meet on Sundays or holidays in restaurants whose menus and rooms are identical at the different price levels, they find that they have become increasingly similar with their increasing isolation. Communication establishes uniformity among men by isolating them.

Mass Society

The cult of celebrities (film stars) has a built-in social mechanism to level down everyone who stands out in any way. They stars are simply a pattern round which the world-embracing garment is cut—a pattern to be followed by the shears of legal and economic justice with which the last projecting ends of thread are cut away.

Note

The opinion that the leveling-down and standardization of men is accompanied on the other hand by a heightened individuality in the "leader" personalities that corresponds to the power they enjoy, is false and an ideological pretense. The modern Fascist bosses are not so much supermen as functions of their own propaganda machine, the focal points at which identical reactions of countless citizens intersect. In the psychology of the modern masses, the Führer is not so much a father-figure as a collective and overexaggerated projection of the powerless ego of each individual—to which the so-called "leaders" in fact correspond.

They look like hairdressers, provincial actors, and hack journalists. Part of their moral influence consists precisely in the fact that they are powerless in themselves but deputize for all the other powerless individuals, and embody the fullness of power for them, without themselves being anything other than the vacant spaces taken up accidentally by power. They are not excepted from the break-up of individuality; all that has happened is that the disintegrated form triumphs in them and to some extent is compensated for its decomposition. The "leaders" have become what they already were in a less developed form throughout the bourgeois era: actors playing the part of leaders. The distance between the individuality of Bismarck and Hitler is scarcely less than that between the prose of *Thoughts and Memories* and the mumbo-jumbo of *Mein Kampf*. One important component of the fight against Fascism is to cut the inflated "Führer" images down to size. Chaplin's *Great Dictator* touched on the core of the problem by showing the similarity between the ghetto barber and the dictator.

Propaganda

How absurd it is to try to change the world by propaganda. Propaganda makes language an instrument, a lever, a machine. It fixes the condition of men, as they have come to be in under social injustice, by setting them in motion. It counts on being able to count on them. Deep down all men know that through this tool they too will be reduced to a tool as in a factory. The anger they feel mounting inside them as they succumb to propaganda is the age-old resentment against the yoke, heightened by the suspicion that the remedy it prescribes is the wrong one. Propaganda manipulates people; when it cries freedom it contradicts itself. Deceit and propaganda are inseparable. A community in which the leader and his followers come to terms through propaganda—whatever the merits of its content—is a community of lies. Truth itself becomes merely a means of enlisting support and is falsified in the very utterance. This is why genuine resistance knows no propaganda. Propaganda is misanthropic. It assumes that to say that policy ought to spring from mutual understanding is not a basic principle but conveniently empty phraseology.

In a society that prudently sets limits to the threat of superfluity, suspicion attaches to whatever one person recommends to another. The warning against commercial advertising—namely, that no business ever gives anything away—applies everywhere, and particularly to the modern fusion of industrial and political interests. The louder the boasts, the poorer the quality. The publicity on which the Volkswagen depends is different to that for the Rolls Royce. Producer and consumer interests are not brought into line, even where the former has something serious to offer. Propaganda for freedom itself can be a source of confusion in that it must bridge the gap between theory and the special interests of its audience. The workers' leaders defeated in Germany were robbed even of the truth of their own action by Fascism, which undermined solidarity through its choice of a method of retaliation. If intellectuals are tortured to death in prison camps, the workers outside do not have to be worse off. Fascism did not mean the same thing to Ossietzky as to the proletariat. But both were betrayed by it.

It is not the portrayal of reality as hell on earth but the slick challenge to break out of it that is suspect. If there is anyone today to whom we can pass the responsibilities for the message, we bequeath it not to the "masses," and not to the individual (who is powerless), but to an imaginary witness—lest it perish with us.

29

Nazi Propaganda and Violence

From *German Radio Propaganda* (1944)

Ernst Kris and Hans Speier

Ernst Kris (1900–1957) came from the same social circles as Paul Lazarsfeld. The son of a Jewish lawyer who was a friend of Sigmund Freud, Kris studied art history and became curator of the Museum of Art in Vienna before turning to psychoanalysis. In 1938, he fled to London, where he helped the BBC analyze Nazi radio propaganda. He moved to New York in 1940 and took a position at the New School for Social Research, known as the "University in Exile" for its accommodation of refugee scholars. Hans Speier (1905–1990), who had studied sociology and economics, came from Germany to the New School in 1933. During the war, he worked for the State Department's Intelligence Service and afterward as head of the Social Sciences Division for the RAND Corporation, where he oversaw numerous research studies on Cold War foreign policy.

German Radio Propaganda (1944) is a huge, multiauthor book funded by the Rockefeller Foundation and based on content analysis of domestic and international propaganda generated by the Nazis. This rich excerpt is from the book's opening, interpretive chapter. It lays out some of the classic criticisms made of the Nazis' propaganda and mass politics: their violence; their planned spontaneity; their bureaucratized mass participation; and their role in creating a charismatic, quasi-magical aura around Hitler.

Words may achieve what bullets do not accomplish, because words do not kill. A ruthless and powerful man would be foolish if he killed opponents he could use for his own purposes. The dead can neither fight nor work. At best, they may be used as examples to frighten others, equally powerless, into yielding in order to keep alive.

Political propaganda in Nazi Germany is a form of coercion; while it lacks the bluntness and irrevocability of physical violence, it derives its ultimate efficacy from the power of those who may, at any moment, cease talking and start killing. Political propagandists are so occupied with their craft that they have no time for executing the threats they utter. They leave the coercion of the recalcitrant who remain unimpressed by verbal threats to men with different skills and weapons. For this reason, the relation between propaganda and physical violence is often obscured. National Socialist propaganda, however, cannot be understood if its relation to National Socialist terror is overlooked. Goebbels at home would be ineffectual without Himmler, and Goebbels addressing foreign audiences would be a comical figure were it not for Germany's armed might. At home, Goebbels bends the Germans; Himmler breaks them.

The effect of Goebbels' eloquence at home is in large but undeterminable measure the effect of State and Party power. The very existence of this power affects action, speech, and attitude. The heart, said Spinoza, is in a certain respect dominated by the supreme authority which has means to effect that people 'believe, love, and hate, etc., what it wills.' And he adds that it is not necessary to prescribe such feelings, but that authority itself engenders them.

The propagandist does not always utter threats. More often he announces what has happened, confining himself, whenever possible, to events that convince the people that their government is strong, profitable, and good. Thus he rallies in admiration of the government all those who fear its power or want to have a share in it, who gain from its actions, or who are pleased by righteousness and devotion to moral principles.

Whether the propagandist utters threats of violence or merely announces what the government has done, he tries to strengthen the authority of the government among the governed, so that the governed will like to do what the government wants them to do, and dislike doing what the government wants to be left undone. Both as a public-relations man of the police and as a celebrator of governmental accomplishments the propagandist eliminates dissent in the political community.

His role is easy when there are accomplishments to celebrate. Then he can tell the truth, letting facts 'speak for themselves.' If he must cope with failure rather than success, he may still choose to tell the truth, either because he assumes that the governed are loyal enough to endure it and that they may even be incited by it to greater exertions, or because he is afraid of endangering his prestige by lying when the truth will spread through other channels. In general, however, no accomplishment is so great as not to tolerate propagandistic enlargement, and no failure so small as not to invite propagandistic efforts to render it even smaller. To a varying degree, the propagandist is constantly tempted to make use of one or several of the many forms of deception: slanting news by selection and emphasis, boasting, empty promises, flattery, the pretense of righteousness, studied enthusiasm, straight-forward lies, inventions, etc.

Ever since September 1939, Goebbels has announced what German soldiers do. This is his primary, though not his sole function; and this is both the source and the main limitation of his strength; his weakness is a consequence of German military defeats. German domestic propaganda has declined as Germany's position has deteriorated on the fields of battle. For the Nazi propagandist plays only a secondary role. He cannot protect German cities from being bombed. He cannot revive dead German soldiers. He cannot produce tanks. He cannot conquer the British Isles, take Stalingrad, or slow down the retreat of his armies. He can only say that German cities will not be bombed. He can try to conceal the number of German casualties. He can talk about 'secret weapons,' predict an invasion of Britain, claim—as Hitler did on 8 November 1942— the Stalingrad *has been* taken, and call retreats 'disengagements.'

When there is a great victory, however, the propagandist has his heyday. He describes it, praises it, and inflates its importance by arranging superb celebrations. Out of victory, he finds the material to comfort his friends and harass his enemies. He exploits what the soldier has achieved, and promises further achievement. In short, the propagandist deals in words and ceremonies within a framework of action and blood.

At home, propaganda supplements victory or is a substitute for it, just as propaganda directed toward the enemy is a substitute for violence before the caissons roll, and a supplement to it when they are rolling.[1] In periods of stalemate or inaction, it is easier for the propagandist to offer substitutes for victory than it is in periods of setback or defeat. In such periods his is the unhappy task of explaining away the situation. He promises what the soldier has not given, or he repeats the stories of past victories. Although he exhorts people not to despair, any military triumph, however small, would be more successful. He attempts to transform military defeats into moral victories— and thus into tokens of future military success. When the Sixth German Army was encircled and beaten before Stalingrad, Goebbels tried to work this miracle.

In the days of limited war, the morale of noncombatants was of little consequence to generals and statesmen, partly because many noncombatants were illiterate, interested in parochial gossip rather than in world news. There was little need to try to make them feel they had a cause in the war of their rulers. In the machine age, with its reduced religiosity and its increased interest in news, mass armies, mass production, and mass exposure to violent death require a larger measure of co-operation from the people. All who are not too ill or too old for work are indispensable in the war effort. Too many bullets would put an end to all co-operation. Propaganda

is a technique for avoiding impractical bloodshed. In Germany today, military officers address workers and award them Knight Crosses to War Merit Crosses. The German radio talks to farmers, housewives, sailors, soldiers in the occupied territories, workers, and foreign workers— all in special programs. All these groups of the population are important in the total war effort.

Napoleon I used to address his whole army, but he did not need to speak to the nation he ruled when he embarked upon a new conquest. In the Franco-Prussian War of 1870-71, Napoleon III and William of Prussia issued proclamations to both the army and the nation, but there was no systematic effort to reach individual groups of the population by continuous and special appeals. In the eighteenth century, Frederick the Great spoke to his generals and officers before a battle, but he declared that he did not wish to bother his civilian subjects about the wars he was waging. Then war was limited; today, war is total.[2]

Like mechanized fighting, domestic propaganda is not a phenomenon peculiar to Nazi Germany. In total war the governments of all belligerent countries must induce a large part of the population to co-operate voluntarily in the total war effort. Major or minor changes in the mode of life are required, their incisiveness depending on the wealth, location, and state of preparedness of the belligerent country. Hardships are imposed and sacrifices demanded everywhere. Whoever is to endure sacrifices or even to give up the pleasures he likes best will do so the more readily, the more firmly he believes he is serving a just cause that is certain to win and one that will bring not only glory to his country but also advantages to himself. In all belligerent countries, the justice of the cause must be taught to those who do not immediately see it clearly. Confidence must be maintained in the face of setbacks, and unity of mind must be preserved.

Does domestic propaganda in Nazi Germany differ from propaganda in other countries at war? The difference is as great as that between dictatorship and democracy—in a sense, even greater, because of the peculiar influence the pre-war history of National Socialism exerts upon National Socialist war propaganda.

Intentionally or unintentionally Goebbels once paraphrased 'formation of public opinion' (*Bildung der oeffentlichen Meinung*) into 'public formation of opinion' (*oeffentliche Meinungsbildung*). He was arguing that *something* should be formed, but the resultant has little in common with what is called public opinion in the non-totalitarian world. It lacks independence and spontaneity, and has no publicly recognized impact on policy. The Nazi elite has coined a new, euphemistic term for dominating the masses by apparently non-violent means. It is *Menschenfuehrung*, which means literally 'guidance of men' and may be freely translated as government through the people, despite the people.

Clearly, the nature of leadership or guidance depends on the leader, his goals and the opinions he holds of the people he leads. Hitler represents both the redemption of Germany's inglorious failures in the past and at the same time the consummation of her glorious heritage. Like a magician giving youth to the aged, wealth to the poor, and health to the sick, Hitler is capable of transforming the substance of the German people. His role in changing and illuminating the hidden meaning of Germany's history is used by Nazi propaganda in presenting German culture as an anticipation of Nazi culture.

Even more important than Hitler's sway over the past, however, is 'the wisdom, the righteousness, the goodness, and the greatness, and especially the genius of his leadership' in regard to the present.[3] There has not been a single successful campaign in this war that has not been attributed to Hitler's strategic genius. He has been credited with planning victory down to the last detail. Likewise, when Germany passes through a 'crisis,' Hitler is usually said to have prevented it's turning into disaster.

Finally, prophetic gifts are attributed to the Fuehrer, which enable him to include the future, too, in the orbit of his power. His infallibility is the core of Nazi news and his intuition governs the predictions the experts make. In the Leader State, propagandists derive whatever they say about the future from Hitler's intuition. Similarly, whatever is said about German success in the present testifies to Hitler's energy. More than that, the insistence of German propagandists on German foresight and initiative in this war is a consequence of Hitler's political position as the leader of the Reich. In a sense, all Nazi news is news of Hitler's forcing fate according to the dictates of his will.

On Hitler's fifty-fourth birthday, after the second Russian winter, Goebbels still spoke of 'the strong magic power of the Fuehrer's personality.' He also made the following statement, extraordinary in both content and style:

When among the many other arguments in favor of the certainty of our final success we also mentioned recently, in a speech at the Berlin Sportpalast, the argument that we believe in victory because we have the Fuehrer, then we received, a few weeks later, torrents of letters, especially from the front, mostly written in fiercely embattled positions, bunkers and fox-holes—letters in which this particular proof was felt to be the most convincing one in comparison with all other, merely factual proofs.

This statement should not be dismissed with the smile of the rationalist who does not believe in beliefs. Hitler's 'magic power' resides in the action of those who believe in his power. And Nazi propagandists do everything possible to nourish this belief, whether they share it or not.

As is well known, Hitler has not hesitated to express, in *Mein Kampf*, his utter contempt for the masses, their lack of intelligence, their forgetfulness, and their 'feminine' character. In the higher Nazi circles, the belief in the manageability of men has replaced the belief in man's perfectibility; the enjoyments of propagandists have superseded the cultural heritage of the West.

For all this professed contempt for the masses, however, the Nazi elite does not disregard the man in the street. Theirs is a post-democratic despotism which must present itself as a truly popular government in order to retain power. No democratic leader claims so often as Hitler to be the spokesman and representative of the people. Nor has any democratic government ever felt so constantly urged to protest that it is loved and admired by a firmly united nation.

The attitudes of the people in Germany are closely watched by the government and the party so that policies can be adapted to pre-established responses. When those responses are missing, popular feeling can be both stimulated and simulated by organized party action. Whenever it has seemed expedient to vent 'the wrath of the people' upon the Jews, synagogues have been burned by the Brown Shirts, and the party press has written of the spontaneous outbursts of popular indignation. The collection of winter clothing for the German troops in Russia during the winter of 1941 was presented as the spontaneous gesture of a people eager to express its gratitude to the soldier. The period of collection which covered Christmas week was extended beyond New Year's Day, ostensibly because of the unexpected wave of enthusiasm which flooded the collection centers. At the time of 'total mobilization' in March 1943, when the middle classes were plowed under, Dr. Goebbels opened a new division in his ministry to handle recommendations on how to conduct the war more efficiently. Suggestions with regard to the conduct of total war were to be addressed by all compatriots to the Reich Ministry of Public Enlightenment and Propaganda, Wilhelmplatz 718, Berlin W-8. The history of National Socialism abounds with cases of planned spontaneity, organized license, and bureaucratized mass participation in politics.

Democratic participation in politics has not been abolished in Germany; rather, it has been perverted. The masses are politically busy, but they are without influence. They are organized for purposes of mutual supervision, of eradicating privacy and leisure, and of stifling real spontaneity. If they look at what they are doing, they must know that they have never been more deeply engaged in politics. But precisely for this reason they participate in the strangulation of their political freedom. The net of Nazi politics in which they are caught is, to a large extent, of their own making.

The masses participate in Nazi politics not only for purposes of mutual control but also for other reasons more truly propagandistic in character. According to carefully planned designs, the masses create, and participate in, a vicarious political reality consisting of parades, meetings, anniversary celebrations, and be-flagged medieval towns. It is a world suggesting the strength and success of the Nazi cause with a degree of persuasiveness that words alone do not have. Music, rhythm, and color play a more important part in it than reason. In this world, which is packed with opportunities for overwhelming sensory experience, success is made visible and audible, righteousness becomes extraordinarily exciting, and strength a crushing immediate experience of organized crowds. Like a carnival, it is a world of physical imagery containing no trace of everyday life with its compromises and worries, but offering instead a miraculously purified reality of elation and triumph. Propaganda through mass meetings is called 'active propaganda' by Nazis.

Words cannot compete with the impact of this vicarious reality upon the masses. Hadamowsky, one of the leading Nazi publicity men, once expressed this by saying that the most nearly perfect newsreel, the most accomplished radio reporting, or the most effective write-up of a mass meeting are merely publicity for the immediate participation in such demonstrations. This Nazi perversion of democratic participation in politics is predicated upon the contempt for man as a reasonable being and the exploitation of his capacity for being fooled by pleasures which prevent him from reasoning soberly.

In part, Nazi propaganda according to the principle of vicarious participation is made possible by the complex social organization of our life. Were our life parochial and our work unspecialized, as it is, for example, on a self-sufficient farm, it would be futile to offer to us an image of reality so spurious and yet so presumptuous as is the vicarious reality of Nazi origin: it would clash with what we know to be true from our life and work. The social world we live in, however, is highly complicated and evades immediate experience. In our strictly specialized existence it takes perspicacity, reliable information, and mental effort to orient ourselves intelligently in this world. We are sure of what we do within the narrow confines of our life, but beyond its pale, the wide world of facts on which we depend easily fades into hazy imagery. Nazi *Menschenfuehrung* exploits this situation in the interest of Nazi rule.

Since the Nazis believe that the immediate sensory experience that participation provides exerts a more powerful influence on man's attitudes than arguments do, they use every verbal propaganda technique that fosters the illusion of immediacy and concreteness. Hence their preference for the spoken rather than the written word, for eye-witness reports rather than summary accounts, for a personalized presentation of the news rather than sober, impersonalized discussion, for illustration rather than explanation. Since the Nazis are also convinced of the suggestive power of the individual, they encourage group listening rather than individual listening. Since they are convinced that the human mind can be manipulated into habits, they prefer repetition to amplification. And frequently they use 'magic' words, the meaning of which is impervious to reason but which evoke a state of emotional gratification.[4]

The same factors that make for the bizarre and spectacular character of Nazi propaganda at home are responsible for its inherent weakness. The Nazis overestimate the importance of propaganda. In part this may be the result of a myth they have been spreading for too many years. Early in their career, they adopted a convenient lie expounded by German generals who could not reconcile themselves to their defeat in the last war. They claimed that Germany had been 'stabbed in the back.' While they never agreed who did the stabbing—the enemy, the Socialists, the home front, the Jews, the Freemasons—or whose back had been stabbed—that of the army, the people at home, the civil authorities, the military leadership—the legend proved too useful in the Nazi Party struggle for power not to be incessantly repeated. The adoption of this legend may have been a major mistake. At least in the present war, its shadow has repeatedly darkened the political horizon in Germany: Nazi leaders must now insist that there will not be another stab in the back because the people are loyal and their leader will not flee to Holland.

Another weakness in Nazi propaganda grows out of their attributing their historic success altogether to their own merits, making no allowance whatever for luck, accident or connivance.

The Nazis developed their propaganda technique in the domestic struggle for power. Until 1933, they engaged in a cutthroat competition with other political parties. These parties were regarded not as political opponents but as enemies, and the history of the party up to 1933 is still being celebrated as a series of martial victories. Casualties did occur at the time. Bullets were fired, and there was knifing, but the main weapons were not made of steel. In those days, Hitler was a drummer racing by car and by plane from beer hall to beer hall. His efforts were bent not on defeating any armies, but on inducing non-Nazis to vote the Nazi ticket, and, above all, on persuading non-voters to become voters— for him. Nazi skill in those days consisted, to

a large extent, in attracting popular attention by organizing mass meetings and parades, and by filling the streets with men who wore uniforms without belonging to any armed force. After the Nazi Party succeeded in gaining power, the professional pride of the propagandists was strengthened. They believed that they had moved a little world by words, and their inclination to overrate the importance of their job is perhaps understandable.

Notes

1. See Speier, Hans, and Otis, Margaret, 'German Radio Propaganda to France during the Battle of France,' *Radio Research*, ed. by P. Lazarsfeld and F. Stanton, Vol. 3, 1942–3. In press.

2. On the problems of total war, see the discussion and bibliographies in Wright, Quincy, *A Study of War*, 2 vols., Chicago, 1943; and Lasswell, H. D., 'The Garrison State,' *American Journal of Sociology*, Vol. 7, 1940, p. 7. For the impact of total war on propaganda, see the following studies by Hans Speier: 'Morale and Propaganda,' in *War in Our Time*, ed. by Speier, Hans, and Kaehler, Alfred, New York, 1939; 'The Social Types of War,' *American Journal of Sociology*, Vol. 46, 1941, pp. 445–54; 'Treachery in War,' *Social Research*, Vol. 7, 1940, pp. 258–79; 'Class Structure and Total War,' in *American Sociological Review*, Vol. 4, 1939, pp. 370–80; 'The Effect of War on the Social Order,' *The Annals of the American Academy of Political and Social Science*, Vol. 218, 1941, pp. 87–96; 'Ludendorff: The German Concept of Total War,' in *Makers of Modern Strategy*, ed. by E. M. Earle, 1943.

3. Goering, 20 May 1942.

4. See Paechter, Heinz, *Magic Thought and Magic Grammar in Totalitarian Propaganda*, mimeographed memorandum, and *Nazi Deutsch*, a dictionary of new terms created since 1933, issued by Office of European Economic Research, New York, 1942. Mimeographed.

30

Biographies in Popular Magazines

From *Radio Research 1942–1943* (1944)

Leo Lowenthal

Leo Lowenthal (1900–1993) illustrates the curious career path followed by left-wing German-Jewish academics in the United States. In the 1920s he was deeply involved in left-wing Jewish circles in Germany, and in the 1930s he became an associate of the Frankfurt Institute for Social Research and later emigrated to the United States. During the Second World War, he worked in the Office of War Information as a U. S. government propaganda analyst, and afterward, during the height of the Cold War, he became an audience research analyst at Voice of America. Professor of sociology at the University of California, Berkeley, from the mid-1950s on, Lowenthal is most famous for his work on the sociology of literature, collected in *Literature, Popular Culture, and Society* (1961). A critical intellectual who "never wanted to play along" (as he titled his autobiographical memoirs), Lowenthal nonetheless engaged in significant amounts of what Lazarsfeld called "administrative research."

"Biographies in Popular Magazines" is famous for its cross-cultural fusion. Its method of content analysis was developed largely in the United States, though its intellectual framework of critical theory was developed largely in Germany. Its central thesis seems compelling: heroes emulated by American society have shifted from self-made men and captains of industry to those elevated by lucky breaks to star status. The argument's evidentiary basis in the magazines, however, deserves to be replicated. In the period Lowenthal examines, news magazines such as *Time* arose, siphoning the male audience away from large-format magazines, such as *Saturday Evening Post* and *Colliers,* perhaps precipitating their shift toward consumerist themes, as editors sought to provide their advertisers with a female audience. Nonetheless, the piece nicely illustrates the critical theorists' disdain for the frivolous, as well as their belief that mass media help maintain an irrational yet highly organized social order whose compensations include the seeming closeness we can feel to celebrities. Leisure for Lowenthal is the continuation of work by other means. His point that "development had ceased to exist" meant that the ideal of self-realization by an integrated personality had lost its cultural purchase, an analysis shared by David Riesman (who cited Lowenthal's essay in *The Lonely Crowd*). This essay is one of many twentieth-century ruminations on the loss of the self before the print and audiovisual barrage of the mass media. Unlike postmodernists in the 1980s, who celebrated this loss as a good thing, Lowenthal held, as did the rest of those in the Frankfurt School, to the classic bourgeois ideal of a coherent self.

Rise of Biography as a Popular Literary Type

The following study is concerned with the content analysis of biographies, a literary topic which has inundated the book market for the last three decades, and has for some time been a regular feature of popular magazines. Surprisingly enough, not very much attention has been paid to this phenomenon, none whatever to biographies appearing in magazines, and little to those published in book form.[1]

It started before the first World War, but the main onrush came shortly afterwards. The popular biography was one of the most conspicuous newcomers in the realm of print since the introduction of the short story. The circulation of books by Emil Ludwig,[2] André Maurois, Lytton Strachey, Stefan Zweig, etc., reached a figure in the millions, and with each new publication, the number of languages into which they were translated grew. Even if it were only a passing literary fad, one would still have to explain why this fashion has had such longevity and is more and more becoming a regular feature in the most diversified media of publications.

Who's Who, once known as a title of a specialized dictionary for editors and advertisers, has nowadays become the outspoken or implied question in innumerable popular contexts. The interest in individuals has become a kind of mass gossip. The majority of weeklies and monthlies, and many dailies too, publish at least one life story or a fragment of one in each issue; theater programs present abridged biographies of all the actors; the more sophisticated periodicals, such as *The New Republic* or *Harper's,* offer short accounts of the main intellectual achievements of their contributors; and a glance into the popular corners of the book trade, including drug store counters, will invariably fall on biographies. All this forces the conclusion that there must be a social need seeking gratification by this type of literature.

One way to find out would be to study the readers' reactions, to explore by means of various interviewing techniques what they are looking for, what they think about the biographical jungle. But it seems to be rather premature to collect and to evaluate such solicited response until more is known about the content structure itself.

As an experiment in content analysis, a year's publication of *The Saturday Evening Post (SEP)* and of *Collier's* for the period from April 1940 to March 1941 was covered.[3] It is regrettable that a complete investigation could not be made for the most recent material, but samples taken at random from magazines under investigation showed that no basic change in the selection or content structure has occurred since this country's entry into the war.[4]

Biographers' Idols

Before entering into a discussion of our material we shall briefly look into the fate of the biographical feature during the past decades.

Production—Yesterday

Biographical sections have not always been a standing feature in these periodicals. If we turn back the pages we find distinct differences in the number of articles as well as in the selection of people treated.

Table 30.1 gives a survey of the professional distribution of the "heroes" in biographies between 1901 and 1941.[5]

Table 30.1 indicates clearly a tremendous increase in biographies as time goes on. The average figure of biographies in 1941 is almost four times as high as at the beginning of the century. The biography has nowadays become a regular weekly feature. Just to illustrate how relatively small the number of biographies was forty years ago: in 52 issues of the *SEP* of 1901-02 we find altogether twenty-one biographies as compared with not less than fifty-seven in 1940-41. The smallness of the earlier figure in comparison to the present day is emphasized by the fact that non-fictional contributions at that time far outnumbered the fictional material. A fair average of distribution in the past would be about three fictional and eight non-fictional contributions; today we never find more than twice as many non-fictional as fictional contributions and in the majority of cases even fewer.

We put the subjects of the biographies in three groups: the spheres of political life, of business and professions, and of entertainment (the latter in the broadest sense of the word). Looking at our table we find for the time before World War I very high interest in political figures and an almost equal distribution of business and professional men, on the one hand, and of entertainers on the other. This picture changes completely after the

Table 30.1 Distribution of biographies according to professions in *Saturday Evening Post* and *Collier's* for selected years between 1901–1941

	1901–1914 (5 sample yrs.)		1922–1930 (6 sample yrs.)		1930–1934 (4 years)		1940–1941 (1 year)	
	No.	%	No.	%	No.	%	No.	%
Political life	81	46	112	28	95	31	31	25
Business and professional	49	28	72	18	42	14	25	20
Entertainment	47	26	211	54	169	55	69	55
Total number	177	100	395	100	306	100	125	100
Yearly average of biographies	36		66		77		125	

war. The figures from political life have been cut by 40 per cent; the business and professional men have lost 30 per cent of their personnel while the entertainers have gained 50 per cent. This numerical relation seems to be rather constant from 1922 up to the present day. If we re-formulate our professional distribution by leaving out the figures from political life we see even more clearly the considerable decrease of people from the serious and important professions and a corresponding increase of entertainers. The social impact of this change comes to the fore strikingly if we analyze the composition of the entertainers. This can be seen from table 30.2.

While at the beginning of the century three quarters of the entertainers were serious artists and writers, we find that this class of people is reduced by half twenty years later and tends to disappear almost completely at present.

Table 30.2 Proportion of biographies of entertainers from the realm of serious arts[a] in *SEP* and *Collier's* for selected years between 1901–1941 (in per cent of total biographies of entertainers in each period)

Period	Proportion entertainers from serious arts	Total no. entertainers
1901–1914 (5 sample yrs.)	77	47
1922–1930 (6 sample yrs.)	38	211
1930–1934 (4 yrs.)	29	169
1940–1941 (1 yr.)	9	69

[a]This group includes literature, fine arts, music, dance, theater.

As an instance of the selection of biographies typical of the first decade of the century, it is notable that out of the twenty-one biographies of the *SEP* 1901-02, eleven came from the political sphere, seven from the business and professions, and three from entertainment and sport. The people in the political group are numerically prominent until before Election Day in the various years: candidates for high office, i.e., the President or senators; the Secretary of the Treasury; an eminent State governor. In the business world, we are introduced to J. P. Morgan, the banker; his partner, George W. Perkins; James J. Hill, the railroad president. In the professions, we find one of the pioneers in aviation; the inventor of the torpedo; a famous Negro educator; an immigrant scientist. Among the entertainers there is an opera singer, Emma Calvé; a poet, Eugene Field; a popular fiction writer, F. Marion Crawford.

If we look at such a selection of people we find that it represents a fair cross-section of socially important occupations. Still, in 1922 the picture is more similar to the professional distribution quoted above than to the one which is characteristic of the present day magazines. If we take, for example, *Collier's* of 1922 we find in a total of 20 biographies only two entertainers, but eight business and professional men and ten politicians. Leaving out the latter ones, we find among others: Clarence C. Little, the progressive President of the University of Maine; Leonard P. Ayres, the very-outspoken Vice-President of the Cleveland Trust Company; Director-General of the United States Railroad Administration, James C. Davis; President of the New York Central Railroad, A. H. Smith; and the City Planner, John Nolen. From the entertainment field, we have a short résumé of the stage comedian, Joe Cook (incidentally, by Franklin P. Adams), and an autobiographical sketch by Charlie Chaplin.

We might say that a large proportion of the heroes in both samples are idols of production, that they stem from the productive life, from industry, business, and natural sciences. There is not a single hero from the world of sports and the few artists and entertainers either do not belong to the sphere of cheap or mass entertainment or represent a serious attitude toward their art as in the case of Chaplin.[6] The first quarter of the century cherishes biography in terms of an open-minded liberal society which really wants to know something about its own leading figures on the decisive social, commercial, and cultural fronts. Even in the late Twenties, when jazz composers and the sports people are admitted to the inner circle of biographical heroes, their biographies are written almost exclusively to supplement the reader's knowledge of the technical requirements and accomplishments of their respective fields.[7] These people, then, are treated as an embellishment of the national scene, not yet as something that in itself represents a special phenomenon which demands almost undivided attention.

We should like to quote from two stories which seem to be characteristic of this past epoch. In a sketch of Theodore Roosevelt, the following comment is made in connection with the assassination of McKinley: "We, who give such chances of success to all that it is possible for a young man to go as a laborer into the steel business and before he has reached his mature prime become, through his own industry and talent, the president of a vast steel association—we, who make this possible as no country has ever made it possible, have been stabbed in the back by anarchy."[8]

This unbroken confidence in the opportunities open to every individual serves as the *leitmotiv* of the biographies. To a very great extent they are to be looked upon as examples of success which can be imitated. These life stories are really intended to be educational models. They are written—at least ideologically—for someone who the next day may try to emulate the man whom he has just envied.

A biography seems to be the means by which an average person is able to reconcile his interest in the important trends of history and in the personal lives of other people. In the past, and

especially before the first World War, the popular biography lived in an optimistic atmosphere where understanding of historical processes and interest in successful people seemed to integrate pleasantly into one harmonious endeavor: "We know now that the men of trade and commerce and finance are the real builders of freedom, science, and art—and we watch them and study them accordingly.... Of course, Mr. Perkins is a 'self-made man.' Who that has ever made a career was not?"[9] This may be taken as a classical formulation for a period of "rugged individualism" in which there is neither the time nor the desire to stimulate a closer interest in the organizers and organization of leisure time, but which is characterized by eagerness and confidence that the social ladder may be scaled on a mass basis.[10]

Consumption—Today

When we turn to our present day sample we face an assortment of people which is both qualitatively and quantitatively removed from the standards of the past.

Only two decades ago people from the realm of entertainment played a very negligible role in the biographical material. They form now, numerically, the first group. While we have not found a single figure from the world of sports in our earlier samples given above, we find them now close to the top of favorite selections. The proportion of people from political life and from business and professions, both representing the "serious side," has declined from 74 to 45 per cent of the total.

Let us examine the group of people representing non-political aspects of life. 69 are from the world of entertainment and sport; 25 from that which we called before the "serious side." Almost half of the 25 belong to some kind of communications professions: there are ten newspapermen and radio commentators. Of the remaining 15 business and professional people, there are a pair of munitions traders, Athanasiades (118)[11] and Juan March (134); Dr. Brinkley (3), a quack doctor; and Mr. Angas (20), judged by many as a dubious financial expert; Pittsburgh Phil (23), a horse race gambler in the "grand style"; Mrs. D'Arcy Grant (25), a woman sailor, and Jo Carstairs (54), the owner of an island resort; the Varian brothers (52), inventors of gadgets, and Mr. Taylor (167), an inventor of fool-proof sports devices; Howard Johnson (37), a roadside restaurant genius; Jinx Falkenburg (137), at that time a professional model; and finally, Dr. Peabody (29), a retired rector of a swanky society prep school.

The "serious" people are not so serious after all. In fact there are only nine who might be looked upon as rather important or characteristic figures of the industrial, commercial, or professional activities, and six of these are newspapermen or radio commentators.

We called the heroes of the past "idols of production": we feel entitled to call the present day magazine heroes "idols of consumption." Indeed, almost every one of them is directly, or indirectly, related to the sphere of leisure time: either he does not belong to vocations which serve society's basic needs (e.g., the heroes of the world of entertainment and sport), or he amounts, more or less, to a caricature of a socially productive agent. If we add to the group of the 69 people from the entertainment and sports world the ten newspaper and radio men, the professional model, the inventor of sports devices, the quack doctor, the horse race gambler, the inventors of gadgets, the owner of the island resort, and the restaurant chain owner, we see 87 of all 94 non-political heroes directly active in the consumers' world.

Of the eight figures who cannot exactly be classified as connected with consumption, not more than three—namely, the automobile producer, Sloan; the engineer and industrialist, Stout; and the air line czar, Smith—are important or characteristic functionaries in the world of production. The two armament magnates, the female freight boat skipper, the prep school head, and the doubtful market prophet remind us of the standardized protagonists in mystery novels and related fictional merchandise: people with a more or less normal and typical personal and vocational background who would bore us to death if we did not discover that behind the "average" front lurks a "human interest" situation.

By substituting such a classification according to spheres of activity for the cruder one according to professions, we are now prepared to present the vocational stratifications of our heroes in a new form. It is shown in table 30.3 for the *SEP* and *Collier's* of 1940–1941.

If a student in some very distant future should use popular magazines of 1941 as a source of information as to what figures the American public looked to in the first stages of the greatest crisis since the birth of the Union, he would come to a grotesque result. While the industrial and

Table 30.3   The heroes and their spheres

	Number of stories	Per cent
Sphere of production	3	2
Sphere of consumption	91	73
Entertainers and sports figures	69	55
Newspaper and radio figures	10	8
Agents of consumers' goods	5	4
Topics of light fiction	7	6
Sphere of politics	31	25
Total	125	100

professional endeavors are geared to a maximum of speed and efficiency, the idols of the masses are not, as they were in the past, the leading names in the battle of production, but the headliners of the movies, the ball parks, and the night clubs. While we found that around 1900 and even around 1920 the vocational distribution of magazine heroes was a rather accurate reflection of the nation's living trends, we observe that today the hero-selection corresponds to needs quite different from those of genuine information. They seem to lead to a dream world of the masses who no longer are capable or willing to conceive of biographies primarily as a means of orientation and education. They receive information not about the agents and methods of social production but about the agents and methods of social and individual consumption. During the leisure in which they read, they read almost exclusively about people who are directly, or indirectly providing for the reader's leisure time. The vocational set-up of the dramatis personae is organized as if the social production process were either completely exterminated or tacitly understood, and needed no further interpretation. Instead, the leisure time period seems to be the new social riddle on which extensive reading and studying has to be done.[12]

The human incorporation of all the social agencies taking care of society as a unity of consumers represents a literary type which is turned out as a standardized article, marketed by a tremendous business, and consumed by another mass institution, the nation's magazine reading public. Thus biography lives as a mass element among the other elements of mass literature.

Our discovery of a common professional physiognomy in all of these portraits encouraged us to guess that what is true of the selection of people will also be true of the selection of what is said about these people. This hypothesis has been quite justified, as we propose to demonstrate in the following pages. Our content analysis not only revealed impressive regularities in the occurrence, omission, and treatment of certain topics, but also showed that these regularities may be interpreted in terms of the very same category of consumption which was the key to the selection of the biographical subjects. Consumption is a thread running through every aspect of these stories. The characteristics which we have observed in the literary style of the author, in his presentation of personal relations, of professions and personalities, can all be integrated around the concept of the consumer.

For classification of the stories' contents, we decided on a four-fold scheme. First there are what one might call the sociological aspects of the man: his relations to other people, the pattern of his daily life, his relation to the world in which he lives. Second, his psychology: what the nature of his development has been and the structure of his personality. Third, his history: what his encounter with the world has been like—the object world which he has mastered or failed to master. Fourth, the evaluation of these data which the author more or less consciously conveys by his choice of language. Granted that this scheme is somewhat arbitrary, we think that our division of subject matter has resulted in a fairly efficient worksheet, especially when we consider the backward state of content analysis of this type.

As we studied our stories,[13] we looked almost in vain for such vital subjects as the man's relations to politics or to social problems in general. Our category of sociology reduces itself to the *private lives* of the heroes. Similarly, our category of psychology was found to contain mainly a static image of a human being to whom a number of things happen, culminating in a success which seems to be none of his doing. This whole section becomes merged with our category of history which is primarily concerned with success data, too, and then takes on the character of a catalogue of *"just Facts."* When we survey the material on how authors evaluate their subjects, what stands out most clearly is the biographers' preoccupation with justifying their hero by means of undiscriminating *superlatives* while still interpreting him in terms which bring him as close as possible to the level of the average man.

Private Lives

The reader may have noticed in public conveyances a poster called "Private Lives" depicting the peculiarities of more or less famous people in the world of science, sports, business, and politics. The title of this feature is a fitting symbol for all our biographies. It would be an overstatement, but not too far from the truth, to say that these stories are exclusively reports on the heroes' private lives. While it once was rather contemptible to give much room to the private affairs and habits of public figures this topic is now the focus of interest. The reason for viewing this as an over-statement is in a way surprising: we learn something, although not very much, about the man's professional career and its requirements, but we are kept very uninformed about important segments of his private life.

Inheritance and Parents—Friends and Teachers
The personal relations of our heroes, on which we are enlightened, are, as a whole, limited to two groups, the parents and the friends. Both groups are taken in a specific sense: the parents comprising other older relations or forebears of former generations, the friends being more or less limited to people who were valuable in the hero's career. In more than half of the stories the father or the mother or the general family background is at least mentioned. Clark Gable's "stubborn determination" seems derived from his "Pennsylvania Dutch ancestors" (6); the very efficient State Department official, Mrs. Shipley, is the "daughter of a Methodist minister" (8); Senator Taft is a "middle-of-the-roader like his father" besides being "an aristocrat by birth and training" (101). We are let in a little bit on the family situation of Brenda Joyce because "somewhere there was a break-up between mamma and papa" (110). The general pattern of the parental home, however, is more on the Joan Carroll side, where we find the "young, quietly dignified mother . . . the successful engineer father . . . a star scout brother six years her senior" (143); we hear in a very sympathetic way about the old Fadimans, "the father a struggling Russian immigrant and pharmacist, the mother a nurse" (47); we learn a good deal about ancestors as in the case of Clark Gable cited above. Of the Secretary of Labor, Frances Perkins, we are told that her "forebears had settled all over New England between 1630-1680" (22); the female freighter skipper, D'Arcy Grant, has "an

ancestral mixture of strong-headed swashbuckling Irish and pioneer Americans" (25); Raymond Gram Swing is the "heir of a severe New England tradition" (42); the Varian brothers have "Celtic blood" (52); in the woman matador, Conchita Cintron, we find "Spanish, Connecticut Irish, and Chilean elements" (116).

The curious fact here is not that the authors mention parentage, but that they have so much to say about it and so little to say about other human relations. It is a good deal as if the author wants to impress on the reader that his hero, to a very considerable extent, must be understood in terms of his biological and regional inheritance. It is a kind of primitive Darwinian concept of social facts: the tendency to place the burden of explanation and of responsibility on the shoulders of the past generations. The individual himself appears as a mere product of his past.

The element of passivity is also found in the second most frequently mentioned group of personal relationships: friends and teachers. Let us look again into some of the material. We hear that the woman diplomat, Mrs. Harriman, was made "Minister to Norway because of her many powerful and loyal friends" (14); of the friendship between the hard-hit restaurateur, Johnson, and his wealthy doctor-friend (37); the movie actress, Brenda Marshall, was somehow saved in her career "by the friendship of a script girl" (161); Senator Byrnes got a good start because "a disillusioned old Charlestonian . . . showed him the ropes" (18); while Miss Perkins is "'protected' by her personal secretary . . . (who) worships her" (22).

There is very rarely an episode which shows our heroes as active partners of friendship. In most cases their friends are their helpers. Very often they are teachers who later on become friends. Perhaps it is stretching a point to say that a vulgarian Darwinism is supplemented at this point by a vulgar distortion of the "milieu" theory: the hero is a product of ancestry and friendship. But even if this may be somewhat exaggerated, it nevertheless helps to clarify the point, namely, that the hero appears in his human relationships as the one who takes, not as the one who gives.

We can supplement this statement by going back to our remark that decisive human relationships, and even those which are decisive for private lives, are missing. The whole sphere of the relations with the opposite sex is almost entirely missing. This is indeed a very strange

phenomenon. We should assume that the predilection for such people as actors and actresses from stage and screen, night club entertainers, etc., would be tied up with a special curiosity in such people's love affairs, but this is not the case at all. The realm of love, passion, even marriage, seem worth mentioning only in terms of vital statistics. It is quite a lot to be informed that Dorothy Thompson "got tangled up in love"; very soon Lewis "asked point blank whether she would marry him" (9); Senator Byrnes "married the charming wife who still watches over him" (18); the industrial tycoon, Sloan, remarks, "Mrs. Sloan and I were married that summer . . . she was of Roxbury, Mass." (24); Mrs. Peabody married the Rector "at the close of the school's first year" (29). We are told about Raymond Gram Swing only that he was married twice (42); as far as Lyons', the baseball player's bachelor situation goes we hear that he "almost married his campus sweetheart" (53); while his colleague, Rizzuto, is "not even going steady" (57). In the high life of politics we are glad to know that Ambassador Lothian "gets on well with women" (115); and that Thomas Dewey is "a man's man, but women go for him" (117); we are briefly informed that Chris Martin "married, raised a family" (121); and that "one girl was sufficiently impressed to marry" Michael Todd, a producer, at the tender age of 17 (131).

These statements of fact, in a matter of fact way, as, for instance, the mention of a marriage or a divorce, is all that we hear of that side of human relations which we were used to look upon as the most important ones. If we again imagine that these popular biographies should at a very distant historical moment serve as the sole source of information, the historian of the future would almost be forced to the conclusion that in our times the institution of marriage, and most certainly the phenomena of sexual passions, had become a very negligible factor. It seems that the fifth-rate role to which these phenomena are relegated fits very well with the emphasis on parentage and friendship. Love and passion require generosity, a display of productive mental and emotional forces which are neither primarily explained nor restrained by inheritance and advice.

A rather amusing observation: we found that the eyes of the hero were mentioned in almost one-third of the stories. It is quite surprising that of all possible physiognomic and bodily features just this one should be so very popular. We take delight in the baseball umpire Bill Klem's "bright blue eyes," in his "even supernaturally good eyes" (104); or in the "modest brown eyes" of General Weygand (107). Miss Cintron, the matador, is "blue-eyed" (116); the night club singer, Moffett, has "very bright blue eyes" (119).

We are not quite certain how to explain our biographers' bodily preferences. The eyes are commonly spoken of as "the windows of the soul." Perhaps it gratifies the more inarticulate reader if the authors let him try to understand the heroes in the same language in which he believes he understands his neighbor's soul. It is just another example of a cliché served up in lieu of a genuine attempt at psychological insight.

Home and Social Life—Hobbies and Food Preferences

The heroes, as we have seen, stem predominantly from the sphere of consumption and organized leisure time. It is fascinating to see how in the course of the presentation the producers and agents of consumer goods change into their own customers. Personal habits, from smoking to poker playing, from stamp collecting to cocktail parties, are faithfully noted in between 30 and 40 per cent of all stories under investigation. In fact, as soon as it comes to habits, pleasures and distractions after and outside of working hours, the magazine biographer turns out to be just a snoopy reporter.

The politicians seem to be an especially ascetic lot—Taft "doesn't smoke" (101); neither does General Weygand (107); the former British Ambassador, Lothian, "hasn't taken a drink in 25 years" (115). There is also the movie actor, Chris Martin, who "doesn't smoke cigars or cigarettes" (121); the German Field Marshal Milch whose "big black Brazilian cigars are his favored addiction" (146). To quote some of the favorite habits or dishes of the crowd: Dorothy Thompson is all out for "making Viennese dishes" while her "pet hates . . . are bungled broth and clumsily buttered tea bread" (9). We are invited to rejoice in Art Fletcher's "excellent digestion" (7). We hope that Major Angas is equally fortunate, for: "Eating well is his secondary career"; he is "perpetually hungry" (20). The circus magnate, North, also seems to have a highly developed sense for food and what goes with it: "His cud-cutters for a three-pound steak are a Martini, a Manhattan, and a beer, in that invariable order, tamped down with a hatful of radishes" (26).

As for the innocent hobbies of our heroes: Art Fletcher likes "the early evening movies" and also "to drive about the country" (7); Senator Byrnes finds recreation in "telling of the long saltily humorous anecdotes which all Southerners love" (18). The pitcher, Paige, is "an expert dancer and singer" (19); Westbrook Pegler "plays poker" (28); and his special pet foe, Mayor Hague, also "likes gambling" (36); his colleague, the London *Times* correspondent, Sir Willmott Lewis, also "plays poker" (49), while Swing takes to badminton (42). More on the serious side is Greer Garson who "reads a great deal and studies the theater every minute she is free" (113). The hobby of golf unites Senator Taft (101), the Fascist, Muti (114), the "Blondie" cartoonist, Chic Young (165), the baseball player, Lyons (53), and Ambassador Lothian (115).

We are furthermore told who likes to be "the life of the party," and who does not; and also how the daily routine in the apartment or private house is fixed. The Fletchers, for instance, "retire early and rise early" (7); while Hank Greenberg "lives modestly with his parents" but also "likes night clubs, bright lights, and pretty girls" (56). We hear of the actress Stickney's charming "town house" (145), of the "fifteen rooms and five baths and the private elevator to the street" of political Boss Flynn (138); of the way in which the Ballet Director Balanchine is "snugly installed in an elaborate Long Island home, and a sleek New York apartment" (152).

As to social gatherings: Nancy Hamilton's parties "aren't glittering at all, but they are fun" (103). The newspaperman, Silliman Evans, "has introduced the Texas-size of large scale outdoor entertainment" (39); while his colleague, Clifton Fadiman, has "very little social life, seldom goes to dinner parties" (47). His habits seem related to those of the private island queen, Jo Carstairs: " . . . A few friends of long standing make up one of the world's shortest guest lists" (54).

And so it goes, through over 200 quotations, changing a study in social relations into consumers' research. It is neither a world of "doers" nor a world of "doing" for which the biographical curiosity of a mass public is evoked. The whole trend goes toward acceptance: the biological and educational heritage; the helpful friends and teachers; the physical protection of the house, and the physiological one of eating and drinking; the security of social standing and prestige, through social entertaining; the complete resting of mind and work-wise energy through the gamut of hobbies. Here we come very close to decisive trends to which the modern individual seems subjected. He appears no longer as a center of outwardly bound energies and actions; as an inexhaustible reservoir of initiative and enterprise; no longer as an integral unity on whose work and efficiency might depend not only his kin's future and happiness, but at the same time, mankind's progress in general. Instead of the "givers" we are faced with the "takers." These new heroes represent a craving for having and taking things for granted. They seem to stand for a phantasmagoria of worldwide social security; for an attitude which asks for no more than to be served with the things needed for reproduction and recreation; for an attitude which has lost any primary interest in how to invent, shape or apply the tools leading to such purposes of mass satisfaction.

We cannot avoid getting something of a distorted picture of society if we look at it exclusively through the personal lives of a few individuals. But in the past an effort was made to show the link between the hero and the nation's recent history. As one of those earlier biographers put it: "Each era, conscious of the mighty works that could be wrought, conscious that we are all under sentence of speedy death, eagerly seeks out the younger man, the obscure man. It has need of all powers and all talents. Especially of the talents for creating, organizing, and directing."[14]

Today the emphasis is on the routine functions of nourishment and leisure time and not on "the talents for creating, organizing, and directing." The real battlefield of history recedes from view or becomes a stock backdrop while society disintegrates into an amorphous crowd of consumers. Greer Garson and Mahatma Gandhi meet on common ground: the one "likes potatoes and stew and never tires of a breakfast of porridge and haddock" (113); the other's "evening meal is simple—a few dates, a little rice, goat's milk" (124); Hitler and Chris Martin "don't smoke . . . "

Just Facts

The 41-year-old quotation above may serve as a transition from the sociology of our heroes to their psychology. With its emphasis on the independence and leadership awaiting the exercise of personal initiative, it expresses the ideal character type of private capitalism.

There are at least two elements in this quotation, the presence of which characterizes the psychological concept of former biographies, and the absence of which is very meaningful for the present situation: development and solitude.

"The young, obscure man" has something of the heritage, however trivial in this case, of the personality as it was conceived during the rise of the middle class culture: the individual as a totality of potentialities, mental, moral, and emotional, which have to be developed in a given social framework. Development, as the essence of human life, was connected with the idea that the individual has to find himself in the soliloquy of the mind. Human existence seemed to be made up of the loneliness of the creature and of his emergence into the outer world by displaying his own gifts. Our quotation is one of the late forms of this concept: the self-developing and fighting individual with all the chances in the world for creation and conquest.

Souls without History

In an essay on present-day man, Max Horkheimer states: "Development has ceased to exist."[15] His remarks on the immediate transition from childhood to adult life, his observation that "the child is grown up as soon as he can walk, and the grown-up in principle always remains the same,"[16] sound as if they were a comment on our biographical heroes. Among our quotations we have a collection of passages which try to tie up the childhood of the hero with his later life. Almost every second story brings some report on the road from childhood to maturity. Does this not seem to contradict our general remark, is this not a variation of the classical concept of the emerging personality? Before answering, let us examine a few representative passages: At the age of twelve "wrestling . . . was the answer to my problem," says the wrestler, Allman (13). The king of horse race betting, Pittsburgh Phil, "began betting when he was fourteen—on his own game chickens" (23). Of the inventor, Stout, it is remarked: "Wherever his family lived, he would rig up a crude shop and try to make things" (41). At twelve, the future actor, Ezra Stone, ran a kid's radio program "directing the actors and paying them off at the end of the week" (108). For the Ringling-Barnum head, J. R. North: "a real circus was his toy" (26). The future film star, Greer Garson, "wanted to be an actress from the time she could walk" (113). The night club singer Hildegarde's parents "weren't surprised when Hildegarde . . . aged eighteen months, hummed a whole aria of an opera they had carried her to" (135).

Childhood appears neither as prehistory and key to the character of an individual nor as a stage of transition to the growth and formation of the abundant diversity of an adult. Childhood is nothing but a midget edition, a predated publication of a man's profession and career. A man is an actor, a doctor, a dancer, an entrepreneur, and he always was. He was not born the tender and unknown potentiality of a human life, of an intellectual, mental, emotional creativeness, effective for himself and for society, rather he came into the world and stayed in it, rubber stamped with and for a certain function. The individual has become a trademark.

In more than a third of the stories an attempt at a "theory of success" seems to be made but no magic formula is offered which an average individual might follow for his own good. The bulk of the answers consists of more or less trivial suggestions that the key may be found in "instinct" or other vague qualities. The golf player, Bobby Jones, "must have been born with the deep love for the game" (11). As to the Senator: "Leadership is Byrnes' real genius" (18). Pittsburgh Phil was "a good horse player by instinct" (23). The businessman, Durand N. Briscoe, "seemed to have an instinct for promotion and speculation" (24). The achievements of the football coach, Kendrigan, are a mystery even to him: "how he did it he never figured" (50). The airline tycoon, Cyrus R. Smith, may count on "an unerring gambler's instinct" (51). This key formula of instinct is supplemented by a collection of almost tautological truisms: The Fascist, Muti, "loves his danger highly spiced" (114). The sociable ambassador, Lothian, "likes newspapermen" (115). Howard Johnson knows what makes a restaurant successful: "A man that is properly supervised never goes haywire" (37). And as far as Clark Gable's success is concerned (and this could be applied to all the 125) "The answer . . . is personality" (6).

We venture to interpret this pseudo-psychology of success as another aspect of the timeless and passive image of modern man. Just as childhood is an abbreviation of the adult's professional career, so is the explanation of this career nothing but an abstract, rather inarticulate, reiteration that a career is a career and a success is a success.

The psychological atmosphere breathes behaviorism on a very primitive level. Childhood as well as that vague realm of instincts represent, so to speak, the biological background from which a variety of human qualities emerge. It is a psychology which shows no need of asking why and, precisely in the same sense in which we tried to show it for sociology, testifies to the transformation from the worship of a spontaneous personality to the adoration of an existence shaped and molded by outside forces. These people live in a limbo of children and victims. The way leads to what we are inclined to call "a command psychology" because people are not conceived as the responsible agents of their fate in all phases of their lives, but as the bearers of certain useful or not so useful character traits which are pasted on them like decorations or stigmas of shame.

There are a few traits which seem to have some bearing on a man's ability to manipulate his environment. We mean the columnist who is a "spotlight stealer" (9); the playwright and actress who never overlooks "good spots for herself" (103); the producer who is "his own ballyhoo artist" (131). We mean the baseball manager who is "chemically opposed to being on the sucker end of a ball game" (2); the smart night club star who sees "no point in disclosing that King Gustave's favorite singer had been born over her father's delicatessen store" (135); the actress who has real "talent for meeting people" (103); the person who shows up "at the right place at the right time" (109); who is a "great man in flying, handshaking and backslapping trips" (21).

The majority of such attitudes are likely to evoke a slyly understanding smile on the part of the observer and reader. These are the "sure-fire" tricks on the road to success, a little doubtful, but not too bad; these are the equipment of the shrewd man and the smart woman. But these psychological gadgets exhaust the list of qualities pertaining to creative and productive abilities. They generate an atmosphere of pseudo-creativeness in an attempt to convince us that a man has contributed his personal, individual share to the general cause of progress. "Something new has been added," insists the advertisement, but beware of inquiring too closely into the nature of the novelty. Thus, the good-natured statements of a certain lack of meticulous innocence on the road to success, become for the sociological interpreter a sad revelation of a lack of originality in productive strength.

This is brought out even more clearly when we turn to the presentation of the actual history of success. Here success is not even attributed to some happy instinct—it merely happens. Success has lost the seductive charm which once seemed to be a promise and a prize for everybody who was strong, clever, flexible, sober enough to try. It has become a rigid matter on which we look with awe or envy as we look at the priceless pictures in our galleries or the fabulous palaces of the rich. The success of our heroes of consumption is in itself goods of consumption. It does not serve as an instigator for more activity, it is introduced as something we have to accept just like the food and drink and the parties; it is nourishment for curiosity and entertainment.

The mythology of success in the biographies consists of two elements, hardship and breaks. The troubles and difficulties with which the road to success is paved are discussed in the form of stereotypes. Over and over again we hear that the going is rough and hard. The baseball umpire goes "the long, rough road up to that night of triumph" (104); the lightweight champion "came up the hard way" (123); a Senator knew in his youth the "long hours of hard work" (149); and the ballet director "worked hard" (152). In identical words we hear that the baseball manager (2) and the great film star (6) "came up the hard way." The "hard way" it was for Dorothy Thompson (9) and for Billy Rose (43). We are reminded of official military communiqués, reporting a defeat or stalemate in a matter-of-fact tone, rather than descriptions of life processes.

The same applies to the reverse side of hardship: to the so-called breaks. All our stories refer to successes and it is fair enough that somehow we must be informed when and how the failures stopped. Here the tendency to commute life data into facts to be accepted rather than understood becomes intensified. Usually, the beginning of the peak is merely stated as an event: A high civil servant was "fortunate in her first assignment" (8); a cartoonist merely gets a "telegram offering him a job on the paper" which later leads to his fame (34); a columnist "bursts into certain popularity" (42); an actor "got a break" (112); another "got the job and it turned out well" (121); for a middleweight champion "the turning point of his career had arrived" (142). If any explanation is offered at all, we are told that the turn occurred in some freakish way: the night club singer gets started by "a king's whim" (135); Clark Gable's appointment as a timekeeper with a telephone company appears as the turning point in his

career (6); a baseball player goes on a fishing trip, loses his old job and thereby gets another one which leads to his success (133a).

These episodes of repetition and freakishness seem to demonstrate that there is no longer a social pattern for the way up. Success has become an accidental and irrational event. The dangers of competition were tied up with the idea of definite chances and there was a sound balance between ambition and possibilities. Appropriately enough, our heroes are almost without ambition, a tacit admission that those dangers of the past have been replaced by the cruelties of the present. It is cruel, indeed, that the ridiculous game of chance should open the doors to success for a handful, while all the others who were not present when it happened are failures. The "facts" of a career are a reflection of the lack of spontaneity. Behind the amusing, fortuitous episode lurks a terrible truth.[17] Hardships and breaks are standard articles for the reader. They are just a better brand of what everyone uses. The outstanding has become the proved specimen of the average. By impressing on the reading masses the idols of our civilization, any criticism or even reasoning about the validity of such standards is suppressed. As a social scientist the biographer represents a pitiless, almost sadistic trend in science, for he demonstrates the recurring nature of such phenomena as hardships and breaks, but he does not attempt to reveal the laws of such recurrence. For him knowledge is not the source of power but merely the key to adjustment.

Catalogue of Adjustment

When we turn to a study of the approval and disapproval which our authors attach to the various character traits they describe, we find a striking and simple pattern.

In tone the catalogue of these traits, like the mythology of success, resembles a digest of military orders of the day: brusque laudations and reprimands. There is no room for nuances or ambiguity. In content it is on a very simple level and the criterion of approval or disapproval is also very simple. The yardstick is social adjustment. Once we realize the subconscious and conscious opinions of present-day society on what an adjusted person should and should not be, we are thoroughly familiar with the evaluation of character traits and their owners. The yardstick has three scales: behavior toward material tasks; behavior toward fellow men; and behavior in relation to one's own emotions. The one who is efficient scores in the first sphere; the one who is sociable, in the second; the one who is always restrained, in the third.

In a separate study of all passages mentioning character traits, we found that of a total of 76 quotations referring to a hero's commendable behavior toward "things to be done," not fewer than 70, or over 90 per cent, mentioned competence, efficiency, and energy; the remaining six referred to ambition. The majority read: "very capable" (154); "sacrifice of time, effort, or my own convenience was too great" (24); "an inordinately hard worker" (48); "was never fired for inefficiency" (167); "thorough and accurate" (16); "being idle is her idea of complete torture" (140).

Out of a total of 48 quotations mentioning commendable behavior in relation to people, all 48 quote "co-operation," "sociability," and "good sportsmanship." There is a constant repetition of such adjectives as "co-operative," "generous," and "sociable." A baseball manager is "easy to meet, sociable, unsparing in his time with interviewers" (27). The "sociable" Chief of the Passport Division (8); the Secretary of Labor, "a delightful hostess" (22); the Republican candidate for the presidency with his "liking for and interest in people" (133); the matador, "genial, friendly, hospitable" (116); a smart actress, "amiable and friendly" (140)—they all belong to one big happy family which knows no limits in being pleasant and agreeable to each other. Like Don James, the barker for sideshows, they all seem to have "hearts so huge and overflowing" (127).

The number of quotations pertaining to disapproved character traits is very small, but conspicuous among them are criticisms of the unrestrained expression of emotion. It is virtually horrible that one of our baseball heroes "is no man for a jest when losing a game" (53); that a movie actress "cannot bear to be teased" (105); or that our Secretary of Labor's "public relations are unfortunate" (22). Unrestrained behavior traits like being "irritable and harsh" (32), "swift, often furious testiness" (117), being "unbalanced" (56), or even possessing a "somewhat difficult personality" (117) are really most unpleasant. Such faults can be tolerated only if they are exceptional—like the man who "for once got his feelings beyond control" (23).

The catalogue of normalcy leaves no room for individuality. This catalogue levels human behavior by the rejection of emotional eruptions; the bad marks given to the poor "joiners" and the temperamental people; the complete lack of creative and passionate behavior among the commendable qualities. The absence of love and passion in our catalogue of human relations finds its counterpart in this catalogue of human qualities. It is a world of dependency. The social implications of such atmosphere seem to be considerable because in their social status the majority of our heroes are either their "own boss" or they have climbed to such a high step in the social ladder that whole worlds separate them from the average employee. Yet the few "big ones" don't differ basically from the many little ones. They demonstrate, taken as a group, not the exception, but the typical cross-section of the socio-psychological condition of modern society.

The foregoing examples from our catalogue of character traits should make clear why we emphasize the double feature of the absence of development and solitude. The average man is never alone and never wants to be alone. His social and his psychological birth is the community, the masses. His human destiny seems to be a life of continuous adjustment: adjustment to the world through efficiency and industriousness; and adjustment to people by exhibiting amiable and sociable qualities and by repressing all other traits. There is no religious or philosophical framework according to which the character traits are classified and evaluated. The concepts of good and bad, of kindness and sin, of truth and falsehood, of sacrifice and selfishness, of love and hate are not the beacons which illuminate our human landscape. The character image on which an affirmative judgment is passed in the biographies is that of a well-trained employee from a well-disciplined lower middle-class family. Our people could occupy an imaginary world of technocracy; everybody seems to reflect a rigid code of flexible qualities: the rigid and mechanized set-up of a variety of useful mechanical institutions. Behind the polished mask of training and adjustment lurks the concept of a human robot who, without having done anything himself, moves just such parts and in just such directions as the makers wished him to do.

Formerly it was only the sick who needed handling because it was known that their symptoms were similar to many others. Now everyone is reduced to the same dependency. The pride of being an individual with his own very personal ways and interests becomes the stigma of abnormality. Interest in the consumption of others is an expression of lack of interest in genuine consumption. The detailed character description is dominated by the same acceptance and passivity which came to the foreground in the concept of souls without development.

Language

Superlatives

Our analysis would not be complete without some discussion of our stories' language which has several characteristic features. The most obvious one is the superlative.[18] Once we are made aware of this stylistic device, it cannot be overlooked. The heroes themselves, their accomplishments and experiences, their friends and acquaintances, are characterized as unique beings and events. The superlative gives a good conscience to the biographer—by applying a rhetorical gadget, he achieves the transformation of the average into the extraordinary. Mr. Muti is "the toughest Fascist of them all" (114); Dr. Brinkley is the "best advertised doctor in the United States" (3); our hero is the "luckiest man in the movies today" (121); another is "not only the greatest, but the first real showman in the Ringling family" (26). There is a general who is "one of the best mathematicians this side of Einstein" (107). There is a columnist with "one of the strangest of courtships" (9); another statesman with "the world's most exciting job" (144). There are also the downward-pointed superlatives. Some sportsman was once "the loudest and by all odds the most abusive of the lot" (2); a newspaper man is "one of the most consistently resentful men in the country" (28); another person is "one of the unhappiest women that ever lived" (154).

As if the biographer had to convince himself and his public that he is really selling an excellent human specimen, he sometimes is not satisfied with the ratio of one superlative per sentence but has to pack a lot of them into a single passage. Pittsburgh Phil is "the most famous and the most feared horse player in America" (23). The German Labor Front is "the best led, most enlightened and most powerful labor organization in Europe" (21). The producer, Lorentz, "demands the best writing, the best music and the best technical equipment available" (126). The baseball manager, Clark Griffith, "was the most

colorful star on the most colorful team in baseball" (2). Tilden is "the greatest tennis player in the world and the greatest guy in the world" (111).

This wholesale distribution of highest ratings defeats its own purpose. Everything is presented as something unique, unheard of, outstanding. Thus nothing is unique, unheard of, outstanding. Totality of the superlative means totality of the mediocre. It levels the presentation of human life to the presentation of merchandise. The most vivacious girl corresponds to the best tooth paste, the highest endurance in sportsmanship corresponds to the most efficient vitamins; the unique performance of the politician corresponds to the unsurpassed efficiency of the automobile. There is a pre-established harmony between the objects of mass production in the advertising columns and the objects of biography in the editorial comment. The language of promotion has replaced the language of evaluation. Only the price tag is missing.

The superlative pushes the reader between two extremes. He is graciously attempting to become conversant with people who are paragons of human accomplishment. He may be proud that to a great extent these wonderful people do nothing but entertain him. He has, at least in his leisure time, the best crowd at his fingertips. But there is no road left to him for an identification with the great, or for an attempt to emulate their success. Thus the superlative, like the story of success itself, brings out the absence of those educational features and other optimistic implications which were characteristic of biographies during the era of liberalism. What on first sight seems to be the rather harmless atmosphere of entertainment and consumption is, on closer examination, revealed as a reign of psychic terror, where the masses have to realize the pettiness and insignificance of their everyday life. The already weakened consciousness of being an individual is struck another heavy blow by the pseudo-individualizing forces of the superlative. Advertisement and terror, invitation to entertainment and summons to humility form their unity in the world of superlatives. The biographer performs the functions of a side show barker for living attractions and of a preacher of human insignificance.

High and Low Language

The use of the superlative is reinforced by frequent references to an assortment of mythical and historical associations, in order, it would seem, to confer pseudo-sanctity and pseudo-safety to the futile affairs of modern mass culture. Clark Gable does not just make a career—he lives the "Gable saga" (6), and the movie actress, Joyce, experiences at least a "little saga" (110). "Historic" is the word for Ilka Chase (140) as well as for Hildegarde (135). What happens to the soft ball player Novikoff is "fabulous" (158); the fate of the actress Morison is "history" (162); of the movie producer Wallis (166) as well as of the baseball player Allen (45) "a miracle"; the baseball manager Griffith experiences "baseball destiny," he accomplishes "a historic piece of strategy" (2). Greek mythology is a favorite; Clark Gable lives in "Olympian regions" (6); the passport administrator Shipley (8) as well as the gadget inventor Taylor (167) have an "Herculean task"; the producer Todd is called an "Archon" (131) and our Taylor "Orpheus" (167). Of course Christianity and the middle ages have to help Dorothy Thompson "like a knight with a righteous sword" (9); the Nazi Ley is the "Jacob of German labor" with "labor itself the Esau" (21). Vice-President Wallace is "Joseph, a dreamer of dreams" (38); Casals is a "good samaritan" (106). There are no limits. Ruth Hussey sometimes "looked a bit like a Buddha" (151); the showman Rose like a "priest of Osiris" (43). And so it goes on with myths, legends, sagas, destinies, miracles.[19] And yet, in the same breath which bestows the blessings of venerable symbols on our heroes, they and we are brought together on the easy level of slang and colloquial speech. McCutcheon, the cartoonist, might be called the "king" of his island possession, but we hear that "kingship is a safe investment" (1); Fletcher, who made history, is also "the soul—or the heel—of honesty" (7); Swing, called "an apostle," has also "radio's best bedside manner" (42). When Taft's father was president, the "crown of Roosevelt I fitted him like a five and ten toupee" (101). There is a boxer who finds it "good business to be brave" (12); there is "gossip—a dime a gross" (23); there is talk of a "personal blitzkrieg" (29); of "votes enough to elect a bee to a beehive" (109); of the "moguls of celluloid" (137); of "that genius business" (152). The historizing hymns of praise and transfiguration correspond to movie "palaces" and the sport "stadiums." It is a colossal façade, a "make-believe ballroom," as one radio station announces its swing program. Behind the façade of language there rules, just as behind the architectural

outside make-up, a versatility of techniques, gadgets and tricks, for which nothing is too expensive or too cheap that may serve the purpose of entertaining or being entertained.

These substitutes and successors of creative production require a language which substitutes for elucidating, revealing, stimulating words a linguistic confusion that strives to produce the illusion of rooted tradition and all-around alertness. Thus this new literary phenomenon complies with the highest artistic criteria: inner, necessary, inseparable connection between form and content, between expression and the expressed—in short, a linguistic creation which will not permit an anatomic clear-cut separation between words and their intentions! These biographies as a literary species are "true."

Especially for You

In an unpublished analysis of songs T. W. Adorno interprets the pseudo-directness with which every one of the millions of girls for whose consumption the hit is manufactured, seems to be addressed. The pseudo-individualization of the heroes corresponds to the pseudo-individualization of the readers. Although the selection of heroes and what is reported about them are as thoroughly standardized as the language of these reports, there is the superlative functioning as the specifying agent for the chosen hero and there is also, as crown and conclusion, the direct speech as the bearer of a personal message to the reader. Affably or condescendingly, everyone is personally invited to attend the spectacle of an outstanding life. Individual meets individual; the biographer takes care of the introduction.

Coach Fletcher and his wife "can be reached only by telegram provided you know the address" (7). Should you happen to be a Brenda Joyce fan: "If you come at the right time, you will see her second-hand car" (110). Watching our election campaign: "If Hull and Mr. Taft are the candidates, your emotion will not be fired, nor will your sleep be disturbed by them" (109). For those interested in film stars: "Let's sit down with Bill Powell and listen to his story" (112); "perhaps, girls, you would like to know how Clark Gable got that way" (6). Reporting McCutcheon's acquisition of an island, the author teases the reader: "so, you want to be a king" (1). For the car owner: "You can't help seeing Johnson's restaurants if you drive along main highways"

(37). There is the London *Times* representative Sir Willmott Lewis: "Meet him on Pennsylvania Avenue. He will stop and talk to you as if you were a five hundred audience" (49). Umpire Klem "knows the multitudinous rules of baseball better than you know the alphabet" (104). Let there be no mistake: the night club singer Moffett "went to the very best schools, my dear" (119). But let's not neglect her colleague Hildegarde: "If you haven't heard her or seen her, don't stand there—go, do something about it" (135). Casals' biographer is a little less imperative: "Meet the blond bowman from Spain" (106). Dependability is the word for Miss Fitzgerald: " . . . you can bank on her for the truth" (105).

The direct apostrophe is similar in function to the superlative: it creates elation and humiliation. The reader, besides being admitted to the intimate details of the hero's habits in eating, spending, playing, has the pleasure of personal contact. There is nothing of the measured distance and veneration which a reader in the classics in biography had to observe before the statesman of the past, or the poet or the scientist. The aristocracy of a gallery of isolated bearers of unusual achievements seems to be replaced by a democratic meeting which requires no special honors and genuflection before the great.

But the ease of admission is not devoid of menacing features. The "You" means not only the friendly gesture of introduction but also the admonishing, calling voice of a superior agency, proclaiming that one has to observe, has to comply. The language of directness betrays the total coverage planned by all modern institutions of mass communication. "Especially for You" means all of you.

The Reader

Magazine biographies have undergone a process of expansion as well as of atrophy. They have become a standard institution in magazines which count their audience by the millions. It is significant that during the present emergency the *Saturday Evening Post* and *Collier's* have been able to double their sales price without incurring any serious setback in circulation. But the scope of this expanding world of biographies has been narrowed down to the highly specialized field of entertainment. If we ask again what social need they serve, we might find the answer in this combination of quantitative increase and qualitative deterioration.

An hypothesis on the pseudo-educational and pseudo-scientific function of the popular biography can be formulated as follows: the task of the social scientist is, in very broad terms, the clarification of the hidden processes and interconnections of social phenomena. The average reader who, like an earnest and independent student, is not satisfied with a mere conglomeration of facts or concepts, but wants to know what it is all about, seems to gain insight from these biographies, and an understanding of the human or social secret of the historical process. But this is only a trick, because these individuals whose lives he studies are neither characteristic of this process, nor are they presented in such a way that they appear in the full light of it. A rather satisfactory understanding of the reader is possible if we look upon the biography as an agent of make-believe adult education. A certain social prestige, the roots of which are planted during one's school days, constantly drives one toward higher values in life, and specifically, toward more complete knowledge. But these biographies corrupt the educational conscience by delivering goods which bear an educational trademark but which are not the genuine article.

The important role of familiarity in all phenomena of mass culture cannot be sufficiently emphasized. People derive a great deal of satisfaction from the continual repetition of familiar patterns. There are but a very limited number of plots and problems which are repeated over and over again in successful movies and short stories; even the so-called exciting moments in sports events are to a great extent very much alike. Everyone knows that he will hear more or less the same type of story and the same type of music as soon as he turns on the radio. But there has never been any rebellion against this fact; there has never been a psychologist who could have said that boredom characterized the faces of the masses when they participate in the routine pleasures. Perhaps, since the average working day follows a routine which often does not show any change during a life-time, the routine and repetition characteristics of leisure-time activities serve as a kind of justification and glorification of the working day. They appear in the guise of beauty and pleasure when they rule not only during the average day, but also in the average late afternoon and evening. In our biographies, the horizon is not extended to the realm of the unknown, but is instead painted with the figures of the known. We have already seen the movie actor performing on the screen and we have seen the cartoons of the competent newspaperman; we have heard what the radio commentator has to say and have noted the talents of boxers and baseball players. The biographies repeat what we have always known.

André Maurois has made a wrong prophecy: "We shall come once more into periods of social and religious certainty in which few intimate biographies will be written and *panegyrics* will take their place. Subsequently we shall again reach a period of doubt and despair in which biographies will reappear as a source of confidence and reassurance."[20] The reader who obviously cherishes the duplication of being entertained with the life stories of his entertainers, must have an irrepressible urge to get something in his mind which he can really hold fast and fully understand. It has been said of reading interests that: "In general, so long as the things of fundamental importance are not presenting one with problems, one scarcely attends to them in any way.[21] This remark has an ironical connotation for our biographies, for it can hardly be said that "things of importance" are not presenting us with problems today. Yet they are scarcely attended to unless we would admit that our heroes' parents, their likes and dislikes in eating and playing and, in the majority of cases, even their professions are important data during the initial stages of this war. But the distance between what an average individual may do and the forces and powers that determine his life and death has become so unbridgeable that identification with normalcy, even with Philistine boredom becomes a readily grasped empire of refuge and escape. It is some comfort for the little man who has become expelled from the Horatio Alger dream, who despairs of penetrating the thicket of grand strategy in politics and business, to see his heroes as a lot of guys who like or dislike highballs, cigarettes, tomato juice, golf and social gatherings—just like himself. He knows how to converse in the sphere of consumption and here he can make no mistakes. By narrowing his focus of attention, he can experience the gratification of being confirmed in his own pleasures and discomforts by participating in the pleasures and discomforts of the great. The large confusing issues in the political and economic realm and the antagonisms and controver-

sies in the social realm—all these are submerged in the experience of being at one with the lofty and great in the sphere of consumption.

Notes

1. Cf. Edward H. O'Neill, *A History of American Biography*, University of Pennsylvania Press, 1935. His remarks on pp. 179 ff. on the period since 1919 as the "most prolific one in American history for biographical writing," are quoted by Helen McGill Hughes, *News and the Human Interest Story*, University of Chicago Press, 1940, p. 285 f. The book by William S. Gray and Ruth Munroe, *The Reading Interests and Habits of Adults*, Macmillan, New York, 1930, which analyzes readers' figures for books and magazines, does not even introduce the category of biographies in its tables on the contents of magazines, and applies it only once for books in a sample analysis of readers in Hyde Park, Chicago. The only comment the authors have to offer is: "There is some tendency to prefer biographies and poetry, especially in moderate doses to other types of reading except fiction" (p. 154). Finally, I want to quote as a witness in this case of scientific negligence, Donald A. Stouffer, *The Art of Biography in Eighteenth Century England*, Princeton University Press, 1941, who in his excellent and very thorough study says: "Biography as a branch of literature has been too long neglected" (p. 3).

2. Up to the spring of 1939, 3.1 million copies of his books were sold: 1.2 million in Germany, 1.1 million in the U.S., 0.8 million elsewhere. (Cf. Emil Ludwig, *Traduction des Œuvres*, Moscia, 1939, p. 2.)

3. It should not be inferred that the results as presented here are without much change applicable to all other magazines which present general and diversified topics. From a few selections taken from less widely circulated and more expensive magazines, ranging from *The New Yorker* to the dollar-a-copy *Fortune*, it seems very likely that the biographies presented there differ in their average content structure and therefore in their social and psychological implications from these lower-priced popular periodicals. The difference in contents corresponds to a difference in readership.

4. Cf. footnote 12 of this article.

5. For the collection of data prior to 1940 the writer is indebted to Miss Miriam Wexner.

6. We have omitted from our discussion and our figures a number of very short biographical features which amounted to little more than anecdotes. These were published fairly regularly by the *SEP* until the late Twenties under the headings "Unknown Captains of Industry," "Wall Street Men," sometimes called "Bulls and Bears," "Who's Who and Why," "Workingman's Wife," "Literary Folk."

7. See, for instance, the *SEP*, September 19, 1925, where the auto-racer, Barney Oldsfield, tells a reporter details of his racing experiences and of the mechanics of racing and automobiles; September 26, 1925, in which the vaudeville actress, Elsie Janis, comments on her imitation acts and also gives details of her techniques. The same holds true for the biography of the band leader, Sousa, in the *SEP*, October 31, 1925, and of the radio announcer, Graham McNamee, May 1, 1926; after a few remarks about his own life and career, McNamee goes on to discuss the technical aspects of radio and his experiences in radio with famous people.

8. *Saturday Evening Post*, October 12, 1901.

9. *Saturday Evening Post*, June 28, 1902.

10. Here and there we find a casual remark on the function of biographies as models for individual imitation. Cf., for instance, Mandel Sherman, "Book Selection and Self Therapy," in *The Practice of Book Selection*, edited by Louis R. Wilson, University of Chicago Press, 1939, p. 172. "In 1890 a book appeared entitled *Acres of Diamonds*, by Russell H. Conwell. This book dealt especially with the problems of attaining success in life. The author attempted to encourage the reader by giving examples of the struggles and triumphs of noted successful men and women. This pattern of encouraging the reader by citing examples of great men has continued, and in recent years a number of books have appeared in which most of the content dealt with case histories of noted individuals. Some psychologists have suggested that interest in autobiographies and biographies has arisen in part from the attempts of the readers to compare their own lives with those about whom they read, and thus to seek encouragement from the evidence of the struggles of successful people."

Helen M. Hughes in her suggestive study has not avoided the tendency to settle the problem of biographies by rather simplified psychological formulae. By quoting generously O'Neill, Bernarr MacFadden, and André Maurois, she points to the differences of the more commemorative and eulogistic elements in earlier biographies and the "anxious groping for certainty of people who live in times of rapid change," which is supposed to be connected with the present interest in biography (see especially p. 285).

11. The figures in parentheses refer to the bibliography of stories studied, Appendix J. Figures 1 to 57 refer to the *SEP* and 101 to 168 to *Collier's*, On the difference between the *SEP* and *Collier's*, see Appendix J, Tables 1, 2.

12. It will be very important to check later how far the present war situation has confirmed, changed, or even reversed the trend. A few casual observations on the present-day situation may be mentioned.

The *New York Times* "Magazine" on July 12, 1942, published an article "Wallace Warns Against 'New Isolationism.'" The Vice-President of the United States is photographed playing tennis. The caption for the picture reads "Mr. Wallace's Serve." This picture and its caption are a very revealing symbol. The word "serve" does not refer to social usefulness, but to a feature in the Vice-President's private life.

This remark can be supplemented by quoting a few issues of the *SEP* and *Collier's*, picked at random from their publications during the summer of 1942. While everywhere else in this study we have limited ourselves to the analysis of strictly biographical contributions, we should like, by quoting some of the topics of the entire issues which we have chosen for this year, to emphasize the overall importance of the spheres of consumption. Not only has the selection of heroes for biographies not changed since America's active participation in the war, but many other of the non-fictional articles are also still concerned with consumers' interests.

Of the ten non-fictional articles in the *SEP*, August 8, 1942, five are connected with the consumers' world: a serial on Hollywood agents; a report on a hometown circus; a report on roadside restaurants; an analysis of women as book readers; and an essay on the horse and buggy. In an issue one week later, August 15, 1942, there is a report on the International Correspondence School; the continuation of the serial on the Hollywood agents; and a biography on the radio idol, Kate Smith. Or let us look at *Collier's*, which as a whole, devotes a much higher percentage of articles to war topics than the *SEP*. Out of nine articles in the issue of July 4, 1942, five belong to the consumers' world. There is again one on the horse and buggy, another one on a baseball hero, a third one on an Army comedian, a fourth one on a Broadway producer, and finally, one on budget buffets. Three weeks later, on July 25, out of ten articles, again five belong to the same category.

In other words, out of 37 articles found in four issues of two leading popular magazines during the present crisis, not less than 17 treat the gustatory and entertainment features of the average citizen.

There appears to be some cause for concern in the fact that so much of the fare presented to the reading public during the times immediately preceding the war and during the war itself is almost completely divorced from important social issues.

13. We proceeded to collect all the passages in the 125 stories pertaining to our four categories. It is not intended here to analyze the 2,400 quotations exhaustively, but merely to present in the following chapters a few observations or hypotheses which their study suggested to us and which we hope may be stimulating to further research in content analysis.

14. D. G. Phillips, "The Right Hand to Pierpont Morgan," *Saturday Evening Post*, June 28, 1902.

15. Max Horkheimer, "The End of Reason," in: *Studies in Philosophy and Social Science*, Vol. IX (1941), #3, p. 381.

16. *Loc. cit.*

17. The spectacle of success, hardships and accidents is attended in the biographies by an assortment of numbers and figures which purport to bestow glamour and exactness to the narration. Calculability is the ideal language of modern biographies. They belong to the scientific mentality which sees its ideal in the transformation from quality into quantity. Life's riddle is solved if caught in a numeric constellation. The majority of figures refer to income, to which may be added relatively few data on capital. The other figures pertain to the spectators of a ball game, to the budget of a city, to the votes of an election, etc.

18. An unpublished study of this writer on popular German biographies in book form shows that the use of superlatives also characterizes them. These books by Emil Ludwig, Stefan Zweig and others, are on a different intellectual level, yet it seems probable that similar sociological implications hold for them as for magazine biographies.

19. Helen McGill Hughes, *loc. cit.*, p. 183, is aware of the fact that the association of "classical" names has a stimulating effect on what she calls "the city demos": "Stated in terms of his popular literature, the mind of modern man lives in the present. And as the present changes, so his news is voluminous and rapidly succeeded by more news. But what fascinates him is the news story—the true story—even though it may duplicate *Bluebeard* or *Romeo and Juliet* so exactly that the headline tells the news just by mentioning the familiar names. The human interest of the common man in the modern world will, and does, ensnare him into reading folktales or even the classics, dull and unreal as he finds them in themselves, if they are paraphrased as the careers of twentieth century Electras, Macbeths and Moll Flanders, for he is pre-occupied with the things that depart from the expected and make news."

20. André Maurois, *Aspects of Biography*, Appleton-Century, New York, 1939, p. 203.

21. Franklin Bobbitt, "Major Fields of Human Concern," quoted in: Gray and Munroe, *loc. cit.*, p. 47.

31

The Negro Press

From *An American Dilemma: The Negro Problem and Modern Democracy* (1944)

Gunnar Myrdal

G unnar Myrdal (1898–1987) was a Swedish economist, sociologist, political leader, and Nobel Prize winner (1974, in economic science). He came to the United States between 1929 and 1930 as a Rockefeller fellow before returning to Sweden and writing (with his wife as coauthor) *Crisis in the Population Question* (1934), an internationally important book influencing thought about new social welfare programs. During the 1930s, Myrdal served as a Social Democratic senator and as a government commissioner, and he helped to build the Swedish welfare state. In 1937, representatives from the Carnegie Corporation approached him as someone whom they believed to be "uninfluenced by traditional attitudes or by earlier conclusions," and invited him to oversee "a comprehensive study of the Negro in the United States, to be undertaken in a wholly objective and dispassionate way as a social phenomenon." Thus began the massive, two-volume *An American Dilemma: The Negro Problem and Modern Democracy*, perhaps the most influential publication on race in the mid-twentieth century and one more example of that era's high hopes for social science as an agent of social clarification and reform.

Like the Lynds' *Middletown*, Myrdal's *An American Dilemma* marshaled a great deal of empirical research to offer a portrait and a criticism of American society, specifically, the condition of African Americans. It involved dozens of researchers (including Louis Wirth, E. Franklin Frazier, Edward Shils, Dorothy Thomas, and Ralph Bunche) and documented aspects of Negro life, ranging from employment to voting, social class, schools, and lynching. The book received wide attention in the periodical press. Its theory of the vicious circle (or "principle of cumulation")—the idea that poverty begets more poverty—was one of the social scientific bases on which arguments were made to dismantle the "separate but equal" doctrine of American education in *Brown v. Board of Education* (1954). In this excerpt, based on a research report by G. James Fleming, Myrdal takes up the classic Chicago view of newspapers as a mode of representing a group to itself, a perspective developed by Cooley, Park, MacGill Hughes, and others. It also nicely sketches institutional and communicative aspects of minority media and the dual social worlds they straddle.

An Organ for the Negro Protest

Most white people in America are entirely unaware of the bitter and relentless criticism of themselves; of their policies in domestic or international affairs; their legal and political practices; their business enterprises; their churches, schools, and other institutions; their social customs, their opinions and prejudices; and almost everything else in white American civilization. Week in and week out these are presented to the Negro people in their own press. It is a fighting press.

Negro papers are first of all race papers. They are first and foremost interested in the advancement of the race. A large percentage of the editorials are concerned with justice to the race, with equal privileges, with facts of race progress, or with complaint against conditions as they are. Of course there occur from time to time well written editorials on topics of general interest, such as world peace, better political adjustment, or the progress of civilization; but it still remains true that most of the editorials are distinctly racial. The articles in these papers are usually propaganda—that is they follow the line of the editorials. A great many are genuinely inflammatory.

The Negro papers offer something not found in the white press:

Through all the Negro press there flows an undercurrent of feeling that the race considers itself a part of America and yet has no voice in the American newspaper. Members of this group want to learn about each other, they want the stories of their success, conflicts, and issues told, and they want to express themselves in public.

The purpose of the press is clearly conceived. P. B. Young, the editor of one of the best Negro papers, the Norfolk *Journal and Guide,* expresses it thus:

Traditionally our press is a special pleader; it is an advocate of human rights.

There are at present about 210 Negro weekly, semi-weekly, or bi-weekly newspapers.[1] Some of these are for the general Negro public; others are organs of Negro religious denominations and labor organizations. Most of the general newspapers have a circulation limited to the locality where they are published. But ten to twenty Negro papers have large circulations extending to whole regions and sometimes to all Negro America. In addition there are some 129 monthly, bi-monthly and quarterly magazines. Two of these have outstanding national importance: *The Crisis,* published by the N.A.A.C.P., and *Opportunity,* published by the National Urban League.[2] The others are almost all organs of Negro religious denominations, fraternal orders, professional groups, colleges and schools. Only four Negro magazines are pictorial or theatrical.

The weekly press alone has a total circulation of around one and a half million.

Practically all Negroes who can read are exposed to the influence of the Negro press at least some of the time. Perhaps a third of the Negro families in cities regularly subscribe to Negro newspapers, but the proportion is much smaller in rural areas. The readers of the Negro press are, however, the most alert and articulate individuals who form Negro opinion. Newspapers are commonly passed from family to family, and they are sometimes read out loud in informal gatherings. They are available in barbershops, and sometimes in churches, lodges and pool parlors. Their contents are passed by word of mouth among those who cannot read. Indirectly, therefore, even aside from circulation figures, this press influences a large proportion of the Negro population.

No unifying central agency directs the opinions expressed in the Negro press. Like white newspapers, Negro newspapers are in keen competition with one another for circulation. Without discounting either the idealistic zeal and the strength of personal opinion of many editors, columnists, and other Negro newspapersmen, or the influence of petty corruption in the Negro papers, by and large the Negro press provides the news and the opinions which its reading public wants. This inference has the corollary conclusion that Negro opinion—at least among the more alert and articulate groups—can be ascertained and studied in the Negro press.

The opinions expressed in the Negro press—directly in the editorials and columns and indirectly in the type of news selected—are remarkably similar all over the country. This is undoubtedly caused by the common demands of the reading public and the similarity of *milieu* of the competing journalists. Negro papers in the South tend to be more cautious and less belligerent. But a large proportion of all Negro papers bought and read in the South are published in the North. This Northern competition explains to some extent why even Southern Negro newspapers give such a relatively blunt expression to the Negro protest. The more basic explanation, however, is that this is what the Southern Negro public wants to read, too. In the South, where concerted action on the part of Negroes is usually so severely checked, and where Negro leadership in all practical matters has to be accommodating, most of the time,[3] the Negro press serves as a safety-valve for the boiling Negro protest.

This is possible—like the great amount of Negro protest within the walls of the Negro church and the Negro school—because the whites seldom know much about it. Whites, apparently, very rarely see Negro papers. Even when they do come across them, there is a certain abstract feeling among all Americans for the freedom of the press which, even in the South covers the Negro newspapers. The Southern Negro press, further, usually takes the precaution of not attaching its protest too much to local issues and news, but to general principles, national issues, and news from distant points. The local pages in Southern Negro papers are usually restrained.

Northern Negro papers are less afraid of carrying the Negro protest into local news and issues. But even in the North most of the local coverage tends to be restricted to news and gossip about the town. Indirectly, however, even the pages devoted to the local community have a protest purpose as well as an informational purpose in both the North and the South. All Negroes, and particularly the ambitious upper and middle classes of Negroes who make up most of the reading public, are aware that white Americans deny them social status and social distinction. This makes class and accomplishment seem tremendously important. The display of Negro "society news" in the Negro press is partly an answer to the social derogation from the whites.

The more important and open expressions of the Negro protest are to be found in the news coverage of the whole American Negro world and, to an extent, the Negro world outside the United States, and also in the columns and editorials on the status of the Negro people. It is a characteristic of the Negro press that if, on the one hand, it is provincial in focusing interest on the race angle, it, on the other hand, embraces the whole race world. *The press defines the Negro group to the Negroes themselves.* The individual Negro is invited to share in the sufferings, grievances, and pretensions of the millions of Negroes far outside the narrow local community. This creates a feeling of strength and solidarity. The press, more than any other institution, has created the Negro group as a social and psychological reality to the individual Negro.

For this reason the Negro press is far more than a mere expression of the Negro protest. By expressing the protest, the press also magni-

fies it, acting like a huge sounding board. The press is also the chief agency of group control. It tells the individual how he should think and feel as an American Negro and creates a tremendous power of suggestion by implying that all other Negroes think and feel in this manner. It keeps the Negro spokesman in line. Every public figure knows he will be reported, and he has to weigh his words carefully. Both the leaders and the masses are kept under racial discipline by the press. This promotes unanimity without the aid of central direction.

The Negro press is thus strongly opinionated. This points to a difference between the Negro press and the foreign-language press supported by the various immigrant groups in America.[4] Both types of "minority press" serve the interest of their groups to read more news about themselves than the "majority press" cares to give them. Many individuals in the immigrant groups are also not familiar with the English language, and a foreign-language paper is to them a practical news agency. Many more feel a certain pride in a non-American origin and culture. But this attachment is usually experienced as a sentimental quality of distinction, besides that of being, or becoming, an American. Immigrants are usually bent on assimilation and, as good prospects are held out to them,[5] they feel little desire to protest.[6]

Negroes, on the contrary, have no language of their own, and their culture is American. But, however much culturally assimilated they are, they are not accepted as full-fledged Americans. They protest, not because they feel themselves different, but because they want to be similar and are forcibly held to be different.[7] The news in the Negro papers is selected and edited to prove the theory that they are similar and that they should be treated as ordinary Americans.

In a sense, the Negro newspapers have, thus, an opposite purpose from the ordinary immigrant papers, which take full assimilation of the group for granted and cater only to temporary language difficulties and to a sentimental pride in keeping up a cherished ethnic and cultural distinction. The foreign-language press is doomed to disappear as the immigrants become fully assimilated and are not replenished by new immigration. The Negro press, on the contrary, is bound to become ever stronger as Negroes are increasingly educated and culturally assimilated but not given entrance to the white world.

In spite of this basic difference in purpose and "function," the two types of press are interesting to compare. In many important technical respects they show similarities. Both the immigrant papers and the Negro papers usually have their reading public spread all over the country, and both tend to become regional or national in circulation. Both, therefore, have difficulty in soliciting advertising, which tends to keep them marginal as economic enterprises. At present, the foreign-language press is often better protected against competition from the majority press; it can support many dailies.[8] With the decrease in the number of persons who read only a foreign language well, even the foreign-language papers will tend to become what the Negro papers already are, namely, papers read in addition to ordinary American newspapers. They will then also tend to be weekly and to be published in English, until they finally disappear altogether.[9]

Notes

1. Florence Murray (editor), *The Negro Handbook* (1942), p. 201. (The figures are taken from a U.S. Bureau of the Census report for 1940.) There have been repeated attempts to launch Negro dailies but they have regularly failed. (See G. James Fleming, "*The Negro Press,*" unpublished manuscript prepared for this study [1940], Chapter IX.) *The Atlanta Daily World* is the only daily newspaper at the present time. In 1940 its daily circulation was about 5,000, but it had a weekly edition with a larger circulation. (*Ibid.*, Chapter IX, pp. 8 ff.)

2. Among the magazines, *The Interracial Review*, an organ for Catholic Action, comes next perhaps in importance. *Silhouette* is a picture monthly, surviving *Flash* and *Candid*, which followed the *Life* pattern. A high place is held by *The Journal of Negro History*, edited by Carter G. Woodson; *Journal of Negro Education*, edited by Charles Thompson of Howard University; and *Phylon, The Atlanta University Review of Race and Culture*, edited by W. E. B. Du Bois. For some further notes on the publications on organization and on the earlier appearances and disap-

pearances of Nero magazines, see Fleming, *op. cit.*, Chapter XII. Also see: Sidney V. Reedy, "The Negro Magazine: A critical Study of Its Educational Significance," *Journal of Negro Education* (October, 1934), pp. 598–604. In this chapter we shall concentrate our attention on the regular Negro weeklies, which, at least directly, are of greatest importance for the formation of Negro opinion. Most of what we have to say is, *mutatis mutandis,* valid for the periodical also.

3. See Chapters 34 and 37.

4. For a sociological analysis of the immigrant press, see Robert E. Park, *The Immigrant Press and Its Control* (1922).

5. See Chapter 3, Section 1.

6. This is true in all ordinary immigrant groups which do not feel very disadvantaged, and who are consequently not in opposition to their treatment in America. Exceptions are the papers of very disadvantaged groups or of extremely radical sub-groups.

7. To the white American their pretensions are preposterous. "The impatient, all but militant and anti-social attitude of an influential section of the Negro press is to be condemned in this connection. These editors show an unfortunate lack of appreciation of the traits of the people they aspire to lead. Their language implies that the Negro is only an Anglo-Saxon who is so unfortunate as to have a black skin. Such a race philosophy only works injustice to the Negro himself and it is high time to discard it." (John M. Mecklin, *Democracy and Race Friction* [1914], p. 46.)

8. In Chicago alone there are some 20 to 25 foreign-language daily newspapers (Elizabeth D. John, "The Role of the Negro Newspaper in the Negro Community," unpublished manuscript made available through the courtesy of the author [1940], p. 24), while the Negroes have not succeeded in keeping up dailies. There is at present only one Negro daily (see footnote a few pages back). This is in spite of the fact that there are nearly 13 million Negroes in the country, as compared to only 11 million foreign-born whites and the latter are split up into many nationalities.

9. This process has proceeded far, for instance, in the Scandinavian language groups.

32

A Social Critique of Radio Music

From the *Kenyon Review* (1945)

Theodor W. Adorno

Theodor Wiesengrund Adorno (1903–1969) was a member of the Frankfurt Institute for Social Research and one of the foremost thinkers of the twentieth century on questions of art, music, and society. An accomplished pianist and composer, Adorno was also a philosopher, sociologist, cultural critic, and musicologist. He was born in Germany to a father who was a wine merchant and to a mother who was an Italian opera singer, whose name he eventually took as his surname in the 1930s. Like many Jewish intellectuals, he left Germany after Hitler took power, spending time first in England (1933–1936) and then in the United States (1937–1949)—principally in New York City and Los Angeles, where he was exposed to the full glories and banalities of American popular culture. Neither America nor Adorno fully understood each other, but the clash produced some sparks that continue to light up contemporary thinking about music and art, media and society, free time and freedom.

Famous for his gnarled and difficult style of writing, Adorno is in this piece refreshingly direct—as he often was when he wrote in English. In what seems almost like a *Reader's Digest* version of his views on popular music, Adorno explains his principles of social criticism, as well as his vision of the deceptions of mass culture, with examples and clarity. In a study derived from work he did at Lazarsfeld's Office of Radio Research, Adorno points out the limits of "administrative research." He is often subtler than he might seem. He does not, for instance, simply say that radio crams musical preferences down the throats of its listeners (as Duncan MacDougald seems to say in his critique of "plugging"). He points not to simple brainwashing but to something more elusive. In professing to uplift listeners with something classic and "ethereal," radio actually does something far worse—it cheapens the possibility of genuine art and, with it, the prospect of human emancipation. It is not simply that people's tastes are manipulated but rather that the true power of music is perverted and brought into the service of domination instead into that of freedom. Adorno is worried not only about people's ears but also their souls.

Some would approach the problem of radio by formulating questions of this type: If we confront such and such a sector of the population with such and such a type of music, what reactions may we expect? How can these reactions be measured and expressed statistically? Or: How many sectors of the population have been brought into contact with music and how do they respond to it?

What intention lies behind such questions? This approach falls into two major operations:

a) We subject some groups to a number of different treatments and see how they react to each.

b) We select and recommend the procedure which produces the effect we desire.

The aim itself, the tool by which we achieve it, and the persons upon whom it works are generally taken for granted in this procedure. The guiding interest behind such investigations is basically one of *administrative* technique: how to manipulate the masses. The pattern is that of market analysis even if it appears to be completely remote from any selling purpose. It might be research of an *exploitive* character, i.e. guided by the desire to induce as large a section of the population as possible to buy a certain commodity. Or it may be what Paul F. Lazarsfeld calls *benevolent* administrative research, putting questions such as, "How can we bring good music to as large a number of listeners as possible?"

I would like to suggest an approach that is antagonistic to exploitive and at least supplementary to benevolent administrative research. It abandons the form of question indicated by a sentence like: How can we, under given conditions, best further certain aims? On the contrary, this approach in some cases questions the aims and in all cases the successful accomplishment of these aims under the given conditions. Let us examine the question: how can good music be conveyed to the largest possible audience?

What is "good music"? Is it just the music which is given out and accepted as "good" according to current standards, say the programs of the Toscanini concerts? We cannot pass it as "good" simply on the basis of the names of great composers or performers, that is, by social convention. Furthermore, is the goodness of music invariant, or is it something that may change in the course of history with the technique at our disposal? For instance, let us take it for granted—as I do—that Beethoven really is good music. Is it not possible that this music, by the very problems it sets for itself, is far away from our own situation? That by constant repetition it has deteriorated so much that it has ceased to be the living force it was and has become a museum piece which no longer possesses the power to speak to the millions to whom it is brought? Or, even if this is not so, and if Beethoven in a musically young country like America is still as fresh as on the first day, is radio actually an adequate means of communication? Does a symphony played on the air remain a symphony? Are the changes it undergoes by wireless transmission merely slight and negligible modifications or do those changes affect the very essence of the music? Are not the stations in such a case bringing the masses in con-

tact with something totally different from what it is supposed to be, thus also exercising an influence quite different from the one intended? And as to the large numbers of people who listen to "good music": *how* do they listen to it? Do they listen to a Beethoven symphony in a concentrated mood? Can they do so even if they want to? Is there not a strong likelihood that they listen to it as they would to a Tchaikovsky symphony, that is to say, simply listen to some neat tunes or exciting harmonic stimuli? Or do they listen to it as they do to jazz, waiting in the introduction of the finale of Brahms's First Symphony for the solo of the French horn, as they would for Benny Goodman's solo clarinet chorus? Would not such a type of listening make the high cultural ideal of bringing good music to large numbers of people altogether illusory?

These questions have arisen out of the consideration of so simple a phrase as "bringing good music to as large an audience as possible." None of these or similar questions can be wholly solved in terms of even the most benevolent research of the administrative type. One should not study the attitude of listeners, without considering how far these attitudes reflect broader social behavior patterns and, even more, how far they are conditioned by the structure of society as a whole. This leads directly to the problem of a social critique of radio music, that of discovering its social position and function. We first state certain axioms.

a) We live in a society of commodities—that is, a society in which production of goods is taking place, not primarily to satisfy human wants and needs, but for profit. Human needs are satisfied only incidentally, as it were. This basic condition of production affects the form of the product as well as the human interrelationships.

b) In our commodity society there exists a general trend toward a heavy concentration of capital which makes for shrinking of the free market in favor of monopolized mass production of standardized goods; this holds true particularly of the communications industry.

c) The more the difficulties of contemporary society increase as it seeks its own continuance, the stronger becomes the general tendency to maintain, by all means available, the existing conditions of power and property relations against the threats which they themselves breed. Whereas on the one hand standardization necessarily follows from the conditions of contemporary economy, it becomes, on the other hand, one of the means of preserving a commodity society at a stage in which, according to the level of the productive forces, it has already lost its justification.

d) Since in our society the forces of production are highly developed, and, at the same time, the relations of production fetter those productive forces, it is full of antagonisms. These antagonisms are not limited to the economic sphere where they are universally recognized, but dominate also the cultural sphere where they are less easily recognized.

How did music become, as our first axiom asserts it to be, a commodity? After music lost its feudal protectors during the latter part of the 18th Century it had to go to the market. The market left its imprint on it either because it was manufactured with a view to its selling chances, or because it was produced in conscious and violent reaction against the market requirements. What seems significant, however, in the present situation, and what is certainly deeply connected with the trend to standardization and mass production, is that *today the commodity character of music tends radically to alter it.* Bach in his day was considered, and considered himself, an artisan, although his music functioned as art. Today music is considered etheral and sublime, although it actually functions as a commodity. Today the terms etheral and sublime have become trademarks. Music has become a means instead of an end, a fetish. That is to say, music has ceased to be a human force and is consumed like other consumers' goods. This produces "commodity listening," a listening whose ideal it is to dispense as far as possible with any effort on the part of the recipient—even if such an effort on the part of the recipient is the necessary condition of grasping the sense of the music. It is the ideal of Aunt Jemima's ready-mix for pancakes extended to the field of music. The listener suspends all intellectual activity when dealing with music and is content with consuming and evaluating its gustatory qualities—just as if the music which tasted best were also the best music possible.

Famous master violins may serve as a drastic illustration of musical fetishism. Whereas only

the expert is able to distinguish a "Strad" from a good modern fiddle, and whereas he is often least preoccupied with the tone quality of the fiddles, the layman, induced to treat these instruments as commodities, gives them a disproportionate attention and even a sort of adoration. One radio company went so far as to arrange a cycle of broadcasts looking, not primarily to the music played, nor even to the performance, but to what might be called an acoustic exhibition of famous instruments such as Paganini's violin and Chopin's piano. This shows how far the commodity attitude in radio music goes, though under a cloak of culture and erudition.

Our second axiom—increasing standardization—is bound up with the commodity character of music. There is, first of all, the haunting similarity between most musical programs, except for the few non-conformist stations which use recorded material of serious music; and also the standardization of orchestral performance, despite the musical trademark of an individual orchestra. And there is, above all, that whole sphere of music whose lifeblood is standardization: popular music, jazz, be it hot, sweet, or hybrid.

The third point of our social critique of radio concerns its ideological effect. Radio music's ideological tendencies realize themselves regardless of the intent of radio functionaries. There need be nothing intentionally malicious in the maintenance of vested interests. Nonetheless, music under present radio auspices serves to keep listeners from criticizing social realities; in short, it has a soporific effect upon social consciousness. The illusion is furthered that the best is just good enough for the man in the street. The ruined farmer is consoled by the radio-instilled belief that Toscanini is playing for him and for him alone, and that an order of things that allows him to hear Toscanini compensates for low market prices for form products; even though he is ploughing cotton under, radio is giving him culture. Radio music is calling back to its broad bosom all the prodigal sons and daughters whom the harsh father has expelled from the door. In this respect radio music offers a new function not inherent in music as an art—the function of creating smugness and self-satisfaction.

The last group of problems in a social critique of radio would be those pertaining to social antagonisms. While radio marks a tremendous technical advance, it has proved an impetus to progress neither in music itself nor in musical listening. Radio is an essentially new technique of musical reproduction. But it does not broadcast, to any considerable extent, serious modern music. It limits itself to music created under pre-radio conditions. Nor has it, itself, thus far evoked any music really adequate to its technical conditions.

The most important antagonisms arise in the field of so-called musical mass-culture. Does the mass distribution of music really mean a rise of musical culture? Are the masses actually brought into contact with the kind of music which, from broader social considerations, may be regarded as desirable? Are the masses really participating in music culture or are they merely forced consumers of musical commodities? What is the role that music actually, not verbally, plays for them?

Under the aegis of radio there has set in a retrogression of listening. In spite of and even because of the quantitative increase in musical delivery, the psychological effects of this listening are very much akin to those of the motion picture and sport spectatoritis which promotes a retrogressive and sometimes even infantile type of person. "Retrogressive" is meant here in a psychological and not a purely musical sense.

An illustration: A symphony of the Beethoven type, so-called classical, is one of the most highly integrated musical forms. The whole is everything; the part, that is to say, what the layman calls the melody, is relatively unimportant. Retrogressive listening to a symphony is listening which, instead of grasping that whole, dwells upon those melodies, just as if the symphony were structurally the same as a ballad. There exists today a tendency to listen to Beethoven's Fifth as if it were a set of quotations from Beethoven's Fifth. We have developed a larger framework of concepts such as atomistic listening and quotation listening, which lead us to the hypothesis that something like musical children's language is taking shape.

As today a much larger number of people listen to music than in pre-radio days, it is difficult to compare today's mass-listening with what could be called the elite listening of the past. Even if we restrict ourselves, however to select groups of today's listeners (say, those who listen to the Philharmonics in New York and Boston), one suspects that the Philharmonic listener of today listens in radio terms. A clear indication is the relation to serious advanced modern music. In the Wagnerian period, the elite listener was eager to follow the most daring musical exploits. Today

the corresponding group is the firmest bulwark against musical progress and feels happy only if it is fed Beethoven's Seventh Symphony again and again.

In analyzing the fan mail of an educational station in a rural section in the Middle West, which has been emphasizing serious music at regular hours with a highly skilled and resourceful announcer, one is struck by the apparent enthusiasm of the listeners' reception, by the vast response, and by the belief in the highly progressive social function that this program was fulfilling. I have read all of those letters and cards very carefully. They are exuberant indeed. But they are enthusiastic in a manner that makes one feel uncomfortable. It is what might be called standardized enthusiasm. The communications are almost literally identical: "Dear X, Your Music Shop is swell. It widens my musical horizon and gives me an ever deeper feeling for the profound qualities of our great music. I can no longer bear the trashy jazz which we usually have to listen to. Continue with your grand work and let us have more of it." No musical item was mentioned, no specific reference to any particular feature was made, no criticism was offered, although the programs were amateurish and planless.

It would do little good to explain these standard responses by reference to the difficulty in verbalizing musical experience: for anybody who has had profound musical experiences and finds it hard to verbalize them may stammer and use awkward expressions, but he would be reluctant, even if he knew no other, to cloak them in rubber stamp phrases. I am forced to another explanation. The listeners were strongly under the spell of the announcer as the personified voice of radio as a social institution, and they responded to his call to prove one's cultural level and education by appreciating this good music. But they actually failed to achieve that very appreciation which stamped them as cultured. They took refuge in repeating, often literally, the announcer's speeches in behalf of culture. Their behavior might be compared with that of the fanatical radio listener entering a bakery and asking for "that delicious, golden crispy Bond Bread."

Another study led to a similar observation. A number of high school boys were subjected to an experiment concerning the role of "plugging" in achieving popularity for popular music. They identified, first, those songs played most frequently on the air during a given period—

that is, those songs rating highest according to the *Variety* figures—with those they regarded as the most popular ones according to general opinion. Further, they identified those songs which they regarded as most popular with those they happened to like themselves. Here it is particularly opportune to make clear the approach of a social critique. If we took such a case in isolattion, it might appear that radio, by a kind of Darwinian process of selection, actually plays most frequently those songs that are best liked by the people and is, therefore, fulfilling their demands. We know, however, from another section of our study, that the "plugging" of songs does not follow the response they elicit but the vested interests of song publishers. The identification of the successful with the most frequently played is thus an illusion—an illusion, to be sure, that may become an operating social force and in turn really make the much-played a success: because through such an identification the listeners follow what they believe to be the crowd and thus come to constitute one.

The standardization of production in this field, as in most others, goes so far that the listener virtually has no choice. Products are forced upon him. His freedom has ceased to exist. This process, however, if it were to work openly and undisguised, would promote a resistance which could easily endanger the whole system. The less the listener has to choose, the more is he made to believe that he has a choice: and the more the whole machine functions only for the sake of profit, the more must he be convinced that it is functioning for him and his sake only or, as it is put, as a public service. In radio we can witness today something very similar to those comic and paradoxical forms of competition between gasolines which do not differ in anything but their names. The consumer is unwilling to recognize that he is totally dependent, and he likes to preserve the illusion of private initiative and free choice. Thus standardiztion in radio produces its veil of pseudo-individualism. It is this veil which enforces upon us scepticism with regard to any first-hand information from listeners. We must try to understand them better than they understand themselves. This brings us easily into conflict with common sense notions, such as "giving the people what they want."

This raises the question of controls and safeguards against biased imagination. Music is not a realm of subjective tastes and relative values, except to those who do not want to undergo the discipline of the subject matter. As soon as one enters the field of musical technology and structure, the arbitrariness of evaluation vanishes, and we are faced with decisions about right and wrong and true and false. I should like to give some examples of what I call musico-technological control of sociological interpretation. I mentioned above the social tendency toward a pseudo-individualism to hide the increase of standardization. This tendency in today's mass-produced music can be expressed in precise technical terms. Musical analysis can furnish us with plenty of materials which manifest, so far as rhythmical patterns, sound combinations, melodic and harmonic structures are concerned, that even apparently divergent schools of popular music, such as Sweet and Wing, are essentially the same. It can further be shown that their differences have no bearing on the musical essence itself. It can be shown that each band has assumed certain mannerisms with no musical function and no other purpose than to make it easier for the listener to recognize the particular band—such as, say, the musically nonsensical staccati with which Guy Lombardo likes to end certain legato phrases.

And now an example from the field of serious music. If we analyze a score of a Beethoven symphony in terms of all the thematic and dynamic interrelationships defined in the music, develop the necessary conditions of fulfilling its prescriptions by a performance, and then analyze the extent to which these prescriptions can be realized by radio, the proposition that symphonic music and the radio are incompatible becomes concretely defined and, so to speak, measurable. Here again the formulation of research problems is affected by our critical outlook. I suspect that people listen to serious music largely in terms of entertainment. Our technical analysis allows us to formulate this suspicion in exact terms. Studies on the Radio Voice have shown that with regard to such categories as the prevalence of sound colors, emphasis on detail, the isolation of the main tune, and similar features, a symphony on the air becomes a piece of entertainment. Consequently it would be absurd to maintain that it could be received by the listeners as anything but entertainment. Entertainment may have its uses, but a recognition of radio music as such would shatter the listener's artificially fostered belief that they are dealing with the world's greatest music.

33

The Social and Cultural Context

From *Mass Persuasion* (1946)

Robert K. Merton

Robert K. Merton (1910–2003) was one of the most influential American sociologists of the twentieth century. The son of working-class Jewish immigrants in Philadelphia, he was a pioneering figure in the sociology of science and a theorist whose embrace of methodologically sophisticated empirical work deeply shaped the mainstream of American sociology in the postwar era. Merton was known for championing "middle-range theory," for developing the structural-functionalist sociology, and for writing eloquently about everything from "the self-fulfilling prophecy" (Merton's concept), to race relations in a public housing project, to the history of the phrase "If I have seen farther, it is by standing on the shoulders of giants."

In the 1940s, Lazarsfeld brought Merton, somewhat reluctantly, into communications research, and Merton responded by producing a small but important body of work. The most significant piece was *Mass Persuasion,* an audience-based study of an eighteen-hour radio bond drive conducted by the popular entertainer Kate Smith, a talk-show host and singer who helped make Irving Berlin's "God Bless America" into a kind of second national anthem. The book combines interviews, survey research, and content analysis to explain the social meaning of the marathon and to situate it within the contexts of American society as Merton saw it. It offers a distinctive blend of empirical sociology and broader social theory (anchored, interestingly, by structuring quotes from classical texts from the rhetorical tradition). For Merton in the 1930s and 1940s, American society was marked by excessive attention to the arts of selling, the profit motive, and short-term instrumental rationality inattentive to the common good. We get a taste of that here in a famous selection on "pseudo-Gemeinschaft."

The rich and emotionally colored images of Smith, as we have seen, did not emerge full-fashioned on the day of the marathon, but for the most part long antedated it. To be sure, responses were affected by what she had to say during that day but they were also strongly influenced by previously established images of Smith and by personal ties to her. Were we to halt our inquiry at this point, without examining the sources of the cultural values which the Smith public image seemingly incorporates, it would be seriously inadequate and partially misleading. We have now to examine the social and cultural context of the sentiments of which Smith was the focus; to consider the nature of the social structure in which these sentiments found support; to investigate, in short, the ramifications of this one episode of mass persuasion into the larger reaches of the society in which it took place.

What, for example, is the social context of the enormous emphasis laid by our informants upon Smith's presumed sincerity? Why does the presence or absence of this quality loom so large among their concerns? It would appear that certain needs were satisfied by the belief in her integrity. What has given rise to these needs? Similar questions can be raised about the further components of the public images of Smith.

So, too, we have learned that Smith's large following played a considerable role in the effectiveness of her bond drive. But need the existence of this following be taken as a brute fact, or can we discover its bases in certain aspects of American culture and social structure? By searching out the functions which Smith fulfills for her adherents, we may partly account for the large measure of their devotion. Whereas in our previous discussion we were chiefly concerned with the dynamics of the persuasion episode itself, we are now looking into the social and cultural bases of the public images which entered so richly into the process of persuasion and of the mass following on which Smith could draw for support in the course of her bond drive.

The Context of Distrust

A heavy emphasis on Smith's sincerity occurs throughout our interviews.[1] It is significant that often this intense belief is expressed by informants who go on to contrast her integrity with the pretenses, deceptions and dissembling which they observe in their daily experience. On every side, they feel themselves the object of manipulation. They see themselves as the target for ingenious methods of control, through propagandas that, utilizing available techniques, guide the unwitting audience into opinions which may or may not coincide with the best interests of themselves or their affiliates; through cumulatively subtle methods of salesmanship which may simulate values common to both salesman and client for private and self-interested motives. In place of a sense of *Gemeinschaft*—genuine community of values—there intrudes *pseudo-Gemeinschaft*—the feigning of personal concern with the other fellow in order to manipulate him the better. Best sellers provide popular instruction in the arts of pseudo-Gemeinschaft: "how to influence people through the pretense of friendship." Drawn from a highly competitive, segmented urban society, our informants live in a climate of reciprocal distrust which, to say the least, is not conducive to stable human relationships. As one informant phrased it, "In my own business I can see how a lot of people in their business deals will make some kind of gesture of friendliness, sincerity and so forth, most of which is phony."

All this gives expression to some of the psychological effects of a society which, focused on capital and the market, tends to instrumentalize human relationships. In such a society, as Marx long since indicated, and as Durkheim and Simmel came to see, there are few dependable ties between each man and others. In such a society "men will tend to look at every relationship through a tradesman's eyes. They will tend more and more to picture natural objects as commodities and look at personal relationships from a mercenary point of view. In this process those much-discussed psychological phenomena, self-estrangement and dehumanization, will develop and a type of man is born for whom a tree is not a tree, but timber."[2] As codes regulating this money-centered behavior decay, there develops acute distrust of the dependability and sincerity of the other. Society is experienced as an arena for rival frauds. There is little belief in the disinterestedness of human conduct. As a devotee of Smith put it, "There are people who wouldn't lift their foot for their country. Everybody wants to make money. This city here is money-mad, dear."

The very same society that produces this sense of alienation and estrangement generates in many a craving for reassurance, an acute need to believe, a flight into faith. For her adherents, Smith has become the object of this faith. She is seen as genuine by those who seek redemption from the spurious. Her motives rise above avarice, ambition and pride of class. The image formed of her is the product of deep-lying needs and serves the function of temporary reassurance.[3]

The emotional emphasis place on Smith's "really meaning what she says" derives from the assumption that advertisers, public relations counsels, salesmen, promoters, script writers, politicians and, in extreme cases, ministers, doctors, and teachers are systematically manipulating symbols in order to gain power or prestige or income. It is the expression of a wish to be considered as a person rather than a potential client or customer. It is a reaction against the feelings of insecurity that stem from the conviction that others are dissembling and pretending to good-fellowship only to gain one's confidence and make one more susceptible to manipulation. It is, finally, the expectable response of persons living in a society which has lost many common values, which has foregone a sense of community ("Gemeinschaft") and has substituted for this community of outlook either the avowed play of atomistic personal interest within narrowly construed legal rules of the game ("Gesellschaft") or, even more disruptive to feelings of security, the mere pretense of common values in order to further private interests ("pseudo-Gemeinschaft"). And, since it is no easy task to discriminate between the pretense and the reality, there is an avid search for cues which testify to the one or the other. Hence, the enormous importance of Smith's "propaganda of the deed" as distinct from her "propaganda of the word." She not only talks, she acts. She not only praises benevolence and generosity, she apparently exemplifies them. It is these behavioral cues that are seized upon as evidence of her full-fashioned sincerity. "If everyone would follow her with their hearts, everything would be all right," a Smith disciple assures us. The phrasing is suggestive: if only Smith, the steadfast symbol of integrity, were taken as the prototype of behavior, insecurities could be allayed. And the reassurance function of the Smith image in an atmosphere of pervasive distrust is further expressed by a follower who exclaims: "I trust *her*. If *she* were a fake, I'd feel terrible."

The Smith following, then, is no mere aggregate of persons who are entertained by a popular singer. For many, she has become the symbol of a moral leader who "demonstrates" by her own behavior that there need be no discrepancy between appearance and reality in the sphere of human relationships. That an entertainer should have captured the moral loyalties of so large a following is itself an incisive commentary on prevailing social and political orientations.[4] But the gratifications which Smith provides for her adherents are not confined to this one type of reassurance. We have seen that Smith presents a kaleidoscopic set of images to her audience: she is at once patriot and philanthropist, mother, spiritual guide and mentor. And, not to be forgotten, she is both a successful careerist and a homebody. Though these images differ in detail, and indeed at times seem to be at odds with one another, they provide a diversity of gratification for those who are themselves not overly secure in a success-oriented culture.

Notes

1. See Chapter 4, pp. 82–89. *Cf.* Ernst Kris, "Some Problems of War Propaganda," *The Psychoanalytic Quarterly*, 1943, 12, 381–99.

2. Karl Mannheim, *Man and Society in an Age of Reconstruction* (New York: Harcourt, Brace & Company, 1940), p. 19.

3. Judging from a recently observed parallel instance, we may conjecture that the concern with "sincerity" becomes widespread precisely in those situations where there is acute danger of one's being manipulated by others for their own private interests. Put too succinctly, perhaps, widespread distrust heightens sensitivity to sincerity as a social value. Thus it has been noticed that among Negroes, "the whole business of 'advancing The Race' offers wide opportunities for fraud, graft and chicanery. There are opportunities for 'selling out to the white folks,' diverting funds from 'the cause,' or making a racket out of race." It is just this social situation which lends itself to manipulation of groups by self-interested persons and that generates an exaggerated concern with sincerity: "When the people are asked to describe a 'real Race Leader' they always stress 'sincerity' as a cardinal virtue . . ." St. Clair Drake and Horace R. Cayton, *Black Metropolis: A Study of Negro Life in a Northern City* (New York: Harcourt, Brace and Company, 1945), pp. 392–93.

4. Compare a recent study which found a shift, during the last generation, in the nature of the "heroes" of biographies in popular magazines. Whereas the earlier subjects of biographies were "idols of production"—stemming from industry, business and scientific research—the latter-day heroes are "idols of consumption"— being drawn almost wholly from the realm of entertainment and sport. "While we found that around 1900 and even around 1920 the vocational distribution of magazine heroes was a rather accurate reflection of the nation's living trends, we observe that today the hero-selection corresponds to needs quite different from those of genuine information. They seem to lead to a dream world of the masses who no longer are capable or willing to conceive of biographies primarily as a means of orientation and education. *They receive information not about the agents and methods of social production but about the agents and methods of social and individual consumption.* During the leisure in which they read, they read almost exclusively about people who are directly, or indirectly, providing for the reader's leisure time. The vocational set-up of the dramatis personae is organized as if the social production process were either completely exterminated or tacitly understood, and needed no further interpretation." Leo Lowenthal, "Biographies in Popular Magazines," in *Radio Research, 1942–1943*, (ed. by P. F. Lazarsfeld and Frank Stanton) (New York: Duell, Sloan & Pearce, 1944), pp. 516–18.

34

The Requirements

From *A Free and Responsible Press* (1947)

Hutchins Commission

The Hutchins Commission was a star-studded group of intellectuals, including Reinhold Niebuhr and Harold Lasswell, bankrolled by *Time* magazine publisher Henry R. Luce and the Encylopedia Britannica to clarify the role of the free press in society. It borrowed its name from its leader, University of Chicago president Robert Maynard Hutchins, who was famous for his educational reforms (which included abolishing the football team) and his tireless campaign on behalf of "the great books." The report is clearly part of an expansive postwar imagination about the media's power for both good and evil—an imagination that is also found in J. S. Huxley's vision of UNESCO and in Wirth's thoughts on mass communication, among others.

The commission produced several documents, including the massive *Government and Mass Communication* (1947), written by First Amendment scholar Zechariah Chaffee. The commission's summary report, from which this excerpt is taken, is called *A Free and Responsible Press: A General Report on Mass Communication: Newspapers, Radio, Motion Pictures, Magazines, and Books*. The book merits reading in its totality. It addresses the news media and other main agencies of mass communication, their structure of ownership, patterns of self-regulation, and attention to "scoops and sensations." In it, the commission argues that concentration of ownership and the failure of media industries "to supply the people with the service they require" imperil the free circulation of significant and competing ideas on which a free society ultimately rests. The commission calls for a press that is both largely independent of government regulation and responsible to the broader public. This excerpt makes "five ideal demands" of the news media in a free society—demands that are still quite relevant to current debates about media ethics. Practicing reporters found much of the report outrageous, and its influence has been less on the world of journalism than on how news media are discussed by scholars.

If the freedom of the press is freighted with the responsibility of providing the current intelligence needed by a free society, we have to discover what a free society requires. Its requirements in America today are greater in variety, quantity, and quality that those of any previous society in any age. They are the requirements of a self-governing republic of continental size, whose doings have become, within a generation, matters of common concern in new and important ways. Its internal arrangements, from being thought of mainly as matters of private interest and automatic market adjustments, have become affairs of conflict and conscious compromise among organized groups, whose powers appear not to be bounded by "natural law," economic or other. Externally, it has suddenly assumed a leading role in the attempt to establish peaceful relationship among all the states on the globe.

Today our society needs, first, a truthful, comprehensive, and intelligent account of the day's events in a context which gives them meaning; second, a forum for the exchange of comment and criticism; third, a means of projecting the opinions and attitudes of the groups in the society to one another; fourth, a method of presenting and clarifying the goals and values of the society; and fifth, a way of reaching every member of the society by the currents of information, thought, and feeling which the press supplies.

The Commission has no idea that these five ideal demands can ever be completely met. All of them cannot be met by any one medium; some do not apply at all to a particular unit; nor do all apply with equal relevance to all parts of the communications industry. The Commission does not suppose that these standards will be new to the managers of the press; they are drawn largely from their professions and practices.

A Truthful, Comprehensive, and Intelligent Account of the Day's Events in a Context Which Gives Them Meaning

The first requirement is that the media should be accurate. They should not lie.

Here the first link in the chain of responsibility is the reporter at the source of the news. He must be careful and competent. He must estimate correctly which sources are most authoritative. He must prefer firsthand observations to hearsay. He must know what questions to ask, what things to observe, and which items to report. His employer has the duty of training him to do his work as it ought to be done.

Of equal importance with reportorial accuracy are the identification of fact as fact and opinion as opinion, and their separation, so far as possible. This is necessary all the way from the reporter's file, up through the copy and makeup desks and editorial offices, to final, published product. This distinction cannot, of course, be made absolute. There is no fact without a context and factual report which is uncolored by the opinions of the reporter. But modern conditions require greater fact and opinion. In a simpler order of society published accounts of events within the experience of the community could be compared with other sources information. Today this is usually impossible. The account of an isolated fact, however is accurate in itself, may be misleading and, in effect, untrue.

The greatest danger here is in the communication of information internationally. The press now bears a responsibility in all countries, and particularly in democratic countries, where foreign policies are responsible to popular majorities, to report international events in such a way that they can be understood. It is no longer enough to report *the fact* truthfully. It is now necessary to report *the truth about the fact.*

In this country a similar obligation rests upon the press in reporting domestic news. The country has many groups which are partially insulated from one another and which need to be interpreted to one another. Factually correct but substantially untrue accounts of the behavior of members of one of these social islands can intensify the antagonisms of others toward them. A single incident will be accepted as a sample of group action unless the press has given a flow of information and interpretation concerning the relations between two racial groups such as to enable the reader to set a single event in its proper perspective. If it is allowed to pass as a sample of such action, the requirement that the press present an accurate account of the day's events in a context which gives them meaning has not been met.

A Forum for the Exchange of Comment and Criticism

The second requirement means that the great agencies of mass communication should regard themselves as common carriers of public discussion.[1] The units of the press have in varying degrees assumed this function and should assume the responsibilities which go with it, more generally and more explicitly.

It is vital to a free society that an idea should not be stifled by the circumstances of its birth. The press cannot and should not be expected to print everybody's ideas. But the giant units can and should assume the duty of publishing significant ideas contrary to their own, as a matter of objective reporting, distinct from their proper function of advocacy. Their control over the various ways of reaching the ear of America is such that, if they do not publish ideas which differ from their own, those ideas will never reach the ear of America.

If that happens, one of the chief reasons for the freedom which these giants claim disappears.

Access to a unit of the press acting as a common carrier is possible in a number of ways, all of which, however, involve selection on the part of the managers of the unit. The individual whose views are not represented on an editorial page may reach an audience through a public statement reported as news, through a letter to the editor, through a statement printed in advertising space, or through a magazine article. But some seekers for space are bound to be disappointed and must resort to pamphlets or such duplicating devices as will spread their ideas to such public as will attend to them.

But all the important viewpoints and interests in the society should be represented in its agencies of mass communication. Those who have these viewpoints and interests cannot count on explaining them to their fellow-citizens through newspapers or radio stations of their own. Even if they could make the necessary investment, they could have no assurance that their publications would be read or their programs heard by the public outside their own adherents. An ideal combination would include general media, inevitably solicitous to present their own views, but setting forth other views fairly. As checks on their fairness, and partial safeguards against ignoring important matters, more specialized media of advocacy have a vital place. In the absence of such a combination the partially insulated groups in society will continue to be insulated. The unchallenged assumptions of each group will continue to harden into prejudice. The mass medium reaches across all groups; through the mass medium they can come to understand one another.

Whether a unit of the press is an advocate or a common carrier, it ought to identify the sources of its fact, opinions, and argument so that the reader or listener can judge them. Persons who are presented with facts, opinions, and arguments are properly influenced by the general reliability of those who offer them. If the veracity of statements is to be appraised, those who offer them must be known.

Identification of source is necessary to a free society. Democracy, in time of peace, at least, has a justifiable confidence that full and free discussion will strengthen rather than weaken it. But, if the discussion is the have the effect for which democracy hopes, if it is to be really full and free,

the names and the characters of the participants must not be hidden from view.

The Projection of a Representative Picture of the Constituent Groups in the Society

This requirement is closely related to the two preceding. People make decisions in large part in terms of favorable or unfavorable images. They relate fact and opinion to stereotypes. Today the motion picture, the radio, the book, the magazine, the newspaper, and the comic strip are principal agents in creating and perpetuating these conventional conceptions. When the images they portray fail to present the social group truly, they tend to pervert judgment.

Such failure may occur indirectly and incidentally. Even if nothing is said about the Chinese in the dialogue of a film, yet if the Chinese appear in a succession of pictures as sinister drug addicts and militarists, an image of China is built which needs to be balanced by another. If the Negro appears in the stories published in magazines of national circulation only as a servant, if children figure constantly in radio dramas as impertinent and ungovernable brats—the image of the Negro and the American child is distorted. The plugging of special color and "hate" words in radio and press dispatches, in advertising copy, in news stories—such words as "ruthless," "confused," "bureaucratic"—performs inevitably the same image-making function.

Responsible performance here simply means that the images repeated and emphasized be such as are in total representative of the social group as it is. The truth about any social group, though it should not exclude its weaknesses and vices, includes also recognition of its values, its aspirations, and its common humanity. The Commission holds to the faith that if people are exposed to the inner truth of the life of a particular group, they will gradually build up respect for and understanding of it.

The Presentation and Clarification of the Goals and Values of the Society

The press has a similar responsibility with regard to the values and goals of our society as a whole. The mass media, whether or not they wish to do so, blur or clarify these ideals as they report the failings and achievements of every day.[2] The

Commission does not call upon the press to sentimentalize, to manipulate the facts for the purpose of painting a rosy picture. The Commission believes in realistic reporting of the events and forces that militate against the attainment of social goals as well as those which work for them. We must recognize, however, that the agencies of mass communication are an educational instrument, perhaps the most powerful there is; and they must assume a responsibility like that of educators in stating and clarifying the ideals toward which the community should strive.

Full Access of the Day's Intelligence

It is obvious that the amount of current information required by the citizens in a modern industrial society is far greater than that required in any earlier day. We do not assume that all citizens at all times will actually use all the material they receive. By necessity or choice large numbers of people voluntarily delegate analysis and decision to leaders whom they trust. Such leadership in our society is freely chosen and constantly changing; it is informal, unofficial and flexible. Any citizen may at any time assume the power of decision. In this way government is carried on by consent.

But such leadership does not alter the need for the wide distribution of news and opinion. The leaders are not identified; we can inform them only by making information available to everybody.

The five requirements listed in this chapter suggest what our society is entitled to demand of its press. We can now proceed to examine the tools, the structure, and the performance of the press to see how it is meeting these demands.

Let us summarize these demands in another way.

The character of the service required of the American press by the American people differs from the service previously demanded, first, in this—that it is essential to the operation of the economy and to the government of the Republic. Second, it is a service of greatly increased responsibilities both as to the quantity and as to the quality of the information required. In terms of quantity, the information about themselves and about their world made available to the American people must be as extensive as the range of their interests and concerns as citizens of self-governing, industrialized community in the closely integrated modern world. In terms of quality, the information provided must be provided in such a form, and with so scrupulous a regard for the wholeness of the truth and the fairness of its presentation, that the American people may make for themselves, by the exercise of reason and of conscience, the fundamental decisions necessary to the direction of their government and of their lives.

Notes

1. By the use of this analogy the Commission does not intend to suggest that the agencies of communication should be subject to the legal obligations of common carriers, such as compulsory reception of all applicants for space, the regulation of rates, etc.

2. A striking indication of the continuous need to renew the basic values of our society is given in the recent poll of public opinion by the National Opinion Research Center at Denver, in which one out of every three persons polled did not think the newspapers should be allowed to criticize the American form of government, even in peacetime. Only 57 per cent thought that the Socialist party should be allowed, in peacetime, to publish newspapers in the United States. Another poll revealed that less than a fourth of those questioned had a "reasonably accurate idea" of what the Bill of Rights is. Here is widespread ignorance with regard to the value most cherished by the press—its own freedom—which seems only dimly understood by many of its consumers.

35

Mass Media

From *UNESCO: Its Philosophy and Purpose* (1947)

Julian Sorrell Huxley

Julian Sorrell Huxley (1887–1975) was from a distinguished British intellectual family, which included his younger brother Aldous, the novelist; and his grandfather Thomas Henry Huxley, founder of Imperial College and known as "Darwin's bulldog" for his ferocious defense of evolutionary theory. A biologist who was involved in the modern synthesis of evolutionary theory, Huxley was a public figure who represented science to the larger world and was the first director general of the United Nations Educational, Social, and Cultural Organization (UNESCO), which would later, especially during the 1970s, be a hotbed of debate and criticism about the injustice of the Euro-American-dominated world communication system. In this excerpt, from his *UNESCO: Its Purpose and Philosophy* (1947), Huxley considers the mass media as agencies of worldwide education. The work expresses the cautious hope for peace and international cooperation that circulated in the immediate postwar period. Mass media might be used both as instruments to help effect this peace by joining hands with "the scientist, the artist, and the educator." In calling for UNESCO to study the effects of radio and film on illiterate peoples, Huxley also signals the start of international mass communication and development research—with a touch of the hubris that sometimes characterized it.

In the first Article of its Constitution, Unesco is expressly instructed to pursue its aims and objects by means of the media of mass communication—the somewhat cumbrous title (commonly abbreviated to "Mass Media") proposed for agencies, such as the radio, the cinema and the popular press, which are capable of the mass dissemination of word or image.

Here Unesco finds itself confronted with something new in human history. It is true that printing with movable type has a respectable antiquity, but the press in the modern sense of the word is a thing of yesterday, or at most of the day before yesterday, depending as it does on the mass production of cheap paper from wood pulp, the technical invention of the rotary printing press and other methods of printing at speed, the further inventions which are at the basis of telecommunication of all sorts—"cable and wireless", together with air transport of mats and the like—and the building up of huge and powerful organisations for the collection and transmission of news. The film and the radio are even more recent, and even more revolutionary in their results.

What are the main effects of these innovations, of which Unesco must take account? First, the possibility of a much wider dissemination of information of every sort, both within and across national boundaries. This means that public opinion can be built up more rapidly and can be better informed than ever before. There is, however, another side to this picture. National public opinion can also be built up by means of propaganda, on the basis of false, distorted or incomplete information, and though the mass media, as I have said, provide the possibility of spreading information across national boundaries, this possibility is often not realised, and indeed often deliberately fought against, by means of censorship, official control of press and radio, and the creation of psychological barriers in the minds of the people.

Thus, although it is true that the mass media provide the first agencies in history through which peoples may speak to peoples, instead of communication between countries being limited to small minorities, yet it is also true that what they say to each other through these agencies may be false, and what they hear may be limited by man-made barriers or its effect distorted by previous propaganda. Accordingly, as one of its earliest aims in this field, Unesco must seek to discover what are the various barriers to free, easy, and undistorted dissemination of news and knowledge between nations, and to see that they are lowered or if possible removed. This, however, is an essentially negative task. Unesco must also avail itself of the force and inspiration which derives from a positive aim. And this, as Grierson says[1] must depend on the indivisibility of interests of the people who populate the world. "Wandering about the world, one finds that while countries differ in their expression and in their local idioms, they are in one respect identical. We are all divided into groups of specialized interests and we are all, at bottom, interested in the same things. There are the same essential groups everywhere. Here is a group interested in town planning, or in agriculture, or in safety in mines, or in stamp collecting. Whatever the different language they speak, they speak the common language of town plannings, agriculture, safety in mines, and stamp collecting." Interests are indivisible and therefore transnational—and so, we may add, are human needs, from simple needs such as food and shelter to more elaborate (but perhaps no less basic) needs like those for intellectual development or emotional and spiritual satisfactions.

Above and beyond all other interests and needs at the moment is the need for peace and the interest of large groups in every country in achieving peace. Merely by preaching peace we shall not achieve much. We can achieve much by indirect methods—by demonstrating the fact that interests and needs transcend national boundaries, and by building a world in which international co-operation is actually operative, and operates to promote better health, and full employment, and the provision of adequate food for all, and safety and ease of travel, and the spread of knowledge. Finally, however, we can achieve a good deal more if we can give people the world over some simple philosophy of existence of a positive nature which will spur them to act in place of the apathy, pessimism or cynicism which is so prevalent to-day, and to act in common instead of in separate groups.

I am sure this can be done if we try hard enough. We need to paint in the scientific background, showing the reality of human progress in the past and its further possibility in the future, reminding men that setbacks like the war and its aftermath are only temporary, and are but some of many in the past which yet have not stood in the way of the secular upward trend. Reminding men also that by all valid criteria humanity is not old but young, and has for all practical purposes unlimited time before it. Demonstrating by concrete examples that scientific discovery has at last made it possible to satisfy the basic needs of all humanity, thus establishing a foundation on which we can proceed to build a superstructure nearer to the heart's desire. Reminding people that one of the basic needs of men is the need for giving, for devotion to something other than self, for service and love of others, so that concentration on satisfaction of selfish needs will spell incompleteness and frustration: showing also, and again by tangible examples, that progress is not automatic or inevitable, but depends on human choice and will and effort. Taking the techniques of persuasion and information and true propaganda that we have learnt to apply nationally in war, and deliberately bending them to the international tasks of peace, if necessary utilising them, as Lenin envisaged, to "overcome the resistance of millions" to desirable change. Using drama to reveal reality and art as the method by which, in Sir Stephen Tallent's words, "truth becomes impressive and a living principle of action," and aiming to produce that concerted effort which, to quote Grierson once more, needs a background of faith and a sense of destiny. This must be a mass philosophy, a mass creed, and it can never be achieved without the use of the media of mass communication. Unesco, in the press of its detailed work, must never forget this enormous fact.

The other main task of Unesco in this field will concern the use of the mass media to foster education, science and culture as such. Regarded from this angle, the mass media fall into the same general category as the libraries and museums—that of servicing agencies for man's higher activities, which offer new technical opportunities to the scientist, the artist and the educator. In this field Unesco will have a great deal of detailed work to do. Granted the services of the mass media to education, science and culture—of the book and the magazine in regard to literature and the spread of ideas; of the daily and weekly press and the radio, in disseminating news and information; of the documentary film as a form of public relations service; of the radio in extending musical interest and raising musical standards: yet the fact remains that they have also rendered many disservices—in the vulgarising of taste, in the debasement of intellectual standards, in the avoidance of real issues, in the erection of false ideals. The gap between possibility and actuality is often all too wide; and Unesco must, in every field of its competence, set out to see that it is narrowed. The techniques and the tactics involved in realising this aim are complex and intricate, and will differ for the different mass media; however, we need not consider them here.

One necessary piece of work which Unesco must undertake is a study of the real effects of radio and film on illiterate peoples hitherto cut off from general thought. At the moment nothing very definite is known about this; yet we must know it if we are to make the best possible use of these revolutionary methods. There are thus two tasks for the Mass Media division of Unesco, the one general, the other special. The special one is to enlist the press and the radio and the cinema to the fullest extent in the service of formal and adult education, of science and learning, of art and culture. The general one is to see that these agencies are used both to contribute to mutual comprehension between different nations and cultures, and also to promote the growth of a common outlook shared by all nations and cultures.

Note

1. "Grierson on Documentary," ed. F. Hardy, London, 1946, pp. 165, 231.

36

The Enormous Radio

From *The Enormous Radio and Other Stories* (1953)

John Cheever

John Cheever (1912–1982) was an American short-story writer and novelist known for his darkly witty tales of middle-class American life. In "The Enormous Radio," first published in the *New Yorker* in 1947, Cheever gives us a mordant vision of the postwar culture of consumption and the strained state of the white middle-class marriage. Here the pleasures and pathologies of radio listening serve as a poignant symbol for the snoopy social surveillance and erosion of private life that so many students of American society in the 1950s such as Riesman, Mills, and Arendt would observe.

Jim and Irene Westcott were the kind of people who seem to strike that satisfactory average of income, endeavor, and respectability that is reached by the statistical reports in college alumni bulletins. They were the parents of two young children, they had been married nine years, they lived on the twelfth floor of an apartment house near Sutton Place, they went to the theatre on an average of 10.3 times a year, and they hoped some day to live in Westchester. Irene Westcott was a pleasant, rather plain girl with soft brown hair and a wide, fine forehead upon which nothing at all had been written and in the cold weather she wore a coat of fitch skins dyed to resemble mink. You could not say that Jim Westcott looked younger than he was, but you could at least say of him that he seemed to feel younger. He wore his graying hair cut very short, he dressed in the kind of clothes his class had worn at Andover and his manner was earnest, vehement, and intentionally naive. The Westcotts differed from their friends, their classmates, and their neighbors only in an interest they shared in serious music. They went to a great many concerts—although they seldom mentioned this to anyone—and they spent a good deal of time listening to music on the radio.

Their radio was an old instrument, sensitive, unpredictable, and beyond repair. Neither of them understood the mechanics of radio—or of any of the other appliances that surrounded them—and when the instrument faltered, Jim would strike the side of the cabinet with his hand. This sometimes helped. One Sunday afternoon, in the middle of a Schubert quartet, the music faded away altogether. Jim struck the cabinet repeatedly, but there was no response; the Schubert was lost to them forever. He promised to buy Irene a new radio, and on Monday when he came home from work he told her that he had got one. He refused to describe it, and said it would be a surprise for her when it came.

The radio was delivered at the kitchen door the following afternoon, and with the assistance of her maid and the handyman Irene uncrated it and brought it into the living room. She was struck at once with the physical ugliness of the large gumwood cabinet. Irene was proud of her living room, she had chosen its furnishings and colours as carefully as she chose her clothes, and now it seemed to her that the new radio stood among her intimate possessions like an aggressive intruder. She was confounded by the number of dials and switches on the instrument panel, and she studied them thoroughly before she put the plug into a wall socket and turned the radio on. The dials flooded with a malevolent green light, and in the distance she heard the music of a piano quintet. The quintet was in the distance for only an instant; it bore down upon her with a speed greater than light and filled the apartment with the noise of music amplified so mightily that

it knocked a china ornament from a table to the floor. She rushed to the instrument and reduced the volume. The violent forces that were snared in the ugly gumwood cabinet made her uneasy. Her children came home from school then, and she took them to the Park. It was not until later in the afternoon that she was able to return to the radio.

The maid had given the children their suppers and was supervising their baths when Irene turned on the radio, reduced the volume, and sat down to listen to a Mozart quintet that she knew and enjoyed. The music came through clearly. The new instrument had a much purer tone, she thought, than the old one. She decided that tone was most important and that she could conceal the cabinet behind a sofa. But as soon as she had made her peace with the radio, the interference began. A crackling sound like the noise of a burning powder fuse began to accompany the singing of the strings. Beyond the music, there was a rustling that reminded Irene unpleasantly of the sea, and as the quintet progressed, these noises were joined by many others. She tried all the dials and switches but nothing dimmed the interference, and she sat down, disappointed and bewildered, and tried to trace the flight of the melody. The elevator shaft in her building ran beside the living room wall, and it was the noise of the elevator that gave her a clue to the character of the static. The rattling of the elevator cables and the opening and closing of the elevator doors were reproduced in her loudspeaker, and realizing that the radio was sensitive to electrical currents of all sort, she began to discern through the Mozart the ringing of telephone bells, the dialing of phones, and the lamentation of a vacuum cleaner. By listening more carefully, she was able to distinguish doorbells, elevator bells, electric razors, and Waring mixers, whose sounds had been picked up from the apartments that surrounded hers and transmitted through her loudspeaker. The powerful and ugly instrument, with its mistaken sensitivity to discord, was more than she could hope to master, so she turned the thing off and went into the nursery to see her children.

When Jim Westcott came home that night, he went to the radio confidently and worked the controls. He had the same sort of experience Irene had had. A man was speaking on the station Jim had chosen, and his voice swung instantly from the distance into a force so powerful that it shook the apartment. Jim turned the volume control and reduced the voice. Then, a minute or two later, the interference began. The ringing of telephones and doorbells set in, joined by the rasp of the elevator doors and the whir of cooking appliances. The character of the noise had changed since Irene had tried the radio earlier; the last of the electric razors was being unplugged, the vacuum cleaners had all been returned to their closets, and the static reflected that change in pace that overtakes the city after the sun goes down. He fiddled with the knobs but couldn't get rid of the noises, so he turned the radio off and told Irene that in the morning he'd call the people who had sold it to him and give them hell.

The following afternoon, when Irene returned to the apartment from a luncheon date, the maid told her that a man had come and fixed the radio. Irene went into the living room before she took off her hat or her furs and tried the instrument. From the loudspeaker came a recording of the "Missouri Waltz." It reminded her of the thin, scratchy music from an old-fashioned phonograph that she sometimes heard across the lake where she spent her summers. She waited until the waltz had finished, expecting an explanation of the recording, but there was none. The music was followed by silence, and then the plaintive and scratchy record was repeated. She turned the dial and got a satisfactory burst of Caucasian music—the thump of bare feet in the dust and the rattle of coin jewelry—but in the background she could hear the ringing bells and a confusion of voices. Her children came home from school then, and she turned off the radio and went to the nursery.

When Jim came home that night, he was tired, and he took a bath and changed his clothes. Then he joined Irene in the living room. He had just turned on the radio when the maid announced dinner, so he left it on, and he and Irene went to the table.

Jim was too tired to make even a pretense of sociability, and there was nothing about the dinner to hold Irene's interest, so her attention wandered from the food to the deposits of silver polish on the candlesticks and from there to the music in the other room. She listened for a few moments to a Chopin prelude and then was surprised to hear a man's voice break in. "For Christ's sake, Kathy," he said, "do you always have to play the piano when I get home?" The music stopped abruptly. "It's the only chance I have," a woman said. "I'm at the office all day." "So am I," the man said.

He added something obscene about an upright piano, and slammed a door. The passionate and melancholy music began again.

"Did you hear that?" Irene asked.

"What?" Jim was eating his dessert.

"The radio. A man said something while the music was still going on—something dirty."

"It's probably a play."

"I don't think it *is* a play," Irene said.

They left the table and took their coffee into the living room. Irene asked Jim to try another station. He turned the knob. "Have you seen my garters?" a man asked. "Button me up," a woman said. "Have you seen my garters?" the man said again. "Just button me up and I'll find your garters," the woman said. Jim shifted to another station. "I wish you wouldn't leave apple cores in the ash-trays," a man said. "I hate the smell."

"This is strange," Jim said.

"Isn't it?" Irene said.

Jim turned the knob again. "'On the coast of Coromandel where the early pumpkins blow,'" a woman with a pronounced English accent said, "'in the middle of the woods lived the Yonghy-Bonghy-Bò. Two old chairs, and half a candle, one old jug without a handle . . .'"

"My God!" Irene cried. "That's the Sweeneys' nurse."

"'These were all his worldly goods,'" the British voice continued.

"Turn that thing off," Irene said. "Maybe they can hear *us*." Jim switched the radio off. "That was Miss Armstrong, the Sweeneys' nurse," Irene said. "She must be reading to the little girl. They live in 17-B. I've talked with Miss Armstrong in the Park. I know her voice very well. We must be getting other people's apartments."

"That's impossible," Jim said.

"Well, that was the Sweeneys' nurse," Irene said hotly. "I know her voice. I know it very well. I'm wondering if they can hear us."

Jim turned the switch. First from a distance and then nearer, nearer, as if borne on the wind, came the pure accents of the Sweeneys' nurse again: "'*Lady Jingly! Lady Jingly!*'" she said, "'*Sitting where the pumpkins blow, will you come and be my wife*, said the Yonghy-Bonghy-Bò . . .'"

Jim went over to the radio and said "Hello" loudly into the speaker.

"'*I am tired of living singly,*'" the nurse went on, "'*on this coast so wild and shingly, I'm a-weary of my life; if you'll come and be my wife, quite serene would be my life . . .*'"

"I guess she can't hear us," Irene said. "Try something else."

Jim turned to another station, and the living room was filled with the uproar of a cocktail party that had overshot its mark. Someone was playing the piano and singing the Whiffenpoof Song, and the voices that surrounded the piano were vehement and happy. "Eat some more sandwiches," a woman shrieked. There were screams of laughter and a dish of some sort crashed to the floor.

"Those must be the Fullers, in 11-E," Irene said. "I knew they were giving a party this afternoon. I saw her in the liquor store. Isn't this too divine? Try something else. See if you can get those people in 18-C."

The Westcotts overheard that evening a monologue on salmon fishing in Canada, a bridge game, running comments on home movies of what had apparently been a fortnight at Sea Island, and a bitter family quarrel about an overdraft at the bank. They turned off their radio at midnight and went to bed, weak with laughter. Sometime in the night, their son began to call for a glass of water and Irene got one and took it to his room. It was very early. All the lights in the neighborhood were extinguished, and from the boy's window she could see the empty street. She went into the living room and tried the radio. There was some faint coughing, a moan, and then a man spoke. "Are you all right, darling?" he asked. "Yes," a woman said wearily. "Yes, I'm all right, I guess," and then she added with great feeling, "but, you know, Charlie, I don't feel like myself any more. Sometimes there are about fifteen or twenty minutes in the week when I feel like myself. I don't like to go to another doctor, because the doctor's bills are so awful already, but I just don't feel like myself, Charlie. I just never feel like myself." They were not young, Irene thought. She guessed from the timbre of their voices that they were middle-aged. The restrained melancholy of the dialogue and the draft from the bedroom window made her shiver, and she went back to bed.

The following morning, Irene cooked breakfast for the family—the maid didn't come up from her room in the basement until ten—braided her daughter's hair, and waited at the door until her children and her husband had been carried away in the elevator. Then she went into the living room and tried the radio. "I don't want to go to school," a child screamed. "I hate school. I won't go to school. I hate school." "You will go to school," an enraged woman said. "We paid eight hundred dollars to get you into that school and you'll go if it kills you." The next number on the dial produced the worn record of the "Missouri Waltz." Irene shifted the control and invaded the privacy of several breakfast tables. She overheard demonstrations of indigestion, carnal love, abysmal vanity, faith, and despair. Irene's life was nearly as simple and sheltered as it appeared to be, and the forthright and sometimes brutal language that came from the loudspeaker that morning astonished and troubled her. She continued to listen until her maid came in. Then she turned off the radio quickly, since this insight, she realized, was a furtive one.

Irene had a luncheon date with a friend that day, and she left her apartment at a little after twelve. There were a number of women in the elevator when it stopped at her floor. She stared at their handsome and impassive faces, their furs, and the cloth flowers in their hats. Which one of them had been to Sea Island, she wondered. Which one had overdrawn her bank account? The elevator stopped at the tenth floor and a woman with a pair of Skye terriers joined them. Her hair was rigged high on her head and she wore a mink cape. She was humming the "Missouri Waltz."

Irene had two Martinis at lunch, and she looked searchingly at her friend and wondered what her secrets were. They had intended to go shopping after lunch, but Irene excused herself and went home. She told the maid that she was not to be disturbed; then she went into the living room, closed the doors, and switched on the radio. She heard, in the course of the afternoon, the halting conversation of a woman entertaining her aunt, the hysterical conclusion of a luncheon party, and a hostess briefing her maid about some cocktail guests. "Don't give the best Scotch to anyone who hasn't white hair," the hostess said. "See if you can get rid of that liver paste before you pass those hot things, and could you lend me five dollars? I want to tip the elevator man."

As the afternoon waned, the conversation increased in intensity. From where Irene sat, she could see the open sky above the East River. There were hundreds of clouds in the sky, as though the south wind had broken the winter into pieces and were blowing it north, and on her radio she could hear the arrival of cocktail guests and the return of children and businessmen from their schools and offices. "I found a good-sized diamond on the bathroom floor this morning," a woman said. "It must have fallen out of that bracelet Mrs. Dunston was wearing last night." "We'll sell it," a man said. "Take it down to the jeweller on Madison Avenue and sell it. Mrs. Dunston won't know the difference, and we could use a couple of hundred bucks . . . " "'Oranges and lemons, say the bells of St. Clement's,'" the Sweeneys' nurse sang. "'Half-pence and farthings, say the bells of St. Martin's. When will you pay me? say the bells at Old Bailey . . .'" "It's not a hat," a woman cried, and at her back roared a cocktail party. "It's not a hat, it's a love affair. That's what Walter Florell said. He said it's not a hat, it's a love affair," and then, in a lower voice, the same woman added, "Talk to somebody, for Christ's sake, honey, talk to somebody. If she catches you standing here not talking to anybody, she'll take us off her invitation list, and I love these parties."

The Westcotts were going out for dinner that night, and when Jim came home, Irene was dressing. She seemed sad and vague, and he brought her a drink. They were dining with friends in the neighborhood, and they walked to where they were going. The sky was broad and filled with light. It was one of those splendid spring evenings that excite memory and desire, and the air that touched their hands and faces felt very soft. A Salvation Army band was on the corner playing "Jesus Is Sweeter" Irene drew on her husband's arm and held him there for a minute, to hear the music. "They're really such nice people, aren't they?" she said. "They have such nice faces. Actually, they're so much nicer than a lot of the people we know." She took a bill from her purse and walked over and dropped it into the tambourine. There was in her face, when she returned to her husband, a look of radiant melancholy that he was not familiar with. And her conduct at the dinner party that night seemed strange to him, too. She interrupted her hostess rudely and stared at the people across the table from her with an intensity for which she would have punished her children.

It was still mild when they walked home from the party, and Irene looked up at the spring stars. "'How far that little candle throws its beams,'" she exclaimed. "'So shines a good deed in a naughty world.'" She waited that night until Jim had fallen asleep, and then went into the living room and turned on the radio.

Jim came home at about six the next night. Emma, the maid, let him in, and he had taken off his hat and was taking off his coat when Irene ran into the hall. Her face was shining with tears and her hair was disordered. "Go up to 16-C, Jim." she screamed. "Don't take off your coat. Go up to 16-C. Mr. Osborn's beating his wife. They've been quarrelling since four o'clock, and now he's hitting her. Go up and stop him."

From the radio in the living room, Jim heard screams, obscenities, and thuds. "You know you don't have to listen to this sort of thing," he said. He strode into the living room and turned the switch. "It's indecent," he said. "It's like looking in windows. You know you don't have to listen to this sort of thing. You can turn it off."

"Oh, it's so horrible, it's so dreadful," Irene was sobbing. "I've been listening all day, and it's so depressing."

"Well, if it's so depressing, why do you listen to it? I bought this damned radio to give you some pleasure," he said. "I paid a great deal of money for it. I thought it might make you happy. I wanted to make you happy."

"Don't, don't, don't, don't quarrel with me," she moaned, and laid her head on his shoulder. "All the others have been quarrelling all day. Everybody's been quarrelling. They're all worried about money. Mrs. Hutchinson's mother is dying of cancer in Florida and they don't have enough money to send her to the Mayo Clinic. At least, Mr. Hutchinson says they don't haveenough money. And some woman in this building is having an affair with the handyman—with that hideous handyman. It's too disgusting. And Mrs. Melville has heart trouble and Mr. Hendricks is going to lose his job in April and Mrs. Hendricks is horrid about the whole thing and that girl who plays the 'Missouri Waltz' is a whore, a common whore, and the elevator man has tuberculosis and Mr. Osborn has been beating Mrs. Osborn." She wailed, she trembled with grief and checked the stream of tears down her face with the heel of her palm.

"Well, why do you have to listen?" Jim asked again. "Why do you have to listen to this stuff if it makes you so miserable?"

"Oh, don't, don't, don't," she cried. "Life is too terrible, too sordid and awful. But we've never been like that, have we, darling? Have we? I mean we've always been good and decent and loving to one another, haven't we? And we have two children, two beautiful children. Our lives aren't sordid, are they, darling? Are they?" She flung her arms around his neck and drew his face down to hers. "We're happy, aren't we, darling? We are happy, aren't we?"

"Of course we're happy," he said tiredly. He began to surrender his resentment. "Of course we're happy. I'll have that damned radio fixed or taken away tomorrow." He stroked her soft hair. "My poor girl," he said.

"You love me, don't you?" she asked. "And we're not hypocritical or worried about money or dishonest, are we?"

"No, darling," he said.

A man came in the morning and fixed the radio. Irene turned it on cautiously and was happy to hear a California-wine commercial and a recording of Beethoven's Ninth Symphony, including Schiller's "Ode to Joy." She kept the radio on all day and nothing untoward came from the speaker.

A Spanish suite was being played when Jim came home. "Is everything all right?" he asked. His face was pale, she thought. They had some cocktails and went in to dinner to the "Anvil Chorus" from "Il Trovatore." This was followed by Debussy's "La Mer."

"I paid the bill for the radio today," Jim said. "It cost four hundred dollars. I hope you'll get some enjoyment out of it."

"Oh, I'm sure I will," Irene said.

"Four hundred dollars is a good deal more than I can afford," he went on. "I wanted to get something that you'd enjoy. It's the last extravagance we'll be able to indulge in this year. I see that you haven't paid your clothing bills yet. I saw them on your dressing table." He looked directly at her. "Why did you tell me you'd paid them? Why did you lie to me?"

"I just didn't want you to worry, Jim," she said. She drank some water. "I'll be able to pay my bills out of this month's allowance. There were the slip-covers last month, and that party."

"You've got to learn to handle the money I give you a little more intelligently, Irene," he said. "You've got to understand that we won't have as much money this year as we had last. I had a very sobering talk with Mitchell today. No one is buying anything. We are spending all our time promoting new issues, and you know how long that takes. I'm not getting any younger, you know. I'm thirty-seven. My hair will be gray

next year. I haven't done as well as I'd hoped to do. And I don't suppose things will get any better."

"Yes, dear," she said.

"We've got to start cutting down," Jim said. "We've got to think of the children. To be perfectly, frank with you, I worry about money a great deal. I'm not at all sure of the future. No one is. If anything should happen to me, there's the insurance, but that wouldn't go very far today. I've worked awfully hard to give you and the children a comfortable life," he said bitterly. "I don't like to see all of my energies, all of my youth, wasted on fur coats and radios and slip-covers and—"

"Please, Jim," she said. "Please. They'll hear us."

"*Who'll hear us*? Emma can't hear us."

"The radio."

"Oh, I'm sick!" he shouted. "I'm sick to death of your apprehensiveness. The radio can't hear us. Nobody can hear us. And what if they can hear us? Who cares?"

Irene got up from the table and went into the living room. Jim went to the door and shouted at her from there. "Why are you so Christly all of a sudden? What's turned you overnight into a convent girl? You stole your mother's jewelry before they probated her will. You never gave your sister a cent of that money that was intended for her—not even when she needed it. You made Grace Howland's life miserable, and where was all your piety and your virtue when you went to that abortionist? I'll never forget how cool you were. You packed your bag and went off to have that child murdered as if you were going to Nassau. If you'd had any reasons, if you'd had any good reasons—"

Irene stood for a minute before the hideous cabinet, disgraced and sickened, but she held her hand on the switch before she extinguished the music and the voices, hoping that the instrument might speak to her kindly, that she might hear the Sweeneys' nurse. Jim continued to shout at her from the door. The voice on the radio was suave and noncommittal. "An early morning railroad disaster in Tokyo," the loudspeaker said, "killed twenty-nine people. A fire in a Catholic hospital near Buffalo for the care of blind children was extinguished early this morning by nuns. The temperature is forty-seven. The humidity is eighty-nine."

37

Mass Communication, Popular Taste, and Organized Social Action

From *The Communication of Ideas* (1948)

Paul F. Lazarsfeld and Robert K. Merton

"Mass Communication, Popular Taste, and Organized Social Action" was a summary piece for mass communications research at Columbia in the immediate postwar period. It is a pieced-together essay that draws from Lazarsfeld's 1942 "Effects of Radio on Public Opinion" (an earlier summary piece) and several speeches given by him, but many of the main sections were composed by Merton.The piece was first published in *The Communication of Ideas* (1948), an important interdisciplinary collection of essays on communication edited by Lyman Bryson, and it has been reprinted in most of the mass communication readers since. The essay features three influential middle-range concepts developed by Merton (status conferral, the enforcement of social norms, and the narcotizing dysfunction) and in its last section lays out an early version of the so-called limited effects hypothesis. Read this nuanced piece carefully and notice the mix of empirical caution and broader, often "critical" themes that run through it (see Simonson and Weimann 2003). For Lazarsfeld's biography see page 166; for Merton's see page 215.

Problems engaging the attention of men change, and they change not at random but largely in accord with the altering demands of society and economy. If a group such as those who have written the chapters of this book had been brought together a generation or so ago, the subject for discussion would in all probability have been altogether different. Child labor, woman suffrage or old age pensions might have occupied the attention of a group such as this, but certainly not problems of the media of mass communication. As a host of recent conferences, books and articles indicate, the role of radio, print and film in society has become a problem of interest to many and a source of concern to some. This shift in public interest appears to be the product of several social trends.

Social Concern with the Mass Media

Many are alarmed by the ubiquity and potential power of the mass media. A participant in this symposium has written, for example, that "the power of radio can be compared only with the power of the atomic bomb." It is widely felt that the mass media comprise a powerful instrument which may be used for good or for ill and that, in the absence of adequate controls, the latter possibility is on the whole more likely. For these are the media of propaganda and Americans stand in peculiar dread of the power of propaganda. As the British observer, William Empson, recently remarked of us: "They believe in machinery more passionately than we do; and modern propaganda is a scientific machine; so it seems to them obvious that a mere reasoning man can't stand up against it. All this produces a curiously girlish attitude toward anyone who might be doing propaganda. 'Don't let that man come near. Don't let him tempt me, because if he does I'm sure to fall.'"

The ubiquity of the mass media promptly leads many to an almost magical belief in their enormous power. But there is another and, probably, a more realistic basis for widespread concern with the social role of the mass media; a basis which has to do with the changing types of social control exercised by powerful interest groups in society. Increasingly, the chief power groups, among which organized business occupies the most spectacular place, have come to adopt techniques for manipulating mass publics through propaganda in place of more direct means of control. Industrial organizations no longer compel eight year old children to attend the machine for fourteen hours a day; they engage in elaborate programs of "public relations." They place large and impressive advertisements in the newspapers of the nation; they sponsor numerous radio programs; on the advice of public relations counsellors they organize prize contests, establish welfare foundations, and support worthy causes. Economic power seems to have reduced direct exploitation and turned to a subtler type of psychological exploitation, achieved largely by disseminating propaganda through the mass media of communication.

This change in the structure of social control merits thorough examination. Complex societies are subject to many different forms of organized control. Hitler, for example, seized upon the most visible and direct of these: organized violence and mass coercion. In this country, direct coercion has become minimized. If people do not adopt the beliefs and attitudes advocated by some power group—say, the National Association of Manufacturers—they can neither be liquidated nor placed in concentration camps. Those who would control the opinions and beliefs of our society resort less to physical force and more to mass persuasion. The radio program and the institutional advertisement serve in place of intimidation and coercion. The manifest concern over the functions of the mass media is in part based upon the valid observation that these media have taken on the job of rendering mass publics conformative to the social and economic *status quo*.

A third source of widespread concern with the social role of mass media is found in their assumed effects upon popular culture and the esthetic tastes of their audiences. In the measure that the size of these audiences has increased, it is argued, the level of esthetic taste has deteriorated. And it is feared that the mass media deliberately cater to these vulgarized tastes, thus contributing to further deterioration.

It seems probable that these constitute the three organically related elements of our great concern with the mass media of communication. Many are, first of all, fearful of the ubiquity and potential power of these media. We have suggested that this is something of an indiscriminate fear of an abstract bogey stemming from insecurity of social position and tenuously held values. Propaganda seems threatening.

There is, secondly, concern with the present effects of the mass media upon their enormous audiences, particularly the possibility that the continuing assault of these media may lead to the unconditional surrender of critical faculties and an unthinking conformism.

Finally, there is the danger that these technically advanced instruments of mass communication constitute a major avenue for the deterioration of esthetic tastes and popular cultural standards. And we have suggested that there is substantial ground for concern over these immediate social effects of the mass media of communication.

A review of the current state of actual knowledge concerning the social role of the mass media of communication and their effects upon the contemporary American community is an ungrateful task, for certified knowledge of this kind is impressively slight. Little more can be done than to explore the nature of the problems by methods which, in the course of many decades, will ultimately provide the knowledge we seek. Although this is anything but an encouraging preamble, it provides a necessary context for assessing the research and tentative conclusions of those of us professionally concerned with the study of mass media. A reconnaissance will suggest what we know, what we need to know, and will locate the strategic points requiring further inquiry.

To search out "the effects" of mass media upon society is to set upon an ill defined problem. It is helpful to distinguish three facets of the problem and to consider each in turn. Let us, then, first inquire into what we know about the effects of the existence of these media in our society. Secondly, we must look into the effects of the particular structure of ownership and operation of the mass media in this country, a structure which differs appreciably from that found elsewhere. And, finally, we must consider that aspect of the problem which bears most directly upon policies and tactics governing the use of these media for definite social ends: our knowledge concerning the effects of the particular contents disseminated through the mass media.

The Social Role of the Machinery of Mass Media

What role can be assigned to the mass media by virtue of the fact that they exist? What are the implications of a Hollywood, a Radio City, and a Time-Life-Fortune enterprise for our society? These questions can of course be discussed only in grossly speculative terms, since no experimentation or rigorous comparative study is possible. Comparisons with other societies lacking these mass media would be too crude to yield decisive results and comparisons with an earlier day in American society would still involve gross assertions rather than precise demonstrations. In such an instance, brevity is clearly indicated. And opinions should be leavened with caution. It is our tentative judgment that the social role played by the very existence of the mass media has been commonly overestimated. What are the grounds for this judgment?

It is clear that the mass media reach enormous audiences. Approximately seventy million Americans attend the movies every week; our daily newspaper circulation is about forty-six million, and some thirty-four million American homes are equipped with radio, and in these homes the average American listens to the radio for about three hours a day. These are formidable figures. But they are merely supply and consumption figures, not figures registering the effect of mass media. They bear only upon what people do, not upon the social and psychological impact of the media. To know the number of

hours people keep the radio turned on gives no indication of the effect upon them of what they hear. Knowledge of consumption data in the field of mass media remains far from a demonstration of their net effect upon behavior and attitude and outlook.

As was indicated a moment ago, we cannot resort to experiment by comparing contemporary American society with and without mass media. But, however tentatively, we can compare their social effect with, say, that of the automobile. It is not unlikely that the invention of the automobile and its development into a mass owned commodity has had a significantly greater effect upon society than the invention of the radio and its development into a medium of mass communication. Consider the social complexes into which the automobile has entered. Its sheer existence has exerted pressure for vastly improved roads and with these, mobility has increased enormously. The shape of metropolitan agglomerations has been significantly affected by the automobile. And, it may be submitted, the inventions which enlarge the radius of movement and action exert a greater influence upon social outlook and daily routines than inventions which provide avenues for ideas—ideas which can be avoided by withdrawal, deflected by resistance and transformed by assimilation.

Granted, for a moment, that the mass media play a comparatively minor role in shaping our society, why are they the object of so much popular concern and criticism? Why do so many become exercised by the "problems" of the radio and film and press and so few by the problems of, say, the automobile and the airplane? In addition to the sources of this concern which we have noted previously, there is an unwitting psychological basis for concern which derives from a socio-historical context.

Many make the mass media targets for hostile criticism because they feel themselves duped by the turn of events.

The social changes ascribable to "reform movements" may be slow and slight, but they do cumulate. The surface facts are familiar enough. The sixty hour week has given way to the forty hour week. Child labor has been progressively curtailed. With all its deficiencies, free universal education has become progressively institutionalized. These and other gains register a series of reform victories. And now, people have more leisure time. They have, ostensibly, greater access to the cultural heritage. And what use do they make of this unmortgaged time so painfully acquired for them? They listen to the radio and go to the movies. These mass media seem somehow to have cheated reformers of the fruits of their victories. The struggle for freedom for leisure and popular education and social security was carried on in the hope that, once freed of cramping shackles, people would avail themselves of major cultural products of our society, Shakespeare or Beethoven or perhaps Kant. Instead, they turn to Faith Baldwin or Johnny Mercer or Edgar Guest.

Many feel cheated of their prize. It is not unlike a young man's first experience in the difficult realm of puppy love. Deeply smitten with the charms of his lady love, he saves his allowance for weeks on end and finally manages to give her a beautiful bracelet. She finds it "simply divine." So much so, that then and there she makes a date with another boy in order to display her new trinket. Our social struggles have met with a similar denouement. For generations, men fought to give people more leisure time and now they spend it with the Columbia Broadcasting System rather than with Columbia University.

However little this sense of betrayal may account for prevailing attitudes toward the mass media, it may again be noted that the sheer presence of these media may not affect our society so profoundly as is widely supposed.

Some Social Functions of the Mass Media

In continuing our examination of the social role which can be ascribed to the mass media by virtue of their "sheer existence," we temporarily abstract from the social structure in which the media find their place. We do not, for example, consider the diverse effects of the mass media under varying systems of ownership and control, an important structural factor which will be discussed subsequently.

The mass media undoubtedly serve many social functions which might well become the object of sustained research. Of these functions, we have occasion to notice only three.

The Status Conferral Function

The mass media *confer* status on public issues, persons, organizations and social movements.

Common experience as well as research testifies that the social standing of persons or social policies is raised when these command favorable attention in the mass media. In many quarters, for example, the support of a political candidate or a public policy by *The Times* is taken as significant, and this support is regarded as a distinct asset for the candidate or the policy. Why?

For some, the editorial views of *The Times* represent the considered judgment of a group of experts, thus calling for the respect of laymen. But this is only one element in the status conferral function of the mass media, for enhanced status accrues to those who merely receive attention in the media, quite apart from any editorial support.

The mass media bestow prestige and enhance the authority of individuals and groups by *legitimizing their status*. Recognition by the press or radio or magazines or newsreels testifies that one has arrived, that one is important enough to have been singled out from the large anonymous masses, that one's behavior and opinions are significant enough to require public notice. The operation of this status conferral function may be witnessed most vividly in the advertising pattern of testimonials to a product by "prominent people." Within wide circles of the population (though not within certain selected social strata), such testimonials not only enhance the prestige of the product but also reflect prestige on the person who provides the testimonials. They give public notice that the large and powerful world of commerce regards him as possessing sufficiently high status for his opinion to count with many people. In a word, his testimonial is a testimonial to his own status.

The ideal, if homely, embodiment of this circular prestige-pattern is to be found in the Lord Calvert series of advertisements centered on "Men of Distinction." The commercial firm and the commercialized witness to the merit of the product engage in an unending series of reciprocal pats on the back. In effect, a distinguished man congratulates a distinguished whisky which, through the manufacturer, congratulates the man of distinction on his being so distinguished as to be sought out for a testimonial to the distinction of the product. The workings of this mutual admiration society may be as non-logical as they are effective. The audiences of mass media apparently subscribe to the circular belief: "If you really matter, you will be at the focus of mass attention and, if you *are* at the focus of mass attention, then surely you must really matter."

This status conferral function thus enters into organized social action by legitimizing selected policies, persons and groups which receive the support of mass media. We shall have occasion to note the detailed operation of this function in connection with the conditions making for the maximal utilization of mass media for designated social ends. At the moment, having considered the "status conferral" function, we shall consider a second: the enforced application of social norms through the mass media.

The Enforcement of Social Norms

Such catch phrases as "the power of the press" (and other mass media) or "the bright glare of publicity" presumably refer to this function. The mass media may initiate organized social action by "exposing" conditions which are at variance with public moralities. But it need not be prematurely assumed that this pattern consists *simply* in making these deviations widely known. We have something to learn in this connection from Malinowski's observations among his beloved Trobriand Islanders. There, he reports, no organized social action is taken with respect to behavior deviant from a social norm unless there is *public* announcement of the deviation. This is not merely a matter of acquainting the individuals in the group with the facts of the case. Many may have known privately of these deviations— e.g., incest among the Trobrianders, as with political or business corruption, prostitution, gambling among ourselves—but they will not have pressed for public action. But once the behavioral deviations are made simultaneously public for all, this sets in train tensions between the "privately tolerable" and the "publicly acknowledgeable."

The mechanism of public exposure would seem to operate somewhat as follows. Many social norms prove inconvenient for individuals in the society. They militate against the gratification of wants and impulses. Since many find the norms burdensome, there is some measure of leniency in applying them, both to oneself and to others. Hence, the emergence of deviant behavior and private toleration of these deviations. But this can continue only so long as one is not in a situation where one must take a public stand for or against the norms. Publicity, the enforced acknowledgment by members of the group that these deviations have occurred, requires each individual to take such a stand. He must either range himself with the non-conformists, thus proclaiming his repudiation of the group norms, and thus asserting that he, too, is outside the moral framework or, regardless of his private predilections, he must fall into line by supporting the norm. *Publicity closes the gap between "private attitudes" and "public morality."* Publicity exerts pressure for a single rather than a dual morality by preventing continued evasion of the issue. It calls forth public reaffirmation and (however sporadic) application of the social norm.

In a mass society, this function of public exposure is institutionalized in the mass media of communication. Press, radio and journals expose fairly well known deviations to public view, and as a rule, this exposure forces some degree of public action against what has been privately tolerated. The mass media may, for example, introduce severe strains upon "polite ethnic discrimination" by calling public attention to these practices which are at odds with the norms of non-discrimination. At times, the media may organize exposure activities into a "crusade."

The study of crusades by mass media would go far toward answering basic questions about the relation of mass media to organized social action. It is essential to know, for example, the extent to which the crusade provides an organizational center for otherwise unorganized individuals. The crusade may operate diversely among the several sectors of the population. In some instances, its major effect may not be so much to arouse an indifferent citizenry as to alarm the culprits, leading them to extreme measures which in turn alienate the electorate. Publicity may so embarrass the malefactor as to send him into flight as was the case, for example, with some of the chief henchmen of the Tweed Ring following exposure by *The New York Times*. Or the directors of corruption may fear the crusade only because of the effect they anticipate it will have upon the electorate. Thus, with a startlingly realistic appraisal of the communications behavior of his constituency, Boss Tweed peevishly remarked of the biting cartoons of Thomas Nast in *Harper's Weekly*: "I don't care a straw for your newspaper articles: my constituents don't know how to read, but they can't help seeing them damned pictures."[1]

The crusade may affect the public directly. It may focus the attention of a hitherto lethargic citizenry, grown indifferent through familiarity to prevailing corruption, upon a few, dramatically simplified, issues. As Lawrence Lowell once observed in this general connection, complexities generally inhibit mass action. Public issues must be defined in simple alternatives, in terms of black and white, to permit of organized public action. And the presentation of simple alternatives is one of the chief functions of the crusade. The crusade may involve still other mechanisms. If a municipal government is not altogether pure of heart, it is seldom wholly corrupt. Some scrupulous members of the administration and judiciary are generally intermingled with their unprincipled colleagues. The crusade may strengthen the hand of the upright elements in the government, force the hand of the indifferent and weaken the hand of the corrupt. Finally, it may well be that a successful crusade exemplifies a circular, self-sustaining process, in which the concern of the mass medium with the public interest coincides with its self-interest. The triumphant crusade may enhance the power and prestige of the mass medium, thus making it, in turn, more formidable in later crusades, which, if successful, may further advance its power and prestige.

Whatever the answer to these questions, mass media clearly serve to reaffirm social norms by exposing deviations from these norms to public view. Study of the particular range of norms thus reaffirmed would provide a clear index of the extent to which these media deal with peripheral or central problems of the structure of our society.

The Narcotizing Dysfunction

The functions of status conferral and of reaffirmation of social norms are evidently well recognized by the operators of mass media. Like other social and psychological mechanisms, these functions lend themselves to diverse forms of application. Knowledge of these functions is power, and power may be used for special interests or for the general interest.

A third social consequence of the mass media has gone largely unnoticed. At least, it has received little explicit comment and, apparently, has not been systematically put to use for furthering planned objectives. This may be called the narcotizing dysfunction of the mass media. It is termed *dys*functional rather than functional on the assumption that it is not in the interest of modern complex society to have large masses of the population politically apathetic and inert. How does this unplanned mechanism operate?

Scattered studies have shown that an increasing proportion of the time of Americans is devoted to the products of the mass media. With distinct variations in different regions and among different social strata, the outpourings of the media presumably enable the twentieth century American to "keep abreast of the world." Yet, it is suggested, this vast supply of communications may elicit only a superficial concern with the problems of society, and this superficiality often cloaks mass apathy.

Exposure to this flood of information may serve to narcotize rather than to energize the average reader or listener. As an increasing meed of time is devoted to reading and listening, a decreasing share is available for organized action. The individual reads accounts of issues and problems and may even discuss alternative lines of action. But this rather intellectualized, rather remote connection with organized social action is not activated. The interested and informed citizen can congratulate himself on his lofty state of interest and information and neglect to see that he has abstained from decision and action. In short, he takes his secondary contact with the world of political reality, his reading and listening and thinking, as a vicarious performance. He comes to mistake *knowing* about problems of the day for *doing* something about them. His social conscience remains spotlessly clean. He *is* concerned. He *is* informed. And he has all sorts of ideas as to what should be done. But, after he has gotten through his dinner and after he has listened to his favored radio programs and after he has read his second newspaper of the day, it is really time for bed.

In this peculiar respect, mass communications may be included among the most respectable and efficient of social narcotics. They may be so fully effective as to keep the addict from recognizing his own malady.

That the mass media have lifted the level of information of large populations is evident. Yet, quite apart from intent, increasing dosages of mass communications may be inadvertently transforming the energies of men from active participation into passive knowledge.

The occurrence of this narcotizing dysfunction can scarcely be doubted, but the extent to which it operates has yet to be determined. Research on this problem remains one of the many tasks still confronting the student of mass communications.

The Structure of Ownership and Operation

To this point we have considered the mass media quite apart from their incorporation within a particular social and economic structure. But clearly, the social effects of the media will vary as the system of ownership and control varies. Thus to consider the social effects of American mass media is to deal only with the effects of these media as privately owned enterprises under profit oriented management. It is general knowledge that this circumstance is not inherent in the technological nature of the mass media. In England, for example, to say nothing of Russia, the radio is to all intents and purposes owned, controlled and operated by government.

The structure of control is altogether different in this country. Its salient characteristic stems from the fact that except for movies and books, it is not the magazine reader nor the radio listener nor, in large part, the reader of newspapers who supports the enterprise, but the advertiser. Big business finances the production and distribution of mass media. And, all intent aside, he who pays the piper generally calls the tune.

Social Conformism

Since the mass media are supported by great business concerns geared into the current social and economic system, the media contribute to the maintenance of that system. This contribution is not found merely in the effective advertisement of the sponsor's product. It arises, rather, from the typical presence in magazine stories, radio programs and newspaper columns of some element of confirmation, some element of approval of the present structure of society. And this continuing reaffirmation underscores the duty to accept.

To the extent that the media of mass communication have had an influence upon their audiences, it has stemmed not only from what is said, but more significantly from what is not said. For these media not only continue to affirm the *status quo* but, in the same measure, they fail to raise essential questions about the structure of society. Hence by leading toward conformism and by providing little basis for a critical appraisal of society, the commercially sponsored mass media indirectly but effectively restrain the cogent development of a genuinely critical outlook.

This is not to ignore the occasionally critical journal article or radio program. But these exceptions are so few that they are lost in the overwhelming flood of conformist materials. The editor of this volume, for example, has been broadcasting a weekly program in which he critically and rationally appraises social problems in general and the institution of radio in particular. But these fifteen minutes in which Mr. Bryson addresses himself to such questions over one network constitute an infinitesimally small drop in the weekly flood of materials from four major networks, from five hundred and seventy or so unaffiliated stations, from hundreds of magazines and from Hollywood.

Since our commercially sponsored mass media promote a largely unthinking allegiance to our social structure, they cannot be relied upon to work for changes, even minor changes, in that structure. It is possible to list some developments to the contrary, but upon close inspection they prove illusory. A community group, such as the PTA, may request the producer of a radio serial to inject the theme of tolerant race attitudes into the program. Should the producer feel that this theme is safe, that it will not antagonize any substantial part of his audience, he may agree, but at the first indication that it is a dangerous theme which may alienate potential consumers, he will refuse, or will soon abandon the experiment. Social objectives are consistently surrendered by commercialized media when they clash with economic gains. Minor tokens of "progressive" views are of slight importance since they are included only by grace of the sponsors and only on the condition that they be sufficiently acceptable as not to alienate any appreciable part of the audience. Economic pressure makes for conformism by omission of sensitive issues.

Impact Upon Popular Taste

Since the largest part of our radio, movies, magazines and a considerable part of our books and newspapers are devoted to "entertainment," this clearly requires us to consider the impact of the mass media upon popular taste.

Were we to ask the average American with some pretension to literary or esthetic cultivation if mass communications have had any effect upon popular taste, he would doubtlessly answer with a resounding affirmative. And more, citing abundant instances, he would insist that esthetic and intellectual tastes have been depraved by the flow of trivial formula products from printing presses, radio stations and movie studios. The columns of criticism abound with these complaints.

In one sense, this requires no further discussion. There can be no doubt that the women who are daily entranced for three or four hours by some twelve consecutive "soap operas," all cut to the same dismal pattern, exhibit an appalling lack of esthetic judgment. Nor is this impression altered by the contents of pulp and slick magazines, or by the depressing abundance of formula motion pictures replete with hero, heroine and villain moving through a contrived atmosphere of sex, sin and success.

Yet unless we locate these patterns in historical and sociological terms, we may find ourselves confusedly engaged in condemning without understanding, in criticism which is sound but largely irrelevant. What is the historical status of this notoriously low level of popular taste? Is it the poor remains of standards which were once significantly higher, a relatively new birth in the world of values, largely unrelated to the higher standards from which it has allegedly fallen, or a poor substitute blocking the way to the development of superior standards and the expression of high esthetic purpose?

If esthetic tastes are to be considered in their social setting, we must recognize that the effective audience for the arts has become historically transformed. Some centuries back, this audience was largely confined to a selected aristocratic elite. Relatively few were literate. And very few possessed the means to buy books, attend theaters and travel to the urban centers of the arts. Not more than a slight fraction, possibly not more than one or two per cent, of the population composed the effective audience for the arts. These happy few cultivated their esthetic tastes, and their selective demand left its mark in the form of relatively high artistic standards.

With the widesweeping spread of popular education and with the emergence of the new technologies of mass communication, there developed an enormously enlarged market for the arts. Some forms of music, drama and literature now reach virtually everyone in our society. This is why, of course, we speak of *mass* media and of *mass* art. And the great audiences for the mass media, though in the main literate, are not highly cultivated. About half the population, in fact, have halted their formal education upon leaving grammar school.

With the rise of popular education, there has occurred a seeming decline of popular taste. Large numbers of people have acquired what might be termed "formal literacy," that is to say, a capacity to read, to grasp crude and superficial meanings, and a correlative incapacity for full understanding of what they read.[2] There has developed, in short, a marked gap between literacy and comprehension. People read more but understand less. More people read but proportionately fewer critically assimilate what they read.

Our formulation of the problem should now be plain. It is misleading to speak simply of the decline of esthetic tastes. Mass audiences probably include a larger number of persons with cultivated esthetic standards, but these are swallowed up by the large masses who constitute the new and untutored audience for the arts. Whereas yesterday the elite constituted virtually the whole of the audience, they are today a minute fraction of the whole. In consequence, the average level of esthetic standards and tastes of audiences has been depressed, although the tastes of some sectors of the population have undoubtedly been raised and the total number of people exposed to communication contents has been vastly increased.

But this analysis does not directly answer the question of the effects of the mass media upon public taste, a question which is as complex as it is unexplored. The answer can come only from disciplined research. One would want to know, for example, whether mass media have robbed the intellectual and artistic elite of the art forms which might otherwise have been accessible to them. And this involves inquiry into the pressure exerted by the mass audience upon creative individuals to cater to mass tastes. Literary hacks have existed in every age. But it would be important to learn if the electrification of the arts supplies power for a significantly greater proportion of dim literary lights. And, above all, it would be essential to determine if mass media and mass tastes are necessarily linked in a vicious circle of deteriorating standards or if appropriate action on the part of the directors of mass media could initiate a virtuous circle of cumulatively improving tastes among their audiences. More concretely, are the operators of commercialized mass media caught up in a situation in which they cannot, whatever their private preferences, radically raise the esthetic standards of their products?

In passing, it should be noted that much remains to be learned concerning standards appropriate for mass art. It is possible that standards for art forms produced by a small band of creative talents for a small and selective audience are not applicable to art forms produced by a gigantic industry for the population at large. The beginnings of investigation on this problem are sufficiently suggestive to warrant further study.[3]

Sporadic and consequently inconclusive experiments in the raising of standards have met with profound resistance from mass audiences. On occasion, radio stations and networks have attempted to supplant a soap opera with a program of classical music, or formula comedy skits with discussions of public issues. In general, the people supposed to benefit by this reformation of program have simply refused to be benefited. They cease listening. The audience dwindles. Researches have shown, for example, that radio programs of classical music tend to preserve rather than to create interest in classical music and that newly emerging interests are typically superficial. Most listeners to these programs have previously acquired an interest in classical music; the few whose interest is initiated by the programs are caught up by melodic compositions and come to think of classical music exclusively in terms of Tschaikowsky or Rimsky-Korsakow or Dvorak.

Proposed solutions to these problems are more likely to be born of faith than knowledge. The improvement of mass tastes through the improvement of mass art products is not as simple a matter as we should like to believe. It is possible, of course, that a conclusive effort has not been made. By a triumph of imagination over the current organization of mass media, one can conceive a rigorous censorship over all media, such that nothing was allowed in print or on the air or in the films save "the best that has been thought and said in the world." Whether a radical change in the supply of mass art would in due course reshape the tastes of mass audiences must remain a matter of speculation. Decades of experimentation and research are needed. At present, we know conspicuously little about the methods of improving esthetic tastes and we know that some of the suggested methods are ineffectual. We have a rich knowledge of failures. Should this discussion be reopened in 1976, we may, perhaps, report with equal confidence our knowledge of positive achievements.

At this point, we may pause to glance at the road we have traveled. By way of introduction, we considered the seeming sources of widespread concern with the place of mass media in our society. Thereafter, we first examined the social role ascribable to the sheer existence of the mass media and concluded that this may have been exaggerated. In this connection, however, we noted several consequences of the existence of mass media: their status conferral function, their function in inducing the application of social norms and their narcotizing dysfunction. Secondly, we indicated the constraints placed by a structure of commercialized ownership and control upon the mass media as agencies of social criticism and as carriers of high esthetic standards.

We turn now to the third and last aspect of the social role of the mass media: the possibilities of utilizing them for moving toward designated types of social objectives.

Propaganda for Social Objectives

This final question is perhaps of more direct interest to you than the other questions we have discussed. It represents something of a challenge to us since it provides the means of resolving the apparent paradox to which we referred previously: the seeming paradox arising from the assertion that the significance of the sheer existence of the mass media has been exaggerated and the multiple indications that the media do exert influences upon their audiences.

What are the conditions for the effective use of mass media for what might be called "propaganda for social objectives"—the promotion, let us say, of non-discriminatory race relations, or of educational reforms, or of positive attitudes toward organized labor? Research indicates that, at least, one or more of three conditions must be satisfied if this propaganda is to prove effective. These conditions may be briefly designated as (1) monopolization (2) canalization rather than change of basic values and (3) supplementary face to face contact. Each of these conditions merits some discussion.

Monopolization

This situation obtains when there is little or no opposition in the mass media to the diffusion of values, policies or public images. That is to say, monopolization of the mass media occurs in the absence of counter propaganda.

In this restricted sense, monopolization of the mass media is found in diverse circumstances. It is, of course, indigenous to the political structure of authoritarian society, where access to the media of communication is wholly closed to those who oppose the official ideology. The evidence suggests that this monopoly played some part in enabling the Nazis to maintain their control of the German people.

But this same situation is approximated in other social systems. During the war, for example, our government utilized the radio, with some success, to promote and to maintain identification with the war effort. The effectiveness of these morale building efforts was in large measure due to the virtually complete absence of counter propaganda.

Similar situations arise in the world of commercialized propaganda. The mass media create popular idols. The public images of the radio performer, Kate Smith, for example, picture her as a woman with unparalleled understanding of other American women, deeply sympathetic with ordinary men and women, a spiritual guide and mentor, a patriot whose views on public affairs should be taken seriously. Linked with the cardinal American virtues, the public images of Kate Smith are at no point subject to a counter propaganda. Not that she has no competitors in the market of radio advertising. But there are none who set themselves systematically to question what she has said. In consequence, an unmarried radio entertainer with an annual income in six figures may be visualized by millions of American women as a hard working mother who knows this recipe for managing life on fifteen hundred a year.

This image of a popular idol would have far less currency were it subjected to counter propaganda. Such neutralization occurs, for example, as a result of preelection campaigns by Republicans and Democrats. By and large, as a recent study has shown, the propaganda issued by each of these parties neutralizes the effect of the other's propaganda. Were both parties to forego their campaigning through the mass media entirely, it is altogether likely that the net effect would be to reproduce the present distribution of votes.

This general pattern has been described by Kenneth Burke in his *Attitudes Toward History* "...businessmen compete with one another by trying to *praise their own commodity* more persua-

sively than their rivals, whereas politicians compete by slandering the *opposition*. When you add it all up, you get a grand total of absolute praise for business and grand total of absolute slander for politics."

To the extent that opposing political propaganda in the mass media are balanced, the net effect is negligible. The virtual monopolization of the media for given social objectives, however, will produce discernible effects upon audiences.

Canalization

Prevailing beliefs in the enormous power of mass communications appear to stem from successful cases of monopolistic propaganda or from advertising. But the leap from the efficacy of advertising to the assumed efficacy of propaganda aimed at deeprooted attitudes and ego involved behavior is as unwarranted as it is dangerous. Advertising is typically directed toward the canalizing of preexisting behavior patterns or attitudes. It seldom seeks to instill new attitudes or to create significantly new behavior patterns. "Advertising pays" because it generally deals with a simple psychological situation. For Americans who have been socialized in the use of a toothbrush, it makes relatively little difference which brand of toothbrush they use. Once the gross pattern of behavior or the generic attitude has been established, it can be canalized in one direction or another. Resistance is slight. But mass propaganda typically meets a more complex situation. It may seek objectives which are at odds with deeplying attitudes. It may seek to reshape rather than to canalize current systems of values. And the successes of advertising may only highlight the failures of propaganda. Much of the current propaganda which is aimed at abolishing deep-seated ethnic and racial prejudices, for example, seems to have had little effectiveness.

Media of media communication, then, have been effectively used to canalize basic attitudes but there is little evidence of their having served to change these attitudes.

Supplementation

Mass propaganda which is neither monopolistic nor canalizing in character may, nonetheless, prove effective if it meets a third condition: supplementation through face to face contacts.

A case in point will illustrate the interplay between mass media and face to face influences. The seeming propagandistic success achieved some years ago by Father Coughlin does not appear, upon inspection, to have resulted primarily from the propaganda content of his radio talks. It was, rather, the product of these centralized propaganda talks *and* widespread local organizations which arranged for their members to listen to him, followed by discussions among themselves concerning the social the social views he had expressed. This combination of a central supply of propaganda (Coughlin's addresses on a nationwide network), the coordinated distribution of newspapers and pamphlets and locally organized face to face discussions among relatively small groups—this complex of reciprocal reinforcement by mass media and personal relations proved spectacularly successful.

Students of mass movements have come to repudiate the view that mass propaganda in and of itself creates or maintains the movement. Nazism did not attain its brief moment of hegemony by capturing the mass media of communication. The media played an ancillary role, supplementing the use of organized violence, organized distribution of rewards for conformity and organized centers of local indoctrination. The Soviet Union has also made large and impressive use of mass media for indoctrinating enormous populations with appropriate ideologies. But the organizers of indoctrination saw to it that the mass media did not operate alone. "Red corners," "reading huts" and "listening stations" comprised meeting places in which groups of citizens were exposed to the mass media in common. The fifty-five thousand reading rooms and clubs which had come into being by 1933 enabled the local ideological elite to talk over with rank and file readers the content of what they read. The relative scarcity of radios in private homes again made for group listening and group discussions of what had been heard.

In these instances, the machinery of mass persuasion included face to face contact in local organizations as an adjunct to the mass media. The privatized individual response to the materials presented through the channels of mass communication was considered inadequate for transforming exposure to propaganda into effectiveness of propaganda. In a society such as our own, where the pattern of bureaucratization has not yet become so pervasive or, at least, not so clearly crystallized, it has likewise been found that mass media prove most effective in conjunction with local centers of organized face to face contact.

Several factors contribute to the enhanced effectiveness of this joining of mass media and direct personal contact. Most clearly, the local discussions serve to reinforce the content of mass propaganda. Such mutual confirmation produces a "clinching effect." Secondly, the central media lessen the task of the local organizer, and the personnel requirements for such subalterns need not be as rigorous in a popular movement. The subalterns need not set forth the propaganda content for themselves, but need only pilot potential converts to the radio where the doctrine is being expounded. Thirdly, the appearance of a representative of the movement on a nationwide network, or his mention in the national press, serves to symbolize the legitimacy and significance of the movement. It is no powerless, inconsequential enterprise. The mass media, as we have seen, confer status. And the status of the national movement reflects back on the status of the local cells, thus consolidating the tentative decisions of its members. In this interlocking arrangement, the local organizer ensures an audience for the national speaker and the national speaker validates the status of the local organizer.

This brief summary of the situations in which the mass media achieve their maximum propaganda effect may resolve the seeming contradiction which arose at the outset of our discussion. The mass media prove most effective when they operate in a situation of virtual "psychological monopoly," or when the objective is one of canalizing rather than modifying basic attitudes or when they operate in conjunction with face to face contacts.

But these three conditions are rarely satisfied conjointly in propaganda for social objectives. To the degree that monopolization of attention is rare, opposing propagandas have free play in a democracy. And by and large, basic social issues involve more than a mere canalizing of preexistent basic attitudes; they call, rather, for substantial changes in attitude and behavior. Finally, for the most obvious of reasons, the close collaboration of mass media and locally organized centers for face to face contact has seldom been achieved by groups striving for planned social change. Such programs are expensive. And it is precisely these groups which seldom have the large resources needed for these expensive programs. The forward looking groups at the edges of the power structure do not ordinarily have the large financial means of the contented groups at the center.

As a result of this threefold situation, the present role of mass media is largely confined to peripheral social concerns and the media do not exhibit the degree of social power commonly attributed to them.

By the same token, and in view of the present organization of business ownership and control of the mass media, they have served to cement the structure of our society. Organized business does approach a virtual "psychological monopoly" of the mass media. Radio commercials and newspaper advertisements are, of course, premised on a system which has been termed free enterprise. Moreover, the world of commerce is primarily concerned with canalizing rather than radically changing basic attitudes; it seeks only to create preferences for one rather than another brand of product. Face to face contacts with those who have been socialized in our culture serve primarily to reinforce the prevailing culture patterns.

Thus, the very conditions which make for the maximum effectiveness of the mass media of communication operate toward the maintenance of the going social cultural structure rather than toward its change.

Notes

1. James Bryce, *The American Commonwealth*, Volume 2. Copyright 1898 by Macmillan and Company; 1910, 1914 by The Macmillan Company; 1920 by The Right Honorable Viscount Bryce.

2. *Ibid.*, Part IV, Chapter LXXX, James Bryce perceived this with characteristic clarity: "That the education of the masses is nevertheless a superficial education goes without saying. It is sufficient to enable them to think they know something about the great problems of politics: insufficient to show them how little they know. The public elementary school gives everybody the key to knowledge in making reading and writing familiar, but it has not time to teach him how to use the key, whose use is in fact, by the pressure of daily work, almost confined to the newspaper and the magazine. So we may say that if the political education of the average American voter be compared with that of the average voter in Europe, it stands high; but if it be compared with the functions which the theory of the American government lays on him, which its spirit implies, which the methods of its party organization assume, its inadequacy is manifest." *Mutatis mutandis*, the same may be said of the gap between the theory of "superior" cultural content in the mass media and the current levels of popular education.

3. *Cf.* Chapter XVI.

38

Table from "Communication Research and the Social Psychologist"

From *Current Trends in Social Psychology* (1948)

Paul F. Lazarsfeld

This table, from Lazarsfeld's "Communication Research and the Social Psychologist" (1948), reveals his vision for the study of communication in the immediate postwar period. He draws his bearings from the Rockefeller Communication Group's memo (chapter 23, p. 136), and offers a relatively spacious view that goes well beyond the study of short-term effects, an area for which he was best known (Katz 2001). For Lazarsfeld's biography, see page 166.

Table 38.1

Kind of Communication Studies	Immediate Response	Kind of Effects		Institutional Changes
		Short Term	Long Term	
Single Unit	11	12	13	14
General Type	21	22	23	24
Economic and Social Structure of Medium	31	32	33	34
General Technological Nature of Medium	41	42	43	44

Source: Table taken from Paul F. Lazarsfeld, "Communication Research and the Social Psychologist," in *Current Trends in Social Psychology,* ed. Wayne Dennis, 218–73. Pittsburgh: University of Pittsburgh Press, 1948.

39

Information, Language, and Society

From *Cybernetics: Control and Communication in the Animal and the Machine* (1948)

Norbert Wiener

Norbert Wiener (1894–1964) was a famously gifted and absent-minded professor of mathematics at the Massachusetts Institute of Technology. Born to a professor of Slavic languages at Harvard who translated Tolstoy into English (after having studied medicine and engineering), Wiener was a child prodigy, graduating from Tufts University with a bachelor's degree in mathematics at age fourteen and receiving his doctorate at age eighteen. He later studied with G. H. Hardy and Bertrand Russell in Cambridge and had wide contacts in the world's mathematics community. Though a spacey genius, he was at the center of the science–war nexus in the twentieth century, making important mathematical contributions to the development of ballistics and antiaircraft techniques.

Wiener's understanding of servomechanisms in this context inspired his brilliant, baffling, and impassioned *Cybernetics: Control and Communication in the Animal and the Machine* (1948). In this book, he warns of the second industrial revolution. The first industrial revolution had replaced the human hand with the machine; the second, he fears, would replace the human brain with the intelligent machine. This conclusion gives us a vision of communication that is not so much concerned with conventional media—the "big five," of radio, television, film, newspapers, and magazines—as it is with other, more subtle forms. Wiener raises the same question that bothered the progressives and has always shadowed mass communication theory: what are the sources of social organization? His vision of the coming computerization fits squarely into an older tradition in which new communication technologies are received in both utopian and dystopian ways, as simultaneously demonic and divine. Similar hopes and fears have been aroused by the written word and the printing press, by the telegraph, and, now, by artificial intelligence. Wiener also anticipated the more-recent debates regarding the "information society," and articulates one important position held in those discussions. Wiener thought that cybernetics necessitated a call to arms for social justice; the contemporaneous "mathematical theory of communication" by Claude Shannon (1948) was far more apolitical and technocratic in its tendency.

The concept of an organization, the elements of which are themselves small organizations, is neither unfamiliar nor new. The loose federations of ancient Greece, the Holy Roman Empire and its similarly constituted feudal contemporaries, the Swiss Companions of the Oath, the United Netherlands, the United States of America, and the many United States to the south of it, the Union of Socialist Soviet Republics, are all examples of hierarchies of organizations on the political sphere. The Leviathan of Hobbes, the Man-State made up of lesser men, is an illustration of the same idea one stage lower in scale, while Leibniz's treatment of the living organism as being really a plenum, wherein other living organisms, such as the blood corpuscles have their life, is but another step in the same direction. It is, in fact, scarcely more than a philosophical anticipation of the cell theory, according to which most of the animals and plants of moderate size and all of those of large dimensions are made up of units, cells, which have many if not all the attributes of independent living organism. The multicellular organisms may themselves be the building bricks of organisms of a higher stage, such as the Portuguese man-of-war, which is a complex structure of differentiated coelenterate polyps, where the several individuals are modified in different ways to serve the nutrition, the support, the locomotion, the excretion, the reproduction, and the support of the colony as a whole.

Strictly speaking, such a physically conjoint colony as that poses no question of organization which is philosophically deeper than those which arise at a lower level of individuality. It is very different with man and the other social animals—with the herds of baboons or cattle, the beaver colonies, the hives of bees, the nests of wasps or ants. The degree of integration of the life of the community may very well approach the level shown in the conduct of a single individual, yet the individual will probably have a fixed nervous system, with permanent topographic relations between the elements and permanent connections, while the community consists of individuals with shifting relations in space and time and no permanent, unbreakable physical connections. All the nervous tissue of the beehive is the nervous tissue of some single bee. How then does the beehive act in unison, and at that in a very variable, adapted, organized unison? Obviously, the secret is in the intercommunication of its members.

This intercommunication can vary greatly in complexity and content. With man, it embraces the whole intricacy of language and literature, and very much besides. With the ants, it probably does not cover much more than a few smells. It is very improbable that an ant can distinguish one ant from another. It certainly can distinguish an ant from its own nest from an ant from a foreign nest, and may cooperate with the one, destroy the other. Within a few outside reactions of this kind, the ant seems to have a mind almost as patterned, chitin-bound, as its body. It is what we might expect *a priori* from an animal whose growing phase and, to a large extent, whose learning phase are rigidly separated from the phase of the mature activity. The only means of communication we can trace in them are as general and diffuse as the hormonal system of communication within the body. Indeed, smell, one of the chemical senses, general and undirectional as it is, is not unlike the hormonal influences within the body.

Let it be remarked parenthetically that musk, civet, castoreum, and the like sexually attractive substances in the mammals may be regarded as communal, exterior hormones, indispensable, especially in solitary animals, for the bringing the sexes together at the proper time, and serve for the continuation of the race. By this I do no mean to assert that the inner action of these substances, once they reach the organ of smell, is hormonal rather than nervous. It is hard to see how it can be purely hormonal in quantities as small as those which are readily perceivable; on the other hand, we know too little of the action of the hormones to deny the possibility of the hormonal action of vanishingly small quantities of such substances. Moreover, the long, twisted rings of carbon atoms found in muskone and civetone do not need too much rearrangement to form the linked ring structure characteristic of the sex hormones, some of the vitamins, and some of the carcinogens. I do not care to pronounce an opinion on this matter; I leave it as an interesting speculation.

The odors perceived by the ant seem to lead to a highly standardized course of conduct; but the value of a simple stimulus, such as an odor, for conveying information depends not only on the information conveyed by the stimulus itself but on the whole nervous constitution of the sender and the receiver of the stimulus as well. Suppose I find myself in the woods with an intelligent savage who cannot speak my language and whose language I cannot speak. Even without any code of sign language common to the two of us, I can learn a great deal from him. All I need to do is to be alert to those moments when he shows the signs of emotion or interest. I then cast my eyes around, perhaps paying special attention to the direction of his glance, and fix in my memory what I see or hear. It will not be long before I discover the things which seem important to him, not because he has communicated them to me by language, but because I myself have observed them. In other words, a signal without an intrinsic content may acquire meaning in his mind by what he observes at the time, and may acquire meaning in my mind by what I observe at the time. The ability that he has to pick out the moments of my special, active attention is in itself a language as varied in possibilities as the range of impressions that the two of us are able to encompass. Thus social animals may have an active, intelligent, flexible means of communication long before the development of language.

Whatever means of communication the race may have, it is possible to define and to measure the amount of information available to the race and to distinguish it from the amount of information available to the individual. Certainly no information available to the individual is also available to the race unless it modifies the behavior of one individual to another, nor is even that behavior of racial significance unless it is distinguishable by other individuals from other forms of behavior. Thus the question as to whether a certain piece of information is racial or of purely private availability depends on whether it results in the individual assuming a form of activity which can be recognized as a distinct form of activity by other members of the race, in the sense that it will in turn affect their activity, and so on.

I have spoken of the race. This is really too broad a term for the scope of most communal information. Properly speaking, the community extends only so far as there extends an effectual transmission of information. It is possible to give a sort of measure to this by comparing the number of decisions entering a group from outside with the number of decisions made in the group. We can thus measure the autonomy of the group. A measure of the effective size of a group is given by the size which it must have to have achieved a certain stated degree of autonomy.

A group may have more group information or less group information than its members. A group of non-social animals, temporarily assembled, contains very little group information, even though its members may possess much information as individuals. This is because very little that one member does is noticed by the others and is acted on by them in a way that goes further in the group. On the other hand, the human organism contains vastly more information, in all probability, than does any one of its cells. There is thus no necessary relation in either direction between the amount of racial or tribal or community information and the amount of information available to the individual.

As in the case of the individual, not all the information which is available to the race at one time is accessible without special effort. There is a well-known tendency of libraries to become clogged by their own volume; of the sciences to develop such a degree of specialization that the expert is often illiterate outside his own minute specialty. Dr. Vannevar Bush has suggested the use of mechanical aids for the searching through vast bodies of material. These probably have their uses, but they are limited by the impossibility of classifying a book under an unfamiliar heading unless some particular person has already recognized the relevance of that heading for that particular book. In the case where two subjects have the same techniques and intellectual content but belong to widely separated fields, this still requires some individual with an almost Leibnizian catholicity of interest.

In connection with the effective amount of communal information, one of the most surprising facts about the body politic is its extreme lack of efficient homeostatic processes. There is a belief, current in many countries, which has been elevated to the rank of an official article of faith in the United States, that free competition is itself a homeostatic process: that in a free market the individual selfishness of the bargainers, each seeking to sell as high and buy as low as possible, will result in the end in a stable dynamics of prices, and with redound to the greatest common good. This is associated with the very comforting view that the individual entrepreneur, in seeking to forward his own interest, is in some manner a public benefactor and has thus earned the great rewards with which society has showered him. Unfortunately, the evidence, such as it is, is against this simple-minded theory. The market is a game, which has indeed received a simulacrum in the family game of Monopoly. It is thus strictly subject to the general theory of games, developed by von Neumann and Morgenstern. This theory is based on the assumption that each player, at every stage, in view of the information then available to him, plays in accordance with a completely intelligent policy, which will in the end assure him of the greatest possible expectation of reward. It is thus the market game as played between perfectly intelligent, perfectly ruthless operators. Even in the case of two players, the theory is complicated, although it often leads to the choice of a definite line of play. In many cases, however, where there are three layers, and in the overwhelming majority of cases, when the number of players is large, the result is one of extreme indeterminacy and instability. The individual players are compelled by their own cupidity to form coalitions; but these coalitions do not generally establish themselves in any single, determinate way, and usually terminate in a welter of betrayal, turncoatism, and deception, which is only too true a picture of the higher business life, or the closely related lives of politics, diplomacy, and war. In the long run, even the most brilliant and unprincipled huckster must expect ruin; but let the hucksters become tired of this and agree to live in peace with one another, and the great rewards are reserved for the one who watches for an opportune time to break his agreement and betray his companions. There is no homeostasis whatsoever. We are involved in the business cycles of boom and failure, in the successions of dictatorship and revolution, in the wars which everyone loses, which are so real a feature of modern times.

Naturally, von Neumann's picture of the player as a completely intelligent, completely ruthless person is an abstraction and a perversion of the facts. It is rare to find a large number of thoroughly clever and unprincipled persons playing a game together. Where the knaves assemble, there will always be fools; and where the fools are present in sufficient numbers, they offer a more profitable object of exploitation for the knaves. The psychology of the fool has become a subject well worth the serious attention of the knaves. Instead of looking out for his own ultimate interest, after the fashion of von Neumann's gamesters, the fool operates in a manner which, by and large, is as predictable as the struggles of a rat in a maze. *This* policy of lies—or rather, of statements irrelevant to the truth—will make him buy a particular brand of cigarettes: *that* policy will, or so the party hopes, induce him to vote for a particular candidate—any candidate—or to join in a political witch hunt. A certain precise mixture of religion, pornography, and pseudo science will sell an illustrated newspaper. A certain blend of wheedling, bribery, and intimidation will induce a young scientist to work on guided missiles or the atomic bomb. To determine these, we have our machinery of radio fan ratings, straw votes, opinion samplings, and other psychological investigations, with the common man as their object: and there are always the statisticians, sociologists, and economists available to sell their services to these undertakings.

Luckily for us, these merchants of lies, these exploiters of gullibility, have not yet arrived at such a pitch of perfection as to have things all their own way. This is because no man is either all fool or all knave. The average man is quite reasonably intelligent concerning subjects which come to his direct attention and quite reasonably altruistic in matters of public benefit or private suffering which are brought before his own eyes. In a small country community which has been running long enough to have developed somewhat uniform levels of intelligence and behavior, there is a very respectable standard of care for the unfortunate, of administration of roads and other public facilities, of tolerance for those who have offended once or twice against society. After all, these people are there, and the rest of the community must continue to live with them. On the other hand, in such a community, it does not do for a man to have the habit of overreaching his neighbors. There are ways of making him feel the weight of public opinion. After a while, he will find it so ubiquitous, so unavoidable, so restricting and oppressing that he will have to leave the community in self-defense.

Thus small, closely knit communities have a very considerable measure of homeostasis; and this, whether they are highly literate communities in a civilized country or villages of primitive savages. Strange and even repugnant as the customs of many barbarians may seem to us, they generally have a very definite homeostatic value, which it is part of the function of anthropologists to interpret. It is only in the large community, where the Lords of Things as They Are protect themselves from hunger by wealth, from public opinion by privacy and anonymity, from private criticism by the laws of libel and the possession of the mans of communication, that ruthlessness can reach its most sublime levels. Of all of these anti-homeostatic factors in society, the control of the means of communication is the most effective and most important.

One of the lessons of the present book is that any organism is held together in this action by the possession of means for the acquisition, use, retention, and transmission of information. In a society too large for the direct contact of its members, these means are the press, both as it concerns books and as it concerns newspapers, the radio, the telephone system, the telegraph, the posts, the theater, the movies, the schools, and the church. Besides their intrinsic importance as means of communication, each of these serves other, secondary functions. The newspaper is a vehicle for advertisement and an instrument for the monetary gain of its proprietor, as are also the movies and the radio. The school and the church are not merely refuges for the scholar and the saint: they are also the home of the Great Educator and the Bishop. The book that does not earn money for its publisher probably does not get printed and certainly does not get reprinted.

In a society like ours, avowedly based on buying and selling, in which all natural and human resources are regarded as the absolute property of the first business man enterprising enough to exploit them, these secondary aspects of the means of communication tend to encroach further and further on the primary ones. This is aided by the very elaboration and the consequent expense of the means themselves. The country paper may continue to use its own reporters to canvass the villages around for gossip, but it buys its national news, its syndicated features, its political opinions, as stereotyped "boiler plate." The radio depends on its advertisers for income, and, as everywhere, the man who pays the piper calls the tune. The great news services cost too much to be available to the publisher of moderate means. The book publishers concentrate on books that are likely to be acceptable to some book club which buys out the whole of an enormous edition. The college president and the Bishop, even if they have no personal ambitions for power, have expensive institutions to run and can only seek their money where the money is.

Thus on all sides we have a triple constriction of the means of communication: the elimination of the less profitable means in favor of the more profitable: the fact that these means are in the hands of the very limited class of wealthy men, and thus naturally express the opinions of that class: and the further fact that, as one of the chief avenues to political and personal power, they attract above all those ambitious for such power. That system which more than all others should contribute to social homeostasis is thrown directly into the hands of those most concerned in the game of power and money, which we have already seen to be one of the chief anti-homeostatic elements in the community. It is no wonder then that the larger communities, subject to this disruptive influence, contain far less communally available information than the smaller communities, to say nothing of the human elements of which all communities are built up. Like the wolf pack, although let us hope to a lesser extent, the State is stupider than most of its components.

This runs counter to a tendency much voiced among business executives, heads of great laboratories, and the like, to assume that because the community is larger than the individual it is also more intelligent. Some of this opinion is due to no more than a childish delight in the large and the lavish. Some of it is due to a sense of the possibilities of a large organization for good. Not a little of it, however, is nothing more than an eye for the main chance and a lusting after the fleshpots of Egypt.

There is another group of those who see nothing good in the anarchy of modern society, and in whom an optimistic feeling that there must be some way out has led to an overvaluation of the possible homeostatic elements in the community. Much as we may sympathize with these individuals and appreciate the emotional dilemma in which they find themselves, we cannot attribute to much value to this type of wishful thinking. It is the mode of thought of the mice when faced with the problem of belling the cat. Undoubtedly it would be very pleasant of us mice if the predatory cats of this world were to be belled, but—who is going to do it? Who is to assure us that ruthless power will not find its way back into the hands of those most avid for it?

I mention this matter because of the considerable, and I think false, hopes which some of my friends have built for the social efficacy of whatever new ways of thinking this book may contain. They are certain that our control over our material environment has far outgrown our control over our social environment and our understanding thereof. Therefore, they consider that the main task of the immediate future is to extend to the fields of anthropology, of sociology, of economics, the methods of the natural sciences, in the hope of achieving a like measure of success in the social fields. From believing this necessary, they come to believe it possible. In this, I maintain, they show an excessive optimism, and a misunderstanding of the nature of all scientific achievement.

All the great successes in precise science have been made in fields where there is a certain high degree of isolation of the phenomenon from the observer. We have seen in the case of astronomy that this may result from the enormous scale of certain phenomena with respect to man, so that man's mightiest efforts, not to speak of his mere glance, cannot make the slightest visible impression on the celestial world. In modern atomic physics, on the other hand, the science of the unspeakably minute, it is true that anything we do will have an influence on many individual particles which is great *from the point of view of that particle*. However, we do not live on the scale of the particles concerned, either in space or in time; and the events that might be of the greatest significance from the point of view of an observer conforming to their scale of existence appear to us—with some exceptions, it is true, as in the Wilson cloud-chamber experiments—only as average mass effects in which enormous populations of particles cooperate. As far as these effects are concerned, the intervals of time concerned are large from the point of view of the individual particle and its motion, and our statistical theories have an admirably adequate basis. In short, we are too small to influence the stars in their courses, and too large to care about anything but the mass effects of molecules, atoms, and electrons. In both cases, we achieve a sufficiently loose coupling with the phenomena we are studying to give a massive total account of this coupling, although the coupling may not be loose enough for us to be able to ignore it altogether.

It is in the social sciences that the coupling between the observed phenomenon and the observer is hardest to minimize. On the one hand, the observer is able to exert a considerable influence on the phenomena that come to his attention. With all respect to the intelligence, skill, and honesty of purpose of my anthropologist friends, I cannot think that any community which they have investigated will ever be quite the same afterward. Many a missionary has fixed his own misunderstandings of a primitive language as law eternal in the process of reducing it to writing. There is much in the social habits of a peo-

ple which is dispersed and distorted by the mere act of making inquiries about it. In another sense from that in which it is usually stated, *traduttore traditore*.

On the other hand, the social scientist has not the advantage of looking down on his subjects from the cold heights of eternity and ubiquity. It may be that there is a mass sociology of the human animalcule, observed like the populations of *Drosophila* in a bottle, but this is not a sociology in which we, who are human animalcules ourselves, are particularly interested. We are not much concerned about human rises and falls, pleasures and agonies, *sub specie aeternitatis*. Your anthropologist reports the customs associated with the life, education, career, and death of people whose life scale is much the same as his own. Your economist is most interested in predicting such business cycles as run their course in less than a generation or, at least, have repercussions which affect a man differentially at different stages of his career. Few philosophers of politics nowadays care to confine their investigations to the world of Ideas of Plato.

In other words, in the social sciences we have to deal with short statistical runs, nor can we be sure that a considerable part of what we observe is not an artifact of our own creation. An investigation of the stock market is likely to upset the stock market. We are too much in tune with the objects of our investigation to be good probes. In short, whether our investigations in the social sciences be statistical or dynamic—and they should participate in the nature of both—they can never be good to more than a very few decimal places, and in short, can never furnish us with a quantity of verifiable, significant information which begins to compare with that which we have learned to expect in the natural sciences. We cannot afford to neglect them; neither should we build exaggerated expectations of their possibilities. There is much which we must leave, whether we like it or not, to the un-"scientific," narrative method of the professional historian.

40

Consensus and Mass Communication

From *American Sociological Review* (1948)

Louis Wirth

Louis Wirth (1897–1952) was a professor of sociology at the University of Chicago. Born in a small German village, in the house where his ancestors had lived for centuries, he emigrated to the United States as a teenager, first to Omaha, Nebraska, and then to study in the swirling urban laboratory of Chicago. His personal trajectory thus follows the classic sociological transition from *Gemeinschaft* (community) to *Gesellschaft* (society), and it is perhaps no accident that he is most remembered for his studies of urbanism and the city as a way of life. Wirth also did important work in the sociology of Jews and Jewish life, race relations, nationalism, and the sociology of knowledge (from 1935 to 1936, Wirth translated, and wrote a preface for, Karl Mannheim's *Ideology and Utopia*).

The following selection consists of sections 1, 2, and 7 of Wirth's 1947 presidential address at the American Sociological Association and clearly shows how progressive themes persist in Chicago sociology. In it, Wirth treats the dangers of social disorganization, the opportunity for social reform, the need for consensus over conflict, and mass society as the outcome of modern social development. But the speech is also very much a creature of its time in comparing the power of mass communication to that of the atom bomb. To many of this era, mass communication, like the bomb, seemed a sign of what was potentially good and evil about the modern world. Like others writing in that time—such as Julian Huxley, Wiener, and the Hutchins Commission—Wirth profoundly saw that the modern media of communication had two-edged possibilities (see Rothenbuhler 2003).

I

Before exploring the nature and conditions of consensus, it seems appropriate to indicate the salient characteristics of mass societies. As we look back upon previous social aggregations, such as those of the ancient kingdoms, or at their greatest extent the Roman Empire, we wonder how, given the primitive communications that obtained, such impressive numbers and territories could be held together under a common regime over any considerable span of time. If we discover, however, that these aggregations were not truly societies but were little more than administrative areas, creatures of military domination along the main arteries of communication from some center of power, and that the economics base of their cohesion rested on exploitation of the outlying territories and peoples by the power holders at a center through their representatives who were scattered thinly over the territory, the magnitude of these aggregations does not seem too impressive. Mass societies as we find them today, however, show greater marks of integration. They are aggregations of people who participate to a much greater degree in the common life, and, at least in democratic parts of the world, comprise people whose attitudes, sentiments, and opinions have some bearing upon the policies pursued by their governments. In this sense mass societies are a creation of the modern age and are the product of the division of labor, of mass communication, and a more or less democratically achieved consensus.

II

Since we shall speak of our society as a mass society and of the communication that it involves as mass communication, it behooves us to depict the characteristics of the mass. Its most obvious trait is that it involves great numbers in contradistinction to the smaller aggregates with which we have become familiar through the study of primitive life and earlier historical forms of human association. Second, and again, almost by definition, it consists of aggregates of men widely dispersed over the face of the earth, as distinguished from the compact local groups of former periods. Third, the mass is composed of heterogeneous members, in that it includes people living under widely different conditions, under widely varying cultures, coming from diverse strata of society, occupying different positions, engaging in different occupations, and hence having different interests, standards of life, and degrees of prestige, power, and influence. Fourth, the mass is an aggregate of anonymous individuals, as may be indicated by the fact that though millions of individuals listening to a radio program, reading a newspaper, or seeing a movie, are exposed to the same images, they are not aware of who the fellow members of the audience are, nor are those who transmit these images certain of the composition of their audience. These anonymous persons who constitute the mass may be, and usually are, of course, aware that they are part of a mass and they make some assumptions as to who their fellow members are and how many of them there are. They are likewise capable of identifying themselves with their anonymous fellows who are exposed to the same images and may even gain some support from the knowledge of their existence. They may even act as if they had their unanimous support as is illustrated by the slogan "Fifty million Frenchmen can't be wrong," or by the much disputed bandwagon effect resulting from the publication of the results of public opinion polls. Fifth, the mass does not constitute an organized group. It is without recognized leadership and a well-defined group. If it acts collectively at all it does so only as a crowd or as a mob, but since it is dispersed in space it cannot even move as these elementary social bodies are capable of action, although it may be far from constituting, as Carlyle thought, "an inert lump." Sixth, the mass has no common customs or traditions, no institutions, and no rules governing the action of the individuals. Hence, it is open to

suggestions, and its behavior, to a greater degree than that of organized bodies, is capricious and unpredictable. And, finally, the mass consists of unattached individuals, or, at best, individuals who, for the time being, behave not as members of a group, playing specific roles representative of their position in that group, but rather as discrete entities. In modern urban industrial society, our membership in each of the multiple organizations to which we belong represents our interests only in some limited aspect of our total personal life. There is no group which even remotely professes to speak for us in our total capacity as men or in all of the roles that we play. Although through our membership in these organized groups we become articulate, contribute to the molding of public opinion, and participate more or less actively in the determination of social policies, there remains for all of us a quite considerable range of ideas and ideals which are subject to manipulation from the outside and in reference to which there is no appreciable reciprocal interaction between ourselves and others similarly situated. It is this idea of life which furnishes the opportunity for others to entrap us or to lead us toward goals with the formulation of which we have had little or nothing whatever to do. Hence, all of us are in some respects characterized in our conduct by mass behavior.

The fragmentation of human interests in heterogeneous, complex modern societies is so far advanced that as Robert E. Park put it, "What a man belongs to constitutes most of his life career and all of his obituary." The trend in group organization is not merely toward the multiplication and diversification of organizations, but also toward bodies of enormously increased size. We have witnessed in recent decades the development of numerous giant organizations in business and industry, in labor, in the professions, in religion, in government, and in social life which seem to dominate our existence and to characterize our civilization.

Many of these organizations have become so colossal that they themselves come to approximate masses. The sense of belonging and of participation which smaller and more compactly organized groups are able to generate is hence largely frustrated by the very size of the typical organizations of our time. This is perhaps a price we must be willing to pay for living in an interdependent and technologically highly advanced world. But it should also constitute a major challenge to the analytical skill and the inventive imagination of social scientists, especially sociologists, for it is to a large extent upon the ability to maintain effective contact between the members and two-way communication between the leaders and the membership of these giant structures that the future of democracy rests.

The problem is complicated by the fact that not only is mass democratic society enormous in scope and intricate in structure, but it presents a dynamic equilibrium in which one of the principal conditions of effective collective action is the accuracy and speed with which the shifting interests and attitudes of great masses of men, whether organized or unorganized, can be ascertained and brought to bear upon the determination of policy.

Another significant feature of modern mass society, and especially of mass democracies, is the instability of the interests and the motives of the members, and the correspondingly frequent changes in leadership and the consequent uncertainty as to the locus of decisive power at any one juncture of events. If the spokesmen in any group are to know whom they are speaking for they must be able to assess how strong or enduring the interests are that they profess to represent, and whether, indeed, the groups for which they speak are at all interested in the issue.

Mass societies, furthermore, involve vast concentrations of power and authority and complicated machinery of administration. Perhaps the most urgent need that goes unmet in such a society is the capacity for prompt decisions in the face of recurrent crises. The fact that concerted action in such societies, if they are to remain democratic, must take into consideration the shifting constellation of public opinion imposes upon them who guide its destinies a responsibility which can only be met by the utilization of all the relevant sources of knowledge and the perfection of very much more advanced techniques than we now seem to possess.

* * *

VII

Before closing, I should like to allude to the problems of consensus as they arise in some of the more crucial spheres of human interaction in contemporary society. The first of these is the sphere of racial and cultural relations, the second is the field of industrial relations, and the third is the area of international relations. I do not mean to suggest that these are the only areas where we face the problems of consensus. I use them merely for illustrative purposes, recognizing that the same problems are also found in family relations, in informal associations, in local community life, and in the operations of government. These three, however, seem to reflect the most characteristic features of mass communication as it impinges upon consensus in modern mass democracies such as our own.

The spread of industrialism and of capitalism with its world markets and its free workers has given rise among other institutions to giant corporations and giant unions, involving great concentrations of power. The competition and conflicting interests within and between these organizations affects every aspect of social life of all society. Management and unions, aware of the crucial influence of public opinion upon their relative positions, have not been slow to utilize the instruments of mass communication, both internally and in relation to one another, and in the effort to mold the attitudes and to affect the decisions of society. In so far as these decisions involve national policies, the effort of each side has been directed to rallying support for itself by molding the attitudes and opinions of the larger public.

The relationship between conflicting groups, such as these, illustrates the significance of consensus within the group for the capacity of each to deal with its opponent. From the standpoint of the larger society the need for a more inclusive consensus involving both of these constellations is indispensable for the maintenance of industrial peace. Propaganda appeals directed toward the larger public, the pressure of government and organized bodies in society, such as the churches and the political parties, are among the indispensable elements in the strategy of collective bargaining, arbitration, labor legislation, and the conduct of strikes. The means of mass communication play no less significant a role in the maintenance of mass production and mass markets.

The rise of self-conscious racial and cultural minorities which has proceeded parallel to the spread of the ideal of quality and the institutions of mass democracy through ever larger areas of the world, has accentuated the problems of racial and cultural relations. The contrast between contemporary society and primitive and earlier historical societies with respect to the contact between diverse racial and cultural groups is startling. Whereas everyone in a primitive, ancient, and medieval society had a more or less fixed place in the social structure, depending to a large extent upon the character and position of his ancestor, today all of us are men on the move and on the make, and all of us by transcending the cultural bounds of our narrower society become to some extent marginal men. More and more the relations of life that were formerly settled by sacred tradition and custom become subjects of discussion, debate, negotiation, and overt conflict. Many of the problems affecting our national solidarity through our loyalties, rest for their orderly adjustment upon the achievement of consensus across the lines of the diverse races and cultures of which America is comprised. The great obstacles encountered by those who attempted to achieve in the face of prejudice and discrimination a national solidarity sufficient to see our nation through the recent war, should recall to all of us the reality of the existence of minorities in our midst. If the experiment of America shows anything, it shows that, despite the many setbacks which the democratic ideal and practice have suffered, we are determined to achieve consensus and have found the road toward it without too much coercion through the idea of cultural pluralism, which is another expression for the toleration of differences.

Nowhere do the problems of racial and cultural relations present themselves more dramatically than they do in our great cities, where the people of varying stocks and cultures live in dense physical concentration. Whereas, in an earlier society it was unusual to meet a stranger, under the conditions of life in great cities, it is an equal rarity to meet someone who is familiar. Although our face may still light up when, in the crowds of the great cities, we see a friend, we have nevertheless learned to live with people of diverse background and character to a degree sufficient at least to achieve the requirements of a fairly orderly, productive, and peaceful society.

What is true of self-conscious minorities impelled by the ideal of the equality of man in our town communities and in our own nation, is increasingly true of the world at large. The so-called backward peoples are increasingly being brought within the orbit of a world society resting upon a world consensus. In this the numerous organized groups and movements, among dominant and minority groups alike, using the instruments of mass communication to bring their ideals before a world public, are increasingly evident.

And finally the question must have occurred to people who are not versed in the language of sociologists and in the serious subjects with which they are preoccupied, why it is that sociologists who claim as their vocation the study of social interaction have paid so little attention to interaction on the grandest scale of all, namely, the interaction between national states and what we call international relations, for in this sphere is exemplified the operation of consensus upon which the future of mankind depends.

We have been making some progress in the building of world consensus. We do have a fairly general recognition of economic interdependence on a world scale. We have a great deal more of traffic across the bounds of nations and of continents than the world has ever seen before. We have even some incipient international institutions whose strength is being tested by the increasing tensions brought about by the very fact that we live in an emerging single world in which we have contacts and conflicts of interest and of ideas with people of whom we were formerly oblivious. We even can see some semblance of emerging world loyalties which makes the expression "world citizenship" sound less utopian than it did before. The instruments of mass communication, particularly the radio, and, it seems soon, television, combining the faithful transmission of the voice with that of the visual image of the human face and gesture, are particularly well suited to supply the means for the furtherance of understanding across the borders of sovereign states.

As long as we do not have a monopoly of power to coerce all of the other nations and people of the earth into our way of life, the only road we can travel is that of continued negotiation, persuasion, and compromise. We should probably, even if we had the power of coercion, not be able to use it on others without destroying the very values which might tempt us to use it.

If our ways of thought and conception of freedom and democracy, our system of economy, and our political and social ideals seem to be, as I am sure they seem to many, irreconcilable with those of the only other remaining power constellation in the world, it is well to recall that there was a time when Catholics and Protestants felt very passionately that they could not live in peace in the same state. Time has fortunately proved them wrong. There have been other conflicts in the history of man which seemed at the time equally irresolvable. The uncomfortable but at the same time reassuring fact, however, is that today in this shrunken world there are more effective ways of interfering with the internal life of any society by those without through the instrumentalities of mass communication, which are no respecters of boundaries and which find ways of surmounting all barriers. What is more, these products of mass communication have a way of reaching the great inert masses of the world, for making them restless and mobilizing them for action, or at least for making the dominant groups in their respective societies more responsive to their pressure.

Mass communication will not, of course, by itself produce the minimum of world consensus requisite for world peace and world society. But it does not operate by itself. It operates through and in conjunction with existing and emerging institutions in a climate of opinion and ultimately through and upon human beings. There are other things in the world besides mass communication, but these other things, some of which I have indicated, are tied increasingly to mass communication and through this tie give it its strategic significance.

The media of mass communication, like all the technological instruments that man has invented, are themselves neutral. They can be used to instill a fighting faith or the will to reconciliation. At any rate, the relationship between nations and people that will allow the fullest use of the world's resources to meet human needs under freedom and order and in peace, calls today for nothing less than the building of a world consensus, for a social psychological integration of the human race commensurate with the interdependent far-flung and rich material resources and human energies of the world.

In mobilizing the instrumentalities of mass communication for the building of that consensus, we cannot fail to remind ourselves that along with the perfection of these means of human intercourse science has also perfected unprecedented means of mass destruction. But in the case of neither the instruments of mass communication nor of atomic energy do the inventors of the instrument dictate the uses to which they shall be put. As a contemporary historian has recently put it: "If our characteristic Western gift [by which he refers to technology] proves to have been a blessing for mankind, it will be a great blessing; and, if a curse, a great curse. If things go well, the epitaph of history on the Franks [by which he means us] may run: 'Here lie the technicians, who united mankind'; and if things go badly: 'Here lie the technicians, who exterminated the human race.'"[1] Except that in the later case, Professor Toynbee, the author of these remarks, fails to point out that there may not be anybody left to carve that epitaph.

If we are uneasy today it is not because of these products of science but because of what men may do with these products of human ingenuity. There is a frightful peril in delay, and the realization of this peril is rapidly leading to intellectual paralysis instead of greater intellectual exertion. The atomic bomb will not, we are told, yield to a physical defense or a counter-weapon which will neutralize its destructive potential. The only defense we have is social—the creation of world consensus. Since the mass media of communication are capable of providing the picture of social reality and the symbolic framework of thought and fantasy and the incentives for human action on an enormous scale, the knowledge of their effective use should become the most important quest of social science, and particularly of sociology. The circumstances under which we live do not any longer allow the saints to sit in their ivory tower while burly sinners rule the world.

I hereby extend a cordial invitation to my fellow sociologists, and such other social scientists, including the statisticians, who care to join us, to return to the subject matter for the cultivation of which society sustains us, though let it be admitted, on a none too luxurious level. That subject matter is the life of man in society and the heart of that subject matter today is the understanding of the processes through which consensus on a world scale is created. Unless we solve that problem, and solve it in a reasonably satisfactory way soon, there will be no opportunity to work on any of the others on which our minds or our hearts are set.

Note

1. Arnold Toynbee: "Technology: Distinguishing Mark of the West," *Listener* November 20, 1947, p. 895.

What "Missing the Newspaper" Means

From *Communications Research* (1949)

Bernard Berelson

Bernard Berelson (1912–1979) studied at Whitman College and at the University of Washington before taking his doctorate in library science from the University of Chicago in 1941. During the war, Berelson worked with Harold Lasswell at the Foreign Broadcast Intelligence Service, learning content analysis techniques that he later applied at Columbia's Bureau of Applied Social Research, where he worked from 1944 to 1946 and from 1960 to 1961. Between those stints, Berelson taught at Chicago from 1946 to 1951 and from 1957 to 1959; and from 1962 to 1974, he was director of the Communication Research Program at the Population Council, where he focused on issues of international development. Berelson assisted Paul Lazarsfeld on his two classic voting studies, *The People's Choice* (1944) and *Voting* (1954); he edited an early reader in communication with Morris Janowitz, *Reader in Public Opinion and Communication* (1950); and he wrote a widely used methodological text, *Content Analysis in Communication Research* (1952).

"What 'Missing the Newspaper' Means" (1949) is an interesting little essay that was researched in the summer of 1945 and was precipitated by a strike of the New York newspapers. Berelson was skeptical about the stereotyped responses that people gave to public opinion pollsters when asked why they read the news; so, he turned to Columbia's focused interview technique to find out more. He draws on broadly psychoanalytic categories to interpret the significance of newspaper reading (at one point speculating that it might "serve some persons as a socially acceptable source of oral pleasure"), and he undercuts any idealized notion of the newspaper as a fundamental source of information for democratic citizens (notice how little time he spends on that use). The article is often remembered as contributing to the "uses and gratifications" approach to media, but read carefully to see how this looked in the 1940s.

In the late afternoon of Saturday, June 30, 1945, the deliverymen of eight major New York City newspapers went on strike. They remained on strike for over two weeks, and during that period most New Yorkers were effectively deprived of their regular newspaper reading. They were able to buy the newspaper *PM* and a few minor and specialized papers at newsstands, and they could buy copies over the counter at central offices of some newspapers. But the favorite papers of most readers were simply inaccessible to them for seventeen days.

These unusual circumstances presented a good opportunity for various interested parties—advertisers, newspaper publishers, radio executives, social scientists—to gauge public attitudes toward the newspaper, and at least three general polls of opinion were independently conducted during the strike. Some if not all findings of two polls have been made public, one by the Elmo

Roper agency and the other by Fact Finders Associates, Inc. This article is a report on the third, an explanatory survey conducted for the Bureau of Applied Social Research, Columbia University.

According to the published findings, the Roper and Fact Finder organizations directed their efforts to determining what people had done in order to keep up with the news, what parts of the newspaper they particularly missed, and how much they missed the newspaper as the strike went on. On no specific question are their results strictly comparable, but in three ways they aimed at the same general attitudes or behavior, although in quite different ways. Both agencies attempted to get at the nature of the substitute for the newspaper, and in both cases respondents stressed that they listened to news broadcasts over the radio. Both attempted, in quite different ways, to discover what parts of the newspaper were particularly missed, and in both cases respondents stressed news (national, local, and war news) and advertising. Finally, both attempted to get at the degree to which the newspapers were actually missed, and in both cases respondents indicated that they missed the paper intensely.

Because the questions used by the two polling agencies differed greatly, the results are not strictly comparable. Furthermore, neither poll is able to interpret its data, which consist altogether of "surface facts," relevant only to the specific question at hand. Saying that one "misses the newspaper," or a part of it, can cover a variety of psychological reactions. What does "missing the newspaper" mean? Why do people miss it? Do they really miss the parts they claim, to the extent that they claim? Why do they miss one part as against another? The Roper and Fact Finders polls bring little or nothing to bear on such questions, which are at the core of the basic problem, namely, to understand the function of the modern newspaper for its reader. Neither poll succeeds in getting at the more complex attitudinal matter operating in the situation.[1]

It was to attack this problem that the present study was conducted. At the end of the first week of the strike, the Bureau of Applied Social Research of Columbia University sponsored a quite different kind of study of people's reactions to the loss of their newspapers. Where the Roper and Fact Finders surveys were extensive, the Bureau's was intensive, designed to secure psychological insight in order to determine just what

not having the newspaper meant to people. It is an axiom in social research, of course, that such studies can most readily be done during a crisis period like that represented by the newspaper strike. People are not only more conscious of what the newspaper means to them during such a "shock" period than they are under normal conditions, but they also find it easier to be articulate about such matters.[2]

Accordingly, the Bureau conducted a small number (60) of intensive interviews.[3] The sample, stratified by rental areas in Manhattan, provided a good distribution by economic status although it was high in education. No attempt was made to secure statistically reliable data on poll questions of the Roper or Fact Finders sort (although for a few similar questions, such as what was missed in the papers, the results are the same as those from the Roper survey). Instead, the Bureau's interviews were designed to supply so-called qualitative data on the role of the newspaper for its readers, as that became evident at such a time. The results are not offered as scientific proof, but rather as a set of useful hypotheses.

In brief, then, the two polls on the subject present certain "surface facts," without knowing just what they mean. This study tries to suggest what "missing the newspaper" really means. Let us start with people's stereotyped responses to questions about missing the newspaper.

II. The Role of the Newspaper: What People Say

Because of people's inclination to produce accepted slogans in answer to certain poll questions, there is always the danger that verbal response and actual behavior may not correspond. This danger was confirmed here. Intensive follow-up interviewing of the respondents demonstrated that practically everyone *pays tribute* to the value of the newspaper as a source of "serious" information about and interpretation of the world of public affairs, although not everyone uses it in that way. During the interview our respondents were asked whether they thought "it is very important that people read the newspapers or not." Almost everyone answered with a strong "Yes," and went on to specify that the importance of the newspaper lay in its informational and education aspects. For most of the respondents, this specification referred to the newspaper as a source of news, narrowly defined, on public affairs.

However, not nearly so many people use the newspaper for this approved purpose, as several previous reading and information studies have shown. The general tribute without supporting behavior was evident in this study as well. When the respondents were given the opportunity to say spontaneously why they missed reading their regular newspaper, only a very few named a specific "serious" news event of the period (such as the Far Eastern war or the British elections) whereas many more answered with some variant of the "to-keep-informed" cliché or named another characteristic of the newspaper (e.g., its departmental features).

At another point in the interview, respondents were asked directly, "What news stories or events which happened last week (i.e., before the strike) did you particularly miss not being able to follow up?" Almost half the respondents were unable to name any such story or event whereas others named such non-"serious" news stories as the then-current Stevens murder case. About a third of the respondents did cite a "serious" news event, most of them the Far Eastern war. Furthermore, directly following this question, the respondents were asked which of a list of six front-page stories of the week before they had missed "not being able to follow up on your regular paper."[4] Here, too, only a little more than a third of the respondents said that they had missed reading about the average serious event in this list. Thus, although almost all the respondents speak highly of the newspaper's value as a channel of "serious" information, only about a third of them seemed to miss it for that purpose.[5]

In brief, there seems to be an important difference between the respondents' *general* protestations of interest in the newspaper's "serious" purposes and their *specific* desires and practices in newspaper reading. The respondents' feeling that the newspaper "keeps me informed about the world" seems to be rather diffuse and amorphous, and not often attached to concrete news events of a "serious" nature. Again, for example, take the answer to our question, "Now that you don't read your regular newspaper, do you feel you know what's going on in the world?" Fully two-thirds of the respondents felt that they did not know what was going on although, as we have seen, only about half that many had any

notion of what in the world they wanted more information about. To miss the newspaper for its "serious" news value seems to be the accepted if not the automatic thing to say.

But this does not mean that the newspapers were not genuinely missed by their readers. There were many spontaneous mentions of the intensity with which the respondents missed their papers, and several of those who missed them a good deal at the beginning of the strike felt even more strongly about it as the week wore on. The question is, *why* did people miss the newspaper so keenly. However, let us first review the several uses to which readers typically put the newspaper. This is the next step in our effort to put content into a check mark on a poll questionnaire by suggesting what "missing the newspaper" really means.

III. The Uses of the Newspaper

The modern newspaper plays several roles for its readers. From the analysis of our intensive interviews, we have attempted to construct a typology of such roles, or functions, of the newspaper. Obviously the types enumerated here, while discrete, are not necessarily mutually exclusive for any one newspaper reader. Undoubtedly, different people read different parts of the newspaper for different reasons at different times. The major problem is to determine the conditions under which the newspaper fulfills such functions as those developed here—and perhaps others— for different kinds of people. In this connection, the special value of a small group of detailed interviews lies in the identification of hypotheses which can then be tested, one way or the other, by less intensive methods. In other words, such "qualitative" interviews suggest the proper questions which can then be asked, in less detail, for "quantitative" verification.

In this section we shall mention briefly several immediate uses of the newspaper which we found in the interviews. These illustrative quotations are typical of those appearing in the interviews. Some of these uses correspond to acknowledged purposes of the newspaper, others do not.

For Information about an Interpretation of Public Affairs

There is a core of readers who find the newspaper indispensable as a source of information about and interpretation of the "serious" world of public affairs. It is important to stress, in this connection, that this interest is not limited simply to the provision of full information about news events. Many people are also concerned with commentaries on current events from both editorials and columnists, which they use as a touchstone for their own opinions. For example:

> I don't have the details now, I just have the result. It's almost like reading the headlines of the newspaper without following up the story. I miss the detail and the explanation of events leading up to the news. I like to get the story behind and the development leading up to—it's more penetrating.... I like to analyze for myself why things do happen and after getting the writers' opinions of it from the various newspapers, in which each one portrays the story in a different manner, I have a broader view and a more detailed view when I formulate my own opinion.

As a Tool for Daily Living

For some people the newspaper was missed because it was used as direct aid in everyday life. The respondents were asked, "Since you haven't been able to get your regular newspaper, have you found some things that you can't do as well without it?" Fully half of them indicated that they had been handicapped in some way. Many people found it difficult if not impossible to follow radio programs without the radio log published in the newspaper. Others who might have gone to a motion picture did not like the bother of phoning or walking around to find out what was on. A few business people missed such merchandising comments as the arrival of buyers; others were concerned about financial and stock exchange information. Several women interested in shopping were handicapped by the lack of advertisements. A few close relatives of returning soldiers were afraid they would miss details of embarkation news. A couple of women who regularly followed the obituary notices were afraid that acquaintances might die without their knowing it. Finally, there were scattered mentions of recipes and fashion notes and even the daily weather forecast in this connection. In short, there are many ways in which many people use the newspaper as a daily instrument or guide and it was missed accordingly.

For Respite

Reading has respite value whenever it provides a vacation from personal care by transporting the reader outside his own immediate world. There is no question but that many newspaper stories with which people readily identify supply this "escape" function satisfactorily for large numbers of people. Exhibit A in this connection is the comics, which people report liking for their story and suspense value. Beyond this, however, the newspaper is able to refresh readers in other ways, by supplying them with appropriate psychological relaxation. The newspaper is particularly effective in fulfilling this need for relief from the boredom and dullness of everyday life not only because of the variety and richness of its "human interest" content or because of its inexpensive accessibility. In addition, the newspaper is a good vehicle for this purpose because it satisfies this need without much cost to the reader's conscience; the prestige value of the newspaper as an institution for "enlightening the citizenry" carries over to buttress this and other uses of the newspapers.

> When you read it takes your mind off other things.

> It [the strike] gave me nothing to do in between my work except to crochet, which does not take my mind off myself as much as reading.

> I didn't know what to do with myself. I was depressed. There was nothing to read and pass the time. I got a paper on Wednesday and felt a whole lot better.

For Social Prestige

Another group of readers seem to use the newspaper because it enables them to appear informed in social gatherings. Thus the newspaper has conversational value. Readers not only can learn what has happened and then report it to their associates but can also find opinions and interpretations for use in discussions on public affairs. It is obvious how this use of the newspaper serves to increase the reader's prestige among his fellows. It is not that the newspapers' content is good in itself but rather that it is good *for* something—and that something is putting up an impressive front to one's associates.

> You have to read in order to keep up a conversation with other people. It is

embarrassing not to know if you are in company who discuss the news.

Not that I am uneasy about what's happening but I like to know about the country so when people ask you questions you don't feel dumb and silly.

It makes me furious, absolutely furious, because I don't know what's going on and all my friends who are getting the papers do know.

For Social Contact

The newspaper's human interest stories, personal advice column, gossip columns, and the like provide some readers with more than relief from their own cares and routine. They also supply guides to the prevailing morality, insight into private lives as well as opportunity for vicarious participation in them, and indirect "personal" contact with distinguished people.

One explanation of the role of the human interest story is that it provides a basis of common experience against which urban readers can check their own moral judgments and behavior (the "ethicizing" effect).[6] The requirements for such stories are that they shall be understandable in terms of the reader's own experience and that they shall be "interesting." (One respondent who read the tabloids although he disliked them remarked that "the *Times* isn't written interestingly enough" and that "*PM* is the most honest paper but should have more interesting stuff like the *Journal-American*.") From the comments of a few respondents, it appears that the human interest stories and the gossip columnists do serve something of this purpose. In fact, a few respondents indicated that they missed the newspaper because, so to speak, some of their friends resided in its pages. A few women who read the gossip columnists and the society pages intensively seemed to take an intimate personal interest in their favorite newspaper characters and to think of them in congenial terms.

I miss Doris Blake's column [advice to the lovelorn]. You get the opinions in Doris Blake of the girls and boys and I find that exciting. It's like true life—a girl expressing her life. It's like everyday happenings.

I always used to condemn the mud-slinging in the *News* and *Mirror,* and many times I swore I'd never buy them if it weren't for

the features I like. But just the other day I said to a friend of mine that I'd never, never talk like that about the papers again, because now I know what it is to be without them.

I missed them [favorite columnists] for their information, their news, their interviews with various people, their interaction with people. It is interesting to know people's reactions. If you read the background of individuals, you can analyze them a little better.

I like the *Daily News*. It's called the "scandal sheet" but I like it. It was the first paper that I bought when I came to New York. When you live in a small town and read the papers you know everybody who's mentioned in the papers. The *News* is the closest thing to them. The pictures are interesting and it makes up for the lack of knowing people.... You get used to certain people; they become part of your family, like Dorothy Kilgallen. That lost feeling of being without papers increases as the days go on. You see, I don't socialize much. There's no place that you can get Dorothy Kilgallen—chitchat and gossip and Louella Parson with Hollywood news.

IV. The Desirability of Reading

This brief review of some uses to which readers typically put the modern newspaper serves to introduce the following sections, in which we shall try to elaborate other (nonconscious) psychological reasons for the genuine interest in newspaper reading. Here again, we shall use material from our intensive interviews as illustrations.

There is some evidence in our interviews to indicate that *reading itself* regardless of content is a strongly and pleasurably motivated act in urban society. The major substitute followed during the period ordinarily given to the reading of the newspaper was some *other* form of reading, of a non-"news" character.[7] For the most part, the content of such substitute reading seemed to be quite immaterial to the respondents, so long as "at least it was something to read":

I read some old magazines I had.

I read whatever came to hand—books and magazines.

I read up on all the old magazines around the house.

I read whatever was lying around and others I hadn't had a chance to read before.

I went back to older magazines and read some parts I didn't usually read.

From such quotations one gets an impression that reading itself, rather than *what* is read, provides an important gratification for the respondents. The fact is, of course, that the act of reading carries a prestige component in American life which has not been completely countered by the rise of "propaganditis." After all, important childhood rewards, from both parent and teacher, are occasioned by success in reading and thus the act has extremely pleasant associations. Not only do the people of this country support libraries to promote the practice of reading; they also give considerable deference to the "well-read" man. In fact, the act of reading is connected with such approved symbols as "education," "good literature," "the full man," "intellectuality," and thus takes on its own aura of respectability and value.[8] And largely because of this aura, it is "better" to read something, anything, than to do nothing. For example, an elderly salesman told us:

Life is more monotonous without the paper. I didn't know what to do with myself. There was nothing to do to pass the time. It just doesn't work, nothing to pass the time.

One might speculate that in addition to the apparent desire of such people not to be left alone with their thoughts—in itself another gratification of reading to which we shall return—the Puritan ethic is at work in such cases. That is, such people may feel that it is somehow immoral to "waste" time and that this does not occur if one reads something, because of the "worthwhileness" of reading. In short, in explaining why people miss their regular newspapers, one must start by noting that the act of reading itself provides certain basic satisfaction, *without primary regard for the content of the reading matter*.

V. Another Use of the Newspaper

Within this context, what of the newspaper? Of the major sources of reading matter, the newspaper is the most accessible. It is also cheap and its contents can be conveniently taken in cap-sules (unlike the lengthier reading units in magazines and books). All in all, the newspaper is the most readily available and most easily consumed source of whatever gratifications derive from reading itself. In addition, there are some other general bases for the *intensity* with which people missed the newspaper.

References by several people to "not knowing what's going on" and to "feeling completely lost" illustrate the sort of *insecurity* of the respondent which was intensified by the loss of the newspaper:

I am like a fish out of water. . . . I am lost and nervous. I'm ashamed to admit it.

I feel awfully lost. I like the feeling of being in touch with the world at large.

If I don't know what's going on next door, it hurts me. It's like being in jail not to have a paper.

You feel put out and isolate from the rest of the world.

It practically means isolation. We're at a loss without our paper.

In some way, apparently, the newspaper represented something like a safeguard and gave the respondents an assurance with which to counter the feelings of insecurity and anomie pervasive in modern society.

This need for the newspaper is further documented by references to the *ritualistic and near-compulsive character* of newspaper reading. Many people read their newspapers at a particular time of the day and as a secondary activity, while they are engaged in doing something else, such as eating, traveling to work, etc. Being deprived of the time-filler made the void especially noticeable and especially effective. At least half the respondents referred to the habit nature of the newspaper: "It's a habit . . . when you're used to something, you miss it . . . . I had gotten used to read it at certain times . . . . It's been a habit of mine for several years . . . . You can't understand it not being there any more because you took it for granted . . . . The habit's so strong . . . . It's just a habit and it's hard to break it . . . . " Some respondents used even stronger terms.

Something is missing in my life.

I am suffering! Seriously! I could not sleep, I missed it so.

There's a place in anyone's life for that, whether they're busy or not.

I sat around in the subway, staring, feeling out of place.

The strength of this near-compulsion to read the newspaper was illustrated in other ways. Such diverse newspapers as the tabloid *News* and *Times* sold thousands of copies daily over the counter at their central offices. One respondent "went from stand to stand until I decided that it was just no use trying to get one." Another walked ten blocks looking for a paper; another went to her newsstand every night during the first week of the strike, hoping to get a paper. One young man reread out-of-date newspapers more thoroughly, "as a resort." Still other respondents admitted to reading the paper regularly even though they believed that they could spend their time more profitably:

It replaces good literature.

I usually spend my spare time reading the papers and put off reading books and studying languages or something that would better for me. . . . [Most of the paper] is just escape trash, except possibly the classified ads and I'm beginning to waste time reading them now, too, when there's no reason for it, just habit.

In this connection, the notion that knowledge is power sometimes appears. One man reported that he felt uneasy "because I don't know what I am missing—and when I don't know I worry." A few people even seemed to suggest that their being informed about the world had something to do with the control of it. A private secretary, for example, recognizing that she was "just a little cog in the wheel," remarked sadly that she "felt cut off" but that "things go on whether you know about it or not." Presumably, the regular contact with the world through the columns of the newspaper gave this person the feeling that she was participating in the running of the world. But when the newspaper was withdrawn, she realized that her little contribution was not being missed.

This sort of analysis throws a new light on the fact that about twice as many people missed the newspaper *more* as this week went on than missed it less. For such people, the absence of the daily ritual was only intensified as the week wore

on. Something that had filled a place in their lives was gone, and the adjustment to the new state of affairs was difficult to make. They missed the newspaper in the same sense they would have missed any other instrument around which they had built a daily routine.

Only a few respondents gave an affirmative answer to our questions, "Are there any reasons why you were relieved at not having a newspaper?" But even they revealed the near-compulsive nature of newspaper reading. In some cases the fascinating attraction of "illicit" content seemed to constitute the compelling factor, e.g., in the case of the middle-aged housewife who reported:

It was rather a relief not to have my nerves upset by stories of murders, rape, divorce, and the war. . . . I think I'd go out more [without the newspaper] which would be good for me. Papers and their news can upset my attitude for the whole day—one gruesome tale after the other. My nerves would be better without the paper.

The typical scrupulousness of the compulsive character is apparent in this case of a middle-aged waiter who went out of his way to read political comment with which he strongly disagreed:

I hate the policy of the *Mirror* [his only newspaper] . . . the editorial writer and also the columnist DeCasseres. It's a pleasure not to read him . . . . I didn't have an opportunity of disagreeing with Winchell.

In still other cases, the compulsion resembled an atonement for guilt feelings about nonparticipation in the war; the comments of two women respondents suggest that they had forced themselves to read the war news, as the least they could do in prosecuting the war:

Under the stress and strain of wartime conditions, my health was beginning to fail and I enjoyed being able to relax a little.

I've been reading war news so much, I'd had enough of it.

A young housewife felt that it was her duty to follow the developments of the war "for the boys—the spirit of it." And such respondents were gratified at the newspaper strike because it provided them with a morally acceptable justification for not reading the newspaper, as they felt compelled to do. Once the matter was taken out of their hands they were relieved.

VI. Summary and Conclusion

In this article we have attempted to elaborate and "deepen" the answers to typical poll questions applied to a complex set of acts and feelings. We have tried to go beyond the general protestations of the newspaper's indispensability and seek out some basic reader-gratifications which the newspaper supplies. In doing so, we have noted certain typical uses of the modern newspaper—both "rational" (like the provision of news and information) and non-"rational" (like the provision of social contacts and, indirectly, social prestige). In addition, however, we have hypothesized that reading has value per se in our society, value in which the newspaper shares as the most convenient supplier of reading matter. In addition, the newspaper is missed because it serves as a (non-"rational") source of security in a disturbing world and, finally, because the reading of the newspaper has become a ceremonial or ritualistic or near-compulsive act for many people. In this way, we have progressively tried to define, in psychological and sociological terms, what missing the newspaper really means.

Notes

1. On the necessity of "probes" to elicit the real "meaning" of straight replies, see Hadley Cantril and Research Associates, *Gauging Public Opinion* (Princeton: Princeton University Press, 1944). "Part One. Problems Involved in Setting the Issues."

2. For an experiment designed to test the intensity of news interest of people relying primarily on newspapers and of those relying primarily on radio, see Paul F. Lazarsfeld, *Radio and the Printed Page* (New York: Duell, Sloan and Pearce, 1940), pp. 246–50. In this experiment, each group of respondents was deprived of its main source of news and their reactions to this situation were studied.

3. A copy of the questionnaire appears in Appendix F, p. 309.

4. The six events were: Changes in President Truman's cabinet; developments in the Far Eastern War; the case of Mrs. Stevens; diplomatic events after the San Francisco Conference; the domestic food situation; the Langford murder case.

It should be mentioned in this connection that the strike occurred during a relatively quiescent news period. And this may have lowered the extent to which people missed reading about specific events.

5. We attempted to get at the effect of the loss of newspapers upon the informational level of the respondents by asking them to identify a series of important news stories, pre-strike and intra-strike. On the whole, they were just as well informed about the intra-strike events as about the pre-strike events. However, this is inconclusive because it does not take into account either the fullness of information about such important stories or the extent of information about middle-sized and small news stories which do not get such extensive radio coverage.

Parenthetically, it is noteworthy that apparently no rumors gained currency during the newspaper strike. We tried to investigate the circulation of rumors by asking the respondents, "Have you heard from other people about any events or happenings which you haven't heard over the radio or read about?" This question drew a complete blank. Apparently access to the radio nipped any possible rumors in the bud.

6. An extensive speculative analysis of this role of the newspaper's human interest story for the urban masses is reported by Helen MacGill Hughes, *News and the Human Interest Story* (Chicago: University of Chicago Press, 1940).

7. The data on substitute activities were secured by asking the respondent to reconstruct the *first* occasion on which he missed the newspaper, with these questions:

"How did you feel the very first time you weren't able to get your paper(s)?"

"When was it that you first missed the newspaper?"

"What did you do then instead of reading the paper?"

Such questions not only help the respondent to recall his feelings and actions but also locate them in concrete behavior. We followed up by asking about substitute activities for the rest of the week.

8. The idea of reading as a nonconscious pleasurable activity can be pushed one step further in our data. There are a few references in psychoanalytic literature which associate reading with oral activity. The fullest development of this

hypothesis appears in an article by James Strachey, "Some Unconscious Factors in Reading," *International Journal of Psychoanalysis,* XI (1930), 322–31, which deals with some oral associations with reading, some possible oral origins of the associations, and some unconscious functions of reading. Similar references appear in Edward Glover, "Notes on Oral Character Formation," *International Journal of Psychoanalysis,* VI (1925), 139. Some notes on the association between sucking activity and eye attention in the first few months of life appear in Margaret A. Ribble, *The Rights of Infants: Early Psychological Needs and Their Satisfaction* (New York: Columbia University Press, 1943), p. 29. In view of this hypothetical background, it is worth noting that one group of responses in the interviews seems to illustrate this notion. Occasionally, in their spontaneous answers to general questions about missing the newspapers, the respondents used a figure of speech in describing how much they missed the newspaper. In almost every such case, the figure was an oral one: "A glass of water . . . a cup of coffee . . . smoking . . . an appetizer to dinner (radio to the newspaper) . . . thirsty for news . . . I felt as though someone had taken candy away from me just as I was going to put it in my mouth." While these remarks are of course not conclusive, they do suggest that the act of reading may serve some persons as a socially acceptable source of oral pleasure. Thus reading material may serve the function of a pacifier for adults.

Part III

∿

The American Dream and Its Discontents
Mass Communication Theory, 1949–1968

The 1950s have gained a somewhat unfair reputation for being boring and conformist when compared with the 1960s. The 1960s did see breakouts in politics and lifestyle, but the 1950s are, on the whole, a much weightier decade in the lastingness of their intellectual and scholarly contributions. Social thinkers did not just celebrate the status quo, despite the popular imagery of white-picket fences and *Father Knows Best*, but they also asked hard and worrisome questions of the American dream. Although the 1950s formed the era of the McCarthy witch-hunts and *Leave It to Beaver,* the decade was also home to the Beat poets, Elvis, and Little Richard. J. D. Salinger's novel of adolescent angst, *A Catcher in the Rye,* was published in 1951. Sloan Wilson's novel, *The Man in the Gray Flannel Suit* (1955), and its film version (1956), portrayed the quiet desperation of middle management and suburban life. William Whyte's *The Organization Man* (1956), an exposé of the inner life and culture of bureaucracy, is the sociological equivalent to Wilson's novel. Thanks to the GI Bill, the universities swelled with new students, who found in sociology and existential philosophy sudden relevance for their experience. The explosion of television into American living rooms in the 1950s, the decline of radio programming from a general to a specialized medium, and the retreat and reorganization of Hollywood after the Paramount decision in 1948 all formed a new media environment. In 1959, art critic Laurence Alloway noted the new complex of devices that had moved from the battlefield to the American home: "The missile and the toaster, the push-button and the repeating revolver, military and kitchen technologies, are the natural possession of the media—a treasury of orientation, a manual of one's occupancy of the twentieth century." His insight—that the media provide orientation to the twentieth century—is the engine of this book.

In the 1950s, like social thought in general, mass communication research wavered between affirmation of the status quo and criticism of it. This vacillation was expressed both institutionally and intellectually. Sociology, the home discipline for much earlier mass communication study, moved in twin directions, becoming more professional and technical on the one hand and more public on the other. Robert K. Merton and Paul Lazarsfeld represented the former strand, David Riesman and C. Wright Mills the latter. A second and distinct political axis ran between Cold War consensus and simmering dissent. Schramm and Riley's piece on propaganda technique in the Korean War is a fine illustration of the Cold War's mobilization of social science in the fight against the "Reds" (p. 310). The effects tradition solidified its identity and continued in work by Katz and Lazarsfeld (p. 358) and by Wright (p. 454), among others; but Riesman, Mills, Breed, and Gerbner (all included here) found ways to ask big questions about media and society. Vance Packard's *The Hidden Persuaders* (1957) more directly attacks the media, especially television and advertising, for using depth psychology to twist our desires into the service of buying. What Edward Bernays thought was a public service, the engineering of consent, Packard attacks as subliminal persuasion. Packard was not a social scientist, nor was he steeped in critical theory, and in many ways his analysis hearkens back to the muckraking propaganda analysis of the 1930s; but it was a characteristic period piece about the dangers of the mass media during a time when the Korean War had made *brainwashing* a household word.

More widely, unease about abundance—a world of Chevrolets and TV dinners—marked American social thought. A famous analysis of the downside of the culture of postwar prosperity came in John Kenneth Galbraith's *The Affluent Society* (1958), which argues, among other things, that the act of consumption did not satisfy but rather stimulated demand, thereby creating a cycle of "dependence." The more people had, the more they wanted. Aldous Huxley made a similar point in "The Arts of Selling," from his collection of essays on contemporary life, *Brave New World Revisited* (1958). The portrait of the "free world" in 1950s American social thought is not an oasis of freedom and plenty but a society nervous about its welfare, quietly simmering with the quest for deeper meaning and liberation among youth, people of color, and women. Rosa Parks refused to get up from her seat in the bus in 1955, symbolically launching the civil rights movement with the *Brown v. Board* decision of the U.S. Supreme Court in 1954. Around the same time, a frustrated housewife named Betty Friedan was taking notes on "the problem without a name," which she would make famous in *The Feminine Mystique* (1963), one chapter of which offered a critical anatomy of popular women's magazines. The 1950s in the United States was not simply a happy time of reaping the fruits of having emerged victor from the rubble of World War II, but it was more a time of jitters—about the Reds, riches, rock 'n' roll. Had the American dream been fulfilled but at the cost of the American soul? Historian Daniel Boorstin asks precisely this question in the subtitle of his first book, *The Image: Or What Happened to the American Dream* (1961).

One contemporary label for this bundle of worries in the 1950s was *mass society theory*. This so-called theory had many precursors. In a sense, it goes back to Plato's denunciation of *hoi polloi* (the many) and the Roman satirist's complaint that all the people need is "bread and circuses" (Giner 1976; Brantlinger 1983). Daniel Bell (p. 364) points out the perennial quality of mass-society worries, suggesting that every age has worried about its direction and its decay. Fair enough, but the 1950s had more proximate sources for their worries. One was a native mass-society theory, found already in the social thought of the progressive era. Robert Park's dissertation, *The Crowd and the Public*, written in 1903 for his German doctorate, contrasted two social formations that would remain key themes in American social thought. Lippmann's works on the public weighed it in the balance and found its intelligence wanting, and Dewey's *The Public and Its Problems* (1927) describes an America torn up by "steam and electricity" whose community soul had been lost. C. Wright Mills's chapter on "the mass society" (p. 387) centrally engages with themes from Dewey and Lippmann, whom Mills struggled with from graduate school onward. The specter of democracy turning sour and breaking up into a society of masses is an old concern within

American thought, raised in one way by Founding Father James Madison in the *Federalist Papers* and noted by the distinguished French visitor Alexis de Tocqueville in his *Democracy in America*. The coming of television simply gave a new urgency to old themes.

Another source for mass-society thinking was imported from Germany by émigré intellectuals in exile, such as Hannah Arendt, Theodor Adorno, Max Horkheimer, and even Paul Lazarsfeld, all of whom came of age intellectually in the Weimar era (1919–1933), one of the most productive, controversial, and dark eras of social thought at any time in history (Kaes, Jay, and Dimendberg 1994). Fritz Lang's classic film *Metropolis* (1927) has continued to provide imagery of just how bad things could get in the future, and much of the imagery and argument deployed in Weimar Germany, echo in the 1950s (and today). Martin Heidegger's *Being and Time* (1927), for instance, perhaps the most influential work in twentieth-century philosophy, portrays the public realm as a place of stupid talk and meaningless noise. Modern society for Heidegger is the rule of *das Man*, a coinage that can be translated as the "They-self" or as the "Anonymous-anyone." Heidegger's point is that it is increasingly difficult to have authentic experience or identity in a time of chatter, and many have followed him in his assessment of modern society.

These older germs of mass-society theory found fertile soil in the postwar era, with its unprecedented prosperity, near Third World birthrate during the baby boom (1945–1964), and criss-crossing currents of the fads and fashions of popular culture (see Meyersohn and Katz, p. 409). Over the course of the 1950s, an average of five million television sets were sold per year in the United States, one of the fastest technological diffusions in modern history (rivaled perhaps only by the cell phone in recent years). The television set was a central symbol of postwar abundance and postwar worry that seemed to reactivate all the ancestral worries. Soldiers had died to make the world free . . . for television? Peggy Lee sang, "Is that all there is?" Conformity, consumption, and mass communication had clear dark sides, and thinkers in the 1950s grappled with all of them.

Riesman's 1950 *Lonely Crowd* (p. 293) helped give an identity to the decade by telling a story of a successful society that had lost its bearings. Riesman is a fascinating figure who has not yet been given his full place in the history of media studies in the United States. A lawyer who clerked for Justice Brandeis of the Supreme Court, Riesman first made his name as a theorist of group defamation in the early 1940s while a law professor at the University of Buffalo. Erich Fromm, a member of the Frankfurt School, was both Riesman's analyst and an important intellectual influence. In its footnotes and intellectual proclivities, *The Lonely Crowd* shows a considerable debt to Frankfurt theory. The book is a good example of works of sociology that got picked up in the periodical press and generated wider fame. From the Lynds' *Middletown* to Myrdal's *American Dilemma* and on to the works of C. Wright Mills, Riesman fits into a lineage of those using sociology as a platform for literate commentary on current social life. *The Lonely Crowd* was a bestseller that gave thinking people an account of their age. To say that Americans had lost their souls exaggerates his thesis, but, like Leo Lowenthal, Riesman observed how Americans were losing the Protestant ethic of what he called *inner-direction* (a gyroscope) in favor of *other-direction* (a radar). Though he did not intend these terms as directly evaluative, they were often received as such, with other-direction being an explanation of why Americans were so likely to look to their neighbor or to the media for guidance and approval, instead of drawing on their inner resources.

A vignette from Ralph Ellison's novel *Invisible Man* (1952), considered by many the greatest American novel from the second half of the twentieth century, shows us the other-directed mind at work. The young African American hero has recently arrived in New York City from the South and is about to go hunt for a job. In his mind's eye, he envisions himself "in a dapper suit of rich material, cut fashionably, like those of the men you saw in magazine ads, the junior executive types in *Esquire*. I imagined myself making a speech and caught in striking poses by flashing cameras, snapped at the end of some period of dazzling eloquence." Of course, none of these fantasies come true in the novel, but the habit of imagining ourselves in the ways others and media images portray us is something we all instinctively understand today. Riesman was one of the first to diagnose this widespread attitude (though it has roots in Cooley's notion of the looking-glass self and Hegel's dialectic of master and slave). Though Riesman always had a conservative streak, which got more pronounced in later years (he later described himself as "a fierce Cold Warrior" in the 1950s), he always considered himself "counter-cyclical," going against the grain and the fashions of the moment. *The Lonely Crowd* is by no means a celebration of American democracy or the benefits of mass media. Whereas Katz and Lazarsfeld (p. 358) find that interpersonal relations offer evidence for the ongoing health of American society against the influence of the media, Riesman gives it a different spin: "The mass media are the wholesalers; the peer groups, the retailers of the communications industry."

Riesman taught for over a decade at the University of Chicago (1948–1959), and much in his analysis in *The Lonely Crowd* is reminiscent of older Chicago themes of communication and community. Two of these themes show up in essays by Kurt Lang and Gladys Engel Lang and by Donald Horton and Richard Wohl. In their study of General MacArthur's parade through Chicago in 1953, the Langs (p. 328) found something curious: the crowds on the street got only a passing glimpse at the great man whereas the masses at home watching on television experienced a coherent event. The Langs made a couple of twists on older assumptions. First, media were not a distortion or a secondhand approximation of experience (as Lippmann had argued), but rather the very means by which an image of reality could be provided whole. Second, the live public, bumping elbows on the street in a classic Chicago picture of milling interaction, was secondary to the home television audience, for whom the event—including the cheering crowds themselves—was staged. In a television age, the notions of society as interaction and of the public as secondary contact, so central to Park and Burgess or Cooley, turns out to be stranger than they had thought.

Horton and Wohl's study of parasocial interaction (p. 373) likewise added a new wrinkle to the old confidence that new means of communication could enable interaction at a distance. It fits into a line of studies about the role of mediated interpersonal relations, especially interaction with celebrities, including Helen MacGill Hughes's study of human interest stories (p. 118), Lowenthal's biographies in popular magazines (p. 188), Merton's dissection of Kate Smith's fans (p. 215), and Berelson's discovery that people missed "social contact" with celebrities during the newspaper strike (p. 253). Charles Horton Cooley had optimistically written in 1909 that the "give-and-take" of new media would allow for more democratic forms of audience participation. However, what Horton and Wohl found in the social relations of broadcasting was a simulation of give-and-take, a pretend intimacy at a distance that radio actively exploited (and that political figures exploited as well, as Leila Sussman shows in her study of fan letters to FDR; p. 401). They showed that people in the listening audience were actively encouraged to regard celebrities as their close friends. Very much in the tradition that goes back to Blumer's Payne Fund movie study (p. 91) and Jane Addams's nervousness about popular theater (p. 25), Horton and Wohl were not as comfortable with fantasy media as factual media. They did not explicitly treat parasocial interaction as a psychopathology, but they clearly leaned in that direction. Their article was published in *Psychiatry*, and the term *parasocial* sounds a bit like *paranoia*: in the first, one thinks that all the people out there are friends; in the second, that they are all enemies! Like Lang and Lang, Horton and Wohl took symbolic interactionist insights in a new direction; both suggested that the immediate physical presence with other people was not the only context in which communication could take place. Mass society, held together by media fantasies and virtual relationships with such figures as General MacArthur and the "Lonely Gal," was a different kind of social creature than the overlapping bundle of urban neighborhoods that the Chicago sociologists had first studied.

This displacement of face-to-face interaction by media fantasy was understood in different ways by different thinkers in the 1950s. The negative viewpoint was stated by the Dutch psychiatrist Joost Meerloo. The title of his 1956 book says it all: *The Rape of the Mind: The Psychology of Thought Control, Menticide, and Brainwashing*. This book is a screed against the machine age and totalitarianism, in the name of liberation from delusion, and it reads like a lesser version of Huxley's *Brave New World Revisited*. We mention it here not as a forgotten classic but as one example of that recurring genre in American social thought: the antimedia jeremiad. The media, according to Meerloo, are a "barrage of stimuli," full of "gibbering maniacs whose voices never stop." Because of the technology that invades our minds, "conversation is becoming a lost art." "What technology gives with one hand—easiness and physical security—it takes away with the other. It has taken away affectionate relationships between men." Mechanical proxies such as form letters take the place of human contact. "Is the ultimate result," he asked, *"living by proxy,* experiencing the world only from the movie or television screen, instead of living and laboring and creating one's own?" (Meerloo 1956, 66, 209–211). Such concerns would likewise animate Mills's chapter "The Mass Society" (p. 387), also from 1956, though the concern for life lived at second hand goes back to Ralph Waldo Emerson and William James.

Another position on media's meaning was perhaps most strongly advocated by Marshall McLuhan, especially in his 1960s writing. As one can still see in his 1950s writings (p. 338 and p. 353), McLuhan started as a high-culture critic of modernist literature. McLuhan had a healthy dose of antimodern longing for the old times, before what T. S. Eliot, an important early influence on McLuhan, called "the dissociation of sensibility." Rather than amputating our human capacities, as Meerloo and many others had argued, the media, as McLuhan came to posit, actually amplified and extended them. McLuhan found in the new audiovisual media, in all their diversity, a redemption from both the sensory restriction and the dry desiccation of a print-based culture. Media were neither the end nor the dematerialization of human contact; they were the harbinger of a new kind of worldwide fraternity, in the "global village." Where Riesman and others half-mourned the loss of the old Protestant, literate character, one self-contained and self-determined, McLuhan said, in effect, good riddance. He welcomed the sound and fury of a wider range of sensory experience, and soon he attained status as a celebrity prophet of youth culture and of the delights and dangers (mostly the delights) of the media.

McLuhan's fellow Canadian, forerunner, and influence, Harold Adams Innis, had a more dour outlook on modern communication. While McLuhan saw electronic media as restoring human civilization, at a higher turn of the spiral to the sensory and social wholeness of oral cultures, Innis was far less certain. Because Innis died in 1952, he never saw the full flowering of electronic culture, but it seems unlikely that he would have celebrated new media the way McLuhan did, had he lived longer. Innis took mass communication as extending the logic of print culture with what he saw as a mechanical impersonality and lack of interaction. Both McLuhan and Innis loved the tradition of speech and human contact, in much the way of James Carey, who drew his bearings partly from both men. For Innis, its epitome was ancient Athens. For McLuhan, history's pinnacle was the thirteenth century, with its soaring cathedrals, stained glass, chants, incense, and fully equipped media sensorium, appealing to sight, sound, smell, and motion in a manner that print culture shattered (as argued in his *Gutenberg Galaxy* [1962], discussed later in this introduction).

The 1950s also saw a series of important studies that focused on the workings of the media as industries and cultural institutions. The way had been prepared by such works as Upton Sinclair's *The Brass Check* (1919) and James Rorty's *Our Master's Voice* (1934) (both written by concerned citizens rather than academics), as well as by the Frankfurt School. The 1950s saw a reemergence of a theme explored in Lippmann's *Public Opinion* (1922) and a good deal of propaganda analysis, namely how the internal workings of media organizations affected the culture and audiences they produced. Hortense Powdermaker's *Hollywood: The Dream Factory* (1950; p. 280 in this reader) applies an anthropological interest to the curious practices of strange people within the Hollywood industry. Dallas Smythe (p. 318), who had worked as an industrial analyst for the Federal Communications Commission (FCC) during the 1940s and is now remembered as one of the founders of critical academic research on the political economy of media institutions, began the academic segment of his career at the University of Illinois, where his leftist politics were eyed warily by the government (with aid, Smythe later alleged, from his colleague Wilbur Schramm). Two other important left-leaning figures also got a start at Illinois in the 1950s and 1960s, George Gerbner (p. 434) and Herbert Schiller (p. 480), the latter of whom arrived at Illinois in the early 1960s, long enough to overlap briefly with Smythe. Meanwhile, two former students at Columbia, Warren Breed (p. 417) and Thelma MacCormack (p. 457), extended some of the critical theoretical veins found in trace elements in Merton and Lazarsfeld.

A final issue in the 1950s was the fate of the field that Paul Lazarsfeld once called "communications research." In a 1959 symposium in *Public Opinion Quarterly* (p. 440), Bernard Berelson pronounced it dead, or at least withering away. In a sense, he was right. He focused on the passing of an older generation; Lewin was dead, Hovland was dying, and Lazarsfeld and Lasswell were doing other things. Berelson was thinking of the interest, sparked by the Rockefeller Foundation and carried further by government-sponsored research during World War II, in communication, propaganda, and persuasion, in which he had played an important part, both at Columbia and the University of Chicago (the latter of which was soon to close down its interdisciplinary Committee on Communications). Operating from a different vantage point was Wilbur Schramm, perched at a shiny new Institute for Communication Research at Stanford University and concerned less about the intellectual vitality of communications than its institutional stability. With the passing of the 1940s guard, Schramm represented a new king in the land who would help make communication research both a recognized field and a department within American universities. (The boom worldwide came in the 1990s). Like almost any year in the early 1960s, 1959 was a turning point, though the real changes that gave birth to our field today came in the 1970s and early 1980s.

Berelson's 1959 coroner's report was paralleled in the world of public policy in 1961 when FCC commissioner Newton Minow denounced American television as a "vast wasteland" (p. 440). In retrospect, the speech by the idealistic thirty-five-year-old Kennedy-appointed lawyer signaled the abandonment of the new medium of television by the intellectual class and indexed a cultural divide that has not been healed since. In the early 1950s, the television industry was based in New York City and was able, thanks in part to its small and elite regional audience, to flourish with significant intellectual and artsy programming, such as theatrical dramas (while also dishing up a healthy dose of Milton Berle and roller derby). By the time of Minow's address, the television industry, with the exception of its news divisions, was in the process of relocating to Los Angeles and had been widely discredited by the quiz show scandals of the late 1950s. Through the rest of the 1960s, American television did its business without the guidance or harrassment of East Coast eggheads. This is in striking contrast to the British case, in which intellectuals of the caliber of Raymond Williams maintained a critical but active relationship with television (likewise for the case of Israel, where the introduction of television was overseen by Elihu Katz). Though recent historians argue that 1960s television is not as placid or dumb as it might appear (Bodroghkozy 2001), the industry in that decade clearly continued to mine the status quo, compared to the much more convulsive 1970s and 1980s, when cable, video, demographics industries, and sharply changed cultural tastes all pushed the medium in new directions, whose aftershocks we are still feeling.

The 1960s and Beyond

The 1960s of popular memory are hardly the 1960s of actual history. LSD, outdoor rock concerts, love-ins, and protest were certainly spectacular events late in the decade, but much of the decade before 1968 looks like the 1950s. White men in positions of power wore crew cuts, white shirts, and black army-issue glasses; indeed, this was even the style of Malcolm X and other political radicals. The 1960s (as popular culture perceives them) did not happen until 1968 or 1971 or maybe even later, as a series of books, movies, and television shows all actively did their bit to shape memory of this curious time. LSD-guru and former Harvard psychology professor Timothy Leary once quipped that if you can remember the 1960s, you weren't there. He was at least partially right in that much of how we regard the 1960s was manufactured after the fact, by people with memories to fill in or axes to grind.

The larger media and historical context of the 1960s shaped thought about mass communication. In 1963, the Kennedy assassination and funeral was one of the first televised media events in American history, thoughtfully analyzed by political scientist Sidney Verba (p. 472). In 1964, the Supreme Court case *Times v. Sullivan* provided the press with reinforced legal protection to investigate and report on public figures. This decision, with its ringing declaration that public debate must be "robust and uninhibited," was part of the background that gave rise to the kind of investigative journalism and culture of inquiry that helped topple President Nixon in the Watergate scandal. The words "robust and uninhibited" are very much creatures of their times; they reflect a faith in letting it all hang out that stretches from the highest court in the land to the drugs, sex, and rock 'n' roll of popular memory. In 1967, President Lyndon Baines Johnson signed into law the Corporation for Public Broadcasting, belatedly giving government support to a medium whose educational efforts had floundered in a blatantly commercial media system. "At its best," Johnson said (1967), "public television would help make our nation a replica of the old Greek marketplace, where public affairs took place in view of all of the citizens."

Such superheated confidence was not in the same spirit as Newton Minow's 1961 denunciation of television as a "vast wasteland," but it served as a reply to such concerns. So did the *Surgeon General's Report into the Causes and Prevention of Violence,* a massive effort that mobilized the talents of many of the country's best and brightest social psychologists and that was finally published in 1972 as the five-volume set, *Television and Social Behavior* (see Rowland 1983). The report did not focus solely on media violence but on violence in general, with television being one key culprit. The small screen did indeed bring home violence, and not only in cartoons and Westerns but also through the televised coverage of the 1968 Democratic Convention, in which bloodied protestors confronted the Chicago police, and coverage of the war in Vietnam, famously (though perhaps not accurately) called the first "living-room war." The 1969 moon landing was one of the first internationally televised media events, witnessed live by millions of viewers around the world. Finally, in the 1969–1970 television season, A. C. Nielsen, the company that provided the broadcasting business with its chief commodity, audience ratings, changed their ways of counting the television audience to be more sensitive to demographics, causing a vast shift in programming practices. The 1960s program *The Beverly Hillbillies*, which still holds the record for four of the ten largest television audiences in American history, was quickly canceled, since it was discovered to have been attracting the "wrong" kind of audience all those years (too young, too old, too rural, too poor). A large audience alone was no longer one guaranteed to be desirable to advertisers (Meehan 1986). Here we find one of several sources for the beginning of the end of the high-water days of national mass television in the United States.

Intellectually, the 1960s are harder to characterize than any other decade we cover in this reader. Though it is always dangerous to offer short summaries of totalities as chaotic as ten years of history, our other decades have at least definable moods. The 1920s have a certain hard-boiled disillusionment, reflected in the acid critiques of democratic ideals by people such as Walter Lippmann, who were chastened by World War I and who sensed the irrelevance of so many progressive dreams. The 1930s breathe the exhilaration of the new, refracted through a sense of world crisis—the idea that modern communications media offered something unprecedented, wonderful, strange, and even foreboding, as in Cantril and Allport's analysis of radio, Mumford's study of the telephone and film, or Sapir's overview of communication in general. The 1940s see a maturation of scientific purpose in communication research with a mixed optimism about the power of communication for the public good and the potential insight of theory to explain the world, along with an even more intense foreboding about what had been loosed on the world, as in Horkheimer and Adorno or Wirth. The 1950s are marked by a mix of battened-down Cold War consensus and jitters about the fallout of the postwar boom and images of a mass society of lonely people connected with media, as Katz memorably put it, but not with each other (a line perhaps borrowed from Dwight Macdonald).

Many things transpired in American social thought about mass communication in the 1960s, but it is perhaps most distinctly remembered as "the development decade." Modernization theory was of course much bigger than communication research, but it was one of the leading narratives, as reflected in our selection from Daniel Lerner (p. 426). In many ways, modernization was *the* establishment social theory of the 1960s. It announced where the world was headed; it gave a blueprint for foreign policy; and it gave communication—literacy, the free press, and national broadcasting systems—a starring role in the story. The theory was in part a story about America's place in the world—the ideal end point and agent for the rest of the world. "Development" was an anticommunist antidote. Industrialization, urbanization, and a cosmopolitan sensibility would sway Third World masses against the seductions of the Marxist–Leninist utopia. Walt Rostow (1916–2003; a special advisor to Presidents Kennedy and Johnson) and Daniel Lerner were enthusiastic propagators of this doctrine. Lucien Pye, Everett Rogers, and Wilbur Schramm, among many others, proposed models of the role of communication in modernization and flew around the world consulting with governments on issues such as water purification, birth control, and antidiarrhea campaigns. There is more than a little hubris in this vision, as anticolonial thinkers and even Rogers (1976) himself later point out. In *The Stages of Economic*

Growth: A Non-Communist Manifesto (1960), Walt Rostow explains the mission of America, the single path of development (consumerist democracy), and the authority of social scientists to know and govern the world. Not incidentally, the modernization theorists are the people who brought us the war in Vietnam. Yet even such a buoyant thinker as Rostow was not above a spot of 1950s melancholy. After all the modernization is over, there remained the question of "what to do when the increase in real income itself loses its charm? Babies, boredom, three-day week-ends, the moon, or the creation of new inner, human frontiers in substitution for the imperatives of scarcity?" (Rostow [1960] 1971, 16; note the Kennedy-esque rhetoric of a new frontier.) Modernization theory and mass society theories were twins separated at birth: one told other nations how they could repeat America's happy past; the other gave warnings about America's ambiguous present and future.

The consensus faith in the civilizing mission of the American empire was waning by the late 1960s and was largely lost by the 1970s (George W. Bush seems eager to rebuild it today). Two characteristic early voices critical of the notion of communication-as-benevolent-development were Herbert Schiller (p. 480) and Herbert Marcuse (p. 485). Schiller assaulted the commercialism of American media as not only a domestic issue but one that reached to the entire planet and to outer space as well. Marcuse saw the violence of the war in Vietnam as intimately tied to the psychosocial habitus of a society of consumption. Whether the potent Freudian–Marxist broth he concocted is still persuasive is less an issue than the withering critique he gave to many of the most closely held confidences of postwar modernization theory.

The mass culture debates continued in the 1960s, giving rise to the thoughtful British response by Stuart Hall and Paddy Whannel, *The Popular Arts* (1964), and to *Mass Culture Revisited* (1971), edited again by Bernard Rosenberg and David Manning White—and now showing the effects of the 1960s, with articles on *Easy Rider,* television violence, hippie values, and radical teachers. Much of the writing of Marshall McLuhan served as an affirmation of mass culture. The flash and clatter of electronic media were not a barbaric yawp, he said, but a harbinger of transformed consciousness, a return to the synaesthetic sensibility of the middle ages or to the oral wholeness of primitive people, compared to the boringly linear consciousness of modern literate rationality. The media also anticipated the possibility of new kinds of social life, leading to a term he made famous, the *global village,* a happily retribalized world community. The French coined the term "mcluhanisme" to refer to an attitude of acceptance to popular culture rather than to any specific doctrine. McLuhan's star—one of the more impressive supernovae of the 1960s—was hitched to a wide-ranging cultural interest in communication as cure and disease, but it had only a spotty impact on the formation of the academic field. Though we believe there is something in his work of lasting value, he behaved like a lot of other 1960s gurus—prophets who saw things no one ever had before, who flattered youth with the sense that they were on the cusp of historical transformation, and whose thought is now largely forgotten save as period pieces: Timothy Leary, Abbie Hoffman, or Grace Slick. John Lilly, the drug-endorsing biologist who studied communication with dolphins, and Gregory Bateson, the cybernetically inclined biologist (whose work still has lasting value as well), are more examples of the free-floating intellectual, buoyed by the media they were in part theorizing, but not anchored to the academic field of communication studies.

Despite Berelson's eulogy, the effects tradition kept sputtering along in the 1960s. Perhaps "sputtering" is unfair if one considers the massiveness of the *Surgeon General's Report,* which showcased both the political power and intellectual limitations of that tradition by scrupulously being unable to specify, in any satisfying way, the social effects of television, save the not very exciting finding that violence can be dangerous for some children under some conditions. Effects research had always had big political and economic stakes, but the *Surgeon General's Report* represented a new level of politicization. There was rigor and care to be found in many specific effects studies but with none of the excitement of intellectual breakthroughs of earlier decades. Effects research in the 1960s was decidedly what Thomas Kuhn would call "normal science."

In retrospect, the most lasting and important work of the 1960s came in 1962, a year of astonishing international convergence on questions of communication and a year that certainly serves as an intellectual watershed for communication theory (unlike the much more heralded 1968, when many were too busy turning the world upside down to write down important ideas). The year 1962 saw the publication of a remarkable array of books, many of them still influential and all of them minor classics, each in some way a philosophical or historical treatment of communication problems. With the exception of Everett Rogers's *Diffusion of Innovations,* a synthesis of research originating in rural sociology about how ideas are adopted and diffused through societies, few of them were written by people who identified themselves as communication scholars:

- *How to Do Things with Words,* by Oxford philosopher John Austin, though given as lectures years earlier, was first published in 1962. Its detailed analysis of "speech acts" inspired much work in philosophy of language, and its notion of "performatives" (speech acts such as "I promise" that both state and enact at the same time) plays a central role in the feminist theory of Judith Butler and in studies of talk in interaction.
- *Language and Thought* (1934), by Russian linguist and semiotician Lev Vygotsky, is translated and published in English for the first time. Vygotsky famously claimed that "the central fact of our psychology is the fact of mediation," and though he did not mean it in the sense of mass media, he was very interested in the "cognitive technologies" (his term) that people use to make sense of their worlds.
- *Structural Transformation of the Public Sphere,* by critical theorist Jürgen Habermas, was published in German in 1962 (though not translated into English until 1989). Its study of the historical, sociological, and philosophical bases of the democratic public is a remarkable synthesis of critical theory with American work, including the effects tradition and dissidents such as Mills and Riesman, and it has been one of the most important books in media studies in the past decade and a half.
- *La Pensée Sauvage,* by French anthropologist Claude Lévi-Strauss, was officially a study of how nonliterate people think about plants (a field known as ethnobotany), but its ambition was nothing less than to explain the structure of the human mind. Indeed, its French title captures this ambiguity well, meaning both "savage thought" and "the wild pansy"; it was translated as *The Primitive Mind.* In the Durkheimian tradition of French sociology, Lévi-Strauss found, in the minutiae of classifications, clues to the underlying structure of human psychology, thus tying cultural categories to cognition.
- Eric Havelock, *Preface to Plato,* was a study of the cultural consequences of the coming of writing to ancient Greece. A wellspring of orality studies, with ties to both Innis and McLuhan, Havelock's book suggests that ancient Greek thought could not be understood apart from its media-environment-in-transition. Plato's dialogues, to take his prominent example, are a literary form and mode of philosophy that are possible only as a compromise between a dying oral tradition and a rising practice of writing. This book is perhaps the most explicit about a theme that marks many of the 1962 books: an interest in orality, the voice, and how writing and speech interact in consciousness and culture.
- Another key text for the development of orality studies was Marshall McLuhan's *Gutenberg Galaxy.* Apart from his 1940s dissertation, this was his most traditional work of scholarship.

The book's title is inspired by McLuhan's name for the cultural complex—of linear reason, nationalism, and individualism—spawned by the printing press. McLuhan offered one of the first extended studies of a theme that went back at least to Cooley: the central role of print media in modern history. As with most of his works, it was quirky in format and argument, and it showed a central debt to Harold Innis, McLuhan's former colleague at Toronto. It was a book declaring the obsolescence of the book medium, a work of scholarship assembled like a surrealist or cubist collage.

- Hugh Dalziel Duncan's *Communication and Social Order* is a forgotten classic that surveys a remarkable range of social theory and philosophy for the sake of theorizing communication. Duncan, in an eclectic spirit pioneered by his hero Kenneth Burke, strives to encompass everything relevant to communication theory in the realm of social theory and philosophy.

- Thomas Kuhn's *Structure of Scientific Revolutions* must rate as one of the most influential books of the late twentieth century. Though it might not seem at first to be a treatment of communication, it is relevant in at least two ways. First, it insists on the social nexus of knowledge production—that is, on the importance of exchange and relationships among researchers. Second, his famous and beleaguered notion of *paradigm* is clearly borrowed from the study of language and perhaps owes something to Wittgenstein's notion of language games. Kuhn, like some sociologists of knowledge before him, helped people to understand science as constituted in the communicative relationships of scientists, not as a pure quest for truth.

- *Communications,* by British cultural theorist and literary critic Raymond Williams, was one of the first wide-ranging popular overviews of media in the modern world, though in this respect it fit with the tradition of work by Cooley, Sapir, Mumford, and Innis. Perhaps not of the lasting importance of his *The Long Revolution* from 1961, *Communications* is still significant for articulating principles of communication as a coherent field of inquiry. Published as a Penguin book, it helped publicize the notion of such a field.

- *The Port Huron Statement,* by Students for a Democratic Society, was a founding document for the New Left. A remarkable social critique for a group of undergraduates, it deals with communication in its call for a participatory democracy in which dialogue and encounter would replace abstraction and interest-group lobbying. It is integrationist in racial politics and anti-imperialist in foreign policy; it is for nuclear disarmament and aggressive foreign aid (though with a strong dose of modernization theory); it is often environmentalist, open to utopian thinking and idealism, and supportive of responsible (i.e., nonmilitary) economic growth and the eradication of poverty; and it is in favor of educational reform. C. Wright Mills and John Dewey's voices clearly echo throughout.

Indeed, as the last entry suggests, much of this work marks the birth of a new—or perhaps reemergent—kind of democratic imagination and politics. The annus mirabilis of 1962 deserves to be brought out of the attic and appreciated as a key moment in twentieth-century social thought about the meaning of communication. Little of this work, however, influenced the institutional formation of communication studies as an academic field. The gods left us with Schramm and company when the greats were pondering our topic in other lands.

Brief Thoughts on Mass Communication Theory since the 1960s

The 1970s, the birth time of the field's current orientation, made the history of communication and media studies more important. Many things of importance occurred; we offer only an inadequate summary here of a few. One was a *Methodenstreit*, a political fight about different kinds of research methods. The clash between qualitative and quantitative tools was often not just as a clash of techniques but a clash of worldviews and a political battle between humanists and scientists. Today the notion that counting is conservative and that storytelling is radical seems rather quaint, but in the 1970s it was part of a pitched battle to overthrow the legacy of Cold War social science. Lazarsfeld's contrast between critical and administrative research helped set the agenda for such debates, and he took on new weight as a symbolically pivotal figure.

The field and its history also became a topic of scholarly discussion in the 1970s: Gitlin's attack on Lazarsfeld (1978) was followed by another salvo by Hall (1982), against the ideology and ethos of modernization theory in American communication research. More nuanced historical work by Kurt Lang (1979) and Hanno Hardt ([1979] 2002) sought to show the deep history of German American exchanges and influences in theorizing communication. James Carey (1989b), in turn, urged greater attention to the American roots of the field, in John Dewey and the progressives. As fields develop, they also imagine and reimagine their histories, and the 1970s just barely started to wriggle free from the field's 1950s narratives, invented by figures such as Schramm, Katz, and Lazarsfeld.

The 1970s saw an international revival of mass communication social theories that had prevailed in the 1930s and 1940s. The decade witnessed a renaissance of cultural Marxism, including the translation of works written between the two World Wars by thinkers such as Lukács, Gramsci, members of the Frankfurt School, and by more recent Marxist thinkers such as Louis Althusser. French theory started to be translated, bringing such eminences as Barthes, Derrida, Foucault, and Lacan to a North American audience. Though French structuralism and poststructuralism had, at first, a glancing effect on North American media studies, they did offer an impressive new array of tools for understanding all texts, including mediated ones. British work came to be more and more appreciated, as it was also a conduit for introducing critical Marxist work to an American audience.

Revisionist theories of media effects arose in the 1970s, which tried to rehabilitate notions of strong effects in subtler and empirically demonstrable ways: agenda setting, spiral of silence, knowledge gap, cultivation (cultural indicators), and third-person effects among them. These were no mere throwbacks to the high hopes of the progressives and to the high horrors of the propaganda critics; rather, they were efforts to think more subtly, and in a sense, explore territories sited by Lazarsfeld but never fully mapped by him or his team. Noelle-Neumann's "spiral of silence" is a good example of continued German American cross-fertilization, and Gerbner's cultural indicators project follows loosely, as Gerbner sees it, in the tradition of Frankfurt critical theory. Both offer critical theories of society, with Gerbner from the Left and Noelle-Neumann from the Right, combined with extensive and sometimes disputed empirical findings.

Many of the intellectual struggles in 1970s media research were centered on the past and its ongoing presence and meaning. The same is true today. The past will not go away; the dead will not leave us alone. Better than simply assuming that older texts have vanished into a well-deserved oblivion, the faith upon which this reader is predicated is the continuing relevance of the past and its ability to surprise, upset, and teach us. Happy reading!

42

Industrialism and Cultural Values

From *The Bias of Communication* (1950)[1]

Harold A. Innis

With his disciple Marshall McLuhan, Harold Adams Innis (1894–1952) was Canada's seminal theorist of communication. First named "Herald" by his devout Baptist mother, much of Innis's career was indeed devoted to questions of proclamation and communication, though he never became a minister, as she had hoped. As an economic historian, he did innovative research in showing the role of staples—such as fur, cod, and lumber—in creating social networks at a distance, a process so important to Canada's history. Toward the end of his life, he started to reinterpret his work explicitly in terms of communication. He defined "media" broadly, to include paper, parchment, canals, roads, speech, books, or any other means of bearing intelligence. Innis was one of the leading academics in Canada and a prominent figure at the University of Toronto, where he taught from 1920 until his death of cancer, in 1952. He received his doctorate in political economy at the University of Chicago in 1920, where he met a graduate student named Mary Quayle, who would be his wife, domestic partner, and (it is increasingly clear) his intellectual partner as well (Black 2003).

In this selection, Innis is featured in his full force, as a non-Marxist critic of modern life and communication. His preference for oral interaction over fixity is clear in his view of writing as dangerous to the health of civilization, of time as being swallowed up in space. Innis had an intense moral vision that, with his sweeping knowledge of world history, led to a potent diagnosis. In his view, modern civilization had dangerously lost its moorings, trading the stability of time for the empire of space and happily rolling toward its self-destruction. His wryly understated final sentence captures both his mode of analysis and his critical vision: "Each civilization has its own methods of suicide" (see Blondheim 2003).

We must all be aware of the extraordinary, perhaps insuperable, difficulty of assessing the quality of a culture of which we are a part or of assessing the quality of a culture of which we are not a part. In using other cultures as mirrors in which we may see our own culture we are affected by the astigma of our own eyesight and the defects of the mirror, with the result that we are apt to see nothing in other cultures but the virtues of our own. During the twentieth century machine industry has made it possible to amass enormous quantities of information evident in encyclopaedias, histories of civilization, and quiz programmes. The concern with the study of civ-

ilization in this century is probably a result of the character of our civilization. Certainly such studies reflect our civilization. Spengler in *The Decline of the West* could not have been unaffected by the position of Germany, nor could Toynbee free himself from the traditions of English-speaking countries, nor could Kroeber escape the influence of the United States and the obsession with the objective qualities of science. I shall assume that cultural values, or the way in which or the reasons why people of a culture think about themselves, are part of the culture.

It is perhaps a unique characteristic of civilization that each civilization believes in its uniqueness and its superiority to other civilizations. Indeed this may be the meaning of culture—i.e., something which we have that others have not. It is probably for this reason that writings on culture can be divided into those attempting to weaken other cultures and those attempting to strengthen their own. The emphasis of St. Augustine on original sin implied an attack on those representing the secular state, as the emphasis of John Locke on the *tabula rasa* was the basis of an attack on ecclesiastical hierarchy, and the work of Spencer on progress was the basis for the claim to supremacy of Anglo-Saxons. "Reason is and ought only to be the slave of the passions and can never pretend to any other office than to serve and obey them"—a statement as true of this quotation and of Hume's writings as of others. Perhaps the obsession of each culture with its uniqueness is the ultimate basis of its decline. Dean Inge has remarked that civilization is a disease almost invariably fatal unless the cause is checked in time. The Hindus and the Chinese have survived by marking time.[2]

A brief survey of cultural development in the West may indicate the peculiarity or uniqueness of culture and elements which make for duration and extension. Cultures will reflect their influence in terms of space and in terms of duration. How large an area did they cover and how long did they last? The limitations of culture, in point of duration, are in part a result of the inability to muster the intellectual resources of a people to the point where stagnation can be avoided and where boredom can be evaded. The history of boredom or stagnation has yet to be written but it might well include the story of the ostracism of Aristides the Just on the ground that the Greeks became weary of hearing him called the Just. Hume wrote that "when the arts and sciences come to perfection in any state, from that moment, they naturally or rather necessarily decline and seldom or never revive in that nation where they formerly flourished." Intense cultural activity is followed by fatigue.

The capacity to concentrate on intense cultural activity during a short period of time and to mobilize intellectual resources over a vast territory assumes to an important extent the development of armed force to a high state of efficiency. Cultural activity, evident in architecture and sculpture, capable of impressing peoples over a wide area, is designed to emphasize prestige. It becomes an index of power. A concern for continuity, the biological limitations of the patriarchal system as a basis for dynasties, and the difficulties of maintaining a high cultural level over a long period of time will involve an emphasis on types of architecture calculated to reflect a control over time as well as over space. The pyramids were an index of power over time but dynasties represented by them were displaced and in turn new dynasties concentrated on new monuments to enhance their prestige. Old capital sites scattered along the Nile valley are a memorial of the demands of successive dynasties for prestige. The Egyptian Empire was a tribute to their success. But such monuments as capitals with tombs, palaces, temples, and sculpture were expensive and did much to bring the Empire to an end. Political power reflected in capitals was supported by such cultural activities as writing evident in successive bureaucracies.

Civilization in the Tigris and Euphrates valleys developed along lines similar to that in the Nile but solutions to the problem of time appear to have been reached before the problem of space and organized force became acute. Religious communities with hierarchical organizations characterized Sumerian civilization. Though architecture dependent on bricks made from the clay of the delta regions became important, writing on clay was a basis for communication, administration, and trade. Organized force represented by Sargon of the Akkadians brought religious communities under control and with access to writing made possible a vast empire. With religion based on writing Sumerian culture proved sufficiently strong to throw off control of a foreign ruler and to support a capital at Ur for a limited number of dynasties. In turn this culture came under the control of fresh conquerors and a new capital of palaces and temples emerged at Babylon. The effectiveness with which control over time reflected in religion was fused with control over space was evident in the long period in which Babylon persisted as a capital under the Kassite dynasty.

The success of organized force was dependent in part on technological advance, notably, in early civilizations, in the use of the horse, the crossing of the light African horse with the heavier Asiatic horse, the introduction of horse riding and cavalry to replace horse driving and chariots, and the use of iron as a substitute for bronze. The Hittites with the use of iron succeeded in building an empire with a capital which emphasized sculpture and architecture but it was checked on the south by Babylon and on the north and west by the Greeks with their control over the sea at Troy. They were followed by the Assyrians who exploited technological advance in warfare are made fresh contributions to its development. With a new capital at Nineveh they succeeded in offsetting the prestige of the Nile and of Babylon and establishing an empire to include the civilizations of both. Prestige was secured not only by architecture and sculpture but also by writing. The library became a great instrument of imperial power and set an example which has influenced the history of the West until the present time. The concern of the Assyrian Empire with the collection of Sumerian documents for the library at Nineveh has been paralleled at Alexandria, Rome, Paris, Berlin, London, Moscow, and Washington. In Canada we are attempting to follow in our own way at Ottawa. The Assyrians attempted to maintain their prestige not only by libraries but also by development of a reputation for war-like ferocity, paralleled in this century. Failure of the Assyrian Empire was in part a result of the tenacity and diversity of civilization in Babylon and Egypt.

Persia succeeded where Assyria had failed by emphasizing the importance of a single capital by architecture and sculpture and of small capitals of districts or satrapies governed from a centre. The beginnings of the principle "divide and rule" were evident in recognition of the religions of Babylon and Egypt and encouragement of the religion of the Hebrews at Jerusalem. But as in the case of Assyria the political organization of Persia was unable to meet the demands of continuity.

Political organizations determined to an important extent by the limitations of armed force and characterized by centralized power emphasized the capital city and left their impress on cultural activity in architecture and sculpture. They emerged in land areas, from the Nile valley to Asia Minor. They provided a shelter for the development of communication facilities and for the growth of trade such as that of Aramaeans on land and of the Phoenicians on the Mediterranean. Communication was subordinated to the demands of centralized power in religion and in political organization; it was characterized by the use of the eye rather than the ear. The scribe occupied a strategic position in centralized bureaucracies.

In attempting to use other civilizations as mirrors by which we may understand our own we are exposed to much greater dangers in study-

ing Greek culture and its successors since our own culture has been profoundly influenced by it. Civilizations of the Nile and Asia Minor had a limited influence on peoples along the north shore of the Mediterranean. Minoan civilization was an attempt to encroach on the sea which failed in the face of opposition from the north. Mycenean civilization on the mainland proved more adaptable but in turn succumbed. The Greeks escaped the centralizing tendencies of river civilizations with their effects on capitals, architecture, and sculpture and on writing with its implications for bureaucracy. In their settlements on the islands and along the coast, the Greeks emphasized cultural aspects suited to their needs. The oral tradition rather than writing provided a basis for the epic and for literature designed to unite scattered groups in a consciousness of Greek culture. The alphabet borrowed from the Phoenicians was given vowels and adapted to the demands of speech. The ear replaced the eye. With the spread of writing the oral tradition developed fresh powers of resistance evident in the flowering of Greek culture in the sixth and fifth centuries. A concern with the Eastern concept of the capital was apparent in the age of tyrants in the sixth century notably in Athens and in the fifth century notably in the Athenian Empire. But as the epic and tragedy reflected the character of Greek civilization so too did architecture and sculpture. "The statues of the classic artists are the relics of ancient dancing" (S. H. Butcher). "After art had been toiling in India, in Persia, and in Egypt to produce monsters, beauty and grace were discovered in Greece" (Sir James Mackintosh). "Nothing over-much" was a maxim which implied distrust of specialization in all phases of cultural life. Greek culture was destroyed in the growth of writing and of individualism in the latter part of the fifth century.

The vitality of Greek culture was evident finally in the flowering of military skill in the conquests of Philip and Alexander. Greek culture with its political organization reflected in the city state came in contact with concepts peculiar to early civilizations and compromised with them in the Hellenistic kingdoms. The capital to a limited extent was restored. In Egypt the Ptolemies established a new capital at Alexandria and created a new deity to destroy the influence of the old capital at Thebes, and built up a library to exploit the limitations of Athens and to offset the influence of Babylon. At Pergamum, the Attalids developed a capital with a library designed to offset the prestige of Alexandria. The Seleucids were eventually defeated by a revival of Persian civilization.

In the east, along the north coast of the Mediterranean, Rome came under the cultural influence of Greece, and after destroying Carthage, which had inherited the commercial traditions of Phoenicia, extended her influence to Hellenistic kingdoms to the east, and to Spain and Gaul in the north and west. The influence of Egypt was evident in the deification of the ruler, in the decline of the Roman Republic and the emergence of the Roman Empire, and in the increasing centralization of a bureaucracy. The attempt to offset the influence of Persian civilization was evident in the orientalization of the emperors and eventually in the establishment of Constantinople as a capital to take advantage of the support of Hellenistic culture including Christianity. The inroads of the barbarians were followed by the decline of Rome and the rise of Constantinople as a political centre. The difficulty of subordinating cultural capitals with their roots in earlier civilizations reflected in the religious controversies of the period led to the emergence of Rome as the religious capital of the West, and to the spread of Mohammedanism in the East. With Mohammedanism new capitals arose at Baghdad and at Cordova in Spain. Access to a medium other than papyrus and parchment, namely paper, enabled these centres to build up libraries and compelled Constantinople to take a fresh interest in learning. In the West the Holy Roman Empire became an institution designed to strengthen the prestige of Rome. In turn the political influence of Rome led to the increasing prestige of Paris as a theological centre. The attempt of the papacy to recapture Jerusalem and the Eastern church in the Crusades was followed by the growth of small Italian city republics notably at Venice, Florence, and Genoa. The final collapse of Constantinople and of the Byzantine Empire in 1453 following the use of artillery brought new efforts to regain prestige in the East at Kiev and in the West at Paris.

The capitals of the northern Mediterranean and Europe while reflecting the influence of the capitals of the Nile and the Tigris and Euphrates valleys were dominated by the oral tradition of Greece. The absolute monarchy of Egypt and the East became the Roman emperor, the English Tudors, Louis XIV, and the czars of Russia, and its influence was evident in the courts of Rome and Constantinople, London, Paris, and St. Petersburg. The city state of Greece was revived in the city republics of Italy and Germany and in the Renaissance, and its influence softened the tyranny of the courts. In some sense the culture represented by the courts had solved the problem of time and space. The Byzantine Empire persisted as a unique achievement in duration, and while the size of its territory fluctuated, its achievement in the solution of problems of space was scarcely less remarkable. Paris became the cultural centre of the West notably under Louis XIV and the influence of the French court was evident in the England of Charles II, in the courts of Russia, and indeed wherever culture in the Western sense raised its head. Antwerp, Amsterdam, London, Berlin, St. Petersburg, Moscow, and Washington were influenced directly and indirectly by the dominance of Paris. French culture persisted after the Revolution and after the occupation of the recent war, and survived the state. Like Paris, London became more dependent on cultural influence than on political organization as is evident in the British Commonwealth of Nations.

After this brief survey of earlier civilizations we can attempt an appraisal of the possibilities in terms of duration and extent of our own civilization. We have emphasized the significance of communication in determining the characteristics of earlier civilizations and of changes in methods of communication. The discovery of printing in the middle of the fifteenth century implied the beginning of a return to a type of civilization dominated by the eye rather than the ear. With printing and an increase in the use and manufacture of paper German cities strengthened their position and facilitated a break from the church in Holland, Germany, and England. Their advance was registered in the concern for the word of the Bible, the Reformation, and the rise of Protestantism. The full impact of printing did not become possible until the adoption of the Bill of Rights in the United States with its guarantee of freedom of the press. A guarantee of freedom of the press in print was intended to further sanctify the printed word and to provide a rigid bulwark for the shelter of vested interests. Printing assumed mass production or reproduction of words and once it escaped from the pattern of the parchment manuscript it compelled the production of vast quantities of new material including material to meet the demands of science and technology. Improvement of communication hastened the development of markets and of industry. The Industrial Revolution followed the printing industry and in turn in the nineteenth century, with the use of steam power in the manufacture of paper and of printed material, supported rapid expansion of the printing industry.

We are perhaps too much a part of the civilization which followed the spread of the printing industry to be able to detect its characteristics. Education in the words of Laski became the art of teaching men to be deceived by the printed word. "The most important service rendered by the press and the magazines is that of educating people to approach printed matter with distrust."[3] But there are unmistakable signs that ours is a civilization which partakes of the character of all civilizations in its belief in its uniqueness and superiority over other civilizations. We are all familiar with the claims of the printing industry to the effect that it has ushered in a new and superior civilization. No other civilization, we are told, has enjoyed our advantages. Democracy, education, progress, individualism, and other blessed words describe our new heaven. At this point the water becomes swift and we are in grave danger of being swept off our feet by the phenomenon we are describing. We are in danger on the one hand of losing our objectivity and on the other hand of being placed under arrest. Freedom of the press has been regarded as a great bulwark of our civilization and it would be dangerous to say that it has become the great bulwark of monopolies of the press. Civilizations have their sacred cows. The Middle Ages burned its heretics and the modern age threatens them with atom bombs.

In contrast with the civilization dominated by Greek culture with its maxim "nothing in excess," modern civilization dominated by machine industry is concerned always with specialization which might be described as always in excess. Economics, beginning with Adam Smith, and indeed other social sciences have an obsession with specialization. Specialization and industrialism support an emphasis on equality. An interest in material goods which characterized the Scottish people, represented notably in Adam Smith, has been followed by an attitude described by Samuel Butler: "All progress is based upon a universal innate desire on the part of every organism to live beyond its income." The concern with specialization and excess, making more and better mousetraps, precludes the possibility of understanding a preceding civilization concerned with balance and proportion. Industrialism implies technology and the cutting of time into precise fragments suited to the needs of the engineer and the accountant. The inability to escape the demands of industrialism on time weakens the possibility of an appraisal of limitations of space. Constant changes in technology particularly as they affect communication, a crucial factor in determining cultural values (for example, the development of radio and television), increase the difficulties of recognizing balance let alone achieving it.

The cultural values of an industrial society are not the cultural values of other societies. The equation of ethical values between cultures is possibly more difficult than the equation of other values, though Professor V. Gordon Childe has described the implications of cultural change in such fields of abstraction as mathematics. The outburst of rich artistic activity in Greece coincided with a decline in the status of women. Dean Inge has reminded us that the extreme sensitivity of modern civilization, for example in the attitude toward cruelty to animals, and the extreme insensitivity toward unbelievable cruelty to human beings have synchronized with the complete collapse of spontaneous and unconscious artistic production.[4] The ugliness of English and American towns and the disappearance of beauty accompanied the invention of machinery and great industries. Von Eicken's thesis that the master key to history lies in the conclusion that human movements provoke violent reactions has much to support it. Roman imperialism created by intense nationalism ended by destroying the nationality of rulers and subjects. The nationalism of the Jews left them without a country. The Catholic church renounced the world and became the heir of the defunct Roman empire. Universal suffrage heralded the end of parliamentary government. The more successful a democracy in levelling population the less the resistance to despotism. The interest of the French Revolution in humanity kindled the fire of patriotism and nationalism in Spain, Germany, and Russia.[5]

Anthropologists, notably Pitt-Rivers, have explored the dangers of the intrusion of one culture on other cultures. Historians have commented on the unsatisfactory results which followed the importation of the parliamentary system to the European continent. The disasters which overtook North American civilization following the coming of Europeans have been described at length. The disturbances which have characterized a shift from a culture dominated by one form of communication to another culture dominated by another form of communication whether in the campaigns of Alexander, the Thirty Years' War, or the wars of the present century point to the costs of cultural change. The impact of Point Four on other cultures, the clash of so-called "backward" and so-called "forward" countries involve such unpaid costs as the enormous loss of life directly through war and indirectly through cultural change. The spread of communism from France to Russia and China is a further illustration of the instability of Western civilization.

Stability which characterized certain periods in earlier civilizations is not the obvious objective of this civilization. Each civilization has its own methods of suicide.

Notes

1. A paper read on December 30, 1950, at the meetings of the American Economic Association at Chicago.
2. W. R. Inge, *Diary of a Dean, St. Paul's 1911–1934* (London, 1950), p. 195.
3. *Further Extracts from the Note-Books of Samuel Butler*, ed. A. T. Bartholomew (London, 1934), p. 261.
4. See his essay in *The Legacy of Greece*, ed. R. W. Livingstone (Oxford, 1923), p. 40.
5. Inge, *Diary of a Dean*, pp. 208, 210.

43

Emerging from Magic

From *Hollywood: The Dream Factory* (1950)

Hortense Powdermaker

Hortense Powdermaker (1900–1970) was probably the first cultural anthropologist to study the mass media. A student of Bronislaw Malinowski and an associate of Edward Sapir, she did field work in New Ireland, Mississippi, Rhodesia—and Hollywood! She had long-standing interests in race relations and psychiatry, among other areas, and she taught at Queens College before spending her last years at the University of California, Berkeley.

This selection is remarkable in several ways. First, it is a forerunner to the slow turn in the field of anthropology, from distant and "primitive" cultures to familiar and complex ones. Second, it is an example of an analysis of the culture industries, and it is one that emphasizes an important finding: that the way that the artifacts look (in this case, film) is a reflection of how their production is socially organized. Powdermaker gives us a production-of-culture study that illustrates how the practices of the industry shape the final text. Finally, Powdermaker uses the concept of magic, something once associated only with primitive or childish thinking, as an explanatory device for the modern world. In this she is in the distinguished company of Sigmund Freud, Max Horkheimer, and Theodor Adorno, and, more recently, Carolyn Marvin (1999), among many others.

Hollywood bustles with frenzied activity, and makes use of the most modern technology. Yet at the same time it gives the impression of being only half awake in its slow emergence from a dim prehistoric past of illusions, fears, and magical thinking. More strikingly than any other section of our society, it seems to span all the ages of mankind. In it, too, are represented all the ages of individual man, from infancy to adult.

In any human society the presence or absence of a particular body of ideas limits and affects the development of behavior as much as do technology and environment.[1] Therefore to comprehend the social organization in which movies are made and to understand the behavior of people in Hollywood, it is necessary to know how they think. All peoples, whether in the South Seas or in Hollywood, try to make the world intelligible to themselves, and to exercise some control over it. The particular ideology of any society shapes its institutions and molds the behavior of its members.

Since its beginning, the human species seems to have been aware that not all phenomena are of the same order. But the division between the animate and inanimate has not always been clear. In order to make the inanimate intelligible, primitive man often ascribed human attitudes and motives to the nonhuman world. (This is called "animism.") It was easier for him to do this than to imagine different processes or to admit his ignorance. As Ruth Benedict has pointed out: "Throughout man's history it has been the mechanistic theory of the universe that he has found fantastic, not the animistic one."[2] So, in many primitive societies, human qualities have been attributed to fishes, birds, trees, rocks, and ancestral spirits, and gods. Men could therefore use towards them attitudes and techniques, such as cajoling, scolding and making gifts which has been found effective in dealing with human beings, and expect similar responses. For instance, primitive peoples sometimes denounce their ancestral spirits and at other times propitiate them with gifts, to gain their help.

Animistic thinking is not restricted to primitive man. Many folk tales of historical civilizations show a confusion between the animate and the inanimate and our own society still exhibits attenuated forms of the same thing. Most everyone who has owned an old car has had the experience of talking cajolingly to it when it mysteriously stalls. A child who hurts himself by falling over a rug may hit the rug in retaliation, as if the rug could feel a spanking. In Hollywood, however, there appears to be a much greater confusion between the animate and inanimate than in the larger society, although it works in an opposite manner from that of primitive man's animism. Hollywood people seem more at home with the inanimate, with property which can be measured in dollars and which can be manipulated to increase itself, than they are with human beings. They therefore attribute the characteristics of what they know best to the unknown— which is, for them, the world of human beings and the art of storytelling. These become intelligible as they take on the characteristics of the known—property—and become functional as they contribute to the goal of wealth. The psychological process appears to be the same one by which primitive man makes his environment intelligible by projecting what he knows about human beings onto his canoe and ancestral spirits.

Much of Hollywood thinking has the characteristics of this inverted form of animism and, as we have seen, the history of movies helps make this possible: props were early used to produce emotional effects. In the legitimate theater, on the other hand, actors were important from the beginning, and elaborate stage settings came later. In literature, the art of storytelling preceded the invention of printing, which has never superseded it. But what the men who founded the movie industry knew best was property, the accumulation of which was their highest goal. Artists and the art of storytelling were strange to them.

Among primitive peoples, magic is one of the techniques used to control supernatural and other forces which they do not understand. The Stone Age agriculturalists in the Southwest Pacific were well aware through observation and experience that the ground had to be cleared before planting their taro, that the plants should be a certain distance apart, that weeds must be pulled out, and that a fence built around the garden would help keep out wild pigs. All these were natural elements controllable by hard work and foresight. But there remained the uncertainties of weather and other factors beyond human control, which also influenced the crop. So before starting a garden, men made magic to coerce or cajole these elements to bring them success. The Melanesians did not think the magic eliminated the need for weeding, or that weeding made the magic unnecessary.

Deep layers of magical thinking still remain in the unconscious of modern men, and sometimes on the conscious level, too. But most of us no longer view magic as an operational tool. We may unconsciously or consciously long for a magical helper and for miracles; but we know that writing a book, getting a job, or making a garden depends on hard work, knowledge, ability and planning, rather than on coercing the supernatural; we usually act on this awareness. We may vaguely feel that disease can be the work of an evil spirit or a punishment for sin, but when we become ill we consult a doctor, who utilizes the latest scientific developments in medicine. Over the centuries of man's development, magical thinking has receded more and more into the unconscious and become less and less a conscious instrument to achieve his ends. The growth of modern civilization has been due, in part, to a constant widening of that area of our thinking based on rational knowledge and experience of reality, and to a corresponding shrinking of the supernatural sphere. It is unlikely that either area will ever disappear, but the proportional significance of each in our conscious thinking and behavior changes considerably.

In Hollywood, however, there appears to be a greater use of magical thinking on a conscious level and as a tool for achieving success than elsewhere in the modern world. The concepts of breaks to secure success, so emphasized in Hollywood, belongs to the supernatural sphere. Most successful people, no matter what their occupation, believe that luck has played some role in their lives. But they usually emphasize far more the contribution of hard work, perseverance, training, or of particular gifts and aptitudes. In Hollywood the quite considerable difference in the degree of emphasis on luck is important, for according to the familiar philosophical principle, a sufficiently large quantitative difference may produce a qualitative one. Almost everyone in

the movie industry from front office executives, producers, actors, directors and writers, to those who play minor roles, such as assistant directors and agents, attribute their own and other people's success to forces lying beyond their control in the world of chance. This belief indeed corresponds with reality as most Hollywood people have known it. An executive without previous training or experience in the art or business of storytelling makes a colossal fortune because he had the breaks; perhaps the breaks for him consisted of coming into the industry when it was very young and success easy. A producer becomes a millionaire and important in the industry, because he had the breaks of knowing in childhood, or later on, an executive. An actress becomes a star because a producer chanced to notice her and gave her a role in a picture which happened to be a hit. A writer has the luck to work with a sympathetic producer, or to hit on a very clever gimmick, or to get credit for the script of a movie which makes big profits for the studio. The profits themselves are believed to be the result of luck, too, since whether or not an audience will like a movie seems unpredictable. Most people who live in Hollywood are wholly committed to this philosophy and regard it as an inherent and necessary part of movie production.

They do not think movies could be made differently.

This type of thinking, whether in New Guinea or Hollywood, produces appropriate attitudes and behavior. The Melanesian puts his faith in coercing the supernatural through using a magical formula, which consists of a spell and rite handed down by tradition. Hollywood people have their formulas too: stars, gimmicks, traditional plots. Just as the Melanesian thinks failure would result from changing the form of a spell, so men in Hollywood consider it dangerous to depart from their formulas. Each group can point to the times it worked and conveniently forget or rationalize the other occasions. The Melanesian placates hostile supernatural forces through a series of taboos; Hollywood attempts to appease its critics and enemies with the MPAA Code. Primitive men often make sacrifices of whatever they consider most valuable—food, animals and occasionally human beings—in order to court the favor of the supernatural. In Hollywood money is more highly valued than anything else and this is sacrificed in large amounts.

It is earnestly believed that the more money spent on a picture the more successful it will be. *How* the money is spent—on the highest paid stars, on the most lavish settings, or on a series of expensive writers, or whether there are realistic returns for it, does not make too much difference. Knowing the right people in Hollywood is also not too unlike the ritual behavior prescribed in family, clans, and other social groups among primitive peoples. In each case the ritual behavior is important: not only the maintaining of one's own status, but the very life of the people, and of society, is believed to depend on it.

In most societies in which supernatural elements are important in attaining success, some form of divination is practiced, because foreknowledge is one way of control. In parts of East Africa, the entrails of chickens are used for divining the future, while among the Karen of Burma it is the gall bladder of a pig; in Hollywood polls are used to determine the mysterious tastes of the audience. Will they like this or that title and this or that plot, with this or that star? The methods now used to determine, a year in advance, the tastes of potential audiences is not too different from trying to foretell the future by examining the spots on an animal's liver.

This comparative *tour de force* can, of course, be carried too far, but success in Hollywood appears to be more closely related to the realm of the supernatural than it does for primitive men. The average producer seems less clear in his thinking about those elements in movie production which are knowable and those where chance plays a role than the Stone Age man is in his occupations. The latter does not confuse the practical work necessary to making his canoe seaworthy with the need for magical rites and taboos. But studio executives have depended more often on formulas, breaks, and following the Code than on the quality of script, directing and acting. But enough good movies (which have also been profitable) *have* been produced with intelligent planning to indicate that the prevailing pattern need not be the only one.

Hollywood seems as wasteful of talent and brains as primitive peoples are neglectful of many of their natural resources. Valuable minerals often remained hidden in the earth which Stone Age men inhabited, because they were ignorant of their presence or use. Natural resources in Hollywood are its talent and brains as well as the technological assets. The industry makes good use of the latter. But the human properties of the artist, his sensitivity, his imagination, his ability to create, are utilized in only a very limited way. Most people have more intelligence and ability than they use, but in Hollywood the discrepancy between potentialities and actualities is more glaring than elsewhere.

The two major characteristics of Hollywood thinking, the belief in chance or breaks, and the confusion between the human and nonhuman, dominate every concept of creativity there. Creativity is not thought of as human in Hollywood. Human sensitivity to the joys and sorrows of life, human imagination, an awareness of human limitations, the decencies of human relations are relatively unimportant, nor is their portrayal regarded as the part of man's capacity to think and plan. As the original founders of the industry, the executives tend to think of themselves as its totemic ancestors, omniscient and omnipotent. They boast about how they manipulate the emotions of millions in the audience, causing them to tense with excitement or to laugh with relief. Even more important is the executive's control and manipulation of everyone connected with production, from star to script girl. The front office knows in some mysterious way—through instinct, they say—everything about script writing, about casting, about cutting, and what the audience will like. Primitive man conveniently forgets the times his magic does not work, and the executives also do not remember when their instinct has been wrong.

The emotional ferment of creativity is an inner one, and there is excitement, with stimulation and satisfaction, in the creative expression of ideas and fantasies. No matter how collaborative or how many contributors, behind every human creation is an idea in one individual's mind. Nor does it spring full blown into being as an instinctual act: preceding it are training, discipline, and work. The artist's intuition is quite different from the showman's instinct. The former rests on deeper than average sensitivity to human beings and to the complexities in the world about him. The artist's reaction is personal and individual, and it is this which he tries to express. He works primarily to please himself, experiments with new ideas and new forms, and leaps ahead into the unknown, not sure of the outcome. When he succeeds he has an inner satisfaction, and he likewise enjoys any honor and payment which society gives him.

The average movie is produced in an entirely different way. The excitement has nothing to do with genuine creation, but is all on the outside. The producer strides up and down his office at the frequent story conferences, phone calls are made at midnight, the front office or star demand changes which precipitate crises, and so on and on. Similarly, in many movies the feeling of excitement is limited to external factors, such as noise, music, props falling, thunderstorms. Rarely does the star's passive face or acting give any indication of an inner emotional ferment. Underlying the studio's bustle and excitement is the tension of the unanswered question, "Will the public like it?" Everyone is aware of the enormous costs of production. Will a large profit be made after these are covered? In this situation, it is rare for writer or actor or director or any other artist to feel the satisfaction of creating something which pleases him and which he respects. He is a cog in the machine.

Although the idea for a film originates in the mind of one person, its execution and final consummation is the result of collaboration with many others, who may be equally creative in their own ways. But collaboration takes different forms. In the production of most pictures, the relationship of one individual to another is direct, one personality impinging on the other in terms of their respective power statuses. In the production of a few pictures, however, the bonds between the individuals are those of mutual connection with a creative activity, and this objective relationship is allowed to take precedence over the power one. Suggestions from writer, executive, director, actors, are discussed in terms of their logic and appropriateness to the film, and the results of the discussion are not foreordained in terms of who has the most money or power. One idea may be recognized as better than the other, or out of the discussion may evolve a totally new idea, containing elements from the several points of view. When problems are discussed in this way and no one person always has the final word, the creative process functions collaboratively. The resulting film is the joint product of many minds, even though the initial idea was conceived by one. Any creative collaboration is of this type. A good teacher-student relationship, at any level from kindergarten to university, is oriented to the objective of knowledge and understanding, rather than to the teacher's using his authority to impose his ideas

on the student, and the latter's critical remark or contribution is as much part of the teaching as are those of the learned lecturer. Actually, all human relationships, including the intimate family ones, are apt to be easier if the ties of the individuals to each other are based on a mutual objective interest, rather than exclusively on age, sex or power difference.

In any factory or business, management does not want too much interference from its employees. Although men on the factory assembly line want some say over conditions of work, such as hours and salaries, most of them take for granted that they work rather mechanically under the foreman's directions, and this does not impair their efficiency. But writers and other artists do their best work only when they have some freedom to try and please themselves. Working on the assembly line and following orders do not bring good results and are basically inefficient from the point of view of profits. Hollywood is an industry, but daydreams are its product and these cannot be successfully produced as if they were cans of beans.

Although Hollywood production has factory characteristics, the general atmosphere pervading the studios is no more that of a factory than it is of a creative human enterprise. Rather it is that of the gamblers' den. The psychology of the gambler has been well described.[3] Outstanding characteristics of all gambling are the importance of chance in determining success or failure, and the lack of emphasis on skill. The neurotic gambler, as Dr. Greenson points out, is driven by unconscious needs and cannot stop. "It [gambling] has an irresistible quality: the tension has to be satisfied by action, not thinking, and immediately, not by postponement."[4] Winning, for the neurotic gambler, means not only the jack pot, but proof that he is favored by Fate, and a token of power.[5] He mistakes his yearnings for omnipotence, for feeling that he is omnipotent. Yet he cannot quite repress his doubts, and so he is always looking for signs to confirm his shaky belief. This longing and belief in omnipotence, is thought to be a regression to early infancy since infants, too, are thought to have a feeling of unlimited omnipotence.[6] "It is this feeling which the neurotic gambler unconsciously is attempting to recapture."[7]

Winning in the Hollywood gamble means being connected with a movie which is a box-office hit. This is then regarded both as a sign of having been favored by Fate and as a token of omniscience and omnipotence. The award of an Oscar is another such sign. It is easy to understand that when an actor, writer, or director dares to question an executive's decision, he is by implication attacking the executive's belief in his own omnipotence, and the reaction is accordingly violent. For to permit omniscience to be questioned would destroy it, and any such attempt therefore arouses great anxiety.

Just as the neurotic gambler cannot stay away from his game, so also there are many people in Hollywood who cannot leave, who cannot imagine any existence apart from it. Successful or unsuccessful, lucky or unlucky, they must remain. Nor is their gambling limited to the making of movies. The same people spend much of their free time gambling with cards and betting on horses. Gambling is for them a way of life, just as acting is for the actor.

This is the atmosphere in which movies are made and which is thought to be inherent and essential to their production. Most people do not imagine that movies could be made differently, any more than Stone Age man can imagine that irrigation might replace rain magic. Since crops do grow and many movies do make money, magic appears to work a sufficient number of times to make giving it up seem risky and dangerous.

Men usually think that their particular way of life is inevitable and such beliefs are strengthened when the way also answers their neurotic needs. It appears easier for primitive men to replace rain magic with irrigation, once they have learned about it, than it is for many Hollywood people to give up their claims to omniscience and omnipotence, and to substitute thinking. Perhaps they mistake their deep emotional needs for the inherent conditions of movie making. Perhaps they oppose change not just for economic reasons, but because the *status quo* suits them on a deep and personal level.

Movie production does give many men the opportunity to live out their deep personality needs for gambling and power, and in so doing to make great fortunes. Yet they can never be satisfied because their needs are insatiable. No matter how large the profits, how many Oscars, they must go on constantly striving to prove to themselves that they are supermen. A pause in the activity—and questioning voices might be heard; the only

way to silence these voices is through further activity.

All gamblers and others with pretensions to omnipotence and omniscience are scared men. For Fate can, and sometimes does, stop smiling; the pretense can never be complete. The only way out is to continue gambling—when not on pictures, then on horses and cards.

While Hollywood provides a situation which meets the needs of gamblers, the conditions for creativity which would satisfy artists are lacking. The artist, as well as the gambler, has deep personality needs. An artist wants to use his talent and training in expressing as well as he can his ideas, his fantasies, his interpretations of life. It is believed that the daydreams which he expresses in his work signify repressed wishes, and that the public acceptance and approval of them reduce his anxieties.[8] In Hollywood, however, the writer does not express his own fantasies, but those of a producer or front-office executive. Even when permitted to use some of his own imaginative thinking, he knows in advance that the script will be changed by other writers, producers, stars, directors, and anyone else with power. He knows that at the end his contribution will probably be distorted beyond recognition. To work as an artist, a gifted director must have a script in which he believes, but he usually has to direct whatever is handed him, whether or not he even respects it. For the actor, it is important that he respects both his role and the script, but he rarely has any choice over either, nor is it possible for him to have a variety of roles and not to become stereotyped. He needs likewise a director who can help him make his role an integrated part of the whole, but rarely does he get this help. The artist can rarely even work toward this goal. Other men, front-office executives and producers, have in their omniscience and omnipotence taken over the artist's functions while the artists have replaced their own values with those of the businessmen.

There is nothing inherently bad or wrong about artists making millions of dollars. Money is not necessarily the root of all evil, as the old proverb says. It can be the source of much pleasure and human good. But the making of money has a nature of its own and follows certain laws. Creativity has another nature and follows other laws. They are not interchangeable. The nature of creativity is such that it is defeated if anything is substituted for its goal. If an artist in expressing himself succeeds also in giving form to the inarticulate dreams or needs of many people, and is later rewarded with a million dollars, that need not affect him, if his creative drive is strong. But if he works on something he does not believe in or respect, *in order* to make a million, then he and his work deteriorate. It is the change of goals which is important. Very few gifted people are always at their best. Everyone has his off periods when he is not up to his own standards—whether giving a lecture, writing a book, composing a score, or performing an experiment in the laboratory. But it is a very different matter for either artist or scientist deliberately to lower his standard in order to make a lot of money. Corruption of both work and man is inevitable, and if it extends over any length of time there is no going back. The artist who thinks he can beat the game, stay in Hollywood and clean up his million, and then return to his own creative works, is usually fooled. There are well-known examples of writers who finally shook the dust of many years of Hollywood from their typewriters, only to turn out mediocre plays and novels which resemble far more the movie scripts on which they had made their million, than their pre-Hollywood work.

This happens much more often to writers than to directors and actors. Of all the creative workers in Hollywood, the writers are the most frustrated because they are allowed to function least as artists. They write to dictation, expressing someone else's fantasies, and even this is later changed and mangled by others. The gifted actor or director, no matter how weak or corny the role or script, can still give it his best. They have at least a partial satisfaction of using initially weak material as well as possible. However, gifted directors also experience some of the writers' frustrations. A director may work hard and creatively on a movie, and at the last minute the front office cuts out certain scenes and so changes others that the effect he has striven for is lost. When the picture is released under his name, he is ashamed of it. An actor doing his best still may not be able to take away the corniness of his role. But the actor and director at least do play their professional roles regardless of the outcome, while the writer rarely even does that.

Of course the truly gifted people for whom the problem of creation is important are few everywhere. Only a small percentage of novelists, painters, musicians, scientists, anywhere in the world, are talented. But there are many more in Hollywood than one would expect from looking at movies. The industry entices them, with big salaries, from New York, London, Paris and Milan. Once Hollywood gets them, it makes them part of that system which prevents their gifts from being utilized to the best advantage. This is costly and wasteful to the studio and to the banks which finance production. It is corrupting to the artists, to the movies they help produce, and a decided disadvantage to the movie-going public.

Many people beside Hollywood artists are frustrated. College professors frequently feel frustrated because of lack of money and the difficulties of bringing up a family and maintaining their social status on the professorial salary. Many artists outside of Hollywood know economic frustrations. While these frustrations are wearing and burdensome, they do not usually cause an individual to lose respect for what he does, or for himself. This is a heavy load for any personality to carry.

The really important people in the development and growth of the movies, as a popular art form and as a profitable industry, are the small group of artists who continuously struggle to function as such, and the occasional executive who appreciates their goals because they are partly or wholly his own. We have therefore stressed their significance which is far greater than their numbers would seem to warrant. It is these men and women, who are not primarily gamblers, who do not confuse the animate with the inanimate—the human with the supernatural—who are responsible for any human creativity that there is in Hollywood. They have a point of view, the expression of which is important to them; they have a capacity for sustained hard work, and they prefer thoughtful planning to constant crises. They regard people as human beings. Although comparatively few, they can be found in all parts of movie production. They struggle constantly for power within the Hollywood system, power not to dominate other human beings, but to bend the system so that creation becomes human. Many times they lose, but sometimes they win; and the fighting, whatever the outcome, relieves some of their frustration.

One strategy for the artist who understands the system and wants to improve it is, first, to meet the front office's standards by making money for the studio, following the conventional formulas. Then by persistent nagging he may gain the opportunity to create something to please himself. This opportunity is granted to keep him in good humor and prevent his going to another studio. If, to the studio's surprise, the humoring of the artist turns out to be good box office, he is given more control over his work. But first the artist must show that he can work within the executive's scheme of values. The executive does not have to prove that he can work within the artist's scale. It is a one-way road.

When occasionally an executive does demonstrate that he understands and appreciates the artist's standards, and is objectively more interested in the movie than in power, he can usually have his pick of talent.

The mediocre would be so in any situation. In Hollywood, they enjoy the illusion of being creative and some of them even emulate the frustrations of artists. They work in a system geared to mediocrity, which enables them, if successful, to earn more money than in any other place in the world. They have the same gambling psychology that the front-office executives have; their faith in breaks is so strong that often they hang on for years and years even when Fate has not yet smiled. As the front office manipulates them, so they manipulate everyone else that they can. Their economic insecurities, however, are greater than those of the front office. But if moderately successful they enjoy material comforts and luxuries far greater than anything they could have outside of Hollywood. For people without marked ability, whether they sit in the front office, in the producer's office or in that of the writer's, whether they direct or act, a system in which success depends upon breaks is far more reassuring than one in which talent or special gifts count. For people without imagination or with understanding of writing, acting and storytelling, a system which mechanizes the whole process is fitting. For people whose whole lives are concerned with the accumulation of property, a system which emphasizes property above everything else is understandable. For people whose drive is toward power over others, a system which encourages manipulation is desirable. For those whose inner need is the excitement of

gambling rather than the stimulation of creation, the system is congenial. It is these people—the majority in Hollywood—who shape and perpetuate that system, in harmony with their own needs rather than with those of movie making.

Yet these people suffer and sometimes have mental breakdowns. Hollywood gives only a neurotic answer to their needs, which are therefore not really satisfied. A man with almost no writing ability becomes an important movie writer because an executive producer is his friend, or for some other reason unconnected with writing. Although he is regarded as a success and enjoys a very big salary, he knows, consciously or unconsciously, that the success has no foundation in ability, and suffers anxiety over whether it can last. He plays the social game in a frenzied fashion to prove to himself and to others that his position is secure. Since in our culture success is supposed to be the result of hard work and ability, he may suffer undue guilt. The anxiety may become too much for him to handle, leading to neurotic symptoms, to breakdown or failure.

The creative person, particularly if he has functioned as such in the past, likewise suffers. He, too, may break down or become maladjusted when his deep aspirations are repeatedly aroused and then left unsatisfied, when his imagination is stirred and then not permitted to function. He, too, knows guilt and anxiety—over his corruption as an artist.

In this collaborative industry, there is also, with a few exceptions, a striking and complete lack of mutual respect as well as trust. The *esprit de corps* of the industry is exceedingly low. People who do not respect each other cannot work cooperatively. Just as morale is necessary to the successful functioning of an army, so is a high level of *esprit de corps* important as a motivating force in any industry. Its absence in Hollywood endangers the industry, injures both the people who work in it and the movies they produce.

In the usual Hollywood production of movies, the quality of the movie is much less important than the assertion of the ego of any individual. When the executive insists on cutting a picture so that the motivation of the leading characters is lost, when he refuses to pay any attention to a director's idea about casting, when the star demands that her footage be increased and that of a minor character cut, when the producer dominates a writer or writers, insisting on carrying out his own ideas, good or bad, when the director refuses to listen to suggestions of a gifted actor about his role, when talented people are fired because they threaten the power of some one higher up—then, of course, it is the movie which goes to pot.

As noted, the kind of thinking which dominates Hollywood stems out of its past. Hollywood is, however, not a sealed chamber. New people, new ideas from literature and the theater, new values, have entered and continue to do so. Also, an increasing number of Hollywood people are now involved in shooting movies in every part of the world. The industry has been quick to accept new technological improvements whether in sound, in color or in some other process, but slow to incorporate those new ideas, which may seriously threaten the power situation. If actors and directors and men of literature are successful in turning out profitable pictures, then the omniscience and omnipotence of studio executives is endangered. If men with talent, ability and intelligent planning can produce better pictures, then the people who have depended on breaks and frenzied activity have no place. Naturally they are not apt to favor such changes.

Whether or not the industry likes new ideas, it is forced to meet unsettled world conditions. Foreign markets and ratios of imported pictures are constantly changing. There is increased foreign competition at home and shifts in audience standards and tastes. Federal court decrees separate production from distribution and exhibition, and costs of production climb upward. The country goes through inflation and recession. All these and many more contemporary changes directly impinge on Hollywood.

One very important consequence is that the margin for error in movie production has very much decreased. In the early days vast profits could be made regardless of mistakes, extravagances, and quality. Movies were at first something of a novelty and for a long time there was little competition. The early audiences were mostly working people who went to see any movie. Much later, during the war years, most people enjoyed larger incomes than ever before and the tensions of war and long hours of work increased their need of entertainment. Today, the situation is very different. While the costs of making movies has spiraled upward, people have less money to spend on entertainment and their standards are changing. They therefore exercise more thought in their choice of what to see.

The upward educational level of the whole country continues. The vast movements in the popularization of knowledge through adult education, museums, books, radio and other media has also done much to broaden the base of the educated public.

But more important than any other change is the loss of homogeneity in the movie audience. Today, this represents as much variety in tastes and backgrounds as does the population of the country. There are still the teen-age girls infatuated with movie heroes who go to see any picture in which their favorite stars perform, and who squirm in their seats when the hero passionately kisses the heroine. But in a preliminary study of audience reactions of high school juniors and seniors a large number, in discussing a movie or one part of it used the phrases and adjectives "weak," "corny," "no motivation," "couldn't happen." Moreover, the audience is not limited to adolescents, critical or otherwise. People over thirty who count movies as one of their pastimes, naturally have different tastes from those of adolescents.

Hollywood has been slow to catch on to this new audience, which asks for something more than movement and excitement. The success all over the country of the so-called "art theater" has startled some of the Hollywood people. In the postwar period there was an influx of foreign pictures and the art theaters were an outlet for the better ones. Today, many regular theaters play foreign movies part of their time. According to *Variety,* there are 57 theaters which are out-and-out art-houses, and 226 which play the foreign-made product part of the time. Ten more are now under construction. It is of interest that the art-houses are called "sureseaters" in this trade paper, which says:

> Despite the dwindling grosses which have hit regular theaters, distribs serving the art-house operation claim that the field is generally a lush one. Out of every 10 sureseaters now doing business several are highly lucrative, two are in a wobbly stage, and one is in the red, it is said.[9]

The same article attributes the success of the art-houses to their low cost of operation without all the "expensive plush" and to their having a steady and stable group of customers. Nor are these art theaters clustered in large cities in the East. Every city of 200,000 or over, except Newark (which suffers because of its proximity to New York) has at least one art theater. Texas is particularly strong in them. In Detroit, four neighborhood movie houses changed into art-houses in 1949. From places as scattered as Syracuse, New York; Salt Lake City, Utah; Tacoma, Washington; Dayton, Ohio, come reports of the openings of new art theaters.[10] These are one indication of changing audience tastes.

Hollywood is not unaware of many of the changes and new trends and has attempted to meet the new situation in various ways. Metro-Goldwyn-Mayer has tried to attract an older audience by casting older people in its movies.

> More than ten Metro pictures are soon to be made with top players over sixty years of age. Eight others are nearing release. It's all part of a drive on Metro's part to lure patrons over 35 back to the theater.[11]

If this plan is carried through to its logical conclusion, Hollywood would merely develop a new formula of teaming the age of the star to the age of the expected audience, which is even more fantastic than some of its past formulas. It is rather doubtful that adults now frequenting the art-houses will rush to see MGM pictures because they star actors over sixty years of age.

Studio executives, trying to analyze the success of *Pinky* and *All the King's Men*, classify them as "gimmick" pictures and are now hunting for other "gimmick pix" to beat the "b.o. Nix."[12] The executives appear unable to break loose from the bonds of their past thinking in terms of gimmicks and formulas.

They might learn from some high school students, who when asked for their favorite type of movie, indicated their preferences—musical, serious, drama, Western—and then added: "But it has to be *good.*"As an example of what they meant by good, some students mentioned *All the King's Men.*

Another suggested solution is improved public relations for the whole industry. Hollywood takes great pride in its showmanship and spends more than any other industry on advertising and publicity. Yet, as is well known, its public relations are

very bad. It is a popular pastime to take a crack at Hollywood at every opportunity. This symbol for sex and lavish wealth to the whole world is a target for continuous criticism and hostility. Anti-Hollywood diatribes are familiar to anyone who reads the American press, and George Seaton, President of the Screen Writers' Guild, returning from a trip to Europe, said there is "too much anti-Hollywood prejudice in the world."[13] Different causes underlie all the hostility towards Hollywood. One is probably the envy of fortunes so easily earned; and there may be resentment or envy, or both, of the supposedly freer sex life of Hollywood people. But perhaps there is a wider awareness, more than Hollywood executives' realize, of the enormous gap between the potentialities and the actual product that is turned out.

The industry knows well that its public relations are bad and suggests many different remedies. An advertising-publicity chief suggested a campaign to combat what he considered the public's misconceptions of the industry: that it is "red," immoral, extravagant, and screwball in its thinking. The office represented by Mr. Eric Johnston emphasizes more the need to effect good will within the various sections of the industry (production, distribution, and exhibition) and the cessation of publicized intra-industry quarreling. He called meetings for this purpose. The Motion Picture Association of America tries to sell what they call "The constructive angle" on Hollywood, and sends out articles—such as "Music in Films," "Literature in Films," "How Films Teach History," to critics and exhibitors and to schools.[14] But what historians, musicians and those concerned with literature would say on these themes, is another story. Plans are made for an American Film Festival similar to those held in Europe, to draw the attention of Americans to their own film industry.[15]

Other plans are for increasing profits through economies in production. "Big name" stars under contract now do more pictures per year. In 1948, Van Johnson made two pictures, *Command Decision* and *The Bride Goes Wild*, while in 1949 he had a schedule of five pictures. Since he received $5000 a week whether he worked or not, the savings to the studio were considerable.[16] But against this new trend, the old one still persists. Deanna Durbin's salary from September 1948 to September 1949 was $300,000 and she did not make a single picture.[17]

As late as 1948 it was news in the trade press that planning in advance produced economies. Mr. Mamoulian emphasized that he was able to make the technicolor musical "Holiday" *(Holiday in Mexico)* for the relatively low budget of $1,800,000 because it was shot in 56 days instead of the average 100–125 for musicals, and that this was possible because of "thorough advance preparation."[18] Rehearsals which had long been desired by the talented directors and actors, but discouraged or forbidden by the front office, gradually have become part of the economy wave. It has been finally discovered that rehearsals actually save money because they prevent the needless extravagance of the cast and highly paid technicians standing around while last minute changes are made. In addition, rehearsals bring some of the advantages of the stage to both actors and directors on the set, cause better pictures to be made, and so probably improve the box-office intake.

Stars are as important as ever and even the economy wave has not reduced their earnings, but there is a move away from picking up pretty-faced newcomers toward one of selecting experienced young Broadway players with talent.[19] It is no longer so easy, but still not impossible, to achieve stardom only through beautiful legs, sensuous appearance, or being brought to the attention of an executive through faked or real publicity.

Many executives and producers repeat the timeworn adage, "There's nothing wrong with the picture business that good pictures can't cure." Yet there is considerable difference of opinion on what is a good picture or how to make one. For some, the best method is still to spend more money. Henry Ginsberg, president of Paramount Pictures, warns against "becoming cost-conscious to the point of forgetting the entertainment needs of a picture," adding that "any picture costing less than $1,000,000 is a B."[20] But other executives have gradually learned that money may not be the whole story. The same paper quoted Adolph Zukor, regarded by many as dean of the motion picture industry, as saying, "Pictures require brains, not money. The talk that high-cost films attract the public is not correct. Give me brains and I'll make good pictures. The others can have the U.S. Treasury behind them but if they don't have the talent, their money will not produce good pictures."[21] Mr. Nicholas M. Schenck, president of Loew's, Incorporated,

also thinks that money is not the most essential factor and is particularly concerned about whether the writers are earning their salaries. He says:

> The motion picture industry cannot throw its weight around and its money around without sincerity of purpose. That purpose must be to give the public the best possible entertainment. This cannot be done merely by cutting costs. It has to be done by making the costs worth while. . . . It means that writers have to try to fully express themselves in their work and not write pictures as a device to get easy money.[22]

Mr. Zukor does not consider the problem of whether the industry knows how to utilize talent, and Mr. Schenck does not raise the questions of *how* the costs can be made worth while and whether writers are permitted, as he says, "to fully express themselves in their work." A talented writer would like nothing better, but this is difficult with the present methods of production.

Both these presidents have gropingly hit only the surface of the problem. They seem not to know that gifted and intelligent people *cannot* function well without a certain amount of freedom to express themselves, and, even, to take some chances and make mistakes. Talented people with more freedom to follow their own goals might find easy money less important to them, because they would have other compensations; and the studios might get more for less money.

Even men of acknowledged talent and the highest prestige, winners of Oscars and responsible for many box-office hits, do not now possess this freedom. Mr. William Wyler is widely regarded by everyone as one of the top directors in Hollywood, and he has additional power as a producer-director. His many successes are a matter of record; he is in the unusual position of sharing with the studio the right to pass on story material. Yet Mr. Wyler, in a newspaper interview, talked about the difficulties he experienced because of the "hyper-caution" of the studios. He . . .

> . . . ruefully added that he had lost considerable time seeking "mutually satisfactory" properties. Half dozen of his suggestions, some of which are now being produced by other companies, have been turned down, he said. . . . "The safest yardstick for any company is to trust someone to make the right choice or else kick him out. If you don't trust

him, the best thing to do is to get rid of him and hire people you can trust."[23]

It is just this quality of trust which is lacking in Hollywood. Almost no one trusts anyone else, and the executives, particularly, trust no one, not even themselves. Trust is impossible to men whose major drive is to exploit and manipulate other human beings. Gamblers who base their play for huge profits on instinct rather than knowledge, are for all their pretensions deeply unsure of themselves. The structure of Hollywood engenders distrust, which in turn breeds the excessive caution of which Mr. Wyler complains, and the enormous cost of a picture reinforces the caution. Even gamblers pause before risking $1,500,000. They are naturally more scared about taking a real chance than a gifted director whose security lies in his actual knowledge of the art of storytelling. This is a better guarantee for financial success than magical claims to omniscience.

To liberate the unused resources of talent in Hollywood entails changes in the way of thinking, in the system of production which reflects the way of thinking and, finally, in the allocation of power. When men give up an exaggerated emphasis on breaks as inherent in movie production and a magical form of thinking, and face the world of realities, which encompass logical thinking, hard work, knowledge and talent; when they cease being primarily gamblers reveling in crises and become good businessmen with a capacity to plan in advance; when they have the courage to try out new ideas as well as new processes in color tinting; when power for the sake of dominating other human beings as if they were property ceases to be the major goal and is supplanted by a human form of collaboration in which the interests of the movies and the movie public are important—then only will the real gold in Hollywood replace the glamorized tinsel.

Change does not take place quickly or by sudden decree. It is slow and happens as the result of many causes rather than of one. The exceptions to the rules are sometimes the beginning of change. A new invention, a new idea, a new form of behavior are usually first introduced as alternatives to already existing ones.[24] To replace them, the new forms must be shown to be better. When automobiles were first introduced, the horse and buggy continued to exist, and for

some time both were used. In the beginning many people were afraid of the new cars. By now the automobile has almost completely replaced the horse and buggy, because of its obviously greater efficiency.

For the exceptional patterns in Hollywood to replace the universal or prevailing ones, they must make more profit. Writers who write to please themselves rather than a producer have turned out some successful scripts, from which box-office hits have been produced. Gifted directors and actors who have gained more control over their work by becoming producers have likewise turned out successful pictures. Of course, neither they nor their pictures are always successful. Sometimes, without even knowing it, they have taken over the standards of their bosses and then their movies do not improve. But they have a high batting average. Pictures which carry a ring of honesty in human relationships rather than phoniness have been box-office hits. Some studios have learned that while beautiful legs for an actress are important, a girl with talent may have them as well as a nitwit, and that there is no reason why legs should preclude other types of actresses. Many different kinds are needed and are not necessarily in competition.

Whether or not these alternatives become universal is more complicated than the matter of automobiles replacing the horse and buggy. It is relatively easy to learn how to drive a car. It is exceedingly difficult for many of the people in Hollywood, who follow the universal patterns, to learn how to use the new alternatives. Their magical thinking, and belief in breaks rather than ability, their lack of real knowledge and training, their claims to omniscience, make it almost impossible for them to change. The alternatives threaten their major goal, the desire for power; and new ideas which threaten existing authority are always resisted.

When a primitive society comes into contact with Western civilization, frequently the old men, who are the powerful ones in the tribe, fight the innovations which the young ones accept. Rarely in the history of mankind has any group with power given it up voluntarily. But bankers and presidents of the industry, who are the powerful ones behind the studio executives, are interested in profits; and if an artist can bring in profits, he is their man. It is they who asked a former writer to become vice president in charge of production at a major studio. An independent studio headed by an executive who has emphasized quality in his films for a long time has been making money. There are other independent men and studios with similar values and the number is increasing. The picture of Hollywood can be painted in many ways, all true to a degree. It is a place of innumerable contradictions, some of which represent the norm and others, the exceptions.

No salary can compensate for being dehumanized. The star and the third assistant director alike realize this, however dimly. They can strive for more and more money yet they cannot accept the denial of their own humanity. The front-office thinking, which attributes nonhuman qualities to human beings, has more far-reaching consequences than primitive man's projection of human qualities on to the inanimate, because mere objects can have no reactions. Human beings *do* react.

The denial of one's human characteristics is the most degrading insult that can be offered any man or woman. All members of minority groups in our culture have suffered it to some degree. In Hollywood, members of minorities can rise to the highest prestige, wealth, and power positions—but the supreme insult is offered to them, and to everyone else.

In one sense the psychological situation is worse than that of slavery. In that situation, owners regarded their slaves as property, but the slaves themselves did not necessarily share this attitude. They were in bondage but they did not sell themselves to the highest bidder. In Hollywood, no master forces men to sell themselves for the duration of a contract. No one even forces people to come to Hollywood. They come of their own will and voluntarily sell their freedom to the highest buyer. Yet men who have known freedom cannot give it up without resentment and bitterness. The fact that they give it up of their own will adds ambivalence and guilt to an already difficult situation.

One of the most hopeful characteristics about the human species is that its members know that man is unique and they do not want to give up their human heritage. The basic problem of Hollywood lies in man. Technological improvements, distribution methods, and foreign markets are all important, and each brings its own problems. But of even deeper significance are the problems concerned with human values, with ways of thinking, with human relationships there and in the movies.

Some element of chance will always exist, just as some tensions and crises are inevitable among people working together. But enough successful pictures have been produced with intelligent planning and the wise use of talent to show that tensions, crises and superficial excitement are not the essential ingredients of good movie making. Enough people with humanistic goals have attained power to prove that successful movie production can be human, and that people working in Hollywood do not have to lose all freedom and dignity. The magical thinking and system of production which flows from it are probably no more necessary to making movies than the corn dance of the Pueblo Indians is needed to making corn grow.

Man in his long history has moved more slowly in some areas than in others. It has always been easier for him to use his intelligence, reason and inventiveness to control his physical environment than to apply them to his human relationships. In the less than fifty years of Hollywood's existence, it has recapitulated much of man's thinking. As it gradually emerges from the age of magic into the present, its future is tied with the future of mankind.

Notes

1. Ralph Linton, *The Study of Man,* Chapter IV. New York: D. Appleton-Century.

2. F. Boas and others, *General Anthropology,* p. 636. Boston: D. C. Heath and Co.

3. Ralph R. Greenson, M.D., "On Gambling," *The American Imago.* Vol. 4, No. 2, April 1947, pp. 61–77.

4. *Ibid.*

5. *Ibid.*

6. Cf. Sandor Ferenczi, *Contributions to Psychoanalysis.* Boston: Richard Badger. Otto Fenichel, *The Psychoanalytical Theory of Neurosis.* New York: W. W. Norton.

7. Greenson, *op. cit.*

8. Hanns Sachs, *The Creative Unconscious,* p. 38. Cambridge, Mass.: Scie-Art Publisher.

9. *Variety,* July 27, 1949.

10. *Ibid.*

11. *Ibid.,* July 13, 1949.

12. *Variety,* March 8, 1950.

13. *Ibid.,* March 16, 1949.

14. *Ibid.*, August 3, 1949.
15. *Ibid.*, July 20, 1949.
16. *Ibid.*
17. *Ibid.*, August 10, 1949.
18. *Ibid.*, April 21, 1948.
19. *Ibid.*, August 10, 1949.

20. *Ibid.*, July 6, 1949.
21. *Ibid.*, July 13, 1949.
22. *Ibid.*, January 5, 1949.
23. *Ibid.*, April 17, 1949.
24. Ralph Linton, *The Study of Man,* Chapter XVI. New York: D. Appleton-Century.

44

Storytellers as Tutors in Technique

From *The Lonely Crowd* (1950)

David Riesman, with Reuel Denney and Nathan Glazer

David Riesman (1909–2002) was one of the great interpreters of American life in the postwar era. Raised by an elite Philadelphia family on Rittenhouse Square, Riesman was trained as a lawyer and never took a doctorate. Riesman served as clerk to Supreme Court justice Louis Brandeis and wrote one of the key articles on group defamation (1942)—which makes him an innovator in one of the key trends in late-twentieth-century American law. He was a professor of social science at the University of Chicago from 1948 to 1959, then he spent the rest of his life at Harvard, where he wrote on U.S. education and many other subjects.

The Lonely Crowd (1950), written with Nathan Glazer and Reuel Denney, is reportedly the best-selling sociology book of all time (with some 1.4 million copies sold). When an abridged version was published in 1953, sales caught fire, and Riesman found himself not only famous but also on the cover of *Time* magazine. The literary critic Lionel Trilling noted that, in the 1950s, sociology did what the novel once had—provide a picture of American life as a whole—and he was surely thinking of his friend Riesman. The book captures the spirit of a moment when Americans were uneasy about the changes wrought by suburbanization, consumption, prosperity, and mass media. It introduces the terms "inner directed" and "outer directed"—that is, those guided by internal mechanisms versus those who look toward other people and mass media for orientation—both of which quickly entered popular consciousness. Described by one observer as "prophetic and casual, respectful of popular culture without imputing to it any fantastic emancipations, [and] refusing sneers" (Gitlin 2002), *The Lonely Crowd* remains instructive today. Though Riesman later retreated from the book's curious theory about personality and population growth, the work as a whole remains relevant in its thoughtful musings on American character and society, its methodological fusion of sociology and psychology, and its embodiment of the creeping feeling of alienation amid success that continues to haunt American life.

A. I like Superman better than the others because they can't do everything Superman can do. Batman can't fly and that is very important.

Q. Would you like to be able to fly?

A. I would like to be able to fly if everybody else did, but otherwise it would be kind of conspicuous.

> —From an interview with a twelve-year-old girl.[1]

Language, as we noted in the previous chapter, becomes a refined and powerful aspect of the organization of the peer-group engaged in consuming its own taste preferences and in marching up its own taste gradients. For the insiders language becomes a chief key to the taste socializations and mood currents that are prevalent in this group at any moment. For the outsiders, including adult observers, language becomes a mysterious opacity, constantly carrying peer-group messages which are full of precisions that remain untranslatable.

When we look more closely at the use of language in the young peer-groups we see how various its aspects are. Language itself becomes a sort of consumption product. It is used neither to direct the work economy, nor to relate the self to others in any really intimate way, nor to recall the past, nor yet as sheer word play. Rather it is used in the peer-groups today much as popular tunes seem to be used: as a set of counters by which one establishes that one is "in" and by which one participates in the peer-group's arduously self-socializing "work." And the peer-groups, while they exercise power more than ever before through the use of words, are more than ever before the victims of words. While they learn to cling desperately to words—most signals are given in words—at the same time they learn to distrust them. As we have seen, verdicts in the peer-group are often quite ambiguous. Some of the older words, such as bastard and skunk, remain, but their meaning is vaguer—they may even be said with a smile! Whole new glossaries crop up every few years.

Mass literacy of course plays a complex part in this process. The peer-group accepts a substantial responsibility in the flow of modern communications. It stands midway between the individuals of whom each group is composed and the messages which flow to the group's opinion leaders from the mass media. The mass media are the wholesalers; the peer-groups, the retailers of the communications industry. But the flow is not all one way. Not only do the peers decide, to a large extent, which tastes, skills, and words, appearing for the first time within their circle, shall be given approval, but they also select some for wider publicity through contiguous groups and eventually back to the mass media for still wider distribution. If we look at this process we see that the individual who develops, say, a particular style of expression, is either ignored by the peers or accepted by them. If he and his style are accepted, his style is taken over by the group, and in at least this sense it is no longer *his*. But the same thing can happen to a given peer-group in its turn. To understand the way in which individual and personal style is siphoned up through these stages of impersonalization we have to understand the work of the main machine in the process—the mass media.

Our interest in this chapter will not be in the commercial purveyors of language and imagery or the storytellers themselves but in the effects on the child audience. And of course these effects cannot be considered in isolation from the constellation of parents, teachers, and peer-groupers who operate on the assembly line of character. If we find, for instance, a child who seems more affected by print than by people, it may be because people are so overwhelming for him that he must take refuge in print. Furthermore, cultures differ very much in the perceptions they stress in teaching the child to differentiate among images and to differentiate among people. But in general it seems fair to say that the storytellers (or more technically the mass media of communication) are indispensable agents of socialization. They picture the world for the child and thus give both form and limits to his memory and imagination.[2]

In exploring this topic we must not confuse the genres of literature with the problem of social-psychological effects. We are going to use "story" broadly in this chapter to include not only poetry and fiction but any fabulous and embroidered account: a "true" newsreel might by this definition be a story. Nor, considering the prestige of the pictorial, shall we confine ourselves to the imagery of language alone.

Societies in the phase of incipient population decline can afford, can technically provide, and have both the time and the need to receive a bounteous flow of imagery from urban centers of distribution. Industrialism and mass literacy seem to go together. These same societies, moreover, rely more heavily than their predecessors on character-forming agencies outside the home. Hence, as we would expect, the storytellers of the mass media play a great role among other-directed children. We can see what has changed in recent generations only by comparing today's experience with that of children in societies depending on tradition-direction and inner-direction.

I. Song and Story in the Stage of Tradition-Direction

The society which depends for conformity on tradition-direction uses as part of its stock in trade its oral traditions, its myths, legends, and songs. These are transmitted by the same family members who play an active part in all the other phases of socializing the young.

Chimney-Corner Media

When we find a society in which stories are transmitted by word of mouth, we put our finger on one of the very indexes by which we know it as a society depending on tradition-direction. In terms of the technique of transmission, the important thing is that the story or fable is told orally, not in print. In terms of the storytelling situation, the important thing is that the story is told, ordinarily, by a family member or by a professional or semiprofessional closely connected with the extended family group. In both cases the result is that the story is modulated for, and built into, the web of values that the storyteller also controls and relates himself to in active ways. One way of expressing this is to say that storytelling is like a handicraft industry: each telling is different from the other, and each is tailored to the taste and disposition of the audience.

These factors are all-important in their effect on audiences. Since the physical and social distance between the teller and listener is slight, the listener is to some extent a participant in the telling. A child can correct the teller or criticize the theme or elaborate the narrative—though more often he is probably confined to asking questions. This means that the listener, even as a child, is in a position to find and develop his own likings. What is more, the unity of the web of social values and personal relations in which the story is transmitted is such that both the story and the vehicle have a resolute meaning. This does not mean that fairy tales and traditional myths lack ambiguity—indeed they possess it to a rich extent

and at many levels—but rather that the ambiguity could often be resolved in a slightly different manner for different audiences. For the act of telling, as we have seen, occurs within a context whose physical and psychological dimensions are largely grasped by tellers and hearers.

It is not surprising that songs and stories rendered in face-to-face performance among relatives and friends are often baldly cautionary tales; they tell what happens to those who disobey the community or the supernatural authorities. Or they illustrate by reference to the illustrious what kind of person one ought to be in the culture in terms of such traits as bravery and endurance. A surprising number of tales, however, in many cultures depending on tradition-direction are not cautionary in this direct sense. As in the Bible, some tales recount rebellions, successful or tragic, against the powers that be—though in many cases the theme of rebellion is disguised.

Tales of Norm and "Abnorm"

As we move over to the consideration of content, we can take the rebellious note struck in these tales to indicate that even in a society depending on tradition-direction there still remain strivings which are not completely socialized. By and large, people accept the harness of their culture, and it is hard for them to conceive of another make of harness. But they are not unaware of constraint, and their stories, as frequently their dreams, are the refuge and succor of this awareness and help to make it possible to go on with ordinary life. The communal load of shame or anxiety is reduced by the common "confession," the common release which the myth permits. There is in these myths, then, a good deal of "realism" about stubborn, unsocialized human nature—this is precisely why they can appeal to us across the centuries and across the cultural boundaries. They show people to be more fierce, more jealous, more rebellious than appears on the surface.

Why is this so? It appears that if people were only "adjusted"—if they never had even a thought which transcended the cultural prohibitions—life would have so little savor as to endanger the culture itself. Cultures depending upon tradition-direction usually manage to institutionalize a degree of rebellion not only for their deviants but for everybody. Sometimes this is done on a life-cycle basis. Thus some cultures permit, even encourage, sauciness from children only to clamp down on the adult; others allow the older women a bawdiness denied the younger ones. Sometimes there are special days—feast days—when bars are down.

Now when the aperture for rebellion lies in the realm of culturally approved fantasy, the socializing function of the tales and stories which are the predecessors of the mass media is clearly a dual one. The elders use the stories to tell the young: you must be like so-and-so if you are to be admired and to live up to the noble traditions of the group. But the young are also told—sometimes in the very same message—that there have been people like so-and-so who broke the rules, who did many worse things than you ever did, and perhaps ever dreamed of, and whether he lived to tell the tale or not, he *did live* and we speak of him.

This very ambivalence of the stories helps the young to integrate their forbidden impulses by recognizing them as part of their legacy as human beings. Stories make it possible for the face-to-face group which is charged with socialization of the young to draw on a cultural warehouse that provides models for behavior not to be found completely in any given face-to-face group. In this tradition-directed form of "popular culture" stories make it possible to form an underground connection, via myth, between repressed sectors of the adults and sectors of the young. Finally, they make it possible to hold the young to both more and less than what they see around them, either of approved behavior or of behavior which, while disapproved, is still done.

And yet it is more complicated than that. Indeed, we may suppose that the change to inner-direction occurs first in circles which, through literacy or otherwise, acquire access to many multiplying ambiguities of direction. As in the mathematical theory of communications all channels mix what is technically called noise with what is technically called information and thus limit the freedom of the sender, so also messages intended or believed to socialize the young cannot help but contain noises which may have diverse effects, effects which may oversocialize or undersocialize them.

II. The Socializing Functions of Print in the Stage of Inner-Direction

When societies enter the phase of transitional growth of population, formal schooling increases, in part to train people for the new, more specialized tasks of industry and agriculture, in part to absorb the young who are no longer needed on farms and whose schooling can be supported by the greater productivity of the society. Of course, these young people learn to read. But the excitement and novelty of literacy in this period affect old as well as young. There is a hunger for the press and for books—a hunger that the technology and distributive facilities of the phase arouse but do not entirely satisfy. This excitement, this hunger, is a sign of the characterological revolution which is accompanying the industrial one.

In the United States, as in other countries of incipient population decline, this hunger has abated; indeed, it has been succeeded for many by a kind of satiety with serious print, coupled with insatiability for the amusements and agenda of popular culture. To remind ourselves of the older pattern we need only look at countries such as Mexico and Russia, now undergoing industrialization, where the old are avid for print and the young admired for learning. Some of this we can still see among the largely self-educated Negroes of the deep South who live among our surviving stratum of white and black illiterates.

How this development aided the shift from tradition-direction to inner-direction can be vividly traced in Thomas and Znaniecki's *Polish Peasant*.[3] These writers describe the way in which the Polish rural press helped to restructure attitudes and values among the peasantry at the turn of the last century. They show that an individual peasant who learned to read at that time did not merely acquire a skill with little impact on his character; rather he made a decisive break with the primary group, with tradition-direction. The press picked him up at this turning point and supported his uncertain steps away from the primary group by criticizing the values of that group and by giving him a sense of having allies, albeit anonymous ones, in this move.

In this way the press helped link the newly individuated person to the newly forming society. The Polish press also supported very specific "character-building" measures, such as temperance and thrift, and fostered scientific farming as the American agricultural extension services have done; science was viewed as a kind of inner-directed morality as against the superstition of the remaining, tradition-directed peasantry. These attitudes, expounded in newspaper nonfiction, were reinforced in newspaper and periodical "edifying" fiction.

In these ways the local reader could escape into print from the criticisms of his neighbors and could test his inner-direction against the models given in the press. And by writing for the press himself, as he occasionally might do as local correspondent, he could bring his performance up for approval before an audience which believed in the magic attached to print itself—much like the Americans who, in the last century, contributed local poetry to their local press. By this public performance, no longer for a face-to-face audience, he confirmed himself on his inner-directed course.

The Whip of the Word

These themes from the *Polish Peasant* might make it appear that literacy and the mass media are the tools of a well-understood shift toward well-understood changes in goal. But the conditions under which print is added to word of mouth and picture as a means of transmitting and mass-transmitting a message are seldom simple. The very existence of print opens up the writer-reader relation to a wider range of goals, even of exploitations. Literacy is indeed a somewhat ambiguous blessing in the early capitalistic period of western history. The tradition-directed person has not only a traditional standard of living but a traditional standard of how hard and long he works; and print serves, along with other agencies of socialization, to destroy both of these standards. The inner-directed man, open to "reason" via print, often develops a character structure which drives him to work longer hours and to live on lower budgets of leisure and laxity than would have been deemed possible before. He can be driven because he is ready to drive himself.

The skeptic may ask how can words, especially printed words, mold character? We might ask him in turn whether he has ever been frightened reading a detective story or excited reading a love story. Words not only affect us temporarily; they change us, they socialize or unsocialize us. Doubtless the printing press alone cannot completely assure any particular form of social coercion—and of course not all children, even in the inner-directed middle class, were readers. But print can powerfully rationalize the models which tell people what they ought to be like. Reaching children directly as well as through their parents and teachers, it can take the process of socialization out of the communal chimney corner of the era depending on tradition-direction and penetrate into the private bedrooms and libraries of the rising middle class: the child is allowed to gird himself for the battle of life in the small circle of light cast by his reading lamp or candle.

To understand this more fully we must realize that the rise of literacy affects not only the content and style of the literary and journalistic genres but also their audience reception. The increased quantitative flow of content brings about an enormous increase in the selectivity of each child, as compared with the era of tradition-direction. With widely increased literacy and extensive print distribution, more and more people begin to read messages not meant for them. And they read them in situations no longer controlled and structured by the teller—or by their own participation. This increase in the number, variety, and "scatter" of the messages, along with the general impersonalization in print which induces these specific effects, becomes one of the powerful factors in social change. The classic instance in western history, of course, is the translation of the Vulgate Bible into the spoken languages, a translation which allowed the people to read a book which only the priests could read before. This shift, repeated in secular form since the days of Erasmus, marks a decisive change in the sociology of audiences.

Some of the genuine difficulties of discussing the shift from the era depending on tradition-direction to that of inner-direction arise from the teleological drift of the language we are likely to use. For example, we are prone to overlook the unintended audience because it is always easier to assume that a given medium was deliberately aimed at the audience it actually succeeded in reaching—and vice versa. Yet there is no proof that the media have ever been so accurate in aim. Indeed, there are reasons for thinking that, in a period dependent on inner-direction, wide misses are possible. The very impersonality of the situation in which print is absorbed helps to increase the chances of underreception or overreception in many of its listeners. Thus the aristocrats were often displeased by what they considered the overreception of mobility strivings in many they would have liked to keep "in their place."

The receptive overeffects I have most in mind, however, are those in individuals whose characterological guilts and tensions were increased by the pressure of print. Their character structure simply could not handle the demand put upon it in a society depending on inner-direction. Their gyroscopes spun wildly and erratically. Not finding justification in print—not finding, as many modern readers do, a "union of sinners," the "One Big Union" of mankind extending back through the past—they experienced print simply as an intensified proof of their maladjustment. The printed sermons of a Colonial divine could cast his readers into hell-fire through print alone—as if every day were Sunday.

Thus, while the myths and symbolism of the societies depending on tradition-direction support the tradition by integrating the rebellious tendencies of the listener into a pattern of the culture, the word-in-print may disorient as well as orient its audience. This is evident in the cry for censorship which goes up as soon as literacy becomes widespread. And not only formal censorship. In America the increasing piety of print, if we compare, for instance, today's press with that of the early republic, may be in part explained by the sheer weight of the informal pressure put on "responsible" editors by near-universal literacy. As the editor of a metropolitan paper used to say if his staff verged on bawdry: "Don't forget, gentlemen, that this paper goes into the *homes.*" Or as the *New York Times* puts it: "All the news that's fit to print."

While it is beyond our ability to measure precisely to what degree the media of the early capitalist period might have been "dysfunctional,"[4] by reaching unintended audiences in unintended ways, we can be sure that print simply contains more noise along its channels than does oral, face-to-face transmission.

This general relation between teller and reader becomes a special case in situations in which the child is the reader. By teaching children to read, a gain is made in the efficiency of the socialization process. The supervising adult cannot be present all the time; but when he is not there, or is unimpressive, the written words and their accompanying illustration speak for him. The child, no longer a listener at the adult's knee, begins to take a more active part in the process of forming his own character by his selection among possible readings and possible interpretations of what is read. In his choice among socializing agencies in the mass communications field, he is soon engaged in inner-directed activity. While in one respect he is socialized from outside, in another he calculates his social possibilities himself as he reads. He begins to make more use of the increase in the number of possible relationships between himself and the storytellers following the change from word of mouth to print.

Models in Print

With this image of the print-influenced child in mind, we can turn to examine the homiletic themes which, in the period dependent on inner-direction, unite the otherwise disparate media of the Protestant and Catholic lands. One main purpose of print is to teach the child something about the variety of adult roles he may enter upon and to permit him to "try on" these roles in fantasy. Life during the period of transitional population growth differs from earlier epochs in that the adult engages in activities which the growing child no longer sees nor understands. This is why he needs not only the rich vicariousness of print but also a mode of internal direction other than tradition to guide him in unaccustomed places and situations. Both the printed media and other forms of popular culture meet this need by adding their own spurs to the parents' admonitions on behalf of ambition as well as by offering more specific guidance about the variety of new paths to success.

These new paths, in both northern and southern lands after the Renaissance, are conceived and described in adult terms. For in the earlier stages of population growth adult life is not long, on the average; the age difference—and perhaps the difference in maturity—between the literate child and the full-grown adult is less than in the period of incipient decline of population. Moreover, while the distribution of imagery and print becomes wider and cheaper than ever before, there are still many people excluded by poverty from the storyteller's market; some of these are also the overworked young. In such a society the adult stories and adult styles of narrative are often made to do for children. Even when the trick, later so prevalent, of using the child's own language, gets started, the storyteller works on the notion that he can more successfully instill *adult* ideas if he uses the language of children.

Among the earliest signposts erected on the printed path to success, aside from the indirect guides of catechism and religious teaching, were the great authorities on etiquette. A volume like Castiglione's *The Courtier*, for example, was meant for adults; but there was nothing else on the subject for the near-adult to read. At the same time people were willing to assume, as Lord Chesterfield did, that the young man was ready in his teens to operate successfully in situations requiring etiquette. In the Protestant lands and classes however, after 1600 or so, the purpose of print is concerned more and more directly with how to succeed not in love or war but in business. Then follows the commercial inspirational literature that reached a sort of climax in Victorian England with the success biographies written by Samuel Smiles—and in the United States with the Horatio Alger books, which come closer to being slanted for the teen-age market.

The variety of such books is great, but it is not unfair to refer their pattern to such an exemplar as Franklin's *Poor Richard's Almanack.* It is the more useful to us because it happens to be the text selected by Max Weber as a typical self-inspirational document of the period of the Protestant ethic. The same themes appear in earlier works, such as *Pilgrim's Progress* or *Robinson Crusoe,* which on the surface do not seem to be concerned with proper conduct for would-be enterprisers. Yet in the first we can trace the motive of social election and salvation which can so easily become secularized, while in the second the motive of economic self-sufficiency is expressed in its classical paradigm. Both works aim to fire the ambition and elan, spiritual and adventurous, of inner-directed youth.

Parallel tasks are undertaken, somewhat less openly, by all fictional literature and much art for the expanding bourgeois market. It would seem that great changes have occurred in the style of myth, as contrasted with the preindustrial era dependent on tradition-direction. In the Middle Ages—to take our example of an era dependent on tradition-direction—the individual learns about human nature from accounts no less realistic because couched in symbolic language—whether Christian, classical, or folk. Often, as is well known, they are not in verbal form at all, like the superabundance of messages in the glass and stone of a cathedral. The child is trained to understand—or, better, he is not trained away from understanding— symbolic meanings. As against this, the rising middle class dependent on inner-direction establishes for itself a new style of realism from which any direct use of symbolism is rigorously excluded.

This documentary style is the literary index of an era increasingly dependent on inner-direction.

There is leisure in such an era for fiction—but little for fantasy. Defoe may be taken as archetypical. He used a variety of techniques, such as first person narration, elaborate descriptions of food, clothing, and shelter, diary-like accounts of money transactions, and collaborative witnesses, to provide a realistic setting for his wildly adventurous tales. In this respect he is certainly the ancestor of the comic book, which excels in exploiting realism of detail as a distraction to hide improbability of situation. Such handling of literary material is connected in subtle ways with the handling of life experiences generally for the inner-directed middle-class Protestant. For him life is lived in its detailed externals; its symbolic meaning seeks richness of expression in the strenuously concrete.

Gradually, the early naturalism of Defoe gives way, both in England and on the continent, to a specifically psychological handling of the complex interpersonal relations of town life that arise in the era of transitional growth of population when people are pouring into the cities. With the growth of social classes in the modern sense, the novel begins to concern itself with subtle class differences between individuals: rises, falls, and collisions of status are perhaps its prime preoccupation. The child is instructed in an ambiguous social world, into which he will later move, by learning to recognize the subtly individualizing traits that bespeak class position and class morality.[5] Thus fiction as well as almanac and manual provide vocational (and status-oriented avocational) guidance.

To us today many of the individuals in the early Victorian novels, or in American Victorian melodrama like *East Lynne* or *Intolerance*—or even in some of Balzac's novels—appear as stereotypes. To their earliest audiences, however, these studies of personality and class in a society of shifting possibilities—a society of more people, and more people moving around—were perhaps not clichés which hindered understanding but explorations of a confusing world, helping to make sense of that world for the young. One can still attend a modern rural high school production of *Aaron Slick of Punkin Crick* and see to what extent an unsophisticated inner-directed audience will respond to the characterological "realism" of the play in terms of the older stereotypes of class, ambition, and virtue.

Biography also allows children, in a society dependent on inner-direction, to move away from family and into a rationalized world—

cooperating in this way with the parental instal-
lation of internal, self-piloting processes. Consider, for instance, the George Washington myth.
Not only are little boys told in the era of inner-
direction that they may grow up to be president
but they are given scales by which to measure and
discipline themselves for the job during boyhood.
If they do not tell lies, if they work hard, and so
on—if, that is, they act in their boyhoods as the
legendary Washington acted in his—then they
may succeed to his adult role. The role, moreover,
by its very nature, is a continuing one; somebody
is always president; thus its heroes do not have
the once-for-all quality of those in the myths and
legends of the earlier era. In fantasy the little boy
not only identifies with young Washington in the
French and Indian wars but also with the adult
role of president—either role will take him far
from home, socially and geographically.

What the story of George Washington was for
the white child the story of Booker Washington
was for the black. The latter's whole effort was
to turn the Negro away from dependence on
tradition-direction toward dependence on inner-
direction. With the role of the freedman as yet
undetermined, he placed enormous emphasis on
character building to enable the Negro to assume
any role once he was established as a middle-
class, respectable American. One of his books
addressed to Negroes was called *Character Building;* and *The Negro Worker,* a journal published at
Tuskegee, with its strong emphasis on thrift, diligence, and manners, is one of the laggard remnants (of course, under violent attack from northern urban Negroes) of a vast literature concerned
not with improving "personality" but with improving "character."

The Oversteered Child
There is, however, a danger for the child in such
pious biographical portraits of exemplary persons and roles because of the very fact that he
can read in isolation, without the intervention either of adults or peers; he can be "oversteered."
This is not so much the danger of being driven
by one's character so that one is easily exploited
by industrialism, but rather the danger of being
set on a course one cannot realistically follow.
The inner-directed child, trying to shape his character according to the ideals presented in print,
does not see these models, any more than he
sees his parents, in a state of undress. There is
none of the familiarity with the hero, even the

gods in the guise of heroes, to be found in the
orally mediated myths of the society depending on tradition-direction. Thus, Washington or
Cromwell, Garibaldi or Bismarck, Edison or Ford,
take on some of the awesomeness of the Calvinist
God. The result for many is a dreadful insecurity
as to whether they live up to their exalted models.
This insecurity not even the parents (when they
do not themselves make matters worse by trying
to be such models) can easily assuage.

Nevertheless, this unmitigated pressure for
inner-directed activity in pursuit of goodness and
fame succeeded, as we know, in producing in
many cases an "adjusted" person because social
conditions rewarded inhibitions and solaced insecurities. In other cases, however, the gap between the demand for inner-direction and the capacity for it became too great and the individual
broke down—the revival meeting represents, at
one class level, the emotional pressures of such
a conflict. While the parents alone, with their demands on all the children, were often responsible for children's emotional collapse, the storytellers tended to reinforce the social pressures
even where the adults might have been more
lenient.

The discussion has emphasized but cannot, indeed, emphasize too much the significance of
putting some of the task of socializing the child
onto other than the face-to-face adults. Just as the
whipping Kachinas of the Hopi Indians can tailor
their punishing or initiatory blows to a particularly sensitive child, so the adults in the era of
tradition-direction can see to it that the bite of the
story is not too grim for any in the audience. The
child in the inner-directed era, however, leaves
home both to go to school and to go to books and
other mass-media products; and here such mediation is no longer possible.

Moreover, the child in a period of rising literacy
is much more likely than his parents to be able to
read. Thus, while some children learn from books
and plays how to act in a career which will be different from that of their parents—or indeed that
it is possible to have such a career—other children, less able to conform in the characterolog-
ically prescribed ways, less self-disciplined and
systematic, for instance, learn from precisely the
same media how lost they are. Perhaps they learn
this especially if their parents are lacking in the
proper ethos and have not been able to give them
the proper early training in inner-direction. But
in other cases they may find that print reinforces

their feelings of inadequacy vis-à-vis their parents if they are characterological black sheep who are not able to live up to steep demands of the home.

Yet it is my impression that the stream of print is seldom without alleviating tendencies, even in the theocratic regimes. Almost always there is an underground of a more picaresque sort in which the growing boy at least can take some refuge. To be sure, the power of the parents in an era dependent on inner-direction may keep out such literature, as the pastors in puritan countries might also keep it out of the community. But they can hardly destroy, even in the worst case, the refuge of print itself—and we must not forget that the great reading-hour storehouse of the era depending on inner-direction is the Bible and that the Bible is not one book but many, with an inexhaustible variety of messages.

On the whole, therefore, the influence of the storytellers in the era of inner-direction is probably a liberating one. Print encourages and permits the child to free himself from his family and primary group; and he learns to criticize what he leaves behind, as did the self-emancipating readers of the Polish peasant press. It opens up to him a whole range of models—the "five-foot wardrobe" from which he can try on new roles. The Renaissance is itself testimony to this potency of the written word. Individualistic strivings find support as well as oversupport in the variety of paths of life described in print and drama. To be alone with a book is to be alone in a new way.

III. The Mass Media in the Stage of Other-Direction

I have assumed that the mass media today—radio, movies, records, comics, books, and magazines for children—play a greater role in shaping character than was the case in previous epochs. Certainly these agencies are more centralized and reach more people more of the time than ever before. Yet with the exception of a few careful and imaginative audience studies, especially by Herta Herzog, T. W. Adorno, Fiske and Wolfe, Lazarsfeld, Merton, and Berelson at the Institute of Social Research and Columbia's Bureau of Applied Social Research, and by Lloyd Warner and William E. Henry at the University of Chicago, we know very little about the audience. It is particularly difficult to study the effects

of nonverbal communication such as popular music or the drawings in the comics perhaps because we researchers have lost the easy sense for symbolic meanings with which I credit tradition-directed folk. Moreover, the sheer mass of the mass media is depressing to a student. Indeed, this would seem to be a field in which the techniques of Mass-Observation, an English organization of nonprofessional social scientists who observe and report on the social and cultural life of their vicinity, might promise results. Meanwhile I set forth armed with what sample soundings I have been able to gather from among isolated Mass-Observers like myself.[6] As in the earlier sections of this chapter, the problem is to see how the situation in which the transmission of the story takes place affects the listener (or reader) and how this situation in turn alters the content of the media. And here, also, the very structure of the critical language employed forces on the discussion certain overcrude distinctions between situation and content, form and content, response and significance.

The Child Market

As we have already seen, in the era of incipient decline of population children begin their training as consumers at an increasingly young age. In America middle-class children have allowances of their own at four or five; they have, as opinion leaders in the home, some say in the family budget. The allowances are expected to be spent, whereas in the earlier era they were often used as cudgels of thrift. Moreover, the monopolistic competition characteristic of this era can afford, and is interested in, building up in the child habits of consumption he will employ as an adult. For he will live long, and so will the monopoly. Monopoly is, in fact, distinguished by this very ability to plan ahead, by providing both specialists who do the planning and resources saved from profits which can pay for the planning and its later implementation. When I was in college we sold a full-page ad in a crew-race program to the American Tobacco Company. I figured that only if almost everyone who saw the program smoked Luckies for the rest of their lives could the company recoup the cost of the ad. But of course the company was interested in opinion leadership among the young or near-young, and so was willing to pay for its message in so fugitive and specialized a medium.

For all these reasons, then, it has become worth while for professional storytellers to concentrate on the child market; and by the same token the controllers of the mass media can afford specialists and market research on the particular age cultures and class cultures involved. The children are more heavily cultivated in their own terms than ever before. But while the educator in earlier eras might use the child's language to put across an adult message, today the child's language may be used to put across the advertiser's and storyteller's idea of what children are like. No longer is it thought to be the child's job to learn the adult world as the adult sees it; for one thing, the world as the adult sees it today is perhaps a more complicated one.[7] Instead, the mass media ask the child to see the world as "the" child—that is, the *other* child—sees it. This is partly, but only partly, the result of the technical advances that make it possible for the movies to create the child world of Margaret O'Brien and her compeers, for the radio to have its array of Hardys, Aldriches, and other juveniles, and for advertising and cover art to make use of professional child models. The media have created a picture of what boyhood and girlhood are like (as during the war they created the picture of the GI, again using the considerably edited language of the soldier) and they force children either to accept or aggressively to resist this picture of themselves.

The child begins to be bombarded by radio and comics from the moment he can listen and just barely read. The bombardment—with of course inevitable over- and undershots—hits specifically at very narrow age grades. For example, there seems to be for many children a regular gradation of comic-reading stages: from the animal stories like *Bugs Bunny* to invincible heroes like *Superman*, and from there to heroes like *Batman* who, human in make-up, are vulnerable, though of course they always win. The authors of "The Children Talk About Comics" find that the children themselves are aware of the progression, aware of those laggards who still read romper media when they should have graduated to blue jeans. Correspondingly, self-manipulation begins early, as we saw when we spoke earlier about the children's radio program on which the youngsters showed awareness of the dialogue on the comics carried on among parents and in the press.

To be sure, the change from the preceding era of inner-direction in America is not abrupt; such changes never are. Formerly the mass media catered to the child market in at least three fields: school texts or homilies, magazines designed for children, and penny dreadfuls. But their appraisal of the market was amateurish in comparison with market research today. Moreover, they aimed generally to spur work drives and role experiments in the mobile, rather than to effect any socialization of taste. The English boys' weeklies, as Orwell describes them,[8] usually opposed liquor and tobacco—as did the clergyman authors of school and church readers. Such admonitions remind us of the "crime doesn't pay" lesson of the comics, a facade for messages of more importance. The boys' weeklies and their American counterparts were involved with training the young for the frontiers of production (including warfare), and as an incident of that training the embryo athlete might eschew smoke and drink. The comparable media today train the young for the frontiers of consumption—to tell the difference between Pepsi-Cola and Coca-Cola, as later between Old Golds and Chesterfields.

We may mark the change by citing an old nursery rhyme:

> "This little pig went to market;
> This little pig stayed at home.
> This little pig had roast beef;
> This little pig had none.
> This little pig went wee-wee-wee
> All the way home."

The rhyme may be taken as a paradigm of individuation and unsocialized behavior among children of an earlier era. Today, however, all little pigs go to market; none stay home; all have roast beef, if any do; and all say "we-we."

Winner Take All?

Yet perhaps the most important change is the shift in the situation in which listening and reading occur. In contrast with the lone reader of the era of inner-direction, we have the group of kids today, lying on the bed or floor, reading and trading comics and preferences among comics, or listening jointly to "The Lone Ranger." When reading and listening are not communal in fact, they are apt to be so in feeling: one is always conscious of the brooding omnipresence of the peer-group. Thus the Superman fan quoted at the head of the chapter cannot allow herself to identify with Superman—the others would think her foolish—while they would not think her foolish for believing that flying is very important.

In a society dependent on tradition-direction children are, as we have seen, introduced to stories by adult storytellers. The latter do not feel themselves to be in critical competition with the young. Hence they can encourage, or at least patronize, children's unsophisticated reactions of alarm or excitement at the tales they are told—and, later on, encourage the youngster's own tall talk and tale embroidery. But the peer-groupers who read or listen together without the protective presence of adults are in no such cozy relation of "listen my children and you shall hear . . ." They cannot afford to let go—to fly.

One correlate is that the comic book differs from the fairy tale in several important respects. In the fairy tale the protagonist is frequently an underdog figure, a younger child, an ugly duckling, a commoner, while the villain is frequently an authority figure, a king, a giant, a stepmother. In the comics the protagonist is apt to be an invulnerable or near-invulnerable adult who is equipped, if not with supernatural powers, at least with two guns and a tall, terrific physique. Magical aid comes to the underdog—who remains a peripheral character—only through the mediation of this figure. Thus, whereas Jack of *Jack and the Beanstalk* gains magical assistance chiefly through his own daring, curiosity, and luck, a comic-book Jack would gain magical assistance chiefly through an all-powerful helper. While vaguely similar themes may be found in the stories of Robin Hood and Sir Galahad, the comics show a quantitative increase in the role of the more or less invulnerable authority-hero.

The relative change in this pattern[9] is not the "fault" of the comics. These merely play into a style of reception that is fitted to peer-group reading. Indeed—and this is both the conclusion of "The Children Talk About Comics" and of my own observations—if other-directed child comic fans read or hear stories that are not comics they will read them as if they were comics. They will tend to focus on who won and to miss the internal complexities of the tale, of a moral sort or otherwise. If one asks them, then, how they distinguish the "good guys" from the "bad guys" in the mass media, it usually boils down to the fact that the former always win; they are good guys by definition.

But of course the child wants to anticipate the result and so looks for external clues which will help him pick the winner. In the comics this is no problem: the good guys *look it*, being square-jawed, clear-eyed, tall men; the bad guys also look it, being, for reasons of piety, of no recognizable ethnic group but rather of a generally messy southern European frame—oafish and unshaven or cadaverous and oversmooth. But in movies (and in some comics with slinky beauties in them) this identification is not easy: the very types that are good guys in most comics may turn out to be villains after all. A striking example I have observed is the bafflement of several comic fans at the movie portrayal of the Countess de Winter (Lana Turner) in *The Three Musketeers*. If she looked so nice, how could she be so mean?

Thus we come to a paradox. The other-directed child is trained to be sensitive to interpersonal relations, and often he understands these with a sophistication few adults had in the era of inner-direction. Yet he is strikingly insensitive to problems of character as presented by his favorite storytellers; he tends to race through the story for its ending, or to read the ending first, and to miss just those problems of personal development that are not telltale clues to the outcome. It looks as though the situation of group reading, of having to sit on the jury that passes out Hooper ratings, forces the pace for the other-directed child. He cannot afford to linger on "irrelevant" detail or to daydream about the heroes. To trade preferences in reading and listening he need know no more about the heroes than the stamp trader needs to know about the countries the stamps come from.

It is not, therefore, the storytellers per se who teach children an emphasis on who wins—an emphasis also found in fairy tales and the Frank Merriwell books. The dime novels and melodramas of the period dependent on inner-direction also emphasized winning; hence it is important to see the precise differences introduced by the contemporary media as well as by the changed focus of the readers.

At the outset it seems helpful to distinguish between the inculcation of ambition and of antagonistic cooperation. "Ambition" I define as an indoctrination of goals in the period of inner-direction; it is a striving for fame or for goodness but always for clear goals: to get the job, to win the battle, to build the bridge. Competition in the era depending on inner-direction is frequently ruthless, but at the same time people are in no doubt as to their place in the race—and that there is a race. If they feel guilt it is when they fail, not when they succeed. By contrast, "antagonistic cooperation" may be defined as an inculcated striving among the groups affected by other-direction. Here the important thing is not the goal but the relationship to the "others"; not one's own victory but the others' failure. In this new-style competition people are often in doubt whether there is a race at all, and if so, what its goals are. Since they are supposed to be cooperative rather than rivalrous, they may well feel guilt about success.[10]

The heroes of boys' literature of the older period were ambitious. They had goals. And the reader identified with them and tried to emulate them, at least in fantasy. Though these heroes might fight Indians or swim icy rivers or detect crime, they were not so remote from the reader as to make identification difficult. These heroes, like the modern ones, always won; but the reader was encouraged to be concerned not only with the final victorious outcome but with the inner struggles that preceded it and made it possible. The virtue which brought victory was frequently an ability to control the self, for instance, to be brave.

While it is often assumed that the comic strip simply continues this older pattern, this is not generally true. For many reasons the child reader does not identify himself with the comic-strip hero so frequently. For one thing, many children prefer the comics where the hero is not man but Superman or Plastic Man—possessing powers that are obviously unique. No correspondence course with Lionel Strongfort will turn one, even in the wildest flight of fantasy, into Superman. What is more important, the realism of petty detail which has reached a fine art in the comics, the radio, and the movies inhibits identification. This realism, with its color effects and sound effects, exceeds by far what Defoe and his direct successors could accomplish. The characters in much fiction of the era dependent on inner-direction are props—stereotypes of the sort indicated in the preceding section. In Jules Verne, for instance, it is the adventures, the mechanical details, not the characters, that are sharply delineated; the latter are loose-fitting uniforms into which many boys could fit themselves. The imaginative, tenebrous illustrations of an artist like Howard Pyle also left openings for identification by the reader who wanted to picture himself as the hero.

Little of this looseness of fit remains for the imagination of the modern reader or listener to fill in. Though comic-strip and comicbook characterization is, if anything, less sharp, externals are pinned down conclusively: every detail of cos- tuming and speech is given. This is the more necessary because, with so many mass-media heroes competing for attention, their portrayers must engage in marginal differentiation in search of their trade-mark. Bodies by Milton Caniff must be as instantly recognizable as bodies by Fisher.

There is paradox in the reception of this realism. On the one hand, every additional brush stroke of the comic-strip artist rules out identifications for millions; the small-breasted girl, for example, may find only disapproval for herself in the comics. On the other hand, the same realism is one source of the fear of being conspicuous in our little Supergirl cited at the chapter head. If she were Superman, she would be instantly recognizable. She would lack the privacy of narcissism permitted the reader of an earlier day who could gloat over the fact that he was M. Vidocq or Sherlock Holmes—only nobody knew it.[11]

These generalizations need not be pushed too far. There are children—at least one has heard of them—who identify with Superman, or, more easily, with Terry or the Saint. Nor is it out of the question to identify, at the same time, on one level of consciousness with the hero and on another level with the person he rescues. And while the heroes of the comics are ageless, having discovered the secret of eternal youth, the growing child can move from one hero to another who better fits his own changing needs and aspirations. These countertendencies are encouraged by the gadgetry—Superman cloaks, box-top items, and so on—that relates children to their radio, movie, and comic-book heroes. But it would be a mistake to assume that each wearer of a Superman cloak identifies with Superman; he may only be a fan, wearing his hero's colors.

Perhaps it is also significant that the comic book compresses into a few minutes' reading time a sequence which, in the earlier era, was dragged out in many pages of print. Think of the Count of Monte Cristo's years in jail, his suffering, his incredible patience, and the industry and study of the abbe's teaching; both his gain and his vengeance are moralized by these prolongations, and he is an old man when, after many chapters, he wins. By contrast, the comic-book or radiodrama hero wins almost effortlessly; the very curtailment of the telling time itself makes this more apparent. To be sure, like his movie counterpart, this hero does frequently get beaten up, but this adds to excitement, not to morality or inner change, and helps justify an even worse beating administered to the "crooks."

Still another aspect of this change is worth looking at. If one does not identify with the winner but is at the very same time preoccupied with the process of winning itself, as the very handle by which one grasps a story, one is prepared for the role of consumer of others' winnings. One is prepared, that is, for the adult role of betting on the right horse, with no interest in the jockey or horse or knowledge of what it takes to be either. The content of the identification is impoverished to the point where virtually the only bond between reader and hero is the fact of the hero's winning. The spectator—the same holds for a quiz game, a sport contest, and, as we shall see, a political contest—wants to become involved with the winner simply in order to make the contest meaningful: this hope of victory makes the event exciting, while the game or contest or story is not appreciated for its own sake.

The victory of the hero, then, is only ostensibly a moral one. To be sure, vestiges of older moralities hang on, often as conventions enforced by censorship or the fear of it. But morality in the sense of a literary character's development, rather than morality in the sense of being on the "right" side, is not depicted. Consequently, morality is an inference from winning. Just as in a whodunit all appear guilty until they are retroactively cleared by finding the real killer, so the victory of the hero retroactively justifies his deeds and misdeeds. "Winner take all" becomes a tautology.

Tootle: A Modern Cautionary Tale

I have spoken as if the comic books, the cheapest and most widespread media, are the chief evidences of the pattern I am describing. It could be easily assumed that, in a home barricaded against the comic books, these patterns of readership would obtain no entrance. On the contrary, however, at least some of the important elements in the pattern are refined, disguised, and introduced into the socializing and informative books of the noncomic variety which are customarily purchased for their children by the middle and upper middle class. Furthermore, a whole range of these media teaches children the lesson given parents and teachers in many recent works on child development. The slant of that lesson is suggested by a passage from a book in use by teachers and PTA groups:

The usual and desirable developmental picture is one of increasing self-control on the part of the individual children, of increasingly smooth social or play technics, and of an emergence at adolescence or early adulthood of higher forms of cooperation. The adolescent should have learned better "to take it" in group activity, should have developed an improved, though not yet perfect, self-control, and should have real insight into the needs and wishes of others.[12]

Tootle the Engine (text by Gertrude Crampton, pictures by Tibor Gergely) is a popular and in many ways charming volume in the "Little Golden Books" series—a series for children with a circulation of well over two million, an audience which includes, it seems, all classes of children. It is a cautionary tale even though it appears to be simply one of the many books about anthropomorphic vehicles— trucks, fire engines, taxicabs, tugboats, and so on—that are supposed to give a child a picture of real life. Tootle is a young engine who goes to engine school, where two main lessons are taught: stop at a red flag and "always stay on the track no matter what." Diligence in the lessons will result in the young engine's growing up to be a big streamliner. Tootle is obedient for a while and then one day discovers the delight of going off the tracks and finding flowers in the field. This violation of the rules cannot, however, be kept secret; there are telltale traces in the cowcatcher. Nevertheless, Tootle's play becomes more and more of a craving, and despite warnings he continues to go off the tracks and wander in the field. Finally the engine schoolmaster is desperate. He consults the mayor of the little town of Engineville, in which the school is located, the mayor calls a town meeting, and Tootle's failings are discussed—of course Tootle knows nothing of this. The meeting decides on a course of action, and the next time Tootle goes out for a spin alone and goes off the track he runs right into a red flag and halts. He turns in another direction only to encounter another red flag; still another—the result is the same. He turns and twists but can find no spot of grass in which a red flag does not spring up, for all the citizens of the town have cooperated in this lesson.

Chastened and bewildered he looks toward the track, where the inviting green flag of his teacher gives him the signal to return. Confused by conditioned reflexes to stop signs, he is only too glad to use the track and tears happily up and down. He promises that he will never leave the track again, and he returns to the roundhouse to be rewarded by the cheers of the teachers and the citizenry and the assurance that he will indeed grow up to be a streamliner.

The story is an appropriate one for bringing up children in an other-directed mode of conformity. They learn it is bad to go off the tracks and play with flowers and that, in the long run, there is not only success and approval but even freedom to be found in following the green lights. The moral is a very different one from that of *Little Red Riding Hood.* She, too, gets off the track on her trip to the grandmother; she is taught by a wolf about the beauties of nature—a hardly veiled symbol for sex. Then, to be sure, she is eaten—a terrifying fate—but the tables are eventually turned, and she and grandmother both are taken from the wolf's belly by the handsome woodchopper. The story, though it may be read as a cautionary tale, deals with real human passions, sexual and aggressive; it certainly does not present the rewards of virtue in any unambiguous form or show the adult world in any wholly benevolent light. It is, therefore, essentially realistic, underneath the cover of fantasy, or, more accurately, owing to the *quality* of the fantasy.

There is, perhaps, a streak of similar realism in *Tootle.* There the adults play the role we have described earlier: they manipulate the child into conformity with the peer-group and then reward him for the behavior for which they have already set the stage. Moreover, the citizens of Engineville are tolerant of Tootle: they understand and do not get indignant. And while they gang up on him with red flags they do so for his benefit, and they reward him for his obedience as if they had played no hand in bringing it about. The whole story, in fact, might have been written by a student of learning theory, so palpably does it deal in terms of conditioned responses.

Yet with all that, there is something overvarnished in this tale. The adult world (the teachers) is *not* that benevolent, the citizenry (the peer-group) *not* that participative and cooperative, the signals are *not* that clear, nor the rewards of being a streamliner that great or that certain. Nevertheless, the child may be impressed because it is all so nice—there is none of the grimness of Red Riding Hood. There is, therefore, a swindle about the whole thing—a fake like that the citizens put on

for Tootle's benefit. At the end Tootle has forgotten that he ever did like flowers anyway—how childish they are in comparison with the great big grown-up world of engines, signals, tracks, and meetings!

While the antagonistic and rebellious elements may be veiled in a folk tale, the children who read *Tootle* or have it read to them are manipulated away from rebellion and taught the lesson of obedience to signals. Strikingly enough, moreover, the story also bears on the presumptive topic of peer-group cooperation: the exercise of consumption preferences. Those middle-class children who read the tale are not going to grow up to be railroad engineers; that is a craft followed by more inner-directed types from the working class. But while neither *Tootle* nor its readers are concerned about what it really means to be an engineer, the book does confirm one of the consumption preferences of the other-directed: big streamliners—if one cannot go by plane—are better than old coal-burning engines.[13] To be sure, *Tootle* has something to teach about train lore. It indicates that there are tracks, signals, roundhouses, just as fairy tales indicate that there are forests, woodchoppers, wolves. On the whole, however, children are attuned to the magic of travel, of communications, not in an adventurous way but in what educators are pleased to call a "realistic" one.

More impalpably, the humanized grimacing engines in *Tootle* symbolize the effort characteristic of the society depending on other-direction to cover over the impersonal mechanisms of production and transport with a personalized veneer—what we shall later discuss under the heading of false personalization. For in the phase of incipient population decline there is sufficient abundance not only for the luxuriant growth of service trades per se but for allowing even the nonservice trades to deliver "service with a smile." Today the conductors (like engineers, inner-directed types in origin) on Vanderbilt's old railroad are trained on the Twentieth Century Limited and other major runs to remember faces and give service "especially for you." The very books such as *Tootle,* or *Scuffy the Tugboat,* by the same writer and illustrator, that are intended to acquaint children with the objects and forces of the industrial society turn out to condition them to their role in the consumers' union.

We return, finally, to the theme of winning dealt with in the preceding section. Tootle does, after all, win; with his winning ways he will grow up to be a big streamliner. The reader's identification with the consumption of others' winnings is, therefore, not betrayed. But it is not made clear in the story what happens to Tootle's school-mates in engine school: do they *all* grow up to be streamliners, too? The peer-group relations of Tootle, either to the other engines or the other citizens of Engineville, are entirely amiable, and Tootle's winning does not mean that others fail. It is akin to the "benevolent conspiracy" of progres-sive parents and teachers who see to it that every child is a leader and that no one is left out, or con-spicuous, thus reinforcing the tendencies toward antagonistic cooperation of the peer-group itself. Who can be sure that Tootle would want to be a streamliner if others were not to be streamliners too?

Areas of Freedom
We have discussed the social situation in which the mass media of today are absorbed by their child readers. We have seen the effects of this sit-uation on the process by which the reader identi-fies with the protagonists and their roles. We have stressed especially the ambiguously competitive nature of these identifications which on the one hand emphasize winning and on the other hand stringently limit all emotional identifications by the code of the peer-group.

If this were all, we would have to conclude that the peer-group, as one of the mediating agencies in child readership and listening, is simply open to manipulation by the professional storytellers. But I want to raise very briefly the alternative pos-sibility: namely, that the peer-group may have a relatively independent set of criteria which helps it maintain not only marginal differentiation but even a certain leeway in relation to the media. Put the question this way: while the self-confirming process of the peer-group pushes preference ex-change to the point of parody, has the peer-group any way of reminding its captives that they are, also, individuals? It is conceivable that, in those peer-groups which succeed in feeding back styles and values to the mass media, there is some feel-ing of achievement, of having one's contribution recognized. To be sure, the feeling of having been invaded and chased by popularity or unpopu-larity off one's island of individuation will also be present, and the total outcome may depend on whether the peer-group feels the mass me-dia to be in pursuit of it or whether the group enjoys playing follow the leader, when it is the leader.

In all probability it is rare enough that a youth-ful peer-group forces the mass media—and hence other peer-groups—to follow its lead. Far more frequent will be the peer-group's opportunity to establish its own standards of media criti-cism. Groups of young hot-jazz fans, for instance, have highly elaborate standards for evaluating popular music, standards of almost pedantic pre-cision. We must go further, then, and ask whether there may be areas of privacy which children learn to find inside a superficial adjustment to the peer-group and under the cover of a super-ficial permeability to the mass media. In other words, we must re-explore the assumption made so far that the other-directed child is almost never alone, that by six or seven he no longer talks to himself, invents songs, or dreams unsupervised dreams.

We are aware that children who have been brought up on the radio can shut out its noise like those automatic devices that can be installed to silence commercials. Perhaps such children can also shut out the noise of the peer-group, even while they are contributing to it. Moreover, the comics themselves may be not only a part of peer-group consumption patterns but on occa-sion a refuge from the peer-group and a defiance against that official adult world which abhors the comics. We shall return in Part III to the ques-tion whether the mass media can foster auton-omy as well as adjustment, independence from the peer-group as well as conformity to it. But before we can tackle these more complex prob-lems of the relation between the peers and the media, we need the groundwork of another per-spective on changing character types in America. We have just scrutinized some aspects of the way in which types of character are formed at the child wave front of population by such typical agents as parents and teachers, the peer-groups, and the media. In the next few chapters let us jump ahead twenty-odd years or more in the life span and approach the structure of character in terms of the spheres of adult life. We can make use of archetypical portraits of the inner-directed and the other-directed man, his work, his play, and his politics.

Notes

1. Katherine M. Wolfe and Marjorie Fiske, "The Children Talk About Comics," *Communications Research 1948–1949,* ed. Paul F. Lazarsfeld and Frank Stanton (New York, Harper, 1949), pp. 26–27.

2. See the remarkable discussion by Ernest Schachtel, "On Memory and Childhood Amnesia," *Psychiatry,* X (1947), I; see also Evelyn T. Riesman, "Childhood Memory in the Painting of Joan Miró," *ETC,* VI (1949). 160.

3. W. I. Thomas and Florian Znaniecki, *The Polish Peasant in Europe and America* (New York, Knopf, 1927), II, 1367–1396.

4. The term is that of Lazarsfeld and Merton, "Mass Communication, Popular Taste and Organized Social Action," *The Communication of Ideas,* ed. Lyman Bryson (New York, Harper, 1948), p. 95, and especially pp. 105 *et seq.*

5. Compare the brilliant discussion by Lionel Trilling in "Art and Fortune," *Partisan Review,* XV (1948), 1271.

6. Including the work of such critics of popular culture as Otis Ferguson, Dwight Macdonald, James Agee, Clement Greenberg, Carl Withers, Bernard Wolfe, David Bazelon, George Orwell, Robert Gorham Davis, Irving Howe, Charles A. Siepmann, and Daniel Bell.

7. Certainly the adult literature is more complicated and/or more salacious on its top levels, as compared with the earlier era when both child and adult could read Mark Twain even at his most bitter, Dickens even at his most crude, H. G. Wells even at his most involved.

8. George Orwell, *Dickens, Dali & Others* (New York, Reynal & Hitchcock, 1946), p. 76.

9. Here, too, the abruptness of the change from inner-direction should not be exaggerated. Eliot Freidson, a graduate student in sociology at the University of Chicago, studying the ability of young children to remember stories, found them much more apt to recall a few traditional fairy tales like *Goldilocks* or *The Three Little Pigs* than either Golden Books or comics or movies. "Myth and the Child: an Aspect of Socialization" (Master's thesis, University of Chicago, 1949).

10. Cf. Karen Horney, *The Neurotic Personality of Our Time* (New York, W. W. Norton, 1937), pp. 192–193.

11. One additional dimension here is that the child literature of today, though written by specialists on the child market, often reaches, as in the case of the comics, millions of more or less childish adults. There are no magazines left, such as *The American Boy* or *St. Nicholas,* which the young boy can read without sharing his readership with adults—for which he can even write, occasionally, as we are reminded by Henry Steele Commager's fine *St. Nicholas Anthology.* (A similar lack of sharp cleavage between child and adult life may be seen in the fact that it is no longer a decisive step for a boy to put on long pants or for a girl to put up her hair. With clothes as with books, when and in what doses to "put away childish things" becomes a matter for the peer-group to decide, within the limits of marginal differentiation.)

12. M. E. Breckenridge and E. L. Vincent, *Child Development* (Philadelphia, W. B. Saunders, 1943), p. 456.

13. This preference is so strong that it influences directorates of railroads in coal-mining territory, concerned not only with public relations but with their own feeling for their road. A fine study could be made of railroad management's belated conversion to glamour, and the influence on this of the development of a new generation of consumers—more eager to be told that their conveyance is up to date than to be comfortable—or, more accurately, eager to be *told* they are comfortable.

45

Our Next Frontier . . . Transoceanic TV

From *Look* (1950)

David Sarnoff

David Sarnoff (1891–1971) was not only an industrial genius but a sales genius as well who transformed RCA and NBC into household names and business empires. Known as "General Sarnoff" because of his service during World War II and his no-nonsense manner, Sarnoff wrote this brief editorial, which was published in *Look* magazine in 1950, to show, first, his characteristic belief that commercial media and democracy naturally go together; and, second, his vision for the strategic role of television as an arm of U.S. foreign policy. What Sarnoff here praises, Herbert Schiller (p. 480) would denounce in 1966.

Television promises today to open up new horizons far beyond anything yet seen in this new and growing means of communication.

It is within the range of possibility now that events across the seas will one day be visible at the moment they happen to anyone within reach of a television set.

We already know the scientific principles for linking the hemispheres by television. When they are worked out and become a practical reality, we shall be able to see as well as hear around the world.

This development will prove to be one of the most revolutionary advances that science has ever offered mankind.

It will make it possible, for example, for the violent reality of distant battlefields to be experienced by people on the home front. Transoceanic TV, too, will make such happenings as international meetings, sports events and human everyday living in distant places almost a first-hand experience to audiences in all parts of the world.

The prospect promises more for real understanding among all peoples, for making human brotherhood a reality, than perhaps anything since the invention of the printing press.

Aviation is hailed today as one of the most effective means of unifying the world. Thousands of people fly to and from Europe every week in luxurious comfort across an ocean that it used to take days and weeks to cross. The distance between the world's continents has come to be measured, not in the thousands of miles, but in the few fleeting hours it takes to cover the distance.

Yet, great as its contribution is, aviation still caters to a minor fraction of the population while television, just a few years olds, is already a mass means of communication. Over 6,000,000 television receivers have a place in American homes today. Within two or three years, maybe over 20,000,000 sets will be in use, with a potential audience of 80,000,000. The growth of the television industry exceeds the strides made by any other new industry in a comparable period.

The United States, of course, has seen a more intensive development of radio than any other country. But even allowing for other nations trailing us in television, as in radio, the potentialities of the new means of communication on an international scale excite the imagination.

TV Can Sell Democracy Overseas

Think, for instance, of the way television, extended across the seas, could sell democracy abroad. In theory, democracy begs for the ear. In action, it challenges the eye. To be believed, the American way of life must be seen as well as heard. Radio can speak about the problems democracy tackles. Television can show the answers.

This means a tremendous opportunity to follow up the great work already being done by the Voice of America in its broadcasts overseas. That service can be expanded to become the "Voice and Vision of America."

Sen. Karl E. Mundt, in fact, recently urged Congressional action for a Vision of America project. He proposed that we help establish a television network in a number of countries in Europe and Asia. The project, he said, would not require the use of individual TV receiving sets but would call for community receivers like those now available and in use here.

A special advantage of such a television network system would be that it could not be easily jammed from remote areas as radio broadcasts are today by Soviet stations.

The range of television signals is at present limited. Therefore a special system would be required for sending television programs across the seas. Several methods for meeting this problem already are known. One is to equip transoceanic planes with microwave radio-relay apparatus

which could operate automatically. This would pass the television signal along from one plane to another until it reached its destination. This system might be called a "radio air lift."

Another method would be to provide a coaxial cable across the ocean. Such radio-air lifts or coaxial cables could carry not only television programs but many ordinary telephone conversations, "ultrafax" or high-speed telegraph communications and similar services. All these could be transmitted simultaneously.

While such services are not yet in existence, I have no doubt about their ultimate practicality.

International television thus is not idle dream. It is nearer than many realize. When nationwide radio broadcasting began, it was only five years before listeners overseas were picking up the broadcasts. Before long, regular international broadcasts had become an established fact. We may expect that international television will follow much of the same pattern of progress.

The reward for such progress will be the greatest opportunity ever given us for creating close ties of understanding among the peoples of the world and for helping to preserve peace.

46

Communication in the Sovietized State, as Demonstrated in Korea

From *Public Opinion Quarterly* (1951)

Wilbur Schramm and John W. Riley Jr.

Born in Marietta, Ohio, Wilbur Lang Schramm (1907–1987) was one of the chief institutionalizers of communication research as an academic field. He left a trail of distinguished institutions in his wake. After undergraduate studies at Marietta College and a master's degree at Harvard, he took his doctorate in American Civilization from the University of Iowa in 1932. He was a whirlwind of energy, a talented musician and athlete who was drawn to Iowa by his one admitted flaw: a stammer. (Wendell Johnson, a key figure in the history of speech pathology, taught at Iowa). Schramm founded the

Iowa Writer's Workshop in the 1930s, which is still one of the premiere creative-writing programs in the United States, and he taught for over a decade at University of Iowa, from 1934 to 1941 as professor of English and from 1943 to 1947 as director of the School of Journalism. From 1941 to 1943, Schramm worked side by side with many distinguished social scientists as the educational director in the Office of Facts and Figures and in the Office of War Information, where he was bitten by the research bug. At the University of Illinois, he founded the Institute of Communications Research in 1948; and at Stanford University, the Institute for Communication Research in 1956. He spent his last years at the East-West Center in Hawaii, acting as the director of its Communication Institute from 1973 to 1975. He believed in "social research for social problems," and his work as an editor and advocate for mass communication research has had a global impact. His clear and easy prose style was indeed one of his greatest assets.

John Winchell Riley Jr. (1908–) received his doctorate in sociology from Harvard University. He taught at Rutgers University from 1937 to 1960, after which he was the first director of the Office of Social Research at the Equitable Life Assurance Company. He married Mathilda White Riley (1911–), a pioneering female sociologist who has made important contributions, especially in the study of age and aging.

This selection shows Schramm and Riley working at the heart of the Cold War, within the ideological context in which Schramm formulated his vision of communication research. This article is a shorter version of Riley and Schramm's book *The Reds Take a City* (1951). Though not one of Schramm's best-known pieces, it captures many of his characteristic themes as a clearly written overview of a society's communication system. Its conclusions about the dulling capacities of mass propaganda seem, curiously, not that distant from the Frankfurt School's gloomiest views of American culture.

Historical note: The title mentions the "Sovietized" state, suggesting a common front, or at least common tactics, between Russia and China (*soviet* means "council" in Russian). Later in the 1950s, quarreling between the two communist megaliths would make such terminology an obvious anachronism.

When the Iron Curtain was rolled back from Korea in 1950, the free world was presented an opportunity to test long-held beliefs and suppositions about the communication system of the sovietized state. Korea was a good place to observe this system because it illustrated the sovietized state in its early stages (the 90-day Communist occupation of South Korea) and in a much later stage of development in North Korea (which had been five years under Communist control). It was quickly apparent to observers that the sovietization of South Korea had proceeded from the same blueprint which had been used in North Korea, and that the North Korean blueprint in turn bore enough resemblance to the patterns in other satellite states to permit a considerable degree of generalization from what was seen in Korea.

The sovietized state as seen in Korea is, of course, an oligarchy that calls itself a people's democracy. Its effectiveness depends upon a meticulously organized power structure, upon control by the state of most or all of the productive resources and facilities, and upon a monopoly of communications sufficient to shut out opposing propaganda and to saturate the people of the state with ideas and attitudes predisposing them to sovietization. One of these controls could hardly endure without the others. If the power system is the most carefully and evidently organized at least in the early stages of the sovietizing process, and if the control of resources produces some of the most spectacular changes observed, certainly the communication program is the most pervasive part of the process.

Literally nothing the Communist government did in Korea was free from association with their ideological propaganda. Every school, every organization, every surviving medium of mass communication became a mouthpiece for the leaders and a tool for the indoctrination of the people. Special attention was paid to official contacts and behavior. The first Communist occupation troops in South Korea, many of whom had fought in the Chinese 8th Route Army, were specially trained in the way they should treat civilians; when they shook hands with South Korean women they used the occasion to emphasize the Communists' promise of equality for women. When they redistributed the land, that too was a text for teaching. When they looted homes for sewing machines and other mechanical devices ostensibly to be used in hospitals, they used that occasion to berate the U.S. forces for their brutality and to explain how the people's democracy cares for its wounded and unfortunate. As a Pyongyang laborer said to us, "Every sheet of paper, every instrument for communicating, and every meeting was for propaganda."

Three principles seem to have governed this ideological program:

1. *Monopoly.* As far as possible, every non-Communist source of information was to be excluded, and every channel of information and opinion was to be in the service of Communism.
2. *Concentration.* Their propaganda was based on a relatively simple line, which was repeated over and over again.
3. *Reinforcement.* As propagandists, they believed in shotgun rather than rifle methods. They used every channel to din their propaganda line into their audiences, and made no effort to avoid repetition. The careful matching of media to message was apparently less important to them than the need to saturate the information channels and to reinforce their message by every possible means.

The Line

The Communist line is quite familiar, and there is no need to detail its contents to this audience. It is perhaps more important to point out the essential simplicity of the line as used in Korea. There is a basic difference in soviet terminology between *propaganda,* which in Leninist terms is the presenting of many ideas about a single subject to a small number of people, and *agitation,* which is defined as the presenting of a few ideas to the mass of

people. In the advanced Communist schools of North Korea and neighboring China, the curriculum was propaganda. The mass media and the many face-to-face channels to the Korean people were used for what the Communists called agitation, and the content of these channels was kept simple and direct.

This content was remarkable not for its difference from Communist lines elsewhere, but rather for its close interlocking with the Chinese and Russian lines. In general, its goals seem to have been four:

1. To promote aggression toward the United States—which was called "capitalist, imperialist aggressor" and accused of trying to colonize Korea for its own economic gain.
2. To divide the people of South Korea from their government—the ROK government was subjected to extremely bitter invective, called traitorous, corrupt, "running dog of the US capitalist imperialists."
3. To promote identification with the USSR—which was given entire credit for liberating Korea from the Japanese, called "peaceful, powerful friend of small nations" and "most powerful nation in the world," and held up as a model for future Korean development.
4. To shape expectations toward rewards under a Communist regime. To dramatize this last purpose, a series of promises were included in the line, among them better living standards, equal status for women, redistribution of farm land so that each farmer would own his equal share, better working conditions and the eight-hour day for laborers, the unification of Korea, and a great future for the country in the Communist family of nations.

It should be added that the line, especially the parts of it directed toward the United States and the ROK government, was in every way as bitter and intense as the Chinese and Russian lines.

The Monopoly Methods

This intense, simple line was dinned incessantly into the people of Korea by means of monopolized communications. The importance of monopoly in the soviet scheme was illustrated by the confiscation of radios in South Korea, despite the fact that the Communists had possession of Radio Seoul, the most powerful broadcasting station in Korea. In other words, the Communists were willing to forego the opportunity of speaking to South Koreans on their own radio in order to be sure that the South Koreans were not able to listen to the Japanese radio!

Control of communications was by means of ownership, supervision, and surveillance. The state owned newspapers, broadcasting stations, theaters. In Seoul the existing papers were suspended by the invaders, and two new papers were established, using some of the plants of the suppressed newspapers. Trusted party members were placed in positions of chief control in all the media. The cultural branches of the ministries supervised content closely. A large quantity of speeches, letters, and statements by leading Communists was furnished to the editors and program directors. TASS was the only news service permitted, and only motion pictures from communist countries could be shown. The influx of printed material from non-Communist countries seems to have been dried up to nothing, and in its place came a large number of books, magazines, posters, pamphlets, and comic books from the sovietized world. The Communist government apparently made every effort not only to prevent non-Communist communication from reaching the Korean people, but also to fill the leisure time of the Koreans with Communist communication so that there would be less opportunity or incentive to seek facts elsewhere.

Finally, the surveillance and penal system operated to make it dangerous for any Korean under Communist domination to receive foreign communication in any circumstance. As many radios as could be found in occupied South Korea were confiscated; many radios in North Korea were sealed to the Pyongyang wave length. To be caught listening to the anti-Communist radio was made an offense punishable by death, as was the picking up of UN leaflets dropped from airplanes or the reading of "capitalist" books. Librarians in occupied South Korea were made responsible for deleting undesirable books from their collections. Citizens were encouraged to denounce fellow-citizens for such offenses, and the secret police operated everywhere to check on offenders who had been rumored to have expressed deviationist sentiments.

Use of the Mass Media

The first requirement of the mass media in this monopoly system is that they shall be politically purposeful. Entertainment is not regarded as an obligation of the media, although, as Alex Inkeles[1] expresses it, "positive and constructive relaxation" is an "accepted but secondary" goal.

In accomplishing the political purposes of the Party, the press takes leadership. A number of South Koreans commented to us that the press during the Communist occupation was "like a textbook." This is, of course, exactly what it was intended to be, and the papers were used as texts for the Party cultural hours. According to Lenin, the Communist press must be at once propagandist, agitator, and organizer. The Korean press was therefore an agitator to the masses, a propagandist to the higher Party members, and a Party journal. A large part of it was neither written by the editors nor furnished by TASS, but consisted of articles by Party dignitaries, officials in the ministries, and politically reliable experts. Another large part consisted of the official statements and directives of the Party—letters, orders, explanations, speeches. The concept of news as event, so common to our newspapers is not common to the Communist press. Rather, news is defined as social process and economic and political meaning. The whole western pattern of fresh news, "scoops," human interest stories, "inside stories" is rather meaningless to the sovietized press, where the criterion is not firstness or freshness or uniqueness or surprise but rather how a news story advances the program of the Party or the state.

The press undoubtedly was given its position of leadership in the Communist pattern because the foreign press can be more easily excluded and because printed material can be studied and re-studied and used as a text for meetings and schools. For this reason, in South Korea for some weeks the newspapers were given free circulation to every *n*th house and the persons who received the papers were ordered after reading to pass them on to the neighbors.

Politically the radio seemed to be used to echo and reinforce the press, rather than to make original contributions of its own. This refers, of course, to domestic radio, not international broadcast. In many cases, the political talks on the radio were reported to be the same as the articles in the newspapers. The same TASS news was printed in the papers and heard on the air. There are many references among Korean listeners to the "talky" quality of the Communist radio, the fact that announcers would read the long political articles in a rather dull way, and that the radio had "no charm." Perhaps the kindest words were said about the children's programs where, in Korea as in Russia, the imagination of radio writers was given freer reign and where agitation was more subtly accomplished. In many cases music on the Communist radio was said to be excellent, and there were some broadcasts of literary material, but all these, like the talks, were required to be politically "purposeful." If the Korean was allowed to relax with his radio program, he was supposed to relax to Party songs or poetic odes to Stalin or a symphony by a solid soviet composer.

The government sought to make sure that motion pictures should be politically purposeful by restricting the showings to films made in Communist countries, which meant chiefly Russia and China. There was some film production in North Korea, supposed to be largely shorts and teaching films. As the official newspapers in occupied Seoul were given free circulation for a time, so were the motion picture theaters for a time opened free to the public. The public approval gained by this gesture was lost, however, when the People's Army began to take young men from the audiences and draft them for military service.

Comics in sovietized Korea were no more for entertainment than were the other media. Indeed, they were no funnier than most American comics. Unlike American comics, however, they tended to be single-frame cartoons rather than continued serials. Some of the cartoons were signed by Russian artists; others not signed were in the familiar biting style of *Pravda*. It is reasonable to suppose that in the production of this material considerable help came from the center of the Communist world. From Russia, too, came beautifully printed magazines carefully following the Party line.

One other point needs to be made about the Communist use of mass media. Having decided that the press should serve them as agitator, they took pains to make the press readable by the masses. In the newspapers as in the schools they used the Korean phonetic alphabet (Hankul) which is mastered much more easily than the Chinese ideographs. Some Korean interviewees reported with gratitude that the papers were also rearranged so that subject matter could be more easily found.

Use of Schools

It seemed to some observers of sovietized communications in Korea that much of the mass communication addressed to adults was intended to dull rather than to arouse, to keep new ideas out rather than to inculcate them. These same observers wondered also whether the Party were not counting on the schools, rather than the mass media, to prepare the ground for conversion. For certainly the Communists, like the Nazis, have much faith in youth and are meticulously careful to expose young people to the kind of schooling the Party considers right. A North Korean farmer told us significantly, "The aged were not required to attend the various political meetings, but the young were forced to."

In South Korea, during the 90-day occupation, the school system broke down and enrollment fell off as much as 90 per cent, not so much because of any changes in the system as because of the dangers of injury from air raids and, in the case of older children, the danger of being impressed into the army. Parents therefore kept their children at home. In North Korea the school system was well developed. Actually there were two systems, but the political schools blended into the civil schools so that at points there was no clear boundary. Political indoctrination appeared in the curriculum of the civil schools, and the political schools for various kinds of Party leaders usually included some general subjects—for example, language and history.

Two things the Communists did with education won the plaudits of most North Koreans. For one thing, they made it easier for children of farmers and laborers to go to school. This they did by building more schools, and designing the first four years around the concept of a "People's School" which should be open to everyone. They also made a real effort to decrease the rate of illiteracy. They put the simple and easy-to-learn Korean Hankul alphabet to use in place of Chinese ideographs, and offered many classes to teach reading. This program extended even into the army, where, as a prisoner of war testified, in peacetime classes were held three hours a day for those who wanted to learn to read. Since the chief lesson material was Communist doctrine, the plan tended to make both literates and Party material.

Curricula in the public schools were little changed. Said a Wonsan school teacher: "Lessons at the high school in North Korea were mathematics, geometry, literature, Russian, trigonometry, astronomy, psychology, logic, philosophy, Korean history, constitution, geography, world history, etc. There wasn't any special hour for Party history. It was mainly instructed at the hour for the constitution." Russian was substituted for English or Japanese, and time was regularly devoted to Communist Party history and Communist songs. But the Party depended on changed methods and materials rather than a change in courses. The government furnished all the textbooks, which were edited so as to be politically satisfactory. The government also examined all the students. Teachers were required to have special indoctrination. In some schools at least, a Party member served as head supervisor, and all lesson plans were submitted to this supervisor for approval or disapproval. Students were given part of their grades on "behavior," which meant not "deportment" in the American sense, but rather political behavior. Teachers were chosen apparently for the political safeness rather than for extensive training, and many complaints were heard that a teacher was required only to have four years of education. It is not surprising, therefore, that one Korean student should report to us: "Courses begin with admiring Communism and conclude with honoring Communism, even though they are Korean history and language courses," nor that a Pyongyang factory manager should say that the goal of all the schools was to "train students to be perfect Communists and eloquent speakers so that they would be able to train the general public to be Communists." It is perhaps unnecessary to say that the young Communists (the Youth Alliance) were carefully and extensively organized throughout the schools.

There was an extensive system of political schools, intended to train Party leaders, labor leaders, cultural officers for the army, and numerous other specialists. It was in specialized and professional training that the political and civil schooling tended most to blur. For example, cultural officer candidates in the army were taught Korean History, Politics, World Political Geography, Mathematics, and Russian. Students in the central political school at Pyongyang, studying to be Party leaders, took Korean History, Politics, World Political Geography, History of the Communist Party, Military Tactics, Physical Training, and Russian. Students in the historical curriculum at Haeju Normal College studied Marxism and Leninism, European History, Korean History, Russian Language, and Russian Teaching Methods. Korean political schools were geared into other Communist systems, so that promising students might study at a Chinese political school, and the most promising of all might have a chance to study in Moscow.

Face-to-Face Methods

Impressive as was the degree of organization revealed by the Communists' use of the mass media and of the schools in Korea, even more impressive was their organization for face-to-face indoctrination.

Through the Communist Party (called the Labor Party in Korea), the Women's Alliance and the Youth Alliance, the Communists reached almost the whole population. The labor unions operated under the wing of the Party. The professional and business associations were required to devote a considerable part of their meeting time to cultural hours teaching Communist doctrine. The school children were organized. The Party's several organizations were active even within the army and navy.

Each of these organizations was the focus of an intensive program of indoctrination through meetings. In addition to these, there were also regular community meetings and industry or office meetings, also for indoctrination. There were, as a Pyongyang ironmonger summarized it, "reading meetings, self-criticism meetings, reflection meetings, and lecture meetings." Reading meetings began with the reading of the newspaper or other Communist text, or with a member reporting on his reading, followed by comment from others present. Self-criticism meetings began usually with denunciations, followed by confessions and expressions of contrition from accused persons. Reflection meetings were "to reflect on one's mistakes and swear not to do the same thing again." Lectures were usually given by higher Party officials or by students from a Party school.

Meetings were going on apparently at all hours of the day, and few sovietized Koreans seem to have escaped going to a least one political meeting a day—at his school, his place of business, his association, or his neighborhood. Evidence on the frequency and ubiquity of these meetings is very extensive, and the indication is that the Communists used the meetings as a part of their saturation technique to fill leisure time and monopolize communication opportunities.

It is worth nothing that these meetings were geared into the mass media. The newspaper served as a text for the reading meeting and the cultural hour. The radio or film sometimes served as a program for the community meeting. In a few cities, loud speakers were installed, through which announcers explained the news. Perhaps most important of all, the tight control on content made sure that the citizens of Korea would be getting the same facts from the media as from face-to-face communication, and that there would thus be a considerable degree of reinforcement.

The meetings were also geared into other face-to-face indoctrination. As a Sunchon clergyman said, "Propaganda officers from the District People's Committee made their rounds once a week preaching Communism." Agitators were active in dealing with individuals and small groups. In Seoul during the occupation, Communist school children were even assigned to visit families in an attempt to persuade them to send their children back to school.

The quality of the planning and organization back of this apparatus of meetings and agitation was most impressive.

Spectacle and Display

Like other totalitarian governments, the government of sovietized Korea knew very well the value of pictorial and spectacular communication.

Posters were much used. They were skillfully drawn and effectively presented. One of the favorite devices of display was to place many of these posters together so as to make a splash of color and a powerful repetition of a theme.

Supposedly, most of these posters were printed in North Korea. Many of them, however, looked exactly like Russian posters except in language. Stalin's picture looked down from many walls in sovietized Korea, and typical Russian poster art was either copied or furnished.

Parades and open-air demonstrations were also favorite devices of the Korean Communists. The Inchon landing in September of 1950 came just in time to cause the cancellation of a great festival scheduled to be held in Seoul celebrating the Communist victory and the reuniting of the country. Choruses, orchestras, dancers, actors, the most distinguished conductors in Korea, all were to participate. The invading Americans found signs of preparation, but the performers had fled. Organized with great speed and efficiency by the Communists, it was intended to celebrate—ironically—the propaganda report that the invaders had been thrown back into the sea. Two days later the Marines came in over the route of the parade.

Special Device—Self-criticism

Among the special devices used with great skill and effect by the Communists as a part of their program of thought control was self-criticism. This is simply a public confession of sins against the philosophy or practice of the state. Sometimes the confession is written, as a part of an indoctrination course or as a test of "reactionism." More often it is oral, and made before a public meeting. Often such a confession follows denunciation. The confessor humbly admits and describes his defections, and promises to do better. The audience then votes as to whether his contribution shall be accepted. The setting and effects are not entirely unlike those of the Oxford movement and other public confessionals in our culture. In the sovietized state, a very large number of the citizens participate in self-criticism in one time or other, and often repeatedly, either as a part of their re-education or as mild therapy. We were given abundant testimony to the effectiveness of the device. There seems little doubt that it would succeed in building anxiety around "undesirable" concepts such as "reactionary," and building expectations of reward around concepts the Communists thought desirable. The mass reinforcements should be considerable.

Surveillance Information

This is not the place to describe in any detail the Korean surveillance system, in which spies spied even upon spies, one government agency on another, and amateur denouncers joined with Party members, inspectors, secret police, security police, and a variety of other groups in reporting to the Party and the central government what they needed to know about potential defection within the ranks. But let it be said that these channels of communication were painstakingly kept open. By many channels this information flowed to Party and government headquarters. "Wherever there were more than two people gathered," said a North Korean, "there was sure to be one spy." The Koreans were careful to whom they talked, what they said, where they were seen. Insecurity and inhibition were built into life in Korea.

How Effective

For obvious reasons, the effectiveness of the Communist use of communication in Korea must be estimated rather than measured. Yet there seems little doubt that the Communists succeeded in dinning their line into the ears of all their Korean subjects. Their concentration on a simple message and their "shotgun" methods were undoubtedly effective. A Seoul physician, for example, told us that he and his family found themselves listening and remembering, even though weary of the repetition, even though predisposed against the Communist position. A housewife told frankly that if the meeting, the self-criticism, the saturation of the press, had gone on a few weeks longer, she felt she would either have been forced to go underground and fight or to become an active Communist. In the face of such an inpouring of communication, she said, a middle ground is difficult if not impossible.

The communication monopoly was thought to have been at least 90% effective, even in occupied South Korea. Yet it was not completely effective, and the cracks in the iron curtain were important. Radio was the most frequently successful way to penetrate the curtain. Short wave radios still were used to hear UN broadcasts even after North Korean receivers were sealed to the Pyongyang wave length and as many South Korean radios as could be found were confiscated. People hid their radios in the wall or ceiling, listened to them a few minutes a day or even a few minutes a week. Sometimes the listener crouched under the floor, and wrapped both himself and the receiver in heavy blankets which both deadened the sound and created a sweatbox. Once a broadcast or a leaflet was received, then there were many grapevines by which the message could circulate. Listeners told their trusted friends, and these friends told others. In the villages, the word was passed around on market days. There is no doubt that channels existed to get at least a small quantity of information from outside to such Koreans as wanted it.

It should be said also that the Communist communication system in Korea worked much better from the government to the people than vice versa. Most governmental systems provide channels whereby citizens can express their opinions, needs and wishes to and about the governing elite, and thus secure changes or at least develop a sense of belongingness. These channels vary from the cracker barrels of the country store through the ward heeler, the *padrone* of Latin American civilizations, the free opposition newspaper, to free elections. By definition, these are omitted from the sovietized state. The devices substituted for them—the front committee, the one-slate election, the letters to the state-owned newspaper, the agitators and political officers—were apparently not entirely satisfactory even in a state where the vast majority of the people had been accustomed to follow direction rather than to participate in making policy. There was considerable evidence in Korea that people saw through the elections, the letters, the "self-governing" committees, and that the oligarchic nature of the state and the covert nature of its authority were understood.

On the other hand, it must be admitted that in getting information *about* the people—by spying, inspection, surveillance, denunciation, self-criticism, personal history, and other means—the Communist communication system was marvelously effective. Just as the central concern of the government in a sovietized state is to keep down a counter-elite, so the provision of information on such a potential elite may be more central to the communication system than either the provision of information to the people or the making of opportunity for the people to speak. Indeed, the impression grows with observation that the Communist elite in Korea were using their elaborate communication system chiefly to dull the people, to fill their communication time and keep them from counter-information or from reflections of their own, looking toward a series of automatic responses at the will of the ruling elite. And meanwhile the ruling elite sat with ears glued to the communication channels that would report the first stirrings of dissatisfaction or rebellion against the automatic response pattern.

Notes

In November, 1950 the Human Resources Research Institute of the Air University, under the direction of Dr. Raymond V. Bowers, sent a team of social scientists to Korea to study certain psychological warfare problems. The authors of this article were members of that team. Other members who were especially helpful in the gathering of material and the discussions from which this article grew include Dr. Frederick W. Williams, chief of the psychological warfare division of the Human Resources Research Institute, and Dr. John C. Peizel, of Harvard. The contribution of 25 Korean social scientists who served

as interviewers and interpreters should also be noted.

This article makes use of material, gathered during the Korean assignment, which the Air Force has declassified. Sources of this material were approximately 75 intensive unstructured interviews with officials in the ministries who had remained in Seoul during the Communist occupation and had been able expertly to watch events in their field; approximately 200 structured interviews with representative citizens of North and South Korea; about 1300 interviews with prisoners of war; about 1400 interviews with refugees; captured documents; and published personal narratives by Koreans who had lived under Communism. Some of these personal narratives may be found in the book by these same authors, *The Reds Take a City*, Rutgers University Press, 1951. Other related material from the Korean assignment has appeared in an article entitled "Flight from Communism: a Report on Korean Refugees," *Public Opinion Quarterly*, summer, 1951.

1. For his discussion of this point see his book, *Public Opinion in Soviet Russia*, Cambridge: Harvard University Press, 1950, chap. 17.

47

The Consumer's Stake in Radio and Television

From *Quarterly of Film, Radio and Television* (1951)

Dallas Smythe

Dallas Smythe (1907–1992) was a leading political economist and theorist of mass communication. Born in Regina, Saskatchewan, he and his family moved to Pasadena in 1918, after a flu epidemic nearly killed them. Smythe attended Pasadena Junior College; the University of California, Los Angeles; and the University of California, Berkeley, where he took his undergraduate and doctoral degrees in economics (1937). He was radicalized by three years of working for the Agricultural Extension Service

(1934–1937), witnessing the migrant labor conditions and the "Okies," as dramatically portrayed in the late-1930s book and movie *The Grapes of Wrath*. From 1937 to 1948, Smythe worked as a government economist in Washington, D.C., in Franklin Roosevelt's New Deal administration, during which time he was active in union efforts. He conducted studies of the telegraph and newspaper industries before joining the Federal Communications Commission in 1943. In 1948, he went to the University of Illinois, where, despite trustee objections based on information provided by the House Committee on Un-American Activities, Smythe was appointed professor of economics and communication. Smythe taught at Illinois until 1963, when, discouraged by the belligerence of American Cold War policy, he returned to Canada and taught at the University of Regina and Simon Fraser until his death. He was best known for a series of provocative and theoretically sophisticated articles in the 1960s and 1970s, addressing the political economy of communications from an increasingly explicit Marxian perspective.

Smythe was one of the earliest television researchers. In 1951, as director of research for the National Association of Educational Broadcasters, he conducted a study of television programming in New York, the first of his several such empirical studies. They helped to provide a basis for Smythe's more critical theoretical insights, one of which is on display in this 1951 article from the *Quarterly of Film, Radio, and Television*. In it, Smythe articulates an early version of his theory of the audience as the product of commercial broadcasting, whose labor is sold to advertisers. He also offers a critical analysis of television programming and an interest in its broad educational possibilities, stylistically distinct from his later, more thoroughgoing devotion to the political economy of media industries.

According to NBC's vice-president in charge of television, "If television is a fad, so is breathing." Even if we discount this salesman's modest enthusiasm for television, it is fairly clear that television is here to stay in a large way.

One of the more popular sports among what used to be called our "intelligentsia" is that game I call "Let's Predict the Effects of Television." Everybody seems to be doing it, especially those who are best qualified by virtue of the fact that "they wouldn't have a television set in the house."

But consumers of radio and television have some specific interests in these media, economic interests which give them the right not only to predict their effects but to examine their techniques. To understand why, it might be well to begin by inquiring in economic terms as to the nature of the "product" which these media offer the consumer. Just what is the "product"?

Radio and television offer a complex of "products." If they had been designed to give nightmares to the economist who tries to measure statistically such things as demand—cross elasticities and all—it could hardly have been better contrived. There are two interrelated kinds of products, each with its unique differentiation of grades and prices.

In the first place there is the group of products and services which relate to the receiving sets. In addition to the sets themselves, there are attachments and antennas. There is electric power. There are replacement parts. And there are the services of the repairman. These are all in a sense intermediate producers' goods, except for whatever utility the radio and television sets may have as furniture.

In the second place there is that product known as station time, and sometimes as audience loyalty (measured by ratings) which stations sell to advertisers. The industry refers to this as a market for time. But it is not that simple. What is sold is a *program for the audience* (in whose continuing loyalty the station management has a vital interest), and *the probability of developing audience loyalty to the advertiser*. And the consideration paid and received is much more than what passes between the advertiser and the station or network—namely the payment for time and talent by the advertiser. In commercial radio and television, our Janus-like product is paid for twice. It is paid for once, as a producer's good, if you please, when the sponsor pays for its production. And it is paid for again, as a consumer's good, when the more or less predictable audience response results in the ringing of cash registers where the sponsor's product is sold to ultimate consumers.

I would feel like apologizing for inflicting on you this application of elementary economics to radio and television were it not for the fact that one of the most prevalent myths in our culture is that radio and television programs are "free." Even so intelligent and acute and observer as Jack Gould helps perpetuate this myth by referring to his lead article in a recent front-page series in the New York *Times* to "society's powerful unknown: the continuous free show available upon the flicking of the switch of a television set." Unless we remember how commercial radio and television articulate with our economic system, subsequent policy considerations may lose perspective.

One significant corollary meets us immediately. Readers of magazines and newspapers usually buy them for their editorial matter, not for their advertising content. The consumer's affirmative or negative reaction to editorial matter runs to the publishers, not to the advertiser. Yet in radio and television the consumer has the advertiser to thank for the program. This phrase falls naturally from our lips, for it realistically locates the effective party responsible for the program. And in saying this I do not derogate at all the legal responsibility of the station for its programs. The troublesome fact is that under our uneasy institutional compromise by which the stations are publicly licensed and commercially operated, the effective, if not the legal, responsibility is divided. And the voice which speaks most often to the consumer is that of the advertiser. Is it any wonder that the consumer is confused and inarticulate in trying to express his judgment as to how these media should conduct themselves? Is it any wonder that our traditional view of our cultural values, including freedom of speech and freedom of the press, may be reshaped increasingly into the likeness of the cultural values of the advertisers?

Having tried to locate the consumer in relation to the place of radio and television in our economic system, let me proceed to examine the principal consumer's interests in radio and television.

One consumer's interest is in the markets relating to the receiving set. Here we are on ground familiar to those engaged in consumer education. The aggregate consumer expenditures on receivers and ancillary services far exceed the expenditures of advertisers and stations on radio and television. Even if we disregard the costs paid by consumers through the prices of advertised goods and services which they buy, it is evident that radio and television, by virtue of his yearly cost of keeping his receiver operating, *alone,* might well be his admission ticket to the policy-making proceedings by the FCC, the FTC, and their Congressional masters.

A second kind of consumer's interest in radio and television is his concern with the technical standards of service. This arises in both the set market and the program market. It is his interest in *when what* kinds of innovation should take place in the art of radio communication. This is his interest in the introduction of FM to supplant in part AM broadcasting. This is his interest in the addition of color to television.

The consumer must look to federal authority to protect this interest. For long ago we decided that federal control was the only way this problem could be handled. When the policy of licensing was applied to the publicly owned radio waves a generation ago, it was realized that a split-up plant in which the lock (the receiver) and the key (the transmitter) are owned by different persons can only operate as a unit if both parts are built to work on the same standards. The FCC has the duty to set these standards with a view to building a nation-wide communications system which will best serve the interest of the public. It has the responsibility of prescribing the nature of the service to be rendered by each class of radio service. Closely related is the FCC's function of allocating wave lengths for the use of the several services. The FCC thus has authority to determine *what* kinds of electronic service should be provided by radio, *how much* of each should be provided, and *where* they should be provided. Through its authority to initiate proceedings at any time, it has ultimately also the control of when the service should be provided. And if no industry group should be interested in promoting a new service which was technically ripe for use, the FCC has the power to study such new uses and encourage them. If it found, for example, that facsimile was such a service, it could recommend to the Congress appropriate developmental legislation (such as grant-in-aid) or remedial legislation to free the new service from possible suppressing influences.

This broad range of federal authority does not represent any one political party viewpoint. In fact these kinds of authority were conferred on the federal administration by historical events which amount to a genuine bipartisan policy. They were originally enacted by a Republican administration (that of President Coolidge) with the eager consent of the radio industry; they were transferred to the FCC by a Democratic administration, that of President Roosevelt.

The consumer's ignorance of the possible practical applications of the techniques covered by the thousands of patents held by the industry—the largest numbers of which are concentrated in the Bell System and RCA—accounts for his helplessness in appraising this aspect of the work of our regulatory agency. Consumers have occasional windfalls of information declassified from corporate security regulations as incidents to patent litigation. But the chances of significant technical developments being disclosed in this way decrease constantly with the growing concentration of patent holdings in large corporate hands and the complexity of science itself. Either consumers must depend passively on corporate decisions to innovate, or they must look to the FCC and to the Congress for protection of their interest in technical innovation.[1]

One reason for talking today about the consumer's interest in innovation is the fact that we are currently witnessing a dramatic example of the scope of this interest. I refer to the controversy over color television.

The great bulk of the capital investment in a nation-wide television system will be made by consumers in their own homes. One thousand television stations, even at a liberal estimate of two million dollars apiece, would represent an investment of two billion dollars. But forty million television sets in as many homes, at an average of $250 each, represent an investment of ten billion dollars, or five times the stations' investment.

We have heard much from RCA and other prominent manufacturers and patent holders in black and white television of the cost to the viewers of making partially obsolete some ten to twelve million black and white receivers through their lack of "compatibility" with the CBS color system. The same manufacturers should take credit at the same time for a major share of the responsibility for creating the problem. When the FCC held its hearings on CBS color in 1946–1947 there were less than half of 1 per cent of the present number of black and white television sets

in the hands of the public. The set manufacturing industry was almost solidly opposed to the adoption of color. Before them loomed a postwar market for perhaps thirty to forty million black and white sets which they were prepared to manufacture. And this was an eager market for consumer durables which had been scarce through four or five years while consumer savings were mounting. Doubtless many able engineers sincerely believed that the development of a satisfactory color system would require many years of research work. But for the set-manufacturing executives who establish corporate policy, and budgets for research and development, the incentive to push color was weak—to put it mildly. Would they not have been derelict in pursuing the goals conventionally attributed to enterprise if they had failed to seek to sell black and white sets to all this vast market—and then brought color sets on the scene as the next step in technical progress?

In any event, the set-manufacturing industry energetically presented many technical arguments to convince the FCC that the CBS color proposals were unsound. And an FCC, perhaps somewhat bemused by the welter of technical language, decided that the bulk of the industry was right and CBS was wrong. As the industry's metaphor put it: black and white got the green light.

Without trying to tell the full story, let me say that the color issue was raised again barely two years after that decision. In the public record of the second hearing, it was evident that the set manufacturers had not pushed the development of color television in their laboratories. And by the time the FCC decided, after an exhaustive year of hearings, in the summer of 1950 that CBS color standards should be adopted, it was possible for most of the set manufacturers to point to the nine or ten billion black and white sets they had sold in the interim and to argue the issue of compatibility which had thus arisen. These manufacturers launched a massive public relations campaign to defeat CBS color. The Supreme Court, with little disagreement, decided this spring, however, that the FCC had both stayed within its powers and given due process to the opponents of CBS color. So we are about to see color television innovated.

What is the moral of this drama? I think it is this. Under Wayne Coy's able chairmanship the FCC ordered an innovation which was probably equally desirable three years earlier. But it is almost inconceivable that this result would have been achieved had there not been an aggressive, large rival—namely CBS—acting as advocate for color. In the present climate of opinion on the relation of government to business, it is doubtful whether the fortitude of the commissioners would be enough to cause the FCC *on its own account* to overrule a major industrial group on an innovation of large significance. The sad history of facsimile broadcasting is probably a case in point.

A related conclusion respecting the color controversy is that ultimately whether one approves of the commission decision or not largely depends on whether one thinks that the final authority in such matters should be that of the Communications Act and its administrators operating under the constitutional due process rules, or that of the large industrial corporations, pursuing their usual policies.

The color controversy illustrates well the inarticulateness of the consumer and of the FCC as well. Under the general Congressional restrictions on government informational activity, the FCC was prevented from presenting to the public its side of the controversy in any way which could compare in effectiveness with the very extensive and expensive public relations program conducted by the set manufacturers. Similarly, the individual members of the public, hearing only one side of the controversy and being unused to communicating with their government agencies, were silent. In an era when much is heard about the necessity of peoples speaking to peoples this may be a bit ironic. Corporations may speak to people but not the FCC; and people speak seldom to either.

A third interest which the consumer has in radio and television is his concern with the quantity and quality of advertising matter which he consumes. Over the past quarter century radio listeners experienced a steady increase in the amount and aggressiveness of advertising matter in their radio programs. Periodically, the commercial broadcasters adopted rather ineffective "codes" relating to the maximum of advertising which stations should carry. The federal regulatory authority, speaking through Herbert Hoover when he was secretary of commerce, the Federal Radio Commission, the Congress, and the FCC, has laid down a series of policy statements, all of which have expressed the view that in the public interest advertising on the radio should be

limited. Just how strictly it should be limited has varied in these policy statements from prohibitions on anything more than the mention of the sponsor's name (Secretary of Commerce Herbert Hoover's first annual radio conference) to the mere requirement that the broadcast stations should inform the FCC of the amount of time they proposed to devote to advertising (in the FCC Blue Book). This is not the time for a careful history of the progressive abuse of this kind of listener interest. Let us leave the policy aspect of the interest with the remark that the bright hope the consumers were entitled to derive from the Blue Book died years ago when the FCC permitted the industry to flout it openly.

In the National Association of Educational Broadcasters' study of New York television programs we did obtain some information about the extent of advertising. But the fact that neither the FCC nor the industry publishes the statistics which it has prevents the public from any objective comparison of the relative saturation of advertising on radio when the Blue Book was issued in 1946, and on radio and television today.

The NAEB study found that the seven New York television stations devoted 10 per cent of their total time on the air to *timeable* commercials. The use of this term "timeable commercials" is itself significant of a development not contemplated when the Blue Book was written. Thus, the FCC in that document restated its obligation to protect this consumer interest in terms which assumed that one could distinguish between the time devoted to the commercial and the time devoted to the program material. Alas, the combination of sight and sound in television permits advertising and program to be blended. For this reason we were forced to regard as program-long advertisements some eighteen programs in which *untimeable* advertisements dominated the program time. If these untimeable programs be included the total television time given to advertising amounted to 14 per cent of time on the air. For individual stations, the total ranged from WABD, 23 per cent, and WNBT, as 22 per cent, at the top to WCBS-TV, 10 per cent, and WATV, 7 per cent, at the bottom. It is very possible, however, that television is less saturated with advertising in New York than in other sections of the country. We found that in New York the weekdays bore a heavier load of advertising than Saturday and Sunday, and that the highest saturation was in the Housewive's Hours (from sign-on to 5 P.M.,

Monday through Friday) when 21 per cent of the time was devoted to advertising.

When the Blue Book was issued the FCC continued the former tradition of making a distinction between commercial and sustaining programs. The doctrine ran something like this: that sustaining programs were the balance wheel through which station management discharged its cultural and civic responsibility to the public and through which an over-all program balance was maintained. We tried in New York to determine, from the position of the viewers sitting before the television set, the proportion of sustaining and commercial programs. We failed. Of course, the telecast of President Truman's message to the new Congress could be identified readily as a sustaining program. But other than this single public event which was televised in the week covered by our study, we had difficulty pointing to examples of sustaining programs which fitted the Blue Book's conception of that type of program. Too often the distinction between sustaining and commercial television programs seems to be the distinction between the program for which a sponsor has not yet been found, and one which is sold. Here is an example. Last summer there was a spectacular oil-tank fire in the Los Angeles harbor area. The fire was telecast in place of one station's regular broadcast of wrestling, which would have been sponsored by a beer company and a men's clothing store. The oil-tank fire might have been expected to be a sustaining program. But it was not: the fire had its own sponsor, an electrical manufacturing company.

We were also frustrated in our attempt in New York to count commercial and sustaining programs by the difficulty in determining whether many short programs had a sponsor or whether they were really sustaining programs thickly hedged in with spot announcements. The multiplicity of back-to-back, cow-catcher, and hitch-hiker spot announcements, many of which contain brief shots of people and scenes, understandably confuses the viewer until he cannot be blamed for not knowing whether any one of these sponsors is to be thanked for the few minutes of program material which is brought to him before the next commercial is due.

One more example of the archaic flavor of the Blue Book doctrine is ironically amusing in the light of television possibilities. You may remember that the Blue Book expressed revulsion at the graphic scope of what it termed physiological commercials *on radio*. There comes to my mind one day last summer when I was looking at my television set in Claremont, California. There was one commercial which *pictorially* and *aurally* presented the sad plight of the young businessman who is tired, has headaches, is ineffective, and so on—and it was all caused by "sluggish bile" for which the cure was obviously a certain laxative. And the same day I saw another advertisement which presented the lack of social and especially male approval which awaits those unfortunate women who have "briar-patch legs" (illustrated visually by superimposing a briar patch on a pair of female legs), for which the remedy was obviously a certain brand of depilatory.

In June, 1951, NBC announced the adoption of a new set of standards for its television programs. It is to be commended for its candor in publishing these standards. I should like to quote several passages from them to illustrate the fact that in the eyes of the television industry all is not advertising that sells.

Stationary backdrops or properties in television presentation, showing the sponsor's name, the name of his product, his trade mark or his slogan, which are used as incidental background for entertainment are not counted as part of the time allowed for advertising. NBC seeks to have such backdrops or properties used judiciously, and reserves the right to count their use as part of the time allowed for advertising where, in NBC's opinion, they are unduly obtrusive and cannot properly be regarded as incidental background to the entertainment presentations of the program. . . .

A lead-in or introductory comedy gag, preceding the direct advertising reference and associated with it, which constitutes entertainment material and would stand by itself even if the advertising message were omitted, is not counted as part of the time allowed for advertising. . . .

Billboards at the opening and closing of programs, identifying sponsorship of the program, are not counted as part of the time allowed for advertising, provided that each such billboard does not exceed 10 seconds in the case of a program sponsored by one advertiser, or 20 seconds in the case of a program sponsored by multiple advertisers.

It is not altogether clear without further interpretation from Radio City whether the following examples from our New York study would be regarded as advertising: (1) the fact that band members and entertainers wear uniforms and the orchestra music racks bear signs prominently displaying the name of the sponsor's product; (2) the fact that a master of ceremonies talks to children in the studio audience about, and then leads them in chanting, the sponsor's advertising message.

Having defined advertising to exclude the kinds I have quoted from its new standards, how much advertising does NBC intend to permit on television? In the case of a thirty-minute program, 10 per cent in the evening and 14 per cent in the daytime; for a five-minute program, 20 per cent in the evening and 25 per cent in the daytime.

The consumer's fourth interest in radio and television is in the programs themselves. Chairman Wayne Coy is quoted in the trade press as having told a meeting of television executives assembled recently to consider criticisms directed against their programming practices:

> I hope also that one of the subjects you will explore will be the problem of advertiser domination of program schedules. Until the broadcaster schedules the kinds of programs that he knows are right and until he builds a schedule that he knows is properly balanced, he cannot realize his full potentialities. Under the law that is his responsibility. Under the law it is not the advertiser's responsibility nor the network's responsibility. Therefore the proper role for the advertiser is not that of the program director.

Lest some skeptic think that this represents merely the bureaucrat's propensity to make life difficult for businessmen, let me quote from a recent article in *Variety*.

> It is claimed that more than one program, which started off with considerable pretensions of showmanship and slick television values eventually bogged down into the inevitable cancellation route. Reason was simply that the salesman-turned-showman who's been picking up the tab for the show, "wanted to play everything the safe way, stripped the program of all its imaginative, fresh elements, and after 26 weeks had practically lost his entire audience." . . .
>
> There are some instances of networks and package owners . . . telling the client off, at the risk of losing the account. But these have been isolated cases. For the most part, nobody's taking chances antagonizing the man with the money belt. . . . (June 6, 1951, p. 27).

You will note that *Variety* is referring not to the resentment of the station management which, as Chairman Coy says, is the responsible party, but to the resentment of the creative artists—the producers—who are employed by the agencies or the package producers. The element of freshness in entertainment is, however, only one of the criteria for evaluating the performance of stations. At the same industry meeting to which I referred earlier, Mr. Coy listed seven "points" which he said covered the essential elements.

1. [The station's] assistance in civic improvements
2. [The station's] promotion of educational and cultural opportunities.
3. The integrity of the station's news.
4. The fairness of [the station's] presentation of controversial issues.
5. [The station's] enterprise and zeal in promoting good community relations and interracial understanding.
6. The wholesomeness of [the station's] entertainers and their sense of responsibility as visitors at the family hearth.
7. Advertising on [the] station; its reliability, its good taste, its listenability, its excesses.

We have already disposed of the last of these criteria. Unfortunately I cannot attempt an evaluation of all television, much less radio programming, in the light of these admirable criteria. The fact is that we citizens, and the industry, and the FCC have not yet laid the groundwork for this over-all evaluation in the year 1951 after a quarter century of experience with this unique institution, broadcasting. Sufficient data have not been collected; the available data on station programs have not been published by the FCC, and the studies which would permit the evaluation which is implicit in the American system of broadcasting have not been done. As a footnote at this point, I might suggest that for graduate students in search of thesis topics there is a fertile field for such evaluative studies right in their home communities.

I can, however, report to you what the NAEB study No. 1 found out about New York television programming in relation to these criteria. Some of Mr. Coy's criteria, however, call for effects studies in depth; others would call for detailed evaluation. For this reason, my comments on the results of the New York study cannot squarely meet all Mr. Coy's criteria. I should explain that in this study, Professor Horton of the University of Chicago and I monitored and inventoried all the programs telecast by all the seven New York stations for one week in January, 1951. We then classified the programs into some fifty-odd classes and subclasses and counted the amount of time given by the stations to each class for the various time segments of the week. We did not attempt either effects studies in depth or detailed evaluation.

Over-all we found that drama was the largest class of program with 25 per cent of the total time on the air, followed by variety (14 per cent) and children's programs (13 per cent). Sports and home-making programs were tied in fourth place with 10 per cent each. Quiz, stunt, and contest programs provided 7 per cent while personalities programs were 5 per cent. News was 5 per cent. When the viewer looked at the subclasses of programs he found that the largest was crime drama with 10 per cent (fifty-seven hours of programs). Informal variety was a close second, with 10 per cent and fifty-five hours. Spectator sports, such as basketball, wrestling, boxing, and roller derbies, came third with 9 per cent. Western drama was 8 per cent (with 6 per cent apparently programmed for adults and 2 per cent for children). The overwhelming bulk of the time was devoted to entertainment programs, for this is the only term which can be applied to those I have named, except for the news, and some of the home-making and children's programs.

Mr. Coy mentions the integrity of the news as one criterion. We were unable, with the means at our disposal, to make such an analysis of the news programs. I must therefore limit my comment on this criterion to noting that we observed a severe deficiency of local and regional news. We also found that one third of the 5 per cent of the total time devoted to news consisted of a single daytime program which was a telegraph-like transmission of news bulletins, accompanied by unrelated recorded music.

Mr. Coy lists three criteria which I should like to take up together: assistance in civic improvements, fairness in the presentation of controversial issues, and enterprise and zeal in promoting good community relations and interracial understanding. While these objectives *might* be served by other kinds of programs, the most obvious place to find such programs would be under our headings of public issues, public events, public institutional, and information.

Public issues programs would be a likely place to find treatments of controversial issues and assistance in civic betterment. Yet we found a total of 1 per cent of the program time given to public issues (of all kinds). About half of that amount was in the form of unilateral presentation of opinion, and the remainder of it in the form of discussion and debate. In all, this 1 per cent represents about eight hours. It consists of few programs, mostly on national and foreign policy topics. Although we did not analyze these programs in detail, it seemed that the half of 1 per cent of the time which was devoted to bilateral or multilateral discussion was hardly a fair representation of the controversial issues of concern to the New York and New Jersey audiences. What we classified as public institutional programs amounted to another six hours, or 1 per cent of total broadcast time. For the most part this time was given over to films relating to national defense and to the activities of the armed forces. The paucity of programs in this category, of course, reflects many unserved interests in the activities of New York and New Jersey's local and state public institutions. We concluded that in providing discussions of current affairs, news, a broadcast of the President's address, and some of the public institutional programs, the television stations performed a necessary public service, although the amount and time of broadcast of these kinds of programs was woefully inadequate.

Conceivably information programs could have been used to assist civic improvement and to develop tolerance and open-mindedness on controversial issues. More obviously, information programs might be the backbone of the stations' promotion of educational and cultural opportunities (which is still another of Mr. Coy's points). As a matter of fact, general information programs amounted to about eighteen hours or 3 per cent of total time on the air, while children's information programs were another five hours or 1 per cent of total time on the air.

What were they like? Only one program, the Johns Hopkins Science Review, was produced under the auspices of an educational institution. There were no extension courses, no vocational courses, no courses for handicapped persons. One of our general information program subclasses was "science information." In it we found, besides the Johns Hopkins program, a film of psychology and a Hayden Planetarium film—a total of one quarter of 1 per cent of total time. The second of our subclasses under information programs was "travelogues." Travelogue programs amounted to 1 per cent of total time. They included standard commercially produced films, intended more for entertainment than to provide a real understanding of foreign lands. Apparently without plan or notice we were taken on visits to Norway, Ottawa, Africa, Latin America, Holland, the Grand Canyon, and we spent a few minutes at Christmas time among the Ukrainians of Manitoba. The last of the general information subclasses was that old standby, "other." It has 2 per cent of total broadcast time. Prominent among films in this class were seven short on wild life, of which the favorite subject was fish. We had films on the habits of salmon, codfish, sticklebacks, trout, and sardines. There were four films on the customs of other peoples, one on rivers and water supply, and one on "spelunking." There were two zoo programs, some institutional advertising films from industry, and four miscellaneous films. Only one genuinely instructional program was observed: a teaching demonstration of art techniques by Joe Gnagy.

Children's information programs were predominately films too. There was a travelogue on Alaska, films on Eskimo dogs, salt mining, how a pump works, how a pulley works, how to change a tire, baby animals, and one on fish. There was also a fifteen-minute violin class, a thirty-minute United Nations Stamp Club, and some western lore in a Chuckwagon program.

Throughout our study we took a broad view of what the term "education" means in connection with television programs—much broader than the identification of the program with some educational institution. We said that while there might be differences of opinion about the characteristics of an optimum educational program, it was possible to find broad agreement on the following minimum requirements of such a program: the educational program would be designed to help the viewer to organize himself, to order his relations with other individuals, and with social groups ranging from the family to the

human race, past and present. More specifically there should be some rational plan for the program with regularity in the time of presentation, continuity in the material, and some progression in its content. There should be some basic theme or problems with some progress achieved in problem solving. There should be emphasis on basic principles with a synthesis of understanding being developed through the series of programs. In the light of these minimum requirements for educational programs, how should one evaluate the educational or cultural contribution which we classed as information programs? With due allowance for the fact that we monitored for only one week, it appeared that these programs were a miscellaneous collection of superficial, unrelated bits of information, presented without plan, without forenotice to the viewer of what was to appear, and seemingly without regularity in the stations' program structures. Shouldn't one conclude that on the whole, and with the exceptions I have noted, the information programs of New York's television stations were insignificant educationally? And as for their serving the objectives of civic improvement and tolerance in social relations named by Mr. Coy, again with the exceptions noted, any such effects would probably be accidental and rather unlikely.

This leaves us the sixth of Mr. Coy's points to apply to New York television programs: "The wholesomeness of the station's entertainers and their sense of responsibility as visitors at the family hearth." There is considerable room for difference of opinion as to what constitutes "wholesomeness," though I suspect that the remainder of this point will command general approval. One view makes a neo-Victorian sense of morality the guide to wholesomeness. For people with this view, it means the absence of certain kinds of vulgarity. Such critics may succeed in imposing on television as they have on motion pictures a censorship policy which prescribes the height of the necklines and kinds of gags which will be acceptable. But if this view prevails there is real danger of throwing out the baby with the dirty bath water. Such a policy will accentuate the already pronounced tendency of the advertising sponsors to avoid program experimentation. Banality and formula entertainers will become even more dominant in television than in the motion pictures where advertising pressures at least are not so directly involved. The contrasting interpretation of wholesomeness might apply this term to entertainment which had the following qualities; respect for human beings with insight into all of their elements of strength and weakness, of humor and grief; spontaneity, candor, imagination, and originality. This last term, originality, I prefer to the notion of "slick values" and "freshness" which *Variety* uses. At the other end of the scale, one might place vulgarity in the sense of degradation, triteness, and certain kinds of formula drama in which people are represented as two-dimensional shadows who move in response to fate, technology, or creaky plot gimmicks. It may be argued convincingly, I think, that the dignity of human beings may be assaulted more grievously and the family hearth more abused by such misrepresentation than by the low-cut gown or the joke which offends some minority pressure group.

If the second of these points of view be adopted, what can be said of New York entertainment programs, as measured by this standard? There are commercial television programs which measure up well on this standard. Without meaning to be invidious, let me mention "Mr. I-Magination" and the highly original "Stud's Place" as two quite different examples. But the weight of the scales in terms of the massive hours given over to entertainment tips heavily toward the formula programs in which pallid representation of character, sadistic and masochistic gimmicks justify generally low ratings for wholesomeness.

Wholesomeness, I think people should tell Mr. Coy and their congressmen, is more than the negative notion of sterilizing the comedian's jokes, and determining the permissible amount of the female body which may be exposed to the hearthside viewer. It is a characteristic of the works of the creative artist judged by some such standards as I have tentatively suggested. And doubtless you could improve on my proposal. In large measure the forms which such entertainment might assume have not yet been created by the television producers, writers, and directors. All the more reason, therefore, not to shackle them so tightly with the twin handcuffs of a censorship code resembling that of the motion pictures and of advertiser pressures for conformity to existing types of shows.

But we might go further and be more specific in suggesting to Mr. Coy and the congressmen existing kinds of wholesome entertainment, more of which could probably be successfully produced on television. We might, for instance, demand that there be more programs for both children and adults presenting some of the enduring forms of art and literature which are part of our proud cultural tradition. In our study we found ten minutes of serious music in the children's listening hours, and seventy-seven minutes in the whole week. The great field of fine arts (including painting, sculpture, architecture, handicraft, and decorative arts) was ignored completely in the children's hours and was given thirty minutes in the whole week. The dance as a serious art was given twelve minutes in the children's hours and thirty-six minutes in the whole week. Classical drama was altogether absent from the children's hours and was given ninety minutes in the whole week.

You will note that I have not spoken of the consumer's interest in the success of the movement by which educational institutions hope to supplement the fare provided by the commercial television and radio stations. That is another story and one I cannot develop now. I am deeply concerned that the drive for educational television should develop soundly and rapidly with all the support which the Congress and the FCC can give it. I believe that this is our best hope of realizing a kind of mass-medium technique which can provide a yardstick of wholesomeness of the sort I have referred to. I am happy to hear that one of our greatest educational foundations is offering to help the commercial television industry improve its instructional and cultural programming. TV needs all the help it can get. Commercial broadcasters should not be cut loose from their present obligations to serve the public interest. And because of the special pressures to which the commercial industry must inevitably be subject, it is clear that the need for educational stations to supply the yardstick of cultural programming and supply the deficiencies in commercial station fare is imminent and real.

In so describing the possibilities of educational television, however, let us be careful lest in stating an attractive plan—a beautiful dream, if you please—we lose sight of the politico-economic

realities surrounding the proposal. It will take unbelievable effort and time in each community to
develop the support required to bring a substantial number of educational stations and to maintain them in vigorous condition. Perhaps the full
quota of stations may not be built as rapidly as
they should be. Even so, the unsuccessful efforts
will themselves yield rich fruit in terms of popular understanding of the problems concerning
the mass media.

Note

1. Parenthetically, a fascinating source of information on how the FCC discharges this and its
other functions is one which I find little known,
even to serious students of communication. I refer to the statements made by the FCC to the
appropriation committees of Congress when it
annually returns to them for its budget. These
Hearings are published annually.

48

The Unique Perspective of Television and Its Effect:
A Pilot Study

From *American Sociological Review* (1952)

Kurt Lang and Gladys Engel Lang

Kurt Lang (1924–) and Gladys Engel Lang (1919–) took their doctorates in sociology from the University of Chicago (1953 and 1954, respectively). Kurt and his family had come to the United States from Germany in 1936, and after serving in the military, he attended the University of Chicago for his bachelor's degree. Before attending the University of Chicago, Gladys attended the University of Michigan (B.A., 1940), wrote a master's thesis on human ecology at the University of Washington (1942), and worked at the Office of War Information (OWI; 1942–1943) and the Office of Strategic Services (OSS; 1943–1949). At the OWI, she studied propaganda directives on daytime soap operas; at the OSS, she engaged in projects ranging from press analysis in Italy and China to observation of the postwar feminist movement and psychological warfare planning. The Langs each wrote pathbreaking dissertations on the new world of televised political life: Gladys, on the 1952 party conventions; and Kurt, on the MacArthur Day parade in Chicago. In the mid-1950s, they both served as advisors to Canadian television researchers—Kurt, as audience researcher for the Canadian Broadcast Corporation (CBC); and Gladys, as a researcher for a Montreal study on television's impact on French Canadian culture. They taught at Queens College as well as at State University of New York, Stonybrook (1972–1984); and at the University of Washington (1984–). In 1961, the Langs published *Collective Dynamics,* a largely forgotten but rich extension of Chicago School sociology, from Park and Burgess through Blumer and Janowitz. Its sections on fashion, rumor, crowds, and mass communication all have passages and bibliographies of continuing interest and value. The Langs are best known for their later, influential books *Politics and Television* (1968) and *The Battle for Public Opinion* (1983), the latter a study of the Watergate drama.

This essay was published while the Langs were in graduate school, and it comes out of the project that became Kurt's dissertation. Using creative research methods, the Langs orchestrated a study of a live event as it appeared to spectators present and to television viewers at home. They found that television did not just report live events but instead created a wholly new view not experienced by anyone at the event itself, and they brought out some of the dangers of that situation, identifying characteristics Kris and Speier (p. 182) had seen in fascism. (A slightly revised version of the essay appears in the Langs' *Politics and Television*.)

This paper aims to investigate a public event as viewed over television or, to put it differently, to study in the context of public life, an event transmitted over video. The concern is not with the effects of television on individual persons, irrespective of the spread of this effect. Our assumption is, on the contrary, that the effect of exposure to TV broadcasting of public events cannot be measured most successfully in isolation. For the influence on one person is communicated to others, until the significance attached to the video event overshadows the "true" picture of the event, namely the impression obtained by someone physically present at the scene of the event. The experience of spectators may not be disseminated at all or may be discounted as the biased version of a specially interested participant. Or, again, the spectator's interpretation of his own experience may be reinterpreted when he finds the event in which he participated discussed by friends, newspapermen, and radio commentators. If the significance of the event is magnified, even casual spectatorship assumes importance. The fact of having "been there" is to be remembered—not so much because the event, in itself, has left an impression, but because the event has been recorded by others. At the opposite extreme, privately significant experiences, unless revived in subsequent interpersonal relations, soon recede into the deeper layers of memory.

By taking MacArthur Day in Chicago,[1] as it was experienced by millions of spectators and video viewers, we have attempted to study an event transmitted over video. The basis of this report is the contrast between the actually recorded experience of participant observers on the scene, on the one hand, and the picture which a video viewer received by way of the television screen, and the way in which the event was interpreted, magnified, and took on added significance, on the other. The contrast between these two perspectives from which the larger social environment can be viewed and "known," forms the starting point for the assessment of a particular effect of television in structuring public events.

The Research Design

The present research was undertaken as an exploration in collective behavior.[2] The design of the communications analysis differs significantly from most studies of content analysis. The usual process of inferring effect from content and validating the effect by means of interviews with an audience and control group is reversed. A generally apparent effect, i.e., the "landslide effect" of national indignation at MacArthur's abrupt dismissal and the impression of enthusiastic support, bordering on "mass hysteria," given to him, was used to make inferences on given aspects of the television content. The concern was with the picture disseminated, especially as it bore on the political atmosphere. To explain how people could have a false imagery (the implication of participant observational data), it was necessary to show how their perspective of the larger political environment was limited and how the occasion of Chicago's welcome to MacArthur, an event mediately known already, was given a particular structure. The concern is how the picture of the events was shaped by selection, emphasis, and suggested inferences which fitted into the already existing pattern of expectations.

The content analysis was therefore focused on two aspects—the selections made by the camera and their structuring of the event in terms of foreground and background, and the explanation and interpretations of televised events given by commentators and persons interviewed by them. Moreover, each monitor was instructed to give his impression of what was happening, on the basis of the picture and information received by way of television. The monitors' interpretations and subjective impressions were separately recorded.

They served as a check that the structure inferred from the two operations of "objective" analysis of content were, in fact, legitimate inferences.[3] At the same time, utilizing the categories of the objective analysis, the devices by which the event was structured could be isolated, and the specific ways in which television reportage differed from the combined observations could be determined.

Thirty-one participant observers took part in the study. They were spatially distributed to allow for the maximum coverage of all the important phases of the day's activities, i.e., no important vantage point of spectatorship was neglected. Since the events were temporally distributed, many observers took more than one station, so that coverage was actually based on more than 31 perspectives. Thus the sampling error inherent in individual participant observation or unplanned mass-observation was greatly reduced. Observers could witness the arrival at Midway Airport and still arrive in the Loop area long before the scheduled time for the parade. Reports were received from 43 points of observation.

Volunteers received instruction sheets which drew their attention to principles of observation[4] and details to be carefully recorded. Among these was the directive to take careful note of any activity indicating possible influences of the televising of the event upon the behavior of spectators, e.g., actions specifically addressed to the cameras, indications that events were staged with an eye towards transmission over television, and the like.

Summary of Findings

The Pattern of Expectations
The mass-observation concentrated on discerning the psychological structure of the unfolding event in terms of present and subsequent anticipations. Certainly the crowd which turned out for the MacArthur Day celebration was far from a casual collection of individuals: the members *intended* to be witnesses to this "unusual event." One may call these intentions specific attitudes, emergent acts, expectations, or predispositions. Whatever the label, materials on these patterns of expectations were taken from two sources: (1) all statements of spectators recorded in the observer reports which could be interpreted as in-

dicative of such expectations (coded in terms of the inferences therein); (2) personal expectations of the 31 study observers (as stated in the personal questionnaire).

Though not strictly comparable—since the observations on the scene contained purely personal, very short-range and factually limited expectations—both series of data provide confirmation of a basic pattern of observer expectations. The persons on the scene *anticipated* "mobs" and "wild crowds." They expected some disruption of transportation. Their journey downtown was in search of adventure and excitement. Leaving out such purely personal expectations as "seeing" and "greeting," the second most frequent preconception emphasizes the extraordinary nature of the preparations and the entertaining showmanship connected with the spectacle.

As a result of an unfortunate collapsing of several questions regarding personal data into one, the response did not always focus properly on what the observers "expected to see." In some cases no evidence or only an incomplete description of this aspect was obtained. Of those answering, 68 per cent expected excited and wildly enthusiastic crowds. But it is a safe inference from the discussion during the briefing session that this figure tends to underestimate the number who held this type of imagery. The main incentive to volunteer resided, after all, in the opportunity to study crowd behavior at first hand.

To sum up: most people expected a wild spectacle, in which the large masses of onlookers would take an active part, and which contained an element of threat in view of the absence of ordinary restraints on behavior and the power of large numbers.

The Role of Mass Media in the Pattern of Expectations
A more detailed examination of the data supports the original assumption that the pattern of expectations was shaped by way of the mass media. For it is in that way that the picture of the larger world comes to sophisticated as well as unsophisticated people. The observers of the study were no exception to this dependence on what newspapers, newsreels, and television cameras mediated. They were, perhaps, better able than others to describe the origin of these impressions. Thus Observer 14 wrote in evaluating his report and his subjective feelings:

I had listened to the accounts of MacArthur's arrival in San Francisco, heard radio reports of his progress through the United States, and had heard the Washington speech as well as the radio accounts of his New York reception. . . . I had therefore expected the crowds to be much more vehement, contagious, and identified with MacArthur. I had expected to hear much political talk, especially anti-Communist and against the Truman administration.

These expectations were completely unfulfilled. I was amazed that not once did I hear Truman criticized, Acheson mentioned, or as much as an allusion to the Communists. . . . I had expected roaring, excited mobs; instead there were quiet, well ordered, dignified people. . . . The air of curiosity and casualness surprised me. Most people seemed to look on the event as simply something that might be interesting to watch.

Other observers made statements of a very similar content.

Conversation in the crowd pointed to a similar awareness. Talk repeatedly turned to television, especially to the comparative merit of "being there" and "seeing it over TV." An effort was consequently made to assess systematically the evidence bearing on the motives for being there in terms of the patterns of expectations previously built up. The procedures of content analysis served as a useful tool, allowing the weighing of all evidence *directly* relevant to this question in terms of confirmatory and contrary evidence. The coding operation involved the selection of two types of indicators: (1) general evaluations and summaries of data; and (2) actual incidents of behavior which could support or nullify our hypothesis.

Insofar as the observers had been instructed to report concrete behavior rather than general interpretations, relatively few such generalizations are available for tabulation. Those given were used to formulate the basic headings under which the concrete evidence could be tabulated. The generalizations fall into two types: namely, the crowds had turned out to see a great military figure and a public hero "in the flesh"; and—its logical supplement—they had turned out not so much "to see *him,* as I noticed, but to see the spectacle (Observer 5)." Six out of eleven concretely stated propositions were of the second type.

Table 48.1   Types of spectator interest

Form of Motivation	Per cent
Active hero worship	9.2
Interest in seeing MacArthur	48.1
Passive interest in spectacle	42.7
Total	100.0

An examination of the media content required the introduction of a third heading, which subdivided the interest in MacArthur into two distinct interpretations: that people had come to find vantage points from which to see the man and his family; or, as the official (media and "Chicago official") version held, that they had come to welcome, cheer, and honor him. Not one single observer, in any generalized proposition, confirmed the official generalization, but there was infrequent mention of isolated incidents which would justify such an interpretation.

The analysis of actual incidents, behavior, and statements recorded is more revealing. A gross classification of the anticipations which led people to participate is given (according to categories outlined above) in table 48.1.

A classification of these observations by area in which they were secured gives a clear indication that the Loop throngs thought of the occasion *primarily* as a spectacle. There, the percentage of observations supporting the "spectacle hypothesis" was 59.7. The percentage in other areas was: Negro district, 40.0; Soldiers Field, 22.9; Airport, 17.6; University district, 0.0. Moreover, of the six generalizations advanced on crowd expectations in the Loop, five interpreted the prevalent motivation as the hope of a wild spectacle.

Thus, a probe into motivation gives a confirmatory clue regarding the pattern of expectations observed. To this body of data, there should be added the constantly overheard expressions—as the time of waiting increased and excitement failed to materialize—of disillusionment with the particular advantage point. "We should have stayed home and watched it on TV," was the almost universal form that the dissatisfaction took. In relation to the spectatorship experience of extended boredom and sore feet, alleviated only by a brief glimpse of the hero of the day, previous and similar experiences over television had been truly exciting ones which promised even greater "sharing of excitement" *if only one were present.*

These expectations were disappointed and favorable allusions to television in this respect were frequent. To present the entire body of evidence bearing on the inadequate release of tension and the widely felt frustration would be to go beyond the scope of this report, in which the primary concern is the study of the television event. But the materials collected present unequivocal proof of the foregoing statements, and this—with one qualified exception—is also the interpretation of each one of the observers.

Moreover, the comparison of the television perspective with that of the participant observers indicates that the video aspects of MacArthur Day in Chicago served to *preserve* rather than disappoint the same pattern of expectations among the viewers. The main difference was that television remained true to form until the very end, interpreting the entire proceedings according to expectations. No hint about the disappointment in the crowd was provided. To cite only one example, taken from what was the high point in the video presentation, the moment when the crowds broke into the parade by surging out into State Street:

> The scene at 2:50 p.m. at State and Jackson was described by the announcer as the "most enthusiastic crowd *ever* in our city. . . . You can feel the tenseness in the air. . . . You can hear that crowd roar." The crowd was described as pushing out into the curb with the police trying to keep it in order, while the camera was still focusing on MacArthur and his party. The final picture was of a bobbing mass of heads as the camera took in the entire view of State Street northward. To the monitor, this mass of people appeared to be pushing and going nowhere. And then, with the remark, "The whole city appears to be marching down State Street behind General MacArthur," holding the picture just long enough for the impression to sink in, the picture was suddenly blanked out.

Observer 26, who was monitoring this phase of the television transmission, reported her impression:

> . . . the last buildup on TV concerning the "crowd" (Cut off as it was, abruptly at 3:00 p.m.) gave me the impression that the crowd was pressing and straining so hard that it was going to be hard to control. My first thought, "I'm glad I'm not in that" and "I hope nobody gets crushed."

But observers near State and Jackson did not mention the event in an extraordinary context. For example, Observer 24 explained that as MacArthur passed:

> Everybody strained but few could get a really good glimpse of him. A few seconds after he had passed most people merely turned around to shrug and to address their neighbors with such phrases: "That's all," "That was it," "Gee, he looks just as he does in the movies," "What'll we do now?" Mostly teenagers and others with no specific plans flocked into the street after MacArthur, but very soon got tired of following as there was no place to go and nothing to do. Some cars were caught in the crowd, a matter which, to the crowd, seemed amusing.

The Structure of the TV Presentation

The television perspective was different from that of any spectator in the crowd. Relatively unlimited in its mobility, it could order events in its own way by using close-ups for what was deemed important and leaving the apparently unimportant for the background. There was almost complete freedom to aim cameras in accordance with such judgments. The view, moreover, could be shifted to any significant happening, so that the technical possibilities of the medium itself tended to play up the dramatic. While the spectator, if fortunate, caught a brief glimpse of the General and his family, the television viewer found him the continuous center of attraction from his first appearance during the parade at 2:21 p.m. until the sudden blackout at 3:00 p.m. For almost 40 minutes, not counting his seven minute appearance earlier in the day at the airport and his longer appearance at Soldiers Field that evening, the video viewer could fasten his eyes on the General and on what could be interpreted as the interplay between a heroic figure and the enthusiastic crowd. The cheering of the crowd seemed not to die down at all, and even as the telecast was concluded, it only seemed to have reached its crest. Moreover, as the camera focused principally on the parade itself, the crowd's applause seemed all the more ominous a tribute from the background.

The shots of the waiting crowd, the interviews with persons within it, and the commentaries, had previously prepared the viewer for this dramatic development. Its resolution was left to the inference of the individual. But a sufficient number of clues had already come over television to leave little doubt about the structure. Out of the three-hour daytime telecast, in addition to the time that MacArthur and party were the visual focus of attention, there were over two hours which had to be filled with visual material and vocal commentary. By far the largest amount of time was spent on anticipatory shots of the crowd. MacArthur himself held the picture for the second longest period; thus the ratio of time spent viewing MacArthur to time spent anticipating his arrival is much greater for the TV observer than for the spectator on the scene.

The descriptive accounts of the commentators (also reflected in the interviews),[5] determined the structure of the TV presentation of the day's events. The idea of the magnitude of the event, in line with preparations announced in the newspapers, was emphasized by constant reference. The most frequently employed theme was that "no effort has been spared to make this day memorable" (eight references). There were seven direct references to the effect that the announcer had "never seen the equal to this moment" or that it was the "greatest ovation this city had ever turned out." The unique cooperative effort of TV received five mentions and was tied in with the "dramatic" proportions of the event. It was impossible to categorize and tabulate all references, but they ranged from a description of crowded transportation and numerical estimates of the crowd to the length of the city's lunch hour and the state of "suspended animation: into which business had fallen. There was repeated mention that nothing was being allowed to interfere with the success of the celebration; even the ball game has been cancelled.[6] In addition to these purely formal aspects of the event, two—and only two—aspects of the spectacle were *stressed*: (1) the unusual nature of the event; (2) the tension which was said to pervade the entire scene. Even the references to the friendly and congenial mood of the waiting crowd portended something about the change that was expected to occur.

Moreover, in view of the selectivity of the coverage with its emphasis on close-ups,[7] it was possible for each viewer to see himself in a *personal* relationship to the General. As the announcer shouted out: "Look at that chin! Look at those eyes!"—each viewer, regardless of what might have been meant by it, could seek a personal interpretation which best expressed, for him, the real feeling underlying the exterior which appeared on the television screen.[8]

It is against the background of this personal inspection that the significance of the telecast must be interpreted. The cheering crowd, the "seething mass of humanity," was fictionally endowed by the commentators with the same capacity for a direct and personal relationship to MacArthur as the one which television momentarily established for the TV viewer through its close-up shots. The net effect of television thus stems from a convergence of these two phenomena; namely, the seemingly extraordinary scope of the event together with the apparent enthusiasm accompanying it and personalizing influence just referred to. In this way the public event was interpreted in a very personal nexus. The total effect of so many people, all shouting, straining, cheering, waving in personal welcome to the General, disseminated the impression of a universal, enthusiastic, overwhelming ovation for the General. The selectivity of the camera and the commentary gave the event a personal dimension, non-existent for the participants in the crowds, thereby presenting a very specific perspective which contrasted with that of direct observation.

Other Indices of the Discrepancy

In order to provide a further objective check on the discrepancies between observer impressions and the event as it was interpreted by those who witnessed it over television, a number of spot checks on the reported amount of participation were undertaken. Transportation statistics, counts in offices, and the volume of sales reported by vendors provided such indices.

The results substantiate the above finding. The city and suburban lines showed a very slight increase over their normal loads. To some extent the paltry 50,000 increase in inbound traffic on the street cars and elevated trains might even have been due to rerouting. The suburban lines had their evening rush hour moved up into the early afternoon—before the parade had begun.

Checks at luncheonettes, restaurants, and parking areas indicated no unusual crowding. Samplings in offices disclosed only a minor interest in the parade. Hawkers, perhaps the most sensitive judges of enthusiasm, called the parade a "puzzler" and displayed unsold wares.

Detailed Illustration of Contrast

The Bridge ceremony provides an illustration of the contrast between the two perspectives.

Seven observers witnessed this ceremony from the crowd.

TV perspective: In the words of the announcer, the bridge ceremony marked "one of the high spots, if not the high spot of the occasion this afternoon.... The parade is now reaching its climax at this point."

The announcer, still focusing on MacArthur and the other participating persons, took the opportunity to review the ceremony about to take place.... The camera followed and the announcer described the ceremony in detail.... The camera focused directly on the General, showing a close-up.... There were no shots of the crowd during this period. But the announcer filled in. "A great cheer goes up at the Bataan Bridge, where the General has just placed a wreath in honor of the American boys who died at Bataan and Corregidor. You have heard the speech... the General is now walking back... the General now enters his car. This is the focal point where all the newsreels... frankly, in 25 years of covering the news, we have never seen as many newsreels gathered at one spot. One, two, three, four, five, six. At least eight cars with newsreels rigged on top of them, taking a picture that will be carried over the entire world, over the Chicagoland area by the combined network of these TV stations of Chicago, which have combined for this great occasion and for the solemn occasion which you have just witnessed."

During this scene there were sufficient close-ups for the viewer to gain a definite reaction, positive or negative, to the proceedings. He could see the General's facial expressions and what appeared to be momentary confusion. He could watch the activities of the Gold Star mothers in relation to MacArthur and define this as he wished—as inappropriate for the bereaved moment or as understandable in the light of the occasion. Taking the cue from the announcer, the entire scene could be viewed as rushed. Whether or not, in line with the official interpretation, the TV viewer saw the occasion as *solemn,* it can be assumed that he expected that the participant on the scene was, in fact, experiencing the occasion in the same way as he.

Actually, this is the way what was meant to be a solemn occasion was experienced by those attending, and which constitutes the crowd perspective. The dedication ceremony aroused little of the sentiment it might have elicited under other conditions. According to Observer 31, "People on our corner could not see the dedication ceremony very well, and consequently after he had passed immediately in front of us, there was uncertainty as to what was going on. As soon as word had come down that he had gone down to his car, the crowd dispersed." Observer 8 could not quite see the ceremony from where he was located on Wacker Drive, slightly east of the bridge. Condensed descriptions of two witnesses illustrate the confusion which surrounded the actual wreath-laying ceremony (three other similar descriptions are omitted here).

It was difficult to see any of them. MacArthur moved swiftly up the steps and immediately shook hands with people on the platform waiting to greet him. There was some cheering when he mounted the platform. He walked north on the platform and did not reappear until some minutes later. In the meantime the crowd was so noisy that it was impossible to understand what was being broadcast from the loud-speakers. Cheering was spotty and intermittent, and there was much talk about Mrs. MacArthur and Arthur... (Observer 2).

Those who were not on boxes did not see MacArthur. They did not see Mrs. MacArthur, but only her back. MacArthur went up on the platform, as we were informed by those on boxes, and soon we heard some sound over the loudspeakers. Several cars were standing in the street with their motors running.... Some shouted to the cars to shut their motors off, but the people in the cars did not care or did not hear.... The people in our area continued to push forward trying to hear. When people from other areas began to come and walk past us to go toward the train, the people in our area shrugged their shoulders. "Well, I guess it's all over. That noise must have been the speech." One of the three men who had stood there for an hour or more, because it was such a good spot, complained, "This turned out to be a lousy spot. I should have gone home. I bet my wife saw it much better over television" (Observer 30).

Regardless of good intentions on the part of planners and despite any recognition of the solemn purpose of the occasion by individuals in the crowd, the solemnity of the occasion was destroyed, if for no other reason, because officials in the parade were so intent upon the time-schedule and cameramen so intent upon recording the solemn dedication for the TV audience and for posterity that the witnesses could not see or hear the ceremony, or feel "solemn" or communicate a mood of solemnity. A crowd of confused spectators, cheated in their hopes of seeing a legendary hero in the flesh, was left unsatisfied.

Reciprocal Effects

There is some direct evidence regarding the way in which television imposed its own peculiar perspective on the event. In one case an observer on the scene could watch both what was going on and what was being televised.

> It was possible for me to view the scene (at Soldiers Field) both naturally and through the lens of the television camera. It was obvious that the camera presented quite a different picture from the one received otherwise. The camera followed the General's car and caught that part of the crowd immediately opposite the car and about 15 rows above it. Thus it caught that part of the crowd that was cheering, giving the impression of a solid mass of wildly cheering people. It did not show the large sections of empty stands, nor did it show that people stopped cheering as soon as the car passed them (Observer 13).

In much the same way, the television viewer received the impression of wildly cheering and enthusiastic crowds before the parade. The camera selected shots of the noisy and waving audience, but in this case, the television camera itself created the incident. The cheering, waving, and shouting was often largely a response to the aiming of the camera. The crowd was thrilled to be on television, and many attempted to make themselves apparent to acquaintances who might be watching. But even beyond that, an event important enough to warrant the most widespread pooling of television facilities in Chicago video history, acquired in its own right some magnitude and significance. Casual conversation continually showed that being on television was among the greatest thrills of the day.

Conclusion

It has been claimed for television that it brings the truth directly into the home: the "camera does not lie." Analysis of the above data shows that this assumed reportorial accuracy is far from automatic. Every camera selects, and thereby leaves the unseen part of the subject open to suggestion and inference. The gaps are usually filled in by a commentator. In addition the process directs action and attention to itself.

Examination of a public event by mass-observation and by television revealed considerable discrepancy between these two experiences. The contrast in perspectives points to three items whose relevance in structuring a televised event can be inferred from an analysis of the television content:

(1) technological bias, i.e., the necessarily arbitrary sequence of telecasting events and their structure in terms of foreground and background, which at the same time contains the choices on the part of the television personnel as to what is important;

(2) structuring of an event by an announcer, whose commentary is needed to tie together the shifts from camera to camera, from vista to close-up, helping the spectator to gain the stable orientation from one particular perspective;

(3) reciprocal effects, which modify the event itself by staging it in a way to make it more suitable for telecasting and creating among the actors the consciousness of acting for a larger audience.

General attitudes regarding television and viewing habits must also be taken into account. Since the industry is accustomed to thinking in terms of audience ratings—though not to the exclusion of all other considerations—efforts are made to assure steady interest. The telecast was made to conform to what was interpreted as the pattern of viewers' expectations. The drama of MacArthur Day, in line with that pattern, was nonetheless built around unifying symbols, personalities, and general appeals (rather than issues). But a drama it had to be, even if at the expense of reality.

Unlike other television programs, news and special events features constitute part of that basic information about "reality" which we require in order to act in concert with anonymous but like-minded persons in the political process. Action is guided by the possibilities for success, and, as part of this constant assessment, inferences about public opinion as a whole are constantly made. Even though the average citizen does, in fact, see only a small segment of public opinion, few persons refrain from making estimates of the true reading of the public temper. Actions and campaigns are supported by a sense of support from other persons. If not, these others at least constitute an action potential that can be mobilized. The correct evaluation of the public temper is therefore of utmost importance; it enters the total political situation as perhaps one of the weightiest factors.

Where no overt expression of public opinion exists, politicians and citizens find it useful to fabricate it. Against such demonstrations as the MacArthur Day, poll data lack persuasiveness and, of necessity, must always lag, in their publication, behind the development of popular attitudes. For the politician who is retroactively able to counter the errors resulting from an undue regard for what at a given time is considered overwhelming public opinion, there may be little significance in this delay. The imagery of momentary opinion may, however, goad him into action which, though justified in the name of public opinion, may objectively be detrimental. It may prevent critics from speaking out when reasoned criticism is desirable, so that action may be deferred until scientific estimates of public opinion can catch up with the prior emergence of new or submerged opinion.

Above all, a more careful formulation of the relations among public opinion, the mass media, and the political process, is vital for the understanding of many problems in the field of politics. The reports and telecasts of what purports to be spontaneous homage paid to a political figure assume added meaning within this context. The most important single media effect coming within the scope of the material relevant to the study of MacArthur Day was the dissemination of an image of overwhelming public sentiment in favor of the General. This effect gathered force as it was incorporated into political strategy, picked up by other media, entered into gossip, and thus came to overshadow immediate reality as it might have been recorded

by an observer on the scene. We have labelled this the "landslide effect" because, in view of the wide-spread dissemination of a particular public welcoming ceremony the imputed unanimity gathered tremendous force.[9] This "landslide effect" can, in large measure, be attributed to television.

Two characteristics of the video event enhanced this effect (misevaluation of public sentiment). (1) The depiction of the ceremonies in unifying rather than in particularistic symbols (between which a balance was maintained) failed to leave any room for dissent. Because no lines were drawn between the conventional and the partisan aspects of the reception, the traditional welcome assumed political significance in the eyes of the public. (2) A general characteristic of the television presentation was that the field of vision of the viewer was enlarged while, at the same time, the context in which these events could be interpreted was less clear. Whereas a participant was able to make direct inferences about the crowd as whole, being in constant touch with those around him, the television viewer was in the center of the entire crowd. Yet, unlike the participant, he was completely at the mercy of the instrument of his perceptions. He could not test his impressions—could not shove back the shover, inspect bystanders' views, or attempt in any way to affect the ongoing activity. To the participant, on the other hand, the direction of the crowd activity as a whole, regardless of its final goal, still appeared as the interplay of certain peculiarly personal and human forces. Political sentiment, wherever encountered, could thus be evaluated and discounted. Antagonistic views could be attributed to insufficient personal powers of persuasion rather than seen as subjugation to the impersonal dynamics of mass hysteria. The television viewer had little opportunity to recognize this personal dimension in the crowd. What was mediated over the screen was, above all, the general trend and the direction of the event, which consequently assumed the proportion of an impersonal force, no longer subject to influence.

This view of the "overwhelming" effect of public moods and the impersonal logic of public events is hypothesized as a characteristic of the perspective resulting from the general structure of the picture and the context of television viewing.

Notes

Condensation of the paper winning the prize for 1952 of the Edward L. Bernays Foundation.

1. "MacArthur Day in Chicago" includes the following occasions which were televised: arrival at Midway Airport, parade through the city including the dedication at the Bataan-Corregidor Bridge, and the evening speech at Soldiers Field.

2. This paper reports only one aspect of a larger study of MacArthur Day in Chicago. A report of the larger study is nearing completion. This writeup is limited to drawing together some of the implications concerning the role of television in public events, this particular study being considered as a pilot study for the framing of hypotheses and categories prerequisite for a more complete analysis of other such events in general. The present study could not test these categories, but was limited to an analysis of the television content in terms of the observed "landslide effect" of the telecast. The authors wish to express their indebtedness to Dr. Tamatsu Shibutani (then of the Department of Sociology, University of Chicago) for lending his encouragement and giving us absolute freedom for a study which, due to the short notice of MacArthur's planned arrival in Chicago, had to be prepared and drawn up in three days, and for allowing his classes to be used for soliciting volunteers. No funds of any sort were at our disposal. Dr. Donald Horton was kind enough to supply us with television sets and tape recorders. In discussions of the general problems involved in the analysis of television content, he has indirectly been of invaluable aid. Finally, we are indebted to the other twenty-nine observers, without whose splendid cooperation the data could never have been gathered.

3. That this check together with our observation of the general impression left by MacArthur day constitutes only a very limited validation is beyond question. Under the conditions of the study—carried on without financial support and as an adjunct to other research commitments—it was the best we could do.

4. Analysis of personal data sheets, filled out by participants prior to MacArthur Day, revealed that "objectivity" in observation was not related to political opinion held, papers and periodicals subscribed to, and previous exposure to radio or TV coverage of MacArthur's homecoming. The significant factor in evaluating the reports for individual or deviant interpretation was found to reside in the degree to which individual observers were committed to scientific and objective procedures. Our observers were all advanced graduate students in the social sciences.

5. An analysis of televised interviews is omitted in this condensation. Interviews obtained for the study by observers posing as press representatives elicited responses similar to those given over TV. Without exception, those questioned referred to the magnitude, import, and other formal aspects of the event. These stand in contrast to results obtained through informal probes and most overheard conversation. One informant connected with television volunteered that television announcers had had specific instructions to emphasize that this was a "dramatic event." Another of Chicago's TV newsmen noted that throughout the telecast the commentary from each position made it sound as if the high points of the day's activity were about to occur or were occurring right on their own spot.

6. The day's activities at a nearby race track were not cancelled. At one point in the motorcade from the airport to the Loop, a traffic block resulted in a partially "captive audience." An irritated "captive" remarked, "I hope this doesn't make me late for the races."

7. In a subsequent interview, a TV producer explained his conception of the MacArthur Day coverage as "being the best in the country." He especially recalled bracketing and then closing in on the General during the motorcade, the assumption being that he was the center of attraction.

8. During the evening ceremonies, MacArthur's failure to show fatigue in spite of the strenuous experiences of the day received special notice. A report from a public viewing of the evening speech indicates the centering of discussion about this "lack of fatigue" in relation to the General's advanced years (Observer 24).

9. It must be re-emphasized that there was no independent check—in the form of a validation—of the specific effect of TV. However, newspaper coverage emphasized the overwhelming enthusiasm. Informal interviews, moreover, even months later, showed that the event was still being interpreted as a display of mass hysteria.

49

Technology and Political Change

From *International Journal* (1952)

Marshall McLuhan

Marshall McLuhan (1911–1980) is best known as the media guru who contributed to the popular lexicon the phrase "the medium is the message" and the term "the global village" and who, in the 1960s, became a celebrity who gave a *Playboy* interview and appeared on the popular television show *Laugh In*—but he arrived at this destination by a twisting, sometimes contradictory path (see Marchand 1989). McLuhan was born in Edmonton and grew up with a mother who was a traveling elocutionist and who dabbled in Christian Science and phrenology. McLuhan studied English at the University of Manitoba and then at Cambridge University (1934–1936), where he worked with the literary critics I. A. Richards and F. R. Leavis. Despite his groovy image, McLuhan had a deep sense of traditionalism—a Catholic convert who attended Mass almost daily, a scholar well-learned in the Western rhetorical and humanist tradition, an admirer of the American South (he was known for a time as an important, though junior member of the literary critics known as the "Southern agrarians"), a great natural participant in the oral tradition (he was an eloquent and charismatic talker), and someone dispositionally appalled by popular culture (like Ezra Pound, who McLuhan deeply admired).

McLuhan commenced his lifelong examination of popular media in 1936 while teaching at Wisconsin, where he transformed a section of first-year English into a critical examination of contemporary advertising, newspapers, and popular fiction (all of which at least partly horrified him). McLuhan took his doctorate from Cambridge in 1939, specializing in Elizabethan literature and reading broadly in the history of rhetoric but also starting an unpublished essay entitled "Dale Carnegie: American Machiavelli." He taught at St. Louis University from 1940 to 1944, where he directed the master's thesis of Walter Ong and read and was influenced by Lewis Mumford's *Technics and Civilization*. In 1946, he transferred to St. Michael's College at the University of Toronto, where he spent most of the rest of his life. He continued to probe popular media and eventually published his first book, *The Mechanical Bride* (1951)—a playful, often incisive criticism of single cultural artifacts (advertisements, comic strips), which was inspired by Leavis's *Culture and Environment*. At Toronto he also started a serious reading of *Finnegan's Wake*, which left a deep impression, evident in McLuhan's mature style. He later met Harold Innis, who, with another colleague, Edmund Carpenter, moved McLuhan toward developing a grand theory of social and cultural change revolving around developments in dominant media of communication, a position he developed in *The Gutenberg Galaxy* (1962) and in *Understanding Media* (1964).

"Technology and Political Change" is one of McLuhan's early pieces on communications media. It is easy to find errors among McLuhan's pronouncements, but the essay also displays some of his real insight and eloquence. His observations about both the blurring of cultural boundaries and "participating in one's own audience participation" anticipate postmodernist themes, while his claims about stereotypes and the advertising industry have interesting similarities with both Walter Lippmann and the Frankfurt School.

"I know about the reasons for the revolution in Mexico," wrote Karel Capek, "but I know nothing at all about the reasons for my next-door neighbour's quarrels. This condition of the man of today is called world citizenship, and it arises from reading the papers." This is to say, among other things, that no matter how much technology reduces the intellectual and social isolation of people, their metaphysical isolation is little affected. But the speed with which we are today abridging the intellectual isolation of people is unquestioned.

Bergson argued that if some cosmic jokester were to speed up the entire universe, we could detect the event by the impoverishment of mind that would ensue. If only on a planetary scale, we are now in a position to observe the effects of such accelerated operations, socially and intellectually, because modern communications, have become geared to the speed of light, and transportation is not too far behind.

It is perhaps useful to consider that any form of communication written, spoken, or gestured has its own aesthetic mode, and that this mode is part of what is said. Any kind of communication has a great effect on what you decide to say if only because it selects the audience to whom you can say it. The unassisted human voice which can reach at most a few dozen yards, imposes various conditions on a speaker. However, with the invention of the alphabet the voice was translated to a visual medium with the consequent loss of most of its qualities and effects. But its range in time and space was thus given enormous extension. At the same time that the distance from the sender of the recipient of a message was extended, the number of those able to decipher the message was decreased. Writing, in other words, was a political revolution. It changed the nature of social communication and control.

Intellectually, the visualization of the word may have made possible the rise of dialectics and logic as they are found in Plato's dialogues. And the Platonic quarrel with the Sophists, from this point of view, may represent the clash of the older oral with the new written mode of communication. For the written form of communication permits the arrest of a mental process for

private analysis and contemplation, whereas the oral form is naturally concerned with the public impact on an audience. The Platonic dialogue may well represent a poise between the aesthetic claims and tendencies of these two forms of expression, between dialectic and rhetoric.

The conflicting claims of dialectic and rhetoric or private and public communication account for a good deal of subsequent intellectual and social history. The Roman world divided the dispute in accordance with the position of Seneca and of Cicero, and the mediaeval world opposed the methods of study and teaching of the Fathers and the Schoolmen. But the invention of printing or letter-press upset the mediaeval equilibrium in this matter. For the mechanization of writing reduced the effect of the spoken word even more than had the invention of writing. And the cheap and rapid multiplication of books not only extended the audience for books, but it changed the methods of study and teaching from a social to a private mode. There arose a cult of privacy. Western culture and religion became centered in the home and the book.

Politically speaking, this social change was felt in the new intensity of commercial exploitation of the vernaculars. Printing fostered nationalism when the printers sought to extend their markets as widely as possible. For any one vernacular market of newly-taught readers was larger than the whole European community of Latin-reading and speaking scholars.

One obvious effect of writing and printing is to bind together long tracts of time by making past writers simultaneously available. Associated with this effect is the republicanism of letters. Anybody, no matter what his origin or condition, has access on equal terms to the written messages of "the mighty dead," so that we can readily link, as most have done, the rise of democratic attitudes to the mechanization of writing.

As the mechanization of writing advanced in speed and cheapness, and the daily newspaper became possible, a whole series of unpredictable social and political consequences appeared. The press became a source of advertising revenue, for one thing. And larger circulation called for a larger range and variety of news. This led to the development of news-gathering agencies and techniques of great scale. And while the newspaper took on the format of a popular daily book, collectively written and produced, it reversed the character of the first printed books.

At first the book had abridged time, making the reader of any period the social equal and contemporary of Homer, Horace, or Petrarch. However, the new book of the people, the newspaper, created a one-day world utterly indifferent to the past, but embracing the whole planet. The newspaper is not a time-binder but a space-binder. Juxtaposed simultaneously in its columns are events from the next block with events from China and Peru. And naturally the technologically determined format of the press has had revolutionary political consequences. It has changed everybody's way of thinking, seeing, feeling. Perhaps the most significant single fact about the newspaper is its date-line.

Aesthetically speaking, a week-old newspaper is of no interest at all, even though intellectually speaking it has exactly the same components as today's paper. Aesthetically the newspaper creates an impact of immediacy and of superrealism. Metaphysically its mode is existential. Its impact is that of the very process of actualization. The entire world becomes, in this way, a laboratory in which everybody can watch the stages of an experiment. Everybody becomes a spectator of the biggest show on earth—namely the entire human family in its most gossipy intimacy. One curious aspect of the press is its willingness to be as surrealist as possible in its handling of geography and space, while sticking rigidly to the convention of a date-line. As soon as the same treatment is accorded time as space, we are in the world of Joyce's *Ulysses* where it is 800 B.C. and 1904 A.D. at the same time. And it is certain from even a casual glance at modern science fiction that the popular mind is decades ahead of the academic mind in being already prepared to drop the date-time on newspapers, and to range as freely in time as in space as a means of intellectual discovery.

This spectator mentality applied not only to the external world but to history includes the habit of seeing oneself as part of the scene, of participating in one's own audience participation, as it were; and it receives a final degree of extension in television where the participants in a show can easily see the broadcast in a studio monitor while

engaged in acting the show. It is noteworthy that the spectator attitude is explicitly associated with one of the early newspapers. For the *Spectator* of Steele and Addison was a commentary on the social and intellectual scene in the days before professional news-gathering had begun. Various inventions like the telescope, the microscope, the spectroscope, and the *camera obscura* coincided with the landscape interest in painting and poetry to foster a spectator attitude to the world. The very idea of "views" as a way of expressing moral and political attitudes arose at this time. Popular metaphors naturally provide an index to changing experience.

For the student of the arts and of politics it is instructive to observe how many of the techniques developed for example, in picturesque poetry, not only appear in the popular novel but in the press. In fact, most current ideas of the opposition between vulgar and sophisticated art, or between popular and esoteric culture, are based on a considerable ignorance of the ways in which communication takes place in society. More specifically, the general concepts of culture have been based on an interest in the moral and intellectual content of art forms, to the neglect of the form itself as a major component of the expression. As attention has widened to see any culture as a communication network, it has become apparent that there are no non-cultural areas in any society. There is no kind of object or activity that has not some *rapport* with the entire network.

The beloved detective story will serve as an example of a supposedly non-cultural type of expression. Built around the character of an omniscient and omni-competent sleuth whose lineage stretches backwards from Holmes to Da Vinci it manages to be popular poetry about the modern city. The sleuth is a master of every facet of the city. With the skill of an organist at a five-keyboard instrument, he can touch any note or level of metropolitan life. He is familiar with all the dives and clubs. He knows the whole range of drinks, foods, clothes, perfumes, as well as every intricacy of transportation routes and schedules. Anybody in the future who wished to acquaint himself with the full range and texture of the modern big town would not be able to find in reputable novels anything comparable to the poetic reportage of the detective story. The raw mechanical power that is imparted to the ordinary metropolitan citizen by his *milieu* is found in the gestures and idiom of the sleuth.

But much more remarkable, as cultural expression, is the form of the detective story. Written backwards, in order that the effect of the story may always be the exact reconstruction of a crime, the form is based on the same method as that employed in laboratory experiment and in modern historiography, archaeology, and mechanical production. But the detective story preceded these sciences in the discovery of this method. It is only one striking instance of popular expression which has its tap-root in the deepest intuitions of our culture.

If the mechanization of writing had some such typical effects as have been suggested, it is not too surprising that its extreme development should have coincided with a tendency to switch from words to pictures. This switch was already under way in the eighteenth century with its spectator outlook and passion for landscape in the arts. By the nineteenth century the demand for illustrations for letter-press became very strong, not only in the book and newspaper but also in the very form taken by the esoteric arts, as for instance Rimbaud's *Illuminations*. Photography and cinema may be seen as the response to prolonged pressure of demand rather than as gratuitous inventions. Perhaps they can be viewed as ultimate or extreme mechanizations of writing. More probably, however, telegraphy has claims to be considered the extreme verge of the mechanization of writing beyond which one enters the Marconi world of the mechanization of speech.

Like any extreme these processes reversed the original effect, and tended to separate people from the printed word. So that in pictorial papers and magazines even words take on the character of landscape. Variety of types is employed to build up the page as a visual unit rather than as a mere linear transmission of printed words. The Chinese never had an alphabet, but their ideograms are pictorial translations of human gestures and relationships. As our press has become more pictorial our whole culture has become more sympathetic to Chinese art and expression. So that the very features of our culture which have intruded disruptively into the East have also brought us a basis for approaching their kinds of communication. Modern advertising is a world of ideograms.

There have been so many domestic and social revolutions associated with the consequences of the mechanization of writing that it is natural to wonder why so little attention has been given to the matter. Without any special awareness of just what revolutions we have been through we have hurried from the age of cinema into the era of television. Between cinema and television we managed to squeeze in radio, the mechanization of speech.

By way of obeisance to our own ingenuity, people have often felt obliged to marvel at radio and television by exclaiming: "Although it's happening over there, it's also happening right here." This kind of self-hypnosis is undertaken in a spirit of uneasy propitiation of the new god. But the real power of these deities is exerted when we aren't looking. The mechanization of speech meant that the most intimate whispers or the most ordinary tones of conversation could be sent everywhere instantly from anywhere. Beside the effects of this revolution in communication even those associated with the invention of writing and printing are trivial events. Radio meant the widest dispersal of the human voice and also the ultimate dispersal of attention. For listening is not hearing any more than looking is reading. And all the networks of human communication are becoming so jammed that very few messages are reaching their destination. Mental starvation in the midst of plenty is as much a feature of mass communication as of mass production.

The stereotypes of advertising have been developed as the nexus between mass consumption and mass production. Advertising has been the means of organizing the mass market. For advertisements are constructed scientifically as machines to stream-line and channel the multiplicity of human desires until they are effectively geared to production. A more effective mode of psychological collectivization could not be imagined than that imposed by the giant stereotypes of the desirable which are insinuated, without argument but with intimate urgency, by the symbolist techniques of visual and auditory appeal in advertisements. These stereotypes are not the product of chance but of careful investigation and experiment with the human recipients. For the present time the realities of political and social change are to be studied in this area. Among other things, these changes mean that events cannot be reported if they involve a degree of complexity in excess of the available stereotypes, so that in modern diplomacy the negotiators will naturally refuse to attempt a working agreement that cannot be followed by or reported to non-professionals. There must be some simple moral or national formula to hand for the diplomats to depend upon, such as will justify them to the half-listening, half-waking world hour by hour and day by day. In this way the new media have compelled history and actuality to feign a simplicity that just isn't there. Thus the magic and mythic power so characteristic of the mass media, having first hypnotized the recipients of their messages, have then, in effect, pronounced the real world to be an illegitimate and reprehensible territory. The same sort of paradox is inherent in the movie as a nighttime therapy applied to the victims of dream routines of daily work.

It would be too much in the spirit of the current effect of the new media to brand these and allied developments as deplorable. For, if the new reality of our time is in the main a collective dream or nightmare brought about by the mechanization of speech (television takes the final step of merchandizing the expressiveness of the human figure and gesture) then we must learn the art of using all our wits in a dream world, as did James Joyce in *Finnegans Wake*.

On looking closely at the newspaper once more, it becomes evident that as a popular art form it embraces the world spatially but under the sign of a single day. The newspaper as a late stage in the mechanization of writing is handicapped in taking the next step, which occurs easily in radio and television, namely to cover not only many spaces, but many times, or history, simultaneously. But even the newspaper has long felt the pressure to take this step. In juxtaposing items from Russia, India, Iran and England, it is plain that there is also a diversity of historical times that are being artificially and arbitrarily elucidated under a single date line. Even in so intimate and influential a fact as dress design, modern archaeology has increased the range of style and idiom to include in a single season types of attire developed many thousands of years apart. The *Time and Western Man* of Mr. Wyndham Lewis is the classic study of the romantic stigmata of the enthusiastic time-traveller. But the further development of communication in space as in historical time, has tended to lessen the romantic appeal of distant times and customs in favour of a direct stylistic interest in their immediate value and relevance. The modern study of the past, as of distant places, has the effect of making them as much a part of the present as our own problems. So that for the modern mind history has become not a receding perspective but a present burden.

This cumulative effect of our techniques of production and of communication has been felt everywhere in the world as an impatience with "the dead hand of the past." As we become more familiar with the components of this revolutionary state of mind we shall discover in our social life as in our private life that there is no past that is dead. And that "the dead hand of the past" is an indispensable guide in the present.

In other words when communication devices have achieved the speed of light, there occurs a social and historical simultaneity as well as a local and temporal one. And since the various societies of our world comprise many ages, as well as many places, the immediate effect of modern communication in overlaying all of these is to create dislocation and distress. The first impulse of reason is to cry out for uniformity at any cost, to prevent further waste, confusion, and madness. A clean sweep, a new start, and the abolition of historical differences seem to be demanded for mere survival.

It would seem that even so superficial and examination of the impact of technology on culture and politics poses some useful matters for study. The great political discovery of the eighteenth century was social equality. The principal insight of this century to date is perhaps the anthropologist's awareness of cultural equality. Modern anthropologists, deeply influenced by our new skills in communication, have arrived at the conviction that all cultures are equal. That is to say, that seen as communication networks, all cultures are equal. That is to say, that seen as communication networks, all cultures past or present represent a uniquely valuable response to specific problems in interpersonal and inter-social communication. This position amounts to no more than saying that any known language possesses qualities of expressiveness not to be found in any other language. But as a matter of practical politics the awareness of cultural equality (a by-product of new techniques of communication) will certainly prove as benign a force as can be imagined, because it frees each society from the odium of inferiority or the arrogance of superiority. Each is free to learn from all the others while possessing itself in quiet.

And by way of abating some of the dread most people feel towards the power of mass communications at present it might be well to consider how with radio or the mechanization of human speech, the hustings and the forum have given way to the round table and face-to-face discussion in the presence of small audiences.

Also, with television has come a weakening of the magic and myth of the movie "star." It appears that the intimacy and immediacy of the flexible television camera and screen are much less favourable to the star system than the movie camera and its giant screen on to which are poured such dreams as money can buy.

50

A Theory of Mass Culture

From *Diogenes* (1953)

Dwight Macdonald

Dwight MacDonald (1906–1982) was one of the leading members of a loose group known as the "New York Intellectuals," who wrote influentially on culture and politics from the 1930s through the 1970s. Many among them were Jewish sons of immigrants who attended New York colleges, but MacDonald was a relatively privileged gentile who went off to Yale (graduating in 1928) and then became a writer—for *Fortune* magazine; *Partisan Review;* and *Politics,* a magazine he founded and ran from 1944 to 1949. Like Daniel Bell and many other young American intellectuals, MacDonald was a socialist in the 1930s. In the 1940s, he turned instead to formulating a radical "third camp" as an alternative to American liberalism and Soviet Stalinism, but in the 1950s, during the Cold War, he turned to other matters—particularly the criticism of mass culture.

In this essay, MacDonald offers classic definitions of *mass culture*—culture that is manufactured from above, that exploits popular tastes, that is homogenized or easily digested—while also anticipating themes of postmodernist cultural theory, such as the "porous" quality of people's tastes and the blurring of cultural boundaries. What postmodernist critics typically celebrate, however, MacDonald criticizes, drawing upon critical theory while making particularly harsh judgments about the Soviet Union. This is a rather dark piece, which shows an incisive intellect deeply alienated from postwar American culture.

For about a century, Western culture has really been two cultures: the traditional kind—let us call it "High Culture"—that is chronicled in the textbooks, and a "Mass Culture" manufactured wholesale for the market. In the old art forms, the artisans of Mass Culture have long been at work:

in the novel, the line stretches from Eugène Sue to Lloyd C. Douglas; in music, from Offenbach to Tin-Pan Alley; in art from the chromo to Maxfield Parrish and Norman Rockwell; in architecture, from Victorian Gothic to suburban Tudor. Mass Culture has also developed new media of its own, into which the serious artist rarely ventures: radio, the movies, comic books, detective stories, science fiction, television.

It is sometimes called "Popular Culture,"[1] but I think "Mass Culture" a more accurate term, since its distinctive mark is that it is solely and directly an article for mass consumption, like chewing gum. A work of High Culture is occasionally popular, after all, though this is increasingly rare. Thus Dickens was even more popular than his contemporary, G. A. Henty, the difference being that he was an artist, communicating his individual vision to other individuals, while Henty was an impersonal manufacturer of an impersonal commodity for the masses.

The Nature of Mass Culture

The historical reasons for the growth of Mass Culture since the early 1800's are well known. Political democracy and popular education broke down the old upper-class monopoly of culture. Business enterprise found a profitable market in the cultural demands of the newly awakened masses, and the advance of technology made possible the cheap production of books, periodicals, pictures, music, and furniture, in sufficient quantities to satisfy this market. Modern technology also created new media such as the movies and television which are specially well adapted to mass manufacture and distribution.

The phenomenon is thus peculiar to modern times and differs radically from what was hitherto known as art or culture. It is true that Mass Culture began as, and to some extent still is, a parasitic, a cancerous growth on High Culture. As Clement Greenberg pointed out in "Avant-Garde and *Kitsch*" (*Partisan Review,* Fall, 1939): "The precondition of *kitsch* (a German term for 'Mass Culture') is the availability close at hand of a fully matured cultural tradition, whose discoveries, acquisitions, and perfected self-conscious *kitsch* can take advantage of for its own ends." The connection, however, is not that of the leaf and the branch but rather that of the caterpillar and the leaf. *Kitsch* "mines" High Culture the way improvident frontiersmen mine the soil, extracting its riches and putting nothing back. Also, as *kitsch* develops, it begins to draw on its own past, and some of it evolves so far away from High Culture as to appear quite disconnected from it.

It is also true that Mass Culture is to some extent a continuation of the old Folk Art which until the Industrial Revolution was the culture of the common people, but here, too, the differences are more striking than the similarities. Folk Art grew from below. It was a spontaneous, autochthonous expression of the people, shaped by themselves, pretty much without the benefit of High Culture, to suit their own needs. Mass Culture is imposed from above. It is fabricated by technicians hired by businessmen; its audiences are passive consumers, their participation limited to the choice between buying and not buying. The Lords of *kitsch,* in short, exploit the cultural needs of the masses in order to make a profit and/or to maintain their class rule—in Communist countries, only the second purpose obtains. (It is very different to *satisfy* popular tastes, as Robert Burns' poetry did, and to *exploit* them, as Hollywood does.) Folk Art was the people's own institution, their private little garden walled off from the great formal park of their masters' High Culture. But Mass Culture breaks down the wall, integrating the masses into a debased form of High Culture and thus becoming an instrument of political domination. If one had no other data to go on, the nature of Mass Culture would reveal capitalism to be an exploitative class society and not the harmonious commonwealth it is sometimes alleged to be. The same goes even more strongly for Soviet Communism and *its* special kind of Mass Culture.

Mass Culture: U.S.S.R.

"Everybody" knows that America is a land of Mass Culture, but it is not so generally recognized that so is the Soviet Union. Certainly not by the Communist leaders, one of whom has contemptuously observed that the American people need not fear the peace-loving Soviet state which has absolutely no desire to deprive them of their Coca-Cola and comic books. Yet the fact is that the U.S.S.R. is even more a land of Mass Culture than is the U.S.A. This is less easily recognizable because their Mass Culture is *in form* just the opposite of ours, being one of propaganda and pedagogy rather than of entertainment. None the less, it has the essential quality of Mass, as against High or Folk, Culture: it is manufactured for mass consumption by technicians employed by the ruling class and is not an expression of either the individual artist or the common people themselves.

Like our own, it exploits rather than satisfies the cultural needs of the masses, though for political rather than commercial reasons. Its quality is even lower: our Supreme Court building is tasteless and pompous, but not to the lunatic degree of the proposed new Palace of the Soviets—a huge wedding cake of columns mounting up to an eighty-foot statue of Lenin; Soviet movies are so much duller and cruder than our own that even the American comrades shun them; the childish level of *serious* Soviet magazines devoted to matters of art or philosophy has to be read to be believed, and as for the popular press, it is as if Colonel McCormick ran every periodical in America.

Gresham's Law in Culture

The separation of Folk Art and High Culture in fairly watertight compartments corresponded to the sharp line once drawn between the common people and the aristocracy. The eruption of the masses onto the political stage has broken down this compartmentation, with disastrous cultural results. Whereas Folk Art had its own special quality, Mass Culture is at best a vulgarized reflection of High Culture. And whereas High Culture could formerly ignore the mob and seek to please only the *cognoscenti,* it must now compete with Mass Culture or be merged into it.

The problem is acute in the United States and not just because a prolific Mass Culture exists here. If there were a clearly defined cultural *élite,* then the masses could have their *kitsch* and the *élite* could have its High Culture, with everybody happy. But the boundary line is blurred. A statistically significant part of the population, I venture to guess, is chronically confronted with a choice between going to the movies or to a concert, between reading Tolstoy or a detective story, between looking at old masters or at a TV show; i.e., the pattern of their cultural lives is "open" to the point of being porous. Good art competes with *kitsch,* serious ideas compete with commercialized formulae—and the advantage lies all on one side. There seems to be a Gresham's Law in cultural as well as monetary circulation: bad stuff drives out the good, since it is more easily understood and enjoyed. It is this facility of access which at once sells *kitsch* on a wide market and also prevents it from achieving quality.[2] Clement Greenberg writes that the special aesthetic qual-

ity of *kitsch* is that it "predigests art for the spectator and spares him effort, provides him with a shortcut to the pleasures of art that detours what is necessarily difficult in genuine art" because it includes the spectator's reactions in the work of art itself instead of forcing him to make his own responses. Thus "Eddie Guest and the Indian Love Lyrics are more 'poetic' than T. S. Eliot and Shakespeare." And so, too, our "collegiate Gothic" such as the Harkness Quadrangle at Yale is more picturesquely Gothic than Chartres, and a pinup girl smoothly airbrushed by Petty is more sexy than a real naked woman.

When to this ease of consumption is added *kitsch's* ease of production because of its standardized nature, its prolific growth is easy to understand. It threatens High Culture by its sheer pervasiveness, its brutal, overwhelming *quantity.* The upper classes, who begin by using it to make money from the crude tastes of the masses and to dominate them politically, end by finding their own culture attacked and even threatened with destruction by the instrument they have thoughtlessly employed. (The same irony may be observed in modern politics, where most swords seem to have two edges; thus Nazism began as a tool of the big bourgeoisie and the army *Junkers* but ended by using *them* as *its* tools.)

Homogenized Culture

Like nineteenth-century capitalism, Mass Culture is a dynamic, revolutionary force, breaking down the old barriers of class, tradition, taste, and dissolving all cultural distinctions. It mixes and scrambles everything together, producing what might be called homogenized culture, after another American achievement, the homogenization process that distributes the globules of cream evenly throughout the milk instead of allowing them to float separately on top. It thus destroys all values, since value judgments imply discrimination. Mass Culture is very, very democratic: it absolutely refuses to discriminate against, or between, anything or anybody. All is grist to its mill, and all comes out finely ground indeed.

Consider *Life,* a typical homogenized mass-circulation magazine. It appears on the mahogany library tables of the rich, the glass end-tables of the middle-class and the oilcloth-covered kitchen tables of the poor. Its contents are as thoroughly homogenized as its circulation.

The same issue will contain a serious exposition of atomic theory alongside a disquisition on Rita Hayworth's love life; photos of starving Korean children picking garbage from the ruins of Pusan and of sleek models wearing adhesive brassieres; an editorial hailing Bertrand Russell on his eightieth birthday ("A GREAT MIND IS STILL ANNOYING AND ADORNING OUR AGE") across from a full-page photo of a housewife arguing with an umpire at a baseball game ("MOM GETS THUMB"); a cover announcing in the same size type "A NEW FOREIGN POLICY, BY JOHN FOSTER DULLES" and "KERIMA: HER MARATHON KISS IS A MOVIE SENSATION"; nine color pages of Renoirs plus a memoir by his son, followed by a full-page picture of a roller-skating horse. The advertisements, of course, provide even more scope for the editor's homogenizing talents, as when a full-page photo of a ragged Bolivian peon grinningly drunk on coca leaves (which Mr. Luce's conscientious reporters tell us he chews to narcotize his chronic hunger pains) appears opposite an ad of a pretty smiling, well-dressed American mother with her two pretty, smiling, well-dressed children (a boy and a girl, of course—children are always homogenized in American ads) looking raptly at a clown on a TV set ("RCA VICTOR BRINGS YOU A NEW KIND OF TELEVISION—SUPER SETS WITH 'PICTURE POWER'"). The peon would doubtless find the juxtaposition piquant if he could afford a copy of *Life* which, fortunately for the Good Neighbor Policy, he cannot.

Academicism and Avantgardism

Until about 1930, High Culture tried to defend itself against the encroachments of Mass Culture in two opposite ways: Academicism, or an attempt to compete by imitation; and Avantgardism, or a withdrawal from competition.

Academicism is *kitsch* for the *élite:* spurious High Culture that is outwardly the real thing but actually as much a manufactured article as the cheaper cultural goods produced for the masses. It is recognized at the time for what it is only by the Avantgardists. A generation or two later, its real nature is understood by everyone and it quietly drops into the same oblivion as its franker sister-under-the-skin. Examples are painters such as Bougereau and Rosa Bonheur, critics such as Edmund Clarence Stedman and Edmund Gosse, the Beaux Arts school of architecture, composers such as the late Sir Edward Edgar, poets such as Stephen Phillips, and novelists such as Alphonse Daudet, Arnold Bennett, James Branch Cabell and Somerset Maugham.

The significance of the Avantgarde movement (by which I mean poets such as Rimbaud, novelists such as Joyce, composers such as Stravinsky, and painters such as Picasso) is that it simply refused to compete. Rejecting Academicism—and thus, at a second remove, also Mass Culture—it made a desperate attempt to fence off some area where the serious artist could still function. It created a new compartmentation of culture, on the basis of an intellectual rather than a social *élite*. The attempt was remarkably successful: to it we owe almost everything that is living in the art of the last fifty or so years. In fact, the High Culture of our times is pretty much identical with Avantgardism. The movement came at a time (1890–1930) when bourgeois values were being challenged both culturally and politically. (In this country, the cultural challenge did not come until World War I, so that our Avantgarde flourished only in the twenties.) In the thirties the two streams mingled briefly, after each had spent its real force, under the aegis of the Communists, only to sink together at the end of the decade into the sands of the wasteland we still live in. The rise of Nazism and the revelation in the Moscow Trials of the real nature of the new society in Russia inaugurated the present period, when men cling to the evils they know rather than risk possibly greater ones by pressing forward. Nor has the chronic state of war, hot or cold, that the world has been in since 1939 encouraged rebellion or experiment in either art or politics.

A Merger Has Been Arranged

In this new period, the competitors, as often happens in the business world, are merging. Mass Culture takes on the color of both varieties of the old High Culture, Academic and Avantgarde, while these latter are increasingly watered down with Mass elements. There is slowly emerging a tepid, flaccid Middlebrow Culture that threatens to engulf everything in its spreading ooze.

Bauhaus modernism has at last trickled down, in a debased form of course, into our furniture, cafeterias, movie theatres, electric toasters, office buildings, drug stores, and railroad trains. Psychoanalysis is expounded sympathetically and superficially in popular magazines, and the psychoanalyst replaces the eccentric millionaire as the *deus ex machina* in many a movie. T. S. Eliot writes *The Cocktail Party* and it becomes a Broadway hit. (Though in some ways excellent, it is surely inferior to his *Murder in the Cathedral*, which in the unmerged thirties had to depend on WPA to get produced at all.)

The typical creator of *kitsch* today, at least in the old media, is an indeterminate specimen. There are no widely influential critics so completely terrible as, say, the late William Lyon Phelps was. Instead we have such gray creatures as Clifton Fadiman and Henry Seidel Canby. The artless numbers of an Eddie Guest are drowned out by the more sophisticated though equally commonplace strains of Benet's *John Brown's Body,* Maxfield Parrish yields to Rockwell Kent, Arthur Brisbane to Walter Lippman, Theda Bara to Ingrid Bergman. We even have what might be called *l'avant-garde pompier* (or, in American, "phoney Avantgardism"), as in the buildings of Raymond Hood and the later poetry of Archibald MacLeish, as there is also an academic Avantgardism in *belles lettres* so that now the "little" as well as the big magazines have their hack writers.

All this is not a raising of the level of Mass Culture, as might appear at first, but rather a corruption of High Culture. There is nothing more vulgar than sophisticated *kitsch*. Compare Conan Doyle's workmanlike and unpretentious Sherlock Holmes stories with the bogus "intellectuality" of Dorothy M. Sayers, who, like many contemporary detective-story writers, is a novelist *manquée* who ruins her stuff with literary attitudinizing. Or consider the relationship of Hollywood and Broadway. In the twenties, the two were sharply differentiated, movies being produced for the masses of the hinterland, theatre for an upper-class New York audience. The theatre was High Culture, mostly of the Academic variety (Theatre Guild) but with some spark of Avantgarde fire (the "little" or "experimental" theatre movement). The movies were definitely Mass Culture, mostly very bad but with some leaven of Avantgardism (Griffith, Stroheim) and Folk Art (Chaplin and other comedians). With

the sound film, Broadway and Hollywood drew closer together. Plays are now produced mainly to sell the movie rights, with many being directly financed by the film companies. The merger has standardized the theatre to such an extent that even the early Theatre Guild seems vital in retrospect, while hardly a trace of the "experimental" theatre is left. And what have the movies gained? They are more sophisticated, the acting is subtler, the sets in better taste. But they too have become standardized: they are never as awful as they often were in the old days, but they are never as good either. They are better entertainment and worse art. The cinema of the twenties occasionally gave us the fresh charm of Folk Art or the imaginative intensity of Avantgardism. The coming of sound, and with it Broadway, degraded the camera to a recording instrument for an alien art form, the spoken play. The silent film had at least the *theoretical possibility*, even within the limits of Mass Culture, of being artistically significant. The sound film, within those limits, does not.

Division of Labor

The whole field could be approached from the standpoint of the division of labor. The more advanced technologically, the greater the division. Cf. the great Blackett-Semple-Hummert factory—the word is accurate—for the mass production of radio "soap operas." Or the fact that in Hollywood a composer for the movies is not *permitted* to make his own orchestrations any more than a director can do his own cutting. Or the "editorial formula" which every big-circulation magazine tailors its fiction and articles to fit, much as automobile parts are machined in Detroit. *Time* and *Newsweek* have carried specialization to its extreme: their writers don't even sign their work, which in fact is not properly theirs, since the gathering of data is done by a specialized corps of researchers and correspondents and the final article is often as much the result of the editor's blue-pencilling and rewriting as of the original author's efforts. The *"New Yorker* short story" is a definite genre—smooth, minor-key, casual, suggesting drama and sentiment without ever being crude enough to actually create it—which the editors have established by years of patient, skilful selection the same way a gardener develops a new kind of rose. They have, indeed, done their work all too well: would-be contributors now deluge them with lifeless imitations, and they have begun to beg writers not to follow the formula *quite* so closely.

Such art workers are as alienated from their brainwork as the industrial worker is from his handwork. The results are as bad qualitatively as they are impressive quantitatively. The only great films to come out of Hollywood, for example, were made before industrial elephantiasis had reduced the director to one of a number of technicians all operating at about the same level of authority. Our two greatest directors, Griffith and Stroheim, were artists, not specialists; they did everything themselves, dominated everything personally: the scenario, the actors, the camera work, and above all the cutting (or *montage*). Unity is essential in art; it cannot be achieved by a production line of specialists, however competent. There have been successful collective creations (Greek temples, Gothic churches, perhaps the *Illiad)* but their creators were part of a tradition which was strong enough to impose unity on their work. We have no such tradition today, and so art—as against *kitsch*—will result only when a single brain and sensibility is in full command. In the movies, only the director can even theoretically be in such a position; he was so in the pre-1930 cinema of this country, Germany, and the Soviet Union.

Griffith and Stroheim were both terrific egoists—crude, naïve, and not without charlatanry—who survived until the industry became highly enough organized to resist their vigorous personalities. By about 1925, both were outside looking in; the manufacture of commodities so costly to make and so profitable to sell was too serious a matter to be entrusted to artists.

"One word of advice, Von," Griffith said to Stroheim, who had been his assistant on *Intolerance,* when Stroheim came to him with the news that he had a chance to make a picture himself. "Make your pictures in your own way. Put your mark on them. Take a stand and stick to your guns. You'll make some enemies, but you'll make good pictures." Could that have been only thirty years ago?

Adultized Children and Infantile Adults

The homogenizing effects of *kitsch* also blurs age lines. It would be interesting to know how many

adults read the comics. We do know that comic books are by far the favorite reading matter of our soldiers and sailors, that some forty million comic books are sold a month, and that some seventy million people (most of whom must be adults, there just aren't that many kids) are estimated to read the newspaper comic strips every day. We also know that movie Westerns and radio and TV programs such as "The Lone Ranger" and "Captain Video" are by no means enjoyed only by children. On the other hand, children have access to such grown-up media as the movies, radio and TV. (Note that these newer arts are the ones which blur age lines because of the extremely modest demands they make on the audience's cultural equipment; thus there are many children's books but few children's movies.)

This merging of the child and grown-up audience means: (1) infantile regression of the latter, who, unable to cope with the strains and complexities of modern life, escape via *kitsch* (which in turn, confirms and enhances their infantilism); (2) "overstimulation" of the former, who grow up too fast. Or, as Max Horkheimer well puts it: "Development has ceased to exist. The child is grown up as soon as he can walk, and the grown-up in principle always remains the same." Also note (a) our cult of youth, which makes 18–22 the most admired and desired period of life, and (b) the sentimental worship of Mother ("Momism") as if we couldn't bear to grow up and be on our own. Peter Pan might be a better symbol of America than Uncle Sam.

Idols of Consumption

Too little attention has been paid to the connection of our Mass Culture with the historical evolution of American Society. In *Radio Research, 1942–43* (Paul F. Lazarsfeld, ed.), Leo Lowenthal compared the biographical articles in *Collier's* and *The Saturday Evening Post* for 1901 and 1940-41 and found that in the forty-year interval the proportion of articles about business and professional men and political leaders had declined while those about entertainers had gone up 50 per cent. Furthermore, the 1901 entertainers are mostly serious artists—opera singers, sculptors, pianists, etc.—while those of 1941 are *all* movie stars, baseball players, and such; and even the "serious" heroes in 1941 aren't so very serious after all: the businessmen and politicians are freaks, oddities, not the really powerful leaders as in 1901. The 1901 *Satevepost* heroes he calls "idols of production," those of today "idols of consumption."

Lowenthal notes that the modern *Satevepost* biographee is successful not because of his own personal abilities so much as because he "got the breaks." The whole competitive struggle is presented as a lottery in which a few winners, no more talented or energetic than any one else, drew the lucky tickets. The effect on the mass reader is at once consoling (it might have been me) and deadening to effort, ambition (there are no rules, so why struggle?). It is striking how closely this evolution parallels the country's economic development. Lowenthal observes that the "idols of production" maintained their dominance right through the twenties. The turning point was the 1929 depression when the problem became how to consume goods rather than how to produce them, and also when the arbitrariness and chaos of capitalism was forcefully brought home to the mass man. So he turned to "idols of consumption," or rather these were now offered him by the manufacturers of Mass Culture, and he accepted them. "They seem to lead to a dream world of the masses," observes Lowenthal, "who are no longer capable or willing to conceive of biographies primarily as a means of orientation and education. . . . He, the American mass man, as reflected in his 'idols of consumption' appears no longer as a center of outwardly directed energies and actions on whose work and efficiency might depend mankind's progress. Instead of the 'givers' we are faced with the 'takers'. . . . They seem to stand for a phantasmagoria of world-wide social security—an attitude which asks for no more than to be served with the things needed for reproduction and recreation, an attitude which has lost every primary interest in how to invent, shape, or apply the tools leading to such purposes of mass satisfaction."

Sherlock Holmes to Mike Hammer

The role of science in Mass Culture has similarly changed from the rational and the purposive to the passive, accidental, even the catastrophic. Consider the evolution of the detective story, a genre which can be traced back to the memoirs of Vidocq, the master-detective of the Napoleonic era. Poe, who was peculiarly fascinated by scientific method, wrote the first and still best detective stories: *The Purloined Letter, The Gold Bug, The Mystery of Marie Roget, The Murders in the Rue Morgue.* Conan Doyle created the great folk hero, Sherlock Holmes, like Poe's Dupin a sage whose wizard's wand was scientific deduction (Poe's "ratiocination"). Such stories could only appeal to—in fact, only be *comprehensible* to—an audience accustomed to think in scientific terms: to survey the data, set up a hypothesis, test it by seeing whether it caught the murderer. The very idea of an art genre cast in the form of a problem to be solved by purely intellectual means could only have arisen in a scientific age. This kind of detective fiction, which might be called the "classic" style, is still widely practiced (well by Agatha Christie and John Dickson Carr, badly by the more popular Erle Stanley Gardiner) but of late it has been overshadowed by the rank, noxious growth of works in the "sensational" style. This was inaugurated by Dashiel Hammett (whom André Gide was foolish enough to admire) and has recently been enormously stepped up in voltage by Mickey Spillane, whose six books to date have sold thirteen million copies. The sensationalists use what for the classicists was the point—the uncovering of the criminal—as a mere excuse for the minute description of scenes of bloodshed, brutality, lust, and alcoholism. The cool, astute, subtle Dupin-Holmes is replaced by the crude man of action whose prowess is measured not by intellectual mastery but by his capacity for liquor, women, and mayhem (he can "take it" as well as "dish it out"—Hammett's *The Glass Key* is largely a chronicle of the epic beatings absorbed by the hero before he finally staggers to the solution). Mike Hammer, Spillane's aptly named hero, is such a monumental blunderer that even Dr. Watson would have seen through him. According to Richard W. Johnston (*Life*, June 23, 1952), "Mike has one bizarre and memorable characteristic that sets him apart from all other fictional detectives: sheer incompetence. In the five Hammer cases, 48 people have been killed, and there is reason to believe that if Mike had kept out of the way, 34 of them—all innocent of the original crime—would have survived." A decade ago, the late George Orwell, apropos a "sensationalist" detective story of the time, *No Orchids for Miss Blandish,* showed how the brutalization of this genre mirrors the general degeneration in ethics from nineteenth-century standards. What he would have written had Mickey Spillane's works been then in existence I find it hard to imagine.

Frankenstein to Hiroshima

The real heirs of the "classic" detective story today, so far as the exploitation of science is concerned, are the writers of science fiction, where the marvels and horrors of the future must always be "scientifically possible"—just as Sherlock Holmes drew on no supernatural powers. This is the approach of the bourgeoisie, who think of science as their familiar instrument. The masses are less confident, more awed in their approach to science, and there are vast lower strata of science fiction where the marvellous is untrammeled by the limits of knowledge. To the masses, science is the modern *arcanum arcanorum,* at once the supreme mystery and the philosopher's stone that explains the mystery. The latter concept appears in comic strips such as "Superman" and in the charlatan-science exploited by "health fakers" and "nature fakers." Taken this way, science gives man mastery over his environment and is beneficent. But science itself is not understood, therefore not mastered, therefore terrifying because of its very power. Taken *this* way, as the supreme mystery, science becomes the stock in trade of the "horror" pulp magazines and comics and movies. It has got to the point, indeed, that if one sees a laboratory in a movie, one shudders, and the white coat of the scientist is as blood-chilling a sight as Count Dracula's black cloak. These "horror" films have apparently an indestructible popularity: *Frankenstein* is still shown, after twenty-one years, and the current revival of *King Kong* is expected to gross over 2 million dollars.

If the scientist's laboratory has acquired in Mass Culture a ghastly atmosphere, is this perhaps not one of those deep popular intuitions? From Frankenstein's laboratory to Maidenek and Hiroshima is not a long journey. Was there a popular suspicion, perhaps only half conscious, that the nineteenth-century trust in science, like the nineteenth-century trust in popular education, was mistaken, that science can as easily be used for antihuman as for prohuman ends, perhaps even more easily? For Mrs. Shelley's Frankenstein, the experimenter who brought disaster by pushing his science too far, is a scientific folk hero older than and still as famous as

Mr. Doyle's successful and beneficent Sherlock Holmes.

The Problem of the Masses

Conservatives such as Ortega y Gasset and T. S. Eliot argue that since "the revolt of the masses" has led to the horrors of totalitarianism (and of California roadside architecture), the only hope is to rebuild the old class walls and bring the masses once more under aristocratic control. They think of the popular as synonymous with cheap and vulgar. Marxian radicals and liberals, on the other hand, see the masses as intrinsically healthy but as the dupes and victims of cultural exploitation by the Lords of *kitsch*—in the style of Rousseau's "noble savage" idea. If only the masses were offered good stuff instead of *kitsch,* how they would eat it up! How the level of Mass Culture would rise! Both these diagnoses seem to me fallacious: they assume that Mass Culture is (in the conservative view) or could be (in the liberal view) an expression of *people,* like Folk Art, whereas actually it is an expression of *masses,* a very different thing.

There are theoretical reasons why Mass Culture is not and can never be any good. I take it as axiomatic that culture can only be produced by and for human beings. But in so far as people are organized (more strictly, disorganized) as masses, they lose their human identity and quality. For the masses are in historical time what a crowd is in space: a large quantity of people unable to express themselves as human beings because they are related to one another neither as individuals nor as members of communities—indeed, they are not related *to each other* at all, but only to something distant, abstract, nonhuman: a football game or bargain sale in the case of a crowd, a system of industrial production, a party or a State in the case of the masses. The mass man is a solitary atom, uniform with and undifferentiated from thousands and millions of other atoms who go to make up "the lonely crowd," as David Riesman well calls American society. A folk or a people, however, is a community, i.e., a group of individuals linked to each other by common interests, work, traditions, values, and sentiments; something like a family, each of whose members has a special place and function as an individual while at the same time sharing the group's interests (family budget) sentiments (family quarrels), and culture (family jokes). The scale is small enough so that it "makes a difference" what the individual does, a first condition for human—as against mass-existence. He is at once more important as an individual than in mass society and at the same time more closely integrated into the community, his creativity nourished by a rich combination of individualism and communalism. (The great culture-bearing *élites* of the past have been communities of this kind.) In contrast, a mass society, like a crowd, is so undifferentiated and loosely structured that its atoms, in so far as human values go, tend to cohere only along the line of the least common denominator; its morality sinks to that of its most brutal and primitive members, its taste to that of the least sensitive and most ignorant. And in addition to everything else, the scale is simply too big, there are just *too many people*.

Yet the collective monstrosity, "the masses," "the public," is taken as a human norm by the scientific and artistic technicians of our Mass Culture. They at once degraded the public by treating it as an object, to be handled with the lack of ceremony and the objectivity of medical students dissecting a corpse, and at the same time flatter it, pander to its level of taste and ideas by taking these as the criterion of reality (in the case of questionnaire-sociologists and other "social scientists") or of art (in the case of the Lords of *kitsch*). When one hears a questionnaire-sociologist talk about how he will "set up" an investigation, one feels he regards people as a herd of dumb animals, as mere congeries of conditioned reflexes, his calculation being which reflex will be stimulated by which question. At the same time, of necessity, he sees the statistical majority as the great Reality, the secret of life he is trying to find out; like the *kitsch* Lords, he is wholly without values, willing to accept any idiocy if it is held by many people. The aristocrat and the democrat both criticize and argue with popular taste, the one with hostility, the other in friendship, for both attitudes proceed from a set of values. This is less degrading to the masses than the "objective" approach of Hollywood and the questionnaire-sociologists, just as it is less degrading to a man to be shouted at in anger than to be quietly assumed to be part of a machine. But the *plebs* have their dialectical revenge: complete indifference to their human *quality* means complete prostration before their statistical *quantity*, so that a movie magnate who cynically "gives the public what it wants"—i.e., assumes it wants trash—sweats with terror if box-office returns drop 10 per cent.

The Future of High Culture: Dark

The conservative proposal to save culture by restoring the old class lines has a more solid historical base than the Marxian hope for a new democratic, classless culture, for, with the possible (and important) exception of Periclean Athens, all the great cultures of the past were *élite* cultures. Politically, however, it is without meaning in a world dominated by the two great mass nations, U.S.A. and U.S.S.R. and becoming more industrialized, more massified all the time. The only practical thing along those lines would be to revive the *cultural élite* which the Avantgarde created. As I have already noted, the Avantgarde is now dying, partly from internal causes, partly suffocated by the competing Mass Culture, where it is not being absorbed into it. Of course this process has not reached 100 per cent, and doubtless never will unless the country goes either Fascist or Communist. There are still islands above the flood for those determined enough to reach them, and to stay on them: as Faulkner has shown, a writer can even use Hollywood instead of being used by it, if his purpose is firm enough. But the homogenization of High and Mass Culture has gone far and is going farther all the time, and there seems little reason to expect a revival of Avantgardism, that is, of a successful countermovement to Mass Culture. Particularly not in this country, where the blurring of class lines, the absence of a stable cultural tradition, and the greater facilities for manufacturing and marketing *kitsch* all work in the other direction. The result is that our intelligentsia is remarkably small, weak, and disintegrated. One of the odd things about the American cultural scene is how many brainworkers there are and how few intellectuals, defining the former as specialists whose thinking is pretty much confined to their limited "fields" and the latter as persons who take all culture for their province. Not only are there few intellectuals, but they don't hang together, they have very little *esprit de corps*, very little sense of belonging to a community; they are so isolated from each other they don't even bother to quarrel—there hasn't been a really good fight among them since the Moscow Trials.

The Future of Mass Culture: Darker

If the conservative proposal to save our culture via the aristocratic Avantgarde seems historically unlikely, what of the democratic-liberal proposal? Is there a reasonable prospect of raising the level of Mass Culture? In his recent book, *The Great Audience*, Gilbert Seldes argues there is. He blames the present sad state of our Mass Culture on the stupidity of the Lords of *kitsch*, who underestimate the mental age of the public; the arrogance of the intellectuals, who make the same mistake and so snobbishly refuse to work for such mass media as radio, TV and movies; and the passivity of the public itself, which doesn't insist on better Mass Cultural products. This diagnosis seems to me superficial in that it blames everything on subjective, moral factors: stupidity, perversity, failure of will. My own feeling is that, as in the case of the alleged responsibility of the German (or Russian) people for the horrors of Nazism (or Soviet Communism), it is unjust to blame social groups for this result. Human beings have been caught up in the inexorable workings of a mechanism that forces them, with a pressure only heroes can resist (and one cannot *demand* that anybody be a hero, though one can *hope* for it), into its own pattern. I see Mass Culture as a reciprocating engine, and who is to say, once it has been set in motion, whether the stroke or the counterstroke is "responsible" for its continued action?

The Lords of *kitsch* sell culture to the masses. It is a debased, trivial culture that voids both the deep realities (sex, death, failure, tragedy) and also the simple, spontaneous pleasures, since the realities would be too real and the pleasures too *lively* to induce what Mr. Seldes calls "the mood of consent," i.e., a narcotized acceptance of Mass Culture and of the commodities it sells as a substitute for the unsettling and unpredictable (hence unsalable) joy, tragedy, wit, change, originality and beauty of real life. The masses, debauched by several generations of this sort of thing, in turn come to demand trivial and comfortable cultural products. Which came first, the chicken or the egg, the mass demand or its satisfaction (and further stimulation) is a question as academic as it is unanswerable. The engine is reciprocating and shows no signs of running down.

Indeed, far from Mass Culture getting better, we will be lucky if it doesn't get worse.

When shall we see another popular humorist like Sholem Aleichem, whose books are still being translated from the Yiddish and for whose funeral in 1916 a hundred thousand inhabitants of the Bronx turned out? Or Finlay Peter Dunne, whose Mr. Dooley commented on the American scene with such wit that Henry Adams was a faithful reader and Henry James, on his famous return to his native land, wanted to meet only one American author, Dunne? Since Mass Culture is not an art form but a manufactured commodity, it tends always downward, toward cheapness—and so standardization—of production. Thus, T. W. Adorno has noted, in his brilliant essay "On Popular Music" (*Studies in Philosophy and Social Science*, New York, No. 1, 1941) that the chorus of every popular song *without* exception has the same number of bars, while Mr. Seldes remarks that Hollywood movies are cut in a uniformly rapid tempo, a shot rarely being held more than forty-five seconds, which gives them a standardized effect in contrast to the varied tempo of European film cutting. This sort of standardization means that what may have begun as something fresh and original is repeated until it becomes a nerveless routine—*vide* what happened to Fred Allen as a radio comedian. The only time Mass Culture is good is at the very beginning, before the "formula" has hardened, before the money boys and efficiency experts and audience-reaction analysts have moved in. Then for a while it may have the quality of real Folk Art. But the Folk artist today lacks the cultural roots and the intellectual toughness (both of which the Avantgarde artist has relatively more of) to resist for long the pressures of Mass Culture. His taste can easily be corrupted, his sense of his own special talent and limitations obscured, as in what happened to Disney between the gay, inventive early Mickey Mouse and Silly Symphony cartoons and the vulgar pretentiousness of *Fantasia* and heavy-handed sentimentality of *Snow White*, or to Westbrook Pegler who has regressed from an excellent sports writer, with a sure sense of form and a mastery of colloquial satire, into the rambling, course-grained, garrulous political pundit of today. Whatever virtues the Folk artist has, and they are many, staying power is not one of them. And staying power is the essential virtue of one who would hold his own against the spreading ooze of Mass Culture.

Notes

1. As I did myself in "A Theory of Popular Culture" *(Politics,* February, 1944) parts of which have been used or adapted in the present article.

2. The success of *Reader's Digest* illustrates the law. Here is a magazine that has achieved a fantastic circulation—some fifteen millions, much of which is accounted for by its foreign editions, thus showing that *kitsch* by no means appeals only to Americans—simply by reducing to even lower terms the already superficial formulae of other periodicals. By treating a theme in two pages which they treat in six, the *Digest* becomes three times as "readable" and three times as superficial.

51

Sight, Sound, and Fury

From *Commonweal* (1954)

Marshall McLuhan

"Sight, Sound, and Fury" represents a transition period in McLuhan's scholarship and in his growing interest in communications media. It displays his early and long-standing interest in poetry and the oral tradition, with other, better-known themes developed more fully in the next decade—including the ideas that the form and experience of media are as important as their content; that changes in media technology bring about broader social and cultural transformation; and that, with radio and television, the world had entered a new era. For McLuhan's biography, see page 338.

On his recent visit to America, Roy Campbell mentioned that when Dylan Thomas had discovered he could read poetry on the radio, this discovery transformed his later poetry for the better. Thomas discovered a new dimension in his language when he established a new relation with the public.

Until Gutenberg, poetic publication meant the reading or singing of one's poems to a small audience. When poetry began to exist primarily on the printed page, in the seventeenth century, there occurred that strange mixture of sight and sound later known as "metaphysical poetry" which has so much in common with modern poetry.

American colonization began when the only culture available to most men was that of the printed book. European culture was then, as now, as much an affair of music, painting, sculpture, and communication as it was of literature. So that to this day North Americans associate culture mainly with books. But, paradoxically, it is in North America that the new media of sight and sound have had the greatest popular sway. Is it precisely because we make the widest separation between culture and our new media that we are unable to see the new media as serious culture? Have four centuries of book-culture hypnotized us into such concentration on the content of books and the new media that we cannot see that the very form of any medium of communication is as important as anything that it conveys?

Ireland is perhaps the only part of the English-speaking world where the oral tradition of culture has strongly persisted in spite of the printed page. And Ireland has given us Wilde, Shaw, Yeats, Synge, and Joyce in recent years—all of them masters of the magic of the spoken word. A Ballynooley farmer who returned to Ireland from America said to his neighbor: "In three years I didn't meet a man who could sing a ballad, let alone compose one on his feet."

The printed page was itself a highly specialized (and spatialized) form of communication. In 1500 A.D. it was revolutionary. And Erasmus was perhaps the first to grasp the fact that the revolution was going to occur above all in the classroom. He devoted himself to the production of textbooks and to the setting up of grammar schools. The printed book soon liquidated two thousand years of manuscript culture. It created the solitary student. It set up the rule of private interpretation against public disputation. It established the divorce between "literature and life." It created a new and highly abstract culture because it was itself a mechanized form of culture. Today, when the textbook has yielded to the classroom project and the classroom as social workshop and discussion group, it is easier for us to notice what was going on in 1500. Today we know that the turn to the visual on one hand, that is, to photography, and to the auditory media of radio and public address systems on the other hand, has created a totally new environment for the educational process.

André Malraux has recently popularized the notion of the art revolution of our time in his *Museum without Walls*. His theme is that the picture book today can embrace a greater range of art than any museum. By bringing such a range of art within portable compass, however, it has changed even the painter's approach to painting. Again, it is not just a question of message, image, or content. The picture-book as a museum without walls has for the artist a new technical meaning, just as for the spectator, pictorial communication means a large but unconscious shift in his ways of thought and feeling.

We have long been accustomed to the notion that a person's beliefs shape and color his existence. They provide the windows which frame, and through which he views, all events. We are less accustomed to the notion that the shapes of a technological environment are also idea-windows. Every shape (gimmick or metropolis),

every situation planned and realized by man's factive intelligence, is a window which reveals or distorts reality. Today, when power technology has taken over the entire global environment to be manipulated as the material of art, nature has disappeared with nature-poetry. And the effectiveness of the classroom has diminished with the decline of the monopoly of book-culture. If Erasmus saw the classroom as the new stage for the drama of the printing press, we can see today that the new situation for young and old alike is classrooms without walls. The entire urban environment has become aggressively pedagogic. Everybody and everything has a message to declare, a line to plug.

This is the time of transition from the commercial age, when it was the production and distribution of commodities which occupied the ingenuity of men. Today we have moved from the production of packaged goods to the packaging of information. Formerly we invaded foreign markets with goods. Today we invade whole cultures with packaged information, entertainment, and ideas. In view of the instantaneous global scope of the new media of sight and sound, even the newspaper is slow. But the press ousted the book in the nineteenth century because the book arrived too late. The newspaper page was not a mere enlargement of the book page. It was, like the movie, a new collective art form.

To retrace some of this ground, it will help to recall that in the *Phaedrus*, Plato argued that the new arrival of writing would revolutionize culture for the worse. He suggested that it would substitute reminiscence for thought and mechanical learning for the true dialectic of the living quest for truth by discourse and conversation. It was as if he foresaw the library of Alexandria and the unending exegesis upon previous exegesis of the scholiasts and grammarians.

It would seem that the great virtue of writing is its power to arrest the swift process of thought for steady contemplation and analysis. Writing is the translation of the audible into the visual. In large measure it is the spatialization of thought. Yet writing on papyrus and parchment fostered a very different set of mental habits from those who associate with print and books. In the first place, silent reading was unknown until the macadamized, streamlined surfaces of the printed page arrived to permit swift traverse of the eye alone. In the second place, difficulty of access to manuscripts impelled students to memorize so far as possible everything they read. This led to encyclopedism, but also to having on tap in oral discourse one's entire erudition.

The child at school in the Middle Ages had first to make his own copies of texts from dictation. He had next to compile his own grammar and lexicon and commonplace book. The arrival of plenty of cheap, uniform, printed texts changed all this. The mechanization of writing by means of the assembly line of movable type speedily expanded the range of available reading and just as quickly reduced the habit of oral discourse as a way of learning. During the sixteenth century, however, a degree of equilibrium persisted between oral and written learning which we associate with the special excellence of Elizabethan drama, sermon, and poetry.

In the reverse direction, much of the vivid energy of American speech and writing in the twentieth century is the result of the movement away from book-culture toward oral communication. This nonliterary direction of speech has been felt to a much smaller degree in England and in Europe during the same period. Radio in particular has encouraged the return to the panel discussion and the round table. But the spontaneous move toward the seminar and class discussion as learning process has been helped by press and photography too, in so far as these have challenged the monopoly of the book.

Above all, the habits of the business community in demanding conference and discussion as the swift way of establishing insight into method and procedure in various specialized branches of business—these have prompted the new reliance on speech as a means of discovery. It is significant, for example, that the atomic physicists found that only by daily, face-to-face association could they get on with their tasks during the past war.

It has long been a truism that changes in material culture cause shifts in the patterns of the entire culture. The ancient road made possible armies and empires and destroyed the isolated city states of Greece. But the road depended in the first place on writing. Behind the imperial command of great land areas stood the written word in easily transportable form. In the nineteenth century, the newspapers, especially after the telegraph, paid for new roads and faster transport by land and sea. The press altered the forms of government, and the telegraph brought secret diplomacy to an end. When events in Egypt or

Russia, London, Paris, or New York were known everywhere at once, the time for secret negotiation was reduced to hours and minutes. And the great national populations of the world, alerted and emotionalized by the press, could confront one another immediately for a showdown.

Printing had from the first fostered nationalism because the vernaculars with their large reading publics were more profitable to commercial publishers than Latin. The press has pushed this nationalism to its ultimate point. There it remains. But photography and movies, like music and painting, are international in their power of appeal. The power of pictures to leap over national frontiers and prejudices is well-known, for good and ill.

One aspect of the press deserves special comment in this same respect. The contents of newspapers, their messages and information, have steadily promoted nationalism. But the form of the newspaper page is powerfully intercultural and international. The unformulated message of an assembly of news items from every quarter of the globe is that the world today is one city. All war is civil war. All suffering is our own. So that regardless of the political line, or the time or the place, the mere format of the press exerts a single pressure. Basic acceptance of this fact is recorded in the steady weakening of interest in political parties everywhere.

From the point of view of its format, the press as a daily cross-section of the globe is a mirror of the technological instruments of communication. It is the popular daily book, the great collective poem, the universal entertainment of our age. As such it has modified poetic techniques and in turn has already been modified by the newer media of movie, radio, and television. These represent revolutions in communication as radical as printing itself. In fact, they are "magic casements opening on the foam of perilous seas," on which few of us have yet ventured in thought, art or living. If Erasmus was the first to size up and exploit the printing press as a new force in art and education, James Joyce was the first to seize upon newspaper, radio, movie, and television to set up his "verbivocovisual" drama in *Finnegans Wake.* Pound and Eliot are, in comparison with Joyce, timid devotees of the book as art form. But most of the difficulties which the ordinary person encounters with the poetry of Pound and Eliot disappear if it is viewed as a historical newsreel of persons, myths, ideas, and events with thematic musical score built in. Joyce had a much greater trust of language and reality than Pound or Eliot. By contrast they give their language and reality the Hollywood glamor treatment. Joyce is closer to a De Sica film with its awareness of the intimate riches of the most ordinary scenes and situations.

But the reader who approaches Pound, Eliot, and Joyce alike as exploiters of the cinematic aspects of language will arrive at appreciation more quickly than the one who unconsciously tries to make sense of them by reducing their use of the new media of communication to the abstract linear forms of the book page.

The basic fact to keep in mind about the movie camera and projector is their resemblance to the process of human cognition. That is the real source of their magical, transforming power. The camera rolls up the external world on a spool. It does this by rapid still shots. The projector unwinds this spool as a kind of magic carpet which conveys the enchanted spectator anywhere in the world in an instant. The camera records and analyzes the daylight world with more than human intensity because of the forty-five degree angle of the camera eye. The projector reveals this daylight world on a dark screen where it becomes a dream world.

The wonderful resemblance in all this to human cognition extends at least this far: in cognition we have to interiorize the exterior world. We have to recreate in the medium of our senses and inner faculties the drama of existence. This is the work of the *logos poietikos*, the agent intellect. In speech we utter that drama which we have analogously recreated within us. In speech we make or *poet* the world even as we may say that the movie parrots the world. Languages themselves are thus the greatest of all works of art. They are the collective hymns to existence. For in cognition itself is the whole of the poetic process. But the artist differs from most men in his power to arrest and then reverse the stages of human apprehension. He learns how to embody the stages of cognition (Aristotle's "plot") in an exterior work which can be held up for contemplation.

Even in this respect the movie resembles the cognitive process since the daylight world which the camera rolls up on the spool is reversed and projected to become the magical dream world of the audience. But all media of communication share something of this cognitive character which only a Thomist vision of existence and cognition dare do justice to.

Television, for example, differs from the movie in the immediacy with which it picks up and renders back the visible. The TV camera is like the microphone in relation to the voice. The movie has no such immediacy of pickup and feedback. As we begin to look into the inevitably cognitive character of the various media we soon get over the jitters that come from exclusive concern with any one form of communication.

In his *Theory of the Film*, Bela Balazs notes how "the discovery of printing gradually rendered illegible the faces of men. So much could be read from paper that the method of conveying meaning by facial expression fell into desuetude. Victor Hugo wrote once that the printed book took over the part played by the cathedral in the Middle Ages and became the carrier of the spirit of the people. But the thousands of books tore the one spirit . . . into thousands of opinions . . . tore the church into a thousand books. The visible spirit was thus turned into a legible spirit and visual culture into a culture of concepts."

Before printing, a reader was one who discerned and probed riddles. After printing, it meant one who scanned, who skipped along the macadamized surfaces of print. Today at the end of that process we have come to equate reading skill with speed and distraction rather than wisdom. But print, the mechanization of writing, was succeeded in the nineteenth century by photography and then by the mechanization of human gesture in the movie. This was followed by the mechanization of speech in telephone, phonograph and radio. In the talkies, and finally with TV, came the mechanization of the totality of human expression, of voice, gesture, and human figure in action.

Each of these steps in the mechanization of human expression was comparable in its scope to the revolution brought about by the mechanization of writing itself. The changes in the ways of human association, social and political, were telescoped in time and so hidden from casual observers.

If there is a truism in the history of human communication it is that any innovation in the external means of communication brings in its train shock on shock of social change. One effect of writing was to make possible cities, roads, armies, and empires. The letters of the alphabet were indeed the dragon's teeth. The printed book not only fostered nationalism but made it possible to bring the world of the past into every study. The newspaper is a daily book which brings a slice of all the cultures of the world under our eyes every day. To this extent it reverses the tendency of the printing press to accentuate merely national culture. Pictorial journalism and reportage tend strongly in the same international direction. But is this true of radio? Radio has strengthened the oral habit of communication and extended it, via the panel and round table, to serious learning. Yet radio seems to be a form which also strengthens the national culture. Merely oral societies, for example, are the ultimate in national exclusiveness.

A group of us recently performed an experiment with a large group of students. We divided them into four sections and assigned each section to a separate communication channel. Each section got the identical lecture simultaneously, but one read it, one heard it as a regular lecture in a studio, one heard it on radio and one heard and saw it as a TV broadcast. Immediately afterwards we administered a quiz to determine apprehension and understanding of this new and difficult material. The TV section came out on top, then the radio section, then the studio, and reading sections at the bottom. This was a totally unexpected result and it is too soon to generalize; but it is quite certain that the so-called mass media are not necessarily ordained to be channels of popular entertainment only.

It is "desirable" in thinking about the new media that we should recall that buildings are mass communications and that the first mechanical medium was print from movable type. In fact, the discovery of movable type was the ancestor of all assembly lines, and it would be foolish to overlook the impact of the technological form involved in print on the psychological life of readers. To overlook this would be as unrealistic as to ignore rhythm and tempo in music. Likewise it is only common sense to recognize that the general situation created by a communicative channel and its audience is a large part of that in which and by which the individuals commune. The encoded message cannot be regarded as a mere capsule or pellet produced at one point and consumed at another. Communication is communication all along the line.

One might illustrate from sports. The best brand of football played before fifty people would lack something of the power to communicate. The large, enthusiastic crowd is necessary to represent the community at large, just as the players enact a drama which externalizes certain motivations and tensions in the communal life

which would not otherwise be visible or available for audience participation. In India huge crowds assemble to experience *darshan,* which they consider to occur when they are massed in the presence of a visible manifestation of their collective life.

The new media do something similar for us in the West. Movies, radio, and TV establish certain personalities on a new plane of existence. They exist not so much in themselves but as types of collective life felt and perceived through a mass medium. L'il Abner, Bob Hope, Donald Duck, and Marilyn Monroe become points of collective awareness and communication for an entire society. And as technology increasingly undertakes to submit the entire planet as well as the contents of consciousness to the purposes of man's factive intelligence, it behooves us to consider the whole process of magical transformation involved in the media acutely and extensively.

From this point of view it should be obvious, for example, that the framers of the Hollywood morality code were operating with a very inadequate set of perceptions and concepts about the nature of the movie medium. Modern discussions of censorship, in the same way, are helplessly tied to conceptions borrowed from book-culture alone. And the defenders of book-culture have seldom given any thought to any of the media as art forms, the book least of all. The result is that their "defense" might as well be staged on an abandoned movie lot for all the effect it has on the actual situation.

When I wrote *The Mechanical Bride* some years ago I did not realize that I was attempting a defense of book-culture against the new media. I can now see that I was trying to bring some of the critical awareness fostered by literary training to bear on the new media of sight and sound. My strategy was wrong, because my obsession with literary values blinded me to much that was actually happening for good and ill. What we have to defend today is not the values developed in any particular culture or by any one mode of communication. Modern technology presumes to attempt a total transformation of man and his environment. This calls in turn for an inspection and defense of all human values. And so far as merely human aid goes, the citadel of this defense must be located in analytical awareness of the nature of the creative process involved in human cognition. For it is in this citadel that science and technology have already established themselves in their manipulation of the new media.

52

Between Media and Mass

From *Personal Influence* (1955)

Elihu Katz and Paul F. Lazarsfeld

Elihu Katz (1926–) is the leading mass communications researcher of his generation. Raised in Brooklyn, he studied sociology at Columbia on the GI Bill after serving as a translator in Japan in the early occupational period. At Columbia, Katz was advised by Paul Lazarsfeld, took classes from Robert Merton, conducted research and wrote a master's thesis with Leo Lowenthal, and inherited an important set of data from C. Wright Mills. Katz also established what would become important, lifelong connections with the new state of Israel (formed 1948), where he has taught part of the year since 1956 (at Hebrew University of Jerusalem) and served as founding director of Israeli Television in 1968 (when the nation first acquired television). Katz has also taught at the University of Chicago (1954–1969), the University of Southern California (1978–1992), and the University of Pennsylvania's Annenberg School (1993–present). He has published key work in diffusion, audience studies, broadcasting in cross-national perspective, Israeli leisure and social life, and broadcast media events.

Personal Influence, published in 1955, is probably the most widely cited and influential book of mass communications research during the postwar era. It began as a classic "administrative" study (see Lazarsfeld, p. 166)—of women in Decatur, Illinois, in 1945, funded by a magazine that wanted to learn more about the decision-making behavior of its target audience. A number of researchers worked on it, including Mills, who left the project in a lasting dispute with Lazarsfeld (one that continued through Mills's severe attack on Lazarfeld in *The Sociological Imagination* [1959]). As a graduate student, Katz inherited the study, which he wrote up and supplemented with an extensive discussion of interpersonal and mass media research. The book solidified the idea of the "two-step flow" of communication—from mass media to opinion leaders, and from them to their friends—which carried a reassuring, democratic quality: contrary to the darker pronouncements about a mass society of isolated people susceptible to propaganda, Katz and Lazarsfeld suggest that people are actually more influenced by their friends and acquaintances than they are by media. This excerpt, from the book's first chapter, represents one of the more influential stories about the history of the field of media study. While evocative and strategically useful, this story neglects the variety of previous research represented in this reader. For Lazarsfeld's biography, see page 166.

When people first began to speculate about the effects of the mass media, they showed two opposite inclinations. Some social commentators thought the mass media would do nothing less than recreate the kind of informed public opinion which characterized the "town meeting," in the sense that citizens would once again have equal access to an intimate, almost first-hand account of those matters which required their decision. People had lost contact with the ever-growing world, went this argument, and the mass media would put it back within reach.[1]

Others saw something quite different. In their view, the mass media looked as agents of evil aiming at the total destruction of democratic society. First the newspaper, and later the radio, were feared as powerful weapons able to rubberstamp ideas upon the minds of defenseless readers and listeners. In the 1920's, it was widely held that the newspapers and their propaganda "got us into the war," while in the 1930's, many saw in the Roosevelt campaign "proof" that a "golden voice" on the radio could sway men in any direction.[2]

From one point of view, these two conceptions of the function of the mass media appear widely opposed. From another viewpoint, however, it can be shown that they are not far apart at all. That is to say, those who saw the emergence of the mass media as a new dawn for democracy and those who saw the media as instruments of evil design had very much the same picture of the *process* of mass communications in their minds. Their image, first of all, was of an atomistic mass of millions of readers, listeners and moviegoers prepared to receive the Message; and secondly, they pictured every message as a direct and powerful stimulus to action which would elicit immediate response. In short, the media of communication were looked upon as a new kind of unifying force—a simple kind of nervous system—reaching out to every eye and ear, in a society characterized by an amorphous social organization and a paucity of interpersonal relations.[3]

This was the "model"—of society and of the processes of communication—which mass media research seems to have had in mind when it first began, shortly after the introduction of radio, in the 1920's. Partly, the "model" developed from an image of the potency of the mass media which was in the popular mind. At the same time, it also found support in the thought of certain schools of social and psychological theory. Thus, classical sociology of the late 19th century European schools emphasize the breakdown of interpersonal relations in urban, industrial society and the emergence of new forms of remote, impersonal social control.[4] Later, random sampling methods, opinion and attitude testing techniques, and a discipline based on an approach to "representative" individuals lifted from the context of their associations link the beginnings of communications research to applied psychology.

Mass Media Research: The Study of "Campaigns"

These were some of the ideas with which mass media research began. And as it proceeded, it became traditional to divide the field of communications research into three major divisions. Audience research—the study of how many of what kinds of people attend to a given communications message or medium—is, historically, the earliest of the divisions, and still the most prolific. The second division is that of content analysis, comprising the study of the language, the logic and the layout of communications messages. And finally, there is what has been called effect analysis or the study of the impact of mass communications.

For some purposes, this three-way division is useful. For other purposes, however—and, notably, for the purpose at hand—it is misleading because it obscures the fact that, fundamentally, all of communications research aims at the study of effect. From the earliest theorizing on this subject to the most contemporary empirical research, there is, essentially, only one underlying problem—though it may not always be explicit—and that is, "what can the media 'do'?" Just as the "model" we have examined poses this question, so too, do the "clients" of mass media research. Consider the advertiser, or the radio executive, or the propagandist or the educator. These sponsors of research are interested, simply, in the effect of their message on the public. And if we find that they commission studies of the characteristics of their audience, or of the content of their message, clearly we have a right to assume that these aspects are connected, somehow, with effects.

Moreover, if we reflect on these patrons of research and their motivations for a moment longer, we can sharpen this notion of effect. We have been talking as if effect were a simple concept when, in fact, there are a verity of possible effects that the mass media may have upon society, and several different dimensions along which effects may be classified.[5] Now of all the different types of effects which have ever been speculated about or categorized, it is safe to say that these sponsors of research—whose goals underlie so much of mass media research—have selected, by and large, just one kind of effect for almost exclusive attention. We are suggesting that the overriding interest of mass media research is in the study of the effectiveness of mass media attempts to influence—usually, to change—opinions and attitudes in the very short run. Perhaps this is best described as an interest in the effects of mass media "campaigns"—campaigns to influence votes, to sell soap, to reduce prejudice. Noting only that there are a variety of other mass media consequences, which surely merit research attention but have not received it,[6] let us proceed with this more circumspect definition clearly in mind: Mass media research has aimed at an understanding of how, and under what conditions, mass media "campaigns" (rather specific, short-run efforts) succeed in influencing opinions and attitudes.

Intervening Variables and the Study of Effect

If it is agreed that the focus of mass media research has been the study of campaigns it can readily be demonstrated that the several subdivisions of research—audience research, content analysis, etc.—are not autonomous at all but, in fact, merely subordinate aspects of this dominant concern. What we mean can be readily illustrated. Consider, for example, audience research—the most prolific branch of mass media research. One way of looking at audience research is to see it only as an autonomous research arena, concerned with what has been called fact-gathering or book-keeping operations. We are suggesting, however, that audience research may be viewed more appropriately as an aspect of the study of effect, in the sense that counting up the audience and examining its characteristics and its likes and dislikes is a first step toward specifying what the potential effect is for a given medium or message. In other words, if we do not lose sight of the end problem which is clearly central to this field, audience research falls right into place as an intermediate step.

And so, it turns out, do each of the other major branches of mass media research. One might say that the intellectual history of mass media research may, perhaps, be seen best in terms of the successive introduction of research concerns—such as audience, content, and the like—which are basically attempts to *impute* effects by means of an analysis of some more readily accessible intermediate factors with which effects are associated.

However, these facts serve not only as a basis for the indirect measurement or imputing of effects: they also begin to specify some of the complexities of the mass communications process. That is to say, the study of intermediate steps has led to a better understanding of what goes on in a mass media campaign—or, in other words, to an understanding of the sequence of events and the variety of factors which "intervene" between the mass media stimulus and the individual's response. Thus, each new aspect introduced has contributed to the gradual pulling apart of the scheme with which research began: that of the omnipotent media, on one hand, sending forth the message, and the atomized masses, on the other, waiting to receive it—and nothing in-between.

Now let us turn to document these assertions somewhat more carefully. A brief view will be taken of each of four factors that come in between—or, as we shall say, that "intervene"—between the media and the masses to modify the anticipated effects of communications. We shall consider four such intervening variables: exposure, medium, content, and predispositions. Each of these has become one of the central foci of research attention (audience research, media comparison studies, content analysis, and the study of attitudes). Each contributes to our understanding of the complexity of mass persuasion campaigns. Treating these factors will set the stage for the introduction of another (the most recently introduced) of these intervening variables, that of interpersonal relations, with which we shall be particularly concerned.

Four Intervening Variables in the Mass Communication Process

The four variables we shall consider contribute, under some conditions, to facilitating the flow of communications between media and masses and, under other conditions, to blocking the flow of communications. It is in this sense, therefore, that we call them intervening.[7]

First, there is the variable of "exposure" (or "access," or "attention") which derives, of course, from audience research.[8] Audience research has shown that the original mass communications "model" is not adequate, for the very simple reason that people are not exposed to specific mass media stimuli as much, as easily, or as randomly as had been supposed. Exposure or non-exposure may be a product of technological factors (as is the case in many pre-industrial countries),[9] political factors (as in the case of totalitarian countries), economic factors (as in the case of not being able to afford a TV set), and especially of voluntary factors—that is, simply not tuning in. In the United States, it is, typically, this voluntary factor that is most likely to account for who is in the audience for a particular communication message. Perhaps the most important generalization in this area—at least as far as an understanding of the process of effective persuasion is concerned—is that those groups which are most hopefully regarded as the target of a communication are often least likely to be in the audience. Thus, educational programs, it has been found, are very unlikely to reach the uneducated; and goodwill programs are least likely to reach those who are prejudiced against another group; and so on.[10] It is in this sense that we consider the mere fact of exposure itself a major intervening variable in the mass communications process.

A second focus of mass media research which developed very early was the differential character of the media themselves. The research which falls into this category asks the general question: What is the difference in the effect of Message X if it is transmitted via Medium A, B or C? The appearance of Cantril and Allport's (1935) book, *The Psychology of Radio*, called attention to a whole set of these "media comparison" experiments. Here, type-of-medium is the intervening variable insofar as the findings of these studies imply that the process of persuasion is modified by the channel which delivers the message.[11]

Content—in the sense of form, presentation, language, etc.—is the third of the intervening variables on our list. And while it is true that the analysis of communications content is carried out for a variety of reasons, by and large, the predominant interest of mass media research in this area relates to the attempt to explain or predict differences in effect based on differences in content. To be more precise, most of the work in this field imputes differences in intervening psychological processes—and thus, differences in effects—from observed differences in content.[12] Content analysis informs us, for example, of the psychological techniques that are likely to be most effective (e.g., repetition, appeal to authority, band-wagon, etc.); the greater sway of "facts" and "events" as

compared with "opinions"; the cardinal rule of "don't argue"; the case for and against presenting "one side" rather than "both sides" of controversial material; the "documentary" vs. the "commentator" presentation; the damaging effect of a script at "cross-purposes" with itself; etc. Important techniques have been developed for use in this field, and the controlled experiment has also been widely adopted for the purpose of observing directly the effect of the varieties of communications presentation and content. The characteristic quality of these techniques is evident: they concentrate on the "stimulus," judging its effectiveness by referring either to more or less imputed psychological variables which are associated with effects or to the actual "responses" of those who have been exposed to controlled variations in presentation.

A fourth set of mediating factors, or intervening variables, emerges from study of the attitudes and psychological predispositions of members of the audience, insofar as these are associated with successful and unsuccessful campaigns. In this area, mass media research has established very persuasively what social psychologists have confirmed in their laboratories—that an individual's attitudes or predispositions can modify, or sometimes completely distort, the meaning of a given message. For example, a prejudiced person whose attitude toward an out-group is strongly entrenched may actively resist a message of tolerance in such a way that the message may been be perceived as a defense of prejudice or as irrelevant to the subject of prejudice entirely.[13]

Just as prior attitudes on issues must be studied, so attitudes toward the media themselves must be accounted for if we are fully to understand the role of psychological predispositions in modifying the effectiveness of communications. Here research on predispositions joins with the previous subject of media differences. Thus, many people regard the radio as more trustworthy than the newspaper, and others have the opposite opinion. In the same way, in many of the highly politicized countries abroad, there is a great intensity of feeling about the relative trustworthiness not just of the several media in general but of each newspaper and each radio station.[14] Similarly, attitudes toward the sources to which information and news are credited are likely to affect the acceptance of a mass media message. The very large number of studies which fall under the heading of "prestige suggestion" bear on this problem.[15]

So far, then, we have examined four intervening factors—exposure and predisposition from the receiving end, media differences and content differences from the transmission end—and each gives a somewhat better idea of what goes on in between the media and the masses to modify the effects of communications.[16] That is, each time a new intervening factor is found to be applicable, the complex workings of the mass persuasion process are illuminated somewhat better, revealing how many different factors have to be attuned in order for a mass communications message to be effective. Thus, the image of the process of mass communications with which researchers set out, that the media play a direct influencing role, has had to be more and more qualified each time a new intervening variable was discovered.

We propose now to turn to the newly accented variable of interpersonal relations. On the basis of several pioneering communications studies, and as we shall see later, on the basis of an exploration of the bearing of the field of small group research on the field of mass media research, it appears that communications studies have greatly underestimated the extent to which an individual's social attachments to other people, and the character of the opinions and activities which he shares with them, will influence his response to the mass media. We are suggesting, in other words, that the response of an individual to a campaign cannot be accounted for without reference to his social environment and to the character of his interpersonal relations. This is the matter which we want to consider most carefully for the reason that it promises to be a key link in the chain of intervening variables, and because it promises also to promote the convergence of two fields of social science research—the one dealing with macroscopic mass communications, the other with microscopic social relations.

Notes

1. Robert E. Park, pioneer American sociologist, and a former journalist himself, attributes his motivation to journalists in his 1925 essay on the newspaper: "The motive, conscious or unconscious, of the writers and the press in all this is to reproduce as far as possible, in the city, the conditions of life in the village. In the village

everyone knew everyone else. . . . In the village gossip and public opinion were the main sources of social control." Similarly, in his 1909 classic, *Social Organization,* C. H. Cooley writes rhapsodically on this subject. ". . . In a general way they [the changes in communication and in the whole system of society' since the beginning of the 19th century] mean the expansion of human nature, that is to say, of its power to express itself in social wholes. They make it possible for society to be organized more and more on the higher faculties of man, on intelligence and sympathy, rather than on authority, caste and routine. They mean freedom, outlook, indefinite possibility. The public consciousness, instead of being confined as regards its more active phases to local groups, extends by even steps with that give-and-take of suggestions that the new intercourse makes possible, until wide nations, and finally the world itself, may be included in one lively mental whole." See Park (1949), p. 11 and Cooley (1950), p. 148. *Note:* Citations appearing in the text and in footnotes will contain only author's name and a date of publication (e.g., Park 1949). The appended bibliography should be consulted for the full reference.

2. Berelson (1950), p. 451.

3. For a comparatively recent statement of this point of view, and for a vivid portrayal of the traditional image of the mass audience, see Wirth (1949). Wirth also deals with the two kinds of mass media impact which we have just described—the "manipulative" and the "democratic"—assuming the inherent potency of the media which underlies both. An equally clear statement is Blumer (1946).

4. In "The Study of the Primary Group," Shils (1951) discusses this main trend in 19th century European sociology which was reflected in the notion that "any persistence of traditionally regulated informal and intimate relations was . . . an archaism inherited from an older rural society or from a small town handicraft society." Discussing early American sociology, Shils indicates that there was a comparatively greater interest in the primary group as a subject for study. He points out, however, that Cooke's well-known contribution and the interest displayed by American sociologists in voluntary associations, pressure groups, etc. were counterbalanced by an emphasis on the disintegration of the primary group in urban society such as may be found in the work of W. I. Thomas, Park and his associates,

and others. Several sections of this and the following chapter will draw extensively on Shils' excellent essay.

5. Lazarsfeld (1948), for example, has distinguished sixteen different types of effects by cross-tabulating four types of mass media "stimuli" and four types of audience "response." The responses are classified along a rough time dimension—immediate response, short term effects, long term effects and institutional change. This classification makes clear, for example, that an investigation of the effect of *Uncle Tom's Cabin* on the outbreak of the Civil War calls for particular kinds of concepts and particular research tools and that this kind of effect must be distinguished from a study of the effect of print on Western civilization, on one hand, and a study of the effect of a subway car-card campaign on prejudiced attitudes, on the other. Many of the substantive statements about mass media research findings in this chapter are based on this paper and on Klapper (1950).

6. The Lazarsfeld (1948) classification cited in the footnote above indicates quite clearly that the study of "immediate" or "short term" responses to concerted mass media "campaigns" is only one of many different dimensions of effect. There are, furthermore, several effects which have been speculated about which do not fall readily within Lazarsfeld's classification. Lists of several such effects—predominantly of a long term sort—which seem accessible to, and deserving of empirical investigation—may be found, for example, in McPhee (1953) and in the appendix to Katz, E. (1953). It is important to note that some of these longer range effects which have barely been looked into promise to reveal the potency of the mass media much more than do "campaign" effects. The latter, as we shall note below, give the impression that the media are quite ineffectual as far as persuasion in social and political (i.e., non-marketing) matters is concerned. The reasons why marketing influences are so much more effective and therefore more easy to come to grips with than other mass media influence attempts are discussed by Wiebe (1951), and under the heading of "canalization" by Lazarsfeld and Merton (1949). Wiebe's paper will be discussed below, p. 29. See also Cartwright (1949).

7. Our use of this phrase should not be confused with the technical usage in the methodology of survey analysis where "intervening variable" refers to a "test" factor which is introduced

to "interpret" a correlation between two factors to which it (the "test" factor) is related. See Lazarsfeld and Kendall (1950) for a full discussion of this usage. For a discussion of the widespread usage of this term in psychology, see Tolman (1951), pp. 281–285.

8. For reviews of some of the major findings of audience research in radio, newspapers, movies and television, see Lazarsfeld and Kendall (1948), Minnesota (194), Schramm and White (1949), Handel (1950), Meyersohn (1953), Lazarsfeld (1948). It is needless perhaps to reiterate that the findings of audience research have an intrinsic value other than the one here discussed, and that the motivation to do audience research is not exclusively to impute effects. Research on, say, the likes and dislikes of an audience may be motivated by a desire to understand what an audience wants in order to pitch a "campaign" in the right way, and/or by a desire to study the characteristics of audience "tastes" for the sake of testing some hypothesis in this realm.

9. See Huth (1952) for a discussion of such factors as barriers to international technical assistance and informational programs.

10. Examples of this phenomenon are documented in Lazarsfeld (1948) and Klapper (1950).

11. In a sense, one of the later sections of this book, "The Impact of Personal Influence," (Part Two, Section Two) contributes to this tradition by comparing the relative effectiveness of personal influence with the influence of radio, newspapers and magazines. See also Lazarsfeld, Berelson and Gaudet (1948). Chaps. 14 and 16.

12. The authoritative work in this field outlining the technique of content analysis and the several uses to which it can be put is Berelson (1951); this book also contains an extensive bibliography of content studies. For a report on the most important series of *experimental* studies to date which, instead of *imputing* effects from content, attempt to measure the relationship between content variation and variation in effects *directly*, see Hovland, Lumsdaine and Sheffield (1949). Statements of some of the "principles" of Propaganda Analysis, e.g., in Lee and Lee, eds. (1939), etc. For further discussion of "principles," see Krech and Crutchfield (1948), Chapter 9.

13. This motivated missing-of-the-point is documented in Cooper and Jahoda (1947). For an illustration in the realm of public opinion on international affairs, see Hyman and Sheatsley (1952) where the ineffectiveness of providing

favorable information to people with initially un-favorable attitudes is demonstrated. For a purely theoretical treatment of this same theme, see Katz, D. (1949).

14. Attitudes toward the comparative trust-worthiness of the media were investigated as part of a study by the Social Science research Council (1947) and in communications studies in the Near and Middle East by the Bureau of Applied Social Research (1951).

15. For a review of these studies, see Asch (1952B).

16. As has been noted earlier, together with the greater precision and increasing predictive power of mass communications research where it

takes account of such factors, there has come an increasing skepticism about the potency of the mass media. As research becomes bolder, it becomes increasingly easy to show that—outside the range of marketing influences—mass media influence-attempts have fallen far short of the expectations of the communicators. This is notoriously the case with regard to persuasion attempts in the civic and political areas. It would be a mistake, however, to generalize from the role of the mass media in such direct short-run effects to the degree of media potency which would be revealed if some longer-run, more indirect effects were conceptualized and subjected to study.

53

The Theory of Mass Society: A Critique

From *Commentary* (1956)

Daniel Bell

Daniel Bell (1919–) is one of the leading American intellectuals of the postwar era. Though sometimes classified as a neoconservative, Bell is a complex and skeptical thinker who resists easy labeling (he once described himself as a "liberal in politics, a conservative in culture, and socialist in economics"). Raised in New York City by a widowed Jewish garment worker, Bell was a young socialist who studied at City College before taking a master's degree in sociology from Columbia (1939), where he often attended evening seminars given by Max Horkheimer, Theodor Adorno, and other Frankfurt Institute exiles (he later participated with Leo Lowenthal in an unpublished study of anti-Semitism in the Amercan labor movement). After writing for the socialist *New Leader* (1938–1944), teaching with Edward Shils and David Riesman at the University of Chicago (1945–1948), and serving as labor columnist for *Fortune* magazine, Bell took a full-time position in 1959 teaching sociology at Columbia (where he had taught part-time from 1952 to 1956). He stayed at Columbia until 1969, when he joined Riesman at Harvard. Bell is most widely known for two collections of essays, each of which served as a kind of marker of its era: *The End of Ideology* (1960) and *The Coming of Post-industrial Society* (1973, but taking its name from an upublished but well circulated 1963 essay). The first book, in which a slightly revised version of the following essay appears, was taken by 1960s radicals as a symbol of the smugness of their elders' generation, but that has more to do with the book's title than its nuanced criticisms of utopian ideologies, inadequate social theories, communism, and consumerist culture.

This essay originated as a paper delivered before the Congress for Cultural Freedom, a Cold War–era organization of artists, scientists, and intellectuals opposed to Stalinist repression. Bell displays his skeptical analytic sense while giving a fine brief overview of theories of mass society. Pointing out differences and internal tensions within the loose family called "mass society theory," Bell resists stereotyped cultural criticisms of 1950s America as an atomized, anonymous, standardized, and highly conforming society. He offers a qualified defense of American society and a critique of mass society theory as inadequate to the task of describing highly complex changes in the structure of modern life.

The sense of a radical dehumanization of life which has accompanied events of the past several decades has given rise to the theory of "mass society." One can say that, Marxism apart, it is probably the most influential social theory in the Western world today. While no single individual has stamped his name on it—to the extent that Marx is associated with the transformation of personal relations under capitalism into commodity values, or Freud with the role of the irrational and unconscious in behavior—the theory is central to the thinking of the principal aristocratic, Catholic, or Existentialist critics of bourgeois society today. These critics—Ortega y Gasset, Karl Mannheim, Karl Jaspers, Paul Tillich, Gabriel Marcel, Emil Lederer, and others—have been concerned, less with the general conditions of freedom, than with the freedom of the *person,* and with the possibility for some *few* persons of achieving a sense of individual self in our mechanized society.

The conception of "mass society" can be summarized as follows: The revolutions in transport and communications have brought men into closer contact with each other and bound them in new ways; the division of labor has made them more interdependent; tremors in one part of society affect all others. Despite this greater interdependence, however, individuals have grown more estranged from one another. The old primary group ties of family and local community have been shattered; ancient parochial faiths are questioned; few unifying values have taken their place. Most important, the critical standards of an educated elite no longer shape opinion or taste. As a result, mores and morals are in constant flux, relations between individuals are tangential or compartmentalized rather than organic. At the same time greater mobility, spatial and social,

intensifies concern over status. Instead of a fixed or known status symbolized by dress or title, each person assumes a multiplicity of roles and constantly has to prove himself in a succession of new situations. Because of all this, the individual loses a coherent sense of self. His anxieties increase. There ensues a search for new faiths. The stage is thus set for the charismatic leader, the secular messiah, who, by bestowing upon each person the semblance of necessary grace, and of fullness of personality, supplies a substitute for the older unifying belief that the mass society has destroyed.

In a world of lonely crowds seeking individual distinction, where values are constantly translated into economic calculabilities, where in extreme situations shame and conscience can no longer restrain the most dreadful excesses of terror, the theory of the mass society seems a forceful, realistic description of contemporary society, an accurate reflection of the *quality* and *feeling* of modern life. But when one seeks to apply the theory of mass society analytically, it becomes very slippery. Ideal types, like the shadows in Plato's cave, generally never give us more than a silhouette. So, too, with the theory of "mass society." Each of the statements making up the theory, as set forth in the second paragraph above, might be true, but they do not follow necessarily from one another. Nor can we say that all the conditions described are present at any one time or place. More than that, there is no organizing principle—other than the general concept of a "breakdown of values"—which puts the individual elements of theory together in a logical, meaningful—let alone historical—manner. And when we examine the way the "theory" is used by those who employ it, we find ourselves even more at a loss.

As commonly used in the term "mass media," "mass" implies that standardized material is transmitted to "all groups of the population uniformly." As understood generally by sociologists, a *mass* is a heterogeneous and undifferentiated audience as opposed to a *class,* or any parochial and relatively homogenous segment. Some sociologists have been tempted to go further and make "mass" a rather pejorative term. Because the mass media subject a diverse audience to a common set of cultural materials, it is argued that these experiences must necessarily lie outside the personal—and therefore meaningful—experiences to which the individual responds directly. A movie audience, for example, is a "mass" because the individuals looking at the screen are, in the words of the American sociologist Herbert Blumer, "separate, detached, and anonymous." The "mass" divorces—or "alienates"—the individual from himself.

As first introduced by the late Ortega y Gasset, however, in his *Revolt of the Masses,* the word "mass" does not designate a *group* of persons—for Ortega, workers do not constitute the "masses"—but calls attention to the *low quality* of modern civilization resulting from the loss of commanding position by an elite. Modern taste, for Ortega, represents the judgment of the unqualified. Modern culture, since it disowns the past, seeks a "free expression of its vital desires"; it becomes, therefore, an unrestrained "spoiled child," with no controlling standards, "no limit to its caprice."

Still another meaning is given to the concept by some German writers, for whom mass society is *mechanized* society. Ernst Jünger asserts that society has become an "apparatus." The machine impresses its style on man, making life calculable, mathematical, and precise; existence takes on a mask-like character: the steel helmet and the welder's face-guard symbolize the individual's disappearance into his technical function. The "regulated man" emerges as a new type, hard and ruthless, a cog in the technological process.

Less romantic, but equally critical, are those theorists who see extreme rationalization and bureaucratization—the *over-organization* of life—as the salient features of the mass society. The idea of "rationalization" goes back to Hegel and Marx, and along with it the notions of "estrangement" or "alienation," "reification," and the "fetishism of commodities"—all of which express the thought that in modern society man has become a "thing," an object manipulated by society, rather than a subject who can remake life in accordance with his own desires. In our time, George Simmel, Max Weber, and Karl Mannheim have developed and elaborated these concepts. In Mannheim's work—notably in his *Man and Society in an Age of Reconstruction*—the diverse strands are all brought together. Mannheim's argument, put schematically, runs as follows: modern large-scale organizations, oriented exclusively toward efficiency, withdraw all decisions from the shop floor and concentrate direction and planning at the top. This concentration of decision-making not only creates conformity, but stunts the initiative of subordinates and leaves them unsatisfied in their personal needs for gratification and esteem. Normally, the routinization of one's job dulls the edge of frustration and provides some security. But when unemployment looms, one's sense of helplessness becomes sharpened, and self-esteem is threatened. Since individuals cannot rationally locate the source of their frustration (i.e., the impersonal bureaucratic system itself), they will under these circumstances seek scapegoats and turn to fascism.

While for Mannheim mass society is equated with monolithic bureaucratization, for Emil Lederer and Hannah Arendt it is defined by the elimination of difference, by uniformity, aimlessness, alienation, and the failure of integration. In Lederer's view, society is made up of many social groups which, so long as society is stratified, can exercise only partial control over the others. As long as this situation obtains, irrational emotions are thus kept within some bounds. But when the lines dividing social groups break down, then the people become volatile, febrile "masses" ready to be manipulated by a leader. Similarly, for Hannah Arendt, the revolt of the masses is a revolt against the "loss of social status along with which [is] lost the whole sector of communal relationships in whose framework common sense makes sense. . . . The masses [become] obsessed by a desire to escape from reality because in their essential homelessness they can no longer bear its accidental incomprehensible aspects." Because modern life sunders all social bonds, and because the techniques of modern communication have perfected the conditions under which propaganda can sway masses, the "age of the masses" is now upon us.

What strikes one first about these varied uses of the concept of mass society is how little they

reflect or relate to the complex, richly striated social relations of the real world. Take Blumer's example of the movie audience as "separate, detached, and anonymous." Presumably a large
number of individuals, because they have been
subjected to similar experiences, now share some
common psychological reality in which the differences between individual and individual become blurred; and accordingly we get the sociological assumption that each person is now
of "equal weight," and therefore a sampling of
what such disparate individuals say they think
constitutes "*mass* opinion." But is this so? Individuals are not *tabulae rasae*. They bring varying
social conceptions to the same experience, and
go away with dissimilar responses. They may
be silent, separate, detached, and anonymous
while watching the movie, but afterward they
talk about it with friends and exchange opinions
and judgments. They are once again members
of particular social groups. Would one say that
several hundred or a thousand individuals home
alone at night, but all reading the same book, constitute a "mass?"

One could argue, of course, that reading a book
is a qualitatively different experience from going to a movie. But this leads precisely to the
first damaging ambiguity in the theory of the
mass society. Two things are mixed up in that
theory: a judgment as to the *quality* of modern
experience—with much of which any sensitive
individual would agree—and a presumed scientific statement concerning the disorganization of
society created by industrialization and by the demand of the masses for equality. It is the second of
these statements with which this essay quarrels,
not the first.

Behind the theory of social disorganization lies
a romantic notion of the past that sees society as
having once been made up of small "organic,"
close-knit communities (called *Gemeinschaften* in
the terminology of the sociologists) that were
shattered by industrialism and modern life, and
replaced by a large impersonal "atomistic" society (called *Gesellschaft*) which is unable to provide the basic gratifications and call forth the loyalties that the older communities knew.[1] These
distinctions are, however, completely riddled by
value judgments. Everyone is against atomism
and for "organic living." But if we substitute,
with good logic, the term "total" for "organic,"
and "individualistic" for "atomistic," the whole
argument looks quite different. In any case, a
great weakness in the theory is its lack of history-

mindedness. The transition to a mass society, if it
be such, was not effected suddenly, explosively,
within a single lifetime, but took generations to
mature. In its sociological determinism, the hypothesis overlooks the human capacity for adap-
tiveness and creativeness, for ingenuity in shaping new social forms. Such new forms may be
trade unions whose leaders rise from the ranks—
there are 50,000 trade union locals in this country
that form little worlds of their own—or the persistence under new conditions of ethnic groups
and solidarities.

Because romantic feeling colors critical judgment, the attacks on modern life often have an unduly strong emotional charge. The image of "facelessness," for example, is given a metaphysical
twist by Gabriel Marcel: "The individual, in order
to belong to the mass . . . has had to . . . divest himself of that substantial reality which was linked
to his initial individuality. . . . The incredibly sinister role of the press, the cinema, the radio has
consisted in passing that original reality through
a pair of flattening rollers to substitute for it a su-
perimposed pattern of ideas, an image with no
real roots in the deep being of the subject of this
experiment." Perhaps terms like "original reality" and "real roots in the deep being" have a
meaning that escapes an empiricist temper, but
without the press, the radio, etc., etc.—and they
are not monolithic—in what way, short of being
everywhere at once, can one learn of events that
take place elsewhere? Or should one go back to
the happy ignorance of earlier days?

Some of the images of life in the mass society
as presented by its critics border on caricature.
According to Ernst Jünger, traffic demands traffic regulations, and so the public becomes conditioned to automatism. Karl Jaspers has written
that in the "technical mass order" the home is
transformed "into a lair or sleeping place." Even
more puzzling is the complaint against modern medicine. "In medical practice . . . patients are
now dealt with in the mass according to the principle of rationalization, being sent to institutes
for technical treatment, the sick being classified
in groups and referred to this or that specialized
department. . . . The supposition is that, like everything else, medical treatment has become a
sort of manufactured article."

The attack on the mass society sometimes
widens into an attack on science itself. For
Ortega, "the scientific man is the prototype of the
mass-man" because science, by encouraging

specialization, has made the scientist "hermetic and self-satisfied within his limitations." Oretga draws from this the sweeping conclusion that "the most immediate result of this unbalanced specialization has been that today, when there are more 'scientists' than ever, there are much less 'cultured' men than, for example, abut 1750." But how is one to verify such a comparison between 1750 and the present. Even if we could establish comparable categories, surely Ortega would have been the first to shy away from statistical comparisons. Moreover, can we assume that, because a man specializes in his work, he is unable in his leisure, and in reflection, to appreciate culture? And what is "culture"? Would not Ortega admit that we have more knowledge of the world than in 1750—knowledge not only of nature, but of the inner life of man? Is knowledge to be divorced from culture, or is "true culture" a narrow area of classical learning in which eternal truths reside?

But more than mere contradictions in usage, ambiguities in terminology, and a lack of historical sense are involved in the theory of the mass society. It is at heart a defense of an aristocratic cultural tradition—a tradition that does carry with it an important but neglected conception of liberty—and a doubt that the large mass of mankind can ever become truly educated or acquire an appreciation of culture. Thus, the theory often becomes a conservative defense of privilege. This defense is so extreme at times as to pose a conflict between "culture" and "social justice." The argument (reminiscent of the title of Matthew Arnold's book, *Culture and Anarchy*) is made that any attempts at social betterment must harm culture. And while mainly directed against "bourgeois" society, the theory also strikes at radicalism and its egalitarian notions.

The fear of the "mass" has its roots in the dominant conservative tradition of Western political thought, which in large measure still shapes many of the political and sociological categories of social theory—i.e., in authoritarian definitions of leadership, and in the image of the "mindless masses." The picture of the "mass" as capable only of violence and excess originates with Aristotle's *Politics*. In his threefold typology, democracy is equated with the rule of *hoi polloi*—who are easily swayed by demagogues—and must degenerate into tyranny. This notion of the

masses as developed in Hellenistic times was deepened by the struggles between *plebs* and aristocracy in the Roman republic and by the efforts of the Caesars to exploit mob support; the image of the insensate mob fed by "bread and circuses" became deeply imprinted in history. Early Christian theory justified its fear of the masses with a theory about human nature. In the religious terms of Augstine—as later in the secularized version of Hobbes—the Earthly City bore an ineradicable stain of blood: property and police were the consequences of the Fall of Man; property and police were evidence, therefore, not of man's civilization, but of his corruption. In heaven there would be neither private property nor government.

It was the French Revolution that transplanted the image of the "mindless masses" into modern consciousness. The destruction of the *ancien regime* and the rallying cry of "equality sharpened the fear of conservative, and especially Catholic, critics that traditional values (meaning political, social, and religious dogma) would be destroyed.[2] For a Tocqueville and an Acton, there was an irreducible conflict between liberty and equality; liberty guaranteed each man the right to be different, whereas equality meant a "leveling" of tastes to the lowest common denominator. For a Max Scheler, as well as an Ortega, the mass society meant a "democracy of the emotions" which could only unleash irrational forces. For the Catholic de Maistre, as for the Anglican T. S. Eliot, the equality of men meant the destruction of the harmony and authority so necessary to a healthy, integrated society.

Important as these conceptions are as reminders of the meaning of excellence, and of liberty, they reflect a narrow conception of human potentialities. The question of social change has to be seen against the large political canvas. The starting point of modern politics, as Karl Mannheim has pointed out, came after the Reformation when chiliasm, or religiously inspired millennial striving to bring about heaven on earth, became an expression of the demands for social and economic betterment of the lower strata of society. Blind resentment of things as they were was thereby given principle, reason, and eschatological force, and directed to definite political goals. The equality of all souls became the equality of all individuals and the right of everyone, as enlightened by progressive revelation, to make a judgment on society. Comte, the father of modern sociology, expressed great horror at the idea of this universal right to one's own opinion. No community could exist, he wrote, unless its members had a certain degree of confidence in one another, and this, he said, was incompatible with the right of everyone to submit the very foundations of society to discussion whenever he felt like it. In calling attention to the dangers of free criticism, Comte pointed to the decline in public morals as evidenced by the increase of divorces, the effacement of traditional class distinctions, and the ensuing impudence of individual ambitions. It was part of the function of government, he thought, to prevent the diffusion of ideas and the anarchic spread of intellectual freedom.

Modern society, apparently, does not bear Comte out: though the foundations of privilege go on being challenged in the name of justice, society does not collapse. Few moralists would now uphold the bleak view once expressed by Malthus that "from the inevitable laws of human nature some human beings will be exposed to want. These are the unhappy persons who in the great lottery of life have drawn a blank." The most salient fact about modern life—capitalist and Communist—is the ideological commitment to social change. And by change is meant the striving for material economic betterment, greater opportunity for individuals to exercise their talents, and an appreciation of culture by wider masses of people. Can any society deny these aspirations?

It is curious that in these "aristocratic" critiques of modern society, refracted as they are through the glass of an idealized feudal past, democracy is identified with equality alone. The role of constitutionalism and of the rule of law which, with universal suffrage, are constituent elements of the Western democratic structure, are overlooked. The picture of modern culture as debauched by concessions to popular taste—a picture that leaves out the great rise in the general appreciation of culture—is equally overdrawn. If it is granted that mass society is compartmentalized, superficial in personal relations, anonymous, transitory, specialized, utilitarian, competitive, acquisitive, mobile, status-hungry, etc., etc., the obverse side of the coin must be shown too— the right to privacy, to free choice of friends and occupation, status on the basis of achievement rather than of ascription, a plurality of norms and standards rather than the exclusive and monopolistic social controls of a single dominant group, etc., etc. For if, as Sir Henry Maine once put it, the movement of modern society has been from status to contract, then it has been, in that light, a movement from a fixed place in the world to possible freedom.

The early theorists of the mass society (Ortega, Marcel) focussed attention on the "deterioration of excellence," while the later theorists (Mannheim, Lederer, Arendt) called attention to the way in which the over-organization and, at the same time, the disruption of the social fabric facilitated the rise of fascism. Recently, in the light of Communist successes, the argument has been advanced that the mass society, because it cannot provide for the individual's real participation in effective social groups, is particularly vulnerable to Communist penetration, and that the mass organization, because it is so unwieldy, is peculiarly susceptible to Communist penetration and manipulation. (See Philip Selznick's study, *The Organizational Weapon*.) Certainly, the Communists have scored enormous successes in infiltration, and their "front" organization may be counted one of the great political inventions of our century. But without discounting Communist techniques, the real problem here lies less with the "mass society" as such (aside from the excuse it affords disaffected intellectuals for attacks on modern culture) than in the capacity or incapacity of the given social order to satisfy the demands for social mobility and higher standards of living that arise once social change is under way. This is the key to any radical appeal.

It is not poverty *per se* that leads people to revolt; poverty most often induces fatalism and despair, and a reliance, embodied in ritual and superstitious practices, on supernatural help. *Social tensions are an expression of unfulfilled expectations.* It is only when expectations are aroused that radicalism can take hold. Radical strength is greatest (and here the appeal of Communism must be seen as a variant of the general appeal of radicalism) in societies where awareness of class differences runs deep, expectations of social advancement outstrip possibilities, and the establishments of culture fail to make room for aspiring intellectuals.

It is among industrial workers rather than apathetic peasants (in Milan rather than Calabria), among frustrated intellectuals rather than workers long unionized (e.g. India), that radicalism spreads. Resentment, as Max Scheler once noted, is among the most potent of human motives; it is certainly that in politics. It is in the advanced industrial countries, principally the United States, Britain, and Northwestern Europe, where national income *has* been rising, where mass expectations of an equitable share in that increase are relatively fulfilled, and where social mobility affects ever greater numbers, that extremist politics have least hold. It may be, as the late Joseph Schumpeter pessimistically believed, that, in newly awakened societies like Asia's, the impatient expectations of key social strata, particularly the intellectuals, may so exceed the actual possibilities of economic expansion that Communism will come to look like the only plausible solution to the majority.[3] Whether this will happen in India and Indonesia is one of the crucial political questions of the next decade. But at any rate it is not the mass society, but the inability, pure and simple, of any society to meet impatient popular expectations that makes for a strong response to radical appeals.

From the viewpoint of the mass society hypothesis, the United States ought to be exceptionally vulnerable to the politics of disaffection. In our country, urbanization, industrialization, and democratization have eroded older primary and community ties on a scale unprecedented in social history. Yet, though large-scale unemployment during the depression was more prolonged and more severe here than in any country in Western Europe, the Communist movement never gained a real foothold in the United States, nor has any fascist movement on a European model arisen. How does one explain this?

It is asserted that the United states is an "atomized" society composed of lonely, isolated individuals. One forgets the truism, expressed sometimes as a jeer, that Americans are a nation of joiners. There are in the United States today at least 200,000 voluntary organizations, associations, clubs, societies, lodges, and fraternities with an aggregate (but obviously overlapping) membership of close to eighty million men and women. In no other country in the world, probably, is there such a high degree of voluntary communal activity, expressed sometimes in absurd rituals, yet often providing real satisfactions for real needs.

"It is natural for the ordinary American," wrote Gunnar Myrdal, "when he sees something that is wrong to feel not only that there should be a law against it, but also that an organization should be formed to combat it." Some of these voluntary organizations are pressure groups—business, farm, labor, veterans, trade associations, the aged, etc., etc.—but thousands more are like the National Association for the Advancement of Colored People, the American Civil Liberties Union, the League of Women Voters, the American Jewish Committee, the Parent-Teachers Associations, local community-improvement groups, and so on, each of which affords hundreds of individuals concrete, emotionally shared activities.

Equally astonishing are the number of ethnic group organizations in this country carrying on varied cultural, social, and political activities. The number of Irish, Italian, Jewish, Polish, Czech, Finnish, Bulgarian, Bessarabian, and other national groups, their hundreds of fraternal, communal, and political groups, each playing a role in the life of America, is staggering. In December 1954, for example, when the issue of Cyprus was first placed before the United Nations, the Justice for Cyprus Committee, "an organization of American citizens," according to its statement, took a full-page advertisement in the New York *Times* to plead the right of that small island to self-determination. Among the groups listed in the Justice for Cyprus Committee were: the Order of Ahepa, the Daughters of Penelope, the Pan-Laconian Federation, the Cretan Federation, the Pan-Messian Federation, the Pan-Icarian Federation, the Pan-Epirotic Federation of America, the Pan-Thracian Association, the Pan-Elian Federation of America, the Deodecanesian League of America, the Pan-Macedonian Association of America, the Pan-Samian Association, the Federation of Sterea Ellas, the Cyprus Federation of America, the Pan-Arcadian Federation, the GAPA, and the Federation of Hellenic Organizations.

We can be sure that if, in a free world, the question of the territorial affiliation of Ruthenia were to come up before the United Nations, dozens of Hungarian, Rumanian, Ukrainian, Slovakian, and Czech "organizations of American citizens" would rush eagerly into print to plead the justice of the claims of their respective homelands to Ruthenia.

Even in urban neighborhoods, where anonymity is presumed to flourish, the extent of local ties is astounding. Within the city limits of Chicago, for example, there are eighty-two community newspapers with a total weekly circulation of almost 1,000,000; within Chicago's larger metropolitan area, there are 181. According to standard sociological theory, these local papers providing news and gossip about neighbors should slowly decline under the pressure of the national media. Yet the reverse is true. In Chicago, the number of such newspapers has increased 165 per cent since 1910; in those forty years circulation has jumped 770 per cent. As sociologist Morris Janowitz, who studied these community newspapers, observed: "If society were as impersonal, as self-centered and barren as described by some who are preoccupied with the one-way trend from '*Gemeinschaft*' to '*Gesellschaft*' seem to believe, the levels of criminalty, social disorganization and psychopathyology which social science seeks to account for would have to be viewed as very low rather than (as viewed now) alarmingly high."

It may be argued that the existence of such a large network of voluntary associations says little about the cultural level of the country concerned. It may well be, as Ortega maintains, the cultural standards throughout the world have declined (in everything—architecture, dress, design?), but nonetheless a greater proportion of the population today participates in worthwhile cultural activities. This has been almost an inevitable concomitant of the doubling—*literally*—of the American standard of living over the last fifty years. The rising levels of education have meant rising appreciation of culture. In the United States more dollars spent on concerts of classical music than on baseball. Sales of books have doubled in a decade. There are over a thousand symphony orchestras, and several hundred museums, institutes, and colleges purchasing art in the United States today. Various other indices can be cited to show the growth of a vast middlebrow society. And in coming years, with steadily increasing productivity and leisure, the United States will become even more actively a "consumer" of culture. (These changes pose important questions for the development of a "high culture," but that problem lies outside the source of this essay—see Clement Greenberg's "The Plight of Our Culture," *Commentary,* June and July 1953.)

It has been argued that the American mass society imposes an excessive conformity upon

its members. But it is hard to discern who is conforming to what. The *New Republic* cries that "hucksters are sugar-coating the culture." The *National Review,* organ of the "radical right," raises the banner of inconoclasm against the liberal domination of opinion-formation in our society. *Fortune* decries the growth of "organization man." Each of these tendencies exists, yet in historical perspective, there is probably less conformity to an over-all mode of conduct today than at any time within the last half-century in America. True, there is less bohemianism than in the twenties (though increased sexual tolerance), and less political radicalism than in the thirties (though the New Deal enacted sweeping reforms). But does the arrival at a political dead-center mean the establishment, too, of a dead norm? I do not think so. One would be hard put to it to find today the "conformity" *Main Street* exacted of Carol Kennicott thirty years ago. With rising educational levels, more individuals are able to indulge a wider variety of interest. ("Twenty years ago you couldn't sell Beethoven out of New York," reports a record salesman. "Today we sell Palestrina, Monteverdi, Gabrielli, and Renaissance and Baroque music in large quantities.")

One hears, too, the complaint that divorce, crime, and violence demonstrate a widespread social disorganization in the country. But the rising number of divorces, as Dennis Wrong pointed out (*Commentary,* April 1950), indicates not the disruption of the family, but a freer, more individualistic basis of choice, and the emergence of the "companionship" marriage. And as regards crime, I have sought to demonstrate (in *Fortune,* January 1955) that there is actually much *less* crime and violence (though more vicarious violence through movies and TV, and more "windows" onto crime, through the press) than was the case twenty-five and fifty years ago. Certainly, Chicago, San Francisco, and New York were much rougher and tougher cities in those years. But violent crime, which is usually a lower-class phenomenon, was then contained within the ecological boundaries of the slum; hence one can recall quiet, tree-lined, crime-free areas and feel that the tenor of life was more even in the past. But a cursory look at the accounts of those days—the descriptions of the gang wars, bordellos, and street-fighting in San Francisco's Barbary Coast, New York's Five Points, or

Chicago's First Ward—would show how much more violent in the past the actual life of those cities was.

At this point it becomes quite apparent that such large-scale abstractions as "the mass society," with the implicit diagnoses of social disorganization and decay that derive from them, are rather meaningless without standards of comparison. Social and cultural change is probably greater and more rapid today in the United States than in any other country, but the assumption that social disorder and *anomie* inevitably attend such change is not borne out in this case.

This may be owing to the singular fact that the United States is probably the first large society in history to have change and innovation "built into" its culture. Almost all human societies, traditionalist and habit-ridden as they have been and still are, tend to resist change. The great efforts to industrialize under-developed countries, increase worker mobility in Europe, and broaden markets—so necessary to the raising of productivity and standards of living—are again and again frustrated by ingrained resistance to change. Thus in the Soviet Union change has been introduced only by dint of wholesale coercion. In the United States—a culture with no feudal tradition; with a pragmatic ethos, as expressed by Jefferson, that regards God as a "workman"; with a boundless optimism and a restless eagerness for the new that has been bred out of the original conditions of a huge, richly endowed land—change, and the readiness to change, have become the norm. This indeed may be why those consequences of change predicted by theorists basing themselves on European precedent find small confirmation.

The mass society is the product of change— and is itself change. But the *theory* of the mass society affords us no view of the relations of the parts of the society to each other that would enable us to locate the sources of change. We may not have enough data on which to sketch an alternative theory, but I would argue that certain key factors, in their country at least, deserve to be much more closely examined than they have been.

The change from a society once geared to frugal saving and now impelled to spend dizzily; the break-up of family capitalism, with the consequent impact on corporate structure and political power; the centralization of decision-making,

politically, in the state and, economically, in a group of large corporate bodies; the rise of status and symbol groups replacing specific interest groups—indicate that new social forms are in the making, and with them still greater changes in the complexion of life under mass society. With these may well come new status anxieties—aggravated by the threats of war—changed character structures, and new moral tempers.

The moralist may have his reservations or give approval—as some see in the break-up of the family the loss of a source of essential values, while others see in the new, freer marriages a healthier form of companionship—but the singular fact is that these changes emerge in a society that is now providing one answer to the great challenge posed to Western—and now world— society over the last two hundred years: how, within the framework of freedom, to increase the living standards of the majority of people, and at the same time maintain or raise cultural levels. American society, for all its shortcomings, its speed, it commercialism, its corruption, still, I believe, shows us the most humane way.

The theory of the mass society no longer serves as a description of Western society, but as an ideology of romantic protest against contemporary society. This is a time when other areas of the glove are beginning to follow in the paths of the West, which may be all to the good as far as material things are concerned; but many of the economically underdeveloped countries, especially in Asia, have caught up the shopworn self-critical Western ideologies of the 19th century and are using them against the West, to whose "materialism" they oppose their "spirituality." What these Asian and our own intellectuals fail to realize, perhaps, is that one may be a thorough going critic of one's own society without being an enemy of its promises.

Notes

1. This antithesis, associated usually with the German sociologist Tonnies, is central in one way or another to almost every major modern social theory: Weber's traditional-rational behavior, Durkheim's mechanical-organic solidarity, Redfield's folk-urban society, and so on.

2. Nazism, in the view of modern conservative and Catholic critics, is not a reaction against, but

the inevitable end-product of, democracy. Hitler was a new version of the classical demagogue, leading the mindless masses in nihilistic revolt against the traditional culture of Europe.

3. As Morris Watnick has pointed out in a pioneering study (in the University of Chicago symposium *The Progress of Underdeveloped Areas*), the Communist parties of Asia are completely the handiwork of native intellectuals. The history of the Chinese Communist party from Li Ta-Chao and Ch'en Tu-hsu, its founders, to Mao Tse-tung and Liu Shao-Chi, its present leaders, "is virtually an unbroken record of a party controlled by intellectuals." This is equally true of India, "where in 1943, 86 of 139 [Communist] delegates were members of professional and intellectual groups." The same pattern also holds true "for the Communist parties of Indochina, Thailand, Burma, Malaya and Indonesia, all of which show a heavy preponderance of journalists, lawyers and teachers among the top leadership."

54

Mass Communication and Para-Social Interaction: Observations on Intimacy at a Distance

From *Psychiatry* (1956)

Donald Horton and R. Richard Wohl

Donald Horton (1910–) received his bachelor's degree at the University of Pennsylvania in 1935 and his doctorate in anthropology from Yale in 1943. He spent four years as a research associate at CBS (1944–1947), and his experience in the industry must have shaped his thinking about the communicative relationships formed via the mass media. He later taught sociology at the University of Chicago and led perhaps the first large-scale content analysis of television: a study of a week's worth of programming in the summer of 1951 (over three hundred hours of broadcasting).

R. Richard Wohl (1921–1957) received his bachelor's and master's degrees from New York University and his doctorate from Harvard in 1951. He taught both at Harvard and at the University of Chicago, and he had an interest in local history and business history, as illustrated in his studies of historical traditions in Kansas City and of the rags-to-riches story in American culture. From 1954 until his death, Wohl directed the Kansas City History Project, partially funded by the Rockefeller Foundation and aimed at documenting the local history of a mid-size American city—one of a long line of the University of Chicago's community studies. Within the context of that study, Wohl was beginning to do important work on the relation of oral and literate historical traditions at the time of his tragically early death (see Wohl and Brown 1960).

Horton and Wohl's study was published in the pages of *Psychiatry*, a journal founded by Harry Stack Sullivan, a friend of Edward Sapir and Harold Lasswell who was interested in the social aspects of psychiatry (and coined the term *interpersonal*). Horton and Wohl are indeed sometimes erroneously referred to as "psychiatrists" in the impressive posthumous life of this essay, which has been translated into many languages and has had a major influence in thinking about media's processes and effects worldwide. Horton and Wohl take symbolic interactionist insights in a new, edgier direction in this creative piece about the mutual simulation of interaction at a distance (see Handelman 2003).

One of the striking characteristics of the new mass media—radio, television, and the movies—is that they give the illusion of face-to-face relationship with the performer. The conditions of response to the performer are analogous to those in a primary group. The most remote and illustrious men are met *as if* they were in the circle of one's peers; the same is true of a character in a story who comes to life in these media in an especially vivid and arresting way. We propose to call this seeming face-to-face relationship between spectator and performer a *para-social relationship.*

In television, especially, the image which is presented makes available nuances of appearance and gesture to which ordinary social perception is cued. Sometimes the 'actor'—whether he is playing himself or performing in a fictional role—is seen engaged with others; but often he faces the spectator, uses the mode of direct address, talks as if he were conversing personally and privately. The audience, for its part, responds with something more than mere running observation; it is, as it were, subtly insinuated into the program's action and internal social relationships and, by dint of this kind of staging, is ambiguously transformed into a group which observes and participates in the show by turns. The more the performer seems to adjust his performance to the supposed response of the audience, the more the audience tends to make the response anticipated. This simulacrum of conversational give and take may be called *para-social interaction.*

Para-social relations may be governed by little or no sense of obligation, effort, or responsibility on the part of the spectator. He is free to withdraw at any moment. If he remains involved, these para-social relations provide a framework within which much may be added by fantasy. But these are differences of degree, not of kind, from what may be termed the ortho-social. The crucial difference in experience obviously lies in the lack of effective reciprocity, and this the audience cannot normally conceal from itself. To be sure,

the audience is free to choose among the relationships offered, but it cannot create new ones. The interaction, characteristically, is one-sided, non-dialectical, controlled by the performer, and not susceptible of mutual development. There are, of course, ways in which the spectators can make their feelings known to the performers and the technicians who design the programs, but these lie outside the para-social interaction itself. Whoever finds the experience unsatisfying has only the option to withdraw.

What we have said so far forcibly recalls the theatre as an ambiguous meeting ground on which real people play out the roles of fictional characters. For a brief interval, the fictional takes precedence over the actual, as the actor becomes identified with the fictional role in the magic of the theatre. This glamorous confusion of identities is temporary: the worlds of fact and fiction meet only for the moment. And the actor, when he takes his bows at the end of the performance, crosses back over the threshold into the matter-of-fact world.

Radio and television, however—and in what follows we shall speak primarily of television—are hospitable to both these worlds in continuous interplay. They are alternately public platforms and theatres, extending the para-social relationship now to leading people of the world of affairs, now to fictional characters, sometimes even to puppets anthropomorphically transformed into "personalities," and, finally, to theatrical stars who appear in their capacities as real celebrities. But of particular interest is the creation by these media of a new type of performer: quiz-masters, announcers, "interviewers" in a new "show-business" world—in brief, a special category of "personalities" whose existence is a function of the media themselves. These "personalities," usually, are not prominent in any of the social spheres beyond the media.[1] They exist for their audiences only in the para-social relation. Lacking an appropriate name for these performers, we shall call them *personae.*

The Role of the Persona

The persona is the typical and indigenous figure of the social scene presented by radio and television. To say that he is familiar and intimate is to use pale and feeble language for the pervasiveness and closeness with which multitudes feel his presence. The spectacular fact about such personae is that they can claim and achieve an intimacy with what are literally crowds of strangers, and this intimacy, even if it is an imitation and a shadow of what is ordinarily meant by that word, is extremely influential with, and satisfying for, the great numbers who willingly receive it and share in it. They "know" such a persona in somewhat the same way they know their chosen friends: through direct observation and interpretation of his appearance, his gestures and voice, his conversation and conduct in a variety of situations. Indeed, those who make up his audience are invited, by designed informality, to make precisely these evaluations—to consider that they are involved in a face-to-face exchange rather than in passive observation. When the television camera pans down on a performer, the illusion is strong that he is enhancing the presumed intimacy by literally coming closer. But the persona's image, while partial, contrived, and penetrated by illusion, is no fantasy or drama; his performance is an objectively perceptible action in which the viewer is implicated imaginatively, but which he does not imagine.

The persona offers, above all, a continuing relationship. His appearance is a regular and dependable event, to be counted on, planned for, and integrated into the routines of daily life. His devotees 'live with him' and share the small episodes of his public life—and to some extent even of his private life away from the show. Indeed, their continued association with him acquires a history, and the accumulation of shared past experiences gives additional meaning to the present performance. This bond is symbolized by allusions that lack meaning for the casual observer and appear occult to the outsider. In time, the devotee-the "fan"—comes to believe that he "knows" the persona more intimately and profoundly than others do; that he "understands" his character and appreciates his values and motives.[2] Such an accumulation of knowledge and intensification of loyalty, however, appears to be a kind of growth without development, for the one-sided nature of the connection precludes a progressive and mutual reformulation of its values and aims.[3]

The persona may be considered by his audience as a friend, counselor, comforter, and model; but, unlike real associates, he has the peculiar virtue of being standardized according to the "formula" for his character and performance which he and his managers have worked out and embodied in an appropriate "production format." Thus his character and pattern of action remain basically unchanged in a world of otherwise disturbing change. The persona is ordinarily predictable, and gives his adherents no unpleasant surprises. In their association with him there are no problems of understanding or empathy too great to be solved. Typically, there are no challenges to a spectator's self—to his ability to take the reciprocal part in the performance that is assigned to him—that cannot be met comfortably. This reliable sameness is only approximated, and then only in the short run, by the figures of fiction. On television, Groucho is always sharp; Godfrey is always warm-hearted.

The Bond of Intimacy

It is an unvarying characteristic of these "personality" programs that the greatest pains are taken by the persona to create an illusion of intimacy. We call it an illusion because the relationship between the persona and any member of this audience is inevitably one-sided, and reciprocity between the two can only be suggested. There are several principal strategies for achieving this illusion of intimacy.

Most characteristic is the attempt of the persona to duplicate the gestures, conversational style, and milieu of an informal face-to-face gathering. This accounts, in great measure, for the casualness with which even the formalities of program scheduling are treated. The spectator is encouraged to gain the impression that what is taking place on the program gains a momentum of its own in the very process of being enacted. Thus Steve Allen is always pointing out to his audience that "we never know what is going to happen on this show." In addition, the persona tries to maintain a flow of small talk which gives the impression that he is responding to and sustaining the contributions of an invisible interlocutor.

Dave Garroway, who has mastered this style to perfection, has described how he stumbled on the device in his early days in radio.

> Most talk on the radio in those days was formal and usually a little stiff. But I just rambled along, saying whatever came into my mind. I was introspective. I tried to pretend that I was chatting with a friend over a highball late in the evening.... Then—and later—I consciously tried to talk to the listener as an individual, to make each listener feel that he knew me and I knew him. It seemed to work pretty well then and later. I know that strangers often stop me on the street today, call me Dave and seem to feel that we are old friends who know all about each other.[4]

In addition to creating an appropriate tone and patter, the persona tries as far as possible to eradicate, or at least to blur, the line which divides him and his show, as a formal performance, from the audience both in the studio and at home. The most usual way of achieving this ambiguity is for the persona to treat his supporting cast as a group of close intimates. Thus all the members of the cast will be addressed by their first names, or by special nicknames, to emphasize intimacy. They very quickly develop, or have imputed to them, stylized character traits which, as members of the supporting cast, they will indulge in and exploit regularly in program after program. The member of the audience, therefore, not only accumulates an historical picture of "the kinds of people they really are," but tends to believe that this fellowship includes him by extension. As a matter of fact, all members of the program who are visible to the audience will be drawn into this by-play to suggest this ramification of intimacy.

Furthermore, the persona may try to step out of the particular format of his show and literally blend with the audience. Most usually, the persona leaves the stage and mingles with the studio audience in a question-and-answer exchange. In some few cases, and particularly on the Steve Allen show, this device has been carried a step further. Thus Allen has managed to blend even with the home audience by the maneuver of training a television camera on the street outside the studio and, in effect, suspending his own show and converting all the world outside into a stage. Allen, his supporting cast, and the audience, both at home and in the studio, watch toge-ther what transpires on the street—the persona and his spectators symbolically united as one big audience. In this way, Allen erases for the moment the line which separates persona and spectator.

In addition to the management of relationships between the persona and performers, and between him and his audience, the technical devices of the media themselves are exploited to create illusions of intimacy.

> For example [Dave Garroway explains in this connection], we developed the "subjective-camera" idea, which was simply making the camera be the eyes of the audience. In one scene the camera—that's you, the viewer—approached the door of a dentist's office, saw a sign that the dentist was out to lunch, sat down nervously in the waiting room. The dentist returned and beckoned to the camera, which went in and sat in the big chair. "Open wide," the dentist said, poking a huge, wicked-looking drill at the camera. There was a roar as the drill was turned on, sparks flew and the camera vibrated and the viewers got a magnified version of sitting in the dentist's chair—except that it didn't hurt.[5]

All these devices are indulged in not only to lure the attention of the audience, and to create the easy impression that there is a kind of participation open to them in the program itself, but also to highlight the chief values stressed in such "personality" shows. These are sociability, easy affability, friendship, and close contact—briefly, all the values associated with free access to and easy participation in pleasant social interaction in primary groups. Because the relationship between persona and audience is one-sided and cannot be developed mutually, very nearly the whole burden of creating a plausible imitation of intimacy is thrown on the persona and on the show of which he is the pivot. If he is successful in initiating an intimacy which his audience can believe in, then the audience may help him maintain it by fan mail and by the various other kinds of support which can be provided indirectly to buttress his actions.

The Role of the Audience

At one extreme, the "personality" program is like a drama in having a cast of characters, which includes the persona, his professional supporting cast, nonprofessional contestants and interviewees, and the studio audience. At the other extreme, the persona addresses his entire performance to the home audience with undisturbed intimacy. In the dramatic type of program, the participation of the spectator involves, we presume, the same taking of successive roles and deeper empathic involvements in the leading roles which occurs in any observed social interaction.[6] It is possible that the spectator's "collaborative expectancy"[7] may assume the more profound form of identification with one or more of the performers. But such identification can hardly be more than intermittent. The "personality" program, unlike the theatrical drama, does not demand or even permit the esthetic illusion—that loss of situational reference and self-consciousness in which the audience not only accepts the symbol as reality, but fully assimilates the symbolic role. The persona and his staff maintain the para-social relationship, continually referring to and addressing the home audience as a third party to the program; and such references remind the spectator of his own independent identity. The only illusion maintained is that of directness and immediacy of participation.

When the persona appears alone, in apparent face-to-face interaction with the home viewer, the latter is still more likely to maintain his own identity without interruption, for he is called upon to make appropriate responses which are complementary to those of the persona. This 'answering' role is, to a degree, voluntary and independent. In it, the spectator retains control over the content of his participation rather than surrendering control through identification with others, as he does when absorbed in watching a drama or movie.

This independence is relative, however, in a twofold sense: First, it is relative in the profound sense that the very act of entering into any interaction with another involves *some* adaptation to the other's perspectives, if communication is to be achieved at all. And, second, in the present case, it is relative because the role of the persona is enacted in such a way, or is of such a character, that an *appropriate* answering role is specified by implication and suggestion. The persona's performance, therefore, is open-ended, calling for a rather specific answering role to give it closure.[8]

The general outlines of the appropriate audience role are perceived intuitively from familiarity with the common cultural patterns on which the role of the persona is constructed. These roles are chiefly derived from the primary relations of friendship and the family, characterized by intimacy, sympathy, and sociability. The audience is expected to accept the situation defined by the program format as credible, and to concede as "natural" the rules and conventions governing the actions performed and the values realized. It should play the role of the loved one to the persona's lover; the admiring dependent to his father-surrogate; the earnest citizen to his fearless opponent of political evils. It is expected to benefit by his wisdom, reflect on his advice, sympathize with him in his difficulties, forgive his mistakes, buy the products that he recommends, and keep his sponsor informed of the esteem in which he is held.

Other attitudes than compliance in the assigned role are, of course, possible. One may reject, take an analytical stance, perhaps even find a cynical amusement in refusing the offered gambit and playing some other role not implied in the script, or view the proceedings with detached curiosity or hostility. But such attitudes as these are, usually, for the one-time viewer. The faithful audience is one that can accept the gambit offered; and the functions of the program for this audience are served not by the mere perception of it, but by the role-enactment that completes it.

The Coaching of Audience Attitudes

Just how the situation should be defined by the audience, what to expect of the persona, what attitudes to take toward him, what to 'do' as a participant in the program, is not left entirely to the common experience and intuitions of the audience. Numerous devices are used in a deliberate "coaching of attitudes," to use Kenneth Burke's phrase.[9] The typical program format calls for a studio audience to provide a situation of face-to-face interaction for the persona, and exemplifies to the home audience an enthusiastic and 'correct' response. The more interaction occurs, the more clearly is demonstrated the kind of man the persona is, the values to be shared in association with him, and the kind of support to give him. A similar model of appropriate response may be supplied by the professional assistants who, though technically performers, act in a subordinate and deferential reciprocal relation toward the persona. The audience is schooled in correct responses to the persona by a variety of other means as well. Other personae may be invited as guests, for example, who play up to the host in exemplary fashion; or persons drawn from the audience may be maneuvered into fulfilling this function. And, in a more direct and literal fashion, reading excerpts from fan mail may serve the purpose.

Beyond the coaching of specific attitudes toward personae, a general propaganda on their behalf flows from the performers themselves, their press agents, and the mass communication industry. Its major theme is that the performer should be loved and admired. Every attempt possible is made to strengthen the illusion of reciprocity and rapport in order to offset the inherent impersonality of the media themselves. The jargon of show business teems with special terms for the mysterious ingredients of such rapport: ideally, a performer should have "heart," should be "sincere";[10] his performance should be "real" and "warm."[11] The publicity campaigns built around successful performers continually emphasize the sympathetic image which, it is hoped, the audience is perceiving and developing.[12]

The audience, in its turn, is expected to contribute to the illusion by believing in it, and by rewarding the persona's "sincerity" with "loyalty." The audience is entreated to assume a sense of personal obligation to the performer, to help him in his struggle for "success" if he is "on the way up," or to maintain his success if he has already won it. "Success" in show business is itself a theme which is prominently exploited in this kind of propaganda. It forms the basis of many movies; it appears often in the patter of the leading comedians and in the exhortations of MC's; it dominates the so-called amateur hours and talent shows; and it is subject to frequent comment in interviews with "show people."[13]

Conditions of Acceptance of the Para-Social Role by the Audience

The acceptance by the audience of the role offered by the program involves acceptance of the explicit and implicit terms which define the situation and the action to be carried out in the program. Unless the spectator understands these terms, the role performances of the participants are meaningless to him; and unless he accepts them, he cannot 'enter into' the performances himself. But beyond this, the spectator must be able to play the part demanded of him; and this raises the question of the compatibility between his normal self—as a system of role-patterns and self-conceptions with their implicated norms and values—and the kind of self postulated by the program schema and the actions of the persona. In short, one may conjecture that the probability of rejection of the proffered role will be greater the less closely the spectator 'fits' the role prescription.

To accept the gambit without the necessary personality 'qualifications' is to invite increasing dissatisfaction and alienation—which the student of the media can overcome only by a deliberate, imaginative effort to take the postulated role. The persona himself takes the role of his projected audience in the interpretation of his own actions, often with the aid of cues provided by a studio audience. He builds his performance on a cumulative structure of assumptions about their response, and so postulates—more or less consciously—the complex of attitudes to which his own actions are adapted. A spectator who fails to make the anticipated responses will find himself further and further removed from the base-line of common understanding.[14] One would expect the 'error' to be cumulative, and eventually to be carried, perhaps, to the point at which the spectator is forced to resign in confusion, disgust, anger, or boredom. If a significant portion of the audience falls in this way, the persona's "error in role-taking"[15] has to be corrected with the aid of audience research, "program doctors," and other aids. But, obviously, the intended adjustment is to some average or typical spectator, and cannot take too much account of deviants.

The simplest example of such a failure to fulfill the role prescription would be the case of an intellectual discussion in which the audience is presumed to have certain basic knowledge and the ability to follow the development of the argument. Those who cannot meet these requirements find the discussion progressively less comprehensible. A similar progressive alienation probably occurs when children attempt to follow an adult program or movie. One observes them absorbed in the opening scenes, but gradually losing interest as the developing action leaves them behind. Another such situation might be found in the growing confusion and restiveness of some audiences watching foreign movies or "highbrow" drama. Such resistance is also manifested when some members of an audience are asked to take the opposite-sex role—the woman's perspective is rejected more commonly by men than vice versa—or when audiences refuse to accept empathically the roles of outcasts or those of racial or cultural minorities whom they consider inferior.[16]

It should be observed that merely witnessing a program is not evidence that a spectator has played the required part. Having made the initial commitment, he may "string along" with it at a low level of empathy but reject it retrospectively. The experience does not end with the program itself. On the contrary, it may be only after it has ended that it is submitted to intellectual analysis and integrated into, or rejected by, the self; this occurs especially in those discussions which the spectator may undertake with other people in which favorable or unfavorable consensual interpretations and judgments are arrived at. It is important to enter a qualification at this point. The suspension of immediate judgment is probably more complete in the viewing of the dramatic program, where there is an esthetic illusion to be accepted, than in the more self-conscious viewing of "personality" programs.

Values of the Para-Social Role
for the Audience

What para-social roles are acceptable to the spectator and what benefits their enactment has for him would seem to be related to the systems of patterned roles and social situations in which he is involved in his everyday life. The values of a para-social role may be related, for example, to the demands being made upon the spectator for achievement in certain statuses. Such demands, to pursue this instance further, may be manifested in the expectations of others, or they may be self-demands, with the concomitant emergence of more or less satisfactory self-conceptions. The enactment of a para-social role may therefore constitute an exploration and development of new role possibilities, as in the experimental phases of actual, or aspired to, social mobility.[17] It may offer a recapitulation of roles no longer played—roles which, perhaps, are no longer possible. The audience is diversified in terms of life-stages, as well as by other social and cultural characteristics; thus, what for youth may be the anticipatory enactment of roles to be assumed in the future may be, for older persons, a reliving and reevaluation of the actual or imagined past.

The enacted role may be an idealized version of an everyday performance—a 'successful' para-social approximation of an ideal pattern, not often, perhaps never, achieved in real life. Here the contribution of the persona may be to hold up a magic mirror to his followers, playing his reciprocal part more skillfully and ideally than do the partners of the real world. So Liberace, for example, outdoes the ordinary husband in gentle understanding, or Nancy Berg outdoes the ordinary wife in amorous complaisance. Thus, the spectator may be enabled to play his part suavely and completely in imagination as he is unable to do in actuality.

If we have emphasized the opportunities offered for playing a vicarious or actual role, it is because we regard this as the key operation in the spectator's activity, and the chief avenue of the program's meaning for him. This is not to overlook the fact that every social role is reciprocal to the social roles of others, and that it is as important to learn to understand, to decipher, and to anticipate their conduct as it is to manage one's own. The function of the mass media, and of the programs we have been discussing, is also the exemplification of the patterns of conduct one needs to understand and cope with in others as well as of those patterns which one must apply to one's self. Thus the spectator is instructed variously in the behaviors of the opposite sex, of people of higher and lower status, of people in particular occupations and professions. In a quantitative sense, by reason of the sheer volume of such instruction, this may be the most important aspect of the para-social experience, if only because each person's roles are relatively few, while those of the others in his social worlds are very numerous. In this culture, it is evident that to be prepared to meet all the exigencies of a changing social situation, no matter how limited it may be, could—and often does—require a great stream of plays and stories, advice columns and social how-to-do-it books. What, after all, is soap opera but an interminable exploration of the contingencies to be met with in "home life?"[18]

In addition to the possibilities we have already mentioned, the media present opportunities for the playing of roles to which the spectator has—or feels he has—a legitimate claim, but for which he finds no opportunity in his social environment. This function of the para-social then can properly be called compensatory, inasmuch as it provides the socially and psychologically isolated with a chance to enjoy the elixir of sociability. The "personality" program—in contrast to the drama—is especially designed to provide occasion for good-natured joking and teasing, praising and admiring, gossiping and telling anecdotes, in which the values of friendship and intimacy are stressed.

It is typical of the "personality" programs that ordinary people are shown being treated, for the moment, as persons of consequence. In the interviews of nonprofessional contestants, the subject may be praised for having children—whether few or many does not matter; he may be flattered on his youthful appearance; and he is likely to be honored the more—with applause from the studio audience—the longer he has been "successfully" married. There is even applause, and a consequent heightening of ceremony and importance for the person being interviewed, at mention of the town he lives in. In all this, the values realized for the subject are those of a harmonious, successful participation in one's appointed place in the social order. The subject is represented as someone secure in the affections and respect of others, and he probably senses the experience as a gratifying reassurance of social solidarity and self-confidence. For the audience, in the studio and at home, it is a model of appropriate role performance—as husband, wife, mother, as "attractive" middle age, "remarkably youthful" old age, and the like. It is, furthermore, a demonstration of the fundamental generosity and good will of all concerned, including, of course, the commercial sponsor.[19] But unlike a similar exemplification of happy sociability in a play or a novel, the television or radio program is real; that is to say, it is enveloped in the continuing reassurances and gratifications of objective responses. For instance there may be telephone calls to "outside" contestants, the receipt and acknowledgement of requests from the home audience, and so on. Almost every member of the home audience is left with the comfortable feeling that he too, if he wished, could appropriately take part in this healing ceremony.

Extreme Para-Sociability

For the great majority of the audience the para-social is complementary to normal social life. It provides a social milieu in which the everyday assumptions and understandings of primary group interaction and sociability are demonstrated and reaffirmed. The "personality" program, however, is peculiarly favorable to the formation of compensatory attachments by the socially isolated, the socially inept, the aged and invalid, the timid and rejected. The persona himself is readily available as an object of love—especially when he succeeds in cultivating the recommended quality of "heart." Nothing could be more reasonable or natural than that people who are isolated and lonely should seek sociability and love wherever they think they can find it. It is only when the para-social relationship becomes a substitute for autonomous social participation, when it proceeds in absolute defiance of objective reality, that it can be regarded as pathological.[20]

The existence of a marginal segment of the lonely in American society has been recognized by the mass media themselves, and from time to time specially designed offerings have been addressed to this minority.[21] In these programs, the maximum illusion of a personal, intimate relationship has been attempted. They represent the extreme development of the para-social, appealing to the most isolated, and illustrate, in an exaggerated way, the principles we believe to apply through the whole range of "personality" programs. The programs which fall in this extreme category promise not only escape from an unsatisfactory and drab reality, but try to prop up the sagging self-esteem of their unhappy audience by the most blatant reassurances. Evidently on the presumption that the maximum of loneliness is the lack of a sexual partner, these programs tend to be addressed to one sex or the other, and to endow the persona with an erotic suggestiveness.[22]

Such seems to have been the purpose and import of *The Lonesome Gal*, a short radio program which achieved such popularity in 1951 that it was broadcast in ninety different cities. Within a relatively short time, the program spread from Hollywood, where it had originated, across the country to New York, where it was heard each evening at 11:15.[23]

The outline of the program was simplicity itself. After a preliminary flourish of music, and an identifying announcement, the main and only character was ushered into the presence of the audience. She was exactly as represented, apparently a lonesome girl, but without a name or a history. Her entire performance consisted of an unbroken monologue unembarrassed by plot, climax, or denouement. On the continuum of para-social action, this is the very opposite of self-contained drama; it is, in fact, nothing but the reciprocal of the spectator's own para-social role. The Lonesome Gal simply spoke in a throaty, unctuous voice whose suggestive sexiness belied the seeming modesty of her words.[24]

From the first, the Lonesome Gal took a strongly intimate line, almost as if she were addressing a lover in the utter privacy of some hidden rendezvous:

> Darling, you look so tired, and a little put out about something this evening. . . . You are worried, I feel it. Lover, you need rest . . . rest and someone who understands you. Come, lie down on the couch, relax, I want to stroke your hair gently. . . . I am with you now, always with you. You are never alone, you must never forget that you mean everything to me, that I live only for you, your Lonesome Gal.

At some time in the course of each program, the Lonesome Gal specifically assured her listeners that these endearments were not being addressed to the hale and handsome, the clever and the well-poised, but to the shy, the withdrawn—the lonely men who had always dreamed, in their inmost reveries, of finding a lonesome girl to comfort them.

The world is literally full of such lonesome girls, she urged; like herself, they were all seeking love and companionship. Fate was unkind, however, and they were disappointed and left in unrequited loneliness, with no one to console them. On the radio, the voice was everybody's Lonesome Gal:

> Don't you see, darling, that I am only one of millions of lonely girls. I belong to him who spends his Sundays in museums, who strolls in Central Park looking sadly at the lovers there. But I am more fortunate than any of these lovers, because I have you. Do you know that I am always thinking about you? . . . You need someone to worry about you, who will look after your health, you need me. I share your hopes and your disappointments. I, your Lonesome Gal, your girl, to whom you so often feel drawn in the big city where so many are lonely. . . .

The Lonesome Gal was inundated with thousands of letters tendering proposals of marriage, the writers respectfully assuring her that she was indeed the woman for whom they had been vainly searching all their lives.

As a character in a radio program, the Lonesome Gal had certain advantages in the cultivation of para-social attachments over television offerings of a similar tenor. She was literally an unseen presence, and each of her listeners could, in his mind's eye, picture her as his fancy dictated. She could, by an act of the imagination, be almost any age or any size, have any background.

Not so Miss Nancy Berg, who began to appear last year in a five-minute television spot called *Count Sheep.*[25] She is seen at 1 A.M. each weekday. After an announcement card has flashed to warn the audience that she is about to appear, and a commercial has been read, the stage is entirely given over to Miss Berg. She emerges in a lavishly decorated bedroom clad in a peignoir, or negligee, minces around the room, stretches, yawns, jumps into bed, and then wriggles out again for a final romp with her French poodle. Then she crawls under the covers, cuddles up for the night, and composes herself for sleep. The camera pans down for an enormous close-up, and the microphones catch Miss Berg whispering a sleepy "Good-night." From out of the distance soft music fades in, and the last thing the viewers see is a cartoon of sheep jumping over a fence. The program is over.

There is a little more to the program than this. Each early morning, Miss Berg is provided with a special bit of dialogue or business which, brief though it is, delights her audience afresh:

> Once, she put her finger through a pizza pie, put the pie on a record player and what came out was Dean Martin singing "That's Amore." She has read, with expression, from "Romeo and Juliet," "Of Time and the River," and her fan mail. She has eaten grapes off a toy ferris-wheel and held an imaginary telephone conversation with someone who, she revealed when it was all over, had the wrong number.[26]

Sometimes she regales her viewers with a personal detail. For instance, she has explained that the dog which appears on the show is her own. Its name is "Phaedeaux," she disclosed coyly, pronounced "Fido."

It takes between twenty and twenty-six people, aside from Miss Berg herself, to put this show on the air; and all of them seem to be rather bemused by the success she is enjoying. Her manager, who professes himself happily baffled by the whole thing, tried to discover some of the reasons for this success in a recent interview when he was questioned about the purpose of the show:

> Purpose? The purpose was, Number 1, to get a sponsor; Number 2, to give people a chance to look at a beautiful girl at 1 o'clock in the morning; Number 3, to do some off-beat stuff. I think this girl's going to be a big star, and this was a way to get attention for her. We sure got it. She's a showman, being slightly on the screwball side, but there's a hell of a brain there. She just doesn't touch things—she caresses things. Sometimes, she doesn't say anything out loud, maybe she's thinking what you're thinking.[27]

The central fact in this explanation seems to be the one which touches on Miss Berg's ability to suggest to her audience that she is privy to, and might share, their inmost thoughts. This is precisely the impression that the Lonesome Gal attempted to create, more directly and more conversationally, in her monologue. Both programs were geared to fostering and maintaining the illusion of intimacy which we mentioned earlier in our discussion. The sexiness of both these programs must, we think, be read in this light. They are seductive in more than the ordinary sense. Sexual suggestiveness is used probably because it is one of the most obvious cues to a supposed intimacy—a catalytic for prompt sociability.

Such roles as Miss Berg and the Lonesome Gal portray require a strict adherence to a standardized portrayal of their "personalities." Their actual personalities, and the details of their backgrounds, are not allowed to become sharply focused and differentiated, for each specification of particular detail might alienate some part of the audience, or might interfere with rapport. Thus, Miss Berg, despite the apparent intimacy of her show—the audience is invited into her bedroom—refuses to disclose her "dimensions," although this is a piece of standard information freely available about movie beauties.

The Lonesome Gal was even more strict regarding personal details. Only once did she appear in a public performance away from her radio show. On that occasion she wore a black mask over her face, and was introduced to her "live" audience on the same mysteriously anonymous terms as she met her radio audience. Rumor, however, was not idle, and one may safely presume that these rumors ran current to provide her with a diffuse glamour of a kind which her audience

would think appropriate. It was said that she lived in Hollywood, but that she originally came from Texas, a state which, in popular folklore, enjoys a lively reputation for improbabilities and extravagances. Whispers also had it that French and Indian blood coursed in her veins, a combination all too likely to suggest wildness and passion to the stereotypes of her listeners. For the rest, nothing was known of her, and no further details were apparently ever permitted.

The Image as Artifact

The encouragement of, not to say demand for, a sense of intimacy with the persons and an appreciation of him as a "real" person is in contradiction to the fact that the image he presents is to some extent a construct—a façade—which bears little resemblance to his private character. The puritanical conventions of the contemporary media make this façade a decidedly namby-pamby one. With few exceptions, the popular figures of radio and television are, or give the appearance of being, paragons of middle-class virtue with decently modest intellectual capacities. Since some of them are really very intelligent and all of them are, like the rest of us, strong and weak, good and bad, the façade is maintained only by concealing discrepancies between the public image and the private life.

The standard technique is not to make the private life an absolute secret—for the interest of the audience cannot be ignored—but to create an acceptable façade of private life as well, a more or less contrived private image of the life behind the contrived public image. This is the work of the press agent, the publicity man, and the fan magazine. How successfully they have done their work is perhaps indicated by the current vogue of magazines devoted to the "dirt" behind the façade.[28]

Public preoccupation with the private lives of stars and personae is not self-explanatory. Sheer appreciation and understanding of their performances as actors, singers, or entertainers does not depend upon information about them as persona. And undoubtedly many members of the audience do enjoy them without knowing or caring to know about their homes, children, sports cars, or favorite food, or keeping track of the ins and outs of their marriages and divorces. It has often been said that the Hollywood stars—and their slightly less glamorous colleagues of radio and television—are modern "heroes" in whom are embodied popular cultural values, and that the interest in them is a form of hero-worship and vicarious experience through identification. Both of these interpretations may be true; we would emphasize, however, a third motive—the confirmation and enrichment of the para-social relation with them. It may be precisely because this is basically an illusion that such an effort is required to confirm it. It seems likely that those to whom para-social relationships are important must constantly strive to overcome the inherent limitations of these relationships, either by elaborating the image of the other, or by attempting to transcend the illusion by making some kind of actual contact with him.

Given the prolonged intimacy of para-social relations with the persona, accompanied by the assurance that beyond the illusion there is a real person, it is not surprising that many members of the audience become dissatisfied and attempt to establish actual contact with him. Under exactly what conditions people are motivated to write to the performer, or to go further and attempt to meet him—to draw from him a personal response—we do not know. The fan phenomenon has been studied to some extent,[29] but fan clubs and fan demonstrations are likely to be group affairs, motivated as much by the values of collective participation with others as by devotion to the persona himself. There are obvious social rewards for the trophies of contact with the famous or notorious—from autographs to handkerchiefs dipped in the dead bandit's blood—which invite toward their possessor some shadow of the attitude of awe or admiration originally directed to their source. One would suppose that contact with, and recognition by, the persona transfers some of his prestige and influence to the active fan. And most often such attempts to reach closer to the persona are limited to letters and to visits. But in the extreme case, the social rewards of mingling with the mighty are foregone for the satisfaction of some deeply private purpose. The follower is actually "in love" with the persona, and demands real reciprocity which the para-social relation cannot provide.

A case in point is provided in the "advice" column of a newspaper.[30] The writer, Miss A, has "fallen in love" with a television star, and has begun to rearrange and reorder her life to conform to her devotion to this man whom she has never actually met. It is significant, incidentally, that the man is a local performer—the probability of actually meeting him must seem greater than would be the case if he were a New York or Hollywood figure. The border between Miss A's fantasies and reality is being steadily encroached upon by the important affective investment she has made in this relationship. Her letter speaks for itself:

> It has taken me two weeks to get the nerve to write this letter. I have fallen head over heels in love with a local television star. We've never met and I've seen him only on the TV screen and in a play. This is not a 16-year-old infatuation, for I am 23, a college graduate and I know the score. For the last two months I have stopped dating because all men seem childish by comparison. Nothing interests me. I can't sleep and my modeling job bores me. Please give me some advice.

The writer of this letter would seem to be not one of the lonely ones, but rather a victim of the 'magic mirror' in which she sees a man who plays the role reciprocal to hers so 'ideally' that all the men she actually knows "seem childish by comparison." Yet this is not the image of a fictional hero; it is a 'real' man. It is interesting that the newspaper columnist, in replying, chooses to attack on this point—not ridiculing the possibility of a meeting with the star, but denying the reality of the image:

> I don't know what you learned in college, but you are flunking the course of common sense. You have fallen for a piece of celluloid as unreal as a picture on the wall. The personality you are goofy about on the TV screen is a hoked-up character, and any similarity between him and the real man is purely miraculous.

This case is revealing, however, not only because it attests to the vigor with which a para-social relationship may become endowed, but also because it demonstrates how narrow the line often is between the more ordinary forms of social interaction and those which characterize relations with the persona. In an extreme case, such as that of Miss A, her attachment to the persona has greatly invaded her everyday life—so much so that, without control, it will warp or destroy her relations with the opposite sex. But the extreme character of this response should not obscure the fact that ordinarily para-social relations do "play back," as it were, into the daily lives of many. The man who reports to his friend the wise thing that Godfrey said, who carefully plans not to make another engagement at the time his favorite is on, is responding similarly, albeit to a different and milder degree. Para-social interaction, as we have said, is analogous to and in many ways resembles social interaction in ordinary primary groups.

The new mass media are obviously distinguished by their ability to confront a member of the audience with an apparently intimate, face-to-face association with a performer. Nowhere does this feature of their technological resources seem more forcefully or more directly displayed than in the "personality" program. In these programs a new kind of performer, the persona, is featured whose main attribute seems to be his ability to cultivate and maintain this suggested intimacy. As he appears before his audience, in program after program, he carries on recurrent social transactions with his adherents; he sustains what we have called para-social interaction. These adherents, as members of his audience, play a psychologically active role which, under some conditions, but by no means invariably, passes over into the more formal, overt, and expressive activities of fan behavior.

As an implicit response to the performance of the persona, this para-social interaction is guided and to some extent controlled by him. The chief basis of this guidance and control, however, lies in the imputation to the spectator of a kind of role complementary to that of the persona himself. This imputed complementary role is social in character, and is some variant of the role or roles normally played in the spectator's primary social groups. It is defined, demonstrated, and inculcated by numerous devices of radio and television showmanship. When it has been learned, the persona is assured that the entire transaction between himself and the audience—of which his performance is only one phase—is being properly completed by the unseen audience.

Seen from this standpoint, it seems to follow that there is no such discontinuity between everyday and para-social experience as is suggested by the common practice, among observers of these media, of using the analogy of fantasy or dream in the interpretation of programs which are essentially dramatic in character. The relationship of the devotee to the persona is, we suggest, experienced as of the same order as, and related to, the network of actual social relations. This,

we believe, is even more the case when the persona becomes a common object to the members of the primary groups in which the spectator carries on his everyday life. As a matter of fact, it seems profitable to consider the interaction with the persona as a phase of the role-enactments of the spectator's daily life.

Our observations, in this paper, however, are intended to be no more than suggestions for further work. It seems to us that it would be a most rewarding approach to such phenomena if one could, from the viewpoint of an interactional social psychology, learn in detail how these para-social interactions are integrated into the matrix of usual social activity.

In this connection, it is relevant to remark that there is a tradition—now of relatively long standing—that spectators whether at sports events or television programs, are relatively passive. This assertion enjoys the status of an accredited hypothesis, but it is, after all, no more than a hypothesis. If it is taken literally and uncritically, it may divert the student's attention from what is actually transpiring in the audience. We believe that some such mode of analysis as we suggest here attunes the student of the mass media to hints *within the program itself* of cues to, and demands being made on, the audience for particular responses. From such an analytical vantage point the field of observation, so to speak, is widened and the observer is able to see more that is relevant to the exchange between performer and audience.

In essence, therefore, we would like to expand and capitalize on the truism that the persona and the "personality" programs are part of the lives of millions of people, by asking how both are assimilated, and by trying to discover what effects these responses have on the attitudes and actions of the audiences who are so devoted to and absorbed in this side of American culture.

Notes

1. They may move out into positions of leadership in the world at large as they become famous and influential. Frank Sinatra, for example, has become known as a "youth leader." Conversely, figures from the political world, to choose another example, may become media "personalities" when they appear regularly. Fiorello LaGuardia, the late mayor of New York, is one such case.

2. Merton's discussion of the attitude toward Kate Smith of her adherents exemplifies, with much circumstantial detail, what we have said above. See Robert K. Merton, Marjorie Fiske, and Alberta Curtis, *Mass Persuasion; The Social Psychology of a War Bond Drive;* New York, Harper, 1946; especially Chapter 6.

3. There does remain the possibility that over the course of his professional life the persona, responding to influences from his audience, may develop new conceptions of himself and his role.

4. Dave Garroway as told to Joe Alex Morris, "I Lead a Goofy Life," *The Saturdy Evening Post,* February 11, 1956; p. 62.

5. Reference footnote 4; p. 64.

6. See, for instance: George H. Mead, *Mind, Self and Society;* Chicago, Univ. of Chicago Press, 1934. Walter Coutu, *Emergent Human Nature;* New York, Knopf, 1949. Rosalind Dymond, "Personality and Empathy," *J. Consulting Psychol.* (1950) 14:343–350.

7. Burke uses this expression to describe an attitude evoked by formal rhetorical devices, but it seems equally appropriate here. See Kenneth Burke, *A Rhetoric of Motives;* New York, Prentice-Hall, 1950; p. 58.

8. This is in contrast to the closed system of the drama, in which all the roles are predetermined in their mutual relations.

9. Kenneth Burke, *Attitudes Toward History, Vol. 1;* New York, New Republic Publishing Co., 1937; see, for instance, p. 104.

10. See Merton's acute analysis of the audience's demand for "sincerity" as a reassurance against manipulation. Reference footnote 2; pp. 142–146.

11. These attributes have been strikingly discussed by Mervyn LeRoy, a Hollywood director, in a recent book. Although he refers specifically to the motion-picture star, similar notions are common in other branches of show business. "What draws you to certain people?" he asks. "I have said before that you can't be a really fine actress or actor without heart. You also have to possess the ability to project that heart, that feeling and emotion. The sympathy in your eyes will show. The audience has to feel sorry for the person on the screen. If there aren't moments when, rightly or wrongly, he moves the audience to sympathy, there's an actor who will never be big box-office." Mervyn LeRoy and Alyce Canfield, *It takes More Than Talent;* New York, Knopf, 1953; p. 114.

12. Once an actor has succeeded in establishing a good relationship with his audience in a particular kind of dramatic role, he may be "typed" in that role. Stereotyping in the motion-picture industry is often rooted in the belief that sustained rapport with the audience can be achieved by repeating past success. (This principle is usually criticized as detrimental to the talent of the actor, but it is a *sine qua non* for the persona whose professional success depends upon creating and sustaining a plausible and unchanging identity.) Sometimes, indeed, the Hollywood performer will actually take his name from a successful role; this is one of the principles on which Warner Brothers Studios selects the names of some of its actors. For instance, Donna Lee Hickey was renamed Mae Wynn after a character she portrayed, with great distinction, in *The Caine Mutiny.* See "Names of Hollywood Actors," *Names* (1955) 3:116.

13. The "loyalty" which is demanded of the audience is not necessarily passive or confined only to patronizing the person's performance. Its active demonstration is called for in charity appeals, "marathons," and "telethons"; and, of course, it is expected to be freely transferable to the products advertised by the performer. Its most active form is represented by the organization of fan clubs with programs of activities and membership obligations, which give a continuing testimony of loyalty.

14. Comedians on radio and television frequently chide their audience if they do not laugh at the appropriate places, or if their response is held to be inadequate. The comedian tells the audience that if they don't respond promptly, he won't wait, whereupon the audience usually provides the demanded laugh. Sometimes the chiding is more oblique, as when the comedian interrupts his performance to announce that he will fire the writer of the unsuccessful joke. Again, the admonition to respond correctly is itself treated as a joke and is followed by a laugh.

15. Coutu, reference footnote 6: p. 294.

16. See, for example, W. Lloyd Warner and William E. Henry, "The Radio Day Time Serial: A Symbolic Analysis," *Genetic Psychol. Monongraphs* (1948) 37: 3–71, the study of a daytime radio serial program in which it is shown that upper-middle-class women tend to reject identification with lower-middle-class women represented in the drama. Yet some people are willing to take unfamiliar roles. This appears to be especially characteristic of the intellectual whose

distinction is not so much that he has cosmopolitan tastes and knowledge, but that he has the capacity to transcend the limits of his own culture in his identifications. Remarkably little is known about how this ability is developed.

17. Most students of the mass media occupy a cultural level somewhat above that of the most popular programs and personalities of the media, and necessarily look down upon them. But it should not be forgotten that for many millions indulgence in these media is a matter of looking up. Is it not also possible that some of the media permit a welcome regression, for some, from the higher cultural standards of their present status? This may be one explanation of the vogue of detective stories and science fiction among intellectuals, and might also explain the escape downward from middle-class standards in the literature of "low life" generally.

18. It is frequently charged that the media's description of this side of life is partial, shallow, and often false. It would be easier and more profitable to evaluate these criticisms if they were formulated in terms of role-theory. From the viewpoint of any given role it would be interesting to know how well the media take account of the values and expectations of the role-reciprocators. What range of legitimate variations in role performance is acknowledged? How much attention is given to the problems arising from changing roles, and how creatively are these problems handled? These are only a few of the many similar questions which at once come to mind.

19. There is a close analogy here with one type of newspaper human-interest story which records extreme instances of role-achievement and their rewards. Such stories detail cases of extreme longevity, marriages of especially long duration, large numbers of children; deeds of heroism—role performance under "impossible" conditions; extraordinary luck, prizes, and so on.

20. Dave Garroway, after making the point that he has many "devout" admirers, goes on to say that "some of them ... were a bit too devout." He tells the story of one lady "from a Western state" who "arrived in Chicago [where he was then broadcasting], registered at a big hotel as Mrs. Dave Garroway, opened several charge accounts in my name and established a joint bank account in which she deposited a large sum of money. Some months later she took a taxi to my hotel and informed the desk clerk she was moving in. He called a detective agency that we had engaged to check up on her, and they persuaded her to return home. Since then there have been others, but none so persistent." Reference footnote 4: p. 62.

21. This group presumably includes those for whom "Lonely Hearts" and "Pen Pal" clubs operate.

22. While the examples which follow are of female personae addressing themselves to male audiences, it should be noted that for a time there was also a program on television featuring *The Continental,* who acted the part of a debonair foreigner and whose performance consisted of murmuring endearing remarks to an invisible female audience. He wore evening clothes and cut a figure in full conformity with the American stereotype of a suave European lover.

23. This program apparently evoked no very great amount of comment or criticism in the American press, and we are indebted to an article in a German illustrated weekly for details about the show, and for the verbatim quotations from the Lonesome Gal's monologue which we have retranslated into English. See "Ich bin bei dir, Liebling ... ," *Weltbild* (Munich), March 1, 1952; p. 12.

24. This is in piquant contrast to the popular singers, the modesty of whose voice and mein is often belied by the sexiness of the words in the songs they sing.

25. The details relating to this show are based on Gilbert Millstein, "Tired of it All?" *The New York Times Magazine,* September 18, 1955; p. 44. See also "Beddy-Bye," *Time,* August 15, 1955; p. 45

26. *The New York Times Magazine,* reference footnote 25.

27. *The New York Times Magazine,* reference footnote 25.

28. Such magazines as *Uncensored* and *Confidential* (which bears the subtitle, "Tells the Facts and Names the Names") enjoy enormous circulations, and may be thought of as the very opposite of the fan magazine. They claim to "expose" the person behind the persona.

29. M. F. Thorp, *America at the Movies;* New Haven, Yale Univ. Press, 1939. S. Stansfeld Sargent, *Social Psychology;* New York, Ronald Press, 1950. K.P. Berliant, "The Nature and Emergence of Fan Behavior: (unpublished M.A. Thesis, Univ. of Chicago).

30. Ann Landers, "Your Problems," *Chicago Sun-Times,* October 25, 1955; p. 36.

55

The Mass Society

From *The Power Elite* (1956)

C. Wright Mills

C. Wright Mills (1916–1962) was one of the great voices of twentieth century life. A Texan who took his doctorate in sociology from the University of Wisconsin, Mills was a cultural outsider at Columbia, where he taught from 1944 until his death. Mills took a quick liking to Paul Lazarsfeld, whose knowledge of methodology initially impressed the more qualitatively trained Texan, but the two had a bitter falling out while Mills was working on the Decatur study, later published by Katz and Lazarsfeld as *Personal Influence* (p. 358). Mills cut a different swath than Lazarsfeld and Merton, rejecting their politically disengaged social science and writing for a broader readership in confident and eloquent tones. In *New Men of Power* (1948), *White Collar* (1951), and *The Power Elite* (1956), Mills successively considered the state of labor, mid-level professionals, and elites in a bureaucratized mass society. In *The Sociological Imagination* (1959), he lampoons (somewhat unfairly) Lazarsfeldian "abstracted empiricism" and Parsonian "grand theory," and he offers an inspiring vision of political engagement and intellectual craftsmanship in an age where freedom was threatened by bureaucratic rationality.

"The Mass Society," one chapter from Mills's *Power Elite,* is a one-man update of Walter Lippmann and John Dewey's 1920s arguments about the modern democratic public. In a book that influenced Jurgen Habermas's *Structural Transformation of the Public Sphere* (1962), Mills argues that publics have been replaced by masses marked by "a sort of psychological illiteracy that is facilitated by the media." He draws on Deweyan concepts of social experience and education, Columbia mass communications research, Weberian sociology, and classic political theory to offer a trenchant critique of media-dominated, postwar American society.

In the standard image of power and decision, no force is held to be as important as The Great American Public. More than merely another check and balance, this public is thought to be the seat of all legitimate power. In official life as in popular folklore, it is held to be the very balance wheel of democratic power. In the end, all liberal theorists rest their notions of the power system upon the political role of this public; all official decisions, as well as private decisions of consequence, are justified as in the public's welfare; all formal proclamations are in its name.

1

Let us therefore consider the classic public of democratic theory in the generous spirit in which Rousseau once cried, 'Opinion, Queen of the World, is not subject to the power of kings; they are themselves its first slaves.'

The most important feature of the public of opinion, which the rise of the democratic middle class initiates, is the free ebb and flow of discussion. The possibilities of answering back, of organizing autonomous organs of public opinion, of realizing opinion in action, are held to be established by democratic institutions. The opinion that results from public discussion is understood to be a resolution that is then carried out by public action; it is, in one version, the 'general will' of the people, which the legislative organ enacts into law, thus lending to it legal force. Congress, or Parliament, as an institution, crowns all the scattered publics; it is the archetype for each of the little circles of face-to-face citizens discussing their public business.

This eighteenth-century idea of the public of public opinion parallels the economic idea of the market of the free economy. Here is the market composed of freely competing entrepreneurs; there is the public composed of discussion circles of opinion peers. As price is the result of anonymous, equally weighted, bargaining individuals, so public opinion is the result of each man's having thought things out for himself and contributing his voice to the great chorus. To be sure, some might have more influence on the state of opinion than others, but no one group monopolizes the discussion, or by itself determines the opinions that prevail.

Innumerable discussion circles are knit together by mobile people who carry opinions from one to another, and struggle for the power of larger command. The public is thus organized into associations and parties, each representing a set of viewpoints, each trying to acquire a place in the Congress, where the discussion continues. Out of the little circles of people talking with one another, the larger forces of social movements and political parties develop; and the discussion of opinion is the important phase in a total act by which public affairs are conducted.

The autonomy of these discussions is an important element in the idea of public opinion as a democratic legitimation. The opinions formed are actively realized within the prevailing institutions of power; all authoritative agents are made or broken by the prevailing opinions of these publics. And, in so far as the public is frustrated in realizing its demands, its members may go beyond criticism of specific policies; they may question the very legitimations of legal authority. That is one meaning of Jefferson's comment on the need for an occasional 'revolution.'

The public, so conceived, is the loom of classic, eighteenth-century democracy; discussion is at once the threads and the shuttle, tying the discussion circles together. It lies at the root of the conception of authority by discussion, and it is based upon the hope that truth and justice will somehow come out of society as a great apparatus of free discussion. The people are presented with problems. They discuss them. They decide on them. They formulate viewpoints. These viewpoints are organized, and they compete. One viewpoint 'wins out.' Then the people act out this view, or their representatives are instructed to act it out, and this they promptly do.

Such are the images of the public of classic democracy which are still used as the working justifications of power in American society. But now we must recognize this description as a set of images out of a fairy tale: they are not adequate even as an approximate model of how the American system of power works. The issues that now shape man's fate are neither raised nor decided by the public at large. The idea of the community of publics is not a description of fact, but an assertion of an ideal, an assertion of a legitimation masquerading—as legitimations are now apt to do—as fact. For now the public of public opinion is recognized by all those who have considered it carefully as something less than it once was.

These doubts are asserted positively in the statement that the classic community of publics is being transformed into a society of masses. This transformation, in fact, is one of the keys to the social and psychological meaning of modern life in America.

I. In the democratic society of publics it was assumed, with John Locke, that the individual conscience was the ultimate seat of judgment and hence the final court of appeal. But this principle was challenged—as E. H. Carr has put it—when Rousseau 'for the first time thought in terms of the sovereignty of the whole people, and faced the issue of mass democracy.'[1]

II. In the democratic society of publics it was assumed that among the individuals who composed it there was a natural and peaceful harmony of interests. But this essentially conservative doctrine gave way to the Utilitarian doctrine that such a harmony of interests had first to be created by reform before it could work, and later to the Marxian doctrine of class struggle, which surely was then, and certainly is now, closer to reality than any assumed harmony of interests.

III. In the democratic society of publics it was assumed that before public action would be taken, there would be rational discussion between individuals which would determine the action and that, accordingly, the public opinion that resulted would be the infallible voice of reason. But this has been challenged not only (1) by the assumed need for experts to decide delicate and intricate issues, but (2) by the discovery—as by Freud—of the irrationality of the man in the street, and (3) by the discovery—as by Marx—of the socially conditioned nature of what was once assumed to be autonomous reason.

IV. In the democratic society of publics it was assumed that after determining what is true and right and just, the public would act accordingly or see that its representatives did so. In the long run, public opinion will not only be right, but public opinion will prevail. This assumption has been upset by the great gap now existing between the underlying population and those who make decisions in its name, decisions of enormous consequence which the public often does not even know are being made until well after the fact.

Given these assumptions, it is not difficult to understand the articulate optimism of many nineteenth-century thinkers, for the theory of the public is, in many ways, a projection upon the community at large of the intellectual's ideal of the supremacy of intellect. The 'evolution of the intellect,' Comte asserted, 'determines the main course of social evolution.' If looking about them, nineteenth-century thinkers still saw irrationality and ignorance and apathy, all that was merely an intellectual lag, to which the spread of education would soon put an end.

How much the cogency of the classic view of the public rested upon a restriction of this public to the carefully educated is revealed by the fact that by 1859 even John Stuart Mill was writing of 'the tyranny of the majority,' and both Tocqueville and Burckhardt anticipated the view popularized in the recent past by such political moralists as Ortega y Gasset. In a word, the transformation of public into mass—and all that this implies—has been at once one of the major trends of modern societies and one of the major factors in the collapse of that liberal optimism which determined so much of the intellectual mood of the nineteenth century.

By the middle of that century: individualism had begun to be replaced by collective forms of economic and political life; harmony of interests by inharmonious struggle of classes and organized pressures; rational discussions undermined by expert decisions on complicated issues, by recognition of the interested bias of argument by vested position; and by the discovery of the effectiveness of irrational appeal to the citizen. Moreover, certain structural changes of modern society, which we shall presently consider, had begun to cut off the public from the power of active decisions.

2

The transformation of public into mass is of particular concern to us, for it provides an important clue to the meaning of the power elite. If that elite is truly responsible to, or even exists in connection with, a community of publics, it carries a very different meaning than if such a public is being transformed into a society of masses.

The United States today is not altogether a mass society, and it has never been altogether a community of publics. These phrases are names for extreme types; they point to certain features of reality, but they are themselves constructions; social reality is always some sort of mixture of the two. Yet we cannot readily understand just how much of which is mixed into our situation if we do not first understand, in terms of explicit dimensions, the clear-cut and extreme types:

At least four dimensions must be attended to if we are to grasp the differences between public and mass.

I. There is first, the ratio of the givers of opinion to the receivers, which is the simplest way to state the social meaning of the formal media of mass communication. More than anything else, it is the shift in this ratio which is central to the problems of the public and of public opinion in latter-day phases of democracy. At one extreme on the scale of communication, two people talk personally with each other; at the opposite extreme, one spokesman talks impersonally through a network of communications to millions of listeners and viewers. In between these extremes there are assemblages and political rallies, parliamentary sessions, law-court debates, small discussion circles dominated by one man, open discussion circles with talk moving freely back and forth among fifty people, and so on.

II. The second dimension to which we must pay attention is the possibility of answering back an opinion without internal or external reprisals being taken. Technical conditions of the means of communication, in imposing a lower ratio of speakers to listeners, may obviate the possibility of freely answering back. Informal rules, resting upon conventional sanction and upon the informal structure of opinion leadership, may govern who can speak, when, and for how long. Such rules may or may not be in congruence with formal rules and with institutional sanctions which govern the process of communication. In the extreme case, we may conceive of an absolute monopoly of communication to pacified media groups whose members cannot answer back even 'in private.' At the opposite extreme, the conditions may allow and the rules may uphold the wide and symmetrical formation of opinion.

III. We must also consider the relation of the formation of opinion to its realization in social action, the ease with which opinion is effective in the shaping of decisions of powerful consequence. This opportunity for people to act out their opinions collectively is of course limited by their position in the structure of power. This structure may be such as to limit decisively this capacity, or it may allow or even invite such action. It may confine social action to local areas or it may enlarge the area of opportunity; it may make action intermittent or more or less continuous.

IV. There is, finally, the degree to which institutional authority, with its sanctions and controls, penetrates the public. Here the problem is the degree to which the public has genuine autonomy from instituted authority. At one extreme, no agent of formal authority moves among the autonomous public. At the opposite extreme, the public is terrorized into uniformity by the infiltration of informers and the universalization of suspicion. One thinks of the late Nazi street-and-block-system, the eighteenth-century Japanese kumi, the Soviet cell structure. In the extreme, the formal structure of power coincides, as it were, with the informal ebb and flow of influence by discussion, which is thus killed off.

By combining these several points, we can construct little models or diagrams of several types of societies. Since 'the problem of public opinion' as we know it is set by the eclipse of the classic bourgeois public, we are here concerned with only two types: public and mass.

In a *public,* as we may understand the term, (1) virtually as many people express opinions as

receive them. (2) Public communications are so organized that there is a chance immediately and effectively to answer back any opinion expressed in public. Opinion formed by such discussion (3) readily finds an outlet in effective action, even against—if necessary—the prevailing system of authority. And (4) authoritative institutions do not penetrate the public, which is thus more or less autonomous in its operations. When these conditions prevail, we have the working model of a community of publics, and this model fits closely the several assumptions of classic democratic theory.

At the opposite extreme, in a *mass,* (1) far fewer people express opinions than receive them; for the community of publics becomes an abstract collection of individuals who receive impressions from the mass media. (2) The communications that prevail are so organized that it is difficult or impossible for the individual to answer back immediately or with any effect. (3) The realization of opinion in action is controlled by authorities who organize and control the channels of such action. (4) The mass has no autonomy from institutions; on the contrary, agents of authorized institutions penetrate this mass, reducing any autonomy it may have in the formation of opinion by discussion.

The public and the mass may be most readily distinguished by their dominant modes of communication: in a community of publics, discussion is the ascendant means of communication, and the mass media, if they exist, simply enlarge and animate discussion, linking one *primary public* with the discussions of another. In a mass society, the dominant type of communication is the formal media, and the publics become mere *media markets:* all those exposed to the contents of given mass media.

3

From almost any angle of vision that we might assume, when we look upon the public, we realize that we have moved a considerable distance along the road to the mass society. At the end of that road there is totalitarianism, as in Nazi Germany or in Communist Russia. We are not yet at that end. In the United Status today, media markets are not entirely ascendant over primary publics. But surely we can see that many aspects of the public life of our times are more the features of a mass society than of a community of publics.

What is happening might again be stated in terms of the historical parallel between the economic market and the public of public opinion. In brief, there is a movement from widely scattered little powers to concentrated powers and the attempt at monopoly control from powerful centers, which, being partially hidden, are centers of manipulation as well as of authority. The small shop serving the neighborhood is replaced by the anonymity of the national corporation: mass advertisement replaces the personal influence of opinion between merchant and customer. The political leader hooks up his speech to a national network and speaks, with appropriate personal touches, to a million people he never saw and never will see. Entire brackets of professions and industries are in the 'opinion business,' impersonally manipulating the public for hire.

In the primary public the competition of opinions goes on between people holding views in the service of their interests and their reasoning. But in the mass society of media markets, competition, if any, goes on between the manipulators with their mass media on the one hand, and the people receiving their propaganda on the other.

Under such conditions, it is not surprising that there should arise a conception of public opinion as a mere reaction—we cannot say 'response'—to the content of the mass media. In this view, the public is merely the collectivity of individuals each rather passively exposed to the mass media and rather helplessly opened up to the suggestions and manipulations that flow from these media. The fact of manipulation from centralized points of control constitutes, as it were, an expropriation of the old multitude of little opinion producers and consumers operating in a free and balanced market.

In official circles, the very term itself, 'the public'—as Walter Lippmann noted thirty years ago—has come to have a phantom meaning, which dramatically reveals its eclipse. From the standpoint of the deciding elite, some of those who clamor publicly can be identified as 'Labor,' others as 'Business,' still others as 'Farmer.' Those who can *not* readily be so identified make up 'The Public.' In this usage, the public is composed of the unidentified and the non-partisan in a world of defined and partisan interests. It is socially composed of well-educated salaried professionals, especially college professors; of non-unionized employees, especially

white-collar people, along with self-employed professionals and small businessmen.

In this faint echo of the classic notion, the public consists of those remnants of the middle classes, old and new, whose interests are not explicitly defined, organized, or clamorous. In a curious adaptation, 'the public' often becomes, in fact, 'the unattached expert,' who, although well informed, has never taken a clear-cut, public stand on controversial issues which are brought to a focus by organized interests. These are the 'public' members of the board, the commission, the committee. What the public stands for, accordingly, is often a vagueness of policy (called open-mindedness), a lack of involvement in public affairs (known as reasonableness), and a professional disinterest (known as tolerance).

Some such official members of the public, as in the field of labor-management mediation, start out very young and make a career out of being careful to be informed but never taking a strong position; and there are many others, quite unofficial, who take such professionals as a sort of model. The only trouble is that they are acting as if they were disinterested judges but they do not have the power of judges; hence their reasonableness, their tolerance, and their open-mindedness do not often count for much in the shaping of human affairs.

4

All those trends that make for the decline of the politician and of his balancing society bear decisively upon the transformation of public into mass.[2] One of the most important of the structural transformations involved is the decline of the voluntary association as a genuine instrument of the public. As we have already seen, the executive ascendancy in economic, military, and political institutions has lowered the effective use of all those voluntary associations which operate between the state and the economy on the one hand, and the family and the individual in the primary group on the other. It is not only that institutions of power have become large-scale and inaccessibly centralized; they have at the same time become less political and more administrative, and it is within this great change of framework that the organized public has waned.

In terms of *scale*, the transformation of public into mass has been underpinned by the shift from a political public decisively restricted in size (by property and education, as well as by sex and age) to a greatly enlarged mass having only the qualifications of citizenship and age.

In terms of *organization*, the transformation has been underpinned by the shift from the individual and his primary community to the voluntary association and the mass party as the major units of organized power.

Voluntary associations have become larger to the extent that they have become effective; and to just that extent they have become inaccessible to the individual who would shape by discussion the policies of the organization to which he belongs. Accordingly, along with older institutions, these voluntary associations have lost their grip on the individual. As more people are drawn into the political arena, these associations become mass in scale; and as the power of the individual becomes more dependent upon such mass associations, they are less accessible to the individual's influence.[3]

Mass democracy means the struggle of powerful and large-scale interest groups and associations, which stand between the big decisions that are made by state, corporation, army, and the will of the individual citizen as a member of the public. Since these middle-level associations are the citizen's major link with decision, his relation to them is of decisive importance. For it is only through them that he exercises such power as he may have.

The gap between the members of the leaders of the mass association is becoming increasingly wider. As soon as a man gets to be a leader of an association large enough to count he readily becomes lost as an instrument of that association. He does so (1) in the interests of maintaining his leading position in, or rather over, his mass association, and he does so (2) because he comes to see himself not as a mere delegate, instructed or not, of the mass association he represents, but as a member of 'an elite' composed of such men as himself. These facts, in turn, lead to (3) the big gap between the terms in which issues are debated and resolved among members of this elite, and the terms in which they are presented to the members of the various mass associations. For the decisions that are made must *take into account* those who are important—other elites—but they must be *sold* to the mass memberships.

The gap between speaker and listener, between power and public, leads less to any iron law of oligarchy than to the law of spokesmanship: as the pressure group expands, its leaders come to organize the opinions they 'represent.' So elections, as we have seen, become contests between two giant and unwieldy parties, neither of which the individual can truly feel that he influences, and neither of which is capable of winning psychologically impressive or politically decisive majorities. And, in all this, the parties are of the same general form as other mass associations.[4]

When we say that man in the mass is without any sense of political belonging, we have in mind a political fact rather than merely a style of feeling. We have in mind (I.) a certain way of belonging (II.) to a certain kind of organization.

I. The way of belonging here implied rests upon a belief in the purposes and in the leaders of an organization, and thus enables men and women freely to be at home within it. To belong in this way is to make the human association a psychological center of one's self, to take into our conscience, deliberately and freely, its rules of conduct and its purposes, which we thus shape and which in turn shape us. We do not have this kind of belonging to any political organization.

II. The kind of organization we have in mind is a voluntary association which has three decisive characteristics: first, it is a context in which reasonable opinions may be formulated; second, it is an agency by which reasonable activities may be undertaken; and third, it is a powerful enough unit, in comparison with other organizations of power, to make a difference.

It is because they do not find available associations at once psychologically meaningful and historically effective that men often feel uneasy in their political and economic loyalties. The effective units of power are now the huge corporation, the inaccessible government, the grim military establishment. Between these, on the one hand, and the family and the small community on the other, we find no intermediate associations in which men feel secure and with which they feel powerful. There is little live political struggle. Instead, there is administration from above, and the political vacuum below. The primary publics are now either so small as to be swamped, and hence give up; or so large as to be merely another feature of the generally distant structure of power, and hence inaccessible.

Public opinion exists when people who are not in the government of a country claim the right to express political opinions freely and publicly, and the right that these opinions should influence or determine the policies, personnel, and actions of their government.[5] In this formal sense there has been and there is a definite public opinion in the United States. And yet, with modern developments this formal right—when it does still exist as a right—does not mean what it once did. The older world of voluntary organization was as different from the world of the mass organization, as was Tom Paine's world of pamphleteering from the world of the mass media.

Since the French Revolution, conservative thinkers have Viewed With Alarm the rise of the public, which they called the masses, or something to that effect. 'The populace is sovereign, and the tide of barbarism mounts,' wrote Gustave Le Bon. 'The divine right of the masses is about to replace the divine right of kings,' and already 'the destinies of nations are elaborated at present in the heart of the masses, and no longer in the councils of princes.'[6] During the twentieth century, liberal and even socialist thinkers have followed suit, with more explicit reference to what we have called the society of masses. From Le Bon to Emil Lederer and Ortega y Gasset, they have held that the influence of the mass is unfortunately increasing.

But surely those who have supposed the masses to be all powerful, or at least well on their way to triumph, are wrong. In our time, as Chakhotin knew, the influence of autonomous collectivities within political life is in fact diminishing.[7] Furthermore, such influence as they do have is guided; they must now be seen not as publics acting autonomously, but as masses manipulated at focal points into crowds of demonstrators. For as publics become masses, masses sometimes become crowds; and, in crowds, the psychical rape by the mass media is supplemented up-close by the harsh and sudden harangue. Then the people in the crowd disperse again—as atomized and submissive masses.

In all modern societies, the autonomous associations standing between the various classes and the state tend to lose their effectiveness as vehicles of reasoned opinion and instruments for the rational exertion of political will. Such associations can be deliberately broken up and thus turned into passive instruments of rule, or they can more slowly wither away from lack of use in the face of centralized means of power. But whether they are destroyed in a week or wither in a generation, such associations are replaced in virtually every sphere of life by centralized organizations, and it is such organizations with all

their new means of power that take charge of the terrorized or—as the case may be—merely intimidated, society of masses.

5

The institutional trends that make for a society of masses are to a considerable extent a matter of impersonal drift, but the remnants of the public are also exposed to more 'personal' and intentional forces. With the broadening of the base of politics within the context of a folk-lore of democratic decision-making, and with the increased means of mass persuasion that are available, the public of public opinion has become the object of intensive efforts to control, manage, manipulate, and increasingly intimidate.

In political, military, economic realms, power becomes, in varying degrees, uneasy before the suspected opinions of masses, and, accordingly, opinion-making becomes an accepted technique of power-holding and power-getting. The minority electorate of the propertied and the educated is replaced by the total suffrage—and intensive campaigns for the vote. The small eighteenth-century professional army is replaced by the mass army of conscripts—and by the problems of nationalist morale. The small shop is replaced by the mass-production industry—and the national advertisement.

As the scale of institutions has become larger and more centralized, so has the range and intensity of the opinion-makers' efforts. The means of opinion-making, in fact, have paralleled in range and efficiency the other institutions of greater scale that cradle the modern society of masses. Accordingly, in addition to their enlarged and centralized means of administration, exploitation, and violence, the modern elite have had placed within their grasp historically unique instruments of psychic management and manipulation, which include universal compulsory education as well as the media of mass communication.

Early observers believed that the increase in the range and volume of the formal means of communication would enlarge and animate the primary public. In such optimistic views—written before radio and television and movies—the formal media are understood as simply multiplying the scope and pace of personal discussion. Modern conditions, Charles Cooley wrote, 'enlarge indefinitely the competition of ideas, and whatever has owed its persistence merely to lack of comparison is likely to go, for that which is really congenial to the choosing mind will be all the more cherished and increased.'[8] Still excited by the break-up of the conventional consensus of the local community, he saw the new means of communication as furthering the conversational dynamic of classic democracy, and with it the growth of rational and free individuality.

No one really knows all the functions of the mass media, for in their entirety these functions are probably so pervasive and so subtle that they cannot be caught by the means of social research now available. But we do now have reason to believe that these media have helped less to enlarge and animate the discussions of primary publics than to transform them into a set of media markets in mass-like society. I do not refer merely to the higher ratio of deliverers of opinion to receivers and to the decreased chance to answer back; nor do I refer merely to the violent banalization and stereotyping of our very sense organs in terms of which these media now compete for 'attention.' I have in mind a sort of psychological illiteracy that is facilitated by the media, and that is expressed in several ways:

I. Very little of what we think we know of the social realities of the world have we found out first-hand. Most of 'the pictures in our heads' we have gained from these media—even to the point where we often do not really believe what we see before us until we read about it in the paper or hear about it on the radio.[9] The media not only give us information; they guide our very experiences. Our standards of credulity, our standards of reality, tend to be set by these media rather than by our own fragmentary experience.

Accordingly, even if the individual has direct, personal experience of events, it is not really direct and primary: it is organized in stereotypes. It takes long and skillful training to so uproot such stereotypes that an individual sees things freshly, in an unstereotyped manner. One might suppose, for example, that if all the people went through a depression they would all 'experience it,' and in terms of this experience, that they would all debunk or reject or at least refract what the media say about it. But experience of such a *structural* shift has to be organized and interpreted if it is to count in the making of opinion.

The kind of experience, in short, that might serve as a basis for resistance to mass media is not an experience of raw events, but the experience of meanings. The fleck of interpretation must be there in the experience if we are to use the word experience seriously. And the capacity for such experience is socially implanted. The individual does not trust his own experience, as I have said, until it is confirmed by others or by the media. Usually such direct exposure is not accepted if it disturbs loyalties and beliefs that the individual already holds. To be accepted, it must relieve or justify the feelings that often lie in the back of his mind as key features of his ideological loyalties.

Stereotypes of loyalty underlie beliefs and feelings about given symbols and emblems; they are the very ways in which men see the social world and in terms of which men make up their specific opinions and views of events. They are the results of previous experience, which affect present and future experience. It goes without saying that men are often unaware of these loyalties, that often they could not formulate them explicitly. Yet such general stereotypes make for the acceptance or the rejection of specific opinions not so much by the force of logical consistency as by their emotional affinity and by the way in which they relieve anxieties. To accept opinions in their terms is to gain the good solid feeling of being correct without having to think. When ideological stereotypes and specific opinions are linked in this way, there is a lowering of the kind of anxiety which arises when loyalty and belief are not in accord. Such ideologies lead to a willingness to accept a given line of belief; then there is no need, emotionally or rationally, to overcome resistance to given items in that line; cumulative selections of specific opinions and feelings become the preorganized attitudes and emotions that shape the opinion-life of the person.

These deeper beliefs and feelings are a sort of lens through which men experience their worlds, they strongly condition acceptance or rejection of specific opinions, and they set men's orientation toward prevailing authorities. Three decades ago, Walter Lippmann saw such prior convictions as biases: they kept men from defining reality in an adequate way. They are still biases. But today they can often be seen as 'good biases'; inadequate and misleading as they often are, they are less so than the crackpot realism of the higher authorities and opinion-makers. They are the lower common sense and as such a factor of resistance. But we must recognize, especially when the pace of change is so deep and fast, that common sense is more often common than sense. And, above all, we must recognize that 'the common sense' of our children is going to be less the result of any firm social tradition than of the stereotypes carried by the mass media to which they are now so fully exposed. They are the first generation to be so exposed.

II. So long as the media are not entirely monopolized, the individual can play one medium off against another; he can compare them, and hence resist what any one of them puts out. The more genuine competition there is among the media, the more resistance the individual might be able to command. But how much is this now the case? *Do* people compare reports on public events or policies, playing one medium's content off against another's?

The answer is: generally no, very few do: (1) We know that people tend strongly to select those media which carry contents with which they already agree. There is a kind of selection of new opinions on the basis of prior opinions. No one seems to search out such counter-statements as may be found in alternative media offerings. Given radio programs and magazines and newspapers often get a rather consistent public, and thus reinforce their messages in the minds of that public. (2) This idea of playing one medium off against another assumes that the media really have varying contents. It assumes genuine competition, which is not widely true. The media display an apparent variety and competition, but on closer view they seem to compete more in terms of variations on a few standardized themes than of clashing issues. The freedom to raise issues effectively seems more and more to be confined to those few interests that have ready and continual access to these media.

III. The media have not only filtered into our experience of external realities, they have also entered into our very experience of our own selves. They have provided us with new identities and new aspirations of what we should like to be, and what we should like to appear to be. They have provided in the models of conduct they hold out to us a new and larger and more flexible set of appraisals of our very selves. In terms of the modern theory of the self,[10] we may say that the media bring the reader, listener, viewer into the sight of larger, higher reference groups— groups, real or imagined, up-close or vicarious, personally known or distractedly glimpsed— which are looking glasses for his self-image. They have multiplied the groups to which we look for confirmation of our self-image.

More than that: (1) the media tell the man in the mass who he is—they give him identity; (2) they tell him what he wants to be—they give him aspirations; (3) they tell him how to get that way— they give him technique; and (4) they tell him how to feel that he is that way even when he is not—they give him escape. The gaps between the identity and aspiration lead to technique and/or to escape. That is probably the basic psychological formula of the mass media today. But, as a formula, it is not attuned to the development of the human being. It is the formula of a pseudo-world which the media invent and sustain.

IV. As they now generally prevail, the mass media, especially television, often encroach upon the small-scale discussion, and destroy the chance for the reasonable and leisurely and human interchange of opinion. They are an important cause of the destruction of privacy in its full human meaning. That is an important reason why they not only fail as an educational force, but are a malign force: they do not articulate for the viewer or listener the broader sources of his private tensions and anxieties, his inarticulate resentments and half-formed hopes. They neither enable the individual to transcend his narrow milieu nor clarify its private meaning.

The media provide much information and news about what is happening in the world, but they do not often enable the listener or the viewer truly to connect his daily life with these larger realities. They do not connect the information they provide on public issues with the troubles felt by the individual. They do not increase rational insight into tensions, either those in the individual or those of the society which are reflected in the individual. On the contrary, they distract him and obscure his chance to understand himself or his world, by fastening his attention upon artificial frenzies that are resolved within the program framework, usually by violent action or by what is called humor. In short, for the viewer they are not really resolved at all. The chief distracting tension of the media is between the wanting and the not having of commodities or of women held to be good looking. There is almost always the general tone of animated distraction, of suspended agitation, but it is going nowhere and it has nowhere to go.

But the media, as now organized and operated, are even more than a major cause of the transformation of America into a mass society. They are also among the most important of those increased means of power now at the disposal of elites of wealth and power; morever, some of the higher agents of these media are themselves either among the elites or very important among their servants.

Alongside or just below the elite, there is the propagandist, the publicity expert, the public-relations man, who would control the very formation of public opinion in order to be able to include it as one more pacified item in calculations of effective power, increased prestige, more secure wealth. Over the last quarter of a century, the attitudes of these manipulators toward their task have gone through a sort of dialectic:

In the beginning, there is great faith in what the mass media can do. Words win wars or sell soap; they move people, they restrain people. 'Only cost,' the advertising man of the 'twenties proclaims, 'limits the delivery of public opinion in any direction on any topic.'[11] The opinion-maker's belief in the media as mass persuaders almost amounts to magic—but he can believe mass communications omnipotent only so long as the public is trustful. It does not remain trustful. The mass media say so very many and such competitively exaggerated things; they banalize their message and they cancel one another out. The 'propaganda phobia,' in reaction to wartime lies and postwar disenchantment, does not help matters, even though memory is both short and subject to official distortion. This distrust of the magic of media is translated into a slogan among the opinion managers. Across their banners they write: 'Mass Persuasion Is Not Enough.'

Frustrated, they reason; and reasoning, they come to accept the principle of social context. To change opinion and activity, they say to one another, we must pay close attention to the full context and lives of the people to be managed. Along with mass persuasion, we must somehow use personal influence; we must reach people in their life context and *through* other people their daily associates, those whom they trust: we must get at them by some kind of 'personal' persuasion. We must not show our hand directly; rather than merely advise or command, we must manipulate.

Now this live and immediate social context in which people live and which exerts a steady expectation upon them is of course what we have called the primary public. Anyone who has seen the inside of an advertising agency or public-relations office knows that the primary public is still the great unsolved problem of the opinion-makers. Negatively, their recognition of

the influence of social context upon opinion and public activity implies that the articulate public resists and refracts the communications of the mass media. Positively, this recognition implies that the public is not composed of isolated individuals, but rather of persons who not only have prior opinions that must be reckoned with, but who continually influence each other in complex and intimate, in direct and continual ways.

In their attempts to neutralize or to turn to their own use the articulate public, the opinion-makers try to make it a relay network for their views. If the opinion-makers have so much power that they can act directly and openly upon the primary publics, they may become authoritative; but, if they do not have such power and hence have to operate indirectly and without visibility, they will assume the stance of manipulators.

Authority is power that is explicit and more or less 'voluntarily' obeyed; manipulation is the 'secret' exercise of power, unknown to those who are influenced. In the model of the classic democratic society, manipulation is not a problem, because formal authority resides in the public itself and in its representatives who are made or broken by the public. In the completely authoritarian society, manipulation is not a problem, because authority is openly identified with the ruling institutions and their agents, who may use authority explicitly and nakedly. They do not, in the extreme case, have to gain or retain power by hiding its exercise.

Manipulation becomes a problem wherever men have power that is concentrated and willful but do not have authority, or when, for any reason, they do not wish to use their power openly. Then the powerful seek to rule without showing their powerfulness. They want to rule, as it were, secretly, without publicized legitimation. It is in this mixed case—as in the intermediate reality of the American today—that manipulation is a prime way of exercising power. Small circles of men are making decisions which they need to have at least authorized by indifferent or recalcitrant people over whom they do not exercise explicit authority. So the small circle tries to manipulate these people into willing acceptance or cheerful support of their decisions or opinions—or at least to the rejection of possible counter-opinions.

Authority *formally* resides 'in the people,' but the power of initiation is in fact held by small circles of men. That is why the standard strategy of manipulation is to make it appear that the people, or at least a large group of them, 'really made the decision.' That is why even when the authority is available, men with access to it may still prefer the secret, quieter ways of manipulation.

But are not the people now more educated? Why not emphasize the spread of education rather than the increased effects of the mass media? The answer, in brief, is that mass education, in many respects, has become—another mass medium.

The prime task of public education, as it came widely to be understood in this country, was political: to make the citizen more knowledgeable and thus better able to think and to judge of public affairs. In time, the function of education shifted from the political to the economic: to train people for better-paying jobs and thus to get ahead. This is especially true of the high-school movement, which has met the business demands for white-collar skills at the public's expense. In large part education has become merely vocational; in so far as its political task is concerned, in many schools, that has been reduced to a routine training of nationalist loyalties.

The training of skills that are of more or less direct use in the vocational life is an important task to perform, but ought not to be mistaken for liberal education: job advancement, no matter on what levels, is not the same as self-development, although the two are now systematically confused.[12] Among 'skills,' some are more and some are less relevant to the aims of liberal—that is to say, liberating—education. Skills and values cannot be so easily separated as the academic search for supposedly neutral skills causes us to assume. And especially not when we speak seriously of liberal education. Of course, there is a scale, with skills at one end and values at the other, but it is the middle range of this scale, which one might call sensibilities, that are of most relevance to the classic public.

To train someone to operate a lathe or to read and write is pretty much education of skill; to evoke from people an understanding of what they really want out of their lives or to debate with them stoic, Christian and humanist ways of living, is pretty much a clear-cut education of values. But to assist in the birth among a group of people of those cultural and political and technical sensibilities which would make them genuine members of a genuinely liberal public, this is at once a training in skills and an education of values. It includes a sort of therapy in the ancient sense of clarifying one's knowledge of one's self; it includes the imparting of all those skills of controversy with one's self, which we call thinking; and with others, which we call debate. And the end product of such liberal education of sensibilities is simply the self-educating, self-cultivating man or woman.

The knowledgeable man in the genuine public is able to turn his personal troubles into social issues, to see their relevance for his community and his community's relevance for them. He understands that what he thinks and feels as personal troubles are very often not only that but problems shared by others and indeed not subject to solution by any one individual but only by modifications of the structure of the groups in which he lives and sometimes the structure of the entire society.

Men in masses are gripped by personal troubles, but they are not aware of their true meaning and source. Men in public confront issues, and they are aware of their terms. It is the task of the liberal institution, as of the liberally educated man, continually to translate troubles into issues and issues into the terms of their human meaning for the individual. In the absence of deep and wide political debate, schools for adults and adolescents could perhaps become hospitable frameworks for just such debate. In a community of publics the task of liberal education would be: to keep the public from being overwhelmed; to help produce the disciplined and informed mind that cannot be overwhelmed; to help develop the bold and sensible individual that cannot be sunk by the burdens of mass life. But educational practice has not made knowledge directly relevant to the human need of the troubled person of the twentieth century or to the social practices of the citizen. This citizen cannot now see the roots of his own biases and frustrations, nor think clearly about himself, nor for that matter about anything else. He does not see the frustration of idea, of intellect, by the present organization of society, and he is not able to meet the tasks now confronting 'the intelligent citizen.'

Educational institutions have not done these things and, except in rare instances, they are not doing them. They have become mere elevators of occupational and social ascent, and, on all levels, they have become politically timid. Moreover, in the hands of 'professional educators,' many schools have come to operate on an ideology of 'life adjustment' that encourages happy acceptance of mass ways of life rather than the struggle for individual and public transcendence.[13]

There is not much doubt that modern regressive educators have adapted their notions of educational content and practice to the idea of the mass. They do not effectively proclaim standards of cultural level and intellectual rigor; rather they often deal in the trivia of vocational tricks and 'adjustment to life'—meaning the slack life of masses. 'Democratic schools' often mean the furtherance of intellectual mediocrity, vocational training, nationalistic loyalties, and little else.

6

The structural trends of modern society and the manipulative character of its communication technique come to a point of coincidence in the mass society, which is largely a metropolitan society. The growth of the metropolis, segregating men and women into narrowed routines and environments, causes them to lose any firm sense of their integrity as a public. The members of publics in smaller communities know each other more or less fully, because they meet in the several aspects of the total life routine. The members of masses in a metropolitan society know one another only as fractions in specialized milieux: the man who fixes the car, the girl who serves your lunch, the saleslady, the women who take care of your child at school during the day. Prejudgment and stereotype flourish when people meet in such ways. The human reality of others does not, cannot, come through.

People, we know, tend to select those formal media which confirm what they already believe and enjoy. In a parallel way, they tend in the metropolitan segregation to come into live touch with those whose opinions are similar to theirs. Others they tend to treat unseriously. In the metropolitan society they develop, in their defense, a blasé manner that reaches deeper than a manner. They do not, accordingly, experience genuine clashes of viewpoint, genuine issues. And when they do, they tend to consider it mere rudeness.

Sunk in their routines, they do not transcend, even by discussion, much less by action, their more or less narrow lives. They do not gain a view of the structure of their society and of their role as a public within it. The city is a structure composed of such little environments, and the people in them tend to be detached from one another. The 'stimulating variety' of the city does not stimulate the men and women of 'the bedroom belt,' the one-class suburbs, who can go through life knowing only their own kind. If they do reach for one another, they do so only through stereotypes and prejudiced images of the creatures of other milieux. Each is trapped by his confining circle; each is cut off from easily identifiable groups. It is for people in such narrow milieux that the mass media can create a pseudo-world beyond, and a pseudo-world within themselves as well.

Publics live in milieux but they can transcend them—individually by intellectual effort; socially by public action. By reflection and debate and by organized action, a community of publics comes to feel itself and comes in fact to be active at points of structural relevance.

But members of a mass exist in milieux and cannot get out of them, either by mind or by activity, except—in the extreme case—under 'the organized spontaneity' of the bureaucrat on a motorcycle. We have not yet reached the extreme case, but observing metropolitan man in the American mass we can surely see the psychological preparations for it.

We may think of it in this way: When a handful of men do not have jobs, and do not seek work, we look for the causes in their immediate situation and character. But when twelve million men are unemployed, then we cannot believe that all of them suddenly 'got lazy' and turned out to be 'no good.' Economists call this 'structural unemployment'—meaning, for one thing, that the men involved cannot themselves control their job chances. Structural unemployment does not originate in one factory or in one town, nor is it due to anything that one factory or one town does or fails to do. Moreover, there is little or nothing that one ordinary man in one factory in one town can do about it when it sweeps over his personal milieu.

Now, this distinction, between social structure and personal milieu, is one of the most important available in the sociological studies. It offers us a ready understanding of the position of 'the public' in America today. In every major area of life, the loss of a sense of structure and the submergence into powerless milieux is the cardinal fact. In the military it is most obvious, for here the roles men play are strictly confining; only the command posts at the top afford a view of the structure of the whole, and moreover, this view is a closely guarded official secret. In the division of labor too, the jobs men enact in the economic hierarchies are also more or less narrow milieux and the positions from which a view of the production process as a whole can be had are centralized, as men are alienated not only from the product and the tools of their labor, but from any understanding of the structure and the processes of production. In the political order, in the fragmentation of the lower and in the distracting proliferation of the middle-level organization, men cannot see the whole, cannot see the top and cannot state the issues that will in fact determine the whole structure in which they live and their place within it.

This loss of any structural view or position is the decisive meaning of the lament over the loss of community. In the great city, the division of milieux and of segregating routines reaches the point of closest contact with the individual and the family, for, although the city is not the unit of prime decision, even the city cannot be seen as a total structure by most of its citizens.

On the one hand, there is the increased scale and centralization of the structure of decision; and, on the other, the increasingly narrow sorting out of men into milieux. From both sides, there is the increased dependence upon the formal media of communication, including those of education itself. But the man in the mass does not gain a transcending view from these media; instead he gets his experience stereotyped, and then he gets sunk further by that experience. He cannot detach himself in order to observe, much less to evaluate, what he is experiencing, much less what he is not experiencing. Rather than that internal discussion we call reflection, he is accompanied through his life-experience with a sort of unconscious, echoing monologue. He has no projects of his own: he fulfills the routines that exist. He does not transcend whatever he is at any moment, because he does not, he cannot, transcend his daily milieu. He is not truly aware of his own daily experience and of its actual standards: he drifts, he fulfills habits, his behavior a result of a planless mixture of the confused standards and the uncriticized expectations that he has taken over from others whom he no longer really knows or trusts, if indeed he ever really did.

He takes things for granted, he makes the best of them, he tries to look ahead—a year or two perhaps, or even longer if he has children or a mortgage—but he does not seriously ask, What do I want? How can I get it? A vague optimism suffuses and sustains him, broken occasionally by little miseries and disappointments that are soon buried. He is smug, from the standpoint of those who think something might be the matter with the mass style of life in the metropolitan frenzy where self-making is an externally busy branch of industry. By what standards does he judge himself and his efforts? What is really important to him? Where are the models of excellence for this man?

He loses his independence, and more importantly, he loses the desire to be independent: in fact, he does not have hold of the idea of being an independent individual with his own mind and his own worked-out way of life. It is not that he likes or does not like this life; it is that the question does not come up sharp and clear so he is not bitter and he is not sweet about conditions and events. He thinks he wants merely to get his share of what is around with as little trouble as he can and with as much fun as possible.

Such order and movement as his life possesses is in conformity with external routines; otherwise his day-to-day experience is a vague chaos—although he often does not know it because, strictly speaking, he does not truly possess or observe his own experience. He does not formulate his desires; they are insinuated into him. And, in the mass, he loses the self-confidence of the human being—if indeed he has ever had it. For life in a society of masses implants insecurity and furthers impotence; it makes men uneasy and vaguely anxious; it isolates the individual from the solid group; it destroys firm group standards. Acting without goals, the man in the mass just feels pointless.

The idea of a mass society suggests the idea of an elite of power. The idea of the public, in contrast, suggests the liberal tradition of a society without any power elite, or at any rate with shifting elites of no sovereign consequence. For, if a genuine public is sovereign, it needs no master; but the masses, in their full development, are sovereign only in some plebiscitarian moment of adulation to an elite as authoritative celebrity. The political structure of a democratic state requires the public; and, the democratic man, in his rhetoric, must assert that this public is the very seat of sovereignty.

But now, given all those forces that have enlarged and centralized the political order and made modern societies less political and more administrative; given the transformation of the old middle classes into something which perhaps should not even be called middle class; given all the mass communications that do not truly communicate; given all the metropolitan segregation that is not community; given the absence of voluntary associations that really connect the public at large with the centers of power—what is happening is the decline of a set of publics that is sovereign only in the most formal and rhetorical sense. Moreover, in many countries the remnants of such publics as remain are now being frightened out of existence. They lose their will for rationally considered decision and action because they do not possess the instruments for such decision and action; they lose their sense of political belonging because they do not belong; they lose their political will because they see no way to realize it.

The top of modern American society is increasingly unified, and often seems willfully coordinated: at the top there has emerged an elite of power. The middle levels are a drifting set of stalemated, balancing forces: the middle does not link the bottom with the top. The bottom of this society is politically fragmented, and even as a passive fact, increasingly powerless: at the bottom there is emerging a mass society.

Notes

1. See E. H. Carr, *The New Society* (London: Macmillan, 1951), pp. 63–6, on whom I lean heavily in this and the following paragraphs.

2. See, especially, the analysis of the decline of the independent middle classes, *Eleven: The Theory of Balance.*

3. At the same time—and also because of the metropolitan segregation and distraction, which I shall discuss in a moment—the individual becomes more dependent upon the means of mass communication for his view of the structure as a whole.

4. On elections in modern formal democracies, E. H. Carr has concluded: 'To speak today of the defense of democracy as if we were defending something which we knew and had possessed for many decades or many centuries is

self-deception and sham—mass democracy is a new phenomenon—a creation of the last half-century—which it is inappropriate and misleading to consider in terms of the philosophy of Locke or of the liberal democracy of the nineteenth century. We should be nearer the mark, and should have a far more convincing slogan, if we spoke of the need, not to defend democracy, but to create it.' (ibid. pp. 75–6)

5. Cf. Hans Speier, *Social Order and The Risks of War* (New York: George Stewart, 1952), pp. 323–39.

6. Gustave Le Bon, *The Crowd* (London: Ernest Benn Ltd., 1952—first English edition, 1896), pp. 207. Cf. also pp. 6, 23, 30, 187.

7. Sergei Chakhotin, *The Rape of the Masses* (New York: Alliance, 1940), pp. 289–91.

8. Charles Horton Cooley, *Social Organization* (New York: Scribner's, 1909), p. 93. Cf. also Chapter IX.

9. See Walter Lippmann, *Public Opinion* (New York: Macmillan, 1922), which is still the best account of this aspect of the media. Cf. especially pp. 1–25 and 59–121.

10. Cf. Gerth and Mills, *Character and Social Structure* (New York: Harcourt, Brace, 1953), pp. 84 ff.

11. J. Truslow Adams, The Epic of America (Boston: Little, Brown, 1931) p. 360.

12. Cf. Mills, 'Work Milieu and Social Structure,' a speech to 'The Asilomar Conference' of the Mental Health Society of Northern California, March 1954, reprinted in their bulletin, *People At Work: A Symposium,* pp. 20 ff.

13. 'If the schools are doing their job,' A. E. Bestor has written, 'we should expect educators to point to the significant and indisputable achievement in raising the intellectual level of the nation—measured perhaps by larger per capita circulation of books and serious magazines, by definitely improved taste in movies and radio programs, by higher standards of political debate, by increased respect for freedom of speech and of thought, by marked decline in such evidences of mental retardation as the incessant reading of comic books by adults.' A. E. Bestor, *Educational Wastelands* (Urbana, Ill.: University of Illinois, 1953), p. 7. Cf. also p. 80.

56

FDR and the White House Mail

From *Public Opinion Quarterly* (1956)

Leila A. Sussmann

Leila Sussmann (1922–1998) was a sociologist of political mass communication and education who taught at Wellesley, the University of Massachusetts, and Tufts. In the mid-1940s, she worked for the Congress of Industrial Organizations (CIO), for whom she studied radio coverage of labor and served as one of the analysts for the Hutchins Commission on Freedom of the Press. She was part of the postwar cohort of graduate students in sociology at Columbia, where she worked with Robert Merton and participated in a number of studies, including a 1948 analysis of letters urging then general Dwight Eisenhower to run for president.

Sussmann's work at Columbia was part of a short tradition of what Merton called "studies centered on communications from audiences directed to those who are dependent on having an audience." Bureau researchers, usually women, examined political letter writing and fan mail—communication *from* the masses instead of toward them. (Leo Lowenthal also conducted one such study, of fan mail directed toward a daytime radio philosopher). This article was part of Sussmann's dissertation project, published in 1962 as *Dear FDR: A Study of Political Letter Writing.* Here Sussmann amplifies communicative and political functions of the mail and gives some sense of the seemingly personal relations that developed between Roosevelt and members of his mass public.

Four hundred and fifty thousand communications from the public came to the White House during Franklin D. Roosevelt's first week in office.[1] This soon settled down to an average of five to eight thousand a day,[2] or ten times the "tremendously big" mail that Hoover had received toward the end of his administration.[3]

The White House mail room, hitherto run by one man, was now staffed by twenty-two regular employees with as many as seventy people working in emergencies.[4] Messages from his family and intimate friends were sent to the President unopened.[5] Official communications were referred to him or the appropriate presidential secretary. All the rest went to the Correspondence Section, a corps of clerks who determined where to forward mail for proper disposition. The bulk of the letters were forwarded to other government agencies.[6] Fan mail for FDR and letters commenting on his policies, however, were answered by the White House.[7]

Mail as Public Relations

Except for pressure mail[8] which got form answers, Presidential Secretary Louis Howe insisted that every letter to Roosevelt must have an individual reply. Howe's policy required a change in traditional White House procedure. According to Mrs. Roosevelt, who followed the same rule in answering her own unprecedented mail:

> We had to work out a completely new system for handling correspondence. Consulting with Ralph W. Magee, head of the correspondence bureau, we had found that most of the

mail in former administrations had been answered by form letters; he even had copies of forms used in President Cleveland's administration. Whether a correspondent asked for a handkerchief for a church bazaar or for a white elephant, she or he was told: "Mrs. _____ has had so many similar requests, it is not possible to accede to your . . ." I decided that the times were too serious and the requests too desperate to have mail answered in that way, so none of my letters was answered by form number so and so.[9]

Periodically, Howe got together with the President and the Executive Clerk to draft "suggested replies" on the subjects discussed most frequently in the current mail. To these guiding paragraphs, usually somewhat reworded, the Correspondence Section added a few sentences alluding to specific remarks in the incoming letter so that the writer would know his reply had been written for him personally, and him alone. Great care was taken to spell names correctly. If these were illegible, the Library of Congress' aid was enlisted to clear up the matter. The Correspondence Section knew that many a White House reply would become a family treasure to be kept and proudly exhibited for a lifetime. When replies went out simultaneously to two writers in the same small community, they were always worded differently:

> . . . because those letters would be compared and they would lose value if people saw that everyone had gotten the same reply. They would say, "It's just a form."[10]

All this was a continuation, with modifications, of methods for handling Roosevelt's mail which had been established years before. Undaunted by the greatest deluge of letters ever seen in the White House, the staff did not budge from their long-standing principle: a personal letter to FDR, no matter from whom it came, deserved a careful, prompt and individual reply. The letter-writers themselves provide evidence that the policy paid political dividends. The following message, sent from Augusta, Georgia during the 1940 campaign, could be duplicated many times over:

Dear Mr. President:
    In 1932, prior to your election as our President, my mother . . . wrote to you, assuring you of her support and well wishes. At that

time she was eighty-six years of age, confined to her bed, suffering the effects of a broken spine, from which she thereafter passed away. Fearing that because of your being extremely busy at that time my mother would receive no reply, I had planned to comfort her by reading to her from a letter as though it had come from you. But this was not necessary; in but a few days your reply came. . . .

    I cannot tell you how greatly pleased was my mother, nor how comforted she was in her pleasure. She highly treasured your letter and instructed us that after her death it was to be kept framed in our home to mark a kindly deed by a noble man.
    In 1936, after my mother had passed away, I worked with all my strength for your reelection, my efforts being urged by thought of your kindness.
    This year, I am working for your reelection. Each day I pray that God will spare to our country your services and guidance.[11]

A considerable number of letters from people unknown to Roosevelt found their way to his desk. At almost any point along the line, the Chief of Mails, the head of the Correspondence Section, the Executive Clerk or any of the presidential secretaries might decide that a particular letter would interest him and send it to his office. Many of these became the basis of press releases:

> Frequently we sent him unusual letters, from which, with a fine knack for publicity, he would pick out material for newspaper stories.[12]

One such story which appeared in the *New York Times* of October, 1933 read in part:

> . . . a letter from one of the 120,000,000 of us may hearten the President far more than its modest writer can reasonably expect. Here is such a letter, all but the signature. . . .
>   "Dear Sir—Enclosed find my pension check, which I am returning to the government. . . . In view of the great work our President has done, I feel this is the least I can do to help. . . . I would have written the Veterans Bureau direct, but I am suspicious that they would find some regulation to countermand my wish. My work takes me all over the country east of the Mississippi. Undoubtedly, I have absorbed some of the

courage and confidence that I have found in the people since the New Deal went into effect and which inspire my action. If my action sounds a note of approval or helps to refresh our President's courage I shall be amply paid."

That letter went from hand to hand throughout the White House. It reached the President's desk and had the effect of a ray of light in a dark hour.[13]

The symbolic functions of these stories are well illustrated here. The article affirms FDR's accessibility to every citizen; even a letter not addressed to him directly may reach him and be read. It asserts the humanity of the President; like ordinary people, he needs the moral support of others. And it celebrates the importance of "modest" men whose words of encouragement can fulfill the President's need. The White House saw to it that some publicity based on mail appeared in the mass media at periodic intervals.

Mail as an Index of Public Sentiment

The letters which White House aids referred to the President's office were out of the ordinary. Roosevelt did not rely on these atypical selections for his overall impressions of the mail. Several methods were employed to ensure that he got a representative picture.

The mail room made a daily count of incoming letters and cards broken down by subject-matter categories, such as "NRA," "Supreme Court Reorganization," "requests for financial aid," and so on. The list of subjects was continually revised to keep step with the changing content of the mail. If a controversial issue began to loom large, the count might be further refined to show the proportion of communications taking specific positions. Pressure mail was always counted and reported separately from the rest.[14]

Unlike Louis Howe's sacred rule of the individual reply, these procedures for keeping tabs on mail were not altogether new at the White House. As far back as the McKinley Administration, pressure mail was counted. At that time letters from the public to the Chief Executive numbered no more than about one hundred on an ordinary day. They were read by the President's secretary who showed him what he thought was important and briefed him informally on the

rest.[15] Only in times of crisis or when a letter-writing campaign was staged by an organized group, did the White House mailbag swell very greatly. For instance, during the period leading up to the war with Spain, church groups organized a letter campaign urging McKinley to keep the country out of war. Voters on the other side of the fence countered with messages urging him to declare war. Together they produced a flow of letters which mounted to over one thousand a day.[16] After the first "wave," the mail room did not bother the President and his secretary with the pressure mail, which varied little in arguments and wording. They were simply kept informed of the number of pieces arriving. Similarly, a coal strike which occurred in Theodore Roosevelt's administration gave rise to a newspaper-sponsored mail campaign urging him to force a settlement. Theodore Roosevelt was given a daily count of the number of newspaper coupons received.[17]

Under the Hoover regime, when incoming correspondence shot up by fifty per cent over its Harding, Coolidge average,[18] the idea of systematic reporting was extended to include non-pressure mail. Unfortunately, there are few details available on the procedure which Hoover instituted. Chief of Mails Ira Smith's brief description leaves the impression that it was more than a mere count. It appears to have involved an analysis of all mail on issues specified by the President:

> He arranged a scientific check of the mail to watch the trend of public opinion on such matters as prohibition, and then on the efforts that were made to combat the depression.[19]

The Roosevelt staff carried systematic analysis one step further. By including *all* messages in their daily subject-matter counts, they were able to use the huge Presidential mail as an indicator of what issues were most on the public mind. The rising and falling flow of communication on various topics was taken to correspond roughly to the trend of public interest in them.[20]

FDR kept close watch over the volume of the mail:

> Whenever there was a decrease in the influx of letters we could expect to hear from him or one of his secretaries, who wanted to know

what was the matter—was the President losing his grip on the public?[21]

The more the public wrote to him, the better he liked it and Roosevelt did not leave this important matter to chance. His early experience in building a political correspondence had taught him the need for taking the initiative. He now lost no opportunity to let the American people know that he wanted to hear from them. The press releases served that purpose in part. By giving official recognition to letter-writing, they helped to "legitimize" it and foster its growth. For example, a front-page *New York Times* story of December 17, 1933 said:

> The President has been especially pleased by the size of the mail. He sees in the volume evidence of an increasing and wholesome reawakening of public interest in the affairs of government.[22]

Repeatedly in fireside chats, Roosevelt invited the audience to write to him or referred to his mail in a way that encouraged letter-writing:

> When he advised millions of listeners in one of his fireside chats to 'tell me your troubles,' most of them believed implicitly that he was speaking to them personally and immediately wrote him a letter. It was months before we managed to swim out of *that* flood of mail.[23]

Like Hoover, Roosevelt frequently called for special analyses of the letters received on important issues. Known as "mail briefs," these analyses gave a count of the "pro" and "con" messages on controversial policies and also included excerpts from the letters to illustrate each category of opinion.[24] Mail briefs were nearly always made on the days immediately following an important policy statement. Along with editorial reaction in the press, they provided the President with his most immediate gauge of public response. In October, 1937, for instance, his "quarantine the aggressors" speech at Chicago brought forth a violent protest:

> The President was attacked by a vast majority of the press.... Telegrams of denunciation came in at once.... "It's a terrible thing," he once said to me, having in mind I'm sure, this occasion, "to look over your shoulder when you are trying to lead—and to find no one there."

With the press and mail response in hand, the President backtracked immediately:

> Having gone too far out on a limb, too fast, he decided the next day at his press conference that he had better get back, or at least not go out any further.[25]

Again, in May 1940:

> As disaster after disaster came to the Allied cause in Europe, and as the propaganda of the isolationists grew louder and more extreme, the President decided to talk to the people directly. He wanted to make sure that the country was behind him in his program of help to those fighting Hitler.

The speech was delivered on May 26:

> The response to the speech was very pleasing. The President felt it showed that the people understood the urgency. Telegrams poured in offering personal services, plants, factories, etc.... Five days later he sent another message to the Congress asking for additional appropriations for national defense.[26]

To take a different kind of example, during the first six months of 1940 Roosevelt received daily briefs on the Third Term mail, which was running very heavy. These showed that the letter-writers were overwhelmingly in favor of his running again and that among them, at least, the argument from the two-term tradition carried little weight.[27] What part of this played in the President's ultimate decision to run can only be a matter of speculation.[28]

While President Roosevelt used content analyses as an aid to getting an accurate picture of his mail, they were no substitute in his eyes for reading letters himself. Not just unusual letters, but "typical" ones as well. As often as his crowded schedule allowed, he read letters chosen haphazardly from the mail to see a representative sample of the day's intake. Louis Howe first described this custom in 1934:

> ... the President has always insisted that he be sent daily a batch of letters picked *at random* from the miscellaneous mail. These are letters which might well be handled by departments directly, but *the President likes to see a cross section of the daily mail,* and not infrequently answers, himself, some of the letters contained in the batch.[29]

An article in the *New York Times* four years later indicated the custom was still being followed, though possibly with less regularity:

> ... the President does frequently dip into his correspondence from the public. He calls for half a dozen or so of the bundles, cuts the cords around them and, for a little while, fingers through them. He reads notes on bond stationery and penciled letters scribbled on dime tablets. And after an hour of such perusal he may have a better idea of the cross-section of American thought than he can gain in a day of conferences with sifted and carefully assorted callers.[30]

Perhaps the chief reason Roosevelt put such high value on his mail was that he considered it one of his best lines of communication with the "common people." He was only too well aware of the biases of the elite-controlled mass media. In his early days in politics he had toyed with a scheme for promoting a chain of Democratic newspapers but gave it up.[31] He was persuaded of the limitations of official information channels. Frances Perkins quotes him as having once told her, "... official channels of communication and information are often pretty rigid ... People making such studies rarely get near the common people."[32]

Today we know that among political letter-writers as well, people of high socio-economic status are likely to be over-represented.[33] However, this was probably less true of Roosevelt's than of most political correspondence.[34] There is evidence, furthermore, that FDR gave special attention to letters from the poor and uneducated:

> It is the scrawled, perhaps illiterate, but always sincere note from the obscure person which interests President Roosevelt most. I have seen him spend precious moments poring over letters scribbled on butcher paper or ruled pages torn from a cheap pad.[35]

If quantitative representation of the opinions of low-income people had been all that was desired, the opinion polls gave a far more accurate picture than the mail could ever do. But the mail had its own unique value. It translated the nation's economic problems into the terms in which concrete people experienced them. It did the same for New Deal legislation. The polls might tell what per cent of each income group favored this law or that, but the letters contained case histories—stories of families being helped, not by one, but by a battery of New Deal measures.[36] Samuel Lubell has written:

> As a reporter in Washington, I had shared the general belief that the New Deal was hastily improvised and animated by no coherent philosophy. When one translated its benefits down to what they meant to the families I was interviewing in 1940, the whole Roosevelt program took on a new consistency.[37]

That consistency was always apparent in Roosevelt's mail.

It is probably not too far-fetched to say that as a guide to public sentiment, the mail was Roosevelt's equivalent of the social researcher's qualitative interviews. It performed the analogous function of giving him insight into the letter-writers' "definition of the situation." Howe makes much the same point:

> When letters are received from the small merchant or the country storekeeper, or the workman in a city factory, or the farmer on a worn out New England homestead, they are always read carefully.... Usually, when they give insight into the problems confronting the writer, or his viewpoint on some of the proposed items in the New Deal program, the whole letter, or at least a summary reaches the President's desk. Some of these letters have undoubtedly influenced the President directly or indirectly in deciding his course. I do not mean that such letters, as a rule, contain solutions of problems which the experts are seeking to solve, although there have been instances of that kind in the past. They do, however, reflect the viewpoints of men whose daily lives and fortunes are most affected by the problem. These viewpoints the President has always regarded as the most important data from which to find the course of most direct benefit. In other words, in searching for a remedy, he attaches chief importance, not to what the experts think is good for the man but what the man himself feels he needs most to help him out of his troubles....[38]

Mail as a Weapon of Pressure

While he was Governor of New York, FDR discovered a way of activating his supporters to bring effective pressure on a recalcitrant legislature. Becoming annoyed with the state legislators' refusal to go along with one of his proposals in 1929, Roosevelt decided to "take the issue to the people" by way of radio:

> ...the results were immediate. Mail came flooding into Albany, most of it in support of the Roosevelt position and most of it addressed to the working level of the legislature.[39]

FDR was not slow to see the implications of this response and exploit them further:

> From time to time during each session of the Legislature he delivered a very simple, direct, chatty radio talk in which he told the people of the state what was currently going on in Albany, and appealed to them for help in his fight with the Legislature.... A flood of letters would deluge the members of the legislature after each talk and they were the best weapon Roosevelt had in his struggle for legislation.[40]

The same technique was later applied in struggles with Congress. For instance, in October 1937, when Roosevelt planned to call an Extraordinary Session of Congress to reconsider legislation which it had refused to pass in the regular session, he first undertook a "softening up" process:

> Before it met, there were two speech-writing jobs to be done. One was the formal message to the Congress; the other was more important—an appeal to the people over the heads of the Congress, a fireside chat.... The fireside chat came...a month before the date set...for the Extraordinary Session.... He thought he could get the people to bring pressure on their Congressman, who were then at home in their own districts. He hoped that by the time they met...they would have been convinced that their constituents wanted action.[41]

And again in 1944 when he wanted to insure that his veto of a bill he considered inflationary would not be overridden by the Congress, he directed his veto message to the public in the hope that the resulting mail response would have the necessary influence on the legislators:

> "I'm going to put it right up to the housewife...," he said to us. "Maybe she can hold the boys in line better than I can."[42]

The stratagem did not always work; once in a while it boomeranged. Early in 1935 the Senate incorporated an amendment into a public works measure over President Roosevelt's protest. The *New York Times* reported:

> It is fairly well agreed among observers, leaders in Congress, administration officials and, so it is understood, the President that a colossal blunder was made from the standpoint of legislative strategy. The Senate leadership...appealed for a public reaction in favor of the President.... Presuming upon a continuing personal popularity in the country, the President let word go out from his Hyde Park retreat that 'thousands' of letters and telegrams were 'flooding' upon the recalcitrant Senators. The fact was, at that time, that there was no such 'deluge' of messages and noticeably so. There has been an increasing number of messages received by Senators since, but even until yesterday the 'flood' of letters and telegrams had not inundated anyone.[43]

It did not require a contest for Roosevelt's influence with the public to be felt by Congress through its mail. Even during the "honeymoon," while the rate of letter-writing to the White House was rising like a fever chart, Congressional mail followed not far behind:

> What was happening in the White House mail room was under way, also, on Capital Hill.... Evidently a good many people— having been urged by the President to write their opinions to him—decided to make a good job of it and give their Congressmen a broadside or two.[44]

What did these Congressional letter writers say? According to the *Times*, the issues discussed were mainly jobs, the depression and New Deal legislation. But there was one recurrent theme:

> The name that appears in the letters more often than any other is that of President Roosevelt. Senators and Representatives, regardless of party affiliation, are urged to 'stand by the President' and are threatened with defeat at the polls if they fail to support his recovery program.[45]

Reading this mail the members of Congress became aware that even in their home districts, it was the President rather than they who was coming to have first claim on the voters' allegiance:

Veterans in the Senate and the House, and even more the newcomers, suddenly realized that their constituents were exclusively theirs no longer; that they were more definitely the constituents of the man in the White House.[46]

Roosevelt had made them "his" constituents partly through skillful use of the mass media. The regular presidential press conference and the fireside chat from coast to coast were his inventions. Through them he could present his policies to the voters directly. Their success decreased his dependence on the intermediate and lower levels of Party leadership for assistance.

The Congressmen were losing ground in another respect as well. No longer could they claim a monopoly of knowledge of what the folks back home had on their minds. Roosevelt had new ways of assessing public opinion, including the polls and the mail. He was considerably less dependent on the Congressmen's information than his predecessors had been:

When Senators or Representatives were called to the President's office, they were seldom asked—as they had been in previous administrations—about the state of the public mind in their particular areas. They were told what the state of the public mind in those areas was.[47]

Roosevelt had learned to employ the mass media, the mass mail and the new techniques of opinion surveying as a circuit of communication which linked him *directly* to a very broad public and them to him. He could appeal to the electorate over the heads of Congress, party officials and local leaders and—by-passing all these as well—the response flowed back to the White House.

The potential power of the Presidency vis-à-vis Congress and the party machines was thereby increased. Because of his extraordinary skill as a mass communicator, FDR was able to cash in that potential. He did it with complete awareness. In a reply written March 28, 1932, to a supporter in Independence, Missouri, he put it in these words:

I was particularly interested in your comment on the importance of the radio. Time after time, in meeting legislative opposition in my own state, I have taken an issue directly to the voters by radio, and invariably I have met a most heartening response. Amid

many developments of civilization which lead away from direct government by the people, the radio is one which tends on the other hand to restore direct contact between the masses and their chosen leaders.[48]

Notes

1. Smith, Ira, *Dear Mr. President*, New York: Julian Messner, Inc., 1949, p. 214. Mr. Smith became a clerk at the White House in 1897 and gradually took over the job of handling incoming mail. He resigned as Chief of Mails in 1948.

2. *Ibid.*, p. 150. Estimates of Roosevelt's presidential mail are only roughly consistent. On p. 12 Mr. Smith says it averaged 7000 a day during the New Deal. On p. 150 he places the average at 5000 to 8000. In an interview on December 2, 1954, Mr. William J. Hopkins, Executive Clerk of the White House who was in the Correspondence Section when Roosevelt became President, estimated FDR's mail average at that time at 4000 to 5000 daily and added that it dropped in later years.

3. Estimates of Hoover's mail also vary. Smith, *op. cit.*, p. 12, places the average at about 800 letters a day. Mr. Hopkins says that in 1931 it was running at 500 to 600 a day and that that was considered a "tremendously big" mail at the time. Although the two men disagree in their figures, each estimated Roosevelt's mail at about ten times Hoover's. That their estimates should differ is not surprising. White House mail fluctuates widely from week to week, making an average not too meaningful. Roosevelt's mail sometimes went as high as 150,000 pieces in one day. Smith, *op. cit.*, p. 186.

4. *Ibid.*, pp. 12 and 186.

5. The mail room staff had to learn to recognize the President's personal mail by handwriting, stationery and, in the case of the Roosevelt family, by keeping track of their itineraries. *Ibid.*, pp. 187–188.

6. Cf. The Alphabetical File, 1933–45, the Franklin D. Roosevelt Library. This file contains a record of every letter received at the White House with the writer's name and address, the date of sending, a summary of the content and a notation of the disposition.

7. If a letter both commented on a policy and made a request calling for action from a government agency, it was answered from the White

House and then forwarded to the appropriate department.

8. Pressure mail was defined as mail inspired by an organization and stereotyped in wording. Mr. Smith explains that it was easily spotted; "Letters and postcards of this type usually arrive in large batches. One delivery might bring 3000 letters on the same subject from, say, Chicago. Because they have all been written at the suggestion of a single organization and say about the same thing, they follow the same post-office channel and are usually delivered in bundles containing about 300 each. These are easily recognized by the experienced clerk who reads the newspapers carefully and is probably expecting them anyway." *Op. cit.*, pp. 211–213.

9. Roosevelt, Eleanor, *This I Remember,* New York: Harper and Bros., 1949, pp. 96–97.

10. This quote comes from an interview with Lela Stiles, December 2, 1954. The information about the Correspondence Section comes from the interview and from Lela Stiles, *The Man Behind Roosevelt: The Story of Louis McHenry Howe,* New York: World Publishing Co., 1954, pp. 241–242. Miss Stiles became Louis Howe's assistant in 1928. On Roosevelt's election, she joined the White House staff and helped to direct the Correspondence Section for many years.

11. Letters to Roosevelt bearing on the 1940 campaign are found at the Franklin D. Roosevelt Library in Official File 2526; the file of Democratic National Committee Campaign Correspondence, 1940; the President's Personal File, 200; and the Alphabetical File.

12. Smith, *op. cit.*, pp. 150–151.

13. *New York Times,* October 15, 1933, VI, 3.

14. This information comes from Smith, *op. cit,* pp. 197–199 and 211; and the interviews with Lela Stiles and William J. Hopkins cited above. According to Miss Stiles, pressure mail was given much less weight per letter than messages which individuals "just sat down and wrote."

15. Smith, *op. cit.*, p. 186.

16. *Ibid.*, p. 46.

17. *Ibid,* pp. 209–210.

18. From the turn of the century, presidential mail increased gradually to an average of about 400 pieces a day which was maintained during the Harding and Coolidge administrations. It then jumped to 600 to 800 daily under Hoover, particularly after the crash. An exception to this pattern was President Wilson's World War I crisis mail, which averaged 800 a day. Cf. The *New York Times,* Oct. 15, 1933, VI:3 and Smith, *op. cit.*, pp. 12 and 136.

19. *Ibid.*, p. 140.

20. This account should make clear that in the realm of politics as in social science the invention of content analysis arose out of the need for summarizing and analyzing increasingly large quantities of communication. Louis Howe was using some quite sophisticated quantitative techniques for analyzing Roosevelt's mail as early as 1928.

21. Smith, *op. cit.*, p. 140.

22. *New York Times,* December 17, 1933, 1:2.

23. Smith, *op. cit.*, p. 156. Presidents Truman and Eisenhower both continued this practice. For instance, in a telecast of June 3, 1953, President Eisenhower introduced a discussion of the national budget this way: "Over here, in this corner, you see a basket of mail. This is a portion of one day's mail at the White House. We've been averaging over 3000 letters a day in an average week—heavy weeks it's more. Now from the whole mass, I'm going to read to you just part of one letter to show you what one citizen in our country is thinking about and it's sort of a challenging letter..." *New York Times,* June 4, 1953, 24:2.

24. Miss Stiles, who was responsible for a good many of these briefs says the excerpts were chosen at her discretion. However, when the "con" mail grew bitter, she did not spare the President excerpts of that type.

25. Rosenman, Samuel I., *Working with Roosevelt,* New York: Harper and Bros., 1952, pp. 166–167.

26. *Ibid.*, pp. 195–198.

27. This was a rare instance when the mail was not answered at once, since it was decided that any reply at all would be interpreted by the press as encouragement. After FDR was nominated, the accumulated Third Term mail was answered with a form. Lela Stiles, interview cited.

28. During this period, the President was getting a similar picture of opinion among his supporters from the polls. Much more interesting would be a case where the press, the polls and the White House mail presented him with contradictory pictures of public opinion. The fight over the Supreme Court Reorganization Plan appears to have been such a case but it cannot be discussed here for lack of space.

29. Howe, Louis, "The President's Mailbag!", *The American Magazine,* June 1934, p. 23, italics supplied.

30. *The New York Times,* May 1, 1938, IV, 7:3.

31. Freidel, Frank, *Franklin D. Roosevelt: The Ordeal,* Little Brown and Co., 1954, pp. 207–208.

32. Perkins, Frances, *The Roosevelt I Knew,* Viking Press, 1946, p. 352.

33. Cf. *Public Opinion, 1935–1946,* edited by Hadley Cantril and Mildred Strunk, Princeton Univ. Press, 1951, p. 703.

34. Mr. Hopkins says it is his impression that Roosevelt received more mail from people of low status than Hoover, Truman or Eisenhower. Interview cited.

35. Howe, *op. cit.,* p. 23.

36. Stories of how a family was "saved" by the New Deal are a very common type of letter in FDR's 1940 campaign mail; a content analysis of this mail is being made by the author.

37. Lubell, Samuel, *The Future of American Politics,* New York: Harper and Bros., 1951, p. 54.

38. Howe, *op. cit.,* p. 23.

39. Tully, Grace, *FDR—My Boss,* New York: Charles Scribbners Sons, 1949, p. 82.

40. Rosenman, *op. cit.,* p. 39. These talks were the original fireside chats, as Rosenman notes.

41. *Ibid.,* p. 170.

42. *Ibid.,* p. 428.

43. *New York Times,* March 3, 1935, V, 12:1.

44. High, Stanley, *Roosevelt—And Then?,* New York: Harper and Bros., 1937, p. 87.

45. *New York Times,* Jan. 21, 1934, IX, 2:7.

46. High, *op. cit.,* p. 87.

47. *Ibid.*

48. FDR to Ralph W. Farrell, Democratic National Committee Campaign Correspondence, 1928–33, the Franklin D. Roosevelt Library.

57

Notes on a Natural History of Fads

From *American Journal of Sociology* (1957)[1]

Rolf Meyersohn and Elihu Katz

Rolf Meyersohn (1926–) is a neglected but interesting figure in the history of the field. His research style draws on several traditions. Born in Germany, he moved to the United States in 1938. He studied and taught in most of the key centers of mass communication in the postwar period: at Harvard (1946–1949, with Samuel Stouffer while he was working on *The American Soldier*); at Columbia (1949–1955, with Lazarsfeld, Merton, and Herbert Hyman); at Chicago (1955–1959, with David Riesman and the Committee for Communication); at Frankfurt's Institute for Social Research (1960–1961, with Horkheimer and Adorno, and where he became close friends with Jurgen Habermas); at the University of Pennsylvania's Annenberg School (1965–1967, hired by George Gerbner); and at Birmingham's Centre for Contemporary Cultural Studies (1967–1968, with Richard Hoggart and Stuart Hall). Meyersohn wrote a number of fine articles on television and leisure, as well as suggestive essays that brought American sociology into conversation with British cultural studies (see Meyersohn 1969).

"Notes on a Natural History of Fads" is a gem. It came out of a course co-taught by Meyersohn, Katz, and David Riesman and brings together Columbia and Chicago school approaches. It is at once a succinct interpretation of popular music and fashion in the mid-1950s and a precursor to today's studies of styles and subcultures. Drawing on Georg Simmel's essay on fashion, Meyersohn and Katz consider, among other things, the flow of music from African American cultures into the broad popular realm, the role of gay men in setting standards of taste, and the nature of fashion leadership in hog breeding. For Katz's biography, see page 358.

The study of fads and fashions[2] may serve the student of social change much as the study of fruit flies has served geneticists: neither the sociologist nor the geneticist has to wait long for a new generation to arrive.

Fads provide an extraordinary opportunity to study processes of influence or contagion, or innovative and cyclical behavior, and of leadership; this has been long recognized by social thinkers, most of whom tended, however, to regard fads and fashions as one form of permanent social change.[3]

To regard change in fads exclusively as a prototype of social change is to overlook several fundamental distinctions. In the first place, the process by which fads operate is typically confined to particular subgroups in society, and, although fads may change violently and swiftly, the subgroup remains the same; the network of fad communication usually remains stable. On the other hand, patterns of communication that create new social movements—for example, a new religious sect— also create a new social structure; here both the content and the network of communication are new. This distinction is well made by Blumer, who points out that social movements, unlike fads, usually leave stable organizations in their wake:

> Not only is the fashion movement unique in terms of its character, but it differs from other movements in that it does not develop into a society. It does not build up a social organization; it does not develop a division of labor among its participants with each being assigned a given status: it does not construct a new set of symbols, myths, values, philosophy, or set of practices, and in this sense does not form a culture; and finally, it does not develop a set of loyalties or form a we-consciousness.[4]

Popular music illustrates this distinction.[5] Every few months a new "content" in the form of new hits flows through the same "network" of distributors (disk jockeys, etc.) and consumers (primarily teen-agers and other radio audiences).

While an occasional song may attract some distributors or consumers who are not regularly a part of the system—for example, the recently popular song "Morität" from Brecht and Weill's *Threepenny Opera* found high-brow listeners outside the regular music audience—these stray elements usually get out as quickly as they came in. The popular music world as a whole remains unchanged and goes on as before to produce its continuous cycle of discontinuous hits.

Each new fad is a *functional alternative* for its predecessor: this hit for that hit, this parlor game for that one. On the other hand, the processes involved in broader social changes, such as religious conversions, and increase in the birth rate, or a movement toward suburban living, are too complex to permit simple substitution. Following Merton, who, in arguing against the functional indispensability of a social structure, points out that the range of possible variation is more relevant,[6] one may say that in fashion the range of functional alternatives is far greater than in other domains of social change.

Perhaps this is so because fashions are found in relatively superficial areas of human conduct—in the trivial or ornamental. Many more changes have occurred in the styling of automobiles (e.g., in the length of tail lights) than in their engines.[7] In a brilliant essay on fashion Simmel discusses the selective process whereby some cultural items are subject to fashion and others not, and he points out that the former must be "independent of the vital motives of human action."

> Fashion occasionally will accept objectively determined subjects such as religious faith, scientific interests, even socialism and individualism; but it does not become operative as fashion until these subjects can be considered independent of the deeper human motives from which they have risen. For this reason the rule of fashion becomes in such fields unendurable. We therefore see that there is good reason why externals—clothing, social conduct, amusements—constitute the specific field of

fashion, for here no dependence is placed on really vital motives of human action.[8]

Triviality, of course, does not refer to the amount of emotion, affect, and functional significance surrounding an object, but rather to its life-expectancy, its susceptibility to being *outmoded*. Every object has a finite and estimable life-span; a pair of nylon stockings may last a few weeks, a dress a few years, an automobile a decade or two, a house much longer. It is one of the characteristics of fashion that replacement is made before the life-span ends. Such objects are acquired without regard for their durability. This is one definition of "conspicuous consumption."

Hence we arrive at one possible indication whether an item is a carrier of fashion. Simmel has illustrated this point very well:

When we furnish a house these days, intending the articles to last a quarter of a century, we invariably invest in furniture designed according to the very latest patterns and do not even consider articles in vogue two years before. Yet it is obvious that the attraction of fashion will desert the present article just as it left the earlier one, and satisfaction or dissatisfaction with both forms is determined by other material criteria. A peculiar psychological process seems to be at work here in addition to the mere bias of the moment. Some fashion always exists and fashion per se is indeed immortal, which fact seems to affect in some manner or other each of its manifestations, although the very nature of each individual fashion stamps it as being transitory. The fact that change itself does not change, in this instance endows each of the objects which it affects with a psychological appearance of duration.[9]

Since most fads are of a minority or subculture, they may of course exhibit contradictory or countervailing trends all at once. While the fashion system as a whole may rely on an incompleted life-span for a part of its *élan*, certain subsystems of fashions operate in the opposite way. Thus, the trend today may be to trade in perfectly usable automobiles; yet there are those who drive nothing but antique automobiles. Such people attempt to *exceed* the structural limits of this particular item, and their possessions are as much a part of the fashion system as the latest, newest, the "most unique."[10]

Several approaches to the study of fads can be distinguished. One is concerned with the function of fashion generally for society, groups, and individuals. There has been considerable interest in the question why one group rather than another is the carrier of certain fashions; for example, in most societies women are the agents of fashion in clothes, though occasionally, and particularly in deviant societies, it is the men. Simmel relates this to the presence or absence of a class system and/or the need to call attention to one.[11]

Fashions have also been examined in terms of their specific content, and many attempts have been made to relate a particular trend, style, or motif to a *Zeitgeist*, a "climate of opinion," or an ideology. The unit under examination is a particular rather than a general fashion, as, for example, in the area of dress, in which a great many attempts have been made to relate style to *Zeitgeist*. Flügel has recorded a number of such connections, such as the shift after the French Revolution from clothes as display of ornament to clothes as display of body—which he attributed to the naturalism of the period.[12]

A third approach to fashion deals not with the content of fashions but with the network of people involved. A fashion "system" may be seen in the interaction among producers, distributors, and consumers, which works as the spiral-like circuit. Studies have been made, on the one hand, of the several "relay stations," the producers of fashions (such as the designers, the "tastemakers"), and the media that serve them. On the other hand, there has been research on the economics of fashion and on the channels of information and advice that impinge on consumer decisions,[13] attention usually focusing on individual choices or "effects" without emphasizing the flow from the mass media to groups and, within groups, from person to person. The latter can be done only by beginning with a specific fashion, A or B, tracing its diffusion, as in a fluoroscopic examination, from one consumer to the next.

A fourth approach to the study of fashions, one which differs from the three cited above, though it operates within their orbits, seeks to determine the origin of a given item, the conditions of acceptance by the first participants (the "innovators"), the characteristics of those whom the innovators influence, the shifts from minority to majority acceptance, its waning, and where it goes to die. This is its natural history. The natural history of any phenomenon which is ephemeral and which comprises a specific content (e.g., popular music) with its particular network (e.g., the flow from song writers to publishing companies to record companies to disk jockeys to teenagers, to juke-box listeners, etc.) can obviously be studied. It is based on the premise that different *stages* of a fad can be isolated and studied. In the past this premise has been used in studies of crowds, race riots, lynching mobs, and even political movements, all of which have been described in terms of discrete evolutionary steps, isolated according to their patterns of person-to-person interaction.[14] Each stage, furthermore, has been described as paving the way for the next stage.

Fads and fashions, too, have been subjected to such analysis. Almost every textbook in social psychology points out how aspirants to social mobility continually try to pre-empt the symbols of higher status, thereby forcing their former holders to search ever for replacements. This is how the story of fashions, and sometimes of all consumer purchasing, is usually told.[15] While it is certainly likely that one function of fashion is in the display of social ascent and that one network for its transmission is from the upper classes downward, the extent to which this traditional view of fashion remains valid cannot be told without refined empirical study—without tracing the diffusion of particular fads and fashions in time and through their relevant social structures.

In the continuing absence of such refined empirical data, this paper presents on the basis of crude observations some notes on the stages in the natural history of any fad; beginning at the point where some change has just begun to occur, it traces very roughly the fad's probable course.

Fads are not born but rediscovered. Where do new fads come from? In many instances they have existed all along but not as fads. For example, in the past several years, a large number of songs that went under the collective title of "Rhythm and Blues" rose to the top of the "hit parade." Now these songs and this type of music were not new. The music industry had known about them for many years, largely under the title "race records." They had been produced for consumption by a Negro audience, a number of small record companies and publishers devoting themselves almost exclusively to this market. Trade journals carried separate ratings for such music, ranking

each new song according to its popularity within this special category.

Then, all of a sudden, "rhythm and blues" songs invaded the general market, and "feedback points" (including the disk jockeys, fan clubs, listings of sheet-music sales, record sales, juke-box sales, etc.) all began to indicate a new trend.[16] This particular new trend had existed for a good long time but in a different audience. It had been a little pocket in the music world as a whole which sustained it not as a fashion but as a "custom." What happened was that minority music was becoming majority music.

These minority social systems seem to feed many kinds of fashions to the majority. This is true not only of racial groups: the word "minority" is here used in the sense of engaging only a small segment of the population. Some "minorities" are more likely to be fashion-feeders, of course; the classic view of fashion assumes that a minority either in the upper classes or tangential to them engages in certain choices, and these are then "discovered" and made fashionable by lower strata.

This process exists in a variety of fields. The hog-breeding industry, for example, has cyclical trends, and in time a number of "dimensions" of hogs are altered in the prize-winning or champion hogs. Hogs may be well larded or have relatively long legs—results produced by variations in breeding. Some hog-breeders seem to ignore the going fashion, but most of them breed "what the public wants," making appropriate annual changes in breeding. But every once in a while the mantle of fashion descends on one of the ignorers of fashion; he becomes the fashion leader, and his hogs set the style.[17]

In areas of life where "new" products are in demand or vital to the continuation of the industry, such "discoveries" are clearly more frequent. Since fashions serve a symbolic function and must be recognized in order to be transmitted, their greatest motility is likely to be found in those areas which are most visible. Thus, changes in dress are likely to be more frequent than in underclothes. Furthermore, the search for something new—what Simmel has called "exceptional, bizarre, or conspicuous"[18]—will be greater there.

In the popular-music industry, where such a search is conducted on a monthly basis, the life-span of a "hit" being approximately that long, new discoveries are essential. Hence, every pocket of the musical world is sooner or later "discovered." "Rhythm and blues" is one of many such pockets, if more successful than some of the others; for a time African songs were hits; South American music has followed this pattern; hillbilly music show the same trend; even classical music was "discovered" when suddenly the first movement of a Tchaikovsky piano concerto exploded all over America.

Minorities not only provide material to majorities but are also an integral part of the total system. Not only do they offer a pretest—"If it goes well in Tangiers, maybe it has a chance here!"—but they are also a shelf and shelter for dangerous or threatening ideas. Mark Benney suggests that bohemias serve this function. For urban societies their bohemias are a kind of social laboratory. Here something new can be tried out—because it is expected—without threatening either the bohemian minority or the urban population as a whole. The city watches, Benney suggests, and confers respectability on what it likes. Wrought-iron furniture, Japanese scrolls, charcoal gray flannel suits, not to mention new literary forms and ideological movements, have indeed been bred in these quarters.

The tastemakers. While the community, the music industry, or the clothing world as a whole may watch and wait for new ideas in many places, the task of scouting seems to fall to one particular set of people. By the nature of their tasks, they must be intimately acquainted with two worlds, the majority and the minority. Fashions, for instance, are often transmitted by the homosexual element in the population or by others who have entrée into different realms, Proustian characters who share the values of several groups.

A good example in the popular-music industry is the success of the current artist and repertoire director (the "A&R Man") at Columbia Records, Mitch Miller. A concert oboist himself, he was thoroughly trained as a serious musician. With an established reputation and a semibohemian personality which manifests itself in harmless ways such as the wearing of a beard and keeping odd hours, he has been able to utilize good judgment in the popular-music world not only by being better educated but by having a far broader range of minorities to draw on for inspiration. Thus he is familiar with the attributes of French horns and harpsichords, with echo chambers and goat bells, and has been able to use all to full advantage. One

reason for his using esoteric "effects" is that in the music industry any popular hit is immediately copied, but his arrangements have been made so complex by the use of such "gimmicks"—as the music industry calls them—that imitation is very difficult. In addition of course, the gimmicks have given Columbia Records a unique reputation.[19]

In any case, certain individuals in society are equipped to scout for new ideas and products to feed the various fashion systems. What is perhaps more important is to examine the fate of the original producer of the particular minority "custom" once it has been "exported" and translated into a fashion.

The exporter becomes self-conscious. At some time in the past Parisian clothes were "discovered" and made fashionable throughout "society" in other countries. Before that, undoubtedly, a stable relationship existed between the Paris *couturières* and their customers, and designs were made with a very particular "audience" in mind. In the course of "discovering" these designs, one element which probably attracted the early innovators was precisely the product which emerged from this relationship. But, once discovered, what happened? As Simmel said, "Paris modes are frequently created with the sole intention of setting a fashion elsewhere."[20] The exporter becomes self-conscious, tries to appeal to his wider circle of customers, and *changes* the product. Another well-known example is found in oriental porcelain. In the nineteenth century, European art collectors "discovered" Chinese and Japanese pottery, and in a very short time the potters began manufacturing "export ware," creating an industry quite separate from the production of domestic "china." Another example is the shift from the 1954 to the 1955 MG car; the most popular British car in this country, the MG had been designed in a somewhat old-fashioned way, with a square hood; but recently the British Motor Company decided to build it more along the lines of the latest American styles.

There are, of course, some occasions when the exporter does not become self-conscious. This would be most true where there is no return for more: composers who work folk songs into concert music, like Mozart, Beethoven, and Béla Bartók, do not affect the folk "producers."

What happens to the original consumers is not clear. Those who find their own customs—pizza or Yiddish melodies or canasta—becoming widely popular undoubtedly enjoy some sense of pride as well as mixed feelings about the inevitable distortions and perhaps yield to the temptation to make some accommodation from then on in the hope of being "picked up " once again.

Statistical versus real fashions: A case of pluralistic ignorance. Who can say that something is a fashion? Who knows about it? It may happen that a number of people in various parts of this country, for a variety of reasons, will all buy a certain item. They may all "go in" for "rhythm and blues" music or good musical sound reproduction or raccoon-skin caps, all unaware that others are doing the same thing.

Such situations, in which no one realizes that others are doing the same thing, probably occur all the time. They are similar to what social psychologists have called "pluralistic ignorance," a state in which nobody knows that others maintain an attitude or belief identical with their own.[21] If this coincidence persists long enough, however, the point will be reached at which one cannot help noticing the unself-conscious "inner-directed" activity of large numbers of people in making identical choices.[22] At this point the phenomenon which had been statistical becomes a real fad; here another important stage is reached—the labeling of a fad.

The label and the coattail. The birth of a fad is really accompanied by two labels; the phenomenon is given a name, and it is named as a fad. The fad is defined as real and in consequence becomes so.

Such a definition, however, must be made not only real but public. It must be translated from the specialized professional, business, or trade vocabulary into more popular terms—in short, into a label or a slogan.

While there are certainly plenty of labels which do not represent fads, there are no unlabeled fads or fashions. It is usually through the label that the fashion acquires fame—even beyond its consumer audience. Thus the "New Look," "hi-fi" "motivation research," "automation," and "charcoal gray."

The ground swell immediately after the labeling is caused partly by the activities of indirectly related enterprises. Machines that yesterday were ordinary phonographs and radios are suddenly called "hi-fi"; coonskin headgear becomes Davy Crockett caps; a lever makes of an industrial machine "automation"; an ordinary open-ended question converts a public opinion survey into "motivation research."

Thus the coattails which dress the fashion. Although the original minorities—whether devotees of recordings of high quality and accurate sound reproduction or Negroes who have been hearing certain kinds of "pop" music for years—may not recognize the $29.95 portable radio as "hi-fi" or the ordinary hit of the week as "rhythm and blues," the respective producers have found something that "works," and every commodity within labeling distance has a chance to be included.

The flow. Where the various fashions find their victims depends on their specific nature. Beginning in the minority, the fad is "discovered," then is labeled, and ultimately reaches the mass audiences. In the case of clothing, there is sometimes a stage, mentioned by Simmel and later by contemporary social psychologists and sociologists, which precedes or accompanies the labeling process, when the fashion is adopted by a group of acknowledged respectability. The fashion is perhaps borrowed from a fringe group within the society, or even outside it, and touted as an "esoteric" discovery. But in a society such as ours very little can be kept private, and providing clues to "better living," tips on the stock market, and advice on clothing, furniture, and virtually every other artifact is the professional job of all the media of communication. Thus, a product associated with a respected group or class is likely to spread, through being publicized, to other groups as well. From here it moves to groups which aspire to be like the advocates. These are not necessarily lower in status, although often so described. It may be that the lower group innovates—as in the "do-it-yourself" fad, a phenomenon which all farmers and lower-income groups have been aware of all their lives—but it is more likely to be a somewhat esoteric group, as the bohemians who flocked to New York's Greenwich Village after World War I, followed by the middle-class New Yorkers after World War II.

Regardless of the direction of the flow, for a time the original possessors of a fashion-to-be will maintain the fashion for themselves and their kind, for people of the same social status are more likely to hear about people of their own level, especially in the upper classes. But after a time the innovation will cross the boundary line of the groups who adopted it and pass into other groups, in the process losing some of its distinguishing characteristics.

The old drives in the new. The story of fads is, then, one of constant change. And the changes themselves do not change, or at least not so much that they cannot be followed.

The process of change occurs necessarily at every point, leaving, as it were, a vacuum when the fashion departs for its next point. Eventually, the vacuum is filled, even to overflowing, by its successor. When a fad has reached full bloom, its distinguishing features become so blurred that some are totally lost. If everything is called "hi-fi," nothing is high-fidelity. Furthermore, if more than just certain classes are *aficionados,* the self-conscious among the class-conscious will want something new for themselves.

Thus, at some point before a dress design hits the Sears-Roebuck catalogue, a sports car the secondhand automobile dealer, and a modern chair the suburban rummage sale, once again it is time for a change.

The feedback.[23] Producers notoriously see an undifferentiated audience before their eyes. They tend so often just to count that they miscalculate demand.

William McPhee and James Coleman have suggested that, while one group may be oversaturated with a fad, another may be very receptive—and only accurate reporting (feedback) about each group can tell the whole story.[24] For example, since teen-agers are the major purchasers of records and sheet music and the major investors in juke boxes and since these three commodities are the major tests of demand consulted by the producers, teen-agers can make or break a song. Disk jockeys also play a role in feedback, but it is primarily the "top" jockeys with the large teenage followings who are the key informants. Yet there is another audience for popular music to whom the producers have almost no access—the daytime radio listeners; the housewives, traveling salesmen, commuters. Their tastes are thus inferred—of all places—from teen-agers!

In other words, the skewed feedback of the music industry is responsible in part for the volatility of its fads; exaggerating as it does the tastes of an already erratic group considered as its primary audience, its fads fluctuate beyond all expectation. With perfect information, a normal distribution of tastes can be expected at most times and for most things. In certain industries, and among certain subgroups, the distribution is less likely to be normal, in part due to the pressures for new commodities, to the superficiality of the appeals themselves, to the publicity accompanying every product, and, in the case of teen-agers, to their unstable moods. When information comes only or largely from teen-agers, who are at the fringes of the distribution curve, so to speak, then the music industry is rendered excessively phrenetic. Kurt and Gladys Lang, in studying the Chicago MacArthur Day parade of 1951, found that the television reporting of this rather slow-moving and dull event was systematically distorted to give the impression of a vast crowd, a glorious spectacle, and an unremitting enthusiasm.[25] Here, as in the case of the popular-music industry, the requirements to hold an audience from switching to another station or channel or losing interest in popular music or a given song force such emphasis on the manic.

Hence, while the feedback from consumer to producer makes, at first, for a frenzied increase in a fashionable product, it may also make for a more rapid saturation than is warranted or, if the gauge is placed somewhere else in society, for an oversupply.

Notes

1. This is a publication of the Center for the Study of Leisure of the University of Chicago which is supported by a grant from the Behavioral Sciences Division of the Ford Foundation. Some of the ideas presented in this paper were formulated several years ago in discussions with colleagues then at the Bureau of Applied Social Research, Columbia University, notably James Coleman, Philip Ennis, William McPhee, Herbert Menzel, and David Sills. We are also grateful to David Riesman and Mark Benney, both at the University of Chicago, for critical comments.

2. We choose to ignore the distinction between the two concepts made by previous writers and perhaps most clearly stated by Sapir, who regarded fads as involving fewer people and as more personal and of shorter duration than fashions. He described a fad, furthermore, as "something unexpected, irresponsible or bizarre and socially disapproved (cf. Edward Sapir, "Fashion," *Encyclopaedia of the Social Sciences*

[New York: Macmillan Co., 1937], III, 139-44). We apply both terms to transitory phenomena that involve a large number of people or a large proportion of members of a subculture.

3. The long-standing interest among social thinkers in fads and fashions is seen, for example, in Tarde, who contrasted fashion with custom and showed that the transformation of tradition and custom is made possible by the form of imitation known as fashion (see Gabriel Tarde *The Laws of Imitation* [New York: Henry Holt & Co., 1903], chap. vii). Sumner regarded a large array of human activities, beliefs, and artifacts as fashions and considered them essential determinants of the *Zeitgeist* (see William Graham Sumner, *Folkways* [Boston: Ginn & Co., 1907], esp. pp. 194-220). Park and Burgess treated fashion as a form of social contagion and as one of the fundamental ways in which permanent social change is brought about (see Robert E. Park and Ernest W. Burgess, *Introduction to the Science of Sociology* [Chicago: University of Chicago Press, 1924], chap. xiii).

4. Herbert Blumer, "Social Movements," in *New Outline of the Principles of Sociology,* ed. A.M. Lee (New York: Barnes & Noble, 1946), pp. 217–18. While fashions do not create social organizations, there is some evidence that a new set of symbols, myths, etc., is apparently often built up in the course of a fashion movement. "Bop talk," for example, could be considered a language built up by the participants of the "bop" fad, and, although extrinsic to the music itself, it nevertheless contributed to "we-consciousness."

5. Examples in this paper which deal with popular music are based in part on the general conclusions of an unpublished study of disk jockeys carried out at the Bureau of Applied Social Research by William McPhee, Philip Ennis, and Rolf Meyersohn.

6. Robert K. Merton, *Social Theory and Social Structure* (Glencoe, Ill.: Free Press, 1949), p. 52.

7. Eric Larrabee and David Riesman, "Autos in America: Manifest and Latent Destiny," in *Consumer Behavior,* Vol. III, ed. Lincoln H. Clark (New York: New York University Press). (In press.)

8. Georg Simmel, "Fashion," *International Quarterly,* X (October, 1904), 135. Reprinted in this issue, p. 544.

9. *Op. cit.,* p. 152. Cf. p. 556 in this issue.

10. It is to such countervailing minority movements that Sapir applies the word "fad." "A taste which asserts itself in spite of fashion and which may therefore be suspected of having something obsessive about it may be referred to as an individual fad" (*op. cit.,* p.139).

11. *Op. cit.,* pp. 130–55. Cf. pp. 541–58 in this issue. See also Talcott Parsons, "An Analytical Approach to the Theory of Social Stratification," reprinted in *Essays in Sociological Theory Pure and Applied* (Glencoe, Ill.: Free press, 1949), pp. 166–84; cf. Bernard Barber and Lyle S. Lobel, "'Fashion' in Women's Clothes and the American Social System," in *Class, Status and Power,* ed. Reinhard Bendix and Seymour M. Lipset (Glencoe, Ill.: Free Press, 1953), pp. 323–32. For an interesting historical discussion relating manners to milieu see Harold Nicolson, *Good Behaviour* (London: Constable & Co., Ltd., 1955).

12. J.C. Flügel, *The Psychology of Clothes* (London: Hogarth Press, 1930), chap. vii.

13. See, e.g., Elihu Katz and Paul F. Lazarsfeld, *Personal Influence* (Glencoe, Ill.: Free Press, 1956).

14. E.g., Blumer enumerated the stages of crowd behavior as follows: from "milling" to "collective excitement" to "social contagion" (*op. cit.,* p. 202).

15. The following may be a typical account: "In recent years status objects of a technical kind have appeared in the home, such as washing, cleaning and polishing machines, and elaborate heating and cooking apparatus. In the United States appliances to provide an artificial climate in the home are the latest in a series of status-conferring devices" (Dennis Chapman, *The Family, the Home and Social Status* [London: Routledge & Kegan Paul, 1955], p.23). A discussion of the importance of fads in television sets may be found in Rolf Meyersohn, "Social Research in Television," in *Mass Culture,* ed. Bernard Rosenberg and David Manning White (Glencoe, Ill.: Free Press, 1957).

16. New trends are reported at least once a week. The uncertainty of prediction in combination with the fact that financial investments are made on the basis of such prediction bring it about that any and all shifts and flutters are exaggerated, and large-scale predictions are made for each and every one of them. This is of course true of all businesses, but many of them (e.g., the stock market) are kept from excesses by various control agencies (e.g., the Securities and Exchange Commission).

17. This example draws on material presented in a term paper dealing with fashions in hog-raising, by Samuel R. Guard, graduate student, Committee on Communications, the University of Chicago.

18. *Op. cit.*, p. 136. Cf. p. 545 in this issue.

19. In a recent essay on jazz and popular music, Adorno argued that its various forms, whether they be called "swing" or "bebop," are identical in all essential respects and distinguishable by only a few trivial variations, formulas, and clichés. He considers jazz a timeless and changeless fashion (Theodor Adorno, "Zeitlose Mode: Zum Jazz," *Prismen: Kulturkritik und Gesellschaft* [Frankfurt: Suhrkamp Verlag, 1955] pp. 144–61).

20. *Op. cit.*, p. 136. Cf. p. 545 in this issue.

21. Cf. Floyd H. Allport, *Social Psychology* (Boston: Houghton Mifflin Co., 1924).

22. An amusing portrayal of the consequences of large masses of people doing the same thing at the same time, such as crossing the George Washington Bridge on a Thursday afternoon, may be found in Robert Coates's short story, "The Law," a description of the law of averages and what might happen to it some day.

23. This word itself has become something of a fad!

24. "Mass Dynamics" (an unpublished research proposal on file at the Bureau of Applied Social Research, Columbia University).

25. "The Unique Perspective of Television," *American Sociological Review,* XVIII (February, 1953), 3–12.

58

Mass Communication and Socio-cultural Integration

From *Social Forces* (1958)[1]

Warren Breed

Warren Breed (1915–1999) was born in San Francisco, took his bachelor's degree at Stanford University, worked at the Bureau of Applied Social Research (including doing a study using focused interviews of newspapers in Harrisburg, Pennsylvania), and received his doctorate in sociology from Columbia in 1952 with a dissertation entitled "The Newspaperman, News, and Society." He is a somewhat neglected figure in the history of the field who wrote several smart and important articles on both the inner workings and the larger social significance of the news media in the 1950s, while he was teaching sociology at Tulane University. He had long-standing research interests on social problems such as suicide, and later in life he engaged in research on alcoholism as a member of the Institute for Scientific Analysis in San Francisco.

"Mass Communication and Socio-cultural Integration" (1958) shows a thoughtful mixture of grander social theory and ingenious research method. It also puts the reader at the heart of 1950s research on communication in communities. Using what he calls "reverse content analysis," Breed reviews the sociological literature about blocked communication in the community press—that is, he examines what cannot be said in the press. Strikingly like later cultural studies of how structured silences serve the interests of elites, Breed shows how systematic avoidance of certain topics in the press, such as a class and religion, serves the latent function of enforcing the status quo (cf. Lazarsfeld and Merton 1948, and p. 230 in this collection).

That a key problem facing any society is the maintenance of order and social cohesion has been the thesis of Durkheim, Weber, and many sociologists, especially the functionalists.[1] Not only is the division of labor and of roles necessary ("functional integration"), but also "normative integration"—consensus over a value system.[2] Should consensus fail, anomie is said to result, such as was found in Harlan County, Kentucky, following the sudden onset of industrialization, France in the 1930's, and Shanghai in 1948.[3]

Just which socio-cultural elements and combinations thereof will provide societal order, then, is a generic problem of great scope. The one independent variable to be analyzed here is the mass media, in cases which find the media facing the dilemma of publishing or not publishing material which may injure popular faith in the society or important parts of it. That controlled communication may promote order has been widely suggested, both in theoretical generalizations in empirical work. Speaking of divisive forces, E. C. Devereux has said, "Such head-on conflicts are prevented also by various barriers to communication embedded in the social structure; tabooed areas simply are not to be discussed, and hence the conflict need not be 'faced'."[4] In discussing cohesive factors in American society, Robin Williams said: "It is as if there is a tacit agreement not to express or to become aware of what would be dysfunctional. We greatly need careful research in this area, for observation already shows the existence of a mass of specific devices for thus suppressing disruptive elements. We suspect that a study of areas of blocked communication would often reveal conflicts that remain nondisabling only so long as they are kept from overt crystallization."[5]

One such study will be reported below. Many previous studies have touched on these "areas of blocked communication" or reflect on them by reporting what is *not* blocked. Thus functions of the media for aiding in the creation of a new consensus in societies undergoing urbanization are shown by Thomas and Znaniecki,[6] Redfield,[7] Helen M. Hughes,[8] and Tocqueville,[9] while Riesman[10] has compared these functions for his three "directedness" types of society.

These and other studies offer a picture of the latent functions of the media somewhat as follows: By expressing, dramatizing, and repeating cultural patterns, both the traditional and the newly emerging, the media reinforce tradition and at the same time explain new roles. Members of the society thus remain integrated within the sociocultural structure. As a form of adult socialization, the media are seen as guarantors that a body of common ultimate values remains visible as a continuing sources of consensus, despite the inroads of change.[11]

The maintenance of cultural consensus is most apparent in simpler societies, where folklore of a single ideology is dominant. For complex societies, the issue is as old as the argument between Plato and Aristotle over the functions of art for man and society, Plato taking the "functionalist" view for stability.[12] More recently, Wirth,[13] and Lazarsfeld and Merton[14] have asserted that the media maintain cultural consensus by reaffirming norms. Janowitz[15] found that Chicago weeklies maintain local consensus by emphasizing common values rather than attempting to solve "values-in-conflict" problems. Similarly, in studying the plots and audience of a daytime serial ("Big Sister"), Warner and Henry concluded that the primary social (as distinguished from psychological) function of the story "is to strengthen and stabilize the basic social structure of our society, the family."[16]

Putting the foregoing in a different way, Albrecht[17] has reviewed studies of literature (popular and classical alike) and classifies the imputed functions into three categories. There is the "reflection" hypothesis (literature reflects society); its converse is that literature "shapes" society with powerful influences. The third is the "social control" hypothesis, that literature maintains and stabilizes society. The latter is most closely under examination here.

Thus writers for years have held that the media serve certain societal and cultural purposes by bringing people into community relations and aiding their socialization into approved forms of behavior. The media have done this by "singing the praises" of vital cultural themes, according to these writers, in a *positive* recounting of the group's ideals.

Such findings are the result of conventional content analysis, which proceeds by studying a given content. The present study turned the question around: What is *not* printed or broadcast? The procedure was to compare newspaper content with another type of description of the American urban scene: the community study. Some eleven studies[18] were perused, and each time a statement was made which to the best of his knowledge the present writer believed would not be featured in that city's press, a note was made. In addition to this "reverse content analysis," data were gathered from other sources, including Dave Breger's book presenting cartoons rejected by popular publications,[19] and data gained in the writer's interviews with newspapermen. Thus two types of data are used: items from the eleven community studies which are believed would not be featured in the media, and cases of known suppression. It is acknowledged that one cannot give a statistical account of such negative and presumed items, but as compiled they present a pattern of regularity fitting a consistent theoretical construction.

"Mass media" is here used broadly, embracing most of the press, radio, television, motion pictures, popular magazines and songs. The "quality press," such as the *New York Times* and *Harper's,* which does not reach the mass, is not included. It is true that most intellectuals consider the media vulgar, trivial, commercial, and oversimplified. Regardless of the validity of this view, it is not pertinent here, the focus being on functions of the media for society.

To review the argument so far, other writers have said the media maintain socio-cultural consensus by precept through dramatizing proper behaviors. Our findings will indicate that they do this also by omission: they omit or bury items which might jeopardize the socio-cultural structure and man's faith in it. This is the hypothesis under investigation. To the extent that a hypothesis containing such global variables can indeed be tested, considerable supporting evidence was found.

Findings

The findings of the "reverse" content check, consisting of more than 250 items, clustered around central institutional areas. By far the most frequent finding focused around the politico-economic area, or more specifically, what we might call "the undemocratic power of business elites." Roughly two-thirds of the items presumably "buried" by the press were of this type. Religion ranked second, with about one-fifth of the total. The remaining notes were concerned with such areas as justice, health, and the family. (Here it should be said that shortly after the perusal of community studies started, the subject of the family was dropped, on the grounds that this is a clearly "private" area, of concern to the sociologist but to much less degree to the newspaper.) A discussion of the several "areas of protection" follows.

Business Elites

The most frequent item screened out of the press dealt with the politico-economic area. More specifically, the typical behavior involved an elite individual or group obtaining a privilege through non-democratic means. This implies two concepts crucial to sociology: power and class. Some examples (the citation and page are given for each case):

Propertied interests prevent tax increases, force low physical and educational standards at high school (E 121-47); Rotarians, with the aid of newspaper, control election to school board (E 123); city grade crossing project abandoned when manufacturers find it would disturb loading (M 488); power and light company owned by prominent men, remains smoke nuisance (M 489); X family buys land, city paves streets (MIT 350-51); banks manipulate wires behind scenes to keep smaller business elements in line (CC 448); businessmen, fearing rise in wages, discourage heavy industry from coming to town (DS 256, 337; M 419; MIT 80); employers insert anti-social security literature in pay envelopes (MIT 361-62); business leaders, promising an open shop to General Motors for bringing its plant back to city, get 50 per cent increase in police force, paid by taxpayers (MIT 35-39); chamber of commerce has power over community affairs, wielded by "contacts" and manipulation (CC 447); leading Democrat holds many mortgages and notes, thus his word on how to vote carries weight (Pvl 89); no sample ballots printed, reportedly for fear of decline in Republican straight-ticket voting (MIT 417-18); small gamblers arrested in "cleanup," large ones let alone (MIT 332-38; SCS 127); X family members hold some censorship power over books, teachers, and speakers at college and YMCA (MIT 83-85); advertising is frankly caveat emptor

(M 475); the press is discreet about manipulation behind the news (MIT 375). Such events need not happen frequently; once may be enough to acquaint the townspeople with the power structure.

More generally, other nondemocratic privileges were cited as follows: favoritism and unequal opportunity, descending by class rank and ethnic prestige—in jobs (M 50-52; MIT 67-73; E 362-74; Pvl 26-27; SCS 273; PT 460-63; DS 424-25 and *passim*; Mvl 341); in schools (M Part III; Mvl 341; E *passim*; YC 361-62; SCS 106); in treatment by police (PT 463; DS 510; YC 373; Mvl 195); in the courts (M 434; DS 510-13; YC 373, 427); in access to health care (M 137; PT 458); in opportunities for upward mobility (M 66-68; MIT 70-72; PT 455; CC 449; Pvl 134-41; E 272-73; DS chap. 8; YC *passim*). Perhaps the most striking fact is that the word "class" is almost entirely absent from the media.

These data suggest that when favors are granted to elite groups and individuals, mostly from the higher levels of business, little "news" results. Further data could be marshalled from many other sources, such as Floyd Hunter's study of the power-wielders in "Regional City"[20] and the several reports in Robert S. Allen's *Our Fair City.*[21]

Religion

Members: low attendance at services (SP 138, 152; Mvl 354; Pvl 142; M 358); extreme differentials in religious participation (SP 55, 68, 188-89); attitudes of skepticism and disbelief of members (Pvl 142; M 329); increasing nonreligious character of church meetings (Pvl 163; M 399-404); upper-class resentment at lower class membership in their church (PF 461).

Clergy: ministers express bitterness over obstacles to their work, shortage of rewards forthcoming (M 347, 350; Pvl 149, 163); ministers forced to play "good fellow" role (M 344); ministers frustrated in reaching out into the community (M 352-54).

Churches in the community: rivalry between churches, replacing earlier "union" spirit (M 333; Pvl 146); churches contributing less to civic charity works (Mvl 359; M 461-62; MIT 296; Pvl 147); churches ranked in hierarchy of class and wealth of church (YC 356-59; Pvl 134; M 402), undertaker sends expensive gifts to pastor at Christmas (SP 129); churches resist scientific training in agriculture and modernized school curricula (Pvl 163, 218).

Other data can be added. Religious cartoons banned for publication ranked third most infrequent in Breger's account; even such a serious film as "Androcles and the Lion" mutes Shaw's irreverence while stressing the boy-girl romance; almost every newspaper has a weekend section devoted to church activities, but religion—doctrine, faith, ritual—is seldom mentioned. It should be noted that religion is of double significance to social integration: it is not only a value in itself but it justifies and rationalizes other sentiments which bring order to a society.

The Family

Since most of the "unprinted news" items related to the categories of business and religion (and "family" items were not counted because of the unlikelihood of their becoming public and therefore news potential), data for the rest of the categories will be drawn from a variety of sources. That the family is an institution without which society would perish is reflected in the media. The most obvious datum is the withholding of the media's blessing to extra-marital sex relations. By far the largest category of unprinted cartoons in Breger's compilation (68 out of 183) dealt with adult sex. Moreover, editors of "slick" magazines, according to Simmons, consider the family "more sacred than church or country."[22] Mother as the "madonna" has long symbolized this sentiment.[23] One datum epitomizes the preferred treatment shown mother. A reporter told the writer how that same day he had covered a story about a baby undergoing an emergency operation. The mother he said, actually showed little concern for the baby, but "made eyes at the interns like she was auditioning for a movie." The baby died, but the story, written by this reporter, spoke of "the soft-voiced young mother, waiting quietly in a beside vigil, praying. ... " The operation for abortion, when performed under proper surgical conditions, has been shown to be safe, a finding reserved for scientific, not popular, publication.[24] Neither has birth control received a good press. The media stress virtues such as duty, obedience, and affection. A number of these conclusions are verified in studies by Warner and Henry, and Albrecht.[25]

Patriotism

Patriotism, or national ethnocentrism, is a value protected by the media. When an individual is accused of disloyalty, favorable discussion of him by the media is sharply checked. He cannot be dramatized as an individual or a leader, only as a "controversial" person under suspicion. The treatment given Dean Acheson is an extreme example. American soldiers overseas may violate norms involving persons and property for which they would be publicly punished in this country, but the press here minimizes overseas derelictions. In other countries, they are "representatives" of our nationality and thus in a quasi-sacred position.[26] United States complicity and intervention in the internal affairs of other countries is not stressed; the Guatemala "revolution" of 1954 is a good example. The media, when depicting history, glorify American deeds and heroes and minimize deviations. Wars are won in the media by courage and character, the role of technical strength being deemphasized. Finally, this value can be epitomized by the Unknown Soldier, to whom ultimate reverence is accorded.

The Community

A tendency toward "local ethnocentrism" or "civic pride" is also found in the media. The progress, growth, and achievements of a city are praised, the failures buried (just as on the national scene stock market gains are featured more than losses). A reporter told the writer that his city's community chest quota had not been reached for several years, but neither he nor any other reporter mentioned it. A southern reporter said he had been assigned to report on the progress of a new citrus venture nearby; he tried to praise the struggling farm, but could not justify it and the story was never printed. The "chamber of commerce attitude" is well exemplified in "Magic Middletown," where the papers carry "booster" pleas from civic clubs and officials such as "You must think that there is no finer town in the whole United States" (M 487). Much of this is caused by the desire for new industry, but not all: "Middletown wants inveterately to believe in itself, and it loses no opportunity to reaffirm its faith in itself" (MIT 433). And, "above all, Middletown people avoid questioning the assumed adequacy of the reigning system under which they live" (MIT 449). Studio audience participants on the air regularly boost their home town. The Hollywood film "Cover Up" surprisingly exemplified this pattern. A town's "meanest man" meets with violent death, and both the sheriff and an outside private detective discover he was murdered by the town's beloved old physician, who died quietly soon thereafter. The detective is persuaded by the sheriff and others to report suicide. The citizens were explicit about the town's need for the doctor as an exemplar of goodness—and besides, the decision to evade came at Christmas time!

Health and Doctors

Health is a vital matter, especially since some therapy is effected not so much by medicine and skill but by the patient's faith in the doctor. Since this faith performs positive functions, the maintenance of the physician's prestige by the media is a contribution. Several reporters have told the writer that physicians are almost never shown in a bad light by the press, and the treatment of doctors in other media such as daytime serials is often worshipful. A Mississippi reporter told how white ambulance drivers took an injured Negro boy to three hospitals late one night before a doctor would examine him, and the boy died at 5 a.m. The reporter wrote the whole story, but the doctors' derelictions were edited out. Suppose the boy had been white? "He probably would have gotten better attention, but I'd say from past experience that doctors are influential in keeping such things out of the paper." Nurses, too, are needed, and recruitment is spurred by glorifying, not mirroring, their role. Our perusal of community studies located two items relevant here: medical society condemns citizens' committee proposal for free out-patient clinic to reduce heavy medical relief costs (MIT 394-96); TB specialist needed, local doctors forbid outsider's entry (M 443).

Other Values

Justice is an undoubted value, particularly in times when courts are deciding between life and death and also on private business and public welfare. Judges are treated with respect by the media, even at times after serious criticism. The bitter criticism of the Supreme Court in 1957 was a marked reversal of form.

The dignity of the individual also seems respected in the media. Libel laws are certainly part of the explanation, in addition to criticism over the invasion of privacy. Media operators attempt "not to hurt anybody"; this was the first rule given the present writer by his first editor. Smalltown papers print "folksy" trivia, but as the Mineville editor pointed out, it was never malicious gossip (Mvl 180-81). Radio and TV commentators frequently offer the irrelevant but warming bouquet about a sports or entertainment celebrity that "he's a great guy." The exceptions are criminals, "characters," and "stuffed shirts." The latter are targets for Groucho Marx, who interestingly to the present thesis has called himself "America's laxative." When published gossip exceeds certain bounds, there is widespread indignation, as with certain columnists and "confidential" magazines.

Other "delicate" areas protected by the media doubtless exist. Newspapers in the South, for example, rarely refer to "white supremacy" or "Jim Crow," whereas northern papers may do so.[27] Other areas of value might include youth, ethnic groups, death, hard work, and certain aspects of education. Hollywood refers to this type of discretion as "licking."

Summarized, it appears that the media typically screen out such items as these: elite individuals or groups, usually business-based, gaining unfair advantage in a privileged, rather than democratic manner; shortcomings in religious behavior, such as lack of piety or respect by parishioners, discontent shown by the clergy, or "human weakness" in church relationships; doctors acting in selfish rather than professional fashion; anything calling into question national or community pride or integrity; shortcomings in mother, judge, or other institutions or unpleasant role deviations. This is a knotty list, making classification difficult. The list is not exhaustive and there certainly are exceptions in the various media, and changes over time.

Discussion

What, then, are the functions of the media for socio-cultural structure? Taking the "social" plane first, it appears that "power" and "class" as structural strata are protected by media performance. Business leaders, doctors, and judges stand high in class rank, and are among the groups which sometimes possess the power to utilize undemocratic means to their ends. This finding is no surprise, as critics have for centuries noted the disproportionate power of elites and the winking by the media at their actions.

Yet power and class are not the whole answer. Do mothers have "power," and overseas GIs, members of churches and the Unknown Soldier? It seems also that *cultural* patterns are likewise given protection by the media. Values

of capitalism, the home, religion, health, justice, the nation and the community are also "sacred cows." Furthermore, the disinclination of the media to talk about social class has a cultural as well as a social aspect: class, being social inequality, is the very antithesis of the American creed.

The media, then, withdraw from unnecessarily baring structural flaws in the working of the institutions. They are an insulating mechanism in the potential clash between two powerful modes of behavior, the normatively ideal way and the persistent pragmatic way.[28] The pattern presents a good fit to the theoretical statements of Devereux and Williams, cited above, as to the nature of "areas of blocked communication." Furthermore, the pattern appears to be a case of Merton's patterned (or institutionalized) evasion,[29] and is likewise related to what Linton and Kluckhohn have called "covert culture."[30]

At the level of community, the media are not only protecting particular "pressure" groups, as is well known, but are also protecting the community *from* particular groups with a disruptive purpose. As Davis[31] has pointed out, the community's ends are more ultimate than those of any constituent group within the community and it therefore must not be partial. Seen as organs of the community, rather than as spokesmen for a subgroup, the media are serving the end of unity.

The media are obviously not the only mechanism promoting consensus; one functional alternative is humor. Edmonson,[32] studying humor among Spanish-Americans of the Southwest, found strong inhibitions on jokes about certain subjects, such as religion, Hispanidad (the glorification of the Spanish tradition), and father and father-in-law (the kinship pattern is patriarchal). In the area of religion jokes were permitted about certain themes, such as religious duties and the saints, but no jokes were uncovered about core areas: the Eucharist, Good Friday, and the *Penitente* movement. While no detailed comparison of these findings with those concerning the media is possible here, they appear to be complementary.

Are media personnel aware that they are performing this function? Perhaps many are, but for present purposes the question is not relevant: subjective motivation and objective consequences need not be related.[33] It is probable that spokesmen for various institutions who do public relations work intensify the existing awareness of media personnel as to the importance of their respective institutions to the society.

The Media Point of View

Since we are studying media performance in relation to cultural values, it is well to consider the particular situation of the media to check on the validity of the comparison. The press will print a "delicate" item when it enters the public ken, as with most police and court records and formal statements or charges brought by a responsible group or individual (i.e., not a "crank"). The press, for instance, could not suppress the 1938 indictment and conviction of Richard Whitney. The news, however, tended to dissociate Whitney from investment bankers as a group, and he was made to seem an exception to the rule; news about other bankers implicated was not featured.[34] Television dramas occasionally portray a businessman as villain, but the focus is on individual morality, not the institution. Newspapers are inclined to print—but not feature—news of structural faults as contained in investigations of campaign financing, lobbying, concentration of economic power, etc.

What has been described as the withdrawal of the media from delicate subjects is typical, not mandatory, and many exceptions occur. Certain media at times broadcast themes which refute the hypothesis presented here (although such an "adult" medium may no longer be a "mass" medium). Functional analysis as used here tends to be static rather than dynamic and processual; it is admitted that many exceptions occur and that shifts of focus toward and away from a given elite or value occur in different periods. Such shifts could be documented elsewhere, but it remains that despite change and variety, certain patterns have been noted which show much constancy. It also appears that an exceptionally frank program like a Mike Wallace interview makes views uncomfortable; "the exception proves the rule" that public media do not challenge basic institutions by exploring flaws in the working of the institutions.

Thus the mass media have very different purposes and contents than the quality press, the protest press (organs of minority groups, etc.), and art. Art (like education) is free to criticize what it will, including institutions and values. Whether or not the consensus that is protected by media may be protecting "bad" as well as "good" values) and calls for further study on the socio-cultural, as well as the individual, plane. Some of the evasions may be arguable as responsible contributions to consensus, while others take the form of rationalizations for the derelictions of elites. One finds much to deplore in the media, but the latent functions claimed here should not continue to be overlooked by students of social integration.

Three Related Observations

1. Besides values and kinds of behavior, we have seen that certain specified individuals receive favorable treatment: doctors, business leaders, judges, mothers, clergymen, GIs overseas, etc. This leads to the proposition that leaders personify or embody the values related to their office.[35] Thus the media, in avoiding criticism of the incumbents, are again supporting the existing cultural structure. Contrariwise, should a leader's deviation become a public scandal, it is possible that a "domino effect" will endanger faith in the institution he represents as well. Whether people respond to such a failing in specific or diffuse ways is an empirical question; exploratory interviews suggest that both occur. For example, to such a "shattering" question as "What would you think if you discovered the Archbishop had a harem?" some respondents expressed shock about the individual only, others said they might question all religion, and one respondent pointed the way to anomie "If they can do it, everybody can." The Hollywood production code follows the diffuse theory: "The reason why ministers of religion may not be comic characters or villains is simply because the attitude taken toward them may easily become the attitude taken toward religion in general."[36]

2. The values of religion, as Durkheim said, are linked to *social processes* taking the form of ritual. Durkheim maintained that rituals, with their repeated, rhythmic, tangible form served to concretize and reinforce religious beliefs. While the analogy is far from perfect, it may be that the mass media also, by the repeated, patterned "ritual" of their dissemination—every month or week, day, hour, etc.—serve a similar function in the conservation of socio-cultural resources. One comes to expect a certain joke from Jack Benny, a "Tiny Tim" story at Christmas, a boy-gets-girl story in magazine and movie, etc. People may not so much "learn" from

the media as they become accustomed to a standardized ritual.[37]

3. In this sense of discretion, we can perceive a similarity between mass communication and personal communication. Tact, the use of the white lie, and the studied avoidance of stating unpleasant facts may be characteristic of all social (as distinguished from scientific) communication. Perfection is a severe model for human behavior, and the use of discretion enables the structure of relationships—however genuine—to survive in the face of strain. What Malinowski called "phatic communion"[38] can thus also be found in formal mass communications.

Notes

Expanded version of paper read at the 1956 meetings of the American Sociological Society. Gratitude is expressed to the Tulane University Council on Research for funds granted, and to William L. Kolb and David Riesman for a critical reading of an earlier draft.

1. See Kingsley Davis, *Human Society* (New York: Macmillan, 1949).

2. Ronald Freedman, Amos Hawley, Werner Landecker, and Horace Miner, *Principles of Sociology* (New York: Holt, 1952), chaps. 4, 5.

3. See P. F. Cressey, "Social Disorganization and Reorganization in Harlan County, Kentucky," *American Sociological Review,* 14 (June 1949), pp. 389–94; Georges Gurvitch, "Social Structure of Pre-War France," *American Journal of Sociology,* 48 (March 1943), pp. 535–54; Robert E. L. Faris, *Social Disorganization* (New York: Ronald, 1955), p. 65.

4. Edward C. Devereux, Some Notes on Structural-Functional Analysis (hectographed), pp. 3–4.

5. Robin M. Williams, Jr., *American Society* (New York: Knopf, 1951), p. 529.

6. W. I. Thomas and Florian Znaniecki, *The Polish Peasant* (New York: Knopf, 1927) II, 1367–96.

7. Robert Redfield, *Tepoztlan* (Chicago: University of Chicago Press, 1930) pp. 1–14.

8. Helen MacGill Hughes, *News and the Human Interest Story* (Chicago: University of Chicago Press, 1940).

9. Alexis de Tocqueville, *Democracy in America* (New York: Knopf, 1948), II, 111–14. For further comment relating the press to early American class structure, see "The American Press: I. How It Has Come into Being," *London Times Literary Supplement* (September 17, 1954), p. lxx.

10. David Riesman, *The Lonely Crowd* (New Haven: Yale University Press, 1950), chaps. 4, 9.

11. Davis has made a parallel statement with regard to the dangers of too much specialization, rationality, and emphasis on achievement, in education. *Op. cit.,* pp. 218–22.

12. See Herbert Weisinger, *Tragedy and the Paradox of the Fortunate Fall* (East Lansing: Michigan State College Press, 1953, pp. 238–73).

13. Louis Wirth, "Consensus and Mass Communication," *American Sociological Review,* 13 (February 1948), pp. 1–15.

14. Paul F. Lazarsfeld and Robert K. Merton, "Mass Communication, Popular Taste and Organized Social Action," in Lyman Bryson (ed.), *The Communication of Ideas* (New York: Harper, 1948), pp. 95–118.

15. Morris Janowitz, *The Community Press in an Urban Setting* (Glencoe: The Free Press, 1952).

16. W. Lloyd Warner and William E. Henry, "The Radio Day Time Serial: A Symbolic Analysis," *Genetic Psychology Monographs,* 37 (February 1948), pp. 3–71, esp. p. 64.

17. Milton C. Albrecht, "The Relationship of Literature and Society," *American Journal of Sociology,* LIX (March 1954), pp. 425–36.

18. The studies, with a code for each, were: A. B. Hollingshead, *Elmtown's Youth* (New York: Wiley, 1949), (E); R. S. and H. M. Lynd, *Middletown* (M) and *Middletown in Transition* (MIT) (New York: Harcourt, Brace, 1929, and 1937); W. L. Warner and P. S. Lunt, *The Social Life of a Modern Community* (New Haven: Yale University Press, 1941), (YC); A. Davis, *et al, Deep South* (Chicago: University of Chicago Press, 1941), (DS); W. F. Whyte, *Street Corner Society* (Chicago: University of Chicago Press, 1943), (SCS); James West, *Plainville, U.S.A.* (New York: Columbia University Press, 1945), (Pvl); Albert Blumenthal, *Small Town Stuff* (Chicago: University of Chicago Press, 1932), (Mvl); Joseph H. Fichter, *Southern Parish* (Chicago: University of Chicago Press, 1951), (SP); John Useem *el al,* "Stratification in a Prairie Town" (PT) and C. Wright Mills, "The Middle Classes in Middle-sized Cities" (CC), both in Logan Wilson and W. L. Kolb (eds.),

Sociological Analysis (New York: Harcourt, Brace, 1949).

19. Dave Breger (ed.), *But That's Unprintable* (New York: Bantam, 1955).

20. Floyd Hunter, *Community Power Structure* (Chapel Hill: University of North Carolina Press, 1953), esp. pp. 87–111, 183–89.

21. New York: Vanguard, 1947. For an exception to the pattern, see Dallas Smythe, "Reality as Presented on Television," *Public Opinion Quarterly*, 18 (Summer 1954), pp. 153–55.

22. Charles Simmons, *Plots That Sell To Top-Pay Magazines* (New York: Funk, 1952), p. 101.

23. Robert F. Winch, *The Modern Family* (New York: Holt, 1952), p. 378.

24. Edwin M. Schur, "Abortion and the Social System," *Social Problems*, 3 (October 1955), pp. 94–99.

25. Milton C. Albrecht, "Does Literature Reflect Common Values?" *American Sociological Review*, 21 (December 1956), pp. 722–29.

26. For some exceptions and discussion, see "The Soldier Reports," and a note by Dwight McDonald, in *Politics* (October 1945), pp. 294–95. The Girard Case in Japan was an outstanding exception.

27. Warren Breed, Comparative newspaper treatment of the Emmett Till Case, *Journalism Quarterly*, 35 (Summer 1958), pp. 291–98.

28. Ignorance as an incentive for continued conforming behavior is discussed in Wilbert E. Moore and Melvin M. Tumin, "Some Social Functions of Ignorance," *American Sociological Review*, 14 (December 1949), pp. 787–95.

29. Robert K. Merton, *Social Theory and Social Structure* (rev.; Glencoe: Free Press, 1957), pp. 343–45. See also Robin M. Williams, *op. cit.*, chap. 10, and Talcott Parsons and Edward A. Shils, *Toward a General Theory of Action* (Cambridge: Harvard University Press, 1951), pp. 174–75.

30. Clyde Kluckhohn, "Covert Culture and Administrative Problems, *American Anthropologist*, 45 (April–June 1943), pp. 213–27. He speaks of "the extraordinary convergence" on this topic, among Sumner, Chapin, Sapir, Sorokin, Warner, Pareto, Parsons, and Whitehead. He could add Merton, and also A. M. Lee ("facades").

31. Davis, *op. cit.*, p. 312.

32. Munro S. Edmonson, Los Manitos, dissertation, Harvard University, 1952. In a paper read at the 1958 meetings of the American Sociological Society, Peter B. Hammond cited anthropologists' interest in "The Functions of Indirection in Communication" such as joking, and suggested further leads. For an analysis of concealment of information, misrepresentation, impression management, symbols of ceremony and many other forms of inhibited communication, see Erving Goffman, *The Presentation of Self in Everyday Life* (Edinburgh: University of Edinburgh Social Sciences Research Center, 1956).

33. Merton, *op. cit.*, pp. 60–61.

34. See I. F. Stone, "Questions on the Whitney Case," *Nation*, 148 (January 14, 1939), pp. 55–58. There are obviously many exceptions and more subtlety than indicated here; see Irving Howe, "Notes on Mass Culture," in Bernard Rosenberg and David M. White (eds.), *Mass Culture* (Glencoe: Free Press, 1957) pp. 501–02.

35. See Orrin E. Klapp, "Heroes, Villains and Fools as Agents of Social Control," *American Sociological Review*, 19 (February 1954), pp. 56–62.

36. For an illuminating discussion of the conservative functions of the various media codes see Wilbur Schramm, *Responsibility in Mass Communication* (New York: Harper, 1957), p. 286 ff.

37. See Bernard Berelson, "What Missing the Newspaper Means," in Paul F. Lazarsfeld and Frank N. Stanton (eds.), *Communications Research 1948–1949* (New York: Harper, 1949), pp. 111–29.

38. Bronislaw Malinowski, in C. K. Ogden and I. A. Richards, *The Meaning of Meaning* (New York: Harcourt, Brace, 1936), pp. 315–16.

59

Modernizing Styles of Life: A Theory

From *The Passing of Traditional Society* (1958)

Daniel Lerner

Daniel Lerner (1918–1980) received all his degrees at New York University. He taught from 1947 to 1953 at Stanford University, where he was also associated with the Herbert Hoover Library, then one of the foremost anticommunist institutions and now still a formidable producer of conservative thought. He published *Sykewar* in 1949, a study of German war propaganda during the Second World War. After a visit to Columbia in 1952, he moved to the Massachusetts Institute of Technology, where he taught sociology and international communications for twenty-five years. Lerner represents Cold War social science at its most optimistic, and more particularly, he expresses the dominant strain of establishment thinking about communication in the late-1950s and 1960s—modernization theory. He was a longtime collaborator with Harold Lasswell. Lerner's *The Passing of Traditional Society: Modernizing the Middle East* (1958), was a landmark of the Cold War era that documented ways in which modern social life was seemingly displacing the ancient regime of tradition. Funded by the Voice of America's Leo Lowenthal, the Near East Study was based on a kind of high level market research conducted by Columbia's Bureau of Applied Social Research (BASR) in Egypt, Turkey, Syria, and other strategically significant states in the global geopolitics of the early 1950s. David Riesman, an ardent Cold Warrior himself, wrote the introduction to the book, which was a central statement of the ideology of development in communication research.

This selection is remarkable for its normative vision of what modernization is all about: for Lerner, it is not just infrastructural development, highways, and hydroelectric dams; rather, it is the development of a certain kind of personality, "a mobile sensibility," tolerant and empathetic, plural and open to the persuasions of new ideas—remarkably like the temperament of literate American or British liberals. This flavor is reinforced by the literary pretensions of the first chapter, a self-described "parable" on the Turkish village of Balgat and its loss of tradition before the force of modernity. Here Lerner occasionally lapses into a bit of Orientalist fantasy and offers melancholy reflections on the destruction of old ways of life by the sweep of modernity. The hubris of the modernization story is captured in an amazing moment in this excerpt: against "a rational and positivist spirit," Lerner approvingly quotes, "Islam is absolutely defenseless." The Iranian revolution of 1979, the Salman Rushdie fatwa, and the September 11 terrorist attacks suggest a very different view of the contours of modernity.

I am thankful that the good God created us all ignorant. I am glad that when we change His plan in this regard we have to do it at our own risk.

—Mark Twain

The United States is presiding at a general reorganization of the ways of living throughout the entire world.

—Andre Siegfried

The passing of Balgat is but an instance of the passing of traditional society in the Middle East. The modernizing of ancient lifeways involves many Tosuns and shepherds, many grocers and chiefs, many sons of chiefs. For the stakes of modernization, as Mark Twain suggests, are deep and personal. Secular enlightenment does not easily replace sacred revelation in the guidance of human affairs. Sacred codes, once revealed and transmitted through the shepherd, provide simple rules of conduct for all the flock—who can remain ignorant, or, more profoundly, innocent. But secular enlightenment each man must get for himself. Many individuals must struggle through the loss of ignorance-as-bliss in the making of a new secular "climate of opinion."

Western men need only reflect on the titanic struggles whereby, over the course of centuries, medieval lifeways were supplanted by modernity. Hindsight now summarizes these struggles as The Age of Exploration, The Renaissance, The Reformation, The Counter-Reformation, The Industrial Revolution. But well we know that this historical sequence worked itself out through millions of individual lives; that many suffered, others prospered, while their world was being reshaped in the modern image. In the end—and the end is not yet—all men of the West had acquired a new style of life.

A similar process is under way in the Middle East. The underlying tensions are everywhere much the same—village *versus* town, land *versus* cash, illiteracy *versus* enlightenment, resignation *versus* ambition, piety *versus* excitement. But the process reaches people in different settings and induces different dilemmas of personal choice. In Turkey a grocer exhilarated by the sight of a city must live out his life in a traditional village; in Iran a newly entrepreneurial peasant proudly owns the first store-bought suit in his walled hamlet but rarely dares to wear it among his envious fellows; in Jordan an illiterate Beduin chieftain professes the tribal law of the desert but

plans to send his son abroad to school; in Lebanon an educated Muslim girl loves the movies but fears her orthodox parents; in Syria an under-educated, over-ambitious clerk dreams of being a Tito; in Egypt a young engineer has eaten pork in the West and seeks atonement in the Muslim Brotherhood. To locate these diverse figures in the modernizing Middle East is our aim. The parable of Balgat conveys some sense of the varied questions and answers, pleasures and pains, which modernization brings into the lives of people so variously situated. But Balgat is a miniature; what we need is a landscape.

Landscaping requires some principle of unity in diversity. The source of Middle East unity is a thorny problem of scholarship, complicated by the recent efforts of ideologues to impose a definition that will be politically usable rather than historically valid. Scholars seem agreed that the current ideologies tend to obscure and evade some real issues. The people of the area today are unified not by their common solutions but by their common problems: how to modernize traditional lifeways that no longer "work" to their own satisfaction. Some seek salvation in past pieties—the recourse to Islamic solidarity providing in this sense a parallel to the Crusades, which, in the name of orthodoxy, hastened the passing of medievalism and coming of modernity in the West. But, underlying the ideologies, there pervades the Middle East a sense that the old ways must go because they no longer satisfy the new wants. A world conference of leading Islamists recently concluded:

> The disorder and poverty which rage in the Middle East ... seem incapable of being remedied except by a greater solidarity among Islamic countries and by a general modernization of these countries. But though modernization is a tangible fact, only the pace of which might require control and acceleration, Muslim solidarity is only a fleeting, variable, uncertain supposition.[1]

Modernization, then, is the unifying principle in this study of the varied Middle East. The term is imposed by recent history. Earlier one spoke of Europeanization, to denote the common elements underlying French influence in Syria-Lebanon and British influence in Egypt and Jordan. More recently, following a century of educational and missionary activity, Americanization became a specific force and the common stimuli of the Atlantic civilization came to be called Westernization. Since World War II, the continuing search for new ways has been coupled with repudiation of the Western aegis. Soviet and other modernizing models, as illustrated by India and Turkey, have become visible in the area. Any label that today localizes the process is bound to be parochial. For Middle Easterners more than ever want the modern package, but reject the label "made in U.S.A." (or, for that matter, "made in USSR"). We speak, nowadays, of modernization.

Whether from East or West, modernization poses the same basic challenge—the infusion of "a rationalist and positivist spirit" against which, scholars seem agreed, "Islam is absolutely defenseless."[2] The phasing and modality of the process have changed, however, in the past decade. Where Europeanization once penetrated only the upper level of Middle East society, affecting mainly leisure-class fashions, modernization today diffuses among a wider population and touches public institutions as well as private aspirations with its disquieting "positivist spirit." Central to this change is the shift in modes of communicating ideas and attitudes—for spreading among a large public vivid images of its own New Ways is what modernization distinctly does. Not the class media of books and travel, but the mass-media of tabloids, radio and movies, are now the dominant modes. Today's Middle East "chaos" is largely due to the shift of modernist inspiration from the discreet discourse of a few in Oxford colleges and Paris salons to the broadcast exhortations among the multitudes by the mass media.

This historic shift stimulated the inquiry begun in 1950, of which this book is the outcome. The role of new messages in the Middle East "transition" raised a breviary of empirical questions: who was changing? from what to what? how fast? with what effects? While the great debate over Permanence *versus* Change often obliges the Middle Easterner to declare himself philosophically on such questions, we investigate them here in a more limited sense. We focus on the personal meaning of social change—the transformations worked into the daily lifeways of individuals by these large historical forces.

That some millions of Turks now live in towns, work in shops, wear trousers and have opinions who, a generation ago, lived in the centuries-old *sholvars* symbolizing the agrarian, illiterate, isolate life of the Anatolian village is what modernization has already done to some people. That other millions throughout the Middle East are

yearning to trade in their old lives for such newer ways is what modernization promises to most people. The rapid spread of these new desires, which provide the dynamic power of modernization, is most clearly perceived in the coming of the mass media. To see why this is so—to comprehend what the Middle Eastern peoples are experiencing under the title of modernization—we remind ourselves of what historically happened in the West. For the sequence of current events in the Middle East can be understood as a deviation, in some measure a deliberate deformation, of the Western model.

This observational standpoint implies no ethnocentrism. As we shall show, the Western model of modernization exhibits certain components and sequences whose relevance is global. Everywhere, for example, increasing urbanization has tended to raise literacy; rising literacy has tended to increase media exposure; increasing media exposure has "gone with" wider economic participation (per capita income) and political participation (voting). The model evolved in the West is an historical fact. That the same basic model reappears in virtually all modernizing societies on all continents of the world, regardless of variations in race, color, creed, will be shown in this chapter. The point is that the secular process of social change, which brought modernization to the Western world, has more than antiquarian relevance to today's problems of the Middle East transition. Indeed, the lesson is that Middle Eastern modernizers will do well to study the historical sequence of Western growth.

Taking the Western model of modernization as a baseline is forced upon us, moreover, by the tacit assumptions and proclaimed goals which prevail among Middle East spokesmen. That some of these leaders, when convenient for diplomatic maneuver, denounce the West is politically important and explains why we have chosen to speak of "modernization" rather than "Westernization." Rather more important, Western society still provides the most developed model of societal attributes (power, wealth, skill, rationality) which Middle East spokesmen continue to advocate as their own goal. Their own declared policies and programs set our criteria of modernization. From the West came the stimuli which undermined traditional society in the Middle East; for reconstruction of a modern society that will operate efficiently in the world today, the West is still a useful model. What the West is, in this sense, the Middle East seeks to become.

But these societies-in-a-hurry have little patience with the historical *pace* of Western development; what happened in the West over centuries, some Middle Easterners now seek to accomplish in years. Moreover, they want to do it their "own way." A complication of Middle East modernization is its own ethnocentrism—expressed politically in extreme nationalism, psychologically in passionate xenophobia. The hatred shown by anticolonialism is harvested in the rejection of every appearance of foreign tutelage. Wanted are modern institutions but not modern ideologies, modern power but not modern purposes, modern wealth but not modern wisdom, modern commodities but not modern cant. It is not clear, however, that modern ways and words can be so easily and so totally sundered. Underlying the variant ideological forms which modernization took in Europe, America, Russia, there have been certain behavioral and institutional compulsions common to all. These historical regularities some Middle East leaders now seek to obviate, trying instead new routes and risky bypasses. We alert ourselves to the novelty of these efforts by recapitulating briefly some essential elements in the modernization of the West.

The Mobile Personality: Empathy

People in the Western culture have become habituated to the sense of change and attuned to its various rhythms. Many generations ago, in the West, ordinary men found themselves unbound from their native soil and relatively free to move. Once they actually moved in large numbers, from farms to flats and from fields to factories, they became intimate with the idea of change by direct experience.[3] This bore little resemblance to the migrant or crusading hordes of yore, driven by war or famine. This was movement by individuals, each having made a personal choice to seek elsewhere his own version of a better life.

Physical mobility so experienced naturally entrained social mobility, and gradually there grew institutions appropriate to the process. Those who gained heavily by changing their address soon wanted a convenient bank in the neighborhood to secure their treasure; also a law-and-police force to guard the neighborhood against disorder and devaluation; also a voice in prescribing standards of behavior for others.[4] So came into operation a "system" of bourgeois values that embraced social change as normal. Rules of the game had to be worked out for adjudicating

conflicts over the direction and rate of change. Who was to gain, how, and how much? As the profits to be gained from mobility became evident to all, conflicts over access to the channels of opportunity became sharper. The process can be traced through the evolution of Western property and tax laws, whose major tendency is to protect the "haves" without disqualifying the "have-nots."[5] It was by protecting every man's *opportunity* to gain that the modern West turned decisively in the direction of social mobility.

Social institutions founded on voluntary participation by mobile individuals required a new array of skills and a new test of merit. Every person, according to the new democratic theory, was equally entitled to acquire the skills needed for shaping his own "future" in the Great Society. The vigorous controversy over public education that agitated the eighteenth century produced a net affirmation of equal opportunity. In every Western country the verdict was pronounced that education should be freely available to all who wanted it, and in some countries whether they wanted it or not. Thus the idea spread that personal mobility is itself a first-order value; the sense grew that social morality is essentially the ethics of social change. A man is what he may become; a society is its potential. These options passed out of the realm of debate into the Western law and mores.

A mobile society has to encourage rationality, for the calculus of choice shapes individual behavior and conditions its rewards. People come to see the social future as manipulable rather than ordained and their personal prospects in terms of achievement rather than heritage. Rationality is purposive: ways of thinking and acting are instruments of intention (not articles of faith); men succeed or fail by the test of what they accomplish (not what they worship). So, whereas traditional man tended to reject innovation by saying "It has never been thus," the contemporary Westerner is more likely to ask "Does it work?" and try the new way without further ado.

The psychic gap between these two postures is vast. It took much interweaving through time, between ways of doing and ways of thinking, before men could work out a style of daily living with change that felt consistent and seamless. The experience of mobility through successive generations gradually evolved participant lifeways which feel "normal" today. Indeed, while past centuries established the public practices of the mobile society, it has been the work of the twentieth century to diffuse widely a *mobile sensibility* so adaptive to change that rearrangement of the self-system is its distinctive mode.

The mobile personality can be described in objective and technical fashion. Since this is what the book is largely about, it will do here to define its main feature and to suggest the main line of its secular evolution. The mobile person is distinguished by a high capacity for identification with new aspects of his environment; he comes equipped with the mechanisms needed to incorporate new demands upon himself that arise outside of his habitual experience. These mechanisms for enlarging a man's identity operate in two ways. *Projection* facilitates identification by assigning to the object certain preferred attributes of the self—others are "incorporated" because they are like me. (Distantiation or negative identification, in the Freudian sense, results when one projects onto others certain disliked attributes of the self.) *Introjection* enlarges identity by attributing to the self certain desirable attributes of the object—others are "incorporated" because I am like them or want to be like them. We shall use the word *empathy* as shorthand for both these mechanisms. This condensation of psycho-analytic terminology has a pragmatic, not theoretic, intent—since our materials are simply not amenable to the more highly differentiated categories of Freudian vocabulary. Our interview data does not permit systematic discrimination between the introjective and projective mechanisms. Nor does empathy denote sympathy or antipathy. In particular cases it may lead to either—"understanding" may breed dislike as well as affection.

We are interested in empathy as the inner mechanism which enables newly mobile persons to *operate efficiently* in a changing world. Empathy, to simplify the matter, is the capacity to see oneself in the other fellow's situation. This is an indispensable skill for people moving out of traditional settings. Ability to emphasize may make all the difference, for example, when the newly mobile persons are villagers who grew up knowing all the extant individuals, roles and relationships in their environment. Outside his village or tribe, each must meet new individuals, recognize new roles, and learn new relationships involving himself. A rich literature of humor and pathos once dealt with the adventures of the country bumpkin in the Big City, the bewildered immigrant in a strange land. They had to learn their way in these new settings. Learn, in swelling numbers, they did. The story of the 19th century West in-

cludes this learning, which now enters the story of the 20th century East. Accordingly, we are interested in the mobile personality mainly as a social phenomenon with a history. Our concern is with the large historical movement, now becoming visible in the Middle East, of which an enlarged capacity for empathy is the distinctive psychic component. Our interest is to clarify the process whereby the high empathizer tends to become also the cash customer, the radio listener, the voter.[6]

It is a major hypothesis of this study that high empathic capacity is the predominant personal style only in modern society, which is distinctively industrial, urban, literate and *participant*. Traditional society is nonparticipant—it deploys people by kinship into communities isolated from each other and from a center; without an urban-rural division of labor, it develops few needs requiring economic interdependence; lacking the bonds of interdependence, people's horizons are limited by locale and their decisions involve only other *known* people in *known* situations. Hence, there is no need for a transpersonal common doctrine formulated in terms of shared secondary symbols—a national "ideology" which enables persons unknown to each other to engage in political controversy or achieve "consensus" by comparing their opinions. Modern society is participant in that it functions by "consensus"—individuals making personal decisions on public issues must concur often enough with other individuals they do not know to make possible a stable common governance. Among the marks of this historic achievement in social organization, which we call Participant Society, are that most people go through school, read newspapers, receive cash payments in jobs they are legally free to change, buy goods for cash in an open market, vote in elections which actually decide among competing candidates, and express opinions on many matters which are not their personal business.

Especially important, for the Participant Style, is the enormous proportion of people who are expected to "have opinions" on public matters— and the corollary expectation of these people that their opinions will matter. It is this subtly complicated structure of reciprocal expectation which sustains widespread empathy. Only in the lowest reaches of America's social hierarchy, for example, is it still discussed whether people *ought* to have opinions. In a climactic scene of *Sweet Thursday*, John Steinbeck relates how the Madam of a whorehouse prepares one of her hustlers, not really made for the business, to go out into the world of respectability. The first rule is to keep her mouth shut:

> Next thing is opinions. You and me is always busting out with opinions. Hell, Suzy, we ain't got no opinions! We just say stuff we heard or seen in the movies. We're scared stiff we'll miss something, like running for a bus. That's the second rule: lay off opinions because you ain't really got any.

As Suzy moves from the anarchic margins of American life into solid citizenry, it is foreseen, she will learn to have opinions along the way. In the Middle East many more people have a much longer way to go. "How can you ask me such a question?" gasped the Balgat shepherd. His gasp resounded often in our interviews around the Middle East.

For, in any society, only when the accepted model of behavior is emulated by the population at large does it become the predominant personal style. The model of behavior developed by modern society is characterized by empathy, a high capacity for rearranging the self-system on short notice. Whereas the isolate communities of traditional society functioned well on the basis of a highly constrictive personality, the interdependent sectors of modern society require widespread participation. This in turn requires an expansive and adaptive self-system, ready to incorporate new roles and to identify personal values with public issues. This is why modernization of any society has involved the great characterological transformation we call psychic mobility. The latent statistical assertion involved here is this: In modern society *more* individuals exhibit *higher* empathic capacity than in any previous society.

As history has not been written in these terms, we were obliged to organize our own forays into historical data to establish a traceline on the evolution of the participant society and the mobile personality. We restrain our account of these forays to some main lines which lead directly to the problem in hand.

The Mobility Multiplier: Mass Media

The historic increase of psychic mobility begins with the expansion of physical travel. Historians conventionally date the modern era from the Age of Exploration. Every Western schoolboy knows the names of Cabot, Columbus, Cortez and is dimly aware that they "opened new worlds." This was an initial phase in the modern expansion of human communication. Gradually the technical means of transporting live bodies improved and physical displacement became an experience lived through by millions of plain folk earlier bounden to some ancestral spot. Geographical mobility became, in this phase, the usual vehicle of social mobility. It remained for a later time to make vivid that each mobile soma of the earlier epoch housed a psyche, and to construct transatlantic history in terms of psychic mobility. It is the contemporary historian who now distinctively perceives the mass immigration into America as a traumatic process of psychic encounter with the new and strange.[7] We accent the contemporaneity of the psychic dimension, because the moral injunction to "look shining at new styles of architecture" is something new in the world.[8]

The expansion of psychic mobility means that more people now command greater skill in imagining themselves as strange persons in strange situations, places and times than did people in any previous historical epoch. In our time, indeed, the spread of empathy around the world is accelerating. The earlier increase of physical experience through transportation has been multiplied by the spread of *mediated* experience through mass communication. A generation before Columbus sailed to the New World, Gutenberg activated his printing press. The technical history of the popular arts suggests the sequence. The typical literary form of the modern epoch, the novel, is a conveyance of disciplined empathy. Where the poet once specialized in self-expression, the modern novelist reports his sustained imagination of the lives of others.[9] The process is carried further in the movies and in radio-television drams. These have peopled the daily world of their audience with sustained, even intimate, experience of the lives of others. "Ma Perkins," "The Goldbergs," "I Love Lucy"— all these bring us friends we never met but whose joys and sorrows we intensely "share." The media create for us what has aptly been called "the world of the daytime serial."[10]

Radio, film and television climax the evolution set into motion by Gutenberg. The mass media opened to the large masses of mankind the infinite *vicarious* universe. Many more millions of persons in the world were to be affected directly, and perhaps more profoundly, by the communication media than by the transportation agencies. By obviating the physical displacement of travel, the media accented the psychic displacement of vicarious experience. For the imaginary universe not only involves more people, but it involves them in a different order of experience. There is a world of difference, we know, between "armchair travel" and actually "being there." What is the difference?

Physical experience of a new environment affronts the sensibility with new perceptions in their complex "natural" setting. The traveler in a strange land perceives simultaneously climate and clothing, body builds and skin textures, gait and speech, feeding and hygiene, work and play—in short, the ensemble of manners and morals that make a "way of life." A usual consequence for the traveler is that the "pattern of culture" among the strangers becomes confused, diverging from his prior stereotype of it and from his preferred model of reality.

Vicarious experience occurs in quite different conditions. Instead of the complexities that attend a "natural" environment, mediated experience exhibits the simplicity of "artificial" settings contrived by the creative communicator. Thus, while the traveler is apt to become bewildered by the profusion of strange sights and sounds, the receiver of communications is likely to be enjoying a composed and orchestrated version of the new reality. He has the benefit of more facile perception of the new experience as a "whole," with the concomitant advantage (which is sometimes illusory) of facile comprehension. The stimuli of perception, which shape understanding, have been simplified.

The simplification of stimuli, however, is accomplished at a certain cost. The displaced traveler's great pragmatic advantage is that he must take responsive action toward the stimuli presented by the new environment. However painful this may be—as when, to take a simple case, he has lost his way and must ask directions in a language of which his mastery is uncertain— overt action does help to discharge the traveler's interior tensions. But the passive audience for mediated communications has no such discharge channel; the radio-listener's personal response to new stimuli remains confined to his own interior. The inhibition of overt active response is a learned behavior and a difficult one. It was common, in the early days of movies, for persons strained beyond endurance to throw themselves

or some object at the screen to stop the villain from strangling the heroine. Even the old media hands among the youngsters of today will sometimes, at a particularly agonizing moment in the television show, hide their faces.

Thus the mass media, by simplifying *perception* (what we "see") while greatly complicating *response* (what we "do"), have been great teachers of interior manipulation. They disciplined Western man in those empathic skills which spell modernity. They also portrayed for him the roles he might confront and elucidated the opinions he might need. Their continuing spread in our century is performing a similar function on a world scale. The Middle East already shows the marks of his historic encounter. As a young bureaucrat in Iran put it: "The movies are like a teacher to us, who tells us what to do and what not." The global network of mass media has already recruited enough new participants in all corners of the earth to make "the opinions of mankind" a real factor instead of a fine phrase in the arena of world politics. There now exists, and its scope accelerates at an extraordinary pace, a genuine "world public opinion." This has happened because millions of people, who never left their native heath, now are learning to imagine how life is organized in different lands and under different codes than their own. That this signifies a net increase in human imaginativeness, so construed, is the proposition under consideration.

The "System" of Modernity[11]

A second proposition of this large historical order derives from the observation that modern media systems have flourished only in societies that are modern by other tests. That is, the media spread psychic mobility most efficiently among peoples who have achieved in some measure the antecedent conditions of geographic and social mobility. The converse of this proposition is also true: no modern society functions efficiently without a developed system of mass media. Our historical forays indicate that the conditions which define modernity form an interlocking "system." They grow conjointly, in the normal situation, or they become stunted severally.

It seems clear that people who live together in a common polity will develop patterned ways of distributing *information* along with other commodities. It is less obvious that these information flows will interact with the distribution of power, wealth status at so many points as to form a system—and, moreover, a system so tightly interwoven that institutional variation in one sector will be accompanied by regular and determinate variation in the other sectors. Yet, just this degree of interaction between communication and social systems is what our historical exploration suggests.

We differentiated two historical systems of public communication, Oral and Media, according to the paradigm: Who says what to whom and how? On these four variables of source, content, audience, channel the ideal types differ as noted in table 59.1. In media systems, the main flow of public information is operated by a corps of professional communicators, selected according to skill criteria, whose job it is to transmit mainly descriptive messages ("news") through impersonal media (print, radio, film) to relatively undifferentiated mass audiences. In oral systems, public information usually emanates from sources authorized to speak by their place in the social hierarchy, i.e., by status rather than skill criteria. Its contents are typically prescriptive rather than descriptive; news is less salient than "rules" which specify correct behavior toward imminent events directly involving the larger population, such as tax collections and labor drafts. (Oral and media systems also differ sharply in recreational content, as we shall see, but we here focus on informational content.) Even these prescriptive messages are normally transmitted via face-to-face oral channels (or via such point-to-point equivalents as letters) to the primary groups of kinship, worship, work and play.

Naturally, few societies in the world today give a perfect fit to either of these idealized sets of paired comparisons. America closely approximates the model of a media system, but people also speak to each other on public issues and the personal influence of the "opinion leader" is strong.[12] Conversely, Saudi Arabia corresponds to the oral system but operates its radio transmitters at Jidda.[13] As we move around the world, subjecting our ideal types to empirical data, various elements in the patterns begin to shift. Most countries are in some phase of transition from one system to the other.

But two observations appear to hold for all countries, regardless of continent, culture, or creed. First the *direction* of change is always from oral to media system (no known case exhibiting change in the reverse direction). Secondly, the *degree* of change toward media system appears to correlate significantly with changes in other key sectors of the social system. If these observations are correct, then we are dealing with a "secular trend" of social change that is global in scope. What we have been calling the Western model of modernization is operating on a global scale. Moreover, since this means that other important changes must regularly accompany the development of a media system, there is some point in the frequent references to a "world communication revolution." We here consider the more moderate proposition that a communication system is both index and agent of change in a total social system. This avoids the genetic problem of causality about which we can only speculate, in order to stress correlational hypotheses which can be tested. On this view, once the modernizing process is started, chicken and egg in fact "cause" each other to develop.

Notes

1. G. E. von Grunebaum (ed.), *Unity and Variety in Muslim Civilization* (1955), p. 3.

2. *Ibid.*, p. 12.

3. See autobiographical literature of human migration, especially W. I. Thomas and F. Znaniecki, *The Polish Peasant in Europe and America*, v. 5 (1927).

4. Robert Park, *Human Communities* (1952).

5. S. Ratner, *American Taxation, Its History as a Social Force in Democracy* (1942).

6. This formulation approaches the typology on American society developed by David Riesman in *The Lonely Crowd* (1950). Cf. my article "Comfort and Fun: Morality in a Nice Society," *The American Scholar* (Spring, 1958).

7. Oscar Handlin, *The Uprooted* (1952).

Table 59.1

	Media Systems	*Oral Systems*
Channel	Broadcast (mediated)	Personal (face-to-face)
Audience	Heterogeneous (MASS)	Primary (groups)
Content	Descriptive (news)	Prescriptive (rules)
Source	Professional (skill)	Hierarchical (status)

8. W. H. Auden, *"Petition."*

9. J. W. Beach, *The Twentieth Century Novel* (1932).

10. P. F. Lazarsfeld and F. N. Stanton, *Radio Research, 1942–1943* (1944).

11. For a fuller discussion of the material in this section, see my paper "Communication Systems and Social Systems: A Statistical Exploration in History and Policy," *Behavioral Science* II (October 1957), pp. 266–75.

12. Elihu Katz and P. F. Lazarsfeld, *Personal Influence* (1955).

13. Be it noted, however, that these State-owned transmitters produce but a single broadcast daily. See UNESCO, *World Communication* (1956), p. 94.

60

The Social-Anatomy of the Romance-Confession Cover Girl

From *Journalism Quarterly* (1959)

George Gerbner

George Gerbner (1919–) was born in Budapest, Hungary, where he developed early interests in literature and folklore. In 1939, Gerbner emigrated, eventually coming to the United States—specifically, New Orleans and California. He studied journalism at the University of California, Berkeley, before enlisting to join the Office of Strategic Services. Benefiting from the GI bill as others in his generation did, he returned to school after the war and took a a doctorate in education from the University of Southern California. In Los Angeles, he met Theodor Adorno and played a role in Adorno's classic 1954 essay "How to Look at Television." In the 1950s, Gerbner taught at the University of Illinois before moving to the University of Pennsylvania's Annenberg School in 1964, where he took over as dean from Gilbert Seldes. Gerbner is best known for his cultural indicators work, begun in 1968, and for his later theory of cultivation analysis, both of which combine extensive empirical research with a moderately critical analysis reminiscent of the Frankfurt School.

In this early essay, Gerbner displays the composite intellectual style that marked his later work as well. He blends textual interpretation with social scientific study of audience and a moderately critical focus on media industries and their market logics. The study is noteworthy as a precursor to cultural studies of romances and other media genres favored by middle- and working-class women. It nicely sketches the contradictions of romance-confession magazine covers and ties them not only to the social psyches of their readers but also to the social conditions that shaped their production.

All mass media are market oriented, but popular magazines must also be *supermarket* oriented. Depending for the bulk of their circulation on single-copy sales through food, drug and variety chains, they have a special task of salesmanship via magazine cover.

How do they tackle this task? How are editorial and distribution requirements reflected in the design and content of magazine covers? And how, in the light of these requirements, are the covers perceived? These questions furnished a starting point for a study of confession magazine covers, selected because of the curious way in which they express both the social appeal of the magazine and the pressures of supermarket distribution.

The market position of the confession industry shapes its content through an editorial prescription designed for working class women with presumably middle-class pocketbooks, anxieties and "behavior problems."[1] The social appeal of the confession pivots on the sympathetic heroine's human frailties in an inhospitable world she cannot fully understand. The heroine's "sinful" resistance, or desperate drift down the line of least resistance, brings further calamity, suffering and the final coming to terms, but not to grips, with the punitive code of her world. Her inevitable "crime" becomes irrelevant as an act of social protest. She is rarely permitted to become conscious of the social origin of her personal troubles. This ingredient of unrelatedness appears to provide the editorial antidote to the risk of strong social medicine involved in evoking sympathy for victims of the brutal society of the confessions.

The unique feature of the confession *cover* is the striking contrast between the "confession type" cover girl and the surrounding verbal context. She appears unrelated to the story titles and blurbs of her menacing verbal world. It is as if the editorial safety-valve of social unrelatedness would find its outward manifestation in the structure of the confession cover. The mechanics of distribution also favor the development of such a cover design, and of a cover girl who has the specific function (as does the heroine) of being a reader-identification image.

The formal aspects of the romance-confession cover design have been surveyed through observation over a period of time and a study of all confession magazine covers on sale in the Campaign, Illinois, area in January 1957. These findings were amplified by soliciting policy statements regarding cover design from confession magazine art editors.[2]

There were 12 different titles on sale at the time, published by nine firms, and distributed by two wholesale news agencies.[3] Close-up pictures of eight blondes and four brunettes dominated the uniformly structured covers. The 11 cover girls (two magazines happened to use the same model) displayed appealing features, flashing smiles, cosmetic perfection and eye-contact with the viewer. There was nothing more "sexy" or revealing than one bare shoulder among them.

The verbal context surrounding the image of the radiantly poised, wholesome cover girl was anything but trouble-free. The story titles and blurbs spoke of women "attacked," "frightened and shamed," confessing "The Most Shameful Night of My Life," exclaiming "Oh, God, Don't Let Me Hurt Him," admitting that "We Didn't Know Our Love Was Abnormal," and so on.

About one out of every three cover titles dealt with sexual problems varying from apparent nymphomania to frigidity, and from taboos to sex-tests and tips. Another third reflected mainly marital and parental troubles such as adultry, bigamy, illegitimacy, miscegenation, etc. The remaining third focused on other forms of anguish, shame, terror, illness and crime.

This is the dark and turbulent verbal world into which confession publishers insert, as a matter of policy, the dominant, concrete and colorful personification of clean-cut all-American girlhood. "There is virtually no relationship between the pictorial element and titles featured" on the cover, explains the art editor of one confession magazine, "The blurbs or cover titles have no relationship to the subject," writes another. Actually, they reason, each unit serves its own purpose, and combined they attempt to satisfy the multiple functions and requirements of the magazine.

The Mechanics of Distribution

In the women's field, the service and fan magazines have enough of a claim on a share of the romance-confession reader market to make competition a factor in cover design. Some outward manifestation of glamour and respectability helps the confession match its rivals' bright atmosphere of supermarket cheer.

The economics of magazine display space, and the rivalry among titles impose further requirements. Chain stores average about 60 magazine titles; but roughly 80% of the dollar volume comes from the top 20 magazines. Their total yearly sales from *all* general magazines put together just about equals that of chewing gums; but the magazines take up more space.[4]

Claims that confession readers spend more on some staples than do others are designed to attract advertisers;[5] they seem to have little effect on retail store managers who consider the magazine display space more a customer convenience than a major profit-maker. Although many of the racks are owned and serviced by the wholesale distributor, the floor manager often rules the display. His judgment, sometimes guided by customer comment, may result in preferential treatment for the magazines whose outward appearances conform to the widest variety of clientele sensibilities. Offenders, especially in the women's field, may suffer by being among those hidden from sight—and sale—behind their rivals on the crowded rack.[6]

There are other reasons, too, why the romance-confession magazine can ill afford to externalize its combustible editorial mixture. It is the only fiction group with both feminine *and* working class readership. Under the soothing but transparent cloak of euphemistic names containing such words of presumably feminine appeal as "secrets," "love," "experience," the strong stuff of working-day life in its torrid aspects is the meat of the "romance-confession" diet. Its editorial formula hits closest to home, both literally and socially. Vivid cover pictures of its embattled and embittered heroine in action (as she *is* portrayed inside the magazine) would dramatize the editorial ingredient of incipient revolt—and by the supposedly more docile of the sexes—against the fabric of restraint of pseudo-middle class life.

So, all cannot be sweetness and light—not in the confessions. Their unique editorial appeal must find its way to the cover without inviting censorship. "Regulations enforced by chain store managements result in penalties to a publisher from banning one issue to losing forever the racks of that chain," writes an art editor. "Local censorship and religious black lists are also important in establishing [cover] format."

The compromise formula adopted by the confession relegates the explosive social appeal to the relatively abstract verbal form. Counterpointing this is the dominant pictorial image of the cover girl, conducive to identification and merchandising euphoria, and seemingly unrelated to the surrounding verbal context.

The confession cover may thus be seen as an objective record of the circumstances of its creation. Underlying the stimulus—whether so intended and recognized or not—is the social history of market-produced editorial functions and distribution requirements. But how does the cover girl actually perform her task of confession magazine salesmanship? How is the apparent contrast between the cover girl and her verbal setting resolved in perception? What *is* her image in the eyes of the viewer? How does her juxtaposition with the contrasting verbal context affect her assumed personality, status, functions?

The experiment discussed below attempted to provide some answers to these questions.

The Cover Girl Experiment

The experiment focused on the romance-confession cover girl, and on the influence of her position in the verbal context. Subject responses were elicited to the 12 covers described previously. There was no attempt to select confession readers as respondents. It was felt that more than average familiarity with the inside contents of the magazine would "contaminate" the judgment of the cover itself as a stimulus.

Each cover was prepared in three different forms to test the influence of the verbal context and the cover girl separately as well as together. One group of subjects received a form of the cover girl showing *only the verbal material*; the cover girl was cut out and replaced by a white sheet of paper. This will be referred to as the verbal form, and the group responding to it as Group V.

Another form showed *only the cover girl's picture* cut out of the verbal form, and pasted on cardboard. This is the pictorial form, shown to Group P.

The cover *without any alteration*, designated as the total form, was given to Group T.

A total of 538 University of Illinois students from five different departments were used as respondents. Testing was done in class. A subject responded only once to one form of one cover. Subjects were told that they would be asked for the views and feelings about *the girl's picture* in front of them. (Group V subjects, who had the girl cut out from the cover, were instructed to respond to the test on the basis of their mental image of the girl whose picture might go on the cover.)

The testing was done in two stages, using two tests that had some features in common. The first

Table 60.1 Mean Scale Positions on the Semantic Differential by Basic Groups

Scale	Group V(N-174)		Group T(N-185)		Group P(N-179)
bad—good	3.77	*	5.25		5.49
cruel—kind	4.39	*	5.32		5.53
false—true	3.64	*	4.67	†	5.06
foolish—wise	3.16	*	4.29		4.58
unsuccessful—successful	3.92	*	5.43	*	5.99
powerless—powerful	3.70	*	4.55		4.58
passive—active	4.97	*	5.61	†	5.98
unimportant—important	3.61	*	4.44		4.68
hard—soft	4.07	*	5.01		5.26
ugly—beautiful	5.59	*	6.13		6.20
cool—warm	5.22	*	5.58		5.40
angular—rounded	5.02	*	5.19		5.30
changeable—stable	2.49	*	3.29		3.53
unpredictable—predictable	2.99	*	3.69		3.68
excitable—calm	2.79	*	3.36		3.23

*The differences between the two means are significant at the 1% level.
†The differences between the two means are significant at 5%.

stage included a total of 140 subjects in the three basic groups. The test used at this stage included a blank page for writing a personality sketch of the cover girl, and 26 "semantic differential" scales.[7] These are 7-point scales defined by contrasting adjectives such as good-bad, wise-foolish, active-passive, etc. Respondents mark their reaction to the stimulus (in this case their form of the cover girl) on these scales according to the intensity of their association with one or the other of the polar adjectives. If undecided, they check the middle.

The second stage of the testing, involved in the balance of the subjects in the three basic groups, was confined to the semantic differential, and three questions asking about the cover girl's age, occupation and "moral principles."

Although the findings reveal some differences *between* certain cover girls, these are fewer and no greater than differences between our forms V, T and P. These and other underlying similarities justify lumping the data for the 12 cover girls together into a composite picture suggestive of the image of "the confession-type cover girl."

Semantic Differential Results

The mean responses on the semantic differential for all subjects in the three groups are plotted on a summary form of the differential in figure 3

[*not shown here—Ed.*]. This summary form includes the 15 scales that appeared to represent the range of discriminating responses. The scales appear grouped into "combined characteristics" rather than in random order and direction as they appeared on the tests.

The results,[8] also shown in table 60.1, suggest possible effects of illustrating, or matching with an overtly appropriate picture, the verbal material on these covers. Such practice would make the cover girl appear significantly more unfavorable on all but two of the 15 characteristics, as she did appear to Group V in comparison with Group T.

In other words, on the basis of story titles and blurbs alone, Group V conceived the cover girl as tending to be a "bad," "false," "foolish," "unsuccessful," "powerless," "unimportant" and almost "hard" creature. Group T, which saw the actual picture of the cover girl in the same verbal context, perceived her as "good," "kind," "true," "successful," "soft," and even a little "wise," "powerful" and "important."

She was rated quite "active" and "beautiful" whether seen or not, but a little more so when seen. She appeared "changeable," "unpredictable" and "excitable" to both groups, but less so when her picture was seen. The picture

Table 60.2 Tabulation of Assertions by Basic Groups

Assertions	V(N-50)	T(N-40)	P(N-50)
Assertions about personality	196	322	306
Average per respondent	3.9	8.0	6.1
Favorable	71	273	267
Average per respondent	1.4	6.8	5.3
Unfavorable	125	49	39
Average per respondent	2.5	1.2	0.8
Assertions about sexiness, promiscuity	83	27	44
Average per respondent	1.7	0.7	0.9

of the cover girl designed to the specifications of the romance-confession market thus transforms the impressions created by the supercharged verbal context of the cover.

Compared to the effects of her image on the verbal material, the effects of the verbal context on her image are subtle. These effects can be examined by comparing the responses of Group T to the actual cover with the responses of Group P which saw only the cover girl's picture.

This comparison reveals that Group P rated her slightly higher on all but two of the scales. However, only three of these differences are significant.

The implications of failure, trouble, and guilt in the verbal setting seem to depress significantly the cover girl's "successful" and "true" ratings, and—probably coupled with her apparent unawareness—make her appear less "active." The verbal context, on the other hand, does not injure significantly her other ratings, least of all her attractiveness. It even appears to enhance slightly her "warmness."

A separate analysis of responses by sex revealed that the appearance of the picture on the cover impressed men most as an indication of her success; it had its greatest effect on women in transforming her image from bad to good. When the verbal context was absent, the girl's success rating went up the most among both men and women.

Other Personality Data

A further assessment of the cover girl's presumed personality was made on the basis of the questionnaire data. One-page personality sketches written by the 140 subjects were analyzed for straightforward assertions. Specific questions yielded additional information.

Analysis of the tabulation of personality assertions (see table 60.2) reveals that those who saw

only the verbal context wrote the least about the cover girl's personality, and most of that was unfavorable. Those who saw the picture *alone* wrote more, and most of that was favorable. But those who saw the confession cover girl in her "natural" verbal habitat wrote the most and came to her defense with the highest number of positive assertions. That this defense was felt necessary in view of her verbal setting is evident from the fact that in that setting she received more critical comment than in the absence of that setting (although not nearly as many as in the absence of her picture).

The high number of favorable assertions in Group T is again indicative of the "contrast effect" of the cover design. For a number of subjects the confession-type cover girls appear "too good" for the confession. As one subject put it, "She has a smile on her face that shows contempt at the thought of the type of magazine that she appears in." Wrote another: "What I can't figure out is what a pleasant, clean-looking American girl is doing on the cover of a scandal sheet." In these cases the threatening implications of the verbal context did less to implicate the cover girl—seemingly oblivious of her setting—than to make them appear perhaps vulnerable but the more virtuous by contrast.

Spontaneous statements about the cover girl's "sexiness" support this possibility. Such assertions occurred *least* often in Group T. Perhaps this "contrast effect" is also due to a feeling on the part of subjects that, in view of the girl's apparent innocence, there is little need to mention what is already vividly spelled out on the cover. But, at any rate, it shows the effectiveness of her role in the cover design as a sop to moralists and censors.

Class Status, Age and Morality

The confession market position requires the editorial prescription of "workshirt" social setting,

Table 60.3 Questionnaire Responses on Class, Occupation

	V(N-50)	T(N-40)	P(N-50)
Class (socio-economic status)			
Middle and higher	55%	89%	84%
Lower	45%	11%	16%
Class status mean on 9 point scale	4.52	5.48	5.36
Occupation and activity			
"Higher type" (including model)	75%	100%	96%
"Lower type"	25%	—	4%

and the woman's middle-class consumer status. The resulting "class structure" of the cover design appears in the responses to a question about the cover girl's socioeconomic position. (See table 60.3.)

The verbal context alone suggested a "lower class" cover girl to four times as many subjects in Group V as did the cover girl when seen in the same context by Group T. Her contrasting verbal setting seemed to enhance her social position; the Group T girl on the cover rated slightly higher than did the Group P girl by herself.

The goal of identification may be served better if the cover girl does not seem too "professional." The test question about occupation or activity yielded a wide variety of guesses. But only about half of all respondents thought of the cover girl as a professional model. Occupational ratings were sorted into "higher type" (including model), such as student, secretary, career girl; and "lower type" ranging from waitress to prostitute. The verbal context alone suggested a lower occupational type to one in four Group V subjects. But none in Group T associated her image with a lower type occupation, and only a few in Group P.

All subjects were asked to judge the cover girl's age and morality. Analysis of these judgments shows that being on the cover enhances the cover girl's youth. More Group T subjects placed her in the 18-or-under and fewer in the 24-or-over category than those of the other groups. Both the verbal context and the appearance of her picture by itself yielded slightly higher mean estimated ages than the actual cover.

A breakdown of subject ages and age ratings by morality judgment indicates 1) that those who judged her to be of "low morality" (a minority, when her picture was seen) were generally younger themselves, and 2) that her moral critics rated her oldest of all groups when they saw only the verbal context, but youngest by a significant margin when they saw the actual cover girl in the same setting.

Summary

The underlying contention is that mass media content reflects, in ways both explicit and implicit, the imprint of concrete circumstances of its production. This led to the hypothesis that the market-produced editorial and distribution requirements shape the functions of the confession cover design, and that these objective functions—whether consciously recognized or not—impart a subtle meaning to content which is implicitly reflected in the response.

The findings of the experiment, as far as they go, suggest that the image of the cover girl, and her juxtaposition with the contrasting verbal context, serve well the editorial and distribution specifications required of the cover girl. She resolves her apparent conflict with the lurid titles of the cover—suggestive of the brutal world of the confessions—to her favor. Her dominant image exhibits the human appeal of the heroine menaced by society, but in an overtly unrelated form, insulating her from most ill effects.

Her implicit involvement in the torrent of troubles raging verbally around her enhances, as if by contrast, some of her qualifications. It makes her appear both more immature and less active, hence probably less implicated by (or responsible for) that surrounding. It enhances her consumer and class status, yet preserves the "working class" setting considered necessary for social appeal to the confession market. Her evident success is tinged with the verbally implied risks of failure, and her apparent virtue spiced with the basically innocent sexual attraction of the good-bad girl.

Art editors conceive of the romance-confession cover girl as a projection of the reader's self-image, "a composite of our reader type." Her function on the cover appears to be analogous to the inside heroine's function of identification. The editorial prescription calls for a heroine who may be outwardly plain and sinful, but not unsympathetic. The inherent human attractiveness of the heroine is reflected in the overt beauty of the cover girl; "badness" is implicit in the verbal background.

The confession story heroine—simple, trustful human being against a brutal world—sins, suffers and repents, without consciously and actively grappling with the social meaning of her difficulties. The cover girl in carefree, suspended animation, her eyes gazing confidently into those of the viewer, appears innocent of insight into the tragic meanings around her.

Notes

1. These conclusions are drawn from a report by this author on "The Social Role of the Confession Magazine," *Social Problems*, Summer 1958 (in press).

2. Letters were received from Edward Rethorn of Ideal Publishing Corporation, Mel Blum, Magazine Management Company, New York, and James B. Fitzpatrick, Fawcett Publications, New York.

3. The magazines are: *True Confessions, Revealing Romances, Life Confessions, Your Romance, Intimate Story, True Revelations, Personal Confessions, Secrets, Personal Romances, True Love Stories, True Romance* and *True Experience.*

4. Chain store magazine sales have been reported by *Chain Store Age,* and summarized in *Advertising Age,* August 12, 1957. The figure on chewing gums can be found in the report on candy and gum sales, *Chain Store Age,* Grocery Edition, Product Study No. 3, September 1956.

5. Cf. *Supermarket Buying and Magazine Dollars,* a study by Crossley, Inc., 1954.

6. This general impression has been confirmed through interviews with 15 store managers in the Champaign-Urbana area.

7. These scales and their uses are described in Charles E. Osgood, "The Nature and Measurement of Meaning," *Psychological Bulletin,* 49:197-237, 1952, and in *The Measurement of Meaning,* by C. E. Osgood, G. J. Suci and P. H. Tannenbaum (University of Illinois Press, 1957).

8. Space limitations preclude publication of all findings and tabular material. However, they may be obtained directly from the author.

61

The State of Communication Research

From *Public Opinion Quarterly* (1959)

Bernard Berelson

Bernard Berelson's "The State of Communication Research" (1959), widely referenced since it first came out, originated as a paper delivered to the American Association of Public Opinion Research. It may have been prompted by the imminent dissolution of the Committee on Communication, begun in the 1940s as one of the University of Chicago's numerous interdisciplinary programs. Chaired by Douglas Waples, the committee had included Berelson, Donald Horton, David Riesman, Elihu Katz, and Rolf Meyersohn, while Kurt and Gladys Lang took courses in the program as graduate students. The elimination of the communication program at a broad-minded and eclectic university such as Chicago no doubt had an adverse effect on the development of the field in the 1960s and after. Attention to communication had taken many forms at Chicago, from Albion Small and Robert Park to Harold Lasswell, Douglas Waples, and David Riesman; but there had been a large-angle continuity, and the university had been the seat of some of the richest thinking on the subject. Berelson takes the committee's dissolution as one small part of a bigger transition in communication research. In the process, he offers an influential characterization of the pre-1959 period, a perceptive account of the major and minor approaches to communication in the 1950s, and an instructive prediction of new approaches to the subject he saw on the horizon. For Berelson's bio, see page 253.

My theme is that, as for communication research, the state is withering away.

The modern version of communication research began about twenty-five years ago with the development of both academic and commercial interest—the former largely coordinated, if not stimulated, by the Rockefeller Foundation seminar of the late 1930's and the latter developed in the response to radio's need to prove its audience. Since then there has been a great deal of research activity on both fronts, so much so that for a time the field exhibited many of the characteristics of a scientific fad. What has it all come to and where do we now stand?

The Past

In the past twenty-five years or so, there have been four major approaches to communication research, and perhaps six minor ones. The four major approaches are so well characterized by their leading proponents that it is convenient and revealing here to identify them by name, as in the chart below. In my view, the major lines of inquiry have been the political approach, represented by Lasswell; the sample survey approach, represented by Lazarsfeld; the small-groups approach, represented by Lewis; and the experimental approach, represented by Hovland. (Whether Lewin really should be counted as a student of "communication research" is a matter of definition with which I am not particularly concerned here.) Lasswell, with his interest in broad sociopolitical considerations, represents a macrocosmic line; Lazarsfeld and Hovland, with their interest in individual responses, represent a microscosmic line; and Lewis, with his interest in the social group, represents something in between.

Chart 61.1 indicates some major characteristics of the four approaches, their similarities and their differences. I shall not elaborate on that presentation except to point out how much of what these innovators did, and the ways they did it, was determined by their disciplinary bases; and to observe that despite their differences in starting point and in methods, their findings have many, and sometimes striking, similarities. Moral: The subject matter or the problem triumphs over the approach and the method.

If these are the major figures and lines of inquiry of the past quarter century, there have been several minor approaches—"minor" not necessarily because they will turn out historically to be less important, but simply because they seem to me to have been less influential in the past twenty years or so. They are the following:

5. The reformist approach: Represented by the Commission on the Freedom of the Press. Concerned with organization, structure, and control of the mass media, and particularly with considerations of public policy. Characterized by commercial hostility on the one hand and academic disinterest on the other (except for schools of journalism; the academic departments apparently found this too value-ridden, and hence not "science").

6. The broad historical approach: Represented by David Riesman and Harold Innis. Again, the field's question has been: Is it science?

7. The journalistic approach: Represented by the professional schools and such people as Casey, Nixon, Schramm, and others. Concern with control aspects of the media, characteristics of communicators, and "practical" interests. Close to the reformist approach, as, for example, in Schramm's valuable analysis of ethical responsibility in mass communications.

Chart 61.1 Lines of Inquiry of Four Innovators in Communication Research

Innovator	Representative Titles	Base	Interest	Typical Categories	Materials and Methods	Typical Propositions
Lasswell—early '30s	World Revolutionary Propaganda The Language of Politics	Political science	Broad politico-historical approach. Concern with power.	Fact and value statements. Symbols of identification (i.e., political).	Documentary Content analysis	"Propaganda pushes the intensity of the situation to extremes: facilitates catharsis if interest is low, and precipitates crisis if interest is high." "Political symbols circulating among the power holder correspond more closely to the power facts than do symbols presented to the domain."
Lazarsfeld—late '30s	The People's Choice Communication Research . . . Voting	Social psychology moving toward Sociology	Specific short-range, empirical problems; tie to market research. Concern with audience and effect.	Demographic and "questionnaire" categories. Social position of respondent and his attitudes (i.e., sociological.)	Mass responses; interview in field; sample survey. Natural setting approximated.	People tend to expose to communications whose content is congenial to their predispositions. Communication exposure "pushes" people to a decision, but mainly in line with their latent attitudes.

442

Lewis—late '30s	*Informal Social Communication* (by his students)	Experimental psychology moving toward Social psychology	Personal relations in small groups. Concern with influence and communication therein.	Autocratic and democratic leadership; press toward uniformity within group (i.e., psychological).	Individual behavior under group pressures. Experimental settings, quasi-natural.	Pressure to communicate within a group on a given topic increases with the discrepancy within the group, the cohesiveness of the group, and the elevance of the issue to group morale. Pressure to communicate to a given individual within a group decreases to the extent the member is not wanted in the group.
Hovland—early '40s	*Communication and Persuasion Experiments in Mass Communication*	Experimental psychology moving toward Social psychology	Psychological analysis of effects.	Characteristics of message and effect, e.g., type of appeal, one-sidedness, source credibility, sleeper, boomerang.	Psychological processes. Experiments in laboratory.	One-sided communications are more effective with those initially favoring the position taken; both-sided communications are more effective with those initially opposed. Recall of factual material fades with time, but initial opinion changes are strengthened, especially when in line with prevailing group attitude (sleeper effect).

8. The mathematical approach: Represented by Shannon and Weaver.

9. The psycho-linguistic approach: Represented by Osgood and Miller.

10. The psychiatric approach: Represented by Ruesch and Bateson.

In the last three, the term "communication" carries different meanings and leads to different problems. In each case, there was considerable hope and some expectation that these approaches would represent new major lines of inquiry, or would at least fortify the old. But also in each case, there has been less help, and even less contact, than envisaged in the first wave of enthusiasm (or perhaps I should say, by the first wave of enthusiasts).

The Contribution

If this is a reasonably fair description of what has happened in communication research in the past two decades or so, how is it to be judged? As far as their contribution to our knowledge of communications is concerned, I believe that the first three are playing out: the innovators have left or are leaving the field, and no ideas of comparable scope and generating power are emerging. The expansion of the field to new centers has certainly slowed down and perhaps even stopped; the Committee on Communication at my own university is in process of dissolution. Some of the newer places are currently repeating what the pioneering places did years ago and are now disappointed with.

Lewin is dead. Lasswell and Lazarsfeld have moved on to other interests, the former to large considerations within political science and the latter to mathematical applications and professional training for social research. Hovland himself may now be moving toward broader issues of cognition and machine simulations. Most of Lasswell's students are no longer working in this field; Lewin's and Lazarsfeld's are, but they seem not to be making a systematic effort to fill in the initiator's picture, or not succeeding at it, and, in any case, not yet going far beyond the master's innovating ideas. The work of Hovland and his associates, for example, is a refinement on the similar studies of Thurstone in the late 1920's, and is providing the field with a body of solid, empirical data; but the approach involves atten-

tion to so many detailed variables that one cannot easily see the end of the line, given the enormous number of comparable variables still to be taken into account.

The observation that this is the typical result of inbred fields, that the concern with communication was too narrowly conceived, is, I think, not really applicable here. In my view, Lazarsfeld was the only one of the four who centered on communication problems *per se*: Lasswell was interested in political power, Lewin in group functioning, and Hovland in cognitive processes, and they utilized this field as a convenient entry to these broader concerns.

It would be wrong to think that this is an unimportant field with unimportant investigators in it. When the history of the behavioral sciences for this period is written, there is no question that these four figures will receive major attention for the contributions as well as for what they represent.

The Future

Where do we go from here? Communication research has had a distinguished past, but what about its future? I am not clear about what the next steps will be, let alone what they ought to be, but I think I can see seven current lines of which some may develop into the major focuses of the years ahead as Lasswell-Lazarsfled-Lewin-Hovland did for the years past. In no particular order, they are:

1. Combinations. For example, the current M.I.T. program might be considered a combination of Lasswell and Lazarsfeld lines (both men were on the original advisory committee), plus some small-group and experimental inquiries. As another example, a few years ago the Committee on Communication at the University of Chicago was contemplating a program centering on standards of evaluation for the mass media that could be seen as a combination of the Lazarsfeld and reformist approaches.

2. Comparative studies. An increase in recent years in studies of international communication is quite likely to continue in the years ahead. Most such work, however, seems to have been in the nature of

geographical rather than conceptual or intellectual extension.

3. Economic analysis. There are those who argue persuasively that the application of economic tools of analysis to communication problems will be particularly rewarding. For example, at different times, Douglas Waples and Daniel Lerner were working on a model of the economic (and social) factors necessary to being into being a mass communication system. Or, since so many programs for reform flounder on the rock of economic necessity, some beginning efforts are now being made to subject the economic factors to traditional economic analysis, for example, the costs of newspaper advertising, which have important implications for the size of the paper, the ratio of advertising to news and comment, etc. As a final example in a closely related field, see Anthony Downs on an economic theory of democracy (first in the *Journal of Political Economy*, Vol. 65, 1957, pp. 135-150, later in book form, *An Economic Theory of Democracy*, New York, Harper, 1957).

4. Socio-historical analysis. By this term I mean attention to "the big issues" without direct and immediate regard to the detailed, empirical underpinning. David Riesman and others have made important contributions along this line already, as a counterbalance to the minute and atomistic inquiry, and I look forward to more such studies in the future.

5. Popular culture. Some interests that earlier would have been called communication are now being followed up under this heading. With aesthetic aspects emphasized, the field has a chance to get some help from humanistic studies, and the cooperation ought to be stimulating. Communication problems have been reflected on a great deal in the past—by very good minds—and such reflection should have a good deal to say to the modern empirical researcher.

6. *Mass* communication. Such "new generation" sociologists as James Coleman and William McPhee tell me that the first word needs more emphasis relative to the second. Their position is that the field is better seen as one of a variety of *mass* activities and that headway will be made by stressing the similarities of such mass phenomena rather than the particularities attaching to a mass communication system. That is, the oblique attack may yield more than the frontal.

7. Practical affairs. One way an intellectual field can advance is by dealing directly with the theoretical problems of the discipline itself. Another is by dealing with practical problems to which the discipline can contribute answers. The former is the academic approach and the latter the professional. Of our four major figures, Lasswell, Lewis, and Hovland were primarily concerned with academic matters, and only Lazarsfeld was sometimes concerned with professional problems. A practical, or more professional, turn may now be indicated.

In sum, then, it seems to me that "the great ideas" that gave the field of communication research so much vitality ten and twenty years ago have to a substantial extent worn out. No new ideas of comparable magnitude have appeared to take their place. We are on a plateau of research development, and have been for some time. There are two ways to look at this phenomenon, assuming that it is correctly gauged. One is to regret that no new "breakthrough" has developed in recent yeas; the other is to be grateful that the field has a period of time to assimilate, incorporate, and exploit the imaginative innovations of the major figures. The reader reads the journals; he can take his choice.

62

The State of Communication Research: Comments

From *Public Opinion Quarterly* (1959)

Wilbur Schramm, David Riesman, and Raymond Bauer

Schramm's reply to Berelson's eulogy focuses more on the hustle and bustle of Schramm's life as an exemplary figure in the field of communication research than on the vitality of the field's ideas. Later, in his work as historiographer of the field, Schramm adopted Berelson's quartet of Lazarsfeld, Lasswell, Lewin, and Hovland as the four founding fathers. His reply here can be read as a symptom of the intellectual price Schramm was willing to pay for the institutional turf of a field of communication research. He focuses on a narrow inheritance instead of the much fuller options that he had at hand (see Peters 1986). One ambiguous part of his legacy is too narrow a vision of the field's ancestry, something that this post-Schrammian reader tries to correct. For Schramm's biography, see page 310.

Riesman's reply draws from previous exchanges between the two men that had occurred on the University of Chicago's Committee on Communication. Holding out earlier exemplars such as Robert K. Merton's *Mass Persuasion* (see p. 215), Leo Lowenthal's examination of popular biographies (p. 188), and Kurt Lang and Gladys Lang's MacArthur Day study (p. 328), Riesman essentially says that if the field is dead, people like Berelson helped kill it. "In the dialectic between impulsivity and restraint, the scientific super-ego became too harsh," Riesman writes, fingering his former colleague as one of the mentors of graduate students who brought this to be. With characteristic intelligence and urbanity, Riesman offers a humane vision of what communication research could be. He also shows his international vision, heading northward to note work by McLuhan and others and to contrast the intellectual situations in Poland and the United States (a section that shows Riesman's own Cold War, anti-Stalinist sensibility). His ideas remain alive today, and his closing swipe at "conceptual schemes" that "alienate the worker from his material" is worth our serious consideration. For a biography of Riesman see page 293.

Raymond Augustine Bauer (1916–1977) was a sociologist who taught at Harvard Business School and gained distinction for his studies of Soviet politics and psychology as well as for his research on persuasion processes in public opinion and advertising. In the 1960s he developed the now well-known notion of "social indicators," to supplement the more traditional and economically oriented view of what statistical measures are important in comparative social research. In communication research, he is especially remembered for his article "The Obstinate Audience" (*American Psychologist* 19 [1964]: 319–28), which examined the sociopsychological defenses that audiences have against persuasive stimuli. Deploying an argument that has taken many forms since the 1950s, from Katz and Lazarsfeld's *Personal Influence*, to uses and gratifications research, and, in quite a different form, British cultural studies, Bauer highlighted the autonomy of audiences as receivers of media influence.

Bauer's reply to Berelson reminds us of broader intellectual contexts of the 1950s, when "communications" was an idea taken up in various fields but, according to Bauer, not adequately conceptualized. He observes that the boundaries of the young academic field were not clear, just as they are not clear today (though for reasons different from those in 1959). Though Bauer claims not to agree with Berelson's argument that the big ideas have deserted the field, he can only offer a modest extension of the media effects paradigm as a "possible point of breakthrough." In this, we might see his reply as an ironic confirmation of Berelson's thesis.

Comments by Wilbur Schramm

When one has been pronounced dead, it is ungracious to rise and make comments. Indeed, it shows a certain lack of faith in the attending physician. Nothing is farther from my wishes than to show any lack of faith in my friend Bernard Berelson, and therefore if he pronounces us dead I am content to believe him.

But it is a somewhat livelier condition than I had anticipated. I have just come from the doctoral examination of a young man who demonstrated depth in psychology, sociology, mathematics, and research method, as well as a deep interest in communication problems, and is clearly better prepared to undertake communication research than, fifteen years ago, almost anyone was. Yesterday I had lunch with a psychologist and a sociologist, Charles Osgood and Morris Janowitz, who have recently made major contributions to communication research: an instrument for the measurement of meaning, and an analysis of the communicating organization. I am about to go to a seminar in which scholars from eight countries will be discussing national differences in the communication system. On the way to my office, just now, I was waylaid by an eager young research man who wanted to tell me of a new finding he has made concerning the messages that are received beneath the threshold of conscious perception. In other words, I can't find the rigor mortis in this field and am led to wonder whether Dr. Berelson might have missed a tiny surge of pulse in the body, or even examined the wrong victim.

If I read Dr. Berelson's coroner's report accurately, we are dead in comparison to Lasswell, Lazarsfeld, Lewin, and Hovland. That is a pretty rough test. These were (still *are,* in the case of the three of them) truly remarkable men. Not only were they great producers in their own right; they were also great "starters." They had the ability to inspire in others a fierce drive for new knowledge, and they cast out hundreds of ideas which later flowered in activities and publications. In fact, I think the greater importance of these men may prove to be, not what they themselves did, but what they got started.

Of course, the second party up Everest, the second man to fly an airplane, always moves in the shadow of the first. The geometrists who followed Lobachewsky and Riemann must have felt the cooling shadow of those founding fathers. But, on the other hand, no inferiority feelings kept Einstein from taking Riemann's geometry into certain realms which the founder had hardly contemplated. In a sense, the summit in study of the blood was reached by Harvey and all later research was a downhill grade; but that has not made blood chemistry a dead field.

Three of the "founding fathers" of communication research are still alive and active and it is rather early, even embarrassing, to talk about what has followed them. But at least we can say that not all has been quiet in their footsteps. The Illinois conference on content analysis in 1955 demonstrated that even this relatively quiet subject has moved beyond where Lasswell had carried it. I suspect that Lazarsfeld was proud of his former students who studied the diffusion of new knowledge amongst physicians. From the founding father Lewin to his pupil Festinger I observe no diminution of research insight and ingenuity. And one can name many important communication experiments in attitude change that have been done away from Yale.

Dr. Berelson may have been handicapped in his diagnosis by his logical insistence on dividing all Gaul into three parts. Thus he names four "approaches"—the Lasswell, Lazarsfeld, Lewin, and Hovland lines—and six "minor approaches," ranging from reform to psychiatry. But what does he mean by approaches? Well, he says, there are "the political approach, represented by Lasswell; the sample survey approach, represented by Lazarsfeld; the small-groups approach, represented by Lewin; and the experimental approach, represented by Hovland." The argument is that these approaches are "playing out," and that therefore the outlook is dark for communication research.

Does this not confuse men with method? There is no question that we now know how to make more reliable sample surveys than Lazarsfeld made in his great years of director of the Bureau of Applied Social Research, but we can't always construct surveys with the insight that Lazarsfeld displayed. Similarly, the experimental method is older than Hovland and will live longer, but not everybody can pick his experimental problem as skillfully as Hovland does. The political approach is a state of mind, rather than a method, and men trained in political science are now picking up some of the tools of quantitative research and beginning to contribute in the areas to which Lasswell first called attention.

What we observe in this young field is precisely what we observe in natural history—the increasing shuffledness which Eddington calls the law that "entropy always increases." These so-called "approaches" tend to be combined in the same man. Hovland's own *Communication and Persuasion* contains a large amount of small-group research, which is supposedly Lewin's "approach." The M.I.T. program in international communication, although strongly influenced by Lasswell and "the political approach," uses both experiment and sample survey, in the spirit of Lazarsfeld and Hovland. Whereas the Bureau of Applied Social Research did indeed for a time specialize in the sample survey, newer centers, like those at Stanford and Illinois, use the sample survey, the experiment, and small-group research side by side, and, along with them, other tools like the semantic differential and depth psychology. Thus the "approach" changes with the field. All that was really unique to Lazarsfeld's approach was Lazarsfeld. If he were starting today, he would doubtless make another "approach," which he would illuminate with his remarkable combination of insight, vigor, and skill. It makes little sense to say of the "founding fathers" that their "approach" is playing out. It is something like saying that personality psychology is playing out because Freud is dead, and who is there in sight to compare with him?

We sometimes forget that communication research is a field, not a discipline. In the study of man, it is one of the great crossroads where many pass but few tarry. Scholars come into it from their own disciplines, bringing valuable tools and insights, and later go back, like Lasswell, to the more central concerns of their disciplines. Merton studies the Kate Smith broadcasts, and returns to

the grand architecture of social theory. Festinger studies communication situations on the way to a theory of cognitive process. Only a relatively few scholars, and those in the last decade or so, have seen fit so to dedicate themselves to communication research that they have equipped themselves with the combination of several social sciences, mathematics, and research method that a man requires to see the field steadily and see it whole. For most scholars who work in communication, the field forces itself on them because some of its problems must be solved before their own discipline will be fully understood. Therefore, we must not look for the unique theory in communication which we are accustomed to see in disciplines, or the kind of career in communication research which we are accustomed to see within disciplines. The test of health will be whether the horizon recedes, and whether the growing knowledge of communication process and institutions contributes to the knowledge of man and society.

In twenty years, communication research has made solid contributions to our understanding of one of the fundamental social processes. It is having a profound effect on the teaching of journalism and other mass communication subjects in our universities, because it has made a bridge between the professional or trade activities of these schools and the ancient and intellectual strengths of the university. It is having an effect also on the concept and teaching of subjects like political science. In half a dozen places in this country, it has drawn together, formally or informally, a group of social scientists dedicated to communication research who contribute to each other knowledge and insights from their disciplines. As we noted, it has led a certain number of young scholars to acquire almost equal competence in psychology and sociology, or politics and psychology, or other such combinations which they felt were necessary in order to work in this broad field. By so doing, and by calling attention to problems and propositions which are broader than disciplines, it has brought a little closer the day when we may have a science of man.

Communication research may be already old enough for us to talk about the great times that used to be, and the giants that once walked the earth, as Dr. Berelson talks about them. But I find it an extraordinarily vital field at the moment, with a competent and intellectually eager group of young researchers facing a challenging set of problems. Who will make the adequate two-person model of communication we need? Who will analyze the communication organization? Who will clarify the economics of mass communication? Who will make sense of the communication "system"? Who will untangle the skein of motivations and gratifications related to mass media use on which a long line of distinguished researchers, including Dr. Berelson, have worked? Who will find out what television is doing to children or, better, what children do with television? Who is going to clarify the diffusion of ideas in a society, or the relation of public opinion to political process?

Let's get on with the problems!

Comments by David Riesman

I first heard Bernard Berelson expound his pessimism concerning the state of the art of communications research when we were both lecturing in a staff seminar of the Committee on Communications at the University of Chicago half a dozen years ago. I thought at that time that there was a possibly self-fulfilling element in his remarks—a danger that students, often already anxious about a borderline field, would lose the little confidence they already had. If the work done so far by the great men who opened up the field had so quickly run into sand, what could be expected of their own miniscule endeavors? While a more rebellious and ripsnorting student body might have reacted by saying, in effect, "I'll show him," Mr. Berelson's views seemed so reasonable, and his claims so modest, as not to invite this sort of counter-attack.

In this situation, I recall saying to the students something like this: "Robert Merton in *Mass Persuasion* got a few people out into the field after a fabulous event, collected a hundred interviews, and wrote a notable book. Isn't it nice to be in a field where there is so much material, and so little known about it and done about it, that this can be done? Isn't Merton's book a standing invitation for many analogous studies: on fan mail, on reactions to films, on political rallies—just as his later work is an invitation to the study of cosmopolitans and locals in institutional as well as geographical settings? Indeed, how many books of the directness and immediacy of *Mass Persuasion* are to be found in other subfields of the social sciences?

"And isn't Mr. Berelson judging contemporary work too readily by the standards of founding fathers who could, in turn, be belittled by comparison with Freud or Aristotle? Lasswell was stimulate by Freud, not obliterated by him—and many have been stimulated by Lasswell [the Program at M.I.T. and the work there of such admirers of Lasswell as Ithiel Pool and Daniel Lerner, which includes not only research on communications in the less electronic countries, but also research on audience reactions, journalistic attitudes, and so forth, seems to me to have been given much too shadowy treatment in Mr. Berelson's paper]. The influence of these progenitors spreads even beyond the boundaries of Mr. Berelson's cineramic view: thus, the magazine *Explorations,* published at the University of Toronto, is a more liberating and lively adventure in mass communications and popular culture than one would gather if one's criterion is the too-frontal one of 'breakthroughs.'

"Work in the field of communications is inviting, at the moment, because of its very ambiguity and lack of structure. It is a somewhat transient way-station where people can meet who don't quite want to commit themselves to the field of literature (as monopolized by English departments) or to the social sciences (as monopolized by departments of sociology or political science)—and, as Mr. Berelson indicates, there is also room for people with an interest in economics and aesthetics. Some of the very best students, and some of the very worst, are attracted by the ability to delay a commitment to one of the established powers of academia. Some institutional rubric is necessary to protect them from those powers and, correspondingly, from the definitions of success or productivity emanating from them. I referred above to *Mass Persuasion* and what could be done with one hundred interviews. In Leo Lowenthal's famous essay in which he traced the shift from heroes of production to heroes of consumption in just two popular magazines, what was necessary was not an elaborate project but a good idea and a library. In Wolfenstein's and Leites' book on the movies (which Mr. Berelson might perhaps not consider as communications research) what was necessary was again a relatively manageable and highly visible amount of data."

It is in some such terms as these, at once hortatory and hopeful, that I sought to persuade Mr. Berelson's audience to be enough provoked by him to prove him wrong. Now, however, looking at the matter again, I am struck by the fact that Mr. Berelson seems to have been proven right by developments, or the lack of them, since then. Moreover, what he says in this article concerning research on communication could hold *pari passu* for other large, exciting, and amorphous fields, such as culture-and-personality, institutional economics (except with respect to the so-called underdeveloped countries), and the kind of critique of character and society which reached its high point with *The Authoritarian Personality* and other volumes in the Study of Prejudice series. In each of these fields, including communications, two developments occurred simultaneously. In the first place, the initial studies with their methodological messiness, their often grandiose generalizations, and their obvious political biases, were met with a barrage of conscientious criticism. And whereas when novelists are criticized by literary critics, they can often brush the attacks off because they do not always move in the same circles and share the same coterie values, most of the authors of the works criticized moved in the same circles as their critics and had internalized many of their values. In the dialectic between impulsivity and restraint, the scientific super-ego became too harsh—a development that was particularly effective in intimidating adventurous research, because the young were learning more about methodological pitfalls than had their elders—from precisely such mentors as Mr. Berelson.

The second development was the opening up of fields of theoretical work which offered at once quick pay-offs for the capable student and elegant models for the meek and timid. A book like *The Invasion from Mars* looks sloppy in comparison with the work of Carl Hovland and his students—just as in economics work on linear programming and various forms of model building is both neater and quicker than the sorts of inquiry that, for instance, Walton Hamilton pursued; and, in anthropology, studies of kinship or linguistics have a clarity lacking in most studies of culture-and-personality or national character.

There is the further advantage to these new fields that they almost guarantee that the effort expended by a talented researcher will not be wasted, but will produce something, whereas a study that goes out into the field to discover something new, empirically, may or may not produce "findings": thus, the economist who would take time off from reading Paul Samuelson to spend two years as assistant comptroller observing concrete decision processes in a particular company might fear that he would have nothing of general interest to show when he came back from his field trip, just as a student of mass communications might fear that he could study a particular campaign in the field and, by the luck of the draw, not add anything to *The People's Choice* or *Voting*. One has to have almost a tropism toward unprocessed data, a passionate curiosity about what is going on, in order to endure the insecurity and lack of structure of pioneering field work.

Consider the situation of sociology in Poland today. The practitioners, old and young alike, have a sense of revolutionary ferment even though their intellectual equipment comes largely from the very sources Mr. Berelson feels have now run out in this country. It is a political act to collect facts in Poland: paradoxically, dictatorship has made it possible to revive the spirit of the Enlightenment. And a great majority of the editors of the now suppressed paper *Pro Prostu* (which played such a great part in the anti-Stalinist movement in Poland) were, I am told, sociologists and sociology students.

In this country, it would seem, we are too sophisticated to be enlightened. Mr. Berelson points to the decline of reformist concerns as represented by the Commission on the Freedom of the Press. Yet we face a situation today in the cold war where the press, while no longer "yellow" in the old-fashioned sense, has become more and more ethnocentric and nationalistic ("white"?) at the very moment when the educated population seems to be becoming more world-minded. How is this to be explained? What can be done about it? Samuel Lubell, with old-fashioned door-to-door methods (he is the Fuller-brush-man of mass communications) has tried to sort out the impact of ethnic heritage, ideologies of status, and economic orientations, in order to help explain the persistence of isolationism and the uneven impact of the media of public information. But we need many more one-man investigations such as his. So too, we are but at the threshold if we ask: What is the impact on Americans of advertising, not in terms of this sale or that choice, but in terms of the visual and literary landscape of America; or: Is there a difference in the Rorschach and TAT responses of those who have been exposed to the modern media and those who have not; or, in general: In what way do the media affect the way we see each other, the landscape, or cities and objects of consumption? Donald Horton recently analyzed the way popular songs provide a language of courtship for teenagers—again a small-scale study without apparatus—and we would understand a lot if we knew some of the kinesic consequences of the way people look and talk in our magazines, movies, and television. In an early paper, Berelson and Salter studied the way popular magazines portrayed, or underplayed, "majority" and "minority" Americans. Today we must ask whether the spectrum has increased in ethnic tolerance—think of Desi Arnez, Frank Sinatra, Leonard Bernstein, and other leading heroes of popular culture—while at the same time eliminating regional and other parochial variations, so that mass media, even more than hitherto, are creating a homogenous national culture? Is there, as a result, a decline of interest in local elections, or at least local issues? And is this national consciousness one factor which both intensifies the cold war and results from it?

And what of the long-term growth of cynicism that may be one consequence of early exposure and over-exposure to the mass media? Cannot we interpret *Personal Influence* as meaning that people are afraid of being gulled by distant persuaders despite all the efforts at folksiness and "para social" intimacy the media make, so that they will only open themselves up to people they know personally and not vicariously? What is the image of the world of a young person today who has watched television commercials—both those so labeled and those not so labeled—since before he could read?

Large-scale questions such as these can still be approached by small-scale empirical sorties. The very omnipresence of the media means that no student is so distant from "sources" that he cannot go down to the local movie house and apply some very rudimentary techniques of "mass observation," or the more refined approaches of Lloyd Warner and William Henry, or Herta Herzog, in their studies of the audiences of soap opera. Such work is "middle level" in the two senses that it does not begin with large conceptual schemes or large data-gathering systems. But, returning to Merton's *Mass Persuasion* again, I see no reason why large implications cannot be drawn, with all appropriate diffidence, from small samples or from the description of an event.

The comparison by Kurt and Gladys Lang of the impression given on TV of General MacArthur's hero's welcome in Chicago and the observed behavior of the crowds at the airport and on the streets is a good example.

I doubt if it is helpful to students to blame them for the inhibitions they have learned from their highly competent professors. But it may help to remind them that there is class persuasion as well as mass persuasion and that conceptual schemes, while essential and inevitable, can serve to alienate the worker from his material as well as to bring him closer to it—much as I suspect that the sophisticated visual imagery in the advertisements of the *New Yorker* infiltrates the way we assimilate the ideas in the magazine's columns and cartoons and stories and, hence, even how we read the *P.O.Q*!

Comments by Raymond A. Bauer

Without checking with the other commentators on Berelson's stimulating paper, I am willing to predict that all of us will take the same basic line: Berelson paints an overly pessimistic picture of the future of communications research. This is the only gambit he has left open to us.

Certainly he is right in his general contention that the lines of demarcation within the field and at its boundaries have become less clearly defined. Psycho-linguists such as George Miller have had a lively interest in information theory. Reformers have done content analysis (although almost always with too little awareness of the limitations of imputing effect from content). "Journalists" such as Schramm have shown a liking for the cybernetic model of communications. Lewin and his students, as Berelson points out, did work that was only marginally classifiable as "communications." Lazarsfeld's disciples are knee-deep in sociometry· and social structure. And Lasswellians are doing sample surveys. In industrial sociology, the word "communications" is banded about quite freely, but it is difficult to tell where "communications" stop and the general process of personal interaction begins. Ruesch and Bateson say they are studying "communications," but at times it is impossible to differentiate what they do from what most psychiatrists and anthropologists would do under different labels. Personally I have found it extremely difficult to distinguish properly the boundaries between a "communications" problem and basic work done on cognition, remembering, personal influence, and reference groups.[1]

If we look at Berelson's own phrase, "the state is withering away," we may agree that it has become more difficult to demarcate the external boundaries of the state and to distinguish clearly the subdivisions within the state. But this does not mean necessarily that the state is atrophying. It may mean that it has expanded, developed, and differentiated in the way of mature organisms (to mix a metaphor).

One of the reasons that I find it difficult to lament the absence of "the great ideas" in present-day communications research is that, with the possible exception of some of Lasswell's work, the early period was not marked by great *ideas* but by diverse methodological approaches to the large common area of communications: content analysis, survey research, small-group dynamics, and systematic psychological experimentation. Each of these approaches was exploited to the point where both its advantages and limitations were revealed. As this has happened, the center of gravity has shifted from the exploitation of a method to the substance of problems which demand diverse methods for their exploitation.

This trend may be illustrated by a number of examples, the most familiar of which has already been eloquently reported in Katz and Lazarsfeld, *Personal Influence*,[2] and is reflected in the more recent studies of physicians' adoption of prescription drugs.[3] The early survey studies of the effects of mass communications started with the implicit assumption that in a "mass media" society informal communications played a minor role. But attempts to establish the effects of mass communications forced Lazarsfeld and his associates (eminent among whom, of course, was Berelson) to accord a larger role to informal personal influence. Immediately their attention was turned to this problem, the experimental work of Lewin and other psychologists took on *theoretical* significance. However, the old methodological device of the sample survey was still employed. Tracing the pattern of personal influence from the data of sample surveys proved a difficult task. The final step has been to adapt the methods of sociometry, together with some of the features of sample surveys, to the study of informal communications and personal influence.

Berelson cites as typical propositions of the Lazarsfeld approach: (1) People tend to expose themselves to communications that are congenial to their predispositions; (2) communication exposure "pushes" people to a decision but mainly in line with their latent attitudes. Perhaps one could go even farther and state that, to date, the chief discovery of field studies of the effects of mass communications is that it is exceedingly difficult to identify such effects. Hovland and others were able in laboratory situations to demonstrate quite readily identifiable changes in attitude. While every attempt was made to approximate "natural" conditions as closely as possible in the laboratory, field studies indicated quite decisively that a direct translation of laboratory findings to field conditions was impossible. Hovland himself has discussed this circumstance in a recent paper to the American Psychological Association,[4] and he and his colleagues are now working on the joint application of laboratory and field studies to the testing of propositions. Again, the focus of attention has shifted from the method to the substance of the problem.

Meanwhile, both field and laboratory studies were demonstrating the untenability of equating the content and the effects of communications. Certain of the "reformers" and "social theorists" have not yet grasped this elemental fact, but few professionals in communications research today do not recognize this imitation on content analysis.

Basically, then, my argument is that the early approaches carried with them necessary oversimplifications which have become clear only because the approaches were pushed to the point where they exposed their own limitations. The result has been not only a recognition of the complexity of the communications process but a shift to primary concern with the substance of the problems with less commitment to a particular device of investigation.

The outlook for new "big ideas" is not necessarily bleak, and I would like to suggest one possible point of breakthrough. Although no one seriously doubts that mass communications have an effect on attitudes, we have to this point, as I suggest above, experienced a peculiar frustration in tracing these effects. The effectiveness of advertising in selling goods has been well demonstrated, but attempts to sell the United Nations, etc., seem to have produced consistently negative results. Wiebe has already made some fruitful suggestions as to why there are such differences;[5] I would like to go a little farther than he has. Most social scientists tend to think of attitudes as "softer" than behavior. By this, I mean that they think it is easier to change attitudes than behavior and, more precisely, that to affect behavior one must first change the attitudes relevant to that behavior. However, the recent work of Festinger,[6] Kelman,[7] and others has shown that often attitudinal changes follow behavioral changes. Perhaps the paradigm we should use in field studies of the effects of communications is to look for instances in which communications have capitalized on existing attitudes to produce behavior which, in turn, produces changes of attitudes.

Suppose we took as our topic the attitudes of Southern whites toward integration. The argument would go that we should avoid discussion in the mass media the basic issue of integration, but on the basis of existing attitudes precipitate behavior which was favorable to integration. Thus, the informational campaign might concentrate exclusively on the need to conform to the law of the land regardless of the issue. The prediction would be that those persons who conformed on this basis would, according to Festinger's *theory of cognitive dissonance,* thereafter accommodate their attitudes toward integration *per se* so as to bring them more closely in line with the actions they had taken.

Any hypothetical example such as this is vulnerable on several counts, but it is my guess that this approach offers a possibility for better insight into the day-to-day effects of the mass media. The main reason that mass communications appear to have such little immediate impact can be traced to the phenomenon of self-selection. What we should look for, then, are instances in which self-selection occurs because of some variable outside the area of *our* primary interest; then we can trace the attitudinal consequences of behavior evoked by peripheral circumstances Perhaps this is the way that mass media change opinions.

Notes

1. Cf. R. A. Bauer, "The Communicator and the Audience," *Conflict Resolution,* Vol. 2, 1958, pp. 66–77.

2. E. Katz and P. Lazarsfeld, *Personal Influence,* Glencoe, Ill., Free Press, 1955.

3. H. Menzel and E. Katz, "Social Relations and Innovation in the Medical Profession," *Public Opinion Quarterly,* Vol. 19, 1955, pp. 337–352.

4. C. I. Hovland, "Reconciling Conflicting Results Derived from Experimental and Survey Studies of Attitude Change," presented to the American Psychological Association, Sept. 1, 1958.

5. G. Wiebe, "Merchandising Commodities and Citizenship on Television," *Public Opinion Quarterly,* Vol. 15, 1951, pp. 679–691.

6. L. Festinger, *A Theory of Cognitive Dissonance,* Evanston, Ill., Row, Peterson, 1957.

7. H. C. Kelman, "Attitude Change as a Function of Response Restriction," *Human Relations,* Vol. 6, 1953, pp. 185–214.

63

What Is Mass Communication?

From *Mass Communication: A Sociological Perspective* (1959)

Charles R. Wright

Charles R. Wright (1927–) grew up outside Philadelphia and attended Columbia as many others did, on the GI bill. Unlike most Columbia graduate students who studied with either Lazarsfeld or Merton, Wright, like Elihu Katz, studied with both. While Katz developed Lazarsfeld's research on opinion leaders, two-step flows of influence, and audience research, Wright spoke more through Mertonian categories of social structures and functions and was a leading figure in extending Mertonian analysis into 1960s communications research. Wright taught sociology at the University of California, Los Angeles (1956–1969) and at Pennsylvania's Annenberg School (1969–present). In addition to his work on mass communication, Wright has written on education, professionalization, opinion leadership, international development, and research methods.

This excerpt comes from Wright's *Mass Communication: A Sociological Perspective,* a book he began at Columbia in the mid-1950s, when he could find no suitable text for his course in the sociology of mass communications. First published in 1959, the book was translated in Argentina, Brazil, Italy, and Japan in the 1960s, when it was taught to a generation of students new to the field. In the excerpt here, Wright offers a classic definition of *mass communication,* in terms of audience, experience, and institutional mode of production.

Communication is the process of transmitting meaning between individuals. For human beings the process is both fundamental and vital. It is fundamental insofar as all human society—primitive to modern—is founded on man's capacity to transmit his intentions, desires, feelings, knowledge, and experience from person to person. It is vital insofar as the ability to communicate with others enhances the individual's chances for survival, while its absence is generally regarded as a serious form of personal pathology. Occasionally children have been discovered who, having spent their earliest years in isolation from other human beings, have lacked verbal communication experience. These isolated children behaved in ways little different from other animals, and shared their lack of cultural control over the natural environment. Not until the rudiments of human communication were established with these individuals did they enter into social relations with other humans and acquire the cultural advantages which most persons accept as a birthright.[1]

It seems inevitable that a process so fundamental and vital to human survival should, in whole or in part, have been a subject for study throughout history. Indeed, from antiquity to modern times the process of human communication has attracted the attention of a long line of authors employing a rich assortment of intellectual orientations, including the artistic, the philosophical, and the political. Only recently, however, has communication become a topic for scientific investigation and, more particularly, for inquiry by social scientists in certain fields, especially anthropology, political science, psychology, and sociology. In keeping with this latest trend, the present Study assumes a *sociological* orientation to the subject.

But the entire field of human communication is not the focus of our work. From the wide span of methods by which meanings are transmitted in human societies, ranging from the most primitive gestures to the most sophisticated electronic techniques, a small but important segment has been selected—that segment of symbolic transmission commonly identified as *mass communication*. What is presented here is an initial step toward a sociological analysis of the process and social consequences of mass communication.

To start, we need a working definition of mass communication. We need to describe a few of the characteristics of mass communication that help to distinguish it from other forms of human communication. Then, in the second section of this chapter, we speculate about some of the social consequences of the mass form of communication.

In popular usage the phrase "mass communication" evokes images of television, radio, motion pictures, newspapers, comic books, etc. But these technical instruments should not be mistaken for the *process* with which we are concerned. Mass communication, as it is used in this Study, is *not* simply a synonym for communication by means of radio, television, or any other modern technique. Although modern technology is essential to the process, its presence does not always signify mass communication. The nation-wide telecast of a political convention is mass communication; the closed-circuit telecast over which industrial assembly line operations are monitored by an engineer is not. Or, to take a more mundane example, a Hollywood motion picture is mass communication; a home movie of vacation scenes is not. Both media in each example use similar modern techniques— electronic transmission of images in one case, film recording of scenes in the other. Nevertheless one of each pair does not qualify as mass communication. The point is perhaps labored; it is not the technical components of modern communications systems that distinguish them as mass media; rather, mass communication is a special kind of communication involving distinctive operating conditions, primary among which are the nature of the audience, of the communication experience, and of the communicator.

Nature of the Audience

Mass communication is directed toward a relatively large, heterogeneous, and anonymous audience. Hence, messages addressed to specific individuals are not customarily regarded as mass communications. Such a criterion excludes letters, telephone calls, telegrams, and the like from our Study. This does not deny that the postal and telecommunications systems play an important role in the communications network of any society. Most certainly they do. Indeed, in some instances they are often linked to the mass media, performing vital functions in the overall communications process, aiding, for example, in the spread of information to areas of the society or segments of the population not reached by the mass media. But the term mass communication is reserved for other activities.

Each of the criteria cited here for a mass audience is relative and needs further specification. For example, what size audience is "large"? Extreme cases are easily classified: a television audience of millions is large; a lecture audience of several dozen is small. But what about an audience of four or five hundred people listening to an evangelist speaking in a tent? Obviously the cutting point must be an arbitrary one. A tentative definition would consider as "large" any audience exposed during a short period of time and of such a size that the communicator could not interact with its members on a face-to-face basis.

The second requirement is that the audience be heterogeneous. Thus communications directed toward an exclusive or elite audience are excluded. For example, the transmission of news (by whatever means) exclusively to members of a governing party or ruling class is not mass communication. Mass-communicated news is offered to an aggregation of individuals occupying a variety of positions within the society— persons of many ages, both sexes, many levels of education, from many geographic locations, and so on.

Finally, the criterion of anonymity means that the individual audience members generally remain personally unknown to the communicator. It does not mean that they are socially isolated. Indeed, there is growing evidence that much of mass communication exposure takes place within the setting of small social groups; and even when physically isolated the audience member, of course, is linked to a number of primary and secondary social groupings which can modify his reaction to the message. But, with respect to the communicator, the message is addressed "to whom it may concern."

Nature of the Communication Experience

Mass communications may be characterized as public, rapid, and transient. They are public because, insofar as the messages are addressed to no one in particular, their content is open for public surveillance. They are rapid because the messages are meant to reach large audiences within a relatively short time, or even simultaneously—unlike works of fine art, which may be examined at leisure over centuries. They are transient because they are usually intended to be consumed immediately, not to enter into permanent records. Of course there are exceptions, such as film libraries, radio transcriptions, and kinescope recordings, but customarily the output of the mass media is regarded as expendable.

As we will note in more detail later, the nature of the communication experience may have important social consequences. Its public character may make it a subject for community censorship and control through legislation, public opinion, and other social mechanisms. The simultaneity of the message—its ability to reach large audiences in a brief time span—suggests potential social power in its impact. Mass communication's transience has led, in some instances, to an emphasis on timeliness and sensation in content.

Nature of the Communicator

Mass communication is organized communication. Unlike the lone artist or writer, the "communicator" in mass media works through a complex organization embodying an extensive division of labor and an accompanying degree of expense. One need only call to mind the vast institutional structure surrounding the production of a Hollywood film or the bureaucratic complexity of television network production to recognize the dissimilarities between such communication and traditional earlier forms. Similarly, modern communications are more costly. For example, it has been estimated that a TV station, say for college productions, would cost approximately $265,000 to equip and another $220,000 annually to operate.[2] Production costs for a network fifteen-minute newscast have been reported as $3400.[3]

These distinctions are not merely academic, but have important consequences for the communication process. The complexity of modern mass media has moved the creative artist many stages away from his final product. And the production expense is decreasing the access to the media of communication for persons wishing to reach the public.

To summarize, recent technological developments have made possible a new form of human communication: mass communication. This new form can be distinguished from older types by the following major characteristics: it is directed toward relatively large, heterogeneous, and anonymous audiences; messages are transmitted publicly, often timed to reach most audience members simultaneously, and are transient in character; the communicator tends to be, or to operate within, a complex organization that may involve great expense. These conditions of communication have important consequences for the traditional activities which are carried out by communicators in society—some of which are considered below.

Notes

1. For a summary of several cases of isolated humans, see R. M. MacIver and C. H. Page, *Society, An Introductory Analysis* (New York: Rinehart and Company, Inc., 1949), pp. 44–45.

2. C. A. Siepmann, *Television and Education in the United States* (Paris: Unesco, 1952), pp. 56–61.

3. *Variety*, November 12, 1952, as cited in *Television, A World Survey* (Paris: Unesco, 1953), p. 68.

64

Social Theory and Mass Media

From *Canadian Journal of Economics and Political Science* (1961)

Thelma McCormack

Thelma McCormack (1921–) is a leading Canadian sociologist. She received her bachelor's degree from the University of Wisconsin and did graduate work at Columbia University, where she was influenced by Paul Lazarsfeld, Robert Lynd, and Robert Merton, as well as by the vibrant community of European scholars in New York. Like many in that era, she worked on research projects as a factotum at the Bureau of Applied Social Research. She has taught at Northwestern University, McGill University, the University of British Columbia, the University of Amsterdam, and York University. At York, she founded the Centre for Feminist Research, where she is an emerita professor in sociology. She is a pioneering academic feminist in North America who has written on topics ranging from research methodology, to polling, pornography and censorship, abortion, and peace studies.

Reminiscent of Merton's work, McCormack's essay puts the chief empirical findings of the Columbia school into contact with the larger insights of Continental social theory.

This paper is an attempt to offer a *functional* theory of the mass media, and to suggest criteria for evaluating the media which emerge from it—criteria which are not taken from other disciplines or from the technology of the media. First, the present stage of communications research is considered; second, the contributions of Marx and Freud; and third, an alternative hypothesis is suggested.

I

Urban sociologists ought to be parties to any discussion of the mass media, for it is difficult to imagine anything more symbolically urban than the mass circulation daily newspaper, the car radio, or the TV antenna. Yet judging from books on urban sociology interest in this aspect of urban life has, in recent years, dwindled to almost nothing. Neglect here is matched by the peculiar evasion in communications research of the urban context. Comparisons are routinely made between rural and urban populations with respect to readership, audiences and programme preferences, but these tabulations are not weighted any differently from comparisons along such dimensions as marital status, sex, education, and others in our standard repertoire. The two bodies of knowledge, then, have developed independently of each other despite the common-sense observation that they are inextricably related.

Stranger fissions of reality have taken place in the history of social science, and many of them have survived their critics. But I want to suggest here that the major challenge to social theory in the field of communications lies in healing the breach. Until data from each of these disciplines are juxtaposed and the empirical contingencies examined, until their particular concepts and generalizations are consolidated under the same propositional roof, both are likely to suffer from a diminution of intellectual force. Some such awareness of the fate accounts, I suspect, for the pessimism of Berelson when he remarked, "as for communication research, the state is withering away."[1]

As all good revolutionaries know, the state does not belong to the sacred order of things, but rather to the profane. And it is in the profane accumulation of contradictory findings that a compelling reason may be found for bringing these two lines of inquiry together. The illustration which comes to mind concerns the process of persuasion.

No generalization is more firmly established or more familiar these days in communications research than that the mass media do not convert people from one opinion to another. They reaffirm, help to crystallize, and intensify the convictions of the believer. Often a predisposition towards one point of view is only latent or incipient, and the mass media are given some of the credit for driving this weak or unacknowledged bias towards a more conscious and more explicit expression. But the mass media cannot be said to persuade those who are genuinely neutral or those for whom non-partisanship is a form of apathy. Indeed, the message does not even reach the latter. Nor can the media persuade those whom life has taught differently. Republicans who vote for Democrats are more apt to have made this decision between campaigns when the mass media were silent than during campaigns when persuasion through the mass media is at its peak.[2] Under certain conditions, when, either by accident or design, an audience is exposed to conflicting opinions—when, for example, members of a trade union are deluged with pamphlets from the Communists and the Catholic church arguing different sides—there may be a lowering of interest, a withdrawal of concern.[3] In the decade which has followed Lazarsfeld's *The People's Choice,* the image of the mass media has shifted from the evangelical preacher, from the powerful political demagogue, from the Great Humanist Mediator of All Social Conflict, to just another humble member of the cast who often achieves an effect by saying nothing.

Had we stopped here, there might have been no difficulty. It was what followed these findings that created the paradox. For when the investigators turned to broader forms of persuasion, they discovered that the real "hidden persuader" was the informal opinion leader. The key situations in which he operates are the job environment, the neighborhood, the family, and other primary face-to-face groups. To read these studies is to relive those early years in American Sociology of Mead[4] and Cooley,[5] when the focus of inquiry was on interpersonal relationships, when communication was seen as role-playing or empathy between persons who confronted each other directly; the days, incidentally, when an anthropologist was invited to write the article on communication for the *Encyclopedia of Social Sciences.*[6] That sense of *deja vu* reached a climax in a recent publication entitled *Political Socialization* in which we rediscover the family, the importance of childhood and the years which precede voting age.[7]

Discussions of urban life present a picture of interpersonal relations in marked contrast. Here the focus is on the secular and bureaucratic development of modern life. Attention is drawn to the gradual disappearance of the face-to-face relationship, the decline of those situations where people could communicate on a non-rational and non-verbal level. So inexperienced are we in traditional patterns of communication that they are now thought of as an "art" or a special discipline to be learned. More typical is a relationship that is purposive, specific, contractual, delimited in time and space, and restricted in common associational references. As for those strategic environments, the work environment has become progressively more formal; the neighborhood more and more a cluster of temporary residents who interact with each other as little as possible. Even the family is no longer recognizable—so many of its conventional functions have been transferred to other social institutions. And these, in turn, have moved in the direction of greater professionalization, more exclusive definitions of role and function. Mass urban society, then, is secular society; and it reveals itself most typically in the erosion and deterioration of the informal face-to-face relationship.

How can we reconcile the two? Communications studies with their current emphasis on the primary group and urban studies which have left this model of the primary group behind—a survival, perhaps, a very important one in terms of certain of our values, but greatly transformed and in danger always of becoming the disingenuous phenomenon which Merton calls the *"pseudo-Gemeinschaft"* relationship. Social theory has nothing to lose, then, and much to gain by being concerned with that stretch of countryside that lies between Chicago and Sandusky, between our concepts of urban life and those of mass communication.

II

In this paper, I want to suggest a hypothesis concerning the function of the mass media in modern societies which is consistent with our theories of secularization and which draws empirical support from our studies of the mass media. First, however, I want to consider some antecedent hypotheses; in particular, those which come to us from Marx and Freud.

Marx set the stage for a social theory of the mass media. It was from Marx and later through Mannheim that ideas were examined as reflections of social systems. Knowledge, according to this view, is not autonomous, outside of culture, but socially determined. To be fully understood it must be examined not in terms of logic, not in terms of linguistic conventions, but as a mirror of the aspirations and anxieties of people living in a given social structure.[8] Later Durkheim was to set forth the same general proposition for primitive religions.[9] They, too, could be read as a record of the particular social organization of the primitive group. If this was true for formal systems of ideas, philosophies and science, if it was true for systems like religion which have a historical continuity, it would be even more true for informal systems of belief which are spontaneous, transient, pragmatic, and close to the vagaries of experience.

The difference, however, between the Marxist line of descent and the anthropological line lies in the kinds of communities studied. Generally speaking, the social unit for an anthropologist is a static culture, a homogeneous population which shares its traditions, configurations of values, and patterns of anxiety. For Marx, however, society is stratified by economic classes whose styles of life are different, whose traditions are dissimilar, whose modes of thought vary, whose economic and political destinies are at cross-purposes. Thus, the modern historical situation is not static, and the ideational universe is inherently pluralistic.

It is from this interpretation of social history that we derive our modern three levels of culture: an elite culture, popular culture, and folk culture. An elite culture represents a class which predates the Industrial Revolution that brought the middle class into power. (Nowadays, its stronghold is not so much the landed aristocracy, but, as Veblen suggested, the institutions of higher learning.[10]) Folk culture is the product of a peasant class with its roots in agricultural life. Hoggart's book, *The Uses of Literacy,* describes how an urban working class, only one generation removed from the land, adapted its folk tradition to the new conditions of life, an adaptation that had now reached its limit.[11] Popular culture, for all its claims to universality, is the distinctive artifact of the bourgeoisie. In style, content, method of production, and transmission, it carries the stamp of capitalism and modern technology.

Marx never doubted that the bourgeoisie would attempt to impose its orientation and *Weltanschauung* on all the rest of society, but he did not expect it to succeed. The expectation was that a folk culture would become transformed into a "genuine" working-class culture. This, perhaps, explains in part the sentimentalism of middle-class liberals for folk music and folklore much of which patently fails to meet their own aesthetic criteria. During the 1930's and '40's there was an energetic drive on the part of Communists (in the United States, at least) to collect and revive folk materials—literature, art, and music: a reactionary strategy, one would have thought, in terms of a Marxist interpretation of history, but one which had at the time a virtue in terms of "grass roots" political strategy.

Just what went on in the Cumberland Mountains when the "folk" and the Third International met face to face, we shall, alas, never know. But it is certain from the number of jukeboxes in these remote districts that the enthusiasm to carry on the folk tradition was not mutual. The current chapter in this historical picture is the voluntary dissociation of the rural proletariat from its agrarian past and its participation in urban popular culture through the mass media. The Negro spirituals, along with other forms of folk wisdom and folk handicraft, have become products for commercial and political exploitations. As Andre Malraux observed, "Folk art no longer exists because the 'folk' no longer exists."[12]

Marx anticipated that the proletariat might succumb to the mythology of the bourgeoisie. The term he used was "false consciousness," a denial of reality in which the ideology of a group runs counter to its economic and social interests. An exception was made for the apostate intellectual who saw the handwriting on the wall, and, having understood it, defected from his own doomed middle class to throw in his lot with the nascent revolutionary proletarian movement.

False consciousness in the proletariat was not due to irrationality. In part it was due to ignorance; in part to the systematic efforts of the ruling class to maintain itself in power. By continuing to define all problems in terms of individual enterprise, the bourgeoisie could divide and subdue the working class. Here is the source, then, of our present-day fear that the mass media tranquilize their audiences, and derision implied in the term "escapist entertainment." Marx and the Protestant ethic (the latter, with its premium on action and distrust of idle speculation or fantasy) combine to create some of the strange anomalies of modern thought. No one is alarmed, for example, if a student finds relaxation in slapstick comedy. It is understood if a mathematician cannot fall asleep at night without a paperback mystery; it is "natural" for a self-made business man to spend evenings entranced by the Horatio Alger myth on TV. But it is a "social problem" when the working classes do this. For in their case it is interpreted as a symptom of despair, frustration, and monotony of economic life. And the consequences are looked upon as far more serious: a displacement of anger from the system to the self; a waste of time that could be used in social action; a damaging misconception that salvation lies in individual rather than collective effort.

To an orthodox Marxist, the good society will need no opiates. A world where workers receive their just reward, where work satisfies "the instinct of workmanship," where leisure time is spent in recreation for the good of the community is a world in which the mass media have no place. The Fabians in our field, however, are not as rigid in their rejection of the mass media. They are prepared to use the mass media for education. Yet they belong to the Marxian rather than the Freudian tradition to the extent that they bring to the mass media a rational criterion.

The Freudian and Marxian hypotheses have much in common. Both start with the assumption that ideational systems, whether dreams, national ideologies, literature, religion, or opinions are derivative, secondary systems, described by Marx as "superstructures," by Freud as "projections." Other factors precede them in time and importance: for Marx, the ownership of the means of production; for Freud, the asocial instinctual desires which must be renounced as a condition for living in organized society. Both differentiate between truth and error: between class consciousness and false consciousness in Marx;

between illusion and delusion in Freud. Further, they both assume that the function of ideational systems is conservative, to maintain the *status quo*. The working class, according to Marx, is deliberately kept quiescent in order to avert insurgent political action. Freud emphasizes the extent to which ideational systems reconcile the individual to the denial of anti-social drives although these continue to exist in the unconscious. In discussing religion, for example, Freud says, "The true believer is in a high degree protected against the danger of certain neurotic afflictions; by accepting the universal neurosis he is spared the task of forming a personal neurosis."[13] Finally, both Marx and Freud see the dynamic factor, whether in history or individual motivation, as conflict. For Marx, it was the conflict of class interests; for Freud, it was a conflict between the internalized norms of society—the superego—and the wishes and infantile instincts of human nature, the id. The leadership or executive function Marx assigned to the intellectuals was assigned by Freud to the ego.

Here the similarity ends. But the two hypotheses overlap to the extent that the mechanisms Freud describes, quite apart from his specific theory of motivation, provide the psychological concepts missing in Marx. Whether or not one accepts the importance Freud placed on the Oedipal conflict is irrelevant. The concept of projection explains how raw experience is transformed by an individual into a set of symbols, images, or ideas. The model here is dream interpretation where, with the help of the analyst, the dreamer sees the connection between unconscious motivation, a forgotten reality, and the dream symbol. Erich Fromm in *The Forgotten Language* provides illustrations of how this model can be used for interpreting a fairy tale like "Red Ridinghood" or a novel like Kafka's *The Trial*,[14] just as Jones did for *Hamlet* and *Opedipus*,[15] and Lasswell did for political propaganda.[16]

Freud provides the key to "false consciousness" in his concept of "identification." According to this view, the child models himself on those in his environment on whom he is dependent. They become his "ego-ideals." They need not be admired or loved; they need not be the source of pleasure or reward. They may be hated and the agents of punishment and rejection. But the helplessness of the individual is a self-propelling force behind the identification. In adult life, the identifications we make repeat the patterns of childhood so that often the underdog identifies with his oppressor, the prisoner with his guards, the "non-com" with his officers, just as they once did with their fathers.

In Freud's concept of "ego-involvement" we find a partial explanation of the failure of the mass media to convert. The attitudes an individual has on public issues have less to do with the issues themselves than they do with the individual's own personality needs. Attitudes are only terminal extensions of a deeper personality organization which seeks to preserve itself. Our approach to experience, then, is selective: we take from it only those parts which nourish and protect the self, resisting anything that evokes guilt, rationalizing in favour of one's self anything that suggests conflict. Hence we have learned that propaganda or informational materials which "threaten" an individual's self-image are ineffective,[17] regardless of how logically persuasive they are or how consistent with class interest. And similarly we have become wary of a "boomerang" effect, when a pamphlet, for example, urging enemy troops to surrender leads to an improvement in their morale.

By examining here the similarities and dovetailing of these two hypotheses, we can understand why both influences, Marx and Freud, have converged in our approach to the mass media. For most purposes, they are not mutually exclusive. For example, in an analysis of the novels of Mickey Spillane, the hero, Mike Hammer, is seen as Senator McCarthy. Both are above and outside the law; both creatures of the contemporary *Zeitgeist*.[18] In another analysis, Mike Hammer is seen as the alter-ego of Inspector Maigret, but either or both constitute a saviour figure in "modern man's Passion Play."[19] What differentiates these two analyses is the level of abstraction and the referent. But they are not inconsistent. Multiple levels of abstraction and referent are used in Merton's study of the Kate Smith marathon broadcast where Kate Smith's appeal to the audience is alternatively explained in terms of a universal mother image and a particular image—the embodiment of sincerity—created by a society where manipulation has become a constant anxiety.[20]

Freudians, like Marxists, are not in agreement about the mass media as such. Some see in the addiction to comic books and television a symptom of individual maladjustment which is not improved and is sometimes worsened by the content of programmes and the habit of withdrawing from reality.[21] Others are satisfied that what we do when we are exposed to the mass media is no different from spontaneous fantasy or dream activity: the media neither further nor obstruct an introspective process that leads to self-awareness.

In summary, the Marxian and Freudian hypotheses have had enormous direct and indirect influence on research in this field of mass communications. Our studies of the institutional development of the media begin in Marx as do many of our studies of the social effects of the media. Our studies of audiences and their motivation have drawn heavily on Freud. Content analysis is the direct outcome of these two orientations. Even our methods of research—the projective question, the depth interview, scale analysis—come from the Freudian tradition. And our criticism of each other's work bears the stamp of Marx or Freud or both.

A much more subtle influence has to do with the criteria for judging the media. From Marx, we acquire our concept of the mass media in the service of knowledge about the social environment; from Freud, our concept of the mass media providing self-insight. From Marx, we inherit our emphasis on documentary information and editorial interpretation; from Freud, our emphasis on illusion or art. Developments in sociology and psychology since Marx and Freud have revised our concept of human nature and of social change. Few, if any, today accept the dichotomy between the rational and irrational definitions of man. Yet we continue in our thinking about the mass media to regard art and rational or scientific knowledge as the goals.

III

Different systems of media control have a great deal to do with how often and how sincerely the effort is made to reach the objectives of knowledge and art and with which these objectives is emphasized. Comparisons between British and American television make this abundantly clear. But even under the most favourable circumstances, the achievement of these standards is rare. And there is a chronic sense of disappointment, of dissatisfaction, of disillusionment among those connected with the mass media as well as among their sympathetic but discerning audiences.

Oddly enough, the media have been compared to folk art. Sometimes with approval; sometimes, not. "The comic books," Fiedler writes, ". . . are seen as inheritors . . . of the inner impulses of traditional folk art . . . Beneath their journalistic commentary . . . they touch archetypal material: those shared figures of our lower minds more like the patterns of dream than fact . . . They are our not quite machine-subdued Grimm, though the Black Forest has become, as it must, the City; the Wizard, the Scientist; and Simple Hans, Captain Marvel."[22]

On a more superficial level, the content of the mass media belongs to the folk tradition in that it projects a *Gemeinschaft* universe. The "soap opera" is the classic example: a small town which never changes, isolated from events in the larger world; characters whose motivation is over-simplified—they are moral or immoral, strong or weak, good or bad; conflicts that are resolved by accident, sudden unexplained character conversions, or by the intervention of supernatural forces; in short, a closed domestic stereotyped world ruled more by fate and by faith than by cause and effect.[23]

Intriguing as this comparison is between folk art and popular culture it is deceptive. If, instead of looking at thematic similarities, we look at function, the difference becomes apparent. Folk art in a primitive society is not regressive. It provides closure; it provides security; it provides continuity and consensus. But it does not interfere with the daily requirements of reality. As Malinowski pointed out, magic and mythology are not alternatives to the scientific knowledge which experience has taught the native about controlling nature.[24] If our popular culture functions chiefly to evade reality, then, despite the textual similarities with folk art, the two are quite different. The parallel drawn between them then is a highly literate plea for a more sensitive and imaginative interpretation of popular culture, and an ideological *tour de force* against the snobbery which often vitiates serious discussions of the mass media.

Folk art and popular culture have one thing in common with each other that they do not share with other art forms. Both are essentially social. Their audiences are never a minority, their appeals never sectarian, their insights never exclusive. It is this public or social character of the mass

media which distinguishes it from what artists call art. And although in practice it is sometimes a difference in degree rather than kind, it provides a clue to the appropriate criterion to apply to the mass media.

The difference along this dimension has long been recognized. Malraux, for example, draws a distinction between the "arts" and the "appeasing arts"; the latter include popular culture. Although he insists that the "appeasing arts" are "in no sense inferior arts,"[25] they are generally regarded as second class. And, given the biases of our society, it is difficult to see how this value judgment can be avoided or what purpose is served by this patronizing air. In any case, such a distinction offers no standard for evaluating popular culture, except a quantitative one. So long as the mass media are seen as the charming other-directed younger son, they will be judged by measures of popularity and success. Not by what they are, not by what they do, but by how many friends they make.

If, instead, we look upon the mass media as a social institution in its own right, we come closer to understanding what differentiates the media from either art or scholarship. The parallel that can be drawn is between the mass media and other institutions like the family and school.

Empirically, there is no doubt that the media meet the minimum requirements of any definition of a social institution. First, some form of media consumption is almost universal in modern societies. Second, the media outlive their audiences. Third, the primary functions of the mass media are socialization and social control.

The fact that some people never read a newspaper, never see a movie, never watch television, does not disprove the point any more than the existence of orphans casts doubt on our concept of the family as an institution. In other words, an expected deviation is part of any definition of a social institution. Deviation here would include not only under-conformity, but over-conformity—media addiction, for example—as well.

In suggesting that the functions of the mass media are socialization and social control, we do not preclude the possibility that the media may also be dysfunctional. The cases which Wertham and others have cited of the mass media contributing to delinquency or mental illness,[26] the suggestion by Klapper that the media introduce children too early to complexities in adult life which they are not prepared to comprehend,[27] the view of Maccoby that the media set up expectations of excitement that real life can never satisfy,[28] of Himmelweit that TV creates an image of an affluent middle-class society which most of its audience have no hope of ever realizing[29]—these, and others, are examples of dysfunction.

The second part of our hypothesis concerns the specific function of the mass media. What is the connection between the mass media and other institutions? One view is that other institutions have failed and that the mass media fill a vacuum created by default. For some, this is the early stages of totalitarianism from which there is no return. But for others, it is just not a very desirable solution to a lamentable situation; a surrogate parent is better than no parent, but one looks forward to the day when the absentee parent will return to resume responsibility. This is the assumption behind various proposed reforms like "group dynamics" to reactivate and reinstate that "comfy" old fashioned face-to-face relationship. It is behind our concern about "feed-back" and the passivity of audiences. It is at the root, too, of the view that artists, intellectuals, and educators can use the mass media to raise the level of public taste and curiosity so that the public will eventually liberate itself from the clutch of the mass media, a day when audience ratings will drop because the audience want authentic art and authentic education. These and similar views are derived from the assumption that the mass media are a temporary substitute for other institutions—institutions which have, for one reason or another, declined but can be made once again to function properly.

The hypothesis I want to suggest here is that this view is not incorrect, but, like the examples I have given of deviation and dysfunction, it is a special and limiting case. Seen in proper perspective, the function the mass media fulfill in modern societies is not the result of the failure of other social institutions, but of their success. Here I am assuming that we live in a society which has become secularized and that the trend in that direction will continue. A high division of labour, a high degrees of role differentiation, a high rate of social mobility and social change, a scientific ethos, and formal organization are among the distinguishing characteristics of this social structure. Experience in such a society is segmented, and the major stress on personality is a pressure towards fragmentation.

Given this context, the unique function of the mass media is to provide both to the individual and to society a coherence, a synthesis of experience, an awareness of the whole which does not undermine the specialization which reality requires. The supreme test of the mass media, then, is not whether it meets the criteria of art or the criteria of knowledge, but how well it provides an integration of experience. Neither art nor knowledge is excluded as standard, but they are secondary. The mass media cannot sacrifice cultural insight to archetypal insight; they cannot sacrifice social urgency to sustained systematic intellectual inquiry; they cannot sacrifice the present for the past. Nor can they sacrifice revelation for production or distribution *finesse*. To expect them to satisfy all of these criteria equally well is unrealistic and places a greater schizophrenic strain on people responsible for the mass media than is placed on any other sector of the population. But different systems of media control and the changing technology of the mass media offer varying degrees of opportunity to realize the order suggested.

To conclude this discussion I want to come back to the original problem: the relation between communications research and our theories of urban society. What I have tried to indicate here is that our present trend in communications research assumes a model of society that is traditional in contrast with the secular model of urban sociology. The hypothesis I have suggested here is that the mass media are a social institution created by the demands, social and psychological, in a secular society, demands for an awareness of the connections in modern experience and our own involvement in them. The greater the specialization, the greater the segmentalization of experience, the greater the stresses toward fragmentation of personality, the greater will be the need for experiences which organize and provide a *Gestalt*. The relation we have with the media as members of an audience is a mediated impersonal one. Ordinarily what is implied in these terms is a quantum of psychological and social distance that effects communication. But whether in a secular society these distances are any greater than those of interpersonal relationships is open to question. They may even be less. But the real problem for both theory and research is not impersonalized but depersonalized relationships. It is my hope that from the frame of reference outlined here attention will shift from comparisons between face-to-face and impersonal communication to the various types of communication in secular society.

Notes

Presented to the Conference of Learned Societies on June 10, 1961 in Montreal.

1. Bernard Berelson, "The State of Communication Research," *Public Opinion Quarterly*, XXIII, no. 1, spring, 1959, 1–9.

2. Paul F. Lazarsfeld, Bernard Berelson and Hazel Gaudet, *The People's Choice* (New York, 1948).

3. Martin Kriesberg, "Cross-Pressures and Attitudes: A Study of the Influence of Conflicting Propaganda on Opinions Regarding American-Soviet Relations," *Public Opinion Quarterly*, XIII, no. 1, spring, 1949, 5–16.

4. George H. Mead, *Mind, Self and Society* (Chicago, 1933).

5. C. H. Cooley, *Human Nature and the Social Order* (New York, 1902).

6. Edward Sapir, "Communication," *Encyclopedia of Social Science*, IV (New York, 1931).

7. Herbert H. Hyman, *Political Socialization* (Glencoe, Ill., 1959).

8. Karl Mannheim, *Ideology and Utopia* (New York, 1940).

9. Emile Durkheim, *The Elementary Forms of the Religious Life* (Glencoe, Ill., 1947).

10. Thorstein Veblen, *The Higher Learning in America* (New York, 1918).

11. Richard Hoggart, *The Uses of Literacy* (London, 1957).

12. André Malraux, "Art, Popular Art, and the Illusion of the Folk," *Partisan Review*, XVIII, no. 5, 487–95.

13. Sigmund Freud, *The Future of an Illusion* (New York, 1949), 77.

14. New York, 1951.

15. Ernest Jones, *Hamlet and Oedipus* (New York, 1954).

16. Harold D. Lasswell, *Psychopathology and Politics* (Chicago, 1930).

17. Eunice Cooper and Marie Jahoda, "The Evasion of Propaganda," *Journal of Psychology*, XXIII, Jan., 1947, 15–25.

18. Christopher La Farge, "Mickey Spillane and His Bloody Hammer," *Saturday Review*, Nov. 6, 1954.

19. Charles J. Rolo, "Simenon and Spillane: The Metaphysics of Murder for the Millions," in Bernard Rosenberg and David Manning White, eds., *Mass Culture* (Glencoe, Ill., 1960), 165–75.

20. Robert K. Merton, *Mass Persuasion* (New York, 1946).

21. Eugene David Glynn, "Television and the American Character—A Psychiatrist Looks at Television," in William Y. Elliott, *Television's Impact On American Culture* (East Lansing, Mich., ed., 1956).

22. Leslie A. Fiedler, "The Middle Against Both Ends," in Bernard Rosenberg and David Manning White, eds., *Mass Culture* (Glencoe, Ill., 1960), 537–47.

23. Rudolf Arnheim, "The World of the Daytime Serial," in Paul F. Lazarsfeld, and Frank N. Stanton, eds., *Radio Research, 1942–1943* (New York, 1944).

24. Bronislaw Malinowski, *Magic, Science and Religion* (New York, 1954).

25. Malraux, "Art, Popular Art, and the Illusion of the Folk."

26. Frederic C. Wertham, *Seduction of the Innocent* (New York, 1954).

27. Joseph T. Klapper, *Children and Television: A Review of Socially Prevalent Concerns* (New York, 1948).

28. Eleanor E. Maccoby, "Television: Its Impact on School Children," *Public Opinion Quarterly*, XV, no. 3, 421–44.

29. Hilde T. Himmelweit, A. N. Oppenheim, and Pamela Vince, *Television and the Child* (London and New York, 1958).

65

Television and the Public Interest (1961)

Newton Minow

In 1961, at the age of thirty-five, Newton Minow (1926–) was appointed chairman of the Federal Communications Commission by John F. Kennedy. During the 1950s, he clerked for Justice Vinson of the U.S. Supreme Court; served as counsel to Governor Adlai Stevenson of Illinois; and played a key role in Stevenson's two unsuccessful presidential election campaigns, during which he became acquainted with people in the upper echelons of the Democratic Party, such as Robert Kennedy. Much of his life has been spent in law and public service, not only professionally, but personally. He is father of media critic and columnist Nell Minow and of law professors Martha Minow and Mary Minow.

Minow's speech, nominated as one of the top one-hundred American speeches of the twentieth century, parallels contemporaneous intellectual debates about the meaning of mass culture. Its boldness reflects in many ways the intellectual idealism of the early Kennedy era. It rests on the faith that government regulators have a moral stewardship over the welfare of public culture, a credo also reflected in a different way in the later *Surgeon General's Report*. The lofty ambitions of the speech also perhaps signal a repudiation of the compromised world of television by American intellectuals. To put it lightly, the speech was not greeted with universal delight by the entertainment industry. A 1961 editorial comment in the advertising trade journal *Printer's Ink* expresses one view of Minow's efforts to reform the media business (which were not restricted to either television or this speech): "He would impose *Hamlet* on the masses with all the ferocious conviction of a medieval torturer turning the screws for the victims' own good." Minow's speech was a symptom of a chasm that would only widen in the 1960s between high and popular culture; gone were the earlier hopes of Dewey, Du Bois, and Locke that public art could simultaneously be popular and profound.

Thank you for this opportunity to meet with you today. This is my first public address since I took over my new job. When the New Frontiersmen rode into town, I locked myself in my office to do my homework and get my feet wet. But apparently I haven't managed to stay out of hot water. I seem to have detected a certain nervous aprehension about what I might say or do when I emerged from that locked office for this, my maiden station break.

First, let me begin by dispelling a rumor. I was not picked for this job because I regard myself as the fastest draw on the New Frontier. Second, let me start a rumor. Like you, I have carefully read President Kennedy's messages about the regulatory agencies, conflict of interest, and the dangers of *ex parte* contacts. And, of course, we at the Federal Communications Commission will do our part. Indeed, I may even suggest that we change the name of the FCC to The Seven Untouchables!

It may also come as a surprise to some of you, but I want you to know that you have my admiration and respect. Yours is a most honorable profession. Anyone who is in the broadcasting business has a tough row to hoe. You earn your bread by using public property. When you work in broadcasting you volunteer for public service, public pressure, and public regulation. You must compete with other attractions and other investments, and the only way you can do it is to prove to us every three years that you should have been in business in the first place.

I can think of easier ways to make a living.

But I cannot think of more satisfying ways. I admire your courage—but that doesn't mean I would make life any easier for you. Your license lets you use the public's airwaves as trustees for 180 million Americans. The public is your beneficiary. If you want to stay on as trustees, you must deliver a decent return to the public—not only to your stockholders. So, as a representative of the public, your health and your product are among my chief concerns.

As to your health: let's talk only of television today. 1960 gross broadcast revenues of the television industry were over $1,268,000,000; profit before taxes was $243,900,000, an average return on revenue of 19.2 per cent. Compared with 1959, gross broadcast revenues were $1,163,900,000, and profit before taxes was $222,300,000, an average return on revenue of 19.1 per cent. So, the percentage increase of total revenues from 1959 to 1960 was 9 per cent, and the percentage increase of profit was 9.7 per cent. This, despite a recession. For your investors, the price has indeed been right.

I have confidence in your health.

But not in your product.

It is with this and much more in mind that I come before you today.

One editorialist in the trade press wrote that "the FCC of the New Frontier is going to be one of the toughest FCC's in the history of broadcast regulation." If he meant that we intend to enforce the law in the public interest, let me make it perfectly clear that he is right—we do. If he meant that we intend to muzzle or censor broadcasting, he is dead wrong. It would not surprise me if some of you had expected me to come here today and say in effect, "Clean up your own house or the government will do it for you." Well, in a limited sense, you would be right—I've just said it.

But I want to say to you earnestly that it is not in that spirit that I come before you today, nor is it in that spirit that I intend to serve the FCC. I am in Washington to help broadcasting, not to harm it; to strengthen it, not weaken it; to reward it, not punish it; to encourage it, not threaten it; to stimulate it, not censor it. Above all, I am here to uphold and protect the public interest.

What do we mean by "the public interest?"

Some say the public interest is merely what interests the public. I disagree. So does your distinguished president, Governor Collins. In a recent speech he said,

> Broadcasting to serve the public interest, must have a soul and a conscience, a burning desire to excel, as well as to sell; the urge to build the character, citizenship and intellectual stature of people, as well as to expand the gross national product.... By no means do I imply that broadcasters disregard the public interest.... But a much better job can be done, and should be done.

I could not agree more.

And I would add that in today's world, with chaos in Laos and the Congo aflame, with Communist tyranny on our Caribbean doorstep and relentless pressure on our Atlantic alliance, with social and economic problems at home of the gravest nature, yes, and with technological knowledge that makes it possible, as our President has said, not only to destroy our world but to destroy poverty around the world—in a time of peril and opportunity, the old complacent, unbalanced fare of action-adventure and situation comedies is simply not good enough.

Your industry possesses the most powerful voice in America. It has an inescapable duty to make that voice ring with intelligence and with leadership. In a few years, this exciting industry has grown from a novelty to an instrument of overwhelming impact on the American people. It should be making ready for the kind of leadership that newspapers and magazines assumed years ago, to make our people aware of their world.

Ours has been called the jet age, the atomic age, the space age. It is also, I submit, the television age. And just as history will decide whether the leaders of today's world employed the atom to destroy the world or rebuild it for mankind's benefit, so will history decide whether today's broadcasters employed their powerful voice to enrich the people or debase them.

If I seem today to address myself chiefly to the problems of television, I don't want any of you radio broadcasters to think we've gone to sleep at your switch—we haven't. We still listen. But in recent years most of the controversies and crosscurrents in broadcast programming have swirled around television. And so my subject today is the television industry and the public interest.

Like everybody, I wear more than one hat. I am the chairman of the FCC. I am also a television viewer and the husband and father of other television viewers. I have seen a great many television programs that seemed to me eminently worthwhile and I am not talking about the much bemoaned good old days of "Playhouse 90" and "Studio One."

I am talking about this past season. Some were wonderfully entertaining, such as "The Fabulous Fifties," "The Fred Astaire Show," and "The Bing Crosby Special"; some were dramatic and moving, such as Conrad's "Victory" and "Twilight Zone"; some were marvelously informative, such as "The Nation's Future," "CBS Reports," and "The Valiant Years." I could list many more—programs that I am sure everyone here felt enriched his own life and that of his family. When television is good, nothing—not the theater, not the magazines or newspapers—nothing is better.

But when television is bad, nothing is worse. I invite you to sit down in front of your television set when your station goes on the air and stay there without a book, magazine, newspaper, profit and loss sheet or rating book to distract you—and keep your eyes glued to that set until the station signs off. I can assure you that you will observe a vast wasteland.

You will see a procession of game shows, violence, audience participation shows, formula comedies about totally unbelievable families, blood and thunder, mayhem, violence, sadism, murder, western bad men, western good men, private eyes, gangsters, more violence, and cartoons. And, endlessly, commercials—many screaming, cajoling, and offending. And most of all, boredom. True, you will see a few things you will enjoy. But they will be very, very few. And if you think I exaggerate, try it.

Is there one person in this room who claims that broadcasting can't do better?

Well, a glance at next season's proposed programming can give us little heart. Of 73 and 1/2 hours of prime evening time, the networks have tentatively scheduled 59 hours to categories of action-adventure, situation comedy, variety, quiz, and movies.

Is there one network president in this room who claims he can't do better?

Well, is there at least one network president who believes that the other networks can't do better?

Gentlemen, your trust accounting with your beneficiaries is overdue.

Never have so few owed so much to so many.

Why is so much of television so bad? I have heard many answers: demands of your advertisers; competition for ever higher ratings; the need always to attract a mass audience; the high cost of television programs; the insatiable appetite for programming material—these are some of them. Unquestionably, these are tough problems not susceptible to easy answers.

But I am not convinced that you have tried hard enough to solve them.

I do not accept the idea that the present over-all programming is aimed accurately at the public taste. The ratings tell us only that some people have their television sets turned on and of that number, so many are tuned to one channel and so many to another. They don't tell us what the public might watch if they were offered half-a-dozen additional choices. A rating, at best, is an indication of how many people saw what you gave them. Unfortunately, it does not reveal the depth of the penetration, or the intensity of reaction, and it never reveals what the acceptance would have been if what you gave them had been better—if all the forces of art and creativity and daring and imagination had been unleashed. I believe in the people's good sense and good taste, and I am not convinced that the people's taste is as low as some of you assume.

My concern with the rating services is not with their accuracy. Perhaps they are accurate. I really don't know. What, then, is wrong with the ratings? It's not been their accuracy—it's been their use.

Certainly, I hope you will agree that ratings should have little influence where children are concerned. The best estimates indicate that during the hours of 5 to 6 P.M. sixty per cent of your audience is composed of children under twelve. And most young children today, believe it or not, spend as much time watching television as they do in the schoolroom. I repeat—let that sink in—most young children today spend as much time watching television as they do in the schoolroom. It used to be said that there were three great influences on a child: home, school, and church. Today, there is a fourth great influence, and you ladies and gentlemen control it.

If parents, teachers, and ministers conducted their responsibilities by following the ratings, children would have a steady diet of ice cream, school holidays, and no Sunday school. What about your responsibilities? Is there no room on television to teach, to inform, to uplift, to stretch, to enlarge the capacities of our children? Is there no room for programs deepening their understanding of children in other lands? Is there no room for a children's news show explaining something about the world to them at their level of understanding? Is there no room for reading the great literature of the past, teaching them the great traditions of freedom? There are some fine children's shows, but they are drowned out in the massive doses of cartoons, violence, and more violence. Must these be your trademarks? Search your consciences and see if you cannot offer more to your young beneficiaries whose future you guide so many hours each and every day.

What about adult programming and ratings? You know, newspaper publishers take popularity ratings too. The answers are pretty clear: it is almost always the comics, followed by the advice to the lovelorn columns. But, ladies and gentlemen, the news is still on the front page of all newspapers; the editorials are not replaced by more comics; the newspapers have not become one long collection of advice to the lovelorn. Yet newspapers do not need a license from the government to be in business—they do not use public property. But in television, where your responsibilities as public trustees are so plain, the moment that the ratings indicate that westerns are popular there are new imitations of westerns on the air faster than the old coaxial cable could take us from Hollywood to New York. Broadcasting cannot continue to live by the numbers. Ratings ought to be the slave of the broadcaster, not his master. And you and I both know that the rating services themselves would agree.

Let me make clear that what I am talking about is balance. I believe that the public interest is made up of many interests. There are many people in this great country and you must serve all of us. You will get no argument from me if you say that, given a choice between a western and a symphony, more people will watch the western. I like westerns and private eyes too, but a steady diet for the whole country is obviously not in the public interest. We all know that people would more often prefer to be entertained than stimulated or informed. But your obligations are not satisfied if you look only to popularity as a test of what to broadcast. You are

not only in show business; you are free to communicate ideas as well as relaxation. You must provide a wider range of choices, more diversity, more alternatives. It is not enough to cater to the nation's whims; you must also serve the nation's needs.

And I would add this: that if some of you persist in a relentless search for the highest rating and the lowest common denominator, you may very well lose your audience. Because, to paraphrase a great American who was recently my law partner, the people are wise, wiser than some of the broadcasters—and politicians—think.

As you may have gathered, I would like to see television improved. But how is this to be brought about? By voluntary action by the broadcasters themselves? By direct government intervention? Or how?

Let me address myself now to my role not as a viewer but as chairman of the FCC. I could not if I would, chart for you this afternoon in detail all of the actions I contemplate. Instead, I want to make clear some of the fundamental principles which guide me.

First: the people own the air. They own it as much in prime evening time as they do at six o'clock Sunday morning. For every hour that the people give you—you owe them something. I intend to see that your debt is paid with service.

Second: I think it would be foolish and wasteful for us to continue any worn-out wrangle over the problems of payola, rigged quiz shows, and other mistakes of the past. There are laws on the books which we will enforce. But there is no chip on my shoulder. We live together in perilous, uncertain times; we face together staggering problems; and we must not waste much time now by rehashing the clichés of past controversy.

To quarrel over the past is to lose the future.

Third: I believe in the free enterprise system. I want to see broadcasting improved, and I want you to do the job. I am proud to champion your cause. It is not rare for American businessmen to serve a public trust. Yours is a special trust because it is imposed by law.

Fourth: I will do all I can to help educational television. There are still not enough educational stations, and major centers of the country still lack usable educational channels. If there were a limited number of printing presses in this country, you may be sure that a fair proportion of them would be put to educational use. Educational television has an enormous contribution to make to the future, and I intend to give it a hand along the way. If there is not a nation-wide educational television system in this country, it will not be the fault of the FCC.

Fifth: I am unalterably opposed to governmental censorship. There will be no suppression of programming which does not meet with bureaucratic tastes. Censorship strikes at the tap root of our free society.

Sixth: I did not come to Washington to idly observe the squandering of the public's airwaves. The squandering of our airwaves is no less important than the lavish waste of any precious natural resource. I intend to take the job of chairman of the FCC very seriously. I believe in the gravity of my own particular sector of the New Frontier. There will be times perhaps when you will consider that I take myself or my job *too* seriously. Frankly, I don't care if you do. For I am convinced that either one takes this job seriously—or one can be seriously taken.

Now, how will these principles be applied? Clearly, at the heart of the FCC's authority lies its power to license, to renew or fail to renew, or to revoke a license. As you know, when your license comes up for renewal, your performance is compared with your promises. I understand that many people feel that in the past licenses were often renewed *pro forma*. I say to you now: renewal will not be *pro forma* in the future. There is nothing permanent or sacred about a broadcast license.

But simply matching promises and performance is not enough. I intend to do more. I intend to find out whether the people care. I intend to find out whether the community which each broadcaster serves believes he has been serving the public interest. When a renewal is set down for hearing, I intend—wherever possible—to hold a well-advertised public hearing, right in the community you have promised to serve. I want the people who own the air and the homes that television enters to tell you and the FCC what's been going on. I want the people—if they are truly interested in the service you give them—to make notes, document cases, tell us the facts. For those few of you who really believe that the public interest is merely what interests the public, hope that these hearings will arouse no little interest.

The FCC has a fine reserve of monitors— almost 180 million Americans gathered around 56 million sets. If you want those monitors to be your friends at court, it's up to you.

Some of you may say, "Yes, but I still do not know where the line is between a grant of a renewal and the hearing you just spoke of." My answer is: Why should you want to know how close you can come to the edge of the cliff? What the Commission asks of you is to make a conscientious, good-faith effort to serve the public interest. Everyone of you serves a community in which the people would benefit by educational, religious, instructive or other public service programming. Every one of you serves an area which has local needs—as to local elections, controversial issues, local news, local talent. Make a serious, genuine effort to put on that programming. When you do, you will not be playing brinkmanship with the public interest.

What I've been saying applies to broadcast stations. Now a station break for the networks:

You know your importance in this great industry. Today, more than one half of all hours of television station programming comes from the networks; in prime time, this rises to more than three quarters of the available hours.

You know that the FCC has been studying network operations for some time. I intend to press this to a speedy conclusion with useful results. I can tell you right now, however, that I am deeply concerned with concentration of power in the hands of the networks. As a result, too many local stations have foregone any efforts at local programming, with little use of live talent and local service. Too many local stations operate with one hand on the network switch and the other on a projector loaded with old movies. We want the individual stations to be free to meet their legal responsibilities to serve their communities.

I join Governor Collins in his views so well expressed to the advertisers who use the public air. I urge the networks to join him and undertake a very special mission on behalf of this industry: you can tell your advertisers, "This is the high quality we are going to serve—take it or other people will. If you think you can find a better place to move automobiles, cigarettes and soap—go ahead and try."

Tell your sponsors to be less concerned with costs per thousand and more concerned with understanding per millions. And remind your stockholders that an investment in broadcasting is buying a share in public responsibility. The networks can start this industry on the road to freedom from the dictatorship of numbers.

But there is more to the problem than network influences on stations or advertiser influences on networks. I know the problems networks face in trying to clear some of their best programs—the informational programs that exemplify public service. They are your finest hours—whether sustaining or commercial, whether regularly scheduled or special—these are the signs that broadcasting knows the way to leadership. They make the public's trust in you a wise choice.

They should be seen. As you know, we are readying for use new forms by which broadcast stations will report their programming to the Commission. You probably also know that special attention will be paid in these reports to public service programming. I believe that stations taking network service should also be required to report the extent of the local clearance of network public service programming, and when they fail to clear them, they should explain why. If it is to put on some outstanding local program, this is one reason. But, if it is simply to carry some old movies, that is an entirely different matter. The Commission should consider such clearance reports carefully when making up its mind about the licensee's over-all programming.

We intend to move—and as you know, indeed the FCC was rapidly moving in other new areas before the new Administration arrived in Washington. And I want to pay my public respects to my very able predecessor, Fred Ford, and my colleagues on the Commission who have welcomed me to the FCC with warmth and cooperation.

We have approved an experiment with pay TV, and in New York we are testing the potential of UHF broadcasting. Either or both of these may revolutionize television. Only a foolish prophet would venture to guess the direction they will take, and their effect. But we intend that they shall be explored fully—for they are part of broadcasting's New Frontier. The questions surrounding pay TV are largely economic. The questions surrounding UHF are largely technological. We are going to give the infant pay TV a chance to prove whether it can offer a useful service; we are going to protect it from those who would strangle it in its crib.

As for UHF, I'm sure you know about our test in the canyons of New York City. We will take every possible positive step to break through the allocations barrier into UHF. We will put this sleeping giant to use and in the years ahead we may have twice as many channels operating in cities where now there are only two or three. We may have a half dozen networks instead of three.

I have told you that I believe in the free enterprise system. I believe that most of television's problems stem from lack of competition. This is the importance of UHF to me: with more channels on the air, we will be able to provide every community with enough stations to offer service to all parts of the public. Programs with a mass market appeal required by mass product advertisers certainly will still be available. But other stations will recognize the need to appeal to more limited markets and to special tastes. In this way, we can all have a much wider range of programs.

Television should thrive on this competition—and the country should benefit from alternative sources of service to the public. And—Governor Collins—I hope the NAB will benefit from many new members.

Another and perhaps the most important frontier: television will rapidly join the parade into space. International television will be with us soon. No one knows how long it will be until a broadcast from a studio in New York will be viewed in India as well as in Indiana, will be seen in the Congo as it is seen in Chicago. But as surely as we are meeting here today, that day will come—and once again our world will shrink.

What will the people of other countries think of us when they see our western badmen and good men punching each other in the jaw in between the shooting? What will the Latin American or African child learn of America from our great communications industry? We cannot permit television in its present form to be our voice overseas.

There is your challenge to leadership. You must reexamine some fundamentals of your industry. You must open your minds and open your hearts to the limitless horizons of tomorrow.

I can suggest some words that should serve to guide you:

Television and all who participate in it are jointly accountable to the American public for respect for the special needs of children, for community responsibility, for the advancement of education and culture, for the acceptability of the program materials chosen, for decency and decorum in production, and for propriety in advertising. This responsibility cannot be discharged by any given group of programs, but can be discharged only through the highest standards of respect for the American home, applied to every moment of every program presented by television.

Program materials should enlarge the horizons of the viewer, provide him with wholesome entertainment, afford helpful stimulation, and remind him of the responsibilities which the citizen has towards his society.

These words are not mine. They are yours. They are taken literally from your own Television Code. They reflect the leadership and aspirations of your own great industry. I urge you to respect them as I do. And I urge you to respect the intelligent and farsighted leadership of Governor LeRoy Collins, and to make this meeting a creative act. I urge you at this meeting and, after you leave, back home, at your stations and your networks, to strive ceaselessly to improve your product and to better serve your viewers, the American people.

I hope that we at the FCC will not allow ourselves to become so bogged down in the mountain of papers, hearings, memoranda, orders, and the daily routine that we close our eyes to the wider view of the public interest. And I hope that you broadcasters will not permit yourselves to become so absorbed in the chase for ratings, sales, and profits that you lose this wider view. Now more than ever before in broadcasting's history the times demand the best of all of us.

We need imagination in programming, not sterility; creativity, not imitation; experimentation, not conformity; excellence, not mediocrity. Television is filled with creative, imaginative people. You must strive to set them free.

Television in its young life has had many hours of greatness—its "Victory at Sea," its Army-McCarthy hearings, its "Peter Pan," its "Kraft Theaters," its "See It Now," its "Project 20," the World Series, its political conventions and campaigns, the Great Debates—and it has had its endless hours of mediocrity and its moments of public disgrace. There are estimates that today the average viewer spends about 200 minutes daily with television, while the average reader spends 38 minutes with magazines and 40 minutes with newspapers. Television has grown faster than a teenager, and now it is time to grow up.

What you gentlemen broadcast through the people's air affects the people's taste, their knowledge, their opinions, their understanding of themselves and of their world. And their future.

The power of instantaneous sight and sound is without precedent in mankind's history. This is an awesome power. It has limitless capabilities for good—and for evil. And it carries with it awesome responsibilities, responsibilities which you and I cannot escape.

In his stirring inaugural address our President said, "And so, my fellow Americans: ask not what your country can do for you; ask what you can do for your country."

Ladies and Gentlemen:

Ask not what broadcasting can do for you. Ask what you can do for broadcasting.

I urge you to put the people's airwaves to the service of the people and the cause of freedom. You must help prepare a generation for great decisions. You must help a great nation fulfill its future.

Do this, and I pledge you our help.

66

The Kennedy Assassination and the Nature of Political Commitment

From *The Kennedy Assassination and the American Public* (1965)

Sidney Verba

Sidney Verba (1932–) is a leading student of American and comparative politics whose theoretically guided, internationally oriented empirical studies extend work of that sort pioneered by Harold Lasswell and others in the 1920s. Born in Brooklyn, Verba attended Harvard and Princeton University, where he took his doctorate in political science (1959). His 1963 book with Gabriel Almond, *The Civic Culture: Political Attitudes and Democracy in Five Nations,* is a classic that takes patterns of communication and persuasion as part of what defines the political cultures of functioning democracies. Verba has taught at Princeton University, Stanford University, the University of Chicago, and Harvard University; and has authored many books on political participation in cross-national perspective, addressing topics from voting to public opinion during Vietnam to equality and inequality.

This selection comes from a collection entitled *The Kennedy Assassination and the American Public: Social Communication in Crisis.* Edited by Michigan State University's Bradley Greenberg and Stanford's Edwin Parker, the book points to a shift in the institutional structure for communications research. Whereas earlier collections on mass communication had been edited by professors of sociology or political science or by researchers affiliated with interdisciplinary institutes of communication, Greenberg and Parker both held appointments in communication *departments,* increasingly the professional home for the field in the United States. As a whole, their book probes the consequences and meaning of the Kennedy assassination and funeral by presenting empirical studies of television news and the press, public opinion, and the face-to-face discussion and diffusion of the shocking events in Dallas. The Kennedy assassination was a watershed moment in American life, when the nation witnessed historic events unfold live on television and when its citizens came together in coordinated emotional and ceremonial patterns of shock and mourning.

Verba's contribution to the volume calls into question the logic that equates modernization with secularization. Instead, he argues that there is a deeply emotional, magical, quasi-religious element to national political life, even in a pluralistic liberal democracy (cf. Merton 1946). The article anticipates work done on media rituals in the past twenty-five years (see, e.g., Couldry 2003), suggesting that there is an aspect of medieval kingliness to the modern presidency and exploring ways that mass-mediated grieving is both a public and private affair.

For God's sake, let us sit upon the ground
And tell sad stories of the death of kings.

Classic political history is the history of the life and death of kings. It is the intensely human drama of great men, for the king is a fallible mortal whom we can see and understand. But it is more than a human drama, for the king is also the symbol of society and nation, and is endowed with the highest religious significance.[1] And the king is the government as well; how he performs in peace and war determines how his nation and subjects live. Thus the life and death of kings merges the history of great institutions with the story of individual men, the secular ruler with the sacred symbol. Political life is endowed with religious significance. It engages us intellectually and emotionally. It is the fit subject for the Shakespearean tragedies.

Political science today studies the complex interaction of many highly differentiated individuals, groups, and governmental institutions; it differentiates between the individual personality and the social role. And the sacred and the secular are no longer linked; politics is viewed as a secular enterprise, at least in the developed nations of the West.[2] The unity of politics embodied in the person of the king is lost.

The events surrounding the Kennedy assassination may offer a unique opportunity for the reintegration of our somewhat fragmented picture of the political system. This paper will attempt to link the more precise behavioral studies of the assassination to the functioning of the larger political system. Such a task is elusive; this essay can only touch some aspects of the problem and must remain more speculative than the studies of the reactions of individuals. But it is a worthwhile enterprise. The way the many aspects of politics were connected in the study of the lives of kings may have been too easy, but some such connection is needed.

The assassination crisis. Political crises are decisive moments in societies. They are moments when political institutions are called upon to function at new levels, when political activities take on a new intensity, and when the salience of political matters rises suddenly and substantially. Crises are often, but not always, generated outside of the political system—by economic collapse, by foreign attack, or in this case, by the violent act of a lone individual. They are important because they place in relief the institutions of the political system and the beliefs of its members; they bring to the fore what may have been implicit and unobserved in a society. Crises are often the major constitutive events of a political system. It is often at times of crisis that new institutions are formed and existing political institutions are tested to the full. It is only at such times of crisis and strain that one can observe the capacity of such institutions, and how they operate under

such tests may determine their fate. Furthermore, it is during crises that most people learn about the nature of their political system. People not ordinarily involved in politics are suddenly deeply involved. They see the operation of the system in an intense light, and what they learn at the moment of crisis will determine what they believe about politics after the crisis.[3]

The particular nature of the Kennedy assassination crisis makes it possible to observe the total American political system in operation—insofar as it is meaningful to talk of observing an abstraction like a political system. This is because the crisis affected so many levels of American politics and society. It involved the top and central institutions of the American government— those having to do with the transfer of power, the succession to high office, and the most crucial decisions of policy that affect our nation. At the same time it involved all the intermediary institutions of the American political process: all levels of government, national, state, and local; various branches of government, military and civilian; and many nongovernmental institutions, notably the American political parties. Furthermore, the great role of the communication media in a modern political system was made explicit in the crisis. And lastly, it involved the micro-units of society—the families and groups of friends that clustered around television sets and reacted as groups to this event—as well as the members of the American society as individuals. Above all, the activities of individuals, of primary groups, of intermediary groups, of the mass media, and of the highest governmental institutions were all focused on the same event. And these various levels were constantly interacting with each other.

Despite all our information about how the members of the political system were affected by the crisis, we know very little about the impact of the crisis on the system itself. The difficulty here is the difficulty of generalizing from a single case. A crisis is a particular event in a particular social setting. Its impact depends in part on the nature of that setting. But using such a crisis as a basis for understanding its setting— in this case, understanding something about the nature of the American political community— involves knowing, ideally, what the impact of such a crisis might be in some other setting. One would want to know—and the question is intriguing—what the reaction to this crisis might have been in an America of 1953, during the height of the McCarthy era, or what the reaction might have been in some other country. We do not, of course, have such clearly comparable situations. But knowledge of succession crises in other societies can help to highlight the important characteristics of this particular succession crisis.

The crisis and institutional performance. Since we wish to examine the meaning for the American political system of the reactions to the assassination, we should mention one of the most obvious (and because obvious perhaps not sufficiently stressed) aspects of the crisis: the rapid and efficient formal transfer of presidential power. The chaos in the Dallas Police Department has tended to obscure the fact that the formal procedures for transferring power went so smoothly. There was almost no time during which the focus of executive power was uncertain, no major period of jockeying for power, and, indeed, little change in personnel or policy direction.

What may be more important is the extent to which the specific mode of institutional transfer was congruent with the basic values and expectations of the American people. We have detailed knowledge of what the American people thought about during the crisis and what inferences they drew from the crisis. At no time does it appear that anyone at any level of the society asked whether the institutions specified in the Constitution should or would operate. Criticism and doubt existed about the general tone of American political life or the activities of particular agencies, but the validity of the central institutional structure seems to have been taken for granted. Indeed, the questions that were not raised during the crisis illustrate how fundamental and implicit is the commitment to these political institutions. Compare succession crises elsewhere. It is not so much that the American military did not attempt to take control of the government; it is that no one even thought to ask where the military's support lay. And though there were many who suspected that a conspiracy lay behind the assassination, it was thought of as a low-level or external conspiracy—that is, few considered it a conspiracy generated within the American government in an attempt to change leadership or the direction of policy.

The reaction to the assassination and political commitment. The assassination crisis increases our understanding of various institutions of American politics because it allows us to see them operating in a time of strain. It increases

our understanding of the American political process also, because it makes apparent certain patterns of political belief and commitment that in ordinary times remain latent and unobservable. The parallel drawn between the assassination crisis and Shakespearean tragedy is, I believe, more than a passing analogy. In Shakespearean tragedy, personal emotion and public performance, the fate of individual men and the fate of nations, the sacred and the secular, are linked. On the weekend of the crisis, these things were also linked in the minds of those observing—in some real sense, participating in—the events of the assassination.

Since *The Lonely Crowd* we have been wont to think of the emotional relationship of Most Americans to the political life of their country as essentially "cool" and detached. Detached amusement or perhaps indignation is the appropriate posture. The assassination and the reaction to it reveal a level of emotional commitment that lay unnoticed beneath the surface. That there was an intense and almost universal emotional reaction to the assassination is amply revealed in the studies in this volume. And though the assassination was extremely important politically, as most observers seem to have been aware, the reactions were highly personal. Family imagery recurs in reactions to the event: people spoke with pain of the shattering of the Kennedy family, or felt as if they had lost a member of their own family. Ideological interpretations of the event and concern with the impact of the event on the American political process were much rarer.

The Kennedy assassination also illustrates the close meshing of the sacred and the secular in the top institutions of a political system. In a society in which the formal ideology is officially secular, in which ceremony is relatively underplayed (compared with societies having monarchic or aristocratic traditions), and in which the assassinated leader was of a minority and controversial religion, the close linkage of religious institutions to the events of the crisis weekend is particularly striking. As illustrated by the data in this volume, a large proportion of the American population responded to the assassination with prayer or attendance at special church services, and religious ceremony and imagery abounded in the events of the weekend.

What this suggests is that complete separation of church and state may be possible in only a formal sense. In a secular society where formal religious commitment is weak, the activities of the state may be the nearest one comes to activities of ultimate importance, activities that fundamentally determine matters of death and life and the quality of life. In short, governmental institutions may have significance of a religious kind. The awe inspired by the ultimate power of the church in more pious times may be akin to the awe inspired in modern secular societies by the ultimate power of the state.

Of even greater importance may be the particular role of the presidency in symbolizing the ultimate nature of state power. Recent studies have shown that the President plays a variety of roles not visualized in the Constitution. He is the symbolic referent for the learning of political commitment; children first become aware of political matters through an awareness of and diffuse attachment to the President.[4] As Durkheim pointed out, complex social collectivities, of which nation-states are the biggest and most complex, are not easily the direct objects of emotional attachment or commitment. Rather some common symbol that stands for the unit and with which people can identify is required. And such attachment is possible to the greatest degree "when the symbol is something simple, definite, and easily representable, while the thing itself [i.e., the social collectivity], owing to its dimensions, the number of its parts, and the complexity of its arrangements, is difficult to hold in the mind."[5] Durkheim was dealing for the most part with relatively simple societies and with the religious symbols that held them together. But what may be most interesting is the way this central symbolic role in a modern secular society is preempted by the political symbols that stand on the highest level for the society—in the American case by the presidency above all.

The presidential role is thus endowed with a religious quality. In many of the new nations of the world, where social change is more rapid and revolutionary than it has usually been in recent western history, scholars have noted the replacement of traditional religious beliefs by belief in a political religion.[6] Commitment to the political, because it replaces the total commitment to traditional religious patterns and arises as part of a general rejection of the traditional patterns, tends to take an all-or-nothing form. Politics demands complete dedication; political deviation is heresy. American society operates on a lower level of intensity. There is little intense commitment in either the religious or the political sphere; there is instead a pluralism of commitments and certainly less expression of political or religious emotion. (Interestingly enough, when there is intense religious commitment, as in some fundamentalist religions, it is often associated with extreme political views). But the relationship between religion and politics in the United States may be analogous to what it is in the new nations. Religion and politics in the United State are closely related to each other, and many of the functions that religion and religious symbolism perform elsewhere in holding society together are performed in the United States by the central political symbols. If in the new states a passionate political religion replaces an intense traditional religious commitment, in a modern society such as the United States a somewhat less intense political religion assumes some of the functions of a less intense religious system.

What I am suggesting is that the absence of ritual in American politics, the absence of an aristocratic or monarchic tradition, and the self-conscious secularization of political life may obscure the extent to which political commitment in the United States contains a prime component of primordial religious commitment. The reactions to the assassination—the intense emotion, the religious observances, and the politico-religious symbolism—are evidence (though hardly proof) that such commitment exists. And the President is the appropriate focus of this commitment, for like the medieval king he is the concrete human individual whom one can see, on whom one can focus attention, and with whom one can share common human emotions, and yet he is something transcending his concrete human aspects, for he is also the symbol of the nation.[7] And as Durkheim stressed, the symbols of nationhood are more than particular objects that are made to stand for something larger; they are major constitutive elements of polities and societies. Relatively simple social units whose functions are not very significant for the participants and that can be easily visualized might survive without some collective representation. But, as the frantic search for symbols by leaders of the new nations indicates, nations are unlikely to survive long without some such central symbols.[8]

But where does this central commitment to the symbols of nationhood—in this case the presidency—and to the nation thus symbolized originate? Early socialization of children is one source, but periodic ceremonies and collective events that allow the members of the society mutually to reinforce each other's commitment by collective activities are another way. In the relatively simple societies of which Durkheim wrote, this was accomplished by periodic reunions and ceremonials. In a complex and widely extended society like the United States, a society without the ceremonies of royalty, such reunions and common observances are somewhat rarer, though national elections and some national holidays may be examples of such events. The assassination crisis is important here because it is probably the nearest equivalent in a large modern nation-state to the kind of intense mutual rededication ceremony that is possible in a smaller and simpler society. There are several features that make it such a ceremony. The fact that it involved almost total participation is important. The figures on the universality of information and involvement are overwhelming as evidence of the ability of the mass media—television in particular—to link a large nation together. Furthermore, the media communicated not only information but shared emotion. It may not be the event itself that is most significant for this ceremonial aspect (though it took a special kind of event to focus so much attention and emotion); the fact that the reaction to the event was shared seems more important. It was in many cases shared by families gathered around television sets, it was shared in church services and other community ceremonials, but it was intensely and widely shared through the media themselves. Not only were the emotions of individual Americans involved, but they were made clearly aware of the emotions of their fellow Americans.

Kennedy the man and Kennedy the symbol. But can one really talk of the assassination crisis in terms of these vast national symbols? Certainly one aspect of the crisis was its immediate human quality. A particularly young and attractive President, the President's family—these are essential features of the event and the reaction to it. Does the intense emotional involvement reported in this volume indicate the importance of national symbolism and a deep emotional commitment to politics? Or does it simply suggest how people might react to the violent death of any personality as well known as President Kennedy?

The question is crucial but unanswerable. The assassination is not one of a recurring set of phenomena; hence one cannot ask whether the same reactions might emerge when the particular setting and participants differ. Indeed, the assassination (when thought of in relation to the overall American political system and not to the millions of individuals who reacted to it) is a prime example of that bane of the student of politics, the nonrecurring single case from which one can learn nothing but that is of such crucial political significance that one must try, nevertheless, to learn from it. One could try to answer the question in two ways. In the first place one could ask if such reactions would have arisen if the President had been a different person. One does not know, but there is evidence that the reaction to the death in office of previous Presidents was intense and by no means commensurate with what one would have expected on the basis of their personal characteristics.[9] Conversely, one could ask if such an intense reaction as followed the Kennedy assassination would have followed the violent death of some equally well-known personage who did not occupy the highest political office. Again one cannot answer definitely, but one suspects not. To some extent the question answers itself, for it is the very fact that Kennedy was the President that made his personal as well as public life so well known. The exposure of nonpolitical figures (say, from the entertainment world) may be great, but it tends to be more heavily stratified and limited to particular groups.

To determine the uniqueness of the event, one would have to partial out the various aspects of the impact of President Kennedy—is personal characteristics, his symbolic and semireligious position, his vast instrumental powers as President. But it is just because these three are in fact so inextricably linked that the assassination of a President is an intense event and the presidency itself such an important unifying institution.

I have focused thus far largely on the linkage between the individual man and the symbolic role of the presidency. Unlike, say, the British Monarch the American President has also a powerful instrumental political role. As Bagehot pointed out, the position of the monarchy above partisan politics enhances its symbolic potential by protecting it from the heat of political controversy. Not so the presidency. Yet there are, I believe, several reasons why the American President can perform a symbolic function despite his actual power position. For one thing, of course, the power itself is a source of the awe that the presidential role inspires. If the actual political power of the President makes the incumbent vulnerable to the sort of criticism that the British Queen's non-political position protects her from, the political power also makes it unlikely that the American presidency would be subjected to many of the criticisms leveled at the royal family for its triviality and lack of function. Bagehot's separation of the instrumental and symbolic parts of the British government may cut both ways. Furthermore, the presidency may be viewed as essentially a nonpartisan office from whose incumbent one may expect at least a reasonably responsible performance. For one thing, the studies of early images of the President among children suggest that one first views him as a benign and diffuse authority figure, not as a figure of partisan controversy. And the reactions to the crisis itself show that there are few sharp differences between the adherents of the two major parties in their reactions to the assassination. It would be hard to find evidence that the crisis was in any important sense a partisan matter.

The effects of the crisis. Crises bring into relief certain aspects of political systems that might otherwise remain implicit and unnoticed. But such events not only make the characteristics of a political system clear, but also have a major effect on the system itself. A crisis, such as the assassination of the President, involves a sudden rise in the salience of politics among the public. Many people who were essentially apolitical or parochial suddenly become deeply concerned with and aroused by political matters. This sudden involvement of all the segments of society, including many whose involvement in politics is rare or intermittent, may involve some danger for the political system. As has been frequently pointed out, the last group mobilized—the group that is immune from all influence and political communication save the most intense—is a group of great volatility. Being somewhat unused to politics and being involved in politics only in the extreme, they are likely to react more emotionally than people with more experience. It is thus during crises that people learn the major lessons of politics, in the sense of forming basic impressions of their political system and of the other groups that make up the system.

Crises may, therefore, have major integrative effects on society or major disintegrative effects.

They are likely to reinforce whichever of the two tendencies is stronger in the society. It has been pointed out, for instance, that the major crises in Italian history have been disintegrative ones—that is, each major crisis from the Risorgimento through the Resistance to the founding of the current Republic has had the effect of alienating one social group from others and from the political elite.[10] Evidence suggests that in American politics great crises tend to have integrative effects—at least in foreign affairs. Anything that increases the salience of the presidency, even such a blunder as the U-2 incident or the Bay of Pigs invasion, seems to lead to a more favorable evaluation of the presidency. This would seem to bear out the basic symbolic importance of the presidency: if events cause one to think about the presidency, the result is increased commitment.

There is little doubt of the integrative effect of the assassination. Partisanship declined in intensity, as the study by Sears shows. The opinions of the American people about Kennedy's presidency soared after the assassination. The crisis had an integrative effect on the American political system in several ways. In the first place, the fundamental institutions of the American political process were put to a test before the entire public. If it is true that such institutions work at least in part because people believe they will work, then the fact that so many people saw them work in this particular case probably increases their future effectiveness. Second, the crisis demonstrated the reliability of a variety of intermediary institutions in our society. In particular, I believe it demonstrated the reliability of the mass media. That a crisis of this sort did not create greater anxiety about the stability of the American government probably depends largely on the fact that channels of mass communication were available that were objective and, what may be more important, were *believed* to be objective by the American public. To see the importance of such rapid and reliable communication facilities, one has only to image what the crisis would have been like without them. Furthermore the other intermediary institutions that were involved in the crisis—such institutions as the American military and the two opposing political parties—all demonstrated their basic commitment to the norms of the democratic system. Lastly, the crisis was integrative in that it involved the collective and largely self-conscious sharing of a significant emotional experience by a national population.

Not only did the individual American mourn, but the mourning went on in groups, and in a communication context that made it apparent to all that they were sharing this experience with most others around the country. In a sense the crisis was the occasion for an unexpected rededication ceremony.

The emotion triggered by the Kennedy assassination was an intensely private emotion, akin to the emotion at the death of a close relative. But it had an important public dimension. It was directed at a public object, it was shared, it was overtly expressed in a society in which such overt expression is rare. That the emotion was so intense and took such a public form was, I believe, due to the particular political nature of the event. It is unlikely that the assassination created emotional commitment on the spot. Rather it brought to the fore a preexisting commitment—a commitment fundamental to the political community in the United States.

There has been a tendency to assume that politics is linked to deep emotional and religious commitments only in traditional societies, in which the sacred and the secular are intertwined, or in societies dedicated to mass mobilization in which commitment to the central institutions of the state becomes dominant and replaces any other. But such deep commitment may also be important, though less apparent and overt, in modern pluralistic societies. The emotional context of the assassination partakes somewhat of the commitment found in smaller traditional societies. It was shared within the primary units of society; it was a primordial and implicit commitment shared by most members of the society and probably acquired during early socialization. Though it was greater in extent—it covered a vast nation and was communicated largely through the "impersonal" mass media—yet one could not describe the reaction as a "mass" response. It was an emotional experience mediated by many nongovernmental institutions, in particular the religious institutions and the family, and above all it was not an emotional commitment that implied a rejection of other commitments.

Perhaps the most important aspect of the reaction to the assassination is the way it illustrates the complex admixture of the rational institutions of politics with the more traditional, religious, and indeed somewhat magical aspects of political commitment. The transfer of power to the new President is a rational-legal procedure in which the limits to individual initiative and on the individual personality are great. Yet it is through this procedure that the symbolic and charismatic aspects of office are also transmitted.

What holds a complicated and pluralistic political society like the United States together? We used to think it was a common democratic ideology, but lately we are not so sure. Americans apparently do not think of politics in any but the vaguest terms; the commitment to democratic values in any overt sense does not appear to extend much below the level of slogans.[11] The reactions to the assassination support this view—there is little overt ideological content to the reactions.

But this may not mean that common beliefs are irrelevant to the political system. What the Kennedy assassination may show is that the level of commitment to politics is both more intense than that revealed by the usual public-opinion-surveying techniques, and of a somewhat different order. For one thing, it is a diffuse emotional commitment not closely related to any particular political ideology, issue, or controversy, which may be why it is so inadequately tapped by the usual issue- or election-oriented public opinion studies; and it is a commitment that lies beneath the surface of ordinary day-to-day politics. As such, it may be the kind of primordial emotional attachment that is necessary for the long-term maintenance of a political system. It is not the rather fragile support that is based solely on a calculation of interests; it is support based on a longer-run, less rational sort of attachment.

And the fact that it is latent and unrecognized under ordinary circumstances is also important. The ordinary operation of politics in a pluralistic country like the United States involves many compromises, much juggling and reconciliation of values, and many activities in which the finer points of principle are ignored. Such may be the price of pluralism. But the man who approached such a political system with his deepest moral commitments close to the surface could only retreat in disgust or remain cynically fascinated with the process he observed. Thus a deep emotional commitment to politics may be unstabilizing if it is constantly in the foreground, but it may also be unstabilizing if it is not somewhere in the background.[12] What the assassination indicated is that such a commitment exists and can be brought to the fore. But a comparison of the emotional tone of political discussion before the crisis and during it—a comparison clearly reflected by the data in this volume—shows that the emotional commitment is not a part of the ordinary day-to-day operation of politics. It also suggests why "business as usual" returned so quickly, and why that quick return is important.

Notes

1. On the dual significance of the king, see Ernst H. Kantorwicz, *The King's Two Bodies: A Study in Medieval Theology* (Princeton, 1957).

2. Edward Shils and Michael Young argue that this is why social scientists have not paid sufficient attention to rituals like the British coronation. See "The Meaning of the Coronation," *Sociological Review* (1953), *1*, 63–81.

3. For a general discussion of the role of salient political crises in the development of political beliefs, see Sidney Verba, "Comparative Political Culture," in Lucian Pye and Sidney Verba, eds., *Political Culture and Political Development* (Princeton, 1965). See also Robert E. Ward and Dankwart A. Rustow, "Conclusion," in Ward and Rustow, eds., *Political Modernization in Turkey and Japan* (Princeton, 1964), pp. 65–68.

4. Robert D. Hess and David Easton, "The Child's Image of the Presidency," *Public Opinion Quarterly* (1960), *24*, 632–44; and Fred I. Greenstein, "The Benevolent Leader: Children's Images of Political Authority," *American Political Science Review* (1960), *54*, 934–43.

5. Emile Durkheim, *The Elementary Forms of Religious Life* (London, n.d.), p. 211.

6. David E. Apter, "Political Religion in the New States," in Clifford Geertz, ed., *Old Societies and New States* (New York, 1963).

7. Kantorowicz stresses the important parallel between the dual human-transcendent nature of the King and the man-God nature of Christ. It is the dual nature that makes the King such a dominant symbol.

8. See, for instance, McKim Marriott, "Cultural Policy in the New States," in Geertz, ed., *Old Societies*.

9. See the references to the reactions to the assassination of President McKinley and the death of Franklin D. Roosevelt in the essay by Sheatsley and Feldman in this volume.

10. See Joseph LaPalombara, "Italy: Fragmentation, Isolation, Alienation," in Pye and Verba, eds., *Political Culture*.

11. See James W. Prothro and C. W. Grigg, "Fundamental Principles of Democracy: Bases of Agreement and Disagreement," *Journal of Politics* (1960), *22*, 276–94; Angus Campbell *et al.*, *The American Voter* (New York, 1960), chap. 10; and Herbert McCloskey, "Consensus and Ideology in American Politics," *American Political Science Review* (1964), *57*, 361–82.

12. For a more general statement of the relationship between commitment and democratic stability, see Gabriel A. Almond and Sidney Verba, *The Civic Culture: Political Attitudes and Democracy in Five Nations* (Princeton, 1963), chap. 15.

67

TV Overseas: The U.S. Hard Sell

From *The Nation* (1966)

Herbert Schiller

Herbert I. Schiller (1919–2000) was one of the most important left-wing American critics of mainstream mass communication research and of commercial mass media in general. Trained as an economist, eventually taking his doctorate from New York University in 1960, he came into communication research through the back door, rather like his colleague Dallas Smythe. Schiller received his bachelor's degree from College of the City of New York in 1940 and his master's from Columbia in 1941, and he served in Berlin as an occupying officer in the U.S. military. Although during his career he held visiting appointments throughout the world, he taught at the Pratt Institute from 1950 to 1963 and at the University of Illinois from 1963 to 1970; and he was a founder of the Department of Communication at the University of California, San Diego, where he was based from 1970 until the end of his life. His leading theme was the corporate domination of cultural expression both within the United States and by the American military–media complex worldwide, a theme pursued in books such as *Mass Communications and American Empire* (1969), *The Mind Managers* (1973), *Who Knows: Information in the Age of the Fortune 500* (1981), *Culture Inc.* (1989), *Information Inequality* (1996), and *Living in the Number One Country* (2000).

Schiller was an intellectual activist who published in journals of opinion, and this 1966 selection from *The Nation* (and later included in *Mass Communications and American Empire*) gives an admirable taste of Schiller's passionate conviction that subordinating the channels of communication to profit was not only an act of international domination but also a violation of humane ideals.

The character and structure of American broadcasting are well-explored features of the domestic landscape. Less well known is the readiness with which a large and growing part of the world community has succumbed to the United States style, and how these developments have been engineered is a story of relatively current vintage.

In the pre-television era, the United States stood alone among advanced industrialized nations in having its radio broadcasting unabashedly commercial. Nowhere else did advertisers pay the bill and direct the destinies of the medium so completely. State broadcasting authorities were the rule in Europe, and the American arrangement was the exception.

With the advent of television, but not because of it, many national broadcasting structures adopted one or another variant of the American pattern. Wilson P. Dizard, author of *Television: A World View*, has written about this shift:

Television has developed primarily as a commercial medium. This was to be expected in the United States and a few other countries, notably in Latin America, where broadcasting was traditionally a private venture. Elsewhere, however, broadcasting was a state monopoly without commercial connections. Theoretically, television should have followed in the established pattern: significantly it did not.... At present, television systems in over fifty countries are controlled, in whole or in part, by private interests under state supervision. Commercial advertising is carried by all but a handful of the world's ninety-five television systems.

For the new countries the emerging pattern is the same. Dizard notes "the virtual domination of local television in developing nations by commercial interests." UNESCO reports the same finding. Even strong, industrialized nations have been forced to modify their long-time, stabilized broadcasting services and accept commercial operations. Britain yielded in 1954; France is now teetering on the edge.

What has powered this almost universal push toward commercialization? Its advocates reply that commercial broadcasting is the most satisfactory method of meeting the financial and programmatic needs of the new media. Dizard, for instance, asserts: "The change [to commercialization] confirmed the effectiveness of American-style broadcasting both as a revenue producer and as a highly acceptable form of entertainment and persuasion."

The revenue-producing capabilities of commercial broadcasting cannot be disputed; the acceptability of the entertainment it offers is a matter that I shall go into in a moment. But neither reason faintly suggests the real force in operation. *Nothing less than the viability of the American industrial economy itself is involved in the movement toward international commercialization of broadcasting.*

The continuing and pressing requirements of United States manufacturers to reach annually higher output levels in order to sustain and increase profit margins activate the process that is relentlessly enveloping electronics (and other) communications in a sheath of commercialization. What happens is a continuing interaction. The direct intrusion of American influence catalyzes developments in the affected nations. Also, those countries with similar industrial structures and organization themselves feel corresponding, if at first weaker, impulses in the same direction.

Evidence of the international explosive thrust in private enterprise's market requirements can be found in the trade press. *Television Magazine,* for instance, describes the interconnections between the advertising, manufacturing, and broadcasting industries (italics added):

About 1959 a gentle curve representing the expansion of American advertising agencies overseas started an abrupt climb which hasn't yet leveled off.... The growth of television abroad had something to do with this upsurge, since the head-start American agencies had in dealing with the medium commercially has given them a highly exportable know how. But television wasn't the prime mover. *That role belongs to the client: The American consumer goods industry.*

The magazine explained this process with a simple illustration:

Take a giant corporation like Procter and Gamble with sales over $2 billion a year. Its position on the open market is based partly on the corporation's growth rate. But to add, say, 10% in sales each year becomes increasingly difficult when already over the two billion mark. *Where do you find that additional $200 million? The answer, for more and more American corporations, is overseas.*

American companies have been crossing the oceans regularly, either through direct acquisition or new plant expansion or leasing arrangements or combinations thereof. United States private direct investments in manufacturing abroad have spurted in the twenty years beginning in 1943 from $2,276 million to $16,861 million. In Western Europe alone, manufacturing investments increased from $879 million to $6,547 million in the period. To assist in marketing the output of these expanding foreign facilities, U.S. advertising agencies have been accompanying the industrial plants overseas. McCann-Erickson has seventy offices employing 4,619 persons in thirty-seven countries. J. Walter Thompson, "the granddaddy of international operations," employs 1,110 people in its key London office alone. There are twenty-one American-associated ad agencies in England, twenty in West Germany, twelve in France. In Latin America, Brazil has fifteen American ad agencies and there are more U.S. agencies in Canada than in any other foreign nation. Even the developing world has begun to be penetrated. "Three enterprising U.S. agencies have tackled the huge market of India ... [and] Africa, too, may be part of a future wave of agency expansion overseas," according to *Television.*

Once the privately directed manufacturing enterprises have begun their goods production, all energies are concentrated on securing the

482 *Part III: The American Dream and Its Discontents*

public's ever-widening acceptance of the out-pouring commodity streams. The insistence of powerful American sellers, temporarily allied with their local counterparts, on obtaining advertising outlets abroad is overwhelming state broadcasting authorities, one after another. The successful campaign to introduce commercial television in England was largely a matter of industry admen manipulating complex political wires. Gerald Beadle, the former director of B.B.C. television, explained with some understatement what happened in Britain:

> . . . there was an unusually strong demand from large sections of British industry in the early nineteen fifties for more opportunities for advertising their goods. Wartime restrictions, especially on paper, had only recently been lifted, and a real boom in consumer goods was developing, but industry felt that there were insufficient opportunities for telling the public about the large range of new goods which were becoming available. Television was obviously an excellent medium for this, and industry was not averse to harnessing the television horse to the industrial chariot.

What is emerging on the international scene bears a striking resemblance to the American routine of uncoordinated expansion of production, promotion of the output through the communications media, higher sales, further plant expansion, and then the cycle's repetition. American society's dissatisfied individual who seeks release in consumption is appearing throughout the expanding orbit of the international free market. According to Erich Fromm, "Twentieth century industrialism has created this new psychological type, *homo consumens,* primarily for economic reasons, i.e., the need for mass consumption which is stimulated and manipulated by advertising. But the character type, once created, also influences the economy and makes the principles of ever-increasing satisfaction appear rational and realistic. Contemporary man, thus, has an unlimited hunger for more and more consumption."

The man in the market economy has become a message receiver beyond all imagination. Bombarded in the United States by an estimated 1,500 advertising messages a day, these "contemporary men" are multiplying rapidly in the North Atlantic community, and are beginning to be discovered as well in Africa, Latin America and

Table 67.1 Advertising Expenditures of U.S. Companies, 1964

	Million
1. Procter and Gamble	$147.8
2. General Motors	137.5
3. Ford Motors	80.6
4. General Foods	74.8
5. Bristol-Myers	74.7
6. R. J. Reynolds Tobacco	68.8
7. Colgate-Palmolive	66.7
8. American Home Products	65.4
9. Chrysler	64.3
10. Lever Brothers (British-owned)	61.4

Asia. In 1964, private enterprise spent $21 billion for advertising in fourteen industrial countries, two-thirds of the amount being spent in the United States. Financing much of this staggering budget for global commercial message-making are the multi-national corporations whose plants and service installations are spread over several countries. (See table 67.1.)

Wherever these "big spenders" penetrate, broadcasting is subverted to salesmanship. It is not only a matter of the ubiquitous, jarring commercial. The entire content that illuminates the home screen is fitted to the marketeer's order. "TV is not an art form or a culture channel: it is an advertising medium," writes Daniel Karp in *The New York Times Magazine.* Therefore, ". . . it seems a bit churlish and un-American of people who watch television to complain that their shows are so lousy. They are not *supposed* to be any good. They are supposed to make money . . . [and] in fact, 'quality' may be not merely irrelevant but a distraction."

As of now, the situation of radio-television in the United States is the extreme case. In Western Europe, the tradition that state broadcasting authorities exercise some social responsibility has not yet been demolished. But the striving of the consumer goods producers to gain the attention of large audiences is unrelenting, and as Fromm observes, once the contact is made, the audience itself searches out further stimuli.

If commercials are still controlled and compressed into special slices of the viewing time in some national systems abroad, the shows themselves often follow the dictates, directly or indirectly, of their sponsors. Certainly, that is the case with the popular and widely shown American productions where the advertising agency may have sat in at each stage of a script's development.

A.B.C., N.B.C. and C.B.S. send their packaged programming to all continents, charging what the freight will bear. In low-income areas in Africa and Asia, old U.S. films and shows are dumped at low prices to secure a foothold in emerging markets, regardless of the relevance or appropriateness of the "entertainment."

In Western Europe, the most stable noncommercial broadcasting structures of sovereign states are unable to resist the forces that are arrayed against them. Here from *Television* is one description of how "commercials" break through national boundaries, especially in the geographically compact North Atlantic region:

Of course, the continued expansion of commercial television, despite powerful opposition, is playing a major role in making unity of diversity. Although many important countries, particularly in Europe, still forbid TV advertising, there is a certain "spillover" effect that tends to spread commercials even to those countries that originally were adamant. Only this year did the 11-year-old governmental-controlled Swiss TV service permit commercials on its three regional networks. The move was in large part prompted by the concern of Swiss manufacturers who knew their customers were viewing Italian and German TV across the border. The same process is expected to unfold in the Netherlands, a large part of which is also open to German programming and advertising messages. If Netherlands TV goes commercial, then Belgium is expected to follow shortly thereafter. Then France and Scandinavia will be the last big holdouts.... If French television goes commercial, an executive at J. Walter Thompson remarks, then there truly will be a common market for the TV advertiser.

If "legitimate" infiltration and demolition of noncommercial state systems of broadcasting is inapplicable for one reason or another, less sophisticated techniques are available. The pirate radio stations located off the coast of England, and some even in the Thames estuary, completely disregard international frequency allocation agreements. They broadcast Pop music interlaced with commercials to European and English audiences who are apparently hungering for the entertainment and not at all displeased with the accompanying consumer messages. Though the pirates are small-scale broadcasters at the moment, large-scale interests stand behind them. Until the government actively intervened, both the Institute of Practitioners in Advertising and the Incorporated Society of British Advertisers lent indirect support to the pirates. A director of the ISBA has stated: "We recognize they fulfill a need. We would be happier, though, if they were on-shore and permanent."

Reacting to an impending governmental regulatory bill, one of the pirates, Radio London, commented: "We expect to get sufficient advertising from overseas to enable us to continue. We have four million overseas listeners, *and much of our revenue is from international companies who would not be affected by British legislation.*" (Italics added.)

Having secured control of communications across a good part of the earth's surface, commerce has now turned its attention to conquering space. At the White House Conference on International Cooperation last winter, the National Citizens Commission's Committee on Space (whose chairman incidentally was Dr. Joseph Charyk, the president of Comsat), listed as the *first* application of communications satellites their future impact on "trade and commerce." The committee's report stated: "It is possible to foresee use of closed circuit television by major companies doing a worldwide business to link together their offices and affiliates in order to kick off a new sales campaign or to demonstrate a new product or to analyze a new marketing situation in the far corners of the world."

Similar sentiment exists in other influential places. The London *Economist* views communications satellites as the chosen business medium of the future. Deploring the British Government's reluctance to participate more actively in ELDO (European Launcher Development Organization), the Europeans' sole hope of matching American communications technological advances, the magazine commented: "But is there only an American or a Russian or a Chinese way of life to be propagated around the world? Will Britain (and Europe) even be able to sell its goods around the world if it cuts itself out of the *advertising medium of the 1970s?*" (Italics added.)

An even better indication of how communications satellites are to be used can be seen in the attitudes of two recent conferences concerned with the space systems. In December, 1965, UNESCO assembled representatives from nineteen member states and other interested international organizations to consider the possible use of space satellites for informational and cultural purposes A few months later, at the 18th World Congress of the Advertising Association in Mexico City, Worldvision, a network including sixty-two television stations in twenty-five countries, organized by the American Broadcasting Company's international subsidiary, A.B.C. International, ran a three-day workship demonstrating how "international advertisers could use TV right now." In the words of Donald W. Coyle, president of A.B.C. International, "Global television is not something that we are going to have to wait for a far-off future to implement. It is upon us now."

The contrast in the two approaches is depressing: UNESCO's vision is of international control of communications satellites for cultural use *in the future*. Worldvision's program for the commercial use of space *has already begun*.

It is a mistake to view these developments as evidence of an international cabal seeking the global commercialization of communications. The forces are openly at work and the success of "consumerism" rests on a varied mix of human and institutional pressures which are at present very powerful. "Both a consumer oriented economy and commercial television seem to have things going for them at this moment of history in a good part of the globe," is the way *Television* puts it.

Western Europe has relied on the existence of national traditions of propriety unobserved in the United States and even on some limitation on American programming to hold back the flood of commercialization. Canada and Great Britain have both tried, not too successfully, to keep the proportion of American to domestic shows within certain limits. But attempts to exclude United states programming and to limit the number and length of national commercials are unlikely to be effective in any one country, no matter how influential that society may be in its own region. The subject matter that is denied local transmission is broadcast from neighboring states, with transmitters sometimes deliberately established for this purpose. Then, too, the business system in Western Europe, Canada, Japan and Australia supports the general principle of commercialization and throws its weight behind an advance of salesmanship.

As for the universe of the global poor, the have-not nations stand practically defenseless before a rampaging Western commercialism. Impoverished as they are, many developing states are able to afford the new communications systems only by accepting commercial packages which "tie" their broadcasting systems to foreign programming and foreign financial sponsorship. In this way their paths of economic development are set, regardless of the intentions and designs of their planners, by the pull of market-directed consumerism. Expectations of new roads to national development which *might* foster motivations and behavior different from contemporary Western styles are being dashed in their infancy.

The gloomy and bitter words of Japanese economist, Shigeto Tsuru, seem to apply everywhere in the wake of Western market enterprise's electronic communications offensive: "In this world of high-powered communications we may even have to speak of a new kind of 'self-alienation' for citizens living under capitalism. If there were a society on this earth somewhere which would make full use of the highly developed techniques of communication of today for the sole purpose of its inhabitants' autonomous cultural needs, it would be an experience of a lifetime for us to visit there—for us who daily, even hourly, cannot escape from the onslaught, either subtle or crude, of modern commercialism in a capitalist society."

68

Aggressiveness in Advanced Industrial Societies, from *Negations* (1968)

Herbert Marcuse

Herbert Marcuse (1898–1979) was not only one of the leading figures in the critical theory of the Frankfurt School but also one of the chief inspirations for the student movement of 1968 (the children of Marx and Coca-Cola, as filmmaker Jean-Luc Godard put it). He was born in Berlin and raised in an upper-middle-class household whose perks included a chauffeur-driven Packard. Like all of his Frankfurt colleagues, he rebelled against the stolidity of bourgeois life, drinking deep from the spring of humanist Marxism that had been replenished in the 1920s with the work of Georg Lukács and the rediscovery of Marx's early unpublished manuscripts from the 1840s, which show the great debt Marx owed to Hegel. Marcuse studied with Martin Heidegger in the late 1920s and early 1930s. Heidegger remained a chief intellectual influence on Marcuse, though he was dismayed at Heidegger's Nazi politics. Marcuse's work combined a rich philosophical background with a utopian hope for a society without repression, a hope he saw foreshadowed in "the aesthetic dimension," as he called one of his last books. Marcuse joined the Frankfurt Institut für Sozialforschung in 1933 and shortly thereafter emigrated to the United States, becoming an American citizen in 1940. From 1942 to 1951, he worked in the Office of Strategic Services in Washington, D.C. (the precusor to the CIA), as an analyst of German and then Russian affairs. (Like Lowenthal, he might be called a 1950s "Marxist anti-Communist.") Marcuse taught at Brandeis University from the mid-1950s to 1965 and then took at chair at the University of California, San Diego, in 1965. His greatest fame met him at an age when most professors are retiring. Though he never liked being called "father of the New Left," he was not only the most gifted of the Frankfurt writers at slogan making but also the most politically outspoken.

His essay "Aggressiveness in Advanced Industrial Society" was first published in English in 1968 in his book *Negations* and represents the spirit of May 1968 well, combining a critique of militarization and affluence in one fell swoop. His characteristic fusion of Marx and Freud is also clear, as are his attack on the imposition of a false normality by an ill society and his criticism of the media for their repetitive manipulation and distortion of language. Outrage at the war in Vietnam is one clear historical pretext for the piece.

I propose to consider here the strains and stresses in the so-called "affluent society," a phrase which has (rightly or wrongly) been coined to describe contemporary American society. Its main characteristics are: (1) an abundant industrial and technical capacity which is to a great extent spent in the production and distribution of luxury goods, gadgets, waste, planned obsolescence, military or semimilitary equipment— in short, in what economists and sociologists used to call "unproductive" goods and services; (2) a rising standard of living, which also extends to previously underprivileged parts of the population; (3) a high degree of concentration of economic and political power, combined with a high degree of organization and government intervention in the economy; (4) scientific and pseudoscientific investigation, control, and manipulation of private and group behavior, both at work and at leisure (including the behavior of the psyche, the soul, the unconscious, and the subconscious) for commercial and political purposes. All these tendencies are interrelated: they make up the syndrome which expresses the normal functioning of the "affluent society." To demonstrate this interrelation is not my task here; I take its existence as the sociological basis for the thesis which I want to submit, namely, that the strains and stresses suffered by the individual in the affluent society are grounded in the normal functioning of this society (and of the individual!) rather than in its disturbances and diseases.

"Normal functioning": I think the definition presents no difficulties for the doctor. The organism functions normally if it functions, without disturbance, in accord with the biological and physiological makeup of the human body. The human faculties and capabilities are certainly very different among the members of the species, and the species itself has changed greatly in the course of its history, but these changes have occurred on a biological and physiological basis which has remained largely constant. To be sure, the physician, in making his diagnosis and in proposing treatment, will take into account the patient's environment, upbringing, and occupation; these factors may limit the extent to which normal functioning can be defined and achieved, or they may even make this achievement impossible, but as criterion and goal, normality remains a clear and meaningful concept. As such, it is identical with "health," and the various deviations from it are to various degrees of "disease."

The situation of the psychiatrist seems to be quite different. At first glance, normality seems to be defined along the same lines the physician uses. The normal functioning of the mind (psyche, psyche-soma) is that which enables the individual to perform, to function in accord with his position as child, adolescent, parent, as a single person or married, in accord with his job, profession, status. But this definition contains factors of an entirely new dimension, namely, that of society, and society is a factor of normality in a far more essential sense than that of external influence, so much so that "normal" seems to be a social and institutional rather than individual condition. It is probably easy to agree on what is the normal functioning of the digestive tract,

the lungs, and the heart, but what is the normal functioning of the mind in lovemaking, in other interpersonal relations, at work and at leisure, at a meeting of a board of directors, on the golf course, in the slums, in prison, in the army? While the normal functioning of the digestive tract or the lung is likely to be the same in the case of a healthy corporation executive and of a healthy laborer, this does not hold true of their minds. In fact, the one would be very abnormal if he regularly thought, felt, and operated like the other. And what is "normal" lovemaking, a "normal" family, a "normal" occupation?

The psychiatrist might proceed like the general physician and direct therapy to making the patient function within his family, in his job or environment, while trying to influence and even change the environmental factors as much as this is in his power. The limits will soon make themselves felt, for example, if the mental strains and stresses of the patient are caused, not merely by certain bad conditions in his job, in his neighborhood, in his social status, but by the very *nature* of the job, the neighborhood, the status itself—in their normal condition. Then making him normal for this condition would mean normalizing the strains and stresses, or to put it more brutally: making him capable of being sick, of living his sickness as health, without his noticing that he is sick precisely when he sees himself and is seen as healthy and normal. This would be the case if his work is, by its very nature, "deadening," stupefying, wasteful (even though the job pays well and is "socially" necessary), or if the person belongs to a minority group which is underprivileged in the established society, traditionally poor and occupied mainly in menial and "dirty" physical labor. But this would also be the case (in very different forms) on the other side of the fence among the tycoons of business and politics, where efficient and profitable performance requires (and reproduces) the qualities of smart ruthlessness, moral indifference, and persistent aggressiveness. In such cases, "normal" functioning would be tantamount to a distortion and mutilation of a human being—no matter how modestly one may define the human qualities of a human being. Erich Fromm wrote *The Sane Society*; it deals, not with the established, but with a future, society, the implication being that the established society is *not* sane but insane. Is not the individual who functions normally, adequately, and healthily as a citizen of a sick society—is not such an individual himself sick? And would not a sick society require an antagonistic concept of mental health, a meta-concept designating (and preserving) mental qualities which are tabooed, arrested, or distorted by the "sanity" prevalent in the sick society? (For example, mental health equals the ability to live as a dissenter, to live a nonadjusted life.)

As a tentative definition of "sick society" we can say that a society is sick when its basic institutions and relations, its structure, are such that they do not permit the use of the available material and intellectual resources for the optimal development and satisfaction of individual needs. The larger the discrepancy between the potential and actual human conditions, the greater the social need for what I term "surplus-repression," that is, repression necessitated not by the growth and preservation of civilization but by the vested interest in maintaining an established society. Such surplus-repression introduces (over and above, or rather underneath, the social conflicts) new strains and stresses in the individuals. Usually handled by the normal working of the social process, which assures adjustment and submission (fear of loss of job or status, ostracism, and so forth, no special enforcement policies with respect to the mind are required. But in the contemporary affluent society, the discrepancy between the established modes of existence and the real possibilities of human freedom is so great that, in order to prevent an explosion, society has to insure a more effective mental coordination of individuals: in its unconscious as well as conscious dimensions, the psyche is opened up and subjected to systematic manipulation and control.

When I speak of the surplus-repression "required" for the maintenance of a society, or of the need for systematic manipulation and control, I do not refer to individually experienced social needs and consciously inaugurated policies: they may be thus experienced and inaugurated or they may not. I rather speak of *tendencies,* forces which can be identified by an analysis of the existing society and which assert themselves even if the policy makers are not aware of them. They express the requirements of the established apparatus of production, distribution, and consumption—economic, technical, political, mental requirements which have to be fulfilled in order to assure the continued functioning of the apparatus on which the population depends, and the continuing function of the social relationships derived from the organization of the apparatus. These objective tendencies become manifest in the trend of the economy, in technological change, in the domestic and foreign policy of a nation or group of nations, and they generate common, supraindividual needs and goals in the different social classes, pressure groups, and parties. Under the normal conditions of social cohesion, the objective tendencies override or absorb individual interest and goals without exploding the society; however, the particular interest is not simply determined by the universal: the former has its own range of freedom, and contributes, in accordance with its social position, to the shaping of the general interest—but short of a revolution, the particular needs and goals will remain defined by the predominant objective tendencies. Marx believed that they assert themselves "behind the back" of the individuals; in the advanced societies of today, this is true only with strong qualifications. Social engineering, scientific management of enterprise and human relations, and manipulation of instinctual needs are practiced on the policy-making level and testify to the degree of awareness within the general blindness.

As for the systematic manipulation and control of the psyche in the advanced industrial society, manipulation and control for what, and by whom? Over and above all particular manipulation in the interest of certain businesses, policies, lobbies—the general objective purpose is to reconcile the individual with the mode of existence which his society imposes on him. Because of the high degree of surplus-repression involved in such reconciliation, it is necessary to achieve a libidinal cathexis of the merchandise the individual has to buy (or sell), the services he has to use (or perform), the fun he has to enjoy, the status symbols he has to carry—necessary, because the existence of the society depends on their uninterrupted production and consumption. In other words, social needs must become individual needs, instinctual needs. And to the degree to which the productivity of this society requires mass production and mass consumption, these needs must be standardized, coordinated, generalized. Certainly, these controls are not a conspiracy, they are not centralized in any agency or group of agencies (although the trend toward centralization is gaining momentum); they are rather diffused throughout the society, exercised by the neighbors, the community, the peer groups, mass media, corporations, and (perhaps least) by the government. But they are exercised with the help of, in fact rendered possible by, science, by the social and behavioral sciences, and especially by sociology and psychology. As industrial sociology and psychology, or, more euphemistically, as "science of human relations," these scientific efforts have become an indispensable tool in the hands of the powers that be.

These brief remarks are suggestive of the depth of society's ingression into the psyche, the extent to which mental health, normality, is not that of the individual but of his society. Such a harmony between the individual and society would be highly desirable if the society offered the individual the conditions for his development as a human being in accord with the available possibilities of freedom, peace, and happiness (that is in accord with the possible liberation of his life instincts), but it is highly destructive to the individual if these conditions do not prevail. Where they do not prevail, the healthy and normal individual is a human being equipped with all the qualities which enable him to get along with others in his society, and these very same qualities are the marks of repression, the marks of a mutilated human being, who collaborates in his own repression, in the containment of potential individual and social freedom, in the release of aggression. And this situation cannot be solved within the framework of any psychology—a solution can be envisaged only on the political level: in the struggle against society. To be sure, therapy could demonstrate this situation and prepare the mental ground for such a struggle—but then psychiatry would be a subversive undertaking.

The question now is whether the strains in contemporary American society, in the affluent society, suggest the prevalence of conditions essentially negative to individual development in the sense just discussed. Or, to formulate the question in terms more indicative of the approach I propose to take: Do these strains vitiate the very possibility of "healthy" individual development— healthy defined in terms of optimal development of one's intellectual and emotional faculties? The question calls for an affirmative answer, that is, this society vitiates individual developments, if the prevailing strains are related to the very structure of this society and if they activate in its members instinctual needs and satisfactions which set the individuals against themselves so that they reproduce and intensify their own repression.

At first glance, the strains in our society seem to be those characteristic of any society which develops under the impact of great technological changes: they initiate new modes of work and of leisure and thereby affect all social relationships, and bring about a thorough transvaluation of values. Since physical labor tends to become increasingly unnecessary and even wasteful, since the work of salaried employees too becomes increasingly "automatic" and that of the politicians and administrators increasingly questionable, the traditional content of the struggle for existence appears more meaningless and without substance the more it appears as unnecessary necessity. But the future alternative, namely, the possible abolition of (alienated) labor seems equally meaningless, nay, frightening. And indeed, if one envisages this alternative as the progress and development of the *established* system, then the dislocation of the content of life to free time suggest the shape of a nightmare: massive self-realization, fun, sport in a steadily shrinking space.

But the threat of the "bogey of automation" is itself ideology. On the one hand it serves the perpetuation and reproduction of technically obsolete and unnecessary jobs and occupations (unemployment as normal condition, even if comfortable, seems worse than stupefying routine work); on the other hand it justifies and promotes the education and training of the managers and organization men of leisure time, that is to say, it serves to prolong and enlarge control and manipulation.

The real danger for the established system is not the abolition of labor but the possibility of nonalienated labor as the basis of the reproduction of society. Not that people are no longer compelled to work, but that they might be compelled to work for a very different life and in very different relations, that they might be given very different goals and values, that they might have to live with a very different morality—this is the "definite negation" of the established system, the liberating alternative. For example, socially necessary labor might be organized for such efforts as the rebuilding of cities and towns, the relocation of the places of work (so that people learn again how to walk), the construction of industries which produce goods without built-in obsolescence, without profitable waste and poor quality, and the subjection of the environment to the vital aesthetic needs of the organism. To be sure, to translate this possibility into reality would mean to eliminate the power of the dominant interests which, by their very function in the society, are opposed to a development that would reduce private enterprise to a minor role, that would do away with the market economy, and with the policy of military preparedness, expansion, and intervention—in other words: a development that would reverse the entire prevailing trend. There is little evidence for such a development. In the meantime, and with the new and terribly effective and total means provided by technical progress, the population is physically and mentally mobilized against this eventuality: they must continue the struggle for existence in painful, costly and obsolete forms.

This is the real contradiction which translates itself from the social structure into the mental structure of the individuals. There, it activates and aggravates destructive tendencies which, in a hardly sublimated mode, are made socially useful in the behavior of the individuals, on the private as well as political level—in the behavior of the nation as a whole. Destructive energy becomes socially useful aggressive energy, and the aggressive behavior impels growth—growth of economic, political, and technical power. Just as in the contemporary scientific enterprise, so in the economic enterprise and in that of the nation as a whole, constructive and destructive achievements, work for life and work for death, procreating and killing are inextricably united. To restrict the exploitation of nuclear energy would mean to restrict its peaceful as well as military potential; the amelioration and protection of life appear as by-products of the scientific work on the annihilation of life; to restrict procreation would also mean to restrict potential manpower and the number of potential customers and clients. Now the (more or less sublimated) transformation of destructive into socially useful aggressive (and thereby constructive) energy is, according to Freud (on whose instinct-theory I base my interpretation) a normal and indispensable process. It is part of the same dynamic by which libido, erotic energy, is sublimated and made socially useful; the two opposite impulses are forced together and, united in this twofold transformation, they become the mental and organic vehicles of civilization. But no matter how close and effective their union, their respective quality remains

unchanged and contrary: aggression activates destruction which "aims" at death, while libido seeks the preservation, protection, and amelioration of life. Therefore, it is only as long as destruction works in the service of Eros that it serves civilization and the individual; if aggression becomes stronger than its erotic counterpart, the trend is reversed. Moreover, in the Freudian conception, destructive energy cannot become stronger without reducing erotic energy: the balance between the two primary impulses is a quantitative one; the instinctual dynamic is mechanistic, distributing an available quantum of energy between the two antagonists.

I have briefly restated Freud's conception inasmuch as I shall use it to discuss the depth and character of the strains prevalent in American society. I suggest that the strains derive from the basic contradiction between the capabilities of this society, which could produce essentially new forms of freedom amounting to a subversion of the established institutions on the one hand, and the repressive use of these capabilities on the other. The contradiction explodes—and is at the same time "resolved," "contained"—in the ubiquitous aggression prevalent in this society. Its most conspicuous (but by no means isolated) manifestation is the military mobilization and its effect on the mental behavior of the individuals, but within the context of the basic contradiction, aggressiveness is fed by many sources. The following seem to be foremost:

1. *The dehumanization of the process of production and consumption.* Technical progress is identical with the increasing elimination of personal initiative, inclination, taste, and need from the provision of goods and services. This tendency is liberating if the available resources and techniques are used for freeing the individual from labor and recreation which are required for the reproduction of the established institutions but are parasitic, wasteful, and dehumanizing in terms of the existing technical and intellectual capabilities. The same tendency often gratifies hostility.

2. *The conditions of crowding, noise, and overtness characteristic of mass society.* As René Dubos has said, the need for "quiet, privacy, independence, initiative, and some open space" are not "frills or luxuries but constitute real biological necessities." Their lack injures the instinctual structure itself. Freud has emphasized the "asocial" character of Eros—the mass society achieves an "oversocialization" to which the individual

reacts "with all sorts of frustrations, repressions, aggressions, and fears which soon develop into genuine neuroses."

I mentioned, as the most conspicuous social mobilization of aggressiveness, the militarization of the affluent society. This mobilization goes far beyond the actual draft of man-power and the buildup of the armament industry: its truly totalitarian aspects show forth in the daily mass media which feed "public opinion." The brutalization of language and image, the presentation of killing, burning, and poisoning and torture inflicted upon the victims of neocolonial slaughter is made in a common-sensible, factual, sometimes humorous style which integrates these horrors with the pranks of juvenile delinquents, football contests, accidents, stock market reports, and the weatherman. This is no longer the "classical" heroizing of killing in the national interest, but rather its reduction to the level of natural events and contingencies of daily life.

The consequence is a "psychological habituation of war" which is administered to a people protected from the actuality of war, a people who, by virtue of this habituation, easily familiarizes itself with the "kill rate" as it is already familiar with other "rates" (such as those of business or traffic or unemployment). The people are conditioned to live "with the hazards, the brutalities, and the mounting casualties of the war in Vietnam, just as one learns gradually to live with the everyday hazards and casualties of smoking, of smog, or of traffic."[1] The photos which appear in the daily newspapers and in magazines with mass circulation, often in nice and glossy color, show rows of prisoners laid out or stood up for "interrogation," little children dragged through the dust behind armored cars, mutilated women. They are nothing new ("such things happen in a war"), but it is the setting that makes the difference: their appearance in the regular program, in togetherness with the commercials, sports, local politics, and reports on the social set. And the brutality of power is further normalized by its extension to the beloved automobile: the manufacturers sell a Thunderbird, Fury, Tempest, and the oil industry puts "a tiger in your tank."

However, the administered language is rigidly discriminating: a specific vocabulary of hate, resentment, and defamation is reserved for opposition to the aggressive policies and for the enemy. The pattern constantly repeats itself. Thus, when students demonstrate against the war, it is a "mob" swelled by "bearded advocates of sexual freedom," by unwashed juveniles, and by "hoodlums and street urchins" who "tramp" the streets, while the counterdemonstrations consist of citizens who gather. In Vietnam, "typical criminal communist violence" is perpetrated against American "strategic operations." The Reds have the impertinence to launch "a sneak attack" (presumably they are supposed to announce it beforehand and to deploy in the open); they are "evading a death trap" (presumably they should have stayed in). The Vietcong attack American barracks "in the dead of night" and kill American boys (presumably, Americans only attack in broad daylight, don't disturb the sleep of the enemy, and don't kill Vietnamese boys). The massacre of hundred thousands of communists (in Indonesia) is called "impressive"—a comparable "killing rate" suffered by the other side would hardly have been honored with such an adjective. To the Chinese, the presence of American troops in East Asia is a threat to their "ideology," while presumably the presence of Chinese troops in Central or South America would be a real, and not only ideological, threat to the United States.

The loaded language proceeds according to the Orwellian recipe of the identity of opposites: in the mouth of the enemy, peace means war, and defense is attack, while on the righteous side, escalation is restraint, and saturation bombing prepares for peace. Organized in this discriminatory fashion, language designates a priori the enemy as evil in his entirety and in all his actions and intentions.

Such mobilization of aggressiveness cannot be explained by the magnitude of the communist threat: the image of the ostensible enemy is inflated out of all proportion to reality. What is at stake is rather the continued stability and growth of a system which is threatened by its own irrationality—by the narrow base on which its prosperity rests, by the dehumanization which its wasteful and parasitic affluence demands. The senseless war is itself part of this irrationality and thus of the essence of the system. What may have been a minor involvement at the beginning, almost an accident, a contingency of foreign policy, has become a test case for the productivity, competitiveness, and prestige of the whole. The billions of dollars spent for the war effort are a political as well as economic stimulus (or cure): a big way of absorbing part of the economic surplus, and of keeping the people in line. Defeat in Vietnam may well be the signal for other wars of liberation closer to home—and perhaps even for rebellion at home.

To be sure, the social utilization of aggressiveness belongs to the historical structure of civilization and has been a powerful vehicle of progress. However, here too, there is a stage where quantity may turn into quality and subvert the normal balance between the two primary instincts in favor of destruction. I mentioned the "bogey man" of automation. In fact the real spectre for the affluent society is the possible reduction of labor to a level where the human organism need no longer function as an instrument of labor. The mere quantitative decline in needed human labor power militates against the maintenance of the capitalist mode of production (as of all other exploitative modes of production). The system reacts by stepping up the production of goods and services which either do not enlarge individual consumption at all, or enlarge it with luxuries—luxuries in the face of persistent poverty, but luxuries which are necessities for occupying a labor force sufficient to reproduce the established economic and political institutions. To the degree to which this sort of work appears as superfluous, senseless, and unnecessary while necessary for earning a living, frustration is built into the very productivity of this society, and aggressiveness is activated. And to the degree to which the society in its very structure becomes aggressive, the mental structure of its citizens adjusts itself: the individual becomes at one and the same time more aggressive and more pliable and submissive, for he submits to a society which, by virtue of its affluence and power, satisfies his deepest (and otherwise greatly repressed) instinctual needs. And these instinctual needs apparently find their libidinal reflection in the representatives of the people. The chairman of the Armed Services Committee of the United States Senate, Senator Russell of Georgia, was struck by this fact. He is quoted as saying:

> There is something about preparing for destruction that causes men to be more careless in spending money than they would be if they were building for constructive purposes. Why that is, I do not know; but I have observed, over a period of almost thirty years in the Senate, that there is something about buying arms with which to kill, to destroy, to wipe out cities, and to obliterate great transportation systems which causes men not to reckon the dollar cost as closely as they do when they think about proper housing and the care of the health of human beings.[2]

I have argued elsewhere the question of how one can possibly gauge and historically compare the aggression prevalent in a specific society; instead of restating the case, I want now to focus on different aspects, on the specific forms in which aggression today is released and satisfied.

The most telling one, and the one which distinguishes the new from the traditional forms, is what I call *technological aggression and satisfaction*. The phenomenon is quickly described: the act of aggression is physically carried out by a mechanism with a high degree of automatism, of far greater power than the individual human being who sets it in motion, keeps it in motion, and determines its end or target. The most extreme case is the rocket or missile; the most ordinary example the automobile. This means that the energy, the power activated and consummated is the mechanical, electrical, or nuclear energy of "things" rather than the instinctual energy of a human being. Aggression is, as it were, transferred from a subject to an object, or is at least "mediated" by an object, and the target is destroyed by a thing rather than by a person. This change in the relation between human and material energy, and between the physical and mental part of aggression (man becomes the subject and agent of aggression by virtue of his mental rather than physical faculties) must also affect the mental dynamic. I submit a hypothesis which is suggested by the inner logic of the process: with the "delegation" of destruction to a more or less automated thing or group and system of things, the instinctual satisfaction of the human person is "interrupted," reduced, frustrated, "super-sublimated." And such frustration makes for repetition and escalation: increasing violence, speed, enlarged scope. At the same time, personal responsibility, conscience, and the sense of guilt is weakened, or rather diffused, displaced from the actual context in which the aggression was committed (i.e. bombing raids), and relocated in a more or less innocuous context (impoliteness, sexual inadequacy, etc.). In this reaction too, the effect is a considerable weakening of the sense of guilt, and the defense (hatred, resentment) is also redirected from the real responsible subject (the commanding officer, the government) to a substitute person: not I as a (morally and physically) acting person did it, but the thing, the machine. The machine: the word suggests that an apparatus consisting of human beings may be substituted for the mechanical apparatus: the bureaucracy, the administration, the party, or organization is the responsible agent; I, the individual person, was only the instrumentality. And an instrument cannot, in any moral sense, be responsible or be in a state of guilt. In this way, another barrier against aggression, which civilization had erected in a long and violent process of discipline is removed. And the expansion of advanced capitalism becomes involved in a fateful psychical dialectic which enters into and propels its economic and political dynamic: the more powerful and "technological" aggression becomes, the less is it apt to satisfy and pacify the primary impulse, and the more it tends toward repetition and escalation.

To be sure, the use of instruments of aggression is as old as civilization itself, but there is a decisive difference between technological aggression and the more primitive forms. The latter were not only quantitatively different (weaker): they required activation and *engagement* of the body to a much higher degree than the automated or semi-automated instruments of aggression. The knife, the "blunt instrument," even the revolver are far more "part" of the individual who uses them and they associate him more closely with his target. Moreover, and most important, their use, unless effectively sublimated and in the service of the life instincts (as in the case of the surgeon, household, etc.), is criminal—individual crime—and as such subject to severe punishment. In contrast, technological aggression is not a crime. The speeding driver of an automobile or motor boat is not called a murderer even if he is one; and certainly the missile-firing engineers are not.

Technological aggression releases a mental dynamic which aggravates the destructive, antierotic tendencies of the puritan complex. The new modes of aggression destroy without getting one's hands dirty, one's body soiled, one's mind incriminated. The killer remains clean, physically as well as mentally. The purity of his deadly work obtains added sanction if it is directed against the national enemy in the national interest.

The (anonymous) lead article in *Les Temps Modernes* (January 1966) links the war in Vietnam with the puritan tradition in the United States. The image of the enemy is that of dirt in its most repulsive forms; the unclean jungle is his natural habitat, disembowelment and beheading are his natural ways of action. Consequently, the burning of his refuge, defoliation, and the poisoning of his foodstuff are not only strategic but also moral operations: removing of contagious dirt, clearing the way for the order of political hygiene and righteousness. And the mass purging of the good conscience from all rational inhibitions leads to the atrophy of the last rebellion of sanity against the madhouse: no satire, no ridicule attends the moralists who organize and defend the crime. Thus one of them can, without becoming a laughingstock, publicly praise as the "greatest performance in our nation's history," the indeed historical achievement of the richest, most powerful, and most advanced country of the world unleashing the destructive force of its technical superiority on one of the poorest, weakest, and most helpless countries of the world.

The decline of responsibility and guilt, their absorption by the omnipotent technical and political apparatus also tends to invalidate other values which were to restrain and sublimate aggression. While the militarization of society remains the most conspicuous and destructive manifestation of this tendency, its less ostensible effects in the cultural dimension should not be minimized. One of these effects is the disintegration of the value of *truth*. The media enjoy a large dispensation from the commitment to truth, and in a very special way. The point is not that the media lie ("lie" presupposes commitment to truth), they rather mingle truth and half-truth with omission, factual reporting with commentary and evaluation, information with publicity and propaganda—all this made into an overwhelming whole through editorializing. The editorially unpleasant truths (and how many of the most decisive truths are not unpleasant?) retreat between the lines, or hide, or mingle harmoniously with nonsense, fun, and so-called human interest stories. And the consumer is readily inclined to take all this for granted—he buys it even if he knows better. Now the commitment to the truth has always been precarious, hedged with strong qualifications, suspended, or suppressed—it is only in the context of the general and democratic activation of aggressiveness that the devaluation of truth assumes special significance. For truth is a value in the strict sense inasmuch as it serves the protection and amelioration of life, as a guide in man's struggle with nature and with himself, with his own weakness and his own destructiveness. In this function, truth is indeed a matter of the sublimated life instincts, Eros, of intelligence becoming responsible and autonomous, striving to liberate life from dependence on unmastered and repressive forces. And with respect to this protective and liberating function of truth, its devaluation removes another effective barrier against destruction.

The encroachment of aggression on the domain of the life instincts also devalues the aesthetic dimension. In *Eros and Civilization* I have tried to show the erotic component in this dimension. Nonfunctional, that is to say, not committed to the functioning of a repressive society, the aesthetic values have been strong protectors of Eros in civilization. Nature is part of this dimension. Eros seeks, in polymorphous forms, its own sensuous world of fulfillment, its own "natural" environment. But only in a protected world—protected from daily business, from noise, crowds, waste, only thus can it satisfy the biological need for happiness. The aggressive business practices which turn ever more spaces of protective nature into a medium of commercial fulfillment and fun thus do not merely offend beauty—they repress biological necessities.

Once we agree to discuss the hypothesis that, in advanced industrial society surplus-aggression is released in quite unsuspected and "normal" behavior, we may see it even in areas which are far removed from the more familiar manifestations of aggression, for instance the style of publicity and information practiced by the mass media. Characteristic is the permanent repetition: the same commercial with the same text or picture broadcast or televised again and again; the same phrases and clichés poured out by the purveyors and makers of information again and again; the same programs and platforms professed by the politicians again and again. Freud arrived at his concept of the death instinct in the context of his analysis of the "repetition compulsion": he associated with it the striving for a state of complete inertia, absence of tension, return to the womb,

annihilation. Hitler knew well the extreme function of repetition: the biggest lie, often enough repeated, will be acted upon and accepted as truth. Even in its less extreme use, constant repetition, imposed upon more or less captive audiences, may be destructive: destroying mental autonomy, freedom of thought, responsibility and conducive to inertia, submission, rejection of change. The established society, the master of repetition, becomes the great womb for its citizens. To be sure, this road to inertia and this reduction of tension is one of high and not very satisfactory sublimation: it does not lead to an instinctual nirvana of satisfaction. However, it may well reduce the stress of intelligence, the pain and tension which accompany autonomous mental activity—thus it may be an effective aggression against the mind in its socially disturbing, critical functions.

These are highly speculative hypotheses on the socially and mentally fateful character of aggression in our society. Aggression is (in most cases) socially useful destructiveness—and yet fateful because of its self-propelling character and scope. In this respect too, it is badly sublimated and not very satisfying. If Freud's theory is correct, and the destructive impulse strives for the annihilation of the individual's own life no matter how long the "detour" via other lives and targets, then we may indeed speak of a suicidal tendency on a truly social scale, and the national and international play with total destruction may well have found a firm basis in the instinctual structure of individuals.

Notes

1. I. Ziferstein, in the UCLA *Daily Bruin*, Los Angeles, May 24, 1966. See also: M. Grotjahn, "Some Dynamics of Unconscious and Symbolic Communication in Present-Day Television," *The Psychoanalytic Study of Society*, III, pp. 356ff., and *Psychiatric Aspects of the Prevention of Nuclear War*, Group for the Advancement of Psychiatry (New York, 1964), passim.

2. Quoted in *The Nation*, August 25, 1962, pp. 65–66, in an article by Senator William Proxmire.

Afterword and Acknowledgments

While doing this project, we have more than once felt the taut pleasures of record geeks making a find at the used vinyl store. Following footnotes, reading old journals, and walking through the stacks, we have experienced the literary equivalents of a music fan's discoveries: rare early recordings by people who later made it big; albums that we were acquainted with that turned out to be different from what we remembered; and crazy, cool sides by musicians we'd barely heard of. We encountered plenty of dull spots and too few novelty numbers (though "Social Anatomy of the Romance-Confession Cover Girl" certainly stands out as a fine exception), but we also discovered plenty of great finds. Both of us have our favorite discoveries and rediscoveries. Ranking high for us are the sections on leisure from the Lynds' *Middletown*, Edward Sapir's entry on communication in the 1931 *Encyclopedia of the Social Sciences*, and Rolf Meyersohn and Elihu Katz's 1957 essay on fads.

Part of the pleasure we felt was being in contact with a tradition that, despite the passage of decades, was still very much alive on the page. Written documents, like record albums, possess an uncanny ability to preserve the voices and thoughts of those who are no longer with us. Coming into contact with yellowed pages, inhaling the sometimes mildewy smell, reading typefaces that are no longer in fashion, discovering quaint and sarcastic marginalia scribbled by readers from previous eras, and blowing dust off bound volumes that had not been consulted in years are some of the secret, strange delights. We wish we could better share the extraordinary feeling of being in touch with departed times and minds that the tangible details of our search have afforded us.

Compiling a reader and assembling a record collection are each a process marked by serendipity, those unanticipated discoveries that prove fruitful (see Merton and Barber 2004). This was particularly the case when we laid hands upon the originals in the stacks of our libraries. While JSTOR and online searches are certainly productive, there is also no substitute for perambulation, proximity, and touch. Physically searching out the originals gave us a new sense of the field as we picked up books shelved near the ones we sought, browsed through early collections, and saw who was publishing together. Before we started this project, we felt as though we had a good sense of the intellectual history of communication, but we made dozens of serendipitous finds that broadened and deepened our knowledge. We incorporate many of them into our essays and short introductions, which probably resemble the liner notes we've always wanted to write. Writing them up helped us to rethink our understandings of the history of the field.

Reading and listening to music are marked by similar patterns. On first hearing unfamiliar music, we tend to respond with tolerant curiosity at best, but more typically with incomprehension and most often with disinterest, discomfort, or disgust. Yet, repeated exposure brings familiarity with patterns and makes the distinctive licks and stylistic touches of particular performances evident to the ear. What was once just noise gradually becomes intelligible as sound, meaning, and temporal performance. What once were quirks become marks of innovative genius moving within larger species of possibility. To the once-annoying strains, we tap our toe or hum along. Discovery in both listening and reading requires a willingness to be exposed and to sacrifice one's mortal minutes to the music. The more one listens within a genre, the richer one finds the individual numbers within it. Music, like writing, is deeply embedded in its traditions and histories. No piece of music or writing is an island; rather, each is a member of a larger, invisible family of sounds and statements. Both of us have acquired a taste for the intellectual sounds recorded on these pages. We may be perverse or idiosyncratic, but we take comfort in the thought that we are not alone. Give it a chance, and you'll be here, too—and then, unlike Dave Hickey's English professor mentioned in our epigraph, we can sit around and talk about how cool David Riesman and Robert Lynd are.

On the other hand, the texts gathered here are not simply intellectual art that provide topics for the quotidian conversation in parlors, pubs, or contemporary classrooms. Many of them had real consequences for real people, and not just those in academia. Since at least the 1920s, propaganda and mass communications research has been intricately tied with institutions of power—government and industries of broadcasting, advertising, public relations, and sales. The relation between ideas and institutions is complex, and we reject simple or overly reductive treatments that cast guilt on any theory or theorist who gets appropriated by forces of power and domination; as the pragmatists argued, ideas can be used for disparate purposes in disparate institutional settings. At the same time, some of the readings here make us shudder as we think about their position within the context of broader forces. In the pieces by David Sarnoff, Wilbur Schramm, and Daniel Lerner, for instance, we see evidence of the entwined realms of Cold War politics, modernization theory, and international media whose consequences were often regrettable, if not disastrous, for people living in the "lesser-developed" world. It is important to read, as Jeffrey Stout (1988) once wrote, "with both eyes open."

Beyond channeling our record-collecting instincts, doing this project taught us a lot, especially about Chicago and Columbia, which are the intellectual settings for most of our texts. Informal oral-history conversations by telephone, by e-mail, and in person were incredibly helpful, not to mention a lot of fun. Sam Becker, George Gerbner, Daniel Bell, Herta Herzog, Elihu Katz, Kurt Lang, Thelma McCormack, Rolf Meyersohn, Charlie Wright, and the late Robert Merton were all very generous in sharing their memories and time with us, and we thank them. We know we have missed things, both worthy texts and important introductory details. If you have suggestions or complaints, please tell us, and we promise to publish an even better reader if we ever decide to do so again. But all in all, we're happy with what we found and think it collectively paints a richer picture of the field's history than many people might have previously imagined.

A project of this magnitude owes much to many people. For expert advice in the early and middle stages, we thank Sam Becker, David Black, James Carey, the late Steve Chaffee,

Brett Gary, Hanno Hardt, Joy Hayes, Susan Herbst, Sue Lafky, Tom Lutz, Michael Schudson, and Robert Wyatt. Ken Cmiel and Eric Rothenbuhler have been long-term supporters of the project, as have Elihu Katz, Tamar Liebes, and Avril Orloff, collaborators with Peters on another volume to which this one is a kind of companion (Katz et al. 2003). John Thompson of Polity Press offered expert advice and put our proposal through an excellent review process: we thank him for his early guidance. Carolyn Marvin and Jonathan Sterne added their enthusiasm at important moments. Andrew Calabrese, the series editor at Rowman and Littlefield, offered the right balance of critique and enthusiasm. Brenda Hadenfeldt was incredibly accommodating and supportive as the acquisitions editor for communication and journalism. Charles Lemert offered helpful advice about preparing large-scale readers. Jim Schwoch went far beyond the call of duty, first by providing us with a constructive review of the book's overall concept and then by helping us track down readings that we would not have thought of ourselves. Jefferson D. Pooley, a rising scholar of the history of mass communication research, generously shared his own bibliography of works on the history of the field (which helped us to form our own, much briefer list) and also made several last-minute suggestions that saved us from some important omissions. We have relied on a team of skilled research assistants and reference librarians, including Hugo Burgos, Jung-Bong Choi, Hee-Eun Lee, Yong Li, Hsin-i Liu, Rosa Monteleone-Amberg, Tracy Routsong, and Ralph Siddall. Peter Schaefer stepped in at the last minute and efficiently guided us through the process of preparing the manuscript. Carey Brezler cheerfully and expertly handled the onerous task of managing the permissions and now knows more about the bowels of the publishing world than anyone should have to. Our families put up with big piles of old books and photocopies for far too long.

We would like to blame all these people for any shortcomings, but decorum prevents it. This project originated in our desire to make texts available that, owing to court decisions in the early 1990s, could not be included in photocopied course packets.[1] This reader emerges from three decades of teaching the treasures and curiosities in American mass communication theory. It is the course packet that we have wanted to give our students over the years, and it is they to whom we dedicate the book.

Note

1. For those who care about such things (Simonson's tenure committee, for instance) and others who by habit or chance come to this note, Simonson was lead author for the Introduction and the 1933–1949 essays, Peters for the 1919–1933 and 1949–1968 essays. Peters had the idea for this Reader and then he and Simonson made it better through interaction at a distance. Behold the Matthew Effect (for Bob Merton—gentleman, scholar, presence).

Other Readers and Historical Collections in American Mass Communication Study and Related Subjects

Berelson, Bernard, and Morris Janowitz, eds. *Reader in Public Opinion and Mass Communication*. New York: Free Press, 1950, 1953, 1966, 1980.

Bryson, Lyman, ed. *The Communication of Ideas: A Series of Addresses*. New York: Harper, 1948.

Davison, Peter, Rolf Meyersohn, and Edward Shils, eds. *Literary Taste, Culture and Mass Communication*. 14 vols. Teaneck, N.J.: Somerset House, 1978.

Dexter, Lewis, and David Manning White, eds. *People, Society, and Mass Communication*. New York: Free Press, 1964.

Durham, Meenakshi Gigi, and Douglas M. Kellner, eds. *Media and Cultural Studies: Keyworks*. Malden, Mass.: Blackwell Publishers, 2001.

Golding, Peter, and Graham Murdock, eds. *The Political Economy of the Media*. 2 vols. Brookfield, Vt.: Edward Elgar, 1997.

Grossberg, Lawrence, Cary Nelson, and Paula A. Treichler, eds. *Cultural Studies*. New York: Routledge, 1992.

Jacobs, Norman, ed. *Culture for the Millions? Mass Media in Modern Society*. Boston: Beacon Press, 1959.

Kaes, Anton, Martin Jay, and Edward Dimendberg, eds. *The Weimar Republic Sourcebook*. Berkeley: University of California Press, 1994.

Lazarsfeld, Paul F., and Frank Stanton. *Radio Research, 1941*. New York: Duell, Sloan and Pearce, 1942.

———. *Radio Research, 1942–3*. New York: Duell, Sloan and Pearce, 1944.

———. *Communications Research, 1948*. New York: Harper & Brothers, 1949.

Lemert, Charles, ed. *Social Theory: The Multicultural and Classic Readings*. Boulder, Colo.: Westview Press, 1993, 1999.

Lowery, Shearon, and Melvin De Fleur, eds. *Milestones in Mass Communication Research: Media Effects*. White Plains, N.Y.: Longmans, 1983, 1988, 1995.

Marris, Paul, and Sue Thornham, eds. *Media Studies: A Reader*. 2nd ed. New York: NYU Press, 2000.

Menand, Louis. *Pragmatism: A Reader*. New York: Vintage, 1997.

Mukerji, Chandra, and Michael Schudson, eds. *Rethinking Popular Culture: Contemporary Perspectives in Cultural Studies.* Berkeley: University of California Press, 1991.

O'Sullivan, Tim, and Yvonne Jewkes, eds. *The Media Studies Reader.* New York: St. Martin's Press, 1997.

Rosenberg, Bernard, and David Manning White, eds. *Mass Culture: The Popular Arts in America.* Glencoe: Free Press, 1957.

———. *Mass Culture Revisited.* New York: Van Nostrand Reinhold, 1971.

Schramm, Wilbur. *Mass Communications: A Book of Readings.* Urbana: University of Illinois Press, 1949, 1960.

———. *The Process and Effects of Mass Communication.* Urbana: University of Illinois Press, 1955.

———. *The Science of Human Communication.* New York: Basic Books, 1963.

Schramm, Wilbur, and Donald F. Roberts, eds. *The Process and Effects of Mass Communication.* Urbana: University of Illinois Press, 1971.

Smith, Alfred G., ed. *Communication and Culture: Readings in the Codes of Human Interaction.* New York: Holt, Rinehart and Winston, 1966.

Smith, Bruce L., Harold D. Lasswell, and Ralph D. Casey, eds. *Propaganda, Communication, and Public Opinion: A Comprehensive Reference Guide.* Princeton, N.J.: Princeton University Press, 1946.

Waples, Douglas, ed. *Print, Radio, and Film in a Democracy.* Chicago: University of Chicago Press, 1942.

Suggested Films

Many films raise questions about the meaning of media for modern social life. Indeed, since the cinema is one of the most important forms of all modern media, the question of how experience is shaped in sound and image is often implicit in most films. Rather than try to list all films that raise media questions—a huge list—the following focuses especially on films that are tied historically or thematically to selections in this reader. Any of these can be an excellent supplement to a course on twentieth-century mass communication theory.

Sherlock Junior (1924)
Buster Keaton's short film about a film projectionist is a masterpiece of reflexivity. Film image and film reality, fantasy and everyday life fold back and forth onto each other in one of the great cinematic treatments of how modern life rearranges time, space, and sensibility.

Metropolis (1926)
Fritz Lang's enormously influential film helped to provide the imagery for the rest of the century's thinking about the dangers of mass society: regimentation, facelessness, fusion of humanity and machines. The film reflects worries in Weimar, Germany, about the shape of modern society—many worries that were imported (like Lang himself) into the United States. In fact, all of Lang's films raise questions about media.

The Big Broadcast (1932)
Radio, stardom, romance, and the record industry. Bing Crosby plays the typecast role of an alcoholic crooner, unreliable but charming. Very subtle treatment of sound and image.

International House (1933)
Goofy comedy starring W. C. Fields, with remarkably prescient and witty treatments of the future of radio and television.

The Invisible Man (1933)
James Whale's film, about a mad scientist who discovers how to make himself invisible, can be read as a treatment of the disembodied voice of radio and film. It includes excellent

sequences involving radio. The idea of "appearing in person," Gordon Allport wrote in 1937, "once seemed redundant, but it is less so now in the days of cinema and radio when partial appearance or appearance *not* in person is possible."

It Happened One Night (1933)
Considered by cultural historian Warren Susman as *the* film about media; every scene, he suggests, is framed by a medium of communication.

Mr. Smith Goes to Washington (1939)
Frank Capra's film pits Jefferson Smith, played by James Stewart, against a corrupt senior senator and a party boss who has monopoly control over communication media. The film is a brilliant capturing of 1930s fears about propaganda, the free press, and the hope of small media. Capra went on in the early 1940s to film the *Why We Fight* film series, the subject of study in *The American Soldier*.

Citizen Kane (1941)
Orson Welles's film, still regarded as one of the greatest of all time, portrays the life and times of a media magnate with political ambitions, a figure still very much on the world stage! The film is a kind of compendium of modern mass media, and part of its brilliance is its integration of contemporaneous media into a single work of art—newspaper, radio, film, newsreel, public relations, photography, papparazzi—they are all there.

Sullivan's Travels (1941)
Exposé of the culture industry (and much more) with striking resemblances to analyses of Adorno, Horkheimer, Macdonald, MacDougald, and others. With the ever-beguiling Veronica Lake.

The Glass Web (1953).
This hard-to-find B movie, about an early television station, plays with the story of murder on (or by) television and has similar reflexivity about what is real and what is fantasy as *Sherlock Junior*. In 3-D!

All That Heaven Allows (1955)
At a poignant moment in this Sirk melodrama, the grown children of a widowed mother (Jane Wyman) give her a television set as a Christmas present to assuage her loneliness and substitute for romance.

The Invasion of the Body-Snatchers (1956)
This campy classic shows, at a popular level, the fear of alienation quite literally—that is, having our bodies possessed by alien beings. A delightfully silly sci-fi flick with overtones of Cold War paranoia, this film's fear that we might turn into "pod-people" captures at a vernacular level some Cold War worries about what media might do to a mass society.

The Man in the Gray Flannel Suit (1956)
The melancholy of the rat race and the dark side of affluence—this treatment of a white middle-class male in the quintessential other-directed profession of public relations

captures much of the mood into which David Riesman's *Lonely Crowd* and theories of mass society resonate. Based on Sloane Wilson's novel of the same name.

Written on the Wind (1956)
Douglas Sirk's melodrama is a classic in its own right, but it is suffused by 1950s pathos regarding advertising, music, and fraught gender relations.

A Face in the Crowd (1957)
Elia Kazan's treatment of media, politics, and demagoguery.

Rock-a-Bye Baby (1958)
Jerry Lewis's typically antic film showcases some humorous routines involving television and parasocial interaction.

The Manchurian Candidate (1962)
John Frankenheimer's thriller, starring Frank Sinatra, has often seemed suspiciously prophetic in its tale of a mob-inspired conspiracy to assassinate the president of the United States (Lee Harvey Oswald is known to have seen it). Its treatment of Cold War psychological brainwashing offers arresting imagery of subliminal control and suggestion.

Fahrenheit 451 (1966)
Based on Ray Bradbury's novel, French New Wave filmmaker François Truffault's film offers some brilliant commentary on the ways that television enters into people's lives as a parasocial "family."

Star Trek: "Bread and Circuses" (1968, episode 43)
Deploying terms of the mass culture debates, this episode of the classic late-1960s sci-fi television series is a clever spoof on modern American television as a latter-day version of the Roman games.

Network (1973)
Paddy Chayevsky's brilliant screenplay superimposes a love triangle, the intrigue of the television news business, and a reflection on the meaning of 1960s-style protest and its commodification.

Videodrome (1982)
Disturbingly brilliant film by Canadian David Cronenburg about the dark side of television. The character of Professor Barry O'Blivion, who lives on after death in his video recordings, is a tribute to, and a spoof of, Marshall McLuhan. Recommended for only the strong of stomach.

Radio Days (1987)
Woody Allen's nostalgic and fond tribute to the golden age of American radio brings to life the broadcast culture of the 1930s and 1940s and, like Herta Herzog's study of radio soap listeners, examines the wide range of roles that radio has played in people's lives.

Avalon (1990)
Barry Levinson's bittersweet treatment of the travails of an extended Jewish family in the United States, with television standing in for suburban alienation and loss of roots.

Quiz Show (1994)
Robert Redford's treatment of the transformation of the television industry in light of the late 1950s quiz show scandals is also a treatment of class, family, and ethnicity in 1950s America.

Vizontele (2001)
Turkish comedy about the introduction of television to a rural village in the early 1970s that dramatizes many of the themes of modernization theory. Offers an ironic and charming redramatization of some of Daniel Lerner's arguments in *The Passing of Traditional Society* (p. 426).

Select Supplementary Reading List

The following are significant books and articles not included in this reader for reasons of space, money, or their easy availability elsewhere. Serious students of the tradition will want to read these titles as well.

1890s–1910s

Cooley, Charles Horton. *A Theory of Transportation* (1894), reprinted in Schubert (1998)
———. *Human Nature and Social Order* (1902)
———.*Social Organization: A Study of the Larger Mind* (1909)
Dewey, John. *Democracy and Education* (1916)
Park, Robert E. *Public and Mass* (1903)
Sinclair, Upton. *The Brass Check: A Study of American Journalism* (1919)
Small, Albion, and George Vincent. *An Introduction to the Study of Society*, esp. chapter 4, "The Psycho-Physical Communicating Apparatus, or the Social Nervous System" (1894)

1920s–1930s

Arnheim, Rudolph. *Radio* (1936)
Bernays, Edward. *Propaganda* (1928)
Burke, Kenneth. *Attitudes toward History*, esp. part III, "Analysis of Symbolic Structure" (1937)
Cooley, Charles Horton, Robert Cooley Angell, and Lowell Juilliard Clark, *Introductory Sociology*, esp. chapters 3 and 12 (extensions of Cooley's writings on communication, updated by Angell and Clark to include consideration of twentieth-century mass communication technologies)
Dewey, John. *The Public and Its Problems* (1927)
———. *Art as Experience* (1935)

Henderson, L. J. "Aphorisms on the Advertising of Alkalies" (1937), reprinted in *L. J. Henderson on the Social System,* edited by Bernard Barber (1970)

Lasswell, Harold, et al. *Propaganda and Promotional Activities: An Annotated Bibliography* (1935)

Lasswell, Harold, and Dorothy Blumenstock. *World Revolutionary Propaganda: A Chicago Study* (1939)

Lippmann, Walter. *Liberty and the News* (1920)

———. *Public Opinion* (1922)

Mead, George Herbert. *Mind, Self, and Society* (1934)

Park, Robert Ezra. Writings on newspapers and communication in the collections edited by Everett Hughes (1950, 1955)

Riegel, O. W. *Mobilizing for Chaos: The Story of the New Propaganda* (1934)

Simpson, George E. *The Negro in the Philadelphia Press* (1936)

Willey, Malcolm. *The Country Newspaper: A Study of Socialization and Newspaper Content* (1926)

1940s

Bryson, Lyman, ed. *The Communication of Ideas* (1948)

Cantril, Hadley. *The Invasion from Mars: A Study in the Psychology of Panic* (1940)

Kracauer, Siegfried. *Propaganda and the Nazi War Film* (1942)

Lazarsfeld, Paul. *Radio and the Printed Page* (1940)

Lowenthal, Leo, and Norbert Guterman. *Prophets of Deceit: A Study of the Techniques of the American Agitator* (1949)

Merton, Robert K. *Social Theory and Social Structure,* part III, "The Sociology of Knowledge and the Sociology of Mass Communications" (1949; reprinted in 2nd and 3rd eds., 1957, 1968)

Schramm, Wilbur, ed. *Communications in Modern Society* (1948)

Shannon, Claude, and Warren Weaver. *The Mathematical Theory of Communication* (1949)

1950s

Adorno, Theodor, et al. *The Authoritarian Personality* (1950)

Arendt, Hannah. *The Human Condition,* section II, "The Public and the Private Realm" (1958)

Huxley, Aldous. *Brave New World Revisited* (1958)

Innis, Harold A. *The Bias of Communication* (1951)

Larrabee, Eric, and Rolf Meyersohn, eds. *Mass Leisure* (1958)

McLuhan, Marshall. *The Mechanical Bride: Folklore of Industrial Man* (1951)

Mills, C. Wright. *The Sociological Imagination* (1959)

Rieff, Philip. "Aesthetic Functions in Modern Politics" (1953), reprinted in Rieff, *The Feeling Intellect: Selected Writings* (1990)

Rosenberg, Bernard, and David Manning White, eds. *Mass Culture: The Popular Arts in America* (1957)

Siebert, Fred, Theodore Peterson, and Wilbur Schramm. *Four Theories of the Press* (1956)

1960s

Boorstin, Daniel J. *The Image, or What Happened to the American Dream* (1962)
Carpenter, Edmund, and Marshall McLuhan, eds. *Explorations in Communication: An Anthology* (1960)
Duncan, Hugh Dalziel. *Communication and Social Order* (1962)
Friedan, Betty. "The Lonely Housewife Heroine," from *The Feminine Mystique* (1963)
Habermas, Jurgen. *Structural Transformation of the Public Sphere* (1962)
Klapper, Joseph. *The Effects of Mass Communication* (1960)
Lowenthal, Leo. *Literature, Popular Culture, and Society* (1961)
Marcuse, Herbert. *One Dimensional Man* (1964)
McLuhan, Marshall. *The Gutenberg Galaxy: The Making of Typographic Man* (1962)
———. *Understanding Media: The Extensions of Man* (1964)
Rogers, Everett. *Diffusion of Innovations* (1962)

The Intellectual History of North American Media Studies, 1919–1968

A Selected Bibliography (Including Works Cited in Interpretive Essays)

Acland, Charles, and William Buxton, eds. 1999. *Harold Innis in the New Century: Reflections and Refractions.* Montreal: McGill-Queens University Press.

Adorno, Theodor. 1969. "Scientific Experiences of a European Scholar in America." In *The Intellectual Migration: Europe and America, 1930–1960,* ed. D. Fleming and B. Bailyn, 338–70. Cambridge, Mass.: Harvard University Press.

Babe, Robert E. 2000. *Canadian Communication Thought: Ten Foundational Writers.* Toronto: University of Toronto Press.

Barton, Allen H. 1982. "Paul Lazarsfeld and the Invention of the University Institute for Applied Social Research." In *Organizing for Social Research,* ed. B. Holzner and J. Nehnevajsa, 17–83. Cambridge, Mass.: Schenkman.

———. 2001. "Paul Lazarsfeld as Institutional Inventor." *International Journal of Public Opinion Research* 13, no. 3: 245–69.

Barton, Judith S. 1984. *Guide to the Bureau of Applied Social Research.* New York: Clearwater.

Baughman, James. 1997. *The Republic of Mass Culture: Journalism, Filmmaking, and Broadcasting in America since 1941.* 2nd ed. Baltimore, Md.: Johns Hopkins University Press.

Becker, Samuel L. 1999. "Looking Forward, Looking Back: A Personal Retrospective." *Communication Studies* 50, no. 1: 22–27.

Beniger, James R. 1987. "Toward an Old New Paradigm: The Half-Century Flirtation with Mass Society." *Public Opinion Quarterly* 51, no. 4: S46–S66.

Beuick, Marshall D. 1927. "The Limited Social Effect of Radio Broadcasting." *American Journal of Sociology* 32:615–22.

Bineham, Jeffery L. 1988. "A Historical Account of the Hypodermic Model in Mass Communication." *Communication Monographs* 55:230–46.

Black, David. 2003. "'Both of Us Can Move Mountains': Mary Quayle Innis and Her Relationship to Harold Innis's Legacy." *Canadian Journal of Communication* 28:4.

Blondheim, Menahem. 1994. *News over the Wires: The Telegraph and the Flow of Public Information in America, 1844–1897.* Cambridge, Mass.: Harvard University Press.

———. 2003. "Harold Adams Innis and His Bias of Communication." In *Canonic Texts in Media Research: Are There Any? Should There Be? How about These?* ed. Elihu Katz, John D. Peters, Tamar Liebes, and Avril Orloff, 156–90. Cambridge, Eng.: Polity.

Bogdroghkozy, Aniko. 2001. *Groove Tube: Sixties Television and the Youth Rebellion.* Durham, N.C.: Duke University Press.

Bramson, Leon. 1961. *The Political Context of Sociology.* Princeton, N.J.: Princeton University Press.

Brantlinger, Patrick. 1983. *Bread and Circuses: Theories of Mass Culture as Social Decay.* Ithaca, N.Y.: Cornell University Press.

Brick, Howard. 1986. *Daniel Bell and the Decline of Intellectual Radicalism: Social Theory and Political Reconciliation in the 1940s.* Madison: University of Wisconsin Press.

Bryson, Lyman, ed. 1948. *The Communication of Ideas: A Series of Addresses.* New York: Harper and Brothers.

Bulmer, Martin. 1981. "Quantification and Chicago Social Science in the 1920s: A Neglected Tradition." *Journal of the History of the Behavioral Sciences* 17:312–31.

Buxton, William. 1994. "From Radio Research to Communications Intelligence: Rockefeller Philanthropy, Communications Specialists, and the American Intelligence Community." In *The Political Influence of Ideas: Policy Communities and the Social Sciences,* ed. A. G. Gagnon and Stephen Brooks, 187–209. Westport, Conn.: Praeger.

———. 1996. "The Emergence of Communications Study—Psychological Warfare or Scientific Thoroughfare?" *Canadian Journal of Communication* 21, no. 4.

Buxton, William, and Stephen P. Turner. 1992. "From Education to Expertise: Sociology as a 'Profession.'" In *Sociology and Its Publics,* ed. Terence C. Halliday and Morris Janowitz, 373–407. Chicago: University of Chicago Press.

Carey, James W. 1989a. "Commentary: Communication and the Progressives." *Critical Studies in Mass Communication* 6:264–282.

———. 1989b. *Communication as Culture.* Boston: Unwin Hyman.

———. 1996. "The Chicago School and Mass Communication Research." In *American Communication Research: The Remembered History,* ed. E. Dennis and E. Wartella, 21–38. Mahwah, N.J.: Lawrence Erlbaum.

———. 1997. "The Roots of Modern Media Analysis: Lewis Mumford and Marshall McLuhan." In *James Carey: A Critical Reader,* ed. Eve Munson and Catherine A. Warren, 34–59. Minneapolis: University of Minnesota Press.

Chaffee, Steven H., and John Hochheimer. 1985. "The Beginnings of Political Communication Research in the United States: Origins of the 'Limited Effects' Model." In *The Media Revolution in America and Western Europe,* ed. Everett M. Rogers and Francis Balle, 267–96. Norwood, N.J.: Ablex.

Cmiel, Kenneth. 1996. "On Cynicism, Evil, and the Discovery of Communication in the 1940s." *Journal of Communication* 46, no. 3: 88–107.

Coleman, James S. 1990. "Columbia in the 1950s." In *Authors of Their Own Lives: Intellectual Autobiographies of Twenty American Sociologists,* ed. Bennett M. Berger, 75–103. Berkeley: University of California Press.

Converse, Jean M. 1987. *Survey Research in the United States: Roots and Emergence, 1890–1960.* Berkeley: University of California Press.

Couldry, Nick. 2003. *Media Rituals: A Critical Approach.* New York: Routledge.

Craig, Robert T., and D. A. Carlone. 1998. "Growth and Transformation of Communication Studies in U.S. Higher Education: Toward Reinterpretation." *Communication Education* 47:67–81.

Czitrom, Daniel J. 1982. *Media and the American Mind: From Morse to McLuhan.* Chapel Hill: University of North Carolina Press.

Darnell, Regna. 1990. *Edward Sapir: Linguist, Anthropologist, Humanist.* Berkeley: University of California Press.

Delia, Jesse. 1987. "Communication Research: A History." In *Handbook of Communication Science,* ed. C. R. Berger and S. H. Chaffee, 20–98. Newbury Park, Calif.: Sage.

Dennis, Everette, and Ellen Wartella, eds. 1996. *American Communication Research: The Remembered History.* Mahwah, N.J.: Lawrence Erlbaum.

Depew, David, and J. D. Peters. 2001. "Community and Communication: The Conceptual Background." In *Communication and Community,* ed. Gregory J. Shepherd and Eric W. Rothenbuhler, 3–21. Mahwah, N.J.: Lawrence Erlbaum.

Dickson, Tom. 2000. *Mass Media Education in Transition.* Mahwah, N.J.: Lawrence Erlbaum.

Douglas, Susan J. 1999. "The Invention of the Audience." In *Listening In: Radio and the American Imagination,* 124–60. New York: Times Books.

Du Bois, W. E. B. [1899] 1967. *The Philadelphia Negro: A Social Study.* New York: Schocken.

Edwards, Violet. 1938. *Group Leader's Guide to Propaganda Analysis.* New York: Institute for Propaganda Analysis.

Fox, Richard Wightman. 1983. "Epitaph for Middletown: Robert S. Lynd and the Analysis of Consumer Culture." In *The Culture of Consumption: Critical Essays in American History, 1880–1980,* ed. Richard Wightman Fox and T. J. Jackson Lears, 101–41. New York: Pantheon Books.

Galliher, John F., and James M. Galliher. 1995. *Marginality and Dissent in Twentieth-Century American Sociology: The Case of Elizabeth Briant Lee and Alfred McLung Lee.* Albany: State University of New York Press.

Gary, Brett. 1999. *The Nervous Liberals: Propaganda Anxieties from World War I to the Cold War.* New York: Columbia University Press.

Giner, Salvador. 1976. *Mass Society.* New York: Academic Press.

Gitlin, Todd. 1978. "Media Sociology: The Dominant Paradigm." *Theory and Society* 6:205–53.

———. 2002. "David Riesman, Thoughtful Pragmatist." *Chronicle of Higher Education* (May 24): B5.

Glander, Timothy. 2000. *Origins of Mass Communications Research during the American Cold War: Educational Effects and Contemporary Implications.* Mahwah, N.J.: Lawrence Erlbaum.

Habermas, Jürgen. [1962] 1989. *The Structural Transformation of the Public Sphere.* Trans. Thomas McCarthy. Cambridge, Mass.: MIT Press.

Hall, Stuart. 1982. "The Rediscovery of 'Ideology': Return of the Repressed in Media Studies." In *Culture, Society, and the Media,* ed. M. Gurevitch et al., 56–90. London: Methuen.

Hall, Stuart, and Paddy Whannel. 1964. *The Popular Arts.* New York: Pantheon.

Handelman, Don. 2003. "Towards a Virtual Encounter: Horton's and Wohl's 'Mass Communication and Para-Social Interaction.'" In *Canonic Texts in Media Research: Are There Any? Should There Be? How about These?* ed. Elihu Katz, John D. Peters, Tamar Liebes, and Avril Orloff, 137–51. Cambridge, Eng.: Polity.

Hardt, Hanno. 1992. *Critical Communication Studies: Communication, History and Theory in America.* London: Routledge.

———. 1998. *Interactions: Critical Studies in Communication, Media, and Journalism.* Lanham, Md.: Rowman and Littlefield.

———. 1999. *In the Company of Media: Cultural Constructions of Communication, 1920s–1930s.* Boulder, Colo.: Westview.

———. [1979] 2002. *Social Theories of the Press: Constituents of Communication Research, 1840s to 1920s.* Lanham, Md.: Rowman and Littlefield.

Heyer, Paul. 2003. *Harold Innis.* Lanham, Md.: Rowman and Littlefield.

Hughes, Helen MacGill. 1973. "Maid of All Work or Departmental Sister-in-Law? The Faculty Wife Employed on Campus." *American Journal of Sociology* 78:767–72.

Illouz, Eva. 2003. "Redeeming Consumption: On Lowenthal's 'Triumph of the Mass Idols.'" In *Canonic Texts in Media Research: Are There Any? Should There Be? How about These?* ed. Elihu Katz, John D. Peters, Tamar Liebes, and Avril Orloff, 90–102. Cambridge, Eng.: Polity.

Institute for Social Research. n.d. "Ten Years on Morningside Heights: A Report on the Institute's History, 1934 to 1944." Personal files of Robert K. Merton.

Jandy, Edward C. 1942. *Charles Horton Cooley: His Life and His Social Theory.* New York: Dryden Press.

Janowitz, Morris. 1969. Introduction to *Introduction to the Science of Sociology,* Robert E. Park and Ernest W. Burgess. 3rd ed. Chicago: University of Chicago Press.

Jay, Martin. 1973. *The Dialectical Imagination: A History of the Frankfurt School and the Institute of Social Research, 1923–1950.* Boston: Little Brown.

Jensen, Joli. 1990. *Redeeming Modernity.* Newbury Park, Calif.: Sage.

Johnson, Lyndon Baines. 1967. "Remarks upon Signing the Public Broadcasting Act of 1967." November 7, Washington, D.C.

Jowett, Garth S. 1976. *Film: The Democratic Art.* Boston: Little Brown.

———. 1991. "Propaganda Critique: The Forgotten History of American Communication Studies." In *Communication Yearbook,* ed. J. A. Anderson, 239–48. Newbury Park, Calif.: Sage.

———. 1992. "Social Science as a Weapon: The Origins of the Payne Fund Studies, 1926–1929." *Communication* 13:211–25.

Jowett, Garth S., Ian C. Jarvie, and Kathryn H. Fuller. 1996. *Children and the Movies: Media Influences and the Payne Fund Controversy.* New York: Cambridge University Press.

Kaes, Anton, Martin Jay, and Edward Dimendberg. 1994. *The Weimar Republic Sourcebook.* Berkeley: University of California Press.

Katz, Elihu. 1987. "Communications Research Since Lazarsfeld." *Public Opinion Quarterly* 51:S25–S45.

———. 1996. "Diffusion Research at Columbia." In *American Communication Research: The Remembered History,* ed. E. Dennis and E. Wartella, 61–70. Mahwah, N.J.: Lawrence Erlbaum.

———. 2001. "Lazarsfeld's Map of Media Effects." *International Journal of Public Opinion Research* 13:270–79.

Katz, Elihu, and Daniel Dayan. 2003. "The Audience Is a Crowd, the Crowd Is a Public: Latter-Day Thoughts on Lang and Lang's 'MacArthur Day in Chicago.'" In *Canonic Texts in Media Research: Are There Any? Should There Be? How about These?* ed. Elihu Katz, John D. Peters, Tamar Liebes, and Avril Orloff, 121–36. Cambridge, Eng.: Polity.

Katz, Elihu, John D. Peters, Tamar Liebes, and Avril Orloff, eds. 2003. *Canonic Texts in Media Research: Are There Any? Should There Be? How About These?* Cambridge, Eng.: Polity. [Composed of thirteen essays by leading scholars evaluating several of the pieces compiled in this reader. A companion volume in many respects to the reader you hold in your hands.]

Katz, Elihu, and Ruth Katz. 1998. "McLuhan: Where Did He Come From? Where Did He Disappear?" *Canadian Journal of Communication* 23:307–19.

Kendall, Patricia, ed. 1982. *The Varied Sociology of Paul F. Lazarsfeld.* New York: Columbia University Press.

Lang, Kurt. 1979. "Critical Functions of Empirical Communication Research: Observations on German-American Influences." *Media, Culture, and Society* 1:83–96.

———. 1996. "The European Roots." In *American Communication Research: The Remembered History,* ed. E. Dennis and E. Wartella, 1–20. Mahwah, N.J.: Lawrence Erlbaum.

Lasch, Christopher. 1991. *The True and Only Heaven: Progress and Its Critics.* New York: Norton.

Lazarsfeld, Paul F. 1942. "The Effects of Radio on Public Opinion." In *Print, Radio, and Film in a Democracy,* ed. Douglas Waples, 66–78. Chicago: University of Chicago Press.

———. 1969. "An Episode in the History of Social Research." In *The Intellectual Migration: Europe and America, 1930–1960,* ed. D. Fleming and B. Bailyn, 270–337. Cambridge, Mass.: Harvard University Press.

———. 1972. *Qualitative Analysis: Historical and Critical Essays.* Boston: Allyn and Bacon.

Lent, John A., ed. 1995. *A Different Road Taken: Profiles in Critical Communication.* Boulder, Colo.: Westview Press. [Includes oral history interviews with Dallas Smythe, George Gerbner, Herbert I. Schiller, and others.]

Lerner, Daniel, and Lyle M. Nelson. 1977. *Communication Research: A Half-Century Appraisal.* Honolulu, Hawaii: East-West Center Press.

Liebes, Tamar. 2003. "Herzog's 'On Borrowed Experience': Its Place in the Debate over the Active Audience." In *Canonic Texts in Media Research: Are There Any? Should There Be? How about These?* ed. Elihu Katz, John D. Peters, Tamar Liebes, and Avril Orloff, 39–54. Cambridge, Eng.: Polity.

Liebowitz, Nathan. 1986. *Daniel Bell and the Agony of Modern Liberalism.* Westport, Conn.: Greenwood Press.

Lindt, Gillian. 1979–1980. "Robert S. Lynd." Special issue, *The Journal of the History of Sociology* (fall–winter).

Marchand, Philip. 1989. *Marshall McLuhan: The Medium and the Messenger.* New York: Ticknor and Fields.

Marvin, Carolyn and David Ingle. 1999. *Blood Sacrifice and the Nation: Totem Rituals and the American Flag.* Cambridge: Cambridge University Press.

McChesney, Robert W. 1993. *Telecommunications, Mass Media, and Democracy: The Battle for Control of U.S. Broadcasting, 1928–1935.* New York: Oxford University Press.

McIntyre, Jerilyn. 1987. "Repositioning a Landmark: The Hutchins Commission on Freedom of the Press." *Critical Studies in Mass Communication* 4:136–60.

Meehan, Eileen R. 1986. "Critical Theorizing on Broadcast History." *Journal of Broadcasting and Electronic Media* 30:393–411.

Meerloo, Joost A. M. 1956. *The Rape of the Mind: The Psychology of Thought Control, Menticide, and Brainwashing.* New York: Grosset and Dunlap.

Menand, Louis. 2002. *The Metaphysical Club: A Story of Ideas in America.* New York: Farrar, Straus, and Giroux.

Merriam, Charles. 1919. "American Publicity in Italy." *American Political Science Review* 13, no. 4: 541–55.

Merton, Robert K. 1945. Draft of *Mass Persuasion.* Bureau of Applied Social Research Archives, Columbia University, folder B0200.

Merton, Robert K. [1946] 2004. *Mass Persuasion: The Social Psychology of a War Bond Drive.* New York: Howard Fertig Publishers.

———. 1968. *Social Theory and Social Structure.* 3rd ed. New York: Free Press.

Merton, Robert K., and Elinor Barber. 2004. *The Travels and Adventures of Serendipity: A Study in Sociological Semantics and the Sociology of Science.* Princeton, N.J.: Princeton University Press.

Meyersohn, Rolf. 1969. "Sociology and Cultural Studies: Some Problems." Reprinted in *Literary Taste, Culture and Mass Communication,* edited by Peter Davison, Rolf Meyersohn, and Edward Shils, 2:3–22. Teaneck, N.J.: Somerset House.

Meyrowitz, Joshua. 2003. "Canonic Anti-text: Marshall McLuhan's *Understanding Media.*" In *Canonic Texts in Media Research: Are There Any? Should There Be? How about These?* ed. Elihu Katz, John D. Peters, Tamar Liebes, and Avril Orloff, 191–212. Cambridge, Eng.: Polity.

Morrison, David. 1978. "*Kultur* and Culture: The Case of Theodor W. Adorno and Paul F. Lazarsfeld." *Social Research* 45:331–55.

———. 1988. "The Transference of Ideas: Paul Lazarsfeld and Mass Communication Research." *Communication* 10:185–209.

———. 1998. *The Search for a Method: Focus Groups and the Development of Mass Communication Research.* Luton, Eng.: University of Luton Press.

Park, Robert Ezra. 1950. *Race and Culture.* Glencoe, Ill.: Free Press.

———. 1955. *Society.* Glencoe, Ill.: Free Press.

Peiss, Cathy. 1987. *Cheap Amusements: Working Women and Leisure in Turn-of-the-Century New York.* Philadelphia: Temple University Press.

Peters, John Durham. 1986. "Institutional Sources of Intellectual Poverty in Communication Research." *Communication Research* 13:527–59.

———. 1989a. "Democracy and Mass Communication Theory: Dewey, Lippmann, Lazarsfeld." *Communication* 11:199–220.

———. 1989b. "Satan and Savior: Mass Communication in Progressive Thought." *Critical Studies in Mass Communication* 6:247–63.

———. 1993. "Genealogical Notes on 'The Field.'" *Journal of Communication* 43, no. 4: 132–39.

———. 1996. "The Uncanniness of Mass Communication in Interwar Social Thought." *Journal of Communication* 46, no. 3: 108–23.

———. 1999. *Speaking into the Air: A History of the Idea of Communication.* Chicago: University of Chicago Press.

———. 2003. "The Subtlety of Horkheimer and Adorno: Reading 'The Culture Industry.'" In *Canonic Texts in Media Research: Are There Any? Should There Be? How about These?* ed. Elihu Katz, John D. Peters, Tamar Liebes, and Avril Orloff, 58–73. Cambridge, Eng.: Polity.

Pietilä, Viekko. 1994. "Perspectives on Our Past: Charting the Histories of Mass Communication Studies." *Critical Studies in Mass Communication* 11:346–61.

Riegel, O. W. 1934. *Mobilizing for Chaos: The Story of the New Propaganda.* New Haven, Conn.: Yale University Press.

Riesman, David. 1990. "Becoming an Academic Man." In *Authors of Their Own Lives: Intellectual Autobiographies of Twenty American Sociologists,* ed. Bennett M. Berger, 22–74. Berkeley: University of California Press.

Riley, John W., Jr., and Wilbur Schramm. 1951. *The Reds Take a City: The Communist Occupation of Seoul, with Eyewitness Accounts.* New Brunswick, N.J.: Rutgers University Press.

Robinson, Gertrude. 1988. "'Here Be Dragons': Problems in Charting the U.S. History of Communication Studies." *Communication* 10:97–119.

———. 1990. "Paul F. Lazarsfeld's Contribution to the Development of U.S. Communication Studies." In *Paul F. Lazarsfeld: Die Wiener Tradition der empirischen Sozial und Kommunikationsforschung,* ed. Wolfgang Langenbucher, 89–112. Munich: Olschlager Verlag.

———. 2001. "Remembering Our Past: Reconstructing the Field of Canadian Communication Studies." *Canadian Journal of Communication* 25:105–25.

Rogers, Everett. 1976. "Communication and Development: The Passing of the Dominant Paradigm." *Communication Research* 3, no. 2: 213–40.

———. 1993. "Looking Back, Looking Forward: A Century of Communication Study." In *Beyond Agendas: New Directions in Communication Research,* ed. Philip Gaunt, 19–39. Westport, Conn.: Greenwood Press.

———. 1994. *A History of Communication Research: A Biographical Approach.* New York: Free Press.

———. 1995. "A History of Diffusion Research." In *Diffusion of Innovations,* 38–94. New York: Free Press.

Rogers, Everett M., and Stephen H. Chaffee. 1994. "Communication and Journalism from 'Daddy' Bleyer to Wilbur Schramm: A Palimpsest." *Journalism Monographs* 148.

Rosenberg, Bernard, and David Manning White. 1971. *Mass Culture Revisited.* New York: Van Nostrand Reinhold.

Ross, Dorothy. 1991. *The Origins of American Social Science.* Cambridge: Cambridge University Press.

Rostow, Walt Whitman. [1960] 1971. *The Stages of Economic Growth.* Cambridge, Mass.: Cambridge University Press.

Rothenbuhler, Eric. 2003. "Community and Pluralism in Wirth's 'Consensus and Mass Communication.'" In *Canonic Texts in Media Research: Are There Any? Should There Be? How about These?* ed. Elihu Katz, John D. Peters, Tamar Liebes, and Avril Orloff, 106–20. Cambridge, Eng.: Polity.

Rowland, Willard D. 1983. *The Politics of TV Violence: Policy Uses of Communication Research.* Thousand Oaks, Calif.: Sage.

———. 1986. "American Telecommunications Policy Research: Its Contradictory Origins and Influences." *Media, Culture and Society* 8, no. 2.

———. 1988. "Recreating the Past: Dilemmas in Rewriting the History of Communication Research." *Communication* 10:121–40.

———. 1993. "The Traditions of Communications Research and the Implications for Telecommunications Study." *Journal of Communication* 43, no. 3: 207–16.

Schiller, Dan. 1993. "Back to the Future: Prospects for the Study of Communication as a Social Force." *Journal of Communication* 43, no. 4: 117–24.

———. 1996. *Theorizing Communication: A History.* New York: Oxford University Press.

Schramm, Wilbur. 1997. *The Beginnings of Communication Study in America: A Personal Memoir,* ed. Steven H. Chaffee and Everett Rogers. Thousand Oaks, Calif.: Sage.

Schubert, Hans-Joachim, ed. 1998. *Charles Horton Cooley on Self and Social Organization.* Chicago: University of Chicago Press.

Shannon, Claude E. 1948. "A Mathematical Theory of Communication." Pts. 1 and 2. *Bell System Technical Journal,* 27 (July): 379–423; (October): 623–56.

Sills, David. 1987. "Paul F. Lazarsfeld: February 13, 1901–August 30, 1976." In *Biographical Memoirs,* 251–82. Washington, D.C.: National Academy Press.

Simonson, Peter. 1996. "Dreams of Democratic Togetherness: Communication Hope from Cooley to Katz." *Critical Studies in Mass Communication* 49:109–22.

————. 2001. "Varieties of Pragmatism and Communication: Visions and Revisions from Peirce to Peters." In *American Pragmatism and Communication Research,* ed. David K. Perry, 1–26. Mahwah, N.J.: Erlbaum.

————. 2003. "Assembly, Ritual, and Widespread Community: Mass Communication in Paul of Tarsus." *Journal of Media and Religion* 2:165–82.

————. [1946] 2004. Introduction to *Mass Persuasion,* by Robert K. Merton. New York: Howard Fertig Publishers.

Simonson, Peter, and Gabriel Weimann. 2003. "Critical Research at Columbia: Lazarsfeld's and Merton's 'Mass Communication, Popular Taste, and Organized Social Action.'" In *Canonic Texts in Media Research: Are There Any? Should There Be? How about These?* ed. Elihu Katz, John D. Peters, Tamar Liebes, and Avril Orloff, 12–38. Cambridge, Eng.: Polity.

Simpson, Christopher. 1993. "U.S. Mass Communication Research, Counterinsurgency, and Scientific 'Reality.'" In *Ruthless Criticism: New Perspectives in U.S. Communication History,* ed. William Simon and Robert McChesney, 313–48. Minneapolis: University of Minnesota Press.

————. 1994. *Science of Coercion: Communication Research and Psychological Warfare, 1945– 1960.* New York: Oxford University Press.

Smith, Bruce Lannes. 1969. "The Mystifying Intellectual History of Harold D. Lasswell." In *Politics, Personality, and Social Science: Essays in Honor of Harold D. Lasswell,* ed. Arnold A. Rogow, 41–105. Chicago: University of Chicago Press.

Smith, Mark C. 1994. *Social Science in the Crucible: The American Debate over Objectivity and Purpose, 1918–1941.* Durham, N.C.: Duke University Press. [Includes excellent chapters on Harold Lasswell and Robert Lynd.]

Smythe, Dallas W., and Thomas H. Guback. 1994. *Counterclockwise: Perspectives on Communication.* Boulder, Colo.: Westview Press.

Splichal, Slavko. 1999. *Public Opinion: Developments and Controversies in the 20th Century.* Lanham, Md.: Rowman and Littlefield.

Sproule, J. Michael. 1987. "Propaganda Studies in American Social Science: The Rise and Fall of the Critical Paradigm." *Quarterly Journal of Speech* 73:60–78.

————. 1989. "Progressive Critics and the Magic Bullet Myth." *Critical Studies in Mass Communication* 6:225–46.

————. 1997. *Propaganda and Democracy: The American Experience of Media and Mass Persuasion.* New York: Cambridge University Press.

Stout, Jeffrey. "Social Criticism with Both Eyes Open." In *Ethics after Babel,* 266–92. Boston: Beacon Press.

Sunstein, Cass. 2001. *Republic.com.* Princeton, N.J.: Princeton University Press.

Tenney, A. A. 1912. "Scientific Analysis of the Press." *The Independent* 73:895–98.

Thrasher, Frederic Milton. 1927. *The Gang: A Study of 1,313 Gangs in Chicago.* Chicago: University of Chicago Press.

Turner, Stephen P. 1991. "The World of the Academic Quantifiers: The Columbia University Family and its Connections." In *The Social Survey in Historical Perspective, 1880–1940,* ed. Martin Bulmer, Kevin Bayles, and Kathryn K. Sklar. Cambridge, Mass.: Cambridge University Press.

Turow, Joseph. 1992. "On Reconceptualizing 'Mass Communication.'" *Journal of Broadcasting & Electronic Media* 36, no. 1: 105–9.

"UNESCO's Program of Mass Communication: I." 1946–1947. *Public Opinion Quarterly* 10:518–39.

Wartella, Ellen, and Everette Dennis, eds. 1996. *American Communication Research: The Remembered History.* Mahwah, N.J.: Lawrence Erlbaum.

Wartella, Ellen, and Byron Reeves. 1983. "Historical Trends in Research on Children and the Media: 1900–1960." *Journal of Communication* 35, no. 2: 118–33.

Wasko, Janet. 1994. Introduction to *Counterclockwise: Perspectives on Communication,* by Dallas Smythe, ed. Thomas Guback. Boulder, Colo.: Westview Press.

Wasser, Frederick. 1998. "Current Views of McLuhan." *Journal of Communication* 43, no. 3: 146–52.

West, Nathanael. [1933] 1975. *The Collected Works of Nathanael West.* Baltimore, Md.: Penguin Books.

Wiggershaus, Rolf. 1994. *The Frankfurt School: Its History, Theories, and Political Significance.* Cambridge, Mass.: Cambridge University Press.

Williams, Raymond. 1958. *Culture and Society.* New York: Columbia University Press.

———. 1974. *Television: Technology and Cultural Form.* New York: Schocken.

Wohl, R. Richard, and A. Theodore Brown. 1960. "The Usable Past: A Study of Historical Traditions in Kansas City." *The Huntington Library Quarterly* 23:237–59.

Wolf, Katherine M., and Marjorie Fiske. 1949. "The Children Talk about Comics." In *Communications Research 1948–49,* ed. Paul F. Lazarsfeld and Frank Stanton, 3–50. New York: Harper and Bros.

Credits

Every effort has been made to obtain permissions for all copyrighted material used in *Mass Communication and American Social Thought*. Please contact the publishers with any updated information.

* * *

Chapter 1 From *Political Science Quarterly*, 12:1 (1897), by Charles H. Cooley, with permission of the publisher, the Academy of Political Science.

Chapter 2 Reprinted from *The Spirit of Youth and the City Streets* (1909) by Jane Addams, Macmillan Co.

Chapter 3 "Godliness," copyright 1950 by Sherwood Anderson, from *Winesburg, Ohio*. Reprinted from *Winesburg, Ohio* (1950), p. 43, by Sherwood Anderson. Copyright 1950 by Random House.

Chapter 4 From *The Introduction to Science of Sociology* (1921), by Robert E. Park and Ernest W. Burgess, with permission of the publisher, the University of Chicago Press.

Chapter 5 *The Collected Works of John Dewey, Later Works, Volume: 1925.* © 1981 by the Board of Trustees, Southern Illinois University and the Center for Dewey Study, reprinted by permission of the publisher.

Chapter 6 Reprinted from *The Phantom Public* (1993), by Walter Lippmann, with permission of the publisher, Transaction Publishers. Original copyright © 1925 by Harcourt and Brace. Renewed with permission by Transaction Publishers.

Chapter 7 Reprinted from *Crisis Magazine* (October 1926) by W. E. B. DuBois. Copyright © 1926 by Crisis Publishing. Reprinted with permission of the NACCP.

Chapter 8 Reprinted from *Propaganda Technique in the World War* (1971), pp. 185–213, by Harold Lasswell, copyright © 1971 by MIT Press. Reprinted with permission of the publisher, MIT Press.

Chapter 9 "Manipulating Public Opinion: The Why and the How," by Edward L. Bernays. From *American Journal of Sociology*, Volume 33, Issue 6 (May 1928), 958–971.

Chapter 10 Excerpt from *Middletown: A Study in Contemporary American Culture,* by Robert S. Lynd and Helen M. Lynd, copyright 1929 by Harcourt, Inc., and renewed 1957 by Robert S. and Helen M. Lynd, reprinted by permission of the publisher.

Chapter 11 "Communication," by Edward Sapir. From *Encyclopaedia of the Social Sciences* (1931). Copyright by Macmillan Press.

Chapter 12 Reprinted from *Movies and Conduct* (1933), pp. 192–200, by Herbert Blumer, published by Macmillan Press.

Chapter 13 Reprinted from *Communication Agencies and Social Life* (1933), 210–214, by Malcolm Willey and Stuart Rice. Copyright © 1933 by McGraw-Hill Companies. Reproduced with permission of the McGraw-Hill Companies.

Chapter 14 From *Opportunity*, Locke, Alain. Vol. 12. No. 11 (1934), pp. 328–331. Copyright © 1934 National League Review.

Chapter 15 Excerpt from *Techniques and Civilization,* by Lewis Mumford, copyright 1934 by Harcourt, Inc., and renewed 1961 by Lewis Mumford, reprinted by permission of the publisher.

Chapter 16 From *Our Master's Voice,* by James Rorty. Copyright 1934 by Harper & Row Publishers, Inc. Published by John Day.

Chapter 17 Pages 19-26 from *The Psychology of Radio,* by Hadley Cantril and Gordon Allport. Copyright 1935 by Harper & Row Publishers, Inc., renewed © 1963 by Hadley Cantril. Reprinted by permission of HarperCollins Publishers, Inc.

Chapter 18 From *Public Opinion Quarterly* 1:1 (1937): 3–5 by the Editors. Copyright 1937 by the University of Chicago Press. Reprinted with permission of the publisher.

Chapter 19 From *Public Opinion Quarterly* 1 (1937): 73–83, by Helen Hughes. Copyright 1937 by the University of Chicago Press. Reprinted with permission of the publisher.

Chapter 20 Reprinted from *The Fine Art of Propaganda* (1939), pp. 14–21, by Alfred Mclung Lee and Elizabeth Briant Lee. Copyright 1943 The Institute for Propaganda Analysis. Published by Harcourt, Brace and Company.

Chapter 21 Reprinted with the permission of Simon & Schuster Adult Publishing Group, from *The Pulse of Democracy: The Public-Opinion Poll and How It Works,* by George H. Gallup and Saul Forbes Rae. Copyright © 1940 by George H. Gallup and Saul F. Rae. Copyright renewed © 1968 by George H. Gallup.

Chapter 22 From the *Public Opinion Quarterly*, Vol. 4, No. 2 (June 1940), pp. 218–220, by Robert Lynd. Copyright 1940 by the University of Chicago Press. Reprinted with permission of the publisher.

Chapter 23 Reprinted from *Needed Research in Communication* (October 10, 1940), with permission of the publisher, the Rockefeller Archive Foundation.

Chapter 24 From *Studies in Philosophy and Social Science* Vol. 9, No. 1 (1941). Pages 65–95. By Herta Hertzog. Copyright 1941 by the Institute of Social Research. Reprinted with permission of the author.

Chapter 25 "Art and Mass Culture." From *Critical Theory,* by Max Horkheimer. English language translation copyright © 1972 by Herder & Herder. Reprinted by permission of the Continuum International Publishing Group.

Chapter 26 From *Studies in Philosophy and Social Science*, Lazarsfeld, Paul F. "Administrative and Critical Communication Research" (1941). Copyright by the Institute of Social Research. Reprinted with permission of the publisher.

Chapter 27 From *Radio Research,* Lazarsfeld, Paul F., and Frank Stanton. "The Popular Music Industry" by D. MacDougald (1941). Copyright 1941 by Duell, Sloan, and Pearce.

Chapter 28 Reprinted from *Dialectic of Enlightenment*, (1972), 221–222, by Max Horkheimer and Theodor Adorno. English translation copyright © 1972 by Herder & Herder. Reprinted by permission of the Continuum International Publishing Group.

Chapter 29 Reprinted from *German Radio Propaganda* (1944), pp. 3–12, by Ernst Kris and Hans Speier, with permission of the publisher, Oxford University Press.

Chapter 48 Reprinted from *American Sociological Review* (1952). "The Unique Perspective of Television," by Kurt Lang and Gladys Engel Lang.

Chapter 49 From the *International Journal*. Vol. 3 (1952):189–195. "Technology in Reverse" by Marshall McLuhan. (Copyright, 1952, Canadian Institute of International Affairs). Reprinted with permission of the publisher.

Chapter 50 From *Diogenes*, Vol. 1 No. 3, Summer, 1953, pp. 1–17, by Dwight MacDonald, with permission of the publisher, *Diogenes*.

Chapter 51 "Sight, Sound, and Fury" by Marshall McLuhan (April 9, 1954). © 1954 Commonweal Foundation, reprinted with permission.

Chapter 52 Reprinted with the permission of the Free Press, a Division of Simon & Schuster Adult Publishing Group, from *Personal Influence* by Elihu Katz and Paul Lazarsfeld. Copyright © 1955 by the Free Press. Copyright © renewed 1983 by Patricia Kendall Lazarsfeld and Elihu Katz.

Chapter 53 Reprinted from *Commentary Vol. 22* (1956), pp. 75–83, by Daniel Bell, with permission of the author.

Chapter 54 From *Psychiatry*, Horton, Donald, and Richard Wohl. "Mass Communication and Para-social Interaction: Observation." Vol. 18 (1956). Pages 215–229. Copyright by Guilford Press. Reprinted with permission of the publisher.

Chapter 55 From *The Power Elite,* new edition, by C. Wright Mills, copyright © 1956, 2000 by Oxford University Press, Inc. Used by permission of Oxford University Press, Inc.

Chapter 56 From *Public Opinion Quarterly,* Sussman, Leila A. "FDR and the White House Mail." 20:1 (1956), 5–16. Copyright by the University of Chicago Press. Reprinted with permission of the publisher.

Chapter 57 From *American Journal of Sociology* 62:6 (1957), 594–601, by R. Meyersohn and E. Katz. Copyright 1957 by the University of Chicago Press. Reprinted with permission of the publisher.

Chapter 58 From *Social Forces*. Vol. 37, No. 2. Copyright © 1958 by the University of North Carolina Press. Used by permission of the publisher.

Chapter 59 Reprinted with the permission of the Free Press, a Division of Simon & Schuster Adult Publishing Group, from *The Passing of Traditional Society,* by Daniel Lerner. Copyright © 1958, copyright renewed 1986 by the Free Press.

Chapter 60 Reprinted from *Journalism Quarterly* Vol. 35 (Summer 1958), pp. 299–306, by George Gerbner, with permission of the publisher, the Association for Education in Journalism and Mass Communication.

Chapter 61 From *Public Opinion Quarterly* 23:1 (1959): 1–6, by Bernard Berelson. Copyright 1959 by the University of Chicago Press. Reprinted with permission of the publisher.

Chapter 62 From *Public Opinion Quarterly* 23:1 (1959): 6–17, by W. Schramm, D. Riesman, and R. Bauer. Copyright by the University of Chicago Press. Reprinted with permission of the publisher.

Chapter 63 Reprinted from *Mass Communication: A Sociological Perspective* (1959), by Charles Wright. Copyright by Random House. Reproduced with permission of the McGraw-Hill Companies.

Chapter 64 From the *Canadian Journal of Economics and Political Science*, Vol. 27, No. 4 (November 1961), pp. 479–489, by Thelma McCormack, by permission of the author and the publisher (Copyright 1961, Canadian Economics Association).

Chapter 65 "Television and Public Interest" (1961), speech by Newton Minow. Reprinted with permission of the author.

Chapter 66 From Greenberg, Bradley, and Parker, Edwin Editors. *The Kennedy Assassination and the American Public: Social Communication in Crisis.* Copyright © 1965 by the Board of Trustees of the Leland Standford Jr. University. Used with permission of the Standford University Press, www.sup.org.

Chapter 67 "T. V. Overseas: The U. S. Hard Sell" by Herbert Schiller. Reprinted with permission from the December 5, 1966 issue of *The Nation.*

Chapter 68 *Negations: Essays in Critical Theory* by Herbert Marcuse. Copyright © 1968 by Herbert Marcuse. Translations from German copyright © 1968 by Beacon Press. Reprinted by permission of Beacon Press, Boston.

Index

administrative research, 85–87, 137, 169,
171–172, 210–211, 274, 358
advertising, 9, 19, 32–33, 49, 52, 53, 55, 60, 62, 63,
66, 67–68, 73, 74, 80–81, 86–87, 97, 106–109,
113–114, 116–117, 118–119, 139, 167, 169–173,
181–182, 188–189, 216, 220, 231–241,
246–247, 254, 264, 270, 289, 319–327,
338–341, 346, 359, 371, 385, 391, 396,
419–420, 436, 440, 445, 446, 450–452, 465,
467–470, 480–484
African-Americans/Negroes, 1, 8, 31, 42–45, 46,
53, 54, 64, 88, 98, 100–102, 206–209, 217, 220,
296, 300, 412, 414, 421, 459
alphabet, 103, 277, 314, 339, 341, 356
American Commonwealth, 59–60
architecture, 102, 104, 276–277, 327, 343, 346,
350, 371, 431
art and aesthetics, 1, 9, 13, 16, 18–19, 21, 24,
26, 28, 29, 35, 40, 42–46, 51, 54, 56, 57, 67,
68, 70, 94, 122, 158–166, 191, 201, 210–214,
237–238, 277, 286, 288–289, 299, 304, 316,
326–327, 339–342, 343–352, 353–357.
See also popular culture/popular taste;
taste
audiences, 20, 22, 139, 165–168, 202, 211,
215–217, 231–233, 236–241, 250, 266, 268,
270, 294–305, 316, 329–337 passim, 339–340,
347–349, 352–353, 356–357, 358–362,
366–367, 374–386, 401–409, 410–417, 418,
421, 431–433, 441–442, 446, 449, 451,
454–456, 457–458, 460–463, 467–468, 482,
493; gratifications of, 89, 142–148, 446;
magazine readers, 188–205, 434–439

(*see also* magazines); movie audiences, 1–2,
9, 26, 66, 282–283, 288–289, 356, 359,
366–367. (*see also* motion pictures/film);
music audiences, 1–2, 63, 301, 410–417
(*see also* music); newspaper, 1–2, 9, 254–260,
298, 320, 330–331, 359, 363n8, 408, 462, 471
(*see also* newspapers); radio audiences, 1–2,
9, 80, 86, 111, 139, 166, 176–178, 215–218,
288, 307, 314, 316–317, 318–328, 331, 357,
359, 361, 410–409 passim, 410–417 passim
(*see also* radio); television viewers, 1–2,
318–328 passim, 328–337 passim, 375–386
passim, 472–473 (*see also* television)
automobiles, 30, 59, 65–68, 71, 97, 200, 204, 232,
291, 410–411, 457, 490–492

books, 70–72, 93, 96, 127, 188–205, 247, 258–259,
275, 288, 296, 300, 301, 313, 339–340, 344,
349, 352, 353, 354, 356, 371, 379, 400n13, 428
broadcasting, 2, 5, 9–10, 19–20, 80, 86, 97, 107,
108, 110–115, 125, 136, 139, 149, 168, 175,
179, 212, 236, 253, 254, 266, 269, 270, 310,
313–314, 317, 319–327, 329, 334, 340, 357,
380, 386n20, 423, 428, 433, 448, 461, 465–471,
480–492
business/big business, 1, 13, 38, 56, 60–74, 96,
106–109, 116–117, 120–121, 125–127,
158–159, 169, 173–176, 189–193, 216–217,
231, 234, 239, 241, 246–250, 270, 280–292
passim, 309, 322, 344–353 passim, 355, 373,
414, 419–423, 460, 465–468, 480–484. *See also*
industry/media industries and
industrialism

Canada, 3, 8, 74, 79, 80, 112, 128, 227, 267, 275, 277, 319, 328, 457, 480, 484

China, 1, 34, 220, 342

civilization, 34, 40, 51, 74–77, 102–107, 180, 206–207, 265, 275–280, 281, 282, 291, 310, 338, 363, 366, 368, 407, 427, 487, 489, 491–493

class, socio-economic, 345, 350–351, 366, 369, 381, 388, 411, 414–415, 419–423, 428; working and lower classes, 8, 60, 61–73, 82, 306, 434–440 passim, 459–464 passim; middle class, 111, 115, 120, 139–140, 158, 160, 163, 172, 196, 199, 208, 297–306, 346, 382, 386–387, 387, 398, 400, 414, 459–464 passim; upper classes, 61–70, 108, 344, 346, 350 420, 428, 459–464 passim

Columbia University, 8, 18, 19, 35, 58, 74, 82, 85, 87, 90, 95, 118, 124, 125, 137, 154n3, 166, 173n2, 173n10, 230, 233, 233–235, 268, 301, 358, 364, 387, 401, 409, 415n1, 417, 426, 454, 457, 480

comics, 89, 220, 257, 299, 301–308, 313–314, 338, 344, 345, 348, 350, 400n13, 455, 461–462, 468

communication research, 3, 6, 7, 10–11, 14, 47, 139, 169–170, 263, 268, 270, 310–311, 426, 440–453, 480

community, including pseudo-community, 19, 26, 33, 35, 38, 41, 58–59, 67–70, 76, 97, 112, 132–133, 160, 162–163, 170–171, 208–209, 216, 219, 221, 244–248, 264–266, 350–351, 357, 365–366, 369–371, 388–392, 399–400, 417, 421, 422; community study, 58, 85, 373, 419

Confucius, 3

consumption/consumers/commodities, 9, 55, 58, 80, 86, 96, 107–108, 138, 141, 173–180, 182, 191–204, 211–214, 221, 232, 239, 264–265, 270–271, 294, 301–302, 305–308, 318–328, 341, 344–345, 348–349, 352, 354, 365–366, 371, 391, 395, 410–416, 429, 432, 439, 449, 451, 453n5, 456, 462, 481–484, 485–494 passim

conversation, 3, 19, 35, 103, 111, 125, 181, 203, 267, 310, 331, 337, 341, 354, 374–375, 381–382, 394. *See also* oratory/speech

Cooley, Charles Horton, 4, 13, 15–17, 21, 30, 75, 81, 82, 83, 96, 118–119, 122, 123n1, 206, 266, 273, 362, 393, 400n8, 458, 464n5

critical research/critical theory, 169–172, 264, 272, 274, 485

crowds, 16, 60, 63, 66, 72, 111–112, 186, 200, 214, 250, 252, 266, 328, 330–337, 350–352, 357, 358, 375, 393, 412, 415, 451

culture, 84, 98, 102–104, 109, 112, 135, 149, 157–166, 169–171, 185, 208, 210, 241, 252, 265, 267, 271, 275–280, 281–292 passim, 293–308 passim, 338–343, 343–353, 353–357, 366–369, 371–373, 410, 416, 429–432, 446, 449–451, 459, 462, 465, 470–471, 472, 480

dating/courtship, 92, 227, 233, 383, 415

democracy/democratic society and institutions, 1, 4, 10, 14–19, 26, 34, 35, 36–42, 46–50, 51, 79, 81–84, 88, 107–108, 110–113, 118–137, 163–165, 184–186, 219–220, 249–254, 264–266, 270–273, 279, 309–312, 344–345, 351–352, 358–359, 362n3, 368–369, 373n2, 387–400, 419–422, 429, 443, 472–479 passim

Dewey, John, 4, 13–15, 17–19, 25, 30, 31, 35, 42, 47, 58, 158, 160, 165, 166n8, 174, 264, 273, 274, 387, 465

Durkheim, Émile, 4, 32, 34, 272, 372n1, 418, 423, 459, 475, 476

education, 22, 32–33, 52–53, 57–58, 67–68, 93–95, 97–98, 108–109, 112, 125–127, 132–133, 136, 162, 164–165, 167, 171–173, 190–192, 206–209, 213, 221, 222–224, 237–238, 247–248, 255, 258, 269, 273, 279, 288, 293, 311, 315–316, 319–328, 344, 349, 354, 361, 371, 389–397, 401, 422–423, 427, 429, 434, 454, 455, 460, 462, 468–470

effects of media/mass communication, 2, 5, 19, 83, 84, 88, 89, 91, 92, 94, 110, 111, 115, 134, 153, 167, 168, 169, 172, 179, 213, 216, 222, 224, 230, 231–241 passim, 242, 248, 274, 277, 281, 294, 296, 297, 301, 307, 316, 319, 325, 326, 329, 335, 339, 341, 348, 358–364 passim, 374, 384, 397, 411, 428, 437–439, 443, 447, 452–453, 461, 477, 492; effects tradition, 89, 264, 271, 272

entertainment and recreation, 17–20, 28–29, 43, 60, 64, 67, 80–81, 83, 93, 108, 112–114, 148, 159, 161, 164–165, 176, 189–209, 214, 217, 237, 288, 290, 313–314, 323–327, 330, 344, 347–349, 354, 355, 357, 381, 433, 460, 467, 471, 481–483, 488

experts/expertise, 37, 39, 54, 85, 113, 134–137, 195, 212, 233, 245, 313, 352, 389, 391, 396, 405

face-to-face communication, 15, 16, 19, 89, 132, 267, 295–298, 300, 312, 315–316, 343, 355, 374–375, 377, 384, 388, 433, 455, 458–459, 464, 472. *See also* conversation; interpersonal communication family, 10, 27, 61–68, 71–76, 113, 141, 148–149, 151–153, 159–161, 163, 170, 193–196, 207, 227, 251, 283–284, 294–295, 299–301, 324, 326, 327, 340, 350–351, 365, 371–372, 377, 391–392, 399, 401, 402, 409n36, 418–420, 458, 462, 467, 474, 476–478, 486

fascism, 1, 9, 109, 112–113, 131, 159, 163–165, 181–182, 329, 351, 366, 369–370. *See also* Nazism

fashion and fads, 7, 25, 32, 51, 54–55, 77, 120, 130, 170, 175, 189, 265–6, 319, 328, 409–417, 428, 441, 450

Frankfurt School, 3, 5, 19, 85–87, 89, 157–158, 167, 174, 188, 210, 265, 268, 274, 311, 339, 364, 409, 417n19, 434, 485

freedom, 22–24, 43–46, 127, 130, 158–159, 163, 172, 182, 210, 214, 220–221, 252–253, 264, 290–292, 296, 306, 307, 332, 362, 365, 369, 387, 395, 468, 471, 487–490, 493; of the press, 18, 127, 208, 218, 278–279, 320

Freud, Sigmund, 4, 47, 80, 86, 89, 139, 161, 182, 271, 281, 365, 389, 430, 448, 449, 457, 459–461, 485, 489, 490, 493

gesture, 22, 34, 75–76, 103, 252, 341, 342, 356, 374–376, 455

government/government regulation, 6, 14, 32, 37–42, 52, 79, 116–117, 130–133, 137–138, 167–168, 183–185, 218, 221, 235–236, 241, 249–251, 268–269, 311–318, 322, 355, 368–369, 392, 404, 407, 465–471 passim, 473–479; Federal Communications Commission (FCC), 83, 180, 268, 319–328 passim, 465–471 passim

Hitler, Adolf, 3, 6, 80, 84, 125–126, 130–131, 161, 181, 183–185, 187, 196, 210, 231, 373n2, 404, 493. *See also* Nazism; fascism

Hollywood, 20, 145, 165, 204, 232, 236, 258, 263, 268, 280–293 passim, 344, 347–348, 351–352, 356, 357–358, 380, 382, 385n12, 422, 423, 455–456, 468. *See also* motion pictures/ film

human interest and popular biography, 18, 33, 45, 61, 105, 118–124, 177, 205, 257, 261, 266, 299, 300, 313, 348–349, 386n19, 424n8, 446

ideology/ideological, 10, 79, 82, 90, 142, 148–149, 166–179 passim, 180–182, 188–205 passim, 212, 239–240, 249, 274, 281, 311–312, 365, 369, 372, 394–397, 411, 413, 418, 426–429, 450, 459–462, 474, 478, 479n11, 488, 490

imitation, 22–25, 33, 75–76, 92–93, 99–100, 161, 204, 376, 413, 476

individual/individuality/individualism, 4, 6, 23–25, 32–33, 40–42, 50–51, 76, 85–86, 93–94, 96–97, 111–113, 125, 130–136, 159–162, 165, 181, 196–197, 199–204, 208, 233–235, 241–245, 250, 273, 276, 279, 283–284, 287, 294, 297–301, 307, 326, 329, 330, 332, 344, 350–351, 359, 365–367, 371, 376, 388–400, 401–402, 413, 421, 423, 429–431, 454–455, 460–461, 473–476, 478, 482, 486–489, 491–493

industrialism/industrial society, 1, 3, 30, 54–57, 58–59, 79, 86–87, 275–280, 294, 296, 300, 301, 306, 344, 351, 359, 367, 370, 427, 430, 455, 459, 482, 485–493

industry/media industries and industrialism, 1, 9, 20, 26–29, 30, 51, 54–57, 58, 79, 81, 86, 87, 89, 91, 96, 102, 106–109, 132, 139, 157–165 passim, 171, 173–180, 182, 188–205 passim, 218–219, 221, 231, 238, 243, 250–251, 266, 268–269, 275–279, 280–293, 294–296, 300, 306, 309, 315, 319–328, 335, 339, 348–349, 351, 367–369, 373, 385, 391, 393, 399, 412–415, 418, 430, 434–440, 465–471, 480–484, 485–493

inner-direction and other-direction, 160, 265, 304, 306

international communication, 121, 309–310, 426, 444–5, 448

interpersonal communication, 9–10, 266, 358–362, 373, 458, 463, 486

jazz, 5, 63, 64, 66, 72, 99–102, 113–115, 123n6, 163, 177, 179, 191, 211–213, 307, 417n19

Jews and Judaism, 8, 49, 57, 82, 84–85, 87, 126, 144–145, 165, 185, 187, 279, 343, 364

Korea/Korean War, 90, 264, 310–318

language, 2, 14, 36, 47, 59, 74–78, 101, 103–104, 110, 160–161, 167, 181, 195, 200–202, 208–209, 227, 244–245, 272–273, 294–295, 297, 299, 301–302, 356, 359, 361, 375, 416n4, 451, 485, 490

lectures as a form of communication, 17, 28, 53, 60–61, 70–71, 286, 315–316, 357, 455

leisure, 58–59, 63–70, 96, 180, 186, 188, 191–192, 195–196, 200, 202, 207, 232–233, 297, 299, 313, 316, 358, 368, 371, 409, 415n1, 460, 488

Lippmann, Walter, 14, 18–19, 36–37, 118, 123n18, 132, 134, 339, 387, 391, 394, 400n9

literacy, 22, 27, 61–63, 71–72, 108, 116, 175, 237, 270, 295, 296–300, 394, 427, 428 loneliness, 29, 105, 115, 124n26, 196, 270, 369, 380–383, 386n21; *The Lonely Crowd*, 188, 265–266, 293, 350, 365, 424, 433, 474; *The Lonesome Gal*, 267, 380–382, 386n23; *Miss Lonelyhearts*, 81

magazines, 30, 33, 45–46, 55, 61–63, 72, 106–108, 118–119, 167, 178, 188–205, 207, 217, 236, 264, 266, 279, 308n11, 314, 341, 345–347, 350, 357, 382, 386n24; confession and romance magazines, 62, 118–119, 434–440

magic, 26, 28, 49, 111, 172, 185–186, 197, 280–293 passim, 297, 306, 342–343, 354–356, 374, 379, 383, 396, 462

mail, including fan mail, 22, 24, 55, 56, 96–97, 106, 108, 213, 376, 378, 381, 401–409

Marx, Karl, and Marxism, 4–5, 34, 47, 51, 80, 82, 86, 88, 106, 216, 270, 271, 274, 275, 315, 319, 350, 351, 365, 366, 388, 389, 457, 459–461, 485, 487

mass communication, concept of, 1–6, 8–10, 11n1, 250–251, 455

mass culture, 19, 157–166, 201, 202, 210, 213, 271, 343–353 passim, 465

masses, the, 1, 10, 19, 33, 80, 192, 200, 211, 213, 233, 237, 250–251, 330, 343–353, 360–362, 366–369, 373n2, 393–400, 401, 407, 417, 432, 465

mass media, definition of, 1, 2, 5, 20, 222, 294, 357, 366, 384, 419, 455, 462, 463

mass society, 9, 181, 234, 249–251, 264–271 passim, 351, 358, 364–373 passim, 387–400 passim

method/research methods, methodology, 17, 18, 19, 47, 50, 52–53, 57, 58, 81–87, 89, 91, 95, 110–111, 125–128, 131–133, 167, 174, 175, 188, 192, 216, 223, 254, 256, 273, 283, 293, 312, 329, 349, 359, 363, 387, 417, 441, 447, 448, 450, 452, 453, 454, 457, 461

minorities, 8, 10, 16, 45, 82, 292, 397, 411–414, 423, 451, 474, 486. *See also* African-Americans/Negroes; Jews and Judaism

modernity, 4, 13, 25, 426, 427, 432; modern communication, 5, 16, 20, 81, 267, 270, 294, 339, 342, 366, 455–456

modernization, theory of, 5, 90, 270–271, 273–274, 426–434, 472

motion pictures/film, 7, 9, 10, 18, 53, 56, 62, 63, 65–67, 71, 73–74, 83, 91–95, 97, 104–106, 117, 132, 161, 164, 181, 222, 280–93 passim, 313–315, 325, 347–348, 350, 352, 356, 367, 419, 420, 421, 432, 433, 449, 455, 456, 483. *See also* Hollywood

music, 1, 18, 28, 29, 43, 45, 56, 63, 66, 67, 68, 87, 111–115, 226, 301, 307, 314, 324, 325, 327, 343, 353, 357, 410–417, 483; classical music, 28, 225, 238, 371, 413; folk music, 99–101, 459; music education/lessons, 63, 72–73. *See also* jazz

nation/nationalism, 3, 18, 28, 37, 39, 47, 53, 70, 76, 79–82, 108, 111–112, 121–122, 133, 252, 273, 276, 279, 320–321, 339, 355–356, 370, 422, 472, 475–476, 489

Nazism, 88, 113, 131, 182–187, 239, 240, 314, 345, 346, 352, 373n2, 390, 485. *See also* Hitler, Adolf; fascism

news and journalism, 5, 6, 9, 10, 18, 30, 31, 32, 36, 62, 67, 68, 97, 246, 247, 269, 298, 313–314, 316, 324–325, 335–336, 340, 355, 357, 361, 371, 395, 417–425 passim, 433, 445, 455, 468–9, 472; radio news, 113, 117, 118–124

newspapers, 1, 24, 32, 84, 95–97, 106–115, 118–123, 253–261, 266, 313–317, 320, 337n8, 339, 340–343, 354–356, 359, 362n1, 383; the black press/Negro newspapers, 18, 88, 206–209; penny press, 13, 119–120

orality/oral tradition, 21–22, 185, 201, 213, 230, 271, 272, 275–280, 338, 339, 353, 354–355, 357, 373, 433–434

oratory/speeches, 29, 37, 38, 39, 42,48, 54, 59–60, 70, 313, 401–408 passim, 465. *See also* lectures as a form of communication

parasocial interaction, 17, 266, 379–384

phonography/phonograph, 63, 73, 96–97, 103–104, 356

photography/camera, 80, 104–105, 329, 330, 332–335, 340, 343, 347, 348, 356, 375–376, 381

Plato, 3, 22, 103, 264, 272, 339, 354, 365, 418

politics, 17, 38, 47, 53, 55, 128–133, 336, 340, 342, 343–353, 368, 370, 393, 405, 432, 446, 472, 473–479, 486, 490; political parties, 129–133, 313–317, 320–321, 328, 350, 355, 373, 388, 392, 406, 407, 455, 465, 473, 477, 487, 492

popular culture/popular taste, 10, 101, 265, 269, 271, 293, 296, 298, 308n6, 338, 344, 353n1

postmodernism and postmodernist theory, 2, 339, 343

printing/printing press, 22, 34, 38, 80, 96–98, 104–105, 107, 110–111, 273, 278–280, 297, 308, 339, 341, 354–357, 431, 468

propaganda, 5, 7, 17, 19–20, 32, 41, 46, 47–50, 51, 52, 55, 81–85, 87–90, 108–109, 116, 124–128, 130–133, 161, 165, 177, 181–187, 188, 207,

216, 217, 222–223, 230–231, 238–239, 240, 251, 264, 268, 274, 311–318 passim, 328, 344, 358, 359, 363n12, 366, 378, 391, 396, 426, 442, 460, 461, 492

public, 116–117, 122, 127, 129, 134–136, 192, 195, 200, 205, 207–209, 218, 219, 220, 233, 234, 235, 238, 246, 252, 254, 264, 265, 266, 270, 272, 284, 320, 336, 351–352, 353, 359, 367, 387–400 passim, 401–409 passim, 456, 465–471 passim, 477; public image, 215–216, 239, 382; public interest, 138, 230, 235, 321, 327, 465–471; public relations, 19, 51–57, 80, 87, 97, 116–117, 138, 216, 224, 231, 396; public service, 19, 214, 264, 325, 465, 469–470

publicity, 4, 19, 31, 32, 39, 45, 49, 57, 67, 97, 186, 234, 289, 290, 294, 378, 382, 396, 402, 403, 415, 492–493

public opinion/public opinion polls, 19, 32–33, 38–41, 51–57, 83, 91, 107–111, 116–117, 128–133, 134–136, 138, 184–185, 221, 222, 246, 250–251, 254, 336, 358, 363n13, 387–393, 396, 403, 407, 408, 414, 432, 446, 449, 456, 472, 478, 490

radio, 1, 5, 9–10, 19–20, 34, 39, 53–54, 59, 60, 63, 65–69, 72–73, 77, 80–81, 83, 85–88, 96–97, 103, 106–107, 110–115, 116–117, 124n26, 125, 126, 128, 130, 132, 138, 139–157, 160, 166–168, 169, 171–173, 174–180, 182–187, 188–205, 210–214, 215–217, 222, 224–229, 230–231, 233, 236, 237, 238–241, 246–247, 252, 254, 256, 260–261,263, 266, 270, 279, 288, 301, 302, 304, 307, 309, 310, 313–314, 316, 317, 318–328, 329, 331, 337, 341–343, 344, 347, 348, 352, 353, 355–357, 359, 361, 363n8, 363n11, 367, 374–376, 380–386, 393–395, 400n13, 401, 406–407, 414, 415, 419, 421, 428, 430, 431, 433, 441, 455, 456, 457, 466, 480, 483

radishes, hatful of, 195

railroad, 15, 39, 77, 181, 190, 229, 305–306, 347

reading, 69–75, 83, 88, 119–126, 167, 171, 203, 205, 257, 297–304, 313–316, 339–341, 348, 353–357, 367, 378, 400n13, 468

Roosevelt, Franklin Delano, 6, 80, 83, 95, 112, 116, 129, 191, 319, 321, 359, 401–409, 479n9

Sarnoff, David, 9, 309–310

science/scientific analysis, 82–90, 105, 111, 116–117, 125–127, 134–137, 203, 222, 223–224, 243, 245, 247, 248, 255, 273, 275, 279, 296, 309, 321, 349–351, 352, 357, 367–368, 417

Simmel, Georg, 16, 31, 32, 33, 216, 366, 410–414

Smith, Kate, 80, 204, 215–217, 239, 266, 385, 448, 461

soap operas, radio serials, 14, 18, 80, 89, 139–154, 172, 236, 237, 238, 328, 347, 379, 451, 462

social norms, 3–5, 9, 13, 15–17, 21–23, 30–34, 75–77

Soviet Union (USSR), 90, 130, 240, 312, 343, 344, 372

standardization, 7, 10, 52, 67, 68–69, 73, 97–98, 112–115, 170, 179, 181, 212, 214, 345, 347, 352, 365, 366, 375, 382, 395, 424, 487

stereotypes, 53, 56, 112–113, 140, 149, 198, 220, 254, 255, 299, 304, 339, 341, 382, 394–395, 398–399, 400n8, 432

survey research, 7, 17, 32, 33, 36, 82–83, 86, 96–97, 110, 128–130, 215, 363, 407, 414, 441, 442, 447, 448, 451, 452, 478

talk, 6, 59, 181, 183, 184, 201, 202, 217, 228, 229, 240, 258, 265, 272, 303, 307, 314, 324, 331, 338, 367, 374–376, 388–389, 404, 406, 451. *See also* conversation; orality/oral tradition

taste, 1, 10, 101, 107, 111–113, 230–241, 294, 295, 302, 324, 345, 347, 351–353, 365–366, 369, 400n13, 410, 416, 463, 467, 471, 489. *See also* popular culture/popular taste

technique, 5, 17, 22, 32, 34, 51, 52–53, 55, 56, 57, 75, 76, 77, 97, 102–105, 111, 131–133, 134, 138, 167, 169, 184, 186, 187, 189, 201, 204, 211, 212, 216, 223, 224, 231, 245, 251, 253, 254, 264, 274, 281, 293–308 passim, 316, 319, 321, 340–343, 355, 361, 363n12, 366, 369, 382, 395, 406, 407, 408n20, 451, 455, 478, 483, 484, 489

telegraph, 22, 24, 34, 76, 96, 97, 103, 110, 243, 246, 310, 319, 325, 341, 355

telephone, 15, 77, 97, 103, 105, 110, 132, 198, 225, 226, 270, 310, 356, 380, 381, 455

television, 4, 6, 9, 96, 103, 252, 263–272, 279, 310, 318–328, 328–337, 338, 340–343, 344, 346, 353, 355–6, 358, 373, 374–376, 380–386, 394, 395, 409, 419, 432, 449, 451, 456, 461, 465–471, 472–473, 476, 480–484

television sets, fads in, 416n15

theater, 17, 26, 27, 28, 65, 66, 73, 91, 95, 112, 164, 170, 195, 237, 246, 266, 281, 288–289, 313–314, 467

Tootle the Engine, 305–307

totalitarianism, 119, 130–131, 267, 316, 350, 390, 463, 490

tradition, 22, 24, 26, 33, 34, 49, 51, 53, 59,62,64,75, 80, 85, 86, 88, 97–101, 136, 175, 194, 201, 206, 243, 250, 252, 275–280, 327, 348, 350, 368, 372, 373, 395, 416n3, 418, 426–434, 456,

458–463, 468, 475, 484, 492;
tradition-direction, 295–303
transportation, 21, 79, 95–97, 333, 339, 340,
431–432, 491
trust/distrust and skepticism, 19, 29, 43, 44, 45,
46, 50, 62, 78, 81–82, 126, 216, 217, 221, 277,
279, 287, 290–291, 293, 313, 317, 350, 361,
364nn14–16, 394, 396, 399, 420, 440, 467, 468,
470

University of Chicago, 8, 14–18, 20, 25–26, 31–32,
35, 38, 47, 75, 82–83, 88, 89, 91, 95, 106, 118,
124, 127, 158, 173n2, 206, 218, 249, 253–254,
266–268, 275, 293, 301, 308n9, 325, 328, 358,
364, 373, 409–410, 415n1, 417n17, 440–441,
444, 446, 449, 472

Veblen, Thorstein, 17, 58, 108, 459
voting and political campaigns, 17, 37–38, 89–90,
130, 173, 178, 201, 205, 206, 254, 150, 173,
177, 178, 179, 187, 239, 241, 246, 359, 402,
423, 428, 458, 472

war and aggression, 5, 9, 15, 20, 23, 26, 29, 37,
47–48, 113, 125, 128–133, 170, 182–183, 184,
185, 186, 187, 188, 189, 190, 203, 204, 205,
223, 239, 246, 252, 254–255, 260, 264,
270–271, 277, 280, 288, 299, 310–318
passim, 346, 355, 372, 426, 473, 485–493
passim
Weber, Max, 4, 299, 366, 372n1, 387, 418
women, including housewives and mothers,
54–55, 69, 80–81, 89, 114, 119–123, 139–140,
141, 142, 143, 146, 147, 148, 149, 150, 151,
152, 153, 160, 172, 184, 193, 204, 227, 237,
239, 256, 257, 260, 264, 279, 296, 312, 315,
317, 323, 346, 348, 349, 358, 380, 385n16, 392,
395, 398, 401, 411, 415, 420–423, 434–440
passim, 461, 490
World War I, 4, 5, 6, 9, 16, 17, 19, 47, 81, 82, 106,
108, 191, 346, 414
World War II, 3, 9, 76–81, 82, 87–90, 182, 184–190,
268, 309, 427

youth/youth cultures, 26, 28, 29, 44, 57, 59, 62,
63, 65–66, 68, 72, 73, 83, 89, 92–95, 96, 111,
113, 153, 159, 160, 161, 213, 220, 229, 264,
267, 271, 272, 293–308, 314–316, 324–327,
346, 348, 378, 380, 384n1, 395, 449, 454, 462,
467–468, 470, 475, 477, 490

About the Editors

John Durham Peters is F. Wendell Miller Distinguished Professor in the Department of Communication Studies at the University of Iowa, where he teaches courses on the cultural history of media and social theory.

Peter Simonson is assistant professor of communication at the University of Pittsburgh, where he teaches courses in the intellectual history of communication and rhetorical and mass communication theory.